The Animal Ethics Reader

The Animal Ethics Reader is an acclaimed anthology containing both classic and contemporary readings, making it ideal for anyone coming to the subject for the first time. It provides a thorough introduction to the central topics, controversies, and ethical dilemmas surrounding the treatment of animals, covering a wide range of contemporary issues, such as animal activism, genetic engineering, and environmental ethics.

The extracts are arranged thematically under the following clear headings:

- Theories of Animal Ethics
- Animal Capacities: Pain, Emotion, Consciousness
- Primates and Cetaceans
- Animals for Food
- Animal Experimentation
- Animals and Biotechnology
- Ethics and Wildlife
- Zoos and Aquariums
- Animal Companions
- Animal Law and Animal Activism

Readings from leading experts in the field including Peter Singer, Bernard E. Rollin, and Jane Goodall are featured, as well as selections from Tom Regan, Donald Griffin, Temple Grandin, Ben A. Minteer, Christine Korsgaard and Mark Rowlands. Classic extracts are well balanced with contemporary selections, helping to present the latest developments in the field.

This revised and updated third edition includes new readings on animal rights, captive chimpanzees, industrial farm animal production, genetic engineering, keeping cetaceans in captivity, animal cruelty, and animal activism. The third edition also is printed with a slightly larger page format and in an easier-to-read typeface.

Featuring contextualizing introductions by the editors, as well as study questions and further reading suggestions at the end of each chapter, this will be essential reading for any students taking a course in the subject.

With a new foreword by Bernard E. Rollin.

Susan J. Armstrong is Professor Emerita and 2004 Outstanding Professor at Humboldt State University in California. She has published widely on animal ethics and affiliated subjects and continues to be very concerned with animal welfare. With Richard G. Botzler, she edited *Environmental Ethics: Divergence and Convergence*.

Richard G. Botzler is Professor Emeritus of Wildlife, Humboldt State University, in California, where he taught courses in wildlife diseases, environmental ethics, and general wildlife. He was HSU's outstanding professor in 1991, and California State University outstanding professor in 1992. His publications include topics in wildlife diseases and, with Susan J. Armstrong, *Environmental Ethics: Divergence and Convergence*.

The Animal Ethics Reader

Third Edition

Edited by Susan J. Armstrong
and Richard G. Botzler

Routledge
Taylor & Francis Group

NEW YORK AND LONDON

First published 2017
by Routledge
711 Third Avenue, New York, NY 10017

and by Routledge
2 Park Square, Milton Park, Abingdon, Oxon, OX14 4RN

Routledge is an imprint of the Taylor & Francis Group, an informa business

Library of Congress Cataloging in Publication Data
A catalog record for this book has been requested

ISBN: 978-1-138-91800-9 (hbk)
ISBN: 978-1-138-91801-6 (pbk)
ISBN: 978-1-315-68871-8 (ebk)

Typeset in Times New Roman
by Apex CoVantage, LLC

Dedicated in gratitude for my children Tom, Summer, Alex and Emily

S.J.A.

Dedicated to:
our many students over the years who have stimulated our thinking and added so richly to our classes, and to my children: Emilisa, Tin, Dorothy, Sarah, and Thomas, with love and pride

R.G.B.

Contents

List of Contributors   xv
Foreword by Bernard E. Rollin   xxiii
Preface for the Third Edition   xxv
Acknowledgments   xxvi

General Introduction: Animal Ethics: A Sketch of How It Developed
and Where It Is Now   1

* indicates that the reading is new to this edition

PART ONE
Theories of Animal Ethics   13

Introduction to Part One 13
   Further Reading 13
   Study Questions 14

1 The Case for Animal Rights   15
   TOM REGAN

2 Reply to Tom Regan   22
   CARL COHEN

3 Are Human Rights *Human*?   26
   PAOLA CAVALIERI

4 Practical Ethics   32
   PETER SINGER

5 Feminism and the Treatment of Animals: From Care to Dialogue   42
   JOSEPHINE DONOVAN

6 Rights, Interests, Desires and Beliefs   50
   R. G. FREY

7 Universal Basic Rights for Animals*   53
   SUE DONALDSON AND WILL KYMLICKA

viii   *Contents*

PART TWO
Animal Capacities: Pain, Emotion, Consciousness   65

Introduction to Part Two 65
  Further Reading 66
  Study Questions 66

Issues/Methods of Study   69

 8 An Integrative and Functional Framework for the Study of
    Animal Emotion and Mood*   71
    MICHAEL MENDL, OLIVER H. P. BURMAN, AND ELIZABETH S. PAUL

 9 Reflections   83
    BARBARA SMUTS

Anthropomorphism   87

10 Anthropomorphism and Cross-Species Modeling   89
    SANDRA D. MITCHELL

11 Thinking without Words: An Overview for Animal Ethics*   99
    JOSÉ LUIS BERMÚDEZ

Consciousness, Emotion, and Suffering   109

12 Animal Pain   111
    BERNARD E. ROLLIN

13 A Neuropsychological and Evolutionary Approach to Animal Consciousness
    and Animal Suffering   116
    BOB BERMOND

14 Animal Pain*   130
    COLIN ALLEN

15 Animal Consciousness: What Matters and Why   133
    DANIEL C. DENNETT

16 New Evidence of Animal Consciousness   140
    DONALD R. GRIFFIN AND GAYLE B. SPECK

17 Self-Awareness in Animals*   149
    DAVID DEGRAZIA

PART THREE
Primates and Cetaceans   161

Introduction to Part Three 161
  Further Reading 162
  Study Questions 162

Primates   165

18 Ape Consciousness–Human Consciousness: A Perspective Informed by
    Language and Culture   167
    SUE SAVAGE-RUMBAUGH, WILLIAM MINTZ FIELDS, AND JARED TAGLIALATELA

19   Are Apes Persons? The Case for Primate Intersubjectivity   175
JUAN CARLOS GÓMEZ

20   Cultures in Chimpanzees   181
A. WHITEN, J. GOODALL, W. C. MCGREW, T. NISHIDA, V. REYNOLDS, Y. SUGIYAMA,
C. E. G. TUTIN, R. W. WRANGHAM, AND C. BOESCH

21   Being a Critter Psychologist*   185
KRISTIN ANDREWS

22   Problems Faced by Wild and Captive Chimpanzees: Finding Solutions   196
JANE GOODALL

Cetaceans   203

23   Culture and Conservation of Non-Humans with Reference to Whales
and Dolphins: Review and New Directions   205
HAL WHITEHEAD, LUKE RENDELL, RICHARD W. OSBORNE, AND BERND WÜRSIG

24   Consciousness in Dolphins? A Review of Recent Evidence*   216
HEIDI E. HARLEY

25   Whales as Persons   235
PAOLA CAVALIERI

PART FOUR
Animals for Food   243

Introduction to Part Four 243
Further Reading 244
Study Questions 244

26   Meat Eating   245
DAVID DEGRAZIA

27   Thinking Like Animals   251
TEMPLE GRANDIN

28   A Major Change   254
TEMPLE GRANDIN

29   Putting Meat on the Table: Industrial Farm Animal Production in America:
A Report of the Pew Commission on Industrial Farm Animal Production*   258

30   The Least Harm Principle May Require that Humans Consume a
Diet Containing Large Herbivores, Not a Vegan Diet   269
STEVEN L. DAVIS

31   The Basic Argument for Vegetarianism   274
JAMES RACHELS

32   The Rape of Animals, the Butchering of Women   281
CAROL J. ADAMS

Religious Issues   287

33   Animal Rights in the Jewish Tradition*   289
DAVID MEVORACH SEIDENBERG

x *Contents*

34 Is Christianity Irredeemably Speciesist?*   294
ANDREW LINZEY

35 Islam   301
MARTIN FORWARD AND MOHAMED ALAM

PART FIVE
Animal Experimentation   305

Introduction to Part Five 305
   Further Reading 305
   Study Questions 306

Laboratory Studies   307

36 The Commonsense Case Against Animal Experimentation*   309
MYLAN ENGEL JR.

37 The Ethics of Animal Research: What Are the Prospects for Agreement?   321
DAVID DEGRAZIA

38 Defending Animal Research: An International Perspective   330
BARUCH A. BRODY

39 Who—or What—Are the Rats (and Mice) in the Laboratory?   339
LYNDA BIRKE

40 Animal Research: A Moral Science: Talking Point on the Use of Animals in
Scientific Research*   347
BERNARD E. ROLLIN

41 The Ethics of Animal Research: Talking Point on the Use of Animals in
Scientific Research*   352
SIMON FESTING AND ROBIN WILKINSON

42 Reasons Scientists Avoid Thinking about Ethics*   358
PAUL ROOT WOLPE

Regulating Animal Experimentation   363

43 Ethical Themes of National Regulations Governing Animal
Experiments   365
F. BARBARA ORLANS

Animals in the Classroom   373

44 Humane Education: The Role of Animal-Based Learning   375
ANDREW J. PETTO AND KARLA D. RUSSELL

Ecological Studies   385

45 Ecological Ethics: Building a New Tool Kit for Ecologists and
Biodiversity Managers*   387
BEN A. MINTEER AND JAMES P. COLLINS

PART SIX
Animals and Biotechnology   395

Introduction to Part Six 395
  Further Reading 395
  Study Questions 396

46 Some Ethical Issues in Biotechnology Involving Animals   397
    DAVID MORTON

Issues in Genetic Engineering   403

47 Crossing Species Boundaries   405
    JASON SCOTT ROBERT AND FRANÇOISE BAYLIS

48 In Defense of the Moral Relevance of Species Boundaries   415
    ROBERT STREIFFER

49 Animal Genetic Manipulation: A Utilitarian Response   418
    KEVIN R. SMITH

50 The Inevitability of Animal Biotechnology? Ethics and the Scientific Attitude   425
    JEFFREY BURKHARDT

51 Dis/Integrating Animals: Ethical Dimensions of the Genetic Engineering of
    Animals for Human Consumption*   434
    TRACI WARKENTIN

***TELOS* as an Influence on Ethical Issues**   447

52 On *Telos* and Genetic Engineering   449
    BERNARD E. ROLLIN

53 Brave New Birds: The Use of "Animal Integrity" in Animal Ethics   456
    BERNICE BOVENKERK, FRANS W. A. BROM, AND BABS J. VAN DEN BERGH

54 Telos and the Ethics of Animal Farming*   463
    JES LYNNING HARFELD

De-Extinction   477

55 Bringing Them Back to Life: The Revival of an Extinct Species Is No Longer a Fantasy*   479
    CARL ZIMMER

56 Reintroduction and De-Extinction*   484
    DOLLY JØRGENSEN

PART SEVEN
Ethics and Wildlife   487

Introduction to Part Seven 487
  Further Reading 487
  Study Questions 488

xii *Contents*

Hunting Controversies   489

57 Game and Wild Life Conservation   491
    ALDO LEOPOLD

58 Hunting as a Moral Good*   494
    LAWRENCE CAHOONE

59 The Killing Game: An Ecofeminist Critique of Hunting   505
    MARTI KHEEL

60 Environmental Ethics and Trophy Hunting   514
    ALASTAIR S. GUNN

Special Problems   523

61 Exotic Species, Naturalisation, and Biological Nativism   525
    NED HETTINGER

62 The Potential Conservation Value of Non-Native Species*   535
    MARTIN A. SCHLAEPFER, DOV F. SAX, AND JULIAN D. OLDEN

63 To Eat the Laughing Animal   548
    DALE PETERSON

64 The Ethic of Care and the Problem of Wild Animals   553
    GRACE CLEMENT

PART EIGHT
Zoos and Aquariums   561

Introduction to Part Eight 561
    Further Reading 561
    Study Questions 562

65 Cetacean Captivity*   563
    LORI MARINO

66 Free Willy—and All His Pals*   573
    MARC SCHEFF

67 Elephants in Captivity*   575
    KRISTIN L. VEHRS

68 Against Zoos   576
    DALE JAMIESON

69 In Defense of Zoos and Aquariums: The Ethical Basis for Keeping Wild
    Animals in Captivity   582
    MICHAEL HUTCHINS, BRANDIE SMITH, AND RUTH ALLARD

70 Opportunities Lost: Zoos and the Marsupial that Tried to Be a Wolf   591
    CHRIS WEMMER

71 Ecological Ethics in Captivity: Balancing Values and Responsibilities in
    Zoo and Aquarium Research Under Rapid Global Change*   594
    BEN A. MINTEER AND JAMES P. COLLINS

PART NINE
Animal Companions 609

Introduction to Part Nine 609
  Further Reading 610
  Study Questions 610

72 Affection's Claim 611
    KONRAD LORENZ

73 The Pet World 613
    PAUL SHEPARD

74 Hand-Raising a Rhino in the Wild 616
    ANNA MERZ

75 Living with Animals 619
    FREYA MATHEWS

76 Killing Animals in Animal Shelters 622
    CLARE PALMER

77 The Structure of Evil* 631
    MARK ROWLANDS

78 An FBI Perspective on Animal Cruelty* 635
    ALAN C. BRANTLEY

79 Ethics and Euthanasia* 639
    BERNARD E. ROLLIN

80 The Miracle of Life and Afterword 646
    DIANE LEIGH AND MARILEE GEYER

81 The Moral Basis of Animal-Assisted Therapy* 650
    TZACHI ZAMIR

PART TEN
Animal Law/Animal Activism 663

Introduction to Part Ten 663
  Further Reading 664
  Study Questions 664

82 A Great Shout: Legal Rights for Great Apes 665
    STEVEN M. WISE

83 Book Review of *Rattling the Cage: Toward Legal Rights for Animals* by
    Steven M. Wise 672
    RICHARD A. POSNER

84 The Dangerous Claims of the Animal Rights Movement 676
    RICHARD A. EPSTEIN

85 U.S. Law and Animal Experimentation: A Critical Primer* 680
    STEPHEN R. LATHAM

xiv *Contents*

86 Personhood, Animals, and the Law*   686
    CHRISTINE M. KORSGAARD

87 Every Sparrow That Falls: Understanding Animal Rights Activism as
    Functional Religion   690
    WESLEY V. JAMISON, CASPAR WENK, AND JAMES V. PARKER

88 Understanding Animal Rights Violence   696
    TOM REGAN

89 Civil Disobedience: A Case Study in Factors of Effectiveness   701
    COURTNEY L. DILLARD

90 Ten Ways to Make a Difference   705
    PETER SINGER

91 The Animal Activist's Handbook: Maximizing Our Positive Impact in
    Today's World*   711
    MATT BALL AND BRUCE FRIEDRICH

    Index   720

Contributors

Carol J. Adams is an American writer, feminist, and animal rights advocate. She had published around 100 articles or entries on vegetarianism, animal rights, domestic violence, and sexual abuse.

Ruth Allard is executive vice president for conservation and visitor experiences at the Phoenix Zoo, Arizona.

Mohamed Alam grew up in Lahore, Pakistan. He now lives in Leicester, where he is President of the Fawal Community and teaches Urdu at a school in Peterborough.

Colin Allen has broad research interests in the general area of philosophy of biology and cognitive science, with particular interests in animal behavior and cognition at Indiana University. Allen has over 100 book chapters, journal articles, and conference proceedings papers.

Kristin Andrews is Associate Professor of Philosophy at York University (Toronto), where she also helps coordinate the Cognitive Science program and the Toronto Area Animal Cognition Discussion Group. Kristin is on the board of directors of the Borneo Orangutan Society Canada and is the author of two books on the philosophy of animal minds.

Matt Ball is a globally recognized authority on animal advocacy, factory farming, vegetarian diets, and applied ethics. He is currently Senior Advisor for VegFund. Before his work for animals, he was a research fellow in the Department of Biology at the University of Pittsburgh.

Françoise Baylis is Professor and Canada Research Chair in Bioethics and Philosophy at Dalhousie University. She also is the founder of the NovelTechEthics research team.

Marc Bekoff is Professor Emeritus in the Department of Ecology and Evolutionary Biology at the University of Colorado at Boulder. His most recent book is *The Emotional Lives of Animals* (2007).

Bob Bermond is a member of the Faculty of Social and Behavioural Sciences Programme group Brain and Cognition, Department of Psychology, University of Amsterdam, the Netherlands. He has published regularly on animal consciousness and emotion, as well as alexithymia, the inability to verbalize emotions, in humans.

José Luis Bermúdez is Dean of Liberal Arts, Texas A&M University. His research interests are at the intersection of philosophy, psychology, and neuroscience. *Thinking without Words* (2003) offered a model for thinking about the cognitive achievements and abilities of prelinguistic infants and nonlinguistiuc humans. He remains an active researcher.

Lynda Birke has taught women's studies as well as courses in biology at Warwick University, Coventry, United Kingdom. She was Senior Lecturer in the Centre for the Study of Women and Gender but is now based in the Institute for Women's Studies at the University of Lancaster.

Christophe Boesch works at the Max-Planck Institute for Evolutionary Anthropology, Leipzig, Germany. He has focused on the flexible adaptations of chimpanzees and gorillas in their natural habitats.

Bernice Bovenkerk is an Assistant Professor at the Social Sciences Group, subdepartment of Communication, Philosophy, and Technology of Wageningen University, the Netherlands. Her research interests concern issues in animal and environmental ethics and political philosophy.

Alan Brantley has served with the National Center for the Analysis of Violent Crime and is a retired FBI Special Agent.

Baruch A. Brody is a Professor of Philosophy at Rice University. He was elected to the Institute of Medicine of the National Academies of Science in 2001. His research interests are focused on the ethical issues raised by intellectual property in biotechnological invention, as well as ethical and methodological issues raised by controlled clinical trials of surgical interventions.

Frans W. A. Brom currently is Head of Technology Assessment at the Rathenau Institute, Netherlands, and has been appointed as the Secretary/Director of the Netherlands Scientific Council for Government Policy. He also occupies an endowed chair of Ethics of Technology Assessment at Utrecht University.

Jeffrey Burkhardt is part of the Ethics and Policy Program, Institute of Food and Agricultural Sciences, University of Florida, Gainesville. His expertise lies in ethics and policy in agriculture and natural resources, as well as in the history and philosophy of economics.

Oliver H. P. Burman is a Reader in Animal Behavior, Cognition, and Welfare, in the Department of Biological Sciences, University of Lincoln, Lincoln, United Kingdom.

Lawrence Cahoone is Professor of Philosophy at the College of the Holy Cross in Worcester, Massachusetts. He has published numerous books on various philosophical topics. His research interests include recent European philosophy, American philosophy, social and political philosophy, metaphysics, and natural science.

Paola Cavalieri is an Italian philosopher, known for her work arguing for extension of human rights to the other great apes.

Grace Clement is an Associate Professor and Chair of the Philosophy Department at Salisbury University, Maryland. She has written a book on feminist ethics, *Care, Autonomy and Justice: Feminism and the Ethic of Care*, and is currently writing on the connections between feminist ethics and animal ethics. Her main areas of interest are moral theory and questions about the foundations and boundaries of ethics.

Carl Cohen is Professor of Philosophy at the University of Michigan in Ann Arbor, Michigan. He is a vigorous civil libertarian and is co-editor of a widely used logic textbook. He is co-author of *The Animal Rights Debate* with Prof. Tom Regan (2001).

James P. Collins is the Virginia M. Ullman Professor of Natural History and the Environment in the School of Life Sciences, Arizona State University, Tempe, Arizona. His professional work includes environmental ethics, as well as the role of host–pathogen interactions in species decline and extinction.

Steven L. Davis is Professor Emeritus of Animal Science at Oregon State University.

David DeGrazia is Professor of Philosophy at George Washington University, as well as a Senior Research Fellow with the Department of Bioethics with the National Institutes of Health. His areas of specialization are ethical theory, biomedical ethics, and personal identity theory.

Daniel C. Dennett is a prominent American philosopher whose research centers on philosophy of mind and philosophy of science, particularly as those fields relate to evolutionary biology and cognitive science. He is Professor of Philosophy and Co-director of the Center for Cognitive Studies as well as the Austin B. Fletcher Professor of Philosophy at Tufts University.

Courtney L. Dillard is in the Department of Communication at Portland State University.

Sue Donaldson is an independent researcher and author. With Will Kymlicka she wrote *Zoopolis: A Political Theory of Animal Rights*.

Josephine Donovan is Emerita Professor at the University of Maine. She is co-editor of *Feminist Care Traditions in Animal Ethics* (2007) as well as numerous other works, including *Animals and Women* (1995).

Mylan Engel, Jr. is a Professor of Philosophy at Northern Illinois University. Engel's specialties are epistemology, philosophy of religion, Scottish philosopher Thomas Reid, animal ethics, and environmental ethics. Engel is a "moral vegetarian" (vegan)—the belief that we are morally obligated to refrain from eating meat.

Richard A. Epstein is an American scholar, educator, lawyer, and author, best known for his writings on classical liberalism.

Simon Festing is the Executive Director at the Research Defence Society, London, United Kingdom.

William Mintz Fields worked in the fields of psychiatry, psychology, engineering, and philosophy in the Department of Biology, Language Research Center, at Georgia State University, Atlanta, Georgia. He died in 2012.

Martin Forward is Professor of Religious Studies and Executive Director of the Aurora University Center for Faith and Action at Aurora University in Aurora, Illinois. His most recent books are *Religion: A Beginner's Guide* (2001) and *Inter-religious Dialogue* (2001).

Bruce Friedrich is Director for engagement and policy at Farm Sanctuary. His articles on farm animal issues appear regularly in the *Huffington Post*, and he has written opinion pieces for a number of other publications. He was named "teacher of the year" for his work as a public school teacher in inner-city Baltimore.

R. G. Frey (1941–2012) was Professor of Philosophy at Bowling Green State University, specializing in moral, political, and legal philosophy.

Juan Carlos Gómez is a Reader at the School of Psychology and Neurosciences, University of St. Andrews, Scotland. His publications include *Apes, Monkeys, Children and the Growth of Mind* (2004). His research interests include the development of intentional communication and social understanding in human children and nonhuman primates, as well as autism, theory of mind, and cognitive development.

Jane Goodall is best known for her 55-year study of social and family interactions of wild chimpanzees in Gombe Stream National Park, Tanzania. She is the founder of the Jane Goodall Institute and the Roots & Shoots program, and she has worked extensively on conservation and animal welfare issues. She has served on the board of the Nonhuman Rights Project since its founding in 1996.

Temple Grandin is an American Professor of animal science at Colorado State University, a best-selling author, autistic activist, and a consultant to the livestock industry on animal behavior.

Donald R. Griffin (1915–2003) was a highly regarded scientist who followed his innovative work on echolocation in bats with groundbreaking work on the question of whether animals possess consciousness. He wrote several books, including *The Question of Animal Awareness*.

Alastair S. Gunn was Professor and Chair of the Department of Philosophy, University of Waikato, Hamilton, New Zealand, until his death in 2012. He wrote and taught about environmental ethics and engineering, as well as hunting and conservation.

Jes Lynning Harfeld is an Assistant Professor at Aalborg University, Denmark. His research areas include philosophy, biomedicine, medicine, and public health.

Heidi Harley is a Professor of Psychology and Director of Environmental Studies at the New College of Florida, Sarasota. She teaches courses in cognitive psychology and comparative cognition. Her research focuses on cognitive processes in dolphins.

Ned Hettinger is Professor of Philosophy, College of Charleston, South Carolina. He specializes in environmental ethics and aesthetics and teaches a range of courses in philosophy, including environmental philosophy, aesthetics, business ethics, introduction to philosophy, and nature, technology, and society.

Michael Hutchins was Director of Conservation and Science, American Zoo and Aquarium Association (AZA). While at AZA, Hutchins and colleagues established the AZA's Animal Welfare Committee and accreditation guidelines regarding welfare and environmental enrichment for captive animals. He currently is the executive director for The Wildlife Society.

Dale Jamieson is Professor of Environmental Studies, Director of Animal Studies Initiative, Professor of Philosophy, and Affiliated Professor of Law at New York University. He is the author of *Morality's Progress: Essays on Humans, Other Animals, and the Rest of Nature*. Current research areas include ethics and environmental philosophy.

Wesley V. Jamison is in the Interdisciplinary and Global Studies Division of Worcester Polytechnic University, Worcester, Massachusetts.

Dolly Jørgensen is a Researcher in the Department of Ecology and Environmental Science, Umeå University, Sverige, Sweden. She has worked on a broad array of environmental history projects and on the historical, social, and political contexts of ecological restoration. She is currently investigating historical animal reintroduction projects in Scandinavia.

Marti Kheel was a long-time animal advocate. In 1982, she co-founded Feminists for Animal Rights. She worked to uncover the emotional basis and presuppositions of the decisions that we make regarding animals until her death in 2011.

Christine M. Korsgaard is Arthur Kingsley Porter Professor of Philosophy at Harvard University. She is the author of four books. Her most recent book is *Self-Constitution: Agency, Identity, and Integrity* (2009).

Will Kymlicka teaches political philosophy at Queen's University in Kingston, Canada. He has received several awards, most recently the Queen Elizabeth II Diamond Jubilee Medal.

Stephen R. Latham is director of the Interdisciplinary Center for Bioethics at Yale University. He has published on a broad range of issues at the intersection of bioethics and law. He is a former board member of the American Society for Bioethics and Humanities, a former graduate fellow of Harvard's Safra Center on Ethics, and a former research fellow of the University of Edinburgh's Institute for Advanced Studies in Humanities. His current research includes a project funded by the Robert Wood Johnson Foundation to create a database of state statutes and cases criminalizing HIV exposure and a project on a legal framework for newborn whole-exome screening.

Diane Leigh and Marilee Geyer are former shelter workers. www.novoiceunheard.org

Aldo Leopold (1887–1948) began his professional career in 1909 when he joined the U.S. Forest Service. In 1924 he became Associate Director of the Forest Products Laboratory in Madison, Wisconsin, and in 1933 the University of Wisconsin created a chair of game management for him.

Andrew Linzey is an Anglican priest, theologian, author, and prominent figure in the Christian vegetarian movement. He is a member of the Faculty of Theology at the University of Oxford and is the founder and director of the Oxford Centre for Animal Ethics.

Konrad Lorenz (1903–1989) was an Austrian ethologist who won the Nobel Prize in Medicine in 1973. His work laid the foundation of an evolutionary approach to mind and cognition.

Lori Marino is a Senior Lecturer in Neuroscience and Behavioral Biology at Emory University. She also is founder and Executive Director of the Kimmela Center for Animal Advocacy and has authored over eighty publications on dolphin and whale neurology, evolution, and self-awareness.

Freya Mathews is Associate Professor of Philosophy at La Trobe University in Australia. Her recent books include *For the Love of Matter* (2003) and *Reinhabiting Reality* (2005).

William C. McGrew is a primatologist in the Department of Zoology and Department of Sociology, Gerontology, and Anthropology, Miami University, Oxford, Ohio.

Michael Mendl is a Professor in the Bristol University School of Medicine and has published extensively on social structure and behavior. He is interested in measures of animal affect (emotion) and welfare and in developing new measures of animal emotion and welfare that can be used under field conditions.

Anna Merz (1930–2013) founded the Ngare Sergoi Rhino Sanctuary in 1983 and pioneered the concept of community game management.

Ben A. Minteer is an Associate Professor, School of Life Sciences, Arizona State University. His work explores the intersection of environmental ethics, ecology, and conservation, especially the impact of global environmental change on our understandings of environmental responsibility.

Sandra Mitchell is Professor of Philosophy and Science, University of Pittsburgh, Pennsylvania. Her research is on epistemological and metaphysical issues in the philosophy of science, including scientific explanations of complex behavior and how we might best represent multilevel, multicomponent complex systems.

David Morton is Professor of Biomedical Science and Ethics, University of Birmingham, Edgbaston, Birmingham, United Kingdom.

Toshisada Nishida worked as a primatology behaviorist in the Laboratory of Human Evolution studies, Kyoto University, Kyoto, Japan. He died in 2011.

Julian Olden is an Associate Professor of the School of Aquatic and Fishery Sciences, University of Washington, Seattle, Washington.

F. Barbara Orlans conducted research at the Johns Hopkins Hospital and at the National Institutes of Health, publishing numerous papers in both British and American journals of physiology, pharmacology, and experimental therapeutics. From 1989 until her death in 2010, she worked as a senior research fellow and then a research assistant professor at the Georgetown University Kennedy Institute of Ethics.

Richard W. Osborne has been the science curator at The Whale Museum, Friday Harbor, Washington, since 1979.

Clare Palmer teaches in the Department of Philosophy at Texas A&M University. Her research interests include environmental and animal ethics and ethics and emerging technologies.

James V. Parker is a retired public-information officer, Oregon National Primate Research Center. He is the author of *Animal Minds, Animal Souls, Animal Rights* (2010) University Press of America.

Elizabeth S. Paul is in the Centre for Behavioural Biology and is interested in understanding the development of human attitudes to animal welfare and the use of animals in society.

Dale Peterson is a Lecturer of English at Tufts University. Recent books include *Eating Apes* (2003), *Jane Goodall: the Woman Who Redefined Man* (2006), and *Elephant Reflections* (2009).

Andrew J. Petto is a Senior Lecturer on science education at the University of Wisconsin–Milwaukee. His areas of interest include scientific literacy and science education, to promote the understanding of the nature and process of scientific inquiry as a context for all the factual information that scientific research generates of modern biology.

Richard A. Posner is Senior Lecturer in Law at the University of Chicago Law School. He has written a number of books, most recently *Antitrust Law* (2nd ed. 2001). He was Chief Judge of the U.S. Court of Appeals for the Seventh Circuit from 1993 to 2000.

James Rachels (1941–2003) taught philosophy at the University of Alabama at Birmingham for twenty-five years. His writings include *Created from Animals: The Moral Implications of Darwinism* (1990) and *Problems for Philosophy* (2008).

Tom Regan is Emeritus Professor of Philosophy at North Carolina State University. His book *The Case for Animal Rights* was central in raising the question of the moral status of animals.

Luke Rendell is EU Postdoctoral Research Fellow at the University of St. Andrews. He has published several papers on behavior and acoustic communication of cetaceans.

Vernon Reynolds works at the Institute of Biological Anthropology, Oxford University, Oxford, UK.

Jason Scott Robert is an Associate Professor, School of Life Sciences, Arizona State University, Tempe, Arizona. He investigates complex political and societal problems that intersect with life sciences.

Bernard E. Rollin is University Distinguished Professor, Professor of Philosophy, Biomedical Sciences and Animal Sciences, and University Bioethicist at Colorado State University, Fort Collins, Colorado. He is the author of numerous books, including *Science and Ethics* (2006), *An Introduction to Veterinary Medical Ethics* (1999), *The Frankenstein Syndrome* (1995), and *Animal Rights and Human Morality* (1992).

Mark Rowlands is a Welsh writer and philosopher. He is Professor of Philosophy at the University of Miami.

Sue Savage-Rumbaugh is a psychologist and primatologist most known for her work with two bonobos, Kanzi and Panbanisha, investigating their linguistic and cognitive abilities using lexigrams and computer-based keyboards. She worked at the Iowa Primate Learning Sanctuary in Des Moines, Iowa, from 2006 until 2013.

Dov F. Sax currently serves as Deputy Director for Education and is part of the Department of Ecology and Evolutionary Biology and Institute at Brown for Environment and Society, Brown University, Providence, Rhode Island.

Marc Scheff is a graphics professional who represented an editorial in *Scientific American*.

Martin A. Schlaepfer was a 2014–2015 Senior Researcher in the Department of Environmental and Forest Biology at the State University of New York College of Environmental Science and Forestry, Syracuse, New York.

Rabbi David Mevorach Seidenberg holds a doctorate in Jewish thought focused in ecology and kabbala. He was ordained at the Jewish Theological Seminary and is a member of the Ohalah organization of renewal rabbis and the Rabbinical Assembly.

Paul Shepard (1925–1996) was a philosopher, essayist, and author of numerous books. In *Thinking Animals* (1998) he argued that animals are indispensable to our being human.

Peter Singer is an Australian moral philosopher. He is currently the Ira W. DeCamp Professor of Bioethics at Princeton University. His book *Animal Liberation* was central in beginning the animal liberation movement.

Brandie Smith is Associate Director for Animal Care Services at the Smithsonian National Zoological Park, Washington, DC.

Kevin Smith is a Senior Lecturer of the School of Science Engineering and Technology at the University of Abertay Dundee, Scotland. His research is in bioethics and theoretical genetics. His work encompasses transgenic bioreactors, xenotransplantation, genetically modified food, gene therapy, and genetic enhancement.

Barbara Smuts is Professor of Psychology and Anthropology at the University of Michigan and is an American anthropologist and psychologist noted for her research into baboons, dolphins, and chimpanzees. She has authored numerous scientific articles on social relationships in wild primates and dolphins.

Gayle B. Speck is in the Vision Sciences Laboratory, Department of Psychology, Harvard University, Cambridge, Massachusetts.

Robert Streiffer is an Associate Professor of Bioethics and Philosophy at the University of Wisconsin–Madison and is affiliated with the Gaylord Nelson Institute for Environmental Studies. His interests include abstract ethical theory and ethical and political issues related to agricultural biotechnology.

Yukimaru Sugiyama works at the Primate Research Institute, Kyoto University, Inuyama, Japan.

Jared Taglialatela works in the fields of neuroscience, plant and animal science, and evolutionary studies at Kennesaw State University, Kennesaw, Georgia.

C. E. G. Tutin works at the Department of Biological and Environmental Sciences, University of Stirling, Stirling, UK.

Babs J. Van den Bergh works on topics in ethics, social and political science, philosophy of science, agricultural science, and animal communications at Wageningen University, Netherlands.

Kristin Vehrs is Executive Director of the Association of Zoos and Aquariums.

Traci Warkentin is an Assistant Professor of Earth and Environmental Sciences of the City University of New York. Her research interests include environmental ethics, environmental and geographic education, human–animal relationships, animal geographies, and environmental feminism.

Chris Wemmer is a Fellow, Ornithology and Mammalogy, of the California Academy of Sciences. Starting in the late 1980s, he directed the National Zoo's Conservation and Research Center. He currently is working on wildlife conservation in Southeast Asia.

Caspar Wenk is Professor of Nutrition Biology at The Institute of Animal Sciences in Zurich.

Hal Whitehead is Killam Professor of Biology at Dalhousie University and has authored over 100 papers on behavior, ecology, population biology, and conservation of whales; he also is coeditor of a book on cetacean societies.

Andrew Whiten is the Wardlaw Professor in the School of Psychology and Neuroscience at the University of St. Andrews, Scotland. He studies and compares human and nonhuman primates, especially chimpanzees.

Robin Wilkinson is the Science Communication Officer at the Research Defence Society, London, UK.

Steven M. Wise, J.D., has taught Animal Rights Law at the Harvard, Vermont, and John Marshall Law Schools and in the Masters Program in Animals and Public Policy at Tufts University School of Veterinary Medicine. He is President of the Center for the Expansion of Fundamental Rights, Inc., in Coral Springs, Florida.

Paul Root Wolpe, is Candler Professor of Bioethics, Schinazi Distinguished Research Chair in Jewish Bioethics, Professor in the Departments of Medicine, Pediatrics, Psychiatry, and Sociology, and Director of the Center for Ethics at Emory University. He is co-editor of the *American Journal of Bioethics* (AJOB), and editor of *AJOB Neuroscience*; he sits on the editorial boards of over a dozen professional journals in medicine and ethics.

Richard W. Wrangham is the Ruth B. Moore Professor of Biological Anthropology, Harvard University, Cambridge, Massachusetts. He has extensive research on primate ecology, nutrition, and social behavior.

Bernd Würsig studies the behavioral ecology of marine mammals, especially small cetaceans, at Texas A&M University, Galveston, Texas.

Tzachi Zamir teaches at the Hebrew University of Jerusalem and is interested in moral aspects of human–animal relations. He wrote *Ethics and the Beast* in 2007.

Carl Zimmer is a popular science writer and blogger, especially regarding the study of evolution and parasites. He has written several books and contributes science essays to publications such as the *New York Times*, *Discover*, and *National Geographic*. He is a fellow at Yale University's Morse College.

Foreword

We should all welcome the third and most recent edition of Armstrong and Botzler's *Animal Ethics Reader*. In most cases, a field of study defines textbooks for that field. More rarely, the appearance of a textbook defines and delineates the field of study, as was the case with Copi's *Introduction to Logic*. It is unquestionable that the Armstrong and Botzler volume performed that function for the field of animal ethics. As the person who wrote one of the first two books on animal ethics published in the 1970s and began to teach that area to students shortly thereafter, I searched in vain for a fair and balanced textbook covering the major topics essential to the field, as I developed courses introducing the material to biology students, philosophy students, and veterinary students, each student population demanding a different set of readings. It was not until the first edition of this book appeared in 2003 that I could rest, comfortable that there would never be a better textbook as useful for introducing major topics in animal ethics to such heterogeneous student groups.

There has been an exponential increase in societal concern for issues in animal ethics since the 1970s. Probably the first milestone occurred in 1985 with the passage of federal law providing some protection for animals used in research. After a literature search I undertook at the request of Congress in 1982 revealed a mere two published papers on analgesia for laboratory animals utilized in research, Congress mandated the control of pain in animal experiments. During the ensuing years, many other changes in animal experimentation were mandated. For example, in 2013 Europe banned cosmetic testing on animals. Research on great apes has been truncated across the world. The book includes discussions of a number of these issues.

Particularly noteworthy has been the increase of public attention to farm animals and their well-being. The referenda developed by the Humane Society of the United States abolishing gestation crates, the raising of veal calves in small boxes, and the production of eggs by chickens kept in extremely cramped, impoverished cages that make no concessions to the natural behavior of chickens or their psychological needs have passed by healthy margins in all states where they have been attempted. In such states as Colorado, the referendum was dropped in favor of legislation supported by both the humane community and the agricultural community, a sure sign of a mainstream issue.

Perhaps the most dramatic step forward has been the relinquishment of gestation crates by the world's largest pork producer, Smithfield Farms. Given what is known of natural behavior in swine, as well as what is known of their intelligence, the small 2′ by 3′ by 7′ cage in which pregnant sows are housed for their entire productive lives was widely perceived by the general public as unacceptable. In 2007, I spent two days in detailed conversation with two prominent Smithfield executives pointing out to them the desirability of phasing out such unnatural accommodations for mother pigs. I indicated to them that, by my calculations, approximately 75% of the general public found this approach to sow housing morally unacceptable. I urged them to examine this question for themselves, and a couple of months later they informed me that I was wrong—it was not 75% of the public that objected to sow stalls; it was 78%! Shortly thereafter, Smithfield announced that in a few months 300,000 sows would be relocated to open housing. They were as good as their word, and it seems clear that such confined housing now has an extremely limited lifespan, despite almost obsessive support from the industry.

At about the same time, the Pew Commission on Industrial Farm Animal Production, staffed by fifteen commissioners with backgrounds in all aspects of agriculture, including environmental considerations, sustainability, public health, animal welfare, rural sociology, air and water pollution, as well as Confined Animal Feeding Operation involvement in human illness, issued its report based upon three years of exhaustive study. In this report, the Commission recommended the rapid abolition of high confinement animal agriculture for reasons of animal welfare and public health. The report received approximately 800 positive editorials in newspapers across the U.S.

It seems clear that public attention to animal welfare will continue to grow. The new edition of this book helps to ensure that people interested in these questions will have up-to-date information and access to excellent ethical thought. This is essential to rational social progress, or else the best intentions of society can be subverted by special interests. This has in fact occurred with the issue of feeding antibiotics to effect growth promotion in confinement agriculture, as well as to compensate for the excessive crowding that is characteristic of such agriculture. The result is in effect to breed for pathogens that are resistant to standard antibiotics, thereby directly endangering human health. (In fact, the Pew Commission began when researchers from Johns Hopkins were studying water quality in the Delaware-Maryland-Virginia poultry production region and were horrified to find the water contaminated with vancomycin, a cutting-edge human antimicrobial apparently being employed in poultry production.) Thus, what was traditionally seen as an issue largely pertaining to animal welfare in fact has major ramifications for human health. Despite extremely strong and repeated recommendations from the Pew Commission to forestall the use of antimicrobials essential for human health in confinement animal agriculture, Congress refused to act, evidencing the political power of food companies to block legislative action for the benefit of human health that is predicated on curtailing the use of antibiotics in the production of food animals. In fact, knowledge of Congress's refusal to act might prompt someone of a cynical nature to declare that the United States has the best legislature money can buy.

The new, third edition includes a considerable amount of novel material that is highly relevant to contemporary, pressing issues. There is a considerable amount of discussion of animal mentation, pain, and consciousness. (Interestingly enough, it was only in 2012 that a consensus conference was held at Cambridge University acknowledging that animals have thoughts and feelings.) The material on primates and cetaceans is very timely, given the debates being conducted internationally on using primates for research and on keeping killer whales in captivity in the wake of the killing of a trainer at Sea World San Diego, and the release of the movie *Blackfish*, which has created an international sensation. Other papers discuss the restoration of extinct species by way of biotechnology. And there is a growing movement in society—utopian though it may be—to reject euthanasia as a solution to irresponsible acquisition of companion animals.

Probably the most profound compliment I can pay to this book is to point out that in my animal ethics classes, I assign a relatively small number of papers from the book as required reading. Yet invariably the students inform me that they read well beyond the required readings, because the material "is so fascinating." They also tell me that "this is a book they intend to keep and never sell." That is high praise indeed!

Bernard E. Rollin
University Distinguished Professor,
Professor of Philosophy,
Professor of Animal Sciences,
Professor of Biomedical Sciences,
University Bioethicist at
Colorado State University

Preface for the Third Edition

This third edition includes thirty-one new articles in the various fields covered by the *Reader*. We hope the book will continue to be of value to undergraduate and graduate students, as well as to their instructors and to the general reader. We appreciate the supportive comments we have received from students in courses which have used the book.

Since the 2008 publication of the second edition, animal ethics has continued to become more prominent, in the discipline of philosophy and in the social and natural sciences, as well as the culture of the world. We have included a new article on basic rights for animals, as well as new articles on assessments of the experiences of animals, including self-awareness and suffering; consciousness in primates and cetaceans; use of animals in research, including reasons why some scientists avoid thinking about ethics; genetic engineering and "de-extinction"; wildlife controversies such as hunting and non-native species; and issues related to zoos and aquariums. We have also included a new report on industrial farm animal production, which details the changes which need to be made. There is also a new discussion of animal rights in the Jewish tradition. The question of whether Christianity is irredeemably speciesist is carefully evaluated by Rev. Andrew Linzey.

Animals are welcomed in the homes of many people. Sometimes that results in cruelty, both to animals and to people. For many of us, euthanasia of an animal must be faced. Animals are also more and more active in assisting the disabled. We have included new articles which address these areas.

The question of whether animals have legal rights continues to be debated. Christine Korsgaard maintains that while animals do not have legal rights, they deserve to be treated as ends in themselves, not subordinated to the interests of people. And animal activism is alive and well in advocating and protesting for animals.

We have made some hard decisions to delete material in favor of incorporating more contemporary thinking and enriching the variety of ideas. The *Reader* contains updated Introductions to each of the Parts, to the Further Reading sections and Study Questions.

We are happy to report that the page format and the type size have been slightly increased for ease of reading.

Acknowledgments

Tom Regan, *The Case for Animal Rights*. Copyright © 2004, The Regents of the University of California Press. Reproduced with permission.

Carl Cohen. 2001. "Reply to Tom Regan," in C. Cohen and T. Regan (eds.), *The Animal Rights Debate*. Reprinted by permission of Rowman & Littlefield Publishers, Inc.

Paola Cavalieri, "Are Human Rights *Human?*" in *Logos: A Journal of Modern Society & Culture*, issue 4.2, 2005. Reprinted by kind permission of the author and journal.

Peter Singer. 1993. *Practical Ethics*, 2nd edn. Copyright © Cambridge University Press, reprinted with permission of the publisher and author.

Josephine Donovan, "Feminism and the Treatment of Animals: From Care to Dialogue," in *Signs* vol. 31, no. 2 © 2006 by The University of Chicago. All rights reserved. Reproduced with permission of The University of Chicago Press.

R. G. Frey. 2008. "Rights, Interests, Desires and Beliefs," in *American Philosophical Quarterly* 16.3. © North American Philosophical Publications. Reprinted by permission of the publisher.

Sue Donaldson and Will Kymlicka, "Universal Basic Rights for Animals," in *Zoopolis: A Political Theory of Animal Rights*. Copyright © 2011 Oxford University Press, reprinted by permission of the publisher.

Michael Mendl, Oliver H. P. Burman, and Elizabeth S. Paul, "An Integrative and Functional Framework for the Study of Animal Emotion and Mood," © 2011 Proceedings of the Royal Society B: 277: 2895–2904. Reprinted with permission.

Barbara Smuts, "Reflections," in J. M. Coetzee (ed.), *The Lives of Animals*. © 1999 Princeton University Press. Reprinted by permission of Princeton University Press.

Sandra D. Mitchell. 2005. "Anthropomorphism and Cross-Species Modeling," in L. Daston and G. Mitman (eds.), *Thinking with Animals in Evolutionary Biology*, Columbia University Press. Reprinted by permission of the publisher.

José Luis Bermúdez. 2007. "Thinking without Words: An Overview for Animal Ethics," in *The Journal of Ethics* 11: 319–335. Reprinted with permission.

Bernard E. Rollin. 1998. "Animal Pain," in *The Unheeded Cry*. Reprinted by kind permission of the author and Blackwell Publishing Ltd.

Bob Bermond, "A Neuropsychological and Evolutionary Approach to Animal Consciousness and Animal Suffering", in *Animal Welfare* 2001, 10: S47–S62. Copyright © 2001 Universities Federation for Animal Welfare. Reprinted by kind permission of UFAW www.ufaw.org.uk.

Colin Allen. 2004. Animal Pain," in *Noûs* 38 (4): 617–643. Reprinted with permission.

Daniel C. Dennett 1995. "Animal Consciousness: What Matters and Why," in Arien Mack (ed.), *Humans and Other Animals*, Ohio State University Press. Reprinted by permission of the publisher.

Donald R. Griffin and Gayle R. Speck, "New Evidence of Animal Consciousness", in *Animal Cognition* (2004) 7: 5–18, Copyright © Springer-Verlag 2004 with kind permission from Springer Science and Business Media.

David DeGrazia. 2009. "Self-Awareness in Animals," pp. 201–217 in R. Lurz (ed.), *The Philosophy of Animal Minds*, Cambridge University Press, Cambridge, UK. Reprinted with permission of Cambridge University Press.

Sue Savage-Rumbaugh, William M. Fields, and Jared Taglialatela. 2000. "Ape Consciousness— Human Consciousness: A Perspective Informed by Language and Culture," in *Integrative and*

Comparative Biology (formerly *American Zoologist*) 40(6): 910–21. Reprinted by kind permission of Oxford University Press and Sue Savage-Rumbaugh.

Juan Carlos Gómez. 1998. "Are Apes Persons? The Case for Primate Intersubjectivity," in *Etica and Animali*. Copyright J.C. Gómez and Paola Cavalieri. Reprinted by kind permission of J. C. Gómez.

A. Whiten, J. Goodall, W. C. McGrew, T. Nishida, V. Reynolds, Y. Sugiyama, C.E.G. Tutin, R. W. Wrangham, and C. Boesch, "Cultures in Chimpanzees," in *Nature* vol. 399: 682–685. Reprinted by permission from Macmillan Publishers Ltd. Copyright © 1999.

Kristin Andrews, 2012. Chapter 12: "Being a Critter Psychologist," pp. 231–248 in *Do Apes Read Minds?: Toward a New Folk Psychology*. MIT Press, Cambridge Massachusetts. Reprinted with permission of MIT Press.

Jane Goodall, "Problems Faced by Wild and Captive Chimpanzees: Finding Solutions," pp. xiii–xxiv. Reprinted from B. B. Beck, T. S. Stoinski, et al. (eds.), *Great Apes and Humans: The Ethics of Coexistence*, Washington, DC: Smithsonian Institution Press. Used by permission of the Smithsonian Institution. Copyright 2001.

Hal Whitehead, Luke Rendell, Richard W. Osborne, and Bernd Wursig, "Culture and Conservation of Non-Humans with Reference to Whales and Dolphins," reprinted from *Biological Conservation* 120: 431–441. Copyright © 2004 Elsevier, reprinted with permission.

Heidi E. Harley. 2013. "Consciousness in Dolphins? A Review of Recent Evidence." *Journal of Comparative Physiology A* 199: 565–582. Reprinted with permission.

Paola Cavalieri. 2006. "Whales as Persons," pp. 28–35 in M. Kaiser and M. E. Lien (eds.), *Ethics and the Politics of Food: Preprints of the 6th Congress of the European Society for Agricultural and Food Ethics*, Wageningen Academic Publishers. Reprinted by permission of the publisher.

David DeGrazia. 2002. "Meat-Eating," in *Animal Rights: A Very Short Introduction*. Reprinted by kind permission of the author and Oxford University Press.

Temple Grandin. 1998. "Thinking Like Animals," in L. Hogan, D. Metzger, B. Petersen (eds), *Intimate Nature: The Bond Between Women and Animals*, Fawcett Books. © Temple Grandin. Reproduced by kind permission of Temple Grandin.

———. 2001. "A Major Change," in *The State of the Animals 2001*, D. J. Salem and A. N. Rowan (eds.), Washington, D.C.: Humane Society Press. Reprinted with permission from THE STATE OF THE ANIMALS: 2001, edited by Deborah J. Salem and Andrew N. Rowan (©2001 The Humane Society of the United States/Humane Society Press, Washington, D.C. 20037).

Putting Meat on the Table: Industrial Farm Animal Production in America: A Report of the Pew Commission on Industrial Farm Animal Production. Reprinted with permission of Pew Charitable Trusts.

Steven L. Davis, "The Least Harm Principle May Require that Humans Consume a Diet Containing Large Herbivores, not a Vegan Diet," *Journal of Agriculture and Environmental Ethics* 16: 387–394, © 2003 Kluwer Academic Publishers with kind permission from Springer Science and Business Media and the author.

James Rachels, "The Basic Argument for Vegetarianism," pp. 70–80 in S. F. Sapontzis (ed.), *Food for Thought: The Debate over Eating Meat*, Amherst, NY: Prometheus Books. Copyright © 2004 by Steve F. Sapontzis. All rights reserved. Reprinted with permission of the publisher.

Carol J. Adams. 1990. "The Rape of Animals, the Butchering of Women," in *Sexual Politics of Meat: A Feminist-Vegetarian Critical Theory*. Reprinted by permission of The Continuum International Publishing Group.

David Mevorach Seidenberg. 2011. "Animal Rights in the Jewish Tradition," in *Encyclopedia of Religion and Nature*. Reprinted with permission of the publisher.

Andrew Linzey. 1998. "Is Christianity Irredeemably Speciesist?" in *Animals on the Agenda*. SCM Ltd., London. Reprinted with permission of SCM Ltd.

Martin Forward and Mohamed Alam. 1994. "Islam," in J. Holm (ed.), *Attitudes to Nature*. Reprinted by kind permission of Jean Holm and Martin Forward.

David DeGrazia, "The Ethics of Animal Research: What Are the Prospects for Agreement?" *Cambridge Quarterly of Healthcare Ethics* (1999) 8: 23–34. Copyright © Cambridge University Press, reprinted with permission of the author and publisher.

Baruch A. Brody, "Defending Animal Research: An International Perspective," pp. 131–147 in E. F. Paul and J. Paul (eds.), *Why Animal Experimentation Matters*. Copyright © 2001 by Transaction Publishers. Reprinted by permission of the publisher and author.

Lynda Birke, "Who—or What—Are the Rats (and Mice) in the Laboratory?", *Society & Animals* 11:3, 2003. Reproduced by kind permission of Koninklijke Brill NV, www.brill.nl.

Bernard E. Rollin. 2007. "Animal Research: A Moral Science," *EMBO Reports* 8 (6): 521–525. Reprinted with permission.

Simon Festing, and Robin Wilkinson. 2007. The Ethics of Animal Research: Talking Point on the Use of Animals in Scientific Research," *EMBO Reports* 8 (6): 526–530. Reprinted with permission.

Paul Root Wolpe. 2006. "Reasons Scientists Avoid Thinking about Ethics," *Cell* 125: 1023–1025. Reprinted with permission from Elsevier.

F. Barbara Orlans, "Ethical Themes of National Regulations Governing Animal Experiments: An International Perspective", pp. 131–147 in J. P. Gluck, T. DiPasquale, and F. Barbara Orlans (eds.), *Applied Ethics in Animal Research*. © 2002 Purdue University Press. Reprinted with permission.

Andrew J. Petto and Karla D. Russell. 1999. "Humane Education: The Role of Animal-based Learning," pp. 167–185 in F. L. Dolins (ed.), *Attitudes to Animals*. Copyright © Cambridge University Press, reprinted with permission of the author and publisher.

Ben A. Minteer and James P. Collins, "Ecological Ethics: Building a New Tool Kit for Ecologists and Biodiversity Managers," *Conservation Biology* 1803–1812. © 2005 Society for Conservation Biology, reprinted by permission of Blackwell Publishing Ltd.

Jason Scott Robert and Francoise Baylis, "Crossing Species Boundaries," *American Journal of Bioethics*, summer 2003, 3(3), reprinted by kind permission of the author and Taylor and Francis Group www.informaworld.com.

Robert Streiffer, "In Defense of the Moral Relevance of Species Boundaries," *American Journal of Bioethics*, summer 2003, 3(3), reprinted by kind permission of the author and Taylor and Francis Group www.informaworld.com.

Kevin R. Smith, "Animal Genetic Manipulation: A Utilitarian Response," *Bioethics* 16(1): 55–71, reprinted by permission of Blackwell Publishing Ltd.

Jeffrey Burkhardt, "The Inevitability of Animal Biotechnology? Ethics and the Scientific Attitude" in A. Holland and A. Johnson (eds.), *Animal Biotechnology and Ethics*. © 1998 Chapman & Hall, with kind permission from Springer Science and Business Media and the author.

Traci Warkentin. 2006. "Dis/integrating Animals: Ethical Dimensions of the Genetic Engineering of Animals for Human Consumption," *AI & Soc.* 20:82–102. Reprinted with permission.

Bernard E. Rollin, "On *Telos* and Genetic Engineering," from in *Animal Biotechnology and Ethics*, in A. Holland and A. Johnson (eds.). © 1998 Chapman & Hall, with kind permission from Springer Science and Business Media and the author.

Bernice Bovenkerk, Frans W. A. Brom, and Babs J. van den Bergh. 2002. "Brave New Birds: The Use of 'Animal Integrity' in Animal Ethics," *Hastings Center Report* 32(1): 16–22. Reprinted by kind permission of Bernice Bovenkerk and The Hastings Center.

Jes Lynning Harfeld. 2013. "Telos and the Ethics of Animal Farming," *Journal of Agricultural and Environmental Ethics* 23 (3): 691–709. Reprinted with permission.

Carl Zimmer. 2013. "Bringing Them Back to Life: The Revival of an Extinct Species Is No Longer a Fantasy," *National Geographic* 223 (4): 28. Reprinted with permission of National Geographic.

Dolly Jørgensen. 2013. "Reintroduction and De-extinction," *BioScience* 63(9): 719–720. Reprinted with permission.

Aldo Leopold, "Game and Wildlife Conservation," *The Condor*, vol. 34, no. 2 (Mar.–Apr., 1932), pp. 103–106, © Cooper Ornithological Society. Reprinted with permission.

Lawrence Cahoone. 2009. "Hunting as a Moral Good," *Environmental Values* 18: 67–89. Reprinted with permission.

Adapted with permission, from Marti Kheel, 1996. "The Killing Game: An Ecofeminist Critique of Hunting," *Journal of the Philosophy of Sport* 23(1):30–44.

Alastair S. Gunn. 2001. "Environmental Ethics and Trophy Hunting," *Ethics and the Environment* 6(1): 68–95. Reprinted by permission of Indiana University Press.

Ned Hettinger, "Exotic Species, Naturalisation, and Biological Nativism," *Environmental Values* 10(2): 193–224, 2001. Reprinted by permission of The White Horse Press.

Martin A. Schlaepfer, Dov F. Sax, and Julian D. Olden. 2010. "The Potential Conservation Value of Non-Native Species," *Conservation Biology* 24 (3): 428–437. Reprinted with permission.

Dale Peterson. 2005. "To Eat the Laughing Animal," in Peter Singer (ed), *In Defense of Animals*, New York: Basil Blackwell. Reprinted by permission of Blackwell Publishing Ltd.

Grace Clement, "The Ethic of Care and the Problem of Wild Animals" from http://cla.calpoly.edu/~jlynch/clement.htm. Reprinted by kind permission of the author.

Ben A. Minteer, and James P. Collins. 2013. "Ecological Ethics in Captivity: Balancing Values and Responsibilities in Zoo and Aquarium Research under Rapid Global Change," *ILAR Journal* 54 (1): 41–51. Reprinted with permission.

Lori Marino. 2014. "Cetacean Captivity," pp. 22–37 in Lori Gruen (ed.), *The Ethics of Captivity.* Oxford University Press, New York, NY. Reprinted with permission by Oxford University Press.

Marc Scheff. 2014. "Free the Elephants and Orcas in Captivity" (Science Agenda editorial). *Scientific American* 310 (3): 10. Reprinted with permission by Scientific American/Macmillan.

Michael Hutchins, Brandie Smith and Ruth Allard. 2003. "In Defense of Zoos and Aquariums: The Ethical Basis for Keeping Wild Animals in Captivity," *Journal of the American Veterinary Medical Association, JAVMA*, vol. 223, no. 7, October 1.

Chris Wemmer, "Opportunities Lost: Zoos and the Marsupial that Tried to be a Wolf," *Zoo Biology*, 21, 2002, Copyright © Chris Wemmer, 2002. Reprinted with permission of John Wiley & Sons, Inc.

Kristin L Vehrs. (Executive Director, Association of Zoos and Aquariums). 2014. "Elephants in Captivity" (reply to Scheff editorial, with Scientific American reply). *Scientific American* 310 (6): 8. Reprinted with permission from Kristin L. Vehrs, Executive Director, Association of Zoos and Aquariums (AZA).

Dale Jamieson. 2005. "Against Zoos," in Peter Singer (ed), *In Defense of Animals*, New York: Basil Blackwell. Reprinted by permission of Blackwell Publishing Ltd.

"Affection's Claim," in Konrad Lorenz: *Man Meets Dog*. Published by Routledge, London and New York. © 1983 Deutscher Taschenbuch Verlag, Munich/Germany. Reprinted with permission by Random House.

"The Pet World," from *THE OTHERS* by Paul Shepard. Copyright © 1996 by the author. Reproduced by permission of Island Press, Washington, D.C.

Anna Merz. 1998. "Hand-Raising a Rhino in the Wild," in L. Hogan, D. Metzger, B. Petersen, (eds.), *Intimate Nature: The Bond between Women and Animals*, Fawcett Books. © Anna Merz. Reproduced by kind permission of Anna Merz.

Freya Mathews, "Living with Animals," *Animal Issues* 1(1): 1–18. Reprinted by permission of the author. See www.freyamathews.com for the full text of the article.

Clare Palmer, "Killing Animals in Animal Shelters," from *Killing Animals*. Copyright 2006 by Board of Trustees of the University of Illinois. Used with permission of the University of Illinois Press.

Mark Rowlands. 2009. "The Structure of Evil," in Andrew Linzey (ed.), *The Link between Animal Abuse and Human Violence*. Sussex Academic Press: Portland, Oregon. Reprinted with permission from Sussex Academic Press.

Alan C. Brantley. 2009. "An FBI Perspective on Animal Cruelty," in in Andrew Linzey (ed.), *The Link between Animal Abuse and Human Violence*. Sussex Academic Press: Portland, Oregon. Reprinted with permission from Sussex Academic Press.

Bernard Rollin. 2009. "Ethics and Euthanasia, *The Canadian Veterinary Journal* 50(10: 1081–1086. Reprinted with permission.

Diane Leigh and Marilee Geyer. 2007. "Miracle of Life" and "Afterword," in *One at a Time: A Week in an American Animal Shelter*, No Voice Unheard; 4th ed. Reproduced by kind permission of the publisher, www.NoVoiceUnheard.org.

Tzachi Zamir. 2006. "The Moral Basis of Animal-Assisted Therapy," *Society and Animals* 14:2: 179–199. Reprinted with permission by Brill.

Steven M. Wise, "A Great Shout: Legal Rights for Great Apes," pp. 274–294 in B. B. Beck, T. S. Stoinski, et al. (eds.), reprinted from *Great Apes and Humans: The Ethics of Coexistence*, Washington, DC: Smithsonian Institution Press. Used by permission of the Smithsonian Institution. Copyright 2001.

Richard A. Posner, "Book Review: *Rattling the Cage: Toward Legal Rights for Animals* by Steven M. Wise," *The Yale Law Journal* 110: 527–41. Reproduced by kind permission of the author.

Richard A. Epstein. 2002. "The Dangerous Claims of the Animal Rights Movement," in *The Responsive Community*. Reprinted by kind permission of the author.

Christine M. Korsgaard (2013). "Personhood, Animals, and the Law," *Think* 12: 25–32. Reprinted with permission by Cambridge University Press.

Wesley V. Jamison, Caspar Wenk, and James V. Parker. 2000. "Every Sparrow that Falls: Understanding Animal Rights Activism as Functional Religion," *Society & Animals* 8:3. Reproduced by kind permission of Koninklijke Brill NV, www.brill.nl.

Tom Regan, "Understanding Animal Rights Violence," from *Defending Animal Rights*. Copyright 2001 by Board of Trustees of the University of Illinois. Used with permission of the University of Illinois Press.

Courtney L. Dillard. 2002. "Civil Disobedience: A Case Study in Factors of Effectiveness," *Society & Animals* 10:1. Reproduced by kind permission of Koninklijke Brill NV, www.brill.nl.

Peter Singer, "Ten Ways to Make a Difference," from *Ethics into Action*, 2000, pp. 194–192. Reprinted by permission of Rowman and Littlefield Publishers, Inc. and the author.

Bruce Friedrich, and Matt Ball. 2009. *The Animal Activist's Handbook: Maximizing Our Positive Impact in Today's World*. Lantern Books, Brooklyn, New York. Reprinted with permission of Lantern Books.

General Introduction

Animal Ethics: A Sketch of How It Developed and Where It Is Now

"All human communities have involved animals."

Mary Midgley, *Animals and Why They Matter* (1984: 112)

Historians estimate that the "hunter-gatherer" stage of human societies began around 500,000 years ago and lasted until about 11,000 years ago (Serpell 1999: 40). While there are problems with using living or recent hunter-gatherers as representatives of our pre-agricultural ancestors, a "remarkable degree of consistency" in attitudes and beliefs toward animals exists among present-day hunter-gatherer societies. Animals are perceived as being fully rational, sentient, and intelligent, with bodies animated by non-corporeal spirits or souls (Serpell 1999: 40). Hunted animals must therefore be treated with proper respect and consideration. Serpell locates the origin of contemporary hunting rules and rituals in these beliefs (Serpell 1999: 41). These respectful beliefs may have been fueled in pre-historic times by the fact that a number of carnivores were large enough to prey on stone-age humans. These carnivores include some of the sabre-tooth cats, as well as the prehistoric wolves, hyenas, and bears (Kruuk 2002: 103–14).

Agriculture and animal husbandry began roughly 11,000 years ago, producing a "dramatic shift in the balance of power between humans and the animals they depended on for food." At first animal guardian spirits were elevated to the status of "zoomorphic gods" (Serpell 1999: 43). For example, the first known written expression of prohibition of cruelty to animals is found in ancient Egypt, and this prohibition seems to be at least partly based on the belief that "all creatures were manifestations of the divine" (LaRue 1991: 3). Some gods assumed animal form. The list of sacred animals included "the vulture, hawks, swallows, turtles, scorpions, serpents" (LaRue 1991: 3). Chapter 125 of the Egyptian *Book of the Dead* prohibited mistreatment of animals (LaRue 1991: 34). While the ancient Egyptians ate animals, humans were expected to treat other creatures with respect and kindness, "for in the afterlife the treatment of animals would be included in actions to be judged" (LaRue 1991: 35). Cattle, particularly bulls, were the preeminent models for power and fertility. In Egypt, as well as other ancient civilizations, both dogs and snakes were strongly associated with death and healing. In early Mesopotamia, sheep began to fulfill an important surrogate religious role as substitute cattle (Schwabe 1994: 48–9).

This respectful relationship was not to last. As Serpell (1999: 43) points out, over time the connections between the gods and animals became more and more tenuous. The gods became increasingly associated with the agricultural cycle, and wholesale animal sacrifice was used as a way to please them. Religious belief systems became increasingly hierarchical.

This change was slow and complex, as can be seen in the intermittent history of vegetarianism (Dombrowski 1984: 1–2). Vegetarian communities may have existed as long as 8,000 years ago in the Mesolithic period.[1] Ryder affirms that by the time of the Middle Kingdom in Egypt, vegetarianism was common at least among priests, and neither pork nor beef was widely eaten (Ryder 1998: 6). The Greek poet Hesiod told of a Golden Age in which the first race of human beings were free from all sorrow, toil, grief, and evil. They were fed out of a boundless cornucopia of fruit. This Age of

Cronus was followed by other, less idyllic ages, but the nostalgia for earlier times remained into the time of the pre-Socratic philosopher Empedocles (495–435 BCE), who said that to kill an animal for food or sacrifice was "the greatest abomination among men" (Dombrowski 1984: 19–22).

The mathematical genius and mystic Pythagoras most probably lived in the sixth century BCE. In common with Hindu, Buddhist, and many Aboriginal societies, Pythagoras taught the doctrine of the transmigration of souls between animals and humans. He seems to have based his vegetarianism on this religious belief, as well as on concerns for health and basic ethics. These ethical concerns included the affirmation of moderation and care for animals. Although there is disagreement over the extent of his vegetarianism (Steiner 2005: 48–50), according to at least one ancient commentator even in moments of great mathematical achievements Pythagoras remained true to his vegetarian principles by sacrificing an ox made of dough (Dombrowski 1984: 38). Pythagoras' ethical concerns were founded on a principle of moderation. He believed that we have no right to cause unnecessary suffering. Animals have the same soul as we do; those who senselessly kill animals are murderers (Dombrowski 1984: 46).

While Socrates (470–399 BCE) was generally indifferent to what he ate (Dombrowski 1984: 55), Plato (428–347 BCE), strongly influenced by Pythagoras, affirmed both that those living in the Age of Cronus were vegetarians and that philosophers should be vegetarians (Dombrowski 1984: 58ff). Animals share with humans the part of the soul which is mortal but not intrinsically irrational (*Timaeus* 69c-77c, 90e-92c). Nevertheless Plato does not condemn hunting, butchering, or raising livestock for consumption.

Aristotle (384–322 BCE) not only permitted meat-eating but seemed to have been opposed to vegetarianism (Dombrowski 1984: 65–6). He affirmed that in each animal "there is something natural and beautiful" (*On the Parts of Animals*, Bk. I, ch. 5) and taught that animals do possess sentient souls. However, because animals lacked reason, for Aristotle they had no moral status (Steiner 2005: 57–92). Augustine and Thomas Aquinas both followed Aristotle in this view, thus greatly influencing the development of the Christian view of animals (Ryder 1998: 8). For example, Thomas Aquinas taught that "[the] life of animals . . . is preserved not for themselves, but for man" (*Summa Theologica*, Q64,1,1466).

Beginning in the first century CE, Stoic philosophers believed that *logos* (reason) was both divine and a cosmic law and that everything serves some purpose. Thus animals cannot be members of our moral community because they lack reason; nevertheless, their usefulness to human beings reflects divine intention (Boersema 2001: 202–3). While the Romans Seneca and Ovid advocated vegetarianism, animals simply did not count morally for most Romans (Dombrowski 1984: 85).

Plutarch (45–125 CE) was a Greek priest at Delphi. Dombrowski notes that he may have been the first to advocate vegetarianism on grounds of universal benevolence, rather than on the basis of transmigration of souls (Dombrowski 1984: 86–7). He strove to convince the Stoics that animals are indeed rational, arguing that sentience implies a reasoning mind through which to experience sentience (Preece 2005: 55). Plutarch was the only early thinker whose beliefs have had a demonstrable influence in later ages (Boersema 2001: 208). Plutarch suggested that sentiency is a matter of degree (Dombrowski 1984: 88). For Plutarch the difference between domesticated and wild (and harmful) animals is morally significant; we may not harm harmless animals. "Plutarch challenged his antagonists to use their teeth to rend a lamb asunder and consume it raw, as true carnivores do" (Boersema 2001: 209). Overall, Plutarch exhibited a love of animals, "but never at the expense of the human race" (Boersema 2001: 210).

The great neo-Platonic philosopher Plotinus (204–270 CE) as well as his distinguished pupil Porphyry (232-c.305 CE) were vegetarians. Plotinus affirmed transmigration of souls and animals' capacity for suffering. But Porphyry went far beyond these affirmations. According to Dombrowski, he deserves recognition for having provided "the most comprehensive and subtly reasoned treatment of vegetarianism by an ancient philosopher" (Dombrowski 1984: 107). He not only offers the best possible reasons for vegetarianism but he collects the best reasons against it (Dombrowski 1984: 109–19). Nevertheless, despite the views of thinkers such as Plutarch and Porphyry, the attitude toward nature and animals in ancient cultures was largely dependent upon whether nature or the animals in question were perceived as helpful or harmful to human beings.

During medieval times, many were deeply ambivalent toward animals.[2] The importance of animals was taken for granted, and as a consequence animal symbolism was pervasive. But over the centuries there were changes in how animals were perceived. For early Christians animals were profoundly different from humans. But by the twelfth century, thinkers began to share the Greco-Roman view of humans as existing on a continuum with animals. Despite these changes, lay culture continued to attribute human traits and feelings to animals throughout the medieval period (Cohen 1994: 68).

Salisbury notes that since saints were considered ideal humans, the stories of the interactions between saints and animals can illuminate the medieval understanding of what it means to be human. Many early Christian saints showed deep concern for animals – for example, in rescuing animals from hunters, talking with animals, sharing their food, and caring for sick or wounded animals. St Benedict (c. 480–547), the founder of the Benedictine order, stated that monks should not eat meat except when sick. (This rule was ignored, however, after the reinterpretation of Christianity by Thomas Aquinas in the thirteenth century.) In the early Middle Ages most interactions between saints and animals demonstrated the power of saints to suspend the bestial nature of animals. Some animals even acquired human qualities. Animals are grateful, kind, and bring food to saints. Because animals were so different from people, "any human-like behaviour on the part of the animal was considered miraculous in itself" (Salisbury 1994: 173). The prevalence of such medieval tales indicates that a mark of saintliness was the caring for our fellow creatures (Waddell 1970).

In the twelfth century, the early medieval paradigm began to break down. Saints continued to overturn beastly behavior, but now animals begin to show evidence of reason. St Francis of Assisi (c. 1181–1226) saw all creatures as mirrors of the creator. Legend tells of him prevailing upon a wolf to stop eating townspeople (Ryder 1989: 33). Saints even save animals' lives without expecting a human return. Thus animal lives had some intrinsic value. The Hermit of Eskedale was killed in 1159 after sabotaging a hunt (Ryder 1998: 34–5). An extreme example of a saint's cult that eliminated the lines between humans and animals is that of Saint Guinefort, a greyhound that was unjustly killed after rescuing a child. He was venerated as a saint that could be called upon to protect children (Salisbury 1994: 175). In the thirteenth century the Inquisition attempted to stamp out the veneration. Animals were kept as pets, considered to possess human virtues, and were even tried by the courts and convicted of crimes. Masses were said for horses, and sick animals were shown the eucharistic bread to cure them (Ryder 1998: 14). Despite these medieval practices, it remains true that the Bible provides conflicting views of the human–animal relationship. Thus the larger question of whether traditional Christianity offers an ethic of compassion toward animals involves the question of whether Christianity is a "fixed set of canonical doctrines or a living phenomenon that can change with the times" (Steiner 2005: 113ff).

The sixteenth and seventeenth centuries in Europe were a time of great social change. The confluence of early capitalism, the beginnings of modern science, the dualistic thinking expressed by Rene Descartes (1596–1650) and others, as well as the emergence of Protestantism, helped ensure that Christians ended any lingering deification of nature. Humans asserted their own importance, throwing off their medieval belief in the unity of creation and seeking to deny their own animal natures by emphasizing the boundaries between man and animals. Renaissance writers insisted on the uniqueness and importance of human beings. Nature, including animals, was no longer an organic whole but dead, soulless matter, indeed a machine, from which the minds and immortal souls of human beings were entirely distinct. All things were created principally for the benefit and pleasure of "man." According to Descartes and many others, human beings were distinguished from animals by the possession of speech and reason, the capacity for moral responsibility, and an immortal soul. Bestiality became a capital offense in 1534 and, except for a brief period, remained so until 1861 (Thomas 1983: 30). Cruel medieval practices such as bear-baiting, bull-baiting, and persecution of cats continued, to be joined by the dissection of living animals (vivisection) for scientific purposes.

Thomas asserts that "the most powerful argument for the Cartesian position was that it was the best possible rationalization for the way man actually treated animals" (1983: 34). The view that there was a total qualitative difference between humans and animals was "propounded in every pulpit" and underlay everyone's behavior (Thomas 1983: 35–6). Yet there were prominent dissenters throughout these centuries, including the vegetarian Leonardo da Vinci, who purchased birds in the marketplace to free them; the essayist Michel de Montaigne, who attacked cruelty in his essays of 1580; and William Shakespeare, who vividly depicted the suffering of animals. Martin Luther and John Calvin expressed concern for God's creatures. Sir Isaac Newton (1642–1727) invented cat flaps, and the great English philosopher John Locke (1632–1704) affirmed that children should be brought up to show kindness to animals. British Chief Justice Sir Matthew Hale wrote in 1661: "I have ever thought that there was a certain degree of justice due from man to the creatures, as from man to man" (Ryder 1998: 13–14). And in 1683 Thomas Tyron, a Christian theologian, produced what may be the first printed use of the term "rights" in connection with animals (Munro 2000: 9).

Despite these examples of compassion for animals, in the seventeenth century the most common view held by intellectuals was that "beasts" had an inferior kind of reason which included sensibility, imagination, and memory but no power of reflection (Thomas 1983: 32–3). Thus, perhaps not surprisingly, the reform movements of the sixteenth and seventeenth centuries were based on the same ideology of human domination as were the oppressions they sought to reform. Slavery was attacked because people were being treated like animals, but the slavery of animals was taken for granted. The main dispute during this period was thus between those who held that all humanity had dominion over the creatures and those who believed that this dominion should be confined to a privileged group of humans (Thomas 1983: 48–9).

But at the same time there were social changes which worked against the idea of human dominion. For example, pet-keeping had been fashionable among the well-to-do as well as among religious orders in the Middle Ages, but it was in the sixteenth and seventeenth centuries that pets seem to have established themselves as a normal feature of the middle-class household (Thomas 1983: 110). Pets included monkeys, tortoises, otters, rabbits, and squirrels, as well as hares, mice, hedgehogs, bats, and toads. Cage-birds were also common, including canaries as well as wild birds of every kind. Gradually, the idea that tamed animals were property was developed. Pets were distinguished by being allowed into the house and by going to church with their human companions, by being given individual personal names, and by never being eaten. The spread of pet-keeping created the psychological foundation for the view that some animals were entitled to moral consideration (Thomas 1983: 110–19).

In England, the growth of towns and the emergence of an industrial order in which animals became increasingly marginal to production were significant factors in the development of concern for animals' rights (Thomas 1983: 181). The reformist ideas were expressed either by well-to-do townspeople or by educated country clergymen (Thomas 1983: 182). The professional middle classes were unsympathetic to the warlike traditions of the aristocracy, which had valued hunting because it simulated warfare, and cock-fighting and bear-baiting because they represented private combat (Thomas 1983: 181). By the later seventeenth century the human-centered (anthropocentric) tradition itself was being eroded. According to Thomas, this erosion is one of the great revolutions in modern Western thought, a revolution to which many factors contributed (Thomas 1983: 166).

Thomas cites factors such as the growth of natural history, which gradually resulted in classifications of animals according to the animals' structure alone, as well as a delight in the world's diversity at least somewhat independent of human standards. Second, people's actual experience of animals on the farms and in their houses conflicted with the theological orthodoxies of the time. Animals were everywhere and consequently were often thought of as individuals, since herds were small. Shepherds knew the faces of their sheep and some farmers could trace stolen cattle by distinguishing their hoof prints (Thomas 1983: 95). Anthropocentrism was still the prevailing outlook, but by the eighteenth century non-anthropocentric sensibilities became much more widely dispersed and were more explicitly supported by the religious and philosophical teaching of the time (Thomas 1983:

174–5). Cruelty to animals began to be regularly denounced. Ryder speculates that one reason for this moral awakening was the extreme cruelty which had been practiced in England for centuries (Ryder 1998: 16). English reformists targeted bull-baiting and bear-baiting, the treatment of horses, the treatment of cattle being driven to slaughter through the streets of London, and the traditional Shrove Tuesday sport of tying a cockerel to a stake and stoning him to death (Ryder 1998: 16). The campaign against cruelty to animals was enhanced by a new emphasis on sensation and feeling as the true basis of moral status (Thomas 1983: 180), as expounded in the utilitarianism of Jeremy Bentham. Once it had been accepted that animals had feelings and therefore should be treated with kindness, it seemed increasingly repugnant to kill them for meat (Thomas 1983: 288). From about 1790 there developed a highly articulate vegetarian movement (Thomas 1983: 295). An increasing number of people felt uneasy about killing animals for food, and so slaughterhouses were concealed from the public eye (Thomas 1983: 300).

By the later eighteenth century the most common view was that animals could indeed think and reason, though in an inferior way. A number of thinkers affirmed the kinship between man and "beast." Humphry Primatt published his dissertation *The Duty of Mercy and the Sin of Cruelty to Brute Animals*, which presented almost all the arguments used in later centuries (Munro 2000: 10). There was an increasing tendency to credit animals with reason, intelligence, language, and almost every other human quality (Thomas 1983: 129). Perhaps most decisive was the revelation by comparative anatomy of the similarity between the structure of human and animal bodies (Thomas 1983: 129). The growing belief in the social evolution of humankind encouraged the view that humans were only animals who had managed to better themselves (Thomas 1983: 132).

Christians continued to be mixed in their attitude toward animals. In 1772 James Granger preached against cruelty to animals and received "almost universal disgust" at his daring to discuss dogs and cats from the pulpit (Passmore 1975: 200). On the other hand, a substantial number of biblical commentators took the view that animals would be eventually restored in heaven to the perfection they had enjoyed before the Fall (Thomas 1983: 139). The idea of animal immortality made more headway in England than anywhere else during this period (Thomas 1983: 140–1). In 1788 the vegetarian John Wesley, founder of the evangelical movement of Methodism, preached a famous sermon entitled "The Great Deliverance." In it Wesley proclaimed that the "whole brute creation" will be delivered into a far higher degree of vigor, strength, and swiftness than they had enjoyed on earth (Preece 2005: 163).

Courts in both Germany and Britain began to punish cruelty to animals on the basis that while animals themselves had no rights, maltreatment of animals violated the direct duty to God (Maehle 1994: 95–8). Eighteenth-century American writers Thomas Paine and Hermann Daggett affirmed the moral status of animals. British politicians introduced a bill to outlaw bull-baiting in 1800, but the bill was defeated. The Lord Chancellor Thomas Erskine, who had once physically attacked a man he found beating a horse, joined with Richard Martin to produce a successful bill in 1822 to make it an offense to wantonly beat, abuse, or ill-treat any horse, donkey, sheep, cow, or other cattle (unless it was the property of the offender). "Known as Martin's Act, this was the first national law against cruelty to animals enacted by full parliamentary process," according to Richard Ryder, though bull-baiting was not stopped until 1835 (1998: 19).

The organized animal welfare movement emerged at this time. One reason for the timing of this emergence was that after the Reformation in northern Europe "good works became increasingly secularized" (Ryder 1998: 25). Also the new general affluence of the period, teamed with increasing democracy, allowed compassionate people to institutionalize their concerns, whether it be opposed to the slave trade or to ill-treatment of animals. In addition, the Industrial Revolution was reducing the dependence on animals, particularly on horses and dogs (Boersema 2001: 237).

In 1824 a group of Members of Parliament as well as three churchmen met to establish two committees: one to publish literature to influence public opinion and the other to adopt measures for inspecting the treatment of animals. In its first year the Society for the Prevention of Cruelty to Animals (SPCA) brought "150 prosecutions for cruelty and engaged in campaigns against bull-baiting, dog-fighting, the abuse of horses and cattle and the cruelties of the main London meat market at Smithfield" (Ryder 1998: 21). The society also condemned painful experiments on animals. Shortly thereafter societies were formed elsewhere in northern Europe. In 1840 Queen Victoria "granted the society the royal prefix," so that it became known as the "Royal Society for the Prevention of Cruelty to Animals" (RSPCA). Four of the society's founders were already well-known reformers who opposed slavery; two opposed the death penalty for minor offenses (Ryder 1998: 21–2). Kalechofsky (1992: 64) notes that throughout the nineteenth century there were "porous boundaries between the various reform causes, and those involved in anti-slavery, prison reform, and child abuse reform were often the same people involved in the women's movement, anti-vivisection, slum clearance, and the hygiene or sanitary movement." This observation works against the thesis argued by Turner (1980: 36–8), and still widely accepted, that concern for animals arose as a displaced compassion for human suffering. Finsen and Finsen (1994: 28ff) name Turner's view the "Displacement Thesis" and propose instead the "Extension Thesis": namely, that those who are concerned about one exploited group will often extend that concern to other groups.

The greatest campaign of the Victorian era in Britain was against the use of live animals in experiments. Such campaigns started as an outcry against demonstrations on cats and dogs by a French experimenter, and were augmented by reports of unanesthetized horses being tied down and slowly dissected by students. Protests were made to the French authorities. In England the Cruelty to Animals Act was passed in 1876, requiring licenses and certificates from the government. The bill was an inconvenience to researchers, though few prosecutions under the act were successful. After much public agitation, a Royal Commission recommended some improvements to the administration of the Act (Ryder 1998: 26–8).

Women were prominent in this anti-vivisection movement, beginning with Descartes' niece, Catherine, who famously rejected his doctrine of the "animal-machine" (Kalechofsky 1992: 61). To undermine women's effectiveness, nineteenth-century scientists viewed women as infantile, animal-like, and belonging to nature rather than to civilization. In contrast, the scientific "intellectual edifice" was identified as masculine, logical, and rational; anyone who opposed animal research was considered irrational, sentimental, and "womanly." These views were shown to be false by the many knowledgeable and intellectually powerful women who combated the scientific cruelty of the time (Kalechofsky 1992: 70).

Finsen and Finsen point to the anti-vivisection movement as the ancestor of the animal rights movement, because the anti-vivisection movement, in contrast to the humane movement as represented by the RSPCA, "challenged an entire institution" (1994: 38). However, at the same time, the medical profession was attaining greater political power due to the successes in experimental medicine in the 1890s in connection with medical microbiology. The medical microbiology revolution required numerous forms of animal experimentation (Finsen and Finsen 1994: 39). For these and other reasons, as detailed by Finsen and Finsen, "the antivivisection movement ceased to be a vital and mass movement after the turn of the century," since it based its case not only on the immorality of vivisection but also on its scientific worthlessness (1994: 41). Complicating the assessment of vivisection is the presence of anthropomorphism within the laboratory as well as outside it: experimental animals were at times assimilated by the investigators to asylum inmates, infants, and patients in a hypnotic trance. The questions of which procedures are legitimate and who has the authority to intervene on behalf of the animal or human were and are entangled (White 2005).

While much of the U.S. concern for animals derives from British precedents, a body of laws protecting animals had in fact been approved by the Massachusetts Bay Colony in 1641. Anti-cruelty laws were passed early in the nineteenth century in several states, but organizations did not form until the 1866 birth of the American Society for the Prevention of Cruelty to Animals (ASPCA). Its founder, Henry Bergh, "rapidly became notorious for defending abused and overworked carriage horses in the streets of New York City." Bergh achieved many successful prosecutions, including those for cruel treatment of livestock, cock-fighting, and dog-fighting. George Angel I founded the Massachusetts SPCA, with an emphasis on humane education. Societies modeled on Bergh's soon cropped up all over the country. Shortly thereafter the American Society for the Prevention of Cruelty to Children was formed. And, as was the case in England, many of the American animal welfare pioneers were active in the anti-slavery movement.

However, the American anti-vivisection movement was unsuccessful. It appears that proponents of animal research had learned from the British lesson and formed an effective lobbying force for vivisection (Finsen and Finsen 1994: 48–9). Some vivisectors portrayed themselves as rational men of science whose work was being retarded by "middle-class, city-based female 'cranks' in humane societies" (Munro 2000: 18). Ryder speculates that the pioneering spirit of America may have welcomed the innovations of science more enthusiastically than did British culture. He notes also that American anti-vivisectionists lacked the equivalent of royal support (Ryder 1998: 28). During this same period, as Munro explains, the animal protection movement in Australia had begun with the 1873 formation of the Animal Protection Society of New South Wales. Due to circumstances peculiar to Australia, the animal protection movement developed in concert with the environmental movement, the first joint campaign being the elevation of the koala from vermin and a commercial fur source to the "national pet" (Munro 2000: 14).

Vegetarianism was adopted by some during this period in both Britain and America, the word itself being coined in 1847 at Ramsgate, England, from the Latin word *vegetare*, meaning "to grow." By the end of the century, vegetarianism was established among a "minority of the middle class," including Henry David Thoreau, George Bernard Shaw, Susan B. Anthony, Anna Kingsford, Howard Williams, and Henry Salt. The great Romantic poet Percy Bysshe Shelley urged, "Never take any substance into the stomach that once had life" (Kenyon-Jones 2001: 121). Mohandas Gandhi in the twentieth century attributed his commitment to vegetarianism to reading Henry Salt's *Plea for Vegetarianism* (1897) (Finsen and Finsen 1994: 25).

After World War I the animal welfare movement seemed to lose its mass appeal in both the U.S. and Britain. There were undoubtedly several reasons for this decline. It may be that incorporating meat into the diet during periods of disease and war was thought to be important for human health. Ryder comments that wars tend to revive the view that worrying about suffering is cowardly; compassion is dismissed as weakness and effeminacy. In any case, those who called for bans on the exploitation of animals tended to be regarded as cranks or extremists (Ryder 1998: 28–9). Animal welfare organizations in Britain and America declined into charities for lost or abandoned dogs and cats, ignoring the "steady increase in the applied technology of cruelty in the laboratory, meat and wild-killing industries" (Ryder 1998: 29), Henry Salt (1851–1939) in Britain being an exception.[3] Although the National Anti-Vivisection Society was founded in 1929, significant progress in the U.S. did not occur until the 1950s, when the Animal Welfare Institute and the Humane Society of the United States were founded. The Society for Animal Protective Legislation, founded in 1955, achieved the passage of the Humane Slaughter Act and the 1959 Wild Horses Act. During this period the International Society for Animal Rights and the Fund for Animals also came into being. In general, however, the postwar period in both Britain and the United States saw little progress in improving conditions for animals. Finsen and Finsen (1994: 3) assert that one reason for this lack of progress was that the humane movement had "promoted kindness and the elimination of cruelty without challenging the assumption of human superiority or the institutions that reflect that assumption," but they also note that the political climate was very conservative during this period.

Beginning with the 1960s in Britain, the humane concern for animals began to be transformed into the animal rights movement, which insists on justice and fairness in our treatment of animals. Guither (1998: 4–5) argues that the modern animal rights movement is "radically different" from the earlier anti-vivisection groups and the traditional humane societies. While this may be an overstatement, it is certainly true that many advocates of animal rights affirm the moral status of animals and oppose all ways in which animals are confined and used by human beings (1998: 4–5). One expression of this demand for justice was the formation of the Hunt Saboteurs in 1963. This British group "appears to be the first organization to speak openly and uncompromisingly of members as proponents of rights of animals in the modern sense" (Finsen and Finsen 1994: 55). The group employed confrontational tactics of direct action; it also represented a significant broadening of the animal movement to the working class. In 1964 Ruth Harrison published *Animal Machines,* a book which initiated much of the public concern for the welfare of farm animals. She is believed to have been the first to label confinement livestock and poultry production as "factory farming," calling attention to the fact that animal agriculture had come to be conducted behind closed doors (Ryder 1998: 30). In response to these concerns, the British Parliament set up an official committee of inquiry made up of scientists and concerned citizens, which issued the influential Brambell Report in 1965. The Report recommended certain mandatory standards and called for the government to establish regulations defining animal suffering; it set the stage for animal welfare reform in the United Kingdom and other northern European countries.

A powerful collection of essays titled *Animals, Men and Morals* was published in 1971 by a group of young philosophers and sociologists at Oxford, employing the new term "speciesism," coined by Richard Ryder. Peter Singer reviewed the book and was invited to expand his review into a book of his own. The resulting work was *Animal Liberation,* published in 1975, known as the first philosophic text to include recipes—vegetarian, of course. The book included clear and powerful argumentation together with well-documented descriptions of the conditions of animals in factory farms and research laboratories. Parliamentarian Douglas Houghton with others led the struggle to "put animals into politics," a campaign which issued in the (British) Animals (Scientific Procedures) Act of 1986 (Ryder 1998: 33).

Overall there was a marked increase in direct action, both legal and illegal, during the 1970s and 1980s. Ronnie Lee launched the Animal Liberation Front (ALF) in England in 1972, leading to raids on animal laboratories, factory farms, and abattoirs all over Europe and North America, and the International Fund for Animal Welfare broadened the move to include wildlife (Ryder 1998: 34). However, the climate of opinion changed in Britain during the years of Margaret Thatcher as prime minister, and the animal rights movement began to be looked at as a subversive threat to capitalism (Ryder 1998: 35). Acts of violence by groups such as the ALF led to a backlash within the animal rights movement as well as to long prison terms (Finsen and Finsen 1994: 101–2).

In the 1990s the British-led European movement again became active. Partly due to the effectiveness of the organization Compassion in World Farming, farm animals succeeded laboratory animals as the main focus among European animal welfarists in the 1990s. "Massive protests in British ports in 1994 against the exports of sheep and calves . . . escalated into self-sustaining grassroots local movements that continued for over a year" (Ryder 1998: 35). Prime Minister John Major invited animal welfarists to Downing Street, and the European Union Commission voted to phase out by 2006 the keeping of calves in crates in Europe. By 1995, 4.5 percent of the British population was vegetarian (Ryder 1998: 37).

In the United States, Peter Singer and Tom Regan emerged as strong voices for animal liberation and animal rights, respectively, in the 1970s and 1980s. A number of organizations were formed, among them People for the Ethical Treatment of Animals (PETA), Trans-Species Unlimited, Farm Animal Reform Movement, Mobilization for Animals, and In Defense of Animals. The principal target of reform in the 1980s in the U.S. was the use of animals in laboratories. Two scandals in 1981 and 1984 helped lead to the upgrading of the oversight of research facilities and some reduction of pain and distress in procedures. Henry Spira led effective protests against the seizure of unwanted dogs from pounds for use in research laboratories.

The U.S. ALF is a group of loosely knit cells which has conducted controversial direct action using illegal tactics. In the United States the ALF has consistently held to a distinction between property damage and violence toward living beings. However, there have been ALF actions in which the methods used placed people in danger, and researchers who have been targeted claim psychological and professional harm (Finsen and Finsen 1994: 98–106). Finsen and Finsen point out that whether or not one agrees with the tactics of the ALF, the information brought to light has in fact increased public awareness of what happens in some laboratories (1994: 106). Nevertheless, the cost is high, not only in property damage but in deaths among some released animals and, in a few cases, physical injury to humans.

Ryder observes (1998: 41) that disputes between those supporting animal rights versus those supporting animal welfare have sapped some of the movement's energies in the United States. Meanwhile, the factory-farming industry has rapidly expanded in both the United States and the world. Billions of farm animals are raised indoors in "conditions largely unknown to the general public" (Finsen and Finsen 1994: 5). Fortunately, not all of these changes in animal agriculture are negative for animal welfare, though many are (Fraser et al. 2001: 93–4). Overall, the U.S. animal welfare movement is a collection of national and local organizations that often do not work together due to concerns for organizational sovereignty and program purity. In the last few years, however, groups such as the Animals Voice and the Institute for Animals and Society have enabled the animal ethics movement to be more effective.[4]

Contemporary Concerns and Future Directions

As noted in the Foreword by Bernard E. Rollin, since the mid-twentieth century, animal agricultural practices have undergone major changes. Ryder (1998: 42) notes that those concerned with animals have come to see the fates of these animals as increasingly determined by the "moral blindness" found in the policies of many multinational corporations and international structures such as the World Trade Organization (WTO) (Ryder 1998: 42). John Hodges, together with many others, identifies the focus on profit, reduced unit costs, and the material prosperity of the individual as key contributors to global animal suffering, particularly in agriculture (Hodges and Han 2000: 260–1).

Fortunately there are many who seek to include environmental and human rights concerns in international trade. It is possible that animal welfare can be taken into account even under existing WTO rules: Article XX of the "General Agreement" says that measures necessary to protect public morals and human, animal, or plant health have priority over other agreements (Appleby 2003: 170). In 2014 the WTO ruled that non-trade concerns, such as animal welfare, can restrict trade and still be in line with international trade law (www.ifaw.org). The WTO upheld the European Union's ban on the import of seal pelts, seal oil, and seal meat on moral grounds.

In general, animal ethics is a subject marked with ambivalence. A 2001 study of meat livestock farmers and consumers in the Netherlands indicated that both groups show ambivalence as a result of discrepancies between perceptions and behavior (Velde et al. 2002). Another study, conducted in Scotland in 1998, found that while 76% of respondents stated that they were concerned about the possible mistreatment or suffering of farm animals, only 34% avoided certain food products on animal welfare grounds. It is estimated that only 10% of U.K. food consumers take an active interest in how their food is produced (McEachern 2002). Complicating the assessment of animal agriculture is the frequent portrayal of the animal producer as wholly driven by the profit motive and hence as much worse than the medical researcher. According to Paul Thompson, this portrayal is inaccurate (Thompson 2004). Lund and Olsson (2006) argue that while many types of modern agriculture do have negative consequences for animal welfare and for the environment, sustainable agriculture can be beneficial for both. However, a 2015 article in the *New York Times*, "U.S. Research Lab Lets Livestock Suffer in Quest for Profit" (http://nyti.ms/1AEPr4J), paints a very disturbing picture of the taxpayer-supported U.S. Meat Animal Research Center in Nebraska, which has one central mission: helping producers of beef, pork, and lamb turn a higher profit. Only the growing consumer demand for humanely raised products seems to have the potential to improve the lives of animals used for meat.

Despite these obstacles to improvements in animal welfare, there are potentially hopeful factors. One important element is the view of the relationship between the divine and animal realms in the various world religions; new attitudes and scriptural interpretation are emerging. Many now believe that the Abrahamic traditions are properly understood not as being anthropocentric, but as theocentric: God, not man, is at the center as the ultimate source of meaning (Patton 2000: 408). Despite the fact that the Jewish and Christian traditions have affirmed that only human beings are created in God's image, numerous passages from the Hebrew and Islamic scriptures convey God's "fierce and tender devotion" to animals (Patton 2000: 409–13, 434). In Patton's felicitous phrase, animals display a "joyous devotion to the One who brought them into being" (Patton 2000: 434). Patton recounts the Russian Orthodox Father Thomas Hopko's affirmation of the "rabbithood of God": "There is an aspect of God's Self that at creation expressed itself as a rabbit, and nothing can better reveal that particular aspect of the divine nature than a real, living rabbit" (Patton 2000: 427). Novel reflections such as these may eventually prove to have a powerful effect on the treatment of animals.

In terms of philosophy, David DeGrazia (1999: 125–9) has identified several areas of "unrealized potential" for the future of animal ethics. One such area is found in the work of feminist theorists, who can contribute their powerful moral opposition to oppression as well as their incisive ability to analyze the ideology of speciesism and the various rationalizations for practices which harm animals. DeGrazia also affirms the value of a virtue ethics approach to animal ethics, developed at length so far only by Steve Sapontzis.[5] Virtue ethics emphasizes the importance of character and attitudes: our actions express what kind of people we are. For example, disrespectful treatment of animals may not always involve harm to an animal but rather may express our own growing willingness to exploit animals (DeGrazia 1999: 125–9). An example can be found in the creation in 2000 of a "transgenic artwork" in the form of a green fluorescent rabbit.[6] The artist, Eduardo Kac, a professor at the School of the Art Institute of Chicago, teamed up with French geneticists to produce the rabbit by injecting rabbit zygotes with a fluorescent protein gene derived from jellyfish. Such use of a living creature as a "new art form" seems to many to be disrespectful and sensationalist. The rabbit died before she could be brought to the U.S. The science writer Emily Anthes has written *Frankenstein's Cat* (1994) and weighs the ethical implications of scientists' experiments to transform animals with biotechnology.

Finsen and Finsen (1994: 257) comment that the animal rights movement has had some impact to date, in the process "arousing intense opposition from [extremely powerful] industries with vested economic interests in the status quo." They join a number of other writers in identifying the reform/ abolition split as the crucial distinction among members of the animal rights movement. This split is often summarized in the question: Should we work for larger cages or empty cages? The reformists usually want to work within the system to improve the conditions for animals, whereas the abolitionists work to eliminate all uses of animals that they see as causing pain and suffering (Guither 1998: 10). In the Foreword to this book, Bernard Rollin allies himself with reform, affirming that the animal ethics movement is dynamic, growing, and influential. A useful computer-supported interactive learning tool has recently been developed for university and professional training which may aid interested persons to identify their own approach to animal ethics (www.aedilemma.net).

The reason for our treatment of animals has never been a mystery. As Ryder comments in his recent book *The Political Animal*, "the simple truth is that we exploit the other animals and cause them suffering because we are more powerful than they are" (1998: 51). The editors hope that this anthology will stimulate reflection on the misuse as well as the appropriate use of human power. Such reflection will both enrich the human relationship with the nonhuman world and contribute to better lives for animals.

Notes

1. Thomas points out that the tradition that humans were originally vegetarian is ancient and worldwide. He states that it "may reflect the actual practice of our remote ancestors, for apes are largely vegetarian" (1983: 288–9).
2. For articles discussing Christian, Jewish, and Islamic interpretations of scripture as it relates to animals, see Part Four of this volume. See also Paul Waudau's (2002) *Discussion of Traditional Christian Views in the Specter of Speciesism: Buddhist and Christian Views of Animals*, New York: Oxford University Press.
3. Both Peter Singer and Tom Regan have identified Henry Salt as an important influence on their thought.

4. The Institute for Animals and Society, www.animalsandsociety.org, is an independent research and educational organization, working to advance the status of animals in public policy and promote the study of human–animal relationships. The Animals Voice publishes the *Animals Voice Magazine*, www.animals-voice.com. A current annotated list of courses concerning animals and society is available at www.crle.org/prog_courses_main.asp.
5. S. F. Sapontzis (1987) *Morals, Reason and Animals*, Philadelphia: Temple University Press.
6. http://www.ekac.org/gfpbunny.html; Eduardo Kac. "Transgenic Art." *Leonardo Electronic Almanac*, vol. 6, n. 11, December 1998. Republished in Gerfried Stock and Christine Schopf (eds). (1999) *Ars Electronica '99-Life Science*, Vienna, New York: Springer, pp. 289–96.

Bibliography

Anthes, Emily. (2014) *Frankenstein's Cat: Cuddling Up to Biotech's Brave New Beasts*, New York: Farrar, Straus and Giroux.

Appleby, Michael C. (2003) "The EU Ban on Battery Cages: History and Prospects." In Deborah J. Salem and Andrew N. Rowan (eds) *The State of the Animals II: 2003*, Washington, DC: Humane Society Press, pp. 159–74.

Beers, Diane L. (2006) *For the Prevention of Cruelty: The History and Legacy of Animal Rights Activism in the United States*, Athens: Ohio University Press.

Boersema, J. J. (2001) *The Torah and the Stoics on Humankind and Nature*, Leiden: Brill.

Cohen, E. (1994) "Animals in Medieval Perceptions: The Image of the Ubiquitous Other." In A. Manning and J. Serpell (eds) *Animals and Human Society: Changing Perspectives*, London and New York: Routledge, pp. 59–80.

DeGrazia, D. (1999) "Animal Ethics around the Turn of the Twenty-First Century." *Journal of Agricultural and Environmental Ethics* 11.2: 111–29.

Dombrowski, D. A. (1984) *The Philosophy of Vegetarianism*, Amherst: University of Massachusetts Press.

Finsen, L. and Finsen, S. (1994) *The Animal Rights Movement in America*, New York: Twayne Publishers.

Fraser, D., Mench, J. and Millman, S. (2001) "Farm Animals and Their Welfare." In D. M. Salem and A. N. Rowan (eds) *The State of the Animals*, Washington, DC: Humane Society Press.

Guither, H. D. (1998) *Animal Rights: History and Scope of a Radical Social Movement*, Carbondale: Southern Illinois University Press.

Hodges, John and Han, I. K. (eds) (2000) *Livestock, Ethics and Quality of Life*, New York: CABI Publishing.

Jasper, J. M. and Nelkin, D. (1992) *The Animal Rights Crusade: The Growth of a Moral Protest*, New York: Macmillan.

Kalechofsky, R. (1992) "Dedicated to Descartes' Niece: The Women's Movement in the Nineteenth Century and Anti-Vivisection." *Between the Species* 8.2: 61–71.

Kenyon-Jones, C. (2001) *Kindred Brutes: Animals in Romantic-Period Writing*, Burlington, VT: Ashgate.

Kruuk, H. (2002) *Hunter and Hunted: Relationships between Carnivores and People*, Cambridge, UK: Cambridge University Press.

LaRue, G. A. (1991) "Ancient Ethics." In P. Singer (ed) *A Companion to Ethics*, Oxford: Blackwell, pp. 29–40.

Lund, Vonne and Olsson, I. Anna S. (2006) "Animal Agriculture; Symbiosis, Culture or Ethical Conflict?" *Journal of Agricultural and Environmental Ethics* 19: 47–56.

Maehle, A. (1994) "Cruelty and Kindness to the Brute Creation: Stability and Change in the Ethics of the Man-Animal Relationship, 1600–1850." In *Manning and Serpell*, pp. 81–105.

Manning, A. and Serpell, J. (eds) (1994) *Animals and Human Society: Changing Perspectives*, London and New York: Routledge.

McEachern, M. G. and Schroder, M.J.A. (2002) "The Role of Livestock Production Ethics in Consumer Values Towards Meat." *Journal of Agricultural and Environmental Ethics* 15.2: 221–37.

Munro, L. (2000) *Compassionate Beasts: The Quest for Animal Rights*, Westport, CT: Praeger.

Passmore, John. (1975) "The Treatment of Animals." *Journal of the History of Ideas* 36.2: 195–218.

Patton, K. C. (2000) "He Who Sits in the Heavens Laughs: Recovering Animal Theology in the Abrahamic Traditions." *Harvard Theological Review* 93A: 401–34.

Preece, Rod. (2005) *Brute Souls, Happy Beasts, and Evolution: The Historical Status of Animals*, Vancouver, Toronto: UBC Press.

Ritvo, H. (1994) "Animals in Nineteenth-Century Britain: Complicated Attitudes and Competing Categories." In *Manning and Serpell*, pp. 106–26.

Rowlands, M. (1998) *Animal Rights: A Philosophical Defence*, New York: St. Martin's Press.

Ryder, R. (1989) *Animal Revolution: Changing Attitudes toward Speciesism*, Oxford: Basil Blackwell.

———. (1998) *The Political Animal: The Conquest of Speciesism*, Jefferson, NC: McFarland.

Salisbury, Joyce E. (1994) *The Beast within: Animals in the Middle Ages*, New York: Routledge.

Schwabe, C. W. (1994) "Animals in the Ancient World." In *Manning and Serpell*.

Serpell, J. A. (1999) "Working Out the Beast: An Alternative History of Western Humaneness." In F. R. Ascione and P. Arkow (eds) *Child Abuse, Domestic Violence, and Animal Abuse*, West Lafayette, IN: Purdue University Press, pp. 38–49.

Serpell, J. A. and Manning, A. (1994) *Animals and Human Society: Changing Perspectives*, pp. 36–58. London and New York: Routledge.

Singer, P. (ed) (1991) *A Companion to Ethics*, Oxford: Basil Blackwell.

Sorabji, R. (1993) *Animal Minds and Human Morals: The Origins of the Western Debate*, Ithaca, NY: Cornell University Press.

Steiner, Gary. (2005) *Anthropocentrism and Its Discontents: The Moral Status of Animals in the History of Western Philosophy*, Pittsburgh, PA: University of Pittsburgh Press.

Thomas, K. (1983) *Man and the Natural World: Changing Attitudes in England 1500–1800*, Magnolia: Peter Smith.

Thompson, Paul B. (2004) "Getting Pragmatic about Farm Animal Welfare." In Erin McKenna and Andrew Light (eds) *Animal Pragmatism*, Bloomington: Indiana University Press, pp. 140–159.

Turner, J. (1980) *Reckoning with the Beast: Animals, Pain, and Humanity in the Victorian Mind*, Baltimore: Johns Hopkins University.

Velde, Hein Te, Aarts, Noelle and van Woerkum, Cees. (2002) "Dealing with Ambivalence." *Journal of Agricultural and Environmental Ethics* 51.2: 203–19.

Waddell, Helen, trans. (1970) *Beasts and Saints*, London: Constable and Co., Ltd.

White, Paul S. (2005) "The Experimental Animal in Victorian Britain." In L. Daston and G. Mitman (eds) *Thinking with Animals: New Perspectives on Anthropomorphism*, New York: Columbia University Press.

Part One

Theories of Animal Ethics

Introduction to Part One

Animal ethics is involved with arguments over several key issues. The most basic issue concerns the basis of the moral value or moral status of animals. Why should animals count morally? This part includes excerpts from several influential theorists in the field of animal ethics.

Tom Regan's answer as well as that of Paola Cavalieri is based on the concepts of rights to which a being is entitled. Regan develops the concept of "subject-of-a-life" as an expansion of Immanuel Kant's focus on rational beings. Cavalieri uses the concept of "intentional beings" as an expansion of universal human rights theory. For Regan and Cavalieri animals have desires, intentions, feelings, and a psychological identity over time—there is "someone home" in an animal. Animals should be included in our moral community as beings with rights. Unlike Regan, Cavalieri grants the same value to the lives of all intentional beings. Carl Cohen rejects Regan's argument. While Cohen does not deny that animals have rudimentary desires and interests, he does deny that having interests is relevant to having moral rights.

Peter Singer rests his argument on the moral principle of the equal consideration of interests, the utilitarian principle which affirms that all sentient individuals, those capable of experiencing pleasure or pain, must be considered when we are contemplating an action. Singer advocates preference utilitarianism, a form of utilitarianism which takes into account what an individual wishes to do. He does not advocate equal treatment but rather equal consideration of animals' interests. Singer states that we have different obligations toward rational and self-conscious animals as contrasted with our obligations to animals lacking such capabilities.

Josephine Donovan critiques the overreliance on reason by Regan and Singer. She maintains that feminist care theory, developed in order to emphasize the significance of emotional responses such as sympathy, empathy, and compassion, also acknowledges the importance of animal communications. She confronts some recent criticisms of care theory.

R. G. Frey critiques Regan and Singer from a different perspective. He maintains that animals, because they lack language, do not have interests in the sense of having desires; thus it is not necessary for scholars to address what relationship there might be between interests and rights.

In many theories of animal ethics, painless death is considered to be morally acceptable. Frederike Kaldewaij challenges this view. She argues that both humans and conscious animals are harmed by death because it deprives them of the goods that continued life would have brought them.

Sue Donaldson and Will Kymlicka argue that all animals who are conscious should be viewed as having inviolable rights. This means that the basic interests of sentient animals cannot be sacrificed for the greater good of others.

Further Reading

Armstrong, S. J. (ed.) (2004) *Animal Ethics, Essays in Philosophy* 5.2 www.humboldt.edu/~essays/archives.html

Carruthers, P. (1992) *The Animals Issue*, Cambridge: Cambridge University Press.

DeGrazia, D. (1998) *Taking Animals Seriously: Mental Life and Moral Status*, Cambridge: Cambridge University Press.

Donovan, J. and C. Adams (eds.) (2007) *The Feminist Care Tradition in Animal Ethics: A Reader*, New York: Columbia University Press.

Jamieson, D. (ed.) (1999) *Singer and His Critics*, Oxford: Blackwell.

McKenna, E. and A. Light (eds.) (2004) *Animal Pragmatism: Rethinking Human-Nonhuman Relationships*, Bloomington: Indiana University Press.

Midgley, M. (1998) *Animals and Why They Matter*, Athens: University of Georgia Press.

Pluhar, E. (1995) *Beyond Prejudice: The Moral Significance of Human and Nonhuman Animals*, Durham, NC: Duke University Press.

Regan, T. (2004) *Empty Cages: Facing the Challenge of Animal Rights*, Lanham, MD: Rowman and Littlefield.

Rollin, B. E. (1992) *Animal Rights and Human Morality*, Amherst, MA: Prometheus Books.

Sapontzis, S. F. (1987) *Morals, Reason and Animals*, Philadelphia, PA: Temple University Press.

Scully, M. (2002) *Dominion: The Power of Man, the Suffering of Animals, and the Call to Mercy*, New York: St. Martin's Press.

Singer, P. (ed.) (2006) *In Defense of Animals: The Second Wave*, Malden, MA: Blackwell.

Sunstein, C. R. and M. C. Nussbaum (eds.) (2004) *Animal Rights: Current Debates and New Directions*, New York: Oxford University Press.

Turner, J. and J. D'Silva (eds.) (2006) *Animals, Ethics and Trade: The Challenge of Animal Sentience*, London: Earthscan.

Warren, M. A. (1997) *Moral Status: Obligations to Persons and Other Living Things*, Oxford: Clarendon Press.

Study Questions

1. Tom Regan bases his argument on the concept of "subject-of-a-life." Do you agree that this concept identifies the crucial difference between a being with moral status and one without status? Explain your reasoning.

2. Carl Cohen identifies what he believes to be an equivocation in Regan's use of "inherent value." Do you agree with Cohen's point? Why or why not?

3. What might be some advantages for animal ethics of Cavalieri's emphasis on rights as protection from institutional interference?

4. Peter Singer uses the principle of equal consideration of interests to guide our practice concerning animals. Do you find this principle more or less convincing than Tom Regan's use of the equal inherent value of moral agents and moral patients? Explain your choice.

5. Do you agree with Donovan that Regan and Singer place too much emphasis on reason? What role should sympathy and compassion play in our treatment of nonhuman animals?

6. Frey argues that having desires requires having the capacity for language-based beliefs. Do you agree? Why or why not?

7. Kaldewaij argues that animals are harmed by premature death, whether it is painless or not. Do you find her reasoning persuasive?

8. In your view, which of the authors in this part presents the best approach to the moral status of animals? Are there significant modifications you would make to the view of the author you chose?

9. Do you agree with Donaldson and Kymlicka that self, being conscious, is the foundation of the recognition of moral rights?

10. The recognition of animals as selves with inviolable rights would have earth-shaking repercussions for many common practices. In what area do you think change is most likely to occur, if it occurs at all?

1   The Case for Animal Rights

Tom Regan

This selection is from the influential The Case for Animal Rights, *published in 1983. Regan explains his concept of "subject-of-a-life" as the basis for inherent value, the distinction between moral agents and moral patients, and two principles to be used in cases of unavoidable conflicts between subjects-of-a-life.*

[. . .]

Moral Agents and Moral Patients

A helpful place to begin is to distinguish between moral agents and moral patients [. . .]. Moral agents are individuals who have a variety of sophisticated abilities, including in particular the ability to bring impartial moral principles to bear on the determination of what, all considered, morally ought to be done and, having made this determination, to freely choose or fail to choose to act as morality, as they conceive it, requires. Because moral agents have these abilities, it is fair to hold them morally accountable for what they do, assuming that the circumstances of their acting as they do in a particular case do not dictate otherwise.

[. . .]

In contrast to moral agents, *moral patients* lack the prerequisites that would enable them to control their own behavior in ways that would make them morally accountable for what they do. A moral patient lacks the ability to formulate, let alone bring to bear, moral principles in deliberating about which one among a number of possible acts it would be right or proper to perform. Moral patients, in a word, cannot do what is right, nor can they do what is wrong. Granted, what they do may be detrimental to the welfare of others—they may, for example, bring about acute suffering or even death; and granted, it may be necessary, in any given case, for moral agents to use force or violence to prevent such harm being done, either in self-defense or in defense of others. But even when a moral patient causes significant harm to another, the moral patient has not done what is wrong. Only moral agents can do what is wrong. Human infants, young children, and the mentally deranged or enfeebled of all ages are paradigm cases of human moral patients. More controversial is whether human fetuses and future generations of human beings qualify as moral patients. It is enough for our purposes, however, that some humans are reasonably viewed in this way.

Individuals who are moral patients differ from one another in morally relevant ways. Of particular importance is the distinction between (a) those individuals who are conscious and sentient (i.e., can experience pleasure and pain) but who lack other mental abilities and (b) those individuals who are conscious and sentient and possess the other cognitive and volitional abilities discussed in previous chapters (e.g., belief and memory). Some animals, for reasons already advanced, belong in category (b); other animals quite probably belong in category (a).

[. . .]

Our primary interest, in this and in succeeding chapters, concerns the moral status of animals in category (b). When, therefore, the notion of a *moral patient* is appealed to in the discussions that follow, it should be understood as applying to *animals in category (b) and to those other moral patients like these animals in the relevant respects*—that is, those who have desires and beliefs, who perceive, remember, and can act intentionally, who have a sense of the future, including their own future (i.e., are self-aware or self-conscious), who have an emotional life, who have a psychophysical identity over time, who have a kind of autonomy (namely, preference-autonomy), and who have an experiential welfare. Some *human* moral patients satisfy these criteria—for example, young children and those humans who, though they suffer from a variety of mental handicaps and thus fail to qualify as moral agents, possess the abilities just enumerated. Where one draws the line between those humans who have these abilities and those who do not is a difficult question certainly, and it may be that no exact line can be drawn. But how we should approach the question in the case of human beings is the same as how we should approach it in the case of animals. Given any human being, what we shall want to know is whether his/her behavior can be accurately described and parsimoniously explained by making reference to the range of abilities that characterizes animals (desires, beliefs, preferences, etc.). To the extent that the case can be made for describing and explaining the behavior of a human being in these terms, to that extent, assuming that we have further reasons for denying that the human in question has the abilities necessary for moral agency, we have reason to regard that human as a moral patient on all fours, so to speak, with animals. As previously claimed, some human beings *are* moral patients in the relevant sense, and *it is only those individuals who are moral patients in this sense (who have, that is, the abilities previously enumerated), whether these individuals be human or nonhuman, who are being referred to, in this chapter and in the sequel, as "moral patients."*

  Moral patients cannot do what is right or wrong, we have said, and in this respect they differ fundamentally from moral agents. But moral patients can be on the receiving end of the right or wrong acts of moral agents, and so in this respect resemble moral agents. A brutal beating administered to a child, for example, is wrong, even if the child herself can do no wrong, just as attending to the basic biological needs of the senile is arguably right, even if a senile person can no longer do what is right. Unlike the case of the relationship that holds between moral agents, then, the relationship that holds between moral agents, on the one hand, and moral patients, on the other, is not reciprocal. Moral patients can do nothing right or wrong that affects or involves moral agents, but moral agents can do what is right or wrong in ways that affect or involve moral patients.

  [. . .]

Individuals as Equal in Value

The interpretation of formal justice favored here, which will be referred to as *equality of individuals*, involves viewing certain individuals as having value in themselves. I shall refer to this kind of value as *inherent value* and begin the discussion of it by first concentrating on the inherent value attributed to moral agents.

  The inherent value of individual moral agents is to be understood as being conceptually distinct from the intrinsic value that attaches to the experiences they have (e.g., their pleasures or preference satisfactions), as not being reducible to values of this latter kind, and as being incommensurate with these values. To say that inherent value is not reducible to the intrinsic values of an individual's experiences means that we cannot determine the inherent value of individual moral agents by totaling the intrinsic values of their experiences. Those who have a more pleasant or happier life do not therefore have greater inherent value than those whose lives are less pleasant or happy. Nor do those who have more "cultivated" preferences (say, for arts and letters) therefore have greater inherent value. To say that the inherent value of individual moral agents is incommensurate with the intrinsic value of their (or anyone else's) experiences means that the two kinds of value are not comparable and cannot be exchanged one for the other. Like proverbial apples and oranges, the two kinds of value do not fall within the same scale of comparison. One cannot ask, How much intrinsic value is the inherent value of this individual worth—how much is it equal to? The inherent value of any given moral agent isn't equal to any sum of intrinsic values, neither the intrinsic value of that individual's experiences nor the total of the intrinsic value of the experiences of all other moral agents. To view moral agents as having inherent value is thus to view them as something different from, and something more than, mere receptacles of what has intrinsic value. They have value in their own right, a value that is distinct from, not reducible to, and incommensurate with the values of those experiences which, as receptacles, they have or undergo.

The difference between the utilitarian-receptacle view of value regarding moral agents and the postulate of inherent value might be made clearer by recalling the cup analogy. On the receptacle view of value, it is *what goes into the cup* (the pleasures or preference-satisfactions, for example) that has value; what does not have value is the cup itself (i.e., the individual himself or herself). The postulate of inherent value offers an alternative. The cup (that is, the individual) has value *and* a kind that is not reducible to, and is incommensurate with, what goes into the cup (e.g., pleasure). The cup (the individual) does "contain" (experience) things that are valuable (e.g., pleasures), but the value of the cup (individual) is not the same as any one or any sum of the valuable things the cup contains. *Individual moral agents themselves have a distinctive kind of value*, according to the postulate of inherent value, but not according to the receptacle view to which utilitarians are committed. It's the cup, not just what goes into it, that is valuable.

[. . .]

All that is required to ensure just treatment, on utilitarian grounds, is that the preferences (pleasures, etc.) of all affected by the outcome be considered and that equal preferences (pleasures, etc.) be counted equally. But if moral agents have a value that is *not* reducible to or commensurate with the value of their own or everyone else's valuable experiences, then how moral agents are to be treated, if they are to be treated justly, cannot be determined *merely* by considering the desires, and the like, of all involved, weighting them equitably, and then favoring that option that will bring about the optimal balance of goods over evils for all involved. To suppose otherwise is to assume that questions of just treatment can be answered by ignoring the value of the individual moral agent, which, if moral agents are viewed as equal in inherent value, simply is not true. Moreover, because all moral agents are viewed as equal in inherent value, if any have such value, what applies to how some may be justly treated applies to all, whatever their race, say, or sex. Given the postulate of inherent value, no harm done to *any* moral agent can possibly be justified merely on the grounds of its producing the best consequences for all affected by the outcome. Thus are we able to avoid the counterintuitive implications of act utilitarianism if we deny the receptacle view of moral agents and postulate their equal inherent value.

[. . .]

It might be suggested that *being-alive* is a *sufficient* condition of an individual's having inherent value. This position would avoid the problems indigenous to the view that being-alive is a necessary condition, but it stands in need of quite considerable analysis and argument if it is to win the day. It is not clear why we have, or how we reasonably could be said to have, direct duties to, say, individual blades of grass, potatoes, or cancer cells. Yet all are alive, and so all should be owed direct duties if all have inherent value. Nor is it clear why we have, or how we reasonably could be said to have, direct duties to collections of such individuals—to lawns, potato fields, or cancerous tumors. If, in reply to these difficulties, we are told that we have direct duties only to some, but not to all, living things, and that it is this subclass of living things whose members have inherent value, then not only will we stand in need of a way to distinguish those living things that have this value from those that do not but more importantly for present purposes, the view that being-alive is a sufficient condition of having such value will have to be abandoned. Because of the difficulties endemic both to the view that being-alive is a necessary condition of having inherent value and to the view that this is a sufficient condition, and granting that moral agents and moral patients share the important characteristic of being alive, it is extremely doubtful that the case could be made for viewing this similarity as the relevant similarity they share, by virtue of which all moral agents and patients have equal inherent value.

Inherent Value and the Subject-of-a-Life Criterion

An alternative to viewing being-alive as the relevant similarity is what will be termed *the subject-of-a-life criterion*. To be the subject-of-a-life, in the sense in which this expression will be used, involves more than merely being alive and more than merely being conscious. To be the subject-of-a-life is to be an individual whose life is characterized by those features explored in the opening chapters of the present work: that is, individuals are subjects-of-a-life if they have beliefs and desires; perception, memory, and a sense of the future, including their own future; an emotional life together with feelings of pleasure and pain; preference- and welfare-interests; the ability to initiate action in pursuit of their desires and goals; a psychophysical identity over time; and an individual welfare in the sense that their experiential life fares well or ill for them, logically independently of their utility for others and logically independently of their being the object of anyone else's interests. Those who satisfy the subject-of-a-life criterion themselves have a distinctive kind of value—inherent value—and are not to be viewed or treated as mere receptacles.

[. . .]

The subject-of-a-life criterion identifies a similarity that holds between moral agents and patients. Is this similarity a relevant similarity, one that makes viewing them as inherently valuable intelligible and nonarbitrary? The grounds for replying affirmatively are as follows: (1) A relevant similarity among all those who are postulated to have equal inherent value must mark a characteristic shared by all those moral agents and patients who are here viewed as having such value. The subject-of-a-life criterion satisfies this requirement. *All* moral agents and *all* those moral patients with whom we are concerned *are* subjects of a life that is better or worse for them, in the sense explained, logically independently of the utility they have for others and logically independently of their being the object of the interests of others. (2) Since inherent value is conceived to be a categorical value, admitting of no degrees, any supposed relevant similarity must itself be categorical. The subject-of-a-life criterion satisfies this requirement. This criterion does not assert or imply that those who meet it have the status of subject of a life to a greater or lesser degree, depending on the degree to which they have or lack some favored ability or virtue (e.g., the ability for higher mathematics or those virtues associated with artistic excellence). One either *is* a subject of a life, in the sense explained, or one *is not*. All those who are, are so equally. The subject-of-a-life criterion thus demarcates a categorical status shared by all moral agents and those moral patients with whom we are concerned. (3) A relevant similarity between moral agents and patients must go some way toward illuminating why we have direct duties to both and why we have less reason to believe that we have direct duties to individuals who are neither moral agents nor patients, even including those who, like moral agents and those patients we have in mind, are alive. This requirement also is satisfied by the subject-of-a-life criterion. Not all living things are subjects of a life, in the sense explained; thus not all living things are to be viewed as having the same moral status, given this criterion, and the differences concerning our confidence about having direct duties to some (those who are subjects) and our not having direct duties to others (those who are not subjects) can be at least partially illuminated because the former meet, while the latter fail to meet, the subject-of-a-life criterion. For these reasons, the subject-of-a-life criterion can be defended as citing a relevant similarity between moral agents and patients, one that makes the attribution of equal inherent value to them both intelligible and nonarbitrary.

[. . .]

Justice: The Principle of Respect for Individuals

[. . .]

If individuals have equal inherent value, then any principle that declares what treatment is due them as a matter of justice must take their equal value into account. The following principle (*the respect principle*) does this: *We are to treat those individuals who have inherent value in ways that respect their inherent value.* Now, the respect principle sets forth an egalitarian, nonperfectionist interpretation of formal justice. The principle does not apply only to how we are to treat some individuals having inherent value (e.g., those with artistic or intellectual virtues). It enjoins us to treat *all* those individuals having inherent value in ways that respect their value, and thus it requires respectful treatment of all who satisfy the subject-of-a-life criterion. Whether they are moral agents or patients, we must treat them in ways that respect their equal inherent value.

[. . .]

It is not an act of kindness to treat animals respectfully. It is an act of justice. It is not "the sentimental interests" of moral agents that grounds our duties of justice to children, the retarded, the senile, or other moral patients, including animals. It is respect for their inherent value. The myth of the privileged moral status of moral agents has no clothes.

[. . .]

Comparable Harm

[. . .]

A distinction [can be] drawn between those harms that are inflictions and those that are deprivations. Harms that are deprivations deny an individual opportunities for doing what will bring satisfaction, when it is in that individual's interest to do this. Harms that are inflictions diminish the quality of an individual's life, not just if or as they deprive that individual of opportunities for satisfaction, though they usually will do this, but because they detract directly from the individual's overall welfare.

[. . .]

[We can now] give content to the notion of comparable harm. Two harms are comparable when they detract equally from an individual's welfare, or from the welfare of two or more individuals. For example, separate episodes of suffering of a certain kind and intensity are comparable harms if they cause an equal diminution in the welfare of the same individual at different times, or in two different individuals at the same or different times. And death is a comparable harm if the loss of opportunities it marks are equal in any two cases.

[. . .]

The Miniride Principle

By making use of the notion of comparable harm, the rights view can formulate two principles that can be appealed to in order to make decisions in prevention cases. The first principle (*the minimize overriding principle*, or *the miniride principle*) states the following:

> Special considerations aside, when we must choose between overriding the rights of many who are innocent or the rights of few who are innocent, and when each affected individual will be harmed in a prima facie comparable way, then we ought to choose to override the rights of the few in preference to overriding the rights of the many.

This principle is derivable from the respect principle. This latter principle entails that all moral agents and patients are directly owed the prima facie duty not to be harmed and that all those who are owed this duty have an equally valid claim, and thus an equal prima facie moral right, against being harmed. Now, *precisely because* this right is equal, no one individual's right can count for any more than any other's, when the harm that might befall either is prima facie comparable. Thus, A's right cannot count for more than B's, or C's, or D's. However, when we are faced with choosing between options, one of which will harm A, the other of which will harm B, C, and D, and the third of which will harm them all, and when the foreseeable harm involved for each individual is prima facie comparable, then numbers count. *Precisely because* each is to count for one, no one for more than one, we cannot count choosing to override the rights of B, C, and D as neither better nor worse than choosing to override A's right alone. Three are more than one, and when the four individuals have an equal prima facie right not to be harmed, when the harm they face is prima facie comparable, and when there are no special considerations at hand, then showing equal respect for the equal rights of the individuals involved requires that we override the right of A (the few) rather than the rights of the many (B, C, D). To choose to override the rights of the many in this case would be to override an equal right three times (i.e., in the case of three different individuals) when we could choose to override such a right only once, and *that* cannot be consistent with showing equal respect for the equal rights of all the individuals involved.

To favor overriding the rights of the few in no way contravenes the requirement that each is to count for one, no one for more than one; on the contrary, special considerations apart, to choose to override the rights of the many rather than those of the few would be to count A's right for more than one—that is, as being equal to overriding the rights of three relevantly similar individuals. Accordingly, because we must not allow any one individual a greater voice in the determination of what ought to be done than any other relevantly similar individual, what we ought to do in prevention cases of the sort under consideration is choose to override the rights of the fewest innocents rather than override the rights of the many. And since this is precisely what the miniride principle enjoins, that principle is derivable from the respect principle.

[. . .]

The Worse-Off Principle

[. . .]

Recall the earlier prevention case where we are called upon to choose between harming A quite radically (−125), or harming a thousand individuals modestly (−1 each), or doing nothing

[. . .]

The miniride principle, since it applies *only* in prevention cases where harms are prima facie comparable, cannot be relied on in cases, such as this one, where the harm all the innocents face is not prima facie comparable. The rights view thus requires a second principle, distinct from but consistent with the miniride principle, and one that is distinct from and not reducible to the minimize harm principle. The following principle (*the worse-off principle*) meets these requirements.

[. . .]

Special considerations aside, when we must decide to override the rights of the many or the rights of the few who are innocent, and when the harm faced by the few would make them worse-off than any of the many would be if any other option were chosen, then we ought to override the rights of the many.

Unfinished Business

Two issues deferred in earlier discussions may now be addressed. The first is the lifeboat case. [. . .] There are five survivors: four normal adults and a dog. The boat has room enough only for four. Someone must go or else all will perish. Who should it be? Our initial belief is: the dog. Can the rights view illuminate and justify this prereflective intuition? The preceding discussion of prevention cases shows how it can. All on board have equal inherent value and an equal prima facie right not to be harmed. Now, the harm that death is, is a function of the opportunities for satisfaction it forecloses, and no reasonable person would deny that the death of any of the four humans would be a greater prima facie loss, and thus a greater prima facie harm, than would be true in the case of the dog. Death for the dog, in short, though a harm, is not comparable to the harm that death would be for any of the humans. To throw any one of the humans overboard, to face certain death, would be to make that individual worse-off (i.e., would cause *that* individual a greater harm) than the harm that would be done to the dog if the animal was thrown overboard. Our belief that it is the dog who should be killed is justified by appeal to the worse-off principle.

[. . .]

Thus has the case for animal rights been offered. If it is sound, then, like us, animals have certain basic moral rights, including in particular the fundamental right to be treated with the respect that, as possessors of inherent value, they are due as a matter of strict justice.

[. . .]

possibility more about empathy than rationality?

2   Reply to Tom Regan

Carl Cohen

In the following passage, Carl Cohen analyzes Regan's use of "subject-of-a-life" and "inherent value" as the foundation for moral rights for animals. According to Cohen, Regan's fallacious logic can be clearly demonstrated.

Why "Subjects-of-a-Life"?

Regan's need is to create some *link* between the imputed subjective experience of animals and the alleged rights of those animals. To this end a class of beings is marked off that Regan calls "subjects-of-a-life." These are the beings who are believed to have some subjective awareness of their own lives, and for whom, as a result, it may be said that things "fare well or badly." Of course we may not conclude, from the fact that things fare well or badly for an animal, that it can formulate the proposition expressing this, or can even grasp that notion in some sub-linguistic way. The judgment that "things are faring well *for me* these days" is not likely to be among the repertoire of chicken reflections. But some crude subjective experience there must be, since the chicken is drawn toward the food tray and runs away from the fox. This indicates, says Regan, that the chicken (like every "subject-of-a-life") has *interests*.

The strategy here is to devise some category into which both animal lives and human lives may be assimilated. Within this newfound category, since it is designed to include humans too, some of the lives led (the human ones) are plainly moral. From this he will go on to infer that *all* the lives in that class, lives so categorized by virtue of his definition, are moral. But this maneuver could succeed only if the criteria for admission to the newly invented category were themselves intrinsically moral—which of course they are not.

"Subjects-of-a-life" is a category of beings that Regan defines by his own stipulation; membership in that class requires only the crudest subjective experience. Having devised the category by fastening upon certain kinds of primitive experience that rats and humans do share, he goes on to assume that moral rights, possessed by humans, arise from just those interests. Some human interests (e.g., in food and sex) are no different in essence from those of rats, and since we all agree that humans do have rights, he infers that rats must have them, too.

In the sense that a sentient animal—even an octopus or a trout—seeks to avoid pain, it does indeed have interests; many animals obviously have interests in that sense. Were Regan to leap directly from the possession of interests to the claim that such interests establish moral rights, his argument—like [the] far-fetched claims of Bernard Rollin and Steven Sapontzis—would be a transparent failure.[1] To avoid this transparency Regan takes a more convoluted path.

A Closer Look at Inherent Value

The rights that are to be established flow, Regan contends, from the *inherent value* of rats and chickens, and their inherent value is held to be a consequence of their being "subjects-of-a-life." So he makes the passage from interests to rights *by way of* "subjects-of-a-life" and then "inherent value."

Both these concepts, as in his 1983 book, are critical links for him: what has subjective experience must have inherent value, and what has inherent value must have rights.[2] This can explain, he argues, why moral respect is owed to rats and chickens.

Reasoning in this way supposes that the rights of rats and chickens are *derived* from the primitive capacities that give them interests. Like Rollin and Sapontzis, Regan is at bottom convinced that rights are the product of animal interests, that a being has rights because it has interests—and he cannot fathom how we could assert of humans, who surely do have interests, that their rights could flow from anything else.

But the conviction that human rights flow from human interests (a conviction shared expressly or tacitly by virtually all animal rights advocates) is one for which there is simply no foundation. The lives we humans lead are indeed moral lives, pervaded by duties and rights. But this moral character of our lives is not a by-product of our subjective awareness. Our rights are not ours because we experience our lives as our own. Nonhuman creatures may have subjective interests like ours in survival and reproduction, and they may be supposed to have subjective experience of some sort. But from those interests moral rights cannot be inferred.

The plausibility of Regan's reasoning depends on the inference that animals have "inherent value" and then on what may be inferred from the possession of such value. The failure of the argument is a consequence of the fact that the "inherent value" that he infers from the reality of subjective experience is not the same "inherent value" from which rights are later derived. An academic shell game is afoot, in which readers are the marks. Having given our assent to what is plausible in one sense of the expression "inherent value," we are told that dramatic conclusions follow respecting rights. But these conclusions do *not* follow from the inherent value that we may have assented to in animals, although they may follow from inherent value in a very different sense of that term.

[. . .]

What is true of inherent value in the one sense is not true of inherent value in the other sense, and by slipping from one to the other meaning of the phrase Regan commits an egregious fallacy.

We earlier distinguished:

1. Inherent value in the very widely applicable sense that every unique life, not replaceable by other lives or things, has some worth in itself. In this sense every rat, and every octopus too, has inherent value. This value may be minimal; it certainly has no awesome moral content— but it is fair to say that being irreplaceable and unique, even primitive living things ought not be destroyed for any reason whatever.
2. Inherent value in the far narrower sense arises from the possession of the capacity to make moral judgments, the value of beings with duties and the consciousness of duties. This is the rich philosophical sense of value made famous by Immanuel Kant and employed by many moral thinkers since; it is the sense of inherent worth flowing from the special *dignity* of those who have a moral will. The value of agents who have a moral will does indeed *inhere* in them and entitles them to be treated as ends, and never as means only. Beings with value in this sense—human beings, of course—have rights.

Now it is plain that most beings with inherent value in the first sense—live creatures in the wild, for example—although they may merit some protection, do not begin to possess inherent value in the second, moral sense. Trees and rats have value in the common sense, and we may plausibly call that value "inherent"—but that is no ground for ascribing moral agency to them. The gap in the argument is here exposed: subjective experiences of rats and chickens lead us to conclude that they really do have interests, but subjective experiences cannot serve to justify the claim that they have rights.

[. . .]

Human beings, on the other hand, have inherent value in both senses. We have worth in that second, Kantian sense, to be sure, but value also in the simpler, common sense as well. [. . .] [The] slippage between these two senses of the same phrase [. . .] is obscured by reaching rights from subjectivity *through* the concept "subject-of-a-life." Within that category lie beings with inherent value in both senses (humans) and beings with inherent value in the first sense only (rats). The stage is set for slippage.

We humans are subjects of our own lives, of course, so we have inherent value in that simple first sense; and surely we do have moral rights. Regan then asks: if the rat is the subject of its own life, must it not also have the same "inherent value" that we have? In the first sense of inherent value it does. And if it does have inherent value as we do, does it not also have moral rights as we do? No, not at all! By moving *into* the concept of "inherent value" in the first sense (in which that value is shared), then drawing inferences *from* inherent value in the second sense (in which it is not shared), Regan pulls the rabbit from the hat, miraculously extending the realm of moral rights to include the rats and the chickens.

Underlying his equivocation is the tacit supposition that we humans have rights only as a *consequence* of our being "subject-of-a-life." But this is false, and we have not the slightest reason to think it true. Having assumed it true, Regan and his friends take themselves to have *amalgamated* the world of human moral experience with the world of rodent experience. That cannot be done with words, or with anything else.

The Argument Step by Step

Here follow the steps of Regan's argument, essentially as he sets them forth, with brief comment on each. Close scrutiny will show that his critical steps rely on double meanings, his objectives reached by using whichever sense of the equivocal term is convenient for the purpose at hand.

1. Humans and rats are both "subjects-of-a-life."
    Comment: If all that is being said here is that other animals as well as humans have subjective interests and awareness, this premise is not in dispute. In having subjective interests "nonhuman animals are like us," Regan says. Yes, in the sense that they also have appetites, feel pain, and so on.
2. Beings that are "subjects-of-a-life" are beings having inherent value.
    Comment: This is the introduction of the central equivocal phrase. Animals with subjective experience do indeed have "inherent value" in the common sense that all living things, including humans, are unique and irreplaceable. But the vast majority of beings having subjective experiences do *not* have "inherent value" in the Kantian sense that would be needed to ground moral rights.
3. Since rats, like humans, have inherent value because they are "subjects-of-a-life," the inherent value that rats possess is essentially no different from the inherent value that humans possess.
    Comment: The distinction between the two very different senses of inherent value being here ignored or obscured, it seems plausible for Regan to assert here what is true (but innocuous) if the words are taken in one way, yet false (and very harmful) if taken in another. In the common sense both rats and humans do have inherent value. But this "inherent value" possessed by them both (sense 1) is profoundly different from the "inherent value" that is bound up with human moral agency (sense 2).

    Regan writes, "The relevant similarity shared by humans who have inherent value is that we are subject-of-a-life" (p. 211). No, that similarity is not relevant to moral matters at all. On the contrary, we may say that the relevant *dissimilarity* between humans and rats is that although both may have value as lives, only humans have inherent value in the sense from which rights may be inferred. Regan conflates the two very different senses of value, referring to both with the same words, and his argument depends upon this conflation.
4. The inherent value that we humans possess is what accounts for our moral rights. (In his words: "All those who possess inherent value possess the equal right to be treated with respect.")

Comment: So long as we understand that it is Kantian inherent value (sense 2) here referred to, the claim that from it great moral consequences flow is not in dispute.

5. Since rats possess inherent value for the same reasons that humans do, rats must have moral rights just as humans do.

    Comment: Not at all! Here the switch is cashed out. Rats possess inherent value *in sense 1* for the same reason humans do, because they have subjective interests as humans also have. But from these primitive interests no moral rights can be inferred. Regan writes, "Relevantly similar cases should be judged similarly" (p. 212). But the circumstances of rats and humans are in the most essential matters *not* relevantly similar. Indeed, with regard to moral status they could hardly be more sharply dissimilar. The argument thrives on repeated equivocation.

6. Regan concludes, "It follows that all those human beings and all those animal beings who possess inherent value share the equal right to respectful treatment" (p. 212).

    Comment: Not on your life! The inherent value shared is value in the common sense, but what can entail respect for rights is *not* shared by rats. What is true of both rats and humans is the fact that they are living beings, the life of each unique, each having interests of its own. From this, nothing about moral rights may be validly inferred.

Infected throughout by the equivocation between inherent value that "subjects-of-a-life" may possess and the entirely different sense of inherent value that may indeed ground human rights, the argument is worthless. The lives of rats and chickens are indeed like the lives of humans in some primitive ways, but it certainly does not follow from those likenesses that rats and chickens share membership in the community of moral beings. Repeatedly we encounter the same fallacious passage from the premise that animals have interests to the conclusion that animals have rights.

[. . .]

Notes

1. Rollin, B. (1992) *Animal Rights and Human Morality*, Amherst: Prometheus Books. Sapontzis, S. F. (1987) *Morals, Reason and Animals*, Philadelphia: Temple University Press.
2. Regan, T. (1983) *The Case for Animal Rights*, Berkeley: University of California Press.

3   Are Human Rights *Human*?

Paola Cavalieri

Cavalieri offers a brief history of Western ethics, according to which animals have been completely excluded from the moral community. She evaluates more recent views in traditional morality according to which nonhuman beings are considered to be moral patients. Concluding that traditional morality is untenable, she bases her argument on the most widespread moral theory: the universal doctrine of human rights. Since the central criterion for the possession of human rights is intentionality, Cavalieri maintains that because animals are intentional beings, they should also be given the protection from institutional interference provided by shifting animals to being subjects of legal rights.

[. . .]

I

Immanuel Kant writes that "so far as animals are concerned, we have no direct duties. Animals are not self-conscious and are there merely as means to an end. That end is man. . . . Our duties towards animals are merely indirect duties towards humanity."[1]

In the idea that nonhumans are nothing but means one can perceive echoes of Aristotle: "the other animals [exist] for the good of man, the domestic species both for his service and for his food, and . . . most of the wild ones for the sake of his food and of his supplies of other kinds."[2] And the thesis of indirect duties betrays a reminiscence of Thomas Aquinas' remarks on the subject of biblical injunctions against cruelty to nonhumans: "this is . . . to remove man's thoughts from being cruel to other men, and lest through being cruel to animals one become cruel to human beings."[3]

Though other views appeared on the philosophical scene—consider for example the Cartesian idea that animals are mere *natural automata* with which we can do entirely as we wish, and on the opposite side the utilitarian ethical concern for all the beings endowed with the capacity for suffering and enjoyment—one might say that these short quotations contain in a nutshell the elements of the most enduring and pervasive thesis about the treatment of nonhumans in all Western culture. In short: animals, as mere means, have zero grade moral status—that is, they are excluded from the moral community. However, there are limits to what can be done to them. Such limits are dictated by the fact that our behavior towards animals can rebound upon our behavior towards the only true objects of moral concern, namely, other human beings.

We can recast such a view in more formal terms. At the center of ethics lies a set of norms to govern behavior towards (at least some) other entities. Asking which are the entities other than the agent that should have their interests protected is tantamount to asking who is a *moral patient*. The moral patient is a being whose *treatment* may be subject to direct moral evaluation.[4] It is apparent that not all entities necessarily belong to this category—for most ethical theories, to shatter a stone or to mow the meadow's grass are wholly irrelevant actions. What the view in question claims is that just like stones and plants, nonhuman animals are not moral patients.

The boundaries of the class of moral patients have often changed in the course of history, and it also happened that many human beings were excluded from ethical consideration—Aristotle himself held that like animals, human slaves too were mere means at their masters' disposal.[5] Today we can easily understand how unsatisfactory such an attitude was, because a long work of rational criticism has dismantled its justifications, revealing the true nature as an implicit appeal to prejudice of the high-sounding claims on behalf of the superiority of a sex to the other, or of one race to all the other races. But if we rightly regard such a critical process as a fundamental component of our moral evolution, a question spontaneously arises: if the justifications on behalf of intra-human discrimination turned out to be indefensible, isn't it possible that the same holds for the justifications put forward on behalf of the discrimination against other-than-human beings? We shall here put to the test this hypothesis.

II

How, then, can one defend the idea that human beings are ends, while nonhuman beings are means? Before tackling this issue, it is necessary to stress that when contemporary philosophers defend the ends/means doctrine, what they are usually referring to is not the traditional Kantian formulation, but instead a softened version of it. According to such a version, nonhuman animals are no longer utterly excluded from the moral community—they are, that is, numbered among moral patients. Nonetheless, the moral community has a stratified, hierarchical structure, and the continued use of nonhuman beings for our benefit is allegedly justified by their being confined to second-class moral status with respect to human beings. Both the traditional and the more recent view are defended by the same arguments. Since it is not possible to offer here a complete survey of such arguments, we shall confine ourselves to considering the most representative ones.

While not being altogether overlooked by philosophers, the first argument is, owing to its simplicity, powerful and widespread mainly at the societal level. To the question of what may draw what we might call, following Bentham, the "insuperable line" between us and the other animals,[6] this argument replies: the fact that they are not human. On such a perspective, what makes the difference is simply the possession, or lack, of a genotype characteristic of the species *Homo sapiens*.

Is it an acceptable reply? One can doubt it. Those who appeal to species membership work in fact within the framework of the intra-human egalitarian paradigm. And yet, it is just the line of reasoning that has led to the defense of human equality which implies, by denying moral relevance to race and sex membership, the rejection of the idea that species membership *in itself* can mark a difference as far as moral status is concerned. If one claims that merely biological characteristics like race and sex cannot play a role in ethics, because ethics is a theoretical inquiry endowed with its own standards of justification, in which criteria imported from other domains cannot be directly relevant,[7] how can one attribute a role to another merely biological characteristic such as species? Ethical views that, while rejecting racism and sexism, accept *speciesism*—as was defined, with a neologism that alludes to the parallel intra-human prejudices, the view that grants to the members of our own species a privileged status with respect to all other creatures—are internally inconsistent. For speciesism and racism are twin doctrines.[8]

Compared with this hardly plausible way of construing the relationships between species and morality, there exist more sophisticated views, to which the theoretical defenders of traditional morality tend to turn. In particular, there are, at least among philosophers, two main ways of describing the alleged difference between humans and the other animals. The appeal to the possession of rationality is central to both of them. We can set aside for the sake of argument the (questionable) assumption that all and only human beings are endowed with this capacity, in order to focus on the importance that is attached to rationality from a moral point of view.

The first argument rests on the idea that rational beings are the existence condition of morality, and might be summarized more or less as follows. Ethical norms are addressed to a particular kind of beings—*moral agents*. In brief, moral agents are those rational beings which can reflect morally on how to act, and whose behavior can be subject to moral evaluation. In this sense, if moral agents did not exist, there could be no ethical norms. As a consequence, ethics is an internal affair of moral agents.[9]

In spite of its apparent plausibility, the argument is based on a misunderstanding. Its conclusion is in fact reached only by the shift from the idea that only rational beings can be morally responsible to the idea that only what is done to rational beings has (full) moral weight. But the *how*, that is, the possibility of morality, is one thing; the *what*, that is, the object of morality, is another.[10] To acknowledge that moral agents make morality possible does not mean to make them the only (full) moral patients. That, on the other hand, we do not really hold this view is shown by the fact that we are far from withdrawing full moral protection from those members of our species who are unable to abide by ethical norms. Small children, or—if one wants to avoid the controversial question of potentiality—severely intellectually disabled individuals (the so-called marginal, or non-paradigmatic, humans),[11] are not on this ground relegated to the no-man's land surrounding the moral community.

A different role is played by rationality within the second argument which is usually advanced in defense of human superiority. Basically, what is ascribed to such a capacity is a particular kind of instrumental value. The core idea is that the introduction into the moral community can be justified by means of some sort of agreement. Since in order to abide by the agreement one must be rational, the agreement will include only rational beings, who will then turn out to be the only moral patients. In this light, moral norms would be the norms with which rational and self-interested individuals would agree to comply on condition that others undertook to do so as well. If the preceding argument can somehow point to the contemporary position of John Rawls, here is apparent the influence of the mutual advantage account of contractarianism of Hobbesian descent.[12]

It is not difficult to understand why not even this approach is acceptable. For, given that self-interested contractors gain no advantage from accepting principles that offer guarantees to individuals who are unable to give any guarantee in return, they can completely ignore the interests of those who are unable to reciprocate. But if the golden rule "treat others as you would have them treat you" is replaced by what we might call the silver rule, "treat others as they would treat you,"[13] mutual advantage has the devastating effect of driving ethical impartiality off the stage. Once more, current morality clearly grasps this point, insofar as it does not deprive of rights those human beings—again, children or the severely intellectually disabled—who cannot have duties.

But if none of the major arguments advanced in defense of the ends/means doctrine[14]—the appeal to the possession of a genotype *Homo sapiens*, the appeal to the possession of rationality as a precondition of morals, and the reference to this very same capacity as a means to intersubjective agreement—can justify maintaining nonhuman animals in their present inferior moral state, it seems plausible to conclude that traditional morality is untenable.

III

If one gives up the doctrine of human superiority, what kind of moral perspective should one adopt in its place? In which ways, and toward which beings, should traditional morality be reformed? In order to tackle this question, many among the authors who have dealt with the animal issue appeal to their own specific normative position—be it utilitarianism, deontologism, virtue ethics or any other. However, only an argument starting from premises that are, as far as possible, shared can grant its conclusions the generality that is needed for moral reform. Because of this reason, we will directly start from what is today the most widespread and accepted among moral theories—the universal doctrine of human rights.[15]

At the center of the theory of human rights lies the protection of the vital interests—in welfare, in freedom, and in life—of some beings. Of which beings, exactly? Though the most common, and apparently tautological, answer is "of *human* beings," such a move is, as we have seen, precluded by the fact that discrimination based on species is analogous to those forms of discrimination that the very doctrine condemns in sexism and racism. Most of the philosophers who confront the issue seem to be somehow aware of this problem. When it is bestowed a role, in fact, reference to species is introduced in a hurried and oblique way.[16] What, then, plays in an effective, and not rhetorical, way the role of explaining the *why* of human rights—of illustrating, that is, what it is that, in the members of our species, justifies the equal attribution of the particular sort of moral claims lumped together under the label of "human rights"?

Among the solutions advanced for this problem, the most defensible, as well as the most theoretically fertile, is no doubt the one put forward by a line of argument that appeared at the beginning of the 1960s,[17] and culminating in the elaboration offered by the American philosopher Alan Gewirth. According to such a line, the criterion for the access to the protection that human rights warrant lies only in being an *agent*, that is, an intentional being that cares about its goals and wants to achieve them. All the beings that fulfill the requisite of intentionality are characterized by the capacity to enjoy freedom and welfare, as well as life which is a precondition for them, both directly and as prerequisites for action; and, for all these beings, the intrinsic value of their enjoyment is the same. To choose as a criterion, instead of intentionality, any other characteristic—be it rationality or any other among the cognitive skills traditionally seen as "superior"—would be arbitrary, since it would exclude from moral consideration interests which are relevantly similar in that they are equally vital for their bearers.[18]

Once articulated, such an answer—which has among other things the important effect of barring the way to discredited perfectionist worldviews—appears obvious. And yet, it involves a corollary which is not equally obvious: that, on the basis of the very doctrine that establishes them, human rights are not *human*. For not only does the more or less avowed acceptance of the idea that species membership is not morally relevant eliminate from the theory any structural reference to the possession of a genotype *Homo sapiens*, but the will to secure equal fundamental rights to all human beings, including the non-paradigmatic ones, implies that the criterion for the ascription of such rights must lie at a cognitive level accessible to a large number of nonhuman animals.

IV

If, in view of all this, we go back to our initial interrogative, it may be safely said that the current divergence in standards between humans and nonhumans is indefensible. All the more so: it is plausible to claim that among those entitled to that minimum of equality and equity that allows one to live a life worth living—among, that is, those moral patients who deserve full moral status—there are many nonhuman beings. But what can it mean, in practice, to extend fundamental rights beyond the boundaries of our species? Confronted with this idea, some opponents tend to make recourse to various reductios, by evoking scenarios that are either concretely impossible, such as the obligation to bring our aid-commitment all the way to the deserts or the sea depths, or socially absurd, such as the revision to its foundations of our whole legal system.

None of this. In order to understand this point, it is worth defining more precisely that particular category of moral rights that we label as "human rights." Such category has in fact two significant peculiarities. Firstly, human rights do not cover the whole of morality but concern the more limited theory of conduct which has been defined as "morality in the narrow sense" and which meets the special class of moral concerns which has to do with the basic protection of individuals from interference.[19] For in spite of the attempts to embody in the doctrine some *positive* rights, or rights to assistance, the ones which prevail are always *negative* rights, or rights to non-interference, that not only are more basic but—being less affected by conditions of scarcity—are less likely to be subject to exceptions.[20] Secondly, human rights clearly developed as an answer to those forms of institutionalized violence and discrimination which have marked the first half of the twentieth century. This implies, as it has been convincingly argued by the American philosopher Thomas Pogge, that the model both of their implementation and of their violation is based not on the interaction between individuals, but on the organization and the action of the state.[21]

Let's therefore reconsider the present situation in the light of these two aspects. Billions of nonhuman animals who meet the requisite of intentionality are tortured, confined, and killed in the pursuit of the most varied human goals. But *codified* killing, confinement, mutilation, and torture are just the opposite of that protection from *institutional interference* that human rights theory aims at granting.

What, then, could an implementation at the social level of the conclusions so far reached mean in such a context? Far from involving impossible practical interventions and complicated legal alchemies, such implementation would merely require a legal change aimed at removing in the status of property the basic obstacle to the enjoyment of the denied rights. In other words, it would imply for these animals the shift from the condition of objects to that of subjects of legal rights,[22] and, as a consequence, the prohibition of all the practices that are today made possible by their current state, from raising for food to scientific experimentation to the most varied forms of commercial use and systematic extermination.

This is, I believe, the conclusion awaiting anyone who wants to seriously reflect on our current behavior toward nonhuman animals. Far from belonging in the different, and lesser, moral category in which they have till now been confined, (most) nonhumans confront us with all the force of a justified ethical demand. And this because it is the very logic of the doctrine that tried to overcome the most serious difficulties for intra-human cohabitation which forces us to extend basic rights beyond the boundaries of the species *Homo sapiens*, thus offering a plausible solution for the problems of a community broader than the human one.

Notes

1. Immanuel Kant, *Lectures on Ethics*, trans. Louis Infield (New York: Harper and Row, 1963), p. 239.
2. Aristotle, *Politics*, I, 3, 1256 b.
3. Thomas Aquinas, *Summa contra Gentiles*, book III, part II, chap. CXII.
4. We owe one of the first formulations of the concept to G. J. Warnock, *The Object of Morality* (London: Methuen, 1971), p. 148. See also Harlan B. Miller, "Science, Ethics, and Moral Status," *Between the Species* 10 (1994), p. 14.
5. See Aristotle, *Politics*, I, 2, 1253 b.
6. See Jeremy Bentham, *An Introduction to the Principles of Morals and Legislation* (New York: Hafner Press, 1948), chap. XVII, IV, note 1.
7. For the autonomy of ethics, see Thomas Nagel, "Ethics as an Autonomous Theoretical Subject," in *Morality as a Biological Phenomenon*, ed. Gunther S. Stent (Berkeley: University of California Press, 1978), pp. 221–232. For the moral irrelevance of biological characteristics, see e.g. Michael Tooley, "Speciesism and Basic Moral Principles," *Etica & Animali* 9 (1998), pp. 5–36.
8. Cf. Peter Singer, *Animal Liberation*, 2nd edn. (New York: The New York Review of Books, 1990), p. 9.
9. Once again, we owe the paradigmatic formulation of this argument, which is particularly widespread in the continental philosophical tradition, to Immanuel Kant. See Immanuel Kant, *Foundations of the Metaphysics of Morals*, trans. Lewis W. Beck (Upper Saddle River, NJ: Prentice-Hall, 1997), p. 45.
10. See Steve F. Sapontzis, *Morals, Reason, and Animals* (Philadelphia: Temple University Press, 1987), pp. 146 ff.
11. A comprehensive survey of the discussion of the case of non-paradigmatic members of our species can be found in Daniel A. Dombrowski, *Babies and Beasts: The Argument from Marginal Cases* (Urbana: University of Illinois Press, 1997).
12. For the similarities and differences between Rawlsian impartial contractarian theory and Hobbesian mutual advantage approach, see Paola Cavalieri and Will Kymlicka, "Expanding the Social Contract," *Etica & Animali* 8 (1996), pp. 5–33.
13. I borrow the expression "silver rule" from Edward Johnson, *Species and Morality* (Ph.D. diss., Princeton University, July 1976 [University Microfilms International, Ann Arbor, MI]), p. 134.
14. For a concise critique of many minor arguments, see Paola Cavalieri, *The Animal Question: Why Nonhuman Animals Deserve Human Rights* (New York: Oxford University Press, 2001), chapters III and IV.
15. For a more articulated version of the following argument, see ibid., chapter VI.
16. Cf., for example, what Adam Bedau writes: "Are human rights to be thought of as possessed by all and only persons, human beings, or human persons? . . . [T]he last alternative . . . is the least controversial way to resolve the problem. The concept of human rights was not designed to embrace non-human persons, and it was clearly intended to exclude infra-human beings, such as animals." See Hugo Adam Bedau, "International Human Rights," in *And Justice for All*, eds. Tom Regan and Donald VanDeVeer (Totowa, NJ: Rowman & Allanheld, 1983), p. 298.
17. Its first seeds are to be found in Gregory Vlastos, "Justice and Equality," in *Social Justice*, ed. Richard B. Brandt (Englewood Cliffs, NJ: Prentice-Hall, 1962), pp. 31–72.
18. See Alan Gewirth, *Reason and Morality* (Chicago: University of Chicago Press, 1978). A summary of the argument can be found in Alan Gewirth, "The Basis and Content of Human Rights," in *Nomos XXIII:*

Human Rights, eds. J. Roland Pennock and John W. Chapman (New York: New York University Press, 1981), pp. 119–47.

19. On the notion of narrow morality, cf. in particular W. K. Frankena, "The Concept of Morality," *Journal of Philosophy* 63 (1966), pp. 688–696; G. J. Warnock, *The Object of Morality* (London: Methuen, 1971), in particular chap. 2 and chap. 5; and J. L. Mackie, *Ethics. Inventing Right and Wrong* (London: Penguin, 1990), pp. 107–108.
20. In his "Human Rights, Old and New," in *Political Theory and the Rights of Man*, ed. D. D. Raphael (London: Macmillan, 1967), pp. 54–67. D. D. Raphael plausibly claims that *positive* rights, rather than as "human rights", are to be classified as "citizen's rights."
21. See Thomas Pogge, "How Should Human Rights Be Conceived?," *Jahrbuch für Recht und Ethik* 3 (1995), pp. 103–120.
22. For a discussion of this problem, see e.g. Gary L. Francione, *Animals, Property, and the Law* (Philadelphia: Temple University Press, 1995).

4 Practical Ethics

Peter Singer

Peter Singer states that there is no moral justification for refusing to take animal suffering seriously. He calls for a boycott of the meat industry on the basis of equal consideration of interests. Singer affirms that experiments on animals should only be carried out if experimenters would be willing to also use human beings at an equal or lower level of consciousness. He then responds to common objections to his views. In a concluding section he presents a strong case against the killing of rational and self-conscious animals such as the great apes.

The argument for extending the principle of equality beyond our own species is simple, so simple that it amounts to no more than a clear understanding of the nature of the principle of equal consideration of interests.[1] We have seen that this principle implies that our concern for others ought not to depend on what they are like or what abilities they possess (although precisely what this concern requires us to do may vary according to the characteristics of those affected by what we do). It is on this basis that we are able to say that the fact that some people are not members of our race does not entitle us to exploit them, and similarly the fact that some people are less intelligent than others does not mean that their interests may be disregarded. But the principle also implies that the fact that beings are not members of our species does not entitle us to exploit them, and similarly the fact that other animals are less intelligent than we are does not mean that their interests may be disregarded.

[. . .] [M]any philosophers have advocated equal consideration of interests, in some form or other, as a basic moral principle. Only a few have recognised that the principle has applications beyond our own species, one of the few being Jeremy Bentham, the founding father of modern utilitarianism. In a forward-looking passage, written at a time when African slaves in the British dominions were still being treated much as we now treat nonhuman animals, Bentham wrote:

> The day may come when the rest of the animal creation may acquire those rights which never could have been withholden from them but by the hand of tyranny. The French have already discovered that the blackness of the skin is no reason why a human being should be abandoned without redress to the caprice of a tormentor. It may one day come to be recognised that the number of the legs, the villosity of the skin, or the termination of the *os sacrum*, are reasons equally insufficient for abandoning a sensitive being to the same fate. What else is it that should trace the insuperable line? Is it the faculty of reason, or perhaps the faculty of discourse? But a fullgrown horse or dog is beyond comparison a more rational, as well as a more conversable animal, than an infant of a day, or a week, or even a month, old. But suppose they were otherwise, what would it avail? The question is not, Can they *reason*? nor Can they *talk*? but, *Can they suffer?*[2]

In this passage Bentham points to the capacity for suffering as the vital characteristic that entitles a being to equal consideration. The capacity for suffering—or more strictly, for suffering and/or enjoyment or happiness—is not just another characteristic like the capacity for language or for higher mathematics. Bentham is not saying that those who try to mark 'the insuperable line' that determines whether the interests of a being should be considered happen to have selected the wrong characteristic. The capacity for suffering and enjoying things is a prerequisite for having interests at all, a condition that must be satisfied before we can speak of interests in any meaningful way. It would be nonsense to say that it was not in the interests of a stone to be kicked along the road by a schoolboy. A stone does not have interests because it cannot suffer. Nothing that we can do to it could possibly make any difference to its welfare. A mouse, on the other hand, does have an interest in not being tormented, because mice will suffer if they are treated in this way.

If a being suffers, there can be no moral justification for refusing to take that suffering into consideration. No matter what the nature of the being, the principle of equality requires that the suffering be counted equally with the like suffering—in so far as rough comparisons can be made—of any other being. If a being is not capable of suffering, or of experiencing enjoyment or happiness, there is nothing to be taken into account. This is why the limit of sentience (using the term as a convenient, if not strictly accurate, shorthand for the capacity to suffer or experience enjoyment or happiness) is the only defensible boundary of concern for the interests of others. To mark this boundary by some characteristic like intelligence or rationality would be to mark it in an arbitrary way. Why not choose some other characteristic, like skin colour?

Racists violate the principle of equality by giving greater weight to the interests of members of their own race when there is a clash between their interests and the interests of those of another race. Racists of European descent typically have not accepted that pain matters as much when it is felt by Africans, for example, as when it is felt by Europeans. Similarly those I would call 'speciesists' give greater weight to the interests of members of their own species when there is a clash between their interests and the interests of those of other species. Human speciesists do not accept that pain is as bad when it is felt by pigs or mice as when it is felt by humans.

That, then, is really the whole of the argument for extending the principle of equality to nonhuman animals; but there may be some doubts about what this equality amounts to in practice. In particular, the last sentence of the previous paragraph may prompt some people to reply: 'Surely pain felt by a mouse just is not as bad as pain felt by a human. Humans have much greater awareness of what is happening to them, and this makes their suffering worse. You can't equate the suffering of, say, a person dying slowly from cancer and a laboratory mouse undergoing the same fate.'

I fully accept that in the case described the human cancer victim normally suffers more than the nonhuman cancer victim. This in no way undermines the extension of equal consideration of interests to nonhumans. It means, rather, that we must take care when we compare the interests of different species. In some situations a member of one species will suffer more than a member of another species. In this case we should still apply the principle of equal consideration of interests, but the result of so doing is, of course, to give priority to relieving the greater suffering. A simpler case may help to make this clear.

If I give a horse a hard slap across its rump with my open hand, the horse may start, but it presumably feels little pain. Its skin is thick enough to protect it against a mere slap. If I slap a baby in the same way, however, the baby will cry and presumably does feel pain, for the baby's skin is more sensitive. So it is worse to slap a baby than a horse, if both slaps are administered with equal force. But there must be some kind of blow—I don't know exactly what it would be, but perhaps a blow with a heavy stick—that would cause the horse as much pain as we cause a baby by a simple slap. That is what I mean by 'the same amount of pain,' and if we consider it wrong to inflict that much pain on a baby for no good reason, then we must, unless we are speciesists, consider it equally wrong to inflict the same amount of pain on a horse for no good reason.

There are other differences between humans and animals that cause other complications. Normal adult human beings have mental capacities that will, in certain circumstances, lead them to suffer more than animals would in the same circumstances. If, for instance, we decided to perform extremely painful or lethal scientific experiments on normal adult humans, kidnapped at random from public parks for this purpose, adults who entered parks would become fearful that they would be kidnapped. The resultant terror would be a form of suffering additional to the pain of the experiment. The same experiments performed on nonhuman animals would cause less suffering, since the animals would not have the anticipatory dread of being kidnapped and experimented upon. This does not mean, of course, that it would be *right* to perform the experiment on animals, but only that there is a reason, and one that is not speciesist, for preferring to use animals rather than normal adult humans, if the experiment is to be done at all. Note, however, that this same argument gives us a reason for preferring to use human infants—orphans perhaps—or severely intellectually disabled humans for experiments, rather than adults, since infants and severely intellectually disabled humans would also have no idea of what was going to happen to them. As far as this argument is concerned, nonhuman animals and infants and severely intellectually disabled humans are in the same category; and if we use this argument to justify experiments on nonhuman animals we have to ask ourselves whether we are also prepared to allow experiments on human infants and severely intellectually disabled adults. If we make a distinction between animals and these humans, how can we do it, other than on the basis of a morally indefensible preference for members of our own species?

There are many areas in which the superior mental powers of normal adult humans make a difference: anticipation, more detailed memory, greater knowledge of what is happening, and so on. These differences explain why a human dying from cancer is likely to suffer more than a mouse. It is the mental anguish that makes the human's position so much harder to bear. Yet these differences do not all point to greater suffering on the part of the normal human being. Sometimes animals may suffer more because of their more limited understanding. If, for instance, we are taking prisoners in wartime we can explain to them that while they must submit to capture, search, and confinement they will not otherwise be harmed and will be set free at the conclusion of hostilities. If we capture wild animals, however, we cannot explain that we are not threatening their lives. A wild animal cannot distinguish an attempt to overpower and confine from an attempt to kill; the one causes as much terror as the other.

It may be objected that comparisons of the sufferings of different species are impossible to make and that for this reason when the interests of animals and humans clash, the principle of equality gives no guidance. It is true that comparisons of suffering between members of different species cannot be made precisely. Nor, for that matter, can comparisons of suffering between different human beings be made precisely. Precision is not essential. As we shall see shortly, even if we were to prevent the infliction of suffering on animals only when the interests of humans would not be affected to anything like the extent that animals are affected, we would be forced to make radical changes in our treatment of animals that would involve our diet, the farming methods we use, experimental procedures in many fields of science, our approach to wildlife and to hunting, trapping, and the wearing of furs, and areas of entertainment like circuses, rodeos, and zoos. As a result, the total quantity of suffering caused would be greatly reduced—so greatly that it is hard to imagine any other change of moral attitude that would cause so great a reduction in the total sum of suffering in the universe.

So far I have said a lot about the infliction of suffering on animals but nothing about killing them. This omission has been deliberate. The application of the principle of equality to the infliction of suffering is, in theory at least, fairly straightforward. Pain and suffering are bad and should be prevented or minimised, irrespective of the race, sex, or species of the being that suffers. How bad a pain is depends on how intense it is and how long it lasts, but pains of the same intensity and duration are equally bad, whether felt by humans or animals. When we come to consider the value of life, we cannot say quite so confidently that a life is a life, and equally valuable, whether it is a human life or an animal life. It would not be speciesist to hold that the life of a self-aware being, capable of abstract thought, of planning for the future, of complex acts of communication, and so on, is more valuable than the life of a being without these capacities. (I am not saying whether this view is justifiable or not; only that it cannot simply be rejected as speciesist, because it is not on the basis of species itself that one life is held to be more valuable than another.) The value of life is a notoriously difficult ethical question, and we can only arrive at a reasoned conclusion about the comparative value of human and animal life after we have discussed the value of life in general. This is a topic for a separate chapter. Meanwhile there are important conclusions to be derived from the extension beyond our own species of the principle of equal consideration of interests, irrespective of our conclusions about the value of life.

Speciesism in Practice

Animals as Food

For most people in modern, urbanised societies, the principal form of contact with nonhuman animals is at meal times. The use of animals for food is probably the oldest and the most widespread form of animal use. There is also a sense in which it is the most basic form of animal use, the foundation stone on which rests the belief that animals exist for our pleasure and convenience.

If animals count in their own right, our use of animals for food becomes questionable—especially when animal flesh is a luxury rather than a necessity. Eskimos living in an environment where they must kill animals for food or starve might be justified in claiming that their interest in surviving overrides that of the animals they kill. Most of us cannot defend our diet in this way. Citizens of industrialised societies can easily obtain an adequate diet without the use of animal flesh. The overwhelming weight of medical evidence indicates that animal flesh is not necessary for good health or longevity. Nor is animal production in industrialised societies an efficient way of producing food, since most of the animals consumed have been fattened on grains and other foods that we could have eaten directly. When we feed these grains to animals, only about 10 per cent of the nutritional value remains as meat for human consumption. So, with the exception of animals raised entirely on grazing land unsuitable for crops, animals are eaten neither for health nor to increase our food supply. Their flesh is a luxury, consumed because people like its taste.

In considering the ethics of the use of animal flesh for human food in industrialised societies, we are considering a situation in which a relatively minor human interest must be balanced against the lives and welfare of the animals involved. The principle of equal consideration of interests does not allow major interests to be sacrificed for minor interests.

The case against using animals for food is at its strongest when animals are made to lead miserable lives so that their flesh can be made available to humans at the lowest possible cost. Modern forms of intensive farming apply science and technology to the attitude that animals are objects for us to use. In order to have meat on the table at a price that people can afford, our society tolerates methods of meat production that confine sentient animals in cramped, unsuitable conditions for the entire duration of their lives. Animals are treated like machines that convert fodder into flesh, and any innovation that results in a higher 'conversion ratio' is liable to be adopted. As one authority on the subject has said, 'Cruelty is acknowledged only when profitability ceases.' To avoid speciesism we must stop these practices. Our custom is all the support that factory farmers need. The decision to cease giving them that support may be difficult, but it is less difficult than it would have been for a white Southerner to go against the traditions of his society and free his slaves; if we do not change our dietary habits, how can we censure those slaveholders who would not change their own way of living?

These arguments apply to animals who have been reared in factory farms—which means that we should not eat chicken, pork, or veal, unless we know that the meat we are eating was not produced by factory farm methods. The same is true of beef that has come from cattle kept in crowded feedlots (as most beef does in the United States). Eggs will come from hens kept in small wire cages, too small even to allow them to stretch their wings, unless the eggs are specifically sold as 'free range' (or unless one lives in a relatively enlightened country like Switzerland, which has prohibited the cage system of keeping hens).

These arguments do not take us all the way to a vegetarian diet, since some animals—for instance, sheep and in some countries cattle—still graze freely outdoors. This could change. The American pattern of fattening cattle in crowded feedlots is spreading to other countries. Meanwhile, the lives of free-ranging animals are undoubtedly better than those of animals reared in factory farms. It is still doubtful if using them for food is compatible with equal consideration of interests. One problem is, of course, that using them as food involves killing them—but this is an issue to which, as I have said, we shall return when we have discussed the value of life in the next chapter. Apart from taking their lives there are also many other things done to animals in order to bring them cheaply to our dinner table. Castration, the separation of mother and young, the breaking up of herds, branding, transporting, and finally the moments of slaughter—all of these are likely to involve suffering and do not take the animals' interests into account. Perhaps animals could be reared on a small scale without suffering in these ways, but it does not seem economical or practical to do so on the scale required for feeding our large urban populations. In any case, the important question is not whether animal flesh *could* be produced without suffering, but whether the flesh we are considering buying *was* produced without suffering. Unless we can be confident that it was, the principle of equal consideration of interests implies that it was wrong to sacrifice important interests of the animal in order to satisfy less important interests of our own; consequently we should boycott the end result of this process.

For those of us living in cities where it is difficult to know how the animals we might eat have lived and died, this conclusion brings us close to a vegetarian way of life. I shall consider some objections to it in the final section of this chapter.

Experimenting on Animals

Perhaps the area in which speciesism can most clearly be observed is the use of animals in experiments. Here the issue stands out starkly, because experimenters often seek to justify experimenting on animals by claiming that the experiments lead us to discoveries about humans; if this is so, the experimenter must agree that human and nonhuman animals are similar in crucial respects. For instance, if forcing a rat to choose between starving to death and crossing an electrified grid to obtain food tells us anything about the reactions of humans to stress, we must assume that the rat feels stress in this kind of situation.

People sometimes think that all animal experiments serve vital medical purposes and can be justified on the grounds that they relieve more suffering than they cause. This comfortable belief is mistaken. Drug companies test new shampoos and cosmetics they are intending to market by dripping concentrated solutions of them into the eyes of rabbits, in a test known as the Draize test. (Pressure from the animal liberation movement has led several cosmetics companies to abandon this practice. An alternative test, not using animals, has now been found. Nevertheless, many companies, including some of the largest, still continue to perform the Draize test.) Food additives, including artificial colourings and preservatives, are tested by what is known as the LD50—a test designed to find the 'lethal dose', or level of consumption that will make 50 per cent of a sample of animals die. In the process nearly all of the animals are made very sick before some finally die and others pull through. These tests are not necessary to prevent human suffering: even if there were no alternative to the use of animals to test the safety of the products, we already have enough shampoos and food colourings. There is no need to develop new ones that might be dangerous.

In many countries, the armed forces perform atrocious experiments on animals that rarely come to light. To give just one example: at the U.S. Armed Forces Radiobiology Institute, in Bethesda, Maryland, rhesus monkeys have been trained to run inside a large wheel. If they slow down too much, the wheel slows down, too, and the monkeys get an electric shock. Once the monkeys are trained to run for long periods, they are given lethal doses of radiation. Then, while sick and vomiting, they are forced to continue to run until they drop. This is supposed to provide information on the capacities of soldiers to continue to fight after a nuclear attack.

Nor can all university experiments be defended on the grounds that they relieve more suffering than they inflict. Three experimenters at Princeton University kept 256 young rats without food or water until they died. They concluded that young rats under conditions of fatal thirst and starvation are much more active than normal adult rats given food and water. In a well-known series of experiments that went on for more than fifteen years, H. F. Harlow of the Primate Research Center,

Madison, Wisconsin, reared monkeys under conditions of maternal deprivation and total isolation. He found that in this way he could reduce the monkeys to a state in which, when placed among normal monkeys, they sat huddled in a corner in a condition of persistent depression and fear. Harlow also produced monkey mothers so neurotic that they smashed their infant's face into the floor and rubbed it back and forth. Although Harlow himself is no longer alive, some of his former students at other U.S. universities continue to perform variations on his experiments.

In these cases, and many others like them, the benefits to humans are either nonexistent or uncertain, while the losses to members of other species are certain and real. Hence the experiments indicate a failure to give equal consideration to the interests of all beings, irrespective of species.

In the past, argument about animal experimentation has often missed this point because it has been put in absolutist terms: would the opponent of experimentation be prepared to let thousands die from a terrible disease that could be cured by experimenting on one animal? This is a purely hypothetical question, since experiments do not have such dramatic results, but as long as its hypothetical nature is clear, I think the question should be answered affirmatively—in other words, if one, or even a dozen animals had to suffer experiments in order to save thousands, I would think it right and in accordance with equal consideration of interests that they should do so. This, at any rate, is the answer a utilitarian must give. Those who believe in absolute rights might hold that it is always wrong to sacrifice one being, whether human or animal, for the benefit of another. In that case the experiment should not be carried out, whatever the consequences.

To the hypothetical question about saving thousands of people through a single experiment on an animal, opponents of speciesism can reply with a hypothetical question of their own: would experimenters be prepared to perform their experiments on orphaned humans with severe and irreversible brain damage if that were the only way to save thousands? (I say 'orphaned' in order to avoid the complication of the feelings of the human parents.) If experimenters are not prepared to use orphaned humans with severe and irreversible brain damage, their readiness to use nonhuman animals seems to discriminate on the basis of species alone, since apes, monkeys, dogs, cats, and even mice and rats are more intelligent, more aware of what is happening to them, more sensitive to pain, and so on, than many severely brain damaged humans barely surviving in hospital wards and other institutions. There seems to be no morally relevant characteristic that such humans have that nonhuman animals lack. Experimenters, then, show bias in favour of their own species whenever they carry out experiments on nonhuman animals for purposes that they would not think justified them in using human beings at an equal or lower level of sentience, awareness, sensitivity, and so on. If this bias were eliminated, the number of experiments performed on animals would be greatly reduced.

Other Forms of Speciesism

I have concentrated on the use of animals as food and in research, since these are examples of large-scale, systematic speciesism. They are not, of course, the only areas in which the principle of equal consideration of interests, extended beyond the human species, has practical implications. There are many other areas that raise similar issues, including the fur trade, hunting in all its different forms, circuses, rodeos, zoos, and the pet business. Since the philosophical questions raised by these issues are not very different from those raised by the use of animals as food and in research, I shall leave it to the reader to apply the appropriate ethical principles to them.

Some Objections

I first put forward the views outlined in this chapter in 1973. At that time there was no animal liberation or animal rights movement. Since then a movement has sprung up, and some of the worst abuses of animals, like the Draize and LD50 tests, are now less widespread, even though they have not been eliminated. The fur trade has come under attack, and as a result fur sales have declined dramatically in countries like Britain, the Netherlands, Australia, and the United States. Some countries are also starting to phase out the most confining forms of factory farming. As already mentioned, Switzerland has prohibited the cage system of keeping laying hens. Britain has outlawed the raising of calves in individual stalls and is phasing out individual stalls for pigs. Sweden, as in other areas of social reform, is in the lead here, too: in 1988 the Swedish Parliament passed a law that will, over a ten-year period, lead to the elimination of all systems of factory farming that confine animals for long periods and prevent them carrying out their natural behaviour.

Despite this increasing acceptance of many aspects of the case for animal liberation, and the slow but tangible progress made on behalf of animals, a variety of objections have emerged, some straightforward and predictable, some more subtle and unexpected. In this final section of the chapter I shall attempt to answer the most important of these objections. I shall begin with the more straightforward ones.

How Do We Know That Animals Can Feel Pain?

We can never directly experience the pain of another being, whether that being is human or not. When I see my daughter fall and scrape her knee, I know that she feels pain because of the way she behaves—she cries, she tells me her knee hurts, she rubs the sore spot, and so on. I know that I myself behave in a somewhat similar—if more inhibited—way when I feel pain, and so I accept that my daughter feels something like what I feel when I scrape my knee.

The basis of my belief that animals can feel pain is similar to the basis of my belief that my daughter can feel pain. Animals in pain behave in much the same way as humans do, and their behaviour is sufficient justification for the belief that they feel pain. It is true that, with the exception of those apes who have been taught to communicate by sign language, they cannot actually say that they are feeling pain—but then when my daughter was very young she could not talk, either. She found other ways to make her inner states apparent, thereby demonstrating that we can be sure that a being is feeling pain even if the being cannot use language.

To back up our inference from animal behaviour, we can point to the fact that the nervous systems of all vertebrates, and especially of birds and mammals, are fundamentally similar. Those parts of the human nervous system that are concerned with feeling pain are relatively old, in evolutionary terms. Unlike the cerebral cortex, which developed fully only after our ancestors diverged from other mammals, the basic nervous system evolved in more distant ancestors common to ourselves and the other 'higher' animals. This anatomical parallel makes it likely that the capacity of animals to feel is similar to our own.

It is significant that none of the grounds we have for believing that animals feel pain hold for plants. We cannot observe behaviour suggesting pain—sensational claims to the contrary have not been substantiated—and plants do not have a centrally organised nervous system like ours.

Animals Eat Each Other, So Why Shouldn't We Eat Them?

This might be called the Benjamin Franklin Objection. Franklin recounts in his *Autobiography* that he was for a time a vegetarian but his abstinence from animal flesh came to an end when he was watching some friends prepare to fry a fish they had just caught. When the fish was cut open, it was found to have a smaller fish in its stomach. 'Well', Franklin said to himself, 'if you eat one another, I don't see why we may not eat you' and he proceeded to do so.

Franklin was at least honest. In telling this story, he confesses that he convinced himself of the validity of the objection only after the fish was already in the frying pan and smelling 'admirably well'; and he remarks that one of the advantages of being a 'reasonable creature' is that one can find a reason for whatever one wants to do. The replies that can be made to this objection are so obvious that Franklin's acceptance of it does testify more to his love of fried fish than to his powers of reason.[3] For a start, most animals who kill for food would not be able to survive if they did not, whereas we have no need to eat animal flesh. Next, it is odd that humans, who normally think of the behaviour of animals as 'beastly' should, when it suits them, use an argument that implies that we ought to look to animals for moral guidance. The most decisive point, however, is that nonhuman animals are not capable of considering the alternatives open to them or of reflecting on the ethics of their diet. Hence it is impossible to hold the animals responsible for what they do, or to judge that because of their killing they 'deserve' to be treated in a similar way. Those who read these lines, on the other hand, must consider the justifiability of their dietary habits. You cannot evade responsibility by imitating beings who are incapable of making this choice.

Sometimes people point to the fact that animals eat each other in order to make a slightly different point. This fact suggests, they think, not that animals deserve to be eaten, but rather that there is a natural law according to which the stronger prey upon the weaker, a kind of Darwinian 'survival of the fittest' in which by eating animals we are merely playing our part.

This interpretation of the objection makes two basic mistakes, one a mistake of fact and the other an error of reasoning. The factual mistake lies in the assumption that our own consumption of animals is part of the natural evolutionary process. This might be true of a few primitive cultures that still hunt for food, but it has nothing to do with the mass production of domestic animals in factory farms.

Suppose that we did hunt for our food, though, and this was part of some natural evolutionary process. There would still be an error of reasoning in the assumption that because this process is natural it is right. It is, no doubt, 'natural' for women to produce an infant every year or two from puberty to menopause, but this does not mean that it is wrong to interfere with this process. We need to know the natural laws that affect us in order to estimate the consequences of what we do; but we do not have to assume that the natural way of doing something is incapable of improvement.

[. . .]

Ethics and Reciprocity

[. . .]

[I]f the basis of ethics is that I refrain from doing nasty things to others as long as they don't do nasty things to me, I have no reason against doing nasty things to those who are incapable of appreciating my restraint and controlling their conduct towards me accordingly. Animals, by and large, are in this category. When I am surfing far out from shore and a shark attacks, my concern for animals will not help; I am as likely to be eaten as the next surfer, though he may spend every Sunday afternoon taking potshots at sharks from a boat. Since animals cannot reciprocate, they are, on this view, outside the limits of the ethical contract.

[. . .]

When we turn to the question of justification, we can see that contractual accounts of ethics have many problems. Clearly, such accounts exclude from the ethical sphere a lot more than nonhuman animals. Since severely intellectually disabled humans are equally incapable of reciprocating, they must also be excluded. The same goes for infants and very young children; but the problems of the contractual view are not limited to these special cases. The ultimate reason for entering into the ethical contract is, on this view, self-interest. Unless some additional universal element is brought in, one group of people has no reason to deal ethically with another if it is not in their interest to do so. If we take this seriously we shall have to revise our ethical judgments drastically. For instance, the white slave traders who transported African slaves to America had no self-interested reason for treating Africans any better than they did. The Africans had no way of retaliating. If they had only been contractualists, the slave traders could have rebutted the abolitionists by explaining to them that ethics stops at the boundaries of the community, and since Africans are not part of their community they have no duties to them.

Nor is it only past practices that would be affected by taking the contractual model seriously. Though people often speak of the world today as a single community, there is no doubt that the power of people in, say, Chad, to reciprocate either good or evil that is done to them by, say, citizens of the United States is limited. Hence it does not seem that the contract view provides for any obligations on the part of wealthy nations to poorer nations.

Most striking of all is the impact of the contract model on our attitude to future generations. 'Why should I do anything for posterity? What has posterity ever done for me?' would be the view we ought to take if only those who can reciprocate are within the bounds of ethics. There is no way in which those who will be alive in the year 2100 can do anything to make our lives better or worse. Hence if obligations only exist where there can be reciprocity, we need have no worries about problems like the disposal of nuclear waste. True, some nuclear wastes will still be deadly for a quarter of a million years; but as long as we put it in containers that will keep it away from us for 100 years, we have done all that ethics demands of us.

These examples should suffice to show that, whatever its origin, the ethics we have now does go beyond a tacit understanding between beings capable of reciprocity. The prospect of returning to such a basis will, I trust, not be appealing. Since no account of the origin of morality compels us to base our morality on reciprocity, and since no other arguments in favour of this conclusion have been offered, we should reject this view of ethics.

[. . .]

Conclusions

[T]here is no single answer to the question: 'Is it normally wrong to take the life of an animal?' The term 'animal'—even in the restricted sense of 'nonhuman animal'—covers too diverse a range of lives for one principle to apply to all of them.

Some nonhuman animals appear to be rational and self-conscious, conceiving themselves as distinct beings with a past and a future. When this is so, or to the best of our knowledge may be so, the case against killing is strong, as strong as the case against killing permanently intellectually disabled human beings at a similar mental level. (I have in mind here the direct reasons against killing; the effects on relatives of the intellectually disabled human will sometimes—but not always—constitute additional indirect reasons against killing the human.)

In the present state of our knowledge, this strong case against killing can be invoked most categorically against the slaughter of chimpanzees, gorillas, and orangutans. On the basis of what we now know about these near-relatives of ours, we should immediately extend to them the same full protection against being killed that we extend now to all human beings. A case can also be made, though with varying degrees of confidence, on behalf of whales, dolphins, monkeys, dogs, cats, pigs, seals, bears, cattle, sheep, and so on, perhaps even to the point at which it may include all mammals—much depends on how far we are prepared to go in extending the benefit of the doubt, where a doubt exists. Even if we stopped at the species I have named, however—excluding the remainder of the mammals—our discussion has raised a very large question mark over the justifiability of a great deal of killing of animals carried out by humans, even when this killing takes place painlessly and without causing suffering to other members of the animal community. (Most of this killing, of course, does not take place under such ideal conditions.)

When we come to animals who, as far as we can tell, are not rational and self-conscious beings, the case against killing is weaker. When we are not dealing with beings aware of themselves as distinct entities, the wrongness of painless killing derives from the loss of pleasure it involves. Where the life taken would not, on balance, have been pleasant, no direct wrong is done. Even when the animal killed would have lived pleasantly, it is at least arguable that no wrong is done if the animal killed will, as a result of the killing, be replaced by another animal living an equally pleasant life. Taking this view involves holding that a wrong done to an existing being can be made up for by a benefit conferred on an as yet non-existent being. Thus it is possible to regard non-self-conscious animals as interchangeable with each other in a way that self-conscious beings are not. This means that in some circumstances—when animals lead pleasant lives and are killed painlessly, their deaths do not cause suffering to other animals, and the killing of one animal makes possible its replacement by another who would not otherwise have lived—the killing of non-self-conscious animals may not be wrong.

Is it possible, along these lines, to justify raising chickens for their meat, not in factory farm conditions but roaming freely around a farmyard? Let us make the questionable assumption that chickens are not self-conscious. Assume also that the birds can be killed painlessly, and the survivors do not appear to be affected by the death of one of their numbers. Assume, finally, that for economic reasons we could not rear the birds if we did not eat them. Then the replaceability argument appears to justify killing the birds, because depriving them of the pleasures of their existence can be offset against the pleasures of chickens who do not yet exist, and will exist only if existing chickens are killed.

As a piece of critical moral reasoning, this argument may be sound. Even at that level, it is important to realise how limited it is in its application. It cannot justify factory farming, where animals do not have pleasant lives. Nor does it normally justify the killing of wild animals. A duck shot by a hunter (making the shaky assumption that ducks are not self-conscious, and the almost certainly false assumption that the shooter can be relied upon to kill the duck instantly) has probably had a pleasant life, but the shooting of a duck does not lead to its replacement by another. Unless the duck population is at the maximum that can be sustained by the available food supply, the killing of a duck ends a pleasant life without starting another, and is for that reason wrong on straightforward utilitarian grounds. So although there are situations in which it is not wrong to kill animals, these situations are special ones and do not cover very many of the billions of premature deaths humans inflict, year after year, on animals.

In any case, at the level of practical moral principles, it would be better to reject altogether the killing of animals for food, unless one must do so to survive. Killing animals for food makes us think of them as objects that we can use as we please. Their lives then count for little when weighed against our mere wants. As long as we continue to use animals in this way, to change our attitudes to animals in the way that they should be changed will be an impossible task. How can we encourage people to respect animals, and have equal concern for their interests, if they continue to eat them for their mere enjoyment? To foster the right attitudes of consideration for animals, including non-self-conscious ones, it may be best to make it a simple principle to avoid killing them for food.

[. . .]

Notes

1. My views on animals first appeared in *The New York Review of Books*, 5 April 1973, under the title 'Animal Liberation'. This article was a review of R. S. Godlovitch and J. Harris (eds.), *Animals, Men and Morals* (London, Harper Collins, 1972). A more complete statement was published as *Animal Liberation*, 2nd ed. (New York, Harper Collins, 1990).
2. Bentham's defence of animals, quoted in the section 'Racism and Speciesism' is from his *Introduction to the Principles of Morals and Legislation*, chap. 18, sec. 1, n.
3. The source for the anecdote about Benjamin Franklin is his *Autobiography* (New York, Modern Library, 1950), p. 41. The same objection has been more seriously considered by John Benson, 'Duty and the Beast', *Philosophy*, vol. 53 (1978): 545–7.

5 Feminism and the Treatment of Animals

From Care to Dialogue

Josephine Donovan

In this essay Josephine Donovan discusses the development of feminist animal care theory from its beginnings in the early 1990s to the present. Feminist animal care theory developed in reaction against the animal rights theory developed by Tom Regan and the utilitarian theory enunciated by Peter Singer. She argues that these theories privilege reason or mathematical calculation. In addition, they are abstract theories which isolate the individual and obscure the particular circumstances of an ethical event. Donovan emphasizes the dialogical nature of care theory: listening to animals and caring about what they are telling us.

In recent years feminists have brought care theory to the philosophical debate over how humans should treat nonhuman animals. Care theory, an important branch of contemporary feminist theory, was originally articulated by Carol Gilligan (1982) and has been elaborated, refined, and criticized extensively since it was first formulated in the late 1970s. Since I and others applied care theory to the animal question in the early 1990s (see esp. Donovan and Adams 1996), it has established itself as a major vein of animal ethics theory (the others being liberal rights doctrine, utilitarianism, and deep ecology theory). It also has received close scrutiny from the philosophical community, which has yielded pertinent criticisms.

This article is an attempt to respond to these criticisms and thereby further refine and strengthen feminist animal care theory. Although focused on the issue of animal treatment, my analysis may have implications for care theory in general. As it is my conclusion that many of the critiques have misapprehended the original message of the feminist animal care theorists, I hope to reposition the discussion to emphasize the dialogical nature of care theory. It is not so much, I will argue, a matter of caring for animals as mothers (human and nonhuman) care for their infants as it is one of listening to animals, paying emotional attention, taking seriously—*caring about*—what they are telling us. As I state at the conclusion of "Animal Rights and Feminist Theory," "We should not kill, eat, torture, and exploit animals because they do not want to be so treated, and we know that" (Donovan 1990, 375). In other words, I am proposing in this article that we shift the epistemological source of theorizing about animals to the animals themselves. Could we not, I ask, extend feminist standpoint theory to animals, including their standpoint in our ethical deliberations?

Feminist Animal Care Theory

Feminist animal care theory developed in reaction against the animal rights/utilitarian theory that had by the 1980s established itself as the dominant vein in animal ethics (Singer 1975; Regan 1983). Rooted in Enlightenment rationalism, liberal rights theory and utilitarianism, feminist care theorists argue, privilege reason (in the case of rights theory) or mathematical calculation (in the case of utilitarianism) epistemologically. Because of their abstract, universalizing pretenses, both rights theory and utilitarianism elide the particular circumstances of an ethical event, as well as its contextual and political contingencies. In addition, rights theory, following Kantian premises, tends to view individuals as autonomous isolates, thereby neglecting their social relationships. It also presumes a society of rational equals, a perspective that ignores the power differentials that obtain in any society but especially in one that includes both humans and animals. Finally, both rights and utilitarianism dispense with sympathy, empathy, and compassion as relevant ethical and epistemological sources for human treatment of nonhuman animals.

Feminist care theory attempted to restore these emotional responses to the philosophical debate and to validate them as authentic modes of knowledge. It also, following Gilligan, urged a narrative, contextually aware form of reasoning as opposed to the rigid rationalist abstractions of the "one-size-fits-all" rights and utilitarian approach, emphasizing instead that we heed the individual particularities of any given case and acknowledge the qualitative heterogeneity of life-forms.

Finally, implicit in feminist animal care theory—though perhaps not sufficiently theorized as such—is a dialogical mode of ethical reasoning, not unlike the dialectical method proposed in standpoint theory, wherein humans pay attention to—listen to—animal communications and construct a human ethic in conversation with the animals rather than imposing on them a rationalistic, calculative grid of humans' own monological construction.

Feminists—indeed most women—are acutely aware of what it feels like to have one's opinion ignored, trivialized, rendered unimportant. Perhaps this experience has awakened their sensitivity to the fact that other marginalized groups—including animals—have trouble getting their viewpoints heard. One of the main directions in feminist legal theory has insisted that legal codes drawn up based on male circumstances often do not fit the lives of women, whose differing realities and needs have not been recognized in the formulation of the law (West 1988, 61, 65; 1997; MacKinnon 1989, 224). Just, therefore, as feminism has called for incorporating the voices of women into public policy and ethical discourse, so feminist animal advocates must call for incorporating the voices of animals as well. Dialogical theory, therefore, means learning to see what human ideological constructions elide; to understand and comprehend what is not identified and recognized in these constructions; to, in short, attempt to reach out emotionally as well as intellectually to what is different from oneself rather than reshaping (in the case of animals) that difference to conform to one's own human-based preconceptions.

Response to Criticisms and Elaborations of Feminist Animal Care Theory

Before further developing the dialogical aspect of feminist animal care theory, I would like first to address recently proposed critiques and refinements of that theory. Such discussion will, I believe, help to elaborate the modifications in care theory I am proposing here.

I begin with the criticisms. A continuing criticism of care theory in general is that the individual experiences of caring on which it is based are not universalizable. Robert Garner, for example, labeled care theory "problematic" because, although he acknowledges that "contextualizing animal suffering in particular cases" (2003, 241) is enriching (citing in this regard Marti Kheel's proposal that all meat eaters should visit slaughterhouses to experience emotionally the circumstances that produce their food [Kheel (1985) 1996, 27]), such an individual experience cannot, he claims, be "universalize[d] to appeal to those who have not had that particular experience" (Garner 2003, 241).

Garner's criticism is a variation of Immanuel Kant's objections to care theory's eighteenth-century counterpart, sympathy theory (see Donovan 1996). Kant argued that sympathy is an unstable base for moral decision making because, first, the feeling is volatile; second, the capacity for sympathy is not evenly distributed in the population; and third, sympathy is therefore not universalizable (Kant 1957, 276–81). Instead, he proposed that one should act ethically out of a sense of duty and that one's sense of what is ethical be determined by imagining what would happen if one's actions were universalized. For example, if one were to universalize one's own lying as an ethical law, it would mean that everyone could lie, which would effect an adverse result, making one realize that lying is wrong. This is the so-called categorical imperative (302).

Kant therefore rooted the idea of universalizability in the individual decision maker—"the moral agent . . . in lonely cogitans" (Walker [1989] 1995, 143)—who attempts to imaginatively universalize his or her own ethical inclination in order to ascertain a moral imperative. Garner, however, seems to imagine an abstract arbiter (the philosopher perhaps) apart from the decision maker who does or does not universalize from the instance of a person revulsed by a slaughterhouse. While there seems to be some confusion among proponents of universalizability as to who is doing the universalizing (see Adler 1987, 219–20), the question is a crucial one for feminists, who have become suspicious of universalizing theories precisely because of who has traditionally done the universalizing and who has been left out. Indeed, many ethic-of-care theorists have dispensed with the universalizability criterion altogether, seeing it as incompatible with the particularistic focus of care (Benhabib 1987; Walker [1989] 1995). Margaret Urban Walker suggests in fact that a rigid application of universalized norms may result in "a sort of 'moral colonialism' (the 'subjects' of my moral decisions disappear behind uniform 'policies' I must impartially 'apply')" ([1989] 1995, 147).

Nevertheless, if generalizing is done from a feminist point of view, as in Kheel's argument—in other words, if we take seriously the perspective or standpoint of a marginalized individual as opposed to contending that such a perspective is invalid because not universalizable—I would argue that it is not illogical to contend that one might easily generalize from an individual ethical reaction, extending that reaction to others similarly situated, thus positing a general or universal precept. Thus, one might reason: if others could see the horrendous conditions in this slaughterhouse, they too would be revulsed and moved to take an ethical stand against such practices—for example, to condemn the slaughter of animals for food as morally wrong, to become vegetarians. Moreover, one can likewise generalize from the treatment of one cow in the slaughterhouse to contend that no cows should be treated in this way. Thus, through the use of the moral imagination one can easily extend one's care for immediate creatures to others who are not present. These remote others are not, however, the abstract disembodied "others of rational constructs and universal principles" envisaged by Kantian rights theorists but rather "particular flesh and blood . . . actual starving children in Africa," as care theorist Virginia Held pointed out with respect to remote suffering humans (1987, 118).

In other words, the injunction to care can be universalized even if all the particular details of an individual case cannot be so extrapolated.[1] The real question that is raised in applying care theory to animals then becomes who is to be included in the caring circle? Or, to put it in other terms, who is to be granted moral status? I will argue below that status should be granted to living creatures with whom one can communicate cognitively and emotionally as to their needs and wishes.[2] [. . .]

Garner offers a second criticism of care theory, namely, that it fails to provide a specific guide for action. He asks, for example, if it prohibits meat eating (2003, 241). It is hard to believe, given the volume of eco-feminist vegan/vegetarian theory that has emerged in the past decade, that anyone could doubt the answer to this question.[3] Garner wonders, however, if animals raised humanely (with care) and slaughtered humanely (but nevertheless slaughtered) would be acceptable under care theory (241), for the animals would be receiving compassionate treatment during their lives. Garner's question points to a misapprehension of care theory that I believe a dialogical theory will help to correct. From the point of view of a dialogical ethic of care, the answer to Garner's question would clearly be no, for if we care to take seriously in our ethical decision making the communicated desires of the animal, it is apparent that no animal would opt for the slaughterhouse. A Jain proverb states the obvious: "All beings are fond of life; they like pleasure and hate pain, shun destruction and like to live, they long to live. To all life is dear" (*Jaina Sûtras* [1884] 1973, I.2.3).[4] Humans know this, and a dialogical ethic must be constructed on the basis of this knowledge. Caring must therefore be extended to mean not just "caring about their welfare" but "caring about what they are telling us."

But what if, Garner continues, one encounters a situation in which there is a "conflict of caring, whose interests should we choose to uphold?" (2003, 241). In particular, he raises the issue of animal research, which may benefit humans and thus satisfy a caring ethic for humans if not for animals. Deborah Slicer, a major feminist animal care theorist, explored this issue thoroughly in her nuanced article, "Your Daughter or Your Dog?" (1991). Slicer makes the salient points in the feminist animal care argument: much of the research is, to be blunt, worthless (i.e., redundant and trivial), and, as is becoming increasingly evident (even more so since Slicer's article appeared), "animals often do not serve as reliable models for human beings and . . . it can be dangerous to extrapolate from results obtained from one species to another" (117).

One might argue that stressing the uselessness of the research evades the basic dilemma posed by Garner. I would counter, however, that a feminist animal care ethic insists that the political context of decision making is never irrelevant and that ethical decisions must include an assessment of that context (in this case, the questions of who benefits from the research economically and how reliable the published research results are by thusly interested parties). [. . .]

A Dialogical Ethic of Care for the Treatment of Animals

Ludwig Wittgenstein once famously remarked that if a lion could speak we couldn't understand him (Wittgenstein 1963, 223e). In fact, as I have been proposing here, lions do speak, and it is not impossible to understand much of what they are saying. Several theorists have already urged that humans need to learn to read the languages of the natural world. Jonathan Bate has proposed that we learn the syntax of the land, not seeing it through our own "prison-house of language," in order to develop appropriate environmental understandings (1998, 65). Similarly, Patrick Murphy has called for an "ecofeminist dialogics" in which humans learn to read the dialects of animals. "Nonhuman others," he claims, "can be constituted as speaking subjects rather than merely objects of our speaking" (1991, 50).[5] Earlier, phenomenologist Max Scheler spoke similarly about the necessity for learning the *universal grammar* of creatural expression ([1926] 1970, 11). Indeed, over a century ago American writer Sarah Orne Jewett speculated about the possibility of learning the language of nonhumans, asking, "Who is going to be the linguist who learns the first word of an old crow's warning to his mate . . .? How long we shall have to go to school when people are expected to talk to the trees, and birds, and beasts in their own language! . . . It is not necessary to tame [creatures] before they can be familiar and responsive, we can meet them on their own ground" (1881, 4–5).

There are those, to be sure, who still raise the epistemological question of how one can know what an animal is feeling or thinking. The answer would seem to be that we use much the same mental and emotional activities in reading an animal as we do in reading a human.[6] Body language, eye movement, facial expression, tone of voice—all are important signs. It also helps to know about the species' habits and culture. And, as with humans, repeated experiences with one individual help one to understand that individual's unique needs and wishes. By paying attention to, by studying, what is signified, one comes to know, to care about, the signifier.[7] In this way, what Carol J. Adams (1990) famously termed the *absent referents* are restored to discourse, allowing their stories to be part of the narrative, opening, in short, the possibility of dialogue with them.

The underlying premise here is that one of the principal ways we know is by means of analogy based on homology. If that dog is yelping, whining, leaping about, licking an open cut, and since if I had an open wound I know I would similarly be (or feeling like) crying and moving about anxiously because of the pain, I therefore conclude that the animal is experiencing the same kind of pain as I would and is expressing distress about it. One imagines, in short, how the animal is feeling based on how one would feel in a similar situation.[8] In addition, repeated exhibitions of similar reactions in similar situations lead one inductively to a generic conclusion that dogs experience the pain of wounds as we do, that, in short, they feel pain and don't like it. The question, therefore, whether humans can understand animals is, in my opinion, a moot one. That they can has been abundantly proved, as Midgley points out, by their repeated success in doing so (1983, 113, 115, 133, 142).

Of course, as with humans, there is always the danger that one might misread the communication of the animal in question, that one might incorrectly assume homologous behavior when there is none. To be sure, all communication is imperfect, and there remain many mysteries in animal (as well as human) behavior. Feminist ethic-of-care theorists have explored some of the difficulties inherent in attempting to assess the needs of an incommunicative human and/or the risks of imposing one's own views or needs on her. But as Alison Jaggar summarizes, care theorists maintain that in general such "dangers may be avoided [or at least minimized, I would add] through improved practices of attentiveness, portraying attentiveness as a kind of discipline whose prerequisites include attitudes and aptitudes such as openness, receptivity, empathy, sensitivity, and imagination" (1995, 190).

Understanding that an animal is in pain or distress—even empathizing or sympathizing with him—doesn't ensure, however, that the human will act ethically toward the animal. Thus, the originary emotional empathetic response must be supplemented with an ethical and political perspective (acquired through training and education) that enables the human to analyze the situation critically so as to determine who is responsible for the animal suffering and how that suffering may best be alleviated. In her recent book *Regarding the Pain of Others* (2003), Susan Sontag warns that people do not automatically act ethically in response to pictures of other people's pain (she doesn't deal with images of animals). While she characterizes as a "moral monster" the person who through a failure "of imagination, of empathy" (8) does not respond compassionately, she nevertheless argues that various ideologies often interfere with the moral response. Too often, she claims, sympathy connotes superiority and privilege without self-reflection about how one is contributing to the suffering one is lamenting. She therefore urges that a heightened humanist political awareness must accompany the sympathetic response in order for truly ethical action to result. Photos of atrocity "cannot be more than an invitation to pay attention, to reflect" (117) on who is responsible for the suffering and similar questions.

Several of the contributors to the feminist animal care collection *Beyond Animal Rights* (Donovan and Adams 1996) argue in this vein for what Deane Curtin terms a "politicized ethic of caring for" ([1991] 1996, 65), one that recognizes the political context in which caring and sympathy take place. In my discussion of the celebrated Heinz hypothetical (in which Heinz has to decide whether to steal a drug, which he cannot obtain any other way, in order to save the life of his dying wife), I propose that "a political ethic-of-care response would include the larger dimension of looking to the political and economic context. . . . Thus the corporate-controlled health care system becomes the primary villain in the piece, and the incident should serve to motivate action to change the system" (Donovan 1996, 161). And, as Adams points out in "Caring about Suffering" (1996, 174), feminist animal care theory necessarily recognizes the "sex-species system" in which animal (and human) suffering is embedded.

In his much-cited article "Taming Ourselves or Going Feral?" (1995), Brian Luke reveals how a massive deployment of ideological conditioning forestalls what he sees as the natural empathetic response most people feel toward animals. Children have to be educated out of the early sympathy they feel for animals, he contends; ideological denial and justifications for animal exploitation and suffering are indoctrinated from an early age. Luke catalogs the ways in which such suffering is rationalized and legitimized by those who profit from it (303–11). To a great extent, therefore, getting people to see evil and to care about suffering is a matter of clearing away ideological rationalizations that legitimate animal exploitation and cruelty. Recognizing the egregious use of euphemism employed to disguise such behavior (copiously documented in Joan Dunayer's book *Animal Equality* [2001]) would seem to be an important step in this direction.

But it is not just a matter of supplementing care with a political perspective; the experience of care can itself lead to political analysis, as Joan Tronto points out in her call for a "political ethic of care" (1993, 155): "Care becomes a tool for critical political analysis when we use this concept to reveal relationships of power" (172). In other words, although Tronto doesn't treat the animal question, if one feels sympathy toward a suffering animal, one is moved to ask the question, Why is this animal suffering? The answer can lead into a political analysis of the reasons for the animal's distress. Education in critical thinking, these thinkers emphasize, is therefore imperative if an ethic of care is to work.

We also need education, as Nel Noddings proposed (1984, 153), in the practices of care and empathy.[9] Years ago, in fact, Gregory Bateson and Mary Catherine Bateson contended that "empathy is a discipline" and therefore teachable (1987, 195). Many religions, they noted, use imaginative exercises in empathetic understanding as a spiritual discipline (195). Such exercises could be adapted for use in secular institutions like schools (including, especially, high school). Certainly a large purpose of such a discipline must be not just emotional identification but also intellectual understanding, learning to hear, to take seriously, to care about what animals are telling us, learning to read and attend to their language. The burgeoning field of animal ethology is providing important new information that will aid in such study.

In conclusion, therefore, a feminist animal care ethic must be political in its perspective and dialogical in its method. Rejecting the imperialist imperative of the scientific method, in which the "scientific subject's voice . . . speaks with general and abstract authority [and] the objects of inquiry 'speak' only in response to what scientists ask them" (as Sandra Harding [1986, 124] characterized the laboratory encounter), humans must cease imposing their voice on that of animals. No longer must our relationship with animals be that of the "conquest of an alien object," Rosemary Radford Ruether notes, but "the conversation of two subjects." We must recognize "that the 'other' has a 'nature' of her own that needs to be respected and with which one must enter into conversation" (1975, 195–6). On that basis and in reflecting upon the political context, a dialogical ethic for the treatment of animals may be established.[10]

Notes

I would like to thank Erling Skorpen, who stimulated my thinking in this direction years ago; Carol Adams for planting the idea of applying standpoint theory to animals; the *Signs* editors and readers for their suggestions; and my dogs Aurora and Sadie, with whom I dialogue daily.

1. Regarding Kant's other points, one might question whether a sense of moral duty and the capacity to reason are any more evenly distributed in the population than the capacity for sympathy. Indeed, care theorists, like most feminist theorists, believe that habits and practices are socially constructed, not innate (Kant's point about sympathy being unevenly distributed implies that only or mostly women have the capacity); thus, they are teachable. I would argue then, following Nel Noddings (1984, 153), that if compassion practice were taught systematically as a discipline in the schools, it would become a widely accepted socially sanctioned basis for moral decision making and therefore not dependent on the whim of various individual responses, thus replying to Kant's concern about subjective volatility.
2. By the term *cognitive* I do not mean restricted to rational discourse but rather including all communicative signs detectable by the human brain.
3. See, e.g., Adams 1995, Donovan 1995, Gaard and Gruen 1995, Lucas 2005.
4. As cited in Chapple (1986, 217). Jainism is an ancient Indian religion, a principal feature of whose practice is the vow of *ahimsa* (to do no harm to other living creatures). All Jains are thus vegetarians.
5. In the past few years a number of other literary theorists have begun exploring the possibility of a dialogical "animal-standpoint criticism." I have just completed an article (not yet published), "Animal Ethics and Literary Criticism," that further develops this concept.
6. This is to disagree somewhat with Thomas Nagel, who in "What Is It Like to Be a Bat?" (1974) argues that we humans cannot apprehend "bat phenomenology" (440); i.e., we can only imagine what it would be like for us to be bats, not what it is like for bats to be bats. To an extent Nagel is correct, of course; it is a truism of epistemology that we are limited by our mental apparatus. However, I believe more effort can be made to decipher animal communications and that while we may never fully understand what it feels like to be a bat, we can understand certain pertinent basics of his or her experience, sufficient for the formulation of an ethical response. For an alternative view to Nagel's, see Kenneth Shapiro's "Understanding Dogs" (1989), which argues that we recognize the validity of interspecies "kinesthetic" communication. Although Val Plumwood proposes a "dialogical interspecies ethic" in her *Environmental Culture* (2002, 167–95) that would seem to be consistent with what I am proposing here, she inconsistently argues that it is ethically permissible to kill and eat nonhumans under this ethic: one can "conceive [them] both as communicative others and as food" (157). This would seem to defeat the purpose of a dialogical ethic, which is to respond ethically to what the "communicative other" is telling one, namely, and invariably, that he does not want to be killed and eaten.
7. Here I am modifying classical structuralist terminology.
8. In the locus classicus on the subject of knowing another's inner states, "Other Minds" ([1946] 1979), J. L. Austin insists that a primary prerequisite for such communication is that one must have had the feeling oneself (104). Austin, however, like Nagel, abjures the possibility of knowing "what it would feel like to be a cat or a cockroach" (105).

9. Noddings (1991) has, however, stipulated reservations about applying care theory to animals. See also my critique of Noddings' position (Donovan 1991).
10. Other theorists who have advocated and explored dialogical ethical theory include Martin Buber, Simone Weil, Iris Murdoch, and Mikhail Bakhtin. See further discussion in Donovan (1996).

References

Adams, Carol J. 1990. *The Sexual Politics of Meat: A Feminist-Vegetarian Critical Theory.* New York: Continuum.

———. 1995. "Comment on George's 'Should Feminists Be Vegetarian?'." *Signs: Journal of Women in Culture and Society* 21(1): 221–25.

Adler, Jonathan E. 1987. "Moral Development and the Personal Point of View." In *Women and Moral Theory,* ed. Eva Feder Kittay and Diana T. Meyers, 205–34. Totowa, NJ: Rowman & Littlefield.

Austin, J. L. (1946) 1979. "Other Minds." In his *Philosophical Papers,* 3rd ed., 76–116. Oxford: Oxford University Press.

Bateson, Gregory, and Mary Catherine Bateson. 1987. *Angels Fear: Towards an Epistemology of the Sacred.* New York: Bantam.

Benhabib, Seyla. 1987. "The Generalized and the Concrete Other: The Kohlberg-Gilligan Controversy and Moral Theory." In *Women and Moral Theory,* ed. Eva Feder Kittay and Diana T. Meyers, 154–76. Totowa, NJ: Rowman & Littlefield.

Chapple, Christopher. 1986. "Noninjury to Animals: Jaina and Buddhist Perspectives." In *Animal Sacrifices: Religious Perspectives on the Use of Animals in Science,* ed. Tom Regan, 213–35. Philadelphia: Temple University Press.

Curtin, Deane. (1991) 1996. "Toward an Ecological Ethic of Care." In *Donovan and Adams,* 60–76.

Donovan, Josephine. 1990. "Animal Rights and Feminist Theory." *Signs* 15(2): 350–75.

———. 1991. "Reply to Noddings." *Signs* 16(2): 423–25.

———. 1996. "Attention to Suffering: Sympathy as a Basis for Ethical Treatment of Animals." In *Donovan and Adams,* 147–69.

Donovan, Josephine, and Carol J. Adams, eds. 1996. *Beyond Animal Rights: A Feminist Caring Ethic for the Treatment of Animals.* New York: Continuum.

Dunayer, Joan. 2001. *Animal Equality: Language and Liberation.* Derwood, MD: Ryce.

Garner, Robert. 2003. "Political Ideologies and the Moral Status of Animals." *Journal of Political Ideologies* 8(2): 233–46.

Gilligan, Carol. 1982. *In a Different Voice: Psychological Theory and Women's Development.* Cambridge, MA: Harvard University Press.

Harding, Sandra. 1986. *The Science Question in Feminism.* Ithaca, NY: Cornell University Press.

Held, Virginia. 1987. "Feminism and Moral Theory." In *Women and Moral Theory,* ed. Eva Feder Kittay and Diana T. Meyers, 111–28. Totowa, NJ: Rowman & Littlefield.

Jacobi, Hermann, Trans. (1884) 1973. *Jaina Sûtras.* Delhi: Motilal Banarsidass.

Jaggar, Alison M. 1995. "Caring as a Feminist Practice of Moral Reason." In *Justice and Care: Essential Readings in Feminist Ethics,* ed. Virginia Held, 179–202. Boulder, CO: Westview.

Jewett, Sarah Orne. 1881. "River Driftwood." In her *Country By-Ways,* 1–33. Boston: Houghton Mifflin.

Kant, Immanuel. 1957. "Theory of Ethics." In his *Selections,* ed. Theodore Meyer-Green, 268–374. New York: Scribner's.

Kelch, Thomas G. 1999. "The Role of the Rational and the Emotive in a Theory of Animal Rights." *Boston College Environmental Affairs Law Review* 27(1): 1–41.

Kheel, Marti. (1985) 1996. "The Liberation of Nature: A Circular Affair." In *Donovan and Adams,* 17–33.

———. 1995. "License to Kill: An Ecofeminist Critique of Hunters' Discourse." In *Animals and Women: Feminist Theoretical Explorations,* ed. Carol J. Adams and Josephine Donovan, 85–125. Durham, NC: Duke University Press.

Luke, Brian. 1995. "Taming Ourselves or Going Feral? Toward a Nonpatriarchal Metaethic of Animal Liberation." In *Animals and Women: Feminist Theoretical Explorations,* ed. Carol J. Adams and Josephine Donovan, 290–319. Durham, NC: Duke University Press.

MacKinnon, Catharine A. 1989. *Toward a Feminist Theory of the State.* Cambridge, MA: Harvard University Press.

Midgley, Mary. 1983. *Animals and Why They Matter*. Athens: University of Georgia Press.

Murphy, Patrick. 1991. "Prolegomenon for an Ecofeminist Dialogics." In *Feminism, Bakhtin, and the Dialogic*, ed. Dale M. Bauer and Susan Jaret McKinstry, 39–56. Albany: State University of New York Press.

Nagel, Thomas. 1974. "What Is It Like to Be a Bat?" *Philosophical Review* 83(4): 435–50.

Noddings, Nel. 1984. *Caring: A Feminine Approach to Ethics and Moral Education*. Berkeley: University of California Press.

———. 1991. "Comment on Donovan's 'Animal Rights and Feminist Theory.'" *Signs* 16(2): 418–22.

Plumwood, Val. 2002. *Environmental Culture: The Ecological Crisis of Reason*. London: Routledge.

Regan, Tom. 1983. *The Case for Animal Rights*. Berkeley: University of California Press.

Ruether, Rosemary Radford. 1975. *New Woman/New Earth: Sexist Ideologies and Human Liberation*. New York: Seabury.

Scheler, Max. (1926) 1970. *The Nature of Sympathy*. Trans. Peter Heath. 3rd ed. Hamden, CT: Archon.

Shapiro, Kenneth J. 1989. "Understanding Dogs through Kinesthetic Empathy, Social Construction, and History." *Anthrozoös* 3(3): 184–95.

Shiva, Vandana. 1994. *Close to Home: Women Reconnect Ecology, Health and Development Worldwide*. Philadelphia: New Society.

Singer, Peter. 1975. *Animal Liberation: A New Ethics for Our Treatment of Animals*. New York: Avon.

Slicer, Deborah. 1991. "Your Daughter or Your Dog?" *Hypatia* 6(1): 108–24.

Sontag, Susan. 2003. *Regarding the Pain of Others*. New York: Farrar, Straus & Giroux.

Tronto, Joan C. 1993. *Moral Boundaries: A Political Argument for an Ethic of Care*. New York: Routledge.

Walker, Margaret Urban. (1989) 1995. "Moral Understandings: Alternative 'Epistemology' for a Feminist Ethics." In *Justice and Care: Essential Readings in Feminist Ethics*, ed. Virginia Held, 139–52. Boulder, CO: Westview.

West, Robin. 1988. "Jurisprudence and Gender." *University of Chicago Law Review* 55(1): 1–71.

Wittgenstein, Ludwig. 1963. *Philosophical Investigations*. Trans. G. E. M. Anscombe. Oxford: Blackwell.

6 Rights, Interests, Desires and Beliefs

R. G. Frey

R. G. Frey argues that the key question is whether animals are the kind of beings who can have rights. He distinguishes two senses of "interest" and maintains that animals have interests only in the sense that things can be good or bad for them, as oil is good or bad for a tractor. Animals do not have desires, because having desires requires the having of beliefs. Beliefs require that the creature be able to distinguish between true and false beliefs, and for this distinction language is required.
[. . .]

The question is not about *which* rights animals may or may not be thought to possess or about *whether* their alleged rights in a particular regard are on a par with the alleged rights of humans in this same regard but rather about the more fundamental issue of whether animals—or, in any event, the "higher" animals—are a kind of being which can be the logical subject of rights. It is this issue, and a particular position with respect to it, that I want critically to address here.

The position I have in mind is the widely influential one which links the possession of rights to the possession of interests. In his *System of Ethics*, Leonard Nelson is among the first, if not the first, to propound the view that all and only beings which have interests can have rights,[1] a view which has attracted an increasingly wide following ever since. [. . .] For Nelson, [. . .] it is because animals have interests that they can be the logical subject of rights, and his claim that animals *do have* interests forms the minor premiss, therefore, in an argument for the moral rights of animals: "All and only beings which (can) have interests (can) have moral rights; animals as well as humans (can) have interests; therefore, animals (can) have moral rights."
[. . .]

[I]t is apparent that the minor premiss is indeed the key to the whole matter. For given the truth of the major premiss, given, that is, that the possession of interests *is* a criterion for the possession of rights, it is nevertheless only the truth of the minor premiss that would result in the inclusion of creatures other than human beings within the class of right-holders. This premiss is doubtful, however, and the case against it a powerful one, or so I want to suggest.
[. . .]

To say that "good health is in John's interests" is not at all the same thing as to say that "John has an interest in good health." The former is intimately bound up with having a good or well-being to which good health is conducive, so that we could just as easily have said, "Good health is conducive to John's good or well-being," whereas the latter—"John has an interest in good health"—is intimately bound up with wanting, with John's wanting good health. That these two notions of "interest" are logically distinct is readily apparent: good health may well be in John's interests, in the sense of being conducive to his good or well-being, even if John does not want good health, indeed, even if he wants to continue taking hard drugs, with the result that his health is irreparably damaged; and John may have an interest in taking drugs, in the sense of wanting to take them, even if it is apparent to him that it is not conducive to his good or well-being to continue to do so. In other words, something can be *in* John's interests without John's *having* an interest in it, and John can *have* an interest in something without its being *in* his interests.

If this is right, and there are these two logically distinct senses of "interest," we can go on to ask whether animals can have interests in either of these senses; and if they do, then perhaps the minor premiss of Nelson's argument for the moral rights of animals can be sustained.

Do animals, therefore, have interests in the first sense, in the sense of having a good or well-being which can be harmed or benefited? The answer, I think, is that they certainly do have interests in this sense; after all, it is plainly not good for a dog to be fed certain types of food or to be deprived of a certain amount of exercise. This answer, however, is of little use to the Nelsonian cause; for it yields the counter-intuitive result that manmade/manufactured objects and even things have interests, and, therefore, on the interest thesis, have or at least are candidates for having moral rights. For example, just as it is not good for a dog to be deprived of a certain amount of exercise, so it is not good for prehistoric cave drawings to be exposed to excessive amounts of carbon dioxide or for Rembrandt paintings to be exposed to excessive amounts of sunlight.

[. . .]

Do animals, therefore, have interests in the second sense, in the sense of having wants which can be satisfied or left unsatisfied? In this sense, of course, it appears that tractors do not have interests; for although being well oiled may be conducive to tractors being good of their kind, tractors do not *have an interest* in being well oiled, since they cannot *want* to be well oiled, cannot, in fact, have any wants whatever. But farmers can have wants, and they certainly have an interest in their tractors being well oiled.

What, then, about animals? Can they have wants? By "wants," I understand a term that encompasses both needs and desires, and it is these that I shall consider.

If to ask whether animals can have wants is to ask whether they can have needs, then certainly animals have wants. A dog can need water. But *this* cannot be the sense of "want" on which having interests will depend, since it does not exclude things from the class of want-holders. Just as dogs need water in order to function normally, so tractors need oil in order to function normally.

[. . .]

This, then, leaves desires, and the question of whether animals can have wants as desires. I may as well say at once that I do not think animals can have desires. My reasons for thinking this turn largely upon my doubts that animals can have beliefs, and my doubts in this regard turn partially, though in large part, upon the view that having beliefs is not compatible with the absence of language and linguistic ability. I realize that the claim that animals cannot have desires is a controversial one; but I think the case to be made in support of it, complex though it is, is persuasive.

[. . .]

Suppose I am a collector of rare books and desire to own a Gutenberg Bible: my desire to own this volume is *to be traced* to my belief that I do not now own such a work and that my rare book collection is deficient in this regard. By "to be traced" here, what I mean is this: if someone were to ask *how* my belief that my book collection lacks a Gutenberg Bible is connected with my desire to own such a Bible, what better or more direct reply could be given than that without this belief, I would not have this desire? For if I believed that my rare book collection *did* contain a Gutenberg Bible and so was complete in this sense, then I would not desire a Gutenberg Bible in order to make up what I now believe to be a notable deficiency in my collection.

[. . .]

The difficulty in the case of animals should be apparent: if someone were to say, e.g., "The cat believes that the door is locked," then that person is holding, as I see it, that the cat holds the declarative sentence "The door is locked" to be true; and I can see no reason whatever for crediting the cat or any other creature which lacks language, including human infants, with entertaining declarative sentences and holding certain declarative sentences to be true.

[. . .]

If what is believed is that a certain declarative sentence is true, then no creature which lacks language can have beliefs; and without beliefs, a creature cannot have desires. And this is the case with animals, or so I suggest; and if I am right, not even in the sense, then, of wants as desires do animals have interests, which, to recall, is the minor premiss in the Nelsonian argument for the moral rights of animals.

But is what is believed that a certain declarative sentence is true? I think there are three arguments of sorts that shore up the claim that this *is* what is believed.

First, I do not see how a creature could have the concept of belief without being able to distinguish between true and false beliefs.

[. . .]

Second, if in order to have the concept of belief a creature must be possessed of the difference between true and false belief, then in order for a creature to be able to distinguish true from false beliefs that creature must—simply must, as I see it—have some awareness of, to put the matter in the most general terms, how language connects with, links up with the world; and I see no reason to credit cats with such an awareness.

[. . .]

Third, I do not see how a creature could have an awareness or grasp of how language connects with, links up with the world, to leave the matter at its most general, unless that creature was itself possessed of language; and cats are not possessed of language.

[. . .]

It may be suggested, of course, that there might possibly be a class of desires—let us call them simple desires—which do not involve the intervention of belief, in order to have them, and which do not require that we credit animals with language. Such simple desires, for example, might be for some object or other, and we as language-users might try to capture these simple desires in the case of a dog by describing its behavior in such terms as "The dog simply desires the bone."

[. . .]

Suppose, then, the dog simply desires the bone: is the dog aware that it has this simple desire or not? If it is alleged to have this desire but to be unaware that it has it, to want but to be unaware that it wants, then a problem arises. In the case of human beings, unconscious desire can be made sense of, but only because we first make sense of conscious desire; but where no desires are conscious ones, where the creature in question is alleged to have only unconscious desires, what cash value can the use of the term "desire" have in such a case?

[. . .]

There is nothing the dog can do which can express the difference between desiring the bone and being aware of desiring the bone. Yet, the dog would have to be capable of expressing this difference in its behavior, if one is going to hold, *on the basis of that behavior*, that the dog is aware that it has a simple desire for the bone, aware that it simply desires the bone.

Even, then, if we concede for the sake of argument that there are simple desires, desires which do not involve the intervention of belief in order to have them, the suggestion that we can credit animals with these desires, without also having to credit them with language, is at best problematic.

[. . .]

I conclude, then, that the Nelsonian position on the moral rights of animals is not a sound one: the truth of the minor premiss in his argument—that animals have interests—is doubtful at best, and animals must have interests if, in accordance with the interest thesis, they are to be a logical subject of such rights. For animals either have interests in a sense which allows objects and things to have interests, and so, on the interest thesis, to have or to be candidates for having moral rights or they do not have interests at all, and so, on the interest thesis, do not have and are not candidates for having moral rights. I have reached this conclusion, moreover, without querying the correctness of the interest thesis itself, without querying, that is, whether the possession of interests *really* is a criterion for the possession of moral rights.

Note

1. Leonard Nelson, *System of Ethics*, tr. by Norbert Guterman (New Haven, 1956), Part I, Section 2, Chapter 7, pp. 136–44.

7 Universal Basic Rights for Animals

Sue Donaldson and Will Kymlicka

An important strand of animal rights theory (ART) starts from the premise that all animals with a subjective existence—that is, all animals who are conscious or sentient beings—should be viewed as the subjects of justice, and as the bearers of inviolable rights. The idea that animals possess inviolable rights is a very distinctive view which goes beyond what is normally understood by the term 'animal rights'. So it is important for us to clarify what we mean by inviolable rights, and why we think animals possess them.

In everyday parlance, anyone who argues for greater limits on the use of animals is said to be a defender of animal rights (AR). Thus, someone who advocates that pigs being raised for slaughter should have larger stalls, so as to improve the quality of their short lives, is described as a believer in animal rights. And indeed we can say that such a person believes that animals have a 'right to humane treatment'. Someone defending a more robust rights view might argue that humans should not eat animals since we have lots of nutritious alternatives but that medical experiments on animals are permissible if this is the only way to advance crucial medical knowledge, or that culling wild animals is permissible if this is the only way to save key habitats. We can say that such a person believes animals have a 'right not to be sacrificed by humans unless an important human or ecological interest is at stake'.

These views, whether they endorse a weaker or more robust conception, are crucially different from the idea that animals have inviolable rights. The idea of inviolable rights implies that an individual's most basic interests cannot be sacrificed for the greater good of others. In Ronald Dworkin's famous phrase, inviolable rights in this sense are 'trumps' which cannot be violated no matter how much others would benefit from their violation (Dworkin 1984). For example, a person cannot be killed in order to harvest her body parts, even if dozens of other humans might benefit from her organs, bone marrow, or stem cells. Nor can she be made a subject of nonconsensual medical experimentation, no matter how much the knowledge gained from experimenting on her would help others. Inviolable rights in this sense are a protective circle drawn around an individual, ensuring that she is not sacrificed for the good of others. This protective circle is usually understood in terms of a set of basic negative rights against fundamental harms such as killing, slavery, torture, and confinement.

The idea that human beings have such inviolable rights is controversial. Utilitarians, for example, believe that morality requires us to bring about the greatest good of the greatest number, even if this means sacrificing one person to do so. If we can save five people by killing one, we should do so, all else being equal. As the great utilitarian Jeremy Bentham famously put it, the idea of inviolable rights is 'nonsense upon stilts' (Bentham 2002). Since utilitarians do not believe that humans are owed inviolable rights, they obviously do not accord such rights to animals either.[1]

Today, however, the idea that humans possess inviolable rights is widely accepted, despite ongoing philosophical debate regarding the grounding for human rights. Inviolability is the basis of our medical ethics, of domestic bills of rights, and of international human rights law. The idea that all human beings are entitled to the protection of certain inviolable rights is part of the 'human rights revolution' in law, and of the shift to 'rights-based' theories in political philosophy. One of the central motivations for Rawls's *A Theory of Justice*, widely seen as heralding the rebirth of political philosophy, was precisely his belief that utilitarianism was unable to account for the wrongness of sacrificing individuals for the good of others, whether that is experimenting on individuals to gain useful medical knowledge or discriminating against racial or sexual minorities to satisfy the preferences of majorities (Rawls 1971). An adequate defence of liberal democracy, he believed, required a more 'Kantian' conception of respect for individuals, which emphasizes that we should never be treated simply as a means for the good of society.[2]

While the idea of inviolability is now widely accepted in relation to human beings, very few people have been prepared to accept that animals too might possess inviolable rights. Even those who accept that animals matter morally and that they deserve to be treated more humanely often think that when push comes to shove, they can be violated—endlessly sacrificed—for the greater good of others. Whereas killing one human to harvest organs to save five other humans is unacceptable, to kill one baboon to save five humans (or five baboons) is permissible, and perhaps even morally required. As Jeff McMahan puts it, animals are 'freely violable in the service of the greater good', whereas human persons are 'fully inviolable' (McMahan 2002: 265). Robert Nozick famously summarized this view under the label 'utilitarianism for animals, Kantianism for people' (Nozick 1974: 39).

The approach we develop rejects this claim that only humans possess inviolable rights. The human rights revolution has been a profound moral achievement, but it is incomplete. As we will see, the arguments for inviolability do not stop at the boundaries of the human species. As Paola Cavalieri puts it, it's time to take the human out of human rights (Cavalieri 2001). If it is wrong to kill a human for her organs, even if we can save five people by doing so, so too is it wrong to kill a baboon for his organs. Killing a chipmunk or a shark is a violation of their basic inviolable right to life, just as killing a human being is.[3]

[. . .]

Why do so many people find the idea of inviolable rights for animals implausible? Some people think it is simply self-evident that the death of a human being is more tragic, and more of a loss to the world, than the death of a baboon and that killing a human being must therefore be a greater wrong than killing a baboon. We hope that our discussion will give readers a livelier sense of the loss when animals die, and of the complexity of making such judgements of comparative loss. But in any event, this entire line of argument is misplaced. After all, we can and do make similar judgements about the relative loss when different human beings die. We may think that it is more of a tragedy when a young person dies in an accident than when a very old person dies, and more of a tragedy when someone who loves life dies than when a misanthrope dies. Yet these judgements about comparative loss have no implications whatsoever for the inviolable right to life. The fact that it may be more tragic when a young person dies does not mean that we can kill the old person to provide organs for the young person. We cannot kill misanthropes to harvest organs to use for people who love life.

Indeed, this is the essential point of inviolable rights and how they differ from utilitarianism. From a strict utilitarian perspective, the strength of people's right to life depends on how much they contribute to the greater good. We are all 'freely violable in the service of the greater good', and so you have to earn your right to life by showing that your continued existence serves the overall good. Those who are young, talented, and gregarious are therefore bound to have a stronger right to life than those who are elderly, infirm, or miserable. The strength of one's right to life varies with the comparative loss from one's death.

The human rights revolution is precisely a repudiation of this way of thinking. The principle of inviolability says that people's right to life is independent of their relative contribution to the overall good and is not violable in the service of the greater good. This is now firmly established in the human case, and we argue that it must extend to animals as well. The death of some individuals may be more of a tragedy or loss than the death of other individuals, within and across species, but they all possess inviolable rights: they all have an equal right not to be sacrificed for the greater good of others.

To say that animals have an equal right not to be sacrificed for the greater good of others raises another set of worries and objections. Does this entail that animals have 'equal rights' with humans, including, say, the right to vote, or to religious freedom, or to post-secondary education? This is often invoked as a *reductio* of the idea of animal rights, but here again, it misunderstands the logic of the rights revolution. Even within the category of human beings, many rights are differentially allocated on the basis of capacities and relationships. Citizens have rights that visitors do not have (e.g., to vote, or to social services); adults have rights that children do not have (e.g., to drive); people with certain rational capacities have rights that those with severe intellectual disabilities do not have (e.g., to decide how to manage their finances). But again, none of these variations has implications for claims to fundamental inviolability. Citizens have rights that foreign tourists do not have, but citizens cannot enslave tourists or kill them to harvest their organs. Adults have rights that children do not have, and competent adults have rights that people with severe intellectual disabilities do not have, but children and the intellectually disabled cannot be sacrificed for the greater good of competent adults. Equal inviolability is compatible with variations in a wide range of other civil, political, and social rights, which track variations in underlying capacities, interests, and relationships. Again, all of this is clear enough in the human case, and we argue that it is equally true in the case of animals.

In short, the issue of inviolable rights needs to be kept clearly in mind and not conflated with a range of other issues regarding our obligations to humans and animals. The issue of inviolability is, to repeat, the question of whether one's basic interests can or cannot be sacrificed for the greater good of others. The human rights revolution says that human beings possess such inviolability. The strong AR position says that sentient animals also possess such inviolability. Some readers may worry that extending inviolability to animals 'cheapens' the hard-won achievements of the rights revolution. We argue, on the contrary, that any attempt to restrict inviolability to human beings can only be done by radically weakening and destabilizing the scheme of human rights protection, leaving many humans as well as animals outside the scope of effective protection.

[. . .]

Animal Selves

The assumption of most mainstream contemporary Western political theory is that the community of justice is coextensive with the community of human beings. Basic justice and inviolable rights are owed to all humans by virtue of their humanity and should be blind to intra-human differences such as race, gender, creed, ability, or sexual orientation. Against this mainstream background, ART poses the question: why just humans? The universalizing impulse of human rights is to extend basic protections across boundaries of physical, mental, and cultural difference, so why should this impulse stop at the boundary of the human species?

The premise of ART—reflected in the writings of Sapontzis (1987), Francione (2000), Cavalieri (2001), Regan (2003), Dunayer (2004), Steiner (2008), and others—is that these protective rights are owed to all conscious or sentient beings, human or animal.[4] Conscious/sentient beings are selves—that is, they have a distinctive subjective experience of their own lives and of the world, which demands a specific kind of protection in the form of inviolable rights. To limit these rights to humans is morally arbitrary or 'speciesist'. Such rights can, and ought to, play a crucial role in protecting all vulnerable beings.

Sentience/consciousness has a distinct moral significance because it enables a subjective experience of the world. According to Francione, 'the observation that animals are sentient is different from saying that they are merely alive. To be sentient means to be the sort of being who is conscious of pain and pleasure; there is an "I" who has subjective experiences' (Francione 2000: 6). Steiner's formulation is that 'sentience is a capacity shared by all beings for whom the struggle for life and flourishing *matters*, whether or not the being in question has a reflective sense of which things matter or how they matter' (Steiner 2008: xi–xii). Beings who experience their lives from the inside and for whom life can go better or worse are selves, not things, whom we recognize as experiencing vulnerability—to pleasure and pain, to frustration and satisfaction, to joy and suffering, or to fear and death.

Recognizing others as sentient in this way changes our attitude towards them. Cora Diamond speaks of recognizing the other as a 'fellow creature' (Diamond 2004). Steiner says that recognizing other beings as sentient creates 'a kinship relation to one another that binds them together in a moral community' (Steiner 2008: xii). Barbara Smuts says 'the "presence" we recognize in another when we meet in mutuality is something we feel more than something we know. . . . In mutuality, we sense that inside this other body, there is "someone home"' (Smuts 2001: 308).[5]

The basic premise of ART is that whenever we encounter such vulnerable selves—whenever we encounter 'someone home'—they need protection through the principle of inviolability, which provides a protective shield of basic rights around every individual. One natural way to express this claim is to say that animals should be recognized as persons, and this is indeed how many AR theorists summarize their position. Francione, for example, entitles his recent book *Animals as Persons* (Francione 2008). Since existing human rights norms are often phrased as 'all persons have the right to X', we can restate the ART position as saying that because animals have selfhood, they too should be included in the category of persons.

Many critics of this ART position reassert the traditional view that only human beings are entitled to the protection of inviolable rights. Some critics appeal to religion. The sacred texts of many faiths, including Judaism, Christianity, and Islam, state that God gave humans dominion over animals, including the right to use them for our benefit, and for some devout religious believers this biblical sanction is sufficient grounds to reject ART.[6] We will set this aside, since we are interested in arguments that draw upon public reasons, not private faith or sacred revelation.

Other critics attempt to deny that animals really do have a subjective experience of the world or that they experience pain, suffering, fear, or pleasure. But the scientific evidence on this point is overwhelming and growing daily. As Palmer notes, it is now accepted by the 'overwhelming majority of biologists and philosophers' (Palmer 2010: 15), so we will set that criticism aside too.[7]

A more serious critique of ART accepts that animals are sentient but denies that sentience is sufficient for being entitled to the protection of inviolable rights. According to this line of argument, inviolable rights are only owed to persons, and personhood is something more than mere selfhood; it requires more than the fact of there being 'someone home'.[8] As we noted earlier, many AR theorists effectively equate selfhood and personhood; since animals are sentient selves, they should be treated as persons. But critics have argued that personhood requires some further capacity found only amongst humans. People disagree about what this further capacity is. Some appeal to language, others to the capacity for abstract reasoning or long-term planning, yet others appeal to the capacity for culture or to enter into moral agreements. According to these views, the fact that there is someone home is not sufficient to trigger inviolable rights: the 'someone' at home must also be capable of complex cognitive functioning. Since allegedly only humans possess these cognitive capacities, only humans deserve inviolable rights. And since animals lack these inviolable rights, they can legitimately be used for the benefit of humans.

The multiple flaws in this attempt to reject ART by appeal to personhood have been extensively discussed in the literature. First, even if we could draw a coherent distinction between 'selves' and 'persons', it would not in fact justify ascribing rights on the basis of species membership. Any attempt to draw a line between selves and persons will cut across the species line, treating some humans and some animals as persons, while relegating other humans and other animals to the status of 'mere' selves. Moreover, the very attempt to make a sharp distinction between personhood and selfhood is not conceptually sustainable. It attempts to draw a single clear line in what is really a continuum, or indeed a series of continua along which individuals move at different stages of life. And this in turn reveals the flimsy moral foundations of the appeal to personhood. There is simply no plausible moral justification for ascribing inviolable rights based on personhood rather than selfhood.

We do not want to rehearse all of these arguments, but it is important to clarify not just the futility, but also the grave risks, of trying to invoke personhood as the basis for privileging humans over animals. We cannot assume a priori that only humans will pass a test of personhood. It is not true that only humans use language, for example, or that only humans engage in planning. Every day we learn more about animal minds and capacities, and every day the line in the sand allegedly establishing a unique human personhood is obliterated. It is on this basis that recent authors have argued, for example, that the great apes (Cavalieri and Singer 1993), dolphins (White 2007), elephants (Poole 1998), and whales (Cavalieri 2006) possess the cognitive and moral capacities that establish personhood.

One could try to overcome this by raising the bar of personhood so that it requires not only language or planning but, say, the capacity to engage in reasoned moral argumentation and to make commitments to comply with principles reached through such argumentation.[9] In this view, personhood requires the ability to articulate one's beliefs verbally in a form that meets certain standards of public accessibility and universalizability, to be able to understand other people's moral arguments, to engage in some process of rational reflection about the relative merits of these different views, and then consciously and deliberatively to conform one's behaviour to the principles that result from such a process of moral reasoning.

It is clear that apes and dolphins are not persons in this Kantian sense. But it is equally clear that many humans are not persons in this sense either. Many humans (e.g., infants, the senile, the mentally disabled, those temporarily incapacitated due to illness, others with severe cognitive impairments) don't possess the alleged prerequisites of personhood, and in some cases their capacities are clearly exceeded by apes and dolphins and other nonhumans. And yet are children and the cognitively impaired not persons? Are they not precisely the most vulnerable kinds of human beings whom the concept of inviolable human rights ought to protect?

In the philosophical literature, this is often described as the 'argument from marginal cases',[10] but this way of stating the objection misses the point. The problem is not that we have a clear majority of 'normal' humans who pass the test of personhood and then a few 'marginal cases' of humans who possess selfhood but not personhood. The problem, rather, is that the capacity for Kantian moral agency is, at best, a fragile achievement that humans have to varying degrees at varying points in their lives. None of us possesses it when we are very young, and we all face periods of shorter or longer duration when it is temporarily or permanently threatened by illness, disability, and aging, or by lack of adequate socialization and education and other forms of social support and nurturance. If personhood is defined as the capacity to engage in rational argumentation and to conform to consciously understood principles, then it is a fluctuating characteristic that varies not only across human beings, but also across time within a life.[11] To ground human rights in the possession of personhood in this sense would be to render human rights insecure for everyone. And this would defeat the purpose of human rights, which is precisely to provide security for vulnerable selves, including (and indeed especially) in those conditions or periods of life when capacities are limited.

AR theorists sometimes make the point about insecurity in another way. If the protected status of personhood is based on humans possessing superior cognitive capacities to animals, then what happens if an even more evolutionarily advanced species from another planet comes to Earth? Imagine that we encounter a species—let's call them Telepaths—who can engage in telepathy, in complex reasoning that exceeds even our most advanced computers, or in forms of moral self-control that exceed the notoriously weak-willed and impulsive human species. And imagine that Telepaths start to enslave humans and use us for food or sport, as beasts of burden, or as subjects of medical experimentation for their health research. And imagine that they justify our enslavement and exploitation on the grounds that our primitive forms of communication, reasoning, and impulse control do not meet their tests of personhood. They recognize us as having selfhood but deny that we have the complex capacities needed for the inviolable rights of personhood.

How would we respond to such enslavement? Presumably we would respond that our alleged inferiority in these respects is irrelevant to our possession of inviolable rights.[12] We might indeed have primitive forms of communication or moral self-discipline in the estimation of Telepaths, but that does not make us mere instruments for the use and benefit of more advanced beings. We have our own lives to lead, our own experience of the world, our own sense of how our lives go better or worse. We are, in short, selves, and it is in virtue of our selfhood that we are owed basic rights, and the presence of allegedly more advanced beings does nothing to reduce our selfhood. Inviolable rights are not a prize awarded to whichever individual or species scores highest on some scale of cognitive capacities, but rather a recognition of the fact that we are subjective beings, and as such should be recognized as having our own lives to lead. But of course we can only respond in this way to the Telepaths if we abandon our quest to deny inviolable rights to animals. The very arguments of cognitive superiority invoked to justify excluding animals are precisely the basis on which Telepaths would justify our enslavement.[13]

In these and other ways, basing human rights on a demanding conception of personhood rather than selfhood would render human rights insecure. Indeed, the evolution of the theory and practice of human rights in the last sixty years has been in the opposite direction, repudiating any limitation based on the rationality or autonomy of the beings involved. We can see this internationally with the adoption of the UN Convention on the Rights of the Child (1990) or the UN Convention on the Rights of Persons with Disabilities (2006), as well as in domestic laws and court cases. For example, in an important case dealing with a profoundly intellectually disabled man who could not understand language or conceptualize death, the Massachusetts Supreme Court in 1977 emphasized that 'the principles of equality under the law' have 'no relation to intelligence' or to an individual's ability to 'appreciate' life in a conceptual sense.[14] None of these developments make sense if we tie human rights to a cognitively demanding conception of personhood. In short, invoking personhood to deny inviolable rights to animals only succeeds in eviscerating the theory and practice of human rights for human beings.

Confronted with these objections, critics of ART have responded in various ways. Some bite the bullet and accept that some human beings will not qualify as persons who are entitled to the protection of inviolability, even as some animals might qualify (Frey 1983). We can identify a range of such imagined geographies of personhood, with various mixes and matches of 'normal' humans and 'higher' animals inside the protected tent, while 'marginal' humans and 'lower' animals are outside.[15] Any intellectually honest attempt to apply a cognitively complex definition of personhood will almost certainly lead to this sort of patchwork quilt of variable and insecure moral status. Some people might think that this is a philosophically respectable position that needs to be taken seriously, but in our view, it is deeply unappealing (not to mention unworkable), and in any event it runs directly counter to the real-world development of human rights theory. The evolving trajectory of human rights has been precisely to erect the strongest of safeguards for the most vulnerable, protecting subordinated groups from dominant groups who question their cognitive capacities, protecting children from adults who can rationalize their abuse, protecting people with disabilities from eugenicists who would deny that their lives have dignity. Anyone who endorses these developments, as we hope our readers do, cannot endorse a theory of moral status that demands cognitively complex personhood.

A surprising number of theorists, however, cling to the hope that personhood can be invoked to reject inviolable rights for (all) animals while preserving the claim to inviolable rights for (all) humans. To preserve this illusory hope, theorists engage in increasingly contorted intellectual gymnastics to defend the privileging of human beings. Some appeal to the idea that all humans, whatever their actual capacities, have the 'species potential' for personhood or that all humans belong to the 'kind' of being that has the potential for personhood (e.g., Cohen and Regan 2001)—forms of argumentation that are widely discredited in all other areas of moral and political philosophy but which get revived in a desperate attempt to preserve the right of humans to exploit animals. When the multiple fallacies of such arguments are pointed out (e.g., Cavalieri 2001, Nobis 2004), the last line of defence is to stipulate that all human beings should be seen as inviolable persons simply because of their species membership, regardless of their actual or potential capacities. In rejecting the idea of animal personhood, Margaret Somerville, for example, says that 'universal human personhood means that every human being has an "intrinsic dignity" that comes simply with being human; having that dignity does not depend on having any other attribute or functional capacity' (Somerville 2010). Here we reach the nadir of appeals to personhood, which become nothing more than the bald assertion of speciesism. For Somerville, we should treat every human as an inviolable person because they are each one of us (whatever their needs, capacities, or interests), and we should deny inviolable personhood to every animal because they are each not one of us (whatever their needs, capacities, or interests).[16]

Much of the literature on animal rights has been consumed with these arguments and counter-arguments around personhood. In our view, however, this way of framing the debate leads us astray. What morally justifies the attribution of inviolable rights is selfhood, not a more cognitively demanding conception of personhood. Indeed, talk of personhood starts us down the wrong path. It suggests we must first develop some canonical list of attributes or capacities that ground inviolable rights and then look around to see which beings possess these attributes. Rather, we believe that respecting inviolability is, first and foremost, a process of intersubjective recognition—that is, the first question is simply whether there is a 'subject' there, whether there is 'someone home'. This process of intersubjective recognition precedes any attempt to enumerate his or her capacities or interests. Once we know there is someone home, we know we are dealing with a vulnerable self, a being with subjective experience whose life can go better or worse as experienced from the inside. And so we know we should respect their inviolable rights, even before we know their variable capacities such as intelligence or moral agency.[17]

All of this is clear enough in the human case. When dealing with sentient humans, we do not assign degrees of basic human rights or inviolability according to differences in mental complexity, intelligence, or emotional or moral range. Simple or brilliant, selfish or saint, torpid or vivacious—we are all entitled to basic human rights because we are all vulnerable selves. Indeed, it is often humans with the most limited capacities who are most vulnerable, and most in need of the protections of inviolability. Moral status does not rest on judgements of mental complexity, but simply on the recognition of selfhood. Talk of personhood obscures this and creates false barriers to the recognition of animal rights.

The idea that inviolable rights are grounded in the capacity for language, moral reflection, or abstract cognitive ability strains common sense and seems disconnected from any plausible account of how we actually reason morally.[18] Focusing on these capacities may be tempting to anyone whose driving motivation is to exclude animals from the protection of inviolable rights. But that end can only be achieved by hollowing out the theory, making a mockery of the idea of protecting the vulnerable and the innocent.[19]

Given the way talk of personhood obscures our moral reasoning and the way it has been used for exclusionary purposes, it might be better to avoid the language of personhood entirely and simply talk, in both the human and animal cases, of selfhood and of the inviolable rights that protect selfhood. But the language of personhood is too deeply woven into our everyday discourses and legal systems to simply be expunged. For many legal and political purposes, advancing an animal rights agenda will require using the pre-existing language of persons and extending it to animals. And so we too, like Francione, will sometimes speak about 'animals as persons'. But it is important to emphasize that, for the rest of this book, we are treating personhood as a synonym for selfhood and that we reject any attempt to distinguish personhood from selfhood as the basis for inviolable rights. Such efforts are conceptually unsustainable, morally unmotivated, and radically destabilizing of the very idea of universal human rights.[20]

Our fundamental position, then, is that animals have inviolable rights in virtue of their sentience or selfhood, the fact that they have a subjective experience of the world. This naturally raises the question of which beings are indeed conscious or sentient in this sense. Which animals are selves? The truth is, we may never be able to fully answer this question. There is something fundamentally unknowable about other minds, and this chasm increases the further we move from forms of consciousness and experience that most resemble our own. Are molluscs conscious? Insects? The evidence to date suggests they are not, but this may just reflect the fact that we are looking for a distinctly human form of subjective experience and not considering other possible forms.[21] Scientists are still learning how to study animal minds, and there will undoubtedly be hard cases and grey areas for a long time to come when trying to identify consciousness. However, this doesn't change the fact that we can readily identify it in many instances. Indeed, the types of animals that are most cruelly abused are precisely those whose consciousness is least in doubt. We domesticate species like dogs and horses precisely because of their ability to interact with us. We experiment on species like monkeys and rats precisely because they share similar responses to deprivation, fear, or rewards. To invoke the difficulty of determining a threshold of basic consciousness as a justification for continuing animal exploitation is dishonest. As Francione argues, even if we don't know enough about animal minds to be sure about whether all animals are sentient/conscious, we know that many of them are and that the ones we routinely exploit most certainly are (Francione 2000: 6; cf. Regan 2003).

Moreover, it is important to emphasize that recognizing selfhood does not require that we be able to unravel the mystery of an animal's mind. The point of the Smuts quote about 'someone home' is that we can recognize consciousness without being able to understand what it is like to be a bat, say, or a deer. (Just as we can recognize the selfhood of other humans whose subjective experience is profoundly different from our own.) This doesn't mean that we shouldn't seek greater understanding of animal minds. Science has made remarkable strides in recent years in demonstrating the range and complexity of animal intelligence and emotion.[22] This understanding has been vital in changing human attitudes towards animals, especially in overturning the old scientific consensus that animals were insentient—a prejudice with remarkable staying power, given the overwhelming evidence (and common sense) to the contrary. Scientific understanding is also vital in helping us understand the specific interests of individual animals and species and in interpreting what they are able to communicate to us about those interests. The better we understand animals, the greater the opportunities for a rich and rewarding (and just) intersubjective relationship. There will always be some animals whose world and experience are so removed from ours—like the eelpout fish living deep in the Pacific Ocean thermal vents—that the best we can do is recognize that there is a self there, respect their basic rights, and leave them to get on with life.[23] But there will be countless others with whom greater understanding and relationship is possible. This is where the science of other minds becomes crucial—not in determining *who* has basic rights, but in helping us to understand *how* best to interact with them.

Thus we eagerly await new developments from the ethical exploration of animal minds. However, the moral claim to basic rights does not hinge on these findings. We already know that in the case of most animals, there is 'someone home'. This, in our view, is sufficient to ground respect for basic inviolable rights. Admittedly, ours is a minority view, and we have no doubt that debates will continue to rage concerning moral status, selfhood, personhood, and universal basic rights. Defenders of human superiority will continue to engage in increasingly contorted intellectual gymnastics to defend the privileging of human beings, and animal advocates will continue to strip the last vestiges of human chauvinism from our moral theories. As we said earlier, our aim in this book is not to reproduce all these arguments and counter-arguments—readers who are interested in them can consult a number of good collections of key texts (Cohen and Regan 2001, Sapontzis 2004, Sunstein and Nussbaum 2004, Donovan and Adams 2007, Armstrong and Botzler 2008, Palmer 2008). And no doubt there will continue to be new and more ingenious efforts to defend speciesism in all its dimensions. But as Peter Singer notes, we have now had thirty years of such attempts, and 'the continuing failure of philosophy to produce a plausible theory of the moral importance of species membership indicates, with increasing probability, that there can be no such thing' (Singer 2003).

Notes

1. Peter Singer is widely seen as one of the founders of the 'animal rights' field, but in fact he is a utilitarian, and so does not believe in inviolable rights for either humans or animals. His arguments for improved treatment of animals are, therefore, based on empirical claims that most of the harms we inflict on animals

do not in fact serve the overall good, rather than on the rights-based claim that it would be wrong to harm animals even when it does serve the greater good. For critiques of Singer's utilitarianism from a rights-based AR perspective, see Regan (1983), Francione (2000), and Nussbaum (2006).

2. For a more extended account of this shift from utilitarian to rights-based theories in political philosophy, see Kymlicka (2002: ch. 2).

3. It is important to note that inviolability is not absolute: there are circumstances, in both the human and animal cases, where inviolable rights can be overridden. The most obvious example of this concerns self-defence, where we recognize the right of individuals to protect themselves from grievous assault by injuring, and even killing, their attacker. Another example is the temporary forcible confinement of an individual with a deadly contagion who poses an immediate threat to others and refuses to undertake voluntary quarantine. In other words, the inviolable rights of individuals can be overridden *in extremis*, when they pose an immediate threat to the basic inviolable rights of others (or, in some cases, when they pose such a threat to themselves). Inviolable rights are 'trumps' against being used for the greater good of others but are not a licence to harm others. This is familiar enough in the human case.

4. Not all AR theorists accept sentience or selfhood as the basis for inviolable rights. Some authors—such as Regan (in his early work, 1983), DeGrazia (1996), Wise (2000), and others—have argued that inviolable rights require some further threshold of cognitive complexity, such as memory, autonomy, or self-consciousness (and hence limit inviolable rights to certain 'higher' animals). We reject such 'mental complexity threshold' views, for reasons explained below. Indeed, it's worth noting that these authors themselves express ambivalence about tying inviolable rights to cognitive complexity. For example, in his later work, Regan shifts to selfhood as the basis for inviolable rights (Regan 2003). And Wise (2004) acknowledges that mental complexity arguments are problematically tied to human-centric standards of mental life.

5. Note the similarity with Eva Feder Kittay's account of the personhood of humans with severe intellectual disabilities. As against philosophical accounts of personhood that require complex cognitive capacities, she insists that 'we know there is a person before us when we see . . . that there is "someone home". . . . In one who can scarcely move a muscle, a glint in the eye at a strain of familiar music establishes personhood. A slight upturn of the lip in a profoundly and multiply disabled individual when a favorite caregiver comes along, or a look of joy in response to the scent of a perfume—all these establish personhood' (Kittay 2001: 568).

6. Such religious arguments have sometimes been invoked by people charged with animal cruelty—see Sorenson (2010: 116).

7. The most recent addition to the literature is the striking new research supporting the likelihood that fish feel pain—see Braithwaite (2010), which also contains a very helpful discussion of the difference between nociception (the unconscious reflexive reaction triggered when pain receptors send information about an injury to the spinal cord) and the subjective sentient experience of pain in the brain. It used to be thought that fish lacked the latter, but as Braithwaite notes, this is simply because no one had actually researched the question—it was only in 2003 that the first studies were conducted on fish pain! As scientific research replaces uninformed prejudice, the evidence for animal sentience continues to expand.

8. A variation on this objection argues that to qualify as a rights-holder, one must have the capacity for rational choice, since to have a right to X is just to have the right to choose whether or not to X. This is often described as the 'choice theory' or 'will theory' of rights. This was once an influential theory of rights, but it is now widely rejected, since it would not only preclude any idea of animal rights, but also any idea that children, the temporarily incapacitated, or future generations might have rights. It would also render unintelligible the idea that we have a right to vote in jurisdictions where voting is mandatory. Most theorists today, therefore, endorse the alternative 'interest theory' of rights, according to which (in Joseph Raz's influential formulation) to say that X is a rights-holder is to say that his or her interests are sufficient reason for imposing duties on others either not to interfere with X in the performance of some action or to secure him or her in something (Raz 1984). Whether animals, children, or the incapacitated have inviolable rights is, therefore, a question that can only be answered by examining the interests at stake.

9. As Stephen Horigan notes, there is a long history in Western culture of people 'responding to the discovery of boundary-threatening abilities in nonhuman animals by contentious reconceptualization of human-definitive powers (such as language) so as to keep the boundary in place' (Horigan 1988, quoted in Benton 1993: 17).

10. For the most sustained discussion, see Dombrowski (1997).

11. Similarly, we reject the idea that humans and animals can be clearly categorized as being either moral agents or moral patients. Moral agency involves a cluster of capacities which vary across species, amongst individuals within species, and over time within individuals. See Bekoff and Pierce 2009; Hribal 2007, 2010; Reid 2010; and Denison 2010.

12. *Star Trek: The Next Generation* fans will be reminded of episode 2 from season 2 ('Where Silence Has Lease') in which the Enterprise is ensnared by a species, represented by Nagilum, who are vastly superior to the Federation, at least in technological terms. The Enterprise crew are turned into rats in a maze and are deeply affronted by this failure to recognize their basic rights and dignity.

13. Telepaths are just science fiction, but they have given even some erstwhile defenders of animal experimentation pause for thought. Michael A. Fox's (1988) book *The Case for Animal Experimentation: An Evolutionary and Ethical Perspective* is often cited as a sophisticated defence of the right of human beings to use animals for their benefit (Fox 1988a). But when Fox realized that his arguments could be used by superior alien species to enslave humans, he repudiated those arguments (Fox 1988b) and now defends a robust AR position (Fox 1999).

14. *Superintendent of Belchertown v Saikewicz* 370 Eastern Reporter 2d Series, 417–35 (Mass. Supreme Court 1977). For discussions of the relevance of this and similar cases for the rights of animals, see Dunayer 2004: 107; Hall and Waters 2000.

15. Sometimes, the moral hierarchy doesn't just have two tiers but looks more like the great chain of being. Consider this recent statement by utilitarian philosopher Wayne Sumner: 'The hierarchy of sentience (capacity to feel pain) and intelligence determines a species' moral weight. Primates outrank other mammals; vertebrates outrank invertebrates. Seals rank with dogs, wolves, sea otters and bears—and ahead of cows' (quoted in Valpy 2010: A6).

16. As Angus Taylor points out, advocates of human exceptionalism, such as Somerville, 'cannot countenance just any ethical view that protects humans, for it is not enough to include all humans within the moral community—one must simultaneously exclude all non-humans. And this is crucial: *human exceptionalism is at least as much about whom we are determined to exclude from the moral community as about whom we wish to include within it*' (Taylor 2010: 228, emphasis in original). This sort of human exceptionalism is not just philosophically suspect, it is also empirically pernicious. The evidence shows that the more people sharply distinguish between humans and animals, the more likely they are to dehumanize human outgroups, such as immigrants. Belief in human superiority over animals is empirically correlated with, and causally connected to, belief in the superiority of some human groups over others. When participants in psychological studies are given arguments about human superiority over animals, the outcome is greater prejudice against human outgroups. By contrast, those who recognize that animals possess valued traits and emotions are also more likely to accord equality to human outgroups. Reducing the status divide between humans and animals helps to reduce prejudice and to strengthen belief in equality amongst human groups (Costello and Hodson 2010).

17. According to Silvers and Francis, 'Gaining an inclusive conception of personhood thus is posterior, not prior, to building out an adequately inclusive conception of justice. In other words, learning how to think more inclusively about personhood is an incremental benefit of building toward justice' (Silvers and Francis 2009: 495–6). See also Kittay 2005a, Vorhaus 2005, and Sanders 1993.

18. The idea that our capacity for moral agency is the foundation of human beings' inviolability (and animals' violability) is particularly perverse. As Stephen Clark notes, this argument says that the characteristic to be valued is our capacity to recognize other points of view than our own, yet the conclusion is that we don't need to consider the interests of others—in other words, 'we are absolutely better than animals because we are able to give their interests some consideration; so we won't' (Clark 1984: 107–8; see discussion in Benton 1993: 6; Cavalieri 2009).

19. Indeed, these often seem like attempts to find a secular basis for older religious ideas about the special place of human beings within God's providential plan. According to the Bible, only humans possess an immortal soul, only humans were made in God's image, and God gave humans dominion over animals. The idea that only humans are entitled to inviolable rights may make sense for anyone who believes in this biblical creation story. But if we seek a secular account of the moral basis of rights, one consistent with evolution, we should not expect or assume that only human beings require the protection of inviolable rights.

20. Some readers may think that in equating selfhood and personhood we are simply losing a word, and that there are good reasons to reserve the term 'person' for that subset of 'selves' who have complex cognitive capacities. We disagree—as we have seen, there is no sharp line that would allow us to stably divide the world into persons and selves—but this is not essential to our argument. Anyone who objects to our references to animal 'personhood' can simply replace the word with 'selfhood', without any change in meaning or argumentation. Even if there are contexts where it is useful to distinguish personhood from selfhood, our claim is simply that this distinction cannot play a role in determining who is a bearer of inviolable rights. See Garner (2005b), who says that while inviolable rights should be based on selfhood, we may nonetheless want an account of personhood for other conceptual purposes.

21. Martin Bell has a helpful discussion of these issues on the Vegan Outreach website: http://www.veganoutreach. org/insectcog.html. See also Dunayer (2004: 103–4, 127–32).

22. By scientific understanding we do not refer primarily to controlled lab experiments on animals, most of which are unethical. We refer to the understanding of animals learned through careful observation and ethical interaction. Many researchers believe that understanding animals' minds is best achieved through ethical interaction, which assumes the existence of mindedness, and indeed helps bring it into existence. Sociological 'interactionist' theory begins from the premise that mindedness and selfhood are established

in relationship with other selves. Irvine (2004), Myers (2003), Sanders (1993), and Sanders and Arluke (1993) have explored animal minds on this interactionist model.

23. We are reminded here of another episode of *Star Trek: The Next Generation* which nicely illustrates aspects of this dilemma. In season 1, episode 18, the crew encounters a 'chrystalline entity' on a distant planet. The species chasm is so wide that merely recognizing that there is 'someone home' is a fraught challenge, and coexistence is not possible. The ship's crew quarantines the entity's planet, to await a possible future when interaction might be possible.

Bibliography

Armstrong, Susan and Richard Botzler (eds) (2008) *The Animal Ethics Reader*, 2nd edn (London: Routledge).

Bekoff, Marc and Jessica Pierce (2009) *Wild Justice: The Moral Lives of Animals* (Chicago: University of Chicago Press).

Bentham, Jeremy (2002) 'Anarchical Fallacies, Being an Examination of the Declarations of Rights Issued During the French Revolution', in Philip Schofield, Catherine Pease-Watkin, and Cyprian Blamires (eds) *The Collected Works of Jeremy Bentham: Rights, Representation, and Reform: Nonsense upon Stilts and Other Writings on the French Revolution* (Oxford: Oxford University Press; first published in 1843).

Benton, Ted (1993) *Natural Relations: Ecology, Animal Rights, and Social Justice* (London: Verso).

Braithwaite, Victoria (2010) *Do Fish Feel Pain?* (Oxford: Oxford University Press).

Cavalieri, Paola (2001) *The Animal Question: Why Nonhuman Animals Deserve Human Rights* (Oxford: University Press).

———— (2006) 'Whales as Persons', in M. Kaiser and M. Lien (eds) *Ethics and the Politics of Food* (Wageningen Academic Publishers).

———— (2009) 'The Ruses of Reason: Strategies of Exclusion', *Logos Journal*. Available at www.logosjournal.com.

———— and Peter Singer (eds) (1993) *The Great Ape Project: Equality Beyond Humanity* (London: Fourth Estate).

Clark, Stephen R.L. (1984) *The Moral Status of Animals* (Oxford: Oxford University Press).

Cohen, Carl and Tom Regan (2001) *The Animal Rights Debate* (Lanham, MD: Rowman and Littlefield).

Costello, Kimberly and Gordon Hodson (2010) 'Exploring the Roots of Dehumanization: The Role of Animal-Human Similarity in Promoting Immigrant Humanization', *Group Processes and Intergroup Relations* 31/1:3–22.

DeGrazia, David (1996) *Taking Animals Seriously: Mental Life and Moral Status* (Cambridge: Cambridge University Press).

Denison, Jaime (2010) 'Between the Moment and Eternity: How Schillerian Play Can Establish Animals as Moral Agents', *Between the Species* 13/10:60–72.

Diamond, Cora (2004) "Eating Meat and Eating People," in Cass Sunstein and Martha Nussbaum (eds) *Animal Rights: Current Debates and New Directions* (Oxford: Oxford University Press), 93–107.

Dombrowski, Daniel (1997) *Babies and Beasts: The Argument from Marginal Cases* (Champaign: University of Illinois Press).

Donovan, Josephine (2007) 'Animal Rights and Feminist Theory', in Josephine Donovan and Carol J. Adams (eds) *The Feminist Care Tradition in Animal Ethics* (New York: Columbia University Press), 58–86.

Dunayer, Joan (2004) *Speciesism* (Derwood, MD: Ryce Publishing).

Dworkin, Ronald (1984) 'Rights as Trumps', in Jeremy Waldron (ed) *Theories of Rights* (Oxford: Oxford University Press), 153–67.

Fox, Michael A. (1988a) *The Case for Animal Experimentation: An Evolutionary and Ethical Perspective* (Berkeley: University of California Press).

———— (1988b) 'Animal Research Reconsidered', *New Age Journal* (January/February):14–21.

———— (1999) *Deep Vegetarianism* (Philadelphia: Temple University Press).

Francione, Gary I. (2000) *Introduction to Animal Rights: Your Child or the Dog?* (Philadelphia: Temple University Press).

———— (2008) *Animals as Persons: Essays on the Abolition of Animal Exploitation* (New York: Columbia University Press).

Frey, Raymond (1983) *Rights, Killing and Suffering* (Oxford: Oxford University Press).

Garner, Robert (2005a) *The Political Theory of Animal Rights* (Manchester: Manchester University Press).

Hall, Lee and Anthony Jon Waters (2000) 'From Property to Persons: The Case of Evelyn Hart', *Seton Hall Constitutional Law Journal* 11/1:1–68.

Horigan, Steven (1988) *Nature and Culture in Western Discourses* (London: Routledge).

Hribal, Jason (2007) 'Animals, Agency, and Class: Writing the History of Animals from Below', *Human Ecology Review* 14/1:101–12.

—— (2010) *Fear of the Animal Planet: The Hidden History of Animal Resistance* (Oakland, CA: Counter Punch Press and AK Press).

Irvine, Leslie (2004) 'A Model of Animal Selfhood: Expanding Interactionist Possibilities", *Symbolic Interaction* 27/1:3–21.

Kittay, Eva Feder (2001) 'When Caring Is Just and Justice is Caring: Justice and Mental Retardation", *Public Culture* 13/3:557–79.

Kymlicka, Will (2002) *Contemporary Political Philosophy*, 2nd edn (Oxford: Oxford University Press).

McMahan, Jeff (2002) *The Ethics of Killing: Problems at the Margins of Life* (Oxford: Oxford University Press).

Myers, Olin E. Jr. (2003) 'No Longer the Lonely Species: A Post-Mead Perspective on Animals and Sociology', *International Journal of Sociology and Social Policy* 23/3:46–68.

Nobis, Nathan (2004) 'Carl Cohen's "Kind" Arguments *for* Animal Rights and *Against* Human Rights', *Journal of Applied Philosophy* 21/1:43–59.

Nozick, Robert (1974) *Anarchy, State and Utopia* (New York: Basic Books).

Nussbaum, Martha (2006) *Frontiers of Justice: Disability, Nationality, Species Membership* (Cambridge, MA: Harvard University Press).

Palmer, Clare (2010) *Animal Ethics in Context* (New York: Columbia University Press).

—— (ed) (2008) *Animal Rights* (Farnham: Ashgate).

Poole, Joyce (1998) 'An Exploration of a Commonality between Ourselves and Elephants', *Etica & Animali* 9:85–110.

Rawls, John (1971) *A Theory of Justice* (Oxford: Oxford University Press).

Raz, Joseph (1984) 'The Nature of Rights', *Mind* 9/3:194–214.

Regan, Tom (1983) *The Case for Animal Rights* (Berkeley: University of California Press).

Reid, Mark D. (2010) 'Moral Agency in *Mammalia*', *Between the Species* 13/20:1–24.

Sanders, Clinton R. (1993) 'Understanding Dogs: Caretakers' Attributions of Mindedness in Canine-Human Relationships', *Journal of Contemporary Ethnography* 22/2:205–26.

—— and Arnold Arluke (1993) 'If Lions Could Speak: Investigating the Animal-Human Relationship and the Perspectives of Non-Human Others', *Sociological Quarterly* 34/3:377–90.

Sapontzis, Steve (ed) (2004) *Food for Thought: The Debate over Eating Meat* (Amherst, NY: Prometheus Books).

Singer, Peter (1975) *Animal Liberation* (New York: Random House).

—— (2003) 'Animal Liberation at 30', *New York Review of Books* 50/8.

Smuts, Barbara (1999) 'Reflections', in J.M. Coetzee and Amy Gutmann (eds) *The Lives of Animals* (Princeton: Princeton University Press), 107–20.

Somerville, Margaret (2010) 'Are Animals People?', *The Mark*, 25 January 2010. Available at http://www.themarknews.com/articles/868-are-animals-people.

Sorenson, John (2010) *About Canada: Animal Rights* (Black Point, Nova Scotia: Fernwood Publishing).

Steiner, Gary (2008) *Animals and the Moral Community: Mental Life, Moral Status, and Kinship* (New York: Columbia University Press).

Taylor, Angus (2010) 'Review of Wesley J. Smith's a Rat Is a Pig Is a Dog Is a Boy: The Human Cost of the Animal Rights Movement', *Between the Species* 10:223–36.

Valpy, Michael (2010) 'The Sea Hunt as a Matter of Morals', *Globe and Mail*, 8 February, A6.

Vorhaus, John (2005) 'Citizenship, Competence and Profound Disability', *Journal of Philosophy of Education* 39/3:461–75.

White, Thomas (2007) *In Defense of Dolphins: The New Moral Frontier* (Oxford: Blackwell).

Wise, Steven (2000) *Rattling the Cage: Toward Legal Rights to Animals* (Cambridge, MA: Perseus Books).

—— (2004) 'Animal Rights, Once Step at a Time', in Martha Nussbaum and Cass Sunstein (eds) *Animal Rights: Current Debates and New Directions* (Oxford: Oxford University Press), 19–50.

Part Two

Animal Capacities

Pain, Emotion, Consciousness

Introduction to Part Two

The capacities of nonhuman animals to experience pain, to have a sense of consciousness embedded with cognitive abilities, and to have emotional lives is a challenging and controversial set of topics. On the one hand, a seemingly boundless set of examples of complex behaviors of these animals that correspond to sophisticated human behaviors are regularly reported by people with interest in and experience with individual animals, including pet owners, zoo personnel, farmers, and ranchers. On the other hand, scientists often have struggled to understand these topics in light of contemporary understandings of neurology, anatomy, biochemistry, physiology, ethology, and behavioral ecology of representatives of these various animal groups. Slowly some coherent pictures are emerging.

Mendl, Burman, and Paul address how to better understand animal emotions by integrating an older discrete emotions approach with a dimensional approach that conceptualizes emotions in terms of universal core affective characteristics.

Smuts found it essential to become immersed in the lives of the baboons she studied over a period of years, coming to know the animals on an individual basis. This leads to the potential complications of anthropomorphism, which long has been a controversial issue in the study of nonhumans.

Mitchell argues that anthropomorphic models are specific claims of similarity between humans and nonhumans that are scientifically accessible and must be substantiated by evidence. In the moral sphere, she argues that the fundamental concern might be establishing what capacities in any creature might be the basis of moral consideration.

Bermúdez believes that at least some animals are "genuine thinkers," in that their behaviors can be explained in psychological terms. He addresses the elements of this perspective most relevant to those addressing animal ethics issues.

Several authors address the notion of consciousness, emotion, and suffering, including pain, in animals. Bermond takes the conservative view that the essential anatomy to have such experiences is lacking in most nonhuman animals, with the possible exception of apes. Rollin addresses what he believes to be the scientific incoherence of denying pain in animals and of denying moral consideration to them. Allen addresses the need for more research to assess the roles and functions of pain among animals.

Dennett argues that consciousness is not an all-or-nothing phenomenon that is present or absent, but a quality that may be present to varying degrees and not entirely a useful question in evolutionary perspectives; its application to mammals might be analogous to the question of whether birds are "wise" or reptiles have "gumption."

Griffin and Speck address the complex topics of animal cognition and consciousness. They argue that humans and other animals probably differ in both the content and the richness of their conscious experiences. They also recognize that animal communication is much richer than previously understood. Finally, DeGrazia argues that the cumulative force of much empirical data and rational and conceptual considerations make it more reasonable to accept than to deny the thesis that many animals are self-aware.

Further Reading

Allen, C. (2005). Deciphering animal pain. In Murat Aydede (ed.). *Pain: New Essays on Its Nature and the Methodology of Its Study*, pp. 351–366. Cambridge MA: Bradford Book/MIT Press.

Baker, S. (2001). *Picturing the Beast: Animals, Identity, and Representation.* Urbana: University of Illinois Press.

Barresi, J., and Moore, C. (1996). Intentional relations and social understanding. *Behavioral and Brain Sciences* 19: 107–154.

Bekoff, M. (2009). Animal emotions, wild justice and why they matter: Grieving magpies, a pissy baboon and empathic elephants. *Emotion, Space and Society* 2(2): 82–85.

Bradshaw, R. H. (1998). Consciousness in non-human animals: Adopting the precautionary principle. *Journal of Consciousness Studies* 5: 108–114.

Butler, A. B., P. R. Manger, B. I. B. Lindahl, and P. Arhem. (2005). Evolution of the neural basis of consciousness: A bird–mammal comparison. *Bio Essays* 27: 923–936.

Carruthers, P. (2005). Why the question of animal consciousness might not matter very much. *Philosophical Psychology* 18: 83–102.

———. (2008). Meta-cognition in animals: A skeptical look. *Mind and Language* 23(1): 58–89.

Cartmill, M. (2000). Animal consciousness: Some philosophical, methodological, and evolutionary problems. *American Zoologist* 40: 835–846.

Crick, F., and C. Koch. (2003). A framework for consciousness. *Nature Neuroscience* 6: 119–126.

Edelman, D. B., and A. K. Seth. (2009). Animal consciousness: A synthetic approach. *Trends in Neurosciences* 32(9): 476–484.

Langford, D. J., S. E. Crager, Z. Shehzad, S. B. Smith, S. G. Sotocinal, J. S. Levenstadt, M. L. Chanda, D. J. Levitin, and J. S. Mogil. (2006). Social modulation of pain as evidence for empathy in mice. *Science* 312: 1967–1970.

Mellor, D. J. (2012). Animal emotions, behavior and the promotion of positive welfare states. *New Zealand Veterinary Journal* 60(1): 1–8.

Mendl, M., O. Burman, R. Parker, and E. S. Paul. (2009). Cognitive bias as an indicator of animal emotion and welfare: Emerging evidence and underlying mechanisms. *Applied Animal Behaviour Science* 118(3–4): 161–181.

Mitchell, R. W., N. S. Thompson, and H. Lyn Miles (eds.). (1997) *Anthropomorphism, Anecdotes, and Animals.* Albany: State University of New York Press.

Ritvo, H. (2000). Animal consciousness: Some historical perspective. *American Zoologist* 40: 847–852.

Rollin, B. E. (2011). Animal pain: What it is and why it matters. *Journal of Ethics* 15: 425–437.

Rutherford, K. M. D. (2002). Assessing pain in animals. *Animal Welfare* 11: 31–53.

Whiteside, G. T., A. Adedoyin, and L. Leventhal. (2008). Predictive validity of animal pain models? A comparison of the pharmacokinetic-pharmacodynamic relationship for pain drugs in rats and humans. *Neuropharmacology* 54: 767–775.

Study Questions

1. Based on Mendl et al.'s article on animal emotion, how likely do you believe it is that cognitive science studies can give a relatively clear answer on the level of emotional experience in nonhuman animals? Give examples and justify your answer.

2. To what degree do you believe that Smuts's objectivity for describing baboon lives might be affected by her interpersonal relations with them? Justify your thinking.

3. Based on Mitchell's presentation, what do you think is the applicability of anthropomorphism for describing behaviors of nonhuman primates? Of other mammals? Of other vertebrates?

4. How do your personal experiences align with the notion that some animals are genuine thinkers, as defined by Bermúdez? Justify your perspective.

5. To what degree are Bermond's and Rollin's positions on animal experience of pain compatible, and incompatible? How do you see Allen's ideas fitting into this framework? Clarify your reasons.

6. How would you compare the perspectives of Bermond and Dennett? What are the key points that Bermond and Dennett might hold in common? On what score do they differ?

7. Compare Griffin and Speck with Dennett, as well as with DeGrazia. What points would you expect that they could agree upon? Give two or three of their most outstanding differences.

Issues/Methods of Study

8 An Integrative and Functional Framework for the Study of Animal Emotion and Mood

Michael Mendl, Oliver H. P. Burman, and Elizabeth S. Paul

Mendl et al. address a better understanding of animal emotions. They challenge a "discrete emotions" approach as piecemeal and incomplete. They also assess the value of "dimensional" approaches in which emotional states are seen as continuums of experience in two- or three-dimensional space, with various values of positivity and negativity. The authors propose a combination to provide a conceptual framework to study animal emotions that offers a structure to integrate disparate discrete emotions, gives a perspective on how "free-floating" mood states arise, and provides new hypothesis-driven measures of animal emotion.

Introduction

A better understanding of animal emotion is highly desirable in disciplines including neuroscience, psycho-pharmacology, pain research, and animal welfare science. To date, much animal emotion research, like Darwin's (1872/2009) pioneering writings on the subject, has focused on 'discrete' emotions. Researchers have investigated how animals respond to situations assumed to induce *specific* emotional states. For example, there is a whole industry devoted to the study of fear and anxiety, largely based on the development of tests designed to induce these states. This approach has yielded detailed information on candidate behavioural and physiological indicators of discrete emotions (e.g. Boissy 1995; Ramos & Mormede 1998; Forkman et al. 2007) and on their putative neural and neurochemical substrates (e.g. LeDoux 1996; Panksepp 1998; Berridge 2003; Dalgleish 2004).

Furthermore, it has been argued that at least in mammals, there are 'basic' discrete emotional systems (e.g., fear, rage, panic, play) rooted in the neural circuitry of particular brain areas, serving specific adaptive functions, and representing the fundamental building blocks of all emotional reactions (Ekman 1992; Panksepp 1998).

[. . .]

The *discrete emotions* approach, however, has inevitably been piecemeal, leaving some emotional states, including positive ones (Boissy et al. 2007), under-studied. It also lacks an overarching framework or 'structure of emotion' that can integrate the wide range of possible emotional states, and provide *a priori* predictions, applicable across species, for how these states are manifest, and hence how they can be measured. Such a framework could be offered by *dimensional theories* that have become increasingly prominent in the study of human emotion (Russell & Barrett 1999; Watson et al. 1999; Carver 2001; Russell 2003). These are largely based on reports of subjective emotional experiences and the temporal relationships between different reported states and suggest that these states can be represented as locations in two- or three-dimensional space. Different theories propose slightly different dimensional axes, but a 'valence' dimension or dimensions (positivity/negativity) is central to all. Some theorists argue that these dimensions, and not basic emotions, are the core building blocks of all emotional experience, are underpinned by specific brain systems, and serve important adaptive functions such as the control of approach and avoidance behaviour (e.g. Watson et al. 1999; Carver 2001; Posner et al. 2005; Barrett 2006; Barrett et al. 2007).

There is ongoing debate between proponents of the discrete/basic and dimensional views of emotion (e.g. Ortony & Turner 1990; Ekman 1992; Barrett 2006; Izard 2007; Panksepp 2007). It is not our aim to argue in support of one or the other. Rather, we believe that they can be brought together to provide a conceptual framework for studying animal emotions that: (i) offers a structure for integrating disparate discrete emotions, providing a functional perspective on the adaptive value of different emotional states, (ii) suggests how 'free-floating' mood states arise from short-term emotional responses to events, and how they may function to guide decision making and (iii) yields novel hypothesis-driven measures of animal emotion.

[. . .]

We start by outlining the dimensional approach, which has received limited attention in animal emotion research (but see Gray 1994), then briefly summarize some disagreements between discrete and dimensional theorists before suggesting how the two approaches may be brought together. We end by considering implications for the assessment of animal emotion, including the development of new measures that may be particularly useful for assessing long-term mood states.

A Dimensional View of the Structure of Emotion: Core Affect

Core Affect and Subjective Emotional Experience

Emotions interest us because of their distinctive conscious manifestation—the *feelings* of joy, relief, anxiety, or depression. The conscious subjective experience of emotions is what we are ultimately concerned about when we consider human and animal welfare, and it is these subjective experiences that define the field of emotion research. In humans, the 'gold standard', albeit indirect, method for measuring these experiences is linguistic self-report. Statistical analyses of these reports suggest that emotions can be defined in terms of two fundamental underlying dimensions (e.g. Stanley & Meyer 2009). Emotional experiences are valenced—they are perceived as positive or negative, rewarding or punishing, pleasant or unpleasant—neutral states are not emotional states. Emotional experiences also vary in reported activation or arousal. For example, the states of elation and contentment are both positively valenced, but the former involves a higher degree of arousal than the latter.

Subjective experiences that can be characterized in terms of these valence and arousal dimensions have been labelled *core affect* (Russell 2003; Barrett et al. 2007). They can be represented in two-dimensional space. Positive affective states lie in the right half of this space (quadrants Q1 and Q2), and negative affective states in the left half (Q3 and Q4). Core affect can thus be conceptualized as the fundamental subjectively reportable manifestation of any emotion or mood state, and core affect space provides us with a way of conceptualizing the structure of subjective emotional experiences. Discrete emotions such as fear, sadness and happiness are located somewhere in this space, although their location *per se* does not fully encapsulate their subjective qualities. For example, a highly aroused negatively valenced state (Q4) accompanied by an urge to flee may characterize fear, while a state of the same valence and arousal accompanied by an urge to attack may characterize anger.

The core affect concept is rooted in an understanding of the subjective experience of emotion. While this may lie at the heart of our interests in animal emotion, it raises challenges given that *direct* measurement of subjective states in another human, let alone another species, is not currently possible. However, the reported subjective experiences of core affect in humans are accompanied by neural, behavioural, physiological and cognitive changes, such as alterations in brain activity, facial expressions, heart rate and attention to threat. These changes *can* be measured objectively. Together with subjective experience, they make up the *components* of emotional or affective states. Researchers can study these *measurable* components of animal emotions and attempt to identify those components that are reliably associated with particular locations in core affect space.

Of course, even if we can use measurable components of emotional responses to locate animals' position in core affect space, we cannot be certain that they experience the *conscious* component too. Whether or not, and to what extent, different species experience conscious affective states remains an area of intense and unresolved debate (e.g. Wemelsfelder 1997; Macphail 1998; Baars 2001; Rolls 2005). For the purposes and scope of this paper, however, we must leave this to one side, discussing animal emotions as states that may or may not be experienced consciously.

Acquiring Rewards and Avoiding Punishment: A Functional View of Core Affect

Could animals have states that equate to core affect (regardless of whether these are consciously experienced)? We think this is plausible because of the likely evolutionary advantage of systems that can represent the organism's overall experience of *reward* and *punishment*. Emotional states occur in response to stimuli or situations that are actually, or potentially, rewarding or punishing. Reward and punishment thus lie at the heart of all emotional states and determine emotional valence (e.g. Lang et al. 1990; Gray 1994; Cacioppo et al. 1999; Watson et al. 1999; Carver 2001; Rolls 2005; Barrett et al. 2007; Nesse & Ellsworth 2009). Inherently rewarding or punishing stimuli include those that enhance fitness (*rewards*—food, water, shelter, mates, etc.) and those that threaten fitness (*punishers*—predator attack, thermal damage, etc.). The affective responses of different animal species to these stimuli are thought to have developed over evolutionary time, and to act as proximate mechanisms guiding and coordinating the organism to achieve two principal survival goals: *maximizing acquisition of fitness-enhancing rewards* and *minimizing exposure to fitness-threatening punishers* (e.g. Rolls 2005; Burgdorf & Panksepp 2006; Nesse & Ellsworth 2009).

Position in core affect space is widely believed to reflect this functionality. Theoretical and empirical studies suggest that positive high arousal affective states in quadrant Q1 (e.g. excitement, happiness) are associated with appetitive motivational states and function to facilitate seeking and obtaining rewards (Cabanac 1992; Carver 2001; Custers & Aarts 2005; Rolls 2005; Burgdorf & Panksepp 2006). In contrast, negative low arousal states in Q3 (e.g. sadness, depression) are associated with experiences of loss or lack of reward and may promote low activity and conservation of energy in conditions where resources are lacking (Nesse 2000). Several researchers propose that an individual's position along this axis may be associated with the activity of underlying, perhaps primitive, biobehavioural systems ('positive activation', 'behavioural activation' (BAS) or 'approach process' systems Gray 1994; Watson et al. 1999; Carver 2001) concerned with the control of approach behaviour and resource acquisition. The mesolimbic dopaminergic system and its role in appetitive and 'wanting' behaviours may be an important neural substrate of such systems (Berridge 1996, 2007; Panksepp 1998; McNaughton & Corr 2008). In humans, activation of left anterior cortical areas may also reflect enhanced activity of these systems (Davidson 1998; Davidson & Irwin 1999).

Negative high-arousal affective states in quadrant Q4 (e.g. fear) are thought to be principally associated with, and to coordinate appropriate responses to, the presence of threat or danger (Gray 1994; Carver 2001; Rolls 2005; Burgdorf & Panksepp 2006). In contrast, positive low-arousal affective states in Q2 (e.g. calm, relaxed) are associated with experience of low levels of threat (Carver 2001), perhaps facilitating the expression of maintenance, consolidation and recovery activities. An individual's position on the Q2–Q4 axis is principally determined by the perceived presence of danger or threat and has been associated with the activation of underlying biobehavioural systems ('negative activation', 'fight flight flee system' [FFFS], 'avoidance process'; Gray 1994; Watson et al. 1999; Carver 2001) that have evolved to facilitate the avoidance of punishment. Gray (1994) also suggests that a 'behavioural inhibition system' (BIS) underpins anxiety states in conditions of conflicting threat/reward (see McNaughton & Corr 2008). Brain structures including the periaqueductal gray, amygdala, anterior cingulate and ventral prefrontal cortex may form the neural substrate of such systems (McNaughton & Corr 2008). In humans, activation of the right anterior cortical areas may also reflect enhanced activity of these systems (Davidson 1998; Davidson & Irwin 1999).

In summary, position in core affect space appears to be functionally related to the experience of success or failure in acquiring rewards and avoiding punishment, and bio-behavioural systems have evolved to serve these two fundamentally important activities. It is worth mentioning that some states (e.g. severe depression) may sometimes be the result of brain pathologies unrelated to experience or, while reflecting the organism's experiences, may be so extreme as to have limited functional value to the organism (i.e. represent a non-adaptive side effect of the proximate mechanisms involved). The border between functionality and pathology in states such as severe depression remains a topic of much debate (Nesse 2000).

Integrating Discrete and Dimensional Approaches

A major disagreement between proponents of discrete and dimensional approaches relates to the relative *primacy* of discrete emotional systems or dimensional core affect systems in generating felt emotional states. Core affect theorists propose that ongoing core affective state (valence and arousal) is combined with evaluations or appraisals of current context/environmental conditions to generate a subjective state that can be described in discrete emotion terms (e.g. Barrett 2006). The experience of specific emotions is thus a *product* of core affect and not vice versa. Discrete/basic emotion theorists take the opposite view and argue that core affect emerges as a cognitive 'distillation' of the overall affective impact of the experience of specific emotions (e.g. Panksepp 2007; see also Tellegen et al. 1999). Given that there is psychological, neural and behavioural evidence for both types of system, an alternative view is to hypothesize that both systems may be present in humans and many animals, that they interact in some way and that they serve different functions. Such a synthesis has been proposed by, among others, Izard (2007) and Panksepp (2007) and we develop it further here.

We first briefly consider the causes and functions of discrete emotions. We then suggest that: (i) core affective components of discrete emotions and other affective states provide a 'common currency' that may function to prioritize actions, (ii) discrete emotions, generated by events, influence position in core affect space, (iii) cumulative experience of location in core affect space underlies longer-term mood and (iv) core affect mood states can, in turn, influence decision making and discrete emotions. Thus, a bi-directional relationship between discrete emotion and core affect systems is proposed.

Causes and Functions of Discrete Emotions

Discrete emotions arise in response to anticipation or experience of rewarding or punishing events. They are thus event-focused (or object-focused) and usually short-lasting. *Appraisal theorists* suggest that a process of 'stimulus checks' of a number of key characteristics (e.g. valence, predictability, familiarity) of eliciting circumstances generates emotions (Ellsworth & Scherer 2003). For example, appraisal of a stimulus as intrinsically unpleasant (punishing), sudden, unpredictable and unfamiliar is likely to induce a 'fear' (Q4) emotion (Scherer 2001). In humans, situations may be appraised in numerous ways depending on, for example, the characteristics of the situation and the subject's previous experiences and current motivations. Consequently, appraisals may result in many different emotional states, including varied nuances of discrete emotions (Ellsworth & Scherer 2003). Human appraisals may involve cognitive processes such as memory (underpinning familiarity/novelty appraisals) and anticipation (underpinning appraisals of predictability), but they can also be simple, rapid and 'automatic' (subconscious; Zajonc 1980; Grandjean & Scherer 2008). It is thus conceivable that similar processes occur in animals (Desiré et al. 2002) and act to trigger discrete emotional states which engage specific neurobehavioural systems.

These discrete emotion systems probably function to organize short-term responses to the eliciting circumstances, recruiting appropriate physiological resources, motivating relevant behaviours and thus facilitating the organism's immediate survival (e.g. Frijda 1994; Rolls 2005). Different discrete emotion systems have evolved to deal with different types of challenge. For example, Panksepp (1998) postulates that a distinct 'panic'/'separation distress' system functions to maintain social bonds between separated individuals by triggering vocalization and search behaviour.

Discrete Emotions, Sensations and Motivations Have Core Affective Characteristics That May Function as a Common Currency in Decision Making

Discrete emotions have an underlying valenced structure—this is what characterizes them as part of the affective/emotional system—and can thus be located in core affective space. Other states such as *sensations* and *motivations* also share these characteristics. Physical sensations mediated by direct neural connections between the sensory apparatus (e.g. receptors for touch, taste, smell) and the brain can be inherently rewarding or punishing and hence also located in core affect space. For example, a taste may give rise to a positively valenced affective response of 'pleasure' that may be located at some point in the Q1 quadrant and function to influence subsequent wanting of the stimulus (Berridge 2007).

Wanting states—*motivation* for a specific reward—can also be located in core affect space. They are determined by internal changes reflecting current physiological need, and external stimuli that have become strongly associated with reward through the animal's developmental or evolutionary past, and, in humans, can be experienced as high-arousal positive states (Q1) associated with reward-seeking behaviour.

Location in core affect space thus represents a *common currency* (cf. McNamara & Houston 1986; Cabanac 1992; Spruijt et al. 2001) that may function to allow comparisons and trade-offs between disparate discrete emotions, sensations and motivations when behavioural decisions are being made. For example, a hungry and thirsty animal needs to be able to weigh up the relative reward values of searching to obtain food or water at any one time, and to calculate when searching behaviour becomes too dangerous because of heightened threats from punishers such as predator attack. Emotions and motivations can only be made use of in such 'expected utility' type decisions if they incorporate the core affective feature of valence that can function as a common currency (cf. Cabanac 1992).

Discrete Emotions and Other States Influence Location in Core Affect Space

Following from the above, discrete emotions, sensations and motivations can be conceptualized as generating short-term changes in an animal's location in core affect space. For example, the onset of feeding motivation may involve the animal moving towards an aroused, positive, seeking state (Q1). Detection of a food item may then lead to a higher arousal state of excitement with successful capture of prey perhaps leading to a temporary state of elation (Q1), followed by a lower arousal consummatory state of sensory pleasure during eating and an even lower arousal post-consummatory positive state of contentment or satisfaction (Q2). On the other hand, failure to detect or obtain a food item may initially lead to a temporary high-arousal negative state of frustration (Q4), which may then subside to a lower arousal negative state of disappointment or sadness (Q3). These trajectories, related to the acquisition of fitness-enhancing rewards (one can imagine similar trajectories related to the search for mates, positive social interactions, etc.), are illustrated. Although, as discussed earlier, they tend to inhabit the Q3–Q1 axis, it is clear that relative success or failure can lead to states in the Q2 and Q4 quadrants too.

The appearance of a fitness-threatening stimulus can intrude into these reward acquisition cycles at any time and rapidly shift the animal's position in core affect space into the Q4 quadrant of high-arousal negative fear and anxiety states. These states are associated with appropriate responses to danger aimed at avoiding punishers. Successful responses will result in the removal of threat and a lower arousal positive state of relief or calm (Q2). Such trajectories, related to the avoidance of fitness reduction, thus primarily inhabit the Q2–Q4 axis and, owing to their potentially life-threatening sequelae, generally assume primacy over Q1–Q3 states associated with the acquisition of fitness-enhancing rewards (e.g. Dawkins & Krebs 1979; cf. Haselton & Nettle 2006).

In this view, movement through core affect space is driven by discrete emotions, sensations and motivations and represents the organism's experiences of success and failure in acquiring rewards and avoiding punishers. We suggest that it forms the basis for longer-term mood states.

[. . .]

The Causes of Longer-Term Core Affect 'Mood' States

In humans, core affective states do not only occur in response to specific events or stimuli. They also occur in the absence of, and without being directed at, any particular object. In this case, they are usually referred to as free-floating *moods*. Moods are typically longer lasting than discrete emotions, sensations or motivations and are a relatively 'pure' form of core affect, lacking the action tendencies and appraisal-induced responses to emotion-eliciting situations that characterize discrete emotions. They include longer-term states of 'happiness' or 'sadness' and, in their more extreme forms, states such as chronic anxiety (Q4), depression (Q3) or mania (Q1). At any one time, an individual's core affective state can be conceptualized as a combination of their longer-term background mood state and their reactions to current emotion-inducing events. Thus, chronically anxious individuals may experience temporary states of positive affect under certain circumstances (e.g. when eating a particularly delicious meal) despite their 'background' state of anxiety. Consequently, ongoing mood states may be most easily revealed when an individual is not currently exposed to strong emotion-inducing events (which may lead to 'ceiling effect' responses that mask background mood state) or when novel or ambiguous events occur whose affective salience is not immediately apparent. They can be conceptualized as the background core affect state that the individual will revert to when specific emotion-inducing events are absent.

In our view, mood states probably reflect a cumulative function of the experience of shorter-term emotional episodes (e.g. discrete emotions, sensations, motivations). For example, if an animal is in an environment in which it experiences frequent threatening events, and hence its emotional state is often in the Q4 quadrant, it may develop a longer-term high-arousal negative mood state that mirrors this cumulative experience. If it is frequently successful at avoiding these events, or it is in a generally safe environment, a longer-term low-arousal positive mood state (Q2: 'relaxed'/'calm') may result. On the other hand, if it is in a plentiful environment and successful at acquiring fitness-enhancing rewards, it is likely to exhibit a mood state that is centred on the Q1 quadrant, whereas a low-resource environment and failure to acquire rewards will lead to a predominantly Q3 mood (cf. Carver 2001).

In relation to the trajectories, we propose that mood states can be likened to a 'running mean' of positions occupied within core affect space over a preceding time period, and thus continually (albeit slowly) change as the result of novel events and experiences. This view of mood states as representing past experience chimes with the findings that, for example, chronic anxiety and depression states usually arise from exposure to specific environmental and emotional circumstances (e.g. chronic stress, major life events; e.g. Eysenck et al. 2006; Young & Korszun 2009).

[. . .]

Functions of Mood States: Their Influence on Decision Making, Appraisals and Discrete Emotions

We suggest that mood states provide information about the type of environment the organism is living in—the presence (or probability) of *threats* and *reward opportunities*—and how well it is coping (see also Carver 2001, 2003; Prinz 2004). This information plays an important role in guiding animals' decisions when appraising new situations or stimuli, especially if there is a degree of ambiguity in their potentially rewarding or punishing consequences (Davidson 1994; Mendl et al. 2009). For example, if an individual is living in an environment where it has experienced *high levels of threat*, its mood state has a greater likelihood of being in the Q4 quadrant. In such an environment where probability of danger is high, it would make adaptive sense to appraise ambiguous stimuli such as a rustle in the grass as more likely to predict a negative event (e.g. predator), and hence to take safety-first avoidant action, in comparison with an individual living in a *low threat* environment with a mood state in the Q2 quadrant for whom a negative judgement is likely to result in wasted time and energy (Nesse 2005).

[. . .]

Different responses to ambiguity may also be observed in individuals whose background mood state is predominantly in quadrant Q1 (resulting from experience of an environment with *high probability of opportunity for gaining fitness-enhancing rewards*) or Q3 (experience *of low reward-opportunity* environments). Those in Q1 are likely to benefit from judging ambiguous stimuli as indicating a positive event (e.g. prey), thus facilitating reward-seeking behaviour, relative to those in Q3 mood states who may benefit from inhibiting reward-seeking behaviour in order to conserve energy until environmental conditions change (Nesse 2000).

Thus, we suggest that Q1 moods are associated with decisions appropriate to high reward-opportunity environments, reflecting a high 'expectation' of positive events, and Q2 moods with decisions reflecting low expectation of negative events. These can be termed 'optimistic' biases in decision making (e.g. judging ambiguous stimuli positively). Conversely, Q3 moods are associated with low expectation of positive events and Q4 moods with high expectation of negative events ('pessimistic' biases). Clearly, environments may not be as simple as this.

[. . .]

Consistent with these ideas, there is a large body of research with humans showing that background mood state does indeed appear to influence decision making (e.g. Schwarz & Clore 1983; Bechara et al. 2000; Loewenstein et al. 2001), including in ways similar to those predicted. People in negative states tend to judge ambiguous stimuli negatively (e.g. MacLeod & Byrne 1996). They also more readily attend to threatening stimuli and recall negative memories than people in positive mood states (see Mineka et al. 1998; Mogg & Bradley 1998). Furthermore, there is evidence that people with a long-term tendency towards (trait) anxiety and/or current (state) anxiety (Q4) judge ambiguous stimuli as more likely to be negative, while people in states of sadness or depression (Q3) judge them as less likely to be positive in line with predictions outlined above (e.g. MacLeod et al. 1997; Stober 2000; MacLeod & Salaminiou 2001). There is also evidence that people in positive moods show optimistic forms of these so-called 'cognitive biases' (e.g. Nygren et al. 1996).

Mood state may thus act as a heuristic device influencing cognitive processes and facilitating appropriate decision-making behaviour. Because appraisals of situations/events may themselves involve cognitive processes, mood states can therefore also affect these appraisals and the resulting short-term emotional responses. The causal link between short-term discrete emotions and longer-term core affect mood is thus bidirectional. It is possible to envisage positive feedback loops in which, for example, a Q4 mood state enhances anticipation of negative events and negative interpretation of ambiguity, and this leads to further negative short-term emotional experiences which, in turn, intensify the Q4 mood. Such processes are implicated in the aetiology of chronic anxiety and depression in humans (Beck 1967, 2008). In the natural environment, they may function to help animals escape from or cope with difficult or threatening conditions (Nesse 2000), until circumstances change and the experience of more positive events leads to a gradual alteration in mood state.

Implications for the Measurement of Animal Emotion

Discrete emotion approaches rely on identifying situations or tests that are assumed to induce a particular emotional state and then measuring behavioural and physiological responses as putative indicators of that state. Such tests may be quick to carry out and, if they accurately identify naturalistic situations that reliably induce a particular state, they may be very useful and ecologically valid. However, there are also some disadvantages to this *ad hoc* approach. For example, different individuals may perceive (appraise) the same situation differently, and different situations thought to induce the same emotion may not do so. This will decrease the likelihood that consistent behavioural and physiological responses are detected. Indeed, in the extensive literature on fear testing, studies sometimes find good cross-test agreement in how they rank order individuals (i.e. in terms of 'fearfulness'), but disagreement is common (e.g. Ramos & Mormede 1998; Miller et al. 2006; Forkman et al. 2007) and behavioural and physiological responses often vary considerably across tests which are all ostensibly designed to measure fear (e.g. Forkman et al. 2007).

One potential solution to this problem is to develop *a priori* hypotheses, based on the conceptual framework outlined above, for the types of event or situation that will generate affective states in each of quadrants Q1–Q4. At a simple level, we can hypothesize that Q1 states occur when a reward is signalled or presented, Q4 states occur when a punisher is signalled or presented, Q3 states occur when a reward is removed or omitted and Q2 states occur when a punisher is removed or omitted (Rolls 2005). Thus, if we can accurately identify species-relevant rewarding and punishing stimuli, we can measure behavioural and physiological responses to their presentation or removal and identify those responses, or response profiles, that occur reliably and hence may be good indicators of the corresponding affective state (e.g. Reefmann et al. 2009)

[. . .]

We have recently developed assays of cognitive bias in animals and started to investigate whether manipulations designed to alter affective states (e.g. living in an unpredictable or threatening environment) are linked to cognitive bias in the ways predicted, and as in humans (Paul et al. 2005). Our 'judgement bias' task (first developed by Harding et al. 2004) involves training an animal to perform a particular response (e.g. press left lever) when presented with a particular stimulus (e.g. tone A) to obtain a positive outcome (e.g. food) and to perform a different response (e.g. press right lever) when presented with a different stimulus (e.g. tone C) to avoid a relatively negative outcome (e.g. no food, noise). The subject is then presented with intermediate, ambiguous stimuli (e.g. tone B), and we hypothesize that, for example, animals in a positive emotional state (Q1/Q2) will be more likely to judge these stimuli as predicting the better outcome (e.g. by pressing the left lever; an optimistic judgement bias), compared with animals in a negative state (Q3/Q4). Recent studies of species, including rats (Harding et al. 2004; Burman et al. 2008, 2009; Enkel et al. 2010), sheep (Doyle et al. 2010), starlings (Bateson & Matheson 2007; Matheson et al. 2008), rhesus monkeys and dogs (see Mendl et al. 2009 for a review) have found evidence in support of these hypotheses, indicating that this new approach for assessing emotional state in animals holds promise.

[. . .]

Conclusions

Does the conceptual framework outlined here help us to better understand and assess affective states in animals? We believe it does in a number of ways.

The framework is grounded in an understanding of the structure of core subjective affective states in humans. It thus links what we are ultimately interested in but cannot yet investigate directly—subjective affective experience—with biologically relevant and tractable phenomena and concepts. This allows predictions to be made about the behavioural, physiological and cognitive changes that may accompany particular affective states, and hence enables the development of novel measures of these states.

The framework attempts to integrate discrete and dimensional approaches to the study of emotion, providing hypotheses for how they interact in a reciprocal fashion. It illustrates how discrete emotions, sensations and motivations contribute to core affect and how core affect in turn may influence decision making, including discrete emotional responses.

The framework brings together all types of affective states. To date, the study of animal emotions has focused largely on Q4 affective states such as fear and anxiety, although there is a substantial literature on the neurobiology of reward processes that underpin Q1 states in particular, and interest in Q3 states such as depression. Q2 states have received very little attention and yet their role in recovery processes and the general well-being of animals may be significant (cf. Porges 2001). Moreover, these different states have generally been studied independently with little reference to each other or to how they may interact. The framework encourages us to investigate them as a whole and to understand how the animal may move between states according to experience.

The framework emphasizes that affective states are strongly influenced by the organism's environment and its experiences within it. It suggests how environmental events can profoundly alter affective state.

By taking a functional perspective on the structure of core affective states (cf. Nesse 2000, 2004, 2005; Carver 2001), the framework allows us to make predictions about the types of situation that will lead to a particular affective state, and the sorts of response that may be a good indicator of that affective state. In particular, the framework emphasizes the role of longer-term mood states in decision-making processes. We believe that the links between affective and cognitive processes, which have been extensively studied in humans, have an important role to play in furthering our understanding of, and ability to assess, affective states in animals.

We thank Richard Parker for discussing these topics with us, Lorenz Gygax and another, anonymous, referee for their comments and BBSRC and UFAW for supporting our work.

References

Baars, B. J. 2001 There are no known differences in brain mechanisms of consciousness between humans and other mammals. *Anim. Welfare* 10, S31–S40.

Barrett, L. F. 2006 Are emotions natural kinds? *Perspect. Psychol. Sci.* 1, 28–58. (doi:10.1111/j.1745-6916.2006.00003.x).

Barrett, L. F., Mesquita, B., Ochsner, K. N. & Gross, J. J. 2007 The experience of emotion. *Ann. Rev. Psychol.* 58, 373–403. (doi:10.1146/annurev.psych.58.110405.085709).

Bateson, M. & Matheson, S. M. 2007 Performance on a categorisation task suggests that removal of environmental enrichment induces 'pessimism' in captive European starlings (*Sturnus vulgaris*). *Anim. Welfare* 16, 33–36.

Bechara, A., Damasio, H. & Damasio, A. R. 2000 Emotion, decision-making and the orbitofrontal cortex. *Cereb. Cortex* 10, 295–307. (doi:10.1093/cercor/10.3.295).

Beck, A. T. 1967 *Depression, clinical, experimental and theoretical aspects*. New York: Harper Row.

Beck, A. T. 2008 The evolution of the cognitive model of depression and its neurobiological correlates. *Am. J. Psychiatry* 165, 969–977. (doi:10.1176/appi.ajp.2008.08050721).

Berridge, K. C. 1996 Food reward: Brain substrates of wanting and liking. *Neurosci. Biobehav. Rev.* 20, 1–25. (doi:10.1016/0149-7634(95)00033-B).

Berridge, K. C. 2003 Comparing the emotional brains of humans and other animals. In *Handbook of affective sciences* (eds R. J. Davidson, K. R. Scherer & H. H. Goldsmith), pp. 25–51. Oxford, UK: Oxford University Press.

Berridge, K. C. 2007 The debate over dopamine's role in reward: The case for incentive salience. *Psychopharmacology* 191, 391–431. (doi:10.1007/s00213-006-0578-x).

Boissy, A. 1995 Fear and fearfulness in animals. *Q. Rev. Biol.* 70, 165–191. (doi:10.1086/418981).

Boissy, A. et al. 2007 Assessment of positive emotions in animals to improve their welfare. *Physiol. Behav.* 92, 375–397. (doi:10.1016/j.physbeh.2007.02.003).

Burgdorf, J. & Panksepp, J. 2006 The neurobiology of positive emotions. *Neurosci. Biobehav. Rev.* 30, 173–187. (doi:10.1016/j.neubiorev.2005.06.001).

Burman, O. H. P., Parker, R. M. A., Paul, E. S. & Mendl, M. T. 2008 A spatial judgement task to determine background emotional state in laboratory rats. *Rattus Norvegicus. Anim. Behav.* 76, 801–809. (doi:10.1016/j.anbehav.2008.02.014).

Burman, O. H. P., Parker, R. M. A., Paul, E. S. & Mendl, M. T. 2009 Anxiety-induced cognitive bias in non-human animals. *Physiol. Behav.* 98, 345–350. (doi:10.1016/j.physbeh.2009.06.012).

Cabanac, M. 1992 Pleasure—the common currency. *J. Theor. Biol.* 155, 173–200. (doi:10.1016/S0022-5193(05)80594-6).

Cacioppo, J. T., Gardner, W. L. & Berntson, G. G. 1999 The affect system has parallel and integrative processing components: Form follows function. *J. Pers. Soc. Psychol.* 76, 839–855. (doi:10.1037/0022-3514.76.5.839).

Carver, C. S. 2001 Affect and the functional bases of behavior: On the dimensional structure of affective experience. *Pers. Soc. Psychol. Rev.* 5, 345–356. (doi:10.1207/S15327957PSPR0504_4).

Carver, C. S. 2003 Pleasure as a sign you can attend to something else: Placing positive feelings within a general model of affect. *Cogn. Emotion* 17, 241–261. (doi:10.1080/02699930302294).

Custers, R. & Aarts, H. 2005 Positive affect as implicit motivator: On the nonconscious operation of behavioral goals. *J. Pers. Soc Psychol.* 89, 129–142. (doi:10.1037/0022-3514.89.2.129).

Dalgleish, T. 2004 The emotional brain. *Nat. Rev. Neurosci.* 5, 582–589. (doi:10.1038/nrn1432).

Darwin, C. 1872/2009 *The expression of the emotions in man and animals.* London, UK: Harper Perennial.

Davidson, R. J. 1994 On emotion, mood, and related affective constructs. In *The nature of emotion* (eds P. Ekman & R. J. Davidson), pp. 51–55. New York: Oxford University Press.

Davidson, R. J. 1998 Affective style and affective disorders: Perspectives from affective neuroscience. *Cogn. Emotion* 12, 307–330. (doi:10.1080/026999398379628).

Davidson, R. J. & Irwin, W. 1999 The functional neuroanatomy of emotion and affective style. *Trends Cogn. Sci.* 3, 11–21. (doi:10.1016/S1364-6613(98)01265-0).

Dawkins, R. & Krebs, J. R. 1979 Arms races between and within species. *Proc. R Soc. Lond. B* 205, 489–511. (doi:10.1098/rspb.1979.0081).

Desiré, L., Boissy, A. & Veissier, I. 2002 Emotions in farm animals: A new approach to animal welfare in applied ethology. *Behav. Proc.* 60, 165–180. (doi:10.1016/S0376-6357(02)00081-5).

Doyle, R. E., Fisher, A. D., Hinch, G. N., Boissy, A. & Lee, C. 2010 Release from restraint generates a positive judgement bias in sheep. *Appl. Anim. Behav. Sci.* 122, 28–34. (doi: 10.1016/j.applanim.2009.11.003).

Ekman, P. 1992 Are there basic emotions. *Psychol. Rev.* 99, 550–553. (doi: 10.1037/0033-295X.99.3.550).

Ellsworth, P. C. & Scherer, K. E. 2003 Appraisal processes in emotion. In *Handbook of affective sciences* (eds R. J. Davidson, K. R. Scherer & H. H. Goldsmith), pp. 572–595. Oxford, UK: Oxford University Press.

Enkel, T., Gholizadeh, D., von Bohlen und Halbach, O., Sanchis-Segura, C., Hurlemann, R., Spanagel, R., Gass, P. & Vollmayr, B. 2010 Ambiguous-cue interpretation is biased under stress and depression-like states in rats. *Neuropsychopharmacology* 35, 1008–1015. (doi:10.1038/npp.2009.204).

Eysenck, M. W., Payne, S. & Santos, R. 2006 Anxiety and depression: Past, present, and future events. *Cogn. Emotion* 20, 274–294. (doi:10.1080/02699930500220066).

Forkman, B., Boissy, A., Meunier-Salauen, M. C., Canali, E. & Jones, R. B. 2007 A critical review of fear tests used on cattle, pigs, sheep, poultry and horses. *Physiol. Behav.* 92, 340–374. (doi:10.1016/j.physbeh.2007.03.016).

Frijda, N. 1994 Emotions are functional, most of the time. In *The nature of emotion* (eds P. Ekman & R. J. Davidson), pp. 112–122. New York: Oxford University Press.

Grandjean, D. & Scherer, K. R. 2008 Unpacking the cognitive architecture of emotion processes. *Emotion* 8, 341–351. (doi:10.1037/1528-3542.8.3.341).

Gray, J. A. 1994 Three fundamental emotion systems. In *The nature of emotion* (eds P. Ekman & R. J. Davidson), pp. 243–247. New York: Oxford University Press.

Harding, E. J., Paul, E. S. & Mendl, M. 2004 Animal behavior—cognitive bias and affective state. *Nature* 427, 312. (doi:10.1038/427312a).

Haselton, M. G. & Nettle, D. 2006 The paranoid optimist: An integrative evolutionary model of cognitive biases. *Pers. Soc. Psychol. Rev.* 10, 47–66. (doi:10.1207/s15327957pspr1001_3).

Izard, C. E. 2007 Basic emotions, natural kinds, emotion schemas and a new paradigm. *Perspect. Psychol. Sci.* 2, 260–280. (doi:10.1111/j.1745-6916.2007.00044.x).

Lang, P. J., Bradley, M. M. & Cuthbert, B. N. 1990 Emotion, attention and the startle reflex. *Psychol. Rev.* 97, 377–395. (doi:10.1037/0033-295X.97.3.377).

LeDoux, J. 1996 *The emotional brain.* New York: Simon and Schuster.

Loewenstein, G. F., Weber, E. U., Hsee, C. K. & Welch, N. 2001 Risk as feelings. *Psychol. Bull.* 127, 267–286. (doi:10.1037/0033-2909.127.2.267).

MacLeod, A. K. & Byrne, A. 1996 Anxiety, depression, and the anticipation of future positive and negative experiences. *J. Abnorm. Psychol.* 105, 286–289. (doi:10.1037/0021-843X.105.2.286).

MacLeod, A. K. & Salaminiou, E. 2001 Reduced positive future-thinking in depression: Cognitive and affective factors. *Cogn. Emotion* 15, 99–107. (doi:10.1080/0269993004200006).

MacLeod, A. K., Tata, P., Kentish, J. & Jacobsen, H. 1997 Retrospective and prospective cognitions in anxiety and depression. *Cogn. Emotion* 11, 467–479. (doi:10.1080/026999397379881).

Macphail, E. M. 1998 *The evolution of consciousness*. Oxford, UK: Oxford University Press.

Matheson, S. M., Asher, L. & Bateson, M. 2008 Larger, enriched cages are associated with 'optimistic' response biases in captive European starlings (*Sturnus vulgaris*). *Appl Anim. Behav. Sci.* 109, 374–383. (doi:10.1016/j.applanim.2007.03.007).

McNamara, J. M. & Houston, A. I. 1986 The common currency for behavioral decisions. *Am. Nat.* 127, 358–378. (doi:10.1086/284489).

McNaughton, N. & Corr, P. J. 2008 The neuropsychology of fear and anxiety: A foundation for reinforcement sensitivity theory. In *The reinforcement sensitivity theory of personality* (ed P. J. Corr), pp. 44–94. Cambridge, UK: Cambridge University Press.

Mendl, M., Burman, O. H. P., Parker, R. M. A. & Paul, E. S. 2009 Cognitive bias as an indicator of animal emotion and welfare: Emerging evidence and underlying mechanisms. *Appl. Anim. Behav. Sci.* 118, 161–181. (doi:10.1016/j.applanim.2009.02.023).

Miller, K. A., Garner, J. P. & Mench, J. A. 2006 Is fearfulness a trait that can be measured with behavioural tests? A validation of four fear tests for Japanese quail. *Anim. Behav.* 71, 1323–1334. (doi:10.1016/j.anbehav.2005.08.018).

Mineka, S., Watson, D. & Clark, L. A. 1998 Comorbidity of anxiety and unipolar mood disorders. *Ann. Rev. Psychol.* 49, 377–412. (doi:10.1146/annurev.psych.49.1.377).

Mogg, K. & Bradley, B. P. 1998 A cognitive-motivational analysis of anxiety. *Behav. Res. Ther.* 36, 809–848. (doi:10.1016/S0005-7967(98)00063-1).

Nesse, R. M. 2000 Is depression an adaptation? *Arch. Gen. Psychiat.* 57, 14–20. (doi:10.1001/archpsyc.57.1.14).

Nesse, R. M. 2004 Natural selection and the elusiveness of happiness. *Phil. Trans. R. Soc. Lond.* B 359, 1333–1347. (doi:10.1098/rstb.2004.1511).

Nesse, R. M. 2005 Natural selection and the regulation of defenses—a signal detection analysis of the smoke detector principle. *Evol. Hum. Behav.* 26, 88–105. (doi:10.1016/j.evolhumbehav.2004.08.002).

Nesse, R. M. & Ellsworth, P. C. 2009 Evolution, emotions, and emotional disorders. *Am. Psychol.* 64, 129–139. (doi:10.1037/a0013503).

Nygren, T. E., Isen, A. M., Taylor, P. J. & Dulin, J. 1996 The influence of positive affect on the decision rule in risky situations. *Org. Behav. Hum. Decis. Process* 66, 79–91. (doi:10.1006/obhd.1996.0038).

Ortony, A. & Turner, T. J. 1990 What's basic about basic emotions. *Psychol. Rev.* 97, 315–331. (doi:10.1037//0033-295X.97.3.315).

Panksepp, J. 1998 *Affective neuroscience: The foundations of human and animal emotion*. New York: Oxford University Press.

Panksepp, J. 2007 Neurologizing the psychology of affects: How appraisal-based constructivism and basic emotion theory can coexist. *Perspect. Psychol. Sci* 2, 281–296. (doi:10.1111/j.1745-6916.2007.00045.x).

Paul, E. S., Harding, E. J. & Mendl, M. 2005 Measuring emotional processes in animals: The utility of a cognitive approach. *Neurosci. Biobehav. Rev.* 29, 469–491. (doi:10.1016/j.neubiorev.2005.01.002).

Porges, S. W. 2001 Is there a major stress system at the periphery other than the adrenals? In *Coping with challenge: Welfare in animals including humans* (ed D. M. Broom), pp. 135–149. Berlin, Germany: Dahlem University Press.

Posner, J., Russell, J. A. & Peterson, B. S. 2005 The circumplex model of affect: An integrative approach to affective neuroscience, cognitive development, and psychopathology. *Dev. Psychopathol.* 17, 715–734. (doi:10.1017/S0954579405050340).

Prinz, J. J. 2004 *Gut reactions: A perceptual theory of emotion*. Oxford, UK: Oxford University Press.

Ramos, A. & Mormede, P. 1998 Stress and emotionality: A multidimensional and genetic approach. *Neurosci. Biobehav. Rev.* 22, 33–57. (doi:10.1016/S0149-7634(97)00001-8).

Reefmann, N., Wechsler, B. & Gygax, L. 2009 Behavioural and physiological assessment of positive and negative emotion in sheep. *Anim. Behav.* 78, 651–659. (doi:10.1016/j.anbehav.2009.06.015).

Rolls, E. T. 2005 *Emotion explained*. Oxford, UK: Oxford University Press. (doi:10.1093/acprof:oso/9780198570035.001.0001).

Russell, J. A. 2003 Core affect and the psychological construction of emotion. *Psychol. Rev.* 110, 145–172. (doi:10.1037/0033-295X.110.1.145).

Russell, J. A. & Barrett, L. F. 1999 Core affect, prototypical emotional episodes, and other things called emotion: Dissecting the elephant. *J. Pers. Soc. Psychol.* 76, 805–819. (doi:10.1037/0022-3514.76.5.805).

Scherer, K. R. 2001 Appraisal considered as a process of multi-level sequential checking. In *Appraisal process in emotion: Theory, methods, research* (eds K. R. Scherer, A. Schorr & T. Johnstone), pp. 92–120. Oxford, UK: Oxford University Press.

Schwarz, N. & Clore, G. L. 1983 Mood, misattribution and judgements of well-being: Informative and directive functions of affective states. *J. Person. Soc. Psychol.* 45, 513–523. (doi:10.1098/rstb.2004.1511).

Spruijt, B. M., van den Bos, R. & Pijlman, F. T. A. 2001 A concept of welfare based on reward evaluating mechanisms in the brain: Anticipatory behaviour as an indicator for the state of reward systems. *Appl. Anim. Behav. Sci.* 72, 145–171. (doi:10.1016/S0168-1591(00)00204-5).

Stanley, D. J. & Meyer, J. P. 2009 Two-dimensional affective space: A new approach to orienting the axes. *Emotion* 9, 214–237. (doi:10.1037/a0014612).

Stober, J. 2000 Prospective cognitions in anxiety and depression: Replication and methodological extension. *Cogn. Emotion* 14, 725–729. (doi:10.1080/02699930050117693).

Tellegen, A., Watson, D. & Clark, L. A. 1999 On the dimensional and hierarchical structure of affect. *Psychol. Sci.* 10, 297–303. (doi:10.1111/1467-9280.00157).

Watson, D., Wiese, D., Vaidya, J. & Tellegen, A. 1999 The two general activation systems of affect: Structural findings, evolutionary considerations, and psychobiological evidence. *J. Pers. Soc. Psychol.* 76, 820–838. (doi:10.1037/0022-3514.76.5.820).

Wemelsfelder, F. 1997 The scientific validity of subjective concepts in models of animal welfare. *Appl. Anim. Behav. Sci.* 53, 75–88. (doi:10.1016/S0168-1591(96)01152-5).

Young, E. & Korszun, A. 2009 Sex, trauma, stress hormones and depression. *Mol. Psychiatry* 15, 23–28. (doi:10.1038/mp.2009.94).

Zajonc, R. B. 1980 Feeling and thinking—preferences need no inferences. *Am. Psychol.* 35, 151–175. (doi:10.1037/0003-066X.35.2.151).

9   Reflections

Barbara Smuts

Smuts reports on her studies with baboons, including the process of exploring the complex topic of human–baboon intersubjectivity. She came to know the 140 baboons in the troop as individuals, with characteristic things to communicate, favorite foods, favorite friends, and unique bad habits. She describes in elegant detail some of the personal relationships she experienced with this troop of baboons.

[. . .]

The heart [. . .] is "the seat of a faculty, sympathy, that allows us to share . . . the being of another." For the heart to truly share another's being, it must be an embodied heart, prepared to encounter directly the embodied heart of another. I have met the "other" in this way, not once or a few times, but over and over during years spent in the company of "persons" like you and me, who happen to be nonhuman.[1]

These nonhuman persons include gorillas at home in the perpetually wet, foggy mountaintops of central Africa, chimpanzees carousing in the hot, rugged hills of Western Tanzania, baboons lazily strolling across the golden grass plains of highland Kenya, and dolphins gliding languorously through the green, clear waters of Shark Bay.[2] In each case, I was lucky to be accepted by the animals as a mildly interesting, harmless companion, permitted to travel amongst them, eligible to be touched by hands and fins, although I refrained, most of the time, from touching in turn.

I mingled with these animals under the guise of scientific research, and, indeed, most of my activities while "in the field" were designed to gain objective, replicable information about the animals' lives. Doing good science, it turned out, consisted mostly of spending every possible moment with the animals, watching them with the utmost concentration, and documenting myriad aspects of their behavior. In this way, I learned much that I could confidently report as scientific findings. [. . .] When I first began working with baboons, my main problem was learning to keep up with them while remaining alert to poisonous snakes, irascible buffalo, aggressive bees, and leg-breaking pig-holes. Fortunately, these challenges eased over time, mainly because I was traveling in the company of expert guides—baboons who could spot a predator a mile away and seemed to possess a sixth sense for the proximity of snakes. Abandoning myself to their far superior knowledge, I moved as a humble disciple, learning from masters about being an African anthropoid.

Thus I became (or, rather, regained my ancestral right to be) an animal, moving instinctively through a world that felt (because it was) like my ancient home. Having begun to master this challenge, I faced another one equally daunting: to comprehend and behave according to a system of baboon etiquette bizarre and subtle enough to stop Emily Post in her tracks. This task was forced on me by the fact that the baboons stubbornly resisted my feeble but sincere attempts to convince them that I was nothing more than a detached observer, a neutral object they could ignore. Right from the start, they knew better, insisting that I was, like them, a social subject vulnerable to the demands and rewards of relationship. Since I was in their world, they determined the rules of the game, and I was thus compelled to explore the unknown terrain of human-baboon intersubjectivity. Through trial and embarrassing error, I gradually mastered at least the rudiments of baboon propriety. I learned much through observation, but the deepest lessons came when I found myself sharing the being of a baboon because other baboons were treating me like one. Thus I learned from personal experience that if I turned my face away but held my ground, a charging male with canines bared in threat would stop short of attack. I became familiar with the invisible line defining the personal space of each troop member, and then I discovered that the space expands and contracts depending on the circumstances. I developed the knack of sweetly but firmly turning my back on the playful advances of juveniles, conveying, as did the older females, that although I found them appealing, I had more important things to do. After many months of immersion in their society I stopped thinking so much about what to do and instead simply surrendered to instinct, not as mindless, reflexive action, but rather as action rooted in an ancient primate legacy of embodied knowledge.

Living in this way with baboons, I discovered what Elizabeth Costello means when she says that to be an animal is to "be full of being," full of "joy." Like the rest of us, baboons get grouchy, go hungry, feel fear and pain and loss. But during my times with them, the default state seemed to be a lighthearted appreciation of being a baboon body in baboon-land. Adolescent females concluded formal, grown-up-style greetings with somber adult males with a somersault flourish. Distinguished old ladies, unable to get a male's attention, stood on their heads and gazed up at the guy upside down. Grizzled males approached balls of wrestling infants and tickled them. Juveniles spent hours perfecting the technique of swinging from a vine to land precisely on the top of Mom's head. And the voiceless, breathy chuckles of baboon play echoed through the forest from dawn to dusk.

During the cool, early morning hours, the baboons would work hard to fill their stomachs, but as the temperature rose, they became prone to taking long breaks in especially attractive locales. In a mossy glade or along the white-sanded beach of an inland lake, they would shamelessly indulge a passion for lying around in the shade on their backs with their feet in the air. Every now and then someone would emit a deep sigh of satisfaction. Off and on, they would concur about the agreeableness of the present situation by participating in a chorus of soft grunts that rippled through the troop like a gentle wave. In the early days of my fieldwork when I was still preoccupied with doing things right, I regarded these siestas as valuable opportunities to gather data on who rested near whom. But later, I began to lie around with them. Later still, I would sometimes lie around without them—that is, among them, but while they were still busy eating. Once I fell asleep surrounded by 100 munching baboons only to awaken half an hour later, alone, except for an adolescent male who had chosen to nap by my side (presumably inferring from my deep sleep that I'd found a particularly good resting spot). We blinked at one another in the light of the noonday sun and then casually sauntered several miles back to the rest of the troop, with him leading the way.

There were 140 baboons in the troop, and I came to know every one as a highly distinctive individual. Each one had a particular gait, which allowed me to know who was who, even from great distances when I couldn't see anyone's face. Every baboon had a characteristic voice and unique things to say with it; each had a face like no other, favorite foods, favorite friends, favorite bad habits. Dido, when chased by an unwelcome suitor, would dash behind some cover and then dive into a pig-hole, carefully peeking out every few moments to see if the male had given up the chase. Lysistrata liked to sneak up on an infant riding on its mother's back, knock it off (gently), and then pretend to be deeply preoccupied with eating some grass when Mom turned to see the cause of her infant's distress. Apié, the alpha male, would carefully study the local fishermen from a great distance, wait for just the right moment to rush toward them, take a flying leap over their heads to land on the fish-drying rack, grab the largest fish, and disappear into the forest before anyone knew what was happening.

I also learned about baboon individuality directly, since each one approached his or her relationship with me in a slightly different way. Cicero, the outcast juvenile, often followed me and sat quietly a few feet away, seemingly deriving some small comfort from my proximity. Leda, the easygoing female, would walk so close to me I could feel her fur against my bare legs. Dakar, feisty adolescent male, would catch my eye and then march over to me, stand directly in front of me, and grab my kneecap while staring at my face intently (thanks to Dakar, I've become rather good at appearing calm when my heart is pounding). Clearly, the baboons also knew me as an individual. This knowledge was lasting, as I learned when I paid an unexpected visit to one of my study troops seven years after last being with them. They had been unstudied during the previous five years, so the adults had no recent experience with people coming close to them, and the youngsters had no such experience at all. I was traveling with a fellow scientist whom the baboons had never met, and, as we approached on foot from a distance, I anticipated considerable wariness toward both of us. When we got to within about one hundred yards, all of the youngsters fled, but the adults merely glanced at us and continued foraging. I asked my companion to remain where he was, and slowly I moved closer, expecting the remaining baboons to move away at any moment. To my utter amazement, they ignored me, except for an occasional glance, until I found myself walking among them exactly as I had done many years before. To make sure they were comfortable with me, as opposed to white people in general, I asked my friend to come closer. Immediately, the baboons moved away. It was I they recognized, and after a seven-year interval they clearly trusted me as much as they had on the day I left.

Trust, while an important component of friendship, does not, in and of itself, define it. Friendship requires some degree of mutuality, some give-and-take. Because it was important, scientifically, for me to minimize my interactions with the baboons, I had few opportunities to explore the possibilities of such give-and-take with them. But occasional events hinted that such relations might be possible, were I encountering them first and foremost as fellow social beings, rather than as subjects of scientific inquiry. For example, one day, as I rested my hand on a large rock, I suddenly felt the gentlest of touches on my fingertips. Turning around slowly, I came face-to-face with one of my favorite juveniles, a slight fellow named Damien. He looked intently into my eyes, as if to make sure that I was not disturbed by his touch, and then he proceeded to use his index finger to examine, in great detail, each one of my fingernails in turn. This exploration was made especially poignant by the fact that Damien was examining my fingers with one that looked very much the same, except that his was smaller and black. After touching each nail, and without removing his finger, Damien glanced up at me for a few seconds. Each time our gaze met, I wondered if he, like I, was contemplating the implications of the realization that our fingers and fingernails were so alike.

I experienced an even greater sense of intimacy when, in 1978, I had the exceptional privilege of spending a week with Dian Fossey and the mountain gorillas she had been studying for many years. One day, I was out with one of her groups, along with a male colleague unfamiliar to the gorillas and a young male researcher whom they knew well. Digit, one of the young adult males, was strutting about and beating his chest in an early challenge to the leading silverback male. My two male companions were fascinated by this tension, but after a while I had had enough of the macho energy, and I wandered off. About thirty meters away, I came upon a "nursery" group of mothers and infants who had perhaps moved off for the same reasons I had. I sat near them and watched the mothers eating and the babies playing for timeless, peaceful moments. Then my eyes met the warm gaze of an adolescent female, Pandora. I continued to look at her, silently sending friendliness her way. Unexpectedly, she stood and moved closer. Stopping right in front of me, with her face at eye level, she leaned forward and pushed her large, flat, wrinkled nose against mine. I know that she was right up against me, because I distinctly remember how her warm, sweet breath fogged up my glasses, blinding me. I felt no fear and continued to focus on the enormous affection and respect I felt for her. Perhaps she sensed my attitude, because in the next moment I felt her impossibly long ape arms wrap around me, and for precious seconds, she held me in her embrace. Then she released me, gazed once more into my eyes, and returned to munching on leaves.

[. . .]

Notes

1. The term *person* is commonly used in two different ways: first, as a synonym for human, and, second, to refer to a type of interaction or relationship of some degree of intimacy involving actors who are individually known to one another, as in "personal relationship," knowing someone "personally," or engaging with another "person to person." Here I use the word in the second sense, to refer to any animal, human or nonhuman, who has the capacity to participate in personal relationships, with one another, with humans, or both. I return to the concept of animal "personhood" later in the essay.

2. Shark Bay is off the coast of Western Australia, the site of a research project on wild bottlenose dolphins.

Anthropomorphism

10 Anthropomorphism and Cross-Species Modeling

Sandra D. Mitchell

In this reading, Mitchell evaluates the concept of anthropomorphism, particularly as it relates to chimpanzees. She argues that broad arguments against anthropomorphism are not supported, but also that there is no easy application of human descriptive concepts to nonhumans. Rather, anthropomorphic models are specific claims of similarity between humans and nonhumans that are scientifically accessible and must be substantiated by evidence. In the moral sphere, she argues that rather than establishing the similarities and differences between humans and nonhumans, a more fundamental concern might be establishing what capacities in any creature might be the basis of moral consideration.

Introduction

"Anthropomorphism" has long been considered a bad word in science.[1] It carries the stale dust of nineteenth-century anecdotal evidence for the continuity of humans with nonhuman animals. Darwin claims that "there can, I think, be no doubt that a dog feels shame . . . and something very like modesty when begging too often for food."[2] But anthropomorphism is neither prima facie bad or necessarily nonscientific. It can be both, but it need not be either.

[. . .]

There has been a recent resurgence of interest in anthropomorphism, attributable to two developments—the rise of cognitive ethology and the requirements of various forms of expanded, environmental ethics.

Some of the most interesting and relevant work in this area has been directed at explaining the behavior of chimpanzees. Since it is generally agreed that the chimp is our phylogenetically closest relative, it makes evolutionary sense that the features of that species are more likely to be similar to features of our species than those of species whose connection is more attenuated. Darwin's and our love of dogs notwithstanding, it is in primate research that the most plausible anthropomorphic theses are to be found. Or, as Daniel Povinelli claims in *Folk Physics for Apes*, "if the argument by analogy cannot be sustained when it comes to behaviors that we share in common with our nearest living relatives, it can hardly be expected to survive more general scrutiny."[3] Indeed, as I will report later, Povinelli argues just this—that a strong version of anthropomorphism cannot be sustained in explaining even some chimpanzee behaviors.

A strong version of anthropomorphism found in some advocates of cognitive ethology aims to explain behaviors of nonhumans by appeal to mental states similar to the ones we take to explain our own behavior. Of particular interest is the thesis that chimps have a "theory of mind," that is, beliefs about the beliefs of others. Such second-order beliefs are invoked to make sense of behavioral variation. For example, a human would respond differently to two actors on the basis of beliefs about what those actors could see. If one of them had a clear view of a source of food, while the other's view of the food was blocked by a barrier, then it would make sense to follow any indication of food given by the one whom you believe can see the food and hence will know where it is. Do chimps do the same thing? Do they do it for the same reasons? As I will discuss below, arguments from analogy and experimental results are brought to bear on answering this type of question.

The second source of interest in the similarities of humans and nonhuman animals arises from the animal rights and environmental ethics movements, which have sought to transform the criteria by which we determine what beings merit moral consideration. Animal welfare and animal rights ethical positions make the nature of nonhuman experience determinate of who and what we must count in judging the moral correctness of our actions. [. . .] Thus, the existence of feelings and cognitive states of nonhuman organisms is no longer just an academic question of whether or not Rumbaugh's Kanzi has language[4] or dolphins can recognize themselves in a mirror[5] but is rather a set of facts about the world that we need to know to ethically decide what to eat and what to wear. Thus, the manner and degree to which nonhuman animals are similar to human beings becomes an even more pressing scientific problem in a context in which the very morality of our actions depends on the answer.

At its basis, anthropomorphism involves claims about the similarity of nonhuman objects or beings to humans and the centrality of human concepts and abilities to classify behaviors across ontological categories. Strong anthropomorphism asserts that some description of a feature of human beings applies in the same way to a feature of a nonhuman animal. Critics of anthropomorphism often attack the presumptive character of such claims, like Darwin's *lack of doubt* of the internal nature of a dog's experience. Observers have been too willing to characterize nonhumans using descriptive language that has humans as its primary referent. By describing a dog as feeling shame when it walks away with its tail between its legs, one is not gathering neutral data with which to test the myriad of theories about the nature of dogs but rather is assuming in that very description that dogs have mental or emotional states like human mental and emotional states. But what is at fault here? Is it the presumptiveness or the anthropomorphism?

After all, similarity between humans and nonhuman animals is just what we should expect on the basis of an evolutionary account of the origin and diversification of life on the planet—but not any willy-nilly similarity. As a scientific claim about the facts of the world, any specific similarity between human immune systems, say, and mouse immune systems, or between human beliefs and chimp beliefs, must be grounded in more than a general truth of the continuum of life and backed by more than an imposition of the same descriptive language.

In what follows I will evaluate the arguments and evidence for a range of stances toward anthropomorphism from global rejections to specific models. The bumper sticker version of this essay could be: Science made too easy is bound to be wrong. In the end I will argue that specific anthropomorphic theses are supported or not supported by the same rigorous experimental and logical reasoning as any other scientific model. However, even though anthropomorphic models can be treated as science as usual, unique problems for these models still will remain. These problems have to do with the way in which language descriptive of our experiences travels back and forth between scientific and social domains.

I will first consider some global objections to anthropomorphism. These attack the logical or conceptual transgressions that the act of describing nonhumans in human terms is supposed to commit. I will then look at empirical arguments for and against specific instances of the anthropomorphism ascribed to nonhuman primates. Finally I will consider some social contextual concerns that arise from the scientific anthropomorphic models.

Logical Objections

A. Anthropomorphism entails a category mistake. To speak of dogs with feelings of shame is like referring to a Bach partita as being purple. This objection is easily dismissed as a relic of the view that humans are a separate and unique species, either created to be such or so far evolved that no predicates true of us could be true of other organisms. Surely the evolution of life on the planet tells against this being a logical claim. For a Cartesian who holds that animals are just complicated machines that lack the souls that make humans human, it might hold sway, but we are centuries beyond that.[6]

B. Anthropomorphism is defined as the *overestimation* of the similarity of humans and nonhumans and hence by definition could not yield accurate accounts.[7] But this is humpty-dumptyism. "When *I* use a word," Humpty Dumpty said, in rather a scornful tone, "it means just what I choose it to mean—neither more nor less."[8]

If we choose to let "anthropomorphism" be so defined, then we merely shift the question to be, *When* is it anthropomorphism, and *when* is it possibly a legitimate similarity? That is, when does a relevant similarity hold such that describing a cognitive state like "believing Sue cannot see the banana" could be equally true of an adult human, a human infant, and a chimpanzee? Such substantive questions cannot be reduced to mere matters of definition.

C. Anthropomorphism is *necessary* or *unavoidable*, since there is no amorphism or neutral language with which to describe behavior. If we do not use the predicates that describe our own human behavior, such as "believing X, wanting Y, deceiving Z" for describing nonhuman animals, then we have to use language appropriate for machines, like "moving toward the object, picking up the banana, looking toward the gate."

This position makes two mistakes. The first is that it presupposes a conceptual and linguistic impoverishment that is not justified. It underestimates our ability to discriminate and refer to multiple states of a system or many-valued parameters. As recent research has suggested, we may end up thinking that chimpanzees do not have the same kind of mental representations that we have but nevertheless think they have mental representations that mediate their behavior. They are not input-output machines but cogitating organisms. They just may not do it the way we do.[9] The second mistake is to confuse anthropocentrism with anthropomorphism. It is true that the descriptions we apply to anything are created *by* us, but they need not be *of* us. That is, we are the source of the terms and predicates, but they need not be terms and predicates that apply principally to our behaviors.

If anthropomorphism is not bad for *logical* reasons, then the extent of the acceptability of claims of similarity must be empirically grounded. This indeed is the conclusion that many recent commentators on anthropomorphism have reached.[10] Do chimpanzees have language, like us? Do they have beliefs about the beliefs of other chimps or of humans? Testing for the presence or absence of mental states, representations internal to the cognizing agent and presumably causally relevant to the behaviors we can observe, is no easy matter. I will now turn to the two main types of observational evidence that are used to justify anthropomorphism; the argument by analogy and experimentation.

Empirical Questions

Argument by Analogy

An *argument by analogy* is invoked to support a claim about the unobserved features of one system—the "target" of the analogy—based on the presence of that feature in another system—the "model system." The relevant similarities between the two systems are what justify the inference. Traditional analyses of analogical arguments render them fairly weak.

Traditional account of analogical argument structure

Premise 1:   System M is observed to have features a, b, c.
Premise 2:   System T is observed to have features a, b, c.
Premise 3:   System M is observed also to have feature d.
Conclusion: Therefore, system T must have feature d.

This inductive argument structure is supposed to capture everyday reasoning. For example, suppose two students in a class have the same study habits and the same grades on the midterm exam. I observe that student M gets an A on the final exam. Suppose student T has not yet taken the exam.

On the basis of the observed similarities, I can infer that student T will also get an A. This is clearly not deductively valid, as student T might be ill or fail to study in the manner she studied in the past or might have lost her book or for any number of reasons not perform the way I expect on the basis of her similarity to student M. Thus there is no deductive guarantee that the conclusion "Student T will get an A on the exam" is true. Nevertheless, the analogy permits inductive support for the inference. Certainly I would have more reason to believe student T would get an A than I would of other students who bear no similarities to student M.

The strength of an analogy is sometimes rendered in terms of the number of similarities between the two systems. The more features in common, the more likely the target system will have the ascribed unobserved feature. But quantifying over similarities is notoriously difficult and, quite frankly, beside the point. The sheer number of similar features does not immediately warrant the relevance of the similarities for the presence or absence of the feature of interest. Humans and mice have a large number of differences, and yet we are comfortable using the results of drug tests on mice to infer the consequences of those drugs on human biochemistry.

A more sophisticated rendering of the logic of analogical arguments, developed by Weitzenfeld[11] and related to structure-based accounts given in the cognitive sciences,[12] suggests that the inference of the presence of the unobserved feature in the target system is based on assumptions about the relations within each of the two analogous structures, rather than just their unstructured sets of properties. For example, according to Weitzenfeld's account, a claim that a human being will have an adverse reaction to saccharine based on experimental studies on mice is entailed by an assumption of the isomorphism obtaining between the causal structures governing mouse and human biochemistry. Thus, when using information about the model system to draw conclusions about the target system—for example, mice to human inferences or, as we shall see, human beliefs in anthropomorphic inferences to chimp beliefs—what establishes the relevant similarities will be the causal or determining structures in those two systems. If they have isomorphic structures, then the inference is sound. If not, then the conclusions are not supported.

There are two important components to this account of analogy. The first is that it is structural isomorphism between the model and target that deductively guarantees an inference from the observed feature of the model to the unobserved feature of the target. However, isomorphism is a rather weak relationship between two structures, since the reason the mapping works may be accidental. Think of the mapping from stellar constellations as seen from earth such as Orion or Ursa Major to the spatial configurations of hunters and bears. For analogical arguments to be informative, the reason the relations in the model structure—for example, mouse ingestion of large quantities of saccharine inducing mouse production of tumors—map onto the relations in the target structure; that is, human ingestion of saccharine in diet foods and subsequent cancers must be nonaccidental, that is, governed by a rule or causal law. This is all rather abstract philosophy. The main point of the structural approach to analogical arguments is to focus attention on the relationships between the variables in each system as well as the relationships between the two systems, rather than on simply the number of features shared by the two systems. Let's bring it back to the case at hand.

A clear reconstruction of the analogical argument for inferring that chimps are like us is provided by Povinelli:

> *P1:   I exhibit bodily behaviors of type B (i.e., those normally thought to be caused by second-order mental states).*
> *P2:   Chimps exhibit bodily behaviors of type B.*
> *P3:   My own bodily behaviors of type B are usually caused by my second-order mental states of type A.*
> *C: Therefore bodily behaviors of type B exhibited by chimps are caused by their second-order mental states of type A, and so* a fortiori *chimps have second-order mental states of type A.*

(*Povinelli, Folk Physics for Apes*, 13)

In the traditional philosophical analysis of analogical arguments, the number of similarities between humans and chimpanzees would determine the strength of support for the conclusion. Phylogenetic proximity is brought to bear to suggest that we have more similarities with chimps than other species, since we are historically closer to them. Divergence occurred more recently from chimpanzees than from other species and hence we expect them to be more like us than would be toads or amoebae. But notice how weak this support actually is. Divergence is presumed, and distinction is required for humans and chimps *not* to be the same species. Many features may be shared, but just the ones we are interested in, second-order mental states, for example, may be the ones that constitute the break in the lineage. So evolutionary proximity may entail more similar features but not necessarily the relevant features.[13]

The more sophisticated analysis of analogical inference suggests a different understanding of the argument. Here, what makes human experience relevant to conclusions about chimp experience is not the number of similarities but the presence of isomorphic causal structures. What causes a human behavior B is, supposedly, a human second-order mental state A. But is this the same causal structure found in chimpanzees? If it is, then even though we cannot ask the chimp what belief motivated its behavior, we can be justified in thinking that if the human and chimp behaviors are the same or similar, then the beliefs that cause them are the same or similar. However, this shifts the question of the legitimacy of analogical reasoning to the determination of whether the causal structures generating behaviors in humans and in chimpanzees are isomorphic. That is the subject of the second type of empirical evidence that I will discuss below.

To summarize so far, anthropomorphic theses can be seen as instances of analogical inferences. We ascribe to other organisms the features we take to be true of us. Phylogenetic relatedness seems to render weak support for the conclusion of such inferences, so weak that they can only garner some modest plausibility for the conclusions. However, a stronger analogical inference is supported when there is justification for isomorphism of causal structures in the two systems generating the features we are interested in. On this account the analogy requires a different type of evidence than evolutionary history alone. Statistical and experimental data are required to support the premises that would entail the inference. So how can empirical evidence help?

Argument from Experimental Data

Advocates of cognitive ethology cry foul when their opponents reject the enterprise from the beginning just for being anthropomorphic. They would rather let the facts decide. But this is not as easy as it might sound. The controversial anthropomorphic theses ascribe to nonhumans just those sorts of features that are not directly accessible to observation. Allen and Hauser want to know whether apes have a concept of death.[14] Premack and Woodruff explore whether apes have a "theory of mind" that is invoked in generating behaviors that appear to be acts of deception.[15] It is obvious that we cannot just look at a chimpanzee, or another human being for that matter, and see its internal mental state. [. . .] We cannot ask a chimpanzee to report to us the content of its cognition. We have access experimentally and observationally only to the very behaviors we take as the effects of the ascribed mental causes. So how can observation and experiment help decide this issue?

It is worth noting that the reason one suggests that concepts and second-order beliefs might be the causes of nonhuman behaviors is because we believe that they are the causes of our own behaviors. This view assumes that there is a causal structure or mechanism that we can investigate that generates behaviors as the effect of beliefs.[16] When I think my husband is joking about where the car keys are, but a friend who is with us is telling the truth, then I do not walk in the direction of the place mentioned by my husband to find my keys. Rather I go to the location cited by my friend. I hear the utterances of each of them, and my behavior is caused not just by those utterances but also by my beliefs about the beliefs of the speakers.

[. . .]

How do I know this? It is introspection or personal self-knowledge that gives me insight into the causal structure that underlies my actions.

If the evidence for beliefs being the cause of behavior is solely the subjective experience of the believer/actor, then I need to ascribe to other human beings the possession of an unobservable mental cause to explain their reasoned behaviors. This is the well-known philosophical problem of "other minds." But the ascription of unobservable mental causes to humans seems to be very much like the ascription to nonhuman beings. Why should it be sanctioned in the case of other humans and not sanctioned in the case of, say, honeybees? And where does that leave the inference when directed toward chimpanzee behavior?

There are two places to look for answers to these questions: background assumptions about the nature of intra- and interspecific similarity and behavioral experiments. I will first consider the background assumptions. There are good grounds to assume that basic causal structures or mechanisms are the same for different members of the same species of organism. Although different individual organisms are spatiotemporally distinct and harbor all sorts of variation in particular features, the basic biological mechanisms most directly connected to surviving and reproducing are most likely to be the same. The reason is that these are the features upon which evolution by natural selection will have been quickest and strongest to act. Variations that have relatively negative effects on survival and reproduction are not kept around. That is how evolution by natural selection works. Even with the caveat of recognizing the continual generation of variation within a species, it nevertheless is a safe assumption that there will be little variation in the basic functioning of organisms within a species. The species is the correct boundary for this degree of similarity because it is the potentially interbreeding population that is the receptacle for the consequences of natural selection.

[. . .]

Nevertheless, there are good, if fallible grounds for believing that other human beings have the same sort of second-order beliefs that are causally relevant to their actions, since we have grounds for believing that the same causal mechanisms are at work in all members of the species.

What is the objection to extending this inference from humans to nonhumans? First of all, we have fewer types of supporting evidence than in the case of human-to-human inference. There is no self-reporting to be acquired from the chimp about the reasons for its actions. There is no shared species membership from which to support causal isomorphism. However, we can look to the similarity or dissimilarity of neurophysiological structure, sensory apparatus, and so on. And, importantly, we can look to behavioral observations and experimentation (see Table 10.1).

The experimental data on whether or not chimpanzees have second-order beliefs, unfortunately, permit multiple interpretations. Povinelli's *Folk Physics for Apes* reports a number of experiments done on captive chimpanzees over a five-year period to investigate how they conceive of the physics that underlies their use of tools in particular or, more generally, to "elucidate the nature of the mental representations that guide this behavior" (1). In service to this goal, Povinelli provides evidence against the strong argument by analogy. A series of experiments were done to determine whether chimpanzees have the concept that others "see." This is a basic second-order belief. I look at another human being and have a visual experience of that person. I look at their eyes and notice that they are directed at the door. I form a belief that the person sees the door, that is, a belief about her

Table 10.1 Grounds for attributing causal isomorphism

	Evolutionary relatedness	Self-reporting	Neurophysiological and other physical features	Behavioral statistics
Human-to-human inference	Strong support	Strong support	Strong support	Strong support
Human-to-chimpanzee inference	Weak support	N/a	Some support	Mixed support

internal visual representation. I can then act on the basis of what I believe that she does or does not see. Povinelli's group studied whether chimpanzees engage in the same kind of cognitive process.

Povinelli dissects forming a belief that another organism sees a particular object into a number of components. The organism must notice the eyes of the other and then follow the gaze of the other toward the object under perception. Interest in eyes and gaze direction are present in a wide range of species, and these abilities may well have emerged as adaptations to predation and social interactions. But how much like humans are the internal states of other organisms that engage in these behaviors? Povinelli puts the point as follows:

> Some researchers interpret the mutual gaze that occurs between infants and adults, as well as among great apes during complex social interactions as *prima facie* evidence of an understanding of the attentional aspect of seeing. And admittedly, there is a certain allure to the idea that, because mutual gaze in adult humans is often attended by representations of the mental states of others, comparable behavior in human infants (or other species) is probably attended by similar representations. But is mutual gaze in apes (for example) really attended by the same psychological representations as in human adults, or is this just a projection of our own way of thinking onto other species?
>
> (22)

In short, is this just wishful anthropomorphism, or can we get evidence that apes have the same or similar cognitive state as humans?

The first step in Povinelli's study was to establish whether chimpanzees had the same behavioral abilities, that is, gaze following, as do human infants and human adults. For the analogical argument to work, the effects—behaviors in this case—expressed in the two systems have to be the same, and then one infers that the causes of these effects are also the same. Experiments show that chimps and one-and-one-half-year-old human infants similarly responded to head movement, eye movement, left/right specificity, gaze following outside of visual field, and so on. So he concluded that chimps and humans engage in similar responses to a series of eye movement stimuli presented to them. Behaviors are the same. But what more is going on?

Povinelli devised ingenious experiments to try to test whether chimps' gaze-following behavior indicated the possession of second-order mental states. He entertained two possible explanations, a low-level and high-level account. The low-level account interprets the chimp's gaze-following behavior to express cognition about behavioral propensities of the person whose gaze they followed, where the high-level account claims chimps form concepts about the internal mental states of the person whose gaze they are following. That is, the low-level model is akin to what happens when a human visually follows the path of a billiard ball being hit by a cue ball. We see the ball being hit and its initial motion and develop expectations of its behavior at a subsequent time. It initially moves towards the corner pocket, hence it will continue to move in a straight line toward the pocket. The high-level model is akin to a human watching another human looking in the direction of the billiard ball. In this case the perceived eye motion induces beliefs about what the observer *sees*. The human's eyes move following the ball, hence the human sees the ball's motion. The Povinelli group hypothesized that the high- and low-level accounts would make different predictions in cases where the observed individual's gaze was obstructed by an opaque barrier. If the low-level account were right, the observing chimp would just scan a line from the eyes of the observed being until something was noticed. This is based on eyes looking right indicating something is right, and a barrier would be irrelevant. If the high-level account were right, the observing chimp would walk around the barrier to see what was being seen. This would be based on eyes looking right indicating there must be something that is seen that is on the other side of the barrier. The results of an opaque-barrier test were unambiguously in support of the high-level model. The chimps walked around the barrier to see what the person in the experiment was looking at. The conclusion naturally drawn was that chimps understand what it is for someone else to see or represent the world; hence they have second-order beliefs just like humans.

However, a dozen other experiments involving seeing supported the low-level model of cognition. In these experiments, the chimps were presented with two humans displaying different capacities to see them, and it was observed whether the chimps responded differently to the two humans. The test response was begging behavior, and the question was did the chimps beg significantly more to the human who did not have his gaze obstructed? The obstruction conditions of the humans in the test included being blindfolded, having a bucket over one's head, having hands over one's eyes, and facing backward in relation to the observing chimpanzee.

In three of the four conditions, the chimps were as likely to gesture to the person who could *not* see them as to the person who could. However, in the front-facing-versus-back-facing case they did beg more to the human with his front facing the chimp. So the low-level account captured three of the experimental conditions, whereas the high-level account was supported by one of the experimental conditions. To try to distinguish whether it was the seeing that mattered or the front position, Povinelli introduced a fifth experimental setup. This time, both humans had their backs to the observing chimp, but one was looking over her shoulder at the chimp, the other was not. "To our surprise and in full support of the low-level model, on the looking-over-the-shoulder trials the apes did not prefer to gesture to the person who could see them" (*Folk Physics*, 34).

Povinelli's group continued to introduce new seeing/not seeing experimental conditions to the chimps using screens and eyes-open/eyes-shut conditions to try to figure out what was going on. In the end, Povinelli rejected the high-level, second-order belief model and suggested that through trial and error the apes learned a set of procedural rules about successful gesturing (1. gesture to person whose front is facing forward; 2. if both fronts present or absent, gesture to person whose face is visible; and 3. if both faces visible or occluded, gesture to person whose eyes are visible). The chimpanzees do not appear to be using a concept of seeing to help them decide to whom to gesture. Instead, the chimpanzees after lots of trial and error behaved "as if" they had our concept of seeing. Important for Povinelli's conclusion is the fact that the behavior at the end of the study was different from the chimps' behavior at the beginning of the study. They learned something, namely, how to gesture to the person *we* would say could see them. In contrast, three-year-old human children compared in these experiments were shown to have the behaviors appropriate to understanding a concept of seeing from the beginning; no variation in behavior occurred for the humans.

Do these experiments tell us whether the similarity of chimp and human behavior indicates a similarity of internal mental cognition? Povinelli concludes that it is still open to interpretation. Indeed, he postulates three different ways to account for the behaviors of the chimps in the experiments. First, they could have entered the test without a concept of seeing but through the testing came to construct the concept. Second, they could have entered the test with a general conception of attention and constructed a notion of visual attention. And third, they could have neither entered nor exited the tests with an understanding of the mental state of visual attention (*Folk Physics*, 42). Rather, they constructed an "as-if" understanding of seeing-as-attention. The third option is like the familiar case of Clever Hans, the horse who appeared to be able to do arithmetic.[17]

An anomaly for Povinelli's preferred low-level interpretation is that the opaque-barrier tests did support the high-level model of cognition for the chimps. Povinelli takes the preponderance of evidence to suggest that the low-level model is much better supported and gives a reinterpretation of the opaque-barrier test that would account for this contrary bit of evidence. On the way, he points out that if we walk into the laboratory with an anthropomorphic attitude, we are much more likely to continually refine and retest experimental results that support the low-level model and accept on its face the results of tests like the opaque barrier test that support an anthropomorphic high-level model.

What conclusion should we draw from these experiments on chimpanzees? Does the fact that their behavior and our behavior are sometimes indistinguishable indicate that the causes of those behaviors in us and in them are also the same? Does the fact that their behavior and our behavior are sometimes different indicate that the cause of their behaviors are not the same as ours? The experimental results are, at best, ambiguous and, according to Povinelli, lean toward a rejection of strong anthropomorphism. Indeed, as you will recall, he said that if the similarity of human and nonhuman behaviors does not license the analogical inference to same causes for chimpanzees, then it can hardly be credible for other species. At least it should be clear how difficult it is to get unambiguous experimental results for anthropomorphic models. There is no consensus in the scientific community about the significance of the Povinelli experiments, with criticisms often focused on the possible crucial dissimilarity between captive chimps, the subjects of Povinelli's studies, and chimps in the wild.[18]

Conclusion

What is the fate of anthropomorphism in contemporary science? I have argued that the global arguments against anthropomorphism cannot be maintained in a post-Darwinian scientific world. Given that humans *are* biologically related to other species, the ascription of concepts whose natural home is in describing human features and behaviors may very well apply to nonhumans. That being said, there is also no global support for the cavalier exportation of human descriptive concepts to nonhumans. Rather, I have suggested that a piecemeal evaluation of the credibility of specific claims of similarity, based on a causal-isomorphism model of analogical reasoning, must be undertaken. There are a variety of types of evidential support for grounding specific anthropomorphic models, and so judgments of its legitimacy in different cases may well vary.

In short, anthropomorphic models are specific, scientifically accessible claims of similarity between humans and nonhumans. As such, they must be substantiated by evidence that there are similar causal mechanisms responsible for generating the apparently similar behaviors that are observed. If experimental and background theoretical support do provide that evidence, then there should be no objection to using the same descriptive language for both humans and nonhumans. If that evidence is not provided, then using the same predicate for a full-fledged human behavior to refer to an "as-if" nonhuman behavior will be misleading and inaccurate.

[. . .]

With respect to the issue of cognitive similarities, the current scientific debates indicate that it is difficult to get definitive evidence either way for even the simplest second-order belief that "A sees X." It would appear to get progressively more difficult when the descriptions carry not just casual assumptions but also social and moral baggage.

Not surprisingly, the most controversial and consequential claims about the similarity between humans and nonhuman animals are the most difficult to substantiate. And yet it is these claims that play a fundamental role in the growing field of cognitive ethology. Perhaps the most telling insights that will be gleaned from careful study of the nature of the cognitive similarity or dissimilarity between humans and nonhumans will be reflexive. That is, characterizing the ways in which nonhuman cognition differs from human cognition may force a reevaluation of our account of human cognition itself.

The same may be true for the advocates of expanding the domain of moral consideration to nonhumans. A deeper understanding of the lives of other animals may shift the focus from the anthropocentric question of whether other beings are sufficiently like humans to warrant the same moral rights as humans to a more generalized analysis of what capacities, whether found in humans or not, ought to be the basis of moral consideration.

Notes

This paper was presented at the Max Planck Society for the History of Science Conference on Thinking with Animals and the Pittsburgh–London Consortium in the Philosophy of Biology and Neuroscience. I wish to thank lively discussions at both those conferences and especially comments by Joel Smith, Lorraine Daston, Elliott Sober, and John Dupré.

1. See J. B. Kennedy, *The New Anthropomorphism* (Cambridge: Cambridge University Press, 1992), for an account of the behaviorist attack on anthropomorphism; Stewart Elliott Guthrie, "Anthropomorphism: A

Definition and a Theory," in *Anthropomorphism, Anecdotes, and Animals: The Emperor's New Clothes?* ed. R. W. Mitchell, N. S. Thompson, and H. L. Miles (Albany: SUNY Press, 1996), 501, cites criticisms of anthropomorphism back to Bacon, Spinoza, and Hume.

2. Charles Darwin, *The Descent of Man, and Selection in Relation to Sex* (1871; reprint, Princeton, NJ: Princeton University Press, 1981), 42; quoted in Elizabeth Knoll, "Dogs, Darwinism, and English Sensibilities," in *Anthropomorphism, Anecdotes, and Animals: The Emperor's New Clothes?* ed. R. W. Mitchell, N. S. Thompson, and H. L. Miles (Albany: SUNY Press, 1996), 14.

3. Daniel J. Povinelli, *Folk Physics for Apes* (Oxford: Oxford University Press, 2000), 9.

4. Sue Savage-Rumbaugh, Stuart G. Shanker, and Talbot J. Taylor, *Apes, Language and the Human Mind* (New York: Oxford University Press, 1998). Kanzi is a bonobo chimpanzee who can manipulate physical symbols in a way that looks very much like human language.

5. Mark Derr, "Brainy Dolphins Pass the Human 'Mirror' Test," *New York Times*, 1 May 2001. http://www.nytimes.com/2001/05/01/science/brainy-dolphins-pass-the-human-mirror-test.html?pagewanted=all.

6. See Emanuela Cenami Spada, "Amorphism, Mechanomorphism, and Anthropomorphism," in *Anthropomorphism, Anecdotes, and Animals: The Emperor's New Clothes?* ed. R. W. Mitchell, N. S. Thompson, and H. L. Miles (Albany: SUNY Press, 1996), 37–50.

7. See Guthrie, "Anthropomorphism: A Definition," 53; and Hugh Lehman, "Anthropomorphism and Scientific Evidence for Animal Mental States," in *Anthropomorphism, Anecdotes, and Animals: The Emperor's New Clothes?* ed. R. W. Mitchell, N. S. Thompson, and H. L. Miles (Albany: SUNY Press, 1996), 105.

8. Lewis Carroll, *Through the Looking Glass* (New York: Putnam, 1972), chapter 6.

9. See Povinelli, *Folk Physics*.

10. See Marc Beckoff, Colin Allen, and Gordon M. Burghardt, eds., *Cognitive Animal: Empirical and Theoretical Perspectives on Animal Cognition* (Cambridge, MA: MIT Press, 2002); and Povinelli, *Folk Physics*.

11. Julian S. Weitzenfeld, "Valid Reasoning by Analogy," *Philosophy of Science* 51 (1984): 137–49.

12. See J. R. Hayes and H. A. Simon, "Understanding Tasks Stated in Natural Language," in *Speech Recognition*, ed. D. R. Reddy (New York: Academic Press, 1975), 443–470; and M. L. Gick and K. J. Holyoak, "Schema Induction and Analogical Transfer," *Cognitive Psychology* 15 (1983): 1–38.

13. See Christopher Lang, Elliott Sober, and Karen Strier, "Are Human Beings Part of the Rest of Nature?" *Biology and Philosophy* 17 (2002): 661–71, for a detailed assessment of the import of phylogenetic proximity for casual similarity.

14. Colin Allen and Marc Hauser, "Concept Attribution in Nonhuman Animals: Theoretical and Methodological Problems in Ascribing Complex Mental Processes," *Philosophy of Science* 58 (1991): 221–40.

15. D. Premack and G. Woodruff, "Does the Chimpanzee Have a Theory of Mind?" *Behavioral Brain Sciences* 1 (1978): 515–26.

16. Of course, there is a debate on whether the folk notion of belief is a part of a scientific account of behavior; alternatives include epiphenomenalism with respect to beliefs as well as eliminativism in favor of physical neural structures. See Owen J. Flanagan, *Science of the Mind*, 2nd ed. (Cambridge, MA: MIT Press, 1991), for an overview of the various positions.

17. Clever Hans was a horse who lived in Berlin at the beginning of the twentieth century who allegedly could do arithmetic, indicating sums by the number of times he tapped his hoof to the ground. Of course, he failed to display this ability when his trainer, from whom he presumably was getting cues for foot tapping, was absent from the scene. See Oskar Pfungst, *Clever Hans (the Horse of Mr. Von Osten)* (Bristol, UK: Thoemmes Press, 1911).

18. See M. D. Hauser, "Elementary, My Dear Chimpanzee," *Science* 291 (2001): 440–41; A. Whiten, "Tool Tests Challenge Chimpanzees," *Nature* 409 (2001): 133; and Colin Allen, "A Skeptic's Progress," *Biology and Philosophy* 17 (2002): 695–702.

11 Thinking without Words
An Overview for Animal Ethics

José Luis Bermúdez

Bermúdez has identified genuine thinkers as creatures behaving in ways that reflect their thoughts about the environment and whose behaviors need to be explained in psychological terms. Here he outlines the elements of the philosophical framework for treating some animals as genuine thinkers that are most relevant to those working in the field of animal ethics. These include varying levels of cognitive sophistication and limits of types of thoughts available among various species.

In *Thinking without Words,* I develop a philosophical framework for treating (at least some) animals and human infants as genuine thinkers.[1] A genuine thinker, I take it, is a creature that behaves in ways that reflect its thoughts about the environment—and hence a creature whose behavior needs to be explained in psychological terms. That many animals are genuine thinkers is taken for granted by much research in cognitive ethology, but scientists and philosophers have often been skeptical of what they take to be anecdotal evidence and tacit anthropomorphism. The aims of my book are

* to set out clear criteria for identifying when psychological explanations are required for non-linguistic creatures;
* to show how precise and determinate thoughts can be attributed to non-linguistic creatures;
* to show how the psychological explanations that we give of animal and infant behavior are continuous with the psychological explanations that we give of language-using creatures;
* to explore the differences between thinking without words and language-based thinking.

This paper outlines the aspects of this account that are of most relevance to those working in animal ethics. There is a range of different levels of cognitive sophistication in different animal species, in addition to limits to the types of thought available to non-linguistic creatures, and it may be important for animal ethicists to take this into account in exploring issues of moral significance and the obligations that we might or might not have to non-human animals.

Psychological and Non-Psychological Explanations of Behavior

Psychological explanations come into play when non-psychological forms of explanation provide insufficient explanatory and predictive leverage. Typical non-psychological forms of explanation appeal to mechanisms of associative conditioning and what are known as "innate releasing mechanisms."

Pavlovian or classical conditioning occurs when an association is reinforced between an *unconditioned stimulus* (e.g., food or pain) and a *conditioned stimulus* (e.g., the sound of a bell). The unconditioned stimulus typically generates an *unconditioned response* (e.g., salivation). As a result of conditioning, the unconditioned response is generated by the conditioned stimulus. Many forms of animal training are based on classical conditioning. It is classical conditioning that makes clicks and whistles effective rewards for dogs and dolphins. In instrumental (or operant) conditioning, the process of reinforcement (or punishment) applies to actions rather than physiological responses.

According to behaviorist models of animal behavior, *all* animal behavior is the product of either classical or instrumental conditioning, and conditioning is certainly the type of animal learning most frequently studied in the laboratory. Ethologists, however, have also appealed to innate releasing mechanisms to explain behavior in the wild.[2] Innate releasing mechanisms are fixed and instinctive sequences of movements. For example, when newly hatched herring gulls encounter stimuli matching the adult herring gull beak in color, length, and movement they respond by pecking. Innate releasing mechanisms have the following characteristics.[3]

- They are triggered by specific stimuli.
- They always take the same form.
- They occur in all members of the relevant species.
- Their occurrence is largely independent of the individual creature's history.
- Once launched they cannot be varied.
- They have only one function.

Innate releasing mechanisms and conditioned responses are both invariant responses to stimuli. When the animal registers the relevant stimulus, the appropriate response results in a way that can in general be fully understood, explained, and predicted without any appeal to an intermediary between stimulus and response. Psychological explanations of behavior only become necessary when no such invariant input–output links can be identified. The essence of a psychological explanation is that it explains behavior in terms of how the creature in question *represents* its environment, rather than simply in terms of the stimuli that it detects. Psychological explanations typically make reference to how the organism perceives its environment, to what it believes about the environment, and to what it desires to achieve. These beliefs, desires, and perceptions allow organisms to respond flexibly and plastically to their environments—the same situations can afford different actions if a creature brings different beliefs and desires to it, or perceives it in different ways.

How are we to determine which animals count as genuine thinkers? By identifying species whose members behave in ways that do not seem to be explicable in non-psychological terms. Any such judgment is provisional and defeasible, since it might always turn out that we have been insufficiently imaginative in thinking about the non-psychological possibilities. What is not provisional and defeasible, however, is the judgment that many species will prove to contain genuine thinkers. The weight of the evidence points strongly to the impossibility of characterizing all animal behavior in non-psychological terms.

There is a basic distinction, then, between creatures that behave in ways that require psychological explanation and those that do not. This may mark a morally significant dividing line. It is worth noting, however, that sentience seems to be required for *some* forms of associative learning. If the unconditioned stimulus is pleasure or pain, or anything whose status as reward/punishment is a function of its phenomenal character, then only sentient creatures are capable of learning through conditioning. If sentience is what matters for moral significance, then it is already built into some non-psychological models of explanation. Nonetheless, it is hard to imagine that moral significance is not a matter of degree—and even if it is not a matter of degree, we will still need to make judgments of relative moral significance. Either way, the distinction between "merely sentient" creatures and thinking creatures is likely to be relevant.

Propositional and Non-Propositional Thinking in Non-Linguistic Creatures

It might be accepted that animals of a certain species at a certain stage of development are thinkers, in the sense that they behave (at least some of the time) in ways that require psychological explanation. But there are different types of thinking at the non-linguistic level. The basic distinction is between propositional and non-propositional thought.

According to Michael Dummett, the types of thinking available to animals are just a subset of the central types of thinking available to language-using creatures.[4] Dummett accepts that there can be non-linguistic thoughts, which can be had both by animals and by language-using creatures, but he calls them "proto-thoughts." These proto-thoughts "do not have the structure of verbally expressed thoughts"; they are not "full-fledged thoughts"; they "cannot float free [of the environment], but can occur only as integrated with current activity"; and the vehicle of non-linguistic thought is "spatial images superimposed on spatial perceptions." There can be non-linguistic thoughts, but these are not "accurately expressible in language." This is what I call the "minimalist conception of non-linguistic thought."

According to the minimalist approach, all non-linguistic thinking is

- context-bound;
- essentially pragmatic and dynamic;
- vehicled by spatial images superimposed on spatial perceptions;
- unstructured.

Proto-thoughts thus construed count as instances of thinking-how rather than thinking-that (to draw an analogy with Gilbert Ryle's well-known distinction between knowing-how and knowing-that).[5] Dummett explicitly assimilates them to complex behavioral skills. Their purpose is essentially the control of responses to the environment, rather than the acquisition of information about it. They do not have a determinate content that can be put into words. In all these respects they are fundamentally different from beliefs, desires, and other propositional attitudes.

One of the central claims of *Thinking without Words* is that the minimalist conception cannot be a complete account of non-linguistic thought. Non-linguistic thought goes beyond perception, because there are forms of animal behavior that we can only explain by thinking of the creatures performing those actions as having full-fledged beliefs and desires. By this I mean that these are beliefs and desires that represent the world in ways that can be accurately reported in sentences of something not too dissimilar to English—but not identical to English, since we will need a vocabulary that reflects the differences between how we "carve up" the world into objects and how the environment is perceived by different types of animal. Psychological explanations of this type are propositional attitude explanations.

The types of behavior that most obviously pose problems for the minimalist conception are those that go beyond the "here and now." When animals represent contingencies between actions and outcomes, perhaps in thinking about how to tailor means to ends, they are going beyond the sensorimotor schemas envisaged by the minimalist conception—similarly when they engage in tool use and other forms of long-range planning. Wild chimpanzees, for example, make two different types of wands for dipping into ant and termite nests from different types of branches.[6] They make wands for dipping into ant swarms by taking a stick several feet long and stripping the side leaves and leafy stem. For dipping into termite nests, on the other hand, they use wands made from vines or more flexible twigs that are considerably shorter and that have a bitten end, unlike the ant wands.

Of course, as with the initial determination of whether we are dealing with thinkers at all, careful experimental work is required to identify when propositional explanations are required. This is probably the most intensively studied and controversial area of animal cognition. It is also potentially the area of most interest to animal ethics. This is also the area where most philosophical work is required to explain the truth-conditions of the thoughts ascribed to non-linguistic creatures and how to go about attributing such thoughts.[7]

If it is argued that moral significance depends upon the capacity for genuine thought, then it is natural (but not, of course, compulsory) to think that there are degrees of moral significance correlated with degrees of cognitive sophistication. The dividing line between thinking of the minimalist kind and thinking of the propositional kind may well be important.

The Limits of Non-Linguistic Thought:
Intentional Ascent and Semantic Ascent

As far as animal ethics is concerned, what animals *cannot* do is likely to be just as important as what animals can do. Many discussions of moral significance make it contingent upon particular types of cognitive achievement. Some of these cognitive achievements could be implicated in the types of non-linguistic thinking we have already discussed. Suppose, for example, that moral significance were thought to be restricted to creatures capable of a concern for their own future. One might take the ability to engage in certain types of long-range planning to be evidence for such concern.

There are a number of ways of thinking about moral considerability that, however, cannot in principle be applied to non-linguistic creatures. In the following sections, I draw out some of the limitations that the unavailability of higher-order thoughts has upon animal cognition.

By a "higher-order thought" I mean a thought that takes another thought as its object. Thoughts about another's mental states count as higher-order thoughts, for example, as does reflection on one's own mental states. W. V. O. Quine once described *semantic ascent* as "the shift from talking in certain terms to talking about them."[8] By analogy we can characterize *intentional ascent* as the shift from thinking in certain ways to thinking about those ways of thinking. My argument, in effect, is that intentional ascent requires semantic ascent—that we can only think about thoughts through thinking about words.

We should distinguish first-order *target thoughts* from the higher-order thoughts that might be directed at them. My belief that *p* is a target thought. It is the object of my higher-order belief that I believe that *p*. Target thoughts must be represented to be the objects of higher-order thoughts. There are all sorts of things going on below the threshold of consciousness when we think (perhaps thinking involves manipulating sentences in a subpersonal language of thought, for example). But these subpersonal events are not what we think about when we think about our own thoughts. There is a difference between thinking about thoughts and thinking about the machinery of thinking. So the question is: How must target thoughts be represented in order for them to be the objects of higher-order thoughts?

There are two possibilities. On the one hand, representation might be secured symbolically through the complex symbols of a natural language. A thought would be represented, therefore, through its linguistic expression and would appear as a potential object of thought *qua* linguistic entity. On the other hand, representation might be secured in an analog manner, through some kind of pictorial model. On this conception of the vehicles of thought, which we find developed in different ways in mental models theory in the psychology of reasoning, and in the conception of mental maps put forward by D. Braddon-Mitchell and F. Jackson, the vehicle of a thought is a pictorial representation of the state of affairs being thought about.[9]

The argument in favor of public language sentences and against pictorial models rests upon considerations of structure and inferential role. I am assuming that thoughts are individuated at least in part by their inferential role. What makes a given thought the thought that *p* is partly a matter of the inferential relations in which it stands to other thoughts. Some of these relations are entailment relations (the thoughts that entail *p* and the thoughts that *p* entails), but they also include evidential relations (the thoughts whose holding true would be good evidence for thinking that *p* holds true, and the thoughts that would be judged more likely to be true if *p* were true). Any thinker capable of thinking a higher-order thought directed at a target thought must, almost by definition, have some grasp of the individuation conditions of the target thought. He must have some grasp of what it is that he is thinking about. There is nothing peculiar here to higher-order thoughts. This is just an application of the very general requirement that to think about anything one must have some sort of "cognitive access" that enables one to pick that thing out. It follows that a higher-order thinker must have some sort of grasp of the entailment and evidential relations in which the target thought stands.[10]

At least some of these entailment and evidential relations are a function of the structure of the thought that *p*. In order to understand the inferential role of a thought we need to be able to view it as made up of distinguishable components that can feature in further thoughts and, moreover, we need to be able to view it as made up from those components in a way that determines its semantic value (thereby capturing the difference between the true thought *Bogotá is the capital of Colombia* and the false thought *Colombia is the capital of Bogotá*). We may say, therefore, that the structure of the thought must be perspicuous in the consciously accessible representation that is the target of the higher-order thought.

The final step in the argument is that the structure of a thought cannot be perspicuous *in the right sort of way* in thoughts that are represented in a pictorial manner. The qualification is important, since pictorial representation in mental maps and mental models does depend upon a notion of structural isomorphism between the models/maps and what they represent. The relations holding between elements of the mental model/map can be mapped onto the relations holding between objects in the represented state of affairs.

[. . .]

Pictorial representations do not have a *canonical structure*. Their structure can be analyzed in many different ways (corresponding to the jigsaw puzzles that one can construct from it), but none of these can properly be described as giving *the* structure of the state of affairs.

Yet, in order to understand the inferential role of a thought one does need to understand the canonical structure of that thought (what is often termed its *logical form*). This canonical structure is perspicuous, although not always perfectly perspicuous, when thoughts are expressed in public language sentences. It is because of this that higher-order thought is language dependent. Only public language sentences can make the canonical structure of a target thought available to thinkers in a way that allows them to grasp the inferential role of the target thought. The conclusion of the argument, then, is that thinking about thinking is only available to language-using creatures.

What the Argument Does *Not* Show: Sentience and Higher-Order Thoughts

Some philosophers have proposed higher-order thought theories of consciousness.[11] According to these theories a mental state is conscious if and only if it is the object of a higher-order thought. Given that sentience just is the capacity to have conscious experiences, higher-order thought theories of consciousness restrict sentience to creatures capable of thinking higher-order thoughts. Any such conclusion is potentially very important for animal ethics, given the weight that is standardly put on animal suffering in thinking about our obligations to non-human animals.

It should be stressed, however, that this conclusion does not in any sense follow from the argument from intentional ascent to semantic ascent. The argument presupposes a theory of consciousness. It does not set out to provide one and it is perfectly compatible with the view that non-human animals can not only have conscious experiences (and so be sentient) but also have conscious beliefs and desires. The object of a conscious belief is a state of affairs in the world (or, in the case of a false belief a merely possible state of affairs) and the argument from intentional ascent to semantic ascent applies only to thoughts that have other thoughts as their objects. As such it offers no direct support to arguments that animals cannot be sentient because they are not capable of having higher-order thoughts.

Intentional Ascent and Understanding Other Minds

Is it possible for non-linguistic creatures to participate in practices of attributing psychological states to their conspecifics or indeed to any other creatures? In the light of the preceding discussion it is not hard to see why a very broad class of psychological attributions should be unavailable to non-linguistic creatures. To attribute a belief, for example, to another creature is essentially to view that creature as standing in a particular relation to a thought—the relation of believing the thought to be true. Clearly, therefore, the attribution of a belief requires thinking about a thought. It is a canonical form of intentional ascent that requires being able to "hold a thought in mind."

This has potential implications for animal ethics, on any view that links moral significance to the capacity to engage in certain types of reflection about the mental states of conspecifics—or to the capacity to engage in types of behavior (perhaps caring behavior) that presupposes and involves such reflection. It is important to recognize, however, that the argument from intentional ascent to semantic ascent does not leave non-linguistic creatures completely "mind-blind." There are types of mental state that can be comprehended and attributed by non-linguistic creatures.

To explain this further, we need to distinguish two ways of thinking about desire.[12] One can desire a particular thing, or one can desire that a particular state of affairs be the case. This is the distinction between *goal-desires* and *situation-desires*. At the level of verbalizable thought, the distinction can be marked in terms of two different ways of completing the sentence "X desires—." A sentence ascribing a goal-desire is completed by the name of an object or by the name of a kind of stuff (e.g., "food"). But when a sentence ascribes a situation-desire, it is completed by a "that—" clause in which the blank is filled by a complete sentence specifying the state of affairs in question.

Goal-desires are more basic than situation-desires. The contrast is effectively between desire construed as a propositional attitude (in situation-desires, which are attributed via that-clauses picking out the thought that is the object of desire) and the more fundamental goal-desires that are directed not at thoughts but rather at objects or features. There is no reason why non-linguistic creatures should not be able to attribute goal-desires to other agents. The argument from intentional ascent cannot get a grip, since goal-desires are relations between a subject and an object/feature, rather than between a subject and a proposition.

The ability to attribute goal-desires goes hand in hand with a basic understanding of intentional, that is to say goal-directed, behavior. Although of course there will be many different degrees of complexity in goal-directed behavior, depending on the richness of the desires and beliefs by which it is driven, a creature capable of attributing goal-desires will be able to make the basic distinction between purposeful behaviors, on the one hand, and random movements and instinctive reactions on the other. A purposive action is an action for which a motivating goal-desire can be identified.

Goal-desires cannot be the only mental states that can be identified and attributed by non-linguistic creatures. It is hard to see, for example, how a goal-desire can be attributed to a creature without some evidence of the information that the creature possesses about its environment. At the bare minimum this information will be perceptual. To know what goal-desire might be motivating a creature at a given moment a creature needs to know, first, what end it is pursuing and, second, how it might reasonably expect that end to be realized by its current behavior. Both of these require knowing to which features of its environment the creature is perceptually sensitive. If, therefore, a non-linguistic creature is to be able to attribute goal-desires to a fellow creature it must be able to formulate hypotheses about what that creature is perceiving.

Here too we can distinguish two ways of thinking about seeing by following F. Dretske, making a distinction between *simple seeing* and *epistemic seeing*. According to Dretske, what we see in simple seeing (or what he calls non-epistemic seeing) "is a function solely of what there is to see and what, given our visual apparatus and the conditions in which we employ it, we are capable of visually differentiating."[13] In contrast, epistemic seeing involves standing in a relation to a proposition (a thought). Epistemic seeing involves seeing *that* something is the case.

The argument from intentional ascent shows that non-linguistic creatures are not capable of understanding epistemic seeing, since this involves thinking about the perceiver's relation to a thought. But this is perfectly compatible with non-linguistic creatures being capable of thinking about the direct perceptual relations in which other creatures stand to objects. This allows non-linguistic creatures to engage in a primitive form of psychological explanation. A creature that knows what a conspecific or predator desires and has some sense of its perceptual sensitivity to the environmental layout (as well as an understanding of its motor capabilities) can expect to be able to predict its behavior with some success.

This restrictive interpretation of the "mind-reading" abilities of some non-linguistic creatures is compatible with much recent research into the extent to which non-human primates can properly be described as possessing a "theory of mind." There are well-documented examples of primate behavior that some prominent students of animal behavior have thought can only be interpreted as examples of interpersonal deception.[14] But the consensus opinion among primatologists is that a more parsimonious interpretation of these behaviors is to be preferred.[15] Many examples of what has come to be termed *tactical deception* can be understood as the manipulation, not of another's propositional attitudes, but simply of their visual perspective. Here is an example of a tactical deception in a troop of baboons in Ethiopia that lends itself to such an interpretation:

> An adult female spent 20 min gradually shifting in a seated position over a distance of about 2 m to a place behind a rock about 50 cm high where she began to groom the subadult male follower of the group—an interaction not tolerated by the adult male. As I was observing from a cliff slightly above [the animals] I could judge that the adult male leader could, from his resting position, see the tail, back and crown of the female's head, but not her front, arms and face: the subadult male sat in a bent position while being groomed, and was also invisible to the leader. The leader could thus see that she was present, but probably not that she groomed.[16]

The behavior of the female baboon, assuming that it is indeed to count as an instance of tactical deception, does not seem to require representing the beliefs of the alpha male. What she is doing is profiting from an understanding of the alpha male's visual "take" on the situation to escape detection. The female baboon needs only to appreciate the alpha male's line of sight and the fact that he would be prevented from seeing the subadult male by the intervening rock. This seems firmly at the level of simple seeing rather than epistemic seeing.

This example (and the discussion of animal "mind-reading" more generally) shows that the argument from intentional ascent to semantic ascent is compatible with taking non-linguistic animals to have fairly sophisticated cognitive abilities. The argument requires theorists to think critically about some contemporary research in animal cognition. It places limits on the conceptual abilities that can be attributed to non-linguistic creatures, but in so doing opens up new ways of interpreting the behaviors revealed by observation and experiment.

Reasoning, Rationality, and Logical Thinking

Explaining animal behavior in psychological terms forces us to consider questions of rationality and reasoning. Psychological explanations work because they identify beliefs and desires in the light of which the action being explained *makes sense* from the agent's perspective. To say that an action makes sense in the light of an agent's beliefs and desires is to say that it is the rational thing to do (or, at least, *a* rational thing to do) given those beliefs and desires. And that in turn means that, in at least some cases, a creature might *reason* her way from those beliefs and desires to acting in the relevant way. Reasoning and rationality are correlative notions. How should we make sense of those notions at the non-linguistic level?

Here is one way in which we *cannot* make sense of them. The argument from intentional ascent stands squarely in the way of treating animals as thinking logically. We can illustrate this with the most basic form of logical thinking—the form of thinking codified in the propositional calculus and involving the basic logical connectives, such as disjunction ("or"), conjunction ("and"), and the material conditional ("if . . . then . . ."). Consider a conditional thought of the sort that might be expressed in the sentence "if A then B." To entertain such a thought is to understand that two thoughts are related in a certain way—namely, that the second thought cannot be false if the first thought is true. But this means that understanding truth-functional compound thoughts is a form of intentional ascent. One cannot think about the truth-values of thoughts without thinking about thoughts and this, by the earlier argument, requires semantic ascent.

Logical thinking depends upon language, therefore, because it presupposes the capacity for intentional ascent, which in turn depends upon semantic ascent. This poses an obvious challenge for how we think about reasoning in animals. The challenge is to identify forms of reasoning at the non-linguistic level and then explain them without assuming that the animal (or prelinguistic infant) is deploying elementary logical concepts. I will illustrate how this challenge can be met for a very basic form of reasoning. This is straightforward conditional reasoning of the type formalized as *modus ponens*—reasoning that is standardly thought to exploit the validity of the inference from "if A then B" and "A" to "B." The detection of patterns of behavior is closely bound up with the possibility of conditional reasoning. A creature that knows that if the gazelles see the lion they will run away and that recognizes (perhaps on the basis of its understanding of the gazelles' visual perspective) that the lion will shortly be detected by the gazelles is in a position to predict that the gazelles will soon take flight.

In *Thinking without Words*, I propose looking for the sources of conditional reasoning in a primitive form of causal reasoning. Whereas conditional reasoning (in the sense codified in the propositional calculus) exploits truth-functional relations between complete thoughts, causal reasoning exploits causal conditions holding between states of affairs. Since causal relationships do not hold between complete thoughts, an understanding of causality presupposes no intentional ascent, and hence does not require language.

One might expect on experimental, observational, and evolutionary grounds that some capacity for causal cognition is very widespread among animals and available at a very early stage in human development.[17] The ability to detect certain types of causal regularity and to distinguish genuine causal relations from accidental conjunctions has obvious survival value. Causal dependence relations are directly observable, highly salient, and pragmatically significant in a way that no other dependence relations are.

How might causality be understood by non-linguistic animals? It seems plausible that the core of the understanding of causation at the non-linguistic level is sensitivity to regularities in the distal environment. A basic sensitivity to environmental regularities must be part of the innate endowment of any creature capable of learning about the environment, and one might expect any creature to be peculiarly sensitive to regularities between its own actions and ensuing changes in its immediate environment (which is why instrumental conditioning works as well as it does). Of course, as regularity theories of causation have been forced to acknowledge, there are many regularities that are not causal, and it is in the capacity to distinguish genuinely causal regularities from accidental regularities that one might expect differences between different species of non-linguistic creature and, for that matter, different stages of development within any given species. The regularities to which non-linguistic creatures are sensitive (unlike those usually stressed in regularity analyses of causation) need not be exceptionless. No creature that only acted on exceptionless regularities would fare well in evading predators and obtaining food.

Proto-causal understanding tracks relationships, which can be either deterministic or probabilistic, between states of affairs. This makes possible a (primitive) grasp of causation at the non-linguistic level. It also explains why primitive versions of certain fundamental inference forms are available at the non-linguistic level. We can term this "proto-conditional reasoning." Instead of treating animals as exploiting full-fledged conditionals (i.e., truth-functional compounds of thoughts) we can think of them as tracking causal relations between states of affairs. I call these *proto-conditionals*. Conditional reasoning in animals can be understood in terms of a proto-conditional together with an understanding, which may take the form of a perception or a memory, that the antecedent holds. The consequent will straightforwardly be detached.

We see, therefore, that the initial argument for the language dependence of logical thinking does not rule out the possibility of non-linguistic reasoning. We cannot, of course, understand non-linguistic reasoning as involving logical concepts (or any form of intentional ascent). But we can identify at the non-linguistic level forms of inference that are analogues of canonical logical inference forms and that can be deployed in practical reasoning without any mastery of logical concepts or capacity for higher-order thinking.

Conclusion

The study of animal cognition offers a rich field for theorists of animal ethics. There are significant continuities between the cognitive life of some non-linguistic animals and the cognitive life of human animals. Some species of animal are genuine thinkers in much the same way that humans count as genuine thinkers. That is, they behave in ways that reflect their desires and their beliefs about the environment. Others are genuine thinkers in a weaker sense—the sense characterized by what I have called the "minimalist conception of non-linguistic thought." Even at the minimalist level we are dealing with forms of behavior that cannot be explained purely in terms of conditioning or innate releasing mechanisms. Ethicists who think that the moral significance of animals is a function of their level of cognitive sophistication will need to take account of the subtle gradations between different types of thinking without words. They will also need to take on board the limits to non-linguistic thought imposed by the argument from intentional ascent. There are serious consequences to making the moral significance of animals depend upon the capacity for higher-order thought (thinking about thinking—or metarepresentation). Nonetheless, the types of cognitive activity that are ruled out by the argument from intentional ascent are more limited than might immediately appear. As I brought out with reference to non-linguistic "mind-reading" and non-linguistic reasoning, non-linguistic animals can get a long way without thinking about thinking!

Notes

1. J. L. Bermúdez, *Thinking without Words* (Oxford: Oxford University Press, 2003).
2. See, for example, N. Tinbergen, *The Study of Instinct* (Oxford: Oxford University Press, 2003).
3. S. E. G. Lea, *Instinct, Environment and Behavior* (London: Methuen, 1984).
4. Michael Dummett, *The Origins of Analytical Philosophy* (London: Duckworth, 1993).
5. Gilbert Ryle, *The Concept of Mind* (London: Hutchinson, 1949), Chapter 2.
6. See R. W. Byrne, *The Thinking Ape* (Oxford: Oxford University Press, 1995), p. 97.
7. See Bermúdez, *Thinking without Words*, Chapters 4 and 5 and for a shorter overview, J. L. Bermúdez, "Ascribing Thoughts to Non-Linguistic Creatures," *Facta Philosophica* 5 (2003), pp. 313–334.
8. W. V. O. Quine, *Word and Object* (Cambridge: Harvard University Press, 1960), p. 271.
9. The theory of mental models was first proposed in K. Craik, *The Nature of Explanation* (Cambridge, UK: Cambridge University Press, 1943) and is most comprehensively developed in P. Johnson Laird, *Mental Models* (Cambridge: Cambridge University Press, 1983). For mental maps, see D. Braddon-Mitchell and F. Jackson, *The Philosophy of Mind and Cognition*, 2nd ed. (London: Black Publishers, 2006), Chapter 10.
10. The thinker who merely thinks such thoughts (as opposed to thinking *about* them) does not have to grasp these entailment and evidential relations. They simply have to think in ways that *respect* them.
11. See, for example, D. Rosenthal, "Two Concepts of Consciousness," *Philosophical Studies* 49 (1986), pp. 329–359.
12. See Bermúdez, *Thinking without Words*, pp. 48–49.
13. F. Dretske, *Seeing and Knowing* (London: Routledge, 1969), p. 76.
14. See, for example, the papers in R. W. Byrne and A. Whiten (eds.), *Machiavellian Intelligence* (Oxford: Oxford University Press, 1995); D. Premack and G. Woodruff, "Does the Chimpanzee Have a Theory of Mind?" *Behavioral and Brain Sciences* 1 (1978), pp. 515–526; and F. de Waal, *Chimpanzee Politics* (London: Jonathan Cape, 1982).
15. E.g., D. Povinelli, "Chimpanzee Theory of Mind," in P. Carruthers and P. K. Smith (eds.), *Theories of Theory of Mind* (Cambridge: Cambridge University Press, 1996), 243–329; and M. D. Hauser, *Wild Minds* (London: Penguin Books, 2000).
16. Report by Hans Kummer quoted in Byrne, *The Thinking Ape,* p. 106.
17. See D. Sperber (ed.), *Causal Cognition* (Oxford: Oxford University Press, 1995).

Consciousness, Emotion, and Suffering

12 Animal Pain

Bernard E. Rollin

Rollin summarizes the rationale for asserting the scientific incoherence of denying pain in animals, the observability of mental states in animals, the commonsense nature of mentation in animals, and the application of morality to animals in light of these understandings. He then points out how the human benefits derived from animals facilitated the rejection of ascribing moral worth to their treatment.

The Scientific Incoherence of Denying Pain in Animals

[. . .]

As Darwinians recognised, it is arbitrary and incoherent, given the theories and information current in science, to rule out mentation for animals, particularly such a basic, well-observed mental state as pain.

[. . .]

One can well believe that only by thinking of animal pain in terms of Cartesian, mechanical processes devoid of an experiential, morally relevant dimension could scientists have done the experimental work which has created the sophisticated neurophysiology we have today. But given that science, the neurophysiological analogies that have been discovered between humans and animals, certainly at least the vertebrates, are powerful arguments against the Cartesianism which made it possible. In a dialectical irony which would surely have pleased Hegel, Cartesianism has been its own undoing, by demonstrating more and more identical neurophysiological mechanisms in humans and animals, mechanisms which make it highly implausible that animals are merely machines if we are not.[1]

Pain and pleasure centres, like those found in humans, have been reported in the brains of birds, mammals, and fish; and the neural mechanisms responsible for pain behaviour are remarkably similar in all vertebrates. Anaesthetics and analgesics control what appears to be pain in all vertebrates and some invertebrates; and, perhaps most dramatically, the biological feedback mechanisms for controlling pain seem to be remarkably similar in all vertebrates, involving serotonin, endorphins and enkephalins, and substance P. (Endorphins have been found even in earthworms.) The very existence of endogenous opiates in animals is powerful evidence that they feel pain. Animals would hardly have neurochemicals and pain-inhibiting systems identical to ours and would hardly show the same diminution of pain signs as we do if their experiential pain were not being controlled by these mechanisms in the same way that ours is. In certain shock experiments, large doses of naloxone have been given to traumatized animals, reversing the effect of endogenous opiates, and it has been shown that animals so treated die as a direct result of uncontrolled pain.[2] In 1987, it was shown that bradykinin antagonists control pain in both humans and animals.

Denial of pain consciousness in animals is incompatible not only with neurophysiology, but with what can be extrapolated from evolutionary theory as well. There is reason to believe that evolution preserves and perpetuates successful biological systems. Given that the mechanisms of pain in vertebrates are the same, it strains credibility to suggest that the experience of pain suddenly emerges at the level of humans. Granted, it is growing increasingly popular, following theorists like Gould and Lewontin, to assume the existence of quantum leaps in evolution, rather than assume that all evolution proceeds incrementally by minute changes. But surely such a hypothesis is most applicable where there is evidence of a morphological trait which seems to suddenly appear in the fossil record. With regard to mental traits, this hypothesis might conceivably apply to the appearance of language in humans, if Chomsky and others are correct in their argument that human language differs in kind, as well as degree, from communication systems in other species. But in other areas of mentation—most areas apart from the most sophisticated intellectual abilities—and surely with regard to basic mental survival equipment like that connected with pain, such a hypothesis is both *ad hoc* and implausible. Human pain machinery is virtually the same as that in animals, and we know from experience with humans that the ability to *feel* pain is essential to survival; that people with a congenital or acquired inability to feel pain or with afflictions such as Hansen's disease (leprosy), which affects the ability to feel pain, are unlikely to do well or even survive without extraordinary, heroic attention. The same is true of animals, of course—witness the recent case of Taub's deafferented monkeys (in whom the sensory nerves serving the limbs had been severed), who mutilated themselves horribly in the absence of the ability to feel. *Feeling* pain and the motivational influence of feeling it are essential to the survival of the system, and to suggest that the system is purely mechanical in animals but not in man is therefore highly implausible. If pain had worked well as a purely mechanical system in animals without a subjective dimension, why would it suddenly appear in man *with* such a dimension? (Unless, of course, one invokes some such theological notion as original sin and pain as divine punishment—hardly a legitimate scientific move!) And obviously, similar argument would hold for discomfort associated with hunger, thirst, and other so-called drives, as well as with pleasures such as that of sexual congress.

So not only does much scientific activity presuppose animal pain, as we have seen *vis-à-vis* pain research and psychological research, it fits better with neurophysiology and evolutionary theory to believe that animals have mental experiences than to deny it. Outside positivistic-behaviouristic ideology, there seems little reason to deny pain (or fear, anxiety, boredom—in short, all rudimentary forms of mentation) to animals on either factual or conceptual grounds. (Indeed, research indicates that all vertebrates have receptor sites for benzodiazepine, which, in turn, suggests that the physiological basis of anxiety exists in all vertebrates.)[3] One may cavil at attributing higher forms of reason to animals, as Lloyd Morgan did, but that is ultimately a debatable, and in large part empirically decidable, question.

The Alleged Unobservability of Mental States

The one lingering doubt which positivism leaves us with concerns the ultimate unobservability of mental states in animals. After all, we cannot experience them, even in principle. Perhaps there is something fundamentally wrong with admitting such unobservable entities to scientific discourse, for would we not be opening a Pandora's box containing such undesirable notions as souls, demons, angels, entelechies, life forces, absolute space, and the rest? Would we not be giving up the hard-won ground by which we demarcate science from other forms of knowing, and opening ourselves to a dissolution of the line between science and metaphysics, science and speculation? Surely that consideration must far outweigh any benefit of admitting animal mentation into legitimate scientific discourse.

Since this is the key (official) reason behind the common sense of science's refusal to talk about animal mentation, it is worth examining in some detail. The first assumption behind this view is obviously that science is, or can be, and surely ought to be, totally empirical—in other words, that science ought to make no assumptions, postulate no entities, and countenance no terms which cannot be cashed empirically. This is, indeed, a mainstay of classical, hard-line positivism.

[. . .]

Mental States as a Perceptual Category

[T]here is no good 'scientific' reason for acquiescing to positivism's demand that only observables be permitted in science—first, because that demand cannot itself be observationally proved, and second, because it would exclude all sorts of basic things like other people and intersubjective physical objects in which science has much stake. Furthermore, it has become increasingly clear since Kant that there is no good reason for believing that facts can be gathered or even observations made independently of a theoretical base. Kant showed that sensory information must be 'boxed' before it becomes an object of experience, that even the notions of 'object' and 'event' are brought to sensation, rather than emerging from it. Indeed, examples demonstrating the role of theory in the broadest sense in perception are endless. To see a fracture or a lesion on a radiograph requires an enormous amount of theoretical equipment and a great deal of training, for which the radiologist is very well paid; though he gets the same sensations on his retina as you or I do, he doesn't see the same thing as we do. This is equally true of the woodland tracker, who spots a trail or some sign of an animal's passage; the artist, who sees dozens of colours in a person's face, whereas most of us see only 'flesh colour'; the horse *aficionado* who sees a thoroughbred, while we see only a horse. And what we see in the standard ambivalent figures like the one which can be seen as a vase or as two faces or the duck-rabbit or the young-old woman depends on what we are thinking about, expecting, hypothesizing, and the like.

Indeed, returning to our main concern, what we perceive or observe in science or consider worthy of calling a fact must be in large measure determined by our metaphysical commitments and their associated values. Aristotle saw the world as an array of facts of function and teleology. Galileo saw a mathematical machine. In so far as common sense has a metaphysics and an epistemology, it surely maintains that we perceive the mental states of others. Contrary to the stories that many philosophers have told in the twentieth century, and which we discussed earlier, I do not believe that common sense uses mental terms like 'happy', 'afraid', 'bored', and so on only to refer to overt behaviour in appropriate contexts. Nor do I believe that common sense simply *infers* mental states by analogy from overt behaviour. I think, rather, that common sense *perceives* mental states in others in exactly the way that it perceives physical states or objects.

[. . .]

On this view, perceiving in terms of mentation is one of the categories by which we commonsensi-cally process reality, and mentation is a fundamental plank upon which our commonsense metaphys-ics is built. And the reason why this notion is so geographically and historically pervasive is because it works so well. Nothing can disconfirm our attribution of mentation to other humans *in general*, because mentation is a (if not *the*) fundamental cognitive category by which we map other humans.

[. . .]

When we use words attributing passion, rage, sadness, joy, depression, and the like to other people, we surely do not do so in the absence of behaviour relevant to and expressive of these mental states. On the other hand, we are not just talking about the behaviour; we are unavoidably referring to what the behaviour is directly and essentially tied to—namely, a feeling which, while perhaps somewhat unlike mine, serves the same function in the other person's life as the feeling in question does in mine.

[. . .]

Morality and the Perception of Mental States

There are doubtless a number of major reasons for our ubiquitous presumption of subjective experi-ences in others. Most obvious is the fact that without this presumption, we could not as readily pre-dict or understand the actions of others. Second, in so far as we are taught moral concern for others, such concern is cogent only on the presumption that others have subjective experiences, that we can more or less know them, that their subjective states matter to them more or less as mine matter to me, and that my actions have major effects on what matters to them and on what they subjectively experience. If we genuinely didn't believe that others felt pain, pleasure, fear, joy, and so on, there would be little point to moral locutions or moral exhortations. Morality presupposes that the objects of our moral concern have feelings. And, what is logically equivalent, if there is no presumption of the possibility of feeling in an entity, there is little reason to speak of it 'in the moral tone of voice'.

Of course, the presumption of feeling is only a necessary condition for moral concern, not a suf-ficient one. One must also believe that the feelings of others warrant our attention. For most people, the mere realization that others experience negative feelings in the same way that they themselves do is enough to generate a stance of moral concern. . . .

[T]he attribution of mental states, especially those associated with pleasure and pain, joy and misery, is connected irrevocably with the possibility of morality. For this reason, only a science with blinders to the moral universe, and, most especially, only a *psychology* provided with such blinders could ever deny not only the legitimacy of talking about mental states, but their fundamental place in the world, which a genuine psychology must seek to explain.

[. . .]

Application of This Theory to Animals

But what of animals? Clearly, common sense and ordinary language have traditionally extended the presumption of mentation to animals. (In some cultures, this was explained by viewing animals as reincarnated humans.) Probably the major reason for doing so was that it works. By assuming that animals feel and have other subjective experiences, we can explain and predict their behaviour (and control it as well). Why beat a dog if it doesn't hurt him? Why does a lion hunt if it isn't hungry? Why does a dog drool and beg for scraps from the table if they don't taste good? Why does a cat in heat rub up against the furniture if it doesn't feel good? Why do animals scratch if they don't itch? Again, common sense continued to think in this way regardless of what scientific ideology dictated, and scientists continued to think in this way in their ordinary moments.

The moral reason for presuming consciousness and mental states in animals does not loom nearly so large. It is an interesting fact that although most cultures in most times and places have attributed mentation to animals, few have clearly set out moral rules for their treatment, and for many, animals do not enter the moral arena. For some philosophers, granting moral status to animals is highly problematic, which is why so many of them have been concerned, like Descartes, to prove that animals are really automata. For others, like Hume, who deem it absurd to deny the full range of mental experience to animals, and who are highly cognizant of the connection between morality and feeling, the question of moral treatment of animals nevertheless does not arise. For ordinary people, though their presumption of mentation in animals is strong, their application of moral notions to animals is minimal or non-existent. Only thus can one explain why for centuries animals were held morally and legally responsible for their actions, subject to trial, punishment, and death, yet at the same time had no legal protection whatever.[4]

Why is this the case? Why has common sense (and until recently the legal system as well) studiously avoided coming to grips with our moral obligations to other creatures?[5] For that matter, why has philosophy, which has notoriously concerned itself with all sorts of questions and which has explored all aspects of ethical theory, been virtually blind to questions concerning animals? (There are, of course, notable exceptions, such as the Pythagoreans; but here we must recall that their concern grew out of the doctrine of transmigration of human souls.) There is no certain answer to this question. Perhaps part of an answer lies in the influence of our theological traditions, most especially the Christian tradition, which has stressed that the proper study of man is man. More plausibly perhaps, a key part of the answer lies in a remark made to me by one of my veterinary students at the end of an ethics course in which I put great stress on moral questions pertaining to animals. 'If I take your teaching seriously', she said,

> no part of my life is untouched, and all parts are severely shaken. For if I ascribe moral status to animals, I must worry about the food I eat, the clothes I wear, the cosmetics I use, the drugs I take, the pets I keep, the horses I ride, the dogs I castrate and euthanize, and the research I do. The price of morality is too high—I'd rather ignore the issue.

Perhaps in a culture which has no choice but to exploit animals in order to survive, one cannot even begin to think about these questions, or even see them as moral choices rather than pragmatic necessities. Or perhaps because the use of animals for our purposes without consideration of their interests is so pervasive and our dependence upon it so great, it becomes invisible to us, in much the same way that exploitation of women and minorities was invisible for too long. Indeed, it is interesting that moral interest in these long-neglected areas arose at virtually the same historical time and place, a point to which we will return.

If I am at all correct, the traditional commonsense view of animals went something like this. On the one hand, common sense took it for granted that animals were conscious and experienced pain, fear, sadness, joy, and a whole range of mental states. Indeed, at times common sense probably gave too much credit to the mental lives of many animals, falling into a mischievous anthropomorphism. Yet in the same breath, common sense consistently ignored the obvious moral problems growing out of attributing thought and feeling to animals, since it had an unavoidable stake in using them in manners which inevitably caused them pain, suffering, and death, and thus, ordinary common sense had its own compartmentalization in this area. Indeed, such animal use was often directed not only at satisfying basic needs such as food and clothing, but more frivolous ones, such as entertainment, as in bear- and bull-baiting, fox-hunting, falconry, bull-fighting, cock-fighting, dog-fighting, gladiatorial contests, and indiscriminate bird shoots. (If the moral issue *was* ever raised, the 'Nature is red in tooth and claw anyway' and 'Animals kill each other' responses quickly dismissed it.)

In this way, though common sense and Darwinism reinforced one another, in general, neither felt the need to draw out the obvious moral implications of its position (allowing, of course, for a few exceptions like M. P. Evans and Henry Salt).[6] And when what we have called the ideology or common sense of science arose, at about the same time that animal experimentation became a crucial part of scientific activity, it had both an ideological and a vested interest in perpetuating blindness to moral issues. Hence, though it violated both common sense and the evolutionary theory which it continued to accept by its denial of animal consciousness, positivistic-behaviouristic ideology, with its denial of the legitimacy of asking moral questions in and about science, buttressed, reinforced, and even to some extent justified and grounded common sense's and Darwinism's systematic disregard of moral issues surrounding animal use and exploitation. Though common sense might balk at science's denial of consciousness to animals, it had no problem at all with science's rejection of moral concern for animals, since scientific use of animals was, after all, like agricultural and other uses of animals, one more area of human benefit. Even lurid, periodic newspaper accounts of 'vivisection' aroused in most people not so much moral indignation as aesthetic revulsion—'I don't want to know about that.' (Most people still react that way to slaughterhouses and packing plants.) Thus, for a long time, there was little social moral opposition to scientific denial or ignoring of animal pain, suffering, and mentation, even as common sense might have objected to the strangeness of quantum theory, but certainly had no moral qualms about it. So, for science, convenience and ideology went hand in hand, and both were unchecked by common sense, which mostly didn't care much about what scientists did. Though it thought their activities odd, it certainly didn't worry about them morally, most especially in biomedical areas, which promised—and delivered—many glittering advances of direct benefit to all of us. And, as we have seen, common sense's tolerant attitude towards biomedical research was not limited to animal subjects; it extended for a long time to human subjects as well, especially when the subjects were not 'us', but 'them'—prisoners, indigents, primitives, lunatics, retarded persons, and the like.

Notes

1. Stephen Walker's recent book *Animal Thought* elegantly documents the neurophysiological similarity between humans and animals.
2. M. Fettman et al., 'Naloxone therapy in awake endotoxemic Yucatan minipigs'.
3. J. A. Gray, *The Neuropsychology of Anxiety*.
4. M. P. Evans, *Criminal Prosecution and Capital Punishment of Animals*.
5. See Rollin, *Animal Rights*, pt. 2.
6. M. P. Evans, *Evolutional Ethics and Animal Psychology*; H. S. Salt, *Animals' Rights Considered in Relation to Social Progress*.

13 A Neuropsychological and Evolutionary Approach to Animal Consciousness and Animal Suffering

Bob Bermond

Bermond reviews the literature for evidence of whether an irreflexive animal consciousness, experienced only in the present and which adds no cognition to the experience, could experience suffering. He argues that irreflexive consciousness and suffering aren't linked because to experience suffering, a well-developed prefrontal cortex is needed. Since the prefrontal cortex is phylogenetically the most recent structure, it is likely that most animals are unable to experience suffering. He concludes that emotional experiences of animals, and therefore suffering, may only be expected in anthropoid apes.

Introduction

At first sight this contribution will be a bit weird for some readers. The reason for this is that the issues of consciousness and suffering both have a long tradition in psychology, therefore most arguments stem not from the field of ethology, but from the field of (neuro)psychology. It follows that, with regard to animals, the arguments presented are only valid if one assumes that if there is animal consciousness or animal suffering, they should not be qualitatively different from human consciousness and human suffering. One could, of course, like Bateson (1991) assume that various animal species have their own type of consciousness and that it may be totally different from human consciousness. There is nothing wrong with assumptions: science flourishes with assumptions. However, such flourishing is only possible if the assumption is specified (in this case by describing how the assumed animal consciousness deviates from the human consciousness), because only then is it possible to analyse the logical consequences of the assumption and only then is it a contribution to science. Since, with the exception of the idea of an irreflexive animal consciousness, I have never seen such specifications in the literature, I have chosen to present two approaches to the question of animal consciousness and animal suffering: first, an analysis of the idea of an irreflexive consciousness, and second, an analysis of the idea of an animal consciousness and animal suffering based upon the assumption that such an animal consciousness and animal suffering are not qualitatively different from the only consciousness and suffering we know anything about, human consciousness and human suffering. With this warning to the readers, I can start with my contribution.

There is no generally accepted theory about consciousness (Lokhorst 1986; Wilkes 1988; de Vries 1991) and there is further serious doubt whether we will have such a theory in the near future (Chalmers 1996). Due to this deficiency, the door is wide open for all kinds of weird theories and assumptions and, if the argument is dominated by social aims, science will be reduced to politics. For instance, Verheijen et al. (1993) wrote: 'to decide whether or not to accept the analogy-postulate, the strength of arguments not only play a role, but also the consequences of acceptance versus rejection'. Dawkins is subtler—referring to 'welfare measurement', she wrote (1998 p 308): 'such gross welfare measures should be made at the level of the individual animal, not the farm unit'. If that were turned into practice, then farm animals would have more social security than people, and farming would become a troublesome business. Dawkins' statement is all the more surprising because in the same article she states that there are no correct welfare measurements at hand (Dawkins 1998 p 323):

> In a thoughtful and provocative essay entitled *The Myth of Animal Suffering*, Bermond (1997) correctly points out that none of the methods proposed so far for assessing 'suffering' in animals actually do so. 'Suffering', as applied to humans, means conscious experience of something very unpleasant. Strictly speaking, none of the measures of 'poor welfare' or 'stress' discussed so far demonstrates the presence of comparable states in nonhuman animals.

Several attempts have been made to substantiate the idea that most animals do have consciousness and are therefore capable of experiencing suffering. The following substantiating arguments for animal suffering are mentioned in the literature: (i) physiological stress responses in animals; (ii) conditioning of animals by negative reinforcers; (iii) emotional behaviour in animals; (iv) registration of behaviours indicating that some animals will overcome various barriers in order to flee from negative situations; (v) information processing by animals on a rather high level; (vi) Romanes' analogy postulate; (vii) the assumption that there are species-specific types of consciousness; and, finally, (viii) Pepperberg's talking parrot. Since I have argued before that all these arguments and assumptions are incorrect (Bermond 1997, 1998), I will not discuss them here and will merely refer to these earlier publications.

In this contribution, 'suffering' is, in accordance with Dawkins (1998), defined as a conscious negative mental state, because suffering does not refer to behaviour but to an experience, and experiences are by definition conscious. Consciousness is, in this contribution, defined as 'knowing that you know'. An irreflexive consciousness is, within this definition, in principle possible. Further, this definition is less severe than that of, for instance, Carruthers (1989), who assumed that there is only consciousness if the knowing that you know results in further conscious cognitions.

An Irreflexive Animal Consciousness?

An irreflexive consciousness is a consciousness with neither past nor future and which does not add any cognition to the experience. For instance, Lijmbach, who assumes such an irreflexive consciousness in animals, states (Lijmbach 1998 pp 5, 149): 'I will emphasise this distinction and say that animal experience, unlike human experience, is impersonal, bodily bound, here-and-now experience', and: 'many ethologists see animal experiences as separated from animal behaviour, namely as causes of behaviour. I do not see them as separated from, and certainly not as causally related to, behaviour'. In other words, an irreflexive consciousness is a minimum, a pure phenomenological consciousness, containing only qualia without accompanying cognitions and without any function for behaviour.

Qualia refer to the quality of perceptions, in particular to those aspects of the perception which are represented in the physical world in a different way. For instance, in the physical world there are electromagnetic waves with different wavelengths. However, we do not see wavelength, we see colours. Likewise, smells are, in the physical world, just certain molecules. The qualia (colours, taste, pain, emotional feelings, odours and sounds) exist, therefore, only in the mind of the conscious perceiver and not in the physical world. This is distinct from the cognitive aspects of a perception. When we see a yellow house, and we are not hallucinating, then there is a house in the outside world, but the yellow is only in our brain or mind.

This definition of qualia could easily lead to the false idea that correct animal motor responses to what humans experience as qualia are proof of animal consciousness. However, since it is known that most human reactions to stimuli are initiated before the stimulus is consciously perceived (see later in this contribution), it is possible that some species react to, for instance, different electromagnetic wavelengths without seeing anything. In fact, this has been described for some humans with lesions in the primary visual cortex. These persons are blind in the sense that they cannot see consciously any more, but they are still capable of giving correct motor responses to the 'unseen' stimuli (Weiskrantz et al. 1974; Sacks 1995). This phenomenon has been named 'blindsight'. It has further been described that such people can, using this blindsight, also differentiate correctly between various colours, although they cannot experience the quale (singular of qualia) of the colours, since they process visual stimuli only at a non-conscious level (Weiskrantz 1997).

The idea of a minimum consciousness has also been a subject in philosophy. Chalmers (1996), who separates qualia from cognition, assumes that such a consciousness could exist and, according to him, it is an epiphenomenon. He assumes that such a consciousness containing only qualia does not emanate from the brain but that it is a basic natural phenomenon in itself which cannot be explained by physics: these ideas do not have many supporters.

Dennett (1996) and Searle (1997) have also speculated about such a minimum consciousness and both reject the idea. Dennett argues that such a minimum consciousness should not only have sensitivity, like a thermostat or photographic paper, but also something extra (X) in order to lift or turn the sensitivity into a conscious experience, and he asks himself (Dennett 1996 p 62):

> What does sentience amount to, above and beyond sensitivity? This is a question seldom asked and has never been properly answered. We shouldn't assume that there's a good answer. We shouldn't assume, in other words, that it's a good question.

According to Dennett, the real question is therefore what this X is, and since there has been no one so far who could even suggest what this X may be, it is therefore better to reject this idea altogether.

Searle sets it aside because, according to him, the qualia and the accompanying cognitions cannot be separated from one another, since if they could there would be no consciousness left (Searle 1997). Likewise, Baars (1997 p 84) states: 'even animals with mainly sensory consciousness must be able to think about events outside the sensory field'. Baars's and Searle's ideas become clearer if we ask ourselves what an irreflexive consciousness could experience if the input was, for instance, a lemon. Certainly not a lemon, because that requires cognitive processing. In fact not even a yellow spot, since that is a cognitive interpretation also. What will be left is the experience of pure 'lemon yellow', whatever that may be. However, although we lack the imagination to conceive of such experiences, it is no proof that such experiences could not exist.

The emotional psychologist Frijda (1986) also makes a plea for an irreflexive consciousness and so a plea for animal consciousness. Frijda states (1986 p 188):

> Irreflexive emotional experience also, by its very nature, is 'projective': the properties are out there. These properties contain the relationship to the subject: emotional experience is perception of horrible objects, insupportable people, oppressive events. They contain that relationship implicitly: the 'to me' or 'for me' dissolves into the property.

This author has an ornate style and is therefore sometimes hard to understand. What is meant here? Firstly, it is assumed that there is a relationship between the subject, the 'I', and the properties in the outside world which induces the emotional feeling. Secondly, it is assumed that this concept of 'I' or 'to me' or 'for me' dissolves into the properties of the outside world. One thing is clear: there is a contradiction—there is a concept of 'I', and at the same time this concept dissolves into thin air! The author does not explain how this dissolving takes place, he just states: 'the notion of irreflexive experience is that of awareness without awareness of itself' (Frijda 1986 p 188). However, we can still imagine something from Frijda's statement. During 'blind rage' or the *'crime passionnel'* we act like a machine, without any reflection; the reflection only comes afterwards, as does remorse. The 'I' concept does not dissolve: it is, during such an act, simply not there. The crucial question here, however, is whether we could become so angry without having ever registered that we are individuals among other individuals. If that were the case, then it would have been impossible to blame someone else for our misfortune and it is this blaming which induces the feeling of anger. In other words, the emotional experience becomes, without the concept of 'I' or 'me', not only aimless but also without content.

Emotions are triggered by stimuli which are, for some reason, important to the perceiver (Frijda 1986). For this reason, conscious reflection is sometimes required, since it is sometimes only after the reflection that the importance becomes clear. Further, we cannot imagine emotional experiences without accompanying conscious cognitions: for instance, the feeling of fear is unthinkable without thoughts like: 'How can I escape?', 'What should I do?', 'Should I defend myself or should I run?', etc. All these thoughts are part of our emotional experience. Finally, the emotional experience needs a subject. It is always an 'I' who is sad, afraid or happy. It is not, as Frijda assumes, projected onto the outside world. 'We' are irate if we are maltreated, but the world around us is not angry. The emotional feeling is part of us, not of the environment. The environment contains the emotion-inducing stimuli not the emotional feeling. However, the emotional behaviour does not require emotional feelings (Bermond 1997, 1998 and later in this contribution). If we add a fear-substance (a substance secreted by some types of fish after they are wounded) into an aquarium, then all other fish of that species will flee and hide, even if there is no predator around (Verheijen 1988; Bateson 1991). The fish's behaviour is induced by a stimulus response mechanism without any cognitive interpretation and, therefore, as we will see later, without any accompanying emotional feelings. In such cases, one could rightly say that the 'fear' is in the aquarium and not in the fish, which only show fear behaviour. However, if we speak about a fear experience, then it is the subject who is loaded with emotions and not the environment. It is for this reason that LeDoux (1989) writes: 'emotional experiences, it is proposed, result when stimulus representations, affect representations, and self-representations coincide in working memory'. In other words, the emotional experience requires the concept of self, or self-consciousness.

Irreflexive Consciousness and Pain or Suffering

Suffering is the experience of pain and negative emotions such as fear, sorrow and guilt. Although pain has already been defined by Aristotle and Plato as an emotion (Menges 1992), most people still think that the pain experience is just a sensorial experience. The fact that all sensorial experiences, except pain, can be induced by electrical stimulation of sensorial cortex (Libet 1982) indicates that pain is more than just a sensorial experience. There are two types of pain: (i) pain as a sensorial registration which is experienced as neither negative nor positive and (ii) pain as a pain experience or pain emotion, which does induce suffering (Trigg 1970; Menges 1992). Likewise, Sherrington, who, early last century, observed pain behaviour in decorticated mammals, which he described as 'pseudo affective', drew a distinction between pain and 'nociception' (Bateson 1991). Furthermore, pain behaviour does not need a conscious pain experience, as is indicated by the pain behaviour of paraplegic patients (Jennett 1989). This observation also indicates that pain behaviour is already partly regulated at the spinal cord level.

The emotional experience, and thus the pain experience, disappears if our natural tendency to reflect upon the pain is blocked, as for instance after destruction of our evolutionarily most recent brain parts, the prefrontal cortex (PFC; Trigg 1970; Damasio et al. 1990). It was for this reason that in the 1940s and 50s, frontal lobotomy was used as a remedy to block chronic pain (Freeman & Watts 1950; Freeman 1971; Kucharski 1984; Kolb & Whishaw 1990). The pain before the operation was overwhelming and permanently the centre of attention, while after the operation patients lost any interest in their pain, although they claimed that the pain itself had not changed. After the operation the sensed pain did not annoy them anymore; the pain left them literally cold (Trigg 1970). The important issue here is that such people can still experience pain as a pain stimulus, but they cannot experience it as a pain emotion, and thus they cannot experience pain suffering anymore (Krystal & Raskin 1970; Trigg 1970).

The fact that pain suffering needs pain-related reflection explains why we can reduce our pain experience by directing our thinking to other issues, a trick used by many people when their molars are drilled out by a dentist. Further, since there are cultural differences in pain expectations, this also explains cultural differences in pain suffering, because the less pain we expect, the less pain-related reflection, and thus the less pain we experience. Lerich, a front surgeon in the First World War, was told by Russian officers that the Cossacks did not need narcotics during operations. Limited in supplies, Lerich tried, although against his 'better' judgement, amputations on Cossacks without narcotics. To his surprise the 'poor victims' showed no signs of pain experience (Menges 1992).

It is interesting that after frontal lobotomy, when the emotional experience has fully disappeared, the frequency of emotional behaviours is increased, whereas the duration of emotional responses is decreased. At the same time, the emotional behaviour becomes, as it is in most animal species, stimulus-bound (Levine & Albert 1948; Freeman & Watts 1950; Jarvie 1954; Nemiah 1962; Trigg 1970; Kucharski 1984; Fuster 1989; Valenstein 1990; Damasio & Anderson 1993; Malloy & Duffy 1994). The behaviour of prefrontal patients is 'captured by salient sensory cues that reflectively elicit strongly associated actions. They are unable to override these impulses' (Miller 2000 p 61). This not only demonstrates that there are different neural circuits for emotional behaviour and emotional feelings, but also that it is the emotional feeling which gives, by emotional rumination, the emotion duration until long after the external emotion-inducing stimuli have disappeared. Since the extended emotion steers our behaviour, it often results in maladapted behaviour. The psychological defence mechanism of displacement (you are angry at your boss, but you are not allowed to show that and therefore you yell, hours later, at your children or spouse) is an example of such maladapted behaviour. Such an extension of the emotional period is absent in most animal species. The lioness does not fall into a depression when her cubs are killed by the new alpha male: after a few days she comes into heat and mates with the killer. The foster parent birds do not hate the cuckoo chick which throws their own young out of the nest: they just keep on feeding the little bastard. It should be kept in mind that subjective feelings in humans require the PFC and are therefore thought to be a relatively late evolutionary development (Plutchik 1994). As stated above, the extension of the emotional period due to the emotional feeling means that the emotion endures after all external emotion-inducing stimuli have disappeared and that the emotion is kept alive with the aid of internal stimuli. Therefore, descriptions of animals which show long-term emotional behaviour while the inducing stimuli are still there cannot be used as an argument for animal consciousness. For instance, the primatologist Frans de Waal describes female monkeys which will often carry around their deceased baby for days, but if they lose the corpse, simply because it has fallen apart due to decay, then immediately all signs of grief disappear (de Waal 1996).

The experience of suffering requires reflection, imagination and understanding of 'duration', of past and future. Dennett writes (1996 pp 166–167):

> Many discussions seem to assume tacitly that suffering and pain are the same thing, on a different scale; that all pain is 'experienced pain'; and that the 'amount of suffering' is to be calculated ('in principle') just by adding up all the pains. . . . What is wrong with this scenario is, of course, that you can't detach pain and suffering from their contexts. What is awful about losing your job, or your leg, or your reputation, or your loved one is not the suffering this event causes in you, but the suffering this event is.

Dennett's aim here is to indicate that the loss of, for instance, a child can only result in the experience of suffering if the context knowledge concerning that child (how life was when the child was still alive) can be retained, or if one can, much later, imagine how life now would be if the child were still around. Without knowledge of past and future, reflection and imagination, which are by definition absent in the irreflexive consciousness, there is no suffering.

In conclusion, we may say that if there is such a thing as an irreflexive consciousness, then it will be free of pain experiences and suffering, although it remains possible that such a consciousness could still non-emotionally register pain stimuli which do not induce pain suffering.

Congenital Pain Indifference

Some people are born with pain indifference. They register pain, like frontal lobotomy patients, only as a stimulus and cannot experience pain as an emotion. They can therefore do all kinds of horrible things to themselves without being troubled by pain. Many of them could earn good money by performing 'pain' inducing theatre acts. One wanted to make a living by showing his own crucifixion. Special gold-plated wire nails were made, which were literally hammered through his hands and feet. Although he had planned several such performances, only one show was staged, since the audience fainted *en masse* during the first performance (Krystal & Raskin 1970). This is what remains of the pain experience if pain can only be registered as a stimulus and not experienced as a pain emotion. The suffering is in the observer, not in the 'self pain inducing' performer. Since we belong to a species which has, on average, a high capacity for empathy, we are inclined to project feelings of pain onto others if we get emotionally aroused by seeing that others are seriously hurt. That is why most of the public fainted while watching the crucifixion. For the same reason, it is almost impossible for us, because we become emotionally aroused if we see animals which are hurt or showing pain behaviour, to consider the possibility that these animals may not be suffering.

How Did Consciousness Develop?

Consciousness as a Natural 'Emergent' Property of Increasing Complexity

Some authors have argued that consciousness is an 'emergent' property of the increasing complexity of the brain, an idea which is now very popular in the field of artificial intelligence. However, Weiskrantz (1997) describes microscopically small lesions which do not make the human brain less complicated and which result in specific losses in consciousness. Weiskrantz therefore states (1997 p 82): 'it is obvious that the answer must lie in the way the nervous system is organised, not in complexity as such'. Further, since no one can indicate which level of complexity should be the turning point, this assumption remains in the domain of belief and is thus not a part of science. How should the question be approached?

Three Questions Concerning Consciousness and Suffering

In order to approach the problem of animal consciousness and animal suffering, we can pose ourselves three questions.

Firstly, we can ask ourselves which evolutionarily latest part of the human brain is a prerequisite for experiencing pain and suffering? Why the evolutionarily most recent brain part? Doesn't correct pain behaviour have an immense fitness value and should it not, for this reason, be assumed that it developed early in evolution? Yes, we should assume that! However, as argued before, pain behaviour is already regulated at the spinal cord level, while human pain emotion and the experience of suffering both need the PFC in order to occur. For these reasons, we have to assume that regulation of pain behaviour developed much earlier in evolution than the experience of pain suffering. Furthermore, brain parts are connected with one another. The longest distance between two neurones is only four synapses (Pöppel & Ruhnau 2000). Due to this high level of interconnection within the brain, inhibition or stimulation of a particular brain centre always results in inhibition or stimulation of other brain structures. This could easily result in wrong conclusions, as, for instance, Baars (1997), who, firstly, correctly states that after bilateral destruction of a rather small nucleus in the brainstem humans lose consciousness and, secondly, that these nuclei are also present in all vertebrates. He then uses these two statements as an argument for the assumption of consciousness in all vertebrates. What is the described function of these brainstem nuclei? They regulate, through their connections with the nuclei reticularis thalami, the amount of sensorial information which is sent to the neocortex

(Heilman et al. 1993). Unilateral destruction of one of these brainstem nuclei induces such a severe reduction in the amount of sensorial information sent to one side of the neocortex that it results in unilateral neglect (stimuli in one side of the 'Umwelt' [environment], although processed correctly on a non-conscious level, cannot reach the consciousness level anymore); bilateral destruction leads to neglect on both sides of the 'Umwelt' (Heilman et al. 1993). No wonder that such patients lose consciousness: since the neocortex is deprived of information and since all sensorial information remains unconscious, there is nothing for their consciousness to react to. Baars's suggestion is like pulling the plug of the television set and then stating that the image-producing device is in the plug and not in the picture tube. Baars's (1997) suggestion is all the more dubious, since elsewhere in the same book he writes that conscious visual perceptions need area 17 of the neocortex.

The higher up one is in the brain, or the information stream, the fewer difficulties one has with the interpretation of the results. One could, of course, when a particular function disappears after lesioning the evolutionarily newest neural structure, assume that this function does emanate from an evolutionarily older structure, lower in the brain, which only needs pre-processed information of the newer structure in order to 'produce' the function being studied. However, if we make such a rather dubious assumption, then it follows that the evolutionarily newer brain structure is still a prerequisite for that particular function to occur. It is for this reason that we have to look for the evolutionarily latest part of the human brain which is a prerequisite for the experience of pain as an emotion and suffering.

The line of reasoning presented here is, however, only correct if the functions of the evolutionarily older brain structures have, for the question being studied, not changed fundamentally. This assumption could very well be correct, since evolution is 'ultraconservative' (Plutchik 1994), and the evolution of the vertebrate brain has mainly consisted of adding new functional elements to what was already there (MacLean 1990). This last argument implies that this approach is, in principle, only suitable within the sub-phylum of vertebrates. However, if we have specified the neural structures concerned we can describe them in functional neural architectural terms and see whether these functional neural architectural interconnections have been described for non-vertebrate animals.

The second question is about which prerequisite cognitive capacities have to be there in order to give consciousness a fitness function. The assumption here is that consciousness is the result of an adaptive development. New developments never occur in isolation. Legs enabling organisms to move around quickly on solid ground are useless if these organisms still have gills instead of lungs. Likewise, consciousness and mental suffering are only useful if they occur in combination with other cognitive powers.

Finally, we can ask ourselves which human capacities are impossible without the interference of consciousness. The assumptions here are, again: (i) that consciousness is not an epiphenomenon; (ii) that it emanates from brain structures; (iii) that evolution is economical, only developing new brain structures if they make something possible which could not be done before; and (iv) that animal consciousness is not qualitatively different from human consciousness.

We start with the last question, because answering this question brings us naturally to the other two questions. It has been demonstrated that almost no human capacity needs consciousness, e.g. conditioning, acquisition of complex procedural knowledge, learning of natural and artificial grammars, breakthroughs in physics and mathematics, solving equations, learning processes and decisions which steer our behaviour in daily situations (Nisbett & Wilson 1977a, b; van Heerden 1982; Lewicki 1985, 1986; Penrose 1989; Greenwald 1992; Carruthers 1996; Mook 1996). It has further been demonstrated that it takes 0.5 second before a stimulus reaches consciousness, while our behavioural reaction to the stimulus takes only 0.25 second (Libet 1982, 1993). It has also been demonstrated that the non-conscious 'brain decision' to act precedes our experience of 'free will' to act by about 0.3 second and that 'free will' can inhibit motor actions but not induce actions (Libet 1985, 1993; Näätänen 1985; Wegner & Wheatley 1999).

I know that the idea of a consciousness which lags behind real time is hard for most people to swallow. However, this lagging behind is to be expected, since only the end products of the neural analyses can reach consciousness (Nisbett & Wilson 1977a, b) and no matter how fast these neural processes are, they still take time. Indeed, there are data which can only be explained by a consciousness with a time lag, like in the famous phenomenon which has been described by Dennett (1991), among others. In this experiment, two light spots are presented shortly after one other at different locations. The trick here is that the first light spot is green and the second red. This results in the perception of a moving light, which halfway along its route changes from green to red. Now we either have to assume that the perceived colour change is a paranormal preview of the near future or that the experience of the present is just a reconstruction of the recent past. Another example is presented by patients with unilateral neglect, induced by lesions in the pre-motor cortex. The one-sided neglect in these persons is not due to disturbances in the processing of sensory stimuli, but due to a disturbance in motor responses in the left side of the 'Umwelt'. It is remarkable that, therefore, the stimuli in the left visual field are also not perceived consciously anymore. This indicates that the motor response to a stimulus adds up to the conscious perception of that stimulus, which in itself is only possible if consciousness lags behind in time. This assumption is confirmed if one presents the stimuli through a mirror device. The stimuli, although in the right part of the environment (where the motor response has to be made), are now seen as mirror reflections in the left visual field. Not only are these patients then able to give a correct motor response to the left visual field stimuli, but these stimuli are now also consciously perceived, whereas the stimuli in the right visual field (requiring a motor response to the left) are now not perceived consciously anymore (Bisiach 1992). Bisiach describes more such examples, and concludes (1992 p 120):

> The division of preconscious labour among several processors with no sole gate-way to consciousness entails a relativity of the timing of consciousness as well as the possibility of ongoing rearrangement of what is being experienced.

The idea that consciousness does not induce behaviour was already assumed by early evolutionists like Huxley (Baars 1997), and this idea has recently been theoretically and experimentally confirmed by, for instance, Wegner and Wheatley (1999) and Gollwitzer (1999). It has further been demonstrated that human consciousness has no access to the unconscious brain modules that steer our behaviour (Nisbett & Wilson 1977a, b; Bargh & Chartrand 1999; Gollwitzer 1999; Wegner & Wheatley 1999). That consciousness fills the information gaps with confabulations, and by doing so gives us false ideas about the reality around us, and the false impression that the behaviour is initiated by our consciousness or our 'free will' (Nisbett & Wilson 1977a, b; Gazzaniga & LeDoux 1978; van Heerden 1982; Farthing 1992; Mook 1996; Bargh & Chartrand 1999; Gollwitzer 1999; Wegner & Wheatley 1999). Furthermore, consciousness does not like loose ends. Information presented to it must make sense; it must fit into the cognitive knowledge which is already there and, if it does not fit, the information is reinterpreted until it does, which also results in confabulations. This tendency is so strong that Mook (1996) calls it 'a coherence motivation'. All these confabulations function as new input to our brains, and so steer our future behaviour (Bargh & Chartrand 1999). And since these confabulations are by definition wrong descriptions of reality, they result in maladapted behaviour, making the question about the fitness value of consciousness all the more important.

It has also been demonstrated that the conscious working memory is far from perfect, since it can contain only between two and five elements (Bower & Hilgard 1981; Schwartz & Reisenberg 1991). It has further been demonstrated that people can easily experience exogenously induced behaviour as being produced by their own free will, and endogenously induced behaviour as being induced by others (Bargh & Chartrand 1999; Gollwitzer 1999; Wegner & Wheatley 1999). Finally, the linear conscious processes are extremely slow compared with the parallel-functioning non-conscious processes, and therefore may exceed the span of consciousness (Kihlstrom 1987). Altogether, these facts indicate that consciousness is an imperfect device and a recent development.

Conscious information processing always requires mental effort (Bargh & Chartrand 1999): we could therefore ask ourselves which cognitive processes cannot take place without mental effort.

Long-term planning, especially the intention to act in the future differently than we are inclined to, and the inhibition of these pre-programmed behavioural intentions, always requires conscious mental effort (Bargh & Chartrand 1999). However, the execution of the planned behaviour itself does not require consciousness (Libet 1985; Bargh & Chartrand 1999). The intention to behave differently in the future requires, besides planning, initiative (Gollwitzer 1999). This brings us to the first question; for planning, inhibition of the behaviour we are inclined to and initiative we need our most recent brain structure—the PFC. Furthermore, the PFC is also required for the emotional experience and the tuning of our behaviour in accordance with the demands of the social situation (Trigg 1970; Valenstein 1990; Damasio & Anderson 1993; Damasio 1994; Malloy & Duffy 1994; Fuster 1997). We use our consciousness, of course, for far more functions: learning languages or complex motor responses, knowing who is a nice person and who is not, etc. However, the point here is, as argued above, that all these processes can also take place non-consciously.

Although a PFC can be identified in higher mammals, only anthropoid apes show a well-developed PFC (Kolb & Whishaw 1990; Kupfermann 1991) and some parts of the PFC are specific to humans (Luria 1980). The PFC is a higher-order association area. Here, information which has already been processed in primary and secondary one-modality sensory neural projection areas, and interpreted on high cognitive levels in multisensory modality-association areas, is once again reprocessed and reinterpreted. Furthermore, the PFC has ample efferent connections to evolutionarily older neural structures and has thus a 'top down' control over these structures (Jones & Powell 1970; Kolb & Whishaw 1990; Miller 2000). Such extremely high neural step-by-step progress, neural processing systems with top down control, have not been described in animals without a PFC. This alone limits tremendously the number of species in which consciousness may be expected.

The Fitness Function of Consciousness and Suffering

Summarizing the literature concerning consciousness, Weiskrantz states (1992 p 8):

> One dominant theme is to attach its benefits to benefits of active thought itself—in allowing the initiation of predictive strategies, in detaching the observer from an immediate dependence on current inputs, by allowing current inputs to be linked, with or without imagery, to other events distant either in space or in time, and in allowing flexible rather than automatic processing

Likewise, Laird and Bresler (1992) reached the conclusion that a specific but very important aspect of consciousness, the emotional feelings, are not epiphenomena, but rather that they force us to reflect. Emotional experiences are, according to these authors, like other conscious contents, constructed from lower-order elements that are themselves not part of consciousness. When we feel an emotion, we are aware of information about the situation and how we are acting. This conscious information can then be processed like any other piece of conscious information. This processing may, by estimating the consequences and the long-term (social) demands of various alternative actions in advance, lead to conscious choices from alternative behaviour patterns. By means of an emotional experience, the stimulus-induced emotional behavioural tendencies can be inhibited so that the actual behaviour can be released from the obvious responses, and eventually a mode of behaviour more suitably matched to this or comparable future situations can be shown. The main functions of consciousness (see earlier in this contribution) and the emotional experience lie, therefore, not as generally assumed by laymen in the induction of (emotional) behaviour, but in the inhibition of the (emotional) behaviour to which we are inclined. The conscious free choice out of behavioural alternatives also enables the organism to manipulate others, by pretending behavioural tendencies or emotions.

The ability to deliberately (under volitional control) induce the wrong impression in others, at the right moment, has a great fitness value (Dennett 1996). It is for this reason that Leakey and Lewin assume that there was, in the early hominids, a selection pressure for the capacity to manipulate others (Leakey & Lewin 1992 p 294): 'the answer, I suggest, is the intense intellectual demands of primate social interactions, with the constant need to understand and outwit others in the drive for reproductive success'. Dennett (1996) comes to essentially the same conclusion, although by a totally different line of thinking (by asking himself how intelligence may have developed in evolution). He argues that higher cognitive powers, through which secret-keeping can emerge, and language (as a tool to take one element out of a cognitive network and place it freely in any other network) are prerequisites for consciousness. According to him, the fitness value of consciousness is given by the fact that it enables the organism to 'bluff' others.

All these ideas are derived from Nicholas Humphrey, who argued in the 1970s that the development of self-consciousness was a stratagem for developing and testing hypotheses about what is going through the minds of others. He suggested that one uses one's self-consciousness as a source of hypotheses about other-consciousness or, because when one gets into the habit of adopting the intentional stance toward others, one notices that one can usefully subject oneself to the same treatment (Dennett 1996). Leakey and Lewin state (1992 pp 296–297):

> The Inner Eye, as Nick Humphrey calls this mental model, must also generate a sense of self, the phenomenon we know as consciousness: the Inner 'I'. In evolutionary terms it must have been a major breakthrough. . . . Imagine the biological benefits to the first of our ancestors who developed the ability to make realistic guesses about the inner life of his rivals; to be able to picture what another was thinking about and planning to do next; to be able to read the minds of others by reading his own.

Frans de Waal (1996), who reacts against the selfish gene idea of Richard Dawkins (1989), assumes that various animals could have moral ideas and therefore morally guided behaviour. He assumes that non-cognitive or non-conscious moral behaviour could develop in groups in which the individuals are mutually dependent upon one another. Real altruism (helping others without benefiting yourself directly or indirectly) is a troublesome phenomenon for neo-Darwinism. De Waal therefore also writes that this moral behaviour could basically very well serve one's own interest. However, according to him, stressing this self-interest, as is done by the selfish gene idea, blocks our view of possible altruistic behavioural mechanisms which could develop on a basis of self-interest. Further, de Waal states that cognitive or conscious empathy is not widespread in the animal kingdom: according to him it is only seen in humans and, possibly, in anthropoid apes. It is a sobering thought, but we have no other option: the original function of consciousness was not social progress, but selfishness and deceit.

Summarizing, we can state that higher cognitive powers like language, the capacity to keep secrets, to have knowledge of the demands of the social environment, to judge the motives of others and to evaluate the consequences of behavioural alternatives in advance are all prerequisites for consciousness in order to get positive fitness value. Due to the consciousness-induced extension of the emotional period and the consciousness-induced confabulations, consciousness would, without these higher cognitive powers, only have a negative fitness value.

Consciousness may therefore only be expected in animals which show these higher cognitive capacities in their behaviour. For the experience of emotional feelings, further knowledge of 'self' is required. Since these capacities have, up to now, only been recorded in the anthropoid apes (Plutchik 1994), they are the only species in which consciousness and suffering may be expected. Plutchik (1994 p 238) states:

> There is little existing evidence, other than anecdotal, for intentionality in animals, and there is even less evidence for self-consciousness. . . . Investigators have replicated this phenomenon of self-recognition (and by implication, self awareness) in orangutans as well as chimpanzees, but every attempt to replicate the phenomenon in lower primates—spider monkeys, capuchins, mandrill and hamadryas baboons, and gibbons—has failed.

De Waal (1996), referring to Gallup (1982), confirms these statements. According to de Waal, Gallup (1982) compared self recognition to higher cognitive capacities like language, knowing what is going on in the minds of others, deceit, reconciliation and empathy and came to the conclusion that humans and anthropoid apes have cognitive powers which set them apart from other animals. De Waal further writes that no matter how much he wanted to record deceit in macaques, he was unable to see a single example of such behaviour.

However, even with the limitation of anthropoid apes only, we have to be careful in our conclusions. Firstly, although there are beautiful descriptions of planning and deceit in chimpanzees (*Pan troglodytes*; Dawkins 1993; de Waal 1996), formal experimental testing has indicated that this ability is limited: only one out of four showed deception of others in a situation in which such deceit paid off (Plutchik 1994). Secondly, the ability to plan also seems limited, in our close relatives, to the direct needs of the situation at hand. Christopher Wills (1989) correctly stated that a chimpanzee has never been observed to select a nice stick to be used for fishing for ants the next day. Thirdly, Dennett (1996) reminds us that the 'AHA Erlebnis' (sudden insight) of Köhler's apes was mainly based on trial and error learning, not on a sudden enlightening insight, and that some of Köhler's apes never saw the light.

Conclusions

Irreflexive consciousness and suffering don't go together. Suffering and pain which is experienced as unpleasant is an emotional experience, and reflection is a prerequisite for such experiences. However, pain perception as a pain stimulus, which does not induce suffering, could still be possible with an irreflexive consciousness.

Standard emotional behaviour is not induced by the emotional experience. On the contrary, the emotional experience derives its fitness function from the fact that it can inhibit the stimulus-bound emotional behaviour so that, by using imagination and information from the past and future, more adaptive behavioural responses can be imagined, planned and later executed.

The PFC, or comparable super higher order association area, is a prerequisite for spontaneous planning of this kind, and for the emotional experience, and thus for the experience of pain as an emotion, or suffering.

Consciousness confabulates, and conscious emotional feelings extend the emotion until long after the disappearance of the external inducing stimuli. Consciousness and emotional feelings are therefore sources of maladapted behaviour.

Higher cognitive powers like language and the capacity to keep secrets, to have knowledge of the demands of the social environment, to judge the motives of others and to evaluate the consequences of behavioural alternatives in advance are all prerequisites for consciousness and the experience of suffering in order to get positive fitness value. Consciousness may therefore only be expected in animals which show these capacities in their behaviour. Since these capacities have, up to now, only been recorded in the anthropoid apes, they are the only species in which consciousness may be assumed. And even then we have to be careful in our conclusions, since there are various indications that anthropoid apes show severe limitations in these capacities. However, as argued before, there is an important difference between the conscious registration of pain as a pain stimulus, which does not induce feelings of suffering, and the experience of pain as an emotion, which does induce suffering. According to the arguments presented in relation to the issue of an irreflexive consciousness, the conscious registration of non-emotion- and non-suffering-inducing pain stimuli could be possible in far more species than anthropoid apes alone.

I would therefore like to end with the following statement. Rejoice! Rejoice! For there is far less animal suffering than our anthropomorphic minds are inclined to believe.

References

Baars B J 1997 *In the Theater of Consciousness: The Workspace of Mind*. Oxford University Press: Oxford, UK.
Bargh J A and Chartrand T L 1999 The unbearable automaticity of being. *American Psychologist 54*: 462–479.

Bateson P 1991 Assessment of pain in animals. *Animal Behaviour 42*: 827–839.

Bermond B 1997 The myth of animal suffering. In: Dol M, Kasanmoentalib S, Lijmbach S, Rivas E and Van den Bos R (eds) *Animal Consciousness and Animal Ethics: Perspectives from the Netherlands* pp. 125–143, Van Gorcum: Assen, the Netherlands.

Bermond B 1998 Consciousness or the art of foul play. *Journal of Agricultural and Environmental Ethics 10*: 227–247.

Bisiach E 1992 Understanding consciousness: Clues from unilateral neglect and related disorders. In: Milner A D and Rugg M D (eds) *The Neurophysiology of Consciousness* pp 113–137. Academic Press: London.

Bower G H and Hilgard E R 1981 *Theories of Learning, 5th edition*. Prentice-Hall Inc: Englewood Cliffs, NJ.

Carruthers P 1989 Brute experience. *The Journal of Philosophy 89*: 258–296.

Carruthers P 1996 *Language Thoughts and Consciousness*. Cambridge University Press: Cambridge, UK.

Chalmers D J 1996 *The Conscious Mind: In Search of a Fundamental Theory*. Oxford University Press: New York.

Damasio A R 1994 *Descartes' Error*. Putnam's and Sons: New York.

Damasio A R and Anderson S W 1993 The frontal lobes. In: Heilman K and Valenstein E (eds) *Clinical Neuropsychology, 3rd edition*. Oxford University Press: New York.

Damasio A R, Tranel D and Damasio H 1990 Individuals with sociopathic behavior caused by frontal damage fail to respond autonomically to social stimuli. *Behavioral Brain Research 41*: 81–94.

Dawkins M S 1993 *Through Our Eyes Only? The Search for Animal Consciousness*. Spektrum/Freeman: Oxford.

Dawkins M S 1998 Evolution and animal welfare. *The Quarterly Review of Biology 73*: 305–328.

Dawkins R 1989 *The Selfish Gene, new edition*. Oxford University Press: Oxford.

Dennett D C 1991 *Consciousness Explained*. Little, Brown and Co: Boston.

Dennett D C 1996 *Kinds of Minds*. Weidenfeld and Nicolson: London.

de Vries R 1991 Van wetenschap tot dierenleed: Wetenschapstheoretische opmerkingen over de plaats van het subjectieve in de natuur. *Antropologische Verkenningen 10*: 64–81.

de Waal F 1996 *Van Nature Goed*. Conact: Amsterdam, the Netherlands (Dutch translation of *Good Natured*).

Farthing G W 1992 *The Psychology of Consciousness*. Prentice-Hall Inc: Englewood Cliffs, NJ.

Freeman W 1971 Frontal lobotomy in early schizophrenia. *British Journal of Psychiatry 119*: 621–624.

Freeman W and Watts W 1950 *Psycho Surgery, 2nd edition*. Charles C Thomas: Springfield, IL.

Frijda N H 1986 *The Emotions: Studies in Emotion and Social Interaction*. Cambridge University Press: Cambridge, UK.

Fuster J M 1989 *The Prefrontal Cortex: Anatomy, Physiology and Neuropsychology of the Frontal Lobe*. Raven Press: New York.

Fuster J M 1997 *The Prefrontal Cortex: Anatomy, Physiology and Neuropsychology of the Frontal Lobe, 3rd edition*. Lippincott-Raven: Philadelphia.

Gallup G 1982 Self-awareness and the emergence of mind in primates. *American Journal of Primatology 2*: 37–248.

Gazzaniga M and LeDoux J E 1978 *The Integrated Mind*. Plenum: New York.

Gollwitzer P M 1999 Implementation intentions. *American Psychologist 54*: 493–503.

Greenwald A G 1992 Unconscious cognition reclaimed. *American Psychologist 47*: 766–779.

Heilman K M, Watson R T and Valenstein E 1993 Neglect and related disorders. In: Heilman K M and Valenstein E (eds) *Clinical Neuropsychology, 3rd edition* pp 279–336. Oxford University Press: New York.

Jarvie H F 1954 Frontal lobe wounds causing disinhibition. *Journal of Neurology, Neurosurgery and Psychiatry 17*: 14–32.

Jennett S 1989 *Human Physiology*. Churchill Livingstone: Edinburgh.

Jones E G and Powell T P S 1970 An anatomical study of converging sensory pathways within the cerebral cortex of the monkey. *Brain 93*: 793–820.

Kihlstrom J F 1987 The cognitive unconscious. *Science 237*: 1445–1452.

Kolb B and Whishaw I Q 1990 *Fundamentals of Human Neuropsychology, 3rd edition*. W H Freeman and Co: New York.

Krystal H and Raskin H A 1970 *Drug Dependence: Aspects of Ego Functions*. Wayne State University Press: Detroit.

Kucharski A 1984 History of frontal lobotomy in the US, 1935–1955. *Neurosurgery 14*: 765–772.

Kupfermann I 1991 Localization of higher cognitive and affective functions: The association cortices. In: Kandel E R, Schwartz J H and Jessell T M (eds) *Principles of Neural Science, 3rd edition* pp 823–838. Elsevier: New York.

Laird J D and Bresler C 1992 The process of emotional experience: A self-perception theory. In: Clark M S (ed) *Emotion Review of Personality and Social Psychology, Volume 13* pp 213–234. Sage Publications: Newbury, UK.

Leakey R and Lewin R 1992 *Origins Reconsidered: In Search of What Makes Us Human.* Doubleday: New York.

LeDoux J E 1989 Cognitive-emotional interactions in the brain. *Cognition and Emotion 3*: 267–289.

Levine J and Albert H 1948 Sexual behavior after lobotomy. *Society Proceedings of the Boston Society of Psychiatry and Neurology* 18 November, 166–168.

Lewicki P 1985 Non conscious biasing effects of single instances on subsequent judgements. *Journal of Personality and Social Psychology 48*: 563–574.

Lewicki P 1986 Information about covariation that cannot be articulated. *Journal of Experimental Psychology: Learning, Memory and Cognition 12*: 135–146.

Libet B 1982 Brain stimulation in the study of neural functions for conscious sensory experience. *Human Neurobiology 1*: 235–242.

Libet B 1985 Unconscious cerebral initiative and the role of conscious will in voluntary action. *Behavioural and Brain Sciences 8*: 529–566.

Libet B 1993 The neural time factor in conscious and unconscious events. In: Nagel T (ed) *Experimental and Theoretical Studies of Consciousness: Ciba Foundation Symposium 174* pp 123–146. Wiley: Chichester, UK.

Lijmbach S 1998 *Animal Subjectivity: A Study Into Philosophy and Theory of Animal Experience.* PhD thesis, University of Wageningen, the Netherlands.

Lokhorst G J C 1986 *Brein en Bewustzijn. De Geest-lichaam Theorieën van Moderne Hersenonderzoekers (1956–1986). Rotterdamse Filosofische Studies.* Erasmus Universiteit Rotterdam & Eburon: Delft, the Netherlands.

Luria A R 1980 *Higher Cortical Functions in Man, 2nd edition.* Plenum Publishing Corporation: New York

MacLean P D 1990 *The Triune Brain in Evolution: Role in Paleocerebral Functions.* Plenum Press: New York.

Malloy P and Duffy J 1994 The frontal lobes in neuropsychiatric disorders. In: Boller F and Graftman J (eds) *Handbook of Neuropsychology, Volume 9* pp 203–232. Elsevier: Amsterdam, the Netherlands.

Menges L J 1992 *Over Pijn Gesproken.* Kok: Kampen, the Netherlands.

Miller E K 2000 The prefrontal cortex and cognitive control. *Nature Reviews/Neuroscience 1*: 59–65.

Mook D G 1996 *Motivation: The Organization of Action.* W.W. Norton and Co: New York.

Näätänen R 1985 Brain physiology and conscious initiation of movements. *Behavioral and Brain Sciences 8*: 549–550.

Nemiah J C 1962 The effect of leucotomy on pain. *Psychosomatic Medicine 24*: 75–80.

Nisbett R E and Wilson T D 1977a Telling more than we can know: Verbal reports on mental processes. *Psychological Review 84*: 231–259.

Nisbett R E and Wilson T D 1977b The halo effect: Evidence for unconscious alteration of judgements. *Journal of Personality and Social Psychology 35*: 250–256.

Penrose R 1989 *The Emperor's New Mind.* Oxford University Press: Oxford, UK.

Plutchik R 1994 *The Psychology and Biology of Emotion.* Harper Collins College Publishers: New York.

Pöppel E and Ruhnau E 2000 Gehirn Bewustsein Zeit. In: *Materie Geist und Bewustsein,* Heinrich Pfusterschmid-Hardtensteinpp (ed.) pp 85–89. Ibera Verlag: Vienna.

Sacks O 1995 *An Anthropologist on Mars.* Picador: London.

Schwartz B and Reisenberg D 1991 *Learning and Memory.* Norton: New York.

Searle J R 1997 *The Mystery of Consciousness.* Granta Books: London.

Trigg R 1970 *Pain and Emotion.* Clarendon Press: Oxford, UK.

Valenstein E S 1990 The prefrontal area and psychosurgery. *Progress in Brain Research 85*: 539–554.

van Heerden J 1982 *De Zorgelijke Staat van het Onbewuste.* PhD thesis, University of Amsterdam, the Netherlands.

Verheijen F J 1988 Pijn en angst bij een aan de haak geslagen vis. *Biovisie 68*: 166–172.

Verheijen F J, de Cock Büning T, Flight W F G, Vorstenbosch J M G and Wendela-Bonga S E 1993 *Brief aan Ir S J Beukema, Ministerie van Landbouw, Natuurbeheer en Visserij* (Letter to the Dutch Ministry of Agriculture) 19 February 1993 obtainable from the Dutch Ministry of Agriculture.

Wegner D M and Wheatley T 1999 Apparent mental causation, sources of the experience of will. *American Psychologist 54*: 480–492.

Weiskrantz L 1992 Dissociated issues. In: Milner A D and Rugg M D (eds) *The Neuropsychology of Consciousness*. Academic Press: London.

Weiskrantz L 1997 *Consciousness Lost and Found*. Oxford University Press: Oxford.

Weiskrantz L, Wattington E K, Sanders M D and Marchal J 1974 Visual capacity in the hemianopic field following a restricted occipital oblation. *Brain 97*: 709–728.

Wilkes K 1988 *Real People*. Clarendon Press: Oxford.

Wills C 1989 *The Wisdom of the Genes*. Basic Books: New York.

14 Animal Pain

Colin Allen

Allen argues that the philosophical information on the topic of pain has relied on overly simple ideas about the function of pain. He argues that a more nuanced view about the biological functions of pain is needed to better understand its nature and distribution among animals and to assess its role in ethical considerations.

Pain and Its Functions

This final section examines claims about the biological (adaptive) functions of pain and argues that, in the light of what's known about the complexity of spinal mechanisms, some common suggestions are not defensible.

At first blush, the idea that conscious pain brings a selective advantage seems so obvious as to need no detailed justification. But while the capacity for conscious pain undoubtedly *seems* very important to survival and reproduction, without independent evidence of selection for the sensation over and above what can be delivered by the nociceptive system (nociception: capacity to sense noxious stimuli), in the absence of consciousness, we should not fool ourselves into thinking that a selectional explanation for conscious pain has been provided. Cases of congenital insensitivity to pain, which are often trotted out by philosophers and scientists to support the claim that the conscious experience of pain is important, fail in this regard precisely because they are cases where several elements of the nociceptive system are also nonfunctional and so the finger cannot be determinately pointed at the absence of conscious pain experiences.[1]

One way to approach the question of what functions are served by the conscious parts of the nociceptive system is to investigate the capacities of the vertebrate spinal cord independent of its connections to the brain. The work by Grau and colleagues indicates that nociception-related learning in the spinal cord shows many advanced features, such as latent inhibition (where repeated presentation of a cue diminishes subsequent associative conditioning to that cue) and overshadowing (where learning about a less salient cue is blocked by presentation of a more salient one). In intact animals, both these phenomena have been explained in cognitive terms as due to attentional processes (indeed they are widely believed to *require* cognitive explanation). But the fact that both occur in detached spinal cords indicates that this form of attention is not mediated by conscious experience and that we should therefore be careful about assuming a role for conscious cognitive systems when similar phenomena are observed in intact organisms (see Grau 2002).

Another area in which statements about the function of pain are often naive is in failing to distinguish different behavioral responses, e.g., withdrawal from the noxious stimulus, and vocalizations. Antinociception is a phenomenon whereby exposure to a noxious stimulus reduces subsequent reactivity to the same or other noxious stimuli. By measuring the amount of time it takes for a rat to flick its tail, it can be shown that prior exposure to a mildly painful stimulus (shock) produces antinociception for up to ten minutes (Grau 2002). But it would be a mistake to infer from this that the animal consciously experiences less pain, for other measures of pain reactivity, such as time to vocalization and motor reactivity, show *increased* sensitivity in the same time frame (King et al.

1996). These results were not simply due to sensitization on the motor side, for the treatment also enhances learning. Interestingly, however, it was also found that with higher intensity shocks, the spinal antinociception was accompanied by reductions in vocalization and fear conditioning, indicating possible hypoalgesia (Meagher et al. 2001).

What can we make of these complicated results? I'll start with a note of caution about Hardcastle's noteworthy attempt to give an account of the functions of pain that goes beyond the usual platitudes about avoiding danger. She makes much of the fact that the pain system consists not only of ascending pathways from nociceptors to the brain (the pain sensory system), but also of descending pathways from the brain to the dorsal horn of the spinal column (the pain inhibitory system). Hardcastle claims that this dual system serves two different (evolutionary) goals: the sensory system provides information about injuries and the potential for injury, while the inhibitory system "shuts down the [pain sensory system] when flight or fleeing is immanent, and then enhances the [pain sensory system] response in moments of control" (Hardcastle 1997, p. 408). Conscious sensation of pain is the joint product of these two sometimes antagonistic, sometimes facilitatory subsystems, on this view. There is something right about this view, but as we have seen, the functional story is not simple. Some behavioral responses are inhibited while others are simultaneously enhanced, thus we cannot just assume that because there is inhibition by some measures, there is also a reduction in conscious pain, or that the function of conscious pain is simply as a warning signal to be suppressed whenever the going gets tough.

Discoveries about the distributed nature of pain processing argue for a more nuanced view about the functions of pain. The conscious experience of pain is most likely not simply an "alarm bell" to be suppressed when it becomes essential to act, but instead has a complicated role in the capacity of organisms to learn how to behave when confronted with actual or possible tissue damage.[2] The variety of different forms of animal learning has been insufficiently appreciated by philosophers. Attention to the details of learning would serve to allow more fine-grained distinctions among organisms of different species. At one level, these details provide a richer base for the analogical argument—a more complete version of Varner's (2000) table, for example. This is useful, and if applied systematically to a wide range of species it would allow us to avoid inappropriate generalizations about entirely too broad taxonomic categories. But, at another level, the approach also has the potential to establish a more theoretical basis for relating the observed capacities and the attribution of consciousness to animals. It appears that certain kinds of associative learning are strongly correlated with phenomenal consciousness in humans, thus strengthening the basic argument by analogy when similar forms of learning are described in nonhuman animals. But they may also be theoretically linked to phenomenal consciousness if the best explanation of such learning involves the organism's ability to notice relationships between its own experiences.

It may seem that the foregoing suggestion constitutes an endorsement of a higher-order account of consciousness. In fact, however, I think we should remain neutral on the ontological question of what constitutes consciousness—the answer to that question cannot be decided without a lot more empirical work. It is nevertheless possible to maintain that evidence for higher-order capacities provides a strong form of evidence for phenomenal consciousness even if those capacities aren't part of any ontological account of phenomenal consciousness, in much the same way that a person's description of his or her deeds can provide strong evidence of those deeds even though the capacity to describe them need not be a necessary condition for the deeds themselves.

While nociception-based learning and centralized modification of peripheral nociception are both found in the marine snail, *Aplysia,* its range of learning abilities is undoubtedly less sophisticated than what is known for at least some mammals and other vertebrates. To my knowledge, work on nociception-related learning in invertebrates with more sophisticated nervous systems, such as cephalopods, simply hasn't been done; in fact, it has only been done for a very limited selection of vertebrates, selected mostly for the convenience of the experimenters. There is a need for serious comparative work in this area, but there are, of course, questions about the ethical propriety of doing more of this kind of work, precisely because it might cause morally objectionable pain.[3] Without it, however, it is dishonest to pretend that we "know where to draw the line," on animal pain, the existing arguments for and against the existence of conscious animal pain remain essentially weak, and legal and moral principles based on such arguments will remain controversial. Although the scientific developments may not resolve all our legal and ethical quandaries, they can surely help us to construct more appropriate regulations and policies than at present.

Finally, although I have criticized some recent attempts by philosophers to bring an evolutionary, functional perspective to bear on questions about pain for being too simplistic, I nonetheless endorse the general approach, for I agree with Hardcastle that it is only by understanding the functions of pain that we can dispel confusion about this most basic of experiences and integrate behavioral and neurological findings. I would add that questions about the distribution of conscious pain in nonhuman animals are central to the evolutionary approach and deserve focused attention from both scientists and philosophers of mind. While the unfolding scientific story about the functions of pain across the animal kingdom is more complicated than we have yet imagined, there is nothing to indicate that it is beyond our comprehension.

Notes

1. Cf. Hardcastle, for example, who writes: "a pain sensory system tied to the somatosensory processors makes good evolutionary sense. As creatures eking out lives in a hostile environment, having a system which could warn us when damage occurred and which could force us to protect damaged parts until they healed would be tremendously beneficial. (Indeed, persons who cannot feel any pain at all often live a nasty, brutish, and short life.)" (Hardcastle 1997, p. 395). I presume that "feel pain" here refers to the capacity for conscious sensations of pain.
2. For a similar thesis about conscious experience in general, see Cotterill (2001); Cotterill also provides a useful reminder of the importance of understanding neural functions in relation to motor systems. Tye's (2000) connection of phenomenal consciousness of pain to modification of beliefs and desires, and to subsequent changes in behavior, also links conscious pain to learning, albeit rather generally.
3. It is worth noting here that the Humane Society of the United States distinguishes between research causing acute and chronic pain to animals, finding the former to be acceptable when conducted within International Association for the Study of Pain guidelines, but calling for a complete termination of the latter by the year 2020.

References

Cotterill, R. M. J. (2001). "Evolution, Cognition and Consciousness," *Journal of Consciousness Studies* 8: 3–17.

Grau, J. (2002). "Learning and Memory without a Brain," in M. Bekoff, C. Allen, & G. M. Burghardt, eds., *The Cognitive Animal*. Cambridge, MA: MIT Press, pp. 77–88.

Hardcastle, V. G. (1997). "When a Pain Is Not." *The Journal of Philosophy*, 94: 381–409.

King, T. E., Joynes, R. L., Meagher, M. W., & Grau, J. W. (1996). "The Impact of Shock on Pain Reactivity II: Evidence for Enhanced Pain." *Journal of Experimental Psychology: Animal Behavior Processes*, 22: 265–278.

Meagher, M. W., Ferguson, A. R., McLemore, S., King, T. E., Sieve, A. N., Crown, E. D., & Grau, J. W. (2001). "Stress-Induced Hyperalgesia: Generality." *Journal of Experimental Psychology: Animal Behavior Processes*, 27: 219–238.

Tye, M. (2000). *Consciousness, Color, and Content*. Cambridge, MA: MIT Press.

Varner, G. (2000). "Sentientism," in D. Jamieson, ed., *A Companion to Environmental Philosophy*. Oxford: Blackwell, pp. 192–203.

15 Animal Consciousness

What Matters and Why

Daniel C. Dennett

Dennett disagrees that nonhumans and even human newborns have consciousness; rather, he argues that in order for a species to be conscious, it is necessary to have a certain informational organization that endows the organisms with a wide set of cognitive powers such as reflection and re-representation and that with these abilities, consciousness emerges by immersion in human culture. He acknowledges that other species undoubtedly achieve some level of similar informational organization but that the differences are so great that most speculative translations of imagination from humans to the other species make no sense.

Are animals conscious? The way we are? Which species, and why? What is it like to be a bat, a rat, a vulture, a whale?

[. . .]

Current thinking about animal consciousness is a mess. Hidden and not so hidden agendas distort discussion and impede research. A kind of comic relief can be found—if you go in for bitter irony—by turning to the "history of the history" of the controversies. I am not known for my spirited defenses of René Descartes, but I find I have to sympathize with an honest scientist who was apparently the first victim of the wild misrepresentations of the lunatic fringe of the animal rights movement. Animal rights activists such as Peter Singer and Mary Midgley have recently helped spread the myth that Descartes was a callous vivisector, completely indifferent to animal suffering *because of* his view that animals (unlike people) were mere automata. As Justin Leiber (1988) has pointed out, in an astringent re-examination of the supposed evidence for this, "There is simply not a line in Descartes to suggest that he thought we are free to smash animals at will or free to do so *because* their behavior can be explained mechanically." Moreover, the favorite authority of Descartes' accusers, Montaigne, on whom both Singer and Midgley also uncritically rely, was a gullible romantic of breathtaking ignorance, eager to take the most fanciful folktales of animal mentality at face value, and not at all interested in *finding out*, as Descartes himself was, how animals actually work!

[. . .]

Certain questions, it is said, are quite beyond science at this point (and perhaps forever). The cloaks of mystery fall conveniently over the very issues that promise (or threaten) to shed light on the *grounds* for our moral attitudes toward different animals. Again, a curious asymmetry can be observed. We do not require absolute, Cartesian certainty that our fellow human beings are conscious—what we require is what is aptly called *moral* certainty. Can we not have the same moral certainty about the experiences of animals? I have not yet seen an argument by a philosopher to the effect that we cannot, with the aid of science, establish facts about animal minds with the same degree of moral certainty that satisfies us in the case of our own species. So whether or not a case has been made for the "in principle" mystery of consciousness (I myself am utterly unpersuaded by the arguments offered to date), it is a red herring. We can learn enough about animal consciousness to settle the questions we have about our responsibilities. The moral agenda about animals is important, and for that very reason it must not be permitted to continue to deflect the research, both empirical and conceptual, on which an informed ethics could be based.

A striking example of one-sided use of evidence is Thomas Nagel's famous paper "What Is It Like to Be a Bat?" (1991). One of the rhetorical peculiarities of Nagel's paper is that he chose bats and went to the trouble to relate a *few* of the fascinating facts about bats and their echolocation, because, presumably, those hard-won, third-person-perspective scientific facts tell us *something* about bat consciousness. What? First and least, they support our conviction that bats *are* conscious. (He did not write a paper called "What Is It Like to Be a Brick?") Second, and more important, they support his contention that bat consciousness is very unlike ours. The rhetorical peculiarity—if not outright inconsistency—of his treatment of the issue can be captured by an obvious question: if a few such facts can establish *something* about bat consciousness, would more such facts not establish more? He has already relied on "objective, third-person" scientific investigation to establish (or at least render rationally credible) the hypothesis that bats are conscious, but not in just the way we are. Why wouldn't further such facts be able to tell us in exactly what ways bats' consciousness isn't like ours, thereby telling us what it *is* like to be a bat? What kind of fact is it that only works for one side of an empirical question?

The fact is that we all do rely, without hesitation, on "third-person" behavioral evidence to support or reject hypotheses about the consciousness of animals. What else, after all, could be the source of our "pretheoretical intuitions"? But these intuitions in themselves are an untrustworthy lot, much in need of reflective evaluation. For instance, do you see "sentience" or "mere discriminatory reactivity" in the Venus Fly Trap, or in the amoeba, or in the jellyfish? What more than mere discriminatory reactivity—the sort of competence many robots exhibit—are you *seeing* when you *see* sentience in a creature? It is, in fact, ridiculously easy to induce powerful intuitions of not just sentience but full-blown consciousness (ripe with malevolence or curiosity or friendship) by exposing people to quite simple robots *made to move in familiar mammalian ways at mammalian speeds.*

Cog, a delightfully humanoid robot being built at MIT, has eyes, hands, and arms that move the way yours do—swiftly, relaxedly, compliantly (Dennett, 1994). Even those of us working on the project, knowing full well that we have not even *begun* to program the high level processes that might arguably endow Cog with consciousness, get an almost overwhelming sense of being in the presence of another conscious observer when Cog's eyes still quite blindly and stupidly follow one's hand gestures. Once again, I plead for symmetry: when you acknowledge the power of such elegant, lifelike motions to charm you into an illusion, note that it ought to be an open question, still, whether you are also being charmed by your beloved dog or cat or the noble elephant. Feelings are too easy to provoke for them to count for much here.

If behavior, casually observed by the gullible or generous-hearted, is a treacherous benchmark, might composition—material and structure—provide some important leverage? History offers a useful perspective on this question. It was not so long ago—Descartes' day—when the hypothesis that a material brain by itself could sustain consciousness was deemed preposterous. Only immaterial souls could *conceivably* be conscious. What was inconceivable then is readily conceivable now. Today, we can readily conceive that a brain, without benefit of immaterial accompanists, can be a sufficient seat of consciousness, even if we wonder just how this could be. This is surely a *possibility* in almost everybody's eyes, and many of us think the evidence for its truth mounts close to certainty. For instance, few if any today would think that the "discovery" that, say, lefthanders don't have immaterial minds but just brains would show unmistakably that they are just zombies.

Unimpressed by this retreat, some people today baulk at the *very idea* of silicon consciousness or artifactual consciousness, but the reasons offered for these general claims are unimpressive to say the least. It looks more and more as if we will simply have to look at what entities—animals in this case, but also robots and other things made of nonstandard materials—*actually can do*, and use that as our best guide to whether animals are conscious and, if so, why and of what.

[. . .]

What I find insupportable is the coupling of blithe assertion of consciousness with the equally untroubled *lack of curiosity* about what this assertion might amount to, and how it might be investigated. Leiber (1988) provides a handy scorecard:

> Montaigne is ecumenical in this respect, claiming consciousness for spiders and ants, and even writing of our duties to trees and plants. Singer and Clarke agree in denying consciousness to sponges. Singer locates the distinction somewhere between the shrimp and the oyster. He, with rather considerable convenience for one who is thundering hard accusations at others, slides by the case of insects and spiders and bacteria; they, *pace* Montaigne, apparently and rather conveniently do not feel pain. The intrepid Midgley, on the other hand, seems willing to speculate about the subjective experience of tapeworms. . . . Nagel . . . appears to draw the line at flounders and wasps, though more recently he speaks of the inner life of cockroaches.

The list could be extended. In a recent paper, Michael Lockwood (1993) supposes, as so many do, that Nagel's "what it is like to be" formula *fixes a sense of consciousness*. He then says: "Consciousness in this sense is presumably to be found in all mammals, and probably in all birds, reptiles and amphibians as well." It is the "presumably" and "probably" to which I want us to attend. Lockwood gives no hint as to how he would set out to replace these terms with something more definite. I am not asking for certainty. Birds aren't just *probably* warm-blooded, and amphibians aren't just *presumably* air-breathing. Nagel confessed at the outset not to know—or to have any recipe for discovering—where to draw the line as we descend the scale of complexity (or is it the cuddliness scale?). This embarrassment is standardly waved aside by those who find it just obvious that there is something it is like to be a bat or a dog, equally obvious that there is *not* something it is like to be a brick, and unhelpful *at this time* to dispute whether it is like anything to be a fish or a spider. What does it mean to say that it is or it isn't?

It has passed for good philosophical form to invoke mutual agreement here that we know what we're talking about even if we can't explain it yet. I want to challenge this. I claim that this standard methodological assumption has no *clear* pretheoretical meaning—in spite of its undeniable "intuitive" appeal—and that since this is so, it is ideally suited to play the deadly role of the "shared" intuition that conceals the solution from us. *Maybe* there really is a huge difference between us and all other species in this regard; *maybe* we should consider "radical" hypotheses. Lockwood says "probably" all birds are conscious, but *maybe* some of them—or even all of them—are rather like sleepwalkers! Or what about the idea that there could be unconscious pains (and that animal pain, though real, and—yes—morally important, was unconscious pain)? *Maybe* there is a certain amount of generous-minded delusion (which I once called the Beatrix Potter syndrome) in our bland mutual assurance that as Lockwood puts it, "*Pace* Descartes, consciousness, thus construed, isn't remotely, on this planet, the monopoly of human beings."

How, though, could we ever explore these "maybes"? We could do so in a constructive, anchored way by first devising a theory that concentrated exclusively on *human* consciousness—the one variety about which we will brook no "maybes" or "probablys"—and then *look and see* which features of that account apply to which animals, and why. There is plenty of work to do, which I will illustrate with a few examples—just warm-up exercises for the tasks to come.

In *Moby Dick*, Herman Melville asks some wonderful questions about what it is like to be a sperm whale. The whale's eyes are located on opposite sides of a huge bulk: "the front of the Sperm Whale's head," Melville memorably tells us, "is a dead, blind wall, without a single organ or tender prominence of any sort whatever" (Ch. 76). As Melville notes: "The whale, therefore, must see one distinct picture on this side, and another distinct picture on that side; while all between must be profound darkness and nothingness to him" (Ch. 74).

> Nevertheless, any one's experience will teach him, that though he can take in an indiscriminating sweep of things at one glance, it is quite impossible for him, attentively, and completely,

to examine any two things—however large or however small—at one and the same instant of time; never mind if they lie side by side and touch each other. But if you now come to separate these two objects, and surround each by a circle of profound darkness; then, in order to see one of them, in such a manner as to bring your mind to bear on it, the other will be utterly excluded from your contemporary consciousness. How is it, then, with the whale? . . . is his brain so much more comprehensive, combining, and subtle than man's, that he can at the same moment of time attentively examine two distinct prospects, one on one side of him, and the other in an exactly opposite direction?

Melville goes on to suggest that the "extraordinary vacillations of movement" exhibited by sperm whales when they are "beset by three or four boats" may proceed "from the helpless perplexity of volition, in which their divided and diametrically opposite powers of vision must involve them" (Ch. 74).

Might these "extraordinary vacillations" rather be the whale's attempt to keep visual track of the wheeling boats? Many birds, who also "suffer" from eyes on opposite sides of their heads, achieve a measure of "binocular" depth perception by bobbing their heads back and forth, giving their brains two slightly different views, and permitting the relative motion of parallax to give them approximately the same depth information we get all at once from our two eyes with their overlapping fields.

Melville assumes that whatever it is like to be a whale, it is similar to human consciousness in one regard: there is a single boss in charge, an "I" or "ego" that either superhumanly distributes its gaze over disparate scenarios, or humanly flicks back and forth between two rivals. But might there be even more radical discoveries in store? Whales are not the only animals whose eyes have visual fields with little or no overlap; rabbits are another. In rabbits there is no interocular transfer of learning! That is, if you train a rabbit that a particular shape is a source of danger by demonstrations carefully restricted to its *left* eye, the rabbit will exhibit no "knowledge" about that shape, no fear or flight behavior, when the menacing shape is presented to its *right* eye. When we ask what it is like to be that rabbit, it appears that at the very least we must put a subscript, *dexter* or *sinister*, on our question in order to make it well formed.

[. . .]

I have argued at length, in *Consciousness Explained* (1991), that the sort of informational unification that is the most important prerequisite for *our* kind of consciousness is not anything we are born with, not part of our innate "hardwiring," but in surprisingly large measure an artifact of our immersion in human culture. What that early education produces in us is a sort of benign "user-illusion"—I call it the Cartesian Theater: the illusion that there is a place in our brains where the show goes on, towards which all perceptual "input" streams, and whence flow all "conscious intentions" to act and speak. I claim that other species—and human beings when they are newborn—simply *are not beset* by the illusion of the Cartesian Theater. Until the organization is formed, there is simply no user in there to be fooled. This is undoubtedly a radical suggestion, hard for many thinkers to take seriously, hard for them even to *entertain*. Let me repeat it, since many critics have ignored the possibility that I mean it—a misfiring of their generous allegiance to the principle of charity.

In order to be conscious—in order to be the sort of thing it is like something to be—it is necessary to have a certain sort of informational organization that endows that thing with a wide set of cognitive powers (such as the powers of reflection and re-representation). This sort of internal organization does not come automatically with so-called sentience. It is not the birthright of mammals or warm-blooded creatures or vertebrates; it is not even the birthright of human beings. It is an organization that is swiftly achieved in one species, ours, and in no other. Other species no doubt achieve *somewhat similar* organizations, but the differences are so great that most of the speculative translations of imagination from our case to theirs *make no sense*.

My claim is not that other species lack our kind of *self*-consciousness, as Nagel (1991) and others have supposed. I am claiming that what must be added to mere responsivity, mere discrimination, to count as consciousness *at all* is an organization that is not ubiquitous among sentient organisms. This idea has been dismissed out of hand by most thinkers.[1] Nagel, for instance, finds it to be a "bizarre claim" that "implausibly implies that babies can't have conscious sensations before they learn to form judgments about themselves." Lockwood is equally emphatic: "Forget culture, forget language. The mystery begins with the lowliest organism which, when you stick a pin in it, say, doesn't merely react, but actually *feels* something."

Indeed, that is where the *mystery* begins if you insist on starting *there*, with the assumption that you know what you mean by the contrast between merely reacting and actually feeling. And the mystery will never stop, apparently, if that is where you start.

In an insightful essay on bats (and whether it is like anything to be a bat), Kathleen Akins (1993) pursues the sort of detailed investigation into functional neuroscience that Nagel eschews, and she shows that Nagel is at best ill-advised in simply *assuming* that a bat *must* have a point of view. Akins sketches a few of the many different stories that can be told from the vantage point of the various subsystems that go to making up a bat's nervous system. It is tempting, on learning these details, to ask ourselves "and where in the brain does the bat *itself* reside?" but this is an even more dubious question in the case of the bat than it is in our own case. There are many parallel stories that could be told about what goes on in you and me. What gives one of those stories about *us* pride of place at any one time is *just this*: it is the story you or I will tell if asked (to put a complicated matter crudely).

When we consider a creature that isn't a teller—has no language—what happens to the supposition that one of *its* stories is privileged? The hypothesis that there is one such story that would tell us (if we could understand it) what it is actually like to be that creature dangles with no evident foundation or source of motivation—except dubious tradition. Bats, like us, have plenty of relatively peripheral neural machinery devoted to "low level processing" of the sorts that are routinely supposed to be entirely unconscious in us. And bats have no machinery analogous to our machinery for issuing public protocols regarding their current subjective circumstances, of course. Do they then have some *other* "high level" or "central" system that plays a privileged role? Perhaps they do and perhaps they don't. Perhaps there is no role for such a level to play, no room for any system to perform the dimly imagined task of elevating merely unconscious neural processes to consciousness. After all, Peter Singer has no difficulty supposing that an insect might keep its act together without the help of such a central system. It is an open empirical question, or rather, a currently unimagined and complex set of open empirical questions, what sorts of "high levels" are to be found in which species under which conditions.

Here, for instance, is one possibility to consider: the bat lacks the brain-equipment for *expressing* judgments (in language), but the bat may nevertheless have to *form* judgments (of some inarticulate sort), in order to organize and modulate its language-free activities. Wherever these inarticulate judgment-like things happen is where we should look for the bat's privileged vantage point. But this would involve just the sort of postulation about sophisticated judgments that Nagel found so implausible to attribute to a baby. If the distinction between conscious and unconscious has nothing to do with anything sophisticated like judgment, what else could it involve?

[. . .]

It turns out that we end up where we began: analyzing patterns of behavior (external and internal—but not "private"), and attempting to interpret them in the light of evolutionary hypotheses regarding their past or current functions.

The very idea of there being a dividing line between those creatures "it is like something to be" and those that are mere "automata" begins to look like an artifact of our traditional presumptions. I have offered (Dennett, 1991) a variety of reasons for concluding that in the case of adult human consciousness there is no principled way of distinguishing when or if the mythic light bulb of consciousness is turned on (and shone on this or that item). Consciousness, I claim, even in the case we understand best—our own—is not an all-or-nothing, on-or-off phenomenon. If this is right, then consciousness is not the sort of phenomenon it is assumed to be by most of the participants in the debates over animal consciousness. Wondering whether it is "probable" that all mammals have *it* thus begins to look like wondering whether or not any birds are *wise* or reptiles have *gumption*: a case of overworking a term from folk psychology that has lost its utility along with its hard edges.

Some thinkers are unmoved by this prospect. They are still unshakably sure that consciousness— "phenomenal" consciousness, in the terms of Ned Block (1992, 1993, 1995, forthcoming)—*is* a phenomenon that is either present or absent, rather as if some events in the brain glowed in the dark and the rest did not.[2] Of course, if you simply will not contemplate the hypothesis that consciousness might turn out *not* to be a property that thus sunders the universe in twain, you will be sure that I must have overlooked consciousness altogether. But then you should also recognize that you maintain the mystery of consciousness by simply refusing to consider the evidence for one of the most promising theories of it.

Postscript: Pain, Suffering, and Morality

[. . .]

The phenomenon of pain is neither homogeneous across species nor simple. We can see this in ourselves, by noting how unobvious the answers are to some simple questions. Are the "pains" that usefully prevent us from allowing our limbs to assume awkward, joint-damaging positions while we sleep experiences that require a "subject" (McGinn, 1995), or might they be properly called unconscious pains? Do they have moral significance in any case? Such body-protecting states of the nervous system might be called "sentient" states without thereby implying that they were the experiences of any self, any ego, any subject. For such states to matter—whether or not we call them pains or conscious states or experiences—there must be an enduring, *complex* subject *to whom* they matter because they are a source of suffering. Snakes (or parts of snakes!) may feel pain—depending on how we choose to define that term—but the evidence mounts that snakes lack the sort of over-arching, long-term organization that leaves room for significant suffering. That does not mean that we ought to treat snakes the way we treat worn out tires, but just that concern for their suffering should be tempered by an appreciation of how modest their capacities for suffering are.

While the distinction between pain and suffering is, like most everyday, nonscientific distinctions, somewhat blurred at the edges, it is, nevertheless, a valuable and intuitively satisfying mark or measure of moral importance. When I step on your toe, causing a brief but definite (and definitely conscious) pain, I do you scant harm—typically none at all. The pain, though intense, is too brief to matter, and I have done no long-term damage to your foot. The idea that you "suffer" for a second or two is a risible misapplication of that important notion, and even when we grant that my causing you a few seconds pain may irritate you a few more seconds or even minutes—especially if you think I did it deliberately—the pain itself, as a brief, negatively signed experience, is of vanishing moral significance. (If in stepping on your toe I have interrupted your singing of an aria, thereby ruining your operatic career, that is quite another matter.)

Many discussions seem to assume tacitly: (1) that suffering and pain are the same thing, on a different scale; (2) that all pain is "experienced pain"; and (3) that "amount of suffering" is to be calculated ("in principle") by just adding up all the pains (the awfulness of each of which is determined by duration-times-intensity). These assumptions, looked at dispassionately in the cold light of day—a difficult feat for some partisans—are ludicrous. A little exercise may help: would you exchange the sum total of the suffering you will experience during the next year for one five-minute blast of no doubt excruciating agony that summed up to the "same amount" of total pain-and-suffering? I certainly would. In fact, I would gladly take the bargain even if you "doubled" or "quadrupled" the total annual amount—just so long as it would be all over in five minutes. (We are assuming, of course, that this horrible episode does not kill me or render me insane—after the pain is over—or have other long-term effects that amount to or cause me further suffering; the deal was to pack all the suffering into one jolt.) I expect anybody would be happy to make such a deal. But it doesn't really make sense. It implies that the benefactor who provided such a service gratis to all, *ex hypothesi*, would be doubling or quadrupling the world's suffering—and the world would love him for it.

It seems obvious to me that something is radically wrong with the assumptions that permit us to sum and compare suffering in any such straightforward way. But some people think otherwise; one person's *reductio ad absurdum* is another's counter-intuitive discovery. We ought to be able to sort out these differences, calmly, even if the best resolution we can reasonably hope for is a recognition that some choices of perspective are cognitively impenetrable.

Notes

1. Two rare—and widely misunderstood—exceptions to this tradition are Julian Jaynes (1976) and Howard Margolis (1987), whose cautious observations survey the field of investigation I am proposing to open:

   A creature with a very large brain, capable of storing large numbers of complex patterns, and capable of carrying through elaborate sequences of internal representations, with this capability refined and elaborated to a very high degree, would be a creature like you and me. Somehow, as I have stressed, consciousness conspicuously enters the scheme at this point of highly elaborate dynamic internal representations. Correctly or not, most of us find it hard to imagine that an insect is conscious, at least conscious in anything approximating the sense in which humans are conscious. But it is hard to imagine that a dog is not conscious in at least something like the way an infant is conscious (Margolis, 1987, p. 55).

2. John Searle also holds fast to this myth. See, for example, Searle (1992), and my review, 1993.

References

Akins, Kathleen, "What Is It Like to be Boring and Myopic?" pp. 124–160, in Bo Dahlbom, ed., *Dennett and His Critics* (Oxford: Blackwell, 1993).

Block, Ned, "Begging the Question Against Phenomenal Consciousness," (Commentary on Dennett and Kinsbourne), *Behavioral and Brain Sciences*, 15 (1992): 205–6.

Block, Ned, "On a Confusion about a Function of Consciousness," *Behavioral and Brain Sciences*, 18 (1995): 272–287.

Block, Ned, "Review of Daniel Dennett, *Consciousness Explained*," *Journal of Philosophy*, 90 (1993): 181–93.

Block, Ned, "What Is Dennett's Theory a Theory of?" in *Philosophical Topics*, Special issue on the work of Dennett, forthcoming.

Dennett, Daniel, *Consciousness Explained* (Boston: Little Brown, 1991).

Dennett, Daniel, "Review of John Searle, 'The Rediscovery of Consciousness'," *Journal of Philosophy*, 90 (1993): 193–205.

Dennett, Daniel, "The Practical Requirements for Making a Conscious Robot," Philosophical Transactions of the Royal Society of London A 349 (1994): 133–46.

Jaynes, Julian, *The Origins of Consciousness in the Breakdown of the Bicameral Mind* (Boston: Houghton Mifflin, 1976).

Leiber, Justin, "Cartesian Linguistics?" *Philosophia*, 118 (1988): 309–46.

Lockwood, Michael, "Dennett's Mind," *Inquiry*, 36 (1993): 59–72.

Margolis, Howard, *Patterns, Thinking, and Cognition* (Chicago: University of Chicago Press, 1987).

McGinn, Colin, "Animal Minds, Animal Morality," *Social Research* 62 (3): 731–747 (1995).

Nagel, Thomas, "What We Have in Mind When We Say We're Thinking," (Review of *Consciousness Explained*), *Wall Street Journal* (November 7, 1991).

16 New Evidence of Animal Consciousness

Donald R. Griffin and Gayle B. Speck

Griffin and Speck propose that the search for neural correlates of consciousness has not found any consciousness-producing structure or process limited to humans. They also argue that appropriate responses to novel challenges for which nonhuman animals have not been prepared by genetic programming or previous experience provide suggestive evidence of animal consciousness. Finally they note that there are increasing numbers of cases of animal communication reporting subjective experiences.

Introduction

Experimental and observational data about the complexity and versatility of animal cognition have been reported and discussed extensively since the subject was reviewed in the first issue of this journal (Griffin 1998). The term "cognition" is ordinarily taken to mean information processing in human and nonhuman central nervous systems that often leads to choices and decisions. But the possibility that nonhuman cognition is accompanied or influenced by consciousness has received relatively little attention, largely because many behavioral scientists have been extremely reluctant to consider nonhuman consciousness on the grounds that it is impossible to obtain objective evidence about subjective experiences. Yet much of the new evidence strengthens that case as well, and it is time to reconsider the long-standing aversion to scientific investigation of animal consciousness. In view of the confusions surrounding terms describing mental states, and despite the fact that some scientists feel that consciousness is a higher and more complex state than awareness, we will follow the common usage of aware and conscious as synonyms that describe subjective experiences. We will assume that these states or processes are produced by the functioning of living nervous systems and not something ethereal and different in kind from anything in the physical universe, as emphasized by Searle (2000, 2002) and Donald (2001).

[. . .]

Consciousness is the subjective state of feeling or thinking about objects and events. The word is often interpreted to mean full-blown human thinking, although of course no animal attains more than a trivial fraction of the scope and versatility of human conscious thinking. But many animals give evidence of what Natsoulas (1983, p. 29) defined as consciousness 3, "the state or facility of being mentally conscious or aware of anything." This has been called perceptual, primary or basic consciousness. However limited its content may be, such awareness is importantly different from unconscious cognition. Consciousness is often considered a complex and "higher" form of cognition; but as Dawkins (2000) has emphasized, the content of human consciousness ranges from very simple to enormously subtle and complex. Insofar as animals are conscious, the content of their awareness probably varies along a continuum from the simplest and crudest feelings to thinking about the challenges they face and alternative actions they might choose.

Computers process information, and robots can even simulate animal behavior; but they can only do what human designers have programmed them to do. It is very unlikely that they have subjective experiences without a living central nervous system. Although no single piece of evidence that an animal is conscious is totally conclusive, and alternate explanations not involving consciousness are always conceivable, suggestive evidence can serve as an entering wedge that stimulates further investigation leading to improved and more conclusive data. Following up on these possibilities provides opportunities and challenges for scientific investigation to evaluate the following hypothesis: Animals are sometimes aware of objects and events, including social relationships, memories, and simple short-term anticipation of likely happenings in the near future, and they make choices of actions they believe are likely to get what they want or avoid what they dislike or fear. Such basic consciousness may but need not include self-awareness or metacognition—thinking about one's thoughts or those of others (Natsoulas' consciousness 4).

[. . .]

The central question about the consciousness of animals is whether they experience anything of the same general kind. And if so, what is the content of their awareness? Whatever they feel and think must be important both to the animals concerned and to our understanding of them and their ways of life.

It is helpful to consider questions about the content of an animal's awareness in terms of the probability of awareness, pA. If we have complete certainty that a given animal has a particular conscious experience, then pA = 1.0, and pA = 0 means that we know with certainty that it does not. If we take literally the claim that it is impossible to learn anything about the so-called private experiences of other species, we are obliged to assume that pA is always 0.5. In practice, however, there has been a tendency to conclude from the impossibility of setting pA at 1.0 that it must be zero.

[. . .]

There are three general categories of evidence that show animals' pA is sometimes well above 0.5: (1) close similarity of basic central nervous system structure and function in a wide variety of animals, indicating that whatever processes lead to conscious experiences are not limited to human brains, (2) versatile adjustment of behavior in response to unpredictable challenges, and (3) animal communication, which often seems to inform receivers about the conscious experiences of the sender and which can also provide information about them to eavesdropping cognitive ethologists. We rely heavily on both verbal and nonverbal communication to infer what our human companions are thinking and feeling, and the same basic approach can be applied to many other species. We will review these three areas in this chapter.

Neural Correlates of Consciousness

As Crick and Koch (1998, p. 105) put it: "The explanation of consciousness is one of the major unsolved problems of modern science. After several thousand years of speculation, it would be very gratifying to find an answer to it." It is theoretically conceivable that only the human nervous system has the capability of producing consciousness. If so, it is an important challenge for the neurosciences to discover the nature of this unique consciousness-producing ability. Some point to the size or the complexity of the human brain, or to specific areas, or else to language ability. But there is no clear evidence that any of these factors is necessary for consciousness. Another theoretical possibility is that simple conscious thinking is an important core function of living central nervous systems and that in small brains it may therefore constitute a larger proportion of brain activity than in animals with very large brains.

Recognition of the importance of these questions has been part of the motivation for an extremely active and talented series of investigations that have recently attempted to identify the neural correlates of consciousness (NCC), as discussed by Crick and Koch (1998, 2000, 2003), Taylor (1999), Metzinger (2000), Searle (2000, 2002), and Baars (2002).

[. . .]

Baars (2002) has lucidly reviewed how modern methods of imaging brain function have provided objective evidence of neural activities correlated with consciousness. In many of these recent investigations of NCC, animals are used for better control of experiments or for invasive procedures, and it is simply taken for granted that they are conscious. Logothetis (1999, p. 70), in his investigations of binocular rivalry, notes that "monkey brains are organized like those of humans, and they respond to stimuli much as humans do. Consequently, we think the animals are conscious in somewhat the same way as humans are." Kanwisher (2001) concurs, stating: "It seems reasonable to assume that when a monkey reports the presence of a particular stimulus, he is aware of the stimulus in something like the way that a human would be. Nevertheless it would be reassuring to find similar results in the human brain." She and her colleagues (Tong et al. 1998) do find similar results in a human experiment that was modeled after the monkey experiments of Logothetis. Engel and Singer (2001), after reviewing numerous studies, some of which involved monkeys and cats, implicitly assume that these animals were conscious. Seward and Seward (2000, p. 86) conclude that "in rodents and lower vertebrates, normal visual awareness is partly due to synchronized oscillatory activities in the optic tectum and partly due to similar activities in the visual cortex."

[. . .]

Blindsight is an intriguing phenomenon that has provided an opportunity to test whether a monkey is or is not conscious of particular visual stimuli. It was given this name by Weiskrantz et al. (1974) from studies of certain human patients who had lesions in the visual cortex that produced large blind areas in the visual field but who could nevertheless respond in limited ways to visual stimuli in their blind fields. If stimuli are presented in these blind areas and the patient is required to guess about them, he is as surprised as anyone that his guesses are far more accurate than expected from chance. [. . .]

Cowey and Stoerig (1995, 1997) and Stoerig et al. (2002) showed similar results in monkeys with large cortical lesions. The monkeys had been trained to touch a small bright square on a touch-sensitive computer screen to obtain food. With sufficient training they were able to do this even when the square fell in their blind field. These monkeys were then trained to touch a different visual pattern when no bright square was presented, and surprisingly they then touched this "no stimulus" pattern when the bright square was presented in their blind field—even though in other experiments they would touch the square to obtain food. It was thus possible to distinguish, under these experimental conditions, whether the monkey was or was not aware of particular stimuli.

Roth (2000) emphasizes brain size: "Among all features of vertebrate brains, the size of cortex or structures homologous to the mammalian cortex, as well as the number of neurons and synapses contained in these structures, correlate most clearly with the complexity of cognitive functions, including states of consciousness" (Roth 2000, p. 94). There is as yet no way to determine the minimum brain size necessary for the most basic level of consciousness, although several thousand neurons would seem adequate for the kinds of NCC that appear most plausible to contemporary neuroscientists. Roth is critical of the idea that language is required for consciousness. If we accepted that suggestion, he points out, "we would be forced to assume that animals are capable of unconsciously mastering cognitive tasks that in humans require highest concentration" (Roth 2000, p. 95).

Damasio (1999) emphasizes the importance of bodily emotions for consciousness. He allows that artifacts such as computers might be created that have the formal mechanisms of consciousness, but they would not be conscious in the full sense. "Feeling is, in effect, the barrier, because consciousness may require the existence of feelings. The 'looks' of emotion can be simulated, but what feelings feel like cannot be duplicated in silicon" (Damasio 1999, p. 314). Damasio (2000) distinguishes what he calls "core consciousness"—which "provides an organism with a sense of self about here and now [but] does not pertain to the future or the past"—from "extended consciousness," which "provides the organism with an identity and a person, an elaborate sense of self, and places that self at a specific point in an individual historical time. . . . [It] offers awareness of the lived past and of the anticipated future, along with the objects in the here and now." Emphasizing that "consciousness depends most critically on evolutionarily old regions (of the vertebrate brain)," Damasio believes that core consciousness is not exclusively human and that "simple levels of extended consciousness are present in some nonhumans" (Damasio 2000, pp. 112–118).

[. . .]

Crick and Koch (2003) propose a "framework" applicable to the visual system of primates, which they believe "knits all these ideas together, so that for the first time we have a coherent scheme for the NCC in philosophical, psychological and neural terms" (Crick and Koch 2003, p. 124). This framework emphasizes "competing coalitions" of neurons and two-way communication between coalitions in the back and front of the brain. They conclude that explicit representations and synchronized activity such as gamma frequency oscillations may be necessary, but not sufficient for consciousness. Reentrant pathways and back projections are widespread in central nervous systems, however, and if they constitute NCC there is no reason to rule out at least simple consciousness in many animals with central nervous systems.

Has this intensive search for NCC disclosed any structure or process necessary for consciousness that is found only in human brains? The short answer is no. But neither has this search identified any specific structure or process that we can yet be sure is both necessary and sufficient to generate human conscious experience. Thus it remains possible that if and when such an essential consciousness-generating neural mechanism is discovered, it might turn out to be something found only in human brains. [. . .]

Versatility

A type of versatility that is particularly relevant as evidence of consciousness is the departure from routine behavior patterns to cope with novel and unpredictable challenges in ways that suggest at least short-range planning of intended actions. Such versatility is helpful in allowing us to distinguish relatively inflexible preprogrammed behavior from being aware of the availability of alternative actions and choosing those the animal believes will have desired consequences. [. . .] Both natural selection and individual experience have doubtless contributed to the development of such versatile thinking and action; but the specific reactions to particular situations can scarcely have been preprogrammed if neither the animal nor its ancestors have previously encountered such situations.

[. . .]

Explicit Learning and Episodic Memory

Students of human learning and memory often distinguish explicit from implicit learning and their resulting memories. The former can be both recalled and reported verbally; the latter entails changes in behavior resulting from prior exposure to stimuli that the subject cannot report because he is currently unaware of them. The concept of explicit memory is similar to declarative memory, which was so named because such memories could be reported or "declared" by human subjects. It is usually assumed that animals cannot have declarative memories because they lack (human) language. This widespread assumption is seriously undermined, however, by twentieth-century discoveries about the versatility of animal communication, which can convey information based on memories by other means than human language, as reviewed by Griffin (2001). [. . .]

Memories of past events that include awareness of oneself perceiving the event on some remembered occasion are termed episodic; and Tulving (1972, 2002) and others have claimed that episodic memory is based on a uniquely human neural system. A strong challenge to the claim of human uniqueness comes from recent experiments by Clayton and Dickinson (1998) and Clayton et al. (2000, 2001, 2003). They first demonstrated that scrub jays (*Aphelocoma coerulescens*) can learn that a particular type of preferred food (wax-moth larvae) become unpalatable five days after the birds had stored them, but that peanuts, a less preferred food, remain edible. The jays were trained to cache these two types of food by burying them in sand in two different locations. When tested four days after caching, and after the sand had been replaced to prevent odor cues from affecting their choices, the jays were more likely to choose the location they knew contained larvae. But after five days they usually went where they had stored peanuts.

Clayton et al. (2001, p. 28) prefer to call this type of memory episodic-like rather than episodic because the latter term has been applied to human "autonoetic" memories, which are verbally reported to include a conscious experience of self. This they claim "has no obvious manifestation in nonlinguistic behaviour" (Griffiths et al. 1999). For this reason, "we regard the what-where-when memory for caching episodes as no more than an analogue of human episodic memory." [. . .] Emery and Clayton (2001, p. 443) discovered that scrub jays "with prior experience of pilfering another bird's caches subsequently re-cached food in new cache sites . . . but only when they had been observed caching. Jays without pilfering experience did not, even though they had observed other jays caching. . . . Jays relate information about their previous experience as a pilferer to the possibility of future stealing by another bird and modify their caching behavior accordingly." These birds appeared to have profited from traveling backward and perhaps also forward in time. A similar example was provided by the dolphins that Pryor et al. (1969) trained to perform on command a completely novel acrobatic action, since they had to remember their complete repertoires in order to create something new. Thus the claim that episodic memory in the full sense of the term is uniquely human rests largely on the assumption that nonhuman animals lack a conscious sense of self.

Knowing What One Knows

Some scientists claim that although animals often know simple facts, they do not know *that* they know. This is a type of metamemory or memory about one's own recollection and would certainly be a higher level of awareness than is usually assumed for animals. With our human companions we assume they know that they know something because they can use human language to express this distinction. But how can we learn, for example, whether an animal not only knows that food is available at a certain time and place but also knows that she knows this? As with many such questions about nonhuman mentality, this one has seemed impossible to answer; but instead of recognizing our ignorance, it has been customary to leap to a negative conclusion.

Goal-Directed Desires and Actions

Dickinson and Balleine (2000, p. 202) reviewed experiments on goal evaluation by laboratory rats, which led them to conclude: "Goal-directed actions of the rat are mediated by intentional representations of the causal relationship between action and outcome and of the value assigned to the outcome. The capacity for goal-directed action requires not only the evolution of intentional representations, but also the co-evolution of an interface between these representations and the animal's biological responses to the goal objects, events, or states. This interface, we suggest, is simple, nonreflexive consciousness in which the biological evaluation of a potential goal is manifested as an affective or hedonic response conjointly with an internal representation of the goal." By "simple, nonreflexive consciousness," Dickinson and Balleine appear to mean what we and others have called primary or perceptual consciousness. And if we understand them correctly, they are using the terms "intention" and "intentional" to include, though perhaps not be limited to, the customary sense of consciously intending to do something, and as one example of the broader philosophical usage of intentional to mean aboutness.

This suggestion by Dickinson and Balleine typifies the degree to which the antimentalistic taboos of behaviorism have been abandoned by leading investigators of animal learning. In addition to suggesting that rats experience simple consciousness, they believe that it plays a crucial role in producing adaptive behavior. Furthermore they propose that emotional feelings play an essential role in goal-directed intentions and the resulting goal-directed behavior. It is certainly reasonable to assume that the animals perceive their goals as desirable; and there is no reason why simple consciousness could not also accompany other forms of perception and influence other types of action.

Tools

The use and especially the making of tools require at least short-term planning and adaptation of behavior to specific and often unpredictable situations. Hart et al. (2001) describe how Asian elephants modify branches to make them useful for fly switching. Many aspects of tool use by chimpanzees are described in detail in Matsuzawa (2001). Sousa and Matsuzawa (2001) demonstrated that captive chimpanzees not only use tokens they have learned to exchange for desired food but also save the tokens for future use. Tonooka (2001) described how some chimpanzees fold leaves to hold drinking water.

New Caledonian crows (*Corvus moneduloides*) have provided perhaps the most surprising and significant new examples of tool use and manufacture, as described and analyzed in detail by Hunt (1996, 2000a, 2000b) and Hunt and Gray (2003). These crows probe for invertebrates in crevices and use different types to probe in different locations. The most complex tools are of two types: twigs stripped of leaves and often of bark and then cut so that a short projecting piece of a branch forms a hook, and long strips torn from pandanus leaves fashioned into tools by removing material from one end to form a hook. The crows then insert these hooks into cavities and drag out prey that would otherwise be difficult or impossible to dislodge. Although most hook tools are discarded after the prey has been obtained, they are sometimes carried about or later retrieved and reused. Young crows make clumsy efforts to obtain food in this way and sometimes try to probe with less effective pieces of vegetation.

[. . .]

Communication Can Report Subjective Experience

After reviewing evidence that visual imagery appears to be very similar in humans and monkeys, Frith et al. (1999, p. 107) conclude that "to discover what someone is conscious of we need them to give us some form of report about their subjective experience. . . . [H]owever we do not need to use language to report our mental experiences. Gestures and movements can be made with a deliberate communicative intent. . . . [T]he same procedure can be used in studies of animals." This realization of the significance of communication as a source of evidence about conscious feelings and thoughts entails a simple transfer to animals of the basic methods by which we infer what our human companions are thinking or feeling, as discussed in detail by Griffin (1976, 1984, 1998, 2001).

There are three general kinds of animal communication that are useful as evidence of conscious experiences:

1. *Systems derived from simple components of human language.* These include manual gestures modified from the sign language of the deaf, as reviewed by Fouts (1997); the keyboard system used by apes at the Yerkes Laboratory, as reviewed by Savage-Rumbaugh et al. (1998); and the imitation of human words used meaningfully by African grey parrots, as reviewed by Pepperberg (1999). Fouts and Jensvold (2002) have video-recorded chimpanzees using manual gestures modeled on the sign language of the deaf to communicate with each other in the absence of any human observer. Savage-Rumbaugh et al. (1998) have added significantly to the already abundant evidence that chimpanzees and bonobos communicate a variety of conscious thoughts and emotional feelings by use of the Yerkes Laboratory keyboard system (which uses symbols for English words). These apes also understand simple levels of human speech. Pepperberg (1999) has provided a coherent account of her extensive studies of how African grey parrots use their imitations of human words to express simple thoughts and answer moderately complex questions. Pepperberg and Lynn (2001) recognize that this type of communication is evidence of perceptual consciousness.

2. *Experimental arrangements by which animals can communicate about their thoughts and feelings by responses to controlled stimulation designed for this purpose.* For many years,

animals have been used in experiments on visual perception, and their manual responses, such as pulling a lever, touching a spot on a computer screen, or making intentional eye movements, have been taken as reporting. In reference to binocular rivalry, for example, Rees et al. (2002, p. 263) remark: "Monkeys can be trained to report their percept during rivalry, and their behaviour is similar to that of humans." Herman (2002) has shown that captive dolphins can learn not only to understand gestural commands from human trainers but also that certain gestures represent body parts. Xitco et al. (2001) report that dolphins can also learn to point by orienting their bodies toward some object. They were observed to do this only when a human companion was present, and the pointing was sometimes related to the dolphin's receiving information about an object via an underwater keyboard of symbols modeled after the keyboards used with apes in the Yerkes Laboratory.

3.   *Natural communicative behavior of animals.* Some of the most important new evidence about natural communication concerns alarm calls. Several new examples have been added to the classic experiments of Seyfarth et al. (1980) on the alarm calls of vervet monkeys (*Cercopithecus aethiops*) that designate which of three major predators has been sighted. [. . .] Manser (2001) has reported that in the social mongoose (*Suricata suricatta*), different call types are given in response to different predators and that the urgency of the danger is also indicated by the noisiness of the call. From these and earlier studies it seems that some animals can communicate both urgency and level of arousal, and to a limited extent the type of predator. Alarm calling is not a stereotyped reaction, for vervet monkeys occasionally withhold them, as discussed by Cheney and Seyfarth (1990, pp. 107–109).

Intriguing and puzzling data about the alarm calls of prairie dogs (*Cynomys gunnisoni*) have been reported in a review by Slobodchikoff (2002). These social rodents that live in a colonial burrow system were presented with real predators, models, and human intruders, and the resulting alarm calls were then recorded. Responses of the prairie dogs to playbacks led Slobodchikoff to conclude: "A call can identify the category of predator, such as coyote, domestic dog, or red-tailed hawk. . . . Each category of predator-specific calls elicits different escape responses. . . . [H]awk and human alarm calls elicit running to the burrows and diving inside. . . . Coyote and domestic dog alarm calls elicit either a running to the lip of the burrow and standing at the burrow entrance (coyote) or standing in place where the animal was feeding (domestic dog)" (Slobodchikoff 2002, p. 258). If confirmed, this level of semantic communication appears comparable to alarm calling by vervet monkeys and calls for further investigation.

[. . .]

Discussion

Although no single piece of evidence provides a "smoking gun" that proves with total certainty that pA, the probability of awareness, is 1.0, the cumulative impact of the data reviewed above, together with abundant evidence previously available, renders it far more likely than not that animal consciousness is real and significant. The basic nature of central nervous system function is much the same in all animals with central nervous systems, despite wide variation in gross anatomy and concentration of particular functions in specific areas of the brain. No uniquely human correlate of consciousness has been discovered.

[. . .]

References

Baars RJ (2002) The conscious access hypothesis: Origins and recent evidence. *Trends Cogn Sci* 6:47–52.
Cheney DL, Seyfarth RM (1990) *How monkeys see the world, inside the mind of other species.* University of Chicago Press, Chicago.

Clayton NS, Dickinson A (1998) Episodic-like memory during cache recovery by scrub jays. *Nature* 398:272–274.

Clayton NS, Griffiths DP, Dickinson A (2000) Declarative and episodic-like memory in animals: Personal musings of a scrub jay. In: Heyes C, Huber L (eds) *The evolution of cognition*. MIT Press, Cambridge, MA, pp 273–288.

Clayton NS, Yu KS, Dickinson A (2001) Scrub jays (*Aphelocoma coerulescens*) form integrated memories of the multiple features of caching episodes. *J Exp Psychol Anim Behav Process* 27:17–29.

Clayton NS, Yu KS, Dickinson A (2003) Interacting cache memories: Evidence for flexible memory use by western scrub-jays (*Aphelocoma californica*). *J Exp Psychol Anim Behav Process* 29:14–22.

Cowey A, Stoerig P (1995) Blindsight in monkeys. *Nature* 373:247–249.

Cowey A, Stoerig P (1997) Visual detection in monkeys with blindsight. *Neuropsychologia* 35:929–939.

Crick F, Koch C (1998) Consciousness and neuroscience. *Cereb Cortex* 8:97–107.

Crick F, Koch C (2000) The unconscious homunculus. In: Metzinger T (ed) *Neural correlates of consciousness, empirical and conceptual questions*. MIT Press, Cambridge, MA, pp 103–110.

Crick F, Koch C (2003) A framework for consciousness. *Nat Neurosci* 6:119–126.

Damasio AR (1999) *The feeling of what happens: Body and emotion in the making of consciousness*. Harcourt, Orlando, FL.

Damasio AR (2000) A neurobiology for consciousness. In: Metzinger T (ed) *Neural correlates of consciousness, empirical and conceptual questions*. MIT Press, Cambridge, MA, pp 111–120.

Dawkins MS (2000) Animal mind and animal emotions. *Am Zool* 40:883–888.

Dickinson A, Balleine BW (2000) Causal cognition and goal-directed action. In: Heyes C, Huber L (eds) *The evolution of cognition*. MIT Press, Cambridge, MA, pp 185–204.

Donald M (2001) *A mind so rare, the evolution of human consciousness*. Norton, New York.

Emery NJ, Clayton NS (2001) Effects of experience and social context on prospective caching strategies by scrub jays. *Nature* 414:443–446.

Engel AK, Singer W (2001) Temporal binding and the neural correlates of sensory awareness. *Trends Cogn Sci* 5:16–26.

Fouts RS (1997) *Next of kin: What chimpanzees have taught me about who we are*. Morrow, New York.

Fouts RS, Jensvold MLA (2002) Armchair delusions versus empirical realities: A neurological model for the continuity of ape and human languaging. In: Goodman M, Moffat MLA (eds) *Probing human origins*. American Academy of Arts and Sciences, Cambridge, MA, pp 87–101.

Frith D, Perry R, Lumer E (1999) The neural correlates of conscious experience: An experimental framework. *Trends Cogn Sci* 3:105–114.

Griffin DR (1976) *The question of animal awareness*. Rockefeller University Press, New York.

Griffin DR (1984) *Animal thinking*. Harvard University Press, Cambridge, MA.

Griffin DR (1998) From cognition to consciousness. *Anim Cogn* 1:3–16.

Griffin DR (2001) *Animal minds, beyond cognition to consciousness*. University of Chicago Press, Chicago.

Griffiths D, Dickinson A, Clayton NS (1999) Episodic memory: What can animals remember about their past? *Trends Cogn Sci* 3:74–80.

Hart BL, Hart LA, McCoy M, Sarath CR (2001) Cognitive behaviour in Asian elephants: Use and modification of branches for fly switching. *Anim Behav* 62:839–847.

Herman LM (2002) Exploring the cognitive world of the bottlenose dolphin. In: Bekoff, M, Allen C, Burghardt GM (eds) *The cognitive animal, empirical and theoretical perspectives*. MIT Press, Cambridge, MA, pp 275–283.

Hunt GR (1996) Manufacture and use of hook-tools by New Caledonian crows (*Corvus moneduloides*). *Nature* 379:249–251.

Hunt GR (2000a) Tool use by the New Caledonian crow (*Corvus moneduloides*) to obtain *Cerambycidae* from dead wood. *Emu* 100:109–114.

Hunt GR (2000b) Human-like, population-level specialization in the manufacture of pandanus tools by New Caledonian crows *Corvus moneduloides*. *Proc R Soc Lond B* 267:403–413.

Hunt GR, Gray RD (2003) Diversification and cumulative evolution in New Caledonian crow tool manufacture. *Proc R Soc Lond B* 270:867–874.

Kanwisher N (2001) Neural events and perceptual awareness. *Cognition* 79:89–113.

Logothetis NK (1999) Vision: A window on consciousness. *Sci Am* Nov:69–75.

Manser MB (2001) The acoustic structure of suricates' alarm calls varies with predator type and the level of response urgency. *Proc R Soc Lond B Biol* 268:2315–2324.

Matsuzawa T (ed) (2001) *Primate origins of human cognition and behavior.* Springer, Berlin Heidelberg New York.

Metzinger T (ed) (2000) *Neural correlates of consciousness, empirical and conceptual questions.* MIT Press, Cambridge, MA.

Natsoulas TN (1983) Concepts of consciousness. *J Mind Behav* 4:13–59.

Pepperberg IM (1999) *The Alex studies, cognitive and communicative abilities of grey parrots.* Harvard University Press, Cambridge, MA.

Pepperberg IM, Lynn SK (2001) Possible levels of animal consciousness with reference to grey parrots (*Psittacus eritiacus*). *Am Zool* 40:893–901.

Pryor, K, Haag R, O'Reilly J (1969) The creative porpoise: Training for novel behavior. *J Exp Anal Behav* 12:653–661.

Rees G, Kreiman G, Koch C (2002) Neural correlates of consciousness in humans. *Nature Rev* 3:261–270.

Roth G (2000) The evolution and ontogeny of consciousness. In: Metzinger T (ed) *Neural correlates of consciousness, empirical and conceptual questions.* MIT Press, Cambridge, MA, pp 77–97.

Savage-Rumbaugh S, Shanker SG, Taylor TJ (1998) *Apes, language, and the human mind.* Oxford University Press, New York.

Searle JR (2000) Consciousness. *Annu Rev Neurosci* 23:557–578.

Searle JR (2002) *Consciousness and language.* Cambridge University Press, New York.

Seward T, Seward MA (2000) Visual awareness due to neuronal activities in subcortical structures: A proposal. *Conscious Cogn* 9:86–116.

Seyfarth D, Cheney D, Marler P (1980) Vervet monkey alarm calls: Evidence for predator classification and semantic communication. *Anim Behav* 28:1070–1094.

Slobodchikoff CN (2002) Cognition and communication in prairie dogs. In: Bekoff, M, Allen C, Burghardt GM (eds) *The cognitive animal, empirical and theoretical perspectives.* MIT Press, Cambridge, MA, pp 257–264.

Sousa C, Matsuzawa T (2001) The use of tokens as rewards and tools by chimpanzees (*Pan troglodytes*). *Anim Cogn* 4:213–221.

Stoerig P, Zontanou A, Cowey A (2002) Aware or unaware: Assessment of cortical blindness in four men and a monkey. *Cereb Cortex* 12:565–574.

Taylor JG (1999) *The race for consciousness.* MIT Press, Cambridge, MA.

Tong F, Nakayama K, Vaughan JT, Kanwisher N (1998) Binocular rivalry and visual awareness in human extrastriate cortex. *Neuron* 21:753–759.

Tonooka R (2001) Leaf-folding behavior for drinking water by wild chimpanzees (*Pan troglodytes*) at Bossou, Guinea. *Anim Cogn* 4:325–334.

Tulving E (1972) Episodic and semantic memory. In: Tulving E, Donaldson W (eds) *Organization of memory.* Academic, New York, pp 382–403.

Tulving E (2002) Episodic memory: From brain to mind. *Annu Rev Psychol* 53:1–25.

Weiskrantz L, Warrington EK, Sanders MD, Marshall J (1974) Visual capacity in the hemianopic field following a restricted cortical ablation. *Brain* 97:709–728.

Xitco MJ Jr, Gory JD, Kuczaj SA, II (2001) Spontaneous pointing by bottlenose dolphins (*Tursiops truncatus*). *Anim Cogn* 4:115–123.

17 Self-Awareness in Animals

David DeGrazia

DeGrazia outlines several types of awareness he argues are found among at least some animals. These include bodily self-awareness, social self-awareness, and likely introspective awareness. He outlines the lines of reasoning to support each.

Introduction

Many animals are self-aware. At any rate, I claim, the cumulative force of various empirical data and conceptual considerations makes it more reasonable to accept than to deny this thesis. Moreover, there are importantly different sorts of self-awareness. If my arguments are on the right track, then scientists and philosophers have significantly underestimated the case for animal self-awareness.

Types of Self-Awareness

The most primitive type of self-awareness is *bodily self-awareness*, an awareness of one's own body as importantly different from the rest of the environment—as directly connected with certain feelings and subject to one's direct control. Because of bodily self-awareness, one does not eat oneself. And one pursues certain goals. Bodily self-awareness includes *proprioception:* an awareness of body parts, their position, their movement, and overall body position. It also involves various *sensations* that are informative about what is happening to the body: pain, itches, tickles, hunger, as well as sensations of warmth, cold, and tactile pressure. These forms of awareness are essential to any creature that can feel features of its body and environment and act appropriately in response. In sum, bodily self-awareness includes both an awareness of one's own bodily condition and an awareness of one's *agency*, of moving around and acting in the world. Somewhat radically, I suggest that most or all sentient animals have this type of self-awareness.

Social self-awareness—awareness of oneself as part of a social unit with differing expectations attaching to different positions—is present in highly social creatures. It enables such animals to interact with each other effectively. By understanding the expectations that come with one's position, and the ways in which particular interactions among group members affect how one can best deal with them, an animal improves her chances of surviving and passing along her genes. Wolf X, for example, understands that he is subordinate to wolf A, the alpha, and that wolf B has recently formed an alliance with A, so X had better not attack B for fear of A's retribution. Social self-awareness in animals presupposes bodily self-awareness insofar as deliberate social navigation is possible only in creatures aware of their own agency.

Introspective awareness is awareness of (some of) one's own mental states, such as feelings, desires, and beliefs. Is this phenomenon exclusive to language users? After all, it requires not just having mental states, but awareness of having them; one might suppose that such mental reflexivity requires the conceptual rocket of language. On the other hand, assuming a rabbit can be hungry—can *have* the sensation of hunger—it may be plausible to hold that the rabbit is also *aware that she has the sensation.* Indeed, insofar as bodily self-awareness rests partly on having various sensations, and noting their connection with one's body, bodily self-awareness may implicate a basic sort of introspective awareness. I leave that possibility open. As we will see, there is independent evidence from metacognition studies involving monkeys that certain non-linguistic creatures are introspectively aware.

Let us turn to the arguments.

Desires and Intentional Action

Many animals have *desires*. That is, they *want* certain things such as food, refuge, or access to a mate. Given a choice between two substances to eat or two places to sleep, they often *prefer* one to the other. The thesis that desire abounds in the animal kingdom seems strongly supported by common sense. But further support is available.

There is a strong case that all animals capable of having pleasant and unpleasant experiences—let's reserve the term *sentient animals* for them—have desires. To find X pleasant entails, *ceteris paribus*, wanting that the experience of X continue. To find Y unpleasant entails, *ceteris paribus*, wanting the experience of Y to discontinue. Hence a conceptual connection between desires and hedonically valenced experiences, assuming many animals have the latter, provides a good reason to believe they have desires.

Their behavior also suggests that many animals have desires. Why does your dog zoom into the kitchen when she hears you pouring food into her dish? Presumably, because she wants to eat. Why does she jump excitedly and head to the back door, where the leash is, when you look at her and say it is time for a walk? Presumably, because she wants to go for a walk. Appeals to animal behavior as evidence for desires, however, must be advanced carefully. Behavior *alone* might suggest that all animals have desires, but that inference would be unwarranted. We would be on questionable ground saying that the spider builds a web because *it* wants to or, worse, that the jellyfish follows its desire in swimming around. At least as I am using the term "desire," one must be capable of conscious states, and in particular pleasant and unpleasant feelings, in order to have desires; unconscious desires are possible, but only in beings capable of having conscious desires.[1] So, desire-like behavior requires independent evidence that the creature in question is sentient for responsible attribution of desires. Here I simply assume that such independent evidence is available in the case of mammals, birds, and probably at least reptiles and amphibians.[2]

Let us now consider studies focusing on animals' preferences. Marian Stamp Dawkins has studied *what* animals want in choice situations and *how much* they want it: "For instance, when a pigeon has learnt to peck a key for food, will it still keep pecking when instead of having to give just one or two pecks per item of food, it has to peck four, eight or even 50 times?" (Dawkins [1993], pp. 147–148). Of course, a pigeon can prefer pecking for food over resting with no food only if he *has* preferences or desires—similarly for any animal who prefers to go into one enclosure over another. For example, when hens were offered a choice between standing on wire floors and standing on a floor of wood shavings, even those hens who had never before encountered the second sort of floor chose it, consistently, as soon as they had the option (ibid, p. 153). Their preference or desire was evident.

Much behavior among sentient animals suggests desires. Much of this same behavior, I submit, is best understood as reflecting *beliefs* that, together with the relevant desires, produce *intentional action.* Your dog heads for the kitchen upon hearing you pour food into her dish not only because she wants to eat, but because she believes that by going to the right place she will be able to eat. Thus she intentionally heads for the kitchen. She goes to the back door when anticipating a walk not only because she wants one, but also because she believes that going there in this situation will enable her to take a walk. So she intentionally heads there. To be sure, there are other ways of interpreting such familiar behaviors without attributing either desires or beliefs, much less intentional action. But these alternative interpretations seem strained in view of the evidence.[3] Better to maintain that cognitive ethology—the study of animal behavior, in the context of evolutionary theory, that attributes intentional states such as beliefs and desires to animals (Jamieson and Bekoff [1993])—is on the right track. If so, then a belief-desire model of intentional action (Davidson [1980]) supports the attribution of the latter to animals.[4]

But now we face an important objection. In the philosophy of mind, desires and beliefs are classified as *propositional attitudes*, mental states that take propositions or sentences as their objects. For example, in desiring food, I desire *that I eat food*. Similarly, I believe *that there is food in the kitchen*. But can my dog, or any non-linguistic creature, mentally entertain such propositions? To do so, he would seem to need *concepts*. Does he really have the concepts of food, eating, kitchen, and so on? Presumably he doesn't have *our* concepts of food as nourishing, eating as applicable to all creatures with mouths, and kitchens as rooms used for cooking. But perhaps he has *his own* concepts that pick out these items even if the conceptual scaffolding differs from that of our concepts—and, from the building blocks of his concepts, we could in principle construct the relevant propositional attitudes. That's one possibility I would take seriously. But one might doubt it. One might reasonably suppose that possession of concepts requires capacities for abstraction that surpass non-linguistic beings. In that case, my dog, lacking concepts, would also lack desires and beliefs as propositional attitudes.

Suppose that's correct. We should still agree that behaviorist and stimulus-response interpretations of relevant animal behavior are less credible than interpretations informed by cognitive ethology. Thus, even if we don't attribute to animals full-blown desires and beliefs, which are concept laden, we may in good epistemological conscience attribute to them *proto-desires* and *proto-beliefs*. These states, we may say, interact in producing *proto-intentional action*. The idea is that these mental states, though not conceptual, nevertheless have *content*. Their content is supplied by something like *generalized features of perceptions*. My dog's proto-desire for food will pick out relevant instantiations of food as things suitable for him to eat even if it does not employ a universal concept of food as stuff that nourishes.

Again, I attribute real desires and beliefs to many animals. But even if I am wrong on this point, I'm on solid ground in attributing at least proto-intentional states to them. And that will suffice for my arguments. (Although I will hereafter drop cumbersome references to *at least proto*-intentional states, let us bear the qualifications in mind.)

Desires to do certain things and intentional actions that involve doing them suggest at least some rudimentary awareness of oneself as persisting through time. Your dog's intentionally running to the back door with a desire to go for a walk requires that she represent herself as being around long enough to go outside. The very desire to do something, even if the action is obstructed, is similarly future oriented and self-implicating. For the desire and intention amount to a rudimentary plan, which necessarily includes a representation of completing the intended action. If this is correct, then a commonsense appreciation of the ordinary behaviors of many animals suggests a kind of self-awareness—namely, bodily self-awareness, here with an emphasis on the agency aspect.

Strengthening the case for intentional action, and therefore for bodily self-awareness, is evidence of more sophisticated behaviors in animals involving planning, complex problem-solving, and/or tool use. In such cases, denying that animals perform intentional actions seems absurd, because the actions are so obviously deliberate. Consider some examples.

Chimpanzees use natural objects in pursuing certain goals—for example, moss as a sponge, rocks as nutcrackers, and stems to probe for insects (McGrew [1992], pp. 44–46). They have also been observed using sticks to cushion the soles of their feet when climbing or walking over thorns (Stanford [2001], p. 126). Such behaviors are clearly intentional, not to mention intelligent. For those who reserve the term "tool use" for instances in which one *fashions* an inanimate object before employing it, several feats will make the grade. Chimpanzees have been observed doing all of the following (Hauser [2000], pp. 35–36): stripping leaves off sticks and inserting them into the homes of ants and termites, waiting for them to climb aboard only to become primate dinner; chewing leaves to create an absorbent sponge, which is used to soak up excess water or sap from tree holes; fashioning sticks to produce a sort of dental probe for an unusual method of grooming group members.

Dolphins also furnish examples of highly deliberate problem-solving. Some dolphins wear cone-shaped sponges over their beaks, apparently a protective measure as they nose along the bottom in search of food (Connor and Peterson [1994], pp. 195–196). They engage in cooperative hunting that is responsive to immediate circumstances (Mann et al. [2000]). There are even reports of dolphins apparently "asking" humans in the water for assistance in removing a fishing hook from a group member's mouth or tail (White [2007], pp. 93–94).

Some examples come from birds, specifically New Caledonia crows, who fashion two different types of twigs to extract insects from different sorts of holes (Hauser [2000], p. 36). One crow was videotaped making a complexly shaped tool out of a wire (Anderson and Kacelnik [2004], p. 46).

[. . .]

Such planning and problem-solving are instances of intentional action. Again, intentional action is possible only if the animal agent has some sense of herself as persisting long enough to complete the action or plan. This sense of self involves, most basically, a sense of one's own body as importantly distinct from the rest of the world and as subject to one's direct control.

Fear

Few will doubt that many animals experience the primitive emotion of fear. Like anger and sexual arousal, fear is associated with the sympathetic autonomic nervous system. This system facilitates action in what we may broadly call *emergency* situations. Fibers in the system increase heart rate, sweating, and general arousal while decreasing digestion and other processes associated with rest. Also implicated is the limbic system, a group of neurological structures (e.g., the amygdala, hippocampus, thalamus) that are essential to motivation and emotion. Importantly, the sympathetic autonomic nervous system and limbic systems are evolutionarily primitive, common to all vertebrates. It seems responsible to assume that any creature that is endowed with these two systems, and sentient, can experience fear.

What is fear? It is an emotional response to the perception of danger, a response that facilitates attention to promote protective action. What is the object of fear? It is something one perceives to pose a threat of harm to oneself. When? Some time in the future. These mundane implications of the concept of fear suggest that those who can be afraid have some sense of themselves as persisting into the (possibly very near) future. That is, anyone who can fear has at least a rudimentary bodily self-awareness. Moreover, if the subject who fears perceives the harm threatened as *being hurt*, this would entail an awareness of the possibility of having pain in the future, a type of introspective awareness. These basic points suggest that an enormous range of animals are self-aware in some way and to some degree.

Anticipation of One's Own Future

Like intentional action involving a plan, fear requires some awareness that one will continue into the future. Is there independent evidence that animals can anticipate their own futures?

Note that from an evolutionary standpoint, a sense of time would be highly adaptive for creatures capable of complex behaviors in a changing environment. Anticipation is useful for getting a jump on predictable events and selecting behaviors accordingly. Moreover, anticipation would presumably work in conjunction with memory. Animals who can anticipate the movement of prey and predators, based partly on memory of their past behavior in similar circumstances, would enjoy a major advantage in determining what to do.

A skeptic might reply, however, that what is adaptive is the capacity to *encode* information gained from experience and *use* that information in modifying future behavior. There is no additional adaptive value, the challenge continues, to representing that information *consciously*, as would be required for any forms of memory or anticipation relevant to self-awareness.

This objection misfires for two reasons. First, there is good reason to think some self-representing memories and anticipations in animals are conscious. There is probably additional adaptive value to being able to represent one's own past and future consciously. In humans, the ability to manage complexity and novelty, to improvise in unfamiliar circumstances, is associated with conscious mental states, whereas unconscious information-processing often suffices in familiar terrain. But, again, animals must deal with variable environments: moving predators and prey, changing weather and food supplies, and—in social species—evolving social dynamics. So conscious anticipation and remembering would be advantageous in novel or highly variable situations. Second, even if the relevant self-representations were all unconscious, they would still manifest self-awareness. There is no reason to require that self-representations be conscious to count as manifesting a rudimentary self-awareness (at least in creatures conscious of some features of their world through pleasure, pain, proprioception, and external senses such as vision and hearing).

In addition to evolutionary considerations, there is specific empirical evidence suggesting certain animals' ability to anticipate their own futures. Squirrel monkeys were initially given a choice between one piece of date (a fruit they like) and four. Naturally, they took four. Then the scientists began to withhold water—for three hours if the monkeys chose four pieces of date, for thirty minutes if they chose one piece. The monkeys learned to anticipate the consequences of their choice. Although not thirsty when choosing, they anticipated becoming thirsty and chose a smaller bounty of food in order to drink more readily when thirsty (Zimmer [2007]). Importantly, in these instances, the animals not only anticipated future events, but anticipated their own situation in the future—being thirsty or not—providing further evidence of bodily (and perhaps introspective) self-awareness.

Memory of One's Own Past

Consider now some data suggesting animals' awareness of their own recent behavior. Researchers trained a dolphin to understand a particular gesture as meaning "repeat": do again what you just did before. The dolphin was able to execute this command, repeating his immediately preceding action when this command was given but not when other commands were given (Mercado et al. [1998]). In an earlier study, rats were trained to press one of four levers right after hearing a buzzer, the correct response depending on their behavior—immobility, face-washing, walking, or rearing—at the time of the buzzer. The rats demonstrated their ability to discriminate among their immediately preceding behavior types (Beninger et al. [1974]). Awareness of what one just did would seem to implicate memory and bodily self-awareness.

Also of interest are studies in which researchers focused on the possibility of *episodic* memories. The latter involve conscious recollection of *experiences from one's past.* Implicit memories, by contrast, are stores of information based on past experiences, where those experiences are not consciously recollected, though the information can influence present behavior. You may remember (having seen) the face of a character in a movie without remembering when you saw it, what the movie was, or whose face it is—implicit memory. If you recall the experience of watching the movie, you have an episodic memory.

Now consider another experiment involving scrub jays, who prefer to eat moth larvae rather than peanuts if the larvae are fresh but prefer peanuts if larvae have been dead a few hours (de Kort et al. [2005]). The jays were given a chance to hide both kinds of food and then were removed to a cage. The birds kept away from their caches for four hours tended to dig up larvae, whereas those who had to wait five days ignored the larvae and dug up peanuts. (The experiment was controlled to rule out the hypothesis that the birds were following their sense of smell.

[. . .]

Does room remain for skepticism? What if the jays, for example, simply remembered *that* they hid food a short time ago or a long time ago without remembering *doing so?* This would be implicit rather than episodic memory. Nevertheless, it would involve an awareness of something one did in the past, manifesting bodily self-awareness.

Imitation

In *imitation*, one intentionally does what someone else has done. More precisely, one individual learns from another *the form of a particular behavior* and copies it. Imitation differs from *goal emulation,* in which one learns from another a particular goal to pursue; from *observational conditioning*, in which one learns from another in what circumstances to apply a behavior already in one's repertoire; and from *stimulus enhancement,* in which one learns from another what in the environment to attend to, leading to one's discovery of an action that resembles that performed by the other (Whiten and Ham [1992]). In genuine imitation, one's intention implies some representation of oneself. For the imperative "Do what that individual did" has an implicit subject: oneself. There is no claim here that the intention and associated representations are linguistic, nor even that they're conscious, just that whatever form they may take, their contents imply an awareness of oneself as an agent capable of acting in the same way.

Convincing instances of imitation include the following. An orangutan was observed using kerosene to start a fire and a trash can lid to tend it after observing the same actions by a human (Russon and Galdikas [1993]). The chimpanzee Washoe "adopted" a young chimp who eventually mastered thirty-nine signs of sign language, without human instruction, by imitating Washoe (Fouts et al. [1984]). Chimpanzees raised in homes have apparently imitated a plethora of actions performed by caretakers (for a list, see Whiten and Ham [1992], pp. 263–264). The same is true of Chantek, a language-trained orangutan, who imitated many signs and actions by the time he was two—including in response to the sign "DO SAME" (Miles [1993], p. 49). Dolphins, meanwhile, have an extraordinary capacity to imitate the actions and postures of conspecifics, humans, and seals, as well as human speech (Connor and Peterson [1994], pp. 188–191; Herman [2002], pp. 277–278). Perhaps the most remarkable instance occurred when two captive dolphins who had been trained to perform for audiences were accidentally put in each other's shows—which had different cues and required different actions. One performed the other's show correctly, without training, based entirely on having observed the other dolphin's training (discussed in White [2007], pp. 88–90). Whether animals other than apes and dolphins can imitate is uncertain.

Self-Recognition with Mirrors

Since Gordon Gallup's pioneering experiments in the 1970s, self-recognition with mirrors has often been cited as evidence of self-awareness in animals. Before considering those experiments, let us note that mirror self-recognition involves more than perceiving oneself in a mirror. Any dog, for example, can perceive an image in the mirror; and when the image is of herself, she can perceive (what happens to be) herself in the mirror. But the sort of recognition that is relevant to bodily self-awareness involves perceiving one's own image as *an image of one's own body.*

In Gallup's studies, primates who had become familiar with mirrors were anesthetized and painted with odorless markers on parts of their heads that were visually inaccessible without the use of mirrors. After awaking, the primates used mirrors to pick at the marks (something they did not do without mirrors). Initially, only chimpanzees and orangutans exhibited the ability to use mirrors for self-examination. Only they—and humans—it seemed, could perceive their reflections as reflections of their own bodies (Gallup [1977]).

More recently, representatives of other species have passed the mirror test, though some controversy remains. Bonobos, or "pigmy chimpanzees," have succeeded (Hyatt and Hopkins [1994]). Among gorillas, Koko, the most proficient language pupil of her species, has apparently made the grade (Patterson and Gordon [1993], p. 71), but it is unclear whether any other gorillas have (Parker [1994]; Gallup et al. [2002], pp. 326–327). Meanwhile, after some early inconclusive studies, a carefully controlled experiment indicated that dolphins can examine themselves in mirrors and other reflective surfaces (Reiss and Marino [2001]). More recently, a well-regarded study confirmed mirror self-recognition in elephants (Plotnik et al. [2006]). Studies on tamarin monkeys suggested they *might* have recognized themselves, but a later attempt to replicate these results failed, leaving uncertain how to interpret the initial data (Hauser [2000], pp. 107–109; Gallup et al. [2002], p. 327).

Thus, certain nonhuman species are clearly capable of recognizing themselves—as themselves—in mirrors, but we don't know how far into the animal kingdom the capacity extends. Although it is silly to maintain, as some commentators have, that mirror self-recognition is the only valid indication of self-awareness in animals, it is surely one relevant consideration in the case for bodily self-awareness.

Taking into Account Another's Spatial Perspective

The behavior of some animals indicates that in pursuing particular objectives they can take into account another individual's spatial (and perceptual?) perspective. In one case (Kummer [1982]), a troop of baboons were resting when, over some twenty minutes, a female gradually moved about two meters, ending up behind a rock where she groomed a male. Had the dominant male observed the grooming, there would have been hell to pay. But from where he sat, he could see only the female's back, tail, and the top of her head. He could not see the male being groomed, who had bent down behind the rock, presumably so the dominant male could not observe the transaction. Jane Goodall (1986, pp. 570, 577–580), meanwhile, provides these instances of suggestive behavior in chimpanzees: A young chimpanzee leads a female out of view of higher-ranking males in order to copulate. A subordinate courting a female covers his erection when a superior male suddenly appears. While fighting a rival, a male hides signs of fear—which might embolden the rival—by suppressing instinctive facial expressions and vocalizations or by manually covering his mouth. A chimpanzee avoids looking at food that only she knows about until other chimpanzees have departed, securing exclusive access to the prize.

In these and similar examples, observers have understood an animal's behavior as evincing an awareness of another individual's spatial perspective, taking it into account in an effort to conceal something about the first animal's situation or behavior—thereby advancing some objective such as a rewarding transaction with a conspecific or exclusive access to food. Wherever such an attribution is correct, it would seem to imply bodily self-awareness. For each case, the other's perspective is salient *in relation to the agent's own physical position or situation*, of which the agent must be aware for the behavior to be effective.

The most rigorous available evidence of animals' taking into account another's spatial perspective suggests a more radical thesis: that the animals have a "theory of mind," that is, some grasp of other individuals' mental states. In a series of carefully controlled studies (Hare et al. [2001]), a subordinate and a dominant chimpanzee competed for food, which was arranged in various ways on the subordinate's side of two opaque barriers. In each setup, the subordinate saw the baiting procedure and could monitor the dominant's visual access to the food. If subordinates could determine what dominants could see, they should preferentially get the food that dominants had not seen hidden or moved. This is exactly what happened. Moreover, when a dominant who witnessed the baiting was replaced with another dominant who had not, subordinates adjusted their behavior accordingly, demonstrating some ability to keep track of who had seen what. A similar set of experiments involving capuchin monkeys (Hare et al. [2003]), interestingly, did not furnish evidence that they are sensitive to what conspecifics can see. Yet later, differently designed experiments suggested that not only chimpanzees, but also tamarins and rhesus monkeys distinguish human investigators' goal-directed and accidental behavior—based on how their actions relate to environmental constraints—in making inferences about the investigators' goals (Wood et al. [2007]). If this interpretation of the data is correct, then monkeys too have a theory of mind.

Besides being interesting in its own right, the question of whether particular animals have a theory of mind is relevant to whether they are capable of true deception (see next section). Moreover, evidence that animals can think about others' mental states makes it more believable that they can think about their own mental states (see discussion in the "Metacognition" section below).

Deception

Do some of the cases described above involve deception? We might initially define deception as an intentional action—or omission—that is misinterpreted by another to the agent's advantage.

The cases of surreptitious grooming and of resisting the urge to look at food seem to meet this standard. And something like this conception is assumed in Byrne and Whiten's attribution of deception to primates' "Machiavellian" manipulations of each other (Byrne and Whiten [1988], chapters 15, 16). Baboons make distinct gestures of "looking" when they see predators or another baboon troop. Other baboons spontaneously follow the gaze. In one instance discussed by the authors, a male attacked a younger baboon, who screamed, provoking several adults to run toward them. The running adults were making aggressive calls, apparently preparing to attack the offending male, who—seeing their approach—suddenly "looked" into the distance, despite the absence of predators or baboons in that direction. The adults stopped and followed his gaze, at which time he escaped. Very effective manipulation, but was it deception?

Deception, as ordinarily understood, involves not merely intentional action that in fact misleads, but *intentional misleading.* The deceiver intends to misrepresent a situation so that another individual will fail to grasp how things really are. Thus, one who deceives has a theory of mind—specifically, a belief or sense that the targets of deception have mental lives (which can be confounded). But it remains debatable whether animals such as those just described have a theory of mind. Whether or not they really see other animals as *conscious subjects* or *thinkers,* surely they see other animals as unlike inanimate objects: they grasp that certain animals will *respond* in predictable ways to particular provocations, not just *move around* the way a ball or balloon might. One might therefore find congenial a suggestion that these animals have a *proto-understanding of agency*:

[. . .]

Even such proto-understanding of agency would suggest a sort of self-awareness: an awareness that one's own behavior can induce certain actions in others. This involves more than the agency aspect of bodily self-awareness, for it implicates an awareness of others as doers or actors, an important component of social self-awareness.

Complex Social Understanding

That your own actions can influence those of others, especially if they are members of your social group, is an insight of social understanding. Many mammals have complex social lives featuring group living, dominance hierarchies or more equitable relations, a sense of kin to particular others, shifting alliances, and the like. Individuals may keep track of salient interactions with others, such as whom they have fought with, whom they have groomed or been groomed by, etc. Each group member has to understand her position in the group and her relation to particular others as well as what behavioral expectations follow from these factors. This understanding manifests social self-awareness. To the extent that memory is involved—for example, that so-and-so recently groomed me, or attacked me—such understanding also implicates a non-trivial awareness of oneself as persisting over time. Examples of complex social understanding in particular species will add flesh to these skeletal remarks.

It is common knowledge that wolf packs feature nuanced social dynamics. Moreover, as many human caretakers notice, domestic dogs (a species that evolved from wolves) engage in pack behavior within a human household; even if there is only one dog, he may assess which human is the "alpha" and work to forge an alliance with him or her. Though less actively social than dogs, domestic cats work out dominance hierarchies among themselves.

Primate social life has been the subject of extensive ethological study. Cheney and Seyfarth's leading work on vervet monkeys, for example, demonstrates that vervets know who is a relative, who is a dominant, who's a relative of a dominant, and how other group members rank against each other (Cheney and Seyfarth [1990]). The authors argue that monkeys' innate disposition to group others in hierarchies and family structures evolved to facilitate the ability to predict the behavior of conspecifics (Seyfarth and Cheney [2002]). This plausible conjecture may apply as well to other highly social mammal species.

Apes recognize group members, remember favors and grudges, have long-term relationships, and build and shift alliances (Goodall [1986]; Stanford [2001]). The structures of social life characterizing different ape species reveal differences, however. For example, while chimps are very hierarchical and not infrequently violent, bonobos cooperate more, communicate with recreational sex, and excel at building alliances (Stanford [2001], chapter 1).

[. . .]

Perhaps the most extensively studied cetacean is the bottlenosed dolphin. As Louis Herman (2002) explains, what young members of the species have to learn about social life is extensive and time-consuming:

> To function effectively within these units, the young dolphin must undergo extensive learning about the conventions and rules of the society, about cooperative and collaborative activities, and about the identities and even personalities of group members. . . . The protracted period of development and dependence of young dolphins on their mothers and other group members allows the time and opportunity for extensive social learning to take place.
>
> (p. 275)

One joint activity is cooperative hunting, which features role specialization: "driver dolphins" herd fish towards the "barrier dolphins." Another example of role specialization is the "broker dolphin," who acts as a link of communication among various subgroups within the larger social unit (Simmonds [2006], p. 110).

These and many other data support the thesis that a wide range of mammalian animals have rich social lives featuring relatively sophisticated social understanding. Such understanding, I have argued, evinces social self-awareness.

Metacognition

Our discussion so far has focused on evidence that strongly suggests bodily self-awareness, social self-awareness, and, cutting across these two types, temporal self-awareness (i.e., an awareness of oneself as persisting over time). What about introspective awareness, an awareness of one's own mental states? Does this require such extensive abstraction that only linguistic beings possess it? There is reason to suppose not.

Of special interest are recent studies on metacognition in animals. Metacognition involves having cognitive states about other cognitive states. Strictly speaking, a theory of mind involves metacognition insofar as, say, X has beliefs about what Y believes, sees, or intends. But what is generally meant by "metacognition" in recent ethology literature is having cognitive states about *one's own* cognitive states. Any creature capable of metacognition (in this sense) is capable of introspective awareness because such meta-states involve awareness of the contents of one's own mind.

Some of the best evidence of metacognition in animals comes from studies of monkeys by David Smith and colleagues (for summaries, see Smith and Washburn [2005]; Phillips [2006]). Monkeys learned to control a joystick to choose answers in discrimination tests about visual patterns on a computer screen. They received food pellets for correct responses and timeouts (delays before further trials)—which they hated—for incorrect responses. Then they learned to choose an on-screen icon for "pass" when a test was too difficult. If they chose pass, they received no food and there was no delay; they simply moved to the next trial, a consequence more desirable than a timeout but less desirable than immediate food. Their ability to use the pass option provided initial evidence that they assessed their own level of confidence and understood that they were unsure—an instance of metacognition.

But what if the monkeys were not assessing their own confidence or understanding, but merely doing something to move faster to another trial? Or, conflicted about which answer was correct, simply selected the pass option by default? Further data render such skepticism more difficult to maintain. First, less cognitively sophisticated animals, rats, never learned the pass option (Smith and Schull [1989]), suggesting that the monkeys might be doing something special. Second, the researchers changed the monkey trials so that they received food or timeouts only after a series of trials, rather than after each trial. Third, the investigators found that some monkeys can use the pass option in a brand new cognitive test rather than having to wait to learn its consequences anew (as would seem necessary for a conditioned response). Moreover, recent trials have had the monkeys demonstrate the ability to *remember* previously shown images rather than discriminate among present images

(Hampton [2001, 2005]). In these trials the monkeys who master the task apparently attempt to recall an image, compare it with current images, and decide whether they can make a match. In addition to providing evidence for introspective awareness, this cognitive achievement strongly suggests episodic memory. Finally, new research suggests that monkeys who learn a pass response in a perception task can immediately apply it not only to different perception tasks but to memory tasks as well (Kornell et al. [2007]). At the same time, it is worth noting that one leading scholar has proffered alternative, "deflationary" explanations for the data (Carruthers [2008]), keeping the issue open.

Conclusion

Our discussion has supported several claims about self-awareness that are not widely accepted. First, self-awareness is not a single phenomenon; rather, it admits of types that are worth distinguishing. Second, and relatedly, self-awareness can exist in quite humble forms. Any creature with an awareness of its own body as importantly different from the rest of the world—as directly connected with certain feelings and as subject to one's direct control—has bodily self-awareness. A vast range of animals, it seems, has this sort of self-awareness. A smaller set of animals, members of highly social species including primates, cetaceans, and many other mammals, possess social self-awareness (which presupposes bodily self-awareness). It is therefore abundantly clear that self-awareness is neither exclusively human nor dependent on linguistic competence. There is also good, if not conclusive, reason to believe that certain nonhuman animals have a degree of introspective awareness.

Notes

1. More formally, A desires X only if (1) A is disposed to bring X about, (2) this disposition is potentially conscious, and (3) A is disposed, *ceteris paribus*, to have pleasant feelings upon attaining X and unpleasant feelings at prolonged failure to attain X (DeGrazia [1996], p. 130).
2. See ibid., chapter 5 for arguments and citations to empirical evidence.
3. See DeGrazia (1996, chapter 6) for my full case.
4. I attribute the model, or its extension to animals, to Davidson.

References

Anderson, A. and Kacelnick, A. (2004). Don't call me bird-brain. *New Scientist*, 12 June, 46–47.
Beninger, R., Kendall, S., and Vanderwolf, C. H. (1974). The ability of rats to discriminate their own behaviours. *Canadian Journal of Psychology*, 28, 79–91.
Byrne, R.W. and Whiten, A. (1988). *Machiavellian Intelligence*. Oxford: Clarendon Press.
Carruthers, P. (2008). Meta-cognition in animals: A skeptical look. *Mind & Language*, 23, 58–89.
Cheney, D. and Seyfarth, R. (1990). *How Monkeys See the World*. Chicago: University of Chicago Press.
Connor, R. and Peterson, D. (1994). *The Lives of Whales and Dolphins*. New York: Holt.
Davidson, D. (1980). *Essays on Actions and Events*. Oxford: Clarendon Press.
Dawkins, M.S. (1993). *Through Our Eyes Only?* Oxford: Freeman Press.
DeGrazia, D. (1996). *Taking Animals Seriously: Mental Life and Moral Status*. Cambridge: Cambridge University Press.
de Kort, S., Dickinson, A., and Clayton, N. (2005). Retrospective cognition by food-caching western scrub-jays. *Learning and Motivation*, 35, 159–176.
Fouts, R., Fouts, D., and Shoenfeld, D. (1984). Sign language conversational interactions between chimpanzees. *Sign Language Studies*, 34, 1–12.
Gallup, G. (1977). Self-recognition in primates: A comparative approach to the bidirectional properties of consciousness. *American Psychologist*, 32, 330–338.
Gallup, G., Anderson, J., and Shillito, D. (2002). The mirror test, pp. 325–334 in M. Bekoff, C. Allen, and G. Burghardt (eds.), The Cognitive Animal. Cambridge, MA: MIT Press.
Goodall, J. (1986). *The Chimpanzees of Gombe*. Cambridge, MA: Harvard University Press.
Hampton, R. (2001). Rhesus monkeys know when they remember. *Proceedings of the National Academy of Sciences USA*, 98, 5359–5362.

Hampton, R. (2005). Can rhesus monkeys discriminate between remembering and forgetting? pp. 272–295 in H. Terrace and J. Metcalfe (eds.), *The Missing Link in Cognition: Origins of Self-Reflective Consciousness*. Oxford: Oxford University Press.

Hare, B., Addessi, E., Call, J., Tomasello, M., and Visalberghi, E. (2003). Do capuchin monkeys, *Cebus apella*, know what conspecifics do and do not see? *Animal Behaviour*, 65, 131–142.

Hare, B., Call, J., and Tomasello, M. (2001). Do chimpanzees know what conspecifics know? *Animal Behaviour*, 61, 139–151.

Hauser, M. D. (2000). *Wild Minds*. New York: Holt.

Herman, L. (2002). Exploring the cognitive world of the bottlenosed dolphin, pp. 275–284 in M. Bekoff, C. Allen, and G. Burghardt (eds.), *The Cognitive Animal*. Cambridge, MA: MIT Press.

Hyatt, C. W. and Hopkins, W. D. (1994). Self-awareness in bonobos and Chimpanzees: A comparative approach, pp. 248–253 in S. Parker, R. Mitchell, and M. Boccia (eds.), *Self-Awareness in Animals and Humans*. Cambridge: Cambridge University Press.

Jamieson, D. and Bekoff, M. (1993). On the aims and methods of cognitive ethology. *Philosophy of Science Association*, 2, 110–124.

Kornell, N., Son, L., and Terrace, H. (2007). Transfer of metacognitive skills and hint seeking in monkeys. *Psychological Science*, 13, 64–71.

Kummer, H. (1982). Social knowledge in free-ranging primates, pp. 113–130, in D. Griffin (ed.), *Animal Mind—Human Mind*. Berlin: Springer-Verlag.

Mann, J., Connor, R., Tyack, P., and Whitehead, H. (2000). *Cetacean Societies*. Chicago: University of Chicago Press.

McGrew, W. C. (1992). *Chimpanzee Material Culture*. Cambridge: Cambridge University Press.

Mercado, E., Murray, R., Uyeyama, R., Pack, A., and Herman, L. (1998). Memory for recent actions in the bottlenosed dolphin (*Tursiops truncates*): Repetition of arbitrary behaviours using an abstract rule. *Animal Learning & Behavior*, 26, 210–218.

Miles, H.L.W. (1993). Language and the orang-utan: The old "person" of the forest, pp. 42–57 in P. Cavalieri and P. Singer (eds.), *The Great Ape Project*. New York: St. Martin's Press.

Parker, S. T. (1994). Incipient mirror self-recognition in zoo gorillas and chimpanzees, pp. 301–307 in S. T. Parker, R. Mitchell, and M. Boccia (eds.), *Self-Awareness in Animals and Humans*. Cambridge: Cambridge University Press.

Patterson, F. and Gordon, W. (1993). The case for the personhood of gorillas, pp. 58–79 in P. Cavalieri and P. Singer (eds.), *The Great Ape Project*. New York: St. Martin's Press.

Phillips, H. (2006). Known unknowns. *New Scientist*, 16 December, 28–31.

Plotnik, J., de Waal, F., and Reiss, D. (2006). Self-recognition in an Asian elephant. *Proceedings of the National Academy of Science*, 103, 17053–17057.

Reiss, D. and Marino, L. (2001). Mirror self-recognition in the bottlenose dolphin: A case of cognitive convergence. *Proceedings of the National Academy of Sciences*, 98, 5937–5942.

Russon, A. and Galdikas, B. (1993). Imitation in free-ranging rehabilitant orangutans (*Pongo pygmaeus*). *Journal of Comparative Psychology*, 107, 147–161.

Seyfarth, R. M. and Cheney, D. L. (2002). The structure of social knowledge in monkeys, pp. 379–384 in M. Bekoff, C. Allen, and G. Burghardt (eds.), *The Cognitive Animal*. Cambridge, MA: MIT Press.

Simmonds, M. (2006). Into the brains of whales. *Applied Animal Behavior Science*, 100, 103–116.

Smith, J. D. and Schull, J. (1989). A failure of uncertainty monitoring in the rat (unpublished raw data). Cited in Shields, W., Smith, J. D., Guttmannova, K., and Washburn, D. (2005). Confidence judgments by humans and rhesus monkeys. *Journal of General Psychology*, 13, 165–186.

Smith, J. D. and Washburn, D. (2005). Uncertainty monitoring and metacognition by animals. *Current Directions in Psychological Science*, 14, 19–24.

Stanford, C. B. (2001). *Significant others: The ape-human continuum and the quest for human nature*. New York: Basic Books.

White, T. (2007). *In Defense of Dolphins*. Oxford: Blackwell.

Whiten, A. and Ham, R. (1992). On the nature and evolution of imitation in the animal kingdom: Reappraisal of a century of research, pp. 239–284 in P. Slater, J. Rosenblatt, C. Beer, and M. Milinski (eds.), *Advances in the Study of Behavior*, Vol. 21. New York: Academic Press.

Wood, J., Glynn, D., Phillips, B., and Hauser, M. (2007). The perception of rational, goal-directed action in nonhuman primates. *Science*, 317, 1402–1405.

Zimmer, C. (2007). Time in the animal mind. *The New York Times*, 3 April, F1, F6. http://www.nytimes.com/2007/04/03/science/03time.html?_r=0

Part Three

Primates and Cetaceans

Introduction to Part Three

This part highlights some of the issues involved with the great apes and cetaceans. One issue is whether study should be laboratory based or observation of great apes and cetaceans in the wild. A second issue is whether our focus should be on species or on individual animals. And a third issue is whether the moral status of an animal should be related to its cognitive abilities.

The great apes exhibit such extraordinary capacities that a number of thinkers, such as Steven Wise, have proposed that they be given basic legal rights. Linguistic capacities and self-awareness of great apes is discussed by Sue Savage-Rumbaugh and her co-authors in their essay. Their pioneering work with chimpanzees and bonobos has been conducted in a laboratory setting, allowing for carefully controlled observations.

Juan Carlos Gómez addresses the specific question of whether or not apes are persons. He rejects definitions of personhood such as that of Daniel Dennett which require that persons exhibit levels of cognitive complexity which require linguistic communication. Based on his studies of great apes, Gómez emphasizes the importance of the second person, of mutual relationships in personhood. Accordingly, we as human beings attain our personhood before we know how to speak. Apes are persons also, though not the same as human persons.

Andrew Whiten and his co-workers discuss their findings from their observations of chimpanzees in the wild. They present their evidence for cultural variations between chimpanzee communities—a feature previously thought to be unique to human communities.

Kristin Andrews addresses the notion of Theory of Mind in relation to chimpanzees. She summarizes evidence that chimpanzees are "folk psychologists" who see others as intentional agents with goals. She addresses the complexity of whether chimpanzees understand others as having representational beliefs.

Jane Goodall discusses problems faced by chimpanzees both in their natural habitats and in captivity. Her comments are based on over thirty years of observations of wild chimpanzees. She states that it is because of knowing chimpanzees who are "wild and free and in control of their own lives" that she is concerned not only with chimpanzees as a species but also with individual chimpanzees in whatever circumstances they find themselves.

Hal Whitehead and his co-authors address the importance of culture as a determinant of behavior in whales and dolphins. They urge that nonhuman culture be integrated into conservation biology, such as the evidence for consciousness in dolphins and some of the problems with interpreting this for dolphins and more broadly for other animals.

Heidi Harley believes current evidence does not provide for a convincing case for consciousness in dolphins and addresses better definitions and methods for studying it.

Paola Cavalieri discusses the gradual emergence of the idea that whales are entitled to life. She argues that recent evidence supports the attribution of "person" to whales.

Further Reading

Beck, B. B., T. S. Stoinski, M. Hutchins, T. L. Maple, B. Norton, A. Rowan, E. F. Stevens, and A. Arluk (eds.). (2001) *Great Apes and Humans: The Ethics of Coexistence*. Washington, DC: Smithsonian Institution Press.

Bickerton, D. (2000) Resolving discontinuity: A minimalist distinction between human and non-human minds. *American Zoologist* 40: 862–873.

Cavalieri, P., and P. Singer (eds.). (1994) *The Great Ape Project: Equality beyond Humanity.* New York: St. Martin's Press.

Cavalieri, P., and P. Singer (eds.). (1996) "The Great Ape Project." *Etica & Animali* 8: 1–178.

De Waal, F. (1996) *Good Natured.* Cambridge, MA: Harvard University Press.

Great Ape Project website: http://www.greatapeproject.org (accessed 28 August 2007).

Gruen, L. (2014) *The Ethics of Captivity*. New York: Oxford University Press.

Hargrove, J., and H. Chua-Owen (2015) *Beneath the Surface: Killer Whales, SeaWorld, and the Truth beyond Blackfish*. New York: Palgrave Macmillan Trade/St. Martin's Press.

Kalin, N. H. (2002) The neurobiology of fear. *Scientific American Special* 12: 77–81.

Keenan, J. P., J. Rubio, C. Racioppi, A. Johnson, and A. Barnacz (2005) The right hemisphere and the dark side of consciousness. *Cortex* 41 (5): 695–704.

Linzey, A., and C. Linzey (eds.). (2015) *Normalising the Unthinkable: The Ethics of Using Animals in Research, Executive Summary*. A Report by the Working Group of the Oxford Dentre for Animal Ethics, Commissioned by the BUAV and Cruelty Free International. Oxford: Oxford Centre for Animal Ethics.

Lyn, H., P. Greenfield, and S. Savage-Rumbaugh (2006) The development of representational play in chimpanzees and bonobos: Evolutionary implications, pretense, and the role of interspecies communication. *Cognitive Development* 21: 199–213.

Marino, L. (2011) Cetaceans and primates: Convergence in intelligence and self-awareness. *Journal of Cosmology* 14: 1063–1079.

Marino, L. (2014) Cetacean captivity, pp. 22–37 in Lori Gruen (ed.). *The Ethics of Captivity*. New York: Oxford University Press.

Matsuzawa, T. (ed.). (2001) *Primate Origins of Human Cognition and Behavior*. Tokyo: Springer.

National Research Council (1997) *Chimpanzees in Research: Strategies for Their Ethical Care, Management, and Use*. Washington, DC: National Academy Press.

National Research Council (1998) *The Psychological Well-Being of Nonhuman Primates*. Washington, DC: National Academy of Sciences.

Payne, R. (2011). Evidence for awareness in whales, pp. 21–24 in *Whale Welfare and Ethics Workshop*, 22–23 March 2011, Eden Project Cornwall, United Kingdom. UK Government Department of Environment, Food and Rural Affairs (DEFRA), World Society for the Protection of Animals (WSPA).

Ross, S. R. (2014). Captive chimpanzees, pp. 57–76 in L. Gruen (ed.). *The Ethics of Captivity*. New York: Oxford University Press.

Sandin, J. (ed.). (2007) *Bonobos: Encounters in Empathy*. Milwaukee, WI: Zoological Society of Milwaukee & The Foundation for Wildlife Conservation, Inc.

Wild Chimpanzee Foundation web site: http://www.wildchimps.org (accessed 28 August 2007).

Study Questions

1. In your view, is it more important to study animals at the species level or on an individual basis? Explain the reasons for your answer.
2. Should the information concerning consciousness and self-awareness in bonobos presented by Savage-Rumbaugh and her co-workers be taken into account in our treatment of bonobos? If so, in what ways?

3. In your view, are apes or dolphins persons? What definition of "person" are you using? Explain why your definition should be adopted.
4. What are the pertinent features defining consciousness? To what degree do you believe that apes and dolphins experience consciousness as you define it?
5. Is the information concerning culture in chimpanzees and in whales and dolphins important for your view of the moral status of these animals? Explain your answer.

Primates

18 Ape Consciousness–Human Consciousness

A Perspective Informed by Language and Culture[1]

Sue Savage-Rumbaugh, William Mintz Fields, and Jared Taglialatela

Savage-Rumbaugh and her co-workers summarize recent findings that provide insights into the occurrence of consciousness in nonhuman animals. They view consciousness as a fundamental property of the universe, much like space, time, mass, etc. In particular they present the evidence for consciousness in bonobos and the findings that they are capable of comprehending human speech and employing a lexical communication system. They find that bonobos have first "person" accounts to offer of their lives. They affirm the significant power of culture on biology and as a force in evolution.

What Is Consciousness?

[. . .]

According to John Searle,

> consciousness refers to the state of sentience or awareness that typically begins when we wake from a dreamless sleep and then continues through the day until we fall asleep again, die, go into a coma, or otherwise become unconscious. Dreams are also a form of consciousness, though in many respects they are quite unlike normal waking states.
>
> (Searle, 1998)

We accept Searle's description of consciousness and agree with the view that subjective experience must be taken seriously as an object of study. Moreover, we would observe that "consciousness cannot be understood unless it is accurately described and that reductive approaches are inherently inappropriate to this descriptive task" (Velmans, 1998). For the time being, we believe that it is useful to assume that "consciousness may be an irreducible fundamental property of the universe in the same category as space and time or mass and electric charge. [. . .] Our position is a simple assumption: consciousness is a property (Searle, 1992) which the brain manipulates in ways we might conceive of as bending, folding, focusing, or magnifying. Such contouring of consciousness is a function of the brain's typology, which we assert has been fashioned by culture. We suggest that reality is a construction of consciousness molded by forces of the brain shaped by culture.

We use the term "culture" in the anthropological sense, a variation of Leslie White's famous definition of culture. That is, culture is a force that has emerged which allows adaptation by the species to the environment at a rate which biology alone would not allow. We further argue that culture, language, and tools ride upon a common neural substrate. As forces, language and tools are subsets of culture.

We suggest that consciousness is quite general among animal species. The differences in what we as humans might interpret as degrees of consciousness are dependent upon the power (size) of the neural substrate to fold or bend consciousness into the appropriate reality. Thus, culture and consciousness co-construct the driving force in the evolutionary mechanism acting upon the highly plastic matter of biological life. [. . .]

Given this co-interactive framework, it is only reasonable to suspect that the culture in which an ape is reared will significantly affect the form of consciousness it develops, as well as its communicative expression of that consciousness. If reared in a human culture, ape consciousness will be molded according to a form that human beings can recognize more easily as similar to their own and thus understandable by them. Such cross-cultural rearing studies can be understood as experiments in the grafting of cultural consciousness across biological platforms. Moreover, the expectations of the human participants in such studies will, unwittingly, affect the outcome. This is because the extent to which they extend their activities of "humanness" to permit the incorporation of alternative biological platforms into their group cultural consciousness will affect the capacity of the developing organism. Thus studies of ape competence on "human tasks" can never be pure measures of ape capacity. The expectancies and culture of the measurer will inevitably affect them. Nonetheless, they inform us with regard to ourselves, the role of our expectancies, and the plasticity of apes.

Ape Language: Insights into Human Bias and Cultural Expectation

[. . .]

When the "Lana Project" began, the chimpanzee Washoe had learned some signs, and serious questions were beginning to surface regarding the amount of imitation that underlay her actions (Terrace *et al.*, 1979). Moreover, her signs were often inarticulate and difficult to decipher for all but those who lived and interacted with her on a daily basis. [. . .] The lexical keyboard system proposed by Duane Rumbaugh, provided a potential means of propelling apes beyond the limitations posed by these other methodologies. In addition, it offered a more accurate means of data collection, as it was linked to a computer, which recorded all utterances of experimenter and ape. [. . .] The first studies left no doubt that Lana could discriminate lexigrams visually and that she could learn the simple ordering rules sufficiently well to apply them to novel sequences. Lana could also associate different symbols with various real world people, places, and things, (Rumbaugh, 1977) and the computer-collected data demonstrated that imitation was not the basis of her performance.

Like many other novel findings in science, the work with Lana raised more questions than it answered. It was not clear that Lana *always* understood what was said to her through lexigrams, particularly if the requests were somewhat unusual. It was also not clear why she sometimes made what seemed to be incomprehensible errors and formed nonsensical strings. [. . .] Lana's errors were more appropriately characterized as "puzzling" and it was often difficult to figure out what Lana was trying to say.

[. . .]

The second generation of language studies with the lexical-keyboard system attempted to compensate for some of the perceived inadequacies in Lana's semantic performance. Her errors had revealed that while she grasped the combinatorial rules of her syntax, she often did not consistently apply semantic content.

[. . .]

Consequently the ensuing effort, with two young male chimpanzees (Sherman and Austin) was directed toward the careful inculcation of single words and a more objective analysis of both semantic and pragmatic word functions as contrasted with lexical "assignment." The "meaning" of words came under intense focus, and *receptive understanding*, along with object labeling, became an important component of the linguistic instruction. The social aspect of language and culture was also enriched far beyond what had been the case for Lana. And lastly, in place of working with a single subject, efforts were concentrated upon communications between two co-reared apes, Austin and Sherman (Savage-Rumbaugh, 1986).

This simple change had profound theoretical implications that are still not widely understood. *It meant that, for the first time in the field of animal language, the experimenter was removed as half of every subject-experimenter interaction.* Such a change fundamentally altered the traditional experimental psychological paradigm in which every action of an animal subject is both preceded by a structured event (usually termed the "stimulus") and followed by a structured event (usually termed the "reinforcer").

Previous animal work with apes, dolphins, and parrots followed the experimental control paradigm. These paradigms are insufficient for either the inculcation or analysis of functional linguistic phenomena. *Linguistic communication necessarily takes place between individuals in a multiplicity of exchanges that cannot be controlled from the outside either by intentionally setting the stage of the preceding stimulus or effecting a particular reinforcing event.* If there can be said to be a "reinforcing event" for the speaker during normal conversation, it can only be that of the comprehension of the listener. If there can be said to be a stimulus event that prompts the verbal selections of the speaker, it can only be the prior utterances of the listener, which are themselves a reflection of the listener's prior comprehension.

In attempting to analyze linguistic exchanges, one inevitably comes to focus upon the exchange of meaning between participants, in a situation where "meaning" is not controlled at the level of either input, output, or reward by any experimentally manipulatable variable. Consequently, as one moves from the experimenter–subject paradigm to the study of communications between two or more participants, the boundaries of the traditional approach to the study of animal behavior are pressed beyond normal limits. Finally, once the exchange of meaning is the focus of investigation, it quickly becomes apparent that what we call "meaning" cannot exist outside of a socio-cultural context. What one party's utterances "mean" to another can only be determined within a socio-culture framework that permits utterances to assume certain inter-individual expectancies and obligations. This leap into the social dynamics of language took the work beyond the "can they talk" phase into something far more complex, and began to open up the issue of what talking is all about as well as how it is that social contracts are constructed. It required new skills on the part of Sherman and Austin, skills that had been missing in Lana, and for which little, if any, behavioral evidence existed.

The work with Sherman and Austin revealed that symbolic communication of a high level, with the use of an abstract code and with mutual understanding and cooperation, was possible between nonhuman creatures [. . .]. It also revealed that the semantic processing of the symbolic components of the communicative system was not just lexically based and dependent upon stimulus-response associative phenomena. It was instead semantically grounded and functionally abstract. Finally, it illustrated, for the first time in the field of animal language, the critical components of listener comprehension and listener co-operation.

[. . .]

The next phase of work pressed the boundaries of scientific method in a different way. The findings with Sherman and Austin brought forth a sensitivity to the process of comprehension as an invisible phenomenon, in the process of language acquisition. Consequently, when research efforts with Kanzi, a young bonobo, began, the emphasis was not on production but comprehension. There is no way to reward comprehension, because, in its initial stages, there is no overt behavioral indication of what is taking place. This made it essential to move away from any type of training.

[. . .]

The bonobo's capacity to acquire high level linguistic skills in essentially the same manner as a child, albeit more slowly, revealed that the burden of linguistic development was carried by comprehension not production (Savage-Rumbaugh *et al.*, 1986). It is especially important that comprehension emerged in contextually meaningful situations, with many variables, not in repetitive training sessions with only a few variables characteristic.

Language competency appeared in Kanzi through an osmotic process in which caretakers passed on their linguistic culture without awareness or intent. These findings raised, for the first time, the serious possibility that bonobos possessed a sentience similar in kind, if not degree, to our own. It also followed logically that this sentience had gone unrecognized in field studies simply because we could not easily grasp the highly abstract and symbolic nature of their communications in the wild (Savage-Rumbaugh *et al.*, 1996).

Because Kanzi's mode of acquisition was very different from that of other linguistically tutored animals, his linguistic output was dramatically changed as well. Analysis of his utterance corpus revealed a basic comprehension of syntactical ordering rules as well as a comprehension of grammatical classes (Greenfield and Savage-Rumbaugh, 1991). But more than this, his understanding encompassed all manner of novel events and even of metaphor. His understanding of language informed his interpretation of real world events, and his broadened capacity to interpret and appropriately classify real world events informed his linguistic comprehension in a boot strapping effect. An example of this was the ease with which Kanzi learned to flake stone tools given a modicum of both visual and verbal instruction. Similar attempts by other apes required long and arduous conditioning and shaping regimens (Toth *et al.*, 1993).

Because Kanzi's achievements went far beyond the accomplishments of Lana, Sherman and Austin, it became essential to determine the degree to which these remarkable capacities were a function of Kanzi's species versus a function of the unique rearing circumstances surrounding his development. Kanzi's rearing had taken place in a free-form captive environment modeled upon the type of existence a young bonobo might experience in the wild. This contrasted with the formal training regimens encountered by Sherman, Austin, and Lana. Kanzi's linguistic accomplishments raised two possibilities. The first was that bonobos and human beings somehow shared a peculiar and unique genetic heritage for linguistic competency and that studies of wild bonobos had simply failed to reveal the true abstract nature of their communication system. The other possibility was that something about the unstructured socio-cultural approach—with its absence of training and its focus upon comprehension—facilitated language in a manner that classical learning approaches did not and could not.

Kanzi's culture was characterized by many objects and by a variety of participants, including human beings who served as caretakers, but also by many others. There were repairmen who cleaned the lab, fixed the cages, and repaired the bridges in the field. [. . .] But Kanzi's world was not solely a human one; it was also "peopled" by Matata, who was raised as a wild bonobo in the Congo. Across time, as Matata produced more offspring, Kanzi's world grew to include many nonlinguistically competent siblings who multiplied in number and began to form a bonobo community.

Kanzi thus developed as a being within a *Pan paniscus/Homo sapiens* socio-cultural world. That is, as a bicultural entity who learned multiple ways of relating to and communicating with others in both his bonobo and human cultures. His linguistic acts were fully, intimately and irrevocably embedded within both these cultures. Moreover, his behavior indicated an awareness that his biological mother could not fully relate to, or trust, many of his human caretakers. The same was true of the majority of his human caretakers; they could not completely understand or adequately relate to the culture and ways of his bonobo mother. Kanzi served, and continues to serve, as something of a liaison between these two cultures in ways that remain to be adequately documented. He will, for example, often employ the keyboard to request food for his mother and siblings who do not know the lexigrams.

Because Kanzi's language development was enmeshed within a culture, his life and communications evidenced a richness and depth that transcended the symbolic communications of Sherman, Austin, and Lana. Kanzi became able to "mean" in a variety of ways. He also appeared to understand that symbolic meaning is something that can be constructed between individuals in the act of social engagement. He seemed to recognize as well that the "meanings" constructed through joint action develop a history, expectancies, and even a certain necessity of being, once undertaken in a legitimate fashion. But Kanzi's very existence made it necessary to determine the relative effects that biology and environment had played in his development.

Consequently, the ensuing research project sought to separate the species variable from the environmental variable by co-rearing a bonobo (Panbanisha) and a chimpanzee (Panzee) in an environment that was essentially the same as that encountered by Kanzi. However, unlike Kanzi, these two apes were always together and therefore always inevitably exerting some indeterminable degree of influence over the development of the other. By introducing two additional apes into the environment built around Kanzi, the cultural aspects of the work expanded greatly. In addition, Kanzi himself provided a model for the behavioral and linguistic development that was very different from the one that Matata had provided for him. He could use the keyboard—she could not. Thus it was not really possible to precisely replicate Kanzi's experiences with additional apes. What we did do was to attempt to avoid the structured training, the emphasis upon production, and the failure to ground the language within a rich socio-cultural environment that had characterized earlier work with Lana, Sherman, and Austin. We concentrated upon comprehension in cultural context, we continued to make natural spoken English the main route of linguistic input, and we spent as much time as possible in the natural forest setting.

Like Kanzi, Panbanisha and Panzee experienced a social environment within which keyboard usage was a daily affair by human caretakers. Because Kanzi was already lexically competent, the keyboard, which had begun with only 1 lexigram in his case, had grown to a board of 256 symbols. Thus the keyboard could not grow with Panbanisha and Panzee, as it did with Kanzi. If Kanzi was to be a part of their linguistic world, his 256 symbols had to be present as well. Consequently, Panbanisha and Panzee were exposed to 256 lexigrams utilized in complex communications from the first week of life. Perhaps for this reason, their acquisition of these symbols was much more rapid than Kanzi's. Similarly, their combinations appeared far earlier and Panbanisha composed more complex utterances of greater duration than Kanzi, although Panzee did not. [. . .] Nonetheless, in mapping onto all the major capacities that were observed in Kanzi but previously absent in Lana, Sherman, and Austin, Panzee clearly demonstrated that Kanzi's skill was not limited to bonobos. Instead, it was a function of his early exposure to the bicultural social environment.

The process by which Kanzi, Panbanisha, and Panzee acquired their lexicons include components of rapid mapping of sound to referent, similar to those utilized by human children (Lyn and Savage-Rumbaugh, 2000; Lyn *et al.*, 1998). In addition, it has been found that no interaction with the ape itself is required, it is sufficient to speak to other individuals about a novel object in front of the ape. New words are learned and understood even when the apes appear to be disinterested in the conversation (Lyn and Savage-Rumbaugh, 2000; Lyn *et al.*, 1998). The cognitive and social processes that were found in Kanzi's proto-grammatical utterances also characterized those of Panbanisha and Panzee, suggesting that there exist, within the genus *Pan*, basic cognitive processes that permit language acquisition in a human culture (Lynn *et al.*, 2010). Work with wild bonobos supports this position through the finding that bonobos employ intentional alteration of vegetation in a symbolic fashion to communicate to other bonobos who are following them (Savage-Rumbaugh *et al.*, 1996). These findings are the first to indicate learned nonhuman intra-species symbolic communication across the domain of time.

Like Kanzi, Panbanisha and Panzee also attempted to produce human-like vocal sounds. Panzee gained far more voluntary motor control over the ability to produce low frequency sounds than either Kanzi or Panbanisha, suggesting that something about the vocal tract of *Pan troglodytes* is more amenable to the lower register than the bonobo vocal tract. Recent work has shown that Panbanisha has the ability to decode some sounds produced by Kanzi and to translate them to us.

It was not only the linguistic aspects of the *Pan paniscus/Homo sapiens* culture that were passed on to Panbanisha and Panzee. They acquired many tool-use skills as well. For example, Panbanisha acquired the capacity to flake stone by observing Kanzi. But unlike Kanzi, she began, with precision, to employ the technique of bimanual percussion. Even though Kanzi had observed his human models demonstrate this technique, and even though he had attempted to emulate the bimanual technique, he did not become proficient in that skill without passing through a number of phases. [. . .] Whereas Kanzi developed this skill over a two-year period, Panbanisha's bimanual technique was oriented toward the edges of the stone almost from the beginning. It may be that observation of a bonobo model provided the needed input to permit Panbanisha to propel rapidly into direct aimed bimanual percussion.

[. . .]

The fact that a competent bonobo model existed for many aspects of Panbanisha's development, coupled with the observation that in nearly every aspect of language and tool use Panbanisha made more rapid progress than Kanzi, may be attributable to the modeling he provided. However, it should be noted that Panbanisha did not appear to be motivated to watch Kanzi or to attempt to do things she observed him do in any sort of imitative manner. She preferred to spend her time with human female caretakers and with her bonobo mother Matata and seemed more prone to actively observe and emulate their actions. [. . .] All three apes that are linguistically competent (Kanzi, Panbanisha, and Panzee) have also been shown to exhibit complex skills in planning travel routes.

PET scans done to compare Lana's linguistic capacity with that of Panzee revealed that Panzee's information processing skills were more highly elaborated and much more human-like than those of Lana. These findings regarding cortical function correspond tightly to the rearing and behavioral differences encountered between Lana and Panzee. They also reveal that the question of "do apes have language" is far too simple. Both Lana and Panzee "have" language to a certain degree, but their functional competencies vary greatly, as does the neurological processing of verbal material.

In sum, the work with Panzee and Panbanisha demonstrated that the powerful variable was that of rearing, not species. In an environment that did not require training, Panzee learned language faster than Sherman, Austin or Lana. She also comprehended spoken English, while they did not. She produced more novel combinations and far more spontaneous utterances. Unlike them, she learned lexigrams independently of keyboard position.

The issue is no longer one of data, the adequacy of data, of potential cueing or experimenter effects, or of conditioning. In addition the issue is no longer that of "apes" in the general sense, but rather that one must take into account, in detail, the socio-cultural experience of *each* ape, in determining how its performance on the continuum of linguistic competency is to be evaluated. The paradigms of the past, in which animal cognition is viewed as riding upon a different substrate than human cognition, are breaking down and the research at LRC has been a component of this change (Tomasello and Call, 1997).

[. . .]

The importance of the research to date is not only that it offers the basic outline of a new paradigm for understanding the mind of the other, but also it provides techniques and data to support the approach.

The long-standing philosophical issue of how meaning emerges has been significantly informed by work with apes, in a manner that could never have occurred if all language studies were limited to *Homo sapiens* (Savage-Rumbaugh, 1990, 1991; Savage-Rumbaugh *et al.*, 1993). This work has clarified the Quinean problem and laid open the road for new insights into that which we give the name of "language." It is beginning to reveal that "meaning" can be packed into any gesture, glance, lexicon, or printed symbol. The packing of "meaning" requires inter-subjectivity—the mutual attribution of intentionality and a joint history informed by mutually shared affective experiences. These components of communication are not limited to *Homo sapiens*, nor are they a peculiarity of the human capacity for reason.

[. . .]

Consciousness in Other Minds

Detecting consciousness: We agree with Searle's principle of connection between consciousness and the intrinsic intentionality that underpins linguistic meaning. The time has come to break away from views which hold that meaning, reference, and intentionality are not measurable phenomena and hence are closed to scientific investigation. Intentionality is systematically observable. While we do not ignore needs, wants, and desires as matters of intentionality, our current research with great apes emphasizes first the

measurable sequence[s] of complex monitoring responses in which the [person]: (a) checks to see that a listener is present before emitting a communicative signal, (b) engages the attention of the listener before emitting this signal, (c) emits a signal that requires a specific behavioral or verbal response on the part of the listener, [and] (d) monitors the listener's response visually and auditorially.

(Savage-Rumbaugh, 1986)

More importantly, we recognize that intentionality has a dynamic quality when intentional processes emerge between speaker and listener. With respect to our research, we do engage dialogs, i.e., intentional processes between listeners and speakers in which both are human and nonhuman primates.

[...]

Regarding the concept of "degree of consciousness" as stated, we reject this notion. We believe that the metaphors of bending and folding that we have applied to consciousness are a process that the neural substrate performs in the creation of reality. We reiterate our introductory remark: Culture controls the topology of the neural substrate and therefore we believe culture is driving speciation. If we are correct, the brain of a nonhuman primate like Kanzi, reared in a *Pan/Homo* culture, capable of understanding spoken English and uttering lexical English counterparts, should possess a brain which is morphologically different than a brain of a feral bonobo or a bonobo reared without human language, culture, and tools.

Our experience with great apes convinces us that they in fact possess consciousness, for they have first "person" accounts to offer of their lives. As a matter critical to the survival of scientific methodology, We accept these first person accounts and the irreducible nature of experience, while at the same time refusing both a dualistic concession and a pessimistic surrender to the debate regarding consciousness issues or animal language research. We emphasize the power of cultural forces upon the neural substrate of biology and the significant role of culture as a force in evolution.

[...]

Note

1. From the symposium *Animal Consciousness: Historical, Theoretical, and Empirical Perspectives* presented at the Annual Meeting of the Society for Integrative and Comparative Biology, 6–10 January 1999, at Denver, Colorado.

References

Greenfield, P. M. and E. S. Savage-Rumbaugh. 1991. Imitation, grammatical development and the invention of protogrammar by an ape. In N. Krasnegor, D. M. Rumbaugh, M. Studdert-Kennedy, and R. L. Schiefelbusch (eds.), *Biological and behavioral determinants of language development*, pp. 235–58. Lawrence Erlbaum Associates, Inc, Hillsdale, NJ.

Lyn, H., E. S. Savage-Rumbaugh, and D. Rumbaugh. 1998. Observational word learning in bonobos (*Pan paniscus*). *American Journal of Primatology*, 45:193 (Abstract).

Lyn, H., and E. S. Savage-Rumbaugh. (2000). Observational word learning in two bonobos (*Pan paniscus*): Ostensive and non-ostensive contexts. *Language & Communication*, 20(3), 255–273.

Lyn, H., P. M. Greenfield, and E. S. Savage-Rumbaugh. 2010. Semiotic combinations in Pan: A comparison of communication in a chimpanzee and two bonobos. *First Language*, 31(3): 300–325.

Rumbaugh, D. M. 1977. *Language learning by a chimpanzee: The Lana project*. Academic Press, New York.

Savage-Rumbaugh, E. S. 1986. *Ape language: From conditioned response to symbol*. Columbia University Press, New York.

Savage-Rumbaugh, E. S. 1990. Language acquisition in a nonhuman species: Implications for the innateness debate. Special Issue: The idea of innateness: Effects on language and communication research. *Developmental Psychobiology*, 23(7):599–620.

Savage-Rumbaugh, E. S. 1991. Language learning in the bonobo: How and why they learn. In Norman A. Krasnegor (ed.), *Biological and behavioral determinants of language development*, pp. 209–33. Lawrence Erlbaum Associates, Inc., Hillsdale, NJ.

Savage-Rumbaugh, E. S., K. McDonald, R. A. Sevcik, W. D. Hopkins, and E. Rubert. 1986. Spontaneous symbol acquisition and communicative use by pygmy chimpanzees (*Pan paniscus*). *Journal of Experimental Psychology: General*, 115(3):211–35.

Savage-Rumbaugh, E. S., J. Murphy, R. A. Sevcik, D. M. Rumbaugh, K. E. Brakke, and S. Williams. 1993. Language comprehension in ape and child. *Monographs of the Society for Research in Child Development*, 58(233):1–242.

Savage-Rumbaugh, E. S., S. L. Williams, T. Furuichi, and T. Kano. 1996. Language perceived: Paniscus branches out. In W. C. McGrew, L. F. Marchant, and T. Nishida (eds.), *Great ape societies*, pp. 173–84. Cambridge University Press, Cambridge and New York.

Searle, J. 1992. *The rediscovery of the mind*. MIT Press, Cambridge, MA.

Searle, J. 1998. How to study consciousness scientifically. In S. R. Hammeroff, A. W. Kaszniak, and A. C. Scott (eds.), *Toward a science of consciousness II: The second Tucson discussions and debates*, pp. 14–29. MIT Press, Cambridge, MA.

Terrace, H. S., L. A. Petitto, R. J. Sanders, and T. G. Bever. 1979. Can an ape create a sentence? *Science*, 206(4421):891–902.

Tomasello, M. and J. Call. 1997. *Primate cognition*. Oxford University Press, New York.

Toth, N., K. D. Schick, E. S. Savage-Rumbaugh, R. A. Secvik, D. M. Rumbaugh. 1993. Pan the tool-maker: Investigations into the stone tool-making and tool-using capabilities of a bonobo (*Pan Paniscus*). *Journal of Archeological Science*, 20:81–91.

Velmans, M. 1998. Goodbye to reductionism. In S. R. Hammeroff, A. W. Kaszniak, and A. C. Scott (eds.), *Toward a science of consciousness II: The second Tucson discussions and debates*, pp. 44–52. MIT Press, Cambridge, MA.

19 Are Apes Persons?

The Case for Primate Intersubjectivity

Juan Carlos Gómez

Gómez argues that apes can perceive others as having intentions (third-person modality) and can perceive themselves in relationships with others involving mutual intentions (second-person modality). Second-person modality is a feature Gómez believes qualifies apes to be characterized as "persons." He does not argue that apes possess a meta-representational ability to be aware of their own personhood, but rather possess a special kind of mutual-awareness. They are persons who do not describe themselves as persons but may act and feel as persons and can recognize themselves and others as individual subjects capable of feeling and behaving intersubjectively.

[. . .]

The philosopher Daniel Dennett (1976) suggests a set of criteria to distinguish persons. His "conditions of personhood" can be summarized into two clusters of cognitive features that are characteristic of persons: a first cluster amounts to being an intentional agent, and a second cluster involves the ability to understand that others are intentional agents as well. Persons are, first of all, *intentional agents*, that is to say, creatures whose behavior is governed not by external stimuli and blindly learned contingencies of reinforcement or punishment, but by internal representations that allow them to follow *goals* with alternative *means* and generate *expectations* about events, and react to these expectations before the actual events have happened. Apes seem to fare reasonably well in relation to these criteria.

But in Dennett's account, persons must also be capable of understanding that other creatures are intentional agents like themselves; that is to say, a person's representations of the external world should include representations of other creatures' representations; or, in other words, a person should understand that the external world is made, among other things, of the *internal worlds*, better known as "minds," of other creatures. This ability of representing representations has come to be known as having a *metarepresentational* ability.

Furthermore, and again following Dennett's detailed discussion, persons should also understand that the representations entertained by their fellow creatures may include representations of other creatures' representations, i.e., that others have a metarepresentational ability too.

[. . .]

Intersubjectivity versus "Theory of Mind"

Dennett's analysis tries to capture an essential feature of persons: their ability to reciprocally recognize each other's intentionality (or, what is the same, each other's mental states). For him, "recognizing" seems to be synonymous with "representing explicitly" each other's mental states. But would it not be possible to engage in this mutual recognition without explicitly representing the intentions of others as internal mental states? Several authors have tried to explore this possibility and have referred to this form of interpersonal mutuality as *intersubjectivity* (Trevarthen, 1979, 1980; Hobson, 1993). The idea is that subjects (intentional agents, in Dennett's terminology) can coordinate their "subjectivities" (i.e., their mental states) with other creatures' subjectivities (i.e., other creatures' mental states) without having recourse to metarepresentations or any other sort of explicit representation of mental states as internal properties of subjects. For example, Trevarthen (1979, 1980) asserts that during their first year of life, human infants achieve intersubjectivity with their caregivers through emotional/expressive interactions that do not require any representations of their underlying mental states. Infants *feel* the subjectivity of others in the emotional and expressive behaviors displayed in their face-to-face interactions with adults. Hobson (1990, 1993) developed a similar view to oppose the "distorting cognitivist frame" advanced by the theory-of-mind approach to intersubjectivity and personhood. In his view, human infants "find themselves relating to people in ways that are special to people" long before they are capable of any metarepresentational ability. Indeed, the metarepresentational understanding of others as persons is built upon the solid foundations provided by this more primitive ability to *relate with* others as persons.

In summary, these authors assert that there is an emotional, expressive, pre-reflective intersubjectivity that precedes the "intellectual," metarepresentational intersubjectivity of Dennett and other students of "theory of mind" abilities (see Gómez, 1999, for a more detailed comparison of approaches). The problem for this approach is to offer a more precise characterization of the mechanisms and features of this earlier form of intersubjectivity. Let me offer you my own version of how this can be achieved in relation to the problem of nonhuman primate intersubjectivity.

As I understand it, this expressive intersubjectivity is not based upon a distinction between external behaviors and internal mental states. For example, an expression of fear is not understood by the young infant as being an index of an internal emotion that causes its external manifestation. Similarly, an expression of attention (e.g., gazing to a target) need not be represented as an indication of an internal mental state that causes that gazing behavior. Fear and attention are experienced as properties of behaviors that are inseparable from those behaviors. They are like colors that are not conceived of as internal essences of objects, but just as properties (dynamic properties, in the case of emotional and cognitive expressions) that may appear or not in the other creatures.

An important characteristic of this intersubjectivity is that it typically appears in face-to-face interactions. The subjectivity of the other is not understood in an abstract, third-person way, but in a concrete, second-person mode. Others are not understood as persons because we infer from their behaviors that they must have intentions and ideas about other people's intentions, but because we are capable of engaging with them in specific patterns of intersubjective interaction that include emotional and expressive behaviors. What matters is that we are capable not only of engaging with them in intersubjective interactions, but also of representing and understanding them as capable of engaging in these interactions. Persons are capable of representing others as "second persons," i.e., as creatures capable of engaging in intersubjective encounters. Let me clarify what I mean with an example involving apes.

Understanding Mental States without Metarepresentations

In Gómez (1990) I presented a study in which I claimed to provide an analysis of the emergence of "attention understanding" in a hand-reared gorilla who, in her interactions with human people, developed the skill to look at the eyes of the person at crucial moments of the interaction. There I made it clear that the kind of "understanding of attention" I was attributing to the gorilla was a *practical* one, equivalent to what Praget (1936) termed "sensorimotor intelligence" in his explanation of early object manipulation and tool use in human infants. This practical understanding of attention implied the gorilla's ability to *see* the expressions of attention of others as causal links that connect her behavior with their behavior. I attributed to the gorilla the possession of a "sensorimotor concept of subjects" not only as entities that are capable of acting by themselves (what some authors call "animacy"), but also as creatures whose executive behavior is causally connected with their perceptual states, as expressed, in this case, in their gaze behavior. Specifically, I proposed that in the same way that apes seem to understand (in a practical or sensorimotor way) that when using a stick to retrieve an object they must establish physical contact between the tool and the object and apply certain forces to them, they also understand (in a similarly practical or sensorimotor way) that to exert an influence upon other organisms by means of gestures, first they must establish "attention contact" with them and then produce gestures and expressions addressed to their attention. There need be no understanding of the attention of the other as an internal mental state, no understanding of the internal cognitive effects provoked by perception, no abstract conception of intentions and internal mental experiences: all they need is a definite differentiation between physical objects and social subjects that incorporates not only the understanding of them as animate and goal-directed (cf. Tomasello and Call, 1997), but also as *subjective* entities.

[. . .]

For example, attention is a mental state. It has, however, the interesting property of being indissociable from the behavior of looking. It is impossible that I am visually attending to an object if I am not physically looking at it.[1] Visual attention is, therefore, a mental state that closely corresponds to external behaviors. In contrast, knowledge and beliefs can never be directly perceived. There is therefore the possibility that an organism without metarepresentational abilities can nonetheless understand and represent attention as an externally expressed subjective state. Such an organism could generate representations of other organisms attending to particular targets, i.e., being in particular *subjective* relations to a target. Apes may see, remember, represent others intending things and attending to things. This would be equivalent to seeing other creatures as intentional agents. This non-metarepresentational way of perceiving and representing others would capture the most basic property of intentionality: being *about* something. Apes would be perceiving others' actions and attentional and expressive displays as being about objects and targets in general. The intentionality is attributed to, seen in, the actions and bodily attitudes of others, not their minds—those mysterious immaterial entities we humans are used to postulate in our dealings with each other.[2]

This view of what it is like to attribute intentionality without metarepresentation could open the doors of personhood *à la* Dennett to apes—and any other animal that demonstrates the ability to perceive others as subjects in the above sense.

However, there is still an obstacle. According to Dennett, what counts for being a person is not only to be able to see others as intentional agents (or subjects, in my own terminology), but also to see others as capable of adopting the intentional stance in mutual relation to oneself. It is the entry into this recursive circle of mutual intentional attributions that singles out real persons from non-persons. Could creatures endowed exclusively with the sort of non-metarepresentational attribution of intentionality that I have suggested cross the doors of mutual recursive intentionality?

Intersubjectivity in the Second Person

Let's return to the case of visual attention. In other types of attention (e.g., auditory, olfactive), the act of someone attending to something can only be perceived in a modality that is different from the one in which the organism is displaying its attention: for example, I cannot hear you listening to me. However, the act of attending visually is visually perceivable itself. Thus when we attend to the visual attention of someone, this very act reveals *ipso facto* our own attention; or conversely, when someone attends to our visual attention, his/her own visual attention is overtly displayed for the benefit of any beholder . . . including whoever is his/her current target of attention. Indeed, when two organisms happen to be attending to each other's direction of attention, a peculiar pattern is generated in which their respective gazes meet; this pattern is known as *eye contact.*

[. . .]

Evolutionarily, many animals seem to have developed a special sensitivity to eye-contact-like patterns. Curiously enough, usually this sensitivity is expressed in the activation of escape and defensive responses, as if the most adaptive way of responding to being the target of attention of another organism is to fly away (Baron-Cohen, 1995). Nonhuman primates clearly show this sensitivity to eye contact: in many species of monkeys, prolonged eye contact is used as an important component of aggressive displays, and may be quite effective as a threat on its own. But something interesting happens in apes in relation to eye contact: instead of reacting to it in a single, predominantly aggressive/defensive way, they seem to make a more generalized use of it as a pivotal component of different kinds of social interactions. For example, for chimpanzees eye contact is not only a component of aggressive displays, but also of their very opposite: reconciliation behaviors. Captive apes have been also reported to use eye contact as part of their interactions with humans (to request food, objects, play bouts, etc.; Gómez, 1991, 1996) and to produce gestures among themselves when the recipients are at least bodily oriented to them (Tomasello *et al.*, 1985).

Of course, the crucial point is not whether apes do or do not make use of eye contact, but how they *understand* eye contact. Do they understand the recursive intentionality embodied in this pattern? I suggest that the answer to this question is "yes" and "no," depending on what kind of understanding we are asking about. If we are asking about a metarepresentational understanding *à la* Dennett, the answer is probably no; not only for the apes, but also probably for adult humans, who do not seem to understand attention contact in metarepresentational terms either (unless they are cognitive scientists engaging in propositional redescriptions with scientific purposes). However, if we are asking about the ability to perceive and represent eye contact as attention contact in a non-metarepresentational way, the answer is most likely yes: I suggest that the special use of eye contact made by apes reflects an adaptation to the detection and elicitation of "attention contact" (Gómez, 1996). Apes, and perhaps to some degree other primates, may have discovered and exploited the potentialities of mutual visual attention, as expressed in eye contact, for intersubjective interaction.

[. . .]

Second Persons: Apes and Humans

I suggest that we have evidence in apes of a non-metarepresentational system of intersubjectivity built upon distinctive adaptations to the emotional and cognitive expressions of others when they are experienced in both a third- and a second-person modality. The third-person modality allows the perception (and representation) of the behavior of others as oriented to targets in the environment (i.e., as *intentional* in the fundamental sense of this word); the second-person modality allows the perception (and representation) of others as intersubjective beings (i.e., as *mutually intentional*). It is this second modality of perception and representation that allows apes to engage in the sort of mutually intentional exchanges that characterize persons.

[. . .]

In this view, apes are intentional agents (subjects) endowed with brain mechanisms specialized in perceiving and treating others as intentional agents (subjects). In a Dennettian mood, we could still ask: but do they understand all this? Are they aware that they are perceiving others as persons and that they themselves are persons? If by "understand" we mean: "Are they capable of elaborating metarepresentations of themselves holding representations of others as subjects?" then the answer is most likely "no," because to begin with, they probably never hold metarepresentations. But this objection would be beside the point. Being aware of being a person is a different phenomenon from being a person. Dennett states that what is crucial for personhood is to possess a special kind of self-awareness. I would rather suggest that what is crucial for personhood is to possess a special kind of *mutual-awareness*. Apes seem indeed to possess such a special kind of mutual-awareness—one that is expressed in the mutuality of attention-contact situations (cf. Gómez, 1994).

Apes are capable of adopting a second-person attitude that is devoid of all the metarepresentational noise of human first- and third-person attitudes. Certainly, in humans, metarepresentations may add a new resonance to the basic psychological processes that make us persons, like the masks of the ancient Greek and Roman actors—the *personae*—could add resonance to their voices. But these additional artefacts cannot create persons on their own. The keys of human personhood will never be found in our metarepresentational fireworks. Apes are not "cheap" versions of persons evolutionarily overcome by the high-tech, metarepresentational minds of humans who are capable of achieving much more sophisticated versions of consciousness and personhood. Our metarepresentional *personae* are mounted upon the solid intersubjective foundations that evolution planted before the advent of *Homo sapiens*. Second-person perceptions and representations are essential parts of ourselves, capable of achieving feats that are not within the reach of third-person representations, that would need to engage in hopeless metarepresentational spirals in a vain attempt to try to imitate what a second-person system achieves in an immediate and direct way (Gómez, 1994, 1996).

In the personhood of apes we may find some of the keys to escape our stubborn persistence in reducing to first- or third-person terms what belongs to the realm of the second-person. I am not a person in so far that I think I am a person; I am not a person in so far as another thinks of me as a person. I am a person in so far as I and another perceive and treat each other as persons.

But we must, on the other hand, avoid the error of "humanizing" the apes. Their mentality, including their mentalizing abilities, are related, but not identical to ours. They are persons that do not describe themselves as persons or perhaps think of themselves as persons: they, however, may act and feel as persons in the most essential sense of the word, which I take to be the ability to recognize others and themselves as individual subjects capable of feeling and behaving intersubjectively. We are not persons because we can claim we are so. Before speaking we already are human persons. Apes, without speaking, perhaps without thinking in the same sense as we do, also are ape persons. We are lucky enough to have a different evolutionary version of persons. Perhaps we, human persons, will be wise enough to preserve and respect these other ape persons.

Notes

1. Some degree of dissociation can be, however, achieved within the scene we are looking at: I may be mentally attending to an object that is in my peripheral vision instead of to the object in front of my eyes, but my visual attention is still constrained by the presence of the object in my visual field. It could be argued that visual attention is, in fact, a combination of two different mental activities: seeing (which would be the one subject to the behavioral constraint of looking) and attending (which could be purely mental and dissociable from external manifestations). The sort of attentiveness I am exploring in the text is the one that remains undifferentiated from the behavior of looking.
2. Cf. Hobson (1993) for a similar account of early infant intersubjectivity.

References

Baron-Cohen, S. (1995), *Mindblindness: An Essay on Autism and Theory of Mind*, MIT Press, Cambridge, MA.

Dennett, D. C. (1976), "Conditions of personhood", pp. 175–196 in A. O. Rorty (ed.), *The Identities of Persons*, University of California Press, Berkeley. [Reprinted in D.C. Dennett (1978), *Brainstorms*, Penguin, London.]

Gómez, J. C. (1990), "The emergence of intentional communication as a problem-solving strategy in the gorilla", in S. T. Parker and K. R. Gibson (eds.), *"Language" and Intelligence in Monkeys and Apes: Comparative Developmental Perspectives*, Cambridge University Press, Cambridge, pp. 333–55.

Gómez, J. C. (1991), "Visual behavior as a window for reading the minds of others in primates", in A. Whiten (ed.), *Natural Theories of Mind: Evolution, Development and Simulation of Everyday Mindreading*, Blackwell, Oxford, pp. 195–207.

Gómez, J. C. (1994), "Mutual awareness in primate communication: A Gricean approach", in S. T. Parker, M. Boccia, and R. Mitchell (eds.), *Self-Recognition and Awareness in Apes, Monkeys and Children*, Cambridge University Press, Cambridge, pp. 61–80.

Gómez, J. C. (1996), "Ostensive behavior in the great apes: The role of eye contact", in A. Russon, S. T. Parker, and K. Bard (eds.), *Reaching into Thought: The Minds of the Great Apes*, Cambridge University Press, Cambridge, pp. 131–51.

Gómez, J. C. (1999), "Do concepts of intersubjectivity apply to non-human primates?", pp. 245–259, in S. Braten (ed.), *Intersubjective Communication and Emotion in Ontogeny: A Source Book*, Cambridge University Press, Cambridge.

Hobson, P. (1990), "On acquiring knowledge about people and the capacity to pretend: Responses to Leslie (1987)", *Psychological Review* 1, 97, pp. 114–21.

Hobson, P. (1993), *Autism and the Development of Mind*, LEA, Hove.

Praget, J. (1936), *La naissance de l'intelligence chez l'enfant*, Delachaux et Niestlée, Neuchatel.

Tomasello, M. and Call, J. (1997), *Primate Cognition*, Oxford University Press, Oxford.

Tomasello, M., George, B., Kruger, A., Farrar, J. and Evans, E. (1985), "The development of gestural communication in young chimpanzees", *Journal of Human Evolution* 14, pp. 175–86.

Trevarthen, C. (1979), "Communication and cooperation in early infancy", in M. Bullowa (ed.), *Before Speech: The Beginnings of Human Communication*, Cambridge University Press, Cambridge, pp. 321–47.

Trevarthen, C. (1980), "The foundations of intersubjectivity: Development of interpersonal and cooperative understanding in infants", in D. R. Olson (ed.), *The Social Foundations of Language and Thought*, Norton, New York, pp. 316–42.

20 Cultures in Chimpanzees

A. Whiten, J. Goodall, W. C. McGrew, T. Nishida, V. Reynolds, Y. Sugiyama, C. E. G. Tutin, R. W. Wrangham, and C. Boesch

Whiten and co-workers summarize numerous years of research on chimpanzee culture. They found that 39 different behavior patterns, including tool use, grooming and courtship, were customary in some communities but absent in others; ecological explanations could be discounted. They noted that the combined repertoire of these behavior patterns was a highly distinctive feature found in human cultures, but previously not observed in nonhuman species.

As an increasing number of field studies of chimpanzees (*Pan troglodytes*) have achieved long-term status across Africa, differences in the behavioural repertoires described have become apparent that suggest there is significant cultural variation.[1-7] Here we present a systematic synthesis of this information from the seven most long-term studies, which together have accumulated 151 years of chimpanzee observation. This comprehensive analysis reveals patterns of variation that are far more extensive than have previously been documented for any animal species except human.[8-11] We find that 39 different behaviour patterns, including tool usage, grooming and courtship behaviours, are customary or habitual in some communities but are absent in others where ecological explanations have been discounted. Among mammalian and avian species, cultural variation has previously been identified only for single behaviour patterns, such as the local dialects of songbirds.[12,13] The extensive, multiple variations now documented for chimpanzees are thus without parallel. Moreover, the combined repertoire of these behaviour patterns in each chimpanzee community is itself highly distinctive, a phenomenon characteristic of human cultures[14] but previously unrecognized in nonhuman species.

Culture is defined in very different ways in different academic disciplines.[15] At one extreme, some cultural anthropologists insist on linguistic mediation, so that culture is constrained to be a uniquely human phenomenon.[16] In the biological sciences, a more inclusive definition is accepted, in which the significance of cultural transmission is recognized as one of only two important processes that can generate evolutionary change: intergeneration transmission of behaviour may occur either genetically or through social learning, with processes of variation and selection shaping biological evolution in the first case and cultural evolution in the second. From this perspective, a cultural behaviour is one that is transmitted repeatedly through social or observational learning to become a population-level characteristic.[17] By this definition, cultural differences (often known as 'traditions' in ethology) are well-established phenomena in the animal kingdom and are maintained through a variety of social transmission mechanisms.[18] Well-documented examples include dialects in songbirds,[12,13] sweet-potato washing by Japanese macaques (*Macaca fuscata*) at Koshima,[19] and stone handling by Japanese macaques at Arashiyama.[20] However, each case refers to variation in only a single behaviour pattern.

Tabulations of population differences amongst chimpanzees have indicated that multiple behavioural variants may exist.[2-7] However, these tabulations have been based on published reports, which, although they record the presence of behaviours, remain problematic in three respects: they are incomplete; they frequently do not clarify the extent to which each behaviour pattern is habitual in the community; and they do not systematically document the absence of behaviour patterns present elsewhere. We therefore adopted a different strategy in our attempt to provide a definitive assessment of what is now known of chimpanzee cultural variation.

Phase 1 of the study established a comprehensive list of candidate cultural variants, which are behaviours suspected by research workers to be specific to particular chimpanzee populations. Beginning with a list drawn from literature review by A.W. and C.B., the research directors of the major chimpanzee field projects . . . added and defined unpublished candidate patterns. The patterns were then split and lumped as appropriate. This complex, collaborative and iterative process produced a listing of candidate cultural variants that were fully and consensually defined. . . . The scope of this list, differentiating 65 categories of behaviour, represents a unique record of the inventiveness of wild chimpanzees.

In phase 2, the research directors assigned to each of these behaviour categories one of the following six codes, as applicable at their site: (1) customary, for which the behaviour occurs in all or most able-bodied members of at least one age-sex class (such as adult males); (2) habitual, for which the behaviour is not customary but has occurred repeatedly in several individuals, consistent with some degree of social transmission; (3) present, for which the behaviour is neither customary nor habitual but is clearly identified; (4) absent, for which the behaviour has not been recorded and no ecological explanation is apparent; (5) ecological explanation, for which absence is explicable because of a local ecological feature; and (6) unknown, for which the behaviour has not been recorded, but this may be due to inadequacy of relevant observational opportunities. These codings were cross-checked and confirmed by senior colleagues at each site. Our results are for the seven chimpanzee groups with the most long-term observation record, so the 'unknown' code was seldom applicable. These studies bring together a total of 151 years of direct observation (range 8–38 years), so our data summarize the enormous increase in our knowledge of chimpanzee behaviour achieved in the latter half of the twentieth century.

[. . .]

The profile of codings of particular interest with respect to cultural variation is that in which behaviours are recorded as customary or habitual in some communities, yet absent in others. Three other classes of profile need to be recognized and discriminated from this.

First, seven behaviours proposed as potential cultural variants in phase 1 were shown instead to be either customary or habitual in all communities. Second, 16 patterns failed to achieve habitual status in any community. The third class includes profiles in which all cases of absence are explicable by local conditions; just three cases were identified. Absence of algae-fishing can be explained by the rarity of algae, and any absence of ground night-nesting by high predator risk. Use of an additional stone to balance an anvil (anvil-prop) occurs only at Bossou, but it is not expected elsewhere because stone anvils are either not used or (at Taï) are embedded in the ground.

The remaining behaviours are absent at some sites but are customary or habitual at others. We found 39 such behavioural variants, significantly more than previously suspected for chimpanzees.[1–6] We know of no comparable variation in other non-human species, although no systematic study of this kind appears to have been attempted.

We arrive at a similar comparative conclusion when we examine the overall profiles of cultural variants in the different communities. Some customary and habitual patterns are unique to certain communities, but others are shared between two or more communities, so the clusters of variants that characterize each community are not mutually exclusive. Nevertheless, the profiles of each community are distinctively different, each with a pattern comprising many behavioural variants. These patterns vary as much between sites associated with the same subspecies [. . .] as between subspecies themselves. The only major difference between the western and eastern populations is that nut-cracking occurs only in the west, although the fact that this behaviour terminates abruptly at the Sassandra-N'Zo river within the range of the *verus* subspecies shows that it is culturally, rather than genetically, transmitted.[21] The patterns can thus be seen to resemble those in human societies, in which differences between cultures are constituted by a multiplicity of variations in technology and social customs.[14] It remains to be shown whether chimpanzees are unique in this respect, or whether any other animal species, if studied in the same way, would reveal qualitatively similar patterns.

Other comparisons between human and non-human animal cultures have focused on the cognitive processes involved, arguing that if processes of human cultural transmission, such as imitative learning and teaching, are not found in animals, then culture in animals is merely an analogue of that in humans, rather than homologous with it.[22,23] Our data agree with experimental studies that have shown that chimpanzees copy the methods used by others to manipulate and open artificial 'fruits' designed as analogues of wild foods.[24,25] These experimental designs show differential copying of each of two quite different methods used to process the foods. Similarly, some of the differences between communities described here represent not only the contrast between habitual versus absent, but also the contrast between different versions of an otherwise similar pattern. Examples include cases of tool use, such as two different methods of ant-dip; in the first of these, a long wand is held in one hand and a ball of ants is wiped off with the other, whereas in the second method a short stick is held in one hand and used to collect a smaller number of ants, which are transferred directly to the mouth. Other examples occur in social behaviour, such as the variants used to deal with ectoparasites discovered during grooming, with leaf-squash, leaf-inspect and index-hit occurring in different communities. It is difficult to see how such behaviour patterns could be perpetuated by social learning processes simpler than imitation, the most commonly suggested alternative to which is stimulus enhancement, in which the attention of an observer is merely drawn to a relevant item such as a stick.[26] But this does not mean that imitation is the only mechanism at work. Experimental studies on the acquisition of tool-use and food-processing skills by both children and captive chimpanzees indicate that there is a complex mix of imitation, other forms of social learning and individual learning.[24,25,27–30]

Our results show that chimpanzees, our closest sister-species, have rich behavioural complexity. However, although this study represents the definitive state of knowledge at present, we must expect that more extended study will elaborate on this picture. Every long-term study of wild chimpanzees has identified new behavioural variants.

Notes

1. McGrew, W. C. and Tutin, C. E. G. Evidence for a social custom in wild chimpanzees? *Man* 13, 234–51 (1978).
2. Goodall, J. *The Chimpanzees of Gombe: Patterns of Behavior* (Harvard Univ. Press, Cambridge, MA, 1986).
3. Nishida, T. *The Chimpanzees of the Mahale Mountains: Sexual and Life History Strategies* (Tokyo Univ. Press, Tokyo, 1990).
4. McGrew, W. C. *Chimpanzee Material Culture Implications for Human Evolution* (Cambridge Univ. Press, Cambridge, 1992).
5. Sugiyama, Y. in *The Use of Tools by Human and Non-Human Primates* (eds Berthelet, A. and Chavaillon, J.) 175–87 (Clarendon, Oxford, 1993).
6. Wrangham, R. W., McGrew, W. C., de Waal, E. B. M. and Heiltne, P. G. (eds) *Chimpanzee Cultures* (Harvard Univ. Press, Cambridge, MA, 1994).
7. Boesch, C. The emergence of cultures among wild chimpanzees. *Proc. Br. Acad.* 88, 251–68 (1996).
8. Bonner, J. T. *The Evolution of Culture in Animals* (Princeton Univ. Press, Princeton, New Jersey, 1980).
9. Mundinger, P. C. Animal cultures and a general theory of cultural evolution. *Ethol. Sociobiol.* 1, 183–223 (1980).
10. Lefebvre, L. and Palamets, B. in *Social Learning: Psychological and Biological Perspectives* (eds Zentail, T. and Galef, B. G. Jr.) 141–64 (Erlbaum, Hillsdale, NJ, 1988).
11. McGrew, W. C. Culture in non-human primates? *Annu. Rev. Anthropol.* 27, 301–28 (1998).
12. Marler, P. and Tamura, M. Song 'dialects' in three populations of white-crowned sparrows. *Science* 146, 1483–86 (1964).
13. Catchpole, C. K. and Slater, P. J. B. *Bird Song: Themes and Variations* (Cambridge Univ. Press, Cambridge, 1995).
14. Murdock, G. P. *Ethnographic Atlas* (Univ. Pittsburgh Press, Pittsburgh, 1967).
15. Kroeber, A. L. and Kluckhohn, C. *Culture: A Critical Review of Concepts and Definitions* (Random House, New York, 1963).

16. Bloch, M. Language, anthropology and cognitive science. *Man* 26, 183–98 (1991).
17. Nishida, T. in *Primate Societies* (eds Smuts, B. B., Cheney, D. L., Seyfarth, R. M., Wrangham, R. W. and Struhsaker, T. T.) 462–74 (Univ. Chicago Press, Chicago, 1987).
18. Whiten, A. and Ham, R. On the nature of imitation in the animal kingdom: Reappraisal of a century of research. *Adv. Study Behav.* 21, 239–83 (1992).
19. Imanishi, K. Identification: A process of enculturation in the subhuman society of *Macaca fuscata*. *Primates* 1, 1–29 (1957).
20. Huffman, M. in *Social Learning in Animals: The Roots of Culture* (eds Heyes, C. M. and Galef, B. G.) 267–89 (Academic Press, London, 1996).
21. Boesch, C., Marchesi, P., Marchesi, N., Fruth, B. and Joulian, F. Is nut cracking in wild chimpanzees a cultural behaviour? *J. Hum. Evol.* 26, 325–38 (1994).
22. Galef, B. G. Jr. The question of animal culture. *Hum. Nature* 3, 157–78 (1992).
23. Tomasello, M., Kruger, A. C. and Ratner, H. H. Cultural learning. *Behav. Brain Sci.* 16, 495–552 (1993).
24. Whiten, A., Custance, D. M., Gotner, J.-C., Teixidor, F. and Bard, K. A. Imitative learning of artificial fruit-processing in children (*Homo sapiens*) and chimpanzees (*Pan troglodytes*). *J. Comp. Psychol.* 110, 3–14 (1996).
25. Whiten, A. Imitation of the sequential structure of actions by chimpanzees (*Pan troglodytes*). *J. Comp. Psychol.* 112, 270–81 (1998).
26. Spence, K. W. Experimental studies of learning and the mental processes in infra-human primates. *Psychol. Bull.* 34, 306–50 (1957).
27. Sumita, K., Kitahara-Frisch, J. and Norikoshi, K. The acquisition of stone tool use in captive chimpanzees. *Primates* 26, 168–81 (1985).
28. Tomasello, M., Davis, Dasilva, M., Camak, L. and Bard, K. Observational learning of tool-use by young chimpanzees. *Hum. Evol.* 2, 175–83 (1997).
29. Paquett, D. Discovering and learning tool-use for fishing honey by captive chimpanzees. *Hum. Evol.* 7, 17–30 (1992).
30. Nagell, K., Olguin, K. and Tomasello, M. Processes of social learning in the tool use of chimpanzees (*Pan troglodytes*) and children (*Homo sapiens*). *J. Comp. Psychol.* 107, 174–86 (1993).

21 Being a Critter Psychologist

Kristin Andrews

Andrews argues that chimpanzees are "folk psychologists" who see others as intentional agents with goals. They predict and coordinate behavior and may even seek explanations for anomalous behaviors. She is not certain about whether chimpanzees understand others as having representational beliefs.

[. . .]

Problems with the Chimpanzee Theory of Mind Research Program

I have argued that being a folk psychologist does not depend on having a theory of mind and that, for the most part, we do not need the ability to attribute propositional attitudes to predict behavior. I have also suggested that the evolution of theory of mind in humans was not driven by a need to improve behavioral predictions. These views have implications for the ongoing research program on chimpanzee theory of mind. This research program, though moribund for twenty years after Premack and Woodruff first introduced the question, has seen an explosion of interest in recent years. However, it is not entirely clear what the current generation of researchers are after when they ask, "Does the chimpanzee have a theory of mind?"

Premack and Woodruff (1978) understood the term *theory of mind* to refer to the ascription of mental states to others to predict and explain their behavior. Premack made this definition explicit in 1988 when he said that he and Woodruff were originally interested in the question "Does the ape do what humans do: attribute states of mind to the other one, and use these states to predict and explain the behavior of the other one?" (Premack 1988, 160). However, given our discussion about the role of belief attribution in prediction and explanation so far, it is clear that Premack and Woodruff's question itself conflates a number of issues, and the question requires some revision.

First, we must address the false presuppositions in the question. In formulating it, Premack and Woodruff assumed that humans attribute mental states when both predicting and explaining behavior. We have seen that this is not necessarily the case. The question also fails to distinguish between prediction and explanation, and I have argued that it is more natural to find mental-state attributions in explanations than in predictions. Yet the research paradigms designed to test the question focus on prediction; to my knowledge, no one has studied chimpanzees' social explanation-seeking behavior.

[. . .]

Another problem with the question is that it is ambiguous. *Theory of mind* has meant both attributing mental states to predict and explain and more specifically attributing belief and desire to predict and explain. Worse, given the philosophical debates about the nature of belief, researchers may be working under different conceptions of what it is to have a belief.

To avoid the ambiguity, some researchers have suggested that we understand the term as a "generic label" for a number of different cognitive processes involved in social cognition (Tomasello et al. 2003b, 239), a view that fits nicely into a Pluralistic Folk Psychology (PFP) approach. Today the dominant view is that chimpanzees understand a variety of nonpropositional mental states, such as seeing (de Waal 1996; Goodall 1986; Hare et al. 2000; Plooij 1978; but see Povinelli and Eddy 1996), hearing (Melis et al. 2006), goals (Uller 2004), intentionality (Tomasello and Carpenter 2005;

Warneken and Tomasello 2006), and even knowledge (Hare et al. 2001; Kaminski et al. 2008). However, even scientists who are happy to explain the behavior of chimpanzees in terms of sophisticated cognitive mechanisms show little willingness to see chimpanzee social cognition as mediated by concepts such as belief. For example, while they think that chimpanzees can ascribe perceptual states to others, Tomasello, Call, and Hare believe that "there is no evidence anywhere that chimpanzees understand the beliefs of others" (Tomasello et al. 2003a, 156). Even David Premack today admits that chimpanzees do not have a theory of mind in the sense of being able to attribute beliefs, because "creatures without language cannot attribute belief" (Premack and Premack 2003, 149).

Not everyone agrees with this position. Some are boosters; given her decades of work with Kanzi and other symbol-trained chimpanzees and bonobos, Sue Savage-Rumbaugh writes, "There is no doubt that Kanzi attributes intentions and feelings to others and that he recognizes the need to communicate things about his own mental state to others" (Savage-Rumbaugh et al. 1998, 56). And some are critics; Daniel Povinelli and his colleagues think that all chimpanzee behavior can be accounted for without postulating that they understand anything about others' mental states. Rather, chimpanzees can solve the purported theory of mind tasks by constructing behavioral abstractions rather than relying on mentalistic concepts such as *seeing* (Povinelli and Vonk 2003, 2004).

The claim that chimpanzees do not understand belief is far too hasty. For one thing, it reflects an implicit commitment to the symmetry thesis, which we have seen to be false. The symmetry thesis states that prediction is backward explanation. If this thesis were true, it would be methodologically appropriate to use only predictive tasks to test chimpanzee theory of mind, since you would also be testing their ability to explain, albeit in a forward-looking way. That researchers have only tested for theory of mind in predictive tasks suggests that they at least implicitly accept the symmetry thesis. Otherwise they would also have attempted to determine whether chimpanzees attribute beliefs to explain behavior. The ability to attribute beliefs will not be fully examined in chimpanzees until someone is able to test chimpanzee explanatory behavior, and while it may be true that we have no evidence that chimpanzees do understand others' beliefs, this may be due to the researchers' theoretical assumptions and not a reflection of the chimpanzees' capacities. When we look for something where we don't expect it to be, we are not really looking at all.

In addition, I am concerned that the definition of the term *belief* (or perhaps just its extension) is more constrained when it comes to questions of chimpanzee belief. We can analyze belief in a number of different ways, and there should be different ways of examining whether chimpanzees understand that others have beliefs given those different accounts.

The lack of agreement about meanings, the ambiguity, and the false presuppositions lead me to conclude that the question "Does the chimpanzee have a theory of mind?" should be rejected and replaced with more specific questions about the nature of chimpanzee social cognition. The original question allows for a yes-no answer, but either answer merely invites more questions about what the answer actually means. I suggest that we replace the original question with other, more productive questions, such as the following: Is the chimpanzee a successful predictor of others' behavior, and in which contexts? Do chimpanzees seek explanations for behavior? Do chimpanzees recognize others as intentional agents? Do chimpanzees have any understanding of representational belief? Do they engage in joint attention with any other chimpanzees (e.g., is joint attention limited to mother-infant dyads?) or with any humans? Do they have any understanding of personality traits? Might chimpanzees construct dispositional stereotypes?

To demonstrate how this investigation might go, I will start by suggesting ways to answer the first four of these questions. My aim is not only to help steer the ongoing debate about the chimpanzee's social cognitive abilities but also to demonstrate the fecundity of the PFP framework for researchers.

Chimpanzee Critter Psychology

Starting from the position that chimpanzees, like other animals, have minds, we can ask whether chimpanzees are critter psychologists, that is, whether they recognize that other critters are intentional agents, and whether they have robust success in any of the folk psychological practices. I argue that like some children younger than three, many chimpanzees can also be considered folk psychologists, given the PFP framework. The requirements for being a folk psychologist in my account are having the ability to recognize that intentional agents exist and having success in some of the folk psychological practices of predicting, explaining, or interpreting the behavior of an intentional agent; such an individual is at least a minimal folk psychologist. We can define a *critter psychologist* as a nonhuman animal who, minimally, understands that others are intentional agents and can successfully engage in some folk psychological practices.

I first argue that chimpanzees recognize that others are intentional agents, and from there I examine the extent to which they engage in predictive, explanatory, and interpretive practices.

Intentional Agency

To see someone as an intentional agent, we must see the agent as the origin of her behavior, as having some flexibility in behavior, and as having behavioral goals. A number of different comparative studies demonstrate that chimpanzees, like human infants, naturally perceive certain kinds of movement as purposeful. We know that chimpanzees perceive a difference between intentional behavior and unintentional body movement and are more impatient with humans who are unwilling to give them food than with those who are unable to give them food (Call et al. 2004). We also know that chimpanzees help humans achieve their goals; in the course of normal social interaction with a human caregiver, chimpanzees pick up an object the caregiver accidentally dropped (Warneken and Tomasello 2006). In addition, we know that chimpanzee infants, like human infants, perform on violation of expectation tasks in ways that suggest an understanding of agency (Uller 2004).

The original chimpanzee theory of mind study is now seen by Premack as evidence that chimpanzees understand goals. In the original study, the chimpanzee Sarah was shown videotapes of humans working to achieve some goal, such as trying to play an unplugged record player or trying to light a gas heater (Premack and Woodruff 1978). In discussing that study, Premack writes:

> To consistently choose photos depicting the proper "solutions" to particular problems, as Sarah did, one must first see a "problem." But what is a "problem"? A videotape depicts merely a sequence of events, not a problem. A "problem" is produced by a reader who interprets a videotape. The reader must see the actor as being goal-directed, as *trying* to reach inaccessible food or *trying* to rectify malfunctioning equipment. Sarah's consistent choice of solutions to the actor's problems demonstrated that she did interpret the videotapes, attributing mental states to the actor.
>
> (Premack and Premack 2003, 146)

Premack's depiction of this study as requiring the perception of a problem is interesting. If Sarah interpreted the human as having a problem, and her action as helping him solve the problem, she must certainly have seen the human as an agent with a goal. However, Premack is too quick to conclude that this means that Sarah attributed a mental state to the actor, since one might be able to see someone as having a goal without seeing them as having a desire; having the concept of desire may not be necessary to recognize behavior as goal oriented.

Another reason to think that chimpanzees understand agency comes from their imitative behavior. Evidence suggests that chimpanzees are able to imitate intentional behaviors and can even act out a model's intended action when that behavior has not been displayed (Myowa-Yamakoshi and Matsuzawa 2000; Tomasello and Carpenter 2005). Further, chimpanzees, like eighteen-month-old human infants, also appear to know when they are being imitated. In a study with a chimpanzee named Cassie, Nielsen and colleagues (2005) found that Cassie responded differently when being imitated by his caregiver than he did when his caregiver engaged in non-imitative behavior. Like human infants, Cassie would systematically vary his behavior while closely watching the imitator. Nielsen and colleagues describe one bout of behavior while Cassie was being imitated: "Cassie poked his finger out of the cage, wiped the ground in front of him, picked up a piece of straw and placed it in his mouth, pressed his mouth to the cage, then poked his finger out of the cage again" (Nielsen et al. 2005, 34). Such repetitive sequences were the norm when Cassie was being imitated, but not when the caregiver engaged in nonimitative behavior or no behavior at all. Cassie's response demonstrates that he was aware that his caregiver was acting purposefully, further evidence that the chimpanzee has a notion of agency.

[. . .]

The studies just discussed offer evidence that chimpanzees have an understanding of agency. Chimpanzees realize that other chimpanzees and humans engage in purposeful action that is goal directed, and while this is sufficient for us to say that they have an understanding of agency, it does not allow us to say much about how they understand agency, what the chimp understanding of agency consists of, and how they discriminate agents from nonagents. Our understanding of the infant understanding of agency is perhaps a bit more developed, but similarly, we do not know, for example, why infants are more likely to see an ungloved hand as an intentional actor, compared with a gloved hand. Comparative research on the folk and the critter understanding of agency is needed if we want to understand whether the mechanisms used by humans and chimpanzees are the same, or whether these behaviors are merely analogous. Regardless of mechanism, however, the function is the same across species: humans and chimpanzees see others as intentional agents engaged in purposeful behavior.

Predicting and Coordinating

Support for the idea that chimpanzees see one another as intentional agents also comes from evidence that they are able to successfully predict and coordinate behavior with others. Of the host of data on predicting and coordinating, the most impressive comes from behavioral observations of chimpanzees in their natural habitat. I will briefly describe two behaviors common among some communities of chimpanzees—hunting and border patrols—as evidence of their ability to predict and coordinate behavior.

During his thirty years observing chimpanzees at Taï National Park, Côte d'Ivoire, the ethologist Christophe Boesch has documented the chimpanzees' sophisticated ability to cooperate to hunt colobus monkeys (Boesch 1994, 2002). Unlike in other chimpanzee communities, where an individual can succeed in a hunt alone, in the Taï forest, single hunters rarely succeed. This drives the Taï chimpanzees to use group hunting strategies, involving up to four individuals in a single hunt. Boesch and colleagues describe the four roles in a group hunt: the driver initiates a hunt by forcing the prey to move through the trees in a single direction; the blocker will climb trees to keep the prey from deviating from the driver's path; the chaser will climb under the prey and attempt to capture it; the ambusher will quietly climb in front of the prey to block escape and form a trap.

When the prey is spotted, each of the hunters takes on one of these roles, based on his/her location in relation to the monkey and the location and behavior of the other chimpanzees. The behavior is carefully synchronized among the chimpanzees, and the hunters have to behave flexibly, for they will change roles as necessary. Each of these roles is quite sophisticated, and it can take the Taï chimpanzees twenty years to become proficient in the more sophisticated hunting roles.

[. . .]

The ability of chimpanzees to coordinate their behavior to achieve a goal that can only be achieved by a group is indicative of their ability to predict behavior—not only the behavior of the prey but also the behavior of the other hunters. This is true both during the hunt, when the movements of all the hunters have to be carefully choreographed, and after the hunt. For example, the driver, who rarely makes contact with the prey and almost never makes the kill, must anticipate that he will be rewarded by those who do make the kill. The group hunting dynamic also suggests that chimpanzees are able to identify when others make good predictions, given that an ambusher who correctly anticipates the movements of the prey and the other hunters is given more meat than one who does not.

Chimpanzees also demonstrate their ability to coordinate behavior in their border patrols. Chimpanzees are one of the few species known to form coalitions to engage in large between-group hostile encounters. Such intergroup aggression has led to the extermination of one known chimpanzee community at Gombe (Goodall et al. 1979). When males form patrol groups, their behavior changes dramatically. John Mitani describes the behavior of chimpanzees in Kibale National Park, Uganda: "Males are silent, tense, and wary. They move in a tight file, often pause to look and listen, sometimes sniff the ground, and show great interest in chimpanzee nests, dung, and feeding remains" (Mitani et al. 2002, 18).

These patrols move along the periphery of their territory, sometimes making incursions into neighboring territories to hunt colobus monkeys, and often they run across members of the other community. Depending on the size of the patrolling group and the size of the group they encounter, the patrol may either back away quietly or attack. When hunting outside their territory, they are silent and quickly take the prey back into their own territory. However, when intergroup encounters result, the chimpanzees have been observed to kill infants and adult males.

[. . .]

These kinds of aggressive intergroup encounters are almost always won by the attacking group. When the patrols cross into another community's territory, it appears that they will attack only when they outnumber the groups they come across; otherwise they retreat. The patrolling chimpanzees are able to coordinate their behavior, as in the case just presented, acting as a group to kill another chimpanzee. The researchers also believe that the chimpanzees are able to recognize low-cost versus high-cost opportunities and that they will make opportunistic attacks when costs are low. If so, chimpanzees are also able to gauge the likelihood of success of their actions.

Given both the naturalistic data and the experimental findings, we can conclude that chimpanzees are critter psychologists, given their ability to predict and coordinate behavior with others they see as agents. However, we still know little about the mechanisms they use to engage in these behaviors. In particular, we do not know whether the means they use to predict behavior can also be used to explain behavior. To better understand the mechanisms that chimpanzees use to engage in these behaviors, we need to know what else they can do. One way of determining whether chimpanzees only anticipate others' behavior in terms of behavioral regularities is to examine whether they also act to understand others' behavior by looking for explanations. If chimpanzees are able to engage in folk psychological practices in anomalous situations in which prior behavioral regularities are lacking, then we have reason to think that chimpanzees may be able to explain behavior.

Explanation Seeking

While it is uncontroversial to say that chimpanzees predict the behavior of conspecifics and prey, explaining behavior is another matter entirely. We don't yet know much about the chimpanzee ability to seek explanations. Little research has been done on this issue, and the studies that have been conducted focused on explanations of physical events (e.g., Povinelli and Dunphy-Lelii 2001).

This oversight should be remedied. Given my account of the elements involved in explaining behavior, we can examine whether chimpanzees seek explanations in terms of (a) having a curiosity state directed at some unexpected state of affairs, and (b) engaging in exploratory behavior associated with the state of affairs. We can also look for evidence that chimpanzees accept an explanation by looking for indications that the curiosity state has been resolved.

[. . .]

We have prima facie reason to suspect that chimpanzees might seek explanations for behavior. Chimpanzees engage in a great deal of exploratory behavior, and they are able to learn from observing others engaging in novel actions. Moreover, the previous discussion of whether chimpanzees understand agency offers suggestive evidence that they might also seek explanations of behavior.

In the Nielsen study, upon noticing the behavior of his caregiver, Cassie began to systematically alter his behavior, all the while watching his caregiver's movements, as though he were trying to figure out whether he was being imitated. Similar studies on children are interpreted as the child's testing the hypothesis that she is being imitated, and are seen to offer convincing evidence of imitation recognition (Asendorpf et al. 1996; Meltzoff 1990). If we interpret the results of this study in the same way, we will be compelled to accept that Cassie engaged in some explanation-seeking behavior. To test a hypothesis about human behavior, he would have been in a curiosity state to drive the hypothesis generation, and he would have created an interpretation of the human's behavior that he could then test.

Though the study is suggestive, the need remains to directly examine whether chimpanzees explain others' behaviors. Evidence that the chimpanzee is explaining someone could come from looking at the topography of chimpanzee behavior: a facial expression or body posture indicating an affective curiosity state; then directed exploratory behavior; and finally a resolution of the curiosity state, as indicated by a satisfaction facial expression or body posture.

Finding evidence of a chimpanzee curiosity state might sound like a difficult task, but current developments in chimpanzee emotion research have simplified this problem. Chimpanzees express emotions by their facial expressions, and following Ekman's work in emotion in human facial expressions, Lisa Parr and Kim Bard have created the Chimpanzee FACS (Facial Action Coding System). They use this system to construct models of chimpanzee expressions to determine the configuration of muscle movements that chimpanzees find salient in their perception of emotion, and the researchers have found that chimpanzees are sensitive to others' emotional responses, as indicated by their facial expressions. For example, Lisa Parr's research demonstrates that chimpanzees are able to categorize facial expressions associated with different emotional responses (Parr 2003).

We have evidence of a chimpanzee affective state that we can categorize as a curiosity state, and we have evidence of chimpanzee affective states of satisfaction, and we have evidence of chimpanzee exploratory behavior. But what we do not yet have is a systematic way to examine whether these three elements arise together in a pattern suggesting explanatory behavior. One way of finding the pattern is to make a formal observational study of chimpanzee behavior in the field and hope to observe incidents that fit the proposed pattern of behavior. This may be our best bet, since we are most likely to see explanatory behavior in the face of anomalous behavior.

It may be possible, however, to set up an anomalous event in an experimental context. This would require making another animal appear deviant to the subject. For example, consider the following scenario. Chimpanzee B observes an anomalous behavior: chimpanzee A screaming at what appears to be a banana. Chimpanzee B is in a curiosity state, as indicated by his facial expression. Next chimpanzee B moves toward chimpanzee A and explores the surroundings. After removing the barrier hiding the snake, chimpanzee B understands why chimpanzee A is screaming, and his curiosity state is resolved.

Some problems arise with the details of this experimental setup. For one, when chimpanzee B sees the snake, he is unlikely to be satisfied; he is more likely to be terrified and run away. And unless chimpanzee A is constrained, it is likely he would run away, too, as soon as he saw the snake. But something like this setup could help to provide experimental evidence that chimpanzees explain behavior. We know that chimpanzees are interested in deviancy. In a personal communication, Frans de Waal says that chimpanzees will run toward their screaming cohorts to see what the trouble is. However, that behavior may be an example of information seeking rather than explanation seeking. What is the difference? When an individual is seeking information, she lacks the affective state that drives the search for an explanation. For example, when a chimpanzee looks in the direction another is looking, or looks to see what is causing someone to make an alarm call but does not express curiosity, she may just be seeking information. Information seeking is not associated either with a puzzled affective state or with a conflict between the situation and the appropriate behavior from the animal's behavioral repertoire. And it is likely that information seeking is not the only goal in anomalous situations. When the actor is truly deviant, and the behavior is outside the norm, an observer may be driven to seek an explanation.

[. . .]

Whether or not chimpanzees seek to explain behavior is an open research question, and an area rich with opportunity for learning about what chimpanzees think about the chimpanzee mind. So far, all the studies of chimpanzee theory of mind have focused on prediction. But prediction is easily accomplished without considering the contents of mind. If we want to know whether chimps understand others' mental states, we should examine their ability to explain behavior.

Belief Attribution

Despite interest in the topic, I believe that the issue of whether chimpanzees understand belief remains underexplored, given the confusion about the nature of belief and the role it plays in human folk psychological practices. The received view is that chimpanzees do not understand belief (or at least no evidence demonstrates that chimpanzees understand belief). For example, in their review of the theory of mind research program, Call and Tomasello (2008) conclude that while chimpanzees understand perceptual states, knowledge, goals, and intentions, they do not understand false belief (which, if true, let me note, would strongly suggest that chimps do not understand true belief, either). Instead Call and Tomasello claim that "chimpanzees understand others in terms of a perception-goal psychology, as opposed to a full-fledged, human-like belief-desire psychology" (187).

If a "full-fledged human-like belief-desire psychology" is what the Standard Folk Psychology (SFP) view says it is, then one concern with Call and Tomasello's conclusion is that they, like Premack and Woodruff, are mistaken about human psychology. However, another worry arises about this conclusion, and that comes from a potential contradiction in the claim that chimpanzees understand seeing and knowledge but do not understand belief.

Let us look at the problem with seeing first. The suggestion is that chimpanzees understand that others have mental representations of their perceptions of the world and that those perceptions can vary from one individual to the next. In addition, chimpanzees are able to use their understanding of others' mental representations to predict their behavior. But to predict behavior, the chimpanzee's understanding of seeing must be holistically connected to a host of other concepts—for example, the chimpanzee must understand that seeing a desirable food item will make an individual want that item, and unless some defeating desire or defeating observation intervenes, the individual will seek out the food item. A defeating desire might be the desire not to be beaten by the alpha, and a defeating observation might be an observation that an alpha is present. What is the difference between this perception-desire account and a belief-desire account? Very little indeed. The story sounds plausible to supporters of a belief-desire psychology simply because the human concept of seeing is intimately connected to believing, so much so that we say "seeing is believing."

Seeing does the same work as *believing*, because someone who sees something happen will then be in a doxastic state regarding that event, whereas someone who does not witness the event will not share that doxastic state (ceteris paribus). Likewise the success of a child's performance in the false-belief task can be ascribed to her developing understanding of seeing just as easily as it can be ascribed to her developing understanding of belief. The child who passes the false-belief task understands that Maxi did not see his mother move the chocolate to the cupboard, and therefore she understands that Maxi will not look for the chocolate in the cupboard.

Our concept of seeing has behaviors associated with it, in addition to having connections with other concepts. Since in humans the category of behaviors we call seeing is associated with the doxastic category of believing, to say that a chimpanzee has anything like the human understanding of seeing, we would be compelled to accept that she also understands belief.

The claim that chimpanzees understand knowledge but not belief is likewise conceptually problematic. According to the traditional account of knowledge as justified true belief, a known proposition must be believed because taking a proposition to be true involves believing it. The act of taking something to be true is an act of believing it, just as the act of rejecting a proposition as false requires believing the negation of it. The justified true belief analysis of knowledge has been challenged, given the Gettier counterexamples (1963), which suggest that justified true belief is not sufficient for knowledge. However, for the most part, epistemologists have not given up on the belief condition for knowledge (but see Williamson 2000).

Thus to claim that chimpanzees understand seeing and knowledge but not belief is fundamentally problematic. One way to resolve this tension would be to reject the claims about the chimpanzee's understanding of seeing and knowledge. However, overwhelming evidence demonstrates that chimpanzees understand seeing. Naturalistic data include reports that adult chimpanzees monitor gaze, while infant chimpanzees do not (Plooij 1978). Infant chimpanzees, like infant children, do not attend to gaze when making requests from their mothers, and do not begin to look at their mother's face before making a request until around ten and a half months. Chimpanzees seem to develop a sophisticated understanding about what others can see, as they are able to anticipate others' behaviors based on what they can and cannot see. For example, low-ranking chimpanzees act differently when they are out of the dominant's sight. When a lowly chimpanzee is invisible, he will take advantage of his situation by mating with a preferred partner or by eating food that would not be available to him if the dominant were present (Whiten and Byrne 1988). As we have seen, chimpanzees express emotion via their facial expressions, which are understood by others. And like humans, chimpanzees sometimes find it useful to hide their expressions from others. De Waal reports that in one case, when a chimpanzee began fear-grinning in response to threatening vocalizations from another chimpanzee, he literally wiped the expression off his face before turning to face his rival. It took him three tries (de Waal 1996). And while laboratory experiments have found mixed results, recent studies defend the claim that chimpanzees do understand seeing (Hare et al. 2000; Tomasello et al. 2003a). Brian Hare and colleagues found that when a subordinate and a dominant chimpanzee are both released into a room baited with food, the subordinate will avoid the food if the dominant can see it. In the conditions under which the dominant chimpanzee cannot see the food, the subordinate will eat it. The chimpanzees are across the room from each other, so the subordinate has to consider a different visual perspective to judge what the dominant can see.

The claim that chimpanzees understand knowledge is based primarily on experimental evidence. Let me briefly describe one study (Kaminski et al. 2008). Two chimpanzees take turns pointing at opaque buckets to gain food rewards that may be hidden inside. In this experiment, the subject observes that two buckets are baited, but the naive competitor only observes the baiting of one bucket. What the researchers found was that when the subject was allowed to make the second request, she tended to choose the bucket that the competitor did not see baited. (Unlike adult humans given a similar task, the chimpanzees allowed to make the first request did not tend to choose the bucket that the competitor knew was baited, thus maximizing their chances of gaining a food reward on their second turn.) Note that neither chimpanzee witnessed the other's first choice, so the subject's choice was influenced not by what her competitor did in fact do but rather by what she expected her competitor to do. The authors claim, "These results suggest that, at least in some situations, chimpanzees know what others know, in the sense of have seen" (Kaminski et al. 2008, 229).

The conclusion that chimpanzees understand knowledge has been derived from studies about auditory awareness as well as visual perception (Melis et al. 2006). Insofar as such claims are warranted, they entail something about the chimpanzee's ability to understand another's epistemic state, and understanding another's epistemic state requires understanding something more general about knowledge that is common to evidence gathering via both visual perception and auditory perception. In the human case, we would say that what is common to our understanding of others' epistemic states, given their perceptual experiences, comes from an understanding of knowledge. And since, in our best analysis, understanding knowledge requires understanding belief, if the chimpanzees understand knowledge, they must also be seen as understanding something about belief.

This argument cuts both ways. Those who think that chimpanzees do not understand the concept *belief* will simply claim that they do not understand the concept *knowledge* or the concept *seeing*, either. The critic might say that these studies show that the chimpanzee is sensitive to another's knowledge or perceptual state without understanding that he is sensitive to it—without any conceptual metacognition involved.

Instead of looking toward the predictive paradigms for evidence of chimpanzees' understanding of belief, we should turn toward the explanatory paradigms. However, here too difficulties arise. In the fearful-banana paradigm described earlier, the topology of explanatory behavior does not indicate the attribution of a belief. Recall that kinds of explanations are pluralistic, too. Chimpanzee B may well explain chimpanzee A's behavior in terms of the situation (there is a snake there) or in terms of a perceptual state (he sees a snake). The best nonverbal evidence that a chimpanzee understands belief would consist of the topology of explanatory behaviors in a situation that does not permit an explanation in terms of anything other than belief state. And to devise an experiment like this requires more knowledge about normal chimpanzee social behavior, and knowledge about instances of deviance in natural chimpanzee society.

Moving Forward

To make greater progress in studying chimpanzee theory of mind, we need better conceptual analysis of the relevant concepts, including knowledge, belief, and seeing. In addition to the conceptual work, methodological work must also be done. We can make progress by recognizing that humans do not appeal to beliefs nearly as often as thought. If humans do not predict much behavior by attributing beliefs, we have no reason to think that other species would. I suggest that we are likely to move ahead on this question of chimpanzee belief attribution only through dedicated field research by primatologists interested in the question of explanation-seeking behavior. The work is laborious and time-consuming, but field researchers are privy to a wider array of natural behaviors than are researchers working with chimpanzees in a laboratory setting. In the field, a variety of social and eco-logical conditions cannot be replicated in a laboratory. For example, the intergroup conflict behavior described earlier is unique to the field; certainly no researcher would be granted ethics approval to reproduce such interactions in captivity, and where serious conflicts do arise among captive chim-panzees, caregivers separate the individuals. In addition, in the field we find seasonal differences—rainy seasons and dry seasons—that affect animal mobility and the availability of different food items. The field is a much richer environment for a chimpanzee, no matter how much enrichment he has in captivity. Differences in terrain, food, building materials, potential tools, social partners, and so on all provide more opportunity for discovering novelty than does a captive situation.

If explanatory behavior is evolutionarily beneficial because it promotes the development of tech-nologies, then looking for the topology of explanatory behavior in the field makes sense. The work on chimpanzee cultures has uncovered technological differences in tool use and construction among different groups of chimpanzees, and these findings indicate that chimpanzees have mechanisms for the social transmission of novel behaviors. A close examination of those mechanisms may help us discover whether the need to explain behavior naturally arises for the chimpanzees. If it doesn't, then we have reason to conclude that chimpanzees do not naturally understand belief. But from that conclusion, it does not follow that chimpanzees cannot be given the opportunity to learn about belief in a human enculturation situation. Savage-Rumbaugh's conviction that Kanzi understands others' minds may indicate something about Kanzi's uniqueness, rather than point to a generality about bonobos. Without fieldwork, however, we cannot know this. We must observe first; then we can think again about experiments testing for belief attribution.

Chimpanzees are folk psychologists who see others as intentional agents with goals. They predict and coordinate behavior, and they may even seek explanations for anomalous behavior. What we don't yet know is whether chimpanzees understand others as having representational beliefs. We need more research to answer this question, but we need to do the right kind of research. Predictive experimental paradigms cannot hope to supply an answer, given the ubiquity of alternative explana-tions. Rather, we must first determine whether chimpanzees seek to explain behavior.

If chimpanzees do not seek to explain behavior, then they will probably not have an understanding of belief, given the fundamental nature of explanation for the development of the belief concept. I have argued that the traditional understanding of the relationship between prediction and explanation should be turned on its head. Prediction in terms of belief is derivative of explanation in terms of belief, and so if someone understands belief, she is also explaining behavior. Given the PFP account, methodological changes are necessary in the chimpanzee theory of mind research program. We should decenter the role of prediction, just as we have decentered the role of propositional attitude attribution in folk psychology. Chimpanzees are folk psychologists, but they may still know nothing about belief.

References

Aspendorpf, Jens B., Veronique Warkentin, and Pierre-Marie Baudonnière. 1996. Self-awareness and other-awareness II: Mirror self-recognition, social contingency awareness, and synchronic imitation. *Developmental Psychology* 32(2): 313–321.

Boesch, Christophe. 1994. Cooperative hunting in wild chimpanzees. *Animal Behavior* 48(3): 653–667.

Boesch, Christophe. 2002. Cooperative hunting roles among Taï chimpanzees. *Human Nature* 13(1): 27–46.

Call, Joseph, Brian Hare, Malinda Carpenter, and Michael Tomasello. 2004. "Unwilling" versus "unable": Chimpanzees' understanding of human intentional action. *Developmental Science* 7(4): 488–498.

Call, Joseph, and Michael Tomasello. 2008. Do chimpanzees have a theory of mind: 30 years later. *Trends in Cognitive Sciences* 12:187–192.

de Waal, Frans. 1996. *Good Natured: The Origins of Right and Wrong in Humans and Other Animals.* Cambridge, MA: Harvard University Press.

Gettier, Edmund. 1963. Is justified true belief knowledge? *Analysis* 23: 121–123.

Goodall, Jane. 1986. *The Chimpanzees of Gombe: Patterns of Behavior.* Cambridge, MA: Harvard University Press.

Goodall, Jane, A. Bandora, E. Bergman, C. Busse, J. Matama, E. Mpongo, A. Pierce, and D. Riss. 1979. Inter-community interactions in the chimpanzee population of the Gombe National Park. In *The Great Apes*, ed. David A. Hamburg and Elizabeth R. McCowen, 13–54. Menlo Park: Benjamin/Cummings.

Hare, Brian, Josep Call, Bryan Agnetta, and Michael Tomasello. 2000. Chimpanzees know what conspecifics do and do not see. *Animal Behaviour* 59(4): 771–785.

Hare, Brian, Josep Call, and Michael Tomasello. 2001. Do chimpanzees know what conspecifics know? *Animal Behaviour* 61(1): 139–151.

Kaminski, Juliane, Josep Call, and Michael Tomasello. 2008. Chimpanzees know what others know, but not what they believe. *Cognition* 109: 224–234.

Melis, Alicia P., Josep Call, and Michael Tomasello. 2006. Chimpanzees conceal visual and auditory information from others. *Journal of Comparative Psychology* 120: 154–162.

Meltzoff, Andrew N. 1990. Foundations for developing a concept of self: The role of imitation in relating self to other and the value of social mirroring, social modeling, and self-practice in infancy. In *The Self in Transition: Infancy to Childhood*, ed. Dante Ciccheti and Marjorie Beeghly, 139–164. Chicago: University of Chicago Press.

Mitani, John C., David P. Watts, and Martin N. Muller. 2002. Recent developments in the study of wild chimpanzee behavior. *Evolutionary Anthropology* 11(1): 9–25.

Myowa-Yamakoshi, Masako, and Tetsuro Matsuzawa. 2000. Imitation of intentional manipulative actions in chimpanzees (Pan troglodytes). *Journal of Comparative Psychology* 114(4): 381–391.

Nielsen, Mark, Emma Collier-Baker, Joanne M. Davis, and Thomas Suddendorf. 2005. Imitation recognition in a captive chimpanzee (Pan troglodytes). *Animal Cognition* 8: 31–36.

Parr, Lisa A. 2003. The discrimination of facial expressions and their emotional content by chimpanzees (Pan troglodytes). In *Emotions Inside Out: 130 Years after Darwin's "The Expression of the Emotions in Man and Animals,"* vol. 100, ed. Paul Ekman, Joseph J. Campos, Richard J. Davidson, and Frans B. M. de Waal, 56–78. New York: Annals of the New York Academy of Sciences.

Plooij, F. X. 1978. Some basic traits of language in wild chimpanzees? In *Action, Gesture, and Symbol: the Emergence of Language*, ed. A. Lock, 111–131. New York: Academic Press.

Povinelli, Daniel J., and Sarah Dunphy-Lelii. 2001. Do chimpanzees seek explanations? Preliminary comparative investigations. *Canadian Journal of Experimental Psychology* 55(2): 185–193.

Povinelli, Daniel J., and Timothy J. Eddy. 1996. What young chimpanzees know about seeing. *Monographs of the Society for Research in Child Development* 61(3): 1–152.

Povinelli, Daniel J., and Jennifer Vonk. 2003. Chimpanzee minds: Suspiciously human? *Trends in Cognitive Sciences* 7(4): 157–160.

Povinelli, Daniel J., and Jennifer Vonk. 2004. We don't need a microscope to explore the chimpanzee's mind. *Mind and Language* 19(1): 1–28.

Premack, David. 1988. "Does the chimpanzee have a theory of mind?" revisited. In *Machiavellian Intelligence: Social Expertise and the Evolution of Intellect in Monkeys, Apes, and Humans*, ed. Richard Byrne and Andrew Whiten, 160–179. New York: Oxford University Press.

Premack, David, and Ann James Premack. 2003. *Original Intelligence: Unlocking the Mystery of Who We Are.* New York: McGraw Hill.

Premack, David, and Guy Woodruff. 1978. Does the chimpanzee have a theory of mind? *Behavioral and Brain Sciences* 1(4): 5515–5526.

Savage-Rumbaugh, Sue, Stuart G. Shanker, and Talbot J. Taylor. 1998. *Apes, Language, and the Human Mind.* New York: Oxford University Press.

Tomasello, Michael, Josep Call, and Brian Hare. 2003a. Chimpanzees understand psychological states—the question is which ones and to what extent. *Trends in Cognitive Sciences* 7(4): 153–156.

Tomasello, Michael, Josep Call, and Brian Hare. 2003b. Chimpanzee versus humans: It's not that simple. *Trends in Cognitive Sciences* 7(6): 239–240.

Tomasello, Michael, and Malinda Carpenter. 2005. The emergence of social cognition in three young chimpanzees. *Monographs of the Society for Research in Child Development* 70(1): 1–131.

Uller, Claudia. 2004. Disposition to recognize goals in infant chimpanzees. *Animal Cognition* 7(3): 154–161.

Warneken, Felix, and Michael Tomaselio. 2006. Altruistic helping in infants and young chimpanzees. *Science* 311(5765): 1301–1303.

Whiten, Andrew, and Richard W. Byrne. 1988. The Machiavellian intellect hypotheses. In *Machiavellian Intelligence*, ed. Richard W. Byrne and Andrew Whiten, 1–9. Oxford: Oxford University Press.

Williamson, Timothy. 2000. *Knowledge and Its Limits.* New York: Oxford University Press.

22 Problems Faced by Wild and Captive Chimpanzees
Finding Solutions

Jane Goodall

Goodall provides a brief summary of her work and experiences with chimpanzees and offers her perspectives on problems faced by these primates in their natural habitats, sanctuaries established by the Jane Goodall Institute to allow orphaned chimpanzees to be raised, the role of zoos, chimpanzees as pets, chimpanzees in circuses or used for entertainment, medical research, and bringing just solutions to "surplus" chimpanzees. She ends with a call to work together to give these animals a good chance to survive and have the best possible quality of life.

In 1960 I began a study of the chimpanzees living in the Gombe National Park in Tanzania. Today I am seldom able to visit more than three or four times a year, for two weeks at a time, but the work continues. Data are collected daily by a team of researchers, making the Gombe project the longest unbroken study of any group of wild animals. Information from this research and from other chimpanzee study sites has provided a wealth of data about these apes. Rich data have also accumulated from studies of gorillas and bonobos in Africa and orangutans in Asia. This information, together with behavioral, psychological, and physiological data from a variety of studies of captive great apes around the world, has served to emphasize their close evolutionary relationship to ourselves. How shocking, then, to learn that these amazing beings are vanishing in the wild and being subjected to abuse in many captive situations.

[. . .]

Chimpanzees show intellectual abilities once thought unique to our own species. They have excellent memories, and they can plan for the immediate future. They are capable of cross-modal transfer of information, generalization and abstraction, and simple problem solving. They are aware of themselves as individuals, and they can interpret the moods and identify the wants and needs of others. They have demonstrated a sense of humor. Moreover, although harder to prove, they undoubtedly feel and express emotions similar to those that we label happiness, sadness, rage, irritation, fear, despair, and mental as well as physical suffering. None of this should surprise us in view of the remarkable similarity between the anatomy of the brain and central nervous system of chimpanzee and human. All of this helps to blur the line, once perceived as so sharp, between humans and the rest of the animal kingdom. Once science admits that it is not, after all, only humans who have personalities, are capable of rational thought, and know emotions similar to happiness, sadness, anger, and despair, this should lead to a new respect for other animals with whom we share the planet, especially for the great apes, our closest living relatives. In fact that respect is seldom apparent.

[. . .]

Problems Faced by Chimpanzees in the Wild

There are still some chimpanzees living in utterly remote wilderness areas who seldom if ever encounter humans—for example, those in the Ndoke National Park area in the People's Republic of Congo (Brazzaville). There are a number of areas, spread across the range of the chimpanzee, that have been given protected status to preserve wildlife. In some countries (e.g., Tanzania and Uganda) efforts are made by wildlife authorities to patrol such areas. Protection is also afforded by wildlife research teams working within these forests. Too often, though, poachers with guns, snares, or spears have easy access, and there are many illegal logging operations with pit saws and illegal mining.

[. . .]

The most severe threat to the Gombe chimpanzees is human population growth in the areas around the tiny 30-square-mile national park. The 120 or so chimpanzees, in three different communities, are isolated, cut off from other conspecifics by cultivated hillsides on three sides, the lake on the fourth. Even 15 years ago chimpanzee habitats stretched far along the eastern shore of Lake Tanganyika. Today the trees have gone as more and more desperate people, including large numbers of refugees from Burundi and Congo, try to grow food on the very steep slopes. In the rainy season the precious thin layer of topsoil is washed down into the lake. In some places the shoreline looks like rocky desert, and the fish breeding grounds have become silted up.

How can we hope to save the forest jewel that is the Gombe National Park, and its famous chimpanzees, when the local people are facing starvation? There are now more people living there than the land can support, there is almost nowhere for them to move to, and they mostly cannot afford to buy food from other areas. In many places the women have to dig up the roots of previously cut trees to get wood to cook their food.

The Jane Goodall Institute has initiated a project in the Kigoma region to try to address this problem. Tree nurseries have been established in 33 villages around Gombe and along the lakeshore. Fruit trees and fast growing trees for building poles, firewood, and charcoal are nurtured as seedlings, then planted in the villages. George Strunden, project manager, has picked a team of qualified Tanzanians who introduce the program into the villages. He has also trained women who demonstrate appropriate tree growing methods. Farming methods that help control and prevent soil erosion are introduced. And there is a strong conservation education element that includes taking small groups of secondary school students to Gombe. There is a big push to increase the self-esteem of women, teaching them skills that will enable them to earn money for themselves. A number of scholarships are offered annually to enable girls from primary schools to benefit from further education. A small microcredit program has been introduced based on the Grameen Bank system. By working with the local medical authorities, TACARE (Lake Tanganika Catchment Reforestation and Education Project) is able to bring primary health care to the village women, along with family planning and AIDS education. Most recently we have formed a partnership with UNICEF that will enable us to bring hygienic latrines and freshwater wells to 33 villages in the area. It should be stressed that the villagers are consulted about their needs, and only projects that have their absolute support are introduced.

Only if we work with the villagers, helping to improve the standard of living of some of the poorest people in Tanzania, do we have a chance to protect the Gombe chimpanzees. Without the goodwill of the local people, the last forests within the park itself, and the tiny remnant forests outside, would surely disappear. A significant factor in our battle to save the Gombe chimpanzees is our employing field staff from communities around the park since 1988. These men follow the chimpanzees, make detailed reports, use 8-mm video cameras, and are proud of their work. They talk about it to family and friends. They care about the chimpanzees as individuals. I believe this is why, until the recent influx of refugees from eastern Congo (people who traditionally eat the meat of monkeys and apes), we had only one case of poaching at Gombe.

Across Africa the great apes face problems caused by the relentless growth of human populations, habitat destruction, and fragmentation of populations. Peasants clear-cut forests to create fields for crops and grazing. They cut down hundreds of trees for the charcoal industry. The forest soils are fragile and soon become infertile and barren when the tree cover is destroyed. So the desert spreads.

In some parts of Africa apes are hunted for the live animal trade and for food. In addition they may be caught in the snares set by village hunters for antelopes and bush pigs. They can usually break the wire, but the tightened noose causes great pain and typically results in gangrene and the loss of the affected hand or foot and sometimes ends in death. Between 40 and 50 percent of all adult chimpanzees in the study communities at Budongo and in the Tai Forest have lost a hand or foot in this way.

Wildlife is sometimes endangered as a result of the ethnic violence so tragically prevalent in many parts of the chimpanzees' range. These conflicts may displace hundreds of refugees who flee their homes, as in Liberia, the Democratic Republic of Congo, Sierra Leone, and Rwanda. Typically they are starving and forced to hunt wild animals for food. Those chimpanzees remaining in Cabinda are endangered by the land mines that have been placed throughout the forests in northwestern Angola.

The great apes are also threatened by the live animal trade, when dealers pay hunters to shoot females simply to steal their infants for export. This trade is by no means as extensive as it was in the days before the Convention on International Trade in Endangered Species of Wild Fauna and Flora (CITES), but there is still a brisk business in some parts of the world, such as the United Arab Emirates, various countries in South America, and parts of eastern Europe. For every infant that arrives at its final destination alive, about ten chimpanzees are estimated to have died in Africa: mothers who escaped only to die later of their wounds, along with their infants; infants killed during capture; other individuals who tried to protect the victims; and captured infants who die of wounds, dehydration, malnutrition, or shock and depression.

Chimpanzees and other wildlife in remote unprotected forests are seriously and increasingly threatened by commercial activities, particularly logging. Even companies that practice sustainable logging have a highly adverse effect on much animal life. Roads made for transportation of logs open up the forests for settlements. People then cut down trees to grow crops, for firewood, for building poles. They set snares to catch antelopes and other animals for food. And they carry human diseases into areas where they have never been before, and the great apes are susceptible to almost all of our infectious diseases. Most serious of all, the roads provide easy access to previously inaccessible areas for commercial hunters who ride the logging trucks. The roads and trucks provide, for the first time, the means for meat, dried or even fresh, to be transported from the heart of the forest to towns far away. Subsistence hunting permitted indigenous people to live in harmony with the forests for hundreds of years. It is the new commercial hunting that threatens the animals of many of the remaining forests. This is the infamous bushmeat trade, exposed by Karl Ammann.

Thus it is clear that wild chimpanzees, gorillas, and bonobos are, only too often, persecuted by their closest relatives, the human apes. The chimpanzee population, which must have numbered more than one million at the beginning of the twentieth century, has been reduced to 200,000 at the very most, spread through 21 countries. It is the rate of decrease of all the great apes that is so alarming. If nothing is done to halt the bushmeat trade, it is estimated that almost no great apes will remain in the Congo Basin in 10 to 15 years. Many organizations have joined the Bushmeat Crisis Task Force in the United States and the Ape Alliance in Europe, which are working on developing methods to slow down and ultimately eliminate this trade.

Sanctuaries

There is not much meat on an infant chimpanzee. Orphans, whose mothers have been shot and sold for meat, are sometimes offered for sale in native or tourist markets. In some areas mothers are shot only so that their infants can be stolen for sale. These pathetic orphans are sometimes bought as pets, to attract customers to a hotel or other place of business, or simply because people feel sorry for them. Paying money for any wild animal for sale serves only to perpetuate a cruel trade. Yet it is hard to turn away from a small infant who looks at you with eyes filled with pain and hopelessness. A solution to this moral dilemma is to persuade government officials to confiscate these victims, because in most African countries there is a law prohibiting the hunting and sale of endangered species, such as the great apes, without a license.

After confiscation, the orphan must be cared for. The Jane Goodall Institute has established sanctuaries in a number of locations. The biggest is in Congo (Brazzaville), where Graziella Cotman cares for 80 at the time of writing (October 2000). The Tchimpounga sanctuary, north of Pointe-Noire on the coast, was built by the petroleum company Conoco, in 1991. It was designed for 25 chimpanzees at most. It has become urgent to add additional enclosures, but we have been delayed by civil war.

In this area, as at Gombe, we employ individuals from the surrounding villages to care for the chimpanzees (and other animals) and as support staff. We also buy fruit and vegetables locally, and this boosts the economy. In addition, we use these orphans as the focus of an environmental education program. The local people are amazed and fascinated when they see the chimpanzees close up. We are trying to establish a wildlife reserve to protect the remaining forest–savanna mosaic in the area. Most of the savanna has been destroyed by eucalyptus plantations, a project of Shell Oil working with a Congolese company, but there is a beautiful unspoiled area around our sanctuary. With permission from the central government, we are working with local government officials and employing ecoguards from each of the seven nearby villages. There are more wild chimpanzees in the area than we believed. When the fighting stops it may be possible to attract tourists and thus bring foreign exchange into the country. Although the building and maintenance of chimpanzee sanctuaries is very expensive, we are not only caring for abandoned orphans but raising awareness through conservation education, and trying to protect the wild chimpanzees.

[. . .]

Zoos

There are approximately 250 chimpanzees living in zoos accredited by the American Zoo and Aquarium Association (AZA) and participating in the chimpanzee Species Survival Plan. There are about 1,700 in all zoos worldwide. There is much controversy regarding zoos, with many animal rights activists believing that they should be closed. Of course, chimpanzees belong in the wild, and if they are lucky enough to live in a protected area, or one remote from people, that is the best life. That life cannot be replicated in captive situations. In the forest they have a great deal of freedom of choice. They can choose whether to travel on their own, in a small group, or to join large excitable gatherings. They can usually choose which individuals to associate with. Females can wander off, with their dependent young, and stay feeding peacefully and grooming together for hours, or even days. Close companions meet often, others may avoid each other. They know the excitement of participating in hunts or boundary patrols, and even aggressive, almost war-like encounters with individuals of neighboring social groups. To survive they must spend much time searching for and sometimes preparing their food—they are occupying their brains, using their skills. They are free. Nevertheless, when compared with the life of chimpanzees living in danger zones in Africa, it sometimes seems to me that those in the really good zoos—those in which there are large enclosures, rich social groups, and an enriched environment—may in fact be better off.

On the other hand, there are still many zoos that should be closed—zoos where chimpanzees are forced to live alone or in pairs in tiny cement-floored, iron-barred, old-fashioned cages. There they suffer terribly from boredom. In African zoos, where sometimes even the keepers can eat only one meal a day, if that, conditions are often appalling for all the animals, and there is much suffering. Lack of water is often a major problem, because there may be no running water and water is delivered very sporadically by keepers who are in the business simply for a job.

[. . .]

The Medical Research Lab

Many ex-pet and ex-entertainment chimpanzees end their days in medical research. It is hard for me to visit the laboratories to see chimpanzees, who have committed no crime, locked into 5 ft × 5 ft × 7 ft high prison cages. They are there because their biology and physiology is so like ours that they can be infected with almost all human diseases. Hundreds have been used in hepatitis and AIDS research. Admittedly some laboratories are improving, developing programs to enrich their prisoners' lives, giving them more space. But there are still hundreds in the United States and other parts of the world in such cells.

Surplus Chimpanzees

A major problem today is the so-called surplus chimpanzee population. [. . .] The following stories of three chimpanzees, two born in the wild and one in captivity, serve to remind us that when we talk of the "surplus" problem we are actually talking of the fate of individuals, each with his or her own personality, each having been exploited by humans.

Gregoire was born in the wild, in the northern forests of Congo (Brazzaville). When I met him he was alone in a dark cage, one in a row of similarly caged, solitary primates at the Brazzaville Zoo. Gregoire had been given to the zoo when his owners left the country, and he had been there since about 1949, some 40 years. He was almost hairless, and I could see nearly every bone in his body. Most of the animals at that zoo were starving; it was cheaper to replace animals who died of malnutrition than to buy an adequate diet. I knew I had to help Gregoire even though he had, somehow, survived without help for so long. A small group of people got together and agreed to save up food and deliver it to the zoo. The Jane Goodall Institute employed its own keeper to care for Gregoire and the other primates. Gregoire put on weight and his hair began to grow. Then the Brigitte Bardot Foundation gave us a small grant (after she saw a video of Gregoire), and we were able to build a small "patio" for him. By this time Graziella Cotman was living in Brazzaville, and she was able to introduce three small orphans to the old male. One was a 2-year-old female, whom I named Cherie. A wonderful relationship, a bit like a grandfather and granddaughter, developed between this little girl and old Gregoire. Things were going well, until civil war broke out again. The zoo, near the airport, was in the middle of the war zone. Fortunately Gregoire, his young companions, and the two adult chimpanzees could be airlifted to the Tchimpounga Sanctuary (along with a group of young gorillas and bonobos). When Gregoire arrived, his back was raw, apparently because he had rushed under his low bed shelf whenever the shelling got too close. But once again this old man adapted, and his hair grew back. Today he is in a group with two adult females and three youngsters.

Sebastian was brought to Kenya (where there are no wild chimpanzees) from West Africa. He ended up in the orphanage run by the Kenya Wildlife Service. There he lived for more than 20 years, becoming the star attraction. When I met him his quarters consisted of a small indoor and private cage that led into a circular mesh enclosure. He lived alone because he had seriously hurt females who had been introduced to him. He was very gentle with humans whom he liked, and loved to manicure my nails with a piece of twig. But when crowds of visitors arrived, especially when these were children who would make faces and tease him, he would display wildly, back and forth in the enclosure, throwing anything he could find. Yet when he was put in a newly built enclosure that prevented the public from approaching closely, he became seriously depressed and refused to eat. Eventually he was returned to his original home, where he quickly recovered. Several years later he again became depressed when the orphanage was temporarily closed for reconstruction. Not until it was again opened to the public, and the daily teasing and displaying sessions resumed, did he recover. Clearly, the crowds provided stimulation and entertainment.

Lucy was born in captivity. As a tiny baby she was adopted by Jane and Maurice Temerlins, a psychoanalyst and his zoologist wife. Lucy was brought up like a human child, clothes and all. The original plan was to find out whether a chimpanzee brought up with love and affection would be able to nurture her first baby despite having no experience of other chimpanzees. But as she reached adolescence the Termerlins decided that their lives had been ruled by Lucy for too long. After considering all options, they decided, with the best of intentions, to give her her freedom, to send her to Africa. Although she went with a trusted human, all that she had learned in her "human" days had to be forgotten. She had learned sign language, but her signs were ignored by the only person she knew, the person with whom, until the nightmare began, she had communicated in sign language. Lucy was introduced to two rambunctious young wild-born chimpanzees. She wanted nothing to do with them. She fell into deep depression. Although she eventually began to behave more like a chimpanzee, I personally believe the exercise was very cruel. Lucy died, years after arriving in Africa and ultimately being released on an island. Her body was found on the island with hands and feet removed. The whole exercise can be compared with taking a middle-class American girl of about 14 years old to live with a group of indigenous people in some far off part of the world. She would leave behind all her clothes, all her comforts, and all her culture. And her American companion would pretend not to understand a word she said.

These three chimpanzees had unnatural life styles to which they adapted. Humans created those situations. We have no right to try to effect change from our arrogant human perspective of "we know what is best." Rather we should try to get inside the mind of the individual chimpanzees and move slowly, a step at a time, toward a solution that is *best for them*.

Conclusions

Clearly chimpanzees today face many problems, both in the wild and in captivity. These problems are all different and need their own unique solutions that take into account all the variables; the country, the different people involved, the resources available, especially financial, and the personalities of the chimpanzees themselves. We cannot draw sweeping conclusions about the correct procedure in all zoos, in all sanctuaries, and in all situations.

Those trying to help the great apes have their own perspectives. There are many differences of opinion. But so long as we all have the same goals—the improvement of conditions for the great apes, in the world and in captivity—we should be able to work together.

[. . .]

I have encountered criticism for starting sanctuaries (they have been called a waste of money to help a few individuals when precious funds are needed to save the species), but for me there was no option. I simply could not look into the eyes of a pathetic orphan and leave it to its fate, because, for so many years, I have been able to look into the eyes of chimpanzees who are wild and free and in control of their own lives.

Let us move forward, united toward our goal of conserving the great apes in the wild, striving for the best treatment for all captive apes, and eliminating them from invasive medical research. Whether we care about the apes as species or as individuals, we all want solutions that will give them a chance to survive and to enjoy the best possible quality of life.

Cetaceans

23 Culture and Conservation of Non-Humans with Reference to Whales and Dolphins

Review and New Directions

Hal Whitehead, Luke Rendell,
Richard W. Osborne, and Bernd Würsig

Whitehead and co-authors address the increasing evidence that culture is an important determinant of behavior in apes and cetaceans (whales and dolphins). They note that culture transmitted within generations ("horizontal" culture) may assist animals to deal with anthropogenic changes. In contrast, culture transmitted principally between generations ("vertical" culture) may impede adaptation to environmental change. The authors argue that non-human culture should be integrated in conservation biology when addressing species with these characteristics.

Introduction

"Conservation," when applied to humans, almost always refers to valued cultural attributes: to art forms, architecture, languages, or "ways of life." For instance, the organization Cultural Survival (2002) declares: "The diversity of cultures around the world is increasingly endangered. This diversity constitutes the wealth of all humanity. We have more than a moral obligation to respect and promote cultural diversity—it is in our interest."

For all other forms of life, conservation has been tightly focused on genetic diversity. We are going to suggest that in some circumstances, for some species, culture should be integrated into conservation biology. We will take most of our examples from cetaceans. However, many of our arguments apply to other non-human species for which culture seems important (see Sutherland, 1998). For instance, culture has begun to be considered in the conservation of chimpanzees, *Pan troglodytes* (Goodall, 1994; McGrew, 2003), and elephants, *Elephantidae* (McComb et al., 2001).

Culture has been defined in many varied ways (e.g., Mundinger, 1980). The definition that we prefer is "information or behavior—shared by a population or subpopulation—which is acquired from conspecifics through some form of social learning" (Rendell and Whitehead, 2001a). Here, "population" could include the whole species, and "subpopulation" any subdivision of a population which contains at least a few individuals in each set. This definition has four important elements: that culture affects behavior and thus phenotypes; that it is a group phenomenon; that it is transmitted from individual to individual and so, like genes, is an inheritance system (Boyd and Richerson, 1985); and that the transmission is through some form of social learning (see Whiten and Ham, 1992 for definitions of social learning). Our definition is similar to that used by most of those who study culture in other non-humans (e.g., Slater, 2001; Laland and Hoppitt, 2003; McGrew, 2003), cultural theorists (e.g., Boyd and Richerson, 1996), and some social scientists (Cronk, 1999). However, some psychologists restrict culture to transmission only through imitation and teaching (Galef, 1992), a restriction that we and others contest (Whiten and Ham, 1992; Boesch, 2001; Rendell and Whitehead, 2001a; Laland and Hoppitt, 2003), and there are anthropologists and other social scientists who use completely different definitions, including elements such as "shared values" (e.g., Ingold, 2001), which cannot currently be applied to non-humans.

Culture, as conceived by us and many others, has some similarities with genetic inheritance. It can mutate and evolve, is subject to the natural selection of both cultural variants and culture-bearers, and often leads to adaptive behavior. However, there are some important differences (see Boyd and Richerson, 1985): individuals can receive culture from a range of donors in addition to their parents; they can choose which culture to adopt; and their own experiences and behavior can influence the form of culture that is transmitted to other individuals, so acquired characters can be inherited. A consequence is that culture can affect behavioral and population biology, and thus conservation issues, in ways that are importantly different from those traditionally expected from a model that includes only genetic inheritance.

Culture is very varied, and this variation has implications for its interactions with conservation. For instance, contrasts have often been drawn between "horizontal" cultures, where transmission is between members of the same generation, and "vertical" or "oblique" cultures, where animals learn behavior from parents or other members of previous generations (Cavalli-Sforza et al., 1982). Horizontal cultural transmission can be highly effective in quickly changing population behavior in adaptive ways, an example being the rapid decrease in the use of certain chemicals by humans once they are shown to be toxic. Conversely, vertical cultures, like some religions, can be highly conservative and can constrain adaptive responses to environmental change.

Using our definition of culture, or any similar one, culture is quite common among animals, especially those that are more cognitively advanced (Boyd and Richerson, 1996). However, in most of the species possessing recognized cultural capacities, only a small proportion of behavior seems to be determined by social learning, and much of this may be functionally neutral, as has been argued for songbirds (Slater, 1986; although see Grant and Grant, 1996). Generally, in these cases, it seems unlikely that culture will be an important factor in population biology or conservation. In contrast, among the great apes and cetaceans, and perhaps in a few other groups (other primates, elephants, bats, and parrots are good candidates; see de Waal and Tyack, 2003), social learning likely determines a large proportion of behavior, including functionally important behavior such as foraging (McGrew, 1992; Whiten et al., 1999; Rendell and Whitehead, 2001b; van Schaik et al., 2003). In these species, culture can affect fitness and population biology in important ways, and so, we argue, have a potential bearing on conservation biology. This is especially the case when the form that culture takes leads to discrete, behaviorally differentiated population segments that can possess quite distinct ecological roles. Luck et al. (2003) argue that population diversity, especially in terms of the range of ecosystem services provided, should be an important element of population and conservation biology. Culture can provide such population diversity.

We will primarily use the cetaceans – whales and dolphins – to make our case. Cetaceans have been studied less thoroughly than the great apes, and less is known of their behavior. However, primatologists have acknowledged that cetaceans have behavior, social learning skills, and cultural capacities which appear at least as advanced as those of the non-human great apes (Dunbar, 2001; Whiten, 2001). Furthermore, the cetacean culture that is emerging from current studies includes a feature that is not known among non-human great apes and that has particular significance for conservation: stable, sympatric, culturally determined groups within populations.

We will briefly summarize the evidence for culture in whales and dolphins, and then show how different forms of culture can have consequences for conservation biology. We provide few solid prescriptions for dealing with these consequences but rather seek to highlight issues that may require further consideration in cultural species.

Cetacean Culture

[. . .]

Despite difficulties in studying the behavior of the whales and dolphins and, compared with primates and songbirds, a lack of knowledge on behavior, communication, and social structure, there is strong evidence for cetacean cultures in the four best studied species (Rendell and Whitehead, 2001b), and some most interesting speculations for some of the others (for instance on spinner dolphins, *Stenella longirostris*, Norris, 1994). Sophisticated social learning abilities exist, at least in bottlenose dolphins and orcas (Boran and Heimlich, 1999). Of the several types of social learning which have been recognized (e.g., Whiten and Ham, 1992), imitation is often singled out as being particularly significant for the promulgation of culture (e.g., Galef, 1992; Boyd and Richerson, 1996 but see Laland and Hoppitt, 2003). The bottlenose dolphin can imitate both vocally and non-vocally and has been shown to understand the broad concept of imitation (Herman and Pack, 2001). Some consider it the most sophisticated non-human imitator (e.g., Whiten, 2001).

This social learning seems to have led to culture, of various types. Among the baleen whales (suborder Mysticeti), there are several known cases of horizontally transmitted cultures (Rendell and Whitehead, 2001b). The best understood horizontal culture of cetaceans is the mating song of the male humpback whale. At any time during the winter breeding season, all the males in any ocean sing more or less the same elaborate song, but this communal song evolves over months and years (Payne, 1999). Songs in different oceans at any time are different but follow the same general syntactical and evolutionary rules.

Horizontal cultures are also found in the suborder Odontoceti, the toothed whales and dolphins. An example is the "dead-salmon carrying" fad of the well-studied "southern resident", fish-eating orcas of the Puget Sound area of the northeastern Pacific. It began with a female in K-Pod carrying around a dead salmon in 1987, spread to the other two pods in the southern resident community over a 5- to 6-week period and then stopped (R. Osborne, personal observation). It was noted a few times the following summer, and then never again.

Probably more significant from the conservation perspective are vertically or obliquely transmitted cultures. Populations of all the well-studied odontocetes are culturally structured, and subpopulations with distinct cultural trait groups are often sympatric. Among the bottlenose dolphins of Shark Bay, Western Australia, there are at least four distinctive foraging specializations, at least some of which are likely transmitted vertically from mother to daughter (Connor, 2001; Mann, 2001; Mann and Sargeant, 2003). Similar population structure by foraging specializations is found in other dolphin communities, for instance in cases of human–dolphin fishing co-operatives. In Brazil there are at least two cases where some, but not all, bottlenose dolphins in a community have a long-standing and complex cooperative relationship with local fishers which is almost certainly vertically transmitted between generations of both dolphins and fishers (Simões-Lopes et al., 1998).

The population of orcas off the west coast of Canada is clearly structured at a number of hierarchical levels, and much of this structuring seems to be cultural. At the highest level, different "types" of orca ("residents" and "transients") are sympatric but show sufficient differences in feeding behavior, vocalizations, social systems, morphology, and genetics that they may be incipient species (Baird, 2000). It has been suggested that this division was originally cultural (Baird, 2000). At lower levels, "communities," "clans," and "pods" of orcas may differ in vocalizations, foraging behavior, and social behavior but often have overlapping ranges (Ford et al., 1999). The complex, stable, and sympatric vocal and behavioral cultures of orca groups have no known parallel outside humans (Rendell and Whitehead, 2001b). The closest analog is with the sperm whale, whose society is also arranged into a multilevel hierarchy, at least two levels of which may support cultural differences among sympatric groups: the approximately 10-member "social units" and ocean-wide "clans" with thousands of members each (Rendell and Whitehead, 2003; Whitehead, 2003).

Some of the attributions of culture to behavioral differences between segments of cetacean populations which are mentioned in this paper are not fully proven and have been contested (see commentaries on Rendell and Whitehead, 2001b). For instance, there is a segment of the scientific community which is unwilling to ascribe culture to a species without experimental proof of social learning (e.g., Galef, 1992). Among cetaceans this is impossible for the larger whales, only exists for the bottlenose dolphin (see above), and, even here, the apparently cultural characteristics of wild populations of this species have not been experimentally tested in the laboratory. However, there are many reasons for questioning such a restriction for culture, including the observation that transmission mechanisms for most human culture have not been experimentally tested in the laboratory (Boesch, 2001; Rendell and Whitehead, 2001a). In all the cases of cetacean behavioral differences cited below, we believe that the evidence strongly points to culture rather than alternative genetic, environmental, or ontogenetic causes (Rendell and Whitehead, 2001a).

The emerging picture, then, is that whale and dolphin behavior is strongly affected by culture. The culture comes in a range of forms, from high-turnover horizontal cultures of the baleen whales to the stable vertical cultures that structure odontocete populations. Cetacean cultural behavior includes vocalizations, foraging and ranging behavior, and social norms, but, in contrast to chimpanzees and orangutans, *Pongo* spp., there is little evidence of material cultures (Rendell and Whitehead, 2001b).

Horizontal Cultures and Conservation

It has been suggested several times that a principal adaptive advantage of culture in humans is to navigate environmental change (e.g., Boyd and Richerson, 1985; Laland et al., 1996): if animals can learn from each other they can adapt to changing environments more quickly than if each individual must learn the optimal behavior independently, and much more quickly than is possible with natural selection of genetically determined behavior. Thus species with cultural capacities possess a potential advantage when environments change, even if they themselves are the agents of the change.

[. . .]

In several areas of the world, cetaceans have learned to remove fish from fishing gear, and given the rapid spread of the behavior within populations, there is little doubt that social learning is responsible for at least some of the recruitment to the population of fish-stealers. Examples include orcas and/or sperm whales taking fish from long-lines in the fisheries for Patagonian tooth-fish, *Dissostichus eleginoides*, off the southern parts of South America, bluenose, *Hyperoglyphe antarchia*, off New Zealand, halibut, *Hippoglossus stenolepis*, and sablefish, *Anoplopoma fimbria*, near Alaska (e.g., Yano and Dahlheim, 1995; Ashford et al., 1996; National Marine Fisheries Service, 1998; Nolan et al., 2000).

[. . .]

In many of these cases of crop-raiding by elephants and fish-stealing by whales the animals suffer hostile repercussions from angry farmers and fishers, including shooting and calls for culls. If elephants and cetaceans did not learn so well from other elephants and cetaceans, it seems highly likely that these problems would be much less severe.

Vertical and Oblique Cultures and Conservation

Vertical and oblique cultures are passed between generations and can be stable over many generations, particularly if enhanced by conformity, the imperative "to do the done thing" (Richerson and Boyd, 1998). Vertical cultures can influence genetic evolution (Laland, 1992; Grant and Grant, 1996; Whitehead, 1999) and may structure populations (e.g., Nettle, 1999; Rendell and Whitehead, 2003).

Cultural Conservatism

While rapidly evolving horizontal cultures may make a species more able to adapt to environmental change, stable vertical cultures can have the opposite effect. They may inhibit the adaptive responses that stimulus-response behavior, individual learning, and innovation would normally produce (although to a lesser extent than overriding genetic determination). For example, if, due to cultural traditions, orcas continued to use areas of their habitat despite excessive vessel traffic, sewage, or underwater noise, their adherence to tradition could potentially override what would otherwise be avoidance of noxious environmental conditions (Osborne, 1999).

For cetaceans perhaps the most important aspect of this cultural conservatism relates to the reestablishment of a species in an ecological niche following extirpation due to whaling. Most large whale populations were enormously reduced by commercial whaling, which began hundreds of years ago but reached its peak during the 1960s (Clapham et al., 1999). These populations are now virtually protected from whaling so that recovery is expected, and in some cases apparent. However, while reasonable, and sometimes growing, population densities are found in some areas, other traditionally important habitat remains deserted. [. . .] While we can document the end of traditional use of a habitat, whaling probably removed other cultural knowledge from populations, and this loss likely inhibits their recovery.

Maladaptive Behavior

More fundamentally, cultural evolution has a greater potential to lead to maladaptive behavior than genetic evolution or individual learning (Boyd and Richerson, 1985). This is particularly the case for conformist cultures in which individuals actively adopt the most common cultural variants in their experience. Conformist cultures can be particularly stable and lead to strong group identification and cultural group selection (Richerson and Boyd, 1998). This process is a leading candidate for explaining genetically maladaptive behavior by humans (Boyd and Richerson, 1985), such as religiously prescribed fertility limitations, or the eating of dead relatives' brains. Conformist cultural evolution can also potentially result in maladaptive behavior in non-humans. This can lead to the appearance of conservation problems, where no anthropogenic threat is actually operating.

[. . .] We have suggested that mass strandings of cetaceans may be linked to conformist cultures (Rendell and Whitehead, 2001b). In this scenario, healthy animals run up on the beaches and die at least partially because the culturally transmitted imperative to remain with the group holds sway over the individual's survival instinct. Although culture has not been studied in pilot whales, they seem to have social structures with similar general attributes to orcas and sperm whales (Heimlich-Boran, 1993; Ottensmeyer and Whitehead, 2003), the types that seem to promote conformist cultures.

The implication is that for cetaceans, like humans, strange and apparently maladaptive behavior may be a product of cultural evolution and not a result of anthropogenic changes to their environment, especially if it is a group phenomenon. Thus not all weird behavior indicates a conservation problem, although some, such as mass strandings of several whale species simultaneously, does (Balcomb and Claridge, 2001; Jepson et al., 2003).

Reintroduction and Translocation

Culture interacts with conservation in the introduction of captive animals into the wild and the forced movement of animals between areas (Sutherland, 1998). Reintroductions and translocations are important conservation tools in some circumstances, and culture will affect their success. The principal issues are whether the animals possess the knowledge to survive and breed in their new habitat.

Cultural aspects undoubtedly affect the success of cetacean reintroductions (see, e.g., Wells et al., 1998), but reintroduction is not generally considered an important tool in cetacean conservation (e.g., Reeves and Mead, 1999). Translocations from the highly impacted Yangtze River to a protected oxbow have been attempted to save the critically endangered baiji (*Lipotes vexillifer*), but these efforts were not successful (Zhang et al., 2003). Cultural aspects may have had a role in this. Translocations of finless porpoises (*Neophocaena phocaenoides*) between the same two habitats have been successful (Ding et al., 2000). This contrast may partially result from differences in the role of cultural knowledge in the two species.

Sympatric Cultural Variants

Conservation biology is complicated by population subdivisions. Anthropogenic threats may affect the different segments in different ways, leading to multiple responses. The situation is particularly complex when the population segments are sympatric. [. . .]

In the ocean, territoriality is much less prevalent than on land, leaving more opportunities for sympatric socially learned behavioral variants within species. A well-studied example is the sea otter, *Enhydra lutris*, in which individuals that share habitat have distinctive foraging styles, which are learned from their mothers, and so may possess distinctive ecological roles (Estes et al., 2003). Among cetaceans, sympatric groups often have distinctive behavioral repertoires resulting from vertical cultural transmission and apparently rendered stable by conformism, a situation which has a range of conservation ramifications. Culturally discrete subpopulations in the same habitat may face different conservation threats or may respond to the same threat in different ways.

In Moreton Bay, Australia, bottlenose dolphins regularly feed from trawler discards (Chilvers and Corkeron, 2001). Among the several hundred dolphins that use Moreton Bay, two sympatric communities have been recognized, one of which generally feeds with trawlers, and the other of which never does (Chilvers and Corkeron, 2001). Although they live in the same area, dolphins from the two communities rarely interact socially, except possibly for some mating (Chilvers and Corkeron, 2001). It may become necessary to restrict trawling to safeguard the resources, peneaid prawns. How will this affect the trawler dolphins? Other impacts, such as the effect of run-off of pollutants into sea-grass beds, may primarily affect the non-trawler dolphins (Chilvers and Corkeron, 2001), so the conservation issues are difficult.

Similar conundrums are emerging for other species. For instance, dusky dolphins (*Lagenorhynchus obscurus*) near the Kaikoura Canyon, New Zealand, feed at night on mesopelagic fishes and squid (Würsig et al., 1989). A subset of those animals, and habitually the same every year, travel about 160 km north to the Marlborough Sounds in winter and there feed in the day on near-surface schooling fishes (Benoit-Bird et al., 2004). Traveling to Marlborough Sounds is thought to be culturally transmitted (B. Würsig, pers. comm.). The Marlborough Sounds users are now facing increasingly choked bays due to extensive mussel farm development in the Marlborough Sounds area, and the dolphins do not use areas with mussel farms (Markowitz et al., 2004).

[. . .]

In orcas, too, sympatric culturally distinguished groupings face different conservation threats. For instance, off southern Vancouver Island, fish-eating "residents" are found in the same waters as mammal-eating "transients." The residents are threatened by declines in salmon stocks and by rampant whale-watching (Osborne, 1999; Trites and Barrett-Lennard, 2001; Erbe, 2002; NOAA, 2002), while for transients extreme concentrations of pollutants linked to their high trophic level (Ross et al., 2000) are probably the major concern.

Sympatric Cultural Variants and Evolutionarily Significant Units

These situations, in which sympatric culturally distinct populations have characteristic conservation issues or may respond differently to threats, indicate the importance of preserving both genetic and cultural diversity (Sutherland, 1998). [. . .]

Conservation is often believed to be promoted through considering the status of populations below the sub-species level, sometimes called "evolutionarily significant units" (ESUs). A consensus definition of an ESU has yet to be achieved, and the practice of assigning them is very much under development. We can now add a further twist to this difficult issue: should culture be considered in the determination of ESUs?

Geographically distinct cultures could be used as part of the process of dividing populations, so that, for example, chimpanzee populations in different parts of Africa might be assigned to different ESUs based upon cultural similarity (Whiten et al., 2001) as well as geographic and genetic proximity. The situation becomes more difficult when population segments overlap geographically and genetically, but are clearly distinguishable based upon culturally transmitted behavior.

A controversial case that contains strong cultural undercurrents is that of the "southern resident" orcas. The southern resident community contains about 80 fish-eating orcas whose range straddles the US–Canadian border. The population has been declining since 1995, but the reasons for this are unclear (NOAA, 2002). The southern residents are sympatric with the mammal-eating "transient" orcas and share some of their range with the "northern resident community," which also eat fish. There are about 200 northern residents, and although they seem less threatened than the southern residents, their population has also started to decline recently (Trites and Barrett-Lennard, 2001). There is little mating between the northern and southern residents, and they are genetically distinct (Barrett-Lennard, 2000). However, genetic divergence is small, just one base pair in the control region of the mitochondrial genome and $F_{ST} = 0.144$ using 11 microsatellite loci (Barrett-Lennard, 2000). The principal, and probably fundamental, differences between the communities are cultural. The Committee on the Status of Endangered Wildlife in Canada (COSEWIC) reviewed orca status in 2001 and divided the orcas into "nationally significant populations" assigning a status of "Endangered" (the highest risk category available for an extant population) to the southern residents, "Threatened" to the northern residents, and "Threatened" to the transients (www.cosewic.gc.ca). In contrast, the US National Marine Fisheries Service (NMFS) in 2002 refused a petition to declare the southern residents "Endangered," listing them only as "Depleted," as they were not considered a "distinct population segment" but were "part of the general killer whale population in the North Pacific, which is considered healthy" (NOAA, 2002; NOAA Press release 02–076; http://www.nwr. noaa.gov/mmammals/whales/srkwnews.pdf). Supporting this decision, NMFS noted that the northern and southern residents use similar habitat types, that loss of the southern residents would not necessarily result in a gap in the species' range, and that the genetic differences between the northern and southern residents is small (NOAA, 2002). NMFS also considered "pod-specific traits, such as acoustic repertoire, that have been described by some biologists as 'cultural' " but concluded "that there was insufficient evidence to indicate whether these 'cultural' traits were inherited or learned, and thus whether they truly signify an evolutionarily important trait" (NOAA, 2002). This reasoning is confused, as cultural traits must be learned and may or may not also be inherited between generations. However, the implication seems to be that traits acquired through learning are not evolutionarily important, and, thus, in apparent contrast to the Canadian listing agency (COSEWIC), NMFS specifically appears to disregard culture in this listing decision.

Where do these practices stand in the light of the evolving theory of ESUs? There have been many approaches to defining ESUs (Fraser and Bernatchez, 2001), but the focus is on genetic separation, not cultural differences. In the definitions of Dizon et al. (1992), Moritz (1994), and Fraser and Bernatchez (2001), ESUs are delineated entirely on the basis of information and inferences about gene flow and differences in allele distributions. There are some broader approaches which do not specifically mention genes in the basic definition. O'Brien and Mayr (1991) and Waples (1991), extending the biological species concept, consider ESUs as population subsets that are substantially reproductively isolated. However, "reproduction" is of genes not cultural variants. One definition of ESU that, on the surface, appears to allow cultural entities to be listed *per se* comes from the cladistic approach of Vogler and DeSalle (1994) in which ESUs are discriminated using characters which cluster individuals or populations to the exclusion of other such clusters. Such characters must be heritable, which admits many culturally determined attributes. However, characters must also "define phylogenetic (i.e., genetically separated) lineages" (Vogler and DeSalle, 1994), and so we are back to genes again.

The emphasis on genetic patterns and processes, or restrictions to reproductively isolated population segments, would probably rule out ESU designation for most known instances of the culturally determined segregation of a sympatric population, such as the Moreton Bay bottlenose dolphins and sperm whale clans. In contrast, the "types" and communities of orcas are largely reproductively isolated and show genetic differences (Barrett-Lennard, 2000), allowing potential discrimination into ESUs under several of the criteria.

Fundamentally we are trying to conserve biodiversity, which may be defined as the "full variety of life on Earth" (Takacs, 1996). A large part of this variety is heritable phenotypic variation. The mechanism by which information is transferred between generations is of secondary significance. There are several mechanisms by which information which determines phenotypes may be transferred between generations, of which genetics is much the most significant, and culture the clear runner-up (Maynard Smith, 1989). Definitions of the ESUs which are neutral as to transmission mechanisms could easily be derived from current proposals. For instance, Fraser and Bernatchez's (2001) "lineage demonstrating highly restricted gene flow from other such lineages within the higher organizational level (lineage) of the species" could become a "lineage demonstrating highly restricted flow of information that determines phenotypes from other such lineages within the higher organizational level (lineage) of the species."

Such an approach would lead to "cultural ESUs" only very rarely: both a large and functionally important part of the behavior of animals would have to be due to social learning and there would need to be little cultural exchange between population segments, despite the segments sharing geographical ranges and most functionally important genes. In most species, cultural variants are either geographically or genetically discrete or of little functional importance, but orcas would probably qualify, and maybe sperm whales and elephants. We believe that preserving significant cultural variants in such species is an important part of conserving the species itself.

Conclusion

We have heard arguments that if we are at the stage of conserving non-human cultures, then the real conservation battles have already been won. We disagree. For a range of non-human animals, culture is a vital determinant of phenotype, and so is how the animals interact with humans and our cultural artifacts. Thus, culture should be an integral element of the conservation biology of these species.

Cultural organisms do not behave like those for which culture has little significance. Clearly maladaptive behavior is often taken as a sign of a threat to individuals or populations, but genetically maladaptive behavior is to be expected in conformist cultures. In cultural societies, individuals with important cultural knowledge may have population significance far in excess of their reproductive capacities (McComb et al., 2001), and populations may be structured in significant ways by cultural knowledge and cultural habit. As we hope we have shown, these mean that conservation takes on an additional dimension. This is manifestly recognized for humans, but we should also consider culture in the conservation of other species—in individual cases by noting how cultural diversity interacts with anthropogenic threats, as well as perhaps more systematically by adding the potential for culture to our concepts of ESUs and other staples of conservation biology.

It has been suggested that the recognition of culture in other animals should affect our perception of them (Fox, 2001). Cultural Survival (2002) believes that there is a "moral obligation" to conserve human cultural diversity. So, in addition to considering culture as a part of the mix of biological attributes that affects how organisms interact with anthropogenic threats, perhaps culture should also be inserted into the roots of our conservation biology: why we wish to conserve organisms, and what we wish to conserve about them. These questions are difficult and perhaps beyond the scope of most practicing conservation biologists. However, this does not mean that the implications of non-human cultures should just be left to the ethicists: non-human culture is not just "chimpanzees/dolphins/elephants reading poetry," it is the source of survival skills fundamental to the daily lives of these animals.

Acknowledgments

Thanks to Bill McGrew for his perspective on the relationship between culture and conservation in chimpanzees, to Marilyn Dahlheim for information about the development of fish-stealing among Alaskan orcas, and to two anonymous reviewers for encouragement and comments.

References

Ashford, J. R., Rubilar, P. S., Martin, A. R., 1996. Interactions between cetaceans and longline fishery operations around South Georgia. *Marine Mammal Science* 12, 452–456.

Baird, R. W., 2000. The killer whale—foraging specializations and group hunting. In: Mann, J., Connor, R. C., Tyack, P., Whitehead, H. (Eds.), *Cetacean Societies*. University of Chicago Press, Chicago, pp. 127–153.

Balcomb, K. C., Claridge, D. E., 2001. A mass stranding of cetaceans caused by naval sonar in the Bahamas. *Bahamas Journal of Science* 5, 2–12.

Barrett-Lennard, L., 2000. Population structure and mating patterns of killer whales (*Orcinus orca*) as revealed by DNA analysis. Ph.D. dissertation, University of British Columbia, Vancouver.

Benoit-Bird, K. J., Würsig, B., & Mfadden, C. J. (2004). Dusky dolphin (Lagenorhynchus obscurus) foraging in two different habitats: active acoustic detection of dolphins and their prey. *Marine Mammal Science*, 20(2), 215–231.

Boesch, C., 2001. Sacrileges are welcome in science! Opening a discussion about culture in animals. *Behavioral and Brain Sciences* 24, 327–328.

Boran, J. R., Heimlich, S. L., 1999. Social learning in cetaceans: Hunting, hearing and hierarchies. *Symposia of the Zoological Society, London* 73, 282–307.

Boyd, R., Richerson, P., 1985. *Culture and the Evolutionary Process*. University of Chicago Press, Chicago.

Boyd, R., Richerson, P. J., 1996. Why culture is common, but cultural evolution is rare. *Proceedings of the British Academy* 88, 77–93.

Cavalli-Sforza, L. L., Feldman, M. W., Chen, K. H., Dornbusch, S. M., 1982. Theory and observation in cultural transmission. *Science* 218, 19–27.

Chilvers, B. L., Corkeron, P. J., 2001. Trawling and bottlenose dolphins' social structure. *Proceedings of the Royal Society of London* B268, 1901–1905.

Clapham, P. J., Young, S. B., Brownell, R. L. J., 1999. Baleen whales: Conservation issues and the status of the most endangered populations. *Mammal Review* 29, 35–60.

Connor, R. C., 2001. Individual foraging specializations in marine mammals: Culture and ecology. *Behavioral and Brain Sciences* 24, 329–330.

Cronk, L., 1999. *That Complex Whole: Culture and the Evolution of Human Behavior*. Westview Press, Boulder, CO.

Cultural Survival, 2002. *Annual Report 2001–2002: Celebrating 30 Years of Cultural Survival*. Cultural Survival, Cambridge, MA.

de Waal, F. B. M., Tyack, P. L., 2003. *Animal Social Complexity: Intelligence, Culture, and Individualized Societies*. Harvard University Press, Cambridge, MA.

Ding, W., Renjun, L., Zhang, X., Jian, Y., Wei, Z., Zhao, Q., Wang, X., 2000. Status and conservation of the Yangtze finless porpoise. In: Reeves, R.R., Smith, B.D., Kasuya, T. (Eds.), *Biology and Conservation of Freshwater Cetaceans in Asia*. IUCN Species Survival Commission, Gland, Switzerland, pp. 81–85.

Dizon, A. E., Lockyer, C., Perrin, W. F., Demaster, D. P., Sisson, J., 1992. Rethinking the stock concept. *Conservation Biology* 6, 24–36.

Dunbar, R. I. M., 2001. Do how do they do it? *Behavioral and Brain Sciences* 24, 332–333.

Erbe, C., 2002. Underwater noise of whale-watching boats and potential effects on killer whales (*Orcinus orca*), based on an acoustic impact model. *Marine Mammal Science* 18, 394–418.

Estes, J. A., Riedman, M. L., Staedler, M. M., Tinker, M. T., Lyon, B. E., 2003. Individual variation in prey selection by sea otters: Patterns, causes and implications. *Journal of Animal Ecology* 72, 144–155.

Ford, J. K. B., Ellis, G. M., Barrett-Lennard, L. G., Morton, A. B., Palm, R. S., Balcomb, K. C., 1999. Dietary specialization in two sympatric populations of killer whales (*Orcinus orca*) in coastal British Columbia and adjacent waters. *Canadian Journal of Zoology* 76, 1456–1471.

Fox, M. A., 2001. Cetacean culture: Philosophical implications. *Behavioral and Brain Sciences* 24, 333–334.

Fraser, D. J., Bernatchez, L., 2001. Adaptive evolutionary conservation: Towards a unified concept for defining conservation units. *Molecular Ecology* 10, 2741–2752.

Galef, B. G., 1992. The question of animal culture. *Human Nature* 3, 157–178.

Goodall, J., 1994. Postscript—conservation and the future of chimpanzee and bonobo research in Africa. In: Wrangham, R. W., McGrew, W. C., de Waal, F. B. M., Heltne, P. G. (Eds.), *Chimpanzee Cultures*. Harvard University Press, Cambridge, MA, pp. 397–404.

Grant, B. R., Grant, P. R. 1996. Cultural inheritance of song and its role in the evolution of Darwin's finches. *Evolution* 50, 2471–2487.

Heimlich-Boran, J. R., 1993. Social organization of the short-finned pilot whale *Globicephala macrorhynchus*, with special reference to the comparative social ecology of delphinids. Ph.D. Dissertation, Cambridge University, Cambridge, UK.

Herman, L. M., Pack, A. A., 2001. Laboratory evidence for cultural transmission mechanisms. *Behavioral and Brain Sciences* 24, 335–336.

Ingold, T., 2001. The use and abuse of ethnography. *Behavioral and Brain Sciences* 24, 337.

Jepson, P. D., Arbelo, M., Deaville, R., Patterson, I. A., Castro, P., Degollada, E., Ross, H. M., Herráez, P., Pocknell, A. M., Rodriguez, F., Howiell, F. E., Espinosa, A., Reid, R. J., Jaber, J. R., Martin, V., Cunningham, A. A., Fernández, A., 2003. Gas bubble lesions in stranded cetaceans. *Nature* 425, 575–576.

Laland, K. N., 1992. A theoretical investigation of the role of social transmission in evolution. *Ethology and Sociobiology* 13, 87–113.

Laland, K. N., Hoppitt, W., 2003. Do animals have culture? *Evolutionary Anthropology* 12, 150–159.

Laland, K. N., Richerson, P. J., Boyd, R., 1996. Developing a theory of animal social learning. In: Heyes, C. M., Galef, B. G. J. (Eds.), *Social Learning in Animals: The Roots of Culture*. Academic Press, San Diego, CA, pp. 129–154.

Luck, G. W., Daily, G. C., Ehrlich, P. R., 2003. Population diversity and ecosystem services. *Trends in Ecology and Evolution* 18, 331–336.

Mann, J., 2001. Cetacean culture: Definitions and evidence. *Behavioral and Brain Sciences* 24, 343.

Mann, J., Sargeant, B., 2003. Like mother, like calf: the ontogeny of foraging traditions in wild Indian Ocean bottlenose dolphins (*Tursiops* sp.). In: Fragaszy, D. M., Perry, S. (Eds.), *The Biology of Traditions: Models and Evidence*. Cambridge University Press, Cambridge, UK, pp. 236–266.

Markowitz, T. M., Harlin, A. D., Würsig, B., McFadden, C. J., 2004. Dusky dolphin foraging habitat: Overlap with aquaculture in New Zealand. *Aquatic Conservation: Marine and Freshwater Ecosystems* 14, 133–149.

Maynard Smith, J., 1989. *Evolutionary Genetics*. Oxford University Press, Oxford, UK.

McComb, K., Moss, C., Durant, S. M., Baker, L., Sayialel, S., 2001. Matriarchs as repositories of social knowledge in African elephants. *Science* 292, 491–494.

McGrew, W. C., 1992. *Chimpanzee Material Culture: Implications for Human Evolution*. Cambridge University Press, Cambridge, UK.

McGrew, W. C., 2003. Ten dispatches from the chimpanzee culture wars: Intelligence, culture, and individualized societies. In: de Waal, F.B.M., Tyack, P. L. (Eds.), *Animal Social Complexity*. Harvard University Press, Cambridge, MA.

Moritz, C., 1994. Defining 'evolutionary significant units' for conservation. *Trends in Ecology and Evolution* 9, 373–375.

Mundinger, P. C., 1980. Animal cultures and a general theory of cultural evolution. *Ethology and Sociobiology* 1, 183–223.

National Marine Fisheries Service, 1998. Sperm whale (*Physeter macrocephalus*): North Pacific stock, Stock Assessment Report, pp. 111–114.

Nettle, D., 1999. Language variation and the evolution of societies. In: Dunbar, R. I. M., Knight, C., Power, C. (Eds.), *The Evolution of Culture*. Rutgers University Press, Piscataway, NJ, pp. 214–227.

NOAA, 2002. *Status Review under the Endangered Species Act: Southern Resident Killer Whales (Orcinus orca)*, NOAA Technical Memorandum NMFS-NWAFSC-54. Seattle, WA.

Nolan, C. P., Liddle, G. M., Elliot, J., 2000. Interactions between killer whales (*Orcinus orca*) and sperm whales (*Physeter macrocephalus*) with a longline fishing vessel. *Marine Mammal Science* 16, 658–664.

Norris, K. S., 1994. Comparative view of cetacean social ecology, culture, and evolution. In: Norris, K. S., Würsig, B., Wells, R.S., Würsig, M. (Eds.), *The Hawaiian Spinner Dolphin*. University of California Press, Berkeley, pp. 301–344.

O'Brien, S. J., Mayr, E., 1991. Species hybridization and protection of endangered animals. *Science* 253, 251–252.

Osborne, R. W., 1999. A historical ecology of Salish Sea resident killer whales (*Orcinus orca*): With implications for management. Ph.D. Dissertation, University of Victoria, Victoria, British Columbia.

Ottensmeyer, C. A., Whitehead, H., 2003. Behavioural evidence for social units in long-finned pilot whales. *Canadian Journal of Zoology* 81, 1327–1338.

Payne, K., 1999. The progressively changing songs of humpback whales: A window on the creative process in a wild animal. In: Wallin, N.vL., Merker, B., Brown, S. (Eds.), *The Origins of Music*. MIT Press, Cambridge, MA, pp. 135–150.

Reeves, R. R., Mead, J. G., 1999. Marine mammals in captivity. In: Twiss, J. R., Reeves, R. R. (Eds.), *Conservation and Management of Marine Mammals*. Smithsonian Institution Press, Washington, DC, pp. 412–436.

Rendell, L., Whitehead, H., 2001a. Cetacean culture: Still afloat after the first naval engagement of the culture wars. *Behavioral and Brain Sciences* 24, 360–373.

Rendell, L., Whitehead, H., 2001b. Culture in whales and dolphins. *Behavioral and Brain Sciences* 24, 309–324.

Rendell, L., Whitehead, H., 2003. Vocal clans in sperm whales (*Physeter macrocephalus*). *Proceedings of the Royal Society of London* B270, 225–231.

Richerson, P. J., Boyd, R., 1998. The evolution of human ultrasociality. In: Eibl-Eibesfeldt, I., Salter, F. K. (Eds.), *Indoctrinability, Ideology and Warfare*. Berghahn Books, London, pp. 71–95.

Ross, P. S., Ellis, G. M., Ikonomou, M. G., Barrett-Lennard, L. G., Addison, R. F., 2000. High PCB concentrations in free-ranging Pacific killer whales (*Orcinus orca*): Effects of age, sex and dietary preference. *Marine Pollution Bulletin* 40, 504–515.

Simões-Lopes, P. C., Fabián, M. E., Menegheti, J. O., 1998. Dolphin interactions with the mullet artisanal fishing on southern Brazil: A qualitative and quantitative approach. *Revista Brasileira de Zoologia* 15, 709–726.

Slater, P.J.B., 1986. The cultural transmission of bird song. *Trends in Ecology and Evolution* 1, 94–97.

Slater, P.J.B., 2001. There's CULTURE and Culture. *Behavioral and Brain Sciences* 24, 356–357.

Sutherland, W. J., 1998. The importance of behavioural studies in conservation biology. *Animal Behaviour* 56, 801–809.

Takacs, D., 1996. *The Idea of Biodiversity: Philosophies of Paradise*. Johns Hopkins University Press, Baltimore, MD.

Trites, A. W., Barrett-Lennard, L. G., 2001. *COSEWIC Status Report on Killer Whales (Orcinus orca)*. Committee on the Status of Endangered Wildlife in Canada, Ottawa.

van Schaik, C. P., Ancrenaz, M., Borgen, G., Galdikas, B., Knott, C. D., Singleton, I., Suzuki, A., Utami, S. S., Merrill, M., 2003. Orangutan cultures and the evolution of material culture. *Science* 299, 102–105.

Vogler, A. P., DeSalle, R., 1994. Diagnosing units of conservation management. *Conservation Biology* 8, 354–363.

Waples, R. S., 1991. Pacific salmon, *Oncorhynchus* spp. and the definition of 'species' under the Endangered Species Act. *Marine Fisheries Review* 53, 11–22.

Wells, R. S., Bassos-Hull, K., Norris, K. S., 1998. Experimental return to the wild of two bottlenose dolphins. *Marine Mammal Science* 14, 51–71.

Whitehead, H., 1999. Culture and genetic evolution in whales. *Science* 284, 2055a.

Whitehead, H., 2003. *Sperm Whales: Social Evolution in the Ocean*. University of Chicago Press, Chicago, IL.

Whiten, A., 2001. Imitation and cultural transmission in apes and cetaceans. *Behavioral and Brain Sciences* 24, 359 360.

Whiten, A., Goodall, J., McGrew, W. C., Nishida, T., Reynolds, V., Sugiyama, Y., Tutin, C. E. G., Wrangham, R. W., Boesch, C., 2001. Charting cultural variation in chimpanzees. *Behaviour* 138, 1481–1516.

Whiten, A., Goodall, J., McGrew, W. C., Nishida, T., Reynolds, V., Sugiyama, Y., Tutin, C. E. G., Wrangham, R. W., Boesch, C., 1999. Cultures in chimpanzees. *Nature* 399, 682–685.

Whiten, A., Ham, R., 1992. On the nature and evolution of imitation in the animal kingdom: Reappraisal of a century of research. *Advances in the Study of Behavior* 21, 239–283.

Würsig, B., Würsig, M., Cipriano, F., 1989. Dolphins in different worlds. *Oceanus* 32, 71–75.

Yano, K., Dahlheim, M. E., 1995. Killer whale, *Orcinus orca*, depredation on long-line catches of bottomfish in the southeastern Bering Sea and adjacent waters. *Fishery Bulletin US* 93, 355–372.

Zhang, X., Wang, D., Liu, R., Wei, Z., Hua, Y., Wang, Y., Chen, Z., Wang, L., 2003. The Yangtze river dolphin or baiji (*Lipotes vexillifer*): Population status and conservation issues in the Yangtze River, China. *Aquatic Conservation: Marine and Freshwater Ecosystems* 13, 51–64.

24 Consciousness in Dolphins?

A Review of Recent Evidence

Heidi E. Harley

Harley reviews studies on topics such as self-recognition/self-awareness and metacognition, notions tied to consciousness, in relation to dolphins. She evaluates some of the challenges in designing, conducting, and interpreting studies on these topics and concludes that the current evidence does not provide a convincing case for consciousness in dolphins. She evaluates a need for clearer definitions of consciousness and better methods for studying it.

For humans, dolphins have a mystique that pervaded the ancient world and continues today. And though oceanarium audiences' clicking cameras and clapping hands indicate that we admire the dolphin's physical prowess, it is primarily their minds that have invited love poems and fights for their rights. Why dolphins have inspired such admiration is not clear. It may be because they are large-brained, highly social mammals with an extended developmental period, flexible cognitive capacities, and powerful acoustic abilities, including a sophisticated echolocation system. Or, it may be their perennial smiles.

Whatever it is that drives our interest in dolphins, it is not their thumbs. Nevertheless, many of the questions we pursue about dolphin cognition are driven by parallel studies with human and nonhuman primates (e.g., Herman et al. 1999; Pack and Herman 2007). Of course, one of the interesting outcomes in pursuing primate-oriented questions with dolphins is that they often do well in these studies. How, then, does one interpret their performance? Do we attribute the same psychological mechanisms to dolphins that humans use to perform the same tasks? Some recent work with dolphins has addressed these questions and concluded that dolphins experience aspects of consciousness. The current article will investigate the recent evidence on which this conclusion is based with specific focus on the areas of study in which the strongest claims for consciousness have been made, i.e., mirror-recognition and metacognition studies.

Characterizations and Interpretations of Consciousness

Scientific work requires a coherent characterization of consciousness, a method for testing for it, and standards for interpreting experimental outcomes in terms of consciousness. These issues have direct relevance to this review, but because consciousness has elicited thoughtful consideration by profoundly influential scholars across millennia (e.g., Aristotle, Descartes, Locke, Darwin, Wittgenstein), resulting in multifaceted insights across fields (e.g., philosophy, biology, psychology, neuroscience), only a brief treatment of the relevant concepts will be presented here.

The path of the study of psychophysics may be (optimistically) illustrative of the study of consciousness today. Psychophysics is the study of the relations between external stimuli and our sensations and perceptions of them, i.e., the correspondence between our perceptions of the world and the world itself. Although perhaps taken for granted now, the study of psychophysics is an acknowledgment that an organism builds its own representation of the world in which it lives based on its needs. Hence, different species live in different perceptual worlds, von Uexküll's (1909) *Umwelten*.

For example, the bee's ability to perceive ultraviolet light means a flower appears quite differently to a bee than it does to a human, a perception that enhances the bee's skill at foraging for pollen in flowers. European citizens of the late Middle Ages/early Renaissance rejected the idea that they did not perceive the world exactly as it is. In fact, people were so convinced that their senses delivered the reality of the world to them that eyeglasses were suspect for several hundred years after their adoption because they distorted their wearers' vision of the world (Coren 2003). Only when Galilei showed the power of the telescope did a majority of people begin to acknowledge that tools might be able to give us a clearer understanding of reality in some cases than our senses alone could provide (Coren 2003).

Psychology originated in part to provide methods to address long-standing philosophical questions; many of psychology's methods were established in psychophysics during the nineteenth century drawing on the work of von Helmholtz, Weber, and Fechner, among others (Fuchs and Milar 2003). A common psychophysics method is a judgment task in which stimuli are compared with a reference stimulus (Pelli and Farell 1995). Often the goal of these studies is to find a detection threshold or just noticeable difference between two stimuli to learn about an organism's sensory capacities, e.g., the range of frequencies a dolphin can hear. At first glance, this method appears rather clear cut, and one might think interpretation of findings would be uncontroversial. In fact, there are many factors to consider when one interprets findings of something as common as a hearing detection task: how does detection vary with stimulus intensity? In noise? Across individuals? Across shifts in a subject's decision criteria? Over time, these issues and more have been addressed through enhancements in methodological and analysis techniques like using spatial gratings for vision and signal detection theory to take receiver operating characteristics into account. Work in psychophysics originated the use of standard control procedures like catch (stimulus-absent) trials, trial randomization, and recruitment of participants naïve to characteristics of the stimuli that could cause biased responding (Fuchs and Milar). Whereas psychophysics has now adopted clear questions and sophisticated techniques for answering them, the scientific study of consciousness is still grappling with problems of characterization as well as those of methods of study and interpretation of results. Pessimism about producing data that confirm or deny consciousness in another species is warranted in that neither sources nor behavioral outcomes of consciousness are clearly identified in any species, including our own. Where then does one look? Current trends addressing these challenges suggest that philosophers may be turning to comparative physiology again as they reevaluate the role of the integration of motor, sensory, and cognitive information to consciousness (Ramachandran and Hirstein 1997).

The facet of consciousness that receives the most focus is often referred to as phenomenal consciousness, i.e., the subjective experiences (also known as *qualia*) of one's own psychological processes, e.g., the way redness or pain feels to oneself. This intimate awareness of one's own mind is the driving force behind humans' study of consciousness. We recognize it in ourselves—and in other people through linguistic communication (e.g., Dennett 1991). However, these subjective experiences do not necessarily provide a veridical reading of how consciousness works or when it is invoked, and so currently much of our explicit knowledge about consciousness is conjecture.

Consciousness is likely not monolithic; it may occur as a continuum, in multiple categories (e.g., phenomenal consciousness, access consciousness, monitoring consciousness, self consciousness), and/or include a variety of processes (e.g., Griffin 1976, 1984, 1992, 1995; Block 1995; Chalmers 1996; Browne 2004). For example, on Dennett's account, consciousness is intrinsic to cognitive processing (see Dennett 1991, 2005, for in-depth discussions of consciousness). For Dennett (1991), "what (the quale) turns out to be in the real world in your brain is just a complex of dispositions" (p. 389). Consciousness does not stand outside of your cognitive processes and then interpret them; consciousness is part of your cognitive processes. On this account, "unconscious driving" ("how did I get here?" you ask yourself after an hour on the road in which you've planned your next vacation) is "better seen as a case of rolling consciousness with swift memory loss" than as "unconscious" (p. 137).

Theories of consciousness are bound up in concepts of self (Descartes' 1637 "Je pense donc je suis"), which are also represented as occurring at different levels or in sundry categories (James 1890/1950; Neisser 1988; Gallagher 2000; Rochat 2001; Rochat and Zahavi 2011; Klein 2012). Due to its subjectivity, a dominant view maintains that phenomenal consciousness is inaccessible to scientific study (see Palmer 1999, and commentaries for views on which aspects of consciousness are accessible to study). For example, Klein (2012) argues that while the "epistemological" (neural, cognitive, behavioral, emotional) self can be studied via the scientific method, the "ontological" (subjective, conscious, phenomenological) self cannot. On his account, researchers who think they are studying the second kind of self are typically only studying the first.

Recently, the view that consciousness cannot be studied scientifically has been contested by cognitive scientists (like Dennett above) who advocate a new understanding of consciousness that does not divorce it from the rest of cognitive processing. In his seminal 1974 article, "What Is It Like to Be a Bat?", Nagel (1974) argued against the usefulness of "the recent wave of reductionist euphoria" (p. 435) to understand the subjective experience of another. However, at the same time, he argued for the importance of understanding this experience, and he suggested the need for a new theoretical framework, "an objective phenomenology not dependent on empathy or the imagination" which might be studied first through the "structural features of perception" (p. 449). This is the direction that some work on consciousness has taken. For example, Hurley and Noë (2003) focus on interesting cases of cortical dominance (e.g., phantom limb responses in which input changes but cortical activation does not) and deference (e.g., visual cortical activation during Braille reading in the congenitally blind) related to the quality of the experiences they provide (e.g., one's subjective experience of "redness" as visual versus auditory). From their perspective, these cases suggest that answers about consciousness may lie in a "dynamic sensorimotor" account in which the emphasis is placed on the external. This "sensorimotor know-how" comes from neural rerouting based on one's interactions with one's environment and subsequent analysis of sensorimotor contingencies, the synchronicity of experiences occurring when sensing and moving. This view draws consciousness into the ecologically based experiences of the organism interacting with the world reminiscent of Gibson's (1979) perceptual theories.

[. . .]

Ramachandran and Hirstein (1998) suggest that body image is a temporary shell built on stimulus contingencies interpreted through Bayesian logic (synchronicity with that precision rarely happens randomly) to create an ephemeral gene-reproduction machine, the self. The authors (1997) also provide an account of qualia that includes three laws: Qualia are irrevocable in that one does not choose the qualities of one's experiences, qualia lead flexibly to a variety of behaviors, and qualia occur in short-term memory. On this account, the function of qualia is to support decisions that require choices, which is why qualia occur between perception and action and are probably located in the temporal lobes, where an executive function (uncharacteristically limbic rather than frontal) that connects motivation/emotion (amygdala-related) to action choices through qualia leads to behavior. This theory lays out predictions of outcomes of experiments and conditions in which qualia should and should not arise.

[. . .]

One consistent approach to interpretation of animal behavior as indicating consciousness has been through the use of analogy: When animals behave as humans would in the same situation, then they are likely using consciousness as humans would. Two difficult problems plague this approach. First, inferring that similar outcomes were created by the same mechanisms is often misleading, as a plethora of examples indicates. For example, bat and bird wings function similarly in that they are used to fly, but they are created rather differently; they evolved independently from a common vertebrate ancestor and are thus homoplasies rather than homologies. Bird song provides a behavioral example. A brown-headed cowbird (a brood parasite) and a starling may be heard singing the same song, but a cowbird raised in isolation (and thus without a model) can produce this species-typical song (although ultimately it is "trained" by female response to its song), whereas starlings can learn songs produced by other species through imitation (West et al. 2004); therefore, both species may produce the same behavior, but the mechanisms that produced that behavior are very different and reflect their natural histories (see Shettleworth 1998/2010 for many good examples of psychological mechanisms underlying behavior). Consciousness could potentially arise via similar mechanisms across species, via different mechanisms, or may not be instantiated as a mechanism (Velmans 1996). We do not know and reasoning by analogy does not help us decode what is happening.

The second problem with reasoning by analogy to determine consciousness in a non-human is that humans perform many of the tasks of their daily lives without the use of consciousness, but they are often misled about their ability to function without it—shaky ground for analogical reasoning. In a classic example, human participants working on a problem-solving task in which they needed to tie two strings together with limited materials were given a hint when a researcher appeared to inadvertently make one of the strings swing (Maier 1931). Not only were successful participants unaware of the influence of the swinging string, but they attributed their success to other causes. (Gazzaniga 2011 also presents examples of erroneous post-decision justifications of behavior.) Therefore, when a person uses metacognitive language to explain a behavior after its execution, the behavior may or may not actually have required consciousness for completion of the original task

[. . .]

Humans often perform complex behaviors without consciousness. For example, humans imitate automatically (see Heyes 2011 for a review). In one study, human participants told to open their hands when they saw blue and to close their hands when they saw red responded more slowly when they also saw contradictory stimuli that were irrelevant to their task, i.e., a task-irrelevant video of a hand closing in the presence of the task-relevant stimulus blue (Stürmer *et al.* 2000). Given that the participants were explicitly trying (and ultimately succeeding) to open their hands to blue, this influence of the videotaped closing hand suggests they were implicitly affected to perform in concert with the video movement regardless of their explicit goals. These implicit effects suggest that humans do not require awareness to engage in this kind of imitation. In addition, evidence showing that people can be re-trained to reduce automatic imitation suggests that general associative learning mechanisms like operant conditioning help create these sensorimotor connections (Heyes 2011). Many experimental data confirm that non-human animals (hereafter "animals") also learn through similar conditioning mechanisms (Shettleworth 1998/2010).

Modern methods to understand animal learning were just emerging at the end of the nineteenth century, so at that time interpreting animal behavior based on human experience was a common method for understanding animals for at least two reasons. First, it was an accessible method. Second, it was a recognition of evolutionary continuity. In the immediate post-Darwinian world, Romanes (1882) felt he had to use his own thoughts as an analogy for those of other species based on the behaviors they performed. His commitment to logical consistency required him to infer "sympathy or rage" in insects, if their behavior, through analogy, led to that conclusion, because "as it is the only analogy available, I shall follow it throughout the animal series" (p. 9). (See Roitblat 1985 and Wynne 2007 for in-depth discussions of this topic.)

In response to this wholesale approach, Morgan (1894) called for a more conservative guideline for interpretation via his Canon: only interpret a behavior as dependent on a higher level of psychological description if a lower one will not suffice. But following this guideline is also tricky. Although Morgan himself recognized that different species would have different psychological strengths (Wynne 2007), his Canon is often interpreted as though it were based on a version of the *scala naturae* in which humans top an evolutionary ladder on which non-human animals are the lower rungs (Hodos and Campbell 1969; Shettleworth 1993). From a cognitive perspective, this implicit view can emerge as an impression that information-related processes have levels of complexity graded from lower to higher: sensation, perception, cognition, consciousness. This sense of grading is probably wrong. Detecting physical energy and turning it into neural energy can be remarkably sophisticated, and the recognition of an object requires interactive processing across multiple systems simultaneously. Recent theories argue that concepts are "grounded" in sensory-motor systems versus being represented amodally (for an accessible review, see Kiefer and Pulvermüller 2012). The role of consciousness in this integrated processing account is not clear, but Cohen and Dennett (2011) argue that a testable theory of consciousness will indicate how cognitive functions interact to create consciousness.

Griffin (1995), who, like many, considers consciousness to come in multiple varieties, takes a fairly uncommon view when he suggests that some forms of consciousness might be especially important for animals with smaller central nervous systems than those with large ones because consciousness may increase efficiency and thus decrease the need for stored information. Hence, for Griffin, consciousness does not necessarily require particularly complex neural equipment. Similarly, complex behavior does not necessarily require consciousness; many remarkable human achievements, e.g., a brilliant performance of Liszt's *Hungarian Rhapsodies*, include a great deal of automatic/non-conscious processing. Although many authors who study animal consciousness through self-awareness or metacognitive awareness (see most of the work highlighted in the following sections of this paper) indicate that consciousness is correlated with neurobehavioral complexity, this hypothesis may or may not be true. For example, it is within the realm of possibility that an explicit representation of self, depending upon its function, could be common across many species. Given how little we actually know (versus surmise) about consciousness, its contribution to or reliance on cognitive power should not be assumed. In addition, although many researchers study consciousness within paradigms that focus on specific cognitive processes (e.g., metacognition), consciousness itself may not be intrinsically linked to these processes. The relation between consciousness and cognition is an open question.

Over the past century or so, the study of sensation, perception, and cognition has produced solid advances in evolutionarily sensitive theoretical and methodological approaches to answering questions in these fields. The answer to Romanes' problem is the application of experimentally sound techniques in search of evidence for one theory over another. Rather than introspecting about bee foraging, we can manipulate spatial configurations, features like color and odor, and other variables of interest to determine what information bees use to accomplish their daily tasks. Through this approach, we have discovered many phylogenetically general processes, e.g., habituation and Pavlovian conditioning, thereby providing a more reasonable structure for interpreting Morgan's Canon (Shettleworth 2010). Concerning the question of animal consciousness, the difficulty lies in determining what consciousness affords that can be detected externally. This problem leads some to dismiss consciousness due to the intractability of its study, and others to call for the tools we need to identify it. Some researchers suggest that we have found those tools in the two methods, the mirror-mark test to show self-awareness and a psychophysical "uncertain" response to show metacognitive awareness of one's own knowledge, used to investigate dolphins as outlined below.

Mirror-Mark Self-Recognition Studies

In 1970, Gordon Gallup (1970) created an innovative method for studying self-recognition in another species. In Gallup's study, each of four wild-caught preadolescent chimpanzees was isolated and exposed to a mirror for 80 h across multiple days. Two observers watched and recorded the behaviors of each chimp every 30 s for two 15-min sessions per day. Behaviors were then classified as social directed, defined by Gallup as behaviors directed to the reflection as referent, e.g., bobbing or vocalizing, or as self-directed, defined as behaviors directed to the self as referent, e.g., picking food from between the teeth while looking in the mirror. Across 10 days, social-directed behaviors became less frequent and self-directed behaviors became more frequent. Then Gallup anesthetized each chimp and dyed part of an eyebrow ridge and ear red. Four hours after the red marks were applied, recovery appeared complete and observers counted the number of touches to the marked skin for a 30-min interval before and after the reintroduction of the mirror. Mark-directed behaviors occurred more frequently with (4–10 times/individual) versus without (1 time) the mirror. Two more young wild-caught chimps without mirror experience were also marked in the same way after which they were exposed to a mirror, but they made no mark-directed responses. Gallup tried the original procedure (although with more mirror exposure) with several other species (stump-tailed macaques, rhesus monkeys, cynomolgus monkeys) but found neither a decrease in social-directed behaviors nor responses to marks. Gallup concluded that the mirror-experienced chimps, but not the monkeys, recognized themselves. He later extended his interpretation of mirror self-recognition to self-awareness, consciousness, metacognition, and theory of mind: "In my view, self-awareness subsumes both consciousness and mind" (Gallup 1982, p. 242). And because great apes, but not monkeys, have been successful at the mirror-mark test, Gallup argues that this finding suggests evolutionary differences between the hominids and other primates (e.g., Anderson and Gallup 2011).

Since 1970, the mirror-mark test has been adopted by many other researchers for studies of mirror self-recognition in children and animals, including the bottlenose dolphin (hereafter referred to as "the dolphin"). In the four studies focusing on the dolphin, methodological constraints have made it impossible to determine whether the dolphins are responding self-referentially or not. Detailed analyses of these four studies follow.

The first of the mirror-mark dolphin studies was conducted by Marten and Psarakos (1994). They marked five dolphins with white zinc oxide (or purple or black ointments) or clear petroleum jelly and videotaped dolphins in three conditions: in front of a mirror, in front of conspecifics, and in the absence of these stimuli. Marks were positioned such that the marked dolphin could not see them without a mirror. Dolphins were tested in a group and were not reinforced with fish for participation. Video analysis included latency to mirror approach (although sometimes the dolphins were called to the mirror), frequency of approaches, time at the mirror, and behaviors at the mirror. Quantitative comparisons across conditions did not use the same units, making them difficult to assess, although the authors state that at least two dolphins adjusted their postures based on the marks much more often in the mark versus no-mark condition and almost not at all during the no-mirror condition. Descriptions of some mirror encounters when the dolphins were and were not marked included behavioral descriptions of dolphins blowing bubbles, manipulating toys, vocalizing, spitting fish out, opening their mouths, hanging sideways, and posturing in front of the mirror as well as butting their melons against the mirror. When marked, all of the dolphins spent some time in front of the mirror with marks visible in the mirror. The subject dolphins' behaviors with other dolphins and a false killer whale on the other side of an underwater gate included blowing bubbles, opening mouths, touching rostra, and vocalizing (Marten and Psarakos 1994, 1995a). The dolphins spent a much larger percentage of total time at the gate when animals were on the other side of it (almost 100%) versus in front of the mirror (<1%). As a final comparison, when two dolphins unfamiliar with each other were placed in the same tank together, the pair spent most of their time swimming together and engaged in rostrum-genital activity. Based on quantitative and qualitative assessments, the authors concluded that their data were "consistent with the hypothesis that these animals are using the mirror to examine themselves" (p. 378). However, due to the difficulties in interpreting the dolphins' responses to the mirror, Marten and Psarakos called for a better method, which they executed in their next study.

The challenge of discriminating social and self-referential behaviors in dolphins prompted Marten and Psarakos (1995a) to adopt a method designed to make it easier to compare behaviors across conditions. In this study, two male dolphins, one 14 years old (Keola) and the other 6 years old (Hot Rod), saw themselves either in real-time video playback in which images of themselves were presented in a mirror-like way (mirror-mode) or in delayed playback in which the mirror-mode recordings were played back at another time. In real-time mirror mode, the images' movements were contingent on the dolphins' movements, but in the delayed playback condition, the images' movements were not simultaneous with the dolphins' current behaviors. (There was also a short narrative concerning a third dolphin, but the data were much less complete for this subject.) As in the first study, dolphins were neither separated nor reinforced with fish for their participation; the two dolphins in this study had also participated in the previous mirror-mark study. Behaviors (e.g., wide open mouth, not very wide open mouth, mouth and head, mouth without head, head without mouth, body spins, watching, bubbles heard, excitement, body twist, touching, swim-by with glance) were compared during 10 min real-time or delayed playback exposures. Behaviors differed in the two playback modes. In particular, Keola opened his mouth and moved his head rhythmically during real-time playback but not during delayed playback. When Keola's teeth were marked with denture adhesive, he opened his mouth wider during real-time playback. When Keola was marked, he presented his marked side to the camera about three times as often during real-time playback versus delayed playback. When unmarked, he was more likely to present his other side to the camera. (Apparently due to the camera angle, he presented his marked side away from the camera most of the time.) The authors reported that Hot Rod's behavior differed more subtly between conditions. The authors concluded that the dolphins used the mirrors and real-time video playback for contingency checking and behaved very differently with mirrors than with other dolphins. They interpreted their findings as "consistent with self-examination" and, across the two studies, as evidence of self-awareness.

Although Marten and Psarakos's use of social controls was an appropriate condition given that the authors were predominantly focused on determining whether their subjects were producing social versus self-oriented behaviors or not, in practice the social condition was difficult to assess, since it allowed the subjects access to chemical, multi-dimensional, and acoustic cues produced by the other dolphins that likely made the social stimuli much more interesting, as the dolphins' strong attention to these live animals suggests (Gallup 1995; Mitchell 1995; Sevcik 1995). Given the peculiar nature of mirror/video images—images that produce no water movements, no interpretable echoes or vocalizations, no chemical information—it is not clear that the dolphins recognized the stimuli as dolphins, either themselves or conspecifics.

Another interesting aspect of this study was the presentation of real-time and delayed video. If the dolphins were interested in watching themselves and recognized that the video images were themselves, then both conditions could have been relevant in terms of self-recognition, but only the real-time video would have promoted self-referential behaviors in terms of immediate contingency checking. Hence, Marten and Psarakos created straightforward conditions for comparisons of the dolphins' sensitivity to the fact that the movement of the video stimulus in the real-time playback was contingent upon their own movements versus in the delayed video playback. The authors also could have analyzed behavior to the stimuli to determine whether the dolphins behaved differentially to themselves or another dolphin in the delayed condition. However, comprehensive analyses were not conducted, leaving data spotty and reliability questionable. For example, inter-rater reliability for interpreting behaviors was not computed. Nevertheless, that the dolphins reportedly behaved at least somewhat differently across the conditions suggests that they may have been sensitive to their control over the images in the real-time playback. Of course, this conclusion does not require that the dolphins recognized that the video images were themselves. Both Marten and Psarakos (1995b) and Reiss and Marino (1995) acknowledge that the dolphins in this study may have found the correlation of their behavior and that of the real-time video images reinforcing whether or not self-recognition occurred. In conclusion, the subjects may have recognized the images as themselves or may have seen them as no more than interesting stimuli that could be manipulated through their own actions during mirror/real-time-video conditions. There is no way to determine which interpretation is more likely using these methods, and hence a claim for self-recognition is not well founded.

Based on their interests in comparing similar abilities across species that are neurobehaviorally complex but belong to distant taxonomic groups, Marino and Reiss conducted their own mirror-mark studies with dolphins to contrast a cetacean's behavior to that of primates (Marino et al. 1994; Reiss and Marino 2001). Their first study assessed the behaviors of two 7-year-old male dolphins (Pan and Delphi) housed in two pools without reflective surfaces until the introduction of a Plexiglas mirror (Marino et al. 1994). The dolphins were exposed to the mirror for differential amounts of time across a 10-day period during which they experienced some sham-marking when a trainer rubbed a towel or hand from their dorsal fins to their pectoral fins. On the eleventh day after the mirror's introduction, each dolphin was marked with zinc oxide between the dorsal and pectoral fins. Videotaped behaviors were coded using a detailed list of 48 behaviors that ranged from barrel rolls to head jerking to whistling. These behaviors were then categorized as self- or mark-directed (also called "suggestive" behaviors), social/aggressive, sexual, or other. Self- and mark-directed behaviors were defined as behaviors observed only during mirror exposure or mark exposure to the mirror, e.g., repetitive body movements. As in Marten and Psarakos's (1994, 1995a) studies, a single coder scored most of the behaviors, and reliability data were not computed. (A later study by Sarko et al. (2002) included a second coder for Pan's behaviors in which initial agreement levels were not reported, but final designations required agreement by both coders.) Again, as in Marten and Psarakos's studies, the authors reported that it was difficult to discriminate self-directed and social behaviors, e.g., open mouths are often used as threats.

What analyses did show was that the dolphins often synchronized their behaviors in front of the mirror and engaged in sexual behavior all over the tank when the mirror was covered but in front of the mirror when it was available; sexual behavior occurred more often with mirror access. The dolphins also increased viewing time across the 10 days before the mark test. While the dolphins were marked, they actually spent less time at the mirror than when unmarked, although each dolphin visited the mirror several times during removal of the zinc oxide mark.

The authors evaluated their results as being inconclusive for several reasons: the difficulty in identifying self-directed behaviors based, at least in part, on the dolphin's morphology; the dolphin's potential lack of interest in marks given that it does not self-groom; and the dolphin's preferential reliance on auditory (versus visual) information compared with a primate. The later re-analysis of behaviors also highlighted the difficulties in classifying behaviors: "Social behaviors remained at extremely low durations throughout the sessions. This may have been due, in part, to the relatively few behaviors from the ethogram that could be definitively designated as social (i.e., only three)" (Sarko et al. 2002, p. 74). Two of the most common "contingency checking" behaviors included vertical head movements (head nodding and headshakes often accompany aggression in dolphins; Overstrom 1983; see Scheer 2010 for a review) and horizontal head movements (commonly correlated with echolocation in dolphins; Au 1993).

In spite of the challenges of interpreting dolphin behavior in front of a mirror, Reiss and Marino (2001) decided to try again using more controls to strengthen their design. This study makes the strongest claims and is the most cited dolphin mirror-mark study (at this writing: 129 citations according to the Web of Science; 259 according to Google); therefore, it is reviewed in some detail here. The subjects were two male bottlenose dolphins, one 13 years old and the other 17 years old, who spent part of each year living in a tank with three reflective glass walls and another part of the year living in a pool without reflective walls. The study was divided into two phases and included several conditions related to marks: The dolphins could be unmarked, marked with black ink, or sham-marked with water in the same way that the black ink was administered. Because the dolphins could not be marked under anesthesia, since they are voluntary breathers, sham-marking was a control to ensure that the mark itself was the relevant stimulus in the mark condition. Coders, naïve to condition, evaluated behavior independently via videotape analysis; behaviors were categorized as self-directed (directed toward marks, the location of sham-marking, exploratory), non-directed, ambiguous, or social. Behaviors were much less precisely described in this study than in the 1994 study (Marino et al. 1994), although some examples were provided: The largest category of location-based behaviors appeared to be self-directed because they included all behaviors directed to the mark, the control sham location, and to no mark when the behaviors were specifically oriented or repetitive, i.e., the exploratory behaviors. This left any-location behaviors like swimming and surfacing as non-directed behaviors; behaviors without a specific orientation or one part of the body exhibited toward the mirror as ambiguous; and fairly specific behaviors as social behaviors, i.e., squawks, jaw claps, "invitations to interact," and tail slaps. This apparent imbalance in the number of behaviors across categories could make it more likely for a behavior to be categorized as self-directed because there were more options in this category. In addition, most of the 15 marking points on the dolphin's body were towards the front and on the side of the body; therefore, if the dolphin positioned itself laterally in front of a reflective surface, its eye would naturally have been near the marks. (Marks occurred in these locations: two on the melon-right or left side of the body; four near the pectoral fins—right or left side; one near the dorsal fin—right or left side; three on the ventral side: between the pectoral fins, on the pectoral fin, and mid-body.) Mark locations were not balanced across trials.

Phase 1 of the study was conducted with the 13-year-old dolphin in the reflective-wall exhibit. Although there were 33 sessions of 15 min (8 pre-feeding no-mark sessions; 9 post-feeding no-mark sessions, one of which included an additional mirror; 3 sham-mark sessions called "early-shams" before there had ever been a mark on the dolphin; 10 mark sessions, 4 of which included an additional mirror; 3 sham-mark sessions called "late-shams" after there had been a mark on the dolphin), the data for most sessions (i.e., the 17 no-mark/no-sham sessions) were not available. In addition, the mark-test results for this phase were presented in a histogram of total time in seconds engaged in mark/sham-mark-directed behaviors in front of a reflective surface, even though there was a much greater chance of spending time in front of a reflective surface when marked because there were 10 mark sessions (9,000 s) versus 3 pre-mark-sham sessions (2,700 s) and 3 post-mark-sham sessions (2,700 s). The authors divided the sham-mark sessions into pre- and post-mark because the dolphin spent more time oriented toward the sham-mark location in the post-mark-sham sessions. When marked, the dolphin spent 549 s of 9,000 s in mark-directed behaviors at a reflective surface (6.1% of the time); when sham-marked (i.e., no mark), it spent 126.8 s of 5400 s in sham-mark-directed behaviors at a reflective surface (2.3%), 8 s (0.3%) in the pre-mark-sham sessions, and 118.8 s (4.4%) in the post-mark-sham sessions. Total time in front of a reflective surface when the dolphin was engaged in non-mark/non-sham-directed behaviors was not provided, perhaps in part because three walls of the tank were reflective. However, of the three of four walls in the tank that were reflective, one wall was most reflective, and the dolphin spent more than 80% of the time he engaged in mark/sham-directed behaviors at this wall; when the mirror was present he engaged in mark/sham-directed behaviors in front of the mirror 16.1% of the time.

Presumably because the reflective surfaces covered three of the four walls in the Phase 1 tank, the researchers investigated both dolphins' interest in engaging with a reflective surface in a second tank that did not have reflective walls but to which a mirror could be added in Phase 2 of the study. They addressed three questions: (1) does the dolphin display social behavior at the mirror? (2) Does the dolphin spend more time at the mirror when marked? (3) Does the dolphin go to the mirror more quickly after being handled (marked/sham-marked) versus not being handled? The data were collected and analyzed separately for each dolphin. For the Phase 1 (13-year-old) dolphin, there were 30 post-feeding 15-min sessions in varying conditions based on availability of the mirror (covered or absent) and whether there was a mark. (Sixteen "nonmarked prefeeding control sessions" were also videotaped, but there does not appear to be available data from these sessions.). Data from postfeeding sessions in five conditions, again unbalanced (eight Mark-Mirror, five Mark-noMirror, nine noMark-noMirror, seven noMark-mirror, one shamMark-mirror), were presented.

The results were organized by question and subject: (1) In the case of the 13-year-old dolphin, he showed no social behaviors at the mirror. (2) He spent more time at the mirror when he was marked, although as evidenced by a reinterpretation of figure 3B (no descriptive statistics were provided, so the figure's logarithmic scale was converted using a ruler for this re-analysis, Reiss and Marino 2001), the variability across sessions was very large, e.g., ranging from 0 to 33 s in the noMark-noMirror condition to a little over 100–900 s (the length of a session) in the no-Mark-Mirror condition. However, though he spent most of the session time at the mirror when he had no mark for several sessions, he tended to spend more time at the mirror during marked sessions (NoMark-Mirror, $M = 238$ s/session; Mark-Mirror, $M = 565$ s/session). The timeline for these sessions is not provided, and so it is not clear whether behavior changed over time. (3) After being handled (marked or, in one case, sham-marked), the dolphin stopped in front of the mirror (the criterion for mirror orientation in this analysis) more quickly than when he was not handled. Again, no descriptive statistics were provided and so means were estimated from a figure. Mean time to stopping at the mirror after being handled was about 19 s; mean time to stopping at the mirror without being handled was about 71 s. Again, variability across trials was large.

Phase 2 also included a second subject, the 17-year-old male, for whom the same three questions were evaluated. The number of sessions analyzed in each condition was not as clear with this animal, but the authors reported that no social behaviors occurred at the mirror; that based on analysis of the first 10 s at the mirror in each session, the dolphin spent more time at the mirror when marked or sham-marked than unmarked (no descriptive statistics or figures were provided); and that the dolphin stopped more quickly at the mirror after being handled (apparently 11 sessions) than not handled (apparently 4 sessions). Based on their quantitative and qualitative analyses, Reiss and Marino (2001) concluded that the dolphins used the mirror to investigate parts of their bodies and thus showed mirror self-recognition.

Within the framework of mirror recognition studies, there was an unexpected problem with this study in that the sham-marking, a control condition, did not turn out to be an adequate control. Before any marking had occurred, there were three "early-sham" trials in which the dolphin participated in 8 s of self-directed behaviors to a reflective surface, i.e., 0.3% of its time. This outcome looks promising for this method in terms of response to a mark or no mark (i.e., a sham mark). The dolphin was not responding to the sham-mark (no mark). After marking trials had begun, the dolphins appeared to respond similarly to the mark and sham-mark (termed "late-shams") conditions. During Phase 2 with the second subject, the authors state: "Mark and sham conditions, i.e., late-shams, were combined because the second subject, like the first, was treating these conditions as equivalent in this setting" (Reiss and Marino 2001, p. 5941). The difficulty here comes in interpreting the results. If the responses to the experimental (mark) and control (sham-mark) conditions are the same, then either the control condition does not work or the experimental condition is ineffective. In this case, the authors determined that the control condition did not work and explained the results: "in the late sham-marking trials, the dolphin used the mirror to investigate the touched area to determine whether it was marked, and upon discovering no mark, abandoned further self-directed behaviors" (p. 5941). In such cases, one usually tries another method in a subsequent study and/or reports a more complete analysis of the control condition (e.g., providing evidence that the sham-marked dolphin did in fact "abandon further self-directed behaviors"). In this case, the authors conducted Phase 2, which provided a little more information in terms of time spent at the mirror. In Phase 2, the first subject spent more time at the mirror when marked than not, but during several sessions he spent as much time at the mirror when he was unmarked as when he was marked, again making interpretation in relation to the dolphin's interest in the mark difficult. The addition of a second subject in Phase 2 is welcome, but the data from this subject are hard to interpret given the absence of descriptive statistics and the lack of detail about what happened in which condition; for example, the sham vs. mark sessions are not separated in any way either before or after marking began. Overall, difficulties in assessing behavioral categories, biased opportunities for responding across conditions, conflation of control and experimental conditions, shifted units across analyses, and other challenges impede our ability to determine that the dolphins in these four studies were responding to their reflections and video images self-referentially.

Clearly, mirror-mark studies are tricky to conduct and interpret with dolphins. One challenge comes with the dolphin's physique (Anderson 1995; Hart and Whitlow 1995; Loveland 1995). Dolphins' bodies are built for swimming (Pabst 1996). Although ancestral marine mammals likely expended much more energy when swimming (Williams 1999), modern dolphins maintain fairly high swimming speeds (e.g., 2.1–3.8 ms^{-1}) with relatively low metabolic costs (Williams et al. 1993). While good for swimming, this streamlined morphology results in a remarkably circumscribed ability for reflexive movement. Whereas most mammals can scratch themselves with their own feet or hands, flick flies off their backs with their tails, lick portions of their bodies with their own tongues, and generally attend to themselves with self-directed actions, dolphins have almost no options for self-directed behavior using their appendages. For these basic services, they interact with environmental surfaces (e.g., breach out of and back onto the water, rub against the sand) or each other.

These behavioral constraints make it particularly difficult to discriminate self-referential and social behaviors in dolphins, a substantive problem for interpreting the mirror-mark test with this species. Another challenge is determining where the dolphin is looking. For example, when dolphins open their mouths in front of a mirror, are they looking inside? If they are at an acute or oblique angle to the mirror, then they probably can see inside their mouths. If they are facing the mirror head on, then maybe not. Dolphins' eyes are on the sides of their heads and thus, although they have a wide visual field, binocular vision is restricted (Dral 1972, 1975; Dawson 1980); because they can protrude their eyes, they may have overlap of 20–30 degrees (Yablakov et al. 1974). Clearest in-air viewing is likely rostroventral, i.e., looking down; for frontal in-air viewing, the dolphin often sits up in the water with its ventral side facing the stimulus of interest (Dral 1974; Mobley and Helweg 1989). Their eyes move independently most of the time (Dawson et al. 1981). For many visual tasks, dolphins engage in lateral viewing with a single eye (Dral 1974; Mobley and Helweg 1989). Poorest vision is probably in front of their heads (Norris et al. 1994). Hence, it can be rather difficult to determine exactly where a dolphin is looking compared with a primate.

[. . .]

All told, coming to conclusions about self-recognition and consciousness based on mirror-mark studies is complicated, and it appears to be much harder with dolphins as subjects. In terms of consciousness, there is a great deal of literature in reference to the mirror-mark test. Although Gallup (e.g., Gallup 1982) has argued that passing the test suggests self-recognition, self-awareness, consciousness, and theory of mind, many others have argued against such strong inferences (e.g., Heyes 1994; Swartz 1997; Delfour 2006). But the question of evidence for dolphin consciousness based on this test is easier to analyze: at present, mirror-mark tests and real-time/delayed video playback with dolphins have not been fruitful in terms of confirming mirror self-recognition, self-awareness, or consciousness. The dolphins often do not spend much of their time at the mirror/screen, and when they do, the results are equivocal. Some data suggest that the dolphins recognize that they can control the visual stimulus on the mirror/screen based on their behaviors there, but it has been impracticable to determine that they recognize the images as their own. Although one avenue might be to continue to refine the methods of mirror studies for dolphins, the authors of the work described in this section tried and tried again. A better approach would be to find a method more suited for dolphins. In terms of awareness, studies of metacognition provide another option.

Metacognition Studies

In contrast to the mirror-mark studies which were designed and used to study representations of self in non-human primates before they were applied to dolphins, a seminal comparative study of metacognition focused on the dolphin. Metacognition refers to the ability to reflect explicitly on one's cognitive processes, i.e., knowing what one knows. For example, I know that I know my daughters' names (even if I interchange them every now and then) and that I do not know the names of all the characters in *War and Peace*. I have knowledge about my knowledge; I have metacognition. In humans, metacognitive studies rely on language, e.g., researchers induce the tip-of-the-tongue phenomenon (knowing one knows the answer but is not quite able to retrieve it) and then investigate it. A study of animal uncertainty could not rely on this linguistically based self-report approach, and so Smith et al. (1995) devised an original and cleverly designed method that took advantage of a long history of documentation concerning the odd behavior related to decision making around sensory thresholds; they enlisted psychophysical techniques to investigate uncertainty in a dolphin. Animals regularly report perception of physical stimuli ("Was a sound present?") or the identification of stimulus classes ("Stripes or no stripes?") by participating in go/no-go or two-alternative procedures (e.g., Bauer et al. 2003; see Schusterman 1980 for a review of behavioral methods with marine mammals), and these tasks typically push animals to their limits because the goals of the studies are to find those limits. Smith et al. took advantage of the ambiguity caused by working at the boundaries of abilities by introducing a third response option, an "uncertainty paddle."

In Smith et al.'s (1995) experiment, a male adult dolphin, Natua, positioned himself at a bar where he heard an underwater tone. If he heard a 2,100-Hz (high) tone, he was rewarded for choosing the paddle to his left; if he heard a lower tone, 1,200–2,099 Hz, he was rewarded for choosing the paddle to his right. He was initially trained to respond to the high tone, after which the low-tone (1,200 Hz) and its paddle were introduced. Trials with tones between 1,200 and 2,100 Hz were considered probe trials and began after two-tone discrimination was stable. Stimulus presentation was nuanced in that probe trial difficulty was yoked with subject performance; trial difficulty increased when performance was above 50% accuracy and decreased when it was below 50%. When error rates increased, the third "uncertainty" paddle became available between the left and right paddles; its use was encouraged by having "broken" trials, i.e., trials in which no response but a press of the middle paddle led to reinforcement. After the dolphin learned to respond to broken trials, he transferred to using the uncertainty paddle as an escape response (he "escaped" having to complete the trial) on his own. Use of the uncertainty paddle led to a delay before the dolphin could be rewarded for the next (always easy) trial, and the delay was longer when the dolphin used the escape response more often. (From a training perspective, the researchers used an interesting technique in that they provided a temporally shifting version of the low tone when the dolphin chose the uncertainty paddle. When the dolphin pressed this paddle, his press was acknowledged by the presentation of the slowly pulsing tone of the next trial, but an answering press of the low-tone paddle was not rewarded until the tone pulses reached their regular pace. Through these means, the dolphin's response was productive, but he still experienced a delay to reward that was indicated by the timing of the next stimulus's pulses).

The dolphin's performance was compared with data collected from five undergraduates who engaged in the same task but on a computer screen with cash for points earned. Dolphin and human performance were similar in terms of operating characteristics; neither species escaped until they hit their psychophysical limits. (For dolphins, tones at 2,086 Hz were no longer differentiable from 2,100 Hz; for humans this was true for tones at 2,090 Hz. Dolphins are most sensitive to frequencies considerably higher than those presented here, whereas humans were working within a range of good sensitivity.) Both species answered low and high, when possible, and maintained a narrow window around perceptual thresholds for use of the escape response. Both would have received better reinforcement ratios if they had accepted fewer difficult trials, i.e., if they had escaped more frequently.

Humans explained their choice strategies: They chose Low when the sound was low; they chose High when the sound was high; they chose Escape when they felt doubt or uncertainty or felt they needed to re-calibrate their determination of low and high. Perhaps they used metacognitive evaluations during the task, or perhaps they applied them later to explain their performance. In any case, the dolphin could not explain his response strategy, and so we are left to interpret his psychological state based on his behaviors. If we reason by analogy, we see that the dolphin and humans behaved very similarly, and so, extending that reasoning to cognitive processes, we might conclude that dolphins have metacognition because humans experienced doubt and uncertainty due to their lack of confidence in classifying the sounds when they used the escape paddle. However, if we reason using behavior alone, there is another explanation for the dolphin's middle-paddle response: He used the Low paddle for a low tone, the High paddle for the high tone, and the Middle paddle for some of the tones between the two. (For an in-depth discussion suggesting that stimulus-based interpretations in metacognitive paradigms are often inappropriate, see Smith et al. 2012). Smith et al. (1995) reported that behaviors preceding the use of the escape response (apparent response competition, slower latencies) indicated that the dolphin may have felt uncertain, and the authors highlight the non-optimality of reinforcement contingencies. That is, the dolphin (and the human participants) should have been less precise about when to answer Low, since trial difficulty was dependent upon performance: do worse, get easier trials and more reinforcement. But neither species did that. Is it because they experienced perceptual uncertainty, were aware they did not know the answer, and so used the uncertain response? Smith et al. state: "Uncertainty would . . . be an intuitive way to explain the dolphin's nonoptimal escapes at threshold, his ancillary behaviors, and all aspects of the close analogy between human and dolphin performance" (p. 401). However, they conclude that characterizing metacognition as conscious, verbal, and abstract (as in an adult human) is bound to mask metacognitive behaviors in young children and animals that may experience it in another way. Tasks like this one begin to create a road toward understanding what that way might be, and the authors suggested multiple arenas, e.g., metamemory, in which this approach could be applied.

Smith et al.'s (1995) study began a period of focus on metacognition in animals in which experimental designs of metamemory have been conducted with monkeys, pigeons, and rats (for reviews, see Shettleworth and Sutton 2006; Hampton 2009; Smith 2009; Smith et al. 2009; Roberts et al. 2012), although they have yet to be applied to dolphins (Smith 2010). Hampton critiques previous work, including Smith et al.'s dolphin study, based on four criteria necessary to show metacognition: (1) an objectively observable primary behavior amenable to accuracy or time measurements (the dolphin's frequency discrimination in the Smith et al. study), (2) an objectively observable secondary behavior with the potential to suggest knowledge awareness (the dolphin's use of the middle paddle), (3) variation in the primary behavior's performance indicators to show how the secondary behavior is functioning (the dolphin's poorer performance with the frequencies close to 2,100 Hz), and (4) analysis of the correlation between the primary and secondary behaviors (the dolphin's use of the middle paddle for these ambiguous frequencies). On this account, the Smith et al. study is strong, but the interpretation is at issue in that Hampton also distinguishes between public and private mechanisms for successfully participating in metacognitive tasks. To demonstrate that an animal has a conscious state of awareness, a motivator for conducting these studies, requires a private mechanism, i.e., introspection by the animal. Public mechanisms are based on publicly available information. Hampton lists three. The first, environmental cue association, includes the stimuli themselves; if specific stimuli (the dolphin's ambiguous high-frequency sounds) lead to predictable outcomes (like worse performance), then the animal can use the stimuli themselves to trigger the metacognitive response (the middle paddle). To test for this explanation, Hampton suggests presenting new stimuli, e.g., a different range of frequencies, to the animal. Good immediate transfer performance would suggest that the stimuli themselves were not dictating performance. Second, behavioral cue associations can be behaviors consistently produced by the subject when the task is difficult, e.g., the dolphin's slower response/dithering may have led him to choose the middle paddle. A method for fixing this problem is to offer performance of the secondary behavior before the actual test of knowledge. Third, response competition could explain a higher use of the secondary option, e.g., when the dolphin heard the difficult frequencies, neither of the primary (low, high) paddles were winners, so he may have defaulted to the other option because it was there. The fix is to avoid presenting both primary and secondary options together. As Hampton points out, the dolphin could have been using introspection, but we cannot know given the other alternatives. (Also see Smith 2009 and Smith et al. 2012 for good reviews of methods and interpretations.)

Hampton himself designed a particularly powerful study of metacognition in rhesus monkeys in which these methodological issues were solved by having regularly changing stimuli, offering the escape paddle before the test occurred, and analyzing performance when no information was offered (no-sample trials) and when the escape option was unavailable across randomly interspersed trials as well as across grades of difficulty in the form of delays (Hampton 2001). One of Hampton's rhesus monkeys clearly responded as predicted based on use of metamemory, but Hampton did not conclude that the monkey had consciousness given the private, subjective nature of this state. Instead, he focused on function in relation to adaptive decision making. Recent work on rhesus monkeys' generalization across multiple tests led to the conclusion that the monkeys were "aware of some memories" (Templer and Hampton 2012, p. 418).

Work on metamemory in animals has been fruitful in providing methodological improvements in comparative cognition and profitable discussions on aspects of consciousness in non-humans. Shea and Heyes (2010), a philosopher and a comparative psychologist, respectively, outlined a case for using studies of metamemory to provide empirical confirmation of phenomenal consciousness in animals. Their goal was to find evidence in animals of "the 'what it's like'-ness of our mental lives" in explicit (versus implicit), declarative (versus procedural) memory beyond cases in which the conclusion would require reasoning analogically from human cognitive processing to animals. They based their design on Hampton's (2001) method but with the addition of requiring that the subject transfer its use of its knowledge to different stimulus types and decisions as well as new tasks. Would transferring require a conscious representation of one's knowledge? It depends: as Fleming et al. (2012), while calling on theorists and empiricists to work together, recently reiterated: "the link between metacognition and consciousness inevitably depends on one's favored definition of each" (p. 1284). Therein continues to lie the rub. On the other hand, work on metacognition in multiple labs (e.g., Foote and Crystal 2007; Sutton and Shettleworth 2008; Beran et al. 2009; McMahon et al. 2010; Templer and Hampton 2012) has expanded our understanding of what animals do and has created a fruitful dialogue about the means through which they might do it.

Studies of Dolphin Consciousness: The Past, the Present, the Future

Recent studies potentially providing evidence of aspects of dolphin consciousness have not confirmed its existence. Dolphin behavior in mirror-mark/video playback studies suggests that dolphins may be sensitive to the contingency between their movements and the simultaneous movements of their mirror images but does not indicate that they recognize those images as themselves. A dolphin's choice of a third paddle designated as an uncertainty response in a psychophysics study holds promise as a method for better understanding what dolphins know about what they know but needs further exploration to determine what motivated the paddle's use. Behaviors in neither area verify self-awareness or consciousness in dolphins.

At present, the dialogue continues. In a current article, Herman (2012) argues that "higher-level interpretations" of animal behavior may be more parsimonious than other interpretations and has re-evaluated some of his previous work on dolphins through this lens. His account highlights the usefulness of considering similar complex behaviors across species as based on similar psychological mechanisms, i.e., inferring consciousness in animals because humans use it in similar circumstances. Herman's argument for dolphins as candidates for this interpretation includes not only the size of the dolphin brain and the complexity of dolphin societies but also primarily its sense of self as evidenced in flexible responses across body part identification studies and imitation of self and others as well as findings by others on mirror self-recognition (Reiss and Marino 2001) and metacognition (Smith et al. 1995). Herman's main thesis is that a dolphin recognizes its body as its own, and the data he presents make a case for an implicit representation by the dolphin of its own body. The tricky question, as he acknowledges, is whether this representation is also explicit. Ultimately, he concludes that "awareness of self in dolphins is extant and that the self is embodied" (p. 540).

An avenue for future work in this area may be an expansion of previous work with dolphins, cited in Herman's (2012) argument for dolphin consciousness, on repeating their past behaviors. Shea and Heyes (2010) recommend enhanced studies of metamemory, but they also highlight episodic memory as offering a potential path for demonstrating consciousness. This line of research has not been well developed with dolphins (although it has with scrub jays as reviewed by Clayton et al. 2006), but some relevant data are available: Two 12-year-old dolphins, a male (Hiapo) and female (Elele), who had been trained to perform specific actions to specific hand movements (e.g., moving an extended thumb up and down indicated that the dolphin should toss an object; pointing an arm at a diagonal into the air indicated a touch) were tested on their ability to repeat an action they had just performed via a hand movement that indicated "repeat" (Mercado et al. 1998). The dolphins performed this task well across multiple conditions, i.e., with familiar behaviors, self-selected first behaviors, combinations of behaviors, and newly trained behaviors. The female was also able to repeat a just-repeated behavior without extra training on 16/16 trials, thereby making it less likely that she was using the hand gesture provided for the first action to guide her repeated behavior but rather was repeating her own action. This interpretation was strengthened by the dolphins' similar performance with more and less complex sequences for hand gestures to elicit the first instance of a behavior that was repeated; if the dolphins were remembering the initial hand gestures, one would expect sequences of hand gestures to be harder to recall than single ones. Performance accuracy was poorer when Elele had to repeat actions with specifically identified objects (Mercado et al. 1999). Potentially, a paradigm like this one could be expanded to study episodic memory explicitly or be incorporated into a metacognitive method as a way to study some facet of consciousness in dolphins related to metamemory or identification of self versus other. However, defining and interpreting what consciousness looks like behaviorally continues to be a stumbling block for finding evidence of consciousness.

Although we are currently experiencing a resurgence of interest in consciousness in other animals, the requirements needed to do a good job of studying it are still in flux. Cognitive scientists are working on characterizing consciousness more clearly, finding methods for studying it more effectively, and considering what it takes to make interpretations of relevant data more credible. While one may argue that we already have that evidence using analogical reasoning from human processing and broadly construed conceptions of psychological terms, does that stance move us forward in our understanding of what people and animals do? To date, this form of anthropomorphism has been a good approach for leading us astray (Blumberg and Wasserman 1995; Povinelli et al. 2000; Wynne 2007; Mercado and DeLong 2010). It has led us to make errors in which we accept data as indicating an ability that it is not actually there (e.g., the horse Clever Hans's mathematical prowess, Pfungst 1911) and to reject evidence of an ability that is in fact there: Before Griffin studied echolocation in bats, eighteenth-century scientists Spallanzani's and Jurine's evidence for bats' use of sound to negotiate the world was mostly dismissed in part because this sensory system was foreign to humans (Hughes 1999). When evaluating dolphins, sensitivity to human expectations about animal cognition is especially relevant because of their mystique. Claims about dolphins' cognitive abilities have occasionally been so strong (e.g., Lilly 1967) that Wilson (1975) felt compelled to highlight dolphins in his 1975 *Sociobiology: The New Synthesis* with the following quote: "It is important to emphasize that there is no evidence whatever that delphinids are more advanced in intelligence and social behavior than other animals" (p. 474). While the data for dolphin's cognitive abilities have certainly been augmented in methodologically sound studies since 1975 (see Herman 2010, and Mercado and DeLong 2010, for recent reviews), Wilson's observations illustrate the human tendency to interpret animal behavior based on humans' implicit attitudes about specific species. Without the careful and persuasive methods and analyses now common in psychophysics, would we have believed that mantis shrimp have tunable eight-channel color vision and can see circular polarized light (Chiou et al. 2008)? Perhaps these gains can also be made for the scientific investigation of consciousness.

In a recent article on episodic memory, comparative psychologist Zentall (2010) writes: "What once seemed to be insurmountably difficult problems to study may be limited only by our inability to discover clever ways" to study animals' psychological processes (p. 239). Perhaps consciousness is too subjective and private to study, or perhaps we can identify specific advantages and behaviors that only consciousness can support and demonstrate its existence in another species. Ongoing work in psychology, philosophy, neuroscience, robotics, and related areas to dissect consciousness will likely help us define it more clearly. Many studies of psychological processing in humans continue to uncover cases of complex cognitive behavior, e.g., goal pursuit, decision making, for which humans do not recruit consciousness, thereby helping us refine models of consciousness in humans (Hassin et al. 2005). Sometimes these behaviors depend on fairly straightforward effects of environmental cues and associative learning. Clarifying mechanisms, including the detection of seemingly simple ones, neither denigrate a species nor preclude complex processing. As Shettleworth (2010) suggests, the identification and careful explication of how simple mechanisms lead to complex behavior is, for the very characteristic of the simplicity of the mechanisms, "awe-inspiring" and relevant to both human and animal behavior by providing a more precise level of description.

Humans do not need consciousness to negotiate many aspects of their lives. This capacity is likely true for non-humans as well. On the other hand, humans have consciousness and use consciousness, and there are surely aspects of our lives that require it. Could humans have written all we have on consciousness without it? *J'en doute!* Can we find a theory clear enough and a method powerful enough to be broadly persuasive in terms of producing evidence of consciousness in another species? One hopes. Currently, we do not have good demonstrations of consciousness in dolphins. Rather, we have mystery which invites inquiry and leads to discovery: For the scientist, an embarrassment of riches, a glass full of blessings.

[. . .]

References

Anderson JR (1995) Self-recognition in dolphins: Credible cetaceans; compromised criteria, controls, and conclusions. *Conscious Cogn* 4:239–243.

Anderson JR, Gallup GG (2011) Which primates recognize themselves in mirrors? *PLOS Bio* 9(3):e1001024

Au WWL (1993) *The sonar of dolphins*. Springer-Verlag, New York.

Bauer GB, Colbert DE, Gaspard JC, Littlefield B, Fellner W (2003) Underwater visual acuity of Florida manatees (*Trichechus manatus latirostris*). *Int J Comp Psychol* 16:130–142.

Beran MJ, Smith JD, Coutinho MVC, Couchman JJ, Boomer J (2009) The psychological organization of "uncertainty" responses and "middle" responses: A dissociation in capuchin monkeys (*Cebus apella*). *J Exp Psychol Anim B* 35:371–381.

Block N (1995) On a confusion about a function of consciousness. *Behav Brain Sci* 18(2):227–287.

Blumberg MS, Wasserman EA (1995) Animal mind and the argument from design. *Am Psychol* 50(3): 133–144.

Browne D (2004) Do dolphins know their own minds? *Biol Philos* 19:633–653.

Chalmers DJ (1996) *The conscious mind*. Oxford University Press, Oxford.

Chiou T, Kleinlogel S, Cronin T, Caldwell R, Loeffler B, Siddiqi A, Goldizen A, Marshall J (2008) Circular polarization vision in a stomatopod crustacean. *Curr Biol* 18:429–434.

Clayton NS, Emery NJ, Dickinson A (2006) The prospective cognition of food caching and recovery by western scrub-jays (*Aphelocoma californica*). *Comp Cogn Behav Rev* 1:1–11.

Cohen MA, Dennett DC (2011) Consciousness cannot be separated from function. *Trends Cogn Sci* 15(8):358–364.

Coren S (2003) Sensation and perception. In: Weiner IB, Freedheim DK (ed) *Handbook of psychology, volume I. History of psychology* Wiley and Sons, Hoboken, pp. 85–108.

Dawson WW (1980) The cetacean eye. In: Herman LM (ed) *Cetacean behavior: Mechanisms and functions*. Krieger Publishing, Malabar, pp. 53–100.

Dawson WW, Carder DA, Ridgway SH, Schmeisser ET (1981) Synchrony of dolphin eye movements and their power density spectra. *Comp Biochem Phys A* 68(3):443–449.

Delfour F (2006) Marine mammals in front of the mirror: Body experiences to self-recognition: A cognitive ethological methodology combined with phenomenological questioning. *Aquat Mamm* 32(4):517–527.

Dennett DC (1991) *Consciousness explained*. Little, Brown and Company, Boston.

Dennett DC (2005) *Sweet dreams: Philosophical obstacles to a science of consciousness*. MIT Press, Cambridge, MA.

Descartes R (1637) Discourse on the method of rightly conducting one's reason, and seeking the truth in sciences. In *Philosophical Works, Volume 2*, translated by E. Haldane and G.R.T. Ross, Cambridge University Press, Cambridge. 388 pp

Dral ADG (1972) Aquatic and aerial vision in the bottle-nosed dolphin. *Neth J Sea Res* 5(4):510–513.

Dral ADG (1974) Problems in image-focusing and astigmatism in cetacea—a state of affairs. *Aquat Mamm* 2:22–28.

Dral ADG (1975) Vision in cetacea. *J Zoo Med* 6(1):17–21.

Fleming SM, Dolan RJ, Frith CD (2012) Metacognition: Computation, biology and function. *Phil Trans R Soc B* 367:1280–1286.

Foote A, Crystal J (2007) Metacognition in the rat. *Curr Biol* 17:551–555.

Fuchs AH, Milar KS (2003) Psychology as a science. In: Freedheim DK, Veiner IB (eds) *Handbook of psychology, volume I: History of psychology*. Wiley and Sons, Hoboken, pp. 1–26.

Gallagher S (2000) Philosophical conceptions of the self: Implications for cognitive science. *Trends Cogn Sci* 4(1):14–21.

Gallup GG Jr (1970) Chimpanzees: Self-recognition. *Science* 167(3914):86–87.

Gallup GG Jr (1982) Self-awareness and the emergence of mind in primates. *Am J Primatol* 2:237–248.

Gallup GG Jr (1995) Mirrors, minds, and cetaceans. *Conscious Cogn* 4:226–228.

Gazzaniga MS (2011) *Who's in charge? Free will and the science of the brain.* Harper Collins, New York.

Gibson JJ (1979) *The ecological approach to visual perception.* Houghton Mifflin, Boston.

Griffin DR (1976) *The question of animal awareness: Evolutionary continuity of mental experience.* Rockefeller University Press, New York.

Griffin DR (1984) *Animal thinking.* Harvard University Press, Cambridge.

Griffin DR (1992) *Animal minds.* University of Chicago Press, Chicago.

Griffin DR (1995) Windows on animal minds. *Conscious Cogn* 4:194–204.

Hampton RR (2001) Rhesus monkeys know when they remember. *Proc Natl A Sci USA* 98(9):5359–5362.

Hampton RR (2009) Multiple demonstrations of metacognition in nonhumans: Converging evidence or multiple mechanisms? *Comp Cog Behav Rev* 4:17–28.

Hart D, Whitlow JW Jr (1995) The experience of self in the bottlenose dolphin. *Conscious Cogn* 4:244–247.

Hassin RR, Uleman JS, Bargh JA (eds) (2005) *The new unconscious: Social cognition and social neuroscience.* Oxford University Press, New York.

Herman LM (2010) What laboratory research has told us about dolphin cognition. *Int J Comp Psychol* 23:310–330.

Herman LM (2012) Body and self in dolphins. *Conscious Cogn* 21:526–545.

Herman LM, Abichandani SL, Elhajj AN, Herman BYK, Sanchez JL, Pack AA (1999) Dolphins (*Tursiops truncatus*) comprehend the referential character of the human pointing gesture. *J Comp Psychol* 113:1–18.

Heyes CM (1994) Reflections on self-recognition in primates. *Anim Behav* 47(4):909–919.

Heyes CM (2011) Automatic imitation. *Psychol Bull* 137:463–483.

Hodos W, Campbell CBG (1969) Scala naturae: Why there is no theory in comparative psychology. *Psychol Rev* 76:337–350.

Hughes HC (1999) *Sensory exotica: A world beyond human experience.* MIT Press, Cambridge.

Hurley S, Noë A (2003) Neural plasticity and consciousness. *Biol Philos* 18:131–168.

James W (1890/1950) *The principles of psychology.* Dover Publications, Oxford.

Kiefer M, Pulvermüller F (2012) Conceptual representations in mind and brain: Theoretical developments, current evidence, and future directions. *Cortex* 48:805–825.

Klein SB (2012) The self and science: Is it time for a new approach to the study of human experience? *Curr Dir Psychol Sci* 21(4):253–257.

Lilly JC (1967) *The mind of the dolphin: A nonhuman intelligence.* Doubleday, New York.

Loveland KA (1995) Self-recognition in the bottlenose dolphin: Ecological considerations. *Conscious Cogn* 4(2):254–257.

Maier NRF (1931) Reasoning in humans: II. The solution of a problem and its appearance in consciousness. *J Comp Psychol* 12:181–194.

Marino L, Reiss D, Gallup GG Jr (1994) Mirror self-recognition in bottlenose dolphins: Implications for comparative investigations of highly dissimilar species. In: Parker ST, Mitchell RW, Boccia ML (eds) *Self-awareness in animals and humans: Developmental perspectives.* Cambridge University Press, Cambridge, pp. 380–391.

Marten K, Psarakos S (1994) Evidence of self-awareness in the bottlenose dolphin (*Tursiops truncatus*). In: Parker ST, Mitchell RW, Boccia ML (eds) *Self-awareness in animals and humans: Developmental perspectives.* Cambridge University Press, Cambridge, pp. 361–379.

Marten K, Psarakos S (1995a) Marten and Psarakos commentary response. *Conscious Cogn* 4:258–269.

Marten K, Psarakos S (1995b) Using self-view television to distinguish between self-examination and social behavior in the bottlenose dolphin (*Tursiops truncatus*). *Conscious Cogn* 4:205–224.

McMahon S, Macpherson K, Roberts WA (2010) Dogs choose a human informant: Metacognition in canines. *Behav Proc* 85:293–298.

Mercado E, DeLong CM (2010) Dolphin cognition: Representation and processes in memory and perception. *Int J Comp Psychol* 23:344–378.

Mercado E III, Murray SO, Uyeyama RK, Pack AA, Herman LM (1998) Memory for recent actions in the bottlenosed dolphins (*Tursiops truncatus*): Repetition of arbitrary behaviors using an abstract rule. *Anim Learn Behav* 26(2):210–218.

Mercado E III, Uyeyama RK, Pack AA, Herman LM (1999) Memory for action events in the bottlenosed dolphin. *Anim Cogn* 2:17–25.

Mitchell RW (1995) Evidence of dolphin self-recognition and the difficulties of interpretation. *Conscious Cogn* 4:229–234.

Mobley JR, Helweg DA (1989) Visual ecology and cognition in cetaceans. In: Thomas JA, Kastelein RA (eds) *Sensory abilities of cetaceans: Laboratory and field evidence*. Plenum Press, New York, pp. 519–536.

Morgan CL (1894) *An introduction to comparative psychology*. Walter Scott Publishing Company, London

Nagel T (1974) What is it like to be a bat? *Philos Rev* 83(4):435–450.

Neisser U (1988) Five kinds of self-knowledge. *Philos Psychol* 1(1):35–59.

Norris KS, Würsig B, Wells RS, Würsig M (1994) *The Hawaiian spinner dolphin*. University of California Press, Berkeley.

Overstrom NA (1983) Association between burst-pulse sounds and aggressive behavior in captive Atlantic bottlenosed dolphins (*Tursiops truncatus*). *Zoo Biol* 2:1–93.

Pabst DA (1996) Morphology of the subdermal connective tissue sheath of dolphins: A new fibre-sound, thin-walled, pressurized cylinder model for swimming vertebrates. *J Zool* 238(1):35–52.

Pack AA, Herman LM (2007) The dolphin's (*Tursiops truncatus*) understanding of human gaze and pointing: Knowing what and where. *J Comp Psychol* 121:34–45.

Palmer SE (1999) Color, consciousness, and the isomorphism constraint. *Behav Brain Sci* 22:923–989.

Pelli DG, Farell B (1995) Psychophysical methods. In: Bass M, Van Stryland EW, Williams DR, Wolfe WL (eds) *Handbook of optics*. McGraw-Hill, New York, pp. 29.1–29.13.

Pfungst O (1911) *Clever Hans: A contribution to experimental animal and human psychology*. Henry Holt, New York

Povinelli DJ, Bering JM, Giambrone S (2000) Toward a science of other minds: Escaping the argument of analogy. *Cogn Sci* 24(3):509–541.

Ramachandran VS, Hirstein W (1997) Three laws of qualia: What neurology tells us about the biological functions of consciousness. *J Conscious Stud* 4(5–6):429–457.

Ramachandran VS, Hirstein W (1998) The perception of phantom limbs: The D. O. Hebb lecture. *Brain* 121:1603–1630.

Reiss D, Marino L (1995) Self-view television as a test of self-awareness: Only in the eye of the beholder? *Conscious Cogn* 4:235–238.

Reiss D, Marino L (2001) Mirror self-recognition in the bottlenose dolphin: A case of cognitive convergence. *Proc Natl A Sci USA* 98(10):5937–5942.

Roberts WA, McMillan N, Musolino E, Cole M (2012) Information seeking in animals: Metacognition? *Comp Cog Behav Rev* 7:85–109.

Rochat P (2001) *The infant's world*. Harvard University Press, Cambridge, MA.

Rochat P, Zahavi D (2011) The uncanny mirror: A re-framing of mirror self-experience. *Conscious Cogn* 20:204–213.

Roitblat HL (1985) *Introduction to comparative cognition*. Freeman, New York.

Romanes GJ (1882) *Animal intelligence*. Appleton, New York.

Sarko D, Marino L, Reiss D (2002) A bottlenose dolphin's (*Tursiops truncatus*) responses to its mirror image: further analysis. *Int J Comp Psychol* 15(1):69–76.

Scheer M (2010) Review of self-initiated behaviors of free-ranging cetaceans directed towards human swimmers and waders during open water encounters. *Interact Stud* 11(3):442–466.

Schusterman RJ (1980) Behavioral methodology in echolocation by marine mammals. In: Busnel R, Fish JF (eds) *Animal sonar systems*. Plenum Press, New York, pp. 11–42.

Sevcik R (1995) Is it live or is it Memorex? *Conscious Cogn* 4:251–253.

Shea N, Heyes C (2010) Metamemory as evidence of animal consciousness: The type that does the trick. *Biol Philos* 25(1):95–110.

Shettleworth SJ (1993) Where is the comparison in comparative cognition? Alternative research programs. *Psychol Sci* 4(3): 179–184.

Shettleworth SJ (1998/2010) *Cognition, evolution, and behavior*. Oxford University Press, Oxford.

Shettleworth SJ (2010) Clever animals and killjoy explanations in comparative psychology. *Trends Cogn Sci* 14(11):477–481.

Shettleworth SJ, Sutton JE (2006) Do animals know what they know? In: Hurley S, Nudds M (eds) *Rational animals*. Oxford University Press, Oxford, pp. 235–246.

Smith JD (2009) The study of animal metacognition. *Trends Cogn Sci* 13(9):389–396.

Smith JD (2010) Inaugurating the study of animal metacognition. *Int J Comp Psychol* 23:401–413.

Smith JD, Beran MJ, Couchman JJ, Coutinho VC, Boomer J (2009) The psychological organization of "uncertainty" responses and "middle" responses: A dissociation in capuchin monkeys (*Cebus apella*). *J Exp Psychol Anim B* 35(3):371–381.

Smith JD, Couchman JJ, Beran MJ (2012) The highs and lows of theoretical interpretation in animal-metacognition research. *Philos T R Soc B* 367:1297–1309.

Smith JD, Schull J, Strote J, McGee K, Egnor R, Erb L (1995) The uncertain response in the bottlenosed dolphin (*Tursiops truncates*). *J Exp Psychol Gen* 124(4):391–408.

Stürmer B, Aschersleben G, Prinz W (2000) Correspondence effects with manual gestures and postures: A study of imitation. *J Exp Psychol Human* 26:1746–1759.

Sutton JE, Shettleworth SJ (2008) Memory without awareness: Pigeons do not show metamemory in delayed matching-to-sample. *J Exp Psychol Anim B* 34:266–282.

Swartz K (1997) What is mirror self-recognition in nonhuman primates, and what is it not? *Ann NY Acad Sci* 818(1):65–71.

Templer VL, Hampton RR (2012) Rhesus monkeys (*Macaca mulatta*) show robust evidence for memory awareness across multiple generalization tests. *Anim Cogn* 15:409–419.

Velmans M (1996) Consciousness and the "causal paradox". *Behav Brain Sci* 19(3):538–542.

Von Uexküll J (1909) *Umwelt und Innenwelt der Tiere*. Springer, Berlin.

West MJ, King AP, Goldstein MH (2004) Singing, socializing, and the music effect. In: Marler P, Slabbekoorn H (eds) *Nature's music: The science of birdsong*. Elsevier, London, pp. 374–387.

Williams TM (1999) The evolution of cost efficient swimming in marine mammals: Limits to energetic optimization. *Philos T R Soc B* 354:193–201.

Williams TM, Friedl WA, Haun JE (1993) The physiology of bottlenose dolphins (*Tursiops truncatus*): Heart rate, metabolic rate, and plasma lactate concentration during exercise. *J Exp Biol* 179:31–46.

Wilson EO (1975) *Sociobiology: The new synthesis*. Harvard University Press, Cambridge.

Wynne CDL (2007) What are animals? Why anthropomorphism is still not a scientific approach to behavior. *Comp Cogn Behav Rev* 2:125–235.

Yablakov AV, Bel'kovich VM, Borisov VI (1974) *Whales and dolphins*. Joint Publications Research Services, Arlington.

Zentall TR (2010) Coding of stimuli by animals: Retrospection, prospection, episodic memory and future planning. *Learn Motiv* 41:225–240.

25 Whales as Persons

Paola Cavalieri

Cavalieri argues that based on the neurological complexity of whales, as well as their elaborate communication skills, whales have a rich inner life and a capacity for self-consciousness that is deemed necessary for personhood. Such a quality fully requires a right to life for them. She further argues that the personhood of whales calls on the international community to enforce the protection of whales both globally and nationally.

I

In the morning of a Sunday of December 2005, in the open water east of the Farallones Islands, about 18 miles off the coast of San Francisco, a female humpback whale on her usual migratory route between the Northern California coast and Baja California became entangled in the nylon ropes that link crab pots. The whale, estimated to weigh 50 tons, was spotted by a person at 8:30 a.m. The combined weight was pulling the whale downward, forcing her to struggle mightily to keep her blow-hole out of the water. Soon, an environmental group was radioed for help. By 2:30 p.m., the rescuers had reached the whale and evaluated the situation. Team members realized the only way to save the endangered leviathan was to dive into the water and cut the ropes. It was a very risky maneuver, because the mere flip of a humpback's massive tail can kill a human being.

"My heart sank when I saw all the lines wrapped around her" the first diver in the water said, "I really didn't think we were going to be able to save her." At least 12 crab traps, weighing 90 pounds each, hung off the whale. Rope was wrapped at least four times around the tail, the back and the left front flipper, and there was a line in the whale's mouth. The crab pot lines were cinched so tight that the rope was digging into the whale's blubber and leaving visible cuts. Four divers spent about an hour cutting the ropes with a special curved knife. The whale floated passively in the water the whole time, they said, giving off a strange kind of vibration. "When I was cutting the line going through the mouth, her eye was there winking at me, watching me, following me the whole time," one rescuer said. "It was an epic moment of my life—I will never be the same."

When the whale realized she was free, she began swimming around in joyous circles. She then came back to each and every diver, one at a time, and nudged them, pushed them gently around and flapped. "It felt to us like she was thanking us, knowing that she was free and that we had helped her," the rescue divers said. "It was the most incredibly beautiful experience of their lives."[1]

In recent centuries, whales have been savagely hunted to near extinction. Even today, despite decades of international restrictions, they are killed by the thousand every year. But, at present, most nations in the world are opposed to whale hunting, millions of people regard the killing of whales as inconsistent with current moral ideals, and a multifarious group of committed individuals wages a continuing war against whale hunters from a small number of countries. Is this new perspective justified?

II

A few years ago, legal scholars Anthony D'Amato and Sudhir Chopra dealt with this question in a dense essay, in which they argued that it is time to extend to whales the most fundamental of all human rights—the right to life.[2] In support they advanced a juridical argument connected with the broadening international consciousness which manifests itself in the history of the policies of the international institutions concerned with "whaling"—as, with an unpleasant locution, whale hunt has come to be defined. Claiming that these policies moved through five stages—free resource, regulation, conservation, protection and preservation—and are now pointing to a sixth, entitlement, D'Amato and Chopra discuss the six stages employing purposive as well as descriptive materials, a reflection of the fact that customary international law is a synthesis of qualitative and quantitative elements. [. . .]

The idea of entitlement clearly implies a major theoretical change: to claim that whales are "entitled" to life means to recognize this right as belonging to the whales themselves. But, though involving a radical philosophical shift, the entitlement stage actually represents simply an incremental advance in the series of the progressive stages in question. Set within the framework of international jurisprudence is that trend in the component of customary international law which is called *opinio juris*. The development of international custom is a dynamic process: the seeds of a future conflict-resolving synthesis are present in the clash of thesis and antithesis constituting the claim conflicts among states. Thus, to anticipate a customary trend is to argue that, in a sense, it already exists. In the case of whales, the practice of states has moved through several stages that are best characterized as increases in international breadth of consciousness—and such combination of practice and consciousness is just what formally constitutes the material and psychological elements of general custom. Since what states do becomes what they legally ought to do, by virtue of a growing sense that what they do is right, proper and natural, the dawning sense of duty to the whales is evidence of a sense of obligation that constitutes the *opinio juris* component of binding customary international law. In this light, the attainment of the final stage—the entitlement of whales to life—in its inevitability has already been anticipated in the law.

The idea of having an entitlement includes a notion of a moral right that can inform existing law or push it in a certain direction. In a legal context, when a court accepts the moral claim of right and recognizes it as somehow subsisting in the law all along, though legal precedent was to the contrary, it is said that the court "articulates" the preexisting right. Along these lines, an international court could articulate a right to life of whales arising from the customary law practice of their preservation. This is because whales' entitlement is already implicit in international law as resulting from progression through the previous stages, and from a sense that further development is morally legitimate.

III

Thus, according to D'Amato and Chopra's argument, the new perspective regarding whales is legally justified. But is the sense that such further development is *morally legitimate* warranted? In other words, is the new perspective also ethically sound? Should we grant whales a right to life? In concluding the presentation of the argument from *opinio juris*, D'Amato and Chopra notice that history has seen the continuous widening of the circle of rights holders, with a progression in ascribing fundamental rights to women, children, the mentally enfeebled and racial minorities. Such ascription, it should be added, has usually occurred through the inclusion in the number of "persons." And it is just the notion of person which can offer a clue to moral enquiry within this context.

Roughly speaking, ethics has as its object two sorts of theory of conduct. Morality in the broad sense is an all-inclusive theory of conduct, which includes precepts about the character traits to be fostered and the values to be pursued. Morality in the narrow sense, or social morality, consists instead of a system of constraints on conduct, usually expressed in terms of negative duties, whose task is to prevent harm to others—first and foremost, in the two main forms of the infliction of suffering and the taking of life.[3] In our philosophical landscape, the notion of person, usually contrasted with the notion of thing, has always played an important role with reference to the protection from such harms.[4] For, while "person" is defined so that it is a descriptive term, whose determinative conditions of application have to do with the presence or absence of certain factual characteristics—most prominently rationality and self-consciousness—the assignment of descriptive content is guided by moral considerations.[5] And if, traditionally, to say of some being that it was a person meant to ascribe it a particular moral status, such as to prevent its use as a mere means to others' ends, the notion has gradually come to be especially tied to the question of the wrongness of killing. Accordingly, in present debates, to say of some being that it is a person is not only, as we have suggested, to ascribe it some rights, but most prominently, to grant it the right to life.[6]

Is the concept of person coextensive with the concept of "member of the species *Homo sapiens*"? Arguably not. On the one hand, the notion of person being a creature of ethical theories, it may be pointed out that, historically, its theological use in connection with God has prevented it from simply becoming another term for human being. On the other, and more theoretically, in recent years an *ad hominem* argument directed at the paradigm of human equality has drawn philosophical attention to the inconsistency of denying a moral role to biological characteristics like race or sex while at the same time attributing a moral role to another biological characteristic such as species.[7] Against this background, an important strand of thinking in contemporary moral philosophy, arguing that the facts which are morally relevant *in themselves* are not biological facts, but rather psychological facts, has claimed that the concept of a person is the concept not of a being belonging to a certain species, but of a being endowed with certain mental traits.[8]

In particular, elaborating on Locke's basic idea that a person is a being that can consider itself as itself in different times and places,[9] many authors have argued that the mental trait which is central to personhood is not so much rationality, as rather the property of being aware of oneself as a distinct entity, existing in time and endowed with a past and a future—in other words, self-consciousness.[10] It is evident that what is at play here is the connection between personhood and the prohibition of killing. For if a being is aware of oneself as a distinct entity, existing in time and endowed with a past and a future, it clearly has the possibility of conceiving of one's death as the discontinuance of one's existence, and of dreading, and being harmed by, this discontinuance; and if the function of rights is to protect interests, the interest of such being in its continued existence ought to be protected by a right to life. In this context, then, our initial question becomes: Are whales self-conscious?

In spite of the difficulty of deciphering the minds of beings as evolutionarily distant from us as whales—suffice it to think of how alien the acoustic-aquatic cetacean cognitive environment is for beings like us, whose natural environment is visual-terrestrial—it can hardly be doubted that whale brains are impressive pieces of biological hardware, supporting a sophisticated type of awareness. Cognitive scientists, emphasizing the psychological mechanism of knowing one's self through interaction, argue that the brain creates the self through relationship. Over millions of years, whale brains evolved through a similar process as those of humans—the need for complex societies and relationships. In the first-ever comprehensive analysis of its kind, a study guided by psychologist Lori Marino used computed tomography to investigate the pattern of encephalization in some fossil cetacean species in the past 47 million years, and analyzed these data along with those for some modern species.[11] Marino's conclusion is that the highly expanded brain size of cetaceans is, in a sense, convergently shared with humans, and that, while evolving along quite different paths, the brains of primates and cetaceans arrived at the same cognitive space.

Despite the fact that logistical problems with observing giant cetaceans in their removed habitats make it difficult to obtain in their case the same detailed evidence—regarding e.g. the capacity for mirror self-recognition or for verbal language apprehension—which is now available for their smaller relatives, the dolphins[12]—conclusions analogous to those stemming from Marino's study have recently been reached by scientists studying whale behavioral patterns. For example, according to biologist Hal Whitehead from the Cetacean Science Center at Dalhousie University, whales learn and live in ways that previously have only been identified as "human."[13]

If culture can be defined as behavior or information affecting behavior that is transmitted between individuals by non-genetic means—namely, social learning—there is ample evidence for culture and cultural transmission in whales. This holds in particular, though by no means exclusively, with reference to the specific patterns of communicative vocalization, better known as whale songs, that are emitted at a much greater wavelength than human-produced sounds and whose transmission speed in the water is four times faster than the transmission speed in the air. Taking an ethnographic, as contrasted with an experimental, approach, biologists found evidence both for horizontal—or within generation—and for vertical—or parent-offspring—cultural processes. Innovations spread rapidly in social units, with many members of the group abandoning traditional feeding habits in favor of new habits introduced by creative individuals, and whale mothers create with their children close bonds which can stretch over decades, devoting time and energy to rearing them.[14] We have now a number of scientific descriptions of imitation and teaching, as well as of complex and stable vocal and behavioural cultures in many groups of whales—cultures which, representing an effect of genes affecting culture, or culture affecting genes, have no parallel outside humans and had previously only been suggested for our species.[15] Indeed, cultural transmission is so crucial that menopause, previously thought a unique human characteristic, has now been detected in several whale species, arguably in connection with the importance of increasing the life span of older females who are the main source of information for the group.

Learning has a strong role in the development of vocal patterns, and cetacean vocalization is an important aspect of their underlying social structure. Male humpback whales produce at any given time nearly identical songs which change yearly, while unknown means of learning enable them to keep singing in unison; and it can happen that when some humpback whales migrate, they teach humpbacks in their new neighbourhood to start singing differently.[16] Female sperm whales display dialects—groups emit typical "codas" of several clicks partially overlapping, and individuals from different vocal clans jointly modify their codas into identical patterns, in a friendly vocal duet.[17] Since dialects will survive for several generations, and since whales in groups with different dialects tend to interact with each other quite often, cetaceans can be said to offer the only nonhuman example of multicultural societies where each individual has its own culture but is also interacting with individuals in a different culture.[18]

Finally, various instances of whale behaviors directly testify to the presence of the backward-, present-, and forward-looking attitudes forming the foundation upon which awareness of oneself as a distinct entity existing in time is mounted. A relevant backward looking attitude is revealed e.g. when hordes of whales returning to their original territory after long-distance trips first sing the old songs of the previous year, and then the new songs. The existence of a conscious self in the present, with the attendant ability to attribute mental states to others, is apparent for example in cases of gray whales doing acrobatic maneuvers to warn approaching vessels of their presence so as to avoid risks of serious damage. And undoubtedly, female killer whales' tutoring of their offspring in the dangerous activity of shallow water hunting offers evidence of the requisite forward looking attitude in the form of a capacity for formulating and carrying out plans.[19]

All considered, then, it can be claimed that the neurological and behavioral complexity of whales, as well as their elaborate communication skills, suggest that cetacean brains can produce not only a rich inner life, but also that capacity for self-consciousness that is deemed necessary for personhood.[20] If so, a consistent application of our moral standards would validate the present *opinio juris*, thus corroborating the reform at which it points—that is, the extension of the right to life to whales.

IV

In the light of all this, it seems plausible to conclude that in any conflict between whales and whalers the latter lack any moral entitlement to kill the whales, and that the international community is bound to enforce the protection of the whales both globally and nationally. Before reaching this conclusion, however, an objection must be met. It is a distinctively legal, as contrasted with ethical, objection. For it might be claimed that since the moment when D'Amato and Chopra's essay was published, in 1991, the trend regarding whaling has slightly changed. Though the great majority of states have responded enthusiastically to the anti-whaling movement, with the United States emerging at the forefront of the controversy as a supporter of the moratorium and unilaterally enacting pieces of legislation intended to augment the enforcement power of the International Whaling Commission (IWC), a pro-whaling bloc not only keeps existing, but is becoming more vocal. [. . .]

Does all this have an adverse impact on the argument from *opinio juris*, with the consequence of relegating the ethical case for whales' personhood and right to life to the abstract level of a merely theoretical aspiration? Arguably not. For it is not really unusual that ethically justified principles or rights backed by that sense of obligation that constitutes the *opinio juris* component of customary international law are not accepted by all nations. The conventions that are today collectively known as the "1949 Geneva Conventions" on the treatment of prisoners of war and of civilians in war, for example, have been subscribed to by only about 150 countries out of 192; and when the Universal Declaration of Human Rights was ratified through a proclamation by the U.N. General Assembly in 1948, 8 nations abstained—including countries as different as Czechoslovakia, Saudi Arabia, South Africa and USSR.[21] But—quite apart from the fact that countries can, and often do, expand their moral consciousness—such lack of consensus, however regrettable, did not, and does not, prevent the involved nations from seeing the principles or rights they agreed to not only as ethically sound but also as binding customary international law, and from endeavouring to enforce them by various means, such as political pressures and economic sanctions. This holds in particular in a moment when the nation-state appears in the process of losing many of its prerogatives in favor of a globalized community.[22] Due to this process, which is clearly testified by the international recognition of the legitimacy of some forms of humanitarian intervention to stop genocides or to impose the respect of human rights within the boundaries of independent countries, the various stances and policies of the individual nation-states, far from being seen as the unchangeable outcomes of wholly autonomous entities, tend now to be considered as the proper objects of international moral censure and correction. In view both of the past record in the field of international jurisprudence and of the ongoing process of globalization, it can be argued that the fact that countries like Japan, Norway and Iceland keep opposing any granting of an entitlement to life to whales is a regrettable reality which cannot—and should not—jeopardize the emerging basic international consensus regarding the whales' status.

If this is so, then the overall argument so far developed stands. But if the new perspective regarding whales is justified, an important change is in order. We have mentioned that when the U.N. demand for a ten-year moratorium of commercial whaling was rejected by the IWC's Scientific Committee, questions were raised about the IWC role, and proposals were made calling for the U.N. to assume jurisdiction. This idea has become more relevant today. It seems plausible that, now that consciousness about whales has broadened, an institution which was initially created with the goal of regulating whales' exploitation can no longer be seen as the best organization to deal with their protection. As humanity as a whole comes to recognize the moral standing of whales, the time is ripe to remove human/cetacean relations from the hands of the former whaling nations. It would be fully in line with the present trend towards greater global governance in a variety of areas—trade and the environment, as well as peace and the protection of human rights—to create a new, *ad hoc* U.N. institution with the task of internationally declaring, and then elaborating in a series of covenants, the whales' right to life.

Among other things, the creation of such an institution would have the important side effect of neutralizing the threat of withdrawal which the pro-whaling nations constantly use as a sort of black-mail towards the IWC. Admittedly, the problem of how to induce compliance would still remain. But this problem—which is common to all fields of international law—would not be altered for the worse in this new scenery. As it was in the past, when pro-whaling nations were prone to base their concrete decisions on their assessment of U.S. intentions, it will still be up to the anti-whaling countries to lead the battle and to provide with their policies of suasion, pressure and sanctions the required enforcement mechanisms for whales' right to life.

Notes

1. Peter Fimrite, "Daring rescue of whale off Farallones", *San Francisco Chronicle*, December 14, 2005, http://sfgate.com/cgi-bin/article.cgi?file=/c/a/2005/12/14/HUMPY.TMP
2. Anthony D'Amato and Sudhir K. Chopra, "Whales: Their emerging right to life", *American Journal of International Law*, 85 (1), 1991.
3. Geoffrey J. Warnock, *The Object of Morality*, Methuen, London, 1971, p. 148; Peter F. Strawson, "Social morality and individual ideal", *Philosophy: The Journal of the Royal Institute of Philosophy*, 36, January 1968.
4. Adolf Trendelenburg, "A contribution to the history of the word person", *Monist*, July 1910. The best-known formulation of the person/thing dichotomy can be found in Kant's moral philosophy; see Immanuel Kant, *Foundations of the Metaphysics of Morals*, trans. Lewis W. Beck, Upper Saddle River, NJ: Prentice-Hall, 1997, p. 45.
5. On this, see generally the special issue of *Etica & Animali* devoted to "Nonhuman Personhood" (vol. 9, 1998).
6. Joel Feinberg, "Abortion", in Tom Regan, ed., *Matters of Life and Death*, 2nd ed., New York: Random House, 1986.
7. Peter Singer, *Animal Liberation*, 2nd ed., New York: The New York Review of Books, 1990, p. 9.
8. Paola Cavalieri, *The Animal Question*, New York: Oxford University Press, 2001, p. 117 ff.
9. John Locke, *An Essay Concerning Human Understanding*, Cleveland: World Publishing Co., 1964, book 2, chap. 9, part 29, p. 211.
10. Such perspective, though grown in the English-speaking world and detailedly developed in the context of contemporary bioethical discussions of the morality of abortion and euthanasia, has antecedents in continental philosophy as well. Leibniz, for example, connects personhood with consciousness of self and recollection of a former state (Gottfried Wilhelm Leibniz, *Epistula ad Wagnerum de vi activa corporis, de anima, de anima brutorum*, 1710), and even Kant, in spite of all his insistence on rationality, claims that it is the fact of being able to represent to themselves their own selves that elevates persons above all living beings (Immanuel Kant, *Anthropology from a Pragmatic Point of View*, trans. Victor Lyle Dowdell, Carbondale: Southern Illinois University Press, 1978, book I, part I).
11. Lori Marino, Mark D. Uhen, Nicholas D. Pyenson and Bruno Frohlich, "Reconstructing cetacean brain evolution using computed tomography", *Anatomical Record (The New Anatomist)*, 272B, 2003.
12. Denise L. Herzing and Thomas I. White, "Dolphins and the question of personhood", *Etica & Animali*, Special issue: "Nonhuman Personhood" 9, 1998; Thomas I. White, *The Sea Peoples*, Oxford: Blackwell, forthcoming.
13. Jonathan Dieli Colburn, "Listening to whales", interview with Hal Whitehead, *San Francisco Chronicle*, January 9, 2003, http://www.sfgate.com/cgi-bin/article.cgi?f=/chronicle/a/2003/01/09/MN184029.DTL
14. Luke Rendell and Hal Whitehead, "Culture in whales and dolphins", *Behavioral and Brain Sciences*, 24 (2), 2001; M. T. Weinrich, M. R. Schilling and C. R. Belt, "Evidence for acquisition of a novel feeding behaviour: Lobtail feeding in humpback whales, *Megaptera novaeangliae*", *Animal Behaviour*, 44, 1992; H. Whitehead, "Cultural selection and genetic diversity in matrilineal whales", *Science*, 282, 1998.
15. Luke Rendell and Hal Whitehead, "Culture in whales and dolphins", cit.
16. Michael J. Noad, Douglas H. Cato and M. M. Bryden, "Cultural displacement and replacement in the songs of Australian humpback whales", *Nature*, 408 (537), 2000.
17. L. S. Weilgart, "Vocalizations of the sperm whale (*Physeter macrocephalus*) off the Galapagos Islands as related to behavioral and circumstantial variables", doctoral dissertation, Dalhousie University, Halifax, Nova Scotia, Canada, 1990.
18. Jonathan Dieli Colburn, "Listening to whales", interview with Hal Whitehead, cit.
19. "Secrets Of Whales' Long-Distance Songs Unveiled", interview with Christopher Clark from Cornell University, March 24, 2005, *Space Daily*, http://www.spacedaily.com/news/life-05t.html; "Gray Whale Migration Update", February 25, 1998, report by Etai Timna, Channel Islands National Marine Sanctuary,

http://www.learner.org/jnorth/spring1998/critters/gwhale/Update022598.html; C. Guinet and J. Bouvier, "Development of intentional stranding hunting techniques in killer whale (*Orcinus orca*) calves at Crozet Archipelago", *Canadian Journal of Zoology*, 73, 1995.

20. This is a conclusion which is also suggested, though in lesser detail, by other authors such as Michael Tooley, *Abortion and Infanticide*, Oxford: Oxford University Press, 1983, p. 412; Peter Singer, *Practical Ethics*, 2nd ed., Cambridge: Cambridge University Press, 1993, pp. 117–119; Harlan B. Miller, "Science, ethics, and moral status", *Between the Species*, 10 (1–2), 1994 etc.

21. University of Minnesota, Human Rights Library, "Human Rights Education", http://www1.umn.edu/humanrts/education/4thR-F97/EleanorRoosevelt.htm

22. Peter Singer, *One World: The Ethics of Globalization*, New Haven, CT: Yale University Press, 2002.

Part Four

Animals for Food

Introduction to Part Four

The use of animals for food is a highly charged topic for many people. For some the emotional lives of animals are reason enough not to eat them. For those who do eat animals, accurate information on how animals for food are raised and slaughtered is important for an informed moral judgment. David DeGrazia describes the conditions of pigs, chickens, and cattle in modern factory farms, which now supply most of the meat and dairy products in the U.S., Great Britain, and most other industrial countries. He argues that factory farming causes more harm to animals than any other human practice.

Temple Grandin has designed 30 percent of the livestock-handling facilities in the U.S. She affirms that we owe animals a decent life and a painless death. Her essay "Thinking Like Animals" explains how her life as a person with autism has enabled her to better understand animal emotions. She has found that cattle are sensitive to the same things that disturb people with autism, and has designed restraint chutes for holding cattle for slaughter with the emotional needs of cattle in mind. In "A Major Change," she describes the improvements made in the handling and stunning of animals between 1997 and 1999, the importance of proper transport of cattle and pigs, and the promotion of better stockmanship.

Two of the authors in Part Four argue for vegetarianism. James Rachels provides what he calls the "basic argument," based on the principle that it is wrong to cause pain unless there is a "good enough reason" for such pain. In "The Rape of Animals, the Butchering of Women," Carol J. Adams argues that both women and animals are "absent referents," made absent through language and metaphor, and in the case of animals, through death. Patriarchal culture transforms women and animals into commodities to be used and consumed.

Several articles argue against vegetarianism. One critique of ethical vegetarianism is that the arguments provided by Regan, Singer, and Adams are discriminatory, applying only to most men and some women aged 20–50 in industrialized countries. This assumption of the "male norm" is mistaken. George advocates "semivegetarianism" and attention to commonsense duties to animals and humans. Steven L. Davis argues that Regan's Least Harm Principle directs us to consume a diet containing both plants and some animal products.

The final three essays in Part Four concern the doctrines of some of the world religions with regard to the slaughter and eating of animals. The Rev. Andrew Linzey argues for vegetarianism from a Christian perspective, based on his reading of Genesis as well as other books of the Bible. Martin Forward and Mohamed Alam explain the Islamic view of animals. Few Muslims are vegetarians, but certain animals are forbidden to Muslims, and all creatures used for food must be killed in a prescribed manner.

Further Reading

Benson, G. J. and Rollin, B. E. (eds.) (2004) *The Well-Being of Farm Animals: Challenges and Solutions*, Ames, IA: Blackwell.

Gregory, N. G. with a chapter by Grandin, T. (1998) *Animal Welfare and Meat Science*, New York: CABI Publishing.

Kaiser, M. and Lien, M. E. (eds.) (2006) *Ethics and the Politics of Food: Preprints of the 6th Congress of the European Society for Agricultural and Food Ethics*, the Netherlands: Wageningen.

Kalechofsky, R. (ed.) (1992) *Judaism and Animal Rights: Classical and Contemporary Responses*, Marblehead, MA: Micah.

Kunkel, H. O. (2000) *Human Issues in Animal Agriculture*, College Station: Texas A & M University Press.

Masri, A.B.A. (1989) *Animals in Islam*, Hants, England: The Athene Trust.

Rosati, A., Tewolde, A., and Mosconi, C. (eds.) (2005) *Animal Production and Animal Science Worldwide*, the Netherlands: Wageningen.

Sapontzis, S. F. (ed.) (2004) *Food for Thought: The Debate over Eating Meat*, New York: Prometheus.

Scully, M. (2002) *Dominion: The Power of Man, the Suffering of Animals, and the Call to Mercy*, New York: St. Martin's.

Turner, J. and D'Silva, J. (eds.) (2006) *Animals, Ethics and Trade: The Challenge of Animal Sentience*, London: Earthscan.

Walters, K. S. and Portmess, L. (eds.) (1999) *Ethical Vegetarianism: From Pythagoras to Peter Singer*, Albany: SUNY.

Webster, J. (2005) *Animal Welfare: Limping Towards Eden: A Practical Approach to Redressing the Problem of Our Dominion over the Animals*, Oxford: Blackwell.

Study Questions

1. Rachels provides an argument for vegetarianism and concludes that it is not an all-or-nothing proposition. Do you agree that we should "focus on the things that cause the most misery"? In your view, what are these things?

2. Rabbi Seidenberg distinguishes between seeing animals in terms of human interests and as living for their own sake. In your view, what is this difference? Rabbi David Seidenberg points out the complexity of rabbinic discussions of animal suffering.

3. To "sacrifice" means to make holy, to offer to a higher end. In your view, why do so many scientists refer to "sacrificing" experimental animals?

4. Do you agree with DeGrazia's evaluation of the harm caused to human beings by factory farming? How might this harm be diminished?

5. Based on DeGrazia's discussion of family farming and your own views, what sort of animal food production (if any) is morally acceptable?

6. Is it morally acceptable to eat fish or other seafood? Why or why not?

7. Do you agree with Andrew Linzey that animals are cherished by God, as are human beings? Why or why not?

8. Have animals taught you about the presence of God? In what ways?

9. Which diet(s) do you believe to be morally acceptable: that of an omnivore, a vegan, or/and a vegetarian? What special circumstances might affect your answer?

10. In your view, is the situation of farm animals described in the "Putting Meat on the Table" article an important moral problem? Why or why not?

11. Why do you think that videos of animals in intensive confinement are generally unavailable?

12. The Pew Commission maintains that animal welfare should be looked at from both a scientific and an ethical point of view. Do you agree? Explain your reasoning.

26 Meat Eating

David DeGrazia

David DeGrazia describes the conditions endured by chickens, pigs, and cows during their lives and deaths as part of the factory farming system in the U.S., Great Britain, and most other industrialized countries. American farm animals have virtually no legal protection. DeGrazia argues that consumers are morally obliged to make a reasonable effort to not provide financial support to institutions that cause extensive unnecessary suffering.

Hen X begins life in a crowded incubator. She is taken to a 'battery' cage made entirely of wire—and quite unlike the outdoor conditions that are natural for her—where she will live her life. (Having no commercial value, male chicks are gassed, ground up alive, or suffocated.) Hen X's cage is so crowded that she cannot fully stretch her wings. Although her beak is important for feeding, exploring, and preening, part of it has been cut off, through sensitive tissue, in order to limit the damage caused by pecking cage mates—a behaviour induced by overcrowding. For hours before laying an egg, Hen X paces anxiously among the crowd, instinctively seeking a nest that she will not find. At egg-laying time, she stands on a sloped, uncomfortable wire floor that precludes such instinctual behaviours as pecking for food, dust bathing, and scratching. Lack of exercise, unnatural conditions, and demands for extreme productivity—she will lay 250 eggs this year—cause bone weakness. (Unlike many hens, Hen X is not subjected to forced moulting, in which water is withheld for one to three days and food for up to two weeks in order to extend hens' productive lives.) When considered spent at age two, she is jammed into a crate and transported in a truck—without food, water, or protection from the elements—to a slaughterhouse; rough handling causes several weak bones to break. At her destination, Hen X is shackled upside down on a conveyor belt before an automated knife slices her throat. Because the (US) Humane Slaughter Act does not apply to poultry, she is fully conscious throughout this process. Her body, which was extensively damaged during her lifetime, is suitable only for pot pies, soup, and the like.

After weaning at four weeks of age, Hog Y is taken to a very crowded, stacked nursery cage. Due to poor ventilation, he breathes in powerful fumes from urine and faeces. Upon reaching a weight of 50 pounds, he is taken to a tiny 'finishing' pen. It is slatted and has a concrete floor with no straw bedding or sources of amusement. Despite being a member of a highly intelligent and social species, Hog Y is separated from other hogs by iron bars and has nothing to do except get up, lie down, eat, and sleep. He sometimes amuses himself by biting a tail in the next crate—until all the hogs' tails are 'docked' (cut off). Both this procedure and castration are performed without anaesthesia. When he is deemed ready for slaughter, Hog Y is roughly herded into a truck with thirty other hogs. The two-day journey is not pleasant for Hog Y, who gets in fights with other hogs while receiving no food, water, rest, or protection from the summer heat. At the slaughterhouse, Hog Y smells blood and resists prodding from the human handlers. They respond by kicking him and smashing him repeatedly from behind with an iron pipe until he is on the restraining conveyor belt that carries him to the stunner. Hog Y is fortunate insofar as the electric stunning procedure is successful, killing him before his body is dropped in scalding water and dismembered. (Although the Humane Slaughter

Act requires that animals other than poultry be rendered unconscious with a single application of an effective stunning device before being shackled, hoisted upside down, and dismembered, many slaughterhouse employees state that violations occur regularly. Fearing that a higher voltage might cause 'bloodsplash' in some carcasses, many slaughterhouse supervisors apparently encourage use of a voltage that is much too low to ensure unconsciousness. Moreover, in numerous slaughterhouses stunners have to stun an animal every few seconds and face extreme pressure not to stop the line of animals.)

Although it is natural for cows and their calves to bond strongly, Cow (then Calf) Z is taken from her mother shortly after birth to begin life as a dairy cow. She never receives colostrum—her mother's milk—which would help her fight disease. She lives in a very crowded 'drylot', which is devoid of grass, and her tail is docked without anaesthesia. In order to produce twenty times more milk than a calf would need, she receives a diet heavy in grain—not the roughage that cows have evolved to digest easily—causing metabolic disorders and painful lameness. And like many dairy cows, she often has mastitis, a painful udder inflammation, despite receiving antibiotics between lactations. To maintain continuous milk production, Cow Z is induced to bear one calf each year. To stimulate additional growth and productivity, she receives daily injections of bovine growth hormone. Her natural life span is twenty or more years, but at age 4 she can no longer maintain production levels and is deemed 'spent'. During transport and handling, Cow Z is fortunate: although deprived of food, water, and rest for over two days, and frightened when prodded, she is not beaten; at the slaughterhouse her instincts—unlike hogs'—allow her to walk easily in a single-file chute. Unfortunately, the poorly trained stun operator has difficulty with the air-powered knocking gun. Although he stuns Cow Z four times, she stands up and bellows. The line does not stop, however, so she is hoisted up on the overhead rail and transported to the 'sticker', who cuts her throat to bleed her out. She remains conscious as she bleeds and experiences some of the dismemberment and skinning process alive. (The federal inspector cannot see what is happening where he is stationed; besides, he's frenetically checking carcasses that whiz by, for obvious signs of contamination.) Cow Z's body will be used for processed beef or hamburger.

The Institution of Factory Farming

The animals portrayed above offer examples of life in modern factory farms, which now supply most of our meat and dairy products in the USA, Great Britain, and most other industrial countries. Since the Second World War, factory farms—which try to raise as many animals as possible in very limited space in order to maximize profits—have driven three million American family farms out of business; over the same time period, Great Britain and other nations have witnessed similar transformations in their agricultural sectors. Scientific developments that have fuelled the emergence of factory farming include the artificial provision of vitamin D (which otherwise requires sunlight for its synthesis), the success of antibiotics in minimizing the spread of certain diseases, and advanced methods of genetic selection for production traits. Since the driving force behind this institution is economic efficiency, factory farming treats animals simply as means to this end—as mere objects with no independent moral importance, or moral status, whatever.

Considering both numbers of animals involved and the extent to which they are harmed, *factory farming causes more harm to animals than does any other human institution or practice*. In the USA alone, this institution kills over 100 million mammals and 5 billion birds annually. American farm animals have virtually no legal protections. The most important applicable federal legislation is the Humane Slaughter Act, which does not cover poultry—most of the animals consumed—and has no bearing on living conditions, transport, or handling. Moreover, as Gail Eisnitz and others have extensively documented, the Act is rarely enforced. Apparently, the US Department of Agriculture supports the major goal of agribusiness: absolute maximization of profit without hindrance. This is not surprising when one considers that since the 1980s, most top officials at USDA either have been agribusiness leaders themselves or have had close political and financial ties to the industry.

By contrast, European nations have curbed some of the excesses typified by American factory farming. For example, Great Britain has banned veal crates and limits to fifteen hours the amount of time animals can go without food and water during transport. The European Community and the Council of Europe have developed requirements for the well-being of farm animals that are translated into law in different member nations. These requirements generally provide animals with more space, greater freedom to engage in species-typical behaviours, and more humane living conditions than those of farm animals in the USA. Despite the more humane conditions that are typical in Europe, however, most European animal husbandry remains sufficiently intensive to merit the term 'factory farming'.

So far this discussion has provided a descriptive sense of factory farms primarily through three cases. Therefore it might be objected that the situations of Hen X, Hog Y, and Cow Z do not represent universal features of factory farming. That is correct. But the experiences of these three animals, the evidence suggests, are not atypical—at least in the USA. Still, while a thorough description of factory farms is impossible here, it may be helpful to add a few general remarks about other types of farm animals. The following generalizations are meant to describe the American situation, although some of them accurately describe the experiences of animals in many other countries as well.

Cattle raised specifically for beef are generally better off than the other animals described here. Many have the opportunity to roam outdoors for about six months. After that, they are transported long distances to feedlots, where they are fed grain rather than grass. Major sources of pain or distress include constant exposure to the elements, branding, dehorning, unanaesthetized castration, the cutting of ears for identification purposes, and a sterile, unchanging environment. We may add, of course, the harms associated with transportation to the slaughterhouse and what takes place therein.

Broiler chickens spend their lives in enclosed sheds that become increasingly crowded as tens of thousands of birds grow at an abnormally fast rate. Besides extreme crowding, major sources of concern include cannibalism, suffocation due to panic-driven piling on top of one another, debeaking, and very unhealthful breathing conditions produced by never-cleaned droppings and poor ventilation. Veal calves' deprivations are similar to many of those that hogs experience. Formula-fed veal calves in particular live in solitary crates too small to permit them to turn around or sleep in a natural position. Denied water and solid food, they drink a liquid milk replacer deficient in iron—making possible the gourmet white flesh and resulting in anaemia. This diet and solitary confinement lead to numerous health problems and neurotic behaviours.

Let us now consider the overall picture: *factory farming routinely causes animals massive harm in the form of suffering, confinement, and death.* Regarding suffering—or experiential harm in general—all evidence suggests that factory farm animals, in the course of their lives, typically experience considerable pain, discomfort, boredom, fear, anxiety, and possibly other unpleasant feelings. Furthermore, factory farms by their very nature *confine* animals in our stipulated sense of the term; that is, they impose external constraints on movement that significantly interfere with living well. (For at least part of their lives, cattle raised specifically for beef are not confined in this sense.) And, of course, factory farming ultimately kills animals raised for meat, adding the harm of death—assuming (. . .) that death harms such beings as cows, pigs, and chickens. Then again, death counts as a harm here only if we consider the sorts of lives these animals *could* have under humane treatment. Given animals' current treatment, death would seem to be a blessing, except possibly in the case of beef cattle. In any event, the general thesis that factory farms cause massive harm to animals is undeniable.

Moral Evaluation

If the first crucial insight into a moral evaluation of factory farms is that they cause massive harm to animals, the second crucial insight is this: *consumers do not need the products of factory farms.* We cannot plausibly regard any of the harms caused to these animals as *necessary*. Unusual circumstances aside—say, where one is starving and lacks alternatives—we do not need to eat meat to survive or even to be healthy. The chief benefits of meat-eating to consumers are *pleasure*, since meat tastes especially good to many people, and *convenience*, since switching to and maintaining a vegetarian diet requires some effort. Putting the two key insights together brings us to the conclusion that *factory farms cause massive unnecessary harm*. Since causing massive unnecessary harm is wrong if *anything* is wrong, the judgement that factory farming is an indefensible institution seems inescapable.

Note that this condemnation of factory farming does not depend on the controversial assumption that animals deserve equal consideration. Even if one accepts a sliding-scale model of moral status, which justifies less-than-equal consideration for animals, one cannot plausibly defend the causing of massive unnecessary harm. Thus, it appears that if one takes animals at all seriously—regarding them as beings with at least some moral status—one must find factory farming indefensible.

But what about the consumer? She isn't harming animals; she's just eating the products of factory farming. Well, imagine someone who says, 'I'm not kicking dogs to death. I'm just paying someone else to do it.' We would judge this person to act wrongly for encouraging and commissioning acts of cruelty. Similarly, while meat-eaters may typically feel distant from meat production and may never even think about what goes on in factory farms and slaughterhouses, the purchase of factory-farmed meat directly encourages and makes possible the associated cruelties—so the consumer is significantly responsible. In general, the following moral rule, although somewhat vague, is defensible: *make every reasonable effort not to provide financial support to institutions that cause extensive unnecessary harm.*

By financially supporting massive unnecessary harm, the purchase of factory-farmed meat violates this principle and is therefore, I argue, morally indefensible. Interestingly, we reached this important conclusion without commitment to any specific ethical theory such as utilitarianism or a strong animal-rights view. In any event, while our case against factory farming and buying its products has so far cited considerations of animal welfare, it is further strengthened by considerations of human welfare. How so?

First, animal products—which are high in fat and protein and contain cholesterol—are associated with higher levels of heart disease, obesity, stroke, osteoporosis, diabetes, and certain cancers. Medical authorities now recommend much less meat and more grains, fruits, and vegetables than Americans, for example, typically consume. Second, American factory farming has driven three million family farms out of business since the Second World War, as huge agribusinesses, enjoying billions of dollars in annual government subsidies, have increasingly dominated; while American consumers frequently hear that factory farming lowers meat prices at the cash register, they are rarely reminded of the hidden cost of tax subsidies. In Britain and many other countries, relatively few large agribusinesses have similarly come to dominate, putting many smaller farms out of business. Third, factory farming is devastating for the environment. It excessively consumes energy, soil, and water while causing erosion of topsoil, destruction of wildlife habitat, deforestation, and water pollution from manure, pesticides, and other chemicals. Fourth, factory farming has a perverse effect on the distribution of food to humans. For example, it takes about 8 pounds of protein in hog feed to generate 1 pound of pork for humans and 21 pounds of protein in calf feed to yield 1 pound of beef. Consequently, most US-produced grain, for example, goes to livestock. Unfortunately, wealthy countries' demand for meat makes plant proteins too costly for the masses in the poorest countries. Poor communities often abandon sustainable farming practices to export cash crops and meat, but profits are short-lived as marginal lands erode, causing poverty and malnutrition. There is, in fact, easily enough grain protein, if used sensibly, to feed every human on Earth. Fifth, perhaps especially in the USA, factory farming is cruel to its employees. It subjects them to extreme work pressures—as seen in a worker who cuts up to ninety chickens per minute, or urinates on the workline for fear of leaving it—and to some of the worst health hazards faced by any American workers (for example, skin diseases, respiratory problems, crippling hand and arm injuries, injury from wild, improperly stunned animals)—all for low pay. Finally, deregulation of the American meat industry since the 1980s, combined with extremely fast production lines, have made it virtually impossible to ensure safe meat. . . .

Thus, receiving further support from considerations of human welfare, the case for boycotting factory farm products is extremely powerful. But let us not ignore the following important objection. One might argue that the continuation of factory farming is economically necessary. Putting this industry out of business—say, through a successful boycott—would obviously be devastating for agribusiness owners, but would also eliminate many jobs and possibly harm local economies. These consequences, the argument continues, are unacceptable. Thus, just as factory farming is necessary, so is the extensive harm it inevitably causes to animals—contrary to my charge of massive *unnecessary* harm.

In reply, we may accept the factual assumption about likely consequences while rejecting the claim that they are unacceptable. First, as Peter Singer notes, the negative costs of ending factory farming would have to be borne only once, whereas perpetuating this institution entails that the costs to animals continue indefinitely. Also, considering how badly factory farm employees are treated, it is hard to believe they would be seriously harmed by having to seek alternative employment, as innumerable 'burnt out' employees do anyway. More generally, the various threats to human well-being posed by factory farming—health risks, environmental destruction, inefficient use and perverse distribution of grain proteins, etc.—could be avoided if this industry is were eliminated (assuming it is not simply replaced by less intensive animal husbandry, which would perpetuate some of these problems). Avoiding these risks and harms, not once but indefinitely, would seem to counterbalance any short-term economic harm. Finally, I submit that *there are moral limits to what we may do to others in the pursuit of profit or employment—and causing sentient beings massive harm in pursuing these goals oversteps those bounds*. (Cases in which people are forced into prostitution, pornography, or slavery vividly exemplify the violation of such limits.) If that is correct, then factory farming cannot be considered necessary. In conclusion, I suggest that these rebuttals, taken together, undercut the argument from economic necessity.

Traditional Family Farming

This chapter has focused on factory farms because most of the animal products we consume come from this source. But people also eat animals from other sources, including traditional family farms.

Because they involve far less intensive rearing conditions, family farms cause much less suffering to animals than factory farms do. Family farms may not even confine animals in our sense of imposing constraints on movement that significantly interfere with living well. But . . . farm animals cannot fully escape harm because they are ultimately killed, entailing the harm of death.

Causing much less harm to animals, and avoiding at least some threats that factory farming poses to human well-being (for example, water pollution, extremely hazardous working conditions), family farming is much more defensible than its dominant competitor. Still, there is a strong moral case against family farming and the practice of buying its products. For one thing, this institution does impose some significant suffering through certain practices: branding and dehorning cattle; castrating cattle and hogs; separating mothers from offspring, which may well cause distress even to birds; and treating animals roughly in transport, handling, and slaughter. And, again, all the animals die. Since meat-eating is—unusual circumstances aside—unnecessary, these harms are unnecessary. It is difficult to defend the routine imposition of unnecessary harm.

A few possible replies, however, may strengthen the case for some forms of family farming. For example, chickens and turkeys can escape most of the harms just described. If a chicken or turkey is able to live a pleasant life—say, with family intact—and is never abused, the only relevant harm would be death.

[. . .]

Alternatively, if one (unlike the present author) accepts the sliding-scale model of moral status, one would grant unequal moral weight to the interests—including the avoidance of suffering—of different beings depending on their cognitive, emotional, and social complexity. Perhaps proponents of this ethical framework would defend practices of family farming that keep the admittedly unnecessary suffering to a minimum. They might argue that it is not always wrong to cause *minimal* unnecessary harm, even to mammals, especially if there are some significant benefits such as employment for farmers. Then again, one would need to consider negative effects on human welfare, such as extremely inefficient use of grain protein, in assessing the plausibility of this line of argument.

Seafood

Much of the meat we consume comes from the sea. Beginning with fish and cephalopods (octopuses and squid), we concluded [in an earlier chapter] that these creatures are sentient, subject to pain and distress; we left somewhat more open whether they can experience suffering in the specific sense: a highly unpleasant emotional state associated with more-than-minimal pain or distress. Now catching fish and cephalopods requires hooking or netting them and causing them to suffocate. Clearly, they experience unpleasant feelings in the process. While traditional fishing methods do not involve confinement—since the animals are at liberty in their natural environment—death is obviously unavoidable. Death harms such creatures to *some degree* on the opportunities-based account of the harm of death, but not on the desire-based view.

There are several ways in which one might argue that fish and cephalopods are harmed only minimally: by claiming that any suffering is very brief; by denying that they suffer at all; or by arguing that the harm of death in their case is negligible to non-existent. Then one might argue that this minimal harm is adequately counterbalanced by certain benefits to humans: pleasure, convenience, rounding out a healthful diet, and employment for fishers. (One who believes that animals have rights in the strongest, utility-trumping sense would reject such reasoning, however.) Naturally, a proponent of the sliding-scale model of moral status will find the production and consumption of seafood easier to defend, since fish and cephalopods would be relatively low in the moral hierarchy.

One complicating factor in our analysis is that many fish today are raised in fish farms. These are so crowded that they amount to confinement and increase the unpleasantness of the fishes' lives. When fish are raised in this way, the case for boycotting these products is stronger.

What about lobsters, crabs, shrimp, and other invertebrates other than cephalopods? Available evidence leaves open the issue of their possible sentience. If they are not sentient, our actions cannot harm them. People might reasonably disagree about whether, in this state of uncertainty, we should give them the benefit of the doubt and assume they are sentient.

As we think about the issue of eating seafood, we must not ignore any harms caused to creatures other than those consumed. For example, suppose you buy tuna fish from a company whose nets often ensnare and kill dolphins—whose cognitive, emotional, and social complexity rivals that of Great Apes. The harms thereby caused to dolphins might make the purchase of tuna from this company as serious a moral matter as buying meat from factory farms.

27 Thinking Like Animals

Temple Grandin

Temple Grandin describes the similarities between autistic emotion and animal emotion and explains how she has designed chute systems for handling cattle in slaughter plants to keep cattle calm. She also discusses how important the attitude of the handler is and the growing role of women in slaughter plants. Grandin affirms that life and death are inseparable and that it is important to accept our own mortality.

Language-based thought is foreign to me. All my thoughts are full-color motion pictures, running like a videotape in my imagination. It was always obvious to me that cattle and other animals also think in pictures. I have learned that there are some people who mainly think in words and I have observed that these verbal thinkers are more likely to deny animals' thought; they are unable to imagine thought without words. Using my visual thinking skills, it is easy for me to imagine myself in an animal's body and see things from their perspective. It is the ultimate virtual reality system. I can imagine looking through their eyes or walking with four legs.

My life as a person with autism is like being another species: part human and part animal. Autistic emotion may be more like an animal's. Fear is the dominant emotion in both autistic people and animals such as deer, cattle, and horses. My emotions are simple and straightforward like an animal's, my emotions are not deep-seated. They may be intense while I am experiencing them, but they will subside like an afternoon thunderstorm.

For the last fifteen years I have designed chute systems for handling cattle in slaughter plants. The conveyorized restraint system I designed is used in slaughtering one third of all the cattle in the United States.

Cattle are not afraid of the same things that people fear. The problem is that many people cannot observe this because they allow their own emotions to get in the way. To design a humane system, I had to imagine what it would be like if I were the animal. I had to become that animal and not just be a person in a cow costume.

Cattle and people are upset by different things. People are repulsed by the sight of blood, but blood does not bother cattle. They are wary of the things that spell danger in the wild, such as high-pitched noise, disturbances of the dirt, and sudden jerky movements. A high-pitched noise may be a distress cry, and dirt or grass that is displaced may mean that there has been a struggle to avoid being eaten. Abrupt motion may be associated with a predator leaping onto its prey. These are all danger signals.

Many times I have observed cattle balking and refusing to move through a chute at a slaughter plant. They may balk at a jiggling gate, a shadow, a shiny reflection, or anything that appears to be out of place. A coffee cup dropped on the floor can make the cattle stop and turn back. But cattle will walk quietly into a slaughterhouse if the things they are afraid of are eliminated. Solid sides on chutes prevent them from seeing people up ahead and muffling devices lessen the shrill sounds that alarm them.

Cattle are sensitive to the same things that disturb people with autism. Immature development in the lower brain systems causes some people with autism to have a heightened sense of hearing, and an intense fear is triggered when anything in their environment is out of place. A curled-up rug, or a book that is crooked on the shelf, causes the same fear as being stalked by a predator. The autistic brain is acutely aware of details that most other people ignore. Sudden high-pitched sounds in the middle of the night cause my heart to race as if a lion was going to pounce.

Like a wild animal, I recoil when people touch me. A light touch sets off a flight reaction and my oversensitive nerve endings do not tolerate hugging. I want the soothing feeling of being held, but the sensations can be too overwhelming, so I pull away. My need for touch started my interest in cattle.

Puberty began the onslaught of hormones that sensitized my nervous system and started the constant fear and anxiety. I was desperate for relief. At my aunt's ranch I observed that when cattle were placed in a squeeze chute for their vaccinations, the pressure from the side panels squeezing against their bodies relaxed them. Pressure over wide areas of the body has a calming effect on many animals. Pressure applied to the sides of a piglet will cause it to fall asleep. Firm touch has a calming effect, while a light tickle touch is likely to set off a flight reaction.

Many parents of autistic children have observed that their child will seek pressure by getting under sofa cushions or a mattress. Therapists often use deep pressure to calm autistic children. I decided to try the squeeze chute and discovered that the intense pressure temporarily made my anxiety go away. When I returned home from the ranch I built a squeezing machine. Early versions pressed against my body with hard wood. When I first started using the machine I flinched and pulled away from it like a wild animal. As I adjusted to being held I used less intense pressure and I remodeled the side panels with foam rubber padding to make the machine more comfortable.

As I became able to tolerate being held I became more interested in figuring out how the cattle felt when they were handled and held in squeeze chutes at the feed yards. Many of the animals were scared because people were rough with them. They chased them, yelled at them, and prodded them. I found that I could coax most cattle to walk through a chute to be vaccinated by moving them quietly, at a slow walk. When an animal was calm I could observe the things that would catch his eye, like shadows or people leaning over the top of the chute. The leader would look at the things that concerned him. He would stop and stare at a coffee cup on the floor or move his head back and forth in time with a small chain that was swinging in the chute. Before moving forward he had to carefully scrutinize the things that attracted his attention. If the handlers tried to force him to move before he had determined that the chain was harmless, he and all the other cattle would panic. Cattle moved quietly and quickly through the chutes as soon as the swinging chain was removed.

I found that the animals were less likely to resist being held by the squeeze chute if pressure was applied slowly. An animal would panic if suddenly bumped. I also discovered the concept of optimum pressure. The chute must apply sufficient pressure to provide the feeling of being held but not cause pain. Many people make the mistake of mashing an animal too tight when it struggles. And the chute always needs solid sides, so that the cattle do not see people deep inside their flight zone. The flight zone is the animal's safety zone. They become anxious and want to get away when people get too close.

Years later, when I designed a restraint chute for holding cattle for slaughter, I was amazed that the animals would stand still and seldom resist the chute. I found that I could just ease their head and body into position by adjusting the chute. When I got really skilled at operating the hydraulic controls, the apparatus became an extension of my arms and hands. It was as if I could reach through the machine and hold each animal very gently. It was my job to hold the animal gently while the rabbi performed the final deed.

During the last ten years, more and more women have been hired to handle cattle and operate chutes in both feed yards and slaughter plants. At first the men were skeptical that women could do the work, but today progressive managers have found that women are gentler and work well with the animals. Some feed yards now hire only women to doctor sick cattle and vaccinate the new arrivals. In slaughter plants, two of the best operators of kosher restraining chutes are women. They were attracted to the job because they couldn't stand to see the guys abusing cattle.

When I first started designing equipment I thought that all the problems of the rough treatment of animals in slaughter plants could be solved with engineering. But engineering is only part of the equation. The most important thing is the attitude of management. A strong manager acts as the conscience of the employees in the trenches. To be most effective in maintaining high standards of animal treatment, the manager has to be involved enough to care, but not so much that he or she overdoses on the constant death. The managers who are most likely to care and enforce humane handling are most likely to have close associations with animals, or are close to the land.

I am often asked how I can care about animals and be involved in their slaughter. People forget that nature can be harsh. Death at the slaughter plant is quicker and less painful than death in the wild. Lions dining on the guts of a live animal is much worse in my opinion. The animals we raise for food would have never lived at all if we had not raised them. I feel that our relationship with animals must be symbiotic. In nature there are many examples of symbiosis. For example, ants raise aphids and use them as "dairy cows." The ants feed the aphids and in return they provide a sugar substance. It is important that our relationship with farm animals is reciprocal. We owe animals a decent life and a painless death.

I have observed that the people who are completely out of touch with nature are the most afraid of death, and places such as slaughter houses. I was moved by Birute Galdikas's book on her research on orangutans. The people in the Borneo rain forests live as a part of nature and have a totally different view of life and death. To the native people, "death is not separate from life." In the jungle they see death every day. Birute states, "For me, as for most middle-class North Americans death was just a tremor far down, far away at the end of a very long road, not something to be lived with every hour of every single day."

Many people attempt to deny the reality of their own mortality. When I designed my first system I had to look my own mortality straight in the eye. I live each day as if I could die tomorrow. I want to make the most of each day and do things to make the world a better place.

28 A Major Change

Temple Grandin

In this article Temple Grandin notes that progress was made in both handling and stunning from 1997 to 1999, largely through the decision of two fast-food companies to audit U.S. plants to make sure they complied with industry guidelines. Grandin describes the animal welfare problems with transporting sick or weak animals. The increase in the numbers of such animals indicates to Grandin that producers may be pushing animals beyond their biological limits. She stresses the importance of continually monitoring animal welfare, using vocalization as an objective measure.

I have worked as a consultant to the meat industry since the early 1970s. I've been in more than 300 slaughter plants in the United States, Canada, Mexico, Europe, Australia, New Zealand, and South America. During the course of my career, I've seen many changes take place, but I'm going to focus in this paper on my work to improve conditions for the slaughter of cattle and calves and later address transport and other animal-handling issues.

[. . .]

I saw more improvement in both handling and stunning from 1997 to 1999 than I had seen previously in my entire career. Two fast-food companies started auditing U.S. plants during 1999 to make sure they complied with the American Meat Institute Guidelines (Grandin 1997c). Both federally inspected beef and pork plants were scored objectively. Many plants now have better stunner maintenance, and electric prod usage has been greatly reduced. One company audited forty-one beef plants in 1999; I was present at about half of the audits. By the end of 1999, ninety percent of beef plants were stunning 95 percent of the cattle they processed with one shot: 37 percent were stunning 99 percent to 100 percent with one shot (Grandin 2000b). If the first shot missed, the animal was immediately restunned. (This was a big improvement over performance noted in the 1996 USDA survey [Grandin 1997a, b].) Large flags were being used to move pigs, and a piece of plastic on a stick was being used to move cattle. These devices had replaced many electric prods.

In beef production, plants were scored on percentage of cattle stunned with one shot, insensibility on the bleed rail, and vocalization during handling. Vocalization (moos and bellows) is a sensitive indicator of welfare-related problems such as excessive electric prod use, slipping and falling, missed stunner shots, and excessive pressure from a restraint device (Grandin 1998a, b).

Researchers have found that vocalization in both cattle and pigs is correlated with physiological indicators of stress (Dunn 1990; Warriss *et al.* 1994; White *et al.* 1995). Vocalization is also correlated with pain (Watts and Stookey 1998; Weary *et al.* 1998). Vocalization scoring can pinpoint handling problems. Beef plants with good handling practices will have 3 percent or less of their cattle vocalizing during handling in the stunning chute (Grandin 1998b). (To keep scoring simple, vocalization is scored on a "yes" and "no" basis—a cow either vocalizes or it does not. Vocalization in the yards where cattle are standing undisturbed is not scored.) In 1999, seventy-four percent of forty-two U.S. beef plants had vocalization scores of 3 percent or less for cattle. In 1996 only 43 percent of the plants had a vocalization score of 3 percent or less.

Excessive electric prod use, due to cattle balking, had raised vocalization scores to as high as 17 percent at some plants.

Vocalization scoring can be used to chart handling improvement within a plant. It also works well on feedlots and ranches. Vocalization scores will often be higher than 3 percent when animals are ear-tagged on ranches or feedlots. In contrast, it is easy to have a 0 percent vocalization rate for animals moving through the chutes, being restrained in the squeeze chute, and being vaccinated.

The presence of distractions, which makes cattle balk, makes a 3 percent or less vocalization score almost impossible. The movement of a small chain hanging in a chute, for example, will make an approaching animal stop and impede the flow of the other animals. Lighting a dark restrainer entrance will often improve animal movement. (Information on debugging systems and removing distractions can be found in Grandin 1996, 1998c).

People manage the things that they measure. Bad practices become "normal" if there is no standard to which they can be compared. Vocalization scoring can be used to chart progress as a plant improves its equipment and practices.

[. . .]

Dairy and Pig Industry Problems

The number-one transport problem in the 1970s—and the number-one transport problem today—is loading onto a truck animals who are not fit for transport. The dairy industry has some of the worst such problems. Baby dairy calves, who are too young to walk, are not fit for transport. Emaciated or lame dairy cows are not fit for transport. Downer dairy cows, those who are unable to walk, are more prevalent now than in 1994. Numbers of beef cattle downers have decreased slightly (Roeber *et al.* 2001; Smith *et al.* 1994, 1995). The 1999 audit by Smith *et al.* indicated that 1.5 percent of all culled dairy cows arrived at a slaughter plant down and unable to walk. In the beef industry, 0.77 percent of the cows were downers.

In the past thirty years, although the handling of beef cattle on ranches and feedlots has improved, welfare problems in the transport of old, culled dairy cows have worsened. Genetics is partly to blame. Selection of individuals for milk production has increased the incidence of lameness. John Webster at Bristol University in the United Kingdom states that the typical cow's foot can no longer support its weight. A dairy veterinarian in Florida told me that the incidence and aspects of lameness in dairy cows are horrendous. Leg conformation is heritable, and good conformation will help prevent lameness (Boettcher *et al.* 1998; Van Dorp *et al.* 1998). Slaughter plant managers and truck drivers have reported that dairies that use bovine somatotropin (BST), bovine growth hormone, in their dairy herds sometimes have more thin, weak cows. Administration of BST reduced body condition score (Jordan *et al.* 1991; West *et al.* 1990). Unless the cow is fed very well, it may lose body condition. The degree of body condition reduction is related to the dose of BST.

Single-trait selection of pigs for rapid growth and leanness has created pigs who are more fragile and likely to die during transport. I have observed that death losses during transport have tripled in the 1990s compared with the 1980s. Some hybrid pigs are very excitable, which makes handling them more difficult (Grandin 2000a). These pigs act as though they have high sympathetic nervous system arousal. A tap on the rump will make them squeal. Normal pigs are much less likely to startle. Pigs who are selected solely for productivity may have a loss of disease resistance. Genetic factors affect susceptibility to disease.

One of my biggest concerns is the possibility that producers are pushing animals beyond their biological limits. The pig industry, for example, has repeated most of the mistakes that the broiler-chicken industry made. Genetic traits are linked in unexpected ways. Some pigs grow so fast that they have very weak bones. These pigs have large bulging muscles but are so fragile that livestock insurance companies will not sell transport insurance to producers to cover them. Fortunately, some breeders are now selecting far more "moderate" pigs, which will have fewer problems. [. . .]

Conclusions

Promoting better stockmanship is essential to improving animal welfare. Large meat-buying customers such as fast-food restaurants in the United States and supermarket chains in the United Kingdom can motivate great change by insisting that suppliers uphold better animal welfare standards. The greatest advances of the last thirty years have been the result of company audits. To maintain such progress, handling and stunning must be continually audited, measured, and managed. Handlers tend to revert to rough handling unless they are monitored and managed. An objective scoring system provides a standard that can be upheld. An overworked employee cannot do a good job of taking care of animals. Good stockmanship requires adequate staffing levels. More efforts are also needed to address problems of faulty stunning equipment, ever-increasing line speed, and enforcement of the Humane Slaughter Act when violations occur.

Attitudes can be changed, and that change can improve both animal welfare and productivity.

References

Boettcher, P. J., J. C. Dekkers, L. O. Warnick, and S. J. Wells. 1998. Genetic analysis of lameness in cattle. *Journal of Dairy Science* 81: 1148–56.

Dunn, C. S. 1990. Stress reactions of cattle undergoing ritual slaughter using two methods of restraint. *Veterinary Record* 126: 522–5.

Grandin, T. 1996. Factors that impede animal movement at slaughter plants. *Journal of the American Veterinary Medical Association* 209: 757–9.

———. 1997a. Assessment of stress during handling and transport. *Journal of Animal Science* 75: 249–57.

———. 1997b. *Survey of handling and stunning in federally inspected beef, pork, veal, and sheep slaughter plants*. ARS Research Project No. 3602–32000–002–08G. Washington, DC: U.S. Department of Agriculture.

———. 1997c. *Good management practices for animal handling and stunning*. Washington, DC: American Meat Institute.

———. 1998a. Objective scoring of animal handling and stunning practices in slaughter plants. *Journal of the American Veterinary Medical Association* 212: 36–93.

———. 1998b. The feasibility of using vocalization scoring as an indicator of poor welfare during slaughter. *Applied Animal Behavior Science* 56: 121–8.

———. 1998c. Solving livestock handling problems in slaughter plants. In *Animal welfare and meat science*, ed. N. G. Gregory. Wallingford, UK: CAB International.

———. 2000a. *Livestock handling and transport*. Second Edition. Wallingford, UK: CAB International.

———. 2000b. 1999 audits of stunning and handling in federally inspected beef and pork plants. Paper presented at the American Meat Institute 2000 Conference on Handling and Stunning, Kansas City, MO.

Jordan, D. C., A. A. Aquilar, J. D. Olson, C. Bailey, G. F. Hartnell, and K. S. Madsen. 1991. Effects of recombinant methionyl bovine somatrophic (sometribove) in high-producing cow's milk three times a day. *Journal of Dairy Science* 74: 220–6.

Roeber, D. L., P. D. Mies, C. D. Smith, K. E. Belk, T. G. Field, J. D. Tatum, J. A. Scanga, and G. C. Smith. 2001. National market cow and bull beef quality audit: 1999: A survey of producer-related defects in market cows and bulls. *Journal of Animal Science* 79: 658–65.

Smith, G. C., J. B. Morgan, J. D. Tatum, C. C. Kukay, M. T. Smith, T. D. Schnell, and G. G. Hilton. 1994. *Improving the consistency and competitiveness of non-fed beef; and improving the salvage value of cull cows and bulls*. The final report of the National Cattlemen's Beef Association. Fort Collins: Colorado State University.

Smith, G. C. et al. 1995. Improving the quality, consistency, competitiveness, and market share of beef: A blueprint for total quality management in the beef industry. *The Final Report of the National Beef Quality Audit*. Fort Collins: Colorado State University.

Van Dorp, T. E., J. C. M. Dekkers, S. W. Martin, and J. P. Noordhuizen. 1998. Genetic parameters of health disorders and relationships with 305-day milk yield and information traits in registered dairy cows. *Journal of Dairy Science* 81: 2264–70.

Warriss, P. D., S. N. Brown, and S. J. M. Adams. 1994. Relationship between subjective and objective assessment of stress at slaughter and meat quality in pigs. *Meat Science* 38: 329–40.

Watts, J. M., and J. M. Stookey. 1998. Effects of restraint and branding on rates and acoustic parameters of vocalization in beef cattle. *Applied Animal Behavior Science* 62: 125–35.

Weary, D. M., L. A. Braithwaite, and D. Fraser. 1998. Vocal response to pain in piglets. *Applied Animal Behavior Science* 56: 161–72.

West, J. W., K. Bondair, and J. C. Johnson. 1990. Effect of bovine somatotropin on milk yield and composition, body weight, and condition score of Holstein and Jersey cows. *Journal of Dairy Science* 73: 1062–8.

White, R. G., J. A. DeShazer, C. J. Tressler, G. M. Borcher, S. Davey, A. Waninge, A. M. Parkhurst, M. J. Milanuk, and E. T. Clems. 1995. Vocalizations and physiological response of pigs during castration with and without anesthetic. *Journal of Animal Science* 73: 381–6.

29 Putting Meat on the Table

Industrial Farm Animal Production in America: A Report of the Pew Commission on Industrial Farm Animal Production

The Pew Commission heard approximately 54 hours of testimony from stakeholders and experts, received technical reports from academics from institutions across the country, and visited operations in five states. Over the past 50 years the production of farm animals for food has shifted from the traditional family farm system to a more concentrated system in which large numbers of animals are confined in enormous operations.

This system has resulted in the disappearance of the open market and has greatly affected the living conditions for farm animals and employees. Many Americans until recently were not aware of these changes. The increase in antibiotic-resistant bacteria, air quality and water quality problems, a grave outlook for rural communities, and animal welfare problems require attention. The Commission report enumerates the changes which should be made.

The Pew Commission on Industrial Farm Animal Production was established through a grant from The Pew Charitable Trusts to The Johns Hopkins Bloomberg School of Public Health to recommend solutions to the problems created by concentrated animal feeding operations in four primary areas: public health, the environment, animal welfare, and rural communities. The Commission heard approximately 54 hours of testimony from stakeholders and experts, received technical reports from academics from institutions across the country, and visited operations in Iowa, California, North Carolina, Arkansas, and Colorado, to gather information on each of the subject areas. In addition, each of the Commissioners brought his or her own unique experiences and expertise to bear during Commission deliberations.

Over the past 50 years, the production of farm animals for food has shifted from the traditional, extensive, decentralized family farm system to a more concentrated system with fewer producers, in which large numbers of animals are confined in enormous operations. While we are raising approximately the same number of swine as we did in 1950, for example, we are doing so on significantly fewer, far larger farms, with dramatically fewer farm workers. This production model—sometimes called industrial farm animal production—is characterized by confining large numbers of animals of the same species in relatively small areas, generally in enclosed facilities that restrict movement. In many cases, the waste produced by the animals is eliminated through liquid systems and stored in open pit lagoons.

The industrial food animal production (IFAP) system, as it exists today, too often concentrates economic power in the hands of the large companies that process and sell the animal products. Until very recently, most people continued to think that their food still came from small farms.

While increasing the speed of production, the intensive confinement production system creates a number of problems. These include contributing to the increase in the pool of antibiotic-resistant bacteria because of the overuse of antibiotics; air quality problems; the contamination of rivers, streams, and coastal waters with concentrated animal waste; animal welfare problems, mainly as a result of the extremely close quarters in which the animals are housed; and significant shifts in the social structure and economy of many farming regions throughout the country. It was on these areas that the Commission focused its attention.

As previously mentioned, one of the most serious unintended consequences of IFAP is the growing public health threat of these types of facilities. In addition to the contribution of IFAP to the major threat of antimicrobial resistance (Smith et al., 2007; Smith et al., 2002), IFAP facilities can be harmful to workers, neighbors, and even those living far from the facilities through air and water pollution and via the spread of disease. Workers in and neighbors of IFAP facilities experience high levels of respiratory problems, including asthma (Donham and Gustafson, 1982; Donham et al., 1989; Donham et al., 1995; Donham et al., 1985; Donham et al., 2007; Merchant et al., 2005; Mirabelli et al., 2006a; Mirabelli et al., 2006b; Sigurdarson and Kline, 2006; Thu, 2002). In addition, workers can serve as a bridging population, transmitting animal-borne diseases to a wider population (Myers et al., 2006; Saenz et al., 2006). A lack of appropriate treatment of enormous amounts of waste may result in contamination of nearby waters with harmful levels of nutrients and toxins, as well as bacteria, fungi, and viruses (Nolan and Hitt, 2006; Peak et al., 2007), all of which can affect the health of people both near and far from IFAP facilities.

Antibiotics are one type of antimicrobial. Antimicrobials are substances that kill bacteria or suppress their multiplication or growth, and include antibiotics, some minerals, metals, and synthetic agents.

The use of antibiotics for growth promotion began with the poultry industry in the 1940s when it discovered that the use of tetracycline-fermentation by-products resulted in improved growth (Stokstad, 1954; Stokstad and Jukes, 1958–1959). Since then, the practice of adding low levels of antibiotics and growth hormones to stimulate growth and improve production and performance parameters has been common among IFAP operations for all species. Because any use of antibiotics results in resistance, this widespread use of low-level antibiotics in animals, along with use in treating humans, contributes to the growing pool of antimicrobial resistance in the environment.

The threat from antimicrobial resistance became more apparent in the 1990s as the number of cases of drug-resistant infections increased in humans. The World Health Organization (WHO) Report on Infectious Diseases published in 2000 expressed alarm at the spread of multidrug–resistant infectious disease agents and pointed to food as a major source of antimicrobial-resistant bacteria. Since the discovery of the growth-promoting and disease-fighting capabilities of antibiotics, farmers, fish-farmers, and livestock producers have used antimicrobials. This ongoing and often low-level dosing for disease prevention and growth inevitably results in the development of resistance in bacteria in or near livestock because a selective pressure that does not kill fosters resistance (WHO, 2000).

While it is difficult to measure what percent of resistant infections in humans are caused by antimicrobial use in agriculture as opposed to other settings, it can be assumed that the wider the use of antimicrobials, the greater the chance for the development of resistance. Reports on the amount of antibiotics used in animals range from 17.8 to 24.6 million pounds per year. The Union of Concerned Scientists estimates that 70% of the antibiotics used in the United States annually are used in farm animals (Mellon et al., 2001).

As the amount of antimicrobials present in the general environmental pool becomes greater, so too does the chance of resistance developing within many different bacterial populations. This is due, in part, to the way resistance is spread among capable bacteria. For example, many bacteria live in the human digestive tract or on human skin. These are not normally harmful (and are often helpful). However, these harmless bacteria may still be capable of passing resistance to other bacteria that *are* harmful, or could then *become* harmful.

Feed formulation further influences risks because the feeds supplied to confined animal populations are significantly different from the foraged feeds traditionally available to poultry, swine, or cattle.

IFAP not only causes concerns about the health of the animals present, but the basic production model creates concerns with respect to human health as well. Health risks are a function of exposure, with those engaged directly in livestock production typically having more frequent and more concentrated exposures to chemical or infectious agents, and others, such as those involved in support services, having lower rates of exposure. Health risks may extend far from the IFAP facility, however.

Groundwater contamination, for example, can extend throughout the aquifer, affecting drinking water supplies far from the source of contamination. Infectious agents arising in IFAP facilities may be transmissible from person to person in a community setting and well beyond. An infectious agent that originates at an IFAP facility may persist through meat processing and contaminate a consumer meat product, resulting in a serious disease far from the IFAP facility.

Agricultural workers may serve as a bridging population between their communities and animal confinement facilities. Because it is categorized as an agricultural process, IFAP is largely exempt from state and federal industrial exposure monitoring, inspection, injury–disease reporting, and surveillance. Without monitoring, it is extremely difficult for public health officials to reduce the occupational health risk associated with IFAP.

The toxic gases and organic dusts associated with IFAP facilities have the potential to produce upper respiratory irritation in confinement facility workers. The emissions from confinement facilities, however, may affect communities proximate to those facilities, as well as populations far away from these operations. In particular, the elderly, those with compromised respiratory systems or chronic conditions that limit their mobility, and children are at most risk of asthma and other respiratory illnesses. Depression and other symptoms have also been attributed to emissions from such facilities (Schiffman et al., 1995).

As with the public health impact, much of IFAP's environmental impact stems from the tremendous quantities of animal waste that are concentrated in and around IFAP facilities. Animal waste in such volumes may exceed the capacity of the land to absorb the nutrients and attenuate pathogens. Thus, what could be a valuable by-product becomes a waste that must be disposed of in an appropriate manner.

In addition, many IFAP facilities have not been sited in areas that are best able to cope with these enormous amounts of nutrients and pathogens. Many are found in vulnerable locations, such as on flood plains or close to communities that utilize well water.

The annual production of manure produced by animal confinement facilities exceeds that produced by humans by at least three times (EPA, 2007). Manure in such large quantities carries excess nutrients, chemicals, and microorganisms that find their way into waterways, lakes, groundwater, soils, and airways. Excess and inappropriate land application of untreated animal waste on cropland contributes to excessive nutrient loading and, ultimately, eutrophication of surface waters.

IFAP runoff also carries antibiotics and hormones, pesticides, and heavy metals. Pesticides are used to control insect infestations and fungal growth. Heavy metals, especially zinc and copper, are added as micronutrients to the animal diet. Tylosin, a widely used antibiotic (macrolide) for disease treatment and growth promotion in swine, beef cattle, and poultry production, is an example of a veterinary pharmaceutical that decays rapidly in the environment but can still be found in surface waters of agricultural watersheds (Song et al., 2007).

Air quality degradation is another problem in and around IFAP facilities, due to localized releases of toxic gases, odorous substances, particulates, and bioaerosols containing a variety of microorganisms and human pathogens (Merchant et al., 2008).

Other environmental issues associated with IFAP include high levels of resource use. IFAP requires a large amount of water for irrigation of animal feed crops, as well as cleaning of many buildings and waste management systems. Much of this water comes from finite groundwater sources that recharge slowly or not at all, and are in demand for human needs. Greenhouse gas emissions from all livestock operations, including IFAP facilities, account for 18 percent of all human-caused greenhouse gas emissions, exceeding the emissions caused from the transportation sector (Steinfeld et al., 2006). Greenhouse gases, primarily methane, carbon dioxide, and nitrous oxide, are produced by animals during the digestion process in the gut. Additional emissions result from degradation processes occurring in uncovered waste lagoons and digesters.

IFAP, as practiced today, is also extremely energy intensive and requires disproportionately large inputs of fossil fuels, industrial fertilizers, and other synthetic chemicals. For example, the ratio of fossil fuel energy inputs per unit of food energy produced averages 3:1 for all US agricultural products combined. For industrially produced meat products, the ratio can be as high as 35:1 (beef produced in feedlots generally has a particularly unfavorable energy balance) (Horrigan et al., 2002).

In the IFAP system, each individual farm animal requires less feed, produces less manure, and reaches market weight far faster than farm animals produced on the small family farm of 50 years ago, which might suggest a *lesser* impact on the environment. Yet IFAP stands in sharp contrast to the more pastoral animal farming methods it has replaced by virtue of the emphasis placed on producing large numbers of animals in close confinement, as rapidly and as cheaply as possible. Until IFAP, agricultural practice and animal husbandry evolved over more than 10,000 years, and proved to be more or less sustainable as measured by the agricultural inputs and outputs and ecosystem health. IFAP systems, on the other hand, are a recent development, dating back approximately 50 years. Rather than seeking a balance between the natural productivity of the land to produce crops to feed animals and absorb wastes produced by those animals, the industrial model concentrates on growing animals as units of protein production. Inputs of feed and feed additives containing antimicrobials ensure that the animals make it to market weight in the shortest period of time possible. Both animals and their waste are concentrated and usually exceed the capacity of the land to produce feed or absorb the waste. Consequently, the rapid ascendance of IFAP has produced an expanding array of deleterious environmental effects on local and regional water, air, and soil resources.

The Commission's recommendations include focusing on appropriate regulation of IFAP facilities in order to prevent further degradation of air, water, and soils and to minimize the impact on adjacent communities.

IFAP methods for raising food animals have produced concern and debate over just what constitutes a decent life for animals and what kind of life we owe the animals in our care. Physical health as measured by absence of some diseases or predation, for example, may be enhanced through confinement, since the animals may not be exposed to certain infectious diseases or sources of injury that would be encountered if the animals were raised outside of confinement. It is clear, however, that good animal welfare can no longer be assumed based only on productivity or the absence of disease. The Commission looked at the issue of animal welfare from both a scientific and an ethical point of view.

The intensive confinement practices that are common in IFAP so severely restrict movement and natural behaviors that the animal may not be able to turn around or walk at all. Gestation and restrictive farrowing crates for sows and battery cages for laying hens are examples of this type of intensive confinement. The stress that results from these situations can result in animals that are more susceptible to disease and more likely to spread disease (Barham et al., 2002; Jones et al., 2001; Kanitz et al., 2002; Losinger and Heinrichs, 1997; Silbergeld et al., 2008). In addition, extremely large group size in an extremely confined area, such as may be seen in broiler houses, can cause the same types of problems. There are alternatives to these types of production systems, including "cage-free" systems for laying hens, and hoop barns, pens, and several less restrictive farrowing systems for hogs. These alternatives can also attenuate many of the health and environmental problems caused by IFAP by naturally spreading the manure over the land in manageable amounts and lessening the animal's susceptibility to disease (and therefore the need for much antibiotic use).

Increasing public awareness of the conditions prevalent in confinement agriculture has led to increased consumer demand for changes in treatment. In anticipation of potentially stronger measures imposed through the regulatory process, the food animal industry has begun to adopt minimum standards of animal treatment codified in voluntary standards that are widely published. In some cases, a third party certifies them. Such standards, however, rarely address the larger concerns for animal well-being relating to freedom of movement and humane treatment in confinement systems and slaughter.

Confinement animals are generally raised indoors and, in some cases (e.g., poultry, laying hens, hogs), the group size when raised indoors is larger than the group size when raised outdoors. In other cases (e.g., veal crates or gestation crates for sows), animals are separated and confined to spaces that provide for only minimal movement. The fundamental welfare concern is the ability of the animal to express natural behaviors: rooting and social behavior for hogs, walking or lying on natural materials, and enough floor space to move around with some freedom at the minimum. Gestation crates, the most restrictive farrowing crates, battery cages, and other intensive confinement systems fail to allow for even these minimal natural behaviors.

Recently, animal scientists in Europe published a set of standards to define basic animal welfare measures. These include five major categories, which must be taken in their entirety: feeding regimens that ensure that animals do not experience prolonged hunger or thirst; housing that ensures resting comfort, a good thermal environment, and freedom of movement; health management that prevents physical injury, disease, and pain; and appropriate means to allow animals to express non-harmful social behaviors and other, species-specific natural behaviors (European Union Animal Welfare Quality Program: http://www.welfarequality.net/everyone/36059) (FAWC, 2007). The animal industry has resisted codifying these standards as common practice for fear of adding new costs to animal production processes.

The Commission believes that ethical treatment of animals raised for food is essential to, and consistent with, achieving a safe and sustainable system for producing food animals. Practices that restrict natural motion, such as sow gestation crates, induce high levels of stress in the animals and threaten their health, which in turn may threaten human health. There is growing public concern for ethical treatment of farm animals that will lead to new laws and regulations governing farm animal treatment unless the industry voluntarily adopts third-party, consensus-based standards for animal well-being. The recommendations made by the Commission are intended to define ethical treatment of animals and what constitutes a decent life for food animals.

Life in rural America has long been challenged by persistent poverty. The causes are many, but among them is the lack of economic diversity in rural economies. Workers have few options in the event of a plant closure or other dislocation, and unemployment rates are high. Consequently, local economic development officials frequently consider IFAP an attractive new source of economic opportunity. But higher rates of poverty are equally prevalent in areas of high IFAP concentration, an association confirmed by Durrenberger and Thu's finding of higher rates of food stamp use in Iowa counties with industrialized hog production (Durrenberger and Thu, 1996).

The industrialization of American agriculture has transformed the character of agriculture itself and, in so doing, the face of rural America. The family-owned farm producing a diverse mix of crops and food animals is largely gone as an economic entity, replaced by ever-larger industrial farms producing just one animal species or growing just one crop, and rural communities have fared poorly. Industrialization has been accompanied by increasing farm size and gross farm sales, lower family income, higher poverty rates, lower retail sales, lower housing quality, and lower wages for farm workers.

As the food animal industry shifted to a system with a reduced number of companies for livestock producers to sell to, as well as one controlled by production contracts, economic power shifted from farmers to livestock processors. Farmers relinquished their once-autonomous animal husbandry decision-making authority in exchange for contracts that provide assured payment but require substantial capital investment. Once the commitment is made to such capital investment, many farmers have *no* choice but to continue to produce until the loan is paid off. Such contracts make it nearly impossible for there to be open and competitive markets for most hog and poultry producers, who must enter into contracts with the so-called integrators (meat packing companies) if they are to sell their product.

Although the proponents of the industrialization of livestock agriculture point to the increased economic efficiency of IFAP operations, the Commission is concerned that the benefits may not accrue in the same way to the rural communities where these operations exist. The Commission's technical report on economics in swine production showed that the current method of intensive swine production is only economically efficient due to the externalization of costs associated with waste management. In fact, industrialization leading to corporate ownership actually draws investment and wealth from the communities in which specific IFAP facilities are located (Abeles-Allison and Connor, 1990).

Merely tweaking our mono-culture confinement farm animal production methods is not likely to reverse the negative impacts on public health, environment, animal welfare, and rural America. At the same time, the Commission believes that there are practical solutions to these problems that can start immediately and will ensure that the productivity of farm animal production can be maintained well into the future. Recommendations address criteria for proper siting of IFAP facilities, increasing market competition, and fairness in production contracts in an effort to improve life in rural America. The Commission does not believe that the nation's demand for food can be met by turning back the clock to the 1950s. At the same time, there is much that can be done to address the problems that industrialization of agriculture has brought. The system of the future may be a mix of small and medium-sized extensive operations as well as large, more humane, sustainable intensive operations such as hoop barns in swine production and intensive rotational grazing in beef production.

There is increasing urgency to chart a new course. Our energy, water, and climate resources are undergoing dramatic changes that, in the judgment of the Commissioners, will require agriculture to transition to much more biologically diverse systems, organized into biological synergies that exchange energy, improve soil quality, and conserve water and other resources.

IFAP systems are largely unregulated, and many practices common to this method of production threaten public health, the environment, animal health and well-being, and rural communities. The use of antibiotics in animals without a diagnosed illness, the mismanagement of the large volumes of farm waste, and the treatment of animals in intensive operations are all of deep concern. The Commission's six primary recommendations address these concerns.

Phase Out and then Ban the Nontherapeutic Use of Antimicrobials

The use of antibiotics and other antimicrobials as growth promoters and in the absence of a diagnosed illness in industrial animal operations is a common practice. In 1998, the National Academies of Science (NAS) estimated that antibiotic-resistant bacteria increased health care costs by a minimum of $5 billion annually, or approximately $13 per person per year (Institute of Medicine, 1998). The next year, the NAS estimated that eliminating all antimicrobials as feed additives would cost each American consumer less than $10 per year (NAS, 1999).

The Commission recommends phasing out and then banning the nontherapeutic use of antimicrobials in food animal production. The Commission defines "nontherapeutic" as any use of antimicrobials in food animals in the absence of clinical disease or documented disease exposure.

The Commission recommends that the first step in this process should be an immediate ban on any new approval of antimicrobials for nontherapeutic uses in food animals and retroactive investigation of antimicrobials previously approved.

Improve Disease Monitoring and Tracking

A voluntary animal tracking system, called the National Animal Identification System (NAIS), has been implemented by the Animal Plant and Health Inspection Service (APHIS) of the United States Department of Agriculture. The goal of the NAIS voluntary system is a 48-hour track back to identify exposures, since that time frame is vital to containing the spread of infection (USDA and APHIS, 2006).

The first two phases of the NAIS are the registration of premises and individual animals or units of animals using a US Animal Identification Number (USAIN) (USDA, 2005). According to the USDA, the USAIN will evolve into the sole national numbering system for the official identification of individual animals in the United States. The Commission views animal identification as an important public health issue. The need for a rapid, accurate trace-back system to protect public health in the event of a disease outbreak is critical.

The Commission recommends the implementation of a disease monitoring program for food animals with a 48-hour track back of those animals at every stage of production in a fully integrated and robust database. A mandatory premise and individual animal or lot registration should be in effect by 2009, with an animal tracing capability in place by 2010. The tracking system should follow food animals from birth to consumption, including movement, illness, breeding, feeding practices implemented, slaughter condition and location, and point of sale.

Federal agency oversight of all aspects of this tracking system with stringent protections from lawsuits for producers is needed. Special funding allocated to small farms to facilitate their participation in the national tracing system is vital.

Improve IFAP Regulation

Waste from IFAP operations contains both desirable and undesirable by-products. Farm waste can be a soil-enriching nutrient when applied in the correct amount and with the right method. But undesirable components of animal waste include pathogenic organisms, antibiotic-resistant bacteria, viruses, industrial chemicals, and heavy metals.

As IFAP facilities have become more concentrated in specific geographic areas around the country, dealing with waste issues has become critical. New regulations must address zoning and siting of IFAP facilities with particular consideration of topography, climate, and population density of a proposed region. New IFAP laws and regulations must mandate development of sustainable waste handling and treatment systems that can utilize the beneficial components but render the less desirable components benign.

The Commission recommends that IFAP be regulated as rigorously as other industrial operations and that a new system of laws and regulations for dealing with farm waste replace the inflexible, patchwork, and broken systems that exist today. Congress and the federal government should work together to formulate laws and regulations outlining baseline waste handling standards for IFAP facilities. These standards would address the minimum level of mandatory IFAP facility regulation and would outline what IFAP regulation states must carry out to prevent pollution and to protect public health and the environment.

Phase out Intensive Confinement

Animals that are raised for human consumption, even under the best of circumstances, are subject to treatment at some point during their lives that causes them pain. Over the past 50 years, there has been a gradual movement away from raising animals in extensive, pasture-based systems to more intensive, confined systems. Not all of the systems that employ such practices are classified as intensive confinement, which can occur in facilities that are not big enough to be classified in that manner. Although the result of this change has been improved speed of production, conditions in many facilities are particularly harsh and stressful, and in many cases may cause undue suffering throughout much of an animal's entire life.

Unbeknownst to most Americans, no federal regulations protect animals while on the farm. The Humane Methods of Slaughter Act was enacted to ensure that animals are rendered "insensible to pain" before slaughter, but poultry are not included under its protection despite the fact that more than 95 percent of the land animals killed for food in this country are birds.

Industry standards for production systems and animal care are generally guided by economics. Welfare issues, such as animal stress and suffering, might be considered in rearing, but only in the context of how they impact performance, efficiency, or profitability. Industrial livestock production systems have often deleteriously affected the welfare of virtually every species of farm animal in the United States (including all forms of poultry [chickens, turkeys, ducks, and geese], dairy cows, veal calves, swine, sheep, and lambs) and raise serious ethical questions regarding the way in which these animals are treated.

The Commission recommends the phase-out, within ten years, of all intensive confinement systems that restrict natural movement and normal behaviors, including swine gestation crates, restrictive swine farrowing crates, cages used to house multiple egg-laying chickens, commonly referred to as battery cages, and the tethering or individual housing of calves for the production of white veal. In addition, the Commission recommends the end to force-feeding of fowl to produce foie gras, tail docking of dairy cattle, and forced molting of laying hens by feed removal. Due to the capital investment in these intensive confinement systems by many contract producers, particularly in swine production, the Commission recommends targeted assistance be made available to contract producers to facilitate the conversion from intensive confinement systems, either through accelerated depreciation or some other mechanism.

Increase Competition in the Livestock Market

The transformation of rural society and the farm economy in many agricultural regions of the country over the past three or four decades has been profound. With the increasing consolidation of agriculture, including livestock production, and the transition to ever larger units of production, small to mid-size family farms in which agricultural activities account for the bulk of family income have rapidly disappeared throughout the nation. Each year, the number of people engaged in agriculture in America grows smaller. What was once a richly textured way of life supported by countless small-town businesses and a corresponding network of health, education, and social services that were once prevalent throughout many rural areas has been dramatically altered. Quite literally, rural life in many parts of the nation has withered, leaving once thriving farm communities with an increasingly ghostlike appearance.

There are multiple factors behind the changing face of rural American society, the rise of industrialized agriculture being only one. However, the increasing concentration and integration of the livestock production process from breeding and insemination to slaughter, processing, and the distribution and sale of meat and dairy products raises issues associated with competitive fairness and economic life in rural areas that continue to spark passionate debate throughout rural America, and are the subject of increasing rancor and confrontation.

The Commission believes that vigorous market competition is of vital importance to consumers and the overall health of the American economy. The nation benefits from an open, competitive, and fair market where the values of democracy, freedom, transparency, and efficiency are in balance.

The Commission recommends the vigorous enforcement of current federal antitrust laws to restore competition in the farm animal market. If enforcing existing antitrust laws is not effective in restoring competition, further legislative remedies should be considered, such as more transparency in price reporting and limiting the ability of integrators to control the supply of animals for slaughter.

Improve Research in Animal Agriculture

IFAP can have a dramatic impact on health, on the environment, and certainly on the lives of the animals themselves. As the Commission traveled across the country, meeting with experts in animal agriculture, the general public, and stakeholders, it heard the recurring theme of the need for independently funded research. The strongest comments came from the academic research community.

The three main areas of concern were:

- Lack of public funding for research into IFAP issues
- Increase in research funding by members of the animal agriculture industry
- Lack of transparency in funding sources in much agricultural research

With declining public research dollars, investigators turn to other funding sources. Increasingly, those sources are the giant multinational agricultural companies that have a vested interest in positive findings. Certainly, companies may want to fund research to help them improve their business, but if such funding is the major source for research, that funding source should be reported. The same may be said if an advocacy organization is the majority funder.

This transparency is particularly important with university extension programs. These programs are the "on the ground" location where research is "translated" into practice. Often, a farmer may be told that something is "best," without any awareness of who funded the research that backs that statement. They may then employ, in good faith, a practice that is not "best," but instead contributes to the environmental, public health, animal welfare, and community issues.

Increasing public research dollars into IFAP should be a major focus, since this form of animal agriculture impacts so many aspects of life. The Commission's effort to gather unbiased information was affected by the industry's undue influence on academic researchers. It is extremely unfortunate that this is the case, because with appropriate independent funding, science may be able to solve many of the problems resulting from IFAP.

Conclusion

Through public testimony from stakeholders, site visits, presentations from experts, technical reports, and the experience and expertise of the Commissioners themselves, the Commission has compiled these recommendations (as well as the more detailed recommendations found in the full report) for improving the sustainability of animal agriculture into the future. The Commission firmly believes that many of the problems associated with IFAP are unintentional, but that does not mitigate the need to move forward in a positive direction. Failure to address these issues will only result in a further lack of confidence in the animal agriculture industry, increased environmental damage, worsening public health, dismal animal welfare, and a grave outlook for rural communities. In this age of increased awareness of the need for economically and environmentally sustainable endeavors, animal agriculture cannot be left behind. The Commission applauds the efforts of many enterprises toward this goal and is certain that a better system is around the corner. The recommendations of the Commission provide examples of steps that should be taken to achieve this larger goal.

References

Abeles-Allison M, Connor I. (1990). *An analysis of local benefits and costs of Michigan hog operations experiencing environmental conflicts.* Department of Agricultural Economics, Michigan State University: East Lansing.

Barham AR, Barham BL, Johnson AK, Allen DM, Blanton JR, Miller MF (2002). Effects of the transportation of beef cattle from the feed yard to the packing plant on prevalence levels of *Escherichia coli* O157 and *Salmonella* 5pp. *Journal of Food Protection* 65: 280–83.

Donham K, Gustafson K (1982). Human occupational hazards from swine confinement. *Annals of the American Conference of Governmental Industrial Hygienists* 2: 137–42.

Donham K, Haglind P, Peterson Y, Rylander R, Belin L (1989). Environmental and health studies of workers in Swedish swine buildings. *British Journal of Industrial Medicine* 46: 31–7.

Donham K, Reynolds S, Whitten P, Merchant J, Burmeister L, Popendorf W (1995). Respiratory dysfunction in swine production facility workers: Dose-response relationships of environmental exposures and pulmonary function. *American Journal of Industrial Medicine* 27: 405–18.

Donham K, Scallon L, Popendorf W, Treuhaft M, Roberts R (1985). Characterization of dusts collected from swine confinement buildings. *American Industrial Hygiene Association Journal* 46: 658–61.

Donham KJ, Wing S, Osterberg D, Flora JL, Hodne C, Thu KM, Thorne PS (2007). Community health and socioeconomic issues surrounding concentrated animal feeding operations. *Environ Health Perspect* 115: 317–20.

Durrenberger PE, Thu KM (1996). The expansion of large scale hog farming in Iowa: The applicability of Goldschmidt's findings fifty years later. *Human Organization* 55: 411–15.

EPA (2007). US EPA 2008 Compliance And Enforcement: Clean Water Act. pp 1–3.

FAWC (2007). Five Freedoms, FAWC (ed).

Horrigan L, Lawrence RS, Walker P (2002). How sustainable agriculture can address the environmental and human health harms of industrial agriculture. *Environmental Health Perspectives* 110: 445–56.

Institute of Medicine (1998). *Antimicrobial drug resistance: Issues and options*. National Academy Press: Washington.

Jones PH, Roe JM, Miller BG (2001). Effects of stressors on immune parameters and on the faccal shedding of enterotoxigenic *Escherichia coli* in piglets following experimental inoculation. *Research in Veterinary Science* 70: 9–17.

Kanitz E, Tuchscherer M, Tuchscherer A, Stabenow B, Manteuffel G (2002). Neuroendocrine and immune responses to acute endotoxemia in suckling and weaned piglets. *Biology of the Neonate* 81: 203–09.

Losinger WC, Heinrichs AJ (1997). Management practices associated with high mortality among preweaned dairy heifers. *Journal of Dairy Research* 64: 1–11.

Mellon MG, Benbrook C, Benbrook KL, Union of Concerned Scientists (2003). *Hogging it: estimates of antimicrobial abuse in livestock*. Union of Concerned Scientists: Cambridge, MA.

Merchant J, Thorne PS, Gray G, Osterberg D, Hornbuckle K, McVey EA (2008). Occupational and Community Health Impacts of Industrial Farm Animal Production. In: *A report to the Pew Commission on Industrial Farm Animal Production*. Pew Commission on Industrial Farm Animal Production: Washington, DC.

Merchant JA, Naleway AL, Svendsen ER, Kelly KM, Burmeister LF, Stromquist AM, Taylor CD, Thorne PS, Reynolds SJ, Sanderson WT, Chrischilles EA (2005). Asthma and farm exposures in a cohort of rural Iowa children. *Environmental Health Perspectives* 113: 350–56.

Mirabelli MC, Wing S, Marshall SW, Wilcosky TC (2006a). Race, poverty, and potential exposure of middle-school students to air emissions from confined swine feeding operations. *Environmental Health Perspectives* 114: 591–96.

Mirabelli MC, Wing S, Marshall SW, Wilcosky TC (2006b). Asthma symptoms among adolescents who attend public schools that are located near confined swine feeding operations. *Pediatrics* 118: 66–75.

Myers KP, Olsen CW, Setterquist SF, Capuano AW, Donham KJ, Thacker EL, Merchant JA, Gray GC (2006). Are swine workers in the United States at increased risk of infection with zoonotic influenza virus? *Clinical Infectious Diseases* 42: 14–20.

NAS (1999). *The use of drugs in food animals: Benefits and risks*. National Academies Press: Washington, DC.

Nolan BT, Hitt KJ (2006). Vulnerability of shallow groundwater and drinking-water wells to nitrate in the United States. *Environmental Science & Technology* 40: 7834–40.

Peak N, Knapp CW, Yang RK, Hanfelt MM, Smith MS, Aga DS, Graham DW (2007). Abundance of six tetracycline resistance genes in wastewater lagoons at cattle feedlots with different antibiotic use strategies. *Environmental Microbiology* 9: 143–51.

Saenz RA, Hethcote HW, Gray GC (2006). Confined animal feeding operations as amplifiers of influenza. *Vector Borne Zoonotic Diseases* 6: 338–46.

Schiffman SS, Miller EA, Suggs MS, Graham BG (1995). The effect of environmental odors emanating from commercial swine operations on the mood of nearby residents. *Brain Research Bulletin* 37: 369–75.

Sigurdarson ST, Kline JN (2006). School proximity to concentrated animal feeding operations and prevalence of asthma in students. *Chest* 129: 1486–91.

Silbergeld E, Graham J, Price L (2008). Antimicrobial Resistance and Human Health. In: *A report to the Pew Commission on Industrial Farm Animal Production*. Pew Commission on Industrial Farm Animal Production: Washington, DC.

Smith DL, Harris AD, Johnson JA, Silbergeld EK, Morris JG, Jr. (2002). Animal antibiotic use has an early but important impact on the emergence of antibiotic resistance in human commensal bacteria. *Proceedings of the National Academy of Sciences of the United States of America* 99: 6434–39.

Smith JL, Drum DJ, Dai Y, Kim JM, Sanchez S, Maurer JJ, Hofacre CL, Lee MD (2007). Impact of antimicrobial usage on antimicrobial resistance in commensal *Escherichia coli* strains colonizing broiler chickens. *Applied Environmental Microbiology* 73: 1404–14.

Song WL, Huang M, Rumbeiha W, Li H (2007). Determination of amprolium, carbadox, monensin, and tylosin in surface water by liquid chromatography/tandem mass spectrometry. *Rapid Communications in Mass Spectrometry* 21: 1944–50.

Steinfeld H, Gerber P, Wassenaar T, Castel V, Rosales M, de Haan C (2006). *Livestock's long shadow—environmental issues and options.* Food and Agriculture Organization of the United Nations: Rome, Italy.

Stokstad EL (1954). Antibiotics in animal nutrition. *Physiological Reviews* 34: 25–51.

Stokstad ELR, Jukes TH (1958–1959). Studies of the growth-promoting effect of antibiotics in chicks on a purified diet. *Antibiotics Annual*: 998–1002.

Thu KM (2002). Public health concerns for neighbors of large-scale swine production operations. *Journal of Agricultural Society and Health* 8: 175–84.

USDA (2005). National Animal Identification System: Draft Strategic Plan.

USDA, APHIS (2006). National Animal Identification System (NAIS).

WHO (2000). Report on Infectious Diseases.

30 The Least Harm Principle May Require that Humans Consume a Diet Containing Large Herbivores, Not a Vegan Diet

Steven L. Davis

Steven L. Davis examines Tom Regan's conclusion that being a vegan is morally required by the animal rights view. Davis points out the large number of animals of the field being killed annually in the production of corn, beans, rice, etc. If pastures were instead used for forage, fewer passages through the field with farm equipment would be necessary. He estimates that significantly fewer animals would die if half of the U.S. land were used for plants for human consumption and half for pasture for cattle.

Although the debate over moral vegetarianism has been going on for millennia (Shapiro, 2000), there has been a resurgence of interest in this issue in the last part of the twentieth century. One of the foundational philosophical works on this subject is *The Case for Animal Rights* (1983). This paper will not critique Regan's theory on animal rights. Rather, for the moment, suppose he is right; animals are subjects-of-a-life with interests of their own that matter as much to them as similar interests matter to humans. Therefore, animals have the right to live their lives without interference from humans. His conclusion follows, therefore, that animal agriculture interferes in the lives of millions of animals annually, so humans are morally obligated to consume a vegan or vegetarian diet. The purpose of this paper is to examine the moral vegan conclusion of Regan's animal rights theory, rather than the rights theory itself. It is also the objective of this paper to examine alternative conclusions. In other words, might there be alternatives to the moral vegetarian conclusion drawn from animal rights theory?

The Concept of Least Harm

As I was thinking about the vegan conclusion, I remembered my childhood on the farm and where our food comes from and how it is produced. Specifically, I remembered riding on farm equipment and seeing mice, gophers, and pheasants in the field that were injured or killed every time we worked the fields. Therefore, I realized that animals of the field are killed in large numbers annually to produce food for humans. Kingsolver (2001) describes these killings very effectively. "I've watched enough harvests to know that cutting a wheat field amounts to more decapitated bunnies under the combine than you would believe." "She stopped speaking when her memory lodged on an old vision from childhood: A raccoon she found just after the hay mower ran it over. She could still see the matted grey fur, the gleaming jaw bone and shock of scattered teeth. . . ." Consequently, a vegan diet doesn't necessarily mean a diet that doesn't interfere in the lives of animals. In fact, production of corn, beans, rice, etc. kills many animals, as this paper will document. So, in 1999, I sent an email to Regan, pointing this out to him. Then I asked him, "What is the morally relevant difference between the animals of the field and those of the farm that makes it acceptable to kill some of them (field mice, etc.) so that humans may eat, but not acceptable to kill others (pigs, etc.) so we may eat?" His reply (Regan, 1999, personal communication) was that we must choose the method of food production that causes the least harm to animals. (I will refer to this concept as the Least Harm Principle, or LHP.) In his book, Regan (1983) calls this the "minimize harm principle" and he describes it in the following way:

> Whenever we find ourselves in a situation where all the options at hand will produce some harm to those who are innocent, we must choose that option that will result in the least total sum of harm.

It seems that Regan is saying that least harm would be done to animals in the production of a plant-based diet, because then at least you wouldn't be killing both the animals of the farm and those of the field, thus supporting the conclusion that humans are morally obligated to consume a vegan diet. But is that conclusion the one that best satisfies the LHP? Are there other ways of accomplishing least harm?

I find Regan's vegan conclusion to be problematic because he seems to think that there are no other alternatives. There is an old adage to the effect: "There is more than one way to skin a cat." Do alternative food production systems exist that may cause even less harm to animals?

How Many Animals of the Field Would Die If a Vegan Diet Were Adopted?

Animals living in and around agricultural fields are killed during field activities, and the greater the number of field activities, the greater the number of field animals that die. A partial list of animals of the field in the USA include opossum, rock dove, house sparrow, European starling, black rat, Norway rat, house mouse, Chukar, gray partridge, ring-necked pheasant, wild turkey, cottontail rabbit, gray-tailed vole, and numerous species of amphibians (Edge, 2000). In addition, Edge (2000) says, "production of most crops requires multiple field operations that may include plowing, disking, harrowing, planting, cultivating, applying herbicides and pesticides as well as harvesting." These practices have negative effects on the populations of the animals living in the fields. For example, just one operation, the mowing of alfalfa, "caused a 50% decline in [the] gray-tailed vole population" (Edge, 2000). Although these examples represent crop production systems in the USA, the concept is also valid for intensive crop production in any country. Other studies have also examined the effect of agricultural tillage practices on field animal populations (Johnson et al., 1991; Pollard and Relton, 1970; Tew et al., 1992).

Although accurate estimates of the total number of animals killed by different agronomic practices from plowing to harvesting are not available, some studies show that the numbers are quite large. Kerasote (1993) describes it as follows: "When I inquired about the lives lost on a mechanized farm, I realized what costs we pay at the supermarket. One Oregon farmer told me that half of the cottontail rabbits went into his combine when he cut a wheat field, that virtually all of the small mammals, ground birds, and reptiles were killed when he harvested his crops. Because most of these animals have been seen as expendable, or not seen at all, few scientific studies have been done measuring agriculture's effects on their populations." In a study that has been done to examine the effect of harvesting grain crops, Tew and Macdonald (1993) reported that mouse population density dropped from 25 per hectare (/ha) preharvest to less than 5/ha postharvest. This decrease was attributed both to migration out of the field and to mortality. They estimated the mortality rate to be 52%. In another study, Nass et al. (1971) reported that the mortality rate of Polynesian rats was 77% during the harvest of sugar cane in Hawaii. These are the estimated mortality rates for only a single species and for only a single operation (i.e., harvesting). Therefore, an estimate somewhere between 52% and 77% (say 60%) for animals of all kinds killed during the production year would be reasonable. If we multiply the population density shown in Tew and Macdonald's (1993) paper (25/ha) times a 60% mortality rate, that equals a mortality of 15 animals/ha each year.

If that is true, how many animals would die annually in the production of a vegan diet? Each year, there are 120 million ha of cropland harvested in the USA (USDA, 1997). If all of that land were used to produce crops to support a vegan diet, and if 15 animals of the field were killed per ha per year, then 15×120 million $= 1800$ million or 1.8 billion animals would be killed annually to produce a vegan diet for the USA.

Would a Pasture/Ruminant Model Kill Fewer Animals?

Production of forages, such as pasture-based forages, would cause less harm to field animals (kill fewer) than intensive crop production systems typically used to produce food for a vegan diet. This is because pasture forage production requires fewer passages through the field with tractors and other farm equipment. The killing of animals of the field would be further reduced if herbivorous animals (ruminants like cattle) were used to harvest the forage and convert it into meat and dairy products. Would such production systems cause less harm to the field animals? Again, accurate numbers aren't available comparing the number of animals of the field that are killed with these different cropping systems, but: "The predominant feeling among wildlife ecologists is that no-till agriculture will have broadly positive effects on mammalian wildlife" populations (Wooley et al., 1984). Pasture-forage production, with herbivores harvesting the forage, would be the ultimate in "no-till" agriculture. Because of the low numbers of times that equipment would be needed to grow and harvest pasture forages, it would be reasonable to estimate that the pasture-forage model may reduce animal deaths. In other words, perhaps only 7.5 animals of the field per ha would die to produce pasture forages, as compared with the intensive cropping system (15/ha) used to produce a vegan diet.

If half of the total harvested land in the US were used to produce plant products for human consumption and half were used for pasture-forage production, how many animals would die annually so that humans may eat?

60 million ha, plant production $\times$ 15 animals/ha = 0.9 billion
60 million ha, forage production $\times$ 7.5 animals/ha = 0.45 billion
Total: 1.35 billion animals

According to this model then, fewer animals (1.35 billion) would die than in the vegan model (1.8 billion). As a result, if we apply the LHP as Regan did for his vegan conclusion, it would seem that humans are morally obligated to consume a diet of vegetables and ruminant animal products.

But what of the ruminant animals that would need to die to feed people in the pasture-forage model? According to USDA numbers quoted by Francione (2000), of the 8.4 billion farm animals killed each year for food in the US, approximately 8 billion of those are poultry and only 37 million are ruminants (cows, calves); the remainder include pigs and other species. Even if the numbers of cows and calves killed for food each year were doubled to 74 million to replace the 8 billion poultry, the total number of animals that would need to be killed under this alternative method would still be only 1.424 billion, still clearly less than in the vegan model.

Other Alternatives

The pasture/ruminant model would have other advantages. For one, it would provide habitat for many species of animals and insects, helping them to survive. In addition, ruminants are capable of surviving and producing on diets containing only forages, which humans cannot digest. This is beneficial in two ways. First, crops such as corn and soybeans could all be fed to humans instead of to animals. Second, pasture forage can be produced on lands that are too rough to be usable to produce crops for human consumption. Grasses are currently grown and harvested by cows in many countries on lands that are too hilly, and/or rocky, and/or dry to be usable for production of crops like corn and soybeans.

Are there other alternatives that would cause "least harm"? As I have discussed this analysis with others, additional alternatives have been suggested. These include the following: [. . .]

1. Another alternative, suggested by Peter Cheeke (personal communication), would be to eliminate intensive agriculture altogether and have everyone produce their own vegan diet on small plots of land using no-till production systems to reduce killing/harm to animals of the field. I believe that this system would also be unpractical and not viable. The human populations are too large, land is concentrated in the hands of the few rather than many, and social systems would need to revert to those of primitive cultures.
2. But if herbivores are used, wouldn't it cause least harm if we used the fewest possible, therefore, the largest herbivores? Elephants might be used, but in practical terms, I believe that the majority of people would object to eating elephants. Large draft horse breeds developed previously as working horses, may be up to twice the size of a cow. Perhaps they could be used to harvest or convert forages into meat and dairy products. Again, I don't believe many humans would support this option; otherwise there would already be more people willing to consume horsemeat.
3. Kerasote (1993) proposed that least harm would be done if humans were to hunt locally, particularly large animals like elk for their own food. But his least harm concept appears to be related as much to least harm to the environment (less fossil fuel consumption) as least harm to animals. Furthermore, this doesn't seem to be a practical idea, because there are too few animals and there would be too many hunters. As Taylor (1999) said, one "issue that arises from Kerasote's argument is whether hunting for one's food is practical on a large scale."

Intended vs. Unintended Deaths

Taylor (1999) says that another issue arises from Kerasote's argument, and that is the matter of intentional infliction of harm versus harm that is the unintentional but foreseeable side effect of one's actions. The animals of the field die not intentionally, but incidentally as a consequence of producing food for humans. On the other hand, farm animals (chickens, pigs, cows, and sheep) are killed intentionally to provide food for humans. Perhaps I don't fully understand the nuances or moral significance of this difference, but it seems to me that the harm done to the animal is the same—dead is dead. Furthermore, many farmers do intentionally kill some animals of the field because their presence causes reduced yields. Taylor (1999) says about the questions of intent, "A utilitarian is likely to see no moral difference between the two, since utilitarianism holds that it is consequences that count and not intentions."

Conclusion

1. Vegan diets are not bloodless diets. Millions of animals of the field die every year to provide products used in vegan diets.
2. Several alternative food production models exist that may kill fewer animals than the vegan model.
3. More research is needed to obtain accurate estimations of the number of field animals killed in different crop production systems.
4. Humans may be morally obligated to consume a diet from plant-based plus pasture-forage-ruminant systems.

References

Comstock, G., *Is There a Moral Obligation to Save the Family Farm?* (Iowa State University Press, Ames, 1987), p. 400.

Edge, W. D., "Wildlife of Agriculture, Pastures, and Mixed Environs," in D. H. Johnson and T. A. O'Neill (eds.) *Wildlife-Habitat Relationships in Oregon and Washington* (Oregon State University Press, Corvallis, 2000), pp. 342–360.

Francione, G. L., *Introduction to Animal Rights: Your Child or the Dog?* (Temple University Press, Philadelphia, PA, 2000), p. xx.

Johnson, I. P., J. R. Flowerdew, and R. Hare, "Effects of Broadcasting and Drilling Methiocarb Molluscicide Pellets on Field Populations of Wood Mice, *Apodemus sylvaticus*," *Bulletin of Environmental Contamination and Toxicology* 46 (1991), 84–91.

Kerasote, T., *Bloodties: Nature, Culture, and the Hunt* (Random House, New York, 1993), pp. 232–233, and 254–255.

Kingsolver, B., *Prodigal Summer* (Harper Collins, New York, 2001), pp. 322–323.

Nass, R. D., G. A. Hood, and G. D. Lindsey, "Fate of Polynesian Rats in Hawaiian Sugar Cane Fields During Harvest," *J. Wildlife Management* 35 (1971), 353–356.

Pollard, E. and T. Relton, "A Study of Small Mammals in Hedges and Cultivated Fields," *Journal of Applied Ecology* 7 (1970), 549–557.

Regan, T., *The Case for Animal Rights* (University of California Press, Berkeley, 1983), pp. 266–329.

Shapiro, L. S., *Applied Animal Ethics* (Delmar Press, Albany, NY, 2000), pp. 25–36.

Taylor, A., *Magpies, Monkeys, and Morals: What Philosophers Say about Animal Liberation* (Broadview Press, Ontario, Canada, 1999), p. 87.

Tew, T. E. and D. W. Macdonald, "The Effects of Harvest on Arable Wood Mice," *Biological Conservation* 65 (1993), 279–283.

Tew, T. E., D. W. Macdonald, and M. R. W. Rands, "Herbicide Application Affects Microhabitat Use by Arable Wood Mice *Apodemus Sylvaticus*," *Journal of Applied Ecology* 29 (1992), 352–359.

USDA, www.nass.usda.gov/Census/Census97/highlights, accessed 2000.

Wooley, Jr., J. B., L. B. Best, and W. R. Clark, "Impacts of No-Till Row Cropping on Upland Wildlife," *Transactions of the North American Wildlife and Natural Resources Conference* 50 (1984), 157–168.

31 The Basic Argument for Vegetarianism

James Rachels

James Rachels identifies Peter Singer's argument that it is wrong to cause pain unless there is a good enough reason as the argument which convinced him to become a vegetarian. Rachels describes some of the facts involved in the meat-production industry and maintains that such facts are a vital part of the argument. Since the facts are well established, how can we account for so many people being unmoved by these facts? According to Rachels, there is a difference between how scientists and animal-rights advocates think about the cognitive abilities of nonhumans. But for Rachels the important issue is animal pain.

I

In 1973 Peter Singer, who was then a young, little-known philosopher from Australia, published an article called "Animal Liberation" in the *New York Review of Books*.[1] The title suggested that there was a parallel between our treatment of animals and the unjust treatment of blacks and women. At first, it was hard to take the comparison seriously. Many proponents of "black liberation" and "women's liberation," as those movements were then known, found the comparison insulting, and most philosophers thought the topic was hardly worth discussing. But Singer kept at it, writing more articles and a now-famous book. It is now commonly said that the modern animal-rights movement grew out of those works. Thanks to Singer, many people, including me, became convinced that a fundamental change in our attitude toward animals was necessary. The indispensable first step was becoming a vegetarian.

The argument that persuaded me to become a vegetarian was so simple that it needs only a little elaboration. It begins with the principle that it is wrong to cause pain unless there is a good enough reason. The qualification is important, because causing pain is not always wrong. My dentist causes me pain, but there's a good reason for it, and besides, I consent. My children's doctor caused them pain when he gave them their shots, and they did not consent, but that was all right, too. However, as the principle says, causing pain is acceptable only when there is a good enough reason for it. Justification is required.

The second step in the argument is to notice that in the modern meat-production business, animals are made to suffer terribly. There is a reason for this suffering, too. We eat the meat, and it helps to nourish us. But there is a catch: we could just as easily nourish ourselves in other ways. Vegetarian meals are also good. Nonetheless, most people prefer a diet that includes meat because they like the way it tastes. The question, then, is whether our enjoyment of the way meat tastes is a good enough reason to justify the amount of suffering that the animals are made to endure. It seems obvious that it is not. Therefore, we should stop eating the products of this business. We should be vegetarians instead.

I will call this the basic argument. It has a limited application. It says nothing about animals raised on old-fashioned family farms or animals killed in hunter-gatherer societies. It addresses only the situation of people like us, in modern industrial countries. But it does point out, in a simple and compelling way, why those of us in the industrial countries should not support the meat-production business as it now exists.

When I emphasize the argument's simplicity, I mean that it does not depend on any controversial claims about health or on any religiously tinged notions of the value of life. Nor does it invoke any disputable ideas about "rights." Further claims of these kinds might strengthen the case for vegetarianism, but the basic argument does not depend on them. Nor does it rest on any contentious philosophical theory about the nature of morality. Philosophers sometimes misunderstand this when they think it is a merely utilitarian argument and that it can be refuted by refuting utilitarianism. But the basic argument is not tied to any particular theory about the nature of ethics. Instead, it appeals to a simple principle that every decent person already accepts, regardless of his or her stand on other issues. The most striking thing about the argument is that it derives such a remarkable conclusion from such a sober, conservative starting point.

The basic argument, then, is common ground for people of various moral and political persuasions. Matthew Scully is in most respects the antithesis of Peter Singer. Scully, a former speechwriter for various Republicans including President George W. Bush, recently surprised his conservative friends by writing a book, *Dominion: The Power of Man, the Suffering of Animals, and the Call to Mercy*,[2] in which he detailed the cruelties of the modern factory farm—cruelties that are, in his words, "hard to contemplate."[3] Scully reports:

> Four companies now produce 81 percent of cows brought to market, 73 percent of sheep, half our chickens, and some 60 percent of hogs. From these latter, the 355,000 pigs slaughtered every day in America, even the smallest of mercies have been withdrawn. In 1967 there were more than a million hog farms in the country; today there are about 114,000, all of them producing more, more, more to meet market demand. About 80 million of the 95 million hogs slaughtered each year in America, according to the National Pork Producers Council, are intensively reared in mass-confinement farms, never once in their time on earth feeling soil or sunshine. Genetically engineered by machines, inseminated by machines, monitored, herded, electrocuted, stabbed, cleaned, cut, and packaged by machines—themselves treated as machines "from birth to bacon"—these creatures, when eaten, have hardly ever been touched by human hands.[4]

Scully visited some of these automated pig farms in North Carolina, and his report is chilling. Sows have been engineered to weigh 500 pounds each. Pigs are crowded twenty each in pens only seven-and-a-half feet square. The close confinement creates problems in managing the animals. Pigs are intelligent and social animals who normally build nests and keep them clean. They will not urinate or defecate in their nests, as they must do in the pens. They form bonds with other animals. They want to suck and chew, but in the pens, being deprived of a normal environment in which they can do these things, they begin to chew on the tails of the animals in front of them. In such close quarters, the victims cannot escape. The chewing causes infection, and sick pigs are no good. The solution is "tail docking," a procedure recommended by the U.S. Food and Drug Administration, in which the pigs' tails are snipped (without anesthetic) by pliers. The point is to make the tails more sensitive to pain, so that the animals will make a greater effort to avoid their neighbors' attacks. Surveying the whole setup, the operator of one such "farm" observes: "It's science driven. We're not raising pets."[5]

When critics of the meat-production industry report such facts, their accounts are often dismissed as "emotional appeals." But that is a mistake. It may be true that such descriptions engage our emotions. However, emotionalism is not the point. The point is to fill in the details of the basic argument. The basic argument says that causing pain is not justified unless there is a sufficiently good reason for it. In order to apply this principle to the case of factory farming, we need to know how much pain is involved. If only a little pain were being caused, a fairly insubstantial reason (such as our gustatory pleasure) might be sufficient. But if there is extensive suffering, that reason is not enough. Thus, these facts are a vital part of the argument, and it is necessary to keep them in mind when considering whether the argument is sound. For those of us who have no firsthand knowledge of the subject, reports by such relatively impartial observers as Matthew Scully are indispensable.

not meant to make emotional appeal but to depict degree of suffering makes factory farming worthwhile but no

Another report recently appeared in the *New York Times Magazine*.[6] The author, Michael Pollan, went to a great deal of trouble to find out what happens to cattle who are raised and slaughtered for beef. "Forgetting, or willed ignorance, is the preferred strategy of many beef-eaters,"[7] he says; but Pollan wanted to see for himself the conditions in which the animals live and die. So he bought a steer—"No. 534"—at the Blair Brothers Ranch in South Dakota and followed its progress to the slaughterhouse. No. 534 spent the first six months of his life in pastures alongside his mother. Then, having been weaned and castrated, he was shipped to Poky Feeders, a feedlot operation in Garden City, Kansas.

"A cattle feedlot," says Pollan, "is a kind of city, populated by as many as 100,000 animals. It is very much a premodern city, however—crowded, filthy and stinking, with open sewers, unpaved roads and choking air."[8] Fecal dust floats in the air, causing irritation to the eyes and lungs. Searching for No. 534, Pollan found his animal standing in a "deep pile of manure."[9] Dried manure caked on the animals is a problem later, in the slaughterhouse, where steps must be taken to ensure that the meat does not become contaminated. In the feedlot itself, disease would kill the animals were it not for massive doses of antibiotics.

At the Blair Brothers Ranch, No. 534 ate grass and was given corn and alfalfa hay to fatten him up. In his last six weeks at the ranch, he put on 148 pounds. After being shipped to Poky Feeders, he would never eat grass again. His diet would be mostly corn and protein supplement, "a sticky brown goop consisting of molasses and urea."[10] Corn is cheap, and it produces "marbled" beef, although it is not what the animals naturally desire. In a grisly sort of forced cannibalism, the animals are also fed rendered cow parts. The animals could not live on this diet for long—it would "blow out their livers," said one of the feedlot operators. But they are slaughtered before this can happen. The diet is effective, however: the animals weigh more than 1,200 pounds when taken to the slaughterhouse.

No. 534 was slaughtered at the National Beef Plant in Liberal, Kansas, a hundred miles down the road from Poky Feeders. This is where Pollan's personal observations come to a stop. He was not allowed to watch the stunning, bleeding, and evisceration process; nor was he permitted to take pictures or talk to the employees.

Opposing cruelty should not be seen as a specifically liberal or conservative cause. Scully, the conservative Republican, emphasizes that one should oppose it "even if one does not accept [the animal rights advocates'] whole vision of the world." He makes a point of distancing himself from Peter Singer, who champions various left-wing causes. Singer is wrong about the other issues, says Scully, but he is right about the animals.[11]

II

The basic argument seems to me obviously correct. But its very obviousness suggests a problem: if it is so simple and obvious, why doesn't everyone accept it? Why doesn't everyone who has this argument explained to them become a vegetarian? Of course, many people do, but most do not. Part of the explanation may be that it is natural for people to resist arguments that require them to do things they don't want to do. If you want to go on eating meat, you may pay no attention to arguments that say otherwise. Moreover, people generally do not respond to ethical appeals unless they see others around them also responding. If all your friends are eating meat, you are unlikely to be moved by a mere argument. It is like an appeal for money to provide vaccinations for third-world children. The argument that the vaccinations are more important than your going to a movie may be irrefutable, considered just as an argument. But when no one around you is contributing, and your friends are all going to the movie, you are likely to ignore the charitable appeal and spend the money on popcorn instead. It is easy to put the children out of mind.

All this may be true. But there is a more pressing problem about the basic argument—at least, a more pressing problem for me, as a philosopher. Many of my professional colleagues are unmoved by this argument, and I am not sure why. Those who study ethics, especially from a nonreligious point of view, often find the argument compelling. But others do not. This is puzzling because professional philosophers—those who teach in colleges and universities—study arguments dispassionately, and while they often disagree, they disagree about arguments only when the issues are tricky or obscure. But there is nothing tricky or obscure about the basic argument. Thus I would expect that, on so simple a matter, there would be widespread agreement. Instead, many philosophers shrug the argument off.

The same is true of other academics who study cognitive science, psychology, and biology. They are at least as smart as I am, if not smarter, and they are morally decent people. Yet, while I think the basic argument is compelling, many of them do not. It is not that they think the argument makes a good point, even though they are unwilling to act on it. Rather, they find the argument itself unconvincing. How can this be?

Sometimes philosophers explain that the argument is unconvincing because it contains a logical gap. We are all opposed to cruelty, they say, but it does not follow that we must become vegetarians. It only follows that we should favor less cruel methods of meat production. This objection is so feeble that it is hard to believe it explains resistance to the basic argument. It is true enough that if you are opposed to cruelty, you should prefer that the meat-production business be made less brutal. But it is also true that if you are opposed to cruelty, you have reason not to participate in social practices that are brutal as they stand. As it stands, meat producers and consumers cooperate to maintain the unnecessary system of pig farms, feedlots, and slaughterhouses. Anyone who finds this system objectionable has reason not to help keep it going. The point would be quickly conceded if the victims were people. If a product—curtains, let's say—were being produced by a process that involved torturing humans, no one would dream of saying: "Of course I oppose using those methods, but that's no reason not to buy the product. After all, the curtains are very nice."

Many in the animal-rights movement believe that scientists are blinded by the need to justify their own practices. The scientists are personally committed to animal experimentation. Their careers, or the careers of their colleagues, are based on it, and they would have to stop this research if they conceded that animals have moral claims on us. Naturally they do not want to do this. Thus they are so biased in favor of current practices that they cannot see the evil in them. This explains why they cannot see the truth even in something so simple as the basic argument.

Perhaps there is something to this, but I do not want to pursue it. On the whole it is a condescending explanation that insults the scientists, cuts off communication with them, and prevents us from learning what they have to teach us. It should be noted, however, that the basic argument about vegetarianism is independent of any arguments about animal experimentation. Indeed, the case against meat eating is much stronger than the case against the use of animals in research. The researchers can at least point out that in many instances, their work has a serious purpose that can benefit humankind. Nothing comparable can be said in defense of meat eating. Thus, even if some research using animals were justified, meat eating would still be wrong.

I believe a better explanation is in terms of the overall difference between how scientists and animal-rights advocates think about the nature of nonhumans. Defenders of animal rights tend to see the differences between humans and nonhumans as slight. They frequently emphasize how much the animals are like us, in order to argue that our ethical responsibilities to the animals are similar to our responsibilities to one another. Animals are pictured as intelligent and sociable creatures who love their children, who experience fear and delight, who sulk, play, mourn their dead, and much more. So how can it be denied that they have rights, just as we do? I have argued in this way myself, more than once.

Many scientists, however, see this as naive. They believe the differences between humans and other animals are vast—so vast, in fact, that putting humans in a separate moral category is entirely justified. Moreover, they feel they have some authority on this score. After all, the scientific study of animals is their professional concern. In light of this, how should we expect them to react when they are confronted by belligerent amateurs who insist they know better? It is only natural that the scientists should disregard the amateurs' arguments.

A case in point is the anthropologist Jonathan Marks, who teaches at the University of North Carolina at Charlotte. In 1993, Peter Singer and Paola Cavalieri, an Italian writer on animal issues, initiated a campaign known as "the Great Ape Project," an effort to secure basic rights for our closest relatives, the chimpanzees, gorillas, and orangutans.[12] The rights being demanded were life, liberty, and freedom from torture. Marks was invited to participate in a debate about these demands, and he recorded his thoughts in an engaging book, *What It Means to Be 98% Chimpanzee*.[13] "Since their brains are closely related to our brains," Marks says, "it should come as no surprise that the apes can approach humans in their cognitive functions."[14] Despite this, "Apes are often objectified by callous and cynical entrepreneurs, who neither regard them nor treat them as the sentient, emotionally complex creatures they are."[15] Marks does not think this is acceptable. "Apes deserve protection," he says, "even rights."[16]

Reading these words, one would expect Marks to be an ally of Singer and Cavalieri. But he is not. The Great Ape Project, he thinks, is completely wrongheaded. Why? Marks's attempt at philosophical argument is unimpressive—he says the critical issues are that chimps, gorillas, and orangutans aren't human, and that in any case we are politically powerless to guarantee such rights even for humans. Of course, these arguments get us nowhere. Everyone knows the animals aren't human; the point is that they are sufficiently like humans to deserve the same basic protections. And the fact that we cannot ensure rights for humans does not mean that we should stop thinking humans ought to have them.

The underlying reason for Marks's scorn of the animal-rights ideology becomes clear when he turns to the scientific study of animal behavior. The similarities between humans and other great apes, he intimates, are only superficial: "Where clever, controlled experimentation has been possible, it has tended strongly to show that in specific ways, ape minds work quite differently from human minds."[17] For support, he cites the work of the psychologist Daniel J. Povinelli, who argues that chimpanzees' conceptions of physical interactions (as, for example, when a hook is used to manipulate an object) are very different from human understanding.[18] Marks does not say how this fits with his earlier assertion that "apes deserve protection, even rights," but clearly, in his view, the latter thought trumps the former.

We find this pattern repeated again and again: The scientists concede that the animal rights advocates have a bit of a point, but then the scientists want to talk about the facts. They think we do not know nearly enough about the details of how animal minds work to justify any firm moral conclusions. Moreover, such knowledge as we do have suggests caution: the animals are more different from us than it seems. The advocates of animal rights, on the other hand, think the facts are well enough established that we can proceed without further ado to the ethical conclusions. Anyone who suggests otherwise is viewed as dragging his/her feet, perhaps to avoid the unpleasant truth about the injustice of our behavior toward the animals.

III

What are we to make of all this? One obvious idea is that we should take seriously what the scientists tell us about what animals are like and adjust our moral conceptions accordingly. This would be an ongoing project. It would take volumes even to begin, by considering what is currently known. But those volumes would be out of date by the time they were completed, because new discoveries are being made all the time.

However, where the basic argument is concerned, the only relevant part of this project would be what science can tell us about the capacity of animals to experience pain. Jeremy Bentham famously said, "The question is not, Can they *reason*? nor Can they *talk*? but *Can they suffer*?"[19] To this we might add that, contrary to Jonathan Marks, it is irrelevant whether chimps have a different understanding of physical interactions. It is irrelevant, that is, if we are considering whether it is acceptable to treat them in ways that cause them pain.

This point is easily misunderstood, so it is worth elaborating just a bit. Of course, the facts about an individual are important in determining how that individual should be treated. (This is true of humans as well as nonhumans.) How an animal should be treated depends on what the animal is like—its nature, its abilities, and its needs. Different creatures have different characteristics, and these must be taken into account when we frame our ethical conceptions. The scientific study of animals gives us the factual information we need. But not every fact about an individual is relevant to every form of treatment. *What facts are relevant* depends on *what sorts of treatment* we are considering. To take a simple example, whether an animal can read is relevant if we are considering whether to admit him to university classes. But the ability to read is irrelevant in deciding whether it is wrong to operate on the animal without anesthesia. Thus, if we are considering whether it is wrong to treat pigs and cattle in the ways we have described, the critical issue is not whether their minds work in various sophisticated ways. The critical issue is, as Bentham said, whether they can suffer.

What does science tell us about this? The mechanisms that enable us to feel pain are not fully understood, but we do know a good bit about them. In humans, nocioceptors—neurons specialized for sensing noxious stimuli—are connected to a central nervous system, and the resulting signals are processed in the brain. Until recently it was believed that the brain's work was divided into two distinct parts: a sensory system operating in the somatosensory cortex, resulting in our conscious experiences of pain, and an affective-motivational system associated with the frontal lobes, responsible for our behavioral reactions. Now, however, this picture has been called into question, and it may be that the best we can say is that the brain's system for processing the information from the nocioceptors seems to be spread over multiple regions. At any rate, the human nocioceptive system also includes endogenous opioids, or endorphins, which provide the brain with its natural pain-killing ability.

The question of which other animals feel pain is a real and important issue, not to be settled by appeals to "common sense." Only a completed scientific understanding of pain, which we do not yet have, could tell us all that we need to know. In the meantime, however, we do have a rough idea of what to look for. If we want to know whether it is reasonable to believe that a particular kind of animal is capable of feeling pain, we may ask: Are there nocioceptors present? Are they connected to a central nervous system? What happens in that nervous system to the signals from the nociceptors? And are there endogenous opioids? In our present state of understanding, this sort of information, together with the obvious behavioral signs of distress, is the best evidence we can have that an animal is capable of feeling pain.

Relying on such evidence, some writers, such as Gary Varner, have tentatively suggested that the line between animals who feel pain and those who do not is (approximately) the line between vertebrates and invertebrates.[20] However, research constantly moves forward, and the tendency of research is to extend the number of animals that might be able to suffer, not decrease it. Nocioception appears to be one of the most primitive animal systems. Nocioceptors have now been identified in a remarkable number of species, including leeches and snails.

The presence of a perceptual system does not, however, settle the question of whether the organism has conscious experiences connected with its operation. We know, for example, that humans have perceptual systems that do not involve conscious experience. Recent research has shown that the human vomeronasal system, which works through receptors in the nose, responds to pheromones and affects behavior even though the person is unaware of it. (It was long believed that this system was vestigial in humans, but it turns out that it is still working.) The receptors for "vomerolfaction" are in the nostrils, alongside the receptors for the sense of smell; yet the operation of one is accompanied by conscious experience, while the operation of the other is not.[21] We do not know why this is so. But this suggests at least the possibility that in some species there may be nocioceptive systems that do not involve conscious experiences. In that case, those animals might not actually feel pain, even though various indications are present. Is this true of leeches and snails? of snakes? of hummingbirds? We may have strong hunches, but we don't really know.

Clearly, then, we still have a great deal to learn about the phenomenon of pain in the animal world, and the scientists who work in this area are right to caution us against quick-and-easy opinions. The

280   *James Rachels*

ongoing study of animal pain is a fascinating subject in itself, and it has enormous importance for ethics. But should this make us less confident of the basic argument? If the issue were our treatment of snails and leeches, perhaps it should. But pigs and cattle are another matter. There is every reason to believe they feel pain—the facts about their nervous systems, their brains, their behavior, and their evolutionary kinship to human beings all point to the same conclusion as common sense: our treatment of them on factory farms and in the slaughterhouses is one of the world's great causes of misery. If further investigation were to prove otherwise, it would be one of the most astonishing discoveries in the history of science.

Strict vegetarians may want more than the basic argument can provide, because the basic argument does not support sweeping prohibitions. If opposition to cruelty is our motive, we will have to consider the things we eat one at a time. Of course we should not eat beef and pork produced in the ways I have described, and we ought also to avoid factory-farm poultry, eggs, and milk. But free-range eggs and humanely produced milk are all right. Eating shrimp may also turn out to be acceptable. Moreover, from this point of view, not all vegetarian issues are equally pressing: eating fish may be questionable, but it is not nearly as bad as eating beef. This means that becoming a vegetarian need not be regarded as an all-or-nothing proposition. From a practical standpoint, it makes sense to focus first on the things that cause the most misery. As Matthew Scully says, whatever one's "whole vision of the world" may be, the pig farms, feedlots, and slaughterhouses are unacceptable.[22]

Notes

1. Peter Singer, "Animal Liberation," *New York Review of Books*, April 5, 1973.
2. Matthew Scully, *Dominion: The Power of Man, the Suffering of Animals, and the Call to Mercy* (New York: St. Martin's Press, 2002).
3. Ibid., p. x.
4. Ibid., p. 29.
5. Ibid., p. 279.
6. Michael Pollan, "This Steer's Life," *New York Times Magazine*, March 31, 2002, pp. 44–51, 68, 71–2, 76–7.
7. Ibid., p. 48.
8. Ibid., p. 50.
9. Ibid., p. 68.
10. Ibid., p. 50
11. Scully, *Dominion*, pp. 326–38.
12. Peter Singer and Paola Cavalieri, *The Great Ape Project: Equality and Beyond* (London: Fourth Estate, 1993).
13. Jonathan Marks, *What It Means to Be 98% Chimpanzee: Apes, People, and Their Genes* (Berkeley: University of California Press, 2002).
14. Ibid., p. 189.
15. Ibid., p. 185.
16. Ibid., p. 188.
17. Ibid., p. 195.
18. Daniel J. Povinelli, *Folk Physics for Apes: The Chimpanzee's Theory of How the World Works* (Oxford: Oxford University Press, 2000).
19. Jeremy Bentham, *The Principles of Morals and Legislation* (New York: Hafner, 1948; originally published in 1789), p. 311.
20. Gary Varner, *In Nature's Interests? Interests, Animals Rights, and Environmental Ethics* (New York: Oxford University Press, 1998).
21. L. Monti-Bloch, C. Jennings-White, and D. L. Berliner, "The Human Vomeronasal Organ: A Review," *Annals of the New York Academy of Sciences* 855 (1998): 373–89.
22. I have learned a great deal from Colin Allen's essay, "Animal Pain" [*NOUS* 2004—ed. note]. It is the best discussion of the question of animal pain known to me.

32 The Rape of Animals, the Butchering of Women

Carol J. Adams

In her powerful essay, Carol J. Adams uses the concept of "absent referent" to describe the erasure of both women and animals used for food. Patriarchal culture strengthens oppression by "always recalling other oppressed groups." She points out how patriarchal culture violently transforms living animals into dead consumable ones both literally and conceptually through words of objectification such as "food-producing unit" to refer to a living animal.

The Absent Referent

Through butchering, animals become absent referents. Animals in name and body are made absent *as animals* for meat to exist. Animals' lives precede and enable the existence of meat. If animals are alive they cannot be meat. Thus a dead body replaces the live animal. Without animals there would be no meat eating, yet they are absent from the act of eating meat because they have been transformed into food.

Animals are made absent through language that renames dead bodies before consumers participate in eating them. Our culture further mystifies the term "meat" with gastronomic language, so we do not conjure dead, butchered animals, but cuisine. Language thus contributes even further to animals' absences. While the cultural meanings of meat and meat eating shift historically, one essential part of meat's meaning is static: One does not eat meat without the death of an animal. Live animals are thus the absent referents in the concept of meat. The absent referent permits us to forget about the animal as an independent entity; it also enables us to resist efforts to make animals present.

There are actually three ways by which animals become absent referents. One is literally: as I have just argued, through meat eating they are literally absent because they are dead. Another is definitional: when we eat animals we change the way we talk about them—for instance, we no longer talk about baby animals but about veal or meat: the word *meat* has an absent referent, the dead animals. [. . .] The third way is metaphorical. Animals become metaphors for describing people's experiences. In this metaphorical sense, the meaning of the absent referent derives from its application or reference to something else.

As the absent referent becomes metaphor, its meaning is lifted to a "higher" or more imaginative function than its own existence might merit or reveal. An example of this is when rape victims or battered women say, "I felt like a piece of meat." In this example, meat's meaning does not refer to itself but to how a woman victimized by male violence felt. That meat is functioning as an absent referent is evident when we push the meaning of the metaphor: one cannot truly *feel* like a piece of meat. Teresa de Lauretis comments: "No one can really *see* oneself as an inert object or a sightless body,"[1] and no one can really feel like a piece of meat because meat by definition is something violently deprived of all feeling. The use of the phrase "feeling like a piece of meat" occurs within a metaphoric system of language.

The animals have become absent referents, whose fate is transmuted into a metaphor for someone else's existence or fate. Metaphorically, the absent referent can be anything whose original meaning is undercut as it is absorbed into a different hierarchy of meaning; in this case the original meaning of animals' fates is absorbed into a human-centered hierarchy. Specifically in regard to rape victims and battered women, the death experience of animals acts to illustrate the lived experience of women.

The absent referent is both there and not there. It is there through inference, but its meaningfulness reflects only upon what it refers to because the originating, literal experience that contributes the meaning is not there.[2] We fail to accord this absent referent its own existence.

Women and Animals: Overlapping but Absent Referents

This chapter posits that a structure of overlapping but absent referents links violence against women and animals. Through the structure of the absent referent, patriarchal values become institutionalized. Just as dead bodies are absent from our language about meat, in descriptions of cultural violence women are also often the absent referent. Rape, in particular, carries such potent imagery that the term is transferred from the literal experience of women and applied metaphorically to other instances of violent devastation, such as the "rape" of the earth in ecological writings of the early 1970s. The experience of women thus becomes a vehicle for describing other oppressions. Women, upon whose bodies actual rape is most often committed, become the absent referent when the language of sexual violence is used metaphorically. These terms recall women's experiences but not women.

When I use the term "the rape of animals," the experience of women becomes a vehicle for explicating another being's oppression. Some terms are so powerfully specific to one group's oppression that their appropriation to others is potentially exploitative: for instance, using the "holocaust" for anything but the extermination of Jewish people, or "slavery" for anything but the forced enslavement of black people. Yet, feminists, among others, appropriate the metaphor of butchering without acknowledging the originating oppression of animals that generates the power of the metaphor. Through the function of the absent referent, Western culture constantly renders the material reality of violence into controlled and controllable metaphors.

Sexual violence and meat eating, which appear to be discrete forms of violence, find a point of intersection in the absent referent. Cultural images of sexual violence, and actual sexual violence, often rely on our knowledge of how animals are butchered and eaten. For example, Kathy Barry tells us of "*maisons d'abattage* (literal translation: houses of slaughter)" where six or seven girls each serve 80 to 120 customers a night.[3] In addition, the bondage equipment of pornography—chains, cattle prods, nooses, dog collars, and ropes—suggests the control of animals. Thus, when women are victims of violence, the treatment of animals is recalled.

Similarly, in images of animal slaughter, erotic overtones suggest that women are the absent referent. If animals are the absent referent in the phrase "the butchering of women," women are the absent referent in the phrase "the rape of animals." The impact of a seductive pig relies on an absent but imaginable, seductive, fleshy woman. Ursula Hamdress is both metaphor and joke; her jarring (or jocular) effect is based on the fact that we are all accustomed to seeing women depicted in such a way. Ursula's image refers to something that is absent: the human female body. The structure of the absent referent in patriarchal culture strengthens individual oppressions by always recalling other oppressed groups.

Because the structure of overlapping absent referents is so deeply rooted in Western culture, it inevitably implicates individuals. Our participation evolves as part of our general socialization to cultural patterns and viewpoints, thus we fail to see anything disturbing in the violence and domination that are an inextricable part of this structure. Consequently, women eat meat, work in slaughterhouses, at times treat other women as "meat," and men at times are victims of sexual violence. Moreover, because women as well as men participate in and benefit from the structure of the absent referent by eating meat, neither achieve the personal distance to perceive their implication in the structure, nor the originating oppression of animals that establishes the potency of the metaphor of butchering.

The interaction between physical oppression and the dependence on metaphors that rely on the absent referent indicates that we distance ourselves from whatever is different by equating it with something we have already objectified. For instance, the demarcation between animals and people was invoked during the early modern period to emphasize social distancing. According to Keith Thomas, infants, youth, the poor, blacks, Irish, insane people, and women were considered beastlike: "Once perceived as beasts, people were liable to be treated accordingly. The ethic of human domination removed animals from the sphere of human concern. But it also legitimized the ill-treatment of those humans who were in a supposedly animal condition."[4]

Racism and the Absent Referent

Through the structure of the absent referent, a dialectic of absence and presence of oppressed groups occurs. What is absent refers back to one oppressed group while defining another. This has theoretical implications for class and race as well as violence against women and animals. Whereas I want to focus on the overlapping oppressions of women and animals, further exploration of the function of the absent referent is needed, such as found in Marjorie Spiegel's *The Dreaded Comparison: Human and Animal Slavery*. Spiegel discusses the connection between racial oppression and animal oppression and in doing so demonstrates their overlapping relationship.[5]

The structure of the absent referent requires assistants who achieve the elimination of the animal, a form of alienated labor. Living, whole animals are the absent referents not only in meat eating but also in the fur trade. Of interest then is the connection between the oppression of animals through the fur trade and the oppression of blacks as slaves rather than Native Americans. Black historians suggest that one of the reasons black people rather than Native Americans were oppressed through the white Americans' institution of slavery is because of the slaughter of fur-bearing animals. As Vincent Harding describes it in *There Is a River: The Black Struggle for Freedom in America*: "One important early source of income for the Europeans in North America was the fur trade with the Indians, which enslavement of the latter would endanger."[6] While the factors that caused the oppression of Native Americans and blacks is not reducible to this example, we do see in it the undergirding of interactive oppressions by the absent referent. We also see that in analyzing the oppression of human beings, the oppression of animals ought not to be ignored. However, the absent referent, because of its absence, prevents our experiencing connections between oppressed groups.

When one becomes alert to the function of the absent referent and refuses to eat animals, the use of metaphors relying on animals' oppression can simultaneously criticize both that which the metaphor points to and that from which it is derived. For instance, when vegetarian and Civil Rights activist Dick Gregory compares the ghetto to the slaughterhouse he does so condemning both and suggesting the functioning of the absent referent in erasing responsibility for the horrors of each:

> Animals and humans suffer and die alike. If you had to kill your own hog before you ate it, most likely you would not be able to do it. To hear the hog scream, to see the blood spill, to see the baby being taken away from its momma, and to see the look of death in the animal's eye would turn your stomach. So you get the man at the packing house to do the killing for you. In like manner, if the wealthy aristocrats who are perpetrating conditions in the ghetto actually heard the screams of ghetto suffering, or saw the slow death of hungry little kids, or witnessed the strangulation of manhood and dignity, they could not continue the killing. But the wealthy are protected from such horror. . . . If you can justify killing to eat meat, you can justify the conditions of the ghetto. I cannot justify either one.[7]

Sexual Violence and Meat Eating

To rejoin the issue of the intertwined oppressions with which this chapter is primarily concerned, sexual violence and meat eating, and their point of intersection in the absent referent, it is instructive to consider incidents of male violence. Men's descriptions of their own violence suggest the structure of overlapping but absent referents. In defense of the "Bunny Bop"—in which rabbits are killed by clubs, feet, stones, and so on—sponsored by a North Carolina American Legion post, one organizer explained, "What would all these rabbit hunters be doing if they weren't letting off all this steam? I'll tell you what they'd be doing. They'd be drinking and carousing and beating their wives."[8]

One common form of domestic violence is the killing of a family's pet. Here the absent referent is clearly in operation: the threatened woman or child is the absent referent in pet murders. Within the symbolic order the fragmented referent no longer recalls itself but something else.[9] Though this pattern of killing pets as a warning to an abused woman or child is derived from recent case studies of domestic violence, the story of a man's killing his wife's pet instead of his wife can be found in an early twentieth-century short story. Susan Glaspell's "A Jury of Her Peers" exposes this function of the absent referent and the fact that a woman's peers, i.e., other women, recognize this function.[10]

Generally, however, the absent referent, because of its absence, prevents our experiencing connections between oppressed groups. Cultural images of butchering and sexual violence are so interpenetrated that animals act as the absent referent in radical feminist discourse. In this sense, radical feminist theory participates in the same set of representational structures it seeks to expose. We uphold the patriarchal structure of absent referents, appropriating the experience of animals to interpret our own violation. For instance, we learn of a woman who went to her doctor after being battered. The doctor told her her leg "was like a raw piece of meat hanging up in a butcher's window."[11] Feminists translate this literal description into a metaphor for women's oppression. Andrea Dworkin states that pornography depicts woman as a "female piece of meat" and Gena Corea observes that "women in brothels can be used like animals in cages."[12] Linda Lovelace claims that when presented to Xaviera Hollander for inspection, "Xaviera looked me over like a butcher inspecting a side of beef."[13] When one film actress committed suicide, another described the dilemma she and other actresses encounter: "They treat us like meat." Of this statement Susan Griffin writes: "She means that men who hire them treat them as less than human, as matter without spirit."[14] In each of these examples, feminists have used violence against animals as metaphor, literalizing *and* feminizing the metaphor. Thus, Mary Daly appropriates the word "butcher" to describe lobotomists, since the majority of lobotomies have been performed on women.[15]

Because of this dependence on the *imagery* of butchering, radical feminist discourse has failed to integrate the *literal* oppression of animals into our analysis of patriarchal culture or to acknowledge the strong historical alliance between feminism and vegetarianism. Whereas women may feel like pieces of meat and be treated like pieces of meat—emotionally butchered and physically battered—animals actually are made into pieces of meat. In radical feminist theory, the use of these metaphors alternates between a positive figurative activity and a negative activity of occlusion, negation, and omission in which the literal fate of the animal is elided. Could metaphor itself be the undergarment to the garb of oppression?

The Cycle of Objectification, Fragmentation, and Consumption

What we require is a theory that traces parallel trajectories: the common oppressions of women and animals and the problems of metaphor and the absent referent. I propose a cycle of objectification, fragmentation, and consumption, which links butchering and sexual violence in our culture. Objectification permits an oppressor to view another being as an object. The oppressor then violates this being by object-like treatment: e.g., the rape of women that denies women freedom to say no, the butchering of animals that converts animals from living, breathing beings into dead objects. This process allows fragmentation, or brutal dismemberment, and finally consumption. While the occasional man may literally eat women, we all consume visual images of women all the time.[16] Consumption is the fulfillment of oppression, the annihilation of will, of separate identity. So too with language: a subject first is viewed, or objectified, through metaphor. Through fragmentation the object is severed from its ontological meaning. Finally, consumed, it exists only through what it represents. The consumption of the referent reiterates its annihilation as a subject of importance in itself.

Since this chapter addresses how patriarchal culture treats animals as well as women, the image of meat is an appropriate one to illustrate this trajectory of objectification, fragmentation, and consumption. The literal process of violently transforming living animals into dead consumable ones is emblematic of the conceptual process by which the referent point of meat eating is changed. Industrialized meat-eating cultures such as the United States and Great Britain exemplify the process by which live animals are removed from the idea of meat. The physical process of butchering an animal is recapitulated on a verbal level through words of objectification and fragmentation.

Animals are rendered being-less not only by technology, but by innocuous phrases such as "food-producing unit," "protein harvester," "converting machine," "crops," and "biomachines." The meat-producing industry views an animal as consisting of "edible" and "inedible" parts, which must be separated so that the latter do not contaminate the former. An animal proceeds down a "disassembly line," losing body parts at every stop. This fragmentation not only dismembers the animal, it changes the way in which we conceptualize animals. In *The American Heritage Dictionary* the definition of "lamb" is illustrated not by an image of Mary's little one but by an edible body divided into ribs, loin, shank, and leg.[17]

After being butchered, fragmented body parts must be renamed to obscure the fact that these were once animals. After death, cows become roast beef, steak, hamburger; pigs become pork, bacon, sausage. Since objects are possessions, they cannot have possessions; thus, we say "leg of lamb" not a "lamb's leg." We opt for less disquieting referent points not only by changing names from animals to meat, but also by cooking, seasoning, and covering the animals with sauces, disguising their original nature.

Only then can consumption occur: actual consumption of the animal, now dead, and metaphorical consumption of the term "meat," so that it refers to food products alone rather than to the dead animal. In patriarchal culture, meat is without its referent point. This is the way we want it, as William Hazlitt honestly admitted in 1826:

> Animals that are made use of as food should either be so small as to be imperceptible, or else we should . . . not leave the form standing to reproach us with our gluttony and cruelty. I hate to see a rabbit trussed, or a hare brought to the table in the form which it occupied while living.[18]

The dead animal is the point beyond the culturally presumed referent of meat.

Notes

1. Teresa de Lauretis, *Alice Doesn't: Feminism, Semiotics, Cinema* (Bloomington: University of Indiana Press, 1984), p. 141.
2. I am indebted to Margaret Homans' discussion of the absent referent in literature for this expanded explanation of the cultural function of the absent referent. See her *Bearing the Word: Language and Female Experience in Nineteenth-Century Women's Writing* (Chicago: University of Chicago Press, 1986), p. 4.
3. Kathy Barry, *Female Sexual Slavery* (Englewood Cliffs, NJ: Prentice Hall, 1979), p. 3.
4. Keith Thomas, *Man and the Natural World: A History of the Modern Sensibility* (New York: Pantheon, 1983), p. 44.
5. Marjorie Spiegel, *The Dreaded Comparison: Human and Animal Slavery* (Philadelphia, PA: New Society Publishers, 1988).
6. Vincent Harding, *There Is a River: The Black Struggle for Freedom in America* (New York: Harcourt Brace Jovanovich, 1981, New York: Vintage Books, 1983), p. 7. Harding's source is Peter H. Wood's *Black Majority: Negroes in Colonial South Carolina from 1670 through the Stono Rebellion* (New York: Alfred A. Knopf, 1974). Wood discusses the reasons that the Proprietors of the Carolina colony protested the enslavement of Indians. They did so not only because they feared "prompting hostilities with local tribes" but also because "they were anxious to protect their peaceful trade in deerskins, which provided the colony's first source of direct revenue to England. With the opening up of this lucrative Indian trade to more people in the 1690s, the European settlers themselves became increasingly willing to curtail their limited reliance upon native American labor." *Black Majority*, p. 39.

7. Dick Gregory, *The Shadow That Scares Me*, ed. James R. McGraw (Garden City, NY: Doubleday & Co., Inc., 1968), pp. 69–70.

8. Commander Pierce Van Hoy quoted in Cleveland Amory, *Man Kind? Our Incredible War on Wildlife* (New York: Harper & Row, 1974), p. 14.

9. Another example of this can be found in the case of Arthur Gary Bishop, a child molester and murderer of five boys, who relived his first murder by buying and killing as many as twenty puppies.

10. Susan Glaspell, *A Jury of Her Peers* (London: Ernest Benn, Ltd., 1927).

11. R. Emerson Dobash and Russell Dobash, *Violence against Wives: A Case against the Patriarchy* (New York: The Free Press, Macmillan, 1979), p. 110.

12. Andrea Dworkin, *Pornography: Men Possessing Women* (New York: Perigee Books, 1981), p. 209; Gena Corea, *The Hidden Malpractice: How American Medicine Mistreats Women* (New York: William Morrow and Co., 1977, New York: Jove-Harcourt Brace Jovanovich Books, 1978), p. 129.

13. Linda Lovelace and Mike McGrady, *Ordeal* (New York: Citadel Press, 1980, Berkley Books, 1981), p. 96. Note that this is one woman looking at another as "meat."

14. Susan Griffin, *Rape: The Power of Consciousness* (San Francisco: Harper & Row, 1979), p. 39.

15. Daly defines "butcher" as "a bloody operator, esp. one who receives professional recognition and prestige for his 'successes' " (*Websters' First New Intergalactic Wickedary of the English Language* [Boston: Beacon Press, 1987], p. 188.) Her failure to include animals in this definition is all the more notable because her book discusses hunting and vivisection, argues for our ability to communicate with animals, and is dedicated to the late Andrée Collard, who had written on violence against animals. (See Andrée Collard and Joyce Contrucci, *Rape of the Wild: Man's Violence against Animals and the Earth* [London: The Women's Press, 1988].)

16. Annette Kuhn remarks: "Representations are productive: photographs, far from merely reproducing a pre-existing world, constitute a highly coded discourse which, among other things, constructs whatever is in the image as object of consumption—consumption by looking, as well as often quite literally by purchase. It is no coincidence, therefore, that in many highly socially visible (and profitable) forms of photography women dominate the image. Where photography takes women as its subject matter, it also constructs 'woman' as a set of meanings which then enter cultural and economic circulation on their own account" (*The Power of the Image: Essays on Representation and Sexuality* [London: Routledge and Kegan Paul, 1985], p. 19). Also see Kaja Silverman, *The Subject of Semiotics* (New York: Oxford University Press, 1983), especially her chapter on "Suture," pp. 194–236.

17. William Morris, ed., *The American Heritage Dictionary of the English Language* (Boston: American Heritage Publishing Co., Inc., and Houghton Mifflin Co., 1969), p. 734.

18. William Hazlitt, *The Plain Speaker* (EL, n.d.), p. 173, quoted in Thomas, *Man and the Natural World*, p. 300.

Religious Issues

33 Animal Rights in the Jewish Tradition

David Mevorach Seidenberg

Rabbi David Mevorach Seidenberg points out that Jewish law defines rights in terms of obligations that people have to any others who have moral standing, human or nonhuman. It is clear in the Torah that animals have moral status. The Torah maintains that domestic and wild animals live for their own sake and not just for ours. The value of human beings comes from the significance of their relationships.

Seidenberg demonstrates the complex and even contradictory values found in rabbinic literature. Today some prominent rabbis prohibit meat from factory farming and advocate vegetarianism as well as the prohibition of using animals for cosmetics testing.

Any discussion of animal rights in the Jewish tradition must start from the recognition that the concept of "rights," based on a modern understanding of individuality, is foreign to Judaism. Rather, Jewish law defines obligations that people have to others, whether those others are people, or animals or the land, or whichever entity has moral standing. The equivalent of a right possessed by a person in Jewish law would be the determination that a Jewish or human obligation existed toward that person. One finds that such obligations exist in Jewish law and theology with respect to animals and not only with respect to human beings.

It is clear in the Torah that animals have moral status. Laws about helping an animal fallen under its load (Ex. 23:5, Deut. 22:4), about not muzzling an animal so that it can eat while it works (Deut. 25:4), as well as many of the laws concerning kosher slaughter or *shechitah,* appear to have consideration for the subjective needs of the creatures. The laws of *shechitah* have two goals: minimizing pain to the animal and draining all the blood from the animal's body. The latter goal is directly connected to a primitive understanding of animal rights, which was expressed in animistic desire to release the animal's soul, which according to the Torah is found in its blood (Gen. 8:3–4; Lev. 17:14; Deut. 12:23–25). Other laws, like the prohibition against taking the life of a mother and child animal on the same day (Lev. 22:8), reflect a concern for the subjectivity of animals as sympathetically understood by human beings. The prohibitions against sterilizing any animal and against crossbreeding between animals also seem to be rooted in needs of species as well as of individual animals.

The Torah maintains that even domestic animals live for their own sake and not just for ours. All the more so, Torah prohibitions that limit the slaughter of wild animals (Lev. 17:13–14), require one to free a wild mother bird if one wishes to take its eggs (Deut. 22:6–7), and assert the need for wild animals to share in the produce of the land (Lev. 25:6–7) reflect a consciousness that animals have their own purposes and needs that are not trumped by human interests.

In the *halakhah* or legal system of the rabbis, the Torah's specific prohibitions were organized into a general valorization of the needs of animals (Schochet 1984: 151). The Talmud established that the Torah forbade causing pain and suffering to animals, *tza'ar ba'alei chayyim,* even though this idea is not articulated in any scriptural verse (BT *Baba Metsi'a* 32b). The laws of Shabbat could be overridden for the sake of this principle (Schochet 1984: 155–157). The rabbis also articulated a near-blanket prohibition of hunting, despite the Torah's acceptance of slaughtering wild animals as long as their blood was buried in the earth.

In general, rabbinic interpretation extended and strengthened laws related to animal welfare. Yet there was an understanding of the needs of animals and all creatures that was far deeper than the notion of "welfare." Emero Stiegman writes that in the rabbinic worldview,

> man is not considered the measure of all things. Nature is not measured against him in metaphysical categories. . . . Things were not forced to coalesce; each was seen, not "objectively", but . . . in its specific, separate relationship to its Maker. . . . [S]uch a view . . . compels an acceptance of creatures, not according to their supposed nature, but according to their concrete relationships, to God not least. Man also, then, is not seen as an essence, but as related.
>
> (1979: 500)

If humans are ends-in-themselves, it is not because they possess some essence which sets them apart over all other species. Rather, their value comes from the significance of their relationships, with humans, other creatures, and God. Many *midrashim* teach that human beings imitate God by extending mercy to other creatures. *Midrash Tanchuma* asks: "Why is Noah called righteous? Because he fed the creatures of the Holy One, and became like his Creator. Thus it says, 'For the Lord is righteous, loving righteous deeds'" '(*Noach* sec. 4, 35). Fundamentally, the meaning of being human is established not only by the way we treat human beings but also by the way we treat the other animals. Stiegman speculates that this emphasis on relationship may be "why the rabbis could affirm man's centrality in creation and his dominion without reducing the world to a mere complex of useful functions."

Since other creatures stand in relation to God and to each other, they have the rabbinic equivalent of intrinsic value, so that the intrinsic needs of animals could override their use-value to humans. These intrinsic needs may be recognized as the equivalent of "animal rights."

Notwithstanding the rules and precepts affirming that animals deserve just treatment, the framework of both the Torah and the rabbis allowed humans to use animals and to kill them to serve human needs. The application of these laws involved finding a balance between using animals for human purposes, and allowing them to fulfill their own purposes. In essence, Judaism recognized the rights of animals to live according to their needs, while recognizing that human beings had the right to use animals as long as the quality of their lives was preserved.

What these laws meant theologically is a more complex subject. In rabbinic Judaism, there was a general acceptance of the idea that animals had souls (*Tanchuma, Noach* sec. 10, 39; *Genesis Rabbah* 30:6) and that they could choose to fulfill God's purpose. A traditional way of framing the latter concept is found in a *midrash* about the animals that were saved in Noah's ark:

> If [God] remembered Noach, why also the animals? May the name of the Holy One be blessed, who never deprives any creature of its reward. If even a mouse has preserved its family [i.e. species] it deserves to receive a reward.
>
> (*Tanchuma, Noach* sec. 11, 41)

This affirmation of animals participating in the moral order is expressed directly in the Noah story itself, where the first covenant that God establishes explicitly includes the animals as partners (Gen. 9:12–16). On a more folkloric level, the rabbis held that animals could be moral actors. Animals like Rabbi Pinchas' donkey, who refused to eat untithed grain, could be especially pious, and animals could show mercy to people, as does the raven in this story:

> Adam and his partner came and cried over Abel, and they didn't know what to do. . . . One raven whose companion died said, "I will teach Adam that this is what to do." He set down his

friend and dug in the earth before their eyes and buried him. Adam said, "Like the raven, this is what we will do."

(*Pirkei d'Rabi Eli'ezer,* sec. 21)

Within the rabbinic worldview, it is not only human beings who have the capacity to show mercy. In general, ethics is in its essence seen by the rabbis as part of the natural order; this is what it means to call normal ethical behavior *derekh eretz,* or "the way of the earth" (Kadushin 1938: 117–130). At the same time, there are passages that suggest that everything, including the animals, was created to serve humanity. Rabbinic literature preserves the wisdom of many schools of thought and often expresses the complexity of its subjects by juxtaposing contradictory values.

Theologically, the rabbis also held a modest understanding of the dominion granted to Adam in Genesis 1:26–28. They understood these verses as allowing human beings to use animals for work, but *not* to kill them (BT *Sanhedrin* 59b). The power of dominion over other animals and the power of conquest over the land, which were present in the blessings of Genesis 1, are noticeably absent in the blessings given to Noah (Gen. 9:1–7), where the permission to eat meat is first articulated. *Genesis Rabbah* (34:12) learns from this that humanity no longer exercised dominion over the animals after the flood; rather, dominion was replaced by fear. According to Rashi's commentary on this passage (eleventh century), the "dominion" of the garden was the opposite of fear because it meant the power to draw the animals close, i.e., "Adam would call the animals and they would come."

One way in which these potentially contradictory values of dominion and compassion were integrated is that animals were understood to fulfill their own needs, on a soul level, by being used for sanctified ends. The ultimate example of this can be found in the animal sacrifices in the Temple, which harvested the intrinsic value of the animal for an end greater than human needs or desires, something we might term its "holiness-value." From a biblical perspective, using animals for sacrifices was a mechanism that affirmed the sacredness of their lives while still allowing them to be eaten. The blood, defined as the *nefesh,* or soul in the animal, was put on the altar to make clear that the essence of the animal was not allowed to be used by human beings.

The rabbis affirmed this system while also occasionally questioning it. When Rabbi Yehudah haNasi, the leading figure of the Talmud, sent a calf that sought refuge with him back to be sacrificed, saying "Go, for you were created for that purpose," the angels afflicted him with sickness and suffering (BT *Baba Metzi'a* 85a). The conflicted message of this story is that even the highest use of an animal's life could not be fully justified from the perspective of righteousness.

Medieval Thought

Rabbinic literature is quite explicit that God cares for animals (e.g., *Deuteronomy Rabbah* 6:1). Nonetheless, later medieval thinkers like Ibn Ezra and Abravanel, influenced by Aristotle's division between rational beings and all other creatures, declared that the only purpose of the laws against *tza'ar ba'alei chayyim* was moral education (Schochet: 212–215). Importantly, Nachmanides, the earliest one to suggest that teaching compassion was the purpose of these laws, emphasized not only that the laws "teach us the trait of compassion" but also that they forbid actions which would cause the extinction of a species (commentary to Deut. 22:7).

Some scholars like David Bleich have interpreted Maimonides as holding this position in *The Guide for the Perplexed* (3:17), though this is incorrect, since Maimonides affirms there that compassion must be shown to the individual animal. This is made clear by the other passages in which Maimonides describes the suffering of animals as the paramount reason for these laws (3:48). In the disagreement between Maimonides and Nachmanides are echoes of the contemporary debate between animal rights and environmental activists over the value of individual lives of animals versus the well-being of species.

In medieval Jewish mysticism and Kabbalah, sensitivity to animals became greatly magnified, in line with the general motive held by the mystics of rejecting the rationalistic thought of the philosophers. For example, *Sefer Chasidim* (Yehudah Hechasid, twelfth century) says that if a person

> causes needless pain to animals . . . he comes to judgment. . . . Thus the sages explained "in that day I will strike every horse" (Zech. 12:4) to mean that the Holy One is destined to punish [human beings] for the humiliation of horses from their riders.
>
> (sec. 43,104)

Similarly, the innocence of animals is invoked in this same work to understand the reason for the commandment to cover the blood of a slaughtered animal:

> [W]hen a person slaughters an animal or bird he should think in his heart, this one that did not sin was slaughtered. . . . He should consider how the Holy One commanded him to cover an animal or bird's blood, lest the angel having authority over them should say, "How is the blood of this one that didn't sin spilled by the hand of a sinner whose sin is like scarlet and worm."
>
> (sec. 373, 273)

Other important figures emphasizing compassion for animals include Rabbis Moshe Cordovero and Moshe Chayyim Luzzato (Sears 2003). With the emphasis on transmigration of the soul in Kabbalah, the belief that both the righteous and the wicked were sometimes reincarnated in animals became widespread. Though some Kabbalists emphasized the practice of strict vegetarianism in response to this belief, most affirmed that an animal's soul could be elevated through being slaughtered and eaten with the right intention by holy people. Moreover, the animal was thought of as yearning for this to happen. Many Chasidic rebbes and teachers also emphasized the deepest compassion for animals; Dovid of Lelov (1746–1814) was especially known for his piety and passion in this regard. Most of this mystical material was not directed at the normally observant Jew but only at the circle of mystics or *tzadikim*. While this material has relevance to ethical questions it is tangential to the formulation of animal rights in Judaism because it was never seen as binding on the entire community.

Modern Applications

Much of the law relevant to contemporary questions is still being worked out. Rabbi David Rosen, the former Chief Rabbi of Ireland, believes that *tza'ar ba'alei chayyim* requires the prohibition of commercially produced meat: "The current treatment of animals in the livestock trade definitely renders the consumption of meat halakhically unacceptable as the product of illegitimate means" (1995: 53). Followers of Rabbi Abraham Isaac Kook like Shear-Yashuv Cohen and David Sears, as well as many early leaders of the Jewish environmental movement in North America, such as Richard Schwartz, have strongly advocated for vegetarianism as the best modern response to laws protecting animals. Prohibitions against using animals for cosmetics testing and similar unnecessary research have also been made here and in Israel.

Further Reading

Cohen Noah J. *Tsa'ar Ba'alei Chayim. The Prevention of Cruelty to Animals.* New York: Feldheim Publishers, 1976.
Isaacs, Ronald. *Animals in Jewish Thought and Tradition.* Northvale, NJ: Jason Aronson, 2000.
Kadushin, Max. *Organic Thinking: A Study in Rabbinic Thought.* New York: Bloch Publishing, 1938.
Rosen, David. "Vegetarianism: An Orthodox Jewish Perspective." In Roberta Kalechofsky (ed.), *Rabbis and Vegetarianism: An Evolving Tradition.* Marblehead, MA: Micah Publications, 1995, 53–60.
Schochet, Rabbi Elijah J. *Animal Life in Jewish Tradition.* New York: Ktav, 1984.
Sears, David. *The Vision of Eden: Animal Welfare and Vegetarianism in Jewish Law and Mysticism.* Spring Valley, NY: Orot, 2003.

Seidenberg, David. "Crossing the Threshold: God's Image in the More-Than-Human World." Doctoral dissertation. Jewish Theological Seminary, New York, NY, 2002.

Stiegman, Emero. "Rabbinic Anthropology." In Hildegard Temporini-Gräfin Vitzthum and Wolfgang Haase (eds.), *Austieg und Niedergang der Romischen Welt: Principat*. II vol. 19.2. Berlin: Walter de Gruyter, 1979, 487–579.

See also: Animals; Eco-Kabbalah; Jewish Environmentalism in North America; Judaism; Maimonides; Vegetarianism and Judaism; Vegetarianism and Rabbi Abraham Isaac Kook; Vegetarianism, Judaism, and God's Intention.

Articles by Rabbi David Seidenberg in *ERN*: "Kabbalah and Ecotheology," "Maimonides," "Animal Rights in the Jewish Tradition," "Judaism and Paganism," and "Jewish Environmentalism in North America"

34 Is Christianity Irredeemably Speciesist?

Andrew Linzey

Linzey notes that Christianity has propagated the view over thousands of years that human beings have dominion over animals. Not all Christians have been speciesist, but in general that tradition has been central in mainstream Christianity. Humanity has not only been given a high place, but it has been defined against animals.

The incarnation has been interpreted as requiring male persons for the Eucharistic role of representing the male Christ. But we should reject this implication and view the incarnation in broader terms: the incarnation is God's Yes to creation. By becoming flesh, the Logos identifies with all creatures of flesh and blood. And the Christian tradition is not a closed book: the doctrine of the Holy Spirit indicates that God's work continues.

'Does God have a daughter?' The question was put to me some years ago by my eight-year-old daughter, Clair. I confess with pride that my daughter is perspicacious about issues in contemporary theology. Even so, her question and my awkward, fumbling, and, I fear, wholly unsatisfactory answers to it have remained with me as a defining moment. For what *was* defined at that moment was a problem that even, and especially, professional theologians rarely see, namely a sense of alienation, of non-inclusion, brought about by the central Christian metaphor of Fatherhood and Sonship—a sense of exclusion so great that even an eight-year-old girl could feel it.

In her widely reviewed book *Theology and Feminism,* Daphne Hampson questions the confidence of many who maintain that Christianity and feminism are compatible. In her view, Christianity cannot help emancipate women, not only because of its historic rejection of equality between men and women, but principally because the foundational stories which give rise to Christian doctrine are inescapably patriarchal. The Christian faith is rooted in stories—indeed, in one particular story of Father and Son—which (so runs the argument) are exclusive of the female gender.[1] In fact, in her latest book, *After Christianity,* Hampson goes further, rejecting not only compatibility between Christianity and feminism but also coexistence. 'Within Christianity', she argues, 'there is no symbolic place for articulate, self-actualizing woman, the equal of man.' In short: the Christian tradition is inimical to the true interests of women.[2]

If such is true of women within Christianity, it is even more so of animals. It may have taken nineteen hundred years for women to arrive firmly on the theological agenda, but at least they *are* now unambiguously on the agenda. The same cannot be said of animals. Mainstream Christianity still propagates a range of ideas about animals which are hugely detrimental to their status and welfare. Animals are 'here for our use', indeed, 'made for us'. Animals have no immortal soul, no rationality, no intrinsic worth. Animals are subordinate to humankind, who have been given 'dominion' (commonly understood as despotism) over them. How far these ideas are distinctly or authentically Christian is beside the point; the fact is that the Christian tradition has propagated them—and still defends them.

Indeed, those who wish to justify the exploitation of animals regard the Christian tradition as the last bastion of anti-progressive sentiment. The editorial of one daily newspaper, recording with distaste the growth of the modern animal rights movement, exclaimed: 'For centuries, it has been an inherent part of the Christian ethic that man is entitled to exploit lesser species for his own advantage, as do many fervently Catholic societies to this day.' Ethical sensitivity to animals, it was supposed, constitutes nothing less than a rejection of Christian values:

> It seems increasingly part of a *post-Christian* ethic, however, to nourish the belief that animals possess dignity, personality and spirit that entitle their interests to be considered in the same fashion as the rest of us.[3]

The question then must be faced: Is Christianity irredeemably speciesist? I do not mean by speciesism the recognition that there are boundaries between species and that each may have differing abilities or characteristics. Neither do I mean a recognition that particular species may have needs, claims, or interests different from others. Rather I define the word here as the '*arbitrary* favouring of one species' interests over another'.[4]

Of course, not all Christianity has been speciesist in this sense. There have been—for want of a better word—'sub-traditions' of thought which have variously commended charity and generosity towards animals. A substantial, if non-canonical, strand from the second to the twelfth centuries associated Jesus and the apostles with peaceable co-operative relations with animals.[5] These 'apocryphal' stories were, it is true, officially disowned by the church and never included in any recognizable canon of scripture. But even after the twelfth century and the hardening of scholastic theology against animals, many canonized saints of East and West exemplified in their lives filial, respectful relations with animals. When in the eighteenth and nineteenth centuries movements sprang up for the protection of animals, they were able to draw inspiration, at least in part, from a tradition, albeit a derided one, that could justifiably claim some Christian antiquity. Elsewhere, I have tried to give some account of this 'alternative' tradition and its unexplored potential for contemporary theology.[6]

Nevertheless, it is true that systematic and moral theology has emerged in such a form that animals are substantially excluded. The thought of Aristotle, Augustine, and Aquinas has been pivotal here. Although devotees of each dismiss the simple charge of 'speciesism' or moral callousness, it remains a fact that Aristotle *did* argue (typically or untypically) that since 'nature makes nothing to no purpose, it must be that nature has made them [animals and plants] for the sake of man'.[7] Augustine *did* maintain (however *ad hoc*) that 'Reason has not been given to them [animals] to have in common with us, and so, by the most just ordinances of the Creator, both their life and their death is subject to our use'.[8] And St Thomas (interpreting Aristotle rightly or wrongly) *did* write: 'It is not wrong for man to make use of them [animals] either by killing or in any other way whatever.'[9] Whatever higher thoughts they may have had—even probably did have—they cannot be entirely absolved of responsibility for the way their words have subsequently been interpreted, as stating that animals should be excluded from proper moral consideration. The lines of St Thomas (above, and others) have been used, it is true, by animal advocates eager to show the callousness of the tradition, but, before that, more often by Catholic authorities, equally eager to absolve us of any direct moral obligation to the brutes.[10]

One discussion published as late as 1960 is revealing. While accepting that the Thomist conception of hierarchy means that 'animals were created to serve the use and benefit of human beings', it maintains that 'wanton' cruelty is sinful. But, most noteworthy, such cruelty is *not* classifiable as a 'sin of injustice' as such. Nor is it, we are assured, *per se* 'a mortal sin'. What kind of sin could it then be? Apparently wanton cruelty is only a 'violation of the virtue of temperance'. And in justification of this—surely the weakest of all delineations—St Thomas' view is offered that cruelty to animals may lead to similar cruelty to humans.[11]

Even now it is difficult to find one mainstream systematic theologian who has given animals space, except as a secondary or peripheral issue in ethics or theology. All the 'great' Christian thinkers (as distinct from doers) both Catholic and Protestant have kept clear of animals. There have of course been 'minor' theologians, writers, and poets who have championed the cause of animals, some impressively so. The eighteenth-century English poet William Cowper 'contented' himself with 'a humble theme', namely the 'worth of brutes', feeling 'recompensed if . . . verse of mine may stand between an animal and woe, and teach one tyrant pity for his drudge',[12] and such imaginative sympathy was characteristic of early humanitarian protest. But there is no evidence that the example of saints or the work of imaginative poets has had any lasting effect on systematic or moral theology, still less on the teachings of the church.

At the very least it must be conceded that contemporary theology remains firmly humanocentric—and that despite increasing ecological awareness. Even creation liturgies as now espoused in some quarters of the church make precious few references to animals, as though their status were little different morally from stones and trees.[13] It is not easy to find a locus, either in systematic theology, or liturgy, or church and synodical pronouncements, for the idea that individual sentient beings have worth before almighty God.

Without exaggeration we might say that contemporary speculative theology is more interested in aliens than animals. One such high-minded discussion recently concluded:

> If, in other worlds, there have evolved forms of intelligent life so different from our own as to entail an utterly different kind of experience, then there seems to be no theological reason why God should not also have assumed those forms of life in order to experience them for himself. And there seems no good reason to wish to deny such other species the opportunity to meet God as one of their own number, incarnate in their own flesh, just as we meet him in Jesus. Any lesser God would be far too small.[14]

Such theological open-mindedness, not to mention open-heartedness, to other non-human alien species is hardly ever directed to other non-human but non-alien animal species. Where has this theological commentator been? we may ask. Has he really not seen that God has already set the human species in the context of hundreds, even thousands, of 'other worlds' where life—some of which is undoubtedly intelligent—exists and abounds before our very eyes? If any 'lesser God' than the one who would meet and relate to them 'would be far too small', how is it that this non-lesser God is only apparently interested in alien non-human life forms, which may or may not actually exist, rather than the thousands of non-human, non-alien species that already do?

We may unravel this conundrum, and the similar ones that contemporary theology presents us with, if we begin to confront directly and honestly the theological investment in *not* addressing the animal issue. Christians are heirs to almost two thousand years of theologizing about the world. That we have been so neglectful of God's other creatures should give us some pause. As I have written elsewhere: Why is it that 'the community of faith which holds to the objective truth of the self-revelation of God in Christ should have advanced its world-affirming doctrine without much more than a passing thought for the millions of non-human inhabitants within creation itself?'[15] Two obvious answers present themselves: one reputable, the other less so.

The first is that throughout the centuries Christianity has demonstrated a penchant for articulating and defending its doctrines in a way that not only gives a high place to humanity but also defines that humanity *against* animals. It is difficult to find one historical or contemporary theological work on the status of humans that doesn't include the words 'unlike animals . . .' or others very similar to them. This—what I have called—'difference-finding tendency'[16] has obscured humanity's relationship to creation and bolstered up a range of 'differences', many of which are now seen to be empirically questionable.

The theological rationale for this tendency is not difficult to discern. It is encapsulated in Karl Barth's view that 'God's eternal Son and Logos did not will to be an angel or animal but man' and that *'this and this alone* was the content of the eternal divine election of grace'.[17] Given this overarching divine election of humanity, it must follow that humankind *is* special, unique, distinct, superior, and so on. It is as if, given this guarantee of divine favour, no claim for specialness—humanly speaking—can be insufficient. The incarnation is used as the trump card to vanquish all other creaturely rights to specialness, intrinsic worth, and respectful treatment. And once perceived as central—as the doctrine of the incarnation surely is—all other doctrines are then reinforced from this centre. The result is a narrowing of theological focus. Contrary to the biblical evidence, the notion of covenant is applied solely to human subjects. Atonement doctrine specifically, if not exclusively, concerns humanity's redemption. The work of the creative Spirit is telescoped into the salvation of human souls. And creation is seen only as the background or theatre to the real work of God performed for, on behalf of, the divinely elected human species which is now viewed as God's exclusive concern.

This christological logic has become so pervasive within the tradition that it is now taken to be the essence of the tradition itself. To be for Christ is to be for humanity: for our true welfare, our final happiness, our salvation. Anything less produces among mainstream Catholics and Protestants a sense of dismay at not having understood the true Christian message. We have become, almost without knowing it, the exponents of humanism's most cherished hope: only human beings really matter in the world.

But what is taken to be the essence of incarnational doctrine is at best only an interpretation of it. Incarnation does not have to be viewed as only the vindication of humanity. The key to realizing this is provided by Barth in his use of the word 'man'. For if the particularity of the incarnation is allowed its full weight, incarnation concerns the election not of men and women but man alone (in fact a Jewish, circumcised male). And true to this particularity there have been Christians throughout the centuries who have seen the election of man in the incarnation as grounds for positing a divine ordering of creation in which women are clearly subordinate. Indeed, some of the most weighty theological objections to the ordination of women have focused on precisely this: the appropriateness of specifically male persons for the eucharistic role of representing the male incarnate Christ.

Once we reject this implication (as we surely should) of the particularity of the incarnation, we are able to view the incarnation in broader terms which transcend even male and female humanity. Far from being God's Yes to male humanity alone, or male and female humanity, the incarnation can be viewed as God's Yes to creation: specifically to fleshly and sentient life. By becoming flesh, the Logos identifies, according to this paradigm, not only with humanity but with all creatures of flesh and blood.

I shall not deal here with the biblical and patristic evidence that justifies this wider view of the incarnation.[18] All that needs to be grasped is that the incarnation doesn't have to be seen as the objective privileging of the human species above all others—at least in a way that is derogatory to other species. It has undoubtedly been read that way. But it doesn't have to be. Indeed, nothing substantial is lost to Christian doctrine by this wider focus, and much, I shall argue, will be gained.

But is Christianity—in this one central doctrine alone—capable of reinterpretation, of embracing a wider paradigm? I think it's a real question. Real in the sense that we do not yet know the answer. If Hampson is right (as I fear she may well be) in rejecting a too-easily forged compatibility between Christianity and feminism, then even more should we be questioning whether historical Christianity is capable of becoming other-than-human species friendly.

Here we come to the second—and less reputable—answer to the question of why mainstream Christianity has been neglectful of animals. It is simply this: humans are not animals. The point is not as trite as it sounds. There is an element of human self-interest in all theological endeavours—not surprisingly perhaps, since, as traditionally conceived, the Christian Gospel means 'good news' for human beings. That allowed, and without supposing that all theology is simply the aggrandisement of the human species, there needs to be some frank acknowledgment that theology can be used for self-serving human ends. The point is easily grasped once it is also appreciated that theology has been used historically to serve specifically male interests—sometimes quite unconsciously so. Feminists have rightly alerted us to the way in which our interpretation of the Bible and the tradition reinforces a patriarchal, man-centred view of the world. And if it is true that some 'hermeneutics of suspicion' are appropriate when considering texts which may have been influenced by patriarchal prejudice, these are even more appropriate when it comes to more widely held speciesist prejudices against animals.

Rejecting humanocentric prejudices about animals may sound—probably *will* sound—like the most ludicrous latest expression of political correctness to those who hold fast to 'historical Christianity' and are fearful of what may be called 'postmodernist innovation'. But, in fact, the promise of real theology has always been that it will liberate us from humanocentrism, that is from a purely human view of the world to a truly God-centred one. Theology at its best has always claimed to be more than a purely human view of the world. Once grasped, the issue about animals is seen for what it is: a central test of the adequacy of Christian theology and its claim to offer an objective God-centred account of the world including some account of the purpose, meaning, and value of non-human creatures. To go on supposing that the meaning and value of other creatures can be determined solely by their relationship with human beings is untheological.[19] Confronting speciesism, then, is not about Christian theology's latest concession to secular fashion, it is an imperative derived from the heart of theology's mission: to render a truthful, non-partial account of the creation God has made.

What might a theology that took animals seriously look like? Recently I made a presentation, with Paul Waldau, at the American Academy of Religion on 'The Dog's Mess: Theology as if Animals Mattered'.[20] The dog's mess is defined by Albert Schweitzer. To describe the place of animals in European thought he used the image of a kitchen floor scrubbed clean by someone who is 'careful to see that the door is shut lest the dog should come in and ruin the finished job with its footprints'.[21] Certainly animals do make a mess of humanocentric theology, but in my view radical insights about the worth of animals can be incorporated into mainstream trinitarian theology, and such doctrines as creation, incarnation, and redemption will themselves be enlarged and improved in the process.

Yes, odd as it may sound to liberals, a theology which took animals seriously would be a more fully trinitarian theology. A theology with real *theos, logos,* and *pneuma* in it. In brief, it would be a theology which

> celebrated God's universal creativity in relation not only to the human species but to all species of life;
>
> recognized the God-givenness of all individual life, human or animal, as something to be honoured and respected;
>
> was open to the work of the Spirit alive and abroad—not just within humankind but in all creation, especially sentient creatures;
>
> affirmed human specialness as a commission to be not the master species but the servant species;
>
> expounded the moral covenant between God and all creatures of all flesh;
>
> celebrated the incarnation as God's love affair with the flesh—not only the flesh of humankind but all embodied, sentient creatures;
>
> saw in the crucified Christ God's identification with all innocent suffering, both human and animal;
>
> grasped that in their innocence and incomprehension sentient creatures represent the unacknowledged faces of Christ in our world;
>
> felt God's own suffering in the pain and misery and futility of unredeemed creation, human and animal, and regarded it as grace that we are able to co-experience with God the passion of the world;
>
> took to itself the Christlike paradigm of inclusive moral generosity to the weak, innocent, and vulnerable and applied that same paradigm to all sentient creatures;
>
> articulated a vision of Christ's reconciling ministry to all suffering creatures and sought to place itself on God's side in the work of redemption and justice; and
>
> looked to the completion and transformation of all things in Christ: the sabbath for all creatures, human and animal.

Doubtless this list is not exhaustive but it does illustrate the orientation required if theology were to move beyond humanocentric parochialism and begin to take God as Creator, Reconciler, and Redeemer seriously.

And is Christianity destined to remain irredeemably speciesist? Certainly non-speciesist theology is a promise in search of fulfilment. Much historical theology is not impartial in relation to animals, and neither is much in the foundational narratives of scripture. The struggle to secure correcting mechanisms in theology's own self-understanding is bound to be a long, slow process—paralleled (though only to a lesser degree) by the challenges presented by feminism itself. In my view, the question remains genuinely open.

But there are many sources of hope, two in particular. The first is expressed by those lines of Alasdair MacIntyre that 'an adequate sense of tradition manifests itself in a grasp of those future possibilities which the past has made available to us in the present', and, again, 'Traditions when vital embody continuities of conflict.'[22] Against the mainstream view that the purpose and value of animals can be wholly defined by reference to the species which controls them, there have been other voices within the tradition urging release from humanocentrism. These voices deserve a hearing, and at least some of them are represented in this collection. The biblical vision of a peaceable kingdom with animals has been largely relegated by Christian theology to the End Time but at least it has kept alive, however futuristically, the possibility of creatures living together in peace. The tradition which has distanced itself from its own vision is also the tradition capable of mediating a sense of its contemporary urgency.

The Christian tradition is not like a closed book with all the lines printed and the plot already worked out. There is an underlying trinitarian dynamic—of Father, Son, *and Holy Spirit*—to be grasped: not all truth is given in the past, the Spirit has something to give us in the present. It is untrinitarian to consistently oppose God's work in the past to what we may learn here and now. For myself, I cannot get away from the dominical promise that the Spirit 'will guide you into all the truth' (John 16.13, NEB). This must mean, *inter alia,* that there are new things to be learnt. The God revealed in Jesus Christ is the same God who reveals now through the Spirit. In the at least half-true words of David Jenkins, 'revelation is always now, or never'.[23] The Spirit which bears witness to the things of Christ is now able to help us learn what living the Christlike life means in relation to God's other sentient creatures.

The other source of hope is represented in a small but not insignificant way by this volume itself. For many centuries, questions about animals have effectively been answered by *not* addressing them. Indeed, the questions have not for the most part even been on the agenda. All disciplines of course are characterized by the asking of some questions to the exclusion of others. The question that most characterizes theology is this: 'What must be true about the nature of the world in the light of God's self-revelation in Jesus Christ?' It is striking that this question has been consistently asked in such a way that animals are rarely included even in the terms of reference. Historical Christianity has thus been marked by the questions it hasn't asked or allowed itself to answer. But the interrogative can be one means by which the Spirit penetrates and disturbs us. As I learnt from my daughter some years ago, the asking of questions can be undermining, even subversive, of standard answers. That theology has formulated its ideas without asking whether its doctrine of God was arbitrary or unjust to animals (and hence inadequate) ought to give us hope that in centuries to come a theology which did at least ask this question would be substantially different.

Theologians have a responsibility in this regard: to articulate a theological understanding in which 'the animal question' can be fairly put and answers assessed. What cannot be right is for practitioners—whether they be biblical scholars, historians, systematizers, or ethicists—to carry on their business as though the world of animals were invisible, and as if urgent and thoughtful questions cannot be raised about our theological understanding of the non-human world. A special word of thanks is therefore appropriate to our contributors, who have the accolade of being, if not the first, certainly among the first to ask questions and formulate answers.[24] The voices represented here have not been selected with any ulterior motive: on the contrary, we have searched out as many contrasting voices from as many traditions—Catholic, Protestant, Anglican, and Evangelical—as we can in order to allow the 'continuities of conflict' to show themselves and in turn stimulate new thought.

My particular hope is that in, say, ten, twenty, or thirty years, most authors will be pleased but also embarrassed by their contribution to this collection. Pleased because most are pioneering essays. Embarrassed because what true pioneers most love is for others to go even further than they have done and leave them behind. That we are still at the beginning of asking theological questions that matter about animals is painfully obvious.

For myself, I love collections. In their overly derided patchiness and disparateness they expose most constructively the strengths and weaknesses of current thinking on a given topic. Constructively because one person's omission or failure is another's creative opportunity. Animals are on the agenda, but the adequacy of theology is on the line.

1. In your view, are animals cherished by God, as are human beings? Why or why not?
2. Have animals taught you about the presence of God? In what ways?

Notes

1. Daphne Hampson, *Theology and Feminism*, Blackwell 1990.
2. Daphne Hampson, *After Christianity*, SCM Press 1996, p. 6. See also Iain Torrance, 'Is Christianity Irredeemably Sexist?' in *Who Needs Feminism? Men Respond to Sexism in the Church*, ed. Richard Holloway, SPCK 1991, and Hampson's comments, *After Christianity*, pp. 287–88.
3. Editorial, *Daily Telegraph*, 10 January 1995, my emphasis. See also my response, 'A Christian Shield for Animals', *The Spectator*, 6 April 1996, pp. 18–19.
4. Andrew Linzey and Paul Waldau, 'Speciesism' in *Dictionary of Ethics, Theology and Society*, ed. Paul Barry Clarke and Andrew Linzey, Routledge 1996, p. 788; my emphasis.
5. For a discussion of this material see Andrew Linzey and Dan Cohn-Sherbok (eds.), *After Noah: Animals and the Liberation of Theology*, Cassell 1997, ch. 4: '*Christ and the Stories of Christlike Compassion*'.
6. I am often accused of focusing only on the negative aspects of the tradition in relation to animals. *After Noah* is an attempt to outline the resources within Judaism and Christianity for a positive view of animals, and ch. 6 shows how 'Animals can liberate Jewish and Christian theology' by rejecting the contemporary deification of humans in theology and ethics. See also my thumbnail sketch of the positive tradition in 'Animals', in *Oxford Companion to Christian Thought*, ed. Adrian Hastings, Oxford: Oxford University Press 2000.
7. Aristotle, *The Politics*, trs. T.A. Sinclair, rev., T.J. Saunders, Penguin Books 1985, p. 79.
8. Augustine, *City of God*, 1.20; cited and discussed by Gillian Clark in ch. 6 below.
9. Thomas Aquinas, *Summa Contra Gentiles*, trs. English Dominican Fathers, Benzger Brothers 1928, Third Book, Part II, ch. cxii; also cited and discussed in Andrew Linzey, *Christianity and the Rights of Animals*, SPCK/Crossroad 1987), pp. 22f.
10. See e.g. P. Palazzini (ed.), *Dictionary of Moral Theology*, comp. F. Roberti, trs. H.Y. Yannone, Burns & Oates 1962), pp. 73f.
11. John Canon McCarthy, *Problems in Theology, Vol. II: The Commandments*, Browne & Nolan 1960, pp. 156–57. Far from falling out of use, the view that the virtue of 'temperance' is sufficient for understanding our obligations to animals was maintained by a leading Dominican at a conference on animals in Oxford in 1996.
12. William Cowper, 'Winter Walk at Noon', extract in *Song of Creation*, ed. Andrew Linzey and Tom Regan, Marshall Pickering 1989, p. 48. Cowper's poem is an impressive essay on the theology of the Fall and restoration of the animal creation.
13. For some recent 'animal blind' discussion of creation liturgy, see Celia Deane-Drummond, *A Handbook in Theology and Ecology*, SCM Press 1996; Deiter T. Hessell, *Theology for Earth Community: A Field Guide*, Orbis Books 1996; and Ralph N. McMichael, Jr. (ed.), *Creation and Liturgy*, The Pastoral Press 1993. I hope to remedy this deficiency in my *Animal Rites: Liturgies for Animal Care*, SCM Press 1999.
14. John Puddefoot, 'Perhaps God Really Is an Alien', *Church Times*, 29 August, 1997, p. 8.
15. Andrew Linzey *Animal Theology*, SCM Press/University of Illinois Press 1994, p. viii.
16. Ibid., p. 47.
17. Karl Barth, 'Church Dogmatics, III/I,' in *The Doctrine of Creation*, ed. G.W. Bromiley and T.F. Torrance, T. & T. Clark 1960, pp. 16, 18; my emphases.
18. For two outstanding discussions on the patristic and biblical evidence see Allan D. Galloway, *The Cosmic Christ*, Nisbet & Co. 1951 and Robert Murray, *The Cosmic Covenant: Biblical Themes of Justice, Peace and the Integrity of Creation*, Sheed & Ward 1992.
19. I develop this point elsewhere: see *After Noah*, ch. 6 and my 'The Theological Basis of Animal Rights', *The Christian Century* 108/28, 9 October 1991, pp. 906–10.
20. Andrew Linzey and Paul Waldau, 'The Dog's Mess: Theology as if Animals Mattered', *AARSBL Abstracts*, 1994 Annual Meeting, Chicago, para. A179.
21. See Albert Schweitzer, *Civilization and Ethics*, trs. C.T. Campion, A. & C. Black 1967, and discussion in Barth, *Church Dogmatics*, III/4, p. 349; also discussed in Linzey, *Animal Theology*, p. 7.
22. Alasdair MacIntyre, *After Virtue*, 2nd edn, Duckworth 1985, pp. 221–22, 223.
23. David Jenkins *God, Miracle and the Church of England*, SCM Press 1987, p. 100. I am grateful to Jenkins for his insightful discussion of MacIntyre. On the need for a new *pneuma*-based paradigm, see my 'On Theology' in *Theology, the University and the Modern World*, ed. P.A.B. Clarke and Andrew Linzey, Lester Crook Academic Press 1988, pp. 29–66.
24. There have been some other theological pioneers—notably Gary Comstock, John B. Cobb, Jr., Jay B. McDaniel, Stephen R.L. Clark, and John Berkman—but not many. There are only two other anthologies on theology and animals: Charles Pinches and Jay B. McDaniel (eds.), *Good News for Animals? Christian Approaches to Animal Well-Being*, Orbis Books 1993, and Andrew Linzey and Tom Regan (eds.), *Animals and Christianity: A Book of Readings*, SPCK/Crossroad 1988.

35 Islam

Martin Forward and Mohamed Alam

Martin Forward and Mohamed Alam explain the Muslim view of the animal–human relationship. Animals are not to be treated as valueless by human beings, but by God's permission human beings have power over the animals and are entitled to use animals for human purposes. Forward and Alam explain the restrictions under which animals may be eaten and the required ritual method of slaughter.

[. . .]

According to the Qur'ān, 'there is not an animal on earth, nor a bird that flies on its wings—but they are communities like you . . . and they shall all be gathered to their Lord in the end' (6: 38). This means that they fulfil the plan which God has allotted to them in his purpose. They are not to be treated as valueless by human beings. It has not usually been taken by commentators of the Qur'ān or jurists to mean that animals share in the bliss (or torment) of life after death. Human beings are distinguished from animals by their capacity to make moral judgements. Only they, of all species of life, can choose to obey or disobey God, and so earn paradise or hell.

Islam is not a sentimental religion. By God's permission, human beings have power over the animals, as over all creation, and they can be used for various purposes.

[. . .]

Islam forbids the keeping of some animals for domestic purposes. Most Muslims do not have dogs as pets. [. . .] Muhammad did not like dogs. [. . .] However, he did not mean that dogs could be mistreated. A prostitute who saw a thirsty dog hanging around a well one day gave it water to drink. For this act of kindness, the Prophet pardoned all her sins.

[. . .]

Other traditions of the Prophet forbid treating animals cruelly. They are not to be caged, or beaten unnecessarily, or branded on the face, or allowed to fight each other for human entertainment. They must not be mutilated while they are alive, which forbids vivisection. Muslims are opposed to battery farming, the slaughter of calves for veal, and all other forms of animal-husbandry which are cruel to creatures or which needlessly kill them. These interdicts arise out of the Islamic emphasis that human beings have a moral obligation towards animals.

[. . .]

A very important function of animals is to provide human beings with food. Few Muslims are vegetarians. But certain animals are forbidden to Muslims, and all creatures used for food need to be killed in a prescribed manner.

Islamic law declares certain things permissible (*Halāl*) for human beings, and other things harmful (*Harām*). This division covers all aspects of life, including what Muslims can eat. Muslims regard all things as *Halāl* unless God has commanded otherwise. There are four forbidden categories of food, which are derived from the Qur'ān (5: 4):

1. Meat of dead animals
2. Blood

3.   Pigs' flesh
4.   Meat over which another name than God's has been invoked.

The meat of dead animals is taken to mean a beast or fowl which dies of natural causes, without being slaughtered or hunted by humans. The qur'ānic verse offers five classifications of dead animals:

1.   The strangled
2.   Those beaten to death
3.   Those fallen from a height
4.   Those gored by other animals
5.   Those partly eaten by wild animals.

Scholars have elaborated a number of reasons for this prohibition. The animal might have died of some disease. Muslims should intend to kill an animal for food, offering it to God, and not thoughtlessly make use of a deceased creature. By this ban, God makes food available to other animals and birds.

Islamic law has exempted fish, whales, and other sea-creatures from the category of dead animals. The Qur'ān says: 'The game of the sea is permitted to you and so is its food' (5: 99). Traditions relate that the Prophet allowed dead food that comes from the sea to be eaten. One story tells of a group of Muslims sent by Muhammad to ambush his enemies. They became very hungry, until the sea threw out a huge, dead whale. They ate its meat, rubbed their bodies with its fat, and, when one of its ribs was fixed over the ground, a rider passed beneath it (Bukhari, in Khan 1984, vol. 7: 293 f.). Many jurists have amplified this permission so that all marine creatures, those which live in the sea and cannot survive outside it, are *Halāl*. It does not matter whether they are taken from the water dead or living, whole or in bits, whether they are caught by a Muslim or someone else.

The interdict on blood is interpreted to mean flowing blood, which was felt by jurists to be repugnant and injurious to health. The law does not forbid eating blood that remains in the animal after the flow has ceased.

Pork is outlawed on a number of grounds. It is dangerous to eat in hot climates, where it quickly goes off. It is regarded as an unclean animal, eating filth and offal, and so its meat is repugnant to decent people. Some scholars have claimed that it incites those who eat it to shameful and lustful thoughts.

Finally, God's name must be invoked when the animal is slaughtered. The man who slits its throat says: *bi-smillāhi, allāhu akbar*, 'in the name of God, God is most great'. It is not acceptable to invoke the name of an idol, as Arab polytheists at the time of Muhammad did. Nor is it all right to say nothing. Killing an animal for food is a devotional act. God gave humans control over all the earth, subjecting animals to them, and allowing them to take an animal's life for food. Pronouncing God's name while killing the creature is a reminder of God's permission and ultimate control over all things.

Other than these four categories, all food can be eaten and enjoyed (2: 172; 6: 119). Indeed, the emphasis in Islam is upon what can be eaten and enjoyed, rather than on what is forbidden. Only a few things are forbidden. There is no virtue in exceedingly strict food laws.

[. . .]

Nowadays, the ritual killing of animals is condemned by many non-Muslim individuals and groups. The bottom line for Muslims is that it is commanded by God, and this order counts for more than the opinions of others. Muslims are not mawkish about such matters. Islam began on the fringes of the desert, where staying alive was the pre-eminent concern of many people, and meat was regarded by them as a necessity, not a luxury. Most Muslims today live in relatively poor countries, where survival counts for more than middle-class values, which can seem excessively indulgent. Islam gives human beings power over, and responsibility for, animals, which should be treated with kindness and consideration, but which, by God's permission, provide food, clothing, and transport.

[. . .]

Bibliography

Khalid, F. with O'Brien, J. (eds.) (1992) *Islam and Ecology*, London, Cassell.

Khan, M. M. (ed.) (1984) *Sahah Al-Bukhari*, vols 1–9, New Delhi, Kitab Bhavan.

Nasr, S. H. (1976) *Islamic Science: An Illustrated Study*, London, Thames and Hudson.

Robson, J. R. (1970 edn) *Mishkat al-Masibih*, vols 1–2, Lahore, Muhammad Ashraf.

Siddiqi, A. H. (ed.) (1977) *Sahih Muslim*, vols 1–4, New Delhi, Kitab Bhavan.

Yusuf Ali, A. (1975 edn) *The Holy Qu'rān: Text, Translation and Commentary*, Leicester, Islamic Foundation.

Part Five

Animal Experimentation

Introduction to Part Five

In this part, we focus on some ethical issues in the context of using nonhuman animals as research subjects in laboratory and fieldwork, and as teaching subjects in educational institutions. Collectively the authors address a wide range of ethical issues on these topics.

Mylan Engel argues that animal-based biomedical research is notoriously unreliable for insights on human medicine. Based on inferences from animal research, he points out that false positive and false negative results from animal models have had severe detrimental effects on humans. David DeGrazia explores areas in which those opposing ("animal advocates") and those favoring ("biomedicine") use of animals in scientific research might find common ground; he also identifies several topics on which agreement appears unlikely. Responding to DeGrazia's description of the biomedicine perspective, Baruch A. Brody articulates a position supporting animal research based on the special obligations humans have to each other, including members of their families, communities, and species. Lynda Birke addresses the conflicting metaphors associated with laboratory rodents, ranging from potent icons of scientific research to "not quite animals."

Bernard Rollin, along with Simon Festing and Robin Wilkinson, have adjacent articles in a journal to assess the ethics of animal research. Rollin argues that scientists purposely have excluded ethical considerations in their "scientific ideology," particularly with invasive research. He argues that animal research needs to evolve into a "moral science." In contrast, Festing and Wilkinson argue that scientists generally accept that animals should be used for research only within an ethical framework, and United Kingdom guidelines all emphasize replacing, reducing, and refining use of animals in research.

While not specifically addressing animal research, Paul Root Wolpe addresses eight general reasons sometimes used by scientists to avoid addressing ethical repercussions of their research. Wolpe then addresses each in detail, affirming that all scientists have moral responsibilities in the work they conduct.

Barbara Orlans assesses the range of legal protection governing animal-based research and briefly summarizes the international variation in levels of animal protection. She also addresses the role of ethical criteria, including animal-harm scales as a means to assess animal research.

Andrew Petto and Karla Russell explore an innovative strategy of fully involving students in making ethical decisions about using animals in their classrooms, including what work can be conducted appropriately as well as the sources, care, and disposal of all animals used.

Ben Minteer and James Collins call for bringing ethicists, scientists, and biodiversity managers together for ethical analysis and problem-solving in ecological field studies.

1. In your view, are animals cherished by God, as are human beings? Why or why not?
2. Have animals taught you about the presence of God? In what ways?

Further Reading

American Association for Laboratory Animal Science (AALAS). *Institutional Animal Care and Use Committees: A comprehensive.* Online at: http://www.iacuc.org.

Balcombe, J. P., N. D. Barnard, and C. Sandusky. 2004. Laboratory routines cause animal stress. *Contemporary Topics in Laboratory Animal Science* 43: 42–51.

Baumans, V. 2004. Use of animals in experimental research: An ethical dilemma? *Gene Therapy* 11: S64–S66.

Bishop, L. J., and A. L. Nolen. 2001. Animals in research and education: Ethical issues. Scope Note 40. *Kennedy Institute of Ethics Journal* 11: 91–112.

Conn, P. M., and J. V. Parker. 2008. *The Animal Research War*. New York: Palgrave/Macmillan.

Dich, T., T. Hansen, A. Algers, A. Hanlon, H. Loor, and P. Sandoe. 2006. Animal Ethics Dilemma: A computer supported learning tool. In *Ethics and the politics of food*, M. Kaiser and M. E. Lien (eds.) Wageningen Academic Publishers, the Netherlands. Online at www.aedilemma.net.

Gluck, J. P., T. DiPasquale, and F. B. Orlans. (eds.) 2002. *Applied Ethics in Animal Research: Philosophy, Regulation, and Laboratory Applications*. West Lafayette, Ind.: Purdue University Press.

Hagelin, J., J. Hau, and H.-E. Carlsson. 2002. The refining influence of ethics committees on animal experimentation in Sweden. *Laboratory Animals* 37: 10–18.

Humane Society of the United States. n.d. *Animals & Society: A List of Courses (Animal Ethics, Animal Rights, Animal Welfare)*. Online at http://www.hsus.org/programs/research/animals_education.html.

Langford, D. J., S. E. Crager, Z. Shehzad, S. B. Smith, S. G. Sotocinal, J. S. Levenstadt, M. L. Chanda, D. J. Levitin, and J. S. Mogil. 2006. Social modulation of pain as evidence for empathy in mice. *Science* 312: 1967–1970.

Mangan, Katherine S. (2000) Can vet schools teach without killing animals? *The Chronicle of Higher Education* 46 (22): A53–4.

New England Anti-Vivisection Society Ethical Science and Education Coalition. n.d. Online at http://www.neavs.org/esec.html and http://www.neavs.org.

Nuffield Council on Bioethics. 2006. *The Ethics of Research Involving Animals*. Online at www.nuffieldbioethics.org.

Phillips, C.J.C., and S. McCulloch. 2005. Student attitudes on animal sentience and use of animals in society. *Journal of Biological Education* 40 (1): 17–24. DOI:10.1080/00219266.2005.9656004

Physicians Committee for Responsible Medicine. Online at www.pcrm.org.

Rollin, B. E. 2006a. The regulation of animal research and the emergence of animal ethics: A conceptual history. *Theoretical Medicine and Bioethics* 27: 285–304.

Rollin, B. E. 2006b. *Science and ethics*. New York, NY: Cambridge University Press.

Shanks, H., and K. Green. 2004. Evolution and the ethics of animal research. *Essays in Philosophy* 5 (2). Online at www.humboldt.edu/~essays/archives.html.

Shanks, N., R. Greek, and J. Greek. 2009. Are animal models predictive for humans? *Philosophy, Ethics, and Humanities in Medicine* 4(2): 20. DOI:10.1186/1747-5341-4-2.

Study Questions

1. Select one of the four issues DeGrazia believes will continue to serve as a point of difference between proponents and opponents of animal use, and explain how you might move the two sides closer together on that issue. How do Engel's arguments affect your outlook on these issues? Justify your answers.

2. How might Brody respond to the claim that animals have a value that cannot be reduced to human utility?

3. How do Rollin, Festing and Wilkinson, and Wolpe address the role of ethics in scientific research? Briefly compare and contrast the position presented in each article with the other two.

4. In light of Orlan's and Birke's discussions, what additional laws regulating animal use, if any, do you believe should be adopted by the U.S.?

5. Based on Minteer and Collins' recommendations for a new field in ecological ethics, give three traits of this ethic you would propose to initiate fruitful discussions.

Laboratory Studies

36 The Commonsense Case Against Animal Experimentation

Mylan Engel Jr.

Engel advocates that there are no good reasons for animal-based biomedical research. From the standpoint of humans, there have sometimes been some devastating effects from applying findings from animal studies to humans—both because of false positive and false negative test results. Because of the greatly compromised value of applying nonhuman animal test results to human medicine, he argues that there is no moral justification for harming or killing research animals in the pursuit of faulty knowledge.

As this volume illustrates, most arguments for the immorality of animal experimentation take one of two forms. Either they follow Peter Singer's lead and maintain that most animal experiments are morally unjustifiable on utilitarian grounds[1] or they follow Tom Regan's deontological rights-based approach and insist that virtually all of the animals experimented on in research facilities around the country possess the very same properties that confer rights on humans, and therefore experimenting on these animals is wrong because it violates their rights.[2] When confronted with Singer's and Regan's arguments opposing animal experimentation, proponents of animal experimentation tend to casually dismiss these arguments by rejecting the ethical theories on which they are predicated. These dismissals take roughly the following form: "Singer's preference utilitarianism[3] is irremediably flawed, as is Regan's theory of moral rights. Since Singer's and Regan's arguments against animal experimentation are predicated on flawed ethical theories, their arguments are also flawed. Until someone can provide me with clear moral reasons for not experimenting on animals, I will continue to experiment on animals as I see fit."

Consider two examples. In an effort to defend animal experimentation, Carl Cohen (2001a, 2001b) goes to great lengths to try to show, contra Regan, that nonhuman animals lack rights and that, therefore, it is permissible to experiment on them (as if the latter followed from the former). In an article published in the *Journal of the American Medical Association*, Richard Vance admits: "Both [Tom Regan and Peter Singer] are exceptionally good philosophers in the analytical tradition. They provide sophisticated defenses of their positions" (1992, 1715). However, Vance rejects their defenses of the immorality of animal experimentation because he rejects the analytical ethical tradition on which they are based. As Vance sees it, Singer's and Regan's arguments against animal experimentation ultimately fail because of the

> limited nature of the philosophical tools they use. Their ultimate theoretical weaknesses are extremely common among analytical ethicists. Unlike more substantive ethical traditions (for example religious or ethnic traditions), analytical ethics cannot draw on a rich array of sources—canonical texts, authoritative readings, overlapping (even contradictory) platitudes, interpretative communities, and the like. In comparison with such traditions, analytical ethics is abstract and thin. Despite claims of rational consistency, no analytical model has been able to claim adequacy.
>
> (1715)

A moment's reflection reveals the self-serving sophistry of such a reply. Since no ethical theory to date is immune to objection, one could fashion a similar reply to "justify" or rationalize virtually any behavior. One could "justify" slavery as follows: An opponent of slavery might appeal to utilitarian, Kantian, or contractarian grounds to establish the immorality of slavery. Our fictitious slavery proponent could then point out that all of these ethical theories are flawed and, ipso facto, so too are all the arguments against slavery. Our slavery proponent might then assert: "Until someone can provide me with clear moral reasons for abolishing slavery, I will continue to own and exploit slaves."

The speciousness of such a "justification" of slavery should be obvious. No one who seriously considered the brutality and inhumanity of slavery could think that *it* is somehow permissible *simply because* all current ethical theories are flawed. But such specious reasoning is often used to "justify" the equally brutal and inhumane breeding, confining, infecting, injuring, mutilating, maiming, blinding, torturing, and killing of animals in animal experiments. My aim in the present chapter is to block this spurious reply by providing an argument for the immorality of animal experimentation that does not rest on any particular highly contentious ethical theory. Rather, it rests on commonsense moral beliefs that we all share.

Before turning to these beliefs, a few prefatory observations are in order. First, unlike other arguments for the immorality of animal experimentation, my argument is not predicated on the wrongness of speciesism,[4] nor does it depend on your believing that all animals are equal or that all animals have a right to life; rather, it is predicated on several commonsense moral principles which you no doubt believe. The significance of this argumentative strategy is two-fold: First and most important, all effective argumentation must start with premises one's interlocutor accepts. The reason Singer's and Regan's arguments sometimes fall on deaf ears is that their arguments do not start with premises their readers share. In contrast, my argument starts with premises the reader already accepts and traces out the moral implications of those premises. Consequently, the reader is already rationally committed to the truth of the resulting conclusion, on pain of inconsistency.

Second, some philosophers remain unmoved by Singer's and Regan's arguments for a different reason than the ones just cited. These philosophers find that the nonspeciesistic implications of Singer's and Regan's arguments just *feel* wrong to them. They sincerely *feel* that humans are more important than nonhumans.[5] Perhaps these feelings are irrational in light of evolutionary theory and our biological kinship with other species, but these feelings are nonetheless real. My argument is neutral with respect to such sentiments. It is compatible with both an anthropocentric and a biocentric worldview. In short, my argument is designed to show that even those steadfastly committed to valuing humans over nonhumans are nevertheless committed to the immorality of animal experimentation, given their other beliefs.

Finally, although animals are used in all sorts of scientific research, including cosmetic testing, household product testing, and psychological experimentation, in what follows I will focus primarily on the use of animals in biomedical research, since if it is wrong to use animals in experiments aimed at the development of vitally important, potentially lifesaving drugs, then it is *a fortiori* wrong to use animals to test unnecessary trivial products like a new floor wax or a new shampoo. Having clarified the scope, significance, and rationale for the argumentative strategy that I will be employing, I now turn to the argument itself. In the following sections, I identify several commonsense moral principles that we all accept, then I use these principles to develop an ethical consistency argument designed to show that using animals as test subjects in biomedical research is wrong.

Common Ground

My argument for the immorality of using animals as test subjects in biomedical research is predicated on several widely accepted, commonsense moral principles—principles that you no doubt already believe. These commonsense principles are so central to our conception of morality that any moral theory that conflicted with them would be rejected as unsatisfactory on reflective equilibrium grounds. Since any adequate moral view must cohere with these principles, we can appeal to these principles directly when making moral evaluations. The principles are these:

(P1) It is wrong to intentionally harm conscious sentient animals *for no good reason.*
(P2) It is wrong to cause conscious sentient animals to suffer *for no good reason.*
(P3) It is wrong to kill conscious sentient animals *for no good reason.*[6]

These principles are not in dispute.[7] Even the staunchest defenders of animal experimentation embrace these commonsense principles. For example, Cohen explicitly endorses (P2) and (P3): "If animals feel pain (and certainly mammals do, though we cannot be sure about insects and worms), *we humans surely ought cause no pain to them that cannot be justified. Nor ought we kill them without reason*" (2001a, 46; emphasis mine).[8] Elsewhere, Cohen reiterates his commitment to (P2) and (P3): "Our obligations to animals arise not from their rights, I believe, but from the fact that they can feel pain and from the fact that *we, as moral agents, have a general obligation to avoid imposing needless pain or death*" (ibid., 226; emphasis mine).[9] Similarly, Peter Carruthers acknowledges that sentient animals deserve some moral consideration when he explicitly endorses (P2): "It will be useful to have a rough idea at the out-set of what our common-sense morality tells us about the status and appropriate treatment of animals. . . . Most people hold that it is wrong to cause animals unnecessary suffering. Opinions will differ as to what counts as necessary. . . . But *all will agree that gratuitous suffering—suffering caused for no good reason—is wrong*" (Carruthers 1992, 8; emphasis mine). These sentiments are not new. In 1813, Le Gallois endorsed (P2): "I own that it would be barbarous to make animals suffer in vain, if the object of the experiment could be obtained without it" (Le Gallois 1813, 20). Thus, even these prominent animal experimentation advocates are on record acknowledging that we owe conscious sentient animals a non-negligible amount of direct moral consideration. How much consideration? At least this much: We cannot harm them, cause them to suffer, or kill them *for no good reason.* If we do harm them, kill them, or cause them to suffer for no good reason, we are doing something morally wrong. We are failing to accord them the moral consideration that they are due. Since we all accept (P1)–(P3), we are all committed to the view that animals deserve at least this much moral consideration.[10]

Principles (P1)–(P3) entail three additional principles directly related to the moral status of animal experimentation. For example, (P1) entails:

(P4) It is wrong to intentionally perform *harmful experiments* on conscious sentient animals *for no good reason.*[11] Principles (P2) and (P3) respectively entail the following principles: (P5) It is wrong to perform *painful* experiments on conscious sentient animals *for no good reason.* (P6) It is wrong to perform *lethal* experiments on conscious sentient animals *for no good reason.*

Anyone committed to (P1)–(P3) is, on pain of inconsistency, also committed to (P4)–(P6), since (P4)–(P6) are simply instantiations of (P1)–(P3), respectively. The relevance of (P4)–(P6) is this: virtually every biomedical experiment performed on animals causes harm to those animals. Many of these *harmful* experiments cause the animal subjects excruciating pain, and virtually all of these experiments are ultimately *lethal,* since the animals are routinely destroyed at the end of the experiment. So, the critical question is this: Is there a good reason to subject animals to these experiments? If not, all of these experiments are wrong and ought to be abolished.

The Scientific Case Against Using Animals in Biomedical Research

There are certain hallmarks of received wisdom. These empirical beliefs have worked their way into mainstream consciousness with no good supporting evidence, and yet, they occupy such a central position in our belief systems that we are loath to give them up. The belief that "milk does a body good" is such a belief. The belief that we need to experiment on animals in order to find cures for human diseases is another. Even people who have become sensitized to the plight of animals needlessly brutalized in factory farms and who have become vegetarians as a result still often think that some animal experimentation can be justified on the basis of its benefits to humanity. Using animals to test new drugs is sacrosanct. It is part of the medical and scientific orthodoxy. Why does almost everyone buy into this orthodoxy? They do so

- in part because the media constantly bombard us with animal research "successes"—for example, the media optimistically report that some drug X tested on rats promises to be a panacea for some horrific human disease but fail to report when X is pulled from the market on the basis of failed clinical trials.
- in part because of scare tactics advanced by researchers and governmental propaganda, with comments like, "If we didn't test these drugs on animals, we'd have to test these drugs on humans, and wouldn't that be terrible?" Not wanting to be guinea pigs ourselves, we happily embrace the orthodoxy. What we neglect to realize is that these drugs will be tested on humans anyway in phase I, phase II, and phase III clinical trials before they are approved by the FDA.
- in part because some claims made by animal experimentation advocates are true, like the claim: "Some questions can be answered *only* by animal research." This claim is true. For example, if you wish to know how much of a given substance X will prove lethal to 50 percent of rats, you must test substance X on rats. Why? Because LD50 [lethal dose 50 percent] results vary from species to species. The amount of substance X that will prove lethal to 50 percent of rats won't be the amount of substance X that will prove lethal to 50 percent of mouse subjects, nor will it be the amount of substance X that will prove lethal to 50 percent of chickens, cats, dogs, or humans. So, if you wish to know how much of substance X will prove lethal to rats, you must use rats. But why should anyone care how much of X proves lethal to 50 percent of rat subjects? This idiosyncratic information has no relevance to human health and well-being. It is no more useful than knowing whether the number of blades of grass in your front yard is odd or even. A real case will illustrate the point. Let X be the substance nicotine. Since some people still smoke tobacco, it *is* important to know the dose of nicotine that is lethal for humans. The lethal dose of nicotine in rats is 53 milligrams per kilogram of body weight. The lethal dose of nicotine in dogs is 9.2 mg/kg. Neither measure is remotely indicative of the dose of nicotine that is lethal in humans, namely, 0.9 mg/kg. Relying on the LD50 results of nicotine in rats (or dogs for that matter) to estimate the lethal dose of nicotine in humans would have had fatal results in humans. Nicotine is not unique in this regard. The lethal dose of mercury (II) chloride in rats and mice is 1 mg/kg and 6 mg/kg, respectively—six times greater in mice. But the lethal dose of paracetamol in rats and mice is 2400 mg/kg and 340 mg/kg, respectively—seven times greater in rats (PCRM 1999, 2). Thirty years ago, two leading toxicologists, Zbinden and Flury-Roversi, concluded: "For the recognition of the symptomatology of acute poisoning in man and for the determination of the human lethal dose, the LD_{50}-test in animals is of very little value" (1981, 96). They further concluded: "The application of the LD_{50}-test for the solution of pharmacokinetic problems must be regarded as one of the semiquantitative pilot procedures that have no place in modern pharmaceutical and chemical research. The use of the LD_{50}-test as basis for selection of doses for sub-acute and chronic toxicity tests and other procedures (e.g., teratogenicity, carcinogenicity studies) is obsolete" (ibid).

Since LD50 tests provide no useful lethal-dose information that can be reliably extrapolated to human beings, all the pain and suffering that animal subjects are forced to endure in LD50 tests is done *for no good reason.* Consequently, (P1)–(P6) entail that conducting LD50 tests on nonhuman animals is wrong and ought to be abolished. Anyone who accepts (P1)–(P6) is committed to the immorality of these tests. But what about other uses of nonhuman animals in scientific and biomedical research? Do we have any good reason to use animals in horrifically painful burn experiments to test potentially therapeutic ointments or drugs? Does *medical advancement* and *treatment of human disease* require using nonhuman animals in painful and ultimately lethal research? Do the human benefits of such research justify subjecting animals to painful, lethal biomedical experiments?

Animal experimentation advocates often try to manipulate us into providing affirmative answers to these questions via appeals to emotional intuition pumps like the following: (Q1) "If experimenting on 10,000 rats were the only way to save your child's life, would you want the experiment to be conducted?" One can, of course, counter one intuition pump with another: (Q2) "If a stranger's child's life could be saved by performing a terribly painful experiment on your animal companion, would you allow the experiment to be performed on your beloved cat or dog?" I doubt many people would volunteer their own animal companions for such an experiment, even if a stranger's child's life were hanging in the balance.

Now consider the following more salient questions:

(Q3)　If your child would die from cancer *because* of animal research that caused the suffering and death of 10,000 rats, would you want that research on rats to be conducted?

(Q4)　If your child would be born with birth defects directly as a result of research that involved the suffering and death of 10,000 rats, would you want that research on rats to be conducted?

Obviously, no parent would want an animal experiment to be conducted if it would result in her/his child's death or deformity. And yet, many animal experiments have had exactly that result. For example, consider the oft-cited thalidomide tragedy. Thalidomide is teratogenic (i.e., causes birth defects) in humans. Moreover, thalidomide's teratogenic effect in humans was recognized early on, on the basis of clinical observation—mothers who had taken thalidomide gave birth to babies without limbs. However, because thalidomide's teratogenicity could not be readily reproduced in other animal species, thalidomide continued to be prescribed to pregnant women. Eventually, after testing thalidomide for teratogenicity in countless animal species, scientists were able to demonstrate a teratogenic effect in one breed of rabbit, but only at doses between 25 and 300 times that given humans. After still more testing, thalidomide was found to have a teratogenic effect in monkeys, but at ten times the normal human dose (Greek and Greek 2000, 45). The crucial point is this: There was a significant time lag—five years!—between the original reliable human clinical data that clearly demonstrated thalidomide's teratogenic effect in humans and scientists' ability to produce a similar teratogenic effect in some other species, a time lag during which thalidomide continued to be prescribed to pregnant women because it hadn't yet been found to be teratogenic in other species. The result: more than ten thousand babies were born without limbs *because* researchers depended on unreliable animal tests and ignored the more reliable human clinical data. Had thalidomide been pulled from the market on the basis of the human clinical data, these birth defects would not have occurred, but it wasn't pulled, pending "confirmation" in other species.

The thalidomide tragedy is a particularly telling illustration of the *human costs* of relying on misleading animal experiments. Animal experiments mislead in at least four ways along two distinct vectors—*the safety vector* and *the efficacy vector.* Consider first one particularly dangerous way animal experiments can mislead along the safety vector: Frequently, animal experiments mistakenly predict that a drug will be *safe* in humans (since it was found safe in animal models in preclinical testing), when in fact that drug is *unsafe* (i.e., toxic, teratogenic, or lethal) in humans. Such misleading results are called "false negatives," because the drugs test "negative" for harmful effects in animals but are subsequently discovered to have seriously harmful effects in humans. Thalidomide is an example of a false negative, but it is hardly unique in this regard. Here is a partial list of false negatives and their harmful consequences for humans, as identified by Greek and Greek (2000):

- Diethylstilbesterol [DES]—animal models predicted that DES would prevent miscarriages; in humans DES caused spontaneous abortion, premature birth, and neonatal death (61).

- Zimeldine—the first selective serotonin reuptake inhibitor (SSRI), caused the paralyzing illness Guillain-Barré syndrome, not predicted by animal tests (62).
- Isuprel—an asthma drug that is highly toxic to humans in the doses that were predicted to be safe for humans based on animal studies. Thirty-five hundred asthmatics died from the drug in Great Britain alone (63).
- Clioquinol—an antidiarrheal drug that tested safe in rats, cats, dogs, and rabbits but caused blindness and paralysis in humans (67).
- Opren—an arthritis drug that tested safe in monkeys but killed sixty-one humans (68).

C. Ray Greek, M.D., and Jean Swindle Greek, D.V.M., go on to identify at least forty other examples of false negatives. Several of these "animal-safe" drugs caused liver failure in humans, others caused seizures in humans, still others caused heart attacks in humans, and still others caused kidney failure or strokes or both in humans (Greek and Greek 2000, 61–68).

[. . .]

Drugs that test safe and effective in animal models can also mislead along the efficacy vector. Drugs found *effective* in animal models often prove *ineffective* in humans. For example, twenty-two drugs have been shown to be therapeutic for spinal cord injury in animal models, but not a single one of these drugs is effective in humans (Greek and Greek 2004, 18). Call such results "false efficacy predictors." False efficacy predictors don't typically result in direct harm to humans; the drugs simply fail to work in humans. There are, however, indirect harms. The billions of research dollars used annually to develop drugs effective in animal models but ineffective in humans are wastefully being pumped into false leads and dead ends. These dollars could be far better spent on effective prevention campaigns.

If false negatives and false efficacy predictors were relatively rare, say 1 out of 1,000 or even 1 out of 100, animal experimentation might still be justified on the basis of its benefits to humans, but false negatives and false efficacy predictors are not rare. In prepared remarks presented January 12, 2006. Andrew C. von Eschenbach, acting commissioner of the Food and Drug Administration, had this to say: "Consider just one stark statistic: Today, nine out of 10 compounds developed in the lab fail in human studies. They fail, in large part because they behave differently in people than they did in animal or laboratory tests" (2006, 1). Actually, the current failure rate of drugs that make their way to phase I human clinical trials on the basis of preclinical animal testing is 92 percent.[12] This *clinical failure rate* is split roughly equally between drugs that are too toxic and drugs that don't work in humans. Accordingly, of all the drugs that make their way to human clinical trials on the basis of preclinical animal testing, approximately 46 percent prove to be false negatives and roughly 46 percent fall into the category of false efficacy predictors, barely better than flipping a coin along either vector. With its 92 percent clinical failure rate, preclinical animal testing is an extraordinarily unreliable method of establishing the safety and effectiveness of pharmaceutical compounds *in humans*. With roughly half of these failures being false negatives, relying on animal models to establish the safety of drugs is also a dangerous way of testing drugs. It puts the human subjects in phase I, phase II, and phase III clinical trials at serious risk of grave harm or death.

Preclinical animal testing can mislead along the safety vector in the other direction as well. Pharmaceutical compounds that are *safe* in humans can test *unsafe* (i.e., toxic, teratogenic, or fatal) in animals. Such test results are called "false positives," because the compounds test "positive" for harmful effects in animals, despite being safe in humans. False positives mistakenly suggest that a drug is unsafe for humans, when in fact that drug is perfectly safe in humans. As for the efficacy vector, drugs that are safe and *effective* in treating disease *X* in humans can be completely *ineffective* in treating *X* in animal models. Call these kinds of misleading results "false inefficacy predictors." By my lights, false positives and false inefficacy predictors are a far greater human cost of animal-based biomedical research than false negatives and false efficacy predictors, because, unlike the latter, false positives and false inefficacy predictors can and do result in drugs that are safe and effective in humans—lifesaving panaceas for human diseases—being pulled from development before ever making it to human clinical trials. As long as we test potential drugs using unreliable animal models and table the development of drugs that might have proven safe and effective in humans on the basis of their deleterious effects in these animal models, we will inevitably continue to forgo certain cures for human diseases. Your child, now dying of cancer, might very well have been saved by a drug that is both safe and effective in treating cancer in humans but was shelved before making it to human clinical trials *because* it made mice and rats sick. Like their false negative counterparts, false positives are not rare. Some safe drugs in common human use that are now known to be examples of false positives include the following:

- Acetaminophen (Tylenol)—causes renal failure and death in cats at low doses.
- Ibuprofen (Advil, Motrin)—causes liver failure in dogs at low doses.
- Acetylsalicylic acid (aspirin)—is teratogenic in mice and rats and causes blood abnormalities in cats.
- Depo-provera (a widely prescribed birth control pill)—causes cancer in dogs and baboons.
- Digitalis (a heart medication routinely used to treat congestive heart failure)—causes high blood pressure in animals.
- Streptomycin (a commonly prescribed antibiotic)—is teratogenic in rats.
- Prednisone (a widely prescribed corticosteroid)—causes cancer in some rodents.
- Cortisone (another regularly prescribed corticosteroid)—is teratogenic in mice.
- Fluoride (a mineral routinely added to toothpaste and tap water to strengthen teeth and help prevent cavities)—causes cancer in rats.

(Greek and Greek 2000, 70–76)

[. . .]

There is no easy way to measure just how many cures for human diseases have been shelved by pharmaceutical companies because the substance in question either proved ineffective in other species or made members of other species sick—partly because that information remains proprietary and partly because drugs that test highly toxic in animal models rarely make it to human clinical trials—but there are good reasons to think that the number is far from negligible. For example, when the National Cancer Institute tested on mice twelve anticancer drugs currently being successfully used in humans, they found that thirty out of forty-eight times, the drugs were ineffective in mice—a false inefficacy predictor rate of 63 percent (Greek and Greek 2004, 17). Animal models also prove terribly unreliable when it comes to testing substances for carcinogenicity. Of twenty compounds known *not* to cause cancer in humans, nineteen *did* cause cancer in animals—a false positive rate of 95 percent (ibid). Couple this information with the fact that 98 percent of the compounds tested in preclinical animal trials are killed by pharmaceutical companies before making their way to human clinical trials, largely on the basis of animal data (Pippin 2007, 2), and one can start to see the magnitude of the risk to human health posed by reliance on unreliable animal models. For every six hundred drugs that enter preclinical testing on animals, only twelve advance to human clinical trials, and only one of these twelve receives FDA approval (ibid). That means for every one FDA-approved drug, 588 drugs are pulled from development by pharmaceutical companies *without ever being tested on humans.* Some of these drugs are pulled because of toxicity in animal models. Some of these drugs are pulled because the compounds are ineffective in animals. Of the 98 percent of chemical compounds that are discarded by pharmaceutical companies due to their toxicity or ineffectiveness in animal models, we will never know how many would have proven safe and effective in humans, but again, there are good reasons to think that the number is probably quite large.

Consider another such reason: Occasionally, drugs that test toxic in animals make their way to human clinical trials anyway (cases where the animal data are simply being ignored). In August 2001, Mark Levin, CEO of Millennium Pharmaceuticals, presented data at the Drug Discovery Technology Conference in Boston that suggests just how prevalent false positives are. In the study that Levin presented, twenty-eight potential new drugs were tested in rats for hepatotoxicity (i.e., liver toxicity). Seventeen of these drugs tested nonhepatotoxic in rats, and eleven tested hepa-totoxic in rats. Twenty-two of these drugs advanced to human clinical trials anyway—fourteen of the seventeen that tested safe and eight of the eleven that tested positive for hepatotoxicity advanced. Of the eight that had tested hepatotoxic in rats, six were found safe (i.e., nonhepato-toxic) in humans (Greek and Greek 2004, 17–18): a false positive rate of 75 percent![13] While it's unlikely that 75 percent of the 98 percent of discarded drugs would have proven safe and effective in humans (since the tests reported by Levin focused solely on one form of toxicity), given the large number of false positives of which we are aware, it is quite likely that a significant percent-age of the discarded drugs would have proven safe and effective in humans had we not relied on misleading animal data. We will never have access to those drugs, because we have relied on misleading animal data. All those people whose diseases would have been cured or ameliorated by those drugs unfortunately must continue to suffer from their illnesses because of our reliance on animal-based biomedical research. In these cases, far from making us better, the animal research is keeping us sick.

What Else Can We Do?

Still, you might wonder, what's the alternative to animal experimentation? We need some way of assessing how a pharmacokinetic agent will behave in humans *before* we administer it to humans in phase I clinical trials, and animal testing seems to be the only game in town. Even though animal experimentation is an unreliable—indeed, often malpredictive—way of assessing the likely effects of pharmacological agents in humans, you might think that it's better than nothing.

Two points are in order: First, given how unreliable animal experiments have proven to be at predicting human response to pharmacological compounds, if animal experimentation were the only game in town, we would be wise to stop playing because, as we have just seen, the animal experimentation game is enormously costly to human health. It is directly responsible for the death or deformity of hundreds of thousands of humans and is also directly responsible for our not having all those curative and ameliorative drugs that would have proven safe and effective in humans but were too toxic or ineffective in animal models to advance to human clinical trials.

Second and more important, animal experimentation is not the only game in town. Scientists are now able to construct, maintain, and analyze complex human-tissue cultures and cell layers in vitro. Testing a pharmacokinetic agent directly on human tissue in vitro provides important information about how that pharmacological compound will be absorbed and metabolized by *human* tissue. In vitro techniques, which were proven to be superior to animal studies at predicting human response over a decade ago, are now being used to identify disease mechanisms, drug targets, drug efficacy, and drug toxicity in virtually all types of human tissue (Pippin 2005, 17). Human stem cells may also be used to test the toxicities and efficacies of chemical compounds and pharmacological agents (ibid.), and once again, the results are specific to humans. Pharmacological compounds can also be tested using computer and mathematical models based on existing clinical knowledge. These *in silico* tests provide important absorption, distribution, metabolism, excretion, and toxic-ity (ADMET) data that allow us to predict how a new compound is likely to behave in humans. In silico technology provides human ADMET predictions whose accuracy rivals that of in vitro methods (ibid., 16). Unlike animal models, all of the alternatives just mentioned provide informa-tion *specific to humans.*

Animal experimentation advocates may well acknowledge the scientific validity and value of human-tissue in vitro testing, human stem-cell research, and in silico testing and may even encour-age the use of these tests, but they will still likely object as follows: "Sometimes drugs behave dif-ferently in intact organisms than they do in isolated tissue cultures. Before a drug can be released to the public, it must be tested on intact organisms. If we did not first test pharmacokinetic agents on animals, we would have to test them directly on humans in order to discover how they will react in intact organisms, and that would be unconscionable."[14]

It is true that if we don't first test drugs on intact animals, then the first intact organisms in which the drugs will be tested will be human beings in phase 0 trials; but such tests can be performed safely using *microdosing technology.* As John Pippin, M.D., explains, microdosing technology uses

> radiolabeled trace doses (1–100 mcg) of candidate drugs to evaluate absorption, distribution, metabolism, and excretion in humans. These doses are less than 1 percent of that required to produce a pharmacological effect, thus there is virtually no risk for adverse effects. The radiation exposure is less than that obtained in a four-hour airplane flight. Positron emission tomography is used to acquire real-time data regarding drug disposition, and accelerator mass spectrometry is used to analyze parent drug and metabolite concentrations in blood, urine, and feces at specific intervals after dosing.
>
> (2005, 16)

Microdosing technology can provide us with accurate information as to how a potential drug will be absorbed, distributed, metabolized, and excreted *in humans*—something that no animal test can do. Is it safe? Yes. Microdosing technology "was endorsed by the European Agency for the Evaluation of Medicinal Products in January 2003 . . . and has already been used to identify drug candidates for human phase I trials" (Pippin 2005, 16). Thus, not only are there alternatives to testing drugs in animal models, there are better, more accurate alternatives.

The bottom line is that the point of preclinical testing is to assess likely *human response* to a candidate drug before administering therapeutic doses of that drug to humans in phase I clinical trials. Animal tests have little or no relationship to human pharmacology and, thus, cannot provide us with that important information, whereas phase 0 microdose testing in humans can. Therefore, we should eliminate animal tests, which are both unhelpful and unnecessary, and replace them with more accurate, more informative microdose tests in humans.

Conclusion

Even if one cared only about humans and their well-being, one would still have good reason to oppose using animals in biomedical research. As we have just seen, the cost to human health of relying on unreliable animal models is staggering. First, drugs highly toxic and even lethal in humans routinely test safe in other animal species. The life-threatening problems posed by these false negatives are often exacerbated by the fact that because of the extensive animal data, human clinical trials are often cursory and brief. The drug is subsequently released to the public at large and because of poor post-release surveillance, it often takes years to recognize the drug's toxicity in humans, especially when that toxicity can't easily be demonstrated in other species. By then thousands of humans may have been permanently harmed, if not killed, by the drug. Second, drugs that would be safe and effective in humans routinely test toxic or ineffective in animals, and as a result, never make it to those human populations that so desperately need them. Had we not relied on misleading animal testing, many of these drugs would have advanced to human clinical trials, where their safety and effectiveness would have been demonstrated. Animal-based research is *directly responsible* for our not having those drugs. And third, there are safe, effective, more accurate alternatives to testing drugs in unreliable, malpredictive animal models, including human tissue in vitro tests, in silico tests, human stem cell research, and microdose tests in humans—alternatives which provide us with reliable information about a candidate drug's absorption, distribution, metabolism, excretion, and toxicity in *humans.* Unlike animal experiments, which have virtually no relationship to human pharmacology, these tests specifically address human response to newly developed pharmacokinetic agents.

So, again, if we cared only about humans, we would have excellent reasons for opposing animal-based biomedical research—but we don't care only about humans. We also care about animals. We accept (P1)–(P6) and think that animals should not be harmed or killed *for no good reason.* There is no good reason to use a research protocol as notoriously unreliable as animal-based biomedical research. Indeed, there are good reasons *not* to use animals as models in biomedical research: (1) People are harmed and even killed because of misleading false negative results in animal models; (2) people are forced to forgo curative, even lifesaving, drugs because of misleading false positive and false inefficacy results in animal models; and (3) there are safe alternative methods of predicting human response to candidate drugs, the results of which are more accurate and more informative than those of outmoded animal experiments. Since there is *no good reason* to perform biomedical experiments on animals and good reason not to, (P1)–(P6) entail that these experiments are wrong and ought to be abolished. This conclusion is not predicated on some highly contentious moral theory that one can easily reject, but rather on beliefs central to and constitutive of our conception of morality—beliefs that we all share, namely, (P1)–(P6). Moreover, this conclusion follows regardless of one's views on speciesism, animal equality, and animal rights. Even those readers sincerely committed to valuing humans over nonhumans are committed to the immorality of using animals in biomedical experiments, given their commitment to (P1)–(P6). Consequently, consistency with our other beliefs demands that we acknowledge the immorality of these experiments and work to bring them to an end.

[. . .]

Notes

1. Singer laid the groundwork for his utilitarian case against animal experimentation in his 1974 article "All Animals Are Equal" and then developed the argument in much greater detail in his later work (Singer 1993, 2002).
2. Regan's rights-based argument against animal experimentation is spelled out in his 1987 article "Ill Gotten Gains" and then developed much more fully in later works (Regan 2001, 2003, 2004).
3. According to *preference utilitarianism,* act *X* is right for agent *A* if and only if, out of all the actions available to *A,* act *X* maximizes the satisfaction of the interests and desires (i.e., the preferences) of all those beings affected by the action. Thus, the preference utilitarian maintains that an action is right if no other action has a better balance of preference satisfaction.
4. *Speciesism* is the widespread view that our species is superior to and more valuable than the other species and that, therefore, members of our species have the right to dominate and exploit members of these other species. While the word "speciesism" and its cognates are often used pejoratively in the animal rights literature, I use them only descriptively.
5. Bonnie Steinbock's (1978, 255–256) criticism of Singer's view seems to be rooted in such a sincerely held feeling.
6. We also accept the following related principles:

    (P1*)   It is wrong to intentionally harm conscious sentient animals unnecessarily.
    (P2*)   It is wrong to cause conscious sentient animals to suffer unnecessarily.
    (P3*)   It is wrong to kill conscious sentient animals *unnecessarily.*

    Strictly speaking, (P1*)–(P3*) are not equivalent to (P1)–(P3), respectively, because there might be a good reason to perform a certain action that strictly speaking isn't *necessary* for some significant human benefit. Suppose *X* and *Y* are equally effective means to achieving some important end *E.* Then, strictly speaking, performing *X* is *not necessary* to bring about *E,* since we might perform *Y* instead. Still, if performing *X* costs considerably less than performing *Y,* we might have a *good reason* to perform *X* to bring about *E.* Conversely, the fact that performing an action *A* is *necessary* for bringing about a certain valuable end *E* doesn't always give us a *good reason* to perform *A.* Suppose the only way I can save my son's life is to kill you and harvest your heart and lungs (suppose you are the only tissue match). In the scenario just imagined, killing you is *necessary* to save my son's life, but that doesn't give me a *good reason* to kill you. I still would not be justified in killing you. Even though *necessity* and *having good reasons* can pull apart in these ways, they typically go hand in hand. Typically, when performing an action is necessary to bring about a significant human benefit, that will give us a good reason to perform it; and more important for present purposes, typically, when there is no good reason to perform an action, performing that action will not be necessary for some significant human benefit. Accordingly, I will treat (P1*)–(P3*) as roughly equivalent to (P1)–(P3), respectively, because nothing in the present chapter will turn on the subtle sorts of situations where *necessity* and *the having of good reasons* pull apart.

7. As I have already noted, these principles are central to our understanding of morality. Together they specify an important part of the underived conceptual role of the concept of *moral wrongness.*

8. To see Cohen's commitment to (P2) here, we need only recognize that justification proceeds in terms of reasons. We are justified in causing an animal pain if and only if we have a good reason for doing so. If there is no good reason to cause an animal pain, then causing that animal pain cannot be justified.

9. Here, strictly speaking, Cohen commits himself to (P2*) and (P3*). See note 10 for details.

10. For further discussion of the moral ramifications of acknowledging that animals deserve non-negligible direct moral consideration, see Engel (2001).

11. Here is why (P1) entails (P4): First, mere laboratory confinement itself is so stressful for the animals as to be properly regarded as a psychological harm (see Balcombe 2004, 6–8). Second, the animals experimented on are virtually always intentionally harmed in some physical way. Some animals are intentionally infected with pathogens. Other animals have diseases thought to model human diseases intentionally induced, including artificially induced coronary artery disease, artificially induced strokes, and artificially induced cancers. Still other animals are irradiated or burned or maimed in other ways, such as intentionally induced spinal cord injuries and intentional limb amputations. Conducting these experiments requires, by its very nature, intentionally harming the animal subjects involved, and the researchers involved are fully aware of that fact. Since, per (P1), it is wrong to *intentionally harm* a conscious sentient animal *for no good reason,* (P1) entails that it is wrong to intentionally conduct *harmful* experiments on conscious sentient animals for no good reason, which is just what (P4) asserts. Principles (P5) and (P6) follow from (P2) and (P3), respectively, in equally straightforward ways.

12. In prepared remarks, Lester Crawford, acting commissioner of the Food and Drug Administration in 2004, reported that only 8 percent of the drugs that test safe and effective in animals prove safe and effective in humans (Crawford 2004, 2). Also see Pippin (2007).

13. Of the fourteen drugs that tested safe (i.e., nonhepatotoxic) in rats that were subsequently tested in humans, six proved hepatotoxic in humans—a false negative rate of 43 percent (Greek and Greek 2004, 17–18).

14. Cohen (2001, 13) offers just such an objection.

References

Balcombe, J. 2004. Lab stress 24/7. *Good Medicine* 13 (4): 6–8.

Carruthers, P. 1992. *The Animals Issue.* Cambridge: Cambridge University Press.

Cohen, C. 2001a. *The Animal Rights Debate* (with Tom Regan). Lanham, MD: Rowman and Littlefield.

Cohen, C. 2001b. The case for the use of animals in biomedical research. In *Biomedical Ethics,* 5th ed., eds. T. Mappes and D. DeGrazia, 281–287. New York: McGraw-Hill.

Crawford, L. 2004. Speech before Global Pharmaceutical Strategies Seminar. Presented May 25. http://www.fda.gov/NewsEvents/Speeches/ucm053539.htm (accessed July 7, 2011).

Engel Jr., M. 2001. The mere considerability of animals. *Acta Analytica* 16: 89–107.

Greek, C. R., and J. S. Greek. 2000. *Sacred Cows and Golden Geese: The Human Cost of Experimenting on Animals.* New York: Continuum.

Greek, J. S., and C. R. Greek. 2004. *What Will We Do If We Don't Experiment on Animals?* Victoria, BC: Trafford.

Le Gallois, J. J. C. 1813. *Experiments on the Principles of Life,* trans., N. C. Nancrede and J. G. Nancrede Philadelphia: Thomas.

Pippin, J. J. 2005. The need for revision of pre-market resting: The failure of animal tests of COX-2 inhibitors. Presented at the FDA Open Public Hearing, February 17. http://www.pcrm.org/news/downloads/Pippin Report.pdf (accessed July 7, 2011).

Pippin, J. J. 2007. Drug development and approval in the United States: Stages, descriptions, timetables, and attrition rates. In manuscript.

PCRM (Physicians Committee for Responsible Medicine). 1999. Inadequacy of the LD50 test. http://www.pcrm.org/resch/PDFs/ae_ld50.pdf (accessed July 7, 2011).

Regan, T. 2001. *The Animal Rights Debate* (with C. Cohen). Lanham, MD: Rowman and Littlefield.

Regan, T. 2003. *Animal Rights, Human Wrongs.* Lanham, MD: Rowman and Littlefield.

Regan, T. 2004. *The Case for Animal Rights.* 2nd ed. Berkeley: University of California Press.

Singer, P. 1993. *Practical Ethics.* 2nd ed. Cambridge: Cambridge University Press.

Singer, P. 2002. *Animal Liberation.* 3rd ed. New York: HarperCollins Publishers.

Steinbock, B. 1978. Speciesism and the idea of equality. *Philosophy* 53: 247–256.

Vance, R. 1992. An introduction to the philosophical presuppositions of the animal rights movement. *Journal of the American Medical Association* 268 (13): 1715.

von Eschenbach, A. C. 2006. FDA teleconference: Steps to advance the earliest phases of clinical research in the development of innovative medical treatments. Speech delivered January 12, http://www.fda.gov/oc/speeches/2006/fdateleconference0112.html (accessed July 17, 2007). The entire text of von Eschenbach's speech is available at http://www.all-creatures.org/saen/articles-nineoutof.html (accessed July 8, 2011).

Zbinden, G., and M. Flury-Roversi. 1981. Significance of the LD50 test for the toxicological evaluation of chemical substances. *Archives of Toxicology* 47: 77–99.

37 The Ethics of Animal Research

What Are the Prospects for Agreement?

David DeGrazia

DeGrazia assesses the perspectives of those favoring and those opposed to animal research. He identifies ten principles where he believes these two perspectives can agree and at least four additional issues he believes will serve as continuing points of difference. He then makes ten suggestions for continuing to build on the various points of agreement.

Few human uses of nonhuman animals (hereafter simply "animals") have incited as much controversy as the use of animals in biomedical research. [. . .] However, a healthy number of individuals within these two communities offer the possibility of a more illuminating discussion of the ethics of animal research.

One such individual is Henry Spira. Spira almost single-handedly convinced Avon, Revlon, and other major cosmetics companies to invest in the search for alternatives to animal testing. Largely due to his tactful but persistent engagement with these companies—and to their willingness to change—many consumers today look for such labels as "not tested on animals" and "cruelty free" on cosmetics they would like to buy.

Inspired by Spira, this paper seeks common ground between the positions of biomedicine and animal advocates. (The term "biomedicine" here refers to everyone who works in medicine or the life sciences, not just those conducting animal research. "Animal advocates" and "animal protection community" refer to those individuals who take a major interest in protecting the interests of animals and who believe that much current usage of animals is morally unjustified. The terms are not restricted to animal activists, because some individuals meet this definition without being politically active in seeking changes.) The paper begins with some background on the political and ethical debate over animal research. It then identifies important points of potential agreement between biomedicine and animal advocates; much of this common ground can be missed due to distraction by the fireworks of the current political exchange. Next, the paper enumerates issues on which continuing disagreement is likely. Finally, it concludes with concrete suggestions for building positively on the common ground.

Background on the Debate over Animal Research

What is the current state of the debate over the ethics of animal research? Let us begin with the viewpoint of biomedicine. It seems fair to say that biomedicine has a "party line" on the ethics of animal research, conformity to which may feel like a political litmus test for full acceptability within the professional community. According to this party line, animal research is clearly justified because it is necessary for medical progress and therefore human health—and those who disagree are irrational, antiscience, misanthropic "extremists" whose views do not deserve serious attention. (Needless to say, despite considerable conformity, not everyone in biomedicine accepts this position.)

In at least some countries, biomedicine's leadership apparently values conformity to this party line more than freedom of thought and expression on the animal research issue (in this paragraph,

I will refer to the American situation to illustrate the point)—hence the unwillingness of major medical journals, such as *JAMA* and *The New England Journal of Medicine*, to publish articles that are highly critical of animal research. Hence also the extraordinary similarity I have noticed in pro-research lectures by representatives of biomedicine. I used to be puzzled about why these lectures sounded so similar and why, for example, they consistently made some of the same philosophical and conceptual errors (such as dichotomizing animal welfare and animal rights and taking the latter concept to imply identical rights for humans and animals). But that was before I learned of the "AMA [American Medical Association] Animal Research Action Plan" and the AMA's "White Paper." Promoting an aggressive pro-research campaign, these documents encourage AMA members to say and do certain things for public relations purposes, including the following: "Identify animal rights activists as anti-science and against medical progress"; "Combat emotion with emotion (e.g [sic], 'fuzzy' animals contrasted with 'healing' children)"; and "Position the biomedical community as moderate—centrist—in the controversy, not as a polar opposite."[1]

It is a reasonable conjecture that biomedicine's party line was developed largely in reaction to fear—both of the most intimidating actions of some especially zealous animal advocates, such as telephoned threats and destruction of property, and of growing societal concern about animals. Unfortunately, biomedicine's reaction has created a political culture in which many or most animal researchers and their supporters do not engage in sustained, critical thinking about the moral status of animals and the basic justification (or lack thereof) for animal research. Few seem to recognize that there is significant merit to the opposing position, fewer have had any rigorous training in ethical reasoning, and hardly any have read much of the leading literature on animal ethics. The stultifying effect of this cultural phenomenon hit home with me at a small meeting of representatives of biomedicine, in which I had been invited to explain "the animal rights philosophy" (the invitation itself being exceptional and encouraging). After the talk, in which I presented ideas familiar to all who really know the literature and issues of animal ethics, several attendees pumped my hand and said something to this effect: "This is the first time I have heard such rational and lucid arguments for the other side. I didn't know there were any."

As for the animal protection community, there does not seem to be a shared viewpoint except at a very general level: significant interest in animal welfare and the belief that much current animal usage is unjustified. Beyond that, differences abound. For example, the Humane Society of the United States opposes factory farming but not humane forms of animal husbandry, rejects current levels of animal use in research but not animal research itself, and condemns most zoo exhibits but not those that adequately meet animals' needs and approximate their natural habitats.[2] Meanwhile, the Animal Liberation Front, a clandestine British organization, apparently opposes all animal husbandry, animal research, and the keeping of zoo animals.[3] Although there are extensive differences within the animal protection community, as far as our paper topic goes, it seems fair to say that almost everyone in this group opposes current levels of animal research.

That's a brief sketch of the perspectives of biomedicine and animal advocates on the issue of animal research. What about the state of animal ethics itself? The leading book-length works in this field exhibit a near consensus that the status quo of animal usage is ethically indefensible and that at least significant reductions in animal research are justified. Let me elaborate.

Defending strong animal rights positions in different ways, Tom Regan and Evelyn Pluhar advocate abolition of all research that involves harming animals.[4] Ray Frey and Peter Singer, by contrast, hold the use of animals to the very stringent utilitarian standard—accepting only those experiments whose benefits (factoring in the likelihood of achieving them) are expected to outweigh the harms and costs involved—where the interests of animal subjects (e.g., to avoid suffering) are given the same moral weight that we give comparable human interests.[5]

Without committing either to a strong animal rights view or to utilitarianism, my own view shares with these theories the framework of equal consideration for animals: the principle that we must give equal moral weight to comparable interests, no matter who has those interests.[6] But unlike the aforementioned philosophers, I believe that the arguments for and against equal consideration are nearly equal in strength. I therefore have respect for progressive views that attribute moral standing to animals without giving them fully equal consideration. The unequal consideration view that I find most plausible gives moral weight to animals' comparable interests in accordance with the animals' cognitive, affective, and social complexity—a progressive, "sliding scale" view. Since I acknowledge that I might be mistaken about equal consideration, my approach tracks the practical implications both of equal consideration and of the alternative just described.

Arguing from pluralistic frameworks, which are developed in different ways, Steve Sapontzis, Rosemary Rodd, and Bernard Rollin support relatively little animal research in comparison with current levels.[7] Drawing significantly from feminist insights, Mary Midgley presents a view whose implications seem somewhat more accepting of the status quo of animal research but still fairly progressive.[8] Of the leading contributors to animal ethics, the only one who embraces the status quo of animal research and does not attribute significant moral status to animals is Peter Carruthers.[9] (It is ironic that while biomedicine characterizes those who are critical of animal research as irrational "extremists," nearly all of the most in-depth, scholarly, and respected work in animal ethics supports such a critical standpoint at a general level.)

In discussing the prospects for agreement between biomedicine and animal advocates, I will ignore political posturing and consider only serious ethical reflection. In considering the two sides of this debate, I will assume that the discussants are morally serious, intellectually honest, reflective, and well informed both about the facts of animal research and about the range of arguments that come into play in animal ethics. I will not have in mind, then, the researcher who urges audiences to dismiss "the animal rights view" or the animal activist who tolerates no dissent from an abolitionist position. The two representative interlocutors I will imagine differ on the issue of animal research, but their views result from honest, disciplined, well-informed ethical reflection. Clearly, their voices are worth hearing.

Points on Which the Biomedical and Animal Protection Communities Can Agree

The optimistic thesis of this paper is that the biomedical and animal protection communities can agree on a fair number of important points and that much can be done to build upon this common ground. I will number and highlight (in bold) each potential point of agreement and then justify its inclusion by explaining how both sides can agree to it, without abandoning their basic positions, and why they should.

The use of animals in biomedical research raises ethical issues. Today very few people would disagree with this modest claim, and any who would are clearly in the wrong.[10] Most animal research involves harming animal subjects, provoking ethical concerns, and the leading goal of animal research, promotion of human health, is itself ethically important; even the expenditure of taxpayers' money on government-funded animal research raises ethical issues about the best use of such money. Although a very modest assertion, this point of agreement is important because it legitimates a process that is sometimes resisted: *discussing* the ethics of animal research.

[. . .]

Sentient animals, a class that probably includes at least the vertebrates, deserve moral protection. Whether because they have moral status or because needlessly harming them strongly offends many people's sensibilities, sentient animals deserve some measure of moral protection. By way of definition, sentient animals are animals endowed with any sorts of feelings: (conscious) sensations such as pain or emotional states such as fear or suffering. [. . .] Lately, strong support has emerged for the proposition that at least vertebrate animals are very likely sentient.[11] This proposition is implicitly endorsed by major statements of principles regarding the humane use of research animals, which often mention that they apply to vertebrates.[12] (Hereafter, the unqualified term "animals" will refer to sentient animals in particular.)

Many animals (at the very least, mammals) are capable of having a wide variety of aversive mental states, including pain, distress (whose forms include discomfort, boredom, and fear),

and suffering. In biomedical circles, there has been some resistance to attributing suffering to animals, so government documents concerned with humane use of animals have often mentioned only pain, distress, and discomfort.[13] Because "suffering" refers to a *highly* unpleasant mental state (whereas pain, distress, and discomfort can be mild and transient), the attribution of suffering to animals is morally significant.

[. . .]

Animals' experiential well-being (quality of life) deserves protection. If the use of animals raises ethical issues, meaning that their interests matter morally, we confront the question of what interests animals have.

[. . .]

Another difficult issue is whether animal well-being can be understood *entirely* in terms of experiential well-being—quality of life in the familiar sense in which (other things equal) pleasure is better than pain, enjoyment better than suffering, satisfaction better than frustration. Or does the exercise of an animal's natural capacities count positively toward well-being, even if quality of life is not enhanced?

[. . .]

Whatever the answers to these and other issues connected with animal well-being, what is not controversial is that animals have an interest in experiential well-being, a good quality of life. That is why animal researchers are normally expected to use anesthesia or analgesia where these agents can reduce or eliminate animal subjects' pain, distress, or suffering.

Humane care of highly social animals requires extensive access to conspecifics. It is increasingly appreciated that animals have different needs based on what sorts of creatures they are. Highly social animals, such as apes, monkeys, and wolves, need social interactions with conspecifics (members of their own species). Under normal circumstances, they will develop social structures, such as hierarchies and alliances, and maintain long-term relationships with conspecifics. Because they have a strong instinct to seek such interactions and relationships, depriving them of the opportunity to gratify this instinct harms these animals.

[. . .]

Some animals deserve very strong protections (as, for example, chimpanzees deserve not to be killed for the purpose of population control). Biomedicine and animal advocates are likely to disagree on many details of ethically justified uses of animals in research, as we will see in the next section. Still, discussants can agree that there is an obligation to protect not just the experiential well-being, but also the lives, of at least some animals. This claim might be supported by the (controversial) thesis that such animals have life interests. On the other hand, it might be supported by the goal of species preservation (in the case of an endangered species), or by the recognition that routine killing of such animals when they are no longer useful for research would seriously disturb many people.[14]

[. . .]

Alternatives should now be used whenever possible and research on alternatives should expand. Those who are most strongly opposed to animal research hold that alternatives such as mathematical models, computer simulations, and in vitro biological systems should replace nearly all use of animals in research. (I say "nearly all" because, as discussed below, few would condemn animal research that does not harm its subjects.) Even for those who see the animal research enterprise more favorably, there are good reasons to take an active interest in alternatives. Sometimes an alternative method is the most valid way to approach a particular scientific question; often alternatives are cheaper.[15] Their potential for reducing animal pain, distress, and suffering is, of course, another good reason. Finally, biomedicine may enjoy stronger public support if it responds to growing social concern about animal welfare with a very serious investment in nonanimal methods. This means not just using alternatives wherever they are currently feasible, but also aggressively researching the possibilities for expanding the use of such methods.

Promoting human health is an extremely important biomedical goal. No morally serious person would deny the great importance of human health, so its status as a worthy goal seems beyond question. What is sometimes forgotten, however, is that a worthy goal does not automatically justify all the means thereto. Surely it would be unethical to force large numbers of humans to serve as subjects in highly painful, eventually lethal research, even if its goal were to promote human health. The controversy over animal research focuses not on the worthiness of its principal goal—promoting human health—but rather on the means, involving animal subjects, taken in pursuit of that goal.

There are some morally significant differences between humans and other animals. [. . .] First, the principle of respect for autonomy applies to competent adult human beings, but to very few if any animals. This principle respects the self-regarding decisions of individuals who are capable of autonomous decision making and action. Conversely, it opposes paternalism toward such individuals, who have the capacity to decide for themselves what is in their interests. Now, many sentient beings, including human children and at least most nonhuman animals, are not autonomous in the relevant sense and so are not covered by this principle.[16] Thus it is often appropriate to limit their liberty in ways that promote their best interests, say, preventing the human child from drinking alcohol, or forcing a pet dog to undergo a vaccination. We might say that where there is no autonomy to respect, the principles of beneficence (promoting best interests) and respect for autonomy cannot conflict; where there is autonomy to respect, paternalism becomes morally problematic.

Second, even if sentient animals have an interest, other things [being] equal, in staying alive (as I believe), the moral presumption against taking human life is stronger than the presumption against killing at least some animals. [. . .] Leaders in animal ethics consistently support—though in interestingly different ways—the idea that, ordinarily, killing humans is worse than killing at least some animals who have moral status.

[. . .]

Some animal research is justified. [. . .] Let me explain by responding to the three likeliest reasons some animal advocates might take exception to the claim.

First, one might oppose all uses of animals that involve *harming them for the benefit of others* (even other animals)—as a matter of absolute principle—and overlook the fact that some animal research does not harm animal subjects at all. Although such nonharmful research represents a tiny sliver of the animal research enterprise, it exists. Examples are certain observational studies of animals in their natural habitats, some ape language studies, and possibly certain behavioral studies of other species that take place in laboratories but do not cause pain, distress, or suffering to the subjects. And if nonsentient animals cannot be harmed (in any morally relevant sense), as I would argue, then any research involving such animals falls under the penumbra of nonharming research.

Moreover, there is arguably no good reason to oppose research that imposes only *minimal* risk or harm on its animal subjects. After all, minimal risk research on certain human subjects who, like animals, cannot consent (namely, children) is permitted in many countries; in my view, this policy is justified. Such research might involve a minuscule likelihood of significant harm or the certainty of a slight, transient harm, such as the discomfort of having a blood sample taken.

Second, one might oppose all animal research because one believes that none of it actually benefits human beings. Due to physical differences between species, the argument goes, what happens to animal subjects when they undergo some biomedical intervention does not justify inferences about what will happen to humans who undergo that intervention. Furthermore, new drugs, therapies, and techniques must always be tried on human subjects before they can be accepted for clinical practice. Rather than tormenting animals in research, the argument continues, we should drop the useless animal models and proceed straight to human trials (with appropriate protections for human subjects, including requirements for informed or proxy consent).

Although I believe a considerable amount of current animal research has almost no chance of benefiting humans, I find it very hard to believe that no animal research does.[17] While it is true that human subjects must eventually be experimented on, evidence suggests that animal models sometimes furnish data relevant to human health.[18] If so, then the use of animal subjects can often decrease the risk to human subjects who are eventually involved in experiments that advance biomedicine, by helping to weed out harmful interventions. This by itself does not justify animal research, only the claim that it sometimes benefits humans (at the very least human subjects themselves and arguably the beneficiaries of biomedical advances as well).

Note that even if animal research never benefited humans, it would presumably sometimes benefit conspecifics of the animals tested, in sound veterinary research.[19] It can't be seriously argued that animal models provide no useful information about animals! Moreover, in successful *therapeutic* research (which aims to benefit the subjects themselves), certain animals benefit directly from research and are not simply used to benefit other animals. For that reason, blanket opposition to animal research, including the most promising therapeutic research in veterinary medicine, strikes me as almost unintelligible.

Almost unintelligible, but not quite, bringing us to the third possible reason for opposing all animal research. It might be argued that whether or not it harms its subjects, all animal research involves *using animals (without their consent) for others' benefit*, since—qua research—it seeks *generalizable knowledge*. But to use animals in this way reduces them to *tools* (objects to be used), thereby *disrespecting* the animals.

Now the idea that we may never use nonconsenting individuals, even in benign ways, solely for the benefit of others strikes me as an implausibly strict ethical principle. But never mind. The fact that some veterinary research is intended to benefit the subjects themselves (as well as other animals or humans down the road) where no other way to help them is known shows that such research, on any reasonable view, is *not* disrespectful toward its subjects. Indeed, in such cases, the animals *would* consent to taking part, if they could, because taking part is in their interests. I fully grant that therapeutic veterinary research represents a minuscule portion of the animal research conducted today. But my arguments are put forward in the service of a goal that I think I have now achieved: demonstrating, beyond a shadow of a doubt, that some animal research is justified.

[. . .]

Points on Which Agreement between the Two Sides Is Unlikely

Even if biomedicine and the animal protection community approach the animal research issue in good faith, become properly informed about animal ethics and the facts of research, and so forth, they are still likely to disagree on certain important issues. After all, their basic views differ. It may be worthwhile to enumerate several likely points of difference.

First, disagreement is likely on the issue of *the moral status of animals in comparison with humans*. While representatives of biomedicine may attribute moral status to animals, they hold that animals may justifiably be used in many experiments (most of which are nontherapeutic and harm the subjects) whose primary goal is to promote human health. But for animal advocates, it is not at all obvious that much animal research is justified. This suggests that animal advocates ascribe higher moral status to animals than biomedicine does.[20]

Second, disagreement is likely to continue on the issue of *the specific circumstances in which the worthy goal of promoting human health justifies harming animals*. Biomedicine generally tries to protect the status quo of animal research. Animal advocates generally treat not using animals in research as a presumption, any departures from which would require careful justification. Clearly, animal advocates will have many disagreements with biomedicine over when it is appropriate to conduct animal research.

Third, in a similar vein, continuing disagreement is likely on the issue of *whether current protections for research animals are more or less adequate*. Biomedicine would probably answer affirmatively, with relatively minor internal disagreements over specific issues (e.g., whether apes should ever be exposed to diseases in order to test vaccines). Animal advocates will tend to be much more critical of current protections for research animals. They will argue, for example, that animals are far too often made to suffer in pursuit of less than compelling objectives, such as learning about behavioral responses to stress or trauma.

In the United States, critics will argue that the basic principles that are supposed to guide the care and use of animals in federally funded research ultimately provide very weak protection for research animals. That is because the tenth and final principle begins with implicit permission to make exceptions to the previous nine: "Where exceptions are required in relation to the provisions of these Principles, . . ."[21] Since no limits are placed on permissible exceptions, this final principle precludes any absolute restraints on the harm that may be inflicted on research animals—an indefensible lack of safeguards from the perspective of animal advocates. (Although similar in several ways to these American principles, including some ways animal advocates would criticize, the *International Guiding Principles for Biomedical Research Involving Animals* avoids this pitfall of a global loophole. One of its relatively strong protections is Principle V: "Investigators and other personnel should never fail to treat animals as sentient, and should regard their proper care and use and the avoidance or minimization of discomfort, distress, or pain as ethical imperatives."[22])

Although protections of research animals are commonly thought of in terms of preventing unnecessary pain, distress, and suffering, they may also be thought of in terms of protecting animal life. A fourth likely area of disagreement concerns *whether animal life is morally protectable*. Return to a question raised earlier: whether a contented animal in good health is harmed by being painlessly killed in her sleep. Since government documents for the care and use of research animals generally require justification for causing pain or distress to animal subjects, but no justification for painless killing, it seems fair to infer that biomedicine generally does not attribute life interests to animals. Although I lack concrete evidence, I would guess that most animal advocates would see the matter quite differently and would regard the killing of animals as a serious moral matter even if it is justified in some circumstances.

The four issues identified here as probable continuing points of difference are not intended to comprise an exhaustive list. But they show that despite the fact that the biomedical and animal protection communities can agree on an impressive range of major points, given their basic orientations they cannot be expected to agree on every fundamental question. Few will find this assertion surprising. But I also suggest, less obviously, that even if both sides cannot be entirely right in their positions, differences that remain after positions are refined through honest, open-minded, fully educated inquiry can be reasonable differences.

What Can be Done Now to Build Upon the Points of Agreement

Let me close with a series of suggestions offered in the constructive yet critical-minded spirit of Henry Spira's work for how to build on the points of agreement identified above. For reasons of space, these suggestions will be stated somewhat tersely and without elaboration.

First, biomedical organizations and leaders in the profession can do the following: openly acknowledge that ethical issues involving animals are complex and important; educate themselves or acquire education about the ethical issues; tolerate views departing from the current party line; open up journals to more than one basic viewpoint; and stop disseminating one-sided propaganda.

Second, the more "militant" animal advocates can acknowledge that there can be reasonable disagreement on some of the relevant issues and stop intimidating people with whom they disagree.

Third, biomedicine can openly acknowledge, as NASA recently did in its principles, that animals can suffer and invite more serious consideration of animal suffering.

Fourth, the animal protection community can give credit to biomedicine where credit is due—for example, for efforts to minimize pain and distress, to improve housing conditions, and to refrain from killing old chimpanzees who are no longer useful for research but are expensive to maintain.

Fifth, animal researchers and members of animal protection organizations can be required by their organizations to take courses in ethical theory or animal ethics to promote knowledgeable, skilled, broad-minded discussion and reflection.

Sixth, the animal protection community can openly acknowledge that some animal research is justified (perhaps giving examples to reduce the potential for misunderstanding).

Seventh, more animal research ethics committees can bring aboard at least one dedicated animal advocate who (unlike mainstream American veterinarians) seriously questions the value of most animal research.

Eighth, conditions of housing for research animals can be improved—for example, with greater enrichment and, for social animals, more access to conspecifics.

Ninth, all parties can endorse and support the goal of finding ways to *eliminate* animal subjects' pain, distress, and suffering.[23]

Tenth, and finally, governments can invest much more than they have to date in the development and use of alternatives to animal research, and all parties can give strong public support to the pursuit of alternatives.

Notes

1. American Medical Association. Animal Research Action Plan (June 1989), 6. See also American Medical Association White Paper (1988).
2. See the Humane Society of the United States (HSUS). *Farm Animals and Intensive Confinement.* Washington, DC: HSUS, 1994; *Animals in Biomedical Research.* Washington, DC: HSUS, revised 1989; and *Zoos: Information Packet.* Washington, DC: HSUS, 1995.
3. Animal Liberation Front. Animal Liberation Frontline Information Service: The A.L.F. Primer. (Website)
4. Regan T. *The Case for Animal Rights.* Berkeley: University of California Press, 1983; Pluhar E. *Beyond Prejudice.* Durham, NC: Duke University Press, 1995.
5. Frey R. G. *Interests and Rights.* Oxford: Clarendon, 1980; Singer P. *Animal Liberation,* 2nd ed. New York: New York Review of Books, 1990.
6. DeGrazia D. *Taking Animals Seriously.* Cambridge: Cambridge University Press, 1996.
7. Sapontzis S. F. *Morals, Reason, and Animals.* Philadelphia: Temple University Press, 1987; Rodd R. *Biology, Ethics, and Animals.* Oxford: Clarendon, 1990; and Rollin B. E. *Animal Rights and Human Morality,* 2nd ed. Buffalo, New York: Prometheus, 1992.
8. Midgley M. *Animals and Why They Matter.* Athens, Georgia: University of Georgia Press, 1983.
9. Carruthers P. *The Animals Issue.* Cambridge: Cambridge University Press, 1992.
10. In a letter to the editor, Robert White, a neurosurgeon well known for transplanting monkeys' heads, asserted that "[a]nimal usage is not a moral or ethical issue . . ." (White R. Animal ethics? [letter]. *Hastings Center Report* 1990, 20(6): 43). For a rebuttal to White, see my letter, *Hastings Center Report* 1991, 21(5): 45.
11. See Rose M., Adams D. Evidence for pain and suffering in other animals. In: Langley G., ed. *Animal Experimentation.* New York: Chapman and Hall, 1989, 42–71; Smith J. A., Boyd K. M. *Lives in the Balance.* Oxford: Oxford University Press, 1991, ch. 4. See also note 7 Rodd 1990: ch. 3; and DeGrazia D., Rowan A. Pain, suffering, and anxiety in animals and humans. *Theoretical Medicine* 1991, 12: 193–211.
12. See, e.g., U.S. Government Principles for the Utilization and Care of Vertebrate Animals Used in Testing, Research, and Training. In: National Research Council. *Guide for the Care and Use of Laboratory Animals.* Washington, DC: National Academy Press, 1996, 117–8; National Aeronautics and Space Administration[0]. *Principles for the Ethical Care and Use of Animals.* NASA Policy Directive 8910.1, effective 23 March 1998; and Council for International Organizations of Medical Sciences. *International Guiding Principles for Biomedical Research Involving Animals.* Geneva: CIOMS, 1985, 18.
13. See note 12, National Research Council 1996; CIOMS 1985.
14. Note that the term "euthanasia," which means a death that is good for the one who dies, is inappropriate when animals are killed because they are costly to maintain or for similarly human-regarding reasons.
15. See note 11, Smith, Boyd 1991: 334.
16. See note 6, DeGrazia 1996: 204–10.
17. That is, except those humans who benefit directly from the conduct of research, such as researchers and people who sell animals and laboratory equipment.
18. See, e.g., note 11, Smith, Boyd 1991: ch. 3.
19. Peter Singer reminded me of this important point.

20. The idea of differences of moral status can be left intuitive here. Any effort to make it more precise will invite controversy. (See note 6, DeGrazia 1996: 256–7.)
21. See note 12, National Research Council 1996: 118.
22. See note 12, CIOMS 1985: 18.
23. This is the stated goal of a new initiative of the Humane Society of the United States, which expects the initiative to expand to Humane Society International.

38 Defending Animal Research
An International Perspective

Baruch A. Brody

Brody compares and contrasts legal and attitudinal differences towards the use of experimental animals between the U.S. and Europe. He believes that as humans we have special obligations to ourselves, our family members, our friends, and our fellow citizens, that go beyond our obligations to members of other species. Those special obligations lend support to human use of animals in research.

Introduction

In a recent article, "The Ethics of Animal Research," philosopher David DeGrazia asks the very important question of whether or not there is room for at least some agreement between "biomedicine" and "animal advocates" on the issue of animal research.[1] This is an important question, but one on which we are unlikely to make any progress until the contents of both positions are clearly understood. This essay is devoted to better articulating the position which supports animal research, the position that DeGrazia labels the "biomedicine" position; I leave the analysis of the animal-advocacy position for other occasions.

My reason for adopting this strategy is as follows: There has been in recent years an extensive philosophical discussion of various versions of the animal-advocacy position, and the variations on this position have been analyzed by several authors.[2] Much less attention has been paid to development of the pro-research position. DeGrazia himself describes the articulation of that position in negative terms:

> It seems fair to say that biomedicine has a "party line" on the ethics of animal research, conformity to which may feel like a political litmus test for full acceptability within the professional community. According to this party line, animal research is clearly justified because it is necessary for medical progress and therefore human health. . . . [M]any or most animal researchers and their supporters do not engage in sustained, critical thinking about the moral status of animals and the basic justification (or lack thereof) for animal research.[3]

Whether or not this is fully accurate, this perception of the status of the pro-research position seems to be widespread. It therefore seems important to attempt a better articulation and defense of a reasonable version of that position.

What do I mean by a reasonable pro-research position on animal research, the type of position that I wish to defend? I understand such a position to be committed to at least the following propositions:

1. Animals have interests (at least the interest in not suffering, and perhaps others as well), which may be adversely affected either by research performed on them or by the conditions under which they live before, during, and after the research.

2. The adverse effect on animals' interests is morally relevant and must be taken into account when deciding whether or not a particular program of animal research is justified or must be modified or abandoned.
3. The justification for conducting a research program on animals that would adversely affect them is the benefits that human beings would receive from the research in question.
4. In deciding whether or not the research in question is justified, human interests should be given greater significance than animal interests.

Some preliminary observations about these propositions are in order. Propositions (1) and (2) commit the reasonable pro-research position to a belief that animal interests are morally relevant and that the adverse impact of animal research on these interests should not be disregarded. This distinguishes the position I am trying to articulate from positions (such as the classical Cartesian position) that maintain that animals have no interests or that those interests do not count morally.[4] In light of their ability to experience pleasures and pains, it is implausible to deny animals interests or to give those interests no moral significance at all. Propositions (3) and (4) distinguish the pro-research position from the animal-advocacy position by insisting that it is permissible for animals to be adversely affected by legitimate research—they do not have a trumping right not to be used adversely for human benefit.[5] Toward this end, proposition (4) asserts that human benefits have greater significance than harms to animals in determining the legitimacy of the research, as animals have less moral significance than humans.[6]

What is the nature of humans' greater significance? [. . .] The reasonable pro-research position is actually a family of positions that differ both theoretically (on their conceptions of the nature of the priority of human interests) and practically (on the resulting types of justified research). What is needed first is a full examination of this family of positions, an examination that explores the plausibility of different views on the priority of human interests. Once we can identify the more plausible of these views, we can begin the attempt to justify one of them.

[. . .]

The U.S. and European Positions

The best statement of the U.S. policy on animal research is found in a 1986 document from the Public Health Service entitled "U.S. Government Principles for the Utilization and Care of Vertebrate Animals Used in Testing, Research, and Training."[7] [. . .] I want to highlight what is and is not present in the U.S. principles; they call upon researchers to:

- use the "minimum number [of animals] required to obtain valid results"
- consider alternatives such as "mathematical models, computer simulation, and in vitro biological systems"
- practice the "avoidance or minimization of discomfort, distress, or pain when consistent with sound scientific practices"
- use "appropriate sedation, analgesia, or anesthesia"
- kill animals painlessly after experiments when the animals "would otherwise suffer severe or chronic pain or distress that cannot be relieved"
- provide living conditions that are "appropriate for their species and contribute to their health and comfort."[8]

All of these principles are compatible with the familiar program, developed by W. M. S. Russell and R. L. Burch in 1959, which has come to be called the 3R program.[9] This program calls for the *replacement* of animal experimentation with other research methods where possible; this is why the U.S. principles request the consideration of alternative research techniques. The program also calls for the *reduction* of the number of animals used; hence, the U.S. principles state a commitment to minimizing the number of animals used as much as is consistent with obtaining scientifically valid results. Finally, the 3R program calls for *refining* both the conduct of the research and the environment in which the research animals live; the aim is to minimize the animals' pain and suffering. This is why the U.S. principles talk about pain relief, euthanasia when necessary, and species-appropriate living conditions.

[. . .]

All of this is very much in the spirit of propositions (1) and (2) of my account of the responsible pro-research position on animal research. It is because animals have interests that may be adversely affected by the research—interests that count morally—that we are called upon to replace, reduce, and refine the use of animals in research. Proposition (3) is also explicitly part of the U.S. principles, which assert that "procedures involving animals should be designed and performed with due consideration of their relevance to human or animal health, the advancement of knowledge, or the good of society."[10] But what about proposition (4)? What sort of greater significance are human interests given over animal interests in the U.S. regulations?

In fact, that question is never directly addressed. This stands in sharp contrast to the U.S. regulations on human subjects in research. These regulations require the minimization of risks, but they also require that the minimized risks be "reasonable in relation to anticipated benefits, if any, to subjects, and the importance of the knowledge that may reasonably be expected to result."[11] Nothing like these strictures occurs in the U.S. principles and regulations governing animal research.

Something else can be inferred from the wording of the U.S. principles on animal research. Discomfort, distress, or pain of the animals should be minimized "when consistent with sound scientific practices." The number of animals used should be minimized to "the number required to obtain valid results." Unrelieved pain necessary to conduct the research is acceptable so long as the animal is euthanized after or during the procedure.[12] What this amounts to in the end is that whatever is required for the research is morally acceptable; the 3R principles are to be applied only as long as they are compatible with maintaining scientifically valid research. There is never the suggestion that the suffering of the animal might be so great—even when it is minimized as much as possible while still maintaining scientific validity—that its suffering might outweigh the benefits from the research. Even when these benefits are modest, the U.S. principles never morally require the abandonment of a research project.

This is a position that gives very strong priority to human interests over animal interests, especially to the human interests that are promoted by scientific research using animals as subjects. Given the wide variety of such animal research projects, which range from developing and testing new lifesaving surgical techniques to developing and testing new cosmetics, the human interests that are given this strong priority over animal interests are very diverse.

[. . .]

The European approach to these issues is quite different. [. . .] [T]he Europeans find these principles incomplete and augment them with additional principles that give greater significance to animal interests by disallowing some research because the costs to the animal subjects are too great.

The 1986 Directive from the Council of the European Communities (now called the European Community) [. . .] stipulates that the relevant authority "shall take appropriate judicial or administrative action if it is not satisfied that the experiment is of sufficient importance for meeting the essential needs of man or animal."[13] This is a limited provision, as it involves animal interests outweighing human interests only in the case of severe and prolonged pain. The provision does not clearly specify what the "appropriate" actions in such cases are, and it implies that even severe and prolonged pain is acceptable if the research is of "sufficient importance." Nevertheless, it goes beyond anything in the U.S. principles and regulations by giving somewhat greater significance to animal interests.

This approach is developed in national legislation in several European countries. [. . .] While these national provisions are both broader in application and more explicit in their implications than is the E.C. directive, they still leave a crucial question unanswered.

Consider a whole continuum of positions, ranging from the claim that animal interests and human interests count equally (the *equal-significance position*) to the claim that even though one may attend to animal interests, human interests always take precedence (the *human-priority position*). In moving from the first position to the second, the significance of animal interests in comparison to human interests is gradually discounted. The intermediate positions move from those that discount animal interests modestly (and are therefore increasingly close to the equal-significance position) to those that discount them significantly (and are therefore increasingly close to the human-priority position). The U.S. position is the human-priority end of this continuum, and the animal rights movement's rejection of proposition (4) of the pro-research position puts that movement at the other end. The European positions are somewhere in-between, but there is no way to tell from their regulations where they are on the continuum.

[. . .]

[P]roposition (4) of the pro-research position, the principle of giving greater significance to human interests than to animal interests, is understood very differently in the United States and in Europe. For the United States, the proposition means that human interests in conducting research always take lexical priority over animal interests. This lexical priority is not characteristic of the European positions, which allow for some balancing of interests. But there is no evidence that the Europeans have rejected proposition (4) and adopted the equal-significance position that is characteristic of the animal-advocacy position. They seem, instead, to have adopted some discounting of animal interests in comparison with human interests, with the crucial discount rate being undetermined.

Are there any reasons for supposing that a lexical-priority approach is a more plausible articulation of proposition (4) than is a discounting approach (or vice versa)? This is the question I will examine in the next section of this essay.

Lexical Priority Versus Discounting

There are two arguments I will consider in this section. The first argument, in favor of a lexical-priority approach to proposition (4), argues that the cross-species comparison of interests that is presupposed by the discounting approach is meaningless and that the discounting approach must, therefore, be rejected in favor of a lexical-priority approach. The second argument, in favor of the discounting approach, asserts that lexical priority is incompatible with significant components of the 3R program, and that pro-research adherents of that program must, therefore, adopt the discounting approach.

[. . .]

The challenge of the first argument . . . has two components. The first component is the claim that there is no basis for placing animal pain and pleasure (if one defines 'interests' hedonistically) or the satisfaction of animal preferences (if one defines 'interests' in terms of preference-satisfaction) on a common metric with human pain and pleasure or human preference-satisfaction. I will refer to this first component of the challenge as the *incommensurability claim.* The second component is the claim that even if there were such a basis, we do not know enough about the sensations or preferences of animals to make such comparisons; I will call this component the *cross-species ignorance claim.*

[. . .]

[E]ven if one accepts this two-pronged challenge, it does not necessarily follow from this that we should adopt the lexical-priority approach to proposition (4). Those who oppose the lexical-priority approach on the intuitive grounds that it does not give sufficient significance to animal interests can simply conclude that some other approach, one which captures those intuitions, must be developed. All that does follow from the first argument's two-pronged challenge is that the lexical-priority approach to proposition (4) is more plausible than is the discounting approach (which, if the incommensurability claim is correct, has no plausibility at all).

But should we grant the challenge's components? I see no reason to accept the incommensurability claim. Human pain and pleasure is quantified on the basis of dimensions such as duration and intensity; animal pain and pleasure can also be quantified on those dimensions. Duration is certainly not conceptually different for different species, and no reason has been offered for why we should treat intensity as differing conceptually for different species. Thus, there is a basis for a common metric for hedonistic comparisons of the impact of research on human and animal interests. I think that the same is true for preference-satisfaction comparisons of the impact of research on human and animal interests, but it is hard to say that with the same degree of confidence, since we still have little understanding of the dimensions on which we quantify preference-satisfaction.

[. . .]

The cross-species ignorance claim is more serious. [. . .] This issue has been faced most directly by a working party of the British Institute of Medical Ethics (an unofficial but respected interdisciplinary group of scholars) in a report published in 1991.[14] The working party's members took note of the fact that the quantification of interests on a common metric seems to be required by the British Animals Act and that there are doubts as to whether this can be done. In response to these concerns, they make two observations, which seem to me to be the beginning of a good answer to these concerns. First, they note that not every reliable judgment must be based upon a mathematically quantifiable balancing of values: it is often sufficient to have confidence in "the procedures which have been used to arrive at that judgment, . . . upon whether [researchers] have taken into account all the known morally relevant factors, and whether they have shown themselves responsive to all the relevant moral interests."[15] Second, the working party claims that it is possible to identify the moral factors relevant to the assessment of animal research and the degree to which they are present in a given case; this knowledge would allow for reliable judgments about the moral acceptability of proposed protocols for animal research. In fact, the working party goes on to create such a scheme and to show by examples how it might work in a reliable fashion.[16]

[. . .]

This brings me to the second argument of this section. There are, this second argument suggests, reasons for doubting that the lexical-priority approach is compatible with even the 3R approach to the reasonable pro-research position. Satisfying the 3R principles, even if done in a way that allows the proposed research to proceed, involves considerable costs. These costs mean that other human interests, in research or otherwise, will not be satisfied. If human interests truly take precedence over animal interests, this seems inappropriate. A lexical-priority approach, then, cannot support even the now widely accepted 3R approach to protecting animal interests; this, it seems to me, makes the lexical-priority interpretation of proposition (4) an implausible version of the pro-research position.

Consider, for example, that aspect of the 3R program's refinement plank that calls for modifications in the environment in which research animals live in order to make those environments species-appropriate and not a source of distress or discomfort. Those modifications, now widely required throughout the world, are often quite costly, and these costs are passed on to the researchers as a cost of doing research. Some poorly funded research never takes place because these extra costs cannot be absorbed. Other, better funded, research projects go on but require extra funding. This extra funding may mean that other research projects are not funded, or that the funded research will not be as complete as originally envisioned. To avoid these outcomes, extra funding would have to be provided to research efforts in general, but this would compromise funding for other human interests. In these ways and others, the adoption of this aspect of the 3R program is not compatible with maintaining the full research effort and/or with meeting other human interests. Hence, human interests are not being given full priority, contrary to the basic premise of the lexical-priority position.

None of this, of course, is a problem for the discounting approach unless the discounting of animal interests is so significant that it approaches the lexical-priority position. If the discounting is not this extensive—if animal interests count a lot, even if not as much as the interests of humans—then it seems reasonable to suppose that the interests of the animals in living in a species-appropriate environment are sufficiently great to justify imposing these burdens on the research effort.

In short, then, those who want a reasonable pro-research position to incorporate the widely adopted 3R program should find the discounting approach more plausible than the lexical-priority approach. But what could possibly justify such a discounting of animal interests? We turn to that question in the next section.

The Rationale for Discounting

Before attempting to develop an approach to justifying discounting, it is important to be clear as to exactly what is claimed by discounting. [. . .] Discounting [. . .] is the claim that the same unit of pain counts less, morally, if it is experienced by an animal than it would if it is experienced by a human being, not because of the human's associated experiences but simply because of the species of the experiencer. Discounting directly denies the equal consideration of interests across species.

I am emphasizing this point to make it clear that *discounting* of animal interests is radically different than the *preference* for human interests that even animal advocates such as Peter Singer accept.

[. . .]

But for Singer and other supporters of the equal-significance position, all that follows from this is that humans may suffer more and that this quantitative difference in the amount of suffering is morally relevant. What discounting affirms, and what they deny, is that even when there is no quantitative difference in the amount of suffering, the human suffering counts more morally.

With this understanding of the claim of discounting, we can easily understand why many would find its claims ethically unacceptable. Why should the moral significance of the same amount of suffering differ according to the species of the sufferer if there are no associated additional differences?

[. . .]

I see no reasonable alternative for the adherent of the discounting position except to challenge the whole idea that we are, in general, morally committed to an equal consideration of interests. This is a plausible move, since equal consideration of interests has come under much challenge in contemporary moral philosophy, totally independently of the debate over the moral significance of the interests of animals. I would trace the beginning of the idea that we should not accept equal consideration of interests to W. D. Ross's contention, as early as 1930, that we have special obligations to ourselves, our family members, our friends, our fellow citizens, etc.[17] Recognizing these special obligations means, of course, giving higher priority to the interests of some (those to whom we have special obligations) than to the interests of others (those to whom we do not). Equally important is the emphasis in the 1980s on the idea that we have a morally permissible prerogative to pay special attention to our own interests in the fulfillment of some of our central projects.[18] Recognizing this prerogative means giving a higher priority to at least some of our interests over the interests of others. Each of these ideas, in separate ways, presupposes a denial of equal consideration of interests, and both are best understood as forms of the discounting of certain interests.

How should we understand the special obligations that we have? One good way of understanding them is that we have special obligations to some people to give a higher priority to their interests than we do to those of others. This may call upon us to promote their interests even at the cost of not promoting the greater interests of strangers. Note, by the way, that it is implausible to see this as a form of lexical priority favoring the interests of those people to whom we have special obligations. When their interests at stake are modest, and when the conflicting interests of strangers are great, we are not obliged to put the interests of those to whom we are specially obligated first; we may not even be permitted to do so. It would appear, then, that special obligations might well be understood as involving a requirement that we discount the interests of strangers when they compete with the interests of those to whom we have special obligations.

The same approach sheds much light upon our prerogative to pursue personal goals even at the cost of not aiding others (or even hindering them) in the pursuit of their interests. This is, once again, hardly a lexical priority. No matter how important a goal may be to me, I may be morally required to put it aside if the competing interests of others are especially great. Our prerogative may best be understood as involving only a permission to discount the interests of strangers when they compete with our interests in attaining our goals.

Note, by the way, that this means that we really have a whole family of theories about special obligations and about personal prerogatives. Different theories will differ on the acceptable discount rate.

Looked at from this perspective, the discounting approach to the animal research position no longer seems anomalous. Rather than involving a peculiar discounting of the interests of animals, in violation of the fundamental moral requirement of the equal consideration of interests, the approach represents one more example of the discounting of the interests of strangers, a feature that is pervasive in morality.

We can see another way of developing this point if we consider the difference between the following two questions:

1A Why should the interests of my children count more than do those of others?
1B Why should the interests of my children count more for me than do those of others?

The former question, asked from an impersonal perspective, is unanswerable. The latter question, which is asked from the personal perspective, is answerable. The same needs to be said about the following pair of questions:

2A Why should the interests of humans count more than do those of animals?
2B Why should the interests of humans count more for human beings than do those of animals?

As with the previous pair of questions, what is unanswerable from one perspective may be very answerable from the other perspective.

There is, of course, an important difference between special obligations, even to oneself, and personal prerogatives. The former *require* you to give certain interests priority, while the latter just *permit* you to do so. This difference is helpful in explaining a certain ambiguity in the reasonable pro-research position. While its adherents often seem to be attempting to justify only the permissibility of animal research, they sometimes talk as though they are arguing that such research is required. Consider, for example, the standard Food and Drug Administration requirement that new drugs be tested on animals before they are tested on humans. I would suggest the following: when adherents justify the permissibility of animal research, they are invoking the analogy to prerogatives, but when they want to require this research, they are invoking the analogy to special obligations. On the latter view, we have an obligation to human beings, as part of our special obligations to members of our species, to discount animal interests in comparison with human interests by testing new drugs on animals first.

This defense of animal research on the ground of species solidarity has been developed elsewhere by the British philosopher Mary Midgley, although her emphasis seems to me to be more on psychological bonds and less on the logical structure of the consideration of interests in moral thought.[19]

[. . .]

Further Issues

[. . .]

There remain, of course, several aspects of the discounting approach that require fuller development. An appropriate discount rate is yet to be determined; the process of cross-species comparisons of gains and losses in interests must be refined; and the conditions under which discounting is merely permissible as opposed to when it is mandatory need to be defined.

In addition to these necessary developments, there is a fundamental challenge that still needs to be confronted. It is a variation on the issue of equal consideration of interests, and it requires much further theoretical reflection. [. . .] Discounting the interests of members of other races or of the other gender seems to be part of the wrong of racism and sexism. Might one not argue that discounting the interests of the members of other species is equally wrong? That is the wrong of "speciesism."

This point can also be put as follows: The charge of speciesism might just be the charge that discounting animal interests is wrong because it violates the principle of equal consideration of interests. This charge is severely weakened by the challenge to the legitimacy of the equal-consideration principle. But the charge might be the very different claim that discounting animal interests is wrong because it is a *discriminatory* version of discounting; this charge is not challenged by the general challenge to the principle of the equal consideration of interests. This version of the charge is articulated by DeGrazia in a critique of Midgley:

> Can appeals to social bondedness in justifying partiality towards humans be convincingly likened to family-based preferences but contrasted with bigotry? Why are racism and sexism unjustified, if species-based partiality is justified?[2]

It is of interest and importance to note that the examples DeGrazia invokes are of partiality toward family members, on the one hand, and toward members of our race or gender, on the other hand. Left out are partiality toward fellow citizens, fellow believers, and fellow members of an ethnic group. All of these seem, *as long as they are not excessive,* to be within the bounds of acceptable partiality toward our fellows and of acceptable discounting of the interests of others. This is why it is appropriate that so much charitable giving is organized by religions and national groups. This is, also, why it is appropriate that nearly all redistribution is done at the individual-country level rather than at the international level. These examples are important in reminding us that the rejection of the equal consideration of interests principle in common morality is very broad and covers large-scale groups that are more analogous to species than to family members. Of course, this by itself is not a refutation of the discrimination charge leveled against the pro-research position. It does, however, place the position in the company of partialities and discountings that are widely accepted in moral theory and in public policy.

What my arguments foreshadow is the need for further ethical reflection on these controversial issues. We have seen that morality can legitimately involve the discounting of even other people's interests when one acts from a prerogative or a special obligation. A question that requires much more exploration is; what differentiates legitimate discounting from discrimination? Only an answer to this question can fully justify the discounting-based, reasonable pro-research position that I have articulated in this essay.

Notes

1. David DeGrazia, "The Ethics of Animal Research," *Cambridge Quarterly of Healthcare Ethics* 8, no. 1 (Winter 1999): 23–34.
2. For summaries of the extensive literature, see, for example, Tom Beauchamp, "The Moral Standing of Animals in Medical Research," *Law, Medicine, and Health Care* 20, nos. 1–2 (Spring/Summer 1992): 7–16; and David DeGrazia, "The Moral Status of Animals and Their Use in Research: A Philosophical Review," *Kennedy Institute of Ethics Journal* 1, no. 1 (March 1991): 48–70.
3. DeGrazia, "The Ethics of Animal Research," 23–4.
4. For a discussion of Descartes' position on these issues, see F. Barbara Orlans, *In the Name of Science: Issues in Responsible Animal Experimentation* (New York: Oxford University Press, 1993), 3–4.
5. This is in opposition to the position articulated in Tom Regan, *The Case for Animal Rights* (Berkeley: University of California Press, 1983).

6. This is in opposition to the position articulated in Peter Singer, *Practical Ethics*, 2nd ed. (New York: Cambridge University Press, 1993).

7. National Institutes of Health—Office for Protection from Research Risks (NIH-OPRR), *Public Health Service Policy on Humane Care and Use of Laboratory Animals* (Bethesda, MD: NIH-OPRR, 1986).

8. Ibid., i.

9. W. M. S. Russell and R. L. Burch, *The Principles of Humane Experimental Technique* (London: Methuen, 1959).

10. NIH-OPRR, *Policy on Humane Care and Use of Laboratory Animals*, principle 2, i.

11. 45 C.F.R. sec. 46.111 (1999).

12. NIH-OPRR, *Policy on Humane Care and Use of Laboratory Animals*, principles 3, 4, and 6, i.

13. Council Directive of November 24, 1986, art. 12, sec. 2, reprinted in Baruch Brody, *The Ethics of Biomedical Research: An International Perspective* (New York: Oxford University Press, 1998), 237–40.

14. Jane A. Smith and Kenneth M. Boyd (eds.), *Lives in the Balance: The Ethics of Using Animals in Biomedical Research—The Report of a Working Party of the Institute of Medical Ethics* (Oxford: Oxford University Press, 1991).

15. Ibid., 141.

16. Ibid., 141–6.

17. W. D. Ross, *The Right and the Good* (Oxford: Oxford University Press, 1930), chap. 2.

18. Samuel Scheffler, *The Rejection of Consequentialism* (Oxford: Oxford University Press, 1982), chap. 3.

19. Mary Midgley, *Animals and Why They Matter* (Harmondsworth, Middlesex: Penguin Books, 1983).

20. David DeGrazia, *Taking Animals Seriously: Mental Life and Moral Status* (New York: Cambridge University Press, 1996), 64.

39 Who—or What—Are the Rats (and Mice) in the Laboratory?

Lynda Birke

Birke traces two intertwined strands of metaphors associated with laboratory rodents. The first focuses on the idea of medical/scientific progress; in this context she views the metaphor of laboratory rodents epitomizing medical triumph or serving as helpers or saviors. In the second strand she addresses the ambiguous status of laboratory rodents who simultaneously are animals and not animals (data). She argues that because of these ambiguous meanings, rodent laboratories are doubly "othered"—first in the way that animals so often are made other to humans and then other in the relationship of the laboratory animal to other animals.

   [. . .]

In this paper, drawing on representations from various sources, I want to explore some of the meanings of "the laboratory rat" or "laboratory rodent." I start with the rats, partly because I am particularly familiar with them in laboratories. However, much of the argument applies also to mice, and I draw also on representations of more generalized rodents. At times, these two different kinds of rodent may be practically interchangeable in their use in scientific research and their histories as specifically bred animals in the laboratory.

   I will begin by sketching how wild rats, harbingers of disease, came to be bred specifically for scientific research (alongside mice); in doing so, they took on new significance. Now, the image of a laboratory rodent conveys a great deal—not so much about the animal who, in many ways, remains a mystery—but about the processes and values of scientific research. The rodent has become a potent icon. So, my main concern here is to examine some of the referents of this icon in order to ask, what does the laboratory rodent signify for us? What does this rodent tell us about the practices of science? And what can we learn from these meanings about human relationships to animals?

Creating the Rodent in the Laboratory

Even when they are white, laboratory rats—the animals bred by the million for various kinds of experimental purposes—are derived from brown rats (*Rattus norvegicus*). [. . .]

   There were, then, two stages in the development of laboratory rodents as we know them. The first was the process of bringing them from the wild into the labs, via the fanciers' breeding rooms. This entailed a transformation from wild to tame and from animals exemplifying certain species (such as brown Norway rats) to multitudes of different types, colors, and strains. It also, of course, required a transformation from being an animal that routinely elicited reactions of disgust and horror from people to becoming an animal that would represent medical progress. The second stage was what might be called a process of greater industrialization, in which lab animals become standardized and increasingly became a production process and part of the apparatus of science (Logan, 2001; Shapiro, 2002). Although many of these generalizations apply also to other species, it was rodents who became particularly standardized and who now exemplify "laboratory work".

Rodents were chosen for early experimental studies for several reasons. They bred quickly, so facilitating studies of inheritance; they were altricial (i.e. they are born immature), so facilitating studies of early development; and rats particularly were thought to have strong sex drives, important to early twentieth century studies of reproduction and sexual behavior (Burian, 1993; Logan, 2001). By the 1930s, rats had become "a kind of generic standard in research on physiology and behavior", so displacing earlier emphases on species diversity in physiological studies (Logan, p. 287). On the contrary, just as studies increasingly came to focus on only one species, more and more subdivisions within that species emerge—a new, but more controlled, form of diversity. [. . .]

Changing Meanings

We may shun the sewer rat or try to exterminate rats and mice from our houses and farms, but, in the laboratory, rats mean a great deal to us. I want now to explore some of these meanings, in two broad, overlapping areas. First, how we understand the laboratory rat today draws on widespread cultural metaphors of medical triumph and the conquest of disease. Laboratory rats may be represented in ways that signify not only successes in conquering diseases but also the triumph of specifically scientific (Western) medicine. Global science relies on a global production of standardized rodents. Yet, rodents in such iconography often seem to become our saviors, standing in for us in their suffering. These metaphors in turn structure how we think about both scientific laboratories and rodents.

Secondly, the transformation into "the" laboratory rat has entailed a loss of the rat understood as an animal or as exemplar of a species. Rather, the laboratory rat has become transformed from what most of us would commonly call an animal into something that stands in for data and scientific analysis. I will explore each of these in turn.

Global Conquest: The Triumphant Rodent

Mapping metaphors in biology are now ubiquitous. We can map the genome of mouse or human, although we have long been mapping the body of rodents through dissection guides and other reference books (there are various "Atlases of the Rat Brain"). We can also map the distribution of hormone receptors, say, within that brain.

It is not, of course, only rodents who are thus "mapped"; indeed, much of the impetus for genome mapping comes from the efforts to sequence the DNA in the human genome. In practice, however, there are very few organisms around whose genomes there is such intensive mapping effort; among these select few are laboratory rats and mice. The significance of their genomes does not lie in understanding them as exemplars of their species but on their role as stand-ins for human disease. Mice and rats attain a particular status thereby; their chromosomes can be compared directly to maps of human ones in relation to the genetics of specific diseases.[1]

Mapping metaphors can be added to Arluke's (1994) classification of three types of images used in advertising laboratory animals: the "classy chemical"; consumer goods (both of which construct the lab animal as analogous to a chemical reagent), and the "team player" in which, typically, cartoon animals are portrayed as "helping" in the service of medicine. Inevitably, the huge interest now in genome mapping is mirrored in advertising. In several advertisements for laboratory rats and mice,[2] the rodent's image appears either juxtaposed to images of gel electrophoresis (the typical "bars" of DNA analysis) or next to a map. In one advertisement,[3] one-half of the (white) rat is shown photographically, but the image merges and its hindquarters appear as diagrammatic isoclines—the mapped rat body.

The mapping metaphor is, as Haraway (1997) has pointed out, a highly pervasive—and persuasive—one, drawing on imagery and rhetoric of global conquest and triumph. Haraway analyzes an image used by New England Biolabs, depicting a young white woman superimposed on a map of Africa, noting the connotations of gender and race. A rat image nearby a world map similarly advertises Charles River Laboratories' (1997) advertisement for the International Genetic Standard

CD Rat. This rat is not morphing into the map, as the woman/Africa image does but stands nearby, the image representing the availability of "total uniformity" for the "global research community." This, then, is the globalized research tool, and the lab rodent thus comes to symbolize the victory of Western science and medicine, not only over disease (the claim that is explicitly made) but also—more implicitly—over other knowledge and forms of medicine.

While scientific medicine becomes triumphant in advertising images and associated narratives, the laboratory animal becomes a willing participant. Arluke (1994) noted the theme of lab animals as "helpers" or "team players" in advertising. This may take the form of jokey, cartoon characters, such as the cartoon mouse dressed as a corporate executive (or perhaps a desk scientist) that was used to advertise GenPharm's transgenic mice. Or, it may portray the animal as victor, as in one of the advertisements Arluke analyzed. [. . .]

The image of laboratory rodents as saviors is a powerful one and figures in many images. One review (Paigen, 1995) of "mouse models" began with a heading: "A Miracle Enough: the Power of Mice," going on to outline ways in which mice are the ideal animals for genomic research, potential saviors who will lead to new therapies and means of preventing human disease. It is the creature, the text claims, to whom we turn experimentally because it is "so important in reaching an understanding of ourselves."

This kind of rhetoric draws partly on the arguments put forward by proponents of animal-based research, who usually emphasize a view of medicine as progress, a progress that has *depended* on the use of animals (Paton, 1993; Quimby, 1994). So, lab animals become constructed as necessary to the creation of all medical advances, thus facilitating their images as our helpers.

In many ways, laboratory rats and mice have been created to bear our diseases—from animals selectively bred to have little or no functional immune system to those who have been genetically engineered with human genes. They have been transformed from bearers of highly contagious diseases such as plague to become benign assistants in the medical fight against infections. In that sense, they become symbols of Christian salvation stories, suggests Haraway (1997). The history of science itself draws heavily on an iconography of salvation (Midgley, 1992), so it perhaps is not surprising that laboratory animals become such symbols. [. . .]

The intertwined metaphors of mapping and of rodents as helpers/saviors signify beliefs in conquest, the triumph of medicine over disease. However problematic the idea of medical triumph and progress may be, laboratory rats and mice are potent icons. Although all kinds of lab animals may be represented as part of the fight against disease, rodents particularly symbolize that fight—not least because of their strong cultural association with disease. It is no accident that advertisements for lab animals so frequently juxtapose statements about fighting disease with images of rodents, for rodent strains are created as bearers of specific diseases. In a sense, the place of rodents as key players in our salvation from illness symbolizes the ultimate triumph of good over evil—a process in which the rodents themselves are transformed from evil, disease-full vermin into sanitized, germ-free angels of mercy.

Not Quite an Animal

To become our saviors in the struggle against ill health, rats and mice also must become something other than the rodent-as-animal: These, after all, are animals we generally loathe. Scientists today use millions of laboratory rats and mice. Rodents are not only medical models for this massive industry (Paton, 1993), but also beings defined as "not quite" animals. The United States Animal Welfare Act has controversially excluded rats, mice, and birds from the definition of "animals" coming under its protection. Legislation in Britain covers all vertebrate animals; information published annually by the Home Office about animal use under current legislation (The Animals [Scientific Procedures] Act, 1986), however, always emphasizes the large percentage of animals who are rodents (approximately 80%). Organizations defending the use of animals in biomedical research make similar arguments, taking the line that most research is for potential medical benefit and most research involves rodents. Somehow, this emphasis implies that it is more acceptable to use animals in research if they are rats or mice.

And to many people, indeed it is. Public opinion is more likely to support painful experiments on rats and mice than on monkeys,[4] while many scientists who would accept using rats or mice in research might draw the line at certain other species (Arluke, 1988; Michael & Birke, 1994). That it is generally more acceptable to cause suffering to rodents reflects the negative view most people have of these animals: Public acceptance is greater just because they are animals we abhor (and this in turn is heeded by antivivisectionist organizations, which rarely use rats or mice in their illustrations).

That scientists, too, draw a line perhaps reflects a need to establish distance from rats or mice as animals in the lab (Arluke, 1988). Accordingly, most laboratory animals (especially rodents) are not named but given only numbers, while references to the naturally behaving animal tend not to enter laboratory reports, even though they may pepper scientists' speech. This schism is particularly noticeable if the animal in question belongs to a species widely accepted as sentient, such as chimpanzees, who typically are given individual names in the laboratory, though not reported as such in subsequent papers (Wieder, 1980).

Rats, however, rarely gain such status as a name. They are more likely to be numbered lots, hidden away in their racked cages, not exposed to view—they no longer have individual histories (Shapiro, 2002). Indeed, in an interview with a technician in one of my own studies, she recounted that the scientists in that lab insisted that she put the rats in opaque cages. They did not like having rats in clear cages because the "animals could look at you." They become a little too like real animals outside the lab when they do that.

Yet at the same time, scientific understanding of the animal and the animal's husbandry relies ultimately on a conception of the animal as an animal. Among other things, the animal might curl around and bite the experimenter. But these features of animalness must not enter written reports, which simplify and mathematicize. It is extremely rare to find a scientific report based on work with rats that refers to the animals in any other way.

Concepts of lab rats as barely animate tools for the job coexist with an (often tacit) understanding of them as being emotional and capable of being influenced by the affect of the researcher (Dewsbury, 1992; Dror, 1999). Partly, this reflects the way in which lab reports are written and by whom. Knowledge of the rat as an animal is explicitly excluded from reports;[5] moreover, it is the animal caretakers rather than the scientists who will have most of this tacit knowledge about everyday rat behavior. Rats have a highly ambiguous status in the laboratory, reflecting in part the ambivalence of the scientists who use them. Meriting special treatment, rats always are both faceless objects of scientific experiment and candidates for simultaneously becoming pets (Arluke, 1988; Herzog, 1988).

In the laboratory, lab animals symbolically must become something other than animals, just as cows and pigs must become something other than animals in order to become food. In his ethnographic study of laboratory neuroscientists, Lynch (1988) described how they sometimes use contrasting models of what is meant by "the animal." The "naturalistic animal" is the animal of common sense, the kind we are familiar with outside the laboratory. But in order to use them experimentally, animals must be made into "analytic animals"; that is, they must become data.

The transformation into analytic animals begins even before the rat enters the laboratory. Sprague-Dawley rats were used in the lab Lynch (1988) studied because of their

> appropriate size, docile disposition, ability to survive stressful operations, and uniformity of brain dimension from one individual to another. . . . The selection and breeding of rats was thus done with an orientation to a generalized 'mathematical' space transcending the brain of any given animal.

(p. 273)

From the beginning, these transformations have been part and parcel of the breeding programs of laboratory strains of rats and mice; rodents have, in a sense, been created to fit their own mathematization.

Rodents are both handy models of human disease and originate in a despised animal; these two aspects of how we see them make it easier to perceive rodents in particular as merely data. Latour (1987), a sociologist of science, has described the ways in which "facts" are created in the course of laboratory work. Latour argues that through processes of persuasion and agreement and reliance on output from accepted devices to produce graphical output, scientists construct stories that become accepted—through repetition and rhetoric—as facts. An initial suggestion that, say, a mammalian brain produces a particular molecule that may be a neurotransmitter can quickly become codified and accepted as evidence that there is such a transmitter (Latour). These transitions begin with an animal. That set of moves, however, from animal to data to inference to established facts, is easier if the first move is foreshortened—if the animal already is not quite an animal.

So, in the production of results from the laboratory, the animals who ate, slept, and played with their friends—hidden from human eyes—disappear. Indeed, for scientists to do their work, the animals must disappear. The lab rat has been metamorphosed from a rat, with particular characteristics of species-typical behavior, to a "laboratory animal" representing numbers. However many millions of rats and mice are used annually in the service of science, we know remarkably little about their characteristics as species.[6] Rather, lab rats—unlike many other kinds of animals studied in the laboratory—no longer stand as exemplars of their species. Looking through back issues of the journal *Animal Behaviour*, I was struck by the difference in how certain animals are described. Most papers refer to studies with a specific species, identified by the Latin binomial and some reference to the habitat in which the animal is found in the wild. Occasionally, studies use rats: Few of these studies are concerned with the Norway rat as such but may use rats to study some specific biological mechanism. In striking contrast to references to other species ("the white-footed mouse," identified in English as a member of a particular species), the studies using rats significantly refer to the animal only as "the laboratory rat." It is as though "the laboratory rat" becomes the species name.[7]

Furthermore, if rats and mice are perceived in the first place as models for human physiology, then their own ratness or mouseness is irrelevant; they already are part way to becoming de-naturalized analytic animals precisely because they are perceived as (and reduced to) "models" (Shapiro, 2002). Models are abstractions. A model of a physiological system in textbooks might mean an abstract diagram or graphical representation of a set of processes. The reader is not meant to think of a living animal while scrutinizing these graphs.

Yet, advertising for laboratory rodents may bring out the "animalness" by using images of the lab rat or mouse without a context. The image in such advertisements (aimed at users of lab animals) may well include representations of data (some emblem of DNA or graphs) but rarely portrays the animal actually in a cage or laboratory or even with a scientist in evidence. Most advertisements, rather, include a photograph of a white rodent, lit from above, casting a shadow and standing over the shadow, so distinguishing the image from the white page. In these images, the animal's eyes are often oriented to the viewer, so becoming, paradoxically, more like a naturalistic animal.

One aspect of being a model for human physiology is that toxicological studies use millions of rodents to test drugs and other chemicals to which we are exposed. Alongside these routine tests, scientists can gain information about chemical exposures from epidemiological studies of our own species as well as "sentinel" species of wildlife or companion animals whose physiological responses to chemicals in the environment can be monitored. The ideal species for such surveys would be one that shares our environment and is equally exposed to our diet—hence, the use of data obtained from companion animals (National Research Council, 1991). The animals who most closely fit these criteria are, of course, the rodents who live so commensally with us in and around our habitations. But we cannot use them as sentinels outside the laboratory for the simple reason that we also are trying to poison them by putting down rodenticides. As indicators of toxicity, laboratory rodents really are a breed apart.

One set of meanings attached to the label "the laboratory rat" is that this rat is, and is not, an animal. This rat's animal status is ambiguous, mirroring the ambivalence of our human relationship to the rat. This rat, when representing animality, may bite or gaze at nervous experimenters. This rat must stand, with shining fur, as though on a plinth, but never appear caged. When not standing for animality, these rats must become part of the equipment of science, fitting literally (cages or stereo-taxic equipment to hold heads in place must fit the animals; but so too must the animals be selected to fit the equipment) or metaphorically by narratives that move them into the realm of data or as models for "man." In these meanings, the rat is not so much an animal as a device for producing an output.[8]

Shape-Changers: (Laboratory) Rats and Other Animals

There are, then, a multitude of overlapping and contradictory meanings attached to "the laboratory rat": The rat neither is quite in nature (having been brought into the lab), nor outside of nature. Like other animals, this rat is "other" to ourselves. Such others include animals we like as well as those we dislike. But what seems to be happening in the story of the laboratory rat is a double othering, whereby first the rat as an animal is other, and then is made other to other kinds of animals in transference to the laboratory. Both moves strip the rat of subject status, of rat persona. And both moves contribute to a double-sidedness, an either/or status.

All lab animals are doubly othered ethically, because things may be done to them in the lab that are not readily permitted outside the lab. Rats and mice may be killed in large number, just as they are in laboratories. However, there is a clear distinction in the way that invasive and sometimes painful procedures may be carried out in labs and in labs alone. Lab rodents in this sense are made, through law and ethics, into others within the others.

Yet, in practice, too, the lab rodent has been doubly othered. These rats are made other to other kinds of animals first in the literal transfer to the laboratory through breeding programs and taming that serve to separate them from the wild *Rattus* or *Mus* counterparts; they are further differentiated from other animals[9] in how they are sequestered in specialized animal houses (from which, of course, wild, naturalistic rodents are scrupulously excluded). They also are made other, symbolically, in the transition from those naturalistic animals. Laboratory animals are, in some senses, already partly non-naturalistic animals. Even in their cages in the animal house, their hiddenness and numbering ensure that they are not quite real animals.

In the processes both of breeding for specific traits of use to scientific experiments and of representation as a "model," laboratory rodents are reduced to something else—particular gene effects or physiological responses. This perhaps makes it easier for us to forget their history and associations with disease and to forget that whatever changes domestication has brought, these laboratory rodents remain living animals. Yet, ironically, they also are represented as our helpers. It is as though, by portraying them as altruistic, we can—metaphorically at least—return to them at least some of their status as animal subjects, even if in practice they have none in laboratories.

Shapiro (2002), writing about the role of the laboratory rat in the history of psychology, notes how, in the process, the animals have been de-individuated and de-animalized as well as de-speciated (in the sense that they no longer represent their original species). This, he notes, very effectively plays down their sentience and consciousness. Yet, alongside the recent development of techniques such as the creation of transgenic organisms, which further reduce laboratory animals to laboratory apparatus, there is renewed interest in the cognitive abilities and awareness of animals.[10] Increasingly, scientists are faced with evidence that not only do laboratory rats and mice have considerable intelligence but that they undoubtedly do suffer a great deal in many (or most) laboratory procedures. This shift of focus begins a process of "re-minding" the laboratory rodent, which might return these rodents to their animal status and so promote the animals' welfare.

The rat, Burt and Ellman (2002) write, is an icon of modernization as well as of the plagues of the past, as rats spread themselves through the networks of modern culture and habitation. The modernized rat is the standardized rat of laboratory breeding. Yet, rats, they note, also can be multiplicities[11] representing post-modernity. That is, what the rat means to us is many things at once—just as the animals can be many things at once in their considerable success at colonizing the world in our wake. The rat and mouse, like the coyote, are shape-changers: They can be much-loved pet and hated adversary; they can be dirt personified, and they can symbolize the eradication of disease. In the laboratory, they are both animals and not quite animals; they are vermin in the pipework under the lab but a useful piece of equipment in the lab; they are equipment, yet we can be mindful of their minds; they are bearers of disease while promising to liberate us from disease. These are contradictory, multiple, and elusive meanings indeed: It seems we can never know who is the laboratory rat.

Notes

1. For example, the JAX website allows one to compare the mouse genome directly with either human or rat, via the Mouse and Human (or rat) Orthology Map. Interestingly, the website directs the viewer toward a genomics dictionary (or atlas) of standardized nomenclature for embryonic stages. The mapping metaphor yields to the language of DNA as a dictionary of life.
2. In journals such as *Science, Laboratory Animals* or *Nature Genetics* or on websites for companies producing laboratory animals, I have examined a range of advertisements for laboratory animals from these journals and websites, which I summarize here. Like Arluke (1994), rats and mice were by far the most commonly portrayed lab animals in the advertisements I analyzed. One significant change since Arluke's study, however, has been the enormous research effort in genome mapping; this is reflected in advertisements, which increasingly make reference to genomes and genome expression.
3. For GeneSpring, www.sigenetics.com; advertisement in *Science,* 292, 2001.
4. A poll for *New Scientist* indicated that, for example, 49% of people polled would disapprove of testing a new drug that might cause pain if the subjects were mice, compared with 61% if the subjects were monkeys.
5. Lederer (1992) has noted how the style of written texts in scientific journals may reflect editorial policies, stemming from fear of antivivisectionist activity.
6. An exception is the ethological studies of Barnett (2001). For a discussion of this point in relation to the history of the use of rats in psychology, see Shapiro (2002).
7. The JAX website, however, notes that the origins of laboratory mice are more multiple, deriving primarily from two subspecies of *Mus musculus*. However, some more recent types may derive also from *M. spretus*. Because of the complex histories, the website advocates that mice "should not be referred to by species name, but rather as laboratory mice or by use of a specific strain or stock" (http:/www. informatics.jax.org, 12th Jan, 2003).
8. Latour (1987) argues that the practices of science prioritize the output of "inscription devices"—apparatuses which generate numbers and graphs. Scientific results can only become truth, suggests Latour, when they are generated by such inscription devices.
9. Some of this applies, to be sure, to other animals bred in laboratories. But, I would argue, lab rodents are the most extreme case in their long history of breeding highly specialized multiple strains for specific purposes.
10. It is ironic that the creature whose own abilities are downplayed in the reductionistic process of creating "models" has to stand as a model in psychology for our much-vaunted human intelligence.
11. Citing the notion of multiplicities in Deleuze and Guattari's concept of becoming (1987).

References

Arluke, A. (1988). Sacrificial symbolism in animal experimentation: Object or pet? *Anthrozoös, 2,* 97–116.

Arluke, A. (1994). We build a better beagle: Fantastic creatures in lab animal ads. *Qualitative Sociology, 17,* 143–158.

Burian, R. M. (1993). How the choice of experimental organism matters: Epistemological reflections on an aspect of biological practice. *Journal of the History of Biology,* 26, 351–367.

Burt, J., & Ellman, M. (2002). *Rat.* Unpublished essay.

Deleuze, G., & Guattari, F. (1987). *A thousand plateaus.* London: Athlone Press.

Dewsbury, D. A. (1992). Studies of rodent-human interactions in animal psychology. In: H. Davis & D. Balfour (Eds.), *The inevitable bond: Examining scientist-animal interactions* (pp. 27–43). Cambridge: Cambridge University Press.

Dror, O. (1999). The affect of experiment: The turn to emotions in Anglo-American physiology, 1900–1940. *Isis, 90,* 205–237.

Haraway, D. (1997). *Modest_witness@second millennium: Female man meets OncoMouse*. London: Routledge.

Herzog, H. A. (1988). The moral status of mice. *American Psychologist, 43*, 473–474.

Latour, B. (1987). *Science in action*. Buckingham: Open University Press.

Lederer, S. (1992). Political animals: The shaping of biomedical research literature in twentieth-century America. *Isis, 83*, 61–79.

Logan, C. A. (2001). 'Are Norway rats . . . things?': Diversity versus generality in the use of albino rats in experiments on development and sexuality. *Journal of the History of Biology, 34*, 287–314.

Lynch, M. (1988). Sacrifice and the transformation of the animal body into a scientific object: Laboratory culture and ritual practice in the neurosciences. *Social Studies of Science, 18*, 265–289.

Michael, M., & Birke, L. (1994). Science and morality in animal experiments: Demarcating the core set. *Social Studies of Science, 24*, 81–95.

Midgley, M. (1992). *Science as: A modern myth and its meaning*. London: Routledge.

National Research Council. (1991). *Animals as sentinels of environmental health hazards*. Washington, DC: National Academy Press.

Paigen, K. (1995). A miracle enough: The power of mice. *Nature Medicine, 1*, 215–217.

Paton, W. (1993). *Man and mouse: Animals in medical research*. Oxford: Oxford University Press.

Quimby, F. W. (1994). Twenty-five years of progress in laboratory animal science. *Laboratory Animals, 28*, 158–171.

Shapiro, K. (2002). A rodent for your thoughts: The social construction of animal models. In: Mary Henninger-Voss (Ed.), *Animals in human histories* (pp. 439–469). Rochester: University of Rochester Press.

Wieder, D. L. (1980). Behavioristic operationalism and the life-world: Chimpanzees and the chimpanzee researchers in face-to-face interaction. *Sociological Inquiry, 50*, 75–103.

40 Animal Research

A Moral Science: Talking Point on the Use of Animals in Scientific Research

Bernard E. Rollin

Rollin critiques the 'scientific ideology' by asserting that true science must be based on experience, observations, or experiments only. Unverifiable statements, such as ethical guidelines, are not relevant to science, including animal research. Science can present facts relevant to making moral decisions, but it steers clear of any ethical debate. Rollin argues that there are no morally relevant differences between humans and animals to justify excluding animals from moral consideration in how they are used and treated, particularly with invasive research.

Historically, the scientific community—at least in the USA—did not perceive the use of animals in research as an ethical issue. Anyone who raised questions about the way animals were kept and treated during experiments ran the risk of being stigmatized as an anti-vivisectionist; a misanthrope preferring animals to people; or an ingrate who did not value the contributions of biomedical science to human health and well-being. I received a full barrage of such charges when I drafted and promoted what eventually became two US federal laws to protect laboratory animals: the 1985 Health Research Extension Act and an 'Animal Welfare' amendment to the 1985 Food Security Act.

[. . .]

In various publications, I have described I what I call scientific ideology: a set of basic, uncriticized assumptions about twentieth-century science (Rollin, 2006). In general, ideologies operate in many different areas: religious, political, sociological, economic and ethnic. Therefore, it is not surprising that an ideology about science would emerge—after all, science has been the dominant method of generating knowledge in Western societies since the Renaissance. The ideology underlying modern—post-medieval—science has grown and evolved along with science itself. An important component of that ideology is a strong positivistic tendency, which is still dominant today, to believe that true science must be based on experience only, because the tribunal of experience is the objective, universal judge of what really happens in the world.

If one asks most working scientists what separates science from religion, speculative metaphysics or shamanistic world-views, they would reply without hesitation that it is an emphasis on validating claims through experience, observation or experiment. This component of scientific ideology can be traced back to Isaac Newton, who proclaimed that he did not feign hypotheses (*'hypotheses non fingo'*) but operated directly from experience. The fact that Newton operated with non-observable ideas such as gravity or, more generally, action at a distance and absolute space and time, did not stop him from issuing an ideological proclamation that one should not do so.

This insistence on experience as the foundation for scientific research persists today, where it reaches its most philosophical articulation in the reductionistic movement known as logical positivism, which was designed to exclude the unverifiable from science. A classic and profound example of this attitude is Albert Einstein's rejection of Newton's concepts of absolute space and time on the grounds that such talk was not testable. Other targets of positivists' criticisms are Henri-Louis Bergson's hypothesis of a life force (*élan vital*) as separating the living from the non-living, and the embryologist Hans Driesch's postulation of 'entelechies' to explain regeneration in starfish.

[. . .]

Although logical positivism took many subtly different and varied forms, the message, as received by working scientists and passed on to students including myself, was that proper science should not tolerate unverifiable statements. This was strengthened further by the British philosopher and logical positivist Sir Alfred Jules Ayer's vastly popular and aggressively polemical book *Language, Truth, and Logic* (Ayer, 1946); it was first published in 1936 and has remained in print ever since. Easy to read and highly critical of wool-gathering, speculative metaphysics and other 'soft' and ungrounded ways of knowing, the book was long used in introductory philosophy courses and, in many cases, represented the only contact with philosophy that aspiring young scientists—or even senior scientists—had.

Be that as it may, the positivist demand for empirical verification of all meaningful claims became a mainstay of scientific ideology from the time of Einstein to the present day. Through it, one could in good conscience dismiss religious or metaphysical claims or other speculative assertions not merely as false and irrelevant to science, but in fact as meaningless. Only what could be verified or falsified empirically was meaningful.

What does all this have to do with ethics? Quite a bit, as it turns out. The philosopher Ludwig Wittgenstein, who greatly influenced the logical positivists, once remarked that, if you took an inventory of all the facts in the universe, you would not find that killing is wrong (Wittgenstein, 1965). You cannot, in principle, test the proposition that killing is wrong—it can be neither verified nor falsified. Consequently, in Wittgenstein's view, ethical judgements are meaningless. From this, it was concluded that ethics—and all judgements regarding values rather than facts—are not part of the scientific universe. The slogan that I learned in my science courses in the 1960s, and which is still taught in too many places, is that science is value-free in general, and ethics-free in particular.

This denial of the relevance of ethics to science was taught both explicitly and implicitly. The widely used Keeton and Gould textbook on biological science—in what one of my colleagues calls the 'throat-clearing introduction,' where the authors pay lip service to the scientific method and provide a bit of history and other 'soft' issues before getting down to biological details—declares that 'science cannot make value judgments [or] moral judgments' (Keeton & Gould, 1986). In the same vein, Sylvia Mader's textbook *Biology* asserts that 'science does not make ethical or moral decisions' (Mader, 1987). The bottom line is that science might provide society with the facts relevant to making moral decisions, but it steers clear of any ethical debate.

That is not, however, the whole story. Positivist thinkers also felt compelled to explain why intelligent people feel inclined to make moral judgements. They argued that when people make assertions such as 'killing is wrong', they are only expressing revulsion. 'Killing is wrong' really expresses 'Killing, yuck!' rather than describing a particular state of affairs. Therefore, a debate over the alleged morality of capital punishment expresses revulsion or approval, and any debate we can engender is really about factual questions such as whether capital punishment acts as a deterrent against murder.

It is therefore not surprising that when scientists are drawn into discussions of ethical issues, they are as emotional as their opponents. The scientific ideology dictates that these issues are nothing but emotional; therefore, the idea of rational ethics is an oxymoron, and he who generates the most effective, emotional response 'wins.'

An ethical issue is one that challenges us to apply our concepts of right, wrong, good, and bad to a new situation. Before the 1970s, U.S. society had a very limited ethic for animal treatment—it prohibited deliberate, sadistic, overt, purposeless cruelty to animals. Under this definition, no regularly accepted use of animals in agriculture or research that was deemed 'to minister to some of the necessities of man' (Colorado Supreme Court, 1896) could be prosecuted, no matter how much pain and suffering it caused. The cruelty ethic and the ensuing laws existed primarily to flush out sadists and psychopaths, who are known to begin inflicting pain and suffering on animals before 'graduating' to people. It is not surprising then, that with 'cruelty' being the only ethical tool available, opponents of animal research labelled researchers as cruel. Researchers, in turn, chafed at being grouped with psychopaths and were further alienated from approaching their critics rationally.

[. . .]

During the 1970s and 1980s, a growing amount of literature in moral philosophy finally provided a rational approach to the ethics of animal treatment. The first such book was Peter Singer's *Animal Liberation* (1975), followed by my book *Animal Rights and Human Morality* (Rollin, 1981), Tom Regan's *The Case for Animal Rights* (1983), and Steve Sapontzis' *Morals, Reason, and Animals* (1987). All of these books discuss animal research from the point of view of moral theory, and argue for a higher moral status for animals. In particular, I pointed out that excluding animals from our moral machinery or concepts could not be justified logically for two reasons.

[. . .]

First, there is no morally relevant difference between humans and animals that justifies excluding animals from what I call 'the moral arena' or the full 'scope of moral concern.' Just as skin colour or gender cannot morally justify discrimination against humans, certain beliefs about animals—for example, that they lack a soul, are 'inferior' to humans in power or evolution, and lack reason or language—cannot morally justify their exclusion.

Second, there are positive reasons for including animals in our 'moral arena.' Most notably, what we do to animals matters to them—as Charles Darwin pointed out, they feel not only pain, but also the full range of emotions that feature in our moral deliberations about humans: fear, loneliness, boredom, frustration, anxiety, and so forth (Darwin, 1896). In addition, following Aristotle, I called attention to the nature or *telos* of an animal: the pigness of a pig; the dogness of a dog. Their *telos* can guide our ethical obligations to animals just as human nature guides us in establishing human rights.

When applied to animal research, this analysis has moral implications for invasive experiments. Our social ethic does not allow us to use humans invasively to advance our knowledge or cure human disease without their explicit and informed consent. General benefit does not surpass concern for the individual in Western democratic systems. Indeed, the US Bill of Rights forbids sacrificing the interests of individuals for the general good. Whether this logic would forbid the painless killing of animals for research is another open question, because it seems that animals do not have the cognitive abilities to value life for its own sake; however, applying our ethical machinery to hurting something—even an animal—against its will forces us to conclude that such behaviour is at least highly problematic.

At the very least, the arguments for including animals in the moral arena should give those engaged in invasive research reason to pause and think. The first issue that arises is what morally justifies hurting animals for human benefit—or even to benefit other animals—when we would not feel morally allowed to do so to humans, even though we have done so. The public decried Nazi medical experiments on concentration-camp inmates, even those that produced benefit, and equally condemned the US Tuskegee syphilis study during which doctors deliberately left African American patients untreated to study the pathology of the disease. In response to the claim that humans can provide informed consent to participate in invasive experiments that benefit other humans, whereas animals cannot, Sapontzis has offered a very clever response: open the cages and we will know if they wish to participate.

Notwithstanding these arguments from philosophers and ethicists, little morally sound discussion has come from the research community. If one presses scientists for a response, it usually takes one of two forms: we are 'superior' to animals and can do as we wish; or invasive animal research is justified because it produces more benefit to humans and/or animals than harm to the animals. With respect to the first response, what does *superior* mean? Does it mean more powerful? If we follow that position, the mugger or rapist is justified in victimizing the weak, which is what much of ethics is designed to prevent. Does it mean intellectually superior? Why should that be morally relevant? Does it mean morally superior? If so, victimizing a sentient organism hardly shows moral superiority.

[. . .]

The second common reply is tendered in terms of cost compared with benefit. Apart from the fact that our consensus social ethic does not accept hurting the minority for the benefit of the majority, this argument is open to a much more practical point: let us assume that invasive animal research is justified only by the benefit produced. It would then seem that the only morally justifiable research would be research that benefits humans and/or animals. But there is in fact a vast amount of research that has not been shown to benefit humans or animals: much behavioural research, weapons research or toxicity testing as a legal requirement are obvious examples, but basic research also often has no clear benefits. Someone might respond that we never know what benefits might emerge in the future, and appeal to serendipity. But if that were a legitimate point, we could not discriminate between funding research likely to produce benefits and that unlikely to do so; however, we do. If we appeal to unknown but possible benefits, we are literally forced to fund everything, which we do not. Even if we disregard the general point about the morality of invasive animal research, we are still left with the fact that much of animal research does not fit with the researchers' own moral justification for it. If one accepts the benefit argument by appealing to utilitarian principles, we are left with the conclusion that the only justifiable animal research is that which produces more benefit than harm—however this is measured.

But this is not all: another moral problem arises. Suppose we ignore both the cost-benefit criteria and the argument questioning the morality of all invasive animal research, which is of course what we do in practice. Would it not then be morally required to treat the animals in the best possible manner commensurate with their use in research? The demand that we do our best to meet their interests and needs, minimize their suffering as much as possible and respect their *telos* seems to be a requirement of common decency, particularly if we are using animals in a way that ignores the moral problems recounted thus far. Sadly, this is not the case.

When I helped to draft the 1985 federal laws for laboratory animals, I needed to know about the deficiencies in animal care to prove to US Congress the need for legislation, which was strongly opposed by much of the research community. What I found could easily be chronicled in a book, but I will restrict myself to two paradigmatic examples: pain control and housing.

Common sense would dictate that one of the worst things one can do to a research animal is to cause unrelieved pain. As animals do not understand sources of pain—particularly the sort of pain inflicted in experiments—they cannot rationalize that it will end soon, and their whole life becomes the pain. This insight has led veterinary pain specialists Ralph Kitchell and Michael Guinan (1989) to surmise that animal pain might be even worse than human pain; after all, humans have hope. Furthermore, pain is a source of stress and can skew the results of experiments in numerous ways. Therefore, for both moral and scientific reasons, one would expect a crucial emphasis on pain control in painful experiments. If someone were conducting fracture research, for example, one would expect the liberal use of pre-emptive and post-surgical or post-traumatic analgesia—pain relief—because the pain is not the point of the experiment, and unmitigated pain actually impedes healing.

[. . .]

A central component of the 1985 legislation was to mandate control of pain in research animals. Although I knew anecdotally that pain control was essentially non-existent in research, Congress demanded that I prove it, as the vocal portion of the research community opposing the legislation proclaimed that pain was already being controlled—and they were a powerful political lobby. I did a literature search, and found only two papers on animal analgesia, and none on laboratory animal analgesia. Of the two papers, one said, in essence, that there should be pain control, whereas the other described, in one page, what very little was known. Fortunately, this convinced Congress to mandate the control of pain and distress. As I expected, the legislative mandate galvanized the research community, and a literature search today would uncover thousands of such articles.

In the same vein, many veterinarians, typically trained before the mid-1980s, still equate anaesthesia with chemical restraint or sedation. The first US textbooks of veterinary anaesthesia (Lumb, 1963; Lumb & Jones, 1973) do not mention pain control as a reason for anaesthesia—instead, it is used to keep the animal still to prevent injury to it or the researcher—and do not mention analgesia at all.

[...]

In the end, the counter-intuitive denial of pain can again be traced back to scientific ideology. The same logic that barred talking about ethics similarly forbade talking about mental states. It was strengthened by the advent of behaviourism in the early twentieth century, which affirmed that, for psychology to become a real science, it needed to eschew discussions about or the study of mental states in humans or animals, and instead study only overt behaviour. This did not significantly affect moral treatment of humans, but certainly reinforced the legitimacy of ignoring pain in animals. The two components of scientific ideology—denial of ethics in science and denial of mental states—worked synergistically to the detriment of laboratory animals and created a formidable barrier to the awareness of the ethical issues inherent in animal research, and the recognition of the pain and distress sometimes created in the process.

As important as reducing the infliction of pain and suffering, which arises only sometimes in research, is the fact that all animals used in research have basic needs and interests, stemming from their biological and psychological natures. It is for this reason that the initial drafts of the 1985 legislation mandated housing and husbandry to meet the nature of all research animals. Unfortunately, this portion of the law was not passed, but it nonetheless created an awareness of 'environmental enrichment' that can only benefit the animals.

In my view, new legislation and, more importantly, the growing societal concern for animals that enabled these laws, have had salubrious consequences for the moral status of animals in research. For one thing, they vividly underscore the fact that society sees invasive animal research as a significant moral issue. For another, they sink the scientific ideology precluding ethical engagement by animal-research scientists. Finally, they have led to what I call the 'reappropriation of common sense' with regard to the reality of animal suffering and the need for its control. One can be guardedly optimistic that animal research will evolve into what it should have been all along: a moral science.

References

Ayer AJ (1946) *Language, Truth, and Logic*. London, UK: V. Gollancz.

Colorado Supreme Court (1896) *Waters v. The People,* 23 Colo 33.**46**: 112–113.

Darwin C (1896) *The Expression of the Emotions in Man and Animals*. New York, NY, USA: D. Appleton.

Keeton WT, Gould JL (1986) *Biological Science*. New York, NY, USA: Norton.

Kitchell R, Guinan M (1989) The nature of pain in animals. In *The Experimental Animal in Biomedical Research*, Vol I, BE Rollin, ML Kesel (eds.), pp. 185–205. Boca Raton, FL, USA: CRC.

Lumb WV (1963) *Small Animal Anesthesia*. Philadelphia, PA, USA: Lea & Febiger.

Lumb WV, Jones EW (1973) *Veterinary Anesthesia*. Philadelphia, PA, USA: Lea & Febiger.

Mader SS (1987) *Biology: Evolution, Diversity, and the Environment*. Dubuque, IO, USA: W.C. Brown.

Regan T (1983) *The Case for Animal Rights*. Berkeley, CA, USA: University of California Press.

Rollin BE (1981) *Animal Rights and Human Morality*. Buffalo, NY, USA: Prometheus Books.

Rollin BE (2006) *Science and Ethics*. Cambridge, UK: Cambridge University Press.

Sapontzis SF (1987) *Morals, Reason, and Animals*. Philadelphia, PA, USA: Temple University Press.

Singer P (1975) *Animal Liberation: A New Ethics for our Treatment of Animals*. New York, NY, USA: Random House.

Wittgenstein L (1965) A lecture on ethics. *Philos Rev* **74**: 3–12.

41 The Ethics of Animal Research

Talking Point on the Use of Animals in Scientific Research

Simon Festing and Robin Wilkinson

Presented alongside Rollin's article, Festing and Wilkinson argue that scientists already have had considerable moral involvement in animal research and that scientists generally accept that animals should be used for research only within an ethical framework. With their experience in the United Kingdom, they note that a high proportion (90%) of people accept using animals in research if the studies are for serious medical purposes, suffering is minimized, and/or alternatives are fully considered. They point out that the principles of replacing, reducing, and refining the use of animals in scientific research are central to UK regulations.

Animal research has had a vital role in many scientific and medical advances of the past century and continues to aid our understanding of various diseases. Throughout the world, people enjoy a better quality of life because of these advances, and the subsequent development of new medicines and treatments—all made possible by animal research. However, the use of animals in scientific and medical research has been a subject of heated debate for many years in the UK. Opponents to any kind of animal research—including both animal-rights extremists and anti-vivisectionist groups—believe that animal experimentation is cruel and unnecessary, regardless of its purpose or benefit. There is no middle ground for these groups; they want the immediate and total abolition of all animal research. If they succeed, it would have enormous and severe consequences for scientific research.

No responsible scientist wants to use animals or cause them unnecessary suffering if it can be avoided, and therefore scientists accept controls on the use of animals in research. More generally, the bio-science community accepts that animals should be used for research only within an ethical framework.

The UK has gone further than any other country to write such an ethical framework into law by implementing the Animals (Scientific Procedures) Act 1986. It exceeds the requirements in the European Union's Directive 86/609/EEC on the protection of animals used for experimental and other scientific purposes, which is now undergoing revision (Matthiessen et al., 2003). The Act requires that proposals for research involving the use of animals must be fully assessed in terms of any harm to the animals. This involves detailed examination of the particular procedures and experiments, and the numbers and types of animal used. These are then weighed against the potential benefits of the project. This cost-benefit analysis is almost unique to UK animal research legislation; only German law has a similar requirement.

[. . .]

In addition, the UK government introduced in 1998 further 'local' controls—that is, an Ethical Review Process at research institutions—which promote good animal welfare and humane science by ensuring that the use of animals at the designated establishment is justified. The aims of this additional review process are: to provide independent ethical advice, particularly with respect to applications for project licences, and standards of animal care and welfare; to provide support to licensees regarding animal welfare and ethical issues; and to promote ethical analysis to increase awareness of animal welfare issues and to develop initiatives for the widest possible application of the 3Rs—replacement, reduction and refinement of the use of animals in research (Russell & Burch, 1959). In practice, there has been concern that the Ethical Review Process adds a level of bureaucracy that is not in proportion to its contribution to improving animal welfare or furthering the 3Rs.

Thanks to some extensive opinion polls by MORI (1999a, 2002, 2005), and subsequent polls by ICM (2006) and YouGov (2006), we now have a good understanding of the public's attitudes towards animal research. Although society views animal research as an ethical dilemma, polls show that a high proportion—84% in 1999, 90% in 2002 and 89% in 2005—is ready to accept the use of animals in medical research if the research is for serious medical purposes, suffering is minimized and/or alternatives are fully considered. When asked which factors should be taken into account in the regulatory system, people chose those that—unknown to them—are already part of the UK legislation. In general, they feel that animal welfare should be weighed against health benefits, that cosmetic-testing should not be allowed, that there should be supervision to ensure high standards of welfare, that animals should be used only if there is no alternative, and that spot-checks should be carried out. It is clear that the UK public would widely support the existing regulatory system if they knew more about it.

[. . .]

Unsurprisingly, medical general practitioners (GPs) are even more aware of the contribution that animal research has made and continues to make to human health. In 2006, a survey by GP Net showed that 96% of GPs agreed that animal research has made important contributions to many medical advances (RDS News, 2006). The opinion poll also sought doctors' views about the safety testing of medicines. Almost nine out of ten GPs (88%) agreed that new medicines should be tested on animals before undergoing human trials.

GP Net also asked whether GPs agreed that 'medical research data can be misleading'; 93% agreed. This result puts into context the results from another poll of GPs in 2004. Europeans for Medical Progress (EMP; London, UK), an anti-vivisection group, found that 82% had a 'concern [. . .] that animal data can be misleading when applied to humans' (EMP, 2004). In fact, it seems that most GPs think that medical research in general can be misleading; it is good scientific practice to maintain a healthy degree of scepticism and avoid over-reliance on any one set of data or research method.

Another law, which enables people to get more information, might also help to influence public attitudes towards animal research. The UK Freedom of Information (FOI) Act came into full force on 1 January 2005. Under the Act, anybody can request information from a public body in England, Wales or Northern Ireland. Public bodies include government departments, universities and some funding bodies such as the research councils. The FOI Act is intended to promote openness and accountability, and to facilitate better public understanding of how public authorities carry out their duties, why and how they make decisions, and how they spend public money. There are two ways in which information can be made available to the public: some information will be automatically published and some will be released in response to individual requests. The FOI Act is retrospective, so it applies to all information, regardless of when it was created.

In response to the FOI Act, the Home Office now publishes overviews of all new animal research projects, in the form of anonymous project licence summaries, on a dedicated website. This means that the UK now provides more public information about animal research than any other country. The Research Defence Society (RDS; London, UK), an organization representing doctors and scientists in the debate on the use of animals in research and testing, welcomes the greater openness that the FOI Act brings to discussions about animal research. With more and reliable information about how and why animals are used, people should be in a better position to debate the issues. However, there are concerns that extremist groups will try to obtain personal details and information that can identify researchers, and use these details and information to target individuals.

As a House of Lords Select Committee report in July 2002 stated, 'The availability to the public of regularly updated, good quality information on what animal experiments are done and why, is vital to create an atmosphere in which the issue of animal experimentation can be discussed productively'

(House of Lords, 2002). Indeed, according to a report on public attitudes to the biological sciences and their oversight, 'Having information and perceived honesty and openness are the two key considerations for the public in order for them to have trust in a system of controls and regulations about biological developments' (MORI, 1999b).

In the past five years, there have been four major UK independent inquiries into the use of animals in biomedical research: a Select Committee in the House of Lords (2002); the Animal Procedures Committee (2003); the Nuffield Council on Bioethics (2005); and the Weatherall Committee (Weatherall et al., 2006), which specifically examined the use of non-human primates in scientific and medical research. All committees included non-scientists and examined evidence from both sides of the debate. These rigorous independent inquiries all accepted the rationale for the use of animals in research for the benefit of human health, and concluded that animal research can be scientifically validated on a case-by-case basis. The Nuffield Council backed the 3Rs and the need for clear information to support a constructive debate, and further stated that violence and intimidation against researchers or their allies is morally wrong.

[. . .]

In addition, the Advertising Standards Authority (ASA; London, UK) has investigated and ruled on 38 complaints made since 1992 about published literature—leaflets and brochures—regarding claims about the validity or otherwise of animal research and the scope of alternative methods. In 34 out of 38 cases, they found against the anti-vivisectionist groups, either supporting complaints about anti-vivisectionist literature, or rejecting the complaints by anti-vivisectionists about the literature from medical organizations. Only four complaints against scientific/medical research literature have been upheld, not because the science was flawed but as a result of either semantics or the ASA judging that the advertisement fell outside the UK remit.

[. . .]

However, seemingly respectable mainstream groups still peddle dangerously misleading and inaccurate information about the use of animals in research.

[. . .]

Approximately 2.7 million regulated animal procedures were conducted in 2003 in the UK—half the number performed 30 years ago. The tight controls governing animal experimentation and the widespread implementation of the 3Rs by the scientific community is largely responsible for this downward trend, as recognized recently by then Home Office Minister, Caroline Flint: '. . . new technologies in developing drugs [have led] to sustained and incremental decreases in some types of animal use over recent years, whilst novel medicines have continued to be produced. This is an achievement of which the scientific community can be rightly proud' (Flint, 2005).

After a period of significant reduction, the number of regulated animal procedures stabilized from 1995 until 2002. Between 2002 and 2005, the use of genetically modified animals—predominantly mice—led to a 1–2% annual increase in the number of animals used (Home Office, 2005). However, between 1995 and 2005, the growth in UK biomedical research far outstripped this incremental increase: combined industry and government research and development (R&D) spending rose by 73% from £2,080 million to £3,605 million (ABPI, 2007; DTI, 2005). Animal research has obviously become a smaller proportion of overall bioscience and medical R&D spending in the UK. This shows the commitment of the scientific community to the development and use of replacement and reduction techniques, such as computer modelling and human cell lines. Nevertheless, animal research remains a small, but vital, part of biomedical research—experts estimate it at about 10% of total biomedical R&D spending.

The principles of replacing, reducing and refining the use of animals in scientific research are central to UK regulation. In fact, the government established the National Centre for the Replacement, Refinement and Reduction of Animals in Research (NC3Rs; London, UK) in May 2004 to promote and develop high-quality research that takes the 3Rs into account. In support of this, then Science Minister Lord Sainsbury announced in 2005 that the Centre would receive an additional £1.5 million in funding over the next three years.

The ultimate aim of the NC3Rs is to substitute a significant proportion of animal research by investigating the development of alternative techniques, such as human studies, and *in vitro* and *in silico* studies. RDS supports this aim, but believes that it is unrealistic to expect this to be possible in every area of scientific research in the immediate future. After all, if the technology to develop these alternatives is not available or does not yet exist, progress is likely to be slow. The main obstacle is still the difficulty of accurately mimicking the complex physiological systems of whole living organisms—a challenge that will be hard to meet. There has been some progress recently imitating single organs such as the liver, but these need further refinement to make them suitable models for an entire organ and, even if validated, they cannot represent a whole-body system. New and promising techniques such as micro-dosing also have the potential to reduce the number of animals used in research, but again cannot replace them entirely.

The development of alternatives—which invariably come from the scientific community, rather than anti-vivisection groups—will necessitate the continued use of animals during the research, development and validation stages.

[...]

The scientific community, with particular commitment shown by the pharmaceutical industry, has responded by investing a large amount of money and effort in developing the science and technology to replace animals wherever possible. However, the development of direct replacement technologies for animals is a slow and difficult process. Even in regulatory toxicology, which might seem to be a relatively straightforward task, about 20 different tests are required to assess the risk of any new substance. In addition, introducing a non-animal replacement technique involves not only development of the method but also its validation by national and international regulatory authorities. These authorities tend to be conservative and can take many years to write a new technique into their guidelines. Even then, some countries might insist that animal tests are carried out if they have not been explicitly written out of the guidelines. Society should push authorities to quickly adopt successfully validated techniques, while realizing that pushing for adoption without full validation could endanger human health.

Despite the inherent limitations of some non-animal tests, they are still useful for pre-screening compounds before the animal-testing stage, which would therefore reduce rather than replace the number of animals used. An example of this is the Ames test, which uses strains of the bacterium *Salmonella typhimurium* to determine whether chemicals cause mutations in cellular DNA. This and other tests are already widely used as pre-screens to partly replace rodent testing for cancer-causing compounds. Unfortunately, the *in vitro* tests can produce false results, and tend to be used more to understand the processes of mutagenicity and carcinogenicity than to replace animal assays. However, there are moves to replace the standard mouse carcinogenicity assay with other animal-based tests that cause less suffering because they use fewer animals and do not take as long. This has already been achieved in tests for acute oral toxicity, where the LD50—the median lethal dose of a substance—has largely been replaced by the Fixed Dose Procedure, which was developed, validated and promoted between 1984 and 1989 by a worldwide collaboration, headed by scientists at the British Toxicological Society (Macclesfield, UK).

[...]

Furthermore, cell-culture based tests have considerably reduced the use of rodents in the initial screening of potential new medicines, while speeding up the process so that 10–20 times the number of compounds can be screened in the same period. A leading cancer charity, Yorkshire Cancer Research (Harrogate, UK), funded research into the use of cell cultures to understand better the cellular mechanisms of prostate cancer—allowing researchers to investigate potential therapies using fewer animals.

Microdosing is an exciting new technique for measuring how very small doses of a compound move around the body. In principle, it should be possible to use this method in humans and therefore to reduce the number of animals needed to study new compounds; however, it too has limitations. By its very nature, it cannot predict toxicity or side effects that occur at higher therapeutic doses. It is an unrealistic hope—and a false claim—that microdosing can completely replace the use of animals in scientific research; 'animal studies will still be required,' confirmed the Fund for the Replacement of Animals in Medical Experiments (FRAME; Nottingham, UK; FRAME, 2005).

However, as with many other advances in non-animal research, this was never classified as 'alternatives research.' In general, there is no separate field in biomedical research known as 'alternatives research'; it is one of the highly desirable outcomes of good scientific research. The claim by anti-vivisection campaigners that research into replacements is neglected merely reflects their ignorance.

Good science and good experimental design also help to reduce the number of animals used in research as they allow scientists to gather data using the minimum number of animals required. However, good science also means that a sufficient number must be used to enable precise statistical analysis and to generate significant results to prevent the repetition of experiments and the consequent need to use more animals. In 1998, FRAME formed a Reduction Committee, in part to publicize effective reduction techniques. The data collected by the Committee so far provides information about the overall reduction in animal usage that has been brought about by the efforts of researchers worldwide (FRAME Reduction Committee, 2005).

For example, screening potential anticancer drugs uses the so-called hollow-fibre system, in which tumour cells are grown in a tube-like polymer matrix that is implanted into mice. Drugs are then administered, the tubes removed and the number of cells determined. This system has increased the amount of data that can be obtained per animal in some studies and has therefore reduced the number of mice used (Double, 2004). In neuroscience, techniques such as cooling regions of the brain instead of removing subsections, and magnetic resonance imaging, have both helped to reduce the number of laboratory animals used (Royal Society, 2004).

[. . .]

Matching the number of animals generated from breeding programmes to the number of animals required for research has also helped to reduce the number of surplus animals. For example, the cryopreservation of sperm and oocytes has reduced the number of genetically modified mice required for breeding programmes (Robinson et al., 2003); mice lines do not have to be continuously bred if they can be regenerated from frozen cells when required.

Although animals cannot yet be completely replaced, it is important that researchers maximize reduction and refinement. Sometimes this is achieved relatively easily by improving animal husbandry and housing, for example, by enriching their environment. These simple measures within the laboratory aim to satisfy the physiological and behavioural needs of the animals and therefore maintain their well-being.

Another important factor is refining the experimental procedures themselves, and refining the management of pain. An assessment of the method of administration, the effects of the substance on the animal and the amount of handling and restraint required should all be considered. Furthermore, careful handling of the animals, and administration of appropriate anaesthetics and analgesics during the experiment, can help to reduce any pain experienced by the animals. This culture of care is achieved not only through strict regulations but also by ensuring that animal technicians and other workers understand and adopt such regulations. Therefore, adequate training is an important aspect of the refinement of animal research, and should continually be reviewed and improved.

In conclusion, RDS considers that the use of animals in research can be ethically and morally justified. The benefits of animal research have been enormous and it would have severe consequences for public health and medical research if it were abandoned. Nevertheless, the use of the 3Rs is crucial to continuously reduce the number and suffering of animals in research. Furthermore, a good regulatory regime—as found in the UK—can help to reduce further the number of animals used. Therefore, we support a healthy and continued debate on the use of animals in research. We recognize that those who oppose animal experimentation should be free to voice their opinions democratically, and we look forward to constructive discussion in the future with organizations that share the middle ground with us.

References

ABPI (2007) *Facts & Statistics from the Pharmaceutical Industry*. London, UK: Association of the British Pharmaceutical Industry. http://www.abpi.org.uk/statistics/section.asp?sect=3

Animal Procedures Committee (2003) *Review of Cost-Benefit Assessment in the Use of Animals in Research*. London, UK: Animal Procedures Committee. www.apc.gov.uk

Double JA (2004) A pharmacological approach for the selection of potential anticancer agents. *Altern Lab Anim* 32: 41–48.

DTI (2005) *Science Funding SET Statistics*. London, UK: Department of Trade and Industry. www.dti.gov.uk

EMP (2004) *Doctors Fear Animal Experiments Endanger Patients*. Press release. London, UK: Europeans for Medical Progress. www.curedisease.net

Flint C (2005) *Report by the Animal Procedures Committee—Review of Cost Benefit Assessment in the Use of Animals in Research: Ministerial Response*. London, UK: Home Office.

FRAME (2005) Human microdosing reduces the number of animals required for pre-clinical pharmaceutical research. *Altern Lab Anim* 33: 439.

FRAME Reduction Committee (2005) *Bibliography of Training Materials on Experimental Design and Statistical Analysis*. Nottingham, UK: Fund for the Replacement of Animals in Medical Experiments. www.frame.org.uk/reductioncommittee/bibliointro.htm

Home Office (2005) *Statistics of Scientific Procedures on Living Animals, Great Britain 2004*. London, UK: Home Office.

House of Lords (2002) *Select Committee on Animals in Scientific Procedures, Volume I—Report*. London, UK: The Stationery Office.

ICM (2006) *Vivisection Survey, Conducted on behalf of BBC Newsnight*. London, UK: ICM Research. www.icmresearch.co.uk

Matthiessen L, Lucaroni B, Sachez E (2003) Towards responsible animal research. *EMBO Rep* 4: 104–107.

MORI (1999a) *Animals in Medicine and Science: Research Study Conducted for the Medical Research Council*. London, UK: MORI. www.ipsos-mori.com

MORI (1999b) *The Public Consultation on Developments in the Biosciences: Executive Summary*. London, UK: MORI. www.ipsos-mori.com

MORI (2002) *The Use of Animals in Medical Research: Research Study Conducted for the Coalition for Medical Progress*. London, UK: MORI. www.ipsos-mori.com

MORI (2005) *Use of Animals in Medical Research: Research Study Conducted for Coalition for Medical Progress*. London, UK: MORI. www.ipsos-mori.com

Nuffield Council on Bioethics (2005) *The Ethics of Research Involving Animals*. London, UK: Nuffield Council on Bioethics.

RDS News (2006) *GPs Back Animal Research*. London, UK: Research Defence Society.

Robinson V et al. (2003) Refinement and reduction in production of genetically modified mice: Sixth report of BVAAWF/FRAME/RSPCA/UFAW Joint Working Group on Refinement. *Lab Anim* 37: 1–51.

Royal Society (2004) *The Use of Non-Human Animals in Research: A Guide for Scientists*. London, UK: The Royal Society.

Russell WMS, Burch RL (1959) *The Principles of Humane Experimental Technique*. London, UK: Methuen.

Weatherall D, Goodfellow P, Harris J, Hinde R, Johnson L, Morris R, Ross N, Skehel J, Tickell C (2006) *The Use of Non-Human Primates in Research*. London, UK: The Royal Society.

YouGov (2006) *Animal Testing*. Daily Telegraph Survey Results. London, UK: YouGov. www.yougov.com

42 Reasons Scientists Avoid Thinking about Ethics

Paul Root Wolpe

While not specifically addressing animal research, Wolpe identifies and addresses the broader reasons sometimes given by scientists for not being more involved with ethical issues. He then addresses each in detail to affirm that all scientists have moral responsibilities in the work they conduct.

All good science is subversive. It challenges beliefs, pushes the boundaries of existing structures of knowledge, and portends a future different from the current one. For that reason, the Controllers, who rule Aldous Huxley's *Brave New World*, forbade new scientific inquiry, declaring "truth's a menace, science is a public danger."

The public, whose taxes fund much scientific work, is keenly interested in where science is going and the integrity of those who are taking us there. The unprecedented ability of scientists to manipulate the building blocks of life, to create altered biological processes, and to understand and re-engineer biological systems promises fundamental changes in how we heal, how we reproduce, and how we relate to the living world. Science tends to be portrayed by the media in extremes, as a series of sensationalized discoveries punctuated by conflicts and scandals. It is certainly understandable that the public would demand careful examination of such powerful technologies.

Scientists, however, are often wary of ethical scrutiny, and generally reluctant to engage the public in moral conversation about their work. Why aren't scientists more engaged in the ethical debates that characterize the public discourse about science? Why are scientists not more effective advocates of their own work? There are a number of reasons that scientists offer, and each is worthy of examination.

"I'm Not Trained in Ethics"

Ethics as an academic field has an established body of knowledge, a set of disciplinary concepts, a canon, and many other trappings of an intellectual discipline. Most scientists are not formally trained in ethics. However, scholars trained in ethics do work with scientists and scientific societies helping to set guidelines, assess the impact of new technologies, and so on.

Scientists can learn the ethos of science by example. Albert Einstein once said, "Most people say that it is the intellect which makes a great scientist. They are wrong: it is character." Behaving ethically is the principal way that mentors transfer the ethical standards of their profession to their trainees. All the formal ethics training in the world cannot compensate for an unethical mentor. However, the failure to integrate training in professional ethics into the basic scientific curriculum impoverishes the educational mission and, ultimately, science itself.

The National Institutes of Health (NIH) now requires that an ethics curriculum discussing protection of human participants in research be taught in the graduate programs it funds. It would be a shame, however, if training in ethics stopped there. To remain true to the highest goals of science, scientists should periodically revisit the big questions: What is science for? What are the values I bring to my scientific work? Why did I become a scientist, and why am I one now? What are the moral motivations, inclinations, and principles at the heart of my scientific pursuits? How do I advance the cause of scientific progress? Whom does my research serve? Serious consideration of those questions qualifies a scientist for participation in the ongoing discussion of scientific values, even without a specialized training in ethics.

"My Scientific Work Has Little to Do with Ethics"

What does the daily work of science have to do with ethics? The ethical norms of science are so embedded in scientific work that we can easily take them for granted. When asked why he made his stem cell lines freely available to other scientists, Harvard's Douglas Melton replied, "because there's a long scientific tradition of making the fruits of one's research available to others" (Dreifus, 2006). Making reagents freely available to colleagues is a fundamental ethical tenet of modem science. The work of historians, philosophers, social scientists, and others shows that the questions scientists choose to pursue, the kinds of data that are considered important, the dynamics of collaboration within a scientific team, the interpretation of results, and many other aspects of scientific work are permeated by ethical assumptions, such as the value of sharing the products of scientific inquiry and the value of mentorship. Science is an eminently social activity.

What distinguishes a profession is not only a body of knowledge or expertise. Professional authority is derived also from a cultural tradition of service carried out with an expectation of high ethical behavior. Professions try to assure such behavior by developing codes of ethics. For example, the American Medical Association was founded in Philadelphia in 1847 by writing and publicly reading a new code of ethics. Many specific scientific societies have developed codes of ethics. Indeed, later this year, the British government's chief scientific advisor will be releasing an ethical code setting out the values and responsibilities of all scientists who work in the United Kingdom (Pincock, 2006).

Clearly plagiarism, fabricating results, misrepresenting contributions to a paper, bypassing informed consent, stealing ideas, and other forms of scientific misconduct have a detrimental effect on science. But it is not just misconduct that is threatening science. A fundamental tenet of academic science and medicine is the ability to replicate published research. In a survey published in JAMA, 47% of geneticists who requested additional information, data, or material from academic colleagues regarding their published research reported being turned down at least once; 28% reported that they had been unable to confirm published results because they had been denied access to requested data or materials (Campbell et al., 2002). Science's claim to self-correction and overall reliability is based on the ability of researchers to replicate the results of published studies. Studies cannot be replicated if scientists will not share additional data, information, or materials from published studies, and upholding such ethical norms is every scientist's responsibility.

"Ethics Is Arbitrary"

From stem cells and cloning to genetic engineering to the sale of organs for transplant, there is no dearth of contentious bioethical debates. Sometimes the debates seem intractable, with all sides convinced of the validity of their ethical position. It is easy to conclude that ethics is essentially arbitrary. Empirical evidence can provide support for ethical conditions, but it cannot ultimately adjudicate between them.

In fact, however, there is widespread consensus on a host of ethical issues in science policy. Consensus tends to be hidden because it is taken for granted; only the controversies make the headlines. For example, developed countries have forged a wide-ranging ethical consensus on research involving human subjects. This includes universal standards of informed consent, risk/benefit analyses, ethics review committees such as Institutional Review Boards, mandatory testing in animals first, protocols to assess toxicity and side effects, conflict of interest declarations, and subject's rights (such as the right to refuse to participate in research without incurring any penalty and to withdraw from research at any time). At the boundaries of the consensus are areas of ethical debate, but that is how it should be. The public discourse eventually may make its way to consensus, but in ethics, process is at least as important as product.

"Ethicists Mostly Say 'No' to New Technologies"

Ethical principles do set limits on technology, but this is unremarkable. We need limits to be set so that new technologies do not cause harm, violate personal privacy or autonomy, damage a collectively owned natural environment, and so on. Although some bioethicists may use ethical arguments to resist technology in general, the majority of biomedical ethics is in the service of good science. Many bioethicists are trained in the biological or social sciences and have academic appointments in medical or life science departments. The irony of being a bioethicist these days is the possibility of being viewed both as a lackey to pharmaceutical and biotechnological interests by the general public and as an overly cautious obstructionist by the scientific community.

Ethicists and scientists should work hand in hand to assure that scientific research is done to the highest ethical standards and to prepare the public for reception of scientific innovation. The cloning of Dolly has become the exemplar of the failure to prepare the public for a scientific breakthrough. After the announcement, polls showed that more than 90% of Americans opposed the cloning of animals. Furthermore, the media were filled with stories about creating human clones for organ transplants, celebrity vanity clones, etc., before scientists could reign in the wild speculation and describe what cloning is and what it can and can't do. Had the ethical discussion kept pace with the research, the global hyperventilation over Dolly might well not have taken place.

"Others Will Make the Ethical Decisions"

Scientists in modern technological societies are professionals, and their work should be viewed through the lens of professional ethics (Chadwick, 2005). Scientists, like all professionals, have ethical responsibilities at three levels: First, scientists must assume personal responsibility for the integrity of their research, their relations with colleagues and subordinates, and their role as representatives of their home institutions. Second, scientists must assume a measure of disciplinary responsibility for the promotion, oversight, and collective activity of their specialized field of inquiry. Finally, scientists must recognize their social responsibility to science as a public enterprise.

Scientists have an obligation, individually as well as collectively, to reflect on the ends, not just the means, of scientific work (Kitcher, 2004). Ethical conversation should be part of "normal science" in every laboratory, academic center, and corporate office.

Sometimes that ethical responsibility may run counter to the practices of an institution or corporation; in those cases, scientific integrity demands that individual scientists respond by speaking out, or trying to change the corporate culture. In rare cases, it may require refusing to participate in a particular project, or in extreme cases, resigning.

"The Public Does Not Know What It Wants"

The public, in general, is not scientifically sophisticated. Yet somehow the public has managed to negotiate its way to a consensus on a variety of scientific issues. Despite the initial reaction to the cloning of Dolly, people eventually settled into a consistent and stable belief that animal cloning is basically acceptable, whereas human reproductive cloning is not. Society invests scientists with public trust and privilege, granting them access to funds, materials, public institutions, and even their bodies as subjects for research. In return, society retains a right to set certain limits on the kind of scientific research that it believes is permissible.

If science serves the collective good, then it must contribute its unique perspective to the moral debates of the day. Scientists should be active participants in that cultural conversation, as they are both citizens with a right to make claims about the common good and experts in the topics in question. In that sense, science's biggest failure lies in its lack of engagement with the public. One study of geneticists (Mathews et al., 2005) found that although most thought that scientists should be more actively involved in public outreach and science policy, many felt ill-equipped themselves and unsupported by their peers and institutions in assuming this responsibility. Scientists who frequently engage the public have often been suspect in the eyes of their peers, yet it is precisely that kind of outreach that will most benefit the scientific enterprise.

"Knowledge Is intrinsically Good"

A working assumption of modern science is that the generation of knowledge is its own justification. But is all knowledge neutral? Is there any piece of information so potentially disturbing or destructive that we should not pursue it? Some scientists may say that all knowledge is fair game. Yet there are precedents for the idea that there is forbidden knowledge. Kempner and colleagues (2005) interviewed about 40 scientists in a variety of disciplines—including cell and molecular biology, neuroscience, and genetics—from a number of prestigious US academic institutions. They asked them to consider their practices and rationales for limiting scientific inquiry or dissemination. Respondents reported that knowledge may be forbidden because the route to obtaining that knowledge is unethical—certain types of human experimentation simply may not be carried out, for example. Some knowledge may be forbidden because the means to knowledge violates religious or moral constraints, as some claim about human embryonic stem cell research.

Kempner and colleagues were most surprised, however, by the power of informal means of limiting scientific inquiry. Researchers are sometimes attacked after publication of their research—as were famous controversial figures such as Kinsey, Milgram, and Herrnstein and Murray—which may dissuade others from pursuing similar lines of research. In the survey, some participants cited the threat of social sanctions as deterring certain types of research, whereas others reported that there were unspoken rules of their scientific community regarding which research to pursue.

Most would agree that there is scientific research that is inherently unethical and ought not to be pursued. However, there is a more nuanced ethical question: is the pursuit of all scientific knowledge equally *worthy*? That question must be asked every time we allocate funds to certain scientific goals and not to others. In that sense, an ethical sensibility is part of the very funding structures that drive science in certain directions in technological societies.

What kinds of research should we prioritize? It is there that the ethical dialog among scientists, ethicists, and the public can be most fruitful.

"If I Don't Do It, Someone Else Will"

Biotechnology has become global, but different societies do not always agree on the same ethical standards. Although there is almost universal agreement to ban human reproductive cloning, for example, there is little international agreement about human embryonic stem cell research. Some countries have banned it altogether, others have severely regulated it, and still others have actively promoted it. With such variation, a common argument for pursuing controversial science is its inevitability; if we don't pursue this line of research, then someone else will. But is that argument, even if true, a justification for pursuing a line of research that a scientist otherwise judges to be ethically questionable?

The argument is ultimately an economic, not an ethical one. If science is to maintain its ethical standards, and if scientists want to be trusted by a wary public, ethical guidelines must be developed and adhered to, even when they cause some economic hardship. The primary ethical responsibility is to one's own moral standing.

Conclusion

Science has become one of the most powerful and pervasive forces for change in modern society. As the professionals at its helm, scientists have a unique responsibility to shepherd that change with careful ethical scrutiny of their own behavior and thoughtful advocacy of scientific research. If scientists find reasons not to do so, the public will find ways to do it for them, and the results may not always be in the best interests of science or society.

References

Campbell, E.G., Clarridge, B.R., Gokhale, M., Birenbaum, L, Hilgartner, S., Holtzman, N.A., and Blumenthal, D. (2002). Data withholding in academic genetics: Evidence from a national survey. *Journal of the American Medical Association 287*, 473–480.

Chadwick, R. (2005). Professional ethics and the 'good' of science. *Interdisciplinary Science Reviews 30*, 247–256.

Dreifus, C. (2006). At Harvard's stem cell center, the barriers run deep and wide. *The New York Times*, January 24, F2. http://www.nytimes.com/2006/01/24/science/at-harvards-stem-cell-center-the-barriers-run-deep-and-wide.html

Kempner, J., Perlis, C.S., and Merz, J.F. (2005). Forbidden knowledge. *Science 307*, 854.

Kitcher, P. (2004). Responsible biology. *Bioscience 54*, 331–336.

Mathews, D., Kalfoglou, A., and Hudson, K. (2005). Geneticists' views on science policy formation and public outreach. *American Journal of Medical Genetics 137A*, 161–169.

Pincock, S. (2006). UK: optimism over new regulator. *The Scientist*. Published online January 10, 2006. http://www.the-scientist.com/news/display/22930

Regulating Animal Experimentation

43 Ethical Themes of National Regulations Governing Animal Experiments

F. Barbara Orlans

Among laws governing use of experimental animals, Orlans identifies eight regulatory dimensions ranging from minimal to extensive protections for laboratory animals; she also reviews and compares the international distribution of animal research laws. Orlans argues that public concerns have led to more stringent protections in recent years. She also believes that this increased regulation has stemmed both from animal rights activities and scientific insights on the intellectual and emotional capabilities of animals.

This essay reports on worldwide progress in the enactment of national laws governing the humane use of laboratory animals in biomedical research, testing, and education. During the last 100 years, national laws to improve the welfare of laboratory animals have become enacted in at least 23 countries. I identify here eight ethical themes for discussion: (1) simple provision of basic husbandry requirements and inspection of facilities; (2) control of animal pain and suffering; (3) critical review of proposed experimental protocols; (4) specification of investigator competency; (5) bans on certain invasive procedures, sources of animals, or use of certain species; (6) application of the Three R alternatives—to refine procedures, reduce animal use, or replace animal procedures with nonanimal use where possible; (7) use of ethical criteria for decision making; and (8) mandatory use of animal-harm scales that rank degrees of increasing ethical cost to the animal. Countries in which all eight themes are addressed have the highest standards of animal care and use.

[. . .]

Countries With and Without Animal Protection Laws

By 2000 at least 23 countries worldwide had enacted laws requiring certain humane standards for experimenting on animals. [. . .] In 1985 the World Health Organization promulgated *Guiding Principles for Biomedical Research Involving Animals*, guidelines designed to provide a framework within which specific legislative or regulatory systems could be built in any country, including less-developed countries. Voluntary acceptance of these modest standards is better than having no provisions at all.

Ethical Issues in Current Laws

The eight issues I have previously listed can be used for comparison among the nations. Within the sequence of this listing is a loose, overall historical pattern. The first enactment of laws in any country typically deals only with the first two topics, basic husbandry requirements and inspection of facilities and control of animal pain and suffering. Only later (in amendments to the law) are refinements addressed that illustrate the next four topics—critical review of protocols, specification of investigator competency, bans on certain activities, and the use of the Three R alternatives. The last two topics, which address the complicated issue of how to justify each specific protocol, represent the cutting edge of new legislation. As yet, they are only found in laws of the most progressive countries concerned with animal welfare.

Husbandry Standards, Inspections, and Record Keeping

Husbandry and Inspections

A basic ethical concern requires that captive animals be housed and cared for humanely. Official government inspection of research facilities maintains standards of sanitation, provision of food and water, space allocation by species' needs, daily care, and other basic requirements. Usually only minimum husbandry standards are mandated, and the tendency has been for animal facilities to conform to the lowest acceptable standards rather than providing optimal housing.

Inspections by government officials are needed to establish compliance. The frequency and adequacy of inspections vary from country to country, as do the standards required. In the United States, inspections are carried out once per year at each of the approximately 1,500 facilities registered with the controlling governing agency. In some countries, inspections are so infrequent and inadequate that the law exists on paper alone.

Historically, standards for housing space have been inadequate. [. . .] However, housing standards for captive animals have been gradually improving in some countries. Reform has been sparked not only by more sympathetic public attitudes to animals but by research demonstrating that poor housing conditions cause stress to the animal, which can confound the experimental results obtained. Also, research has demonstrated that abnormal, stereotypic behaviors (such as pacing, cage biting, etc.) of laboratory, zoo, and farm animals do not occur if the animals are housed in enriched environments—ones as close as possible to those conditions experienced by free-living animals.

In the United States, Congress enacted an amendment to the Animal Welfare Act in 1985 that requires promotion of the "psychological well-being" of primates. This legal provision sparked new funding for environmental enrichment studies and has been profoundly effective in improving the housing conditions of primates. There is a trend toward increased space allocation, group-housing animals of similar species, and the addition of branches, toys, and exercise apparatus to the cages where appropriate. European countries and Australia have been in the forefront of enriching the housing of many common laboratory species, not only primates but also dogs, cats, rabbits, guinea pigs, and rats.

Record Keeping

Public reporting of the numbers and species of animals used is a basic requirement of effective oversight and accountability of animal experiments. The rationale is that the public has a right to know what is happening in this socially controversial area of harming animals for human good. [. . .] Worldwide, estimates of the total number of animals used range as high as 50 to 100 million annually, since many animals are uncounted.

It is unclear whether the total number of animals used worldwide is declining, as animal advocates hope, or increasing. A few countries, including the Netherlands, have reported a decline. In the United States, very probably the largest user of animals worldwide, inadequate data make trends impossible to assess.

[. . .]

Controls on Animal Pain and Suffering

National laws also require that every effort be made to reduce or eliminate pain and suffering that result from an experimental procedure. Anesthetics, analgesics, and postoperative care should be used wherever needed, and animals in extreme pain should be put to death. It is generally considered a matter of plain humanity that the degree of animal pain and suffering be minimized. Indeed, it is a moral imperative.

But such provisions have not necessarily come with the first enactment of a national law. For instance, in the United States, animal pain was not addressed in 1966 when the law was first passed. Indeed, at that time, whether animals actually perceived pain was widely doubted. Not until 1976 was the Animal Welfare Act, the federal law governing laboratory animals, amended to require for the first time the use of anesthetics and analgesics. As a result, research on animal pain and its alleviation accelerated. Textbooks devoted to the physiology and relief of animal pain were published, new anesthetics and analgesics were developed, and postsurgical care became an important topic. Great progress has been made, and by now it is well recognized in national policies throughout the world that vertebrate animals do indeed feel pain.

Methods of killing of animals represent another aspect of control of pain. In the 1980s, the American Veterinary Medical Association established standards for recommended euthanasia practices to ensure that methods used are as rapid and painless as possible. These standards, which are now law in the United States, have been repeatedly updated, and other countries have adopted similar standards.

Critical Review of Protocols

Not all countries include legal provisions for review of investigators' proposed protocols. Sometimes investigators are subjected to either no formal procedure for protocol review or review only by their peers within their own discipline (for instance, in departmental review at a university or pharmaceutical company).

Nonetheless, there has been considerable growth in the establishment of oversight review committees that function as gatekeepers for approval of proposed experiments. These committees are variously called Animal Care and Use Committees (ACUCs) or Ethical Committees.

[. . .]

The ethical rationale behind such review is that investigators should be accountable in what they do, not only to their peers but also to the public. These committees may be institutional or regional. They typically operate with considerable autonomy, being only loosely regulated by national bodies. The resulting framework is often characterized as "enforced self-regulation."

The composition of these committees varies among countries, but most include representation of several viewpoints. Committee membership typically includes animal researchers, veterinarians, and lay (nonscientist) members of the public. Representatives from the animal-protection movement should be included because this is the constituency most concerned about humane standards. Experience has shown that to avoid rubber stamping, committee membership should not be dominated by animal researchers, and the chair should be an independent person and not an animal researcher.

The value of public representation on these committees is well established, and most committees would benefit with increased public representation.

[. . .]

The purpose of oversight committee review is to ensure compliance with established standards of care and use by modifying (to improve the animal's welfare) or disapproving proposed projects. This does not necessarily mean that ethical debate that questions the fundamental justification of a project occurs. Indeed, most commonly there is an assumption of fundamental justification of a project. Thus there is room for considerable improvement in the level of debate within most of these oversight committees. I discuss this further in the section "Ethical Criteria for Decision Making."

Specification of Investigator Competency

The question concerning investigator competency is "What training is required before a person is allowed to conduct *any* animal experiment?" Untrained persons are likely to inflict greater harm on an animal than trained persons attempting the same procedure and furthermore are unlikely to produce experimental results that are of scientific value. So the benefits are less and the harms greater. Establishment of competency standards is important, yet only a few countries have adequately addressed these issues.

[. . .]

In addition to controls over qualifications for persons working in animal-research facilities, several countries place controls over what is permitted by beginning biology students in early stages of their education. [. . .] Historically, a real problem existed in U.S. junior and senior high schools in the 1960s to early 1980s. Youths from age 11 to 17 sought to impress judges of science-fair competitions by attempting highly invasive experiments on live animals. Often the students conducted these experiments in their homes, and supervision was absent or cursory. Extreme animal suffering occurred. Typical were high school student projects of attempted mammalian surgery, blinding, injection of lethal substances, and starving animals to death. Because the public protested strongly about these abuses, improvements have been made. But still today there is inadequate control over the use of animals in junior and senior high school education in the United States, as well as insufficient encouragement to use nonharmful alternatives. Federal laws do not exist. Unsatisfactory 1995 guidelines (which are voluntary and unenforceable) of the National Association of Biology Teachers include no provisions to ban the infliction of animal pain or suffering on sentient creatures and encourage dissection. Further reforms are still urgently needed.

As for the use of animals in U.S. colleges, there has been limited progress. The 1985 amendment to the Animal Welfare Act required for the first time that oversight committees review the use of animals in undergraduate college courses at some (but by no means all) tertiary educational institutions. [. . .] Rats, mice, and birds, the species most used in college classes, are not covered under the Animal Welfare Act. Thus, a number of colleges fall outside the law, so that much of the use of animals in U.S. biology classes is unregulated.

There are a number of ethical rationales for prohibiting students from harming or killing animals: (1) nonpainful, nonharmful animal projects, nonharmful human studies, and other projects that carry no ethical burden are readily available that are equally or more instructive; (2) because projects at this educational level are primarily demonstrations of known facts, they lack the major ethical justification for harming animals that is based on the reasonable likelihood of obtaining significant, original knowledge; (3) unskilled students are likely to inflict greater harm than trained researchers; and (4) allowing emotionally immature youth to harm animals under the guise of education desensitizes students' feeling of empathy with animals. It can be argued that these points apply not only to primary and secondary school students but also to undergraduate college-level students. It is usually not until graduate school that a student makes a serious career commitment, and even then, not all careers in the biological sciences require expertise in animal experimentation techniques.

Bans on Certain Activities

Experimental procedures that cause intense and prolonged animal suffering have been the focus of the greatest public protest and demands for prohibition. Even if useful scientific results might be obtained, the lack of justification holds.

Some success in banning such activities has been achieved. A 1986 amendment to a German law, the Animal Protection Act, forbids experimentation on animals for development and testing of weapons, as well as the testing of tobacco products, washing powders, and cosmetics. The Netherlands and the United Kingdom also ban the use of animals for cosmetic testing. Recently, the British government announced its commitment to stop licensing any further testing of tobacco or alcohol products on animals. Indeed, in the whole field of animal testing, with the bans on the notorious LD50 test (the lethal dose that painfully kills 50% of the animals) and the Draize eye irritancy test (which can cause blindness in rabbits), considerable progress has been made.

Recently, three European countries (the Netherlands, Switzerland, and the United Kingdom) have banned the use of the ascites method of monoclonal antibody production. This procedure, used on mice, causes considerable suffering, including respiratory distress, circulatory shock, difficulty walking, anorexia, and other disabilities. It is estimated that in the United States up to one million animals a year are killed using this experimental method, but efforts to ban it in the United States have failed.

[. . .]

Another issue, apart from the experimental procedure, is the source of the subject animal. There are three potential sources: former animal pets, either stolen for research or abandoned by their owners; free-living wild animals; or purpose-bred animals (those specifically raised by commercial breeders for research). All sources have come under criticism (antivivisectionists object to every source), but most criticism has focused on the use of one-time companion animals and on the capture of wild animals, especially nonhuman primates.

Of the three possible sources, the use of purpose-bred animals is preferred. The ethical reasoning is that purpose-bred animals are likely to suffer less; they do not have to make a stressful transition from a free life to a life in captivity. Purpose-bred animals know no other life than living in confined quarters; they have been singly caged all their lives with little or no opportunity to make decisions for themselves over what exercise they take, what they eat, whom they spend time with, and so on. But former pets and free-living wild animals are different; they have usually lived rich social lives where they were accustomed to expressing their own free will. To lose this freedom can be traumatic. The period of transition can cause considerable suffering, including the stresses that come with transportation (sometimes for thousands of miles, as with some nonhuman primates, and which can result in death), close confinement, and social and other forms of deprivation.

In addition, the experimental results from purpose-bred animals are more reliable because, unlike former pets and wild animals, their genetic and health backgrounds are known. This reduces the number of variables that can confound experimental results.

[. . .]

Three R Alternatives

The Three R principles (refine, reduce, replace), first enunciated by Russell and Burch in 1959, state that experimental procedures should be refined to lessen the degree of pain or distress, that the numbers of animals used should be reduced consistent with sound methodological design, and where possible, that nonanimal methods should be used in preference to those that do use animals. Legal mandates requiring the Three Rs facilitate the acceptance of these concepts by investigators and oversight reviewers. The countries that specifically address all Three Rs in their legislation include the United States, the Netherlands, Sweden, Switzerland, and New Zealand.

The Three R principles are increasingly becoming accepted worldwide by both the humane and scientific communities. Although antivivisectionists focus on replacement alternatives exclusively, others believe that incremental improvements in laboratory animal welfare are best achieved at this time by pursuing all Three Rs.

Promising advancements can be made in refining experimental methods by improving anesthetic and other pain-relieving regimens, using humane experimental end points, and employing only rapid and painless methods of euthanasia. To a lesser extent, reductions in numbers are feasible through the better use of statistics in methodological design. Replacement alternatives may not be applicable, but increasingly, nonanimal alternatives are being developed, especially in animal testing and in teaching biology to students.

[. . .]

Although the concept of the Three Rs is now fairly well accepted on a universal basis as an ideal, it has proved very difficult to persuade regulatory bodies to stop requiring safety tests that involve use of whole animals before a new product can be approved. Although validated nonanimal tests are available in many cases, the regulatory bodies continue to mandate whole-animal testing. The nonanimal tests are thereby unreasonably being held to a much higher standard of validation than animal tests.

The evaluation of progress in implementing the Three Rs is a new topic and is in its infancy; most countries do not have adequate data for analysis. However, the Netherlands provides a unique model. Analysis of official data shows a significant decline in the percentage of total experiments that involve severe animal pain, from 29.3 percent in 1984 to 18.8 percent in 1997 (Orlans 2000). In addition, over the same period, the number of animals used has dropped by about half: in 1984 the total was 1,242,285 and in 1997 it was 618,432 (Orlans 2000).

[. . .]

Ethical Criteria for Decision Making

In general, existing laws do not address the fundamental ethical question, "Should this particular animal experiment be done at all?" The usual presumption of the law is that animal experimentation is justified and that proposed projects should be approved so long as the individual investigator believes that useful scientific knowledge might be gained. Indeed, oversight committees tend to approve almost everything that investigators propose, even highly invasive procedures on primates. Although some projects are modified (typically by application of a refinement), rarely is any proposal totally disapproved. It is thus a step forward when national policies specifically acknowledge that ethical decisions are involved in assessing the justification of an animal experiment, giving credence to the possibility that a proposed work is not justified.

Several countries have taken the lead in requiring a cost-benefit analysis that links animal pain (and other harms) to the scientific worthiness and social significance of the experiment's purpose. [. . .] The concept of making a cost-benefit analysis sounds reasonable but is difficult to apply because the costs and benefits are incommensurable. Almost all the harms fall on the animals and all the benefits on humans. Nevertheless, the cost-benefit view has gained considerable acceptance as a tool for clarifying ethical choices.

[. . .]

Use of Animal-Harm Scales

An important issue on the cutting edge of new reforms in national laws is the requirement to assess and rank the sum total of animal harms for any particular procedure. The ranking systems are variously called severity banding, invasiveness, or more colloquially and inaccurately, pain scales. First mandated in the Netherlands in 1979, such systems are now found in other countries (in chronological order, the United Kingdom, Finland, Canada, Switzerland, and New Zealand). This spread attests to the usefulness of these schemes. Pressure exists in the United States and other countries to adopt similar systems.

According to these systems, the degree of pain or distress is ranked according to a severity banding of either minor, moderate, or severe. For example, in the minor category are such procedures as biopsies or cannulating blood vessels; in the moderate category are major surgical procedures under general anesthesia and application of noxious stimuli from which the animal cannot escape; in the severe category are trauma infliction on conscious animals and cancer experiments with death as an end point. At some point (according to one's point of view), procedures become unethical because of the severity of animal pain.

Mandatory use of these ranking systems forces laboratory personnel to think carefully about the condition of the animal and its state of well-being or adversity throughout the experiment. It also encourages laboratory personnel to learn how to identify clinical signs of well-being and adversity.

In recent years, adoption of harm scales by various countries has acted as a significant stimulus to clinical investigations of animals in assessing signs of well-being and adverse states. A notable contribution that has attracted worldwide attention is that of Mellor and Reid (1994). Their categorization system, which represents a major step forward in assessing the condition of animals, has been adopted with minor modification as national policy in New Zealand and is the gold standard by which other harm rankings should be measured.

Summary

Laboratory animals are much benefited by enforcement of legally established standards for humane care and use. Nonetheless, an absence of laws in many countries where animal experimentation takes place needs to be corrected. New provisions along the lines of the topics discussed here are also needed, as is enforcement of many existing laws. It takes a great deal of effort to enact legal protections for animals, but the value of such laws has been indisputably established, as evidenced by the vast improvements that have come about in the standards of animal care and use found in today's laboratories compared with those of previous years. I also believe that improved conditions that serve to support the welfare of animals serve also to improve immeasurably the quality of the resulting science.

References

Mellor, D.J., and C.S.W. Reid. 1994. Concepts of animal well-being and predicting the impact of procedures on experimental animals. In *Improving the well-being of animals in the research environment*, R. M. Baker, G. Jenkin, and D. J. Mellor (eds.), pp. 3–18. Glen Osmond, South Australia: Australian and New Zealand Council for the Care of Animals in Research and Teaching.

Orlans, F.B. 2000. Public policies on assessing and reporting degrees of animal harm: International perspectives. In *Progress in the reduction, refinement, and replacement of animal experimentation*, edited by M. Balls, A.-M. van Zeller, and M.F. Halder, 1075–82. Amsterdam: Elsevier Science.

Russell, W.M.S., and R.L. Burch. 1959. *The principles of humane experimental technique*. London: Methuen. Reprinted 1992 by Universities Federation for Animal Welfare, 8 Hamilton Close, South Mimms, Potters Bar, Herts, UK ENG 3QD.

World Health Organization. 1985. *Guiding principles for biomedical research involving animals*. Geneva: Council for International Organizations of Medical Sciences.

Animals in the Classroom

44 Humane Education
The Role of Animal-Based Learning

Andrew J. Petto and Karla D. Russell

Petto and Russell address the complex issue of incorporating animal use in education and outline a process for involving students as well as teachers in making humane decisions about animal studies in the curriculum. Issues addressed by students would include decisions on whether and how animals ought to be introduced into the curriculum as well as various practical issues such as acquisition, classroom care and use, and disposition of animals at completion of the studies. While oriented toward secondary and early levels of education, many of their suggestions are also applicable to university levels.
[. . .]

Concept of the 'Humane'

'Humane' is a cognitive concept for humans and subject to the same constraints as other cognitive concepts held by humans (Atran, 1990). It is universal in the sense that all cultures seem to have a concept that some actions and attitudes toward animals (and toward other humans) are desirable and others are unacceptable. However, often the set of acceptable and proscribed actions towards non-human animals differs greatly from one culture to another, and, even within a culture, attitudes toward treatment of animals can vary by class or socio-economic status (Driscoll, 1992; Löfgren, 1985).

[. . .]

The challenge for anyone trying to describe a process through which one learns about animals and with animals as 'humane education,' then, is to focus not only on the final rules for behaviours toward animals but also to examine the pathways to those rules. There are two main goals of this examination. The first is to find opportunities in the learning process to understand better both the 'natural' and the 'cultural' animal (sensu Lévi-Strauss, 1965) and to discover what we can learn from all the different ways in which our culture and others know these animals. The second is to reline the pedagogical process so that we develop in our students a humane attitude that includes appreciation of the animal's natural life, role in the environment, and the costs (to animals and humans) of its capture and study.

The process of considering these issues for animals in education has three stages. The first stage focuses on pedagogical issues and is generally the domain of the teacher. The main issues in this stage relate to the objectives of the lesson, integration of the animal-based activities with other aspects of the curriculum, the design and presentation of the materials, actions and reactions of the learners, and an evaluation of the learning by each individual as well as of the lesson or activity as a whole. The second stage focuses on the impact on the animals themselves. The main issues in this stage relate to the acquisition, care and use, and disposition of the animals being used for education. Finally, the third stage focuses on the wider social impact. The main issues in this stage relate to the outcome(s) of the process on the educational climate in the schools, the community, and in society in general.

We do not believe that this approach will or must lead to an abolition of animals in the classroom nor that it should do so. Rather, we hold that humane education is embodied in the process of considering a variety of issues including the nature of the lesson to be taught, the opportunities for multiple approaches to that knowledge, the active consideration of the life (sensu Regan, 1993) of the animal subject as an important issue, the conservation of resources, and the outcome of the exercise for the teacher, the student, and the animal.

Our use of the term 'active consideration' throughout this chapter is meant to convey a sense that each choice to use animals in education is explored and investigated by the teachers and students as appropriate to the students' experience and abilities; that this exploration is not merely a perfunctory checklist of health, safety, and physical comfort issues but an integral part of the educational experience; that the conclusions and choices to be made are not a foregone conclusion before the process begins; and that executing this exploration requires a set of learning activities that may take the student beyond the immediate lesson and classroom environment to do background research, to check sources of information, to document past educational uses and their outcomes, etc. If successful, the members of the learning community—teachers and students—have turned the hit-or-miss experiences of the classroom 'pet' into an integrated, multi-disciplinary exploration of the biology, psychology, economics, and anthropology of educational use of non-human animals.

The experience of this process is the essence of humane education. The absence of real experience with non-human animals in the context of a humane educational setting eliminates an important opportunity to develop the concept of 'humane' in our students. Unless all members of the learning community are actively engaged in learning how information about animals is obtained and used in the classroom, we cannot fully demonstrate to the community in practice how to foster an environment of respect for those animals. We illustrate the values of humane education by accepting the responsibility to think clearly and responsibly about the role(s) that animals may play in our planned educational activities and the impact of those activities on the lives of animals.

Issues in Teaching and Learning

There are many ways in which animals may appear in an educational setting, but we will be concerned with just two subject areas—biological and behavioural sciences. [. . .] [M]ost of the examples that we will use and most of the discussion will centre on secondary and introductory level university students. We believe that the approach and concepts apply through a lifelong education, but our examples drawn from our own teaching and learning experiences draw us to this more restricted phase in our student's formal education.

The first step in a humane approach to animals in education is for the teacher to identify the best pathway to meet the lesson's objectives. The teacher must take into account the learners' stage of cognitive development, prior or collateral knowledge that the learners bring to the lesson, resources available to plan and execute the lesson, plans for evaluating the success of the lesson and the learners, the internal environment of the classroom, and the external environment imposed by systemic or other standard for mastery of life sciences content and concepts at this and subsequent stages of education (see Table 44.1).

[. . .]

If the lesson or any learning activity will include the use of live animals or animal products, the teacher first should be able to provide a compelling and significant pedagogical justification for such use. That means that the use of animals in the classroom provides an added component to the learning that is non-trivial and unique or unattainable in other ways and that there is substantive evidence to support this assertion.

[. . .]

Most educational uses of live animals or animal tissues are based on the demonstrated value of a practical or 'hands-on' component to the lesson. The power of adding visual and 'bodily-kinaesthetic' components to what Gardner (1993, 8) called the 'linguistic' and 'logical-mathematical' biases of nineteenth and twentieth-century education is illustrated in many disciplines. This approach has been most appreciated, perhaps not surprisingly, in arts education (e.g. Arnheim, 1969; Lowenfeld and

Table 44.1 Issues in teaching and learning with animals

Learning styles (intelligence)

Does the proposed activity allow or encourage acquisition and construction of knowledge by learners in a variety of ways?

Does this proposed activity engage the learner actively in the process of discovery, learning, evaluation, and assimilation of knowledge?

(Cognitive) developmental stage/age/level

Is the proposed activity appropriate to the abilities of the learners to understand and assimilate the main points of the lesson?

Is the proposed activity better performed at an earlier or later developmental stage?

Has the prior preparation for the proposed activity been adequate and appropriate to both the developmental stage of the learners and to the expected learning outcomes or culminations?

Lesson objectives

When the lesson objectives and goals are clearly formulated, how does the proposed activity support their attainment? What skills or knowledge are being developed, and how and when are they necessary for future learning?

What other pathways to the objective might be used, and how would they affect the educational outcome of the activities?

Will the proposed activity be a superficial, one-time event, or will it reflect and support the main theme throughout a curriculum unit or longer-term educational effort?

Career stage

How does the development of specific skills and knowledge translate into a potential for future study or career choices for learners?

Conversely, how would lack of specific skills inhibit the student's future plans and expectations?

What are the best ways to learn these skills and to what depth at this stage in the learner's academic career?

Brittain, 1970; Petto, 1994). In these disciplines, both learning and its evaluation take into account a rich array of interactions among the teacher, the learner, and the subject matter, including sensory, emotional, spatial, interpersonal, and kinaesthetic.

There is no question that what educators call active learning throughout multiple modalities makes learning better in at least two ways. First, students learn more when they confront learning problems that engage them in inquiry, problem posing, problem solving, and defence of their ideas before their classmates (Jungck, 1985; Peterson and Jungck, 1988). In most cases, teachers are referring to their personal experiences as well as a reflection on their intuitive (emotional or interpersonal, sensu Gardner, 1993, 9) sense that hands-on laboratory activities with animals add significantly to learning biology (e.g. Keiser and Hamm, 1991; Mayer and Hinton, 1990; Offner, 1993). This is not merely a matter of developing manual dexterity or hand–eye co-ordination or facility and self-confidence with some laboratory technique, as some have described it (e.g. Kinzie et al., 1993; Quentin-Baxter and Dewhurst, 1992). Rather, these practical or hands-on lessons provide non-linguistic ways of learning, and for some students the movement, proprioception, and emotional reaction to the learning and to other learners cannot be replaced by linguistic, visual, or symbolic (i.e. logical-mathematical) representations of the problem.

Secondly, this approach to learning engages more students in the process (e.g. Gardner, 1993; Markova and Powell, 1992; Petto, 1994). Such a wider engagement allows more students to participate in, and contribute to, the learning experience and may give them more of a sense of control or self-direction in constructing their own learning. In addition, Petto (1994) reports that the personalization of the learning activity through the incorporation of the emotional response to the activity, materials, and even the other learners is a key factor in both the retention of learned material and the ability of students to relate that material or lesson to other knowledge or life experience.

Furthermore, the perspectives of those students whose learning is not primarily linguistic or logical-mathematical contribute insights into the learning that may be overlooked by fellow learners, including the teacher. Even the learners who prefer expository teaching and declarative evaluation of their learning, learn more and better when using multiple modalities, as illustrated in a recent study on reinforcing the lessons learned through dissection by using prior preparation with an interactive video demonstration (Kinzie et al., 1993).

[. . .]

Finally, the main issue in humane education with animals is that biology is the study of the living (Lock, 1994; Orlans, 1991). In teaching and learning about living animals, one might consider, for example, their way of life, social and environmental needs (in nature and in captivity), feeding strategies and nutritional needs, and their role in the ecosystem. [. . .] This approach raises a paradox for the learning community, since almost any proposed educational use of animals will disrupt the animals' lives to varying extents.

One solution to this apparent paradox was proposed by Donnelley and colleagues (1990) under the term 'moral ecology.' Considering the moral ecology of the proposed use of an animal in education (or research) includes asking about the life that the animals (would) lead outside the educational context and how any proposed use would contribute to the educational objectives of the lesson. This is where the educational use of animals becomes humane. First, the teachers and students examine what needs to be learned and how an animal might contribute to that learning. Next, they review the needs of the animals and the impact on that animal of the proposed learning activity, considering, perhaps, alternatives that include using the animals in a different way, using different animals, or using non-animal resources. Then they should discuss the source of the animals, their acquisition, and their disposition after the educational activity.

[. . .]

Such a process places a heavy responsibility, however, on science teachers who may not have had any formal training in bioethics, particularly in exploring complex ethical issues with children (Downie, 1993; Downie and Alexander, 1989). Lock (1993, 114), in particular, points out the responsibility of the teacher to demonstrate 'a caring and humane approach in all their work with living things.' The responsibility for the teacher, then, is to be sure that the students have accurate, up-to-date information from a variety of sources about the animals they propose to study, including information relevant to the moral ecology of the use of particular animals in specific learning activities and projects.

In summary, the justification of any educational use of animals must have a strong pedagogical basis. This justification must include consideration of the choice of species, the type of learning activity, the developmental readiness and scholastic abilities of the students, the necessity for adequate foundations for future study, and advanced preparation and study by the students and teachers. A part of this justification is to balance the needs of, and outcomes for, the learners against the impact of the proposed educational usages on the animals.

Effects on Animals

After careful consideration of the pedagogical issues, if the teacher concludes that there is an appropriate educational role for animals in the lesson, then s/he must determine whether there are any animals suitable for the lesson and the classroom environment. The main issues pertain to the acquisition, care and use, and disposition of the animals used in the lesson.

[. . .]

Moral ecology may be viewed as an attempt at operationalization of the 'subject-of-a-life' criterion proposed by Regan (1993). It presents a set of principles against which we might explore by what criteria we may judge the subjective lives of animals and the impact on their 'individual experiential welfare' (Regan, 1993, 203) of various uses of these animals by humans. Moral ecologists recognize that the life's experience and the expectations for future life differ greatly among individuals of the same species (e.g. Rodd, 1990; Sapontzis, 1987). Therefore, the impact upon their individual experiential welfare of their interactions with humans in an educational setting may also be different.

[. . .]

[A] humane approach requires that everyone involved in the educational use of animals explores explicitly the effects of the proposed use on the animal subjects. Indeed, such background research before any classroom activity is a hallmark of the proposed standards for life sciences education from the US National Research Council (NRC, 1994).

[. . .]

The issues in Table 44.2 expand the sphere of inquiry of the effects of educational use on the animals beyond whether the subject animals will live or die. This process includes learning about their lives before the animals come to the classroom (in nature or in any other environment), how the animals will be cared for and by whom, how the proposed use will affect the animals and the learners, and what the effects of this activity might be on the animal's future life once the project is over. It also requires us to identify and evaluate the sources of this information and to determine what message each of these is bringing to the lesson at hand.

Although no such list can ever include all the issues that could be raised, we believe that the process of considering explicitly the impact of educational usage on the animals themselves is vital to

Table 44.2 Inventory of issues for use of animals in education

Acquisition

How are the acquisition and use of the animals to be introduced to the students?

How and from where will the animals be acquired?

Can they be studied in their natural habitats, or must they be introduced to the classroom?

Can they be acquired and placed in an appropriate classroom habitat without harm to the animals?

Does the acquisition pose any harm to the students?

Care and use

Habitat

Is the classroom habitat safe for the animal? Are temperature and humidity appropriate?

Is proposed classroom activity appropriate to activity cycle?

Are materials appropriate for digging, nesting, foraging, tunnelling, etc.?

Does the habitat provide appropriate options for movement, rest?

Social life

Is habitat appropriate to the type, frequency, intensity of social contact typical of this species?

If there is more than one individual in an enclosure, how should they be matched or mixed by age, sex, size, or other important variables?

Is there adequate opportunity for access to food, water, hiding places for all individuals in a social group?

Life cycle needs

Is there adequate opportunity for physical growth and development or social maturation?

Can normal life cycle functions such as reproduction and birth/hatching be carried out?

If reproduction is successful, can the offspring survive and thrive in the classroom habitat?

How and up to what point will this population growth be sustained?

Disposition

What will happen to the animals after the completion of the lesson(s)?

Can they return to their natural habitat?

Is any sort of preparation, training, or rehabilitation required before the animal can return to nature or its previous way of life? Is so, how will this be carried out and by whom?

How will the disposition of the animal(s) be introduced to and discussed with the students?

the development of a humane ethic in education. The desire to add other items to the list is a healthy expression of a learning community that takes seriously the need for such a development. Perhaps most importantly, this list is applicable to all animals and to any proposed use in education from behavioural observations of free-ranging animals in the schoolyard to dissection of mammalian species.

(Human) Social Issues

An important question in the use of animals in education that is often overlooked is the effect on human society and on the learners that experience it. Both the lore of scientific training and the criticisms from the animal rights literature point out the distancing, the deadening of emotion, the objectification of the animals, and the desensitization to suffering and death that educational uses of animals can have on the people who use them (e.g. Davis and Balfour, 1992; Shapiro, 1990, 1991). These emotional 'adaptations' are expected for all uses of animals, but are particularly pronounced when the animal use results in death or dismemberment or involves suffering. These studies argue that being forced to partake in these activities may require a psychological adjustment by the learners that degrades or devalues animal life. Similar reactions to the plight of human subjects in scientific research has been well documented for decades (e.g. Milgram, 1974). Under social pressure from peers and authority figures, experimental assistants new to the project were rather easily convinced to administer what they believed were painful procedures to unseen subjects for the sake of the experimental protocol.

However, the contributors to the volume by Davis and Balfour (1992) demonstrate that this outcome is not unavoidable. Furthermore, researchers and research technicians are frequent contributors to the journal *Humane Innovations and Alternatives* (Cohen and Block, 1991; O'Neill, 1987; Petto et al., 1992). In recent years, some winners of the journal's annual recognition award have also been on the research staff in biomedical research facilities (Anon., 1992, 1993).

Furthermore, one may argue that confronting the animal subject of our learning 'face-to-face' can be the basis of a sensitizing process in which the students learn about the real needs of non-human animals and the animals' observable reactions to handling, care, and educational activities of various sorts. The presence of living animals in the classroom can be a valuable way to increase the appreciation of learners for the real animal and its experience of life.

[. . .]

Rather than desensitizing the students to the animals that will enrich their education, this process requires the students to confront the real needs that living animals have in their environments. Direct, personal interactions with living animals provide the best opportunity for the bonding and empathetic responding between student and non-human animal that is universally acknowledged from Davis and Balfour (1992) to Shapiro (1990, 1991) to Weatherill (1993) and Ascione (1992). Because there are real and observable consequences in such a situation for making poorly informed choices about learning activities, habitat construction, or even choice of appropriate animal subject, students and teachers must confront and accept the consequences of their actions through interactions with living animals. Davis and Balfour (1992) argue that these interactions also bring benefits to human scientific and educational activities.

Another consequence of educational animals use is the development of an industry that serves the needs of thousands of schools that will use animals in some way. This is an important issue in Hepner's (1994) examination of the role of animals in education. The sheer volume of animals that must be killed, skeletonized, and/or preserved in some form every year in North America alone would probably surprise most educators. It is not only a matter of volume, but a matter of the effect on our expectations of the educational experience with animals.

[. . .]

If the process to acquire each of the animals supplied from these sources took an approach similar to the one we propose here, then the existence of large, centralized supply houses that kill and preserve millions of animals annually might be somewhat less worrisome. However, the sheer volume of this industry's output should be enough to make us reconsider how our choices to use animals in education relates to this phenomenon. The realities of the animal supply business must be a part of the process of choosing to use animals in education.

If there is a determined need for animals or animal tissues in the classroom, the humane educational process is enhanced by the explicit discussion by teachers and learners of the questions of source and supply. Is it better to use purpose-bred animals, or specimens from slaughter-houses, or body parts from hunters or taxidermists? And, what social, economic, and moral implications does each of these choices have? How should, or could, we decide among them and on what basis?

The process of recognizing the social implications of animal use beyond the classroom adds another important dimension to humane education. The whole learning community makes an informed and conscious choice for specific learning activities in which at least one component is animal based. It is vitally important that the learning community take this discussion beyond the blanket prescription or proscription of animal use.

Conclusions

What we have proposed here is an outline for making the choice to include animals in the curriculum a humane learning activity. All members of the learning community should be actively engaged in the process of constructing the humane ethic that will govern the choice to use animals in the classroom and the decisions on how they will be used. It must be clear from the start that there is a choice to be made. We wish to avoid the phenomenon described by McGinnis (1992) of beginning with the conclusion that animal use in education is automatically either 'noa' or 'taboo'—prescribed or forbidden. When the outcome of this consideration is not a foregone conclusion, the process of making these choices adds a valuable dimension to the educational process for all members of the learning community.

For the whole learning community, this process of considering the various practical issues of acquisition, classroom care and use, and disposition of animals used in educational activities is the essence of humane education, because it requires the students to confront these issues explicitly. In so doing, it shows that the teacher and the school value the animals as entities in themselves worthy of such consideration and not only as a means to an end.

In the end, taking this process seriously may mean, perhaps, that some activities using animals in the classroom will not be done at particular times and places—even when they clearly have pedagogical value. It may mean that there will be several learning activities and that not all students will participate in each of them. It may mean that the curricular activities involving animals will be developed around different choices. However, none of what we have described as the process of humane education means that these learning activities will never be done. In the end, 'humane' education is a process that increases, not decreases, sensitivity of all the members of the learning community to the impact of their learning. This, we believe, can be accomplished through a process of active consideration of these impacts in the various dimensions that are affected by these choices.

References

Anon. (1992). PSYeta's *Human Innovations and Alternatives* Annual Award, 1992. Viktor Reinhardt. *Humane Innovations and Alternatives*, 6, 317.

Anon. (1993). PSYeta's *Human Innovations and Alternatives* Annual Award, 1993. Peggy O'Neill Wagner. *Humane Innovations and Alternatives*, 7, 423.

Arnheim, V. (1969). *Visual Thinking*. Berkeley: University of California Press.

Ascione, F. R. (1992). Enhancing children's attitudes about the humane treatment of animals: Generalization to human-directed empathy. *Anthrozoös*, 5, 176–91.

Atran, S. (1990). *Cognitive Foundations of Natural History: Towards an Anthropology of Science.* New York: Cambridge University Press.

Cohen, P. S. and Block, M. (1991). Replacement of laboratory animals in an introductory-level psychology laboratory. *Humane Innovations and Alternatives*, 5, 221–5.

Davis, H. and Balfour, D. (1992). *The Inevitable Bond: Examining Scientist-Animal Interactions.* New York: Cambridge University Press.

Donnelley, S., Dresser, R., Kleinig, J. and Singleton, R. (1990). Animals in science: The justification issue. In *Animals, Science, and Ethics*, ed. S. Donnelley and K. Nolan, Hastings Center Report, Suppl. 20(3), 8–13.

Downie, R. (1993). The teaching of bioethics in the higher education of biologists. *Journal of Biological Education*, 27(1), 34–8.

Downie, R. and Alexander, L. (1989). The use of animals in biology teaching in higher education. *Journal of Biological Education*, 23(2), 103–11.

Driscoll, J. W. (1992). Attitudes toward animal use. *Anthrozoös*, 5(1), 32–9.

Gardner, H. (1993). *Multiple Intelligences: The Theory in Practice.* New York: Basic Books.

Hepner, L. A. (1994). *Animals in Education: The Facts, Issues, and Implications.* Alberquerque, NM: Richmond Publishers.

Jungck, J. R. (1985). A problem-posing approach to biology education. *The American Biology Teacher*, 47(5), 264–6.

Keiser, T. D. and Hamm, R. W. (1991). Forum: Dissection: The case for. *The Science Teacher*, 58(1), 13, 15.

Kinzie, M. B., Strauss, R. and Foss, J. (1993). The effects of interactive dissection simulation on the performance of high school biology students. *Journal of Research in Science Teaching*, 30(8), 989–1000.

Lévi-Strauss, C. (1965). *Le Totémisme Aujourd'hui.* Paris: Presses Universitaires de France.

Lock, R. (1993). Animals and the teaching of biology/science in secondary schools. *Journal of Biological Education*, 27(2), 112–14.

Lock, R. (1994). Biology—the study of living things? *Journal of Biological Education*, 28(2), 79–80.

Löfgren, O. (1985). Our friends in nature: Class and animal symbolism. *Ethnos*, 50(3–4), 184–213.

Lowenfeld, V. and Brittain, W. L. (1970). *Creative and Mental Growth*, 5th edn. New York: Macmillan.

Markova, D. and Powell, A. R. (1992). *How Your Child Is Smart: A Life-Changing Approach to Learning.* Berkeley, CA: Conari Press.

Mayer, V. I. and Hinton, N. K. (1990). Animals in the classroom: Considering the options. *The Science Teacher*, 57(3), 27–30.

McGinnis, J. R. (1992). The taboo and the 'noa' of teaching science-technology-society (STS): a constructivist approach to understanding the rules of conduct teachers live by. Paper presented at the annual meeting of the Southeastern Association for the Education of Teachers of Science, Wakulla Springs FL. Feb 14–15.

Milgram, S. (1974). *Obedience to Authority.* New York: Harper and Row.

National Research Council, National Committee on Science Education Standards and Assessment. (1994). *National Science Education Standards.* Washington, DC: National Academy Press.

Offner, S. (1993). The importance of dissection in biology teaching. *The American Biology Teacher*, 55(3), 147–9.

O Neill, P. L. (1987). Enriching the lives of primates in captivity. *Humane Innovations and Alternatives*, 1, 1–5.

Orlans, F. B. (1991). Forum: Dissection: The case against. *The Science Teacher*, 58(1), 12, 14.

Peterson, N. S. and Jungck, J. R. (1988). Problem posing, problem solving, and persuasion in biology education. *Academic Computing*, 2(6), 14–17, 48–50.

Petto, A. J., Russell, K. D., Watson, L. M. and LaReau-Alves, M. L. (1992). Sheep in wolves' clothing: Promoting psychological well-being in a biomedical research facility. *Humane Innovations and Alternatives*, 6, 366–70.

Petto, S. G. (1994). Time and time again: Holistic learning through a multimodal approach to art history. MFA Thesis. Boston University.

Quentin-Baxter, M. and Dewhurst, D. (1992). An interactive computer-based alternative to performing rat dissection in the classroom. *Journal of Biological Education*, 26(1), 27–33.

Regan, T. (1993). Ill-gotten gains. In *The Great Ape Project: Equality beyond Humanity*. eds. P. Cavalieri and P. Singer. New York: St Martin's Press, pp. 194 – 205.

Rodd, R. M. (1990). *Biology, Ethics, and Animals*. Oxford: Oxford University Press.

Sapontzis, S. F. (1987). *Morals, Reason, and Animals*. Philadelphia: Temple University Press.

Shapiro, K. (1990). The pedagogy of learning and unlearning empathy. *Phenomenology and Pedagogy*, 8, 43–8.

Shapiro, K. (1991). The psychology of dissection. *The Animals' Agenda*, 11: 9, 20–21.

Weatherill, A. (1993). Pets at school: Child animal bond sparks learning and caring. *Inter Actions*, 11(1), 7–9.

Ecological Studies

45 Ecological Ethics
Building a New Tool Kit for Ecologists and Biodiversity Managers

Ben A. Minteer and James P. Collins

Ben A. Minteer and James P. Collins argue that the ethical questions that develop in areas of ecological research and biodiversity management call for bringing ethicists, scientists, and biodiversity managers together in a collaborative effort to study and inform the methods of ethical analysis and problem solving in these fields. They present some cases to illustrate the kinds of ethical questions generated by practicing scientists and managers and call for an extensive case database and a new ethical framework they call 'ecological ethics.'
[. . .]

Introduction

When they confront difficult ethical questions in their work, biomedical scientists and clinicians can turn to bioethics, a recognized field within applied philosophy with a rich literature, for scholarly insight and practical guidance. Bioethics has a strong institutional presence in hospitals and research centers; scientists and clinicians often can and sometimes must consult directly with ethics committees or qualified bioethical personnel in their home institutions. Bioethics is embedded within these research and clinical communities, providing a recognized forum for the discussion of ethical issues, an established scholarly area of research yielding new research findings, and a support network to assist researchers and clinicians in making practical ethical decisions.

There is, however, no analogous subfield of applied or practical ethics devoted expressly to investigating the special kind of ethical issues raised within ecological research and biodiversity management contexts. Environmental ethics comes closest to filling this need, but it has not developed any special focus on the design and conduct of ecological field and laboratory experiments or (with a few notable exceptions) paid sufficient attention to the ethical dilemmas that often plague decision making in biodiversity management (including natural areas, botanical gardens, zoos, and aquaria). There is a need for a novel approach within practical ethics that cannot be met by simply stretching the current disciplinary boundaries of bioethics or environmental ethics as some have argued (e.g., Ehrlich 2003).

Experimental ecologists and biodiversity managers need a network and an ethical support system analogous to the one linking bioethics with biomedical scientists and clinicians. In recent years there have been increasing pleas for scientists to play a more active role in environmental policy discussions and to be more responsive to citizens' interests in maintaining biologically diverse, healthy, and productive ecosystems (e.g., Lélé & Norgaard 1996; Lubchenco 1998; Wilson 2002). These arguments are not entirely new, but their increasing frequency and moral seriousness suggest that more than ever ecologists are being asked to provide citizens and policy makers with the knowledge and tools for conserving biological resources and planning for sustainable development. In attempting to meet their end of this "social contract," ecological researchers confront an expanding set of ethical challenges that are in part a function of their field's growing technical acumen and increasing, though by no means complete or infallible, predictive power. Indeed, designing and conducting ecological research and managing biological resources often raise ethical considerations relating not only to an ecologist's responsibilities to public welfare and the scientific community but also to his or her obligations to wild animals, species, and ecosystems.

Consider the following case (recently documented in *Science*). Six of the Channel Islands of California have endemic subspecies of the island fox (*Urocyon littoralis*), an endangered species, and feral pig (*Sus scrofa*) populations. Golden Eagles (*Aquila chrysaetos*), a federally protected species, recently colonized the islands and drove two fox subspecies to extinction and reduced a third species to < 100 animals (Courchamp et al. 2003). Eradicating pigs was planned for early 2004, but population models demonstrate that eagles will then feed more heavily on foxes and trigger their extinction. Translocation alone will not eradicate the eagles, so lethal removal is suggested as the way to save the fox. What values should guide the decision regarding the appropriate conservation target in this case? Should both species be saved at any cost? If not, why does one species deserve to be saved and not the other? Is there a principled way to resolve these questions?

We believe that ecological scientists, biodiversity managers, and practical ethicists have for the most part devoted little systematic effort to exploring these sorts of issues. Exceptions include a handful of researchers who have investigated the social roles and ethical responsibilities of conservation biologists, including their obligations to ecological systems (e.g., Shrader-Frechette & McCoy 1999; Potvin et al. 2001; Lodge & Shrader-Frechette 2003) and related discussions regarding the ethical context of ecological restoration (e.g., Light & Higgs 1996; Gobster & Hull 2000). Still others have considered some of the animal and environmental ethical questions raised by zoo conservation strategies and techniques (Norton et al. 1995), the conceptual and moral considerations surrounding in situ and ex situ conservation of plants (Rolston 2004), and the ethical obligations of scientists who study wildlife in the field (Bekoff & Jamieson 1996; Monamy & Gott 2001; Swart 2004).

[. . .]

Although we can point to these and related attempts to focus more intently on the moral dimensions of ecological research and management, this work has not been coordinated in such a manner that it forms a self-conscious intellectual community with an explicit research agenda. Consequently, there needs to be a more concerted attempt to organize and integrate the discussion across the sciences, humanities, and conservation professions. Writing in these pages some years ago, Farnsworth and Rosovsky (1993) advocated a multidisciplinary dialog among field biologists and philosophers that would address some of the ethical questions we have identified. Our reading and experience, however, suggest this dialog has still not happened (Marsh & Kenchington 2004).

[. . .]

Scientists, managers, and ethicists can all learn by studying jointly the ethical issues confronting practicing ecologists and biodiversity managers. Doing so will help ecologists respond more effectively to the ethical challenges encountered in their research and help them lead discussions of proper research design and management rather than waiting for more slow-moving, ambiguous, and often unwieldy legal guidelines and prohibitions to point the way (Angulo & Cooke 2002). In short, we need a new approach in practical ethics, one we term "ecological ethics."

We offer a few exemplary cases in ecological research and biodiversity management and discuss some of the specific ethical considerations they raise for scientists and managers. We also outline the relevant literature in theoretical and applied ethics that speak to the duties and responsibilities of these same communities. We end with a call for the collaborative development of a pluralistic ethical framework for making decisions, one that will be a heuristic and analytical instrument informed by multiple domains within theoretical and applied ethics.

Ethical Dilemmas in Ecology and Conservation Biology

[. . .]

Using Genetically Modified Organisms to Conserve and Control Species

European wild rabbits (*Oryctolagus cuniculus*) from southwestern Europe are widely introduced into other countries worldwide and can be pests. Angulo and Cooke (2002) summarize a case with complexities that extend beyond those usually associated with deliberate release of genetically modified organisms (GMOs). Rabbits native to Europe support predators, including endangered Imperial Eagle (*Aquila adalberti*) and Iberian lynx (*Lynx pardinus*) populations. In the last 50 years, rabbit populations have declined mainly because of the viral myxomatosis and rabbit hemorrhagic diseases. One solution being pursued is releasing a genetically modified virus based on an attenuated myxoma (MV) strain that protects against both viruses. Only a few rabbits must be vaccinated to immunize the larger population because the strain can be transmitted horizontally among rabbits in the field. The same rabbit species is an Australian pest. A control strategy being considered is releasing a genetically modified MV that reduces rabbit fertility through transmissible (virally vectored) immunocontraception; in other words, an introduced contagious virus would disseminate a contraceptive agent through the exotic populations of rabbits. This is not a solitary case. Opossums, foxes, cats, and rodents are also candidates for control by virally vectored immunocontraception (Angulo & Cooke 2002).

Some regulations focus on research and release of genetically modified organisms, but few agreements specifically address safe research, handling, and release of these organisms internationally (Angulo & Cooke 2002). What are the human, animal, and ecological consequences of releasing genetically modified MV? Is it wise to genetically modify viruses for conservation and pest control? Tyndale-Briscoe (1994) considers some of the ethical implications of this practice, but in general what are we to make of an applied research program for rabbit management with opposing goals: conserving a declining species in Europe and killing the same species in Australia?

[. . .]

Choosing between Protected and Endangered Species

The declining desert bighorn sheep (*Ovis canadensis*) population in New Mexico prompted the state's game commission to pass a new regulation in 2002 allowing hunters to kill its primary predator, the mountain lion (*Puma concolor*), during the hunting season. Both animals are rare: the sheep are federally listed as an endangered species, and the mountain lion is a state-protected species. Critics of the lion management plan (including animal protective associations) argue that the kill quotas are too high and that hunting threatens the long-term survival of the population. Others argue that evidence of predation on the endangered sheep does not warrant the increased hunting quotas (West 2002).

Is it right to favor protection of the sheep over the lions in this case, or does this decision reflect an inappropriate and longstanding prejudice against predators? How much influence should stakeholders (e.g., hunters, animal protection associations, environmentalists) have in the decision-making processes of the New Mexico Department of Game and Fish compared with that of the department's (and nondepartmental) scientists? What should be the evidentiary standards for concluding that lion predation on sheep requires active management intervention? Should managers be compelled to pursue nonlethal lion population controls even if these are more costly and difficult to administer?

Ethical Tools for Ecological Problem Solving

Ecological researchers and biodiversity managers need to be able to seek appropriate guidance in answering questions such as those we posed here. In particular, they need to be able to identify and use relevant ethical principles and related considerations in problematic situations. Following the pragmatic insights of philosopher John Dewey, we hold the view that moral principles are best understood as tools for practical problem solving. The various expressions of value, duty, and obligation in these areas of ethical theory, that is, will prove useful in revealing the moral responsibilities in specific decision contexts and may be used as deliberative resources in the process of determining what should be done in concrete research and management situations (Dewey 1982, 1989; Minteer 2001; Minteer 2004). This pragmatic approach places much greater emphasis on the process of moral reasoning and moral deliberation—the experimental rehearsal, testing, and revision of principles and decision scenarios in the imagination and public debate—than it does on the adherence to any single principle that might be thought of as uniquely authoritative or privileged in moral reflection.

Four primary domains of theoretical and applied ethics are the most relevant to the ethical questions raised by work in ecology and biodiversity management: [. . .] (traditional) normative ethical theory, research ethics, animal ethics, and environmental ethics. Each domain and its constituent principles may contribute to our understanding of the moral responsibilities of the ecological researcher and biodiversity manager to the public good; the scientific and professional community; and to individual plants, animals, and ecosystems. In our view, however, each tradition is limited to the extent that it typically highlights only a particular dimension of the moral situation.

For example, the discussion in environmental ethics focuses largely on establishing the moral standing of parts or processes of nature (e.g., nonhuman individuals, species, and ecosystems). Although this may help identify general obligations and responsibilities to natural parts and wholes in ecological research and biodiversity management, scientific researchers and biodiversity managers also have significant obligations beyond the duties that they may be said to owe to species and ecosystems. These include obligations to uphold scientific integrity and avoid conflicts of interest and responsibilities to the greater public good or welfare. These latter obligations may entail both "negative" duties such as refraining from any activities that may produce social harms and "positive" duties such as the protection and promotion of biological diversity and environmental quality for an array of human cultural values. In addition to traditional environmental ethical considerations, then, these other responsibilities may also figure prominently in the deliberations in reaching an ethical judgment about what should be done in a particular research or management context.

We believe a pluralistic ethical framework is therefore the best and most effective way to conceive of the moral resources required by practicing researchers and managers (Norton 1991; Minteer & Manning 1999). The primary task of creating this pluralistic framework lies with the identification and organization of practical ethical principles across the theoretical and applied ethics literatures in ways that will help ecologists and biodiversity managers delineate the moral aspects of specific research and management dilemmas. The framework would distill from this work multiple sets of moral principles—rendered in the form of clear prescriptive statements—relevant to ecological research and biodiversity management in the laboratory and field. Such statements should include both traditional normative ethical principles speaking to ecologists' and biodiversity managers' duties to avoid social harms and promote the general public good (now and in the future), principles relating to their obligations to the scientific or professional community, and ethical principles speaking to their responsibilities to organisms, species, and ecosystems.

The best way to go about creating this framework is to form and cultivate a "deliberative community" of academic researchers and managers that can give shape to this new conceptual and practical tool kit. This community should be interdisciplinary and include ethicists, social scientists, research ecologists, and biodiversity managers tasked with exploring and debating the ethical dimensions of ecological research and biological conservation practices. The group would perform the creative functions of identifying and assembling a comprehensive ethical framework relevant to ecological research and biodiversity management and fulfill the critical role of providing peer review of this framework as a tool to aid moral deliberation and practical problem solving.

The resulting ecological ethics framework we envision will not produce absolute and definitive answers to the specific moral quandaries encountered in environmental research and management settings, but it would provide an important service by offering an instrument for clarifying and reasoning through the relevant principles and values that bear on problematic research and management situations. Still, one of the great difficulties that haunts any pluralistic model of ethics is the challenge of developing a method of integrating multiple principles, or, alternatively, of articulating one or more rules to direct the selection and application of one or more principles in particular situations. Along these lines, there have been some important attempts by other interdisciplinary teams of scholars to identify and integrate, on largely a conceptual level, various environmental and social values and duties in conservation contexts. Two of the more notable examples are Shrader-Frechette and McCoy's (1999) "two-tier" method of moral decision making in conservation biology (incorporating both general utilitarian and deontological principles) and Mumford and Callicott's (2003) conceptual assimilation of multiscalar environmental and community values, an analysis based on their study of stakeholders in the Great Lakes region.

Our own preference (keeping with our pragmatist leanings) is to emphasize the contextual and situational dimension of ethical integration and decision making within problematic research and management situations rather than the more conceptual aspects of this process. Ethical integration is not only a theoretical or intellectual activity (i.e., the philosophical assimilation of multiple values, duties, and interests) but also a form of practical reasoning, one performed by conflicted moral agents in complex and often morally and empirically ambiguous situations. We believe the most important "integrative" tasks in any sound model of ethical analysis are therefore action oriented and methodological in nature: improving individuals' sensitivity to the ethical context of specific practices (and their awareness of the relevant moral principles that bear on these practices) and facilitating the sharpening of individuals' imaginative and analytical skills so that they may learn to take a more reflective, creative, and systematic approach to moral problems.

This more pragmatic and "particularist" approach to ethics does not deny the role of general principles in ethical problem solving so much as it attempts to place them within a larger experimental process of moral deliberation and inquiry, a process that can also lead to the transformation of values as inquirers rehearse potential courses of action and share information and trade arguments with others over what should be done in specific environmental research and management contexts (Dewey 1982, 1989; Wallace 1996; Minteer 2004).

Of course, such pluralistic and dynamic moral models are notoriously messy; principles can and do often come into significant conflict despite our best attempts to achieve either conceptual or pragmatic integration. In such cases, hard decisions will undoubtedly have to be made. At the same time, however, we should remember that there are often opportunities for moral deliberation to settle on practical actions and decisions that reflect the convergence rather than the divergence of different interests and values (Norton 1991; Minteer & Manning 2000). On this point, there may be much to learn from established dispute resolution and "negotiated agreement" approaches (e.g., Fisher & Ury 1983; Susskind & Cruikshank 1987). Especially relevant to the vision of practical ethics we have outlined here are these methods' emphasis on the search for shared interests and mutual gain and their focus on the development of novel tactics and solutions to complex problems through organized negotiation and consensus-building activities (Minteer 2004).

Finally, in addition to creating a pluralistic ecological ethics framework, our proposed project leads to the preparation of a wide-ranging set of case studies in ecological research and biodiversity management (such as more developed versions of the kinds of cases presented above) that would become a useful database for scientists, managers, and students interested in learning how ethical questions emerge in the course of field and laboratory practices and about the moral claims that may be placed on them in a given situation (e.g., Dubycha & Geedey 2003). As we have witnessed with the rapid growth of the field of bioethics, such a case database can be an important educational and analytical tool, sharpening our understanding of ethical issues, our critical thinking, and our problem-solving skills (e.g., Crigger 1998; Murphy 2004; Pence 2004).

The development of a similarly detailed and organized case literature in ecological ethics would allow scientists, managers, and students to compare a variety of ethical, research, and managerial issues across experiential and value contexts, and would provide them with an opportunity to learn from the specific differences and similarities of the issues and cases. Such cases, developed as full educational modules complete with discussion questions, background readings, and supporting materials, could then be housed on a website that would serve as an integrative focus for interdisciplinary work and dialog in this new area of practical ethics. Through these kinds of activities, we hope to facilitate the interdisciplinary conversation and preparation of the ecological ethics "tool kit" for environmental researchers and managers.

Conclusion

We call for a new approach in practical ethics—"ecological ethics"—and a new conceptual and analytical tool kit for ecologists and biodiversity managers that will help them deal with the moral questions raised by their work. These questions have to date not been addressed in a systematic fashion within the established areas of applied ethics. A comprehensive ethical framework and case study database is therefore needed to help research scientists and biodiversity managers better understand and respond to the ethical issues they face in their research and conservation activities. These tools not only will provide critical assistance to researchers and managers as they deliberate within specific decision-making contexts but also will ultimately help create a larger and necessary forum for discussion of the complex ethical dimensions of ecological research and conservation practices.

References

Angulo, E., and B. Cooke. 2002. First synthesize new viruses then regulate their release? The case of the wild rabbit. *Molecular Ecology* **11**: 2703–2709.

Bekoff, M., and D. Jamieson. 1996. Ethics and the study of carnivores: Doing science while respecting animals. Pages 15–45 in J. L. Gittleman, editor. *Carnivore behavior, ecology, and evolution.* Cornell University Press, Ithaca, New York.

Courchamp, F., R. Woodroffe, and G. Roemer. 2003. Removing protected populations to save endangered species. *Science* **302**: 1532.

Crigger, B. J. 1998. *Cases in bioethics: Selections from the Hastings Center Report.* St. Martin's Press, Boston.

Dewey, J. 1982 (orig. 1920). Reconstruction in philosophy. Pp. 77–202, collected in volume 12 of J. A. Boydston, editor. *John Dewey: The middle works.* Southern Illinois University Press, Carbondale.

Dewey, J. 1989 (orig. 1932). Ethics. Pp. 1–18, collected in volume 7 of J. A. Boydston, editor. *John Dewey: The later works,* Southern Illinois University Press, Carbondale.

Dubycha, J. L., and C. K. Geedey. 2003. Adventures of the mad scientist: Fostering science ethics in ecology with case studies. *Frontiers in Ecology and the Environment* **1**: 330–333.

Ehrlich, P. R. 2003. Bioethics: Are our priorities right? *BioScience* **53**: 1207–1216.

Farnsworth, E. J., and J. Rosovsky. 1993. The ethics of ecological field experimentation. *Conservation Biology* **7**: 463–472.

Fisher, R., and W. Ury. 1983. *Getting to yes.* Penguin Books, New York.

Gobster, P. H., and R. B. Hull, editors. 2000. *Restoring nature: Perspectives from the social sciences and the humanities.* Island Press, Washington, DC.

Lélé, S., and R. B. Norgaard, 1996. Sustainability and the scientist's burden. *Conservation Biology* **10**: 354–365.

Light, A., and E. Higgs. 1996. The politics of ecological restoration. *Environmental Ethics* **18**: 227–247.

Lodge, D. M., and K. Shrader-Frechette. 2003. Nonindigenous species: Ecological explanation, environmental ethics, and public policy. *Conservation Biology* **17**: 31–37.

Lubchenco, J. 1998. Entering the century of the environment: A new social contract for science. *Science* **279**: 491–497.

Marsh, H., and R. Kenchington. 2004. The role of ethics in experimental marine biology and ecology. *Journal of Experimental Marine Biology and Ecology* **300**: 5–14.

Minteer, B. A. 2001. Intrinsic value for pragmatists? *Environmental Ethics* **23**: 57–75.

Minteer, B. A. 2004. Beyond considerability: A Deweyan view of the animal rights-environmental ethics debate. Pages 97–118 in E. McKenna and A. Light, editors. *Animal pragmatism: Rethinking human-nonhuman relationships.* Indiana University Press, Bloomington.

Minteer, B. A., and R. E. Manning. 1999. Pragmatism in environmental ethics: Democracy, pluralism, and the management of nature. *Environmental Ethics* **21**: 191–207.

Minteer, B. A., and R. E. Manning. 2000. Convergence in environmental values: An empirical and conceptual defense. *Ethics, Place, and Environment* **3**: 47–60.

Minteer, B. A., E. A. Corley, and R. E. Manning. 2004. Environmental ethics beyond principle? The case for a pragmatic contextualism. *Journal of Agricultural & Environmental Ethics* **17**: 131–156.

Monamy, V., and M. Gott. 2001. Practical and ethical considerations for students conducting ecological research involving wildlife. *Austral Ecology* **26**: 293–300.

Mumford, K., and J. B. Callicott. 2003. A hierarchical theory of value applied to the Great Lakes and their fishes. Pages 50–74 in D. G. Dallmeyer, editor. *Values at sea: Ethics for the marine environment.* University of Georgia Press, Athens.

Murphy, T. F. 2004. *Case studies in biomedical research ethics.* MIT Press, Cambridge, MA.

Norton, B. G. 1991. *Toward unity among environmentalists.* Oxford University Press, New York.

Norton, B. G., M. Hutchins, E. F. Stevens, and T. L. Maple, editors. 1995. *Ethics on the ark: Zoos, animals welfare, and wildlife conservation.* Smithsonian Institution Press, Washington, DC.

Pence, G. E. 2004. *Classic cases in medical ethics: Accounts of cases that have shaped medical ethics, with philosophical, legal, and historical backgrounds.* 4th edition. McGraw-Hill, New York.

Potvin, C. J., M. Kraenzel, and G. Seutin, editors. 2001. *Protecting biological diversity: Roles and responsibilities.* McGill-Queen's University Press, Montreal.

Rolston, H., III. 2004. In situ and ex situ conservation: Philosophical and ethical concerns. Pages 21–39 in E. O. Guerrant Jr., K. Havens, and M. Maunder, editors. *Ex situ plant conservation: Supporting species in the wild.* Island Press, Washington, DC.

Shrader-Frechette, K., and E. D. McCoy. 1999. Molecular systematics, ethics, and biological decision making under uncertainty. *Conservation Biology* **13**: 1008–1012.

Susskind, L., and J. Cruikshank. 1987. *Breaking the impasse.* Basic Books, New York.

Swart, J. A. A. 2004. The wild animal as a research animal. *Journal of Agricultural & Environmental Ethics* **17**: 181–197.

Tyndale-Briscoe, C. H. 1994. Virus-vectored immunocontraception of feral mammals. *Reproduction, Fertility and Development* **6**: 281–287.

Wallace, J. D. 1996. *Ethical norms, particular cases.* Cornell University Press, Ithaca, New York.

West, K. 2002. Lion vs. lamb. *Scientific American* **286**(5): 20–21.

Wilson, E. O. 2002. *The future of life.* Alfred A. Knopf (distributed by Random House), New York.

Part Six

Animals and Biotechnology

Introduction to Part Six

Authors of this part grapple with some of the very difficult issues associated with biotechnology. David Morton argues that protection of animals and the environment matter most and if humans have the right motivation and intention right actions will follow. Some of the moral issues associated with genetic engineering are addressed in the next five papers: Robert and Baylis in one paper, and Streiffer in the next, present some opposing views on whether human-to-animal embryonic chimeras would introduce inexorable moral confusion in our existing relationships with non-humans. Arguing from a utilitarian perspective, Kevin Smith believes that there is no clear moral mandate against genetic sequence alteration; likewise, he argues that within the concept of "replaceability," killing of transgenic animals is acceptable for animals not identified with "personhood." Smith does advocate a general prohibition on studies that entail significant suffering for animals. Jeffrey Burkhardt argues that most of the arguments raised in opposition to biotechnology lack ethical force because most scientists and science policy makers lack the moral education necessary to fully understand the significance of the arguments made. Burkhardt calls for ethical training to become an established part of the training and thinking of scientists and science policy makers. Finally, Traci Warkentin presents a strong moral challenge to the notion of genetic engineering of animals for purposes of human consumption, with an emphasis of pigs and chickens.

Using the Maxim to Respect Telos, Bernard E. Rollin agrees with Kevin Smith that there is no clear justification to preclude genetic engineering of animals; he notes that genetic modifications should be assessed in relation to the Principle of Conservation of Welfare. Bernice Bovenkirk, Frans Brom and Babs van den Bergh respond to Rollin's perspective by introducing the notion of integrity as a set of characteristics of an animal humans believe important to preserve; they call for moral discussion to identify these features and note that, even if there is not full agreement on what constitutes integrity for an animal, the discussions can provide a basis for evaluating existing practices. Jes Lynning Harfeld addresses what kinds of beings fare well under confinement agriculture, and defines what that sense of wellness is for them.

Carl Zimmer and Dolly Jørgensen address "de-extinction," the work of bringing a species back from extinction through cloning viable cellular nucleic acids collected from a member of that species. Zimmer explores some of the practical and moral issues of this approach. Jørgensen looks at the practical issues of reintroducing a previously extinct species back into its former habitat and proposes using the same guidelines as for reintroducing a current species to former habitat.

Further Reading

Best, S., and D. Kellner. 2002. Biotechnology, ethics and the politics of cloning. *Democracy and Nature* 8: 439–465.

Christiansen, S. B., and P. Sandoe. 2000. Bioethics: Limits to the interference with life. *Animal Reproduction Science* 60–61: 15–29.

DeSalle, R., and G. Amato. 2004. The expansion of conservation genetics. *Nature Reviews (Genetics)* 5: 702–712.

De Vries, R. 2006. Genetic engineering and the integrity of animals. *Journal of Agricultural and Environmental Ethics* 19: 469–493.

Holt, W. V., A. R. Pickard, and R. S. Prather. 2004. Wildlife conservation and reproductive cloning. *Reproduction* 127: 317–324.

Fiester, Autumn. 2005. Ethical issues in animal cloning. *Perspectives in Biology and Medicine* 48 (3): 328–343.

Lassen, J., M. Gjerris, and P. Sandøe. 2006. After Dolly—ethical limits to the use of biotechnology on farm animals. *Theriogenology* 65 (5): 992–1004.

Loi, Pasqualino, Barbara Barboni, and Grazyna Ptak. 2002. Cloning advances and challenges for conservation. *Trends in Biotechnology* 20 (6): 233.

Munro, Lyle. 2001. Future animals: Environmental and animal welfare perspectives on the genetic engineering of animals. *Cambridge Quarterly of Healthcare Ethics* 10: 314–324.

Rojas, M., F. Venegas, E. Montiel, J. L. Servely, X. Vignon, and M. Guillomot. 2005. Attempts at applying cloning to the conservation of species in danger of extinction. *International Journal of Morphology* 23: 329–336.

Rollin, Bernard E. 2006. *Science and ethics*. Cambridge University Press, New York, NY.

Rosati, A., A. Tewolde, and C. Mosconi (eds.). 2005. *Animal production and animal science worldwide*, Wageningen Academic Publishers, The Netherlands.

West, Chad. 2006. Economics and ethics in the genetic engineering of animals. *Harvard Journal of Law & Technology* 19 (2): 414–442.

Study Questions

1. Do you believe that increased knowledge of genetic engineering will inevitably lead to increased human genetic manipulation? Justify your response.

2. What is your view on developing genetically engineered animal strains with a telos that would make them well adapted to the conditions associated with intensive farming and production? Give some examples of good adaptations. What limits do you propose for work along this line? Justify your response.

3. In light of Burkhardt's discussion, do you agree that ethical preparation is lacking in scientific education? If so, what approach do you propose for best incorporating ethical training into science education? If not, clarify your reasons.

4. What is your position on proceeding with "de-extinction" of previously extinct species? Under what circumstances might you support it, and under what circumstances do you believe it would be inappropriate? Justify your response.

46 Some Ethical Issues in Biotechnology Involving Animals

David Morton

Morton argues that biotechnological discoveries have given rise to ethical issues, particularly concerning the welfare of animals and the protection of the environment with regard to other animal species. He argues that protection of animals and the environment should have the highest concern and, further, that if humans have good motivation and intentions, then appropriate good actions will follow.

Introduction

This paper provides a personal view of some of the ethical issues that have arisen in light of some biotechnological discoveries or ideas, particularly concerning the welfare of animals and the protection of the environment with regard to other animal species. It does not address broader and important legal and consumer concerns. [. . .] In this paper, it is argued that protection of animals and the environment matter most, and that given the right motivation and intention of human beings then the right actions will follow. It is hoped that this essay will generate some discussion that will enable readers to question their own views and attitudes.

Benefits of Genetic Manipulation

Recent advances in our understanding of how cells work at the molecular level have sparked a plethora of ideas as to how to harness this knowledge to our (human) advantage. Adding genes to animals from the same or other species (transgenesis), removing other genes through knock-out technology, and cloning animals using embryonic and somatic cells have been fundamentally important advances, and some of these advances have led, or may lead, to significant improvements in the health and welfare of both humans and animals. For example, the genetic modification of farm animals to be resistant to zoonotic diseases such as *Salmonella* and spongiform encephalopathy (e.g., bovine SE or new variant CJD, scrapie) would improve both human and animal welfare. (Note that if animals are sick, their welfare is compromised, and so health is one important welfare measure.)

Changing the sentience of animals through gene deletion so that they suffer less stress during their lives could be seen, on the one hand, as a desirable outcome and another aspect of domestication. On the other hand, it might be seen as an undesirable outcome and inherently objectionable, as it goes against the very essence of what an animal is.[1] Genetically engineering animals to produce leaner meat, to grow faster, and to utilise feed more efficiently would be good for both consumers and farmers, but would it be good for animal welfare? The production and isolation of therapeutic proteins from the milk of sheep carrying and expressing human genes (e.g., human essential clotting factors, alpha-1-anti-trypsin) would help those with haemophilia and emphysema, and possibly those with cystic fibrosis, to have a better quality of life with little impact on the welfare of the sheep.

Genetically manipulating (GM) pigs to provide a supply of organs and tissues for those waiting for a human transplant would save lives, and would probably involve little more harm to the animals other than killing it humanely. Note that it is not only mammals that are being utilised in this way. GM salmon that grow six times faster than ordinary salmon have been created, and if they escape (and some GM fish have), they could theoretically make the native salmon population extinct in 40 generations. Similarly, adding cold resistant genes could help create tropical fish for food in other than their natural waters and 'pet' fish (as well as other animals) could be manipulated for size, shape, colour, etc., for the amusement of their owners.

Finally, in this medley of potential benefits, the 'ultimate' goal of making new organs, tissues, and cells from somatic stem cells taken from the diseased patient herself, thus avoiding the need for immunosuppression, would be a significant advance. These advances in stem cell technology, together with a better understanding of cell differentiation, cell signaling, and cellular integration in whole organs, provide for exciting prospects for the development of even more ingenious therapeutic modalities.

Ethical Issues

However, all of these developments have ethical dimensions that should make us think twice before rushing headlong into what seems to be such worthwhile efforts. The persuasive power of the dollar, euro, etc., in our society tends sometimes to conflict with ethical concerns, as making money can appear to be the primary, rather than a secondary, goal at the expense of the sick humans or the welfare of animals. The motivation and intentions of those carrying out these genetic manipulations—or implicated in other ways, such as funding and giving ethical approval—has also to be questioned. There surely needs to be a strong element of good intention if we are to indirectly affect the welfare of animals or disturb the environment in a serious way before the work starts. Even if finance was not directly involved, there are perhaps some things that we should not do to humans or animals, like altering their sentience (i.e., ability to experience pain and pleasure) or their gross shape [. . .]. Our current predominantly anthropocentric view of life (putting human interests first) in our ecosystem with respect to the environment and animals is increasingly being challenged so that the possible outcomes of our actions should also be fully considered before going ahead. This is not a Luddite statement but rather that we should be giving careful and serious thought to what we do before we do it.[1-4] The fact that we '*can*' do something does not mean we '*ought*' to do it.

The ethical issues revolve around what we might do to other humans, to animals, and to the environment, and this short paper focuses on animals. Before that it is worth a comment on ethics in science. Scientists often claim that science is ethically neutral; they provide facts and the ethical issues are really about how those facts are used, and not linked to their discovery. But there are ethical considerations to be taken into account before certain lines of investigation are followed. We should consider how that scientific information might be used before carrying out experiments, or the direct impact of an experiment on the animals or environment (or on the scientists themselves). Scientists, just as other moral agents, are responsible for their actions and, apart from lines of investigation, it is important that scientific research is conducted in an ethical manner. The following examples illustrate this point.

The very act of transferring a piece of human DNA into animals has been questioned on religious grounds as some believe that it is unethical to do so because being 'human' denotes something God-given and, therefore, special and not to be tampered with. On the other hand, humans have many gene sequences in common with bananas, rats, and chimpanzees (nearly 99 per cent), and so the claim that human genes are unique cannot be sustained. However, there may be some unique human genes, for example for self-awareness: would it be right to transfer these into animals?

With shared genes, considerable benefits could accrue from transgenic technology, for example the production of therapeutic proteins in animals—so-called gene pharming. This 'artificial' production of proteins that can be given to humans and animals deficient in them would produce considerable benefits. An example is the production of human insulin in yeast for the treatment of diabetes (an increasingly common disease in the developed countries). More recently, the production and purification of human proteins from the milk of transgenic sheep is being trialled to treat humans with emphysema, and other proteins being researched include those involved in the clotting process in order to treat people with haemophilia.[5]

There are also considerable advantages in gene pharming as yields are higher than conventional methods (purification from human plasma) since the resultant products are free from potential human infections such as HIV and hepatitis. So in the instance of therapeutic proteins one might argue that the benefits for humans far outweigh the harms done to the sheep (and maybe cattle) that produce the milk and it is reasonable to do so. But it should not be forgotten that there are hidden costs to this approach. These are in the *development* of the transgenic animal lines that produce these proteins and include superovulation and death of the donor animals, embryo transfer into a recipient, sometimes Caesarean sections for the dam, and even then some neonates die or are abnormal at birth. However, those animals born alive and that survive to a reproductive age may well go on to found the production line. These founder animals and their offspring are likely to have a good quality of life and, almost certainly, a longer life compared with their cohorts that are slaughtered for food, simply because of their economic and scientific value.

Cloning is also being used to generate animals from the transgenic line and although recently there has been some evidence that they have a higher rate of abnormal and overweight lambs than normal animals, and that they may age quicker (by no means unequivocal), these adverse effects may be overcome in the longer term. In terms of what 'society' regards as acceptable for animals, it is relevant to note that these harms are far fewer overall (both in type, intensity and duration) than those caused to millions of intensively farmed animals such as chickens and pigs.

Some companies are writing codes of ethics for their employees to follow. For example, the Genetic Savings & Clone (GSC) company—a biotechnology company which markets genetic services to the public via the Internet—has a Code of Ethics for all its employees. All GSC employees are contractually bound to follow this code which governs the treatment of all the animals involved in the development of their technology and also the future application of their technology.[6]

[. . .]

In the UK, the law controlling animal research (the Animals [Scientific Procedures] Act 1986) uses a utilitarian approach when considering whether to grant a project licence for a programme of research work. In the present context, an application for a project licence would have to detail the consequences of developing a transgenic line with descriptions of how it is to be done including any uncertainties, and the anticipated benefits. Both these statements of benefits and harms are, of course, predictions at this stage, and under the 1986 Act the scientist, the local ethics committee (or ethical review process), and the Home Office Inspectorate have then to decide whether the work should go ahead. The Inspector is the final arbiter (although there is an appeal process) and if s/he agrees with the submission then a licence is granted, although often with amendments concerning experimental design and refinement of the scientific protocol.

[. . .]

Another conundrum that some philosophers have raised (notably Singer[7]) when opposing the use of animals in science is whether humans have the right to carry out research on animals that would not be carried out on humans. The question is phrased somewhat differently: 'What are the morally relevant differences between animals and humans that make it acceptable to carry out research on animals but not on humans?' To condone current practice, the answer has to place all humans in one 'box' and all non-human animals in another. One answer might be that we are human beings and not animals, but this really gets us no further forward, for what is it about being a human being that separates us from all the other species? Indeed the very reason for using animals as models for ourselves is our close genetic, physiological, and anatomical similarities. Some might argue that we use animals in this way simply because it is custom and practice, so why should any change be necessary? But the fact is that all human cultures continually evolve, and had this answer been accepted in the past, then we would still have slavery, women would not have the right to vote, and so on. The fact that something happens at present does not make it right. Perhaps animal research can be justified because humans are stronger than animals; in which case, should women be used as research subjects? Or if the criterion is intelligence, then perhaps men! But seriously, our ability to reflect on these questions potentially sets us apart as a species, but is this a *morally relevant* difference? Would it protect mentally retarded children, for example? Perhaps we should protect the vulnerable and give as much consideration to chimpanzees as to mentally retarded children (who may even be less intelligent than the chimpanzee) and so do research on neither. But do we know where to draw the line between the species—at primates, pigs, dogs, mammals, parrots, chickens, reptiles, amphibians, fish, octopus, etc.? The evidence is lacking for our present legal position, but it errs on the side of caution over physical pain and distress.

Another proposition is that 'suffering' is the key objection to animal research and humans would suffer mentally more than animals—e.g., we can think about the future as well as experience pain, distress, and so on. But are we sure that only humans have this ability? As it happens, there is increasing evidence that many non-human primates, and even non-primate species, have some limited degree of self-awareness and can anticipate the future.[8,9] But to what degree and to what end (their death?) we can only ascertain indirectly and in a very limited way. The recent debate over stag and fox hunting in the UK illustrates this point well. Descartes (1596–1650) was sure that using animals was acceptable on the basis that they could not speak and were irrational, and so they could not suffer; whereas Jeremy Bentham (1748–1832) asked, 'Surely the question is not whether they can talk, or whether they can reason, but whether they can suffer?'

Do religious beliefs help here, even though many people do not have a faith? Religions differ widely on this matter.[10] Compare Buddhists who believe in not harming any living creature as well as in reincarnation, with the Hindus who protect cows, with the traditional Judeo-Christian belief that animals are put on this earth for us and we have dominion over them. (Linzey disputes this interpretation of 'dominion'; see, e.g., Linzey and Turner[11] and Linzey.[12]) Overall, there seems to be no universal agreement that can be gained from religion on this matter.

To summarise then, the use of animals in research when we would not use humans has been termed *speciesism*[13] and has been likened to racism, sexism, and ageism. It is simply a prejudice, and not a justifiable position. We should either use both animals and humans in the same way[14] or we should use neither. There are other philosophical arguments against the use of animals in research, and utilitarians argue that the benefits of the research should outweigh the harms. Where this is not the case, or the anticipated benefit is so unlikely, or the predicted harm is so great, then the work should not proceed. Some research indeed may have no benefit but simply help us understand better how the body works, but that in itself is a benefit, even if less predictable.[15] Whatever animal research is carried out for the direct or indirect prevention of human and animal suffering, it will always require careful justification.

Going further with the utilitarian line of thought, it can be understood that balancing harms against benefits can still be subject to certain ethical rules in order to minimise the harms and maximise the benefits. Indeed, these rules would be seen as good things to do in themselves. Animal welfarists believe it is wrong to cause animals to suffer or to take their lives, but their caveat is that it is only permissible when it is unavoidable, i.e., least harm is caused, and is done for a good reason. In other words, it has to be backed by good reasons.

Before deciding whether a particular experiment is acceptable or not, utilitarians might draw on other ethical considerations and ask questions to help them decide. For example, is the work worth doing? Is it going to answer a scientifically valuable question? Could the scientific objective be achieved without using animals or by using animals that are not likely to suffer such as bacteria, or invertebrates, or lower forms of vertebrates with a less well-developed neuro-physiological sensitivity? Could cell cultures or computer modelling be used instead—that is, could the use of sentient animals be *replaced* in some way? Has the number of animals to be used been *reduced* to the minimum for the work, and has good statistical advice been taken? Is the level of suffering to be caused to the animals the minimum required to achieve the scientific objective, for example through the use of good anaesthetic and analgesic regimes, through good experimental design?[16]

This *refinement* of experiments to cause only that degree of animal suffering which is necessary is key to a humane and responsible scientific process (and is part of scientific ethics and a scientist's integrity). The application of these three Rs, as Replacement, Reduction, and Refinement are known, were first described by Russell and Burch as long ago as 1959[17] and are part of the scientific licensing process in the UK under the 1986 Act.[18] But it should be appreciated that applying the three Rs is not the end of the matter, as the 'basic' question still remains, should the work proceed even though there are no replacements, the number of animals has been reduced to the minimum, and there is no avoidable suffering? A weighing of the predicted harms against the anticipated benefits has then to be carried out to try to ensure that the harms done to the animals are in proportion to the benefits, but it is like comparing chalk with cheese: animal suffering versus human benefit. How can it be carried out in practice? This is the subject of current debate and is the meat of ethical discussion that would normally involve scientists, veterinarians, medics, lay members, even an ethicist(!). There is some general agreement that the greater the scientific benefit, such as developing a vaccine against AIDS or cancer, or making new replacement organs, might merit a higher degree of animal suffering than say for a gain in fundamental knowledge with no anticipated medical benefit.[19] [. . .]

The Future

However, let us return to some of our earlier futuristic biotechnological considerations. The prospect of improved and novel therapeutic approaches through gene pharming almost certainly will be welcomed by most as the balance of good over harm would seem to be significantly greater even though during the developmental phase a relatively high price had been paid. Similarly, most would welcome the manipulation of animals to promote a genetically determined disease resistance, but how about increased agricultural efficiency and meat quality at the expense of animal well-being or animal integrity? How would you react if lumps of chicken or sheep flesh or steaks were grown in test tubes or plates in a laboratory to contain different flavours or have varying degrees of tenderness? What if chicken eggs were produced by isolated ovaries cultured in test tubes? Many of these 'advances' would certainly be more welfare-friendly than all current farming practices and avoid the pain, fear, and distress and other adverse effects that are presently caused. But should we do it? Is there not something rather unnatural about these means of food production? What about making animals that removed something unwanted, such as meat with no gristle, leading to animals that could not walk but feel no pain, and that made no noise. This might mean that those animals could only feed, even be force-fed by machine (like foie gras), and if they did not feel pain in a controlled and protected environment, then would it matter?

Interfering with the integrity of animals for such commercial purposes is not new; after all, humans have deliberately bred through genetic selection farm and companion animals in this way for centuries. The new technologies may speed this up, or may enable us to produce food in the different ways described above. Perhaps they are 'a step too far' and would cause a public outcry—at the present. 'At the present' as new developments tend to go ahead of public opinion but with time, public opinion changes and a practice becomes acceptable as has already happened with kidney transplantation, freezing semen, IVF, cloning animals, gene therapy. [. . .] The question is, should we do it? Or even start to research it? And what does it say about us as human beings if we do?

References

1. Rollin, B. E. (1995), 'The Frankenstein Syndrome: Ethical and Social Issues in the Genetic Engineering of Animals', Cambridge University Press, New York.
2. Bryant, J., La velle, L. B. and Searle, J. (2002), 'Bioethics for Scientists', John Wiley & Sons Ltd, Chichester.
3. Benson, J. (2000), 'Environmental Ethics: An Introduction with Readings', based on the Open University coursebook, Routledge, London.

4. Rollin, B. E. (2001), 'Livestock production and emerging social ethics for animals', in 'Eursafe 2001: Proceedings of the Third Congress of the European Society for Agricultural and Food Ethics', Florence, 3–5 October, pp. 79–85.

5. Walsh, G. (2000), 'Biopharmaceutical benchmarks', *Nature Biotechnology*, Vol. 18(8), pp. 831–833.

6. URL: http://www.savingsandclone.com/ethics_codeofethics.cfm?div/

7. Singer, P. (1975), 'Animal Liberation', Jonathan Cape/Thorsons Ltd., Wellingborough; 2nd edn. (1990) HarperCollins, London.

8. Morton, D. B. (2000), 'Self-consciousness and animal suffering', *The Biologist*, Vol. 47, pp. 77–80.

9. Dawkins, M. S. (1993), 'Through Our Eyes Only: The Search for Animal Consciousness', W.H. Freeman, Spektrum, Oxford.

10. Kraus, A. L. and Renquist, D. (eds.) (2000), 'Bioethics and the Use of Laboratory Animals: Ethics in Theory and Practice', Gregory C. Benoit Publishing, Dubuque, for the American College of Laboratory Animal Medicine.

11. Linzey, A. and Turner, J. (1998), 'Bioethics: Making animals matter', *Biologist*, Vol. 45, pp. 209–211.

12. Linzey, A. (1994), 'Animal Theology', SCM Press Ltd., London.

13. Ryder, R. D. (1975), 'Victims of Science—The Use of Animals in Research', National Anti-vivisection Society, Davis-Pointer Ltd., London.

14. Frey, R. G. (1988), 'Moral standing, the value of lives and speciesism', *Between the Species*, Vol. 4, pp. 191–201.

15. LaFollette, H. and Shanks, N. (1996), 'Brute Science: Dilemma of Animal Experimentation', Routledge, London.

16. Morton, D. B. (1998), 'The importance of non-statistical design in refining animal experimentation'. *ANZCCART Facts Sheet, ANZCCART News*, Vol. 11(2), June, insert. 14 pp.

17. Russell, W. M. S. and Burch, R. L. (1959), 'The principles of humane experimental technique', Special Edition (1992), Wheathampstead.

18. HMSO (2000), Home Office Guidance on the Operation of the Animals (Scientific Procedures) Act 1986, The Stationery Office, London, HC 321.

19. Home Office (2001), Guidance on the Operation of the Animals (Scientific Procedures) Act 1986 HMSO HC 321.

Issues In Genetic Engineering

47 Crossing Species Boundaries

Jason Scott Robert and Françoise Baylis

Robert and Baylis evaluate the biology of species identity and the morality of crossing species boundaries in the context of emerging research that involves combining human and nonhuman animals at the genetic or cellular level. They review biological and philosophical problems of defining species as well as earlier attempts to forbid crossing species boundaries. While not attempting to establish the immorality of crossing species boundaries, they suggest that such crosses will result in important moral concerns and confusion about social and ethical obligations to novel interspecies beings.

Introduction

Crossing species boundaries in weird and wondrous ways has long interested the scientific community but has only recently captured the popular imagination beyond the realm of science fiction. [. . .] As part of the project of harnessing the therapeutic potential of human stem cell research, researchers are now involved in creating novel interspecies whole organisms that are unique cellular and genetic admixtures (Dewitt 2002). A human-to-animal embryonic chimera is a being produced through the addition of human cellular material (such as pluripotent or restricted stem cells) to a nonhuman blastocyst or embryo. To give but four examples of relevant works in progress, Snyder and colleagues at Harvard have transplanted human neural stem cells into the forebrain of a developing bonnet monkey in order to assess stem cell function in development (Ourednik et al. 2001); human embryonic stem cells have been inserted into young chick embryos by Benvenisty and colleagues at the Hebrew University of Jerusalem (Goldstein et al. 2002); and most recently it has been reported that human genetic material has been transferred into rabbit eggs by Sheng (Dennis 2002), while Weissman and colleagues at Stanford University and StemCells, Inc., have created a mouse with a significant proportion of human stem cells in its brain (Krieger 2002).

Human-to-animal embryonic chimeras are only one sort of novel creature currently being produced or contemplated. Others include: *human-to-animal fetal or adult chimeras* created by grafting human cellular material to late-stage nonhuman fetuses or to postnatal nonhuman creatures; *human-to-human embryonic, fetal, or adult chimeras* created by inserting or grafting exogenous human cellular material to human embryos, fetuses, or adults (e.g., the human recipient of a human organ transplant, or human stem cell therapy); *animal-to-human embryonic, fetal, or adult chimeras* created by inserting or grafting nonhuman cellular material to human embryos, fetuses, or adults (e.g., the recipient of a xenotransplant); *animal-to-animal embryonic, fetal, or adult chimeras* generated from nonhuman cellular material whether within or between species (excepting human beings); *nuclear-cytoplasmic hybrids*, the offspring of two animals of different species, created by inserting a nucleus into an enucleated ovum (these might be intraspecies, such as sheep–sheep; or interspecies, such as sheep–goat; and, if interspecies, might be created with human or nonhuman material); *interspecies hybrids* created by fertilizing an ovum from an animal of one species with a sperm from an animal of another (e.g., a mule, the offspring of a he-ass and a mare); and *transgenic organisms* created by otherwise combining genetic material across species boundaries.

For this paper, in which we elucidate and explore the concept of species identity and the ethics of crossing species boundaries, we focus narrowly on the creation of interspecies chimeras involving human cellular material—the most recent of the transgressive interspecies creations. Our primary focus is on human-to-animal *embryonic* chimeras, about which there is scant ethical literature, though the scientific literature is burgeoning.

Is there anything ethically wrong with research that involves the creation of human-to-animal embryonic chimeras? A number of scientists answer this question with a resounding "no." They argue, plausibly, that human stem cell proliferation, (trans)differentiation, and tumorigenicity must be studied in early embryonic environments. For obvious ethical reasons, such research cannot be carried out in human embryos. Thus, assuming the research must be done, it must be done in nonhuman embryos—thereby creating human-to-animal embryonic chimeras. Other scientists are less sanguine about the merits of such research. Along with numerous commentators, they are quite sensitive to the ethical conundrum posed by the creation of certain novel beings from human cellular material, and their reaction to such research tends to be ethically and emotionally charged. But what grounds this response to the creation of certain kinds of part-human beings? In this paper, we make a first pass at answering this question. We critically examine what we take to be the underlying worries about crossing species boundaries by referring to the creation of certain kinds of novel beings involving human cellular or genetic material. In turn, we highlight the limitations of each of these arguments. We then briefly hint at an alternative objection to the creation of certain novel beings that presumes a strong desire to avoid introducing moral confusion as regards the moral status of the novel being. In particular, we explore the strong interest in avoiding any practice that would lead us to doubt the claim that humanness is a necessary (if not sufficient) condition for full moral standing.

Species Identity

Despite significant scientific unease with the notion of *species identity*, commonplace among biologists and commentators are the assumption that species have particular identities and the belief that the boundaries between species are fixed rather than fluid, established by nature rather than by social negotiation. Witness the ease with which biologists claim that a genome sequence of some organism—yeast, worm, human—represents the identity of that species, its blueprint or, alternatively, instruction set. As we argue below, such claims mask deep conceptual difficulties regarding the relationship between these putatively representative species-specific genomes and the individual members of a species.

The ideas that natural barriers exist between divergent species and that scientists might some day be able to cross such boundaries experimentally fuelled debates in the 1960s and 1970s about the use of recombinant DNA technology (e.g., Krimsky 1982). There were those who anticipated the possibility of research involving the crossing of species boundaries and who considered this a laudable scientific goal. They tried to show that fixed species identities and fixed boundaries between species are illusory. In contrast, those most critical of crossing species boundaries argued that there were fixed natural boundaries between species that should not be breached.

At present, the prevailing view appears to be that species identity is fixed and that species boundaries are inappropriate objects of human transgression. The idea of fixed species identities and boundaries is an odd one, though, inasmuch as the creation of plant-to-plant[1] and animal-to-animal hybrids, either artificially or in nature, does not foster such a vehement response as the prospective creation of interspecies combinations involving human beings—no one sees rhododendrons or mules (or for that matter goat-sheep, or geep) as particularly monstrous (Dixon 1984). This suggests that the only species whose identity is generally deemed genuinely "fixed" is the human species. But, what is a *species* such that protecting its identity should be perceived by some to be a scientific, political, or moral imperative? This and similar questions about the nature of species and of species identities are important to address in the context of genetics and genomics research (Ereshefsky 1992; Claridge, Dawah, and Wilson 1997; Wilson 1999b).

Human beings (and perhaps other creatures) intuitively recognize species in the world, and cross-cultural comparative research suggests that people around the globe tend to carve up the natural world in significantly similar ways (Atran 1999). There is, however, no one authoritative definition of species. Biologists typically make do with a plurality of species concepts, invoking one or the other depending on the particular explanatory or investigative context.

One stock conception, propounded by Mayr (1940) and Dobzhansky (1950), among others, is the *biological species concept* according to which species are defined in terms of reproductive isolation, or lack of genetic exchange. On this view, if two populations of creatures do not successfully interbreed, then they belong to different species. But the apparent elegance and simplicity of this definition masks some important constraints: for instance, it applies only to those species that reproduce sexually (a tiny fraction of all species); moreover, its exclusive emphasis on interbreeding generates counterintuitive results, such as the suggestion that morphologically indistinguishable individuals who happen to live in neighboring regions but also happen never to interbreed should be deemed members of different species. (Imagine viewing populations of human beings "reproductively isolated" by religious intolerance as members of different species, and the biological species concept fails to pick out *Homo sapiens* as a discrete species comprising all human beings.)

Such results can be avoided by invoking other definitions of species, such as the *evolutionary species concept* advanced by G. G. Simpson and E. O. Wiley, which emphasizes continuity of populations over geological time: "a species is a single lineage of ancestral descendant populations of organisms which maintains its identity from other such lineages and which has its own evolutionary tendencies and historical fate" (Wiley 1978, 18; see also Simpson 1961). Unlike the biological species concept, this definition of species applies to both sexually and asexually reproducing creatures and also underscores shared ancestry and historical fate—and not merely capacity to interbreed—as what unifies a group of creatures as a species. The evolutionary species concept is by no means unproblematic, however, mainly because it is considerably more vague than the biological species concept, and so also considerably more difficult to operationalize.

A third approach to defining species has lately received considerable attention among philosophers of biology. This approach is known as the *homeostatic property cluster* view of species, advocated in different ways by Boyd (1999), Griffiths (1999), and Wilson (1999a). Following Wilson (1999a, 197–99) in particular, the homeostatic property cluster view of species is properly understood as a thesis about natural kinds, of which a species is an instance. The basic idea is that a species is characterized by a cluster of properties (traits, say) no one of which, and no specific set of which, must be exhibited by any individual member of that species, but some set of which must be possessed by all individual members of that species. To say that these property clusters are "homeostatic" is to say that their clustering together is a systematic function of some causal mechanism or process; that an individual possesses any one of the properties in the property cluster significantly increases the probability that this individual will also possess other properties in the cluster. So the list of distinguishing traits is a property cluster, wherein the properties cluster as a function of the causal structure of the biological world. Of course, an outstanding problem remains, namely that of establishing the list of traits that differentiate species one from the other. Presumably this would be achieved by focusing on reproductive, morphological, genealogical, genetic, behavioral, and ecological features, no one of which is necessarily a universal property of the species and no set of which constitutes a species essence. We return below to the homeostatic property cluster view of species when we consider how best to characterize *Homo sapiens*.

To these definitions of species many more can be added: at present, there are somewhere between nine and twenty-two definitions of species in the biological literature.[2] Of these, there is no one species concept that is universally compelling. Accordingly, rather than asking the generic question, "How is 'species' defined?" it might be useful to focus instead on the narrower question "How is a species defined?" In response to the latter question Williams (1992) proposes that a species be characterized by a description comprising a set of traits differentiating that species from all others. It is no small task, however, to devise a satisfactory species description for any particular group of beings. Take, for example, *Homo sapiens*. Significantly, not even a complete sequence of *the* human genome can tell us what particular set of traits of *Homo sapiens* distinguishes human beings from all other species.

[. . .]

Although human beings might share 99.9% commonality at the genetic level, there is nothing as yet identifiable as *absolutely* common to all human beings. According to current biology, there is no genetic lowest common denominator, no genetic essence, "no single, standard, 'normal' DNA sequence that we all share" (Lewontin 1992, 36). [. . .]

What Is *Homo Sapiens*?

What, then, is *Homo sapiens*? Though clearly there is no one authoritative definition of species, notions of "species essences" and "universal properties of species" persist, always in spirit if not always in name, in discussions about breaching species boundaries. For this reason, on occasion, attempts to define *Homo sapiens* are reduced to attempts to define *human nature*. This is a problem, however, insofar as the literature exhibits a wide range of opinion on the nature of *human nature*; indeed, many of the competing conceptions of *human nature* are incommensurable (for a historical sampling of views, see Trigg 1988). On one view, the claim that there is such a thing as human nature is meant to be interpreted as the claim that all members of *Homo sapiens* are essentially the same. But since everything about evolution points toward variability and not essential sameness, this would appear to be an inherently problematic claim about human nature (Hull 1986). One way of avoiding this result is to insist that talk of human nature is not about essential sameness but rather about universality and then to explain universality in terms of distinct biological attributes—a functional human nervous system, a human anatomical structure and physiological function, or a human genome (Campbell, Glass, and Charland 1998). A classic example of the latter strategy, explaining universality genetically, appears in an article on human nature by Eisenberg (1972), who writes that "one trait common to man everywhere is language; in the sense that only the human species displays it, the capacity to acquire language must be genetic" [. . .]. In this brief passage Eisenberg moves from the claim that language is a human universal, to the claim that the ability to have a language is unique and species specific, to the claim that this capacity is genetic (Hull 1986). But, of course, language is not a human universal—some human beings neither speak nor write a language, and some are born with no capacity whatsoever for language acquisition. Yet, in a contemporary context, no one would argue that these people, simply by virtue of being nonverbal and/or illiterate, are not members of the same species as the rest of us.

And therein lies the rub. We all know a human when we see one, but, really, that is all that is known about our identity as a species. Of course we all know that human beings are intelligent, sentient, emotionally-complex creatures. We all know the same of dolphins, though. And, of course, not all human beings are intelligent, sentient, or emotionally complex (for instance, those who are comatose); nevertheless, most among us would still consider them human.

The homeostatic property cluster approach to species avoids the problem of universality but at the possible expense of retaining an element of essentialism. Recall that, according to the homeostatic property cluster view, membership in a species is not determined by possession of *any particular* individual homeostatically clustered property (or *any particular sets* of them) but rather by possession of *some* set of homeostatically clustered properties. Nevertheless, although possession of property x (or of property set x-y-z) is not *necessary* for species membership, possession of *all* the identified homeostatically clustered properties is *sufficient* for membership, which suggests that a hint of essentialism persists (Wilson 1999a).

[. . .]

Moral Unrest with Crossing Species Boundaries

[. . .]

Scientifically, there might be no such thing as fixed species identities or boundaries. Morally, however, we rely on the notion of fixed species identities and boundaries in the way we live our lives and treat other creatures, whether in decisions about what we eat or what we patent. Interestingly, there is dramatically little appreciation of this tension in the literature, leading us to suspect that (secular) concern over breaching species boundaries is in fact concern about something else, something that has been mistakenly characterized in the essentialist terms surveyed above. But, in a sense, this is to be expected. While a major impact of the human genome project has been to show us quite clearly how similar we human beings are to each other and to other species, the fact remains that human beings are much more than DNA and moreover, as we have witnessed throughout the ages, membership within the human community depends on more than DNA. [. . .]

Although in our recent history we have been able to broaden our understanding of what counts as human, it would appear that the possible permeability of species boundaries is not open to public debate insofar as novel part-human beings are concerned. Indeed, the standard public-policy response to any possible breach of human species boundaries is to reflexively introduce moratoriums and prohibitions.[3]

But why should this be so? Indeed, why should there be *any* ethical debate about the prospect of crossing species boundaries between human and nonhuman animals? After all, hybrids occur naturally, and there is a significant amount of gene flow between species in nature.[4] Moreover, there is as yet no adequate biological (or moral) account of the distinctiveness of the species *Homo sapiens* serving to capture all and only those creatures of human beings born. As we have seen, neither essentialism (essential sameness, genetic or otherwise) nor universality can function as appropriate guides in establishing the unique identity of *Homo sapiens*. Consequently, no extant species concept justifies the erection of the fixed boundaries between human beings and nonhumans that are required to make breaching those boundaries morally problematic. Despite this, belief in a fixed, unique, human species identity persists, as do moral objections to any attempt to cross the human species boundary—whatever that might be.

[. . .]

[Some] maintain that combining human genes or cells with those of nonhuman animals is [. . .] inherently unnatural, perverse, and so offensive. Here the underlying philosophy is one of repugnance. [. . .] For many, the mainstay of the argument against transgressing species "boundaries" is a widely felt reaction of "instinctive hostility" (Harris 1998, 177) commonly known as the "yuck factor." [. . .]

A robust explanation for the instinctive and intense revulsion at the creation of human-to-animal beings (and perhaps some animal-to-human beings) can be drawn from Douglas's work on taboos (1966). Douglas suggests that taboos stem from conceptual boundaries. Human beings attach considerable symbolic importance to classificatory systems and actively shun anomalous practices that threaten cherished conceptual boundaries. This explains the existence of well-entrenched taboos, in a number of domains, against mixing things from distinct categories or having objects/actions fall outside any established classification system. Classic examples include the Western response to bi-sexuality (you can't be both heterosexual and homosexual) and intersexuality. Intersexuality falls outside the "legitimate" (and exclusive) categories of male and female, and for this reason intersex persons have been carved to fit into the existing categories (Dreger 2000). Human-to-animal chimeras, for instance, are neither clearly animal nor clearly human. They obscure the classification system (and concomitant social structure) in such a way as to constitute an unacceptable threat to valuable and valued conceptual, social, and moral boundaries that set human beings apart from all other creatures. Following Stout, who follows Douglas, we might thus consider human-to-animal chimeras to be an abomination. They are anomalous in that they "combine characteristics uniquely identified with separate kinds of things, or at least fail to fall unambiguously into any recognized class." Moreover, the anomaly is loaded with social significance in that interspecies hybrids and chimeras made with human materials "straddle the line between *us* and *them*" (Stout 2001, 148). As such, these beings threaten our social identity, our unambiguous status as human beings.

But what makes for unambiguous humanness? Where is the sharp line that makes for the transgression, the abomination? According to Stout, the line must be both sharp and socially significant if trespassing across it is to generate a sense of abomination: "An abomination, then, is anomalous or ambiguous with respect to some system of concepts. And the repugnance it causes depends on such factors as the presence, sharpness, and social significance of conceptual distinctions" (Stout 2001, 148). As we have seen, though, there is no biological sharp line: we have no biological account of unambiguous humanness, whether in terms of necessary and sufficient conditions or of homeostatic property clusters. Thus it would appear that in this instance abomination is a social and moral construct.

Transformative technologies, such as those involved in creating interspecies beings from human material, threaten to break down the social dividing line between human beings and nonhumans. Any offspring generated through the pairing of two human beings is by natural necessity—reproductive, genetic, and developmental necessity—a human. But biology now offers the prospect of generating offspring through less usual means; for instance, by transferring nuclear DNA from one cell into an enucleated egg. Where the nuclear DNA and the enucleated egg (with its mitochondrial DNA) derive from organisms of different species, the potential emerges to create an interspecies nuclear-cytoplasmic hybrid.

In 1998, the American firm Advanced Cell Technology (ACT) disclosed that it had created a hybrid embryo by fusing human nuclei with enucleated cow oocytes. The goal of the research was to create and isolate human embryonic stem cells. But if the technology actually works (and there is some doubt about this) there would be the potential to create animal–human hybrids (ACT 1998; Marshall 1998; Wade 1998). Any being created in this way would have DNA 99% identical with that of the adult from whom the human nucleus was taken; the remaining 1% of DNA (i.e., mitochondrial DNA) would come from the enucleated animal oocyte. Is the hybrid thus created simply part-human and part-nonhuman animal? Or is it unequivocally human or unequivocally animal (see Loike and Tendler 2002)? These are neither spurious nor trivial questions. [. . .]

It has recently been suggested that human stem cells should be injected into mice embryos (blastocysts) to test their pluripotency (Dewitt 2002). If the cells were to survive and were indeed pluripotent, they could contribute to the formation of every tissue. Any animal born following this research would be a chimera—a being with a mixture of (at least) two kinds of cells. Or, according to others, it would be just a mouse with a few human cells. But what if those cells are in the brain, or the gonads (Weissman 2002)? What if the chimeric mouse has human sperm? And what if that mouse were to mate with a chimeric mouse with human eggs?

All of this to say that when faced with the prospect of not knowing whether a creature before us is human and therefore entitled to all of the rights typically conferred on human beings, we are, as a people, baffled.

One could argue further that we are not only baffled but indeed fearful. Hybrids and chimeras made from human beings represent a metaphysical threat to our self-image. [. . .] Hybrids and chimeras made from human materials blur the fragile boundary between human beings and "unreasoning animals," particularly when one considers the possibility of creating "reasoning" nonhuman animals (Krieger 2002). But is protecting one's privileged place in the world solid grounds on which to claim that hybrid- or chimera-making is intrinsically or even instrumentally unethical?

Moral Confusion

Taking into consideration the conceptual morass of species-talk, the lack of consensus about the existence of God and His role in Creation, healthy skepticism about the "yuck" response, and confusion and fear about obscuring, blurring, or breaching boundaries, the question remains as to why there should be any ethical debate over crossing species boundaries. We offer the following musings as the beginnings of a plausible answer, the moral weight of which is yet to be assessed.

All things considered, the engineering of creatures that are part human and part nonhuman animal is objectionable because the existence of such beings would introduce inexorable moral confusion in our existing relationships with nonhuman animals and in our future relationships with part-human hybrids and chimeras. The moral status of nonhuman animals, unlike that of human beings, invariably depends in part on features other than species membership, such as the intention with which the animal came into being. With human beings, the intention with which one is created is irrelevant to one's moral status. In principle it does not matter whether one is created as an heir, a future companion to an aging parent, a sibling for an only child, or a possible tissue donor for a family member. In the case of human beings, moral status is categorical insofar as humanness is generally considered a necessary condition for moral standing. In the case of nonhuman animals, though, moral status is contingent on the will of regnant human beings. There are different moral obligations, dependent on social convention, that govern our behavior toward individual nonhuman animals depending upon whether they are bred or captured for food (e.g., cattle), for labor (e.g., oxen for subsistence farming), for research (e.g., lab animals), for sport (e.g., hunting), for companionship (e.g., pets), for investment (e.g., breeding and racing), for education (e.g., zoo animals), or whether they are simply cohabitants of this planet. In addition, further moral distinctions are sometimes drawn between "higher" and "lower" animals, cute and ugly animals, useful animals and pests, all of which add to the complexity of human relationships with nonhuman animals.

These two frameworks for attributing moral status are clearly incommensurable. One framework relies almost exclusively on species membership in *Homo sapiens* as such, while the other relies primarily on the will and intention of powerful "others" who claim and exercise the right to confer moral status on themselves and other creatures. For example, though some (including ourselves) will argue that the biological term *human* should not be conflated with the moral term *person*, others will insist that all human beings have an inviolable moral right to life simply by virtue of being human. In sharp contrast, a nonhuman animal's "right to life" depends entirely upon the will of some or many human beings, and this determination typically will be informed by myriad considerations.

It follows that hybrids and chimeras made from human materials are threatening insofar as there is no clear way of understanding (or even imagining) our moral obligations to these beings—which is hardly surprising given that we are still debating our moral obligations to some among us who are undeniably biologically human, as well as our moral obligations to a range of nonhuman animals. If we breach the clear (but fragile) *moral* demarcation line between human and nonhuman animals, the ramifications are considerable, not only in terms of sorting out our obligations to these new beings but also in terms of having to revisit some of our current patterns of behavior toward certain human and nonhuman animals.[5] As others have observed (e.g., Thomas 1983), the separateness of humanity is precarious and easily lost; hence the need for tightly guarded boundaries.

Indeed, asking—let alone answering—a question about the moral status of part-human interspecies hybrids and chimeras threatens the social fabric in untold ways; countless social institutions, structures, and practices depend upon the moral distinction drawn between human and nonhuman animals. Therefore, to protect the privileged place of human animals in the hierarchy of being, it is of value to embrace (folk) essentialism about species identities and thus effectively trump scientific quibbles over species and over the species status of novel beings. The notion that species identity can be a fluid construct is rejected, and instead a belief in fixed species boundaries that ought not to be transgressed is advocated.

[. . .]

Our point is not that the creation of interspecies hybrids and chimeras adds a huge increment of moral confusion, nor that there has never been confusion about the moral status of particular kinds of beings, but rather that the creation of novel beings that are part human and part nonhuman animal is sufficiently threatening to the social order that for many this is sufficient reason to prohibit any crossing of species boundaries involving human beings. To do otherwise is to have to confront the possibility that humanness is neither necessary nor sufficient for personhood (the term typically used to denote a being with full moral standing, for which many—if not most—believe that humanness is at least a necessary condition).

In the debate about the ethics of crossing species boundaries, the pivotal question is: Do we shore up or challenge our current social and moral categories? Moreover, do we entertain or preclude the possibility that humanness is not a necessary condition for being granted full moral rights? How we resolve these questions will be important not only in determining the moral status and social identity of those beings with whom we currently coexist (about whom there is still confusion and debate), but also for those beings we are on the cusp of creating. Given the social significance of the transgression we contemplate embracing, it behooves us to do this conceptual work now, not when the issue is even more complex—that is, once novel part-human beings walk among us.

Conclusion

To this point we have not argued that the creation of interspecies hybrids or chimeras from human materials should be forbidden or embraced. We have taken no stance at all on this particular issue. Rather, we have sketched the complexity and indeterminacy of the moral and scientific terrain, and we have highlighted the fact that despite scientists' and philosophers' inability to precisely define *species*, and thereby to demarcate species identities and boundaries, the putative fixity of putative species boundaries remains firmly lodged in popular consciousness and informs the view that there is an obligation to protect and preserve the integrity of human beings and *the* human genome. We have also shown that the arguments against crossing species boundaries and creating novel part-human beings (including interspecies hybrids or chimeras from human materials), though many and varied, are largely unsatisfactory. Our own hypothesis is that the issue at the heart of the matter is the threat of inexorable moral confusion.

With all this said and done, in closing we offer the following more general critique of the debate about transgressing species boundaries in creating part-human beings. The argument, insofar as there is one, runs something like this: species identities are fixed, not fluid; but just in case, prohibiting the transgression of species boundaries is a scientific, political, and moral imperative. The scientific imperative is prudential, is recognition of the inability to anticipate the possibly dire consequences for the species *Homo sapiens* of building these novel beings. The political imperative is also pruden- tial, but here the concern is to preserve and protect valued social institutions that presume pragmati- cally clear boundaries between human and nonhuman animals. The moral imperative stems from a prior obligation to better delineate moral commitments to both human beings and animals before undertaking the creation of new creatures for whom there is no apparent a priori moral status.

As we have attempted to show, this argument against transgressing species boundaries is flawed. The first premise is not categorically true—there is every reason to doubt the view that species iden- tity is fixed. Further, the scientific, political, and moral objections sketched above require substantial elaboration. In our view, the most plausible objection to the creation of novel interspecies creatures rests on the notion of moral confusion—about which considerably more remains to be said.

Notes

1. A possible exception is the creation of genetically modified crops. But here the arguments are based on human health and safety concerns, as well as on political opposition to monopolistic business practices, rather than on concern for the essential identity of plant species.
2. Kitcher (1984) and Hull (1999) each discuss nine concepts. Mayden (1997) discusses twenty-two.
3. See, for example, s6(2)(b) Infertility (Medical Procedures) Act 1984 (Victoria, Australia); s3(2)(a)–(b) and s3(3)(b) Human Fertilisation and Embryology Act 1990 (United Kingdom); and Article 25 Bill containing rules relating to the use of gametes and embryos (Embryo Bill), September 2000 (the Netherlands). See also Annas, Andrews, and Isasi (2002).

4. A particularly well-documented example of gene flow between species is Darwin's finches in the Galapagos Islands. For a recent account, see Grant and Grant (2002).

5. Animal-rights advocates might object to the creation of part-human hybrids on the grounds that this constitutes inappropriate treatment of animals solely to further human interests. Obviously, proponents of such a perspective will not typically have a prior commitment to the uniqueness and "dignity" of human beings. For this reason we do not pursue this narrative here.

References

Advanced Cell Technology. 1998. Advanced Cell Technology announces use of nuclear replacement technology for successful generation of human embryonic stem cells. Press release, 12 November. Available from: http://www.advancedcell.com/pr_11–12–1998.html.

Annas, G. J., L. B. Andrews, and R. M. Isasi. 2002. Protecting the endangered human: Toward an international treaty prohibiting cloning and inheritable alterations. *American Journal of Law & Medicine* 28: 151–78.

Atran, S. 1999. The universal primacy of generic species in folkbiological taxonomy: Implications for human biological, cultural, and scientific evolution. In *Species: New interdisciplinary essays*, ed. R. A. Wilson, 231–61. Cambridge: MIT Press.

Boyd, R. 1999. Homeostasis, species, and higher taxa. In *Species: New interdisciplinary essays*, ed. R. A. Wilson, 141–85. Cambridge: MIT Press.

Campbell, A., K. G. Glass, and L. C. Charland. 1998. Describing our "humanness": Can genetic science alter what it means to be "human"? *Science and Engineering Ethics* 4: 413–26.

Claridge, M. F., H. A. Dawah, and M. R. Wilson, eds. 1997. *Species: The units of biodiversity*. London: Chapman and Hall.

Dennis, C. 2002. China: Stem cells rise in the East. *Nature* 419: 334–36.

Dewitt, N. 2002. Biologists divided over proposal to create human–mouse embryos. *Nature* 420: 255.

Dixon, B. 1984. Engineering chimeras for Noah's ark. *Hastings Center Report* 10: 10–12.

Dobzhansky, T. 1950. Mendelian populations and their evolution. *American Naturalist* 84: 401–18.

Douglas, M. 1966. *Purity and danger*. London: Routledge and Kegan Paul.

Dreger, A. D. 2000. *Hermaphrodites and the medical invention of sex*. Cambridge: Harvard University Press.

Eisenberg, L. 1972. The *human* nature of human nature. *Science* 176: 123–28.

Ereshefsky, M., ed. 1992. *The units of evolution: Essays on the nature of species*. Cambridge: MIT Press.

Goldstein, R. S., M. Drukker, B. E. Reubinoff, and N. Benvenisty. 2002. Integration and differentiation of human embryonic stem cells transplanted to the chick embryo. *Developmental Dynamics* 225: 80–86.

Grant, P. R., and B. R. Grant. 2002. Unpredictable evolution in a 30-year study of Darwin's finches. *Science* 296: 633–35.

Griffiths, P. 1999. Squaring the circle: Natural kinds with historical essences. In *Species: New interdisciplinary essays*, ed. R. A. Wilson, 209–28. Cambridge: MIT Press.

Harris, J. 1998. *Clones, genes, and immortality: Ethics and the genetic revolution*. New York: Oxford University Press.

Hull, D. L. 1986. On human nature. *Proceedings of the Biennial Meeting of the Philosophy of Science Association* 2: 3–13.

———. 1999. On the plurality of species: Questioning the party line. In *Species: New Interdisciplinary essays*, ed. R. A. Wilson, 23–48. Cambridge: MIT Press.

Kitcher, P. 1984. Species. *Philosophy of Science* 51: 308–33.

Krieger, L. M. 2002. Scientists put a bit of man into a mouse. *Mercury News*, 8 December. Available from: http://www.bayarea.com/mld/mercurynews/4698610.htm.

Krimsky, S. 1982. *Genetic alchemy: The social history of the recombinant DNA controversy*. Cambridge: MIT Press.

Lewontin, R. C. 1992. The dream of the human genome. *New York Review of Books*, 28 May, pp. 31–40.

Loike, J. D., and M. D. Tendler. 2002. Revisiting the definition of Homo sapiens. *Kennedy Institute of Ethics Journal* 12: 343–50.

Marshall, E. 1998. Claim of human–cow embryo greeted with skepticism. *Science* 282: 1390–91.

Mayden, R. L. 1997. A hierarchy of species concepts: The denouement in the saga of the species problem. In *Species: The units of biodiversity*, ed. M. F. Claridge, H. A. Dawan, and M. R. Wilson, 381–424. London: Chapman and Hall.

Mayr, E. 1940. Speciation phenomena in birds. *American Naturalist* 74: 249–78.

Ourednik, V., J. Ourednik, J. D. Flax, W.M. Zawada, C. Hutt, C. Yang, K. I Park, S. U. Kim, R. L. Sidman, C. R. Freed, and E. Y. Snyder. 2001. Segregation of human neural stem cells in the developing primate forebrain. *Science* 293: 1820–24.

Simpson, G. G. 1961. *Principles of animal taxonomy*. New York: Columbia University Press.

Stout, J. 2001. *Ethics after Babel: The languages of morals and their discontents*. Boston: Beacon Books, 1988. Reprint, in expanded form and with a new postscript, Princeton: Princeton University Press.

Thomas, K. 1983. *Man and the natural world: Changing attitudes in England, 1500–1800*. London: Allen Lane.

Trigg, R. 1988. *Ideas of human nature: An historical introduction*. Oxford, UK: Basil Blackwell.

Wade, N. 1998. Researchers claim embryonic cell mix of human and cow. *New York Times*, 12 November, p. A1. Available from: http://query.nytimes.com/search/article-page.html?res=9C04E3D71731F931A25752 C1A96E 958260.

Weissman, I. 2002. Stem cells: Scientific, medical, and prolitical issues. *New England Journal of Medicine* 346: 1576–79.

Wiley, E. O. 1978. The evolutionary species concept reconsidered. *Systematic Zoology* 27: 17–26.

Williams, M. B. 1992. Species: Current usages. In *Keywords in evolutionary biology*, ed. E. F. Keller and E. A. Lloyd, 318–23. Cambridge: Harvard University Press.

Wilson, R. A. 1999a. Realism, essence, and kind: Resuscitating species essentialism? In *Species: New Interdisciplinary essays*, ed. R. A. Wilson, 187–207. Cambridge: MIT Press.

———. 1999b. *Species: New interdisciplinary essays*. Cambridge: MIT Press.

48 In Defense of the Moral Relevance of Species Boundaries

Robert Streiffer

Streiffer argues that it is premature to conclude, as Robert and Baylis do, that the arguments against crossing species boundaries have been shown to be largely unsatisfactory. He notes that there continues to be considerable disagreement about the propriety of crossing species boundaries but acknowledges that there still are no satisfactory principles that provide oversight on the matter.

Public Opinion and Biotechnology

Jason Scott Robert and Françoise Baylis (2003) hypothesize that what explains public worries about human-to-animal embryonic chimeras (henceforth, "chimeras") is the concern that "the existence of such beings would introduce inexorable moral confusion in our existing relationships with nonhuman animals and in our future relationships with part-human hybrids and chimaeras." Thus, what worries people is a consequentialist concern, namely, that the creation of chimeras will undermine the usefulness of perceived, even if fictitious, boundaries.

Robert and Baylis offer no empirical evidence to support this claim, and there is substantial evidence against it. The U.S. Office of Technology Assessment's (OTA) report on public perceptions of biotechnology, which remains the most comprehensive study of its kind, found that consequentialist concerns were cited by only a meager 1% (for environmental concerns) to 8% (for unforeseen consequences) of the respondents who believed that creating cross-species plants or animals was morally wrong (OTA 1987). Concerns about playing God and tampering with nature were much more prevalent, and the concern Robert and Baylis hypothesize apparently didn't even merit reporting by the OTA.

At any rate, it would be both surprising and disappointing if oversight bodies gave weight to the concern about moral confusion that Robert and Baylis say is at the heart of the public controversy. To prevent scientific research on the grounds that it would force people to reexamine a particular moral view by demonstrating the falsity of its underlying factual assumptions would be to prevent not only scientific progress but moral progress as well.

Crossing Species Boundaries

Public opinion aside, what about Robert and Baylis's substantive criticisms of the argument that creating chimeras is wrong because it involves crossing species boundaries? Their first criticism arises from their claim that there are intractable disagreements surrounding how to define "the species *Homo sapiens*." Their second criticism arises from their claim that species boundaries are fluid, not fixed.

Conceding both claims, if only for the sake of argument, it still remains that Robert and Baylis provide little explanation as to how those claims provide reasons against the idea that crossing species boundaries is morally problematic. Indeed, I doubt that these claims actually do provide any such reasons.

There are, after all, intractable disagreements about how to delineate many key concepts relevant to ethics: killing and letting die, life and death, consciousness, rationality, equality, respect, rights, goodness. This does not imply that these concepts are morally irrelevant. The presence of those intractable disagreements will tempt some to moral relativism, but my view, which I won't argue for here, is the opposite: intractable disagreement typically means that there is an objective fact of the matter (Streiffer 2003).

Nor does the moral relevance of species boundaries require "the erection of fixed boundaries" between species. It is clear, for example, that the groups constituting one's family and one's fellow citizens change over time (and, it might be added, are subject to numerous indeterminacies and controversies), and yet the boundaries of those groups retain robust moral significance. Thus, fixed boundaries are not necessary for moral relevance.

Robert and Baylis make a third criticism: "Indeed, why should there be *any* ethical debate about the prospect of crossing species boundaries between human and nonhuman animals? After all, hybrids occur naturally, and there is a significant amount of gene flow between species in nature" (emphasis in original). The unstated assumption is that if something happens in nature, then there is nothing wrong with our doing it. Clearly this is false.

Perhaps the following is a more charitable interpretation of their remarks: Some people object to crossing species boundaries on the grounds that it is unnatural. But given that horizontal gene flow between species occurs in nature, it isn't unnatural.

But naturalness is relative to the agent who is performing the action. It can be natural for fish to live underwater without its being natural for human beings to live underwater. Similarly, it can be natural for bacteria to move genes across species boundaries without it being natural for human beings to do so.

The Yuck Factor

Even though Robert and Baylis's criticisms of the unnaturalness objection fail, there are difficulties in providing a positive defense of the objection as well, both in defining "unnatural" and in defending the alleged relationship between something's being unnatural and its being morally problematic. Robert and Baylis note that no one objects to mules even though they are unnatural. These difficulties have led some to reject the unnaturalness objection as muddled thinking.

But we should be wary of dismissing the objection too quickly. I have already noted the difficulties in arguing that if a concept is hard to delineate, it is morally irrelevant. And there seem to be clear examples of wrong actions where the only explanation of their wrongness appears to be that they are unnatural. Bestiality and pedophilia are wrong even when they cause no physical or psychological harm. Merely pointing to the lack of valid consent certainly won't explain their wrongness: children and animals cannot give valid consent to *anything* done to them.

At this stage in the dialectic, the unnaturalness objection can be supplemented by considerations of the "yuck factor." Proponents of the yuck factor argue that the revulsion some people experience in contemplating certain activities sometimes suffices for knowing that the activity is wrong, even in the absence of satisfactory justification for the revulsion. So proponents of the unnaturalness objection can insist that in spite of the above difficulties, they still know that crossing species boundaries is wrong.

Some think that the yuck factor has been discredited because it has been used to rationalize discrimination (Thompson 2000). Racists claimed to "know simply by looking" that interracial marriages were wrong. But the fact that an argument has been used inappropriately in some areas does not mean that it is inappropriate in other areas. Paternalistic arguments were used to rationalize unjust treatment of women, but that doesn't mean that they are inappropriate when applied to children.

Even opponents of the yuck factor must concede that, sometimes, we know that an action is wrong merely on the basis of our reaction to it, even if we cannot satisfactorily justify that reaction. We know it is wrong to kill a healthy person so that his organs can be used to save five lives, even though we presently lack any theoretically satisfactory way of distinguishing that case from the various trolley cases prominent in the killing/letting-die literature. Robert and Baylis's epistemological claim that intuitions must be justified if they are to "have any moral force" is mistaken.

Should the repugnance some feel at the crossing of species boundaries be dismissed (as the reaction of a racist should be), or does it constitute yet another intuition in a long line of intuitions where our difficulties in providing satisfactory theoretical explanations merely indicate theoretical inadequacy? Given the poor state of the arguments on both sides of this debate, it is too early to tell.

Conclusion

It therefore seems premature to conclude, as Robert and Baylis do, that the arguments against crossing species boundaries have been "shown" to be "largely unsatisfactory." This issue deserves continued investigation to provide guidance to those conducting, overseeing, and funding the relevant research. Two examples illustrate this need.

First, at a recent conference to discuss standards for human embryonic stem (HES) cell research, scientists failed to reach a consensus because of disagreement about how to handle chimeras (Dewitt 2002).

Second, during our deliberations in the University of Wisconsin (UW) Bioethics Advisory Committee (2001), we flagged research involving the introduction of HES cells into animals early in fetal development as requiring "special review." But we have yet to satisfactorily articulate the principles that should govern that review. Because of the Wisconsin Alumni Research Foundation's patents on HES cell lines and because UW's HES cell lines are considered the gold standard, UW's policy will constrain HES cell researchers worldwide. Thus, it is obviously important that progress be made on this issue.

Acknowledgments

Thanks to Alan Rubel for helpful discussion. This material is based upon work supported by the Cooperative State Research, Education, and Extension Service, U.S. Department of Agriculture, under Agreement No. 00-52100-9617. Any opinions, findings, conclusions, or recommendations expressed in this publication are those of the author and do not necessarily reflect the views of the U.S. Department of Agriculture.

References

Dewitt, N. 2002. Stem-cell proposal stirs debate. *Wall Street Journal*, 22 November, p. A7, European edition.
Office of Technology Assessment. 1987. *New developments in biotechnology: Background paper: Public perceptions of biotechnology*. OTA-BP-BA–45. Washington: GPO.
Robert, J. S., and F. Baylis. 2003. Crossing species boundaries. *The American Journal of Bioethics* 3(3): 1–13.
Streiffer, R. 2003. *Moral relativism and reasons for action*. New York: Routledge.
Thompson, P. 2000. *Food and agricultural biotechnology: Incorporating ethical considerations*. Ottawa: Canadian Biotechnology Advisory Committee.
University of Wisconsin. Bioethics Advisory Committee. 2001. *Second report of the bioethics advisory committee on human embryonic stem cell research at the university of Wisconsin-Madison*. Madison: University of Wisconsin.

49 Animal Genetic Manipulation
A Utilitarian Response

Kevin R. Smith

Smith considers several objections to genetically manipulating animals. He rejects the belief that deliberate genetic sequence change is intrinsically wrong, and the belief that such knowledge will inevitably lead to human genetic manipulation. Smith proposes that the concept of replaceability can justify the killing of transgenic animals, but he supports a general prohibition on transgenic studies that entail significant suffering of animals.

Is it morally acceptable to genetically manipulate animals? I shall address this question by outlining the process and outcomes of animal genetic manipulation with reference to its morally salient features, followed by a discussion of various objections to the genetic manipulation of animals.

Background to Animal Genetic Manipulation

[. . .]

Biologists view transgenic animals as essential research tools. This is particularly so for research into complex systems, involving interactions between different cells or organs. Transgenic animals are especially valued for their medical use as models of human disease. Such animal models are valued as means for the exploration of abnormal functioning and as testbeds for new therapies.

The agricultural biotechnology industry uses transgenic research in pursuit of quantitative and qualitative changes in animal products. Potential quantitative changes include more milk, more meat and more wool, while potential qualitative changes include altered milk composition (for example, to make cow's milk more suitable for human babies), leaner meat and pest-resistant wool.

Truly novel uses of transgenic animals are also under development. For example, transgenic animals as 'bioreactors' are able to produce human proteins. Such proteins, produced in the milk, have potential medical uses. Another example is research aimed at producing transgenic animals with human-compatible organs for human transplantation ('xenotransplantation').

A final point concerns the types of animals used for transgenesis. Although transgenesis has been successfully carried out on a very wide range of animals, ranging from insects to primates, more than 99 per cent of transgenic animals currently produced are laboratory mice.

The Process of Transgenesis

Consideration of the morality of animal genetic manipulation requires an understanding of the actual steps involved in transgenesis. This section aims to furnish such an understanding. Aspects that have moral salience are emphasised, and technical (scientific) language is minimised as far as possible.

General Features of Transgenesis

Foreign DNA molecules (termed 'transgenes') are introduced to a host embryo such that the resident genetic sequence (the 'genome') of the embryo—and hence that of the resulting animal—is altered by the incoming transgene genetic sequences. In most forms of transgenesis (see below), host embryos must be removed from the reproductive tracts of 'donor' females. Donor females are prepared for embryo collection by a course of hormone injections. Embryos may be collected from large agricultural animals by the relatively non-invasive procedure of 'flushing' the upper portions of the reproductive tract via the vagina. For smaller animals, surgery is used or, as is the case with mice, donor females are killed to allow efficient embryo collection. Genetically manipulated embryos are transferred to the reproductive tract of a 'recipient' female. Recipients must be in a 'pseudopregnant' state; this is induced by hormone injections and/or by mating the recipients with vasectomised males. In most animal types, including mice, embryo transfer requires surgery under general anaesthesia. When the potentially transgenic offspring are born, tissue samples (typically blood or skin) must be taken to enable laboratory determination of transgeneity. Most methods of transgenesis are less than 100 per cent efficient: the majority of potentially transgenic offspring test negative for transgene genetic sequences. Such animals are routinely killed. Finally, depending on the degree of precision of genetic manipulation associated with each method of transgenesis, further killing occurs when transgenic animals do not satisfy desired criteria.

Specific Methods of Transgenesis

There are several available methods for the genetic manipulation of animals. [. . .] See below for a tabulation of transgenic methods and their associated *prima facie* morally salient features (Table 49.1).

Table 49.1 Transgenic Methods and Associated *Prima Facie* Morally Salient Features

Method of Transgenesis	Donor Females as Egg/ embryo Source?	Physical Manipulation of Host Embryos?	Pseudo-pregnant Females as Recipients?	Killing of Non-Transgenic Offspring?	Wastage through Lack of in vitro Selection?
Retroviral Transfer	Yes, 8-cell embryos	Not usually required	Yes	Yes, only ca. 30% transgenic	Yes
Pronuclear Microinjection	Yes, one-cell embryos	Yes, by injection into one-cell embryos	Yes	Yes, only ca. 25% transgenic	Yes
ESCs* Transgenesis	Yes, early embryos (and as original source of ESCs)	Yes, by addition of ESCs to embryos	Yes	Yes, only ca. 40% germline transgenic	No
Nuclear Transfer Transgenesis	Yes, unfertilised eggs	Yes, transfer of cell nuclei into enucleated eggs	Yes	No, all selected embryos transgenic	No
Sperm-Mediated Transgenesis	Only for non-AI* methods	Only for ICSI* methods	Only for non-AI methods	Yes, not all animals expected to be transgenic	Yes

* ESCs = embryonic stem cells; AI = artificial insemination; ICSI = intra cytoplasmic sperm injection

Outcomes of Transgenesis

The outcomes of genetic manipulation, comparing transgenic animals with their non-manipulated counterparts fall into three main categories: 1. No physiological changes expected; 2. Physiological changes that do not cause suffering; 3. Physiological changes that are likely to cause suffering.

Some transgenic experiments do not aim to alter physiology. An example would be attempts to direct a transgene to a particular non-essential part of the genome, as part of fundamental studies of gene targeting.

[. . .]

Transgene-induced physiological changes need not necessarily cause suffering to the host animals. For example, human proteins produced in the milk of transgenic ewes have no detrimental effects on the lactating animals. [. . .] There are many more examples of such transgene-induced physiological changes, in which suffering is not entailed. Utilitarians have no clear grounds for objecting to such outcomes of transgenesis.

[. . .]

Certain transgene-induced physiological changes may cause animal suffering as an incidental effect of the purpose of the experimentation. [. . .] Suffering is more certain in animals manipulated to develop a specific disease that, in humans, has pain as a central feature. Many such transgenic disease 'models' have been created. For example, transgenic mice have been produced which reliably develop certain cancers. The induction of pain, such as that resulting from invasive tumours, is only justifiable to utilitarians if outweighed by the avoidance of a greater amount of suffering elsewhere. Of course, a central defence of transgenic disease models is that 'the end justifies the means,' in that animal suffering is claimed to be outweighed by alleviation of suffering from cancer arising from experiments on transgenic models. I shall take up this issue later.

[. . .]

Moral Objections to Transgenesis

I am not persuaded by arguments from pro-animal absolutism, and this discussion of objections to transgenesis will start from the assumption, shared by most forms of utilitarianism, that *some* research with animals is morally permissible.

I will consider the following claims:

1. Transgenesis is objectionable because it is intrinsically wrong to deliberately alter genetic sequences.
2. Transgenesis is objectionable because it may lead to the genetic manipulation of humans.
3. Transgenesis is objectionable because it necessitates the killing of animals.
4. Transgenesis is objectionable because it involves the infliction of suffering on animals.

Intrinsic Wrongness of Deliberate Sequence Alteration

Genetic manipulation entails the deliberate alteration of genetic sequences within the genome. The same fundamental process of sequence alteration occurs as a result of genetic selection, both natural (as with evolution) and artificial (as with selective breeding of domesticated plants and animals). In terms of sequence alteration, the only significant difference between genetic manipulation and genetic selection is that the former process is much faster than the latter. Thus, an assault on the ethics of transgenesis based on a notion of the intrinsic wrongness of sequence manipulation would be sustainable only as a subset of a much broader assault on all forms of *deliberate sequence altera-tion* (DSA). A coherent anti-DSA argument would entail the approval or acceptance of sequence alterations occurring naturally (from evolution) and the rejection of deliberate forms of alteration (breeding and genetic manipulation). Thus, to assume an ethical stance against DSA would be to subscribe to an unsubtle 'naturalistic fallacy.' Further, it is difficult to see how any form of utilitarian argument could be made against DSA in respect of its actual historical consequences, considering the vast expansion of thriving humanity that would not have been possible without centuries of selective breeding of domesticated plants and animals.

[. . .]

Thus, I hold that genetic sequence alteration *per se* is ethically neutral. [. . .] Assuming genetic sequence alteration *per se* to be ethically acceptable, it follows that the genetic sequence alteration inherent in animal transgenesis must also be considered ethically acceptable.

Risks of Genetic Manipulation Being Applied to Humans

Some people object to transgenic research because they take the view that such work represents the 'thin end of a wedge' towards human genetic manipulation. Without doubt, the spectre of human genetic manipulation raises a plethora of moral questions. However, the fact is that most current transgenic techniques could (in principle) be readily applied to humans. Therefore, if the 'wedge' argument represents a valid objection to transgenesis, time has rendered such an objection passé.

However, the following variant of the 'wedge' objection avoids the charge of outmodedness: If transgenesis is allowed to proceed, it will increasingly be applied to 'higher' animals including primates, until the 'highest' primates—humans—become the next easy step. [. . .] The first premise for this objection is difficult to contest: higher animals *will* undoubtedly be used with increasing frequency, assuming continued progress in transgenic science. In addition, there may well be moral grounds for objecting to (at least some aspects of) transgenesis when particular non-human animals are concerned, where such animals have attributes of 'persons.'

However, the preceding 'wedge' argument depends crucially upon a claimed 'easy step' from non-human to human transgenesis. Is this notion of an 'easy step' valid? It is difficult to make a coherent case in its favour. Peoples of all cultures appear well able to discern a firm human/non-human line in terms of what is deemed permissible within each category.

I conclude that, if transgenesis really is the 'thin end of a wedge' on the way to human genetic manipulation, the onus must rest with the proponents of such a position to come forward with persuasive arguments.

Wrongness from Killing

The production of transgenics undoubtedly necessitates the *killing* of many animals (such as animals that either fail to become transgenic or fail to express the transgene appropriately). The argument may be advanced that, since it is wrong *prima facie* to kill, it is wrong to produce transgenics. However, this position is opposed by the 'replaceability argument,' which holds that it is not wrong to kill if a death is 'balanced' by the bringing into existence of another (equally happy) life. This situation is generally the case with transgenic science, where animals killed are replaced by breeding.

Assuming that significant suffering is not inflicted from an instance of killing (whether directly to the individual being killed or to others as a 'side-effect'[1]), it is difficult for utilitarians to argue against the replaceability argument. One objection to replaceability runs as follows: replaceability does not apply to humans, therefore to invoke the replaceability argument in the case of non-human animals is speciesist. A more sophisticated variant of this objection is the appeal to 'personhood,' which starts by dividing sentient life into 'self-conscious' *vs.* 'non-self-conscious' beings.[2] The designation 'self-consciousness' denotes entities that are aware of themselves as distinct entities with a past and a future—entities that we may readily describe as 'persons.' Human beings (except for those with severe neurological deficits) are undoubtedly self-conscious, while very simple life forms (e.g. insects, assuming these to be sentient) are probably non-self-conscious. Proponents of this approach hold that replaceability may be applied to non-self-conscious entities but not to self-conscious entities—those with personhood. This personhood approach is plausible, but it contains at least two major weaknesses. Firstly, it is difficult to give strong reasons for viewing self-conscious entities as non-replaceable. Possibly the least flawed reason is the 'life as a journey' metaphor, where a self-conscious life is held to be inherently non-replaceable, because to end such a life would be to interrupt a coherent life narrative (complete with plans and hopes for the futures) prior to its completion. However, it is not clear why one such 'journey' may not be potentially replaceable by another, equally enjoyable 'journey,' or why one large 'journey' may not be replaced by several smaller 'journeys.'

A second weakness of the personhood approach is the very real problem of attributing personhood. [. . .] [A]t the present time, it is impossible to say with confidence which, if any, of the animals commonly used for transgenesis (i.e. mice, sheep, pigs) merit the designation 'persons.'

Thus, the debate on killing and replaceability has not been resolved. [. . .] [A]n 'intermediate position' is highly desirable, in which a *provisional* line is drawn between animals deemed 'persons' and others not so designated, pending ongoing research into personhood. This provisional division would need to be based on (a) the (few) specific research findings presently available, and (b) on general observations of animal behaviour. On this approach, my own tentative preference would be to attribute personhood to (for example) pigs, rats and all higher primates, and withhold it from (for example) mice, sheep and chickens. However, such preferences are inevitably highly subjective. There is no perfect way to avoid such subjectivity, but a 'jury' approach, in which a group of 'disinterested' people is asked to provisionally attribute/withhold personhood, may be the best way forward.

I conclude that, categorisation difficulties notwithstanding, if the moral validity of personhood is accepted, transgenesis (in so far as killing is concerned) ought to be restricted to non-self-conscious animals.

Wrongness from Suffering

I suggest that animal suffering gives the strongest grounds for objection to transgenesis. Specifically, I propose that *prohibition* should be considered in cases where either of the following negative consequences are entailed:

A. Significant suffering arising in any animals used in the process of transgenesis.
B. Significant suffering arising in transgenics from the development of a pathological condition engineered into the animals' genetic makeup.

I use the term '*significant suffering*' to exclude suffering likely to occur to an animal in a non-experimental situation. [. . .] If the extent of suffering unavoidably entailed by a particular transgenic approach is clearly less than that likely to occur inevitably in the life of the animal, utilitarians have no clear grounds for objection.

Other occurrences of suffering may be associated with transgenesis, such as suffering arising from failures in basic welfare provision (unsuitable animal accommodation, lack of veterinary care, etc.), and suffering arising from subsequent experimentation on transgenics (invasive surgery, stressful procedures, etc.). These occurrences of suffering have clear moral content. Moreover, the stringency of steps necessary to genuinely ensure adequate welfare may be formidable. For example, the happiness of some higher primates depends *inter alia* on the existence of environmental features such as extensive climbing opportunities, and on the freedom to engage in social groupings, all of which ought (morally) to be provided for such animals, as a prerequisite for any experimentation. Even laboratory mice require extensive welfare provision, such as adequately large cages with features to allow exploration. However, because such welfare issues are not the special reserve of *transgenic* animal science, I will not consider them in this discussion.

Although I propose that prohibition should be considered for negative consequences A and B (above), this should not be taken to mean transgenic cases entailing A or B ought automatically to be prevented. Rather, it is necessary, at least in principle, to weigh costs (significant suffering) against potential benefits (for example, a contribution to the development of a new anticancer drug).

Conclusion

Although conceptually simple, the calculus described above is notoriously difficult to conduct in practice. In the following sections, I shall consider the methods and outcomes of transgenesis from the perspective of significant suffering. I shall argue that there ought to be a strong presumption in favour of prohibition, in transgenic cases involving significant suffering where the extent, value or likelihood of realisation of a potential benefit is uncertain.

Methods of Transgenesis

From the perspective of suffering, there are two key morally salient features of genetic manipulation that can lead to negative mental states, such as pain and fear. These features are (i) invasive procedures to recover and transfer embryos, and (ii) killing of animals involved in or arising from transgenesis.[3]

The first question should be: Can the degree of suffering arising from (i) and (ii) be *reduced*, without jeopardising the scientific purposes of transgenic experiments? An affirmative answer is possible for cases in which one method of transgenesis could be substituted for another. The various methods of transgenesis are not all equal in respect of features (i) and (ii). From Table 49.1, it is apparent that both the 'traditional' methods of transgenesis (pronuclear microinjection and ESCs) entail features (i) and (ii). This is in contrast with the more 'novel' methods (nuclear transfer and sperm-mediated transgenesis). Given that nuclear transfer transgenesis allows the pre-selection of transgene-positive embryos, this method should largely avoid the need to kill non-transgenic offspring. However, invasive procedures (for the recovery and transfer of embryos) are still necessitated by nuclear transfer transgenesis. Conversely, sperm-mediated transgenesis, coupled with artificial insemination, retains the need for killing while avoiding the need for invasive procedures. Thus, substitution of a 'novel' method of transgenesis for one of the 'traditional' methods may permit a reduction in suffering. If such a substitution can be made without undermining experimental objectives, then it follows that such substitutions ought to be made wherever possible. However, it is important to emphasise that, as discussed previously, nuclear transfer transgenesis is in its infancy and sperm-mediated transgenesis is very far from being established as a viable method. Therefore, reducing suffering by choice of transgenesis method should be seen as a future possibility rather than as a practical proposition at present.

Thus, it seems undeniable that the process of transgenesis inevitably entails *some* (significant) suffering. The question now becomes: is this suffering outweighed by good consequences? I suggest that—assuming impeccable welfare provisions—an affirmative answer should be given. The 'good consequences' arising from transgenesis may be summarised under the heading of 'scientific progress.' As discussed previously, the scientific value of transgenesis can be in no doubt. Most forms of utilitarianism view scientific progress (in terms of an increased understanding of nature, and of the possible beneficial uses from such understanding) as morally desirable. Thus, prevention of transgenic research *per se* would only be justifiable on the grounds of major negative consequences. I contend that the inevitable significant suffering entailed by transgenesis is insufficiently large to outweigh the benefits to society arising from the contribution of transgenesis to scientific progress. The amount of significant suffering implicit in transgenesis cannot be quantified. However, the suffering actually entailed by the invasive procedures and killing used in transgenesis ought to be relatively minimal. Typically, donor and recipient animals are used only once in their lifetimes: this is in marked contrast to the many protracted experiments that 'ordinary' laboratory animals endure.

424 Kevin R. Smith

Moreover, the procedures themselves are not of a severe nature: at worst (but under proper welfare conditions), embryo collection or transfer is akin to the sterilisation operations commonly used with household pet animals. Similarly, euthanasia is the most frequent fate of pet animals.

In summary: although all possible steps ought to be taken to reduce the amount of suffering entailed in the process of transgenesis, it would be wrong to prohibit animal genetic manipulation *per se*.

Outcomes of Transgenesis

As discussed previously, the outcomes of transgenesis that have relevance here are those that are likely to cause suffering. Taking this category of transgenic outcomes in general, the consequences are of the same type as those for transgenesis *per se*, scientific progress is the benefit; and suffering is the cost. However, the degree of suffering implicit in this category of outcomes is greater than is the case for the process of transgenesis. On *prima facie* grounds, I contend that transgenic outcomes that cause significant suffering are contenders for prohibition. I suggest that utilitarians take a 'default' position in which experimentation entailing such negative transgenic outcomes is deemed unacceptable, unless (on a case-by-case basis) a watertight argument has been made to the effect that suffering is clearly outweighed by good consequences. For example, the generation of transgenics that develop an analogue of a painful human cancer ought to be permissible only if the experimenters could clearly demonstrate a major, tangible, high probability payoff in terms of a specific advance in cancer treatment. The difficulties in practice of convincingly demonstrating such benefits should not be underestimated: the majority of research using transgenic disease models is *not* expected to yield discernible immediate medical benefits. Moreover, there are many forms of transgenic experimentation for which a cost-benefit justification is *impossible*: for example, pain research may well fall into this category.

What I am suggesting is that, in the case of protracted or acute significant suffering arising in transgenic animals, the general 'scientific progress' benefit (although undeniable) is simply too nebulous to justify such experimentation. By contrast, there are circumstances in which one might envisage very direct benefits to humans that are both highly probable and highly proximate. In such exceptional cases, where it can be firmly demonstrated that the significant suffering of transgenic animals would be outweighed by the prevention of such suffering in humans (or by the saving of many human lives that would otherwise be lost), the prohibition ought to be lifted.

This 'default prohibition' position has radical implications because its application would entail the proscription of many transgenic experiments. However, unless the misconceived equation of utilitarianism with the notion 'the end always justifies the means' is accepted, or speciesism is resorted to, default prohibition appears to be the only coherent position compatible with utilitarianism. The alternative is that we would have to accept the doctrine of 'anything goes' in the name of scientific progress: I assume it axiomatic that no utilitarian would accept such a doctrine.

Notes

1. For example, other animals might become terrified as a consequence of their awareness of a nearby killing.
2. See P. Singer. 1993. *Practical Ethics*, 2nd ed. Cambridge, Cambridge University Press: 110–31.
3. Although killing may in principle be free of suffering, I suggest that this is so difficult to achieve in practice that the safest option is to assume *some* suffering, even under the most humane conditions.

50 The Inevitability of Animal Biotechnology?

Ethics and the Scientific Attitude

Jeffrey Burkhardt

Burkhardt believes that a moral or ethical re-education of scientists and science policy makers is essential if ethical thinking is to enter the scientific establishment. He further believes that fundamental changes in the scientific attitude would be necessary for any ethical arguments to have force and that there probably will be considerable resistance to inclusion of ethical matters in scientific training. He argues that only when ethics becomes an established part of scientific thinking can the issues of the morality of using animals or the propriety of biotechnology be understood by scientists.

Introduction

Most observers of biotechnology are aware that the main standard critiques of animal biotechnology are based on either animal rights/welfare arguments, ecological-oriented arguments, or socioeconomic consequences arguments. In this chapter, I want to suggest that despite the logic or seeming appropriateness of many of these critiques, they lack *ethical force*. By this I mean that the arguments (and the arguers) are unlikely to actually change the minds of those engaged in biotechnology practices and policy-making (Stevenson, 1944; Olshevsky, 1983). This is because of the orientation or attitude of those entrusted with doing and overseeing biotechnological work with non-human animal species. I will argue that this orientation must change before ethical arguments concerning animal biotechnology, indeed ethics generally (in the philosophical sense as opposed to legalistic or professional courtesy senses), mean anything to the scientific community. [. . .]

There are philosophical reasons, but more important, practical reasons for the proposal in this chapter. Philosophically, while some of the ethical objections to animal biotechnology or to particular biotechnology practices may be justifiable, behind many of them is a misplaced Platonic assumption that the problem with those engaged in animal biotechnology is that they do not know 'the good.' That is, if the scientists or policy makers knew or understood the philosophical objections, then they would stop doing what they are doing. The problem with this assumption is that scientists would have to accept the fundamental criteria for justifiability or reasonableness upon which philosophical argument rests before they would even fathom these criticisms as reasonable ones. This relates to my practical concern.

Practically, the rights/welfare, environment/ecology, and socioeconomic approaches are usually bound to fall on deaf ears. Arguments concerning 'ethics and animal biotechnology' are generally irrelevant, at best, to the actual members of the bioscience community or 'Science Establishment.' Scientists and policy makers may fathom some ethical concerns when their scientific or policy-making 'hats' are off. But to scientists and science-oriented policy makers *qua* scientists and science-oriented policy makers, proponents of animal rights/welfare arguments, environmental/ecological ethics arguments, or social justice arguments, can easily be relegated to the role of 'philosophers crying in the wind' (or howling at the moon). Ethical arguments which do not first assume the *a priori* legitimacy of whatever the scientific enterprise has decided to pursue are bound to be 'external' and 'externalized.' [. . .] My belief is that we should accept the inevitability of continued animal biotechnology research and development, and hope that the legalistic-type controls now in place in many nations continue to work or work even better. In the meantime, we should also 'sympathetically' impress on scientists the value of ethical reflection on their work.

Why the Standard Ethical Critiques Fail

Animal Welfare, Rights, and Natural Kinds Arguments

Animal rights or animal welfare arguments regarding animal biotechnology arise because in all of these biotechnology activities, non-human animals are *involved*. The strongest argument objects to the use of animals *per se*. The rights argument, articulated so forcefully initially by Regan (1985), maintains that individuality and 'subject-of-a-life'-hood of non-human animals (in particular larger mammals) ethically demands their being treated in a quasi-Kantian manner: as ends in themselves, with appropriate stakes in life, liberty, and self-actualization. Genetically altering an individual non-human animal, either before or after conception, *ipso facto* intrudes upon the autonomy of the being.

[. . .]

The philosophical underpinnings to the rights objection to animal biotechnology are easily countered by the scientific community. Most direct genetic engineering of animals (i.e. altering an animal's genetic structure) is performed either so early in the fetal developmental process that a distinct individual animal (in terms of moral autonomy) is indiscernible, or, more often, occurs even before conception takes place. Under any or all of Regan's criterion of the animal's having some rudimentary consciousness, or Singer's criterion of sentience, or Fox's criterion of 'telos-possession' (Fox, 1990), there is no 'subject of a life' (Rachels, 1990) whose inherent value or rights or unique purpose are disrespected through the engineering process.

[. . .]

Rights or welfare arguments may be appropriate to an appraisal of some biotechnology techniques, nonetheless. In particular, the use of biotechnologically produced hormones, pharmaceuticals, and other agents may be seen as in some way disrespecting animals' rights or may cause a decrease in welfare. Using a chemical which artificially increases milk production in dairy cows, but which also increases incidences of disease (mastitis) and shortens an individual cow's productive life (and by implication, its life), may be bad for the cow in both rights and welfare terms. The issue here is, however, less an animal biotechnology matter than a simple matter of people using cows in dairy production systems.

[. . .]

One final point on the rights/welfare approaches: if any ethical concession is to be made to the fact that animals are used by humans, then some animal biotechnology may in fact be more ethical than some other research and production practices currently employed. If, as various humane societies have argued, better treatment of non-human animals ought to be our goal, biotechnology might be precisely the means to achieve that goal. This would, of course, depend on exactly what is being done with or to the animals, individually or by species (see, for example, NABC, 1992).

The natural kinds argument is the other main kind of animal-based objection to genetic engineering. Rifkin (1983) argued that the very ideology of genetic engineering—'algeny'—challenged the naturalness of those species which were either created by God or evolved through natural selection. Independent of the potentially disastrous ecological consequences of tampering with these long-standing kinds, there is a fundamentally immoral audacity in those people who would 'play God' and change the natural order for whatever purposes they intended.

[. . .]

Again, there are science-based replies to natural kinds arguments. Simply stated, humans have used animals for millennia, and in many respects, the very animal species which they used now exist only because of their use.

[. . .]

In terms of ethical force, the appropriate ethical critiques of animal biotechnology are not, at least as animal biotechnology is currently practised, either the animal rights/welfare sorts of argument or the natural kinds approach advanced by Rifkin. These kinds of criticisms, which I refer to as 'intrinsic' critiques, can generally be met with reasonable points about either the nature of the practices performed on animals, or the extent to which they produce suffering, or the extent to which they are no different in principle from any other animal-using scientific practice. I suggest that other, 'extrinsic' or consequentialist critiques may be more appropriate and forceful challenges to biotechnology, to the extent that there is science-based (and hence, 'reasonable') evidence to support their claims. I will argue, nevertheless, that these criticisms can also fail because they miss major points about what biotechnology, and animal biotechnology in particular, can potentially do.

Consequentialist Critiques and Irreversibility Arguments

Consequentialist-type arguments regarding animal biotechnology usually focus on ecological or socioeconomic cultural ills associated with biotechnology in general, and animal biotechnology in particular. One common theme among these arguments, and, perhaps, underlying fear among their proponents, is that these consequences are or may tend to be irreversible: that is, once the technology or its products have been developed, adopted, or widely used or released into the world, severe negative effects will obtain which will be difficult or impossible to stop or reverse (Comstock, 1990).

The ecological arguments are most straightforward, though most originally were advanced with respect to microorganisms and plant species with little thought given to (larger) animal implications. According to this line of argument, a genetically altered individual or species of organism is necessarily different from its natural or wild counterpart. In fact, the reason behind genetic engineering is to design plants, animals, or organisms with traits which would allow the organism to cope with the environment in ways different from the non-engineered kin, for instance withstand different and hostile climatic conditions, resist pests, better absorb nutrients from the environment. [. . .] These creatures of bioengineering were intended to perform in their environments in ways to be preferred to those of their natural relatives.

The prime concern of the ecological-ethical critique is that bioengineered organisms, once outside controlled laboratory conditions, might behave in ecologically inappropriate ways. For instance, the engineered species might out-compete its natural relatives to the point of the extinction of the latter; or new predator species might evolve in response to the changes in the original species; or the new species just might grow out of control; or the new species might simply upset the 'biotic community' (Holland, 1990). [. . .] Note that it is again not bioengineering *per se* that is at issue. Rather, it is the *results* of bioengineering.

[. . .]

There may be sound moral premises behind this critique, such as, 'We morally should not risk ecosystemic disruption because of risks to present or future people or to the ecosystem itself.' Once we have allowed these organisms into the environment, we cannot get them back. Even so, there is again a reasonable reply in this case. We risk ecosystemic disruption all the time, and in fact *cause* ecosystemic disruption through many things much more dangerous than genetically engineered animals or animal products. So, unless the point is that we should leave the ecosystem alone, a practical impossibility, these potential ecosystemic disruptions are not necessarily immoral. [. . .] Because we know the genetic makeup of the engineered species even better than that of the non-engineered ones, we are in fact in a better position to control the new species or even eradicate those individuals who begin to get out of control.

[. . .]

Risk and irreversibility are also behind the economic and social consequentialist arguments vis-à-vis biotechnology. The argument here is that, unlike ecosystemic behaviour, we have clear precedents with respect to how new technologies affect social or economic behaviour, relationships, or structures (Burkhardt, 1988). On this basis, it is argued that animal biotechnology is potentially socially disastrous, and hence likely to be immoral in that regard.

[. . .]

Despite the force of ethical precedents, the reply to socioeconomic criticisms is straightforward. [. . .] The objection to biotechnology's socioeconomic consequences is really an objection to technology in general, or perhaps to capitalist socioeconomic arrangements. [. . .] [A]ny [. . .] particular product or process might change socioeconomic relations, but that is not the fault of the technology, only the system into which it is introduced (Burkhardt, 1991).

[. . .]

There is one further consequentialist argument to attend to here. This might be called the 'cultural consequence' argument. [. . .] [W]idespread diffusion of biotechnological products (from altered animals and plants to bioengineered chemicals and food products) might open the door for general public acceptance of the ethical appropriateness of engineering *people*. [. . .] As more biotechnology becomes the norm, a whole culture might come to accept whatever is bioengineered as even morally preferable to the non-engineered. Given *real* slippery slopes in attitudes, and *real* risks to longstanding human values such as freedom of choice and perhaps diversity among people, biotechnology accordingly is a cultural threat.

Like the potential ecological consequences critique, this last concern plays up the element of uncertainty. Unlike the environmental/ecological position, however, it is less a matter of how bioengineered organisms or ecosystems will behave or be affected than a matter of how people will act and react toward biotechnology. The question is whether there are any reasons for the public or policy makers to be concerned about the standard science-based reply to this position, namely, it will not happen. I will argue in the next section that the answer is predicated on whether there is indeed any reason for us to be concerned that biotechnology will continue to be employed without prior or at least concomitant ethical reflection. There may be little reason to fear biotechnology progressing, but only if biotechnology is either regulated and monitored, or ethics becomes an intrinsic part of the scientific attitude—the fundamental ideological/epistemological basis for science.

The Biotechnology Culture and the Scientific Attitude

[. . .]

A realistic appraisal of biotechnology, in general, has to begin with this fact: something in the biotechnology area has occurred, and likely will continue to occur. Philosophers and social analysts have long pointed to the power that science has in modern society. This notion was given contemporary expression and force by Rosenberg (1976) in his notion of 'Scientism'—the ideology of science solving all human problems. Scientism, it is argued, has become another dominant '-ism' of our day.

[. . .]

The extent to which Scientism undergirds both the biotechnology enterprise as practised as well as public policy regarding biotechnology is astounding. It is this fact which lends credibility to the cultural critique described above.

[. . .]

In the public policy arena, moreover, we have witnessed a gradual but steady strengthening of the power of biotechnology or bioscience in general (Busch et al., 1991). Even as funding for some specific kinds of basic research (e.g., AIDS) has been questioned by members of the United States' Congress, the general level of support for biotechnology has grown. In addition, much of the regulatory oversight which grew up in the early years of biotechnology—the late 1970s and early 1980s—has gradually devolved (NABC, 1994). Public policy priorities have shifted from concerns about the potential negative effects of biotechnological research to concerns that the advances in bioscience and especially bioengineered products are not coming fast enough. [. . .] [T]here is little reason to believe that anything short of an environmental catastrophe caused by a bioengineered product or experiment gone awry could actually cause a reduction in the enthusiasm with which biotechnology has been embraced at nearly all levels of research management, oversight, or policy-making.

[. . .]

There are a number of reasons or causes to which the biotechnology craze might be attributed. One might simply be the excitement or enchantment that members of the scientific establishment experience when, as I mentioned above, what was conceivable becomes possible, or what was possible becomes actual.

[. . .]

There are other, perhaps less noble, reasons for the degree of excitement and commitment to biotechnology in general and agricultural (plant and animal) biotechnology in particular. [. . .] The motivation also appears to have been the time element involved: whereas a new plant variety or pharmaceutical product might take several years or even decades to develop under older research methods, the new biotechnologies offered hope for quicker new products and processes. Again, in an increasingly competitive environment, the quicker the better.

Whatever the reason for the interest in and excitement about biotechnology, there is one additional glaring fact about the scientific attitude concerning biotechnology: ethical considerations such as those discussed above matter little, if at all. This orientation has permeated the science establishment. This lack of concern for deeper ethical matters, as opposed to legalities or professional courtesies, may permeate all society as well (save theologians and philosophers trying to conserve older ways of thinking about what is or is not moral). So long as science continues to deliver or at least forecast new promises—for corporations, for policy makers, and ultimately for the general public—ethics is irrelevant.

The Scientific Attitude

Biologist Frederick Grinnell, in *The Scientific Attitude* (1987), described what I take to be the underlying reason why 'ethics and science' or 'ethics and biotechnology' have been seen as beyond the pale in terms of attitudes and practices of members of the scientific community. [. . . Grinnell] hits on the idea that science must become, for scientists, a 'way of seeing' and a 'way of being.'

By 'way of seeing,' Grinnell means that the material with which much physical and biological science operates (though perhaps true of social sciences such as economics as well) is only visible once one has come to appreciate and accept the appropriate theoretical or ideological foundation.

[. . .]

The 'way of being' of the scientist is of more direct and critical concern. For, as Grinnell suggests, this means adopting 'the scientific attitude,' which in essence is to come to believe in Scientism: Rosenberg's (1976) book was aptly titled *No Other Gods*. And believing in Scientism means always being willing to act on making what is conceivable possible, and what is possible actual. In other words, to *be* a scientist (in this ideal typology), one must accept the *doctrine* that science defines what is real. Those who do not accept either that reality or its technological ramifications (the tools employed or the products created) are wrong at best, *irrational* at worst. This becomes the crux of the matter.

That this sort of attitude might engender a degree of arrogance or self-righteousness is clear (Feyerabend, 1978). However, not all individual scientists, or even most, need to or do display those personality traits. It is enough that the science establishment—research administrators, policy setters, leading scientific spokespersons—has the power to define what is or is not real, reasonable or rational. This is power in sociologist Stephen Lukes' (1986) sense of a 'third dimension' of power (the first two being physical force and persuasive ability)—the ability to define the terms in which rational discourse takes place. The work, perceptions, and professional communications of members of the scientific community all take as a given the reality and importance of scientific rationality, and whatever emanates from rational scientific work.

Scientists, including biotechnologists, may in fact be quite humble in the face of new problems, new theories, new frontiers. Nevertheless, there is a sort of moral imperative in the widely shared attitude that 'the work (of science) *must go on*' (J. Burkhardt, L. Busch and W. Lacy, personal interview, 1988). Moreover, significantly, whatever appears to impede or constrain the work of science must be based on some irrational or non-scientific force. As such, lack of funding (to the extent that some of this work lacks funding) is unreasonable. Even more unreasonable, and immoral by this doctrine, are rules, regulations, oversight committees, and reporting requirements. [. . .] In a word, constraints are unreasonable.

This characterization of the scientific attitude and Scientism undoubtedly overstates the case, and may even be questioned for grossly caricaturing science and the scientist. However, the ease with which the science establishment, and many individual scientists, can dismiss criticism or the kinds of objections to biotechnology discussed above is telling. There is not only nothing wrong with biotechnology (that is not wrong with any part of science), but to suggest otherwise is to either fail to understand science or simply be irrational. This refers back to my earlier point: any criticism or ethical concern which does not *a priori* assume the legitimacy of the scientific enterprise and the necessity of using science (including biotechnology) to solve problems must be ignored or, better, rendered impotent. One way to emasculate those criticisms is to fall back on the power that the science establishment has long had in Western society: change the terms of the discourse.

The Culture of Biotechnology

The case of bovine somatotrophin, one of the first commercial animal-affecting products to emerge from the biotechnology enterprise, is a telling example of the power of the bioscience community to actually change the terms of discourse—to the advantage of the biotechnology enterprise, of course. Bovine somatotrophin is a naturally occurring compound, produced in the pituitary glands of cows, which regulates growth and indirectly affects milk production. [. . .] Scientists at a number of United States universities, under grants or contracts with Dow Chemical and Monsanto corporations, became able in the early 1980s to produce the compound using recombinant DNA methods. The product could now be produced in greater quantities, and much more cheaply and efficiently.

Bovine somatotrophin was originally named 'bovine growth hormone' (BGH) when scientists and company representatives began touting the chemical for its potential use in animal agriculture. Quite soon afterwards, however, representatives of the bioscience establishment began to be met with resistance from consumer advocacy groups, and eventually lawsuits were even filed to prevent the US Food and Drug Administration from permitting the use of BGH in agriculture. Emphasis was placed on the nature of this compound as a *hormone*, despite scientists' and the industry's assurances that it was a non-steroidal-type hormone and would not in any adverse way affect consumers of milk from BGH-treated cows. About the same time, however, the term 'BGH' disappeared from scientific publications and company promotions. Bovine somatotrophin became known by its real abbreviation, 'BST.' The resistance and criticisms of the substance did not disappear overnight, but the bioscience establishment managed to diffuse a significant amount of consumer activists' policy-affecting power by simply redirecting the concern away from a 'hormone' to just another productivity-increasing 'treatment' (Browne, 1987).

The whole BGH/BST story is much more complicated and drawn out (Burkhardt, 1992), but just this name change element in the story is sufficient to suggest my point. With nothing more than a semantic sleight of hand, the bioscience establishment was able to effectively control the public forum as well as public policy agenda. There are undoubtedly many and more glaring cases of science winning a public relations battle or war. The only times the science establishment does not win hands down, it seems, is when it faces an equally formidable foe, for example the tobacco industry in the US, or organized religion, especially the Roman Catholic Church.

[. . .]

Critics of the agricultural research establishment have for a number of years pointed to a 'circle the wagons' mentality among people in the science establishment (Busch and Lacy, 1983). Always mindful of potential criticisms—from environmentalists, animal-rightists and animal welfarists, and small-farm and labour activists—the establishment (it was claimed) sought to dismiss or ignore the reasonableness of criticisms. In the case of the new generation of the bioscience/biotechnology community, the strategy seems more intended to pre-empt or co-opt criticisms than to ignore or dismiss them. The result is, nevertheless, that critics become marginalized, unless, again, there is significant political or social power behind them. Given the inherent (and self-defined) 'reasonableness' of the views, activities, and arguments of the scientific community, even formidable social challenges are likely to fail.

These points may suggest nothing more than that the bioscience community, including practitioners of animal biotechnology, probably have little or no reason to fear that their activities will be fundamentally challenged in the actual public arena. Moreover, to the extent that the scientific establishment is becoming more sophisticated about 'science education,' the likelihood of even a powerful challenge diminishes greatly. Science writers, science popularizers, and spokespersons for universities and corporations are out in force, promoting the legitimacy and safety of biotechnology. Surveys suggest that as the public becomes more 'informed' and 'educated' about science, concern diminishes significantly. Further, as policy makers become more informed and educated as to the relative benefits and risks of biotechnology (as defined by scientists themselves), strong legislative action is unlikely. Indeed, as mentioned above, the result of all this information and education may well be simply greater levels of funding for the biotechnology enterprise. The only conclusion to be reached is that 'the beast will go on.' The spectre of a broader, social 'culture of biotechnology,' with attendant human genetic engineering, is real.

Conclusion: Ethics by Regulation, Committee, or (Re-)Education

In the early 1970s, a gathering of concerned scientists was held in Asilomar, California, to discuss the risks and benefits of genetic engineering. What emerged from those meetings was a set of biosafety guidelines concerning biotechnology. Many of those guidelines made their way into federal regulations and general governmental oversight. Though fairly stringent at the time, the guidelines and subsequent rules have been gradually weakened. Scientists argue that, as their knowledge about bioengineering has grown, what were reasonable concerns are now known to be unfounded fears. Recall that the USDA abolished its biotechnology oversight committee. Apparently it was thought to be an unnecessary public expenditure. Most universities have in-house biosafety committees, and corporations, it has been argued, exercise extreme caution because of the risk of lawsuits or prosecution under environmental or human safety regulations.

[. . .]

The scientific establishment continues to engage in genetic engineering practices involving animals. And, technologies will continue to have impacts, some of them negative, on particular socioeconomic groups in society. Barring some sort of major catastrophe or major gestalt shift, animal biotechnology, biotechnology in general, and even more generally, technological research and development will undoubtedly continue. If ethical considerations are to fit anywhere in this scientific enterprise, it would seem that it would have to be through the current system of oversight and control or through the force of higher levels of government action. Given the power of science and Scientism, the latter is unlikely, though not impossible.

One conclusion that can be reached is this: if ethics in a substantive sense is to make its way into the scientific establishment, and the bioscience community in particular, it will have to be at least in part if not exclusively through the moral or ethical re-education of scientists and science policy makers. And the moral or ethical education of young scientists and students would also be a key. Indeed, the ethical force of particular kinds of arguments pertaining to animal biotechnology is dependent on *any* ethical argument having force. And for any ethical argument to have force, fundamental changes in the scientific attitude would be necessary. As Grinnell noted, the way of seeing and way of being of science are *learned* orientations. *Seeing* ethical considerations as inherently part of the scientific enterprise, as well as *being* an ethically aware scientist or policy maker, must also be learned.

Just as there is considerable resistance on the part of the science establishment to external control—to the point of pre-empting *rational* discussion of criticisms—there may also be considerable resistance to the inclusion of ethics as part of the indoctrination into the scientific attitude. Nevertheless, there are enough scientists who do engage in ethical reflection when their scientific 'hats are off' that there is at least some promise for ethics to be a part of the scientific mind-set. Already, there are college and university courses, colloquia, and informal discussion among members of the bioscience community about 'science ethics.' With considerable effort on the part of theologians, philosophers, and social scientists—duly respectful of the ability of science to define the terms of rational discussion—more such inclusion of ethics might continue.

Only when ethics becomes a legitimate—and rational—part of the scientific attitude will concerns about particular aspects of animal biotechnology be taken seriously, or taken at all. Only when ethics is a routine concern among scientists will considerations of whether we should be using animals, or engaging in biotechnology, even be fathomed. I do not believe that we will stop using animals in research (or for food purposes) in the near future. Nor do I believe that the scientific establishment will stop engaging in biotechnology any time soon, if at all. I do believe, however, that any critique which does not first address the need for including discussion of ethics in the very process of 'doing science' is doomed to failure. It does little practical or political good to challenge science from the outside. Rather, rational, informed, science-based discussion of ethical considerations has to be the key to whether continued biotechnological research and development, whether in the animal, plant, or human domains, will simply be inevitable.

Note

A considerable amount of the 'evidence' for the theses in this chapter is based on 'research' performed by the author, a professional philosopher, but whose appointment is in the agricultural science college at a major state university in the US. Although the author wishes to indict no particular scientists or administrators for espousing 'the scientific attitude,' or especially indict them for 'ethical insensitivity,' both orientations have been found to be extant (though the former far more prevalent) among the physical and biological scientists with whom the author interacts on a daily basis.

References

Browne, W. (1987) Bovine Growth Hormone and the Politics of Uncertainty: Fear and Loathing in a Transitional Agriculture. *Agriculture and Human Values,* **4** (1): 75–80.
Burkhardt, J. (1988) Biotechnology, Ethics, and the Structure of Agriculture. *Agriculture and Human Values,* **4** (2): 53–60.
———. (1991) The Value Measure in Public Agricultural Research, Chpt 4, pp. 79–105, in *Beyond the Large Farm* (eds P. Thompson and W. Stout), Westview Press, Boulder, CO.
———. (1992) On the Ethics of Technical Change: The Case of bST. *Technology and Society,* **14**: 221–243.
Busch, L. and Lacy, W. (1983) *Science, Agriculture, and the Politics of Research,* Westview Press, Boulder, CO.
Busch, L., Lacy, W. B., and Burkhardt, J. (1988). Ethical and policy issues. In *Biotic diversity and germplasm global imperatives. Invited papers presented at the symposium held May 9–11, Beltsville, MD,* Kluwer Academic Publishers, Dordrecht and Boston.
Busch, L., Lacy, W., Burkhardt, J. and Lacy, L. (1991) *Plants, Power and Profit,* Blackwell, Oxford.
Comstock, G. (1990) The Case against bGH, pp. 309–339, in *Agricultural Bioethics* (eds S. Gendel, A. Kline, D. Warren and F. Yates), Iowa State University Press, Ames.
Feyerabend, P. (1978) *Science in a Free Society,* NLB, London.
Fox, M. (1990) Transgenic Animals: Ethical and Animal Welfare Concerns, pp. 31–50, in *The Bio-Revolution* (eds P. Wheale and R. McNally), Pluto Press, London.

Grinnell, F. (1987) *The Scientific Attitude*, Westview Press, Boulder, CO.

Holland, A. (1990) The Biotic Community: A Philosophical Critique of Genetic Engineering, pp. 166–174, in *The Bio-Revolution* (eds P. Wheale and R. McNally), Pluto Press, London.

Lukes, S. (1986) *Power*, New York University Press, New York.

NABC (National Agricultural Biotechnology Council, USA) (1992) *Animal Biotechnology: Opportunities and Challenges*, NABC Report 4, Ithaca, NY.

———. (1994) *Agricultural Biotechnology and the Public Good*, NABC Report 6, Ithaca, NY.

Olshevsky, T. (1983) *Good Reasons and Persuasive Force*, University Presses of America, New York.

Rachels, J. (1990) *Created from Animals*, Oxford University Press, Oxford.

Regan, T. (1985) *The Case for Animal Rights*, University of California Press, Berkeley, CA.

Rifkin, J. (1983) *Algeny*, Viking Press, New York.

Rosenberg, C. E. (1976) *No Other Gods*, Johns Hopkins University Press, Baltimore, MD.

Stevenson, C. (1944) *Ethics and Language*, Yale University Press, New Haven, CT.

51 Dis/Integrating Animals

Ethical Dimensions of the Genetic Engineering of Animals for Human Consumption

Traci Warkentin

Warkentin evaluates the moral implications of genetic engineering 'domesticated' animals, especially pigs and chickens, for human consumption. She focuses on issues of growing human organs in pigs for xenotransplantation and the ultimate ends of the intensive factory farming of chickens. She addresses the provocative questions of sufficient genetic modification of animal bodies so as to end the suffering of domestic food animals.

A biotechnological age is here, and contemporary Western society is steeped in its controversies of possibilities and problems. Debates on its potential for inspiring hope, as a tool for environmental salvation, and for rousing fear, as in opening Pandora's box and creating Frankensteins, have raged for long enough now to even become cliché. News of a new medical finding or agricultural epidemic makes headlines daily. Indeed, as I write, this week's leading headline on the *Scientific American* website reads: "Mouse Research Bolsters Controversial Theory of Aging," and is accompanied by an all-too-familiar image of a white mouse, an icon of laboratory research.

The first paragraph reads:

> Aging is a process we humans tend to fight every step of the way. The results of a mouse study underscore the potential of antioxidants as a tool in that battle: animals genetically modified to produce more antioxidant enzymes lived longer than control animals did.
>
> (Graham 2005)

While this news article may seem commonplace now, it is headlines such as this one that inspired Margaret Atwood to write a book of speculative fiction on how genetic engineering may continue to shape life on Earth in the future. Her novel, *Oryx and Crake,* published in 2003, opens with a description of an ominous and barren landscape, and it becomes immediately apparent that Atwood's vision of the biotechnological future is dystopian to say the least. The take-home messages are deeply humbling as Atwood presents her readers with provocative and disturbing possibilities. As such, *Oryx and Crake* provides a transitional narrative space for the discussion of current biotechnological philosophies and practices in Western society and where they might lead to in the not-so-distant future. While the book covers many aspects of society and technology worthy of discussion, this paper will focus on issues of genetically modified organisms (GMOs), particularly 'transgenic organisms.'[1] A transgenic organism is one that has been microgenetically engineered so that its genome contains genetic material derived from a different species (Wheale and McNally 1990, p 285). For example, a 'geep' is a sheep and goat hybrid, containing genetic material from both species (Wheale and McNally 1990, p 276).

Focussing on transgenic animals, I explore the complex concepts and assumptions of value embedded within such practices of genetically engineering animal bodies. For instance, Leesa Fawcett calls the use of animals as medical models of human disease, the ultimate practical expression of anthropomorphism (personal communication, 5 April 2005). The mouse model in the aging study quite literally becomes a metaphor for human physiology. This is particularly important in terms of challenging dominant Western understandings of humans and animals, of nature and culture, and related patriarchal dualisms,[2] which tend to define who and what we are. Thus, as Lynda Birke asserts, these Western scientific ideas and practices have integral connections with social and political, not to mention economic, issues and deserve attention from an ecofeminist perspective (1994, pp 10–11). This treatment of animal bodies as biofactories is a clear expression of the strong reductionist trend in Western sciences in general, and biotechnologies in particular, which has resulted in a predominant view of organisms as machines. The body as machine metaphor is prolific and powerful, and further exemplified in an application—which enjoys the most attention in this paper—in which the bodies of animals are modified to grow in ways that result in commercially valuable and consumable 'parts' and processes for medicinal or agricultural purposes. The production of these biofactories, of commodified transgenic flesh and viscera, is now a chilling reality, and may have even more startling implications with regard to both animal welfare and human moral sensibilities in its future development.

As such, research at the intersections of feminism, biology and philosophy (like Lynda Birke's and Leesa Fawcett's) provides dynamic starting grounds for this discussion of genetic technologies and animals. With a focus on animal bodies, I will examine moral implications of the genetic engineering of 'domesticated' animals—primarily pigs and chickens—for purposes of human consumption. Concepts of natural and artificial, contamination and purity, integrity and fragmentation and mind and body will feature in the discussion. In this respect, Atwood's *Oryx and Crake* serves as a cogent medium for exploring these highly contentious practices and ideas as it provides hypothetical narratives of possibility. Moreover, it is used to highlight contemporary hegemonic assumptions and values in ways that make them visible, for example, by taking a current biotechnological process/ practice to a seemingly absurd end. Particular attention is paid to issues of growing human organs in pigs for xenotransplantation (resulting, for Atwood, in 'pigoons') and the ultimate end of the intensive factory farming of chickens through the genetic engineering of 'mindless' chicken tumours (or, as Atwood calls them, 'ChickieNobs'). Integral to these philosophical considerations is the provocative question of employing the genetic engineering of animal bodies as a means to end the suffering of domestic food animals. This discussion ultimately leads to its implications for the future of human experience and morality.

Dis/Integrity Is a Virtue?

In a brief survey of literature that discusses genetic engineering and animals, two prevailing concerns emerge, those that focus on issues of animal welfare and those that focus on issues of animal rights. Advocates of animal rights claim that animals, particularly vertebrates, should not be used at all, while those taking up animal welfare accept the uses of animals to varying extents and direct their concerns to *how* animals are treated and whether harm can be justified by the benefits to humankind (Becker and Buchanan 1996, p 8). The moral equation of utilitarianism is commonly employed to calculate the overall 'greater good' by subtracting the costs from the benefits, which is always done from an anthropocentric, or human-centred, perspective. That is to say that the benefits always relate to human needs and desires because only humans are morally responsible to other human beings. This is the ethical position that typically forms the basis of policy (Bowring 2003, p 127).[3]

However, the idea that there is indeed something inherently wrong with the genetic manipulation of animals is taken up in a different, yet equally popular, philosophical approach known as deontological ethics. This ethical approach, most commonly developed from the philosophy of Immanuel Kant and applied to animals rather than just human beings, is drawn upon to argue that living beings should never be treated as merely a means to an end (Bowring 2003, p 134; Holland 1990, p 170). In a similar line of argument, others claim that it is wrong to treat animals as instruments solely for human purposes because they have value unto themselves, an intrinsic value, regardless of any instrumental value they may hold for human beings. But, it is not just that animals are considered instruments, the bigger problem is that they are viewed as mechanical instruments (Holland 1990, p 170). Stressing the full implications of this view, Val Plumwood states that 'a nature represented in mechanistic terms as inferior, passive and mindless, whose only value and meaning is derived from the imposition of human ends is simply replaceable by anything else which can serve those ends equally well' (2002, p 49).

This is an important contention because it exposes the extremely reductionist, value-laden nature of Western technoscience, with its fundamental ideology and language of mechanism which essentially makes genetic engineering possible. As Bowring succinctly sums up:

> the idea that the functioning of organisms can be distilled to discreet and transferable units of information is the dominant fiction which underpins and legitimizes the practice of genetic engineering.

> (2003, p 1)

Rather than attributing or recognizing human characteristics in animals, known as 'anthropomorphism,' technoscience favours "mechanomorphism," labelling animal bodies, and describing behaviour, in mechanical terms (Cenami Spada 1997, pp 43–44). This mechanistic way of thinking and talking about organic life results ultimately in a dramatic reduction of actual bodies in biotechnological practices. Bowring further adds:

> the disturbing image engendered by these developments is thus of a scientific community indifferent to the natural patterns, features and divisions of organic life, and which is content to address the alter instead as an assemblage of inherently disposable artefacts to be manipulated and reconstructed according to human whim.

> (2003, 118)

It may be that what makes this mechanical reduction so disturbing is that it represents a deliberate corruption of an integrity of being, or telos. This notion of integrity makes the fragmentation, the mutilation of bodies into machine-like components, unsettling in subtle and sometimes dramatic ways. It appears to be an organic quality arising in an organism through its own bio-physical processes of development and through interaction with the environment within which it is immersed. It is also aligned with a notion of intrinsic value, which, as opposed to instrumental value, is independent of any human judgment of utility. Of course, the word 'integrity' itself is loaded with meaning and particular moral value in English language and in Western culture, which likely heightens the discomfort felt by many when confronted with the threats to organic integrity that biotechnology is said to pose. This way of thinking is grounded in the pervasive Western assumption of a radical discontinuity between human beings and nature. By this logic, anything that human beings do is unnatural, and anything 'manmade' [sic]—such as a transgenic animal—is therefore also unnatural or artificial. The assumption that 'natural is good' is remarkably prevalent in the literature on transgenics even though it is contested and problematized across cultures, ethnicities and religions. While many stick to this designation in their arguments, some make a distinction between the process and the animal itself. So, where the process of genetic engineering, the way in which a being is modified, is understood as unnatural because it is biologically impossible outside of a laboratory, the organism itself still possesses integrity of its own and is neither natural nor unnatural in definitive terms (Holland 1990, p 169)

Taking this understanding further, in her essay 'The Promises of Monsters: A Regenerative Politics for Inappropriate/d Others,' Donna Haraway disrupts any and all divisions between natural and artificial when she states that:

> if organisms are natural objects, it is crucial to remember that organisms are not born; they are made in world-changing technoscientific practices by particular collective actors in particular times and places.

> (2004, p 65)

Moreover, Haraway insists that although life may seem to be overwhelmingly 'denatured' by these human practices, 'it is not a *denaturing* so much as *a particular production* of nature' (2004, p 66). Haraway proposes that nature is continually co-constructed by various organic and technological actors, some human and some non-human (2004, p 66). In spite of this, notions of natural goodness maintain a tenacious hold on Western imaginations and the debate often turns to the integrity of *species,* rather than the individual.

Pigoons, Purity and Perversions of Boundaries

Interestingly, the possibilities of actually transgressing the 'natural' boundaries between species via genetic engineering effectively call into question the very definition and concept of species (Becker and Buchanan 1996, p 7). It points to a certain cultural arbitrariness both in scientific definitions of species as well as in the moral stances that species boundaries support.

[. . .]

If I may be allowed some cultural and historical generalizations, in the West there has been an acceptance of the idea that all organisms can be categorized into different species based upon bio-logical characteristics, particularly in terms of mating. So defined, species have become relatively fixed and bounded phenomena, and there is a long history regarding the ideological and practical maintenance of such boundaries in Western society. Much has been written on this history of ideas already, of great chains of being and of cultural taboos, too much to summarize here; rather, I will take up the underlying notions of purity and contamination in the discussion as they relate to atti-tudes and values regarding transgenic animals and xenotransplantation. Both involve the deliberate crossing of the so-called species barriers and both result in the actual combination of genetic material from two or more different species.

In the fictional world created by Atwood in *Oryx and Crake*, such transgenic animals, called 'pigoons' (or by their Latin title '*sus multiorganifer*'), play a pivotal role in human medical and com-mercial enterprise. At first they are used to provide various means of human physical enhancement and prolonging life, yet, ironically, in the end they become a tangible threat to human survival. For Jimmy, the principle character in the story, pigoons represent his family's livelihood. His father is employed as a genetic engineer at OrganInc Farms, a huge biotechno-industrial compound, which also serves as a gated-community for all of its employees and their families.

As Atwood explains in the narrative:

> The goal of the pigoon project was to grow an assortment of fool-proof human-tissue organs in a transgenic knockout pig host—organs that would transplant smoothly and avoid rejection, but would also be able to fend off attacks by opportunistic microbes and viruses, of which there were new strains every year. A rapid maturity gene was spliced in so the pigoon kidneys and livers and hearts would be ready sooner, and now they were perfecting a pigoon that could grow five or six kidneys at a time. Such a host animal could be reaped of its extra kidneys; then, rather than being destroyed, it could keep on living and grow more organs, much as a lobster could grow another claw to replace a missing one.
>
> (2003, pp 22–33)

It is interesting to note that in naming them 'pigoons,' Atwood hints at the idea that since they have undergone dramatic genetic modifications they are no longer 'pigs,' that they have become a new animal altogether. This is contrary to the language currently employed in biotech rhetoric, where genetically modified pigs are still called pigs, and yet it also points to another controversial aspect in biotechnology: the patenting of genetically modified organisms (GMOs). A patent is only granted if an organism is considered to be completely novel and artefactual, which is what the renaming actually represents. To be sure, the boundary between reality and fiction is porous. As Atwood stated in the passage at the beginning of this paper, this is not merely the stuff of speculative, or science, or fiction, and there are presently many examples in which human genetic material is being inserted into the genomes of other animals. For example, transgenic pigs, known as 'Beltsville' pigs, were produced from single-cell embryos that had been injected with a human growth hormone gene (Bowring 2003, p 124). The corporeal results of this experiment failed dramatically in terms of animal welfare, as Bowring explains:

> The pigs showed improved weight gain, greater feed efficiency, and reduced subcutaneous fat, but at the cost of a wide range of pathological side-effects, including 'gastric ulceration, severe synovitis [joint inflammation], degenerative joint disease, percarditis and endocarditis [inflammation of the outer and inner lining of the heart], cardiomegaly [enlargement of the heart], parakeratosis [cracking of the skin], nephritis [inflammation of the kidney] and pneumonia. In addition,' the researchers disclose, 'gilts were anoestrus [infertility due to quiescence or involution of the reproductive tract] and boars lacked libido.'
>
> (Bowring 2003, p 125)

Clearly, there is no moral consideration for the individual pigs involved, only the potential human benefits of increased agricultural efficiency are of value. Strangely enough, however, these transgenic pigs present a challenge to such blatant anthropocentrism, and may serve to undermine species-based morality (Ryder 1990, p 190). It comes back to ideas of purity and species boundaries and we are forced to ask at what point does a pig with human genes stop being a pig and become something more human, or a porcine-human hybrid? Richard Ryder (1990) raises this provocative idea in his essay, 'Pigs *Will* Fly,' when he poses questions like:

> How many human genes make a sufficiently human creature to have human rights in the eyes of the law? How many human genes can you give a humanized pig before you feel obliged to send it to school rather than to the slaughterhouse?
>
> (p 190).

Ryder is hopeful that the perforation of species boundaries 'spotlights the absurdity of our species-based morality,' particularly by drawing attention to practices in which human growth hormone genes:

> have already been injected into the embryos of pigs. The aim was to produce bigger and juicier pork chops. But wait a minute. This would mean eating human genetic material! It might only be a minute proportion of the chop, but all the same, would it not be a partial cannibalism?
>
> (Ryder 1990, p 190)

Playing up the revulsion of this very real possibility in her fiction, Atwood has Jimmy reflect on the same questions while dining at the OrganInc Farms cafeteria where, 'to set the queasy at ease, it was claimed that none of the defunct pigoons ended up as bacon or sausages: no one would want to eat an animal whose cells might be identical with at least some of their own' (2003, pp 23–44). Beyond their role as living pork factories, and like the pigoons, present day pigs are also being genetically modified to provide a 'source of replacement organs (the so-called "spare parts factories") for humans' (Bowring 2003, p 121). To this end, the use of biotechnology is vital.
[. . .]
   The purpose of this process is to make a pig's body less pig-like so that it can become more compatible with human bodies, and in essence then, more human (at least on a physiological level). The impetus for ridding the pig's organ of all traces of its 'pigness' perhaps also arises in part out of sentiments of a general distaste, a 'feeling that there is something undignified for the recipient in receiving a pig's heart' (Aldridge 1996, p 132).
[. . .]

While fears of contamination appear justified[4] and provide reason for caution, general concepts of blood purity and contamination may be more dangerous in terms of racism and classism. Notions of pedigree have been around for centuries, revered in royal family lineage and designations of 'pure blood' and 'blue blood,' and have extended to breeding practices of 'domesticated' animals, such as dogs, cats and horses. This is not an unfamiliar idea, and so does not require elucidation. A more novel and complex implication of 'blood purity' however, is its exposure of how certain beliefs arise out of bodily experiences which may not be reconcilable with what are considered to be rational truths and facts (Kirmayer 1992, p 329). Such beliefs and fears can play out even when the species barrier is not transgressed, for instance, in cases of human-to-human blood transfusion. For example, Laurence Kirmayer illustrates what he calls 'the body's insistence on meaning' through a challenging case study of a man, called 'Mr. Y,' who refuses to undergo a life-saving blood transfusion because of his belief that the 'foreign' blood will contaminate him with the donor's, 'genetic material that carries personality traits' (1992, p 325).

Promises of Failure and Risks of Success (or, It's All about Perspective!)

With this kind of visceral discrimination, I can only imagine the horror of Mr. Y's reaction to the idea of receiving blood or organs from an animal of another species. Nevertheless, biotechnological research in this area gallops on with great fervour and promise for medical progress. Meanwhile, there is a greater uncertainty to this work that I have yet to see specifically addressed in the literature on transgenics. While there is much written about the fears of failure in which the GMO is unable to survive out in the world due to unforeseen problems (such as increased susceptibility to disease that was coded for on a gene that was removed for other reasons (Rollin 1995, p 110), and about welfare arguments concerned with failure (as in the Beltsville pigs' case) there is very little about the risks of *success*. Admittedly, concerns of ecological risk have received some attention, but they all tend to focus on microscopic organisms, invertebrates (mainly insects) and transgenic plants, that have been modified for agricultural purposes. The conventional warning is that, 'unlike chemical substances, genetically engineered organisms have the capacity to mutate, migrate and multiply' (Holland 1990, p 173) and that 'a genetically engineered organism once free in the environment is impossible to recall' (Bereano 1996, p 30).

As with the fear of blood contamination due to xenotransplantation, this fear of 'polluting' an ecological system with a 'foreign' organism has an experiential basis; experiments in biological pest control have provided all too many lessons learned, the hard way, of what can happen. So the logic follows that any novel (i.e. transgenic) organism has no natural habitat, no place of origin in this world, and therefore always presents an ecological risk if released from the laboratory. But, what of those transgenic animals never intended for release? Although human beings are capable of altering the genetic makeup and phenotypic expression of that modified genotype, we are not actually in control of evolution, and even transgenic animals kept in a laboratory or otherwise confined may change and adapt over time, through mutation and reproductive processes. What, indeed, might be the potential long-term implications of splicing human genetic material into pig embryos? Has the scientific mind become so accustomed to a severely reductionist view of the world that it can only 'see' animals as passive machine-like objects, an assemblage of inert parts to be tinkered with? Some humility and wonder is in order; a respect for all that is still not known or understood about bodies and whole biological systems, and the findings of biological sciences which suggest their dynamic complexity and chaotic nature. For all of its sophistication, the science of genetic engineering is founded upon an overzealous faith in the technology itself, and upon an over-simplified idea of living processes and bodies. The former, known as technological determinism, creates a hold upon scientific thought and effectively eliminates worries of risk. The latter, known as biological determinism, defines animals as only the physical products of their DNA.

In this regard, Atwood's pigoon becomes not only a kind of allegory for the ecological risks of transgenic organisms but also a warning for what may come to pass, quite literally. In Jimmy's own lifetime and as a result of deliberate human action, a microorganism wipes out all human life on Earth. In this post-apocalyptic world, pigoons have escaped from the laboratories and now roam freely. Possibly emphasizing the agency of all transgenic animals, Atwood writes: 'They were always escape artists, the pigoons: if they'd had fingers they'd have ruled the world' (p 267). In this scenario, from the pigoon's perspective of course, they are very successful in terms of ecological adaptation and ability to thrive.

On the other hand, from a human perspective, pigoons become an experimental failure, or monstrous mistake, as they now express both the desire and talents to hunt and eat human flesh. Apparently, the practice of mixing human and pig genetic material for numerous generations has endowed pigoons with a certain amount of human similarity.

[. . .]

The idea of pig-human hybrids running rampant in the streets may be taking current genetically modified organisms to an absurdly extreme end of the range of possibility. However, experience does suggest that organisms can and will respond to biological and ecological changes in unpredictable ways. Atwood's pigoons remind us of this agency of animals, which tends to be ignored or denied all too often. Therefore, although 'mechanical models express the denial to nature of any uniqueness, agency and power' (Plumwood 2002, p 49), warnings of ecological risk speak loudly and clearly of the *agency and power* of transgenic organisms. Such agency is expressed when genetically modified wheat suddenly appears in an organic farmer's field several kilometres away, and when the Beltsville pig's body develops severe arthritis. Unfortunately, the denial of animal agency is underpinned by a reification of the 'gene' itself, the ultimate reduction of life into its smallest component part, which guides genetic engineering. Birke cautions that 'reifying them allows us to see *only* the genes, devoid of their physiological context, the organism itself and *its* environment' (1994, p 83). Once removed from their original context, how can scientists be sure of how the gene will function in an essentially alien one? Expressing this concern, Birke questions: 'what happens to the inserted gene *apart from* its attributed role of molecule factory. How does it interact with the sheep's genes? Or with its cells? Or with its wider environment? And what are the consequences of those actions?' (1994, p 83).

Thinking of a gene as just interchangeable DNA matter brings the discussion back to the question of species hierarchy, presenting a challenge to the superiority dominantly attributed to the human species over all others. Success in genetic engineering depends upon similarity between and among different individuals and species, otherwise it could not work. As a result, 'the boundaries start to dissolve,' and Birke recognizes that 'to avoid that worrying prospect, we can label the genes as embodying essence. *Human* genes must have something special about them, an essence of humanness, that gives them a territorial boundary' (1994, pp 83–84). This presents us with an apparent paradox in which 'genetics as a system of representation both challenges concepts of species as fixed (in the practice of, for example, transgenics) and reinforces them (by incorporating notions of essence)' (Birke 1994, p 84).

Rather than struggling with the contradiction, it appears that biotechnoscience is content to ignore it and to maintain one set of rules for defining human beings and another set for all other animals. To continue this hierarchy of species by defining animals as only products of their biology, poses perhaps the greatest threat to animal agency and welfare, resulting in the actualization of the 'animal is machine' metaphor.

[. . .]

Designed for Deprivation

Factory farming is already based upon thinking of animals as machines to be tinkered with so they can be made more efficient. For instance, cows are thought of as milk machines and given genetically engineered bovine growth hormones, known as Bovine Somatotropin (BST), to increase their production of milk (Wenz 2001, p 222; Wheale and McNally 1990). As the conditions within industrial animal agriculture intensify, the occurrences of disease and disharmony among the animals themselves increase dramatically (Bowring 2003, p 131). Unfortunately, rather than changing the conditions of production, many look to genetic engineering for quick-fix solutions. As Caroline Murphy points out, 'the "Trojan horse" of disease resistance may provide a means whereby genetic engineers can design animals to cope with conditions that no animal, genetically engineered or not, should be expected to endure' (1990, p 16).

Modifications to animal bodies via genetic engineering thus effectively enable continued, and possibly even increased, deprivation as animals are treated as nothing more than meat factories, confined to 'cramped and unsanitary conditions' (Bowring 2003, p 132). This in itself is cause enough for alarm in terms of animal welfare, yet becomes even more horrifying as proponents attempt to alleviate all causes of suffering through changing the very nature of the animals. Those in favour of redesigning animals to be even better adapted to factory environments call it simply the 'latest stage in the historical process of "domesticating" animals' (Bowring 2003, p 132), insisting that it is no different, in theory, from pastoral practices of domestication through selective breeding. But the stakes are much higher, as Bowring explains, this means that now: 'one could, therefore, produce chickens which lack a desire to nest' (2003, p 136). What's more, advocates insist that since transgenic animals could, in principle, be created without causing suffering, and for that matter engineered . . . to suffer *less,* there is in the eyes of most scientists nothing inherent in genetic engineering which makes it an unethical tool (Bowring 2003, p 132).

By contrast, opponents assert that this would be morally reprehensible, and turn again to the argument that the telos of beings should not to be violated under any circumstances (Bowring 2003, pp 133–134; Fox 1990, pp 32–33; Holland 1990, pp 170–171). Expanding upon his earlier deontologic argument, Holland claims that:

> there is a distinction between using another creature's ends as your own—which is acceptable—and disregarding that other creature's ends entirely—which is not. A problem, however, which Kant's notion does not seem to address . . . comes when the genetic engineer starts to *redesign* those ends.
>
> (1990, p 170; emphasis added)

The End of Animal Suffering = the End of Animals?

Incidentally, this is precisely what Bernard Rollin advocates in his 'new social ethic for animals' (1995). Rollin argues that if animals can be modified to be 'happier' in the confinement conditions of factory farms, there should be no moral opposition to it. It is interesting that he does not argue that it should be a moral *imperative*, only that it should *not be immoral* to alleviate suffering using genetic modification to better fit animals to their conditions. In response to claims of the inviolability of telos, Rolling addresses his critics by emphasizing that he believes there is nothing wrong with changing the nature, or telos, of an animal as long as the animal's interests—which emerge from that telos—are not violated (1995, p 171). For example, he supports changing the nature of a chicken, when normally confined in a battery cage, which suffers frustration at not being able to nest to lay her eggs so that the 'new kind of chicken' no longer expresses the urge to nest and instead experiences satisfaction at laying eggs in a cage (Rollin 1995, p 172). Rollin admits that public apprehension to his argument may emerge from 'a queasiness that is at root aesthetic. The chicken sitting in a nest is a powerful aesthetic image. . . . A chicken without that urge jars us' (1995, p. 175).

However, he is quick to point out that this pastoral image is already forsaken to an immense degree in current practices of factory farming, which should cause as much if not more concern than hypothetical applications of genetic engineering. Indeed, his argument becomes harder to dispute as he recounts that Western culture has 'a historical tradition as old as domestication for changing (primarily agricultural) animal telos (through artificial selection) to fit animals into human society to serve human needs. We selected for non-aggressive animals, animals disinclined or unable to leave our protection and so on' (Rollin 1995, p 174). Here, Rollin's argument begins to appear very pragmatic in the face of the West's 'current exploitative business context' (1995, p 182) of intensive industrial animal agriculture.

He is not without sympathy, nor ignorant of the full ramifications of what he suggests; rather, he presents himself as a realist—justifiably cynical of society's lack of will to change such strongly rooted economic, political and social practices—admitting that to change the nature of an animal to fit a poor environment rather than changing the environment itself is merely the 'lesser of two evils' (Rollin 1995, p 192), but a necessary one when the likelihood of the system changing to fit animals' needs is slim.

Up to here, Rollin presents a fairly persuasive case. However, he takes it too far when he suggests:

> if we could genetically engineer essentially decerebrate food animals, animals that have merely a vegetative life but no experiences, I believe it would be better to do this than to put conscious beings into environments in which they are miserable.
>
> (1995, p 193)

To suggest genetically modifying a chicken which lacks the urge to nest is provocative enough, but to suggest a chicken which lacks a brain is downright shocking. And it is here where we come to the most extreme manifestation of the mechanical metaphor, and the division of mind and body, with the proposed production of actual meat machines.

This prospect is celebrated among some scientists in the field and has apparently been around for quite some time. In fact, Rollin's comment on 'decerebrate food animals' was inspired by a conversation with a genetic engineer who claims that, 'in the long run, biotechnology will make the whole debate about agricultural animal welfare moot. Eventually, he told [Rollin], we will be able to create the relevant animal proteins in fermentation vats produced by bacteria genetically coded to do so. Thus we will be able to have animal products without animals' (1995, p 193).

[. . .]

Beyond Suffering; 'ChickieNobs Bucket O'Nubbins'

Bringing this terrifying prospect to life in the world of *Oryx and Crake*, Atwood confronts her readers with an evocative image that they will surely find unforgettable. Jimmy is visiting his best friend, Crake, at his new high school called the Watson-Crick Institute. As its name implies, it's an institute of genetic technology, with students specializing in areas such as 'Botanical Transgenics,' 'NeoGeologicals,' and 'Décor Botanicals.' Crake takes Jimmy on a tour of these departments, winding up in 'Neo Agriculturals' or 'AgriCouture' as it is nicknamed. Here, Jimmy is presented with 'a large bulblike object that seemed to be covered with stippled whitish-yellow skin. Out of it came twenty thick fleshy tubes, and at the end of each tube another bulb was growing' (Atwood 2003, p 202). He is told that they are essentially chicken parts, some just breasts, others just drumsticks. They have been modified to have no head, just a mouth into which nutrients are dumped.

> 'This is horrible,' said Jimmy. The thing was a nightmare. It was like an animal-protein tuber.
> 'Picture the sea-anemone body plan,' said Crake. 'That helps.'
> 'But what's it thinking?' said Jimmy.
>
> (Atwood 2003, p 202)

In response, Jimmy is told by one of the student scientists involved that it's not supposed to think that 'they'd removed all the brain functions that had nothing to do with digestion, assimilation and growth' (Atwood 2003, p 203).

> 'No need for added growth hormones,' said the woman, 'the high growth rate's built in. . . . And the animal-welfare freaks won't be able to say a word, because this thing feels no pain.'
>
> (Atwood 2003, p 203)

Jimmy's immediate response of horror and his question of 'what's it thinking' speak to an agency in chickens that has been dramatically violated and distorted. Atwood then makes allusions to the already tight relationship between present-day research in biotechnology and big business through its commercial applications:

> 'Those kids are going to clean up,' said Crake after they'd left. The students at Watson-Crick got half the royalties from anything they invented there. Crake said it was a fierce incentive. 'ChickieNobs, they're thinking of calling the stuff.' 'Are they on the market yet?' asked Jimmy weakly. He couldn't see eating a ChickieNob. It would be like eating a large wart.
>
> (Atwood 2003, p 203)

As unpalatable as they seem to Jimmy at first, eventually they become familiar, cheap and convenient enough for him to overcome his revulsion. With his acquiescence to ChickieNobs Bucket O'Nubbins, Atwood is definitely commenting upon the power of marketing and on contemporary society's cultural amnesia regarding many once controversial environmental issues. As warnings of global warming and species extinction become increasingly monotonous and commonplace in the news and everyday life, it seems that the public tends to either tire of them or finds them so completely overwhelming that it becomes preferable to ignore them and let the politicians work it out. Ironically, this seemingly pervasive apathy in dominant Western society is exactly what Rollin had been referring to for supporting the non-fictional production of ChickieNobs.

To get beyond these circular arguments of suffering, Holland stresses freedom as grounds for objection, which he defines as 'the capacity to exercise options;' he abhors the idea that an animal might be modified to have a diminished capacity in this respect (1990, p 171; also see Fox 1990, p 34). With sober wit he acknowledges that if capacity is to be modified, a kind of genetic lobotomy is the inevitable result since:

> the genetic engineer is unlikely to deal with the problem of the unhappy pig by increasing the animal's sophistication to the level where it is capable of being philosophical about its condition and learns not to mind. Rather, the capacities of the animal would be reduced to the state where it was, from a sentient point of view, more vegetable than animal.
>
> (Holland 1990, p 172)

Depriving Ourselves: Mechanomorphosis and Other Ethical Consequences

Alternatively, it may be more generative to argue that genetic engineering presents a violation of 'being' in terms of living processes rather than seemingly static qualities such as capacities. To this end, Bowring cautions that the continued treatment of animals as malleable artefacts is as much a threat to 'human's own vital sensibilities' as it is to animal welfare, and that it will 'progressively erode the scope for and substance of human's moral existence' (Bowring 2003, p 3). In other words, through the philosophy and practices embedded within genetic engineering that ultimately reduce all animal life into biological machines, human beings are distorting their own experience of the world, and thus their values and belief systems along with them. In phenomenological terms, human beings are situated within our own unique bodies, which connect us with the world, enabling sensory experiences of it, while simultaneously limiting what and how we know to our own embodied experiences (Merleau-Ponty 1962, p 82). There can be no absolute objectivity, nor isolated subjectivity, as we are always in relation to other beings, materials and processes. To borrow Maurice Merleau-Ponty's fabric metaphor of existence, I imagine numerous threads stretching from my body out to everything and everyone around me (Gill 1991, p 4). And just as each thread stretches in both directions, so too is perception reciprocal, facilitating my experiences as both an observer and as one who is observed by others. Extending this reciprocity of perception to animals, David Abram provides an elegant example of an ant walking upon his arm. He senses the ant visually and through the touch of the ant's feet upon his skin, and realizes that the ant also senses him as he notices the ant respond to his arm movements (Abram 1996, p 67). Counter to a mechanical view of nature, a phenomenological perspective enables such experiences of intentionality and agency in others, particularly other animals. Emphasizing the importance of human-animal interaction through direct embodied experiences, Bowring stresses that:

> While there are . . . obvious dangers involved in romanticising traditional agricultural practices for being 'closer to nature,' it may still be argued that the genetic approach to farming, and the reductionist science which underpins it, marks a watershed in the development of humans' relationship to nature in so far as it involves a decisive degradation in their subjective qualities of feeling and perception.
>
> (Bowring 2003, p 138)

In doing so, we are losing the capacity to relate to other animals, our own bodies and other human beings. Such an impoverishment of experience is, as evident in the discussion throughout this paper, intimately connected with an inanimate language, reinforcing and reinforced by a dominant mechanical worldview. To speak of organisms as machines legitimizes our treatment of them as artefacts, as completely knowable and transparent objects and of their lives as having no ethical significance. As such, Bowring warns that

> genetic engineers' favoured language of 'bioreactors,' 'spare-parts factories,' 'nutraceutical fruits,' 'live-stock pharming,' 'biofacture' and so on, are not just commercially sanitised descriptions of what remain stubbornly recalcitrant natural phenomena. . .: this mechanistic language and philosophy is also disturbing for the way they seem to express the degradation of scientists' own physical and moral sensibilities, and a diminishing care for the integrity of life which has troubling ramifications for human relations themselves.
>
> (2003, p 142)

Behind commercial profits from the commodification of bodies and lingering enlightenment fantasies of revealing all the secrets of nature, there lurks the ominous promise of our own sensory and moral deprivation. Ultimately, by transforming nature into an insensate, decerebrate, wholly objectified product, devoid of independent well-being, the biotech programme may thus deliver its golden promise by relieving us of care. The mechanization of nature will lead to the mechanization of ourselves, our sentiments, judgments, fears and dreams (Bowring 2003, p 143).

In this respect, Bowring worries that 'this process is already foreshadowed by the cultural fetishization of the cyborg, and of course in the assertion that human nature itself should now become the object of the biotech enterprise' (2003, p 143). While I can appreciate Bowring's fear of the cyborg, I do not find it to be problematic in itself. Truth be told, I find the reality of the cyborg metaphor much more appealing than the current mechanical one, particularly in terms of Haraway's understanding of the cyborg's potential to expose and dissolve hierarchical divisions between mind and body, nature and culture and so on that are the direct result of a mechanical (and patriarchal) worldview (1991). For, as Haraway reminds us in her infamous 'cyborg manifesto,' a cyborg is a 'hybrid of machine and organism, a creature of social reality as well as a creature of fiction' (1991, p 149). If we are already cyborgs, as Haraway contends and Bowring fears, then we are least still partly human animals. As cyborgs, we retain some form of organic sensory perception while also enjoying technological augmentations. Thinking of ourselves in this way may enable the humility so desperately needed in our social relations with other animals, particularly as it encourages us to engage our imaginations, to recognize both the generative and destructive fictions in our worldviews, as we struggle to comprehend our ontological predicament (the meaning of life, the universe and everything).

If we continue along the biotechnological path without questioning its ideological basis, we risk much more than becoming actual cyborgs, we risk manifesting our mechanomorphism via mechanomorphosis. That is, we gamble with becoming machines ourselves, in the most reductionist sense, inheriting only the mechanistic part of our cyborg heritage and leaving all traces of humanimality behind. With the loss of embodied sensibility, of our modes of social relatedness, we run the risk of eliminating our ability to ponder metaphysics, to question our own actions and fundamental beliefs, and with it the desire or need for ethics at all. In due course, we need to resist our conversion into insensate automatons and imagine what is at stake. Will the dis/integration of our corporeal-selves and other animals, and re/integration through mechanomorphosis lead to amoral relationships? Do we really want to achieve a future without suffering by way of disembodiment?

Notes

1. For an accessible scientific explanation of genetic engineering and the processes of producing transgenic organisms, please see Susan Aldridge's (1996) *The Thread of Life: The story of Genes and Genetic Engineering*. Cambridge University Press, Cambridge.
2. For cogent explanations of the patriarchal (male hierarchy) basis of modern, Western sciences, please see Val Plumwood's (1993) *Feminism and the Mastery of Nature*. Routledge, London and her *Environmental Culture: The Ecological Crisis of Reason*, Routledge, London (Val Plumwood 2002); also see Donna Haraway's (1989) Primate Visions. Routledge, London.
3. 'Most advisory reports in the UK and the European Union on the "ethical implications" of biotechnology have thus taken the utilitarian view that there is nothing inherently wrong with the genetic manipulation of animals, but scientists involved in such practices must demonstrate that there are tangible human benefits to be gained from their work' (Bowring 2003, p 127).
4. Beyond such aesthetic revulsion, there is a definite and well-grounded fear that disease and its vectors will also transgress the species barrier in dangerous and unpredictable ways. Bowring warns of the 'widespread concerns amongst ecologists and medical researchers that xeno-transplantation will allow new and unknown microorganisms, harmless to their natural hosts, to cross the species barrier, causing infectious disease, spreading cancer-causing retroviruses, and potentially creating mutant viruses as deadly as HIV, Ebola, or BSE. Pigs are already known to harbour endogenous retroviruses which have been found to infect human cells in vitro' (2003, pp 303–304). Bowring further notes that 'the Ebola and Marburg monkey viruses have caused large disease outbreaks in humans, and HIV is widely believed to have derived from a monkey retrovirus, and millions of people in the 1950s were infected with the non-virulent monkey virus SV40 after vaccines were contaminated by the monkey kidney cells in which they were produced' (2003, pp 303–304).

References

Abram D (1996) *The spell of the sensuous*. Random House Inc., New York.
Aldridge S (1996) *The thread of life: The story of genes and genetic engineering*. Cambridge University Press, Cambridge.
Atwood M (2003) *Oryx and crake*. McClelland & Stewart Ltd, Toronto.
Becker G, Buchanan JP (eds) (1996) *Changing nature's course: The ethical challenge of biotechnology*. Hong Kong University Press, Hong Kong.
Bereano P (1996) Some environmental and ethical considerations of genetically engineered plants and foods. Pp. 27–36, in: Becker G, Buchanan JP (eds) *Changing nature's course: The ethical challenge of biotechnology*. Hong Kong University Press, Hong Kong.

Birke L (1994) *Feminism, animals and science: The naming of the shrew*. Open University Press, Buckingham.

Bowring F (2003) *Science, seeds and cyborgs: Biotechnology and the appropriation of life*. Vergo, London.

Cenami Spada E (1997) Amorphism, mechanomorphism, and anthropomorphism. Pp. 37–49, in: RW Mitchell, NS Thompson, and HL Miles (eds) *Anthropomorphism, anecdotes, and animals*. State University of New York Press, Albany.

Fox M (1990) Transgenic animals: Ethical and animal welfare concerns. Pp. 31–50, in: Wheale P, McNally R (eds) *The bio-revolution: Cornucopia or Pandora's box?* Pluto Press, London.

Gill J (1991) *Merleau-Ponty and metaphor*. Humanities Press International Inc, New Jersey.

Graham S (2005) Mouse research bolsters controversial theory of aging, *Scientific American.com*. [retrieved May 6, 2005 from http://www.sciam.com/article.cfm?chanID=sa003&articleID=0004094A-849D-127A-849D83414B7F0000]

Haraway D (1991) *Simians, cyborgs, and women: The reinvention of nature*. Routledge, New York.

Haraway D (2004) *The Haraway reader*. Routledge, New York.

Holland A (1990) The biotic community: A philosophical critique of genetic engineering. In: Wheale P, McNally R (eds) *The bio-revolution: Cornucopia or Pandora's Box?* Pluto Press, London.

Kirmayer L (1992) The body's insistence on meaning: Metaphor as presentation and representation in illness experience. *Medical Anthropolology Quarterly* 6: 323–346.

Merleau-Ponty M (1962) *Phenomenology of perception*. C Smith (Trans) Routledge & Kegan Paul Ltd, London.

Murphy C (1990) Genetically engineered animals. In: Wheale P, McNally R (eds) *The bio-revolution: Cornucopia or Pandora's Box?* Pluto Press, London.

Plumwood V (2002) *Environmental culture: The ecological crisis of reason*. Routledge, London.

Rollin B (1995) *The Frankenstein syndrome: Ethical and social issues in the genetic engineering of animals*. Cambridge University Press, Cambridge.

Ryder R (1990) Pigs will fly. In: Wheale P, McNally R (eds) *The bio-revolution: Cornucopia or Pandora's box?* Pluto Press, London.

Wenz PS (2001) *Environmental ethics today*. Oxford University Press, Oxford.

Wheale P, McNally R (eds) (1990) *The bio-revolution: Cornucopia or Pandora's box?* Pluto Press, London.

TELOS as an Influence on Ethical Issues

52 On *Telos* and Genetic Engineering

Bernard E. Rollin

Rollin addresses the notion of telos, *the essence and purpose of a creature, and proposes that there is no direct reasoning to argue that the notion of* telos *in animals and the Maxim to Respect* Telos *should preclude genetic engineering of animals. He notes that for domestic animals, each proposed modification should be assessed in relation to the Principle of Conservation of Welfare. For non-domestic animals, he believes that such modifications also may be valuable. He exercises proceeding cautiously so as to avoid possible ecological impacts or affecting other animals adversely.*

Telos

Aristotle's concept of *telos* lies at the heart of what is very likely the greatest conceptual synthesis ever accomplished, unifying common sense, science, and philosophy. By using this notion as the basis for his analysis of the nature of things, Aristotle was able to reconcile the patent fact of a changing world with the possibility of its systematic knowability. [. . .] Though individual robins come and go, 'robin-ness' endures, making possible the knowledge that humans, in virtue of their own *telos* as knowers, abstract from their encounters with the world. Common sense tells us that only individual existent things are real; reflective deliberation, on the other hand, tells us that only what is repeatable and universal in these things is knowable.

[. . .]

For Aristotle, as for common sense, the fact that animals had *tele* was self-evident—the task of the knower was to systematically characterize each relevant *telos*. [. . .] [T]he notion of *telos* has in fact been refined and deepened by the advent of molecular genetics, as a tool for understanding the genetic basis of animals' physical traits and behavioural possibilities. At the same time, the classical notion of *telos* is seen as threatened by genetic engineering, the operational offspring of molecular genetics. For we may now see *telos* neither as eternally fixed, as did Aristotle, nor as a stop action snapshot of a permanently dynamic process, as did Darwin, but rather as something infinitely malleable by human hands.

Contemporary Agriculture

Despite the fact that the concept of *telos* has lost its scientific centrality, there are two major and conceptually connected vectors currently thrusting the notion of *telos* into renewed philosophical prominence, both of which are moral in nature. These vectors are social concern about the treatment of animals, and the advent of practicable biotechnology. The former concern reflects our recently acquired ability to use animals without respecting the full range of their *telos*; the latter concern reflects our in-principle ability to drastically modify animal *telos* in unprecedented ways. There obtain significant conceptual connections between the two concerns, but before these are dealt with one must understand the social conditions militating in favour of a revival of the concept of *telos*.

[. . .]

The overwhelmingly preponderant use of animals in society since the dawn of civilization has unquestionably been agricultural—animals were kept for food, fibre, locomotion and power. Presupposed by such use was the concept of husbandry; placing the animals in environments congenial to their *telos*—the Biblical image of the shepherd leading his animals to green pastures is a paradigm case—and augmenting their natural abilities by provision of protection from predators, food and water in times of famine and drought, medical and nursing attention, etc. In this ancient contract, humans fared well if and only if their animals fared well, and thus proper treatment of animals was guaranteed by the strongest possible motive—the producer's self-interest. Any attempt to act against the animals' interests as determined by their natures resulted in damage to the producers' interests as well. In this contract, both sides benefited—the animals' ability to live a good life was augmented by human help; humans benefited by 'harvesting' the animals' products, power or lives. One could not selectively accommodate some of the animals' interests to the exclusion of others, but was obliged to respect the *telos* as a whole.

[. . .]

All of this changed drastically in the mid-twentieth century with the advent of high-technology agriculture, significantly portended as university departments of animal husbandry underwent a change in nomenclature to departments of 'animal science.' In this new approach to animal agriculture, one no longer needed to accommodate the animal's entire *telos* to be successful. [. . .] Technology has allowed animal producers to divorce productivity from total or near-total satisfaction of *telos*.

High-technology agriculture was not the only mid-twentieth century force significantly deforming the ancient contract with animals. Large-scale animal use in biomedical research and toxicology is, like intensive agriculture, a creature of the mid-twentieth century. Like confinement agriculture, too, successful use of animals in biomedicine does not necessitate accommodating the animals' *tele*.

[. . .]

Thus, both the advent of industrialized agriculture and large-scale animal use in science created an unprecedented situation in the mid-twentieth century by inflicting significant suffering on animals which was nonetheless not a matter of sadism or cruelty. Agriculturalists were trying to produce cheap and plentiful food in a society where only a tiny fraction of the population was engaged in agricultural production; scientists were attempting to cure disease, advance knowledge and protect society from toxic substances. As society became aware of these new animal uses neither bound by the ancient contract nor conceptually captured by the anti-cruelty ethic, and concerned about the suffering they engendered, it necessarily required an augmentation in its moral vocabulary for dealing with animal treatment.

[. . .]

It is th[e] notion of rights, based on plausible reading of the human *telos*, which has figured prominently in mid-century concerns about women, minorities, the handicapped and others who were hitherto excluded from full moral concern. It is therefore inevitable that this notion would be exported, *mutatis mutandis*, to the new uses of animals. In essence, society is demanding that if animals are used for human benefits, there must be constraints on that use, equivalent to the natural constraints inherent in husbandry agriculture. These constraints are based in giving moral inviolability to those animal interests which are constitutive of the animals' *telos*. If we are to use animals for food, they should live reasonably happy lives, i.e. lives where they are allowed to fulfil the interests dictated by their *telos*. [. . .] For the baboon used in biomedicine, this means creating a housing system which, in the words of US law, enhances the animals' 'psychological well-being,' i.e. social non-austere containment for these animals that accommodates 'species-specific behaviour' (Rollin, 1989, pp. 177–81). For the zoo animals, it means creating living conditions which allow the animals to express the powers and meet the interests constitutive of its *telos* (Markowitz and Line, 1989).

Thus, *telos* has emerged as a moral norm to guide animal use in the face of technological changes which allow for animal use that does not automatically meet the animals' requirements flowing from their natures. In this way, one can see that the social context for the re-emergence of the notion of *telos* is a pre-eminently moral one: *telos* provides the conceptual underpinnings for articulating social moral concern about new forms of animal suffering. From this moral source emerge epistemological consequences which somewhat work against and mitigate the reductionistic tendencies in science alluded to earlier. For example, it is moral concern for *telos* which is sparking a return of science to studying animal consciousness, animal pain and animal behaviour, areas which had been reduced out of existence by the mechanistic tendencies of the twentieth-century science that affords pride of place to physicochemistry (Rollin, 1989). In an interesting dialectical shift, moral concern for animals helps revive the notion of *telos* as a fundamental scientific concept, in something of a neo-Aristotelian turn.

Genetic Engineering

If our analysis of the moral concerns leading to the resurrection of the notion of *telos* is correct, we can proceed to rationally reconstruct the concept and then assess its relevance to the genetic engineering of animals. By rationally reconstruct, I mean first of all provide an articulated account of *telos* which fills the moral role society expects of it. Second, I mean to protect it from fallacious accretions which logically do not fit that role but which have attached, or are likely to attach to it for purely emotional, aesthetic or other morally irrelevant reasons. A simple example of such a conceptual barnacle might be those who would restore the notion of 'Divine purpose' to the concept of *telos*, and then argue that any genetic engineering is wrong simply because it violates that Divine purpose.

What sense can we make out of the notion of *telos* we have offered? In that sense, the *telos* of an animal means 'the set of needs and interests which are genetically based, and environmentally expressed, and which collectively constitute or define the "form of life" or way of living exhibited by that animal, and whose fulfilment or thwarting matter to the animal.' The fulfilment of *telos* matters in a positive way, and leads to well-being or happiness; the thwarting matters in a negative way and leads to suffering (see Rollin, 1992, Part I). Both happiness and suffering in this sense are more adequate notions than merely pleasure and pain, as they implicitly acknowledge qualitative differences among both positive and negative experiences. The negative experience associated with isolating a social animal is quite different from the experience associated with being frightened or physically hurt or deprived of water. Since, as many (but not all) biologists have argued, we tend to see animals in terms of categories roughly equivalent to species, the *telos* of an animal will tend to be a characterization of the basic nature of a species. On the other hand, increased attention to refining the needs and interests of animals may cause us to further refine the notion of *telos* so that it takes cognisance of differences in the needs and interests of animals at the level of sub-species or races, or breeds, as well as of unique variations found in individual animals, though, strictly speaking, as Aristotle points out, individuals do not have natures, even as proper names do not have meaning.

Thus, we may attempt to characterize the general *telos* of the dog as a pack animal requiring social contact, a carnivore requiring a certain sort of diet, etc. At this level we should also characterize gender- and age-specific needs, such as nest-building for sows, or extensive play for puppies and piglets.

[. . .]

This is perfectly analogous to moral notions we use vis-à-vis humans. Our *ur*-concern is that basic human interests as determined by human nature are globally protected—hence the emphasis on general human rights. We may also concern ourselves with refinement of those interests regarding subgroups of humans, although these subgroups are as much cultural as genetic.

[. . .]

Thus, *telos* is a metaphysical (or categorial) concept, serving a moral and thus value-laden function, and is fleshed out in different contexts by both our degree of empirical knowledge of a particular kind of animal and by our specificity and degree of moral concern about the animals in question. For example, the earliest stages of moral concern about the *telos* of laboratory animals focused only on very basic needs: food, ambient temperature, water, etc. As our moral concern grew, it focused on the less obvious aspects of the animals' natures, such as social needs, exercise, etc. As it grew still more, it focused on even less evident aspects.

[. . .]

Thus, the notion of *telos* as it is currently operative is going to be a dynamic and dialectical one, not in the Darwinian sense that animal natures evolve but, more interestingly, in the following sense: as moral concern for animals (and for more kinds of animals) increases in society, this will drive the quest for greater knowledge of the animals' natures and interests, which knowledge can in turn drive greater moral concern for and attention to these animals.

It is not difficult to find this notion of *telos* operative internationally in current society. Increasing numbers of people are seeking enriched environments for laboratory animals, and this is even discussed regularly in trade journals for the research community. Indeed, one top official in the US research community has suggested that animals in research probably suffer more from the way we keep them (i.e. not accommodating their natures) than from the invasive research manipulations we perform. The major thrust of international concern about farm animals devolves around the failure of the environments they are raised in to meet their needs and natures, physical and psychological.

[. . .]

Respect for *Telos* and the Conservation of Well-Being

This, then, is a sketch of the concept of *telos* that has re-emerged in society today. Though it is partially metaphysical (in defining a way of looking at the world), and partially empirical (in that it can and will be deepened and refined by increasing empirical knowledge), it is at root a moral notion, both because it is morally motivated and because it contains the notion of what about an animal we *ought* at least to try to respect and accommodate.

What, then, is the relationship between *telos* and genetic engineering? One widespread suggestion that has surfaced is quite seductive (Fox, 1986). The argument proceeds as follows. Given that the social ethic is asserting that our use of animals should respect and not violate the animals' *telos*, it follows that we should not alter the animals' *telos*. Since genetic engineering is precisely the deliberate changing of animal *telos*, it is *ipso facto* morally wrong.

[. . .]

Seductive though this move may be, I do not believe it will stand up to rational scrutiny, for I believe it rests upon a logical error. What the moral imperative about *telos* says is this:

Maxim to Respect *Telos*:

> If an animal has a set of needs and interests which are constitutive of its nature, then, in our dealings with that animal, we are obliged to not violate and to attempt to accommodate those interests, for violation of and failure to accommodate those interests matters to the animal.

However, it does not follow from that statement that we cannot change the *telos*. The reason we respect *telos*, as we saw, is that the interests comprising the *telos* are plausibly what matters most to the animals. If we alter the *telos* in such a way that different things matter to the animal, or in a way that is irrelevant to the animal, we have not violated the above maxim. In essence, the maxim says that, given a *telos*, we should respect the interests which flow from it. This principle does not logically entail that we cannot modify the *telos* and thereby generate different or alternative interests.

The only way one could deduce an injunction that it is wrong to change *telos* from the Maxim to Respect *Telos* is to make the ancillary Panglossian assumption that an animal's *telos* is the best it can possibly be vis-à-vis the animal's well-being, and that any modification of *telos* will inevitably result in even greater violation of the animal's nature and consequently lead to greater suffering. This ancillary assumption is neither *a priori* true nor empirically true, and can indeed readily be seen to be false.

Consider domestic animals. One can argue that humans have, through artificial selection, changed (or genetically engineered) the *telos* of at least some such animals from their parent stock so that they are more congenial to our husbandry than are the parent stock. I doubt that anyone would argue that, given our decision to have domestic animals, it is better to have left the *telos* alone, and to have created animals for whom domestication involves a state of constant violation of their *telos*.

By the same token, consider the current situation of farm animals mentioned earlier, wherein we keep animals under conditions which patently violate their *telos*, so that they suffer in a variety of modalities yet are kept alive and productive by technological fixes. As a specific example, consider the chickens kept in battery cages for efficient, high-yield, egg production. It is now recognized that such a production system frustrates numerous significant aspects of chicken behaviour under natural conditions, including nesting behaviour (i.e. violates the *telos*), and that frustration of this basic need or drive results in a mode of suffering for the animals (Mench, 1992). Let us suppose that we have identified the gene or genes that code for the drive to nest. In addition, suppose we can ablate that gene or substitute a gene (probably *per impossibile*) that creates a new kind of chicken, one that achieves satisfaction by laying an egg in a cage. Would that be wrong in terms of the ethic I have described?

If we identify an animal's *telos* as being genetically based and environmentally expressed, we have now changed the chicken's *telos* so that the animal that is forced by us to live in a battery cage is satisfying more of its nature than is the animal that still has the gene coding for nesting. Have we done something morally wrong?

I would argue that we have not. Recall that a key feature, perhaps *the* key feature, of the new ethic for animals I have described is concern for preventing animal suffering and augmenting animal happiness, which I have argued involves satisfaction of *telos*. I have also implicitly argued that the primary, pressing concern is the former, the mitigating of suffering at human hands, given the proliferation of suffering that has occurred in the twentieth century. I have also argued that suffering can be occasioned in many ways, from infliction of physical pain to prevention of satisfying basic drives. So, when we engineer the new kind of chicken that prefers laying in a cage and we eliminate the nesting urge, we have removed a source of suffering. Given the animal's changed *telos*, the new chicken is now suffering less than its predecessor and is thus closer to being happy, that is, satisfying the dictates of its nature.

This account may appear to be open to a possible objection that is well known in human ethics. As John Stuart Mill queried in his *Utilitarianism*, is it better to be a satisfied pig or a dissatisfied Socrates? His response, famously inconsistent with his emphasis on pleasure and pain as the only morally relevant dimensions of human life, is that it is better to be a dissatisfied Socrates. In other words, we intuitively consider the solution to human suffering offered, for example, in *Brave New World*, where people do not suffer under bad conditions, in part because they are high on drugs, to be morally reprehensible, even though people feel happy and do not experience suffering. Why then, would we consider genetic manipulation of animals to eliminate the need that is being violated by the conditions under which we keep them to be morally acceptable?

[. . .]

In the case of animals, [. . .] there are no *ur*-values like freedom and reason lurking in the background. We furthermore have a historical tradition as old as domestication for changing (primarily agricultural) animal *telos* (through artificial selection) to fit animals into human society to serve human needs. We selected for non-aggressive animals, animals that depend on us not only on themselves, animals disinclined or unable to leave our protection, and so on. Our operative concern has always been to fit animals to us with as little friction as possible—as discussed, this assured both success for farmers and good lives for the animals.

If we now consider it essential to raise animals under conditions like battery cages, it is not morally jarring to consider changing their *telos* to fit those conditions in the same way that it jars us to consider changing humans.

Why then does it appear to some people to be *prima facie* somewhat morally problematic to suggest tampering with the animal's *telos* to remove suffering? In large part, I believe, because people are not convinced that we cannot change the conditions rather than the animal.

[. . .]

On the other hand, suppose the industry manages to convince the public that we cannot possibly change the conditions under which the animals are raised or that such changes would be outrageously costly to the consumer. And let us further suppose, as is very likely, that people still want animal products, rather than choosing a vegetarian lifestyle. There is no reason to believe that people will ignore the suffering of the animals. If changing the animals by genetic engineering is the only way to assure that they do not suffer (the chief concern of the new ethic), people will surely accept that strategy, though doubtless with some reluctance.

From whence would stem such reluctance, and would it be a morally justified reluctance? Some of the reluctance would probably stem from slippery slope concerns—what next? Is the world changing too quickly, slipping out of our grasp? This is a normal human reflexive response to change—people reacted that way to the automobile. The relevant moral dimension is consequentialist; might not such change have results that will cause problems later? Might this not signal other major changes we are not expecting?

Closely related to that is a queasiness that is, at root, aesthetic. The chicken sitting in a nest is a powerful aesthetic image, analogous to cows grazing in green fields. A chicken without that urge jars us. But when people realize that the choice is between a new variety of chicken, one *without* the urge to nest and denied the opportunity to build a nest by how it is raised, and a traditional chicken *with* the urge to nest that is denied the opportunity to build a nest, and the latter is suffering while the former is not, they will accept the removal of the urge, though they are likelier to be reinforced in their demand for changing the system of rearing and, perhaps, in their willingness to pay for reform of battery cages. This leads directly to my final point.

The most significant justified moral reluctance would probably come from a virtue ethic component of morality. Genetically engineering chickens to no longer want to nest could well evoke the following sort of musings: 'Is this the sort of solution we are nurturing in society in our emphasis on economic growth, productivity and efficiency? Are we so unwilling to pay more for things that we do not hesitate to change animals that we have successfully been in a contractual relationship with since the dawn of civilization? Do we really want to encourage a mind-set willing to change venerable and tested aspects of nature at the drop of a hat for the sake of a few pennies? Is tradition of no value?' In the face of this sort of component to moral thought, I suspect that society might well resist the changing of *telos*. But at the same time, people will be forced to take welfare concerns more seriously and to decide whether they are willing to pay for tradition and amelioration of animal suffering, or whether they will accept the 'quick fix' of *telos* alteration. Again, I suspect that such musings will lead to changes in husbandry, rather than changes in chickens.

We have thus argued that it does not follow from the Maxim to Respect *Telos* that we cannot change *telos* (at least in domestic animals) to make for happier animals, though such a prospect is undoubtedly jarring. A similar point can be made in principle about non-domestic animals as well. Insofar as we encroach upon and transgress against the environments of all animals by depositing toxins, limiting forage, etc. and do so too quickly for them to adjust by natural selection, it would surely be better to modify the animals to cope with this new situation so they can be happy and thrive rather than allow them to sicken, suffer, starve and die, though surely, for reasons of uncertainty on how effective we can be alone as well as aesthetic reasons, it is far better to preserve and purify their environment.

In sum, the Maxim to Respect *Telos* does not entail that we cannot change *telos*. What it does entail is that, if we do change *telos* by genetic engineering, we must be clear that the animals will be no worse off than they would have been without the change, and ideally will be better off. Such an unequivocally positive *telos* change from the perspective of the animal can occur when, for example, we eliminate genetic disease or susceptibility to other diseases by genetic engineering, since disease entails suffering. The foregoing maxim which does follow from the Maxim to Respect *Telos*, we may call the Principle of Conservation of Well-Being. This principle does of course exclude much of the genetic engineering currently in progress, where the *telos* is changed to benefit humans (e.g. by creating larger meat animals) without regard to its effect on the animal. A major concern in this area which I have discussed elsewhere is the creation of genetically engineered animals to 'model' human genetic disease (Rollin, 1995b, Chapter 3).

There is one final caveat about genetic engineering of animals which is indirectly related to the Maxim to Respect *Telos*, and which has been discussed, albeit in a different context, by biologists. Let us recall that a *telos* is not only genetically based, but is environmentally expressed. Thus, we can modify an animal's *telos* in such a way as to improve the animal's *telos* and quality of life, but at the expense of other animals enmeshed in the ecological/environmental web with the animal in question. For example, suppose we could genetically engineer the members of a prey species to be impervious to predators. While their *telos* would certainly be improved, other animals would very likely be harmed. While these animals would thrive, those who predate them could starve, and other animals who compete with the modified species could be choked out. Thus, we would, in essence, be robbing Peter to pay Paul. Furthermore, while the animals in question would surely be better off in the short run, their descendants may well not be—they might, for example, exceed the available food supply and may also starve, something which would not have occurred but for the putatively beneficial change in the *telos* we undertook. Thus, the price of improving one *telos* of animals in nature may well be to degrade the efficacy of others. In this consequential and environmental sense, we would be wise to be extremely circumspect and conservative in our genetic engineering of non-domestic animals, as the environmental consequences of such modifications are too complex to be even roughly predictable (Rollin, 1995a, Chapter 2).

Conclusion

In conclusion, there is no direct reason to argue that the emerging ethical/metaphysical notion of *telos* and the Maxim to Respect *Telos* logically forbid genetic engineering of animals. In the case of domestic animals solidly under our control, one must look at each proposed genetic modification in terms of the Principle of Conservation of Welfare. In the case of non-domestic animals, there is again no logical corollary of the maxim of respect for *telos* which forestalls genetically modifying their *telos*, and, on occasion, such modification could be salubrious. Given our ignorance, however, of the systemic effects of such modifications, it would be prudent to proceed carefully, as we could initiate ecological catastrophe and indirectly affect the functionality of many other animals' *tele*.

References

Fox, M.W. (1986) On the genetic engineering of animals: A response to Evelyn Pluhar. *Between the Species*, **2** (1), 51–2.

Markowitz, H. and Line, S. (1989) The need for responsive environments, in *The Experimental Animal in Biomedical Research*, vol. I (eds B.E. Rollin and M.L. Kesel), CRC Press, Boca Raton, Florida, pp. 153–73.

Mench, J.A. (1992) The welfare of poultry in modern production systems. *Critical Reviews in Poultry Biology*, **4**, 107–28.

Rollin, B.E. (1989) *The Unheeded Cry: Animal Consciousness, Animal Pain and Science*, Oxford University Press, Oxford.

Rollin, B.E. (1992) *Animal Rights and Human Morality*, Prometheus Books, Buffalo, NY.

Rollin, B.E. (1995a) *Farm Animal Welfare: Ethical, Social, and Research Issues*, Iowa State University Press, Ames, IA.

Rollin, B.E. (1995b) *The Frankenstein Syndrome: Ethical and Social Issues in the Genetic Engineering of Animals*, Cambridge University Press, New York.

53 Brave New Birds

The Use of "Animal Integrity" in Animal Ethics

Bernice Bovenkerk, Frans W. A. Brom, and Babs J. van den Bergh

Bovenkirk, Brom, and van den Bergh use the terms integrity *and* naturalness *to address the notions of bioengineering and* telos *raised by Rollin. They note that the concept of integrity refers to a set of characteristics of a species humans define and believe is important to preserve and that the identity of such characteristics can be elucidated by moral discussion. Even in the absence of full agreement, such discussions can help clarify the issues and evaluate existing practices.*

Besides providing us with new biological knowledge and opening up some intriguing possibilities in medicine and agriculture, genetic engineering provides philosophers with some interesting thought experiments. Inspired by Bernard Rollin's remark in *The Frankenstein Syndrome*[1] about the creation of wingless, legless, and featherless chickens, Gary Comstock urges us to imagine just that: the transition of chickens into living egg machines.[2]

[. . .]

What if we could make these animals adjust better to their environment and genetically engineer them into senseless humps of flesh, solely directed at transforming grain and water into eggs. [. . .] Intuitively, treating an animal in this way—or rather creating an animal for these purposes—is morally problematic. This intuition is also prompted by uses of biotechnology that are already feasible and indeed are already in use, but the "brave new birds" provide a paradigmatic case.

In public debate in The Netherlands, these sorts of cases evoke appeals to such notions as integrity and naturalness.[3] In the case of the egg machines, for example, we might say that the chickens' integrity has been violated because we have interfered with their physical makeup, not for their own good, but for ours. We have tampered with the characteristics that make a chicken a chicken.

Why Animal Integrity?

This intuition that changing chickens into senseless, living egg machines is problematic and cannot be elaborated solely with the help of traditional moral concepts such as animal interests or animal rights.

"Welfarists," like Rollin, take animals to have interests because, and only insofar as, they are sentient. In other words, Rollin holds that animals have interests by virtue of their sentience, and therefore that only welfare matters from a moral point of view.

[. . .]

Since the chickens are senseless, Rollin cannot raise any objection to the use of genetic engineering to turn these animals into machines. But even though Rollin asserts that he "sees no moral problem if animals could be made happier by changing their natures," elsewhere he seems to acknowledge that creating living egg machines is not a desirable course of action. Rather, it is the lesser of two evils "while it is certainly a poor alternative to alter animals to fit questionable environments, rather than alter the environments to suit the animals, few would deny that an animal that does mesh with a poor environment is better off than one that does not." This assertion seems to acknowledge the moral intuition that changing an animal's nature is objectionable, while holding that the circumstances may make it necessary. Clearly, however, suffering is not the main issue here. In other words, Rollin's concept of interest is too narrow to analyze our moral intuition.[4]

Animal rights proponents, such as Tom Regan, argue that raising animals for food is wrong not primarily because it causes animal suffering but because it is wrong in principle. This is because animals, like humans, are valuable in themselves and not only by virtue of their value to others. In other words, they possess inherent value and therefore have moral standing.[5] According to Regan, the basis for this inherent value is that animals are "subjects-of-a-life."[6] Regan regards mammals that possess a certain amount of awareness as paradigmatic subjects-of-a-life. If so, the senseless egg machines in our example are probably not subjects-of-a-life, and it is probably not wrong in principle to change chickens into them.

[. . .]

Animal ethicists in the Netherlands have proposed the notion of animal integrity precisely because of the inability of interests and rights to accommodate the moral intuition that we should adjust the farm environment to the animal and not vice versa. Integrity has been described by Bart Rutgers as the "wholeness and intactness of the animal and its species-specific balance, as well as the capacity to sustain itself in an environment suitable to the species."[7]

Some Objections

"Integrity" seems to be helpful because it has an objective, biological aspect. It implies that the animal is intact or whole, which is an attribute of the animal itself, not just some value we have placed on it. Integrity therefore could play an important role in elaborating moral concerns not only about genetic engineering but also about other interventions in animal life, like cross-breeding or intensive animal husbandry.

It is important to note that we would not speak of the violation of integrity in all cases in which an animal's intactness is violated. Rutgers holds that docking a dog's tail for aesthetic reasons constitutes a violation of the dog's integrity, but when the dog's tail must be docked for medical reasons, he claims that its integrity has not been violated. In effect, docking a dog's tail for these two reasons could be regarded as two different actions, depending on the intention with which the action is carried out.

But this raises a problem. If the physiological result of the two different kinds of docking is the same, then it seems that integrity is not a biological aspect of the animal itself after all. The concept then loses its objective, biological character and becomes a moral rather than an empirical notion. It does not refer to a notion of factual intactness or wholeness so much as to a *perceived* intactness. It refers to how we feel an animal *should* be.[8] That leaves us wondering how objective the notion of integrity really is.

A second difficulty with the notion of integrity is the problem of "gradation." If we are to judge the acceptability of, say, a certain scientific experiment on animal subjects, then we need to be able to weigh the moral good against the moral wrong.[9] Only when we can deem one type of experiment more acceptable than another will "integrity" have meaning in the context of ethical deliberation. If gradation were impossible, then every intervention constituting a violation of integrity would have to be dealt with similarly: either they would all have to be condemned, no matter how trivial the purpose, or none of them could be condemned, no matter how severe the consequences.

Gradation could be achieved in three different ways. First, violations of integrity could be graded based on the good that the violation aims at. The problem with this first position is that all the work has to be done by weighing goals and not by grading the moral wrongs. Integrity itself is not graded at all.

Second, one could consider respect for integrity as a prima facie duty that must be weighed against other prima facie duties. The problem with this strategy is that we must know more about integrity to do the weighing, which leads us back to the question about integrity's content.

The third way would be to describe different kinds of violations of integrity, some more severe than others. The problem with the third way is that, unlike the notions of well-being and health, integrity—conceived of as intactness or wholeness—seems to be an absolute notion.[10] A body is either intact or not, and so either has integrity or not. It's like being pregnant: a woman is either pregnant or she is not; she cannot be more or less pregnant. The *violation* of integrity is not necessarily this absolute. Docking a dog's tail, for instance, does not seem to be as harsh a violation of its integrity as, say, the removal of one of its legs. The question is what basis we have for judging the weight of a violation of integrity. What criteria can we use to establish which of two violations is worse? And what criteria can be used to argue that the violation is bad enough to reject the possible good it constitutes (as in the case of scientific experiments)? We need grounds to make this kind of gradation possible. In other words: how can we measure integrity?

Human Integrity

Thus the notion of integrity is problematic. It carries a false pretense of objectivity, of being "empirically determinable," and it is not clear how it can be of practical use, as this would entail criteria to measure it. Do these problems render the concept of animal integrity useless? To answer this question, it is helpful to look at two parallel discussions in which integrity plays a role: human integrity and ecosystem integrity.

A widely shared moral intuition exists that no matter what the benefits, every human being has the right not to be physically violated without his or her consent. The concept of human integrity is often employed to give voice to this intuition.

Physical and mental integrity concerns the inviolability or intactness of a person's body and mind. Historically, the concept originates in the debate about the relationship between the state and its citizens. The most important human right is the right not to be imprisoned arbitrarily or to have the integrity of one's person or body violated in any other way. This right has now been extended to the medical sphere, where it plays a central role in defining the relationship between physicians and their patients, obliging doctors to request the patient's informed consent before carrying out an invasive action.[11] More precisely, informed consent is based on two complexly interrelated pillars—autonomy over and integrity of one's mind and body. Sometimes, but not always, they support each other. Protection from invasive action cannot be lifted without the permission of the patient. However, permission is not always a sufficient condition for integrity not to be violated. The concept of integrity provides some restraint on self-determination: some violations might be objectionable even if the person wants them.

If a patient is not able to give permission for whatever reason, others have to see to the protection of her body from invasive action. This is where integrity becomes most important; it establishes the inviolability of the bodies of people who cannot dispose of their bodies themselves, including children, prisoners, and those who are mentally handicapped or comatose. The same intuition plays a role in decisions about people who out of sheer poverty feel forced to "donate" their organs. Socioeconomic circumstances prevent these people from exercising their autonomy. When we want to argue against allowing them to sell their organs, we could appeal to their physical integrity.

[. . .]

It is important to note that the law not only concerns violations of the body resulting in suffering or in adverse health conditions, but that it also deals with infringements on the body without such detrimental effects. In fact, as with animals, it is this dimension of inviolability that is best expressed by the notion of integrity. Even though the person with Down syndrome who receives a contraceptive injection can hardly be said to suffer a great deal of pain or illness as a result of the injection, the notion of integrity allows one to argue that she has been violated and that the administration of contraceptive injection is—at the very least—morally problematic and in need of justification.

Plainly the concept of integrity is well established in the field of medical ethics as a way of structuring discussions. Yet here, too, it is not free of problems. The problems can be illustrated by considering the implications of Article 11 of the Dutch Constitution, which states that every person has the right, apart from limitations imposed by law, to the inviolability of her body. The clause is part of the right to protection of personal privacy and contains two elements: (1) the right to be protected from harm of and infringement upon the body by a third party, and (2) the right to self-determination of the body. Thus in its explanation of what "integrity" involves, the law makes a distinction between a person and her body and allows a person to dispose of her body freely.

This distinction is controversial in philosophy, but it is undeniably useful for understanding and regulating the doctor-patient relationship. If the distinction is admitted, however, then protecting the integrity of a *person* can lead to a violation of the integrity of the person's *body*. The right to physical integrity contends that every person has the right to remain free from infringements upon the body by others, but it also states that every person has a right to determine the disposition of one's body.

If the body has integrity of its own that could be violated, then a trans-sexual who undergoes a sex-change may very well be violating her own physical integrity. If we do not want to draw this conclusion, then we must hold that an intervention into the body is not a violation when it is approved of by the person. We could say that as the operation seems to bring the person more in harmony with her body, in the overall picture the person's integrity has not been violated.[12] Integrity as a moral notion can therefore be diametrically opposed to integrity as an empirical notion. Here, as with animal integrity, we see that an intervention constitutes a violation of integrity only if it is *perceived* as such. Clearly the problem of objectivity is present in the domain of human integrity as well as in that of animal integrity.

Ecosystem Integrity

The notion of integrity has also been applied within the science of ecology in order to help protect environmental resources. Aldo Leopold employed the concept in relation to ecosystems. In what must be the most quoted passage in ecological ethics, he asserted that "A thing is right when it tends to preserve the integrity, stability, and beauty of the biotic community. It is wrong when it tends to do otherwise."[13]

Ecological integrity refers to the wholeness, unity, or completeness of an ecosystem. Immediately, of course, the question arises what we are to make of the stability and wholeness of an ecosystem when it is a central feature of ecosystems that they change continuously. Parts of an ecosystem can be destroyed while the ecosystem as a whole seems to flourish. There is an uninterrupted movement through life cycles; some individuals die and others are born, but the ecosystem as a whole remains. How can we determine whether or not the integrity of an evolving ecosystem has been violated?

James Kay's definition of ecosystem integrity takes this dynamic character into account and calls attention to certain processes found within ecosystems. According to Kay, constitutive elements of ecosystem integrity are the ability of ecosystems to maintain optimum operations, to cope with environmental stress, and to self-organize.[14] Laura Westra adds a human element to this definition; she asserts that an ecosystem must be able to maintain its "conditions as free as possible from human intervention" and to withstand anthropocentric stresses upon the environment.[15] Westra also distinguishes ecosystem integrity from ecosystem health. An ecosystem can be healthy even when it is intensively managed by people, but it possesses integrity only "when it is wild, that is, free as much as possible today from human intervention, when it is an 'unmanaged' ecosystem, although not a necessarily pristine one."[16]

When the first European settlers came to Australia in 1788, they encountered a more or less harmonious ecosystem, characterized by native flora and fauna that were well adapted to their environment. Delicate relations between the land and its vegetation and between different kinds of plants and animals kept all in balance. Understandably, however, the settlers felt homesick in this alien land. Also, it did not at first sight seem to offer very many food crops. Thus the settlers thought it would be a good idea to bring some of their own native plants and animals to Australia, in order both to sustain themselves and to remind them of their homeland. Little did they know what havoc they were to cause by this introduction of exotic species.

[. . .]

Biodiversity was lost, and the ecosystem can no longer be said to be free and unmanaged in Westra's sense. The native vegetation has been overgrown, and animals that fed on the native plants have lost a food source. In effect, an altogether new ecosystem has evolved. The initial ecosystem could not respond well.

Several attempts have been made to put the concept of ecological integrity to practical use. This has proven to be difficult, but it is also very important, as it could help guide policy. For instance, managers of different national parks adhere to different approaches about whether or not to prevent naturally occurring fires. Westra's account of ecosystem integrity gives us some criteria to employ in thinking about this problem. Her account suggests that while the health of a forest might be damaged by naturally occurring fires, its integrity cannot be said to be violated because the effects are not the result of human action.

The problems that beset the concept of ecosystem integrity include those of both objectivity and gradation. There is no easy way of establishing objectively whether or not a violation of an ecosystem has occurred. All that seems clear is that ecosystems' integrity is violated when we destroy the whole world, for then it is quite clear that the ecosystem has not been able to cope with anthropocentric stress. As John Lemons notes,

> it could be said that any ecosystem that can maintain itself without collapsing has integrity. . . .
> There is no scientific reason why a changed ecosystem necessarily has less ability to maintain optimum operations under normal environmental conditions, cope with changes in environmental conditions less effectively, or be limited in its ability to continue the process of self-organisation on an ongoing basis.[17]

Thus ecological integrity does not allow us to demarcate precisely which intervention does and which does not violate the integrity of an ecosystem.

Moreover, as with animal integrity, it is difficult to find criteria to determine how severely the ecosystem's integrity has been violated. How, for example, can we determine the severity of the damage caused by blackberries in Australia? A new balance was found between different plants and animals within the ecosystem, and in a sense, optimum operations were restored. It is because we find the change undesirable that we say the ecosystem's integrity has been violated. In short, whether or not an ecosystem's integrity has been violated "must be based on human judgement regarding the acceptability of a particular change."[18]

As we saw before in the case of animal integrity, whether or not such a change is rendered acceptable largely depends on the purpose for which the intervention is carried out. The example of the forest destroyed by naturally occurring fire makes clear that integrity is primarily a moral term, referring to human action. Only when the fire has been lit by humans do we speak of a violation of the forest's integrity. Moreover, setting the forest on fire could actually benefit it,[19] and in that case, even a human-induced fire would probably not be counted as a violation of integrity. It is the ends an act serves that makes us judge it favorably or not.

Flawed but Workable

As we have seen, arguments about "integrity" are problematic not only in the animal domain but in parallel discussions as well. The concept refers not to a state of affairs that can be assessed empirically but rather to our own ideals for a human, an animal, or an ecosystem. Violations of integrity cannot be objectively proven, nor can their severity be established.

Yet despite these problems, "integrity" is used in the ecological and human domains to structure discussions and to reach agreements. In these domains, it serves a useful critical function. It has proven especially valuable in the field of medicine, and at least in continental Europe seems to be widely accepted, alongside the concepts of autonomy and dignity.[20] These other concepts are also rather obscure, but nevertheless they have been translated into principles whose usefulness is widely accepted, despite disputes about their exact meaning.

In the field of environmental policy, too, "integrity" seems to be a sound notion. Appeals to integrity frequently pop up in the management of national parks. Even though it is sometimes hard to establish whether or not a policy will amount to a violation of an ecosystem's integrity, the concept hands policymakers and park managers a tool to structure and clarify their discussion. Here, as in the case of medical interventions, an appeal to integrity gives us the opportunity to criticize certain proposed actions that have repercussions for an ecosystem's functioning. Again, the concept of integrity generates no knock-down arguments, but it nonetheless appears to be quite workable in a practical context. It gives us a way to communicate moral reservations we might have about environmental policies.

When we envision a future in which we buy eggs from a warehouse housing hundreds of rows of flesh-colored humps created from what we once knew as chickens, a feeling of discomfort comes over us. We—or many of us, anyway—have a moral intuition that changing chickens into living egg machines is wrong. The moral notion that gives voice to this intuition is "integrity." Integrity goes beyond considerations of an animal's health and welfare, and it applies not only to present but also to future animals. An animal's integrity is violated when through human intervention it is no longer whole or intact, if its species-specific balance is changed, or if it no longer has the capacity to sustain itself in an environment suitable to its species. However, when the intervention is directed toward the animal's own good, we do not speak of a violation of its integrity.

One of the main appeals of the use of integrity seems to be its objective, biological aspect. As we have shown, however, integrity is not as objective a notion as it appears at first sight. Should we therefore do away with the concept of animal integrity? Not necessarily, or rather, necessarily not. The concept has been introduced to fill a gap between moral theory and moral experience. It is important to do justice to this moral experience, and not to reject the concept too swiftly because of difficulties in setting out precisely what it involves. In the light of ongoing technological developments, we are confronted ever more frequently with moral dilemmas that traditional moral concepts cannot deal with, and we have a responsibility to try to refine our moral thinking and to develop criteria that help us act in a morally justifiable way.

So let's take a closer look at the problems with the concept of integrity. We argued that the purpose of potential violation of integrity is crucial for judging whether or not the action actually constitutes a violation of integrity. When we dock a dog's tail, for example, our reason for docking it is decisive in deciding whether the dog's integrity has been violated. The concept of integrity thus does not refer to an objective state of affairs, but to one that *we* feel is important to preserve.

Yet we need not regard the concept as completely subjective, either. While it does not refer to empirically ascertainable biological facts, we can still establish intersubjective criteria for its application. Through moral discussion, we can reach agreement about which sorts of actions do and do not lead to violations of integrity. And even if we could not reach this agreement, the notion of integrity still has an important function, namely to clarify the moral debate and criticize existing practices. Integrity can give opponents of Rollin's thought experiment a way to voice their criticism of the creation of living egg machines without having to appeal to traditional moral concepts like welfare, interests, or rights, none of which seem to capture what is important in Rollin's scenario. "Integrity" should therefore remain a part of our moral discussion. Its content can be continually refined through an ongoing learning process.

Notes

1. B.E. Rollin, *The Frankenstein Syndrome: Ethical and Social Issues in the Genetic Engineering of Animals* (New York: Cambridge University Press, 1995).
2. G. Comstock, *What Obligations Have Scientists to Transgenic Animals?*, discussion paper by the Center for Biotechnology, Policy and Ethics, 8, College Station, Tex.: Texas A&M University, 1992.

3. In this article we will limit ourselves to a discussion of the former. F.W.A. Brom, J.M.G. Vorstenbosch, and E. Schroten, "Public Policy and Transgenic Animals: Case-by-Case Assessment as a Moral Learning Process," in *The Social Management of Genetic Engineering*, ed. P. Wheale, R. von Schomberg, and P. Glasner (Aldershot: Ashgate, 1998), 249–64.

4. Other welfarists, such as Nils Holtug, object to changing animals into senseless machines by arguing that attention to welfare should not be limited to the prevention of suffering, but should also be directed to the promotion of positive experiences. By making animals senseless we would deny animals the possibility to enjoy positive experiences. See N. Holtug, "Is Welfare All that Matters in our Moral Obligations to Animals?" *Acta Agriculturae Scandinavica Sect. A, Animal Science Supplement* 27 (1996): 16–21. However, welfarists need to invoke an extra premise, not reducible to mere sentience, to explain why positive experiences matter to the animal. See F.W.A. Brom, "Animal Welfare, Public Policy and Ethics," in *Animal Consciousness and Animal Ethics: Perspectives from the Netherlands*, ed. M. Dol, S. Kasanmoentalib, S. Lijmbach, E. Rivas, and R van den Bos. (Assen: Van Gorcum, 1997), 208–22.

5. T. Regan, *The Case for Animal Rights* (London: Routledge and Kegan Paul, 1983).

6. To be a "subject-of-a-life" is to "have beliefs and desires; perception, memory, and a sense of the future, including their own future; an emotional life together with feelings of pleasure and pain; preference and welfare-interests; the ability to initiate action in pursuit of their desires and goals; a psychophysical identity over time; and an individual welfare in the sense that their experiential life fares well or ill for them, independently of their utility to others." See Regan, *The Case for Animal Rights*, 243.

7. L.J.E. Rutgers, F.J. Grommers, and J.M. Wijsmuller, "Welzijn-Intrinsieke waarde-Integriteit," *Tijdschrift voor Diergeneeskunde* (1995): 490–4; and L.J.E. Rutgers and F.R. Heeger, "Inherent Worth and Respect for Animal Integrity," (41–51) in *Recognizing the Intrinsic Value of Animals: Beyond Animal Welfare*, ed. M. Dol, M. F. Van Vlissingen, S. Kasanmoentalib, T. Visser, and H. Zwart (Assen: Van Gorcum, 1999).

8. F.W.A. Brom, "Animal Welfare," and F.W.A. Brom, "The Good Life of Creatures with Dignity," *Journal for Agricultural and Environmental Ethics* 13, nos. 1–2 (2000): 53–63.

9. We intentionally do not use the terms "benefits" and "advantages" because they imply a utilitarian framework, whereas our discussion depends on a deontological one.

10. J.M.G. Vorstenbosch, "The Concept of Integrity: Its Significance for the Ethical Discussion on Biotechnology and Animals," *Livestock Production Science* 36 (1993): 109–12.

11. T.L. Beauchamp and J.F. Childress, *Principles of Biomedical Ethics*, 4th ed. (New York: Oxford University Press, 1994), 128.

12. On the other hand, as integrity is not an absolute notion, it might well be that it is a violation that is justified, because the appeal to integrity is in this case overruled by an appeal to autonomy. However, we doubt that transsexuals even experience their bodies' integrity as being violated by the sex change.

13. A. Leopold, *A Sand County Almanac* (Oxford: Oxford University Press, 1949), 224–5.

14. J. Kay (1992), quoted in J. Lemons, pp. 177–201, "Ecological Integrity and National Parks," in *Perspectives on Ecological Integrity*, ed. L. Westra and J. Lemons (Dordrecht: Kluwer Academic Publishers, 1995).

15. Lemons, "Ecological Integrity," 180.

16. L. Westra, "Ecosystem Integrity and Sustainability: The Foundational Value of the Wild," in *Perspectives on Ecological Integrity*, ed. L. Westra and J. Lemons (Dotdrecht: Kluwer Academic Publishers, 1995), 12.

17. Lemons, "Ecological Integrity."

18. Lemons, "Ecological Integrity."

19. This is the case with fire-prone and fire-resistant trees, such as gum trees in Australia, that need fire in order to regenerate. Moreover, if regular burning is not conducted in some Australian forests, a fuel buildup on the forest floor will lead to unintended raging bush fires. See on this subject A.M. Gill, R.H. Groves, and I.R. Noble, eds. *Fire and the Australian Biota* (Canberra: Australian Academy of Science, 1981).

20. Beauchamp and Childress, *Principles of Biomedical Ethics*.

54 Telos and the Ethics of Animal Farming

Jes Lynning Harfeld

Harfeld addresses what kinds of animals fare well in confinement agriculture and what is meant by their doing well. Harfeld addresses contemporary philosophical and ethical analysis of animals based on the notion of telos, *as posed by Rollin. Harfeld then goes on to address some of the welfare problems in modern animal agriculture and how they relate to the* telos *concept, focusing on boredom and loneliness in confined animals.*

Introduction

Everybody is talking about animal welfare. In the Danish public media alone there were more than 4,000 articles mentioning "animal welfare" in 2009.[1] These articles focus on animal welfare issues in many different areas of society, such as companion animals, zoological gardens, and animals used in laboratories. The majority of public interest and concern, however, focuses on the lives and (lack of) welfare of animals in agriculture. This is most likely a result of at least two factors: First of all, the sheer number of animals in the different areas of use tends to give the agricultural industry a noticeable primacy. Copenhagen Zoo, one of the largest in Denmark, has about 4,000 individuals,[2] Danish laboratories have been using about 350,000 animals a year the last 10 years (Alstrup and Hansen 2009), and the present number of pets (including horses) in Denmark is around 1.7 million.[3] These numbers are, nonetheless, dwarfed by the two main areas of animal agriculture alone, where production numbers for poultry[4] and pigs reach 145 million individuals (120 and 25 million respectively) every year.[5] A second factor is of course the different aims of animal keeping in the different areas. The aim of pet owners, very generalized, is to have a companion—personally or for the family—and intrinsic to this companion relation rests, in most cases, an idea of care for the animal for the animal's sake. Many pet owners will endure a great deal, both financially and personally, to care for their animals. In some aspects, this is analogous to the zoo animals: although the animals in zoos are fundamentally kept for the pleasure of audiences, the animal keepers in most modern zoos strive for good welfare for the animals—irrespective of any audience presence. In laboratory research and agriculture, however, the sole aim for the keeping of the animals is located, so to speak, outside the animals themselves? This is not to say that farmers and lab workers cannot or do not care for their animals. It is merely to say that the use and treatment of animals in laboratories and in food productions is in no way, or insignificantly so, for the animals.

Both scholars and, as we have seen, the public media increasingly discuss animal welfare—but what is this thing called *animal welfare*? What does it mean for an animal to fare well and how does it relate to ethics? In this article, I intend to explore the notion of animal welfare and ethics in animal agriculture through an idea of the active flourishing of positive natural capabilities. Such a manner of welfare would entail a view of and use of animals in agriculture that would have to situate the aim of animal lives not only outside the animals but also in the animals themselves. Furthermore, it will be theorized that the practical effects of such a changed view would also, through the necessity for different housing systems, reduce the number of animals that could possibly be kept and produced. For this purpose, the ancient Greek idea of telos will be explored in its modern philosophical sense as a theoretical instrument as an investigation into the concepts of *good life* and *welfare* and it will be argued that telos provides us with a comprehensive, non-reductionist and ethologically viable picture of the good animal life—including strictly individual as well as relational welfare. The fundamental premises of this article are twofold. First, I shall assume what may seem obvious, and mostly uncontroversial. Namely that we, by an account of ethics, are presuming to speak of something that is intrinsically linked to the notions of *good* and *bad/evil*. Secondly, and decidedly more controversial, I shall assume that these notions of good and bad are intrinsically linked to entities. This notion infers that good and bad in an ethical sense is something that is good or bad for a certain entity. Thus, it is not good or bad because, for example, the law deems it so, because a religious belief (or God) commends or condemns it, or because it is somehow rationally right or wrong. The entities in question throughout this article are animals in general and animals in agriculture in particular, and the focus will be on establishing what the relevant factors of these entities are with regard to the good and the bad for them.

The article will commence with an analysis and critique of the concept of telos through the works of Bernard E. Rollin. This, together with an argument for an emphasis on the lived life, will be followed by two examples—boredom and loneliness—which will serve to demonstrate how to better understand animal welfare problems in the light of telos-theory. Conclusively the article highlights some of the benefits of adopting a telos-based animal welfare paradigm opposed to other theories; a paradigm that would, if realized, fundamentally change the way animal agriculture is done.

Telos and the Nature of an Animal

The concept of telos is a gateway to understanding what it means to be a certain being and fare well as such a being. We will now look into the theoretical sources and, through the work of Rollin, how these sources have been used in a contemporary applied ethical theory. This will help us better understand the practical examples of telos in the later sections on boredom and loneliness.

[. . .]

Aristotle (2004) relates his concept of humans—and, by rational and natural extension, animals—as beings that have certain inalienable characters that shape their existence within the framework of quite specific possibilities. This end purpose—or telos—is perhaps best understood through a parallel about an inanimate object such as a tool. A hammer is a certain object with certain characteristics. I can surely describe the hammer (shape, color, weight, materials) without saying anything about its end purpose, but it will be a poor description without actually explaining about the hammer's final objective that, depending on the type of hammer, is to hammer a nail into a piece of wood or chiseling stones into road material. So in order to truly understand "hammer" my understanding must transcend "object with wooden handle and metal head of a certain shape and size" and include the actualization of the hammers potential and form. The hammer-telos is a concept about what the hammer is meant to do or be, not about its purely physical attributes. However, the focus of this article is neither inanimate tools such as hammers, nor, indeed, is it the humans which, to a significant extent, was Aristotle's objective. The focus is (1) on farm animals and how the concept of telos applies to their lives in man-made confinement agriculture and (2) the concept of *the good* that arguably follows this. First off, it is important to understand that the telos of living beings is, obviously, somewhat more complicated than that of a simple tool, and the telos of farm animals—the actualization of a pig's form and potential—involves a series of complex questions which will include many quite different capabilities and potentials. In the following, I will present such an account by Bernard E. Rollin.

Rollin and the Telos of Animals

In *Animal Rights and Human Morality* (first edition 1981) Rollin describes the telos of an animal (in this case a spider) as:

> a nature, a function, a set of activities intrinsic to it, evolutionarily determined and genetically imprinted, that constitutes its "living spiderness."
>
> (Rollin 2006, p. 100)

Several perspectives spring from this quote. First, it is obvious that we, in this type of telos, are unable to speak of the telos of a hammer in any other fashion than that of a metaphor. Telos is uniquely a concept that can be attributed to living beings that are part of the evolutionary chain (in a modern understanding of the concept) and which are capable of activities. A hammer might be said to have a telos to it as described in the previous page, but only in an extrinsic sense of the word; meaning that its function is imposed upon it from outside itself—by human hands in this case. The telos of an animal is, on the contrary, an intrinsic nature imposed on the animal only through its genetic composition. It is, in other words, internal to the animal and, in an important sense, its own. In Rollin's view uncovering the telos of an animal is ". . . to characterize each type of living thing according to the unique way it meets the set of characteristics constitutive of all living things" (Rollin 1998a, pp. 156–157). Such a set of characteristics can involve many aspects that are shared with other beings and, therefore, it is through an understanding of the animal's plurality of features as a whole or a unity that we get to the telos of a specific animal. It is, so to speak, the collective constitution of the animal's distinctive and active "being-in-the-world"[6] and argues Rollin, its fulfilment or lack thereof matters positively or negatively to the animal in question.

Now, how do we go about determining the telos of a particular animal? Rollin answers within the biological and naturalistic tradition of Aristotle that we must look to the biological sciences. Both ethology (study of animal behavior) and genetic science provide us with evidence to the specific natures and purposes of living beings.

> The genetic code of a given species provides us with a clear, scientific, testable, physicalistic locus of *telos*.
>
> (Rollin 2006, p. 121)

This species specific-code then determines behavior and physical attributes which can subsequently be understood through ethological studies or what Rollin calls "sympathetic observation" (Rollin 2006). Such a combination of biological and commonsensical approaches presents us with a significant and workable foundation on which we can describe a certain animal's telos and, states Rollin, infer its primary interests. However, this is not a static understanding of telos, as originally argued by Aristotle. Modern biology, originating with Charles Darwin's theories, has taught us that living nature—and thus telos—is a varying and evolving phenomenon; both a consequence of natural evolution and—in the case of domestic animals—a consequence of changes imposed on the animal types by human actions. This does not mean that a certain species of animal does not, at a certain time, have a certain telos. It simply means that, as any creature evolves so does its telos, or, as Rollin points out: ". . . what we called *telos* is a snapshot of a dynamic process" (Rollin 2006, p. 124) and ". . . ought always be open to revision" (Rollin 2006, p. 120).

Rollin does not provide us with a comprehensive list of capabilities or characteristics that would serve as a guideline to recognizing the telos of a specific type of animal. He does, however, give some general examples of telos-dependent features such as the giraffe's ability (freedom) to stretch its neck, the bird's ability (freedom) to fly, and the possibility for a working dog to work. Furthermore, he gives a couple of extended examples, notably one on the rearing of pigs. Citing the work of Stolba and Wood-Gush on domestic pig behavior in semi-natural environments (Stolba and

Wood-Gush 1981), Rollin emphasizes (among other things) such characteristics as the forming of complex social bonds, rooting and nesting as behavioral aspects against which we can measure the possibilities of pig-telos in our current farming systems (Rollin 2006, p. 341)

The connection between telos and what Rollin calls interests is key to understanding his philosophical ethology and, indeed, his primary endeavor: animal ethics. Telos is to this extent a moral norm in Rollin's theory, and it is by allowing the animals to fulfill the interests determined by their specific telos that they are able to live good lives. In other words, the morally relevant interests of animals are those "which are constitutive of the animals' *telos*" (Rollin 1998a, p. 161). We can thus elaborate Rollin's concept of telos as being the platform from which the interests of the animals come into view or materialize. However, to be a being capable of interests is to be more than merely alive. To have an interest is to have a conscious awareness enabling the being to mind what happens to it; put differently, things must matter to the being in question and it must be aware that it matters. Thus, the form of telos proposed by Rollin adheres to more than simply living beings as first suggested. It adheres to living beings with certain mental capabilities that include a reflective consciousness of its own mental states and an attitude—positive, negative, or neutral—towards these.

Telos and the Lived Life

Bernard E. Rollin develops his theories from a neo-Aristotelian standpoint. The theory of species relevant flourishing, in particular, has many advantages and is, as will be shown, of great value to the construction of a comprehensive and valid animal ethic. The previous sections have given us a basic understanding of the concept of telos. Through Rollin we are given a number of definitions pertaining to what telos encompasses and what kind of beings are relevant in discussing telos and welfare. In the following, I will sketch out a further development of the Aristotelian ideas of telos and flourishing as they apply to animals within the framework of normative ethics. This will be done by initially focusing on not only the kind of beings that telos relates to but on the kind of life that telos is relevant to. Following this we will, in sections on boredom and loneliness, turn to the applicational aspects of such a lived life's telos.

First, however, my issue is with the concepts of life and death—and how Rollin's idea of interest-driven welfare and telos relates to these. I will commence with a categorization of life into two distinct notions: life as being alive and life as living. The former pertains to a state of existence that involves certain biological processes and applies to all living beings including, e.g., bacteria and brain dead human being. However, life as living—or the lived life—is an existence beyond merely being alive. It is an existence where there is a conscious entity that is actively and purposefully living its life and it would thus, by definition, rule out, e.g., bacteria and brain dead human beings. I will return to some of the further definitions and implications of this distinction later, but for now it will suffice as a minimum characteristic of the beings/animals that I will be discussing. In my view, it does not make sense to speak of such a thing as a right or an entitlement to life (as in being alive)—neither one that springs from nature itself nor from any societal or other structure. Non-permanence, the fact that we, as the individuals we are, do not live forever, is an intrinsic part of existence as a living being. Life is a temporary state, which will inevitably conclude in death and the end of individual existence. Now, this simple fact secures our focus and that our concern for animal life is not for life itself but for the actively lived life of the animal. In one of his earlier books, *Animal Rights & Human Morality*, Rollin argues that the killing of animals could indeed be a violation of the rights of the animal since it is an unnecessary and often painful obstruction of the animal's life and "its current and future positive experiences" (Rollin 2006, p. 113). Nevertheless, in the same chapter Rollin forms the first version of a counter argument against *the right to life*, which would come to be the model for his later works. He argues, very much like Peter Singer (1993), that death itself is inconceivable to the animal and that it inherently lacks the ability to mind it.

In short, while an animal's actions may ultimately be aimed at survival, it does not understand this, and thus survival in and of itself does not matter to it (Rollin 2006, p. 113).

This view of course relates very well to Rollin's concept of telos. There certainly is no natural imperative in the pigness of a pig that excludes death. On the contrary, it is in the very nature, the very telos, of any animal to die at some time or another. However, this death *at some time or another* is, I argue, not equivalent to irrelevancy concerning the duration of the animal's life. If, as I believe, the concept of Aristotle's telos is to be one of the benchmarks by which we identify and evaluate the good life of animals—and subsequently our ethical obligations involving them—we must adhere to a broader paradigm of telos and thus include a necessary certain life span. As it is, the telos of an acorn to become an oak tree with all the characteristics of a full grown tree, so it is equally the telos of animals (non-human and human alike) to grow from boy child, wolf cub, and piglet into fully developed man, wolf, and pig. Thus, even if we recognize the argument that the killing of animals as such—in agriculture and hunting-—is not intrinsically problematical in an animal ethics perspective, we are compelled by the notion of telos to allocate certain durations of life to the animals. Durations—or life spans—that enable them to actualise the potentials that are needed to "flourish *qua* member of its particular species" (MacIntyre 1999, p. 64). This, I contend, is obviously impossible in modern intensive farming practices, but it is also, maybe less obviously, impossible in most extensive systems of animal agriculture. Customarily raised beef cattle, for example, live average lives of about 1½ years. They are, typically, born in the spring time, graze on pasture for a year, and then spend their last (approx.) five months in the feedlot before slaughter. Grass fed cattle, which do not spend time in the feedlot, need a bit more time on the pasture in order to reach the appropriate weight for slaughter and are normally a little more than two years old when they are killed. But neither of these two types of beef cattle appears to meet the necessary life span conditions for any kind of true telos. The average life of a buffalo is 25–30 years, and cows in captivity have lived beyond 20 years, so it is obvious that a steer or heifer killed when they have only lived a tenth of this time is deprived of many of the aspects of a full cow life—there is, so to speak, a shortfall in the cowness of the cow's life. Many of the positive natural aspects of being a cow, a pig, or a chicken are hindered, even in extensive agriculture, due to the lack of sufficient life spans. The possible implementation of genetically programmed behaviors like breeding and parenting are thwarted together with more complex social capabilities like friendships and other affiliations. Thus, the argument of telos compels us towards an animal agriculture where the animals are provided with a life span adequate to their nature—or in other words, an agriculture where the acorn's telos is respected and oak saplings are not uprooted.

Boredom, Choosing, and Telos

[. . .]

Where the previous section ended with a telos-argument for the quantity of an animal's life in our agricultural system, the next two sections will investigate some of the qualitative aspects of an animal life that would be necessary in order to respect the telos of farm animals.

The matter of personal choice and (part) ownership to your actions and lived life is of crucial importance to the makings of a good life for people and—as I hope will become clear—animals. The good life, in any sense and crucially in what we could call a neo-Aristotelian eudaimonic form, is a life that necessarily has to be lived through active volitions by the being whose life it is. A good life, therefore, cannot be achieved without the active and meaningful participation of the subject in question, but the possibility of such a life can still be hindered or furthered by certain environments or other subjects. The following section addresses boredom as a specific hindrance to a good life in intensive animal husbandry.

The terminology of boredom is derived from the world of human psychology where it is employed to express a distressing attention deficit and restlessness originating from either interior or exterior phenomena—or a combination of both (Martin et al. 2006). The phenomenon of boredom in humans is a fairly new area of research and as a result there is, to some extent, still disagreement on its definition, and the understanding of boredom's impact is still limited. The field is, however, developing and flourishing—which is in stark contrast to temporary animal science where the phenomenon and terminology of boredom is only slowly being accepted as applicable. Indeed, together with altruism, happiness, and similar terms, boredom has been and is by some people regarded as problematically anthropomorphic and non-applicable to other beings. On the other hand, concepts like fear and stress have made their way into everyday animal science, along with definitions and analysis of their impact on animal welfare. This has happened despite the notion of stress, along with similar concepts, having been derived from human psychology and notwithstanding that an animal could not possibly experience human stress qua its decidedly un-human nature. In other words, no animal can experience the boredom that human beings experience, because they are not human beings. The divide between how it is to be a human and how it is to be an animal (of a certain kind) does, however, not disqualify us from using certain terminologies.[7] Indeed, some of the newest research on emotions in farm animals accept the terminology used here and conclude "that sheep are able to experience emotions such as fear, anger rage, despair, boredom, disgust and happiness . . ." (Veissier et al. 2009). The question we must continually ask is whether the addressed type of condition and suffering of the animals is relevantly similar to the type of condition and suffering which researchers in human psychology and medicine address in their work. If so, then it gives good reason not to dismiss entirely the terminology off hand.

An investigation into the notions of boredom and suffering would serve as a tool in both a further definition of the concept of animal telos and in exemplifying relevant problems associated with the obstruction of telos. Edinburgh based researcher Françoise Wemelsfelder is the foremost proponent of the use of animal boredom as a significant focus in the assessment of animal welfare and has published several articles focusing on this subject. Her stated objective is to:

> explore that richness [i.e., the many layers of the meaning of boredom] and develop a sense of what boredom is about—and to consider how this applies to the welfare of captive animals.
> (Wemelsfelder 2005, p. 79)

I believe the notion of *captive*—or *confinement*—is critical in this objective since it describes the negative framework within which the suffering of boredom has a possibility of developing and existing. To be confined for extended periods by either crammed physical quarters or a certain societal structure is at the heart of boredom's influence on a being's ability to fulfil its telos. We will return to this idea later in the article. First, however, there is the ever-present difficulty of adequately defining the concept with which one works. Boredom is, in this case, no exception, and because of the intrinsic complexity of animal boredom and the limited work that has been done on the subject we will most likely be left with a definition which is a bit "fuzzy" along the edges. This is, nevertheless, the circumstances under which many of our biological concepts are defined, and it does not in itself dismiss the usefulness or the relevance of a certain terminology. Wemelsfelder initially lists three versions of boredom—or three ways of defining it—that all originate in human psychology. First, there is the kind of boredom that develops from repetitive and monotonous activities and is associated with—among other things—lessened alertness, restlessness, and fatigue. This is called transient boredom and is brought on by external factors during a certain period and will be rectified if these external factors are prevented. Second, there is the more severe chronic boredom that manifests itself through symptoms such as apathy, depression, and feelings of loneliness. These indicators are, to varying degrees, associated with loss of purpose and "the boredom-prone person finds it difficult to experience meaning in the activities with which he or she is engaged" (Wemelsfelder 2005, p. 80). This kind of boredom arises in other contexts than those where the presence of highly repetitive tasks is the catalyst. Whereas the infliction of transient boredom was mainly due to externally induced monotonous tasks, chronic boredom is better defined by an internal state brought on by circumstances under which the possibility of choosing meaningful activities is inhibited. These circumstances can be of varying types and categories, although a characteristic example would be confinement in a barren environment of some sort—e.g., certain kinds of prison systems or, in the case of animals, intensive housing systems or laboratory cages. Included in but not restricted to the problem of barren environments, it has been suggested that environments and housing systems in which the levels of predictability are too extreme could have adverse effects on the animals (Van Rooijen 1991). These are, on the other hand, not the only circumstance under which chronic boredom can arise. It would also be a possibility in a situation exactly opposite of a barren environment; namely, in an environment with such a rich array of stimulations that it overloads the ability of the involved agent, rendering him or her incapable of engaging in anything. Finally, the environment in question does not have to be of a purely physical nature. The chronically bored individual can be confined within a number of social structures and thus have their ability to creatively and actively break out of their boredom obstructed, not by the walls of rooms or cages, but by the walls of social systems or authoritative relations. The essential nature of both categories of walls is to render the activities and sensations of the individual meaningless by disconnecting them from the individual's voluntary choices. This disconnection, Wemelsfelder contends, can lead to a state of "flow deprivation" in which the affected agent looses the ability to have, what she calls, attentive awareness. This sort of disruptive condition estranges the individual from both himself and the flow of time, capturing him in a mode of being—inactive or active—that he, in a deep sense, does not see as his own.

Now, how do these two ways of defining boredom, originally used only for humans, help us in identifying and defining boredom in animals? Wemelsfelder's answer revolves around an interpretation of animal actions as going beyond mere functional purpose and that (at least some) animals act towards other animals and objects in the world in ways that show both innovation and volition—and which is, to a greater or lesser extent, motivated by the action itself.

[. . .]

These properties of volition and attentional flow are that that can be thwarted and lead to sufferings of the kind that Wemelsfelder called chronic boredom. According to her, some of the clearest cases of such effects are evident in the close confinement systems in laboratories and industrialized agriculture. Small and barren captive environments lead to animals being bored to such an extent that they simply give up trying to be active and thus their behavior becomes increasingly passive and apathetic. Under these conditions, the animals might furthermore misdirect their attention towards objects as well as themselves or other objects. This results in, for example, self-inflicted injuries—direct or through misuse of objects—and sucking or chewing on other animals in the confinement area. However, behaviors such as these cannot be considered choice or volitional in the sense in which described earlier. Mutilations and self-mutilations among confined animals are, Wemelsfelder argues, equivalent to the actions of for instance an unwilling human drug addict who engages in the action of taking drugs, not because of choice but specifically because of the lack of choice. The same holds true for stereotypical behaviors like excessive pacing that represent an un-self-motivated coping with a disruption of the animal's attentional flow and ability to choose. Of course, several problems arise from the very dynamic concept of attentional flow and complex and many-sided notion of boredom. How are we to recognise the signs of boredom in animals and what, if any, solutions do we have available to counteract the sufferings associated with chronic boredom? The answer to the former part of the question hinges on a specific method for the assessment of animal welfare—in a comparative and distinctively non-reductionist method.

> when we see the animal come to life in enriched conditions, we may realize how "not its normal self" it previously was.
>
> Addressing attentional flow requires a more qualitative approach that evaluates the behavior of animals as a dynamic, coherent whole.
>
> (Wemelsfelder 2005, p. 86)

Thus, Wemelsfelder argues for a kind of animal welfare assessment that does not merely look at the former and present condition of the animals in a certain environment, but one which, by taking into account the capabilities of the animals, establishes an idea of welfare founded on how the environment could have been and what kind of active animal life could have been lived within it.

The above notion about animals as selves living dynamic lives with personal choices is not unduly far away from similar notions in both ancient and modern philosophy about humans, both descriptively in philosophical anthropology and in the normative realm of ethics. A prominent example of this is the Canadian philosopher Charles Taylor's theory of self-formation and identity making through active, ongoing choices and self evaluation (Taylor 1985). His, and others', theories explain the foundation of such everyday complaints as "he is a bit besides himself right now" and "I am not myself today." These sayings are of course not to be understood literally but indicate that the person in question is in a situation that has shaken his self to such a degree that he is suffering. Animals most likely do not have the capacity for the highly reflective strong evaluations that are central to the definition (and good life) of persons in Taylor's philosophy. Nor do they presumably have the mental depths needed for an existential identity crisis the like of those prevalent throughout human society, from teenage rebellions to retirement anxiety. Nonetheless, animals—certainly mentally well-endowed farm animals such as for example pigs—do have the capabilities associated with living open-ended and versatile lives of their own choosing; an activity that additionally continually reshapes the identity of the animal. This is the reason why suffering by boredom is a clear indication of a telos interconnected problem. According to Wemelsfelder, boredom in confinement agriculture is brought on by environments and circumstances that do not provide the animals with sufficient possibilities for volitional action. The idea of telos similarly hinges on the idea of choice and—to some extent—autonomy. The way in which the telos of an animal can possibly be actualized is, indeed, through the choosing by the animal. To unfold and flourish in its natural life is only achievable in a life that has choices, since the animal is such a being whose basic nature it is to choose (Krebs 1979) and thus to live what could only then be considered its own life. Without choice there can be no telos—no matter how much else is done for the animal. One cannot unfold a life and make it flourish for someone else. This is the essence of what was earlier in this article called a *lived life*. There is of course no living being with a limitless amount of options and choices—even the most powerful and most free beings (both human and animal) are restricted by their own physical existence, nature, society, and so on. But a limitless number of options is, on the other hand, not the goal here. To be able to actively live a good life in accordance with one's telos is to live a life in a world in which one is presented with a number of choices adequate to the kind of being one is.

Loneliness—Telos and the Pain of Isolation

The concept of loneliness is, much like that of boredom, often seen as too vague or too anthropomorphic to be valid in ethological research and welfare assessment. Instead terms like "stress from social isolation'" and "psychosocial stress" (Tuchscherer et al. 2006) are preferred and used widely throughout the available literature. There are—at least—two problems with this view. First of all, the anthropomorphic nature of loneliness is actually an asset in the understanding of animals suffering from it (Harfeld 2011)—and secondly, that the notion of stress itself is notoriously vague and also widely disagreed on (Broom and Johnson 1993; McEwen 2000). We know from ourselves that which a human being suffers due to a lack of adequate social interactions is substantially and qualitatively different than the stress that she feels from having her leg broken in a skiing accident or the stress of being behind schedule at work. So stress does not say much about the quality of the feelings involved—only that some sort of "negative feelings" are involved. The understanding of our own types of stresses is obviously not directly transferable to other non-human animals, but it does not indicate that other similarly developed beings could very well be capable of experiencing stress, suffering, discomfort, etc., of distinctly different kinds depending on the situation they are in. And in the case of a social animal (human or non-human) being alone for an extended period of time, this suffering is loneliness.

Most traditional farm animals—pigs, cattle, sheep, and poultry—are innately highly social beings and loneliness, by any terminology, has been well documented to affect these and other social animals both behaviorally and physiologically (Hermes et al. 2009; Munksgaard and Simonsen 1996; Ruis et al. 2001). Loneliness is, in the context of this article, defined as the chronic psychological suffering from prolonged social isolation.[8] This suffering is relevant to animals that have been separated from a social setting in which they have hitherto lived as well as to animals that have never actively lived in a social context.[9] Furthermore, loneliness can be experienced by animals who actually do live in social settings, but where the settings are either incorrectly constructed (inappropriate species or type within species) or changed at a, for the animal, overwhelming rate (Færevik et al. 2006).[10] To investigate problematic separation from or absence of important social relations imposes the initial question of the nature of these social relations. In this article, social relations are defined as interactions between individuals over time that establish a longer lasting connection between the individuals. This entails a focus on animals in established pairs or, as is the case with the type of animals in agriculture, in groups that are cohesive over time. The definition excludes the temporary and infrequent social interactions of normally solitary animals during mating seasons or similar events. Social relations and bonds of different kinds are prevalent among traditional farm animals and include—among others—the bonds between mothers and offspring, sibling bonds, and preferential relationships and bonding between genetically unrelated individuals (Arnold 1985). Within these different types of relations are a number of different types of interactive behaviors—some of which are particular to certain specific relations and some of which are overlapping between the different types of relations. These behaviors include things like playing, grooming/allogrooming, reciprocated and unreciprocated protection, and even such subtle behaviors such as close mutual proximity (McFarland 1981). Traditionally, the question as to why animals form social relations and groups has been answered in terms of evolutionary theory or a combination of the four classic question of Nikolaas Tinbergen. Why does an animal behave in a certain way in terms of the behavior's (1) function, (2) evolution, (3) causation, and (4) development (Manning and Dawkins 1998)? These questions then lead to answers focused largely on social relations as behavior that help groups by, for example, improving predator detection and avoidance and maybe facilitating feeding by way of collective searching or hunting. Such a focus then supports viewing social relations as behavior directed at the ability to support and enhance the general evolutionary fitness and species survival. In other words: individual group animals that are capable at a certain kind of social relations with other individuals outcompete their less socially inept co-species members in the evolutionary struggle to pass on their genes. Though evolutionary explanations are interesting and the sort of thriving that enables survival and sexual reproduction is, in my view, relevant to the notion of *telos*, the questions and answers just mentioned do not satisfy the sort of questions and answers that we are looking for when dealing with animal welfare and ethics. First, I believe, we must ask the question "Why do animals engage in social relations?" as if we were putting the question to the animals themselves. Clearly, no farm animal would be able to linguistically explain its motivations to us as we would have a human being do in a psychology experiment. This, however, does not disqualify the question and merely points to that more interpretation will be needed to gain anything from the answers. If we were to ask a fellow human being as to why he behaves in a certain social way—e.g., engaging in a behavior like friendship—he would probably not explain that his bond with and behavior towards his friend helps him secure the passing on of his genes. He would be more likely to explain the friendship in terms of personal value and affection with statements like: "He's a caring person and helps me," "He's there for me and I can trust him," "He makes me laugh and feel happy," "I can relax around him," and "I just really like him."

Using our knowledge of human beings, we can then carefully apply a bit of reasonable anthropomorphism and consider whether any of these human values and affections could validly be applied in the case of social relations between animals. That the animals in question are capable of both negative and positive emotions is well documented (Bekoff 2000; Veissier et al. 2009), and several experiments have shown these emotional responses in respect to social relations—stress-related responses in situations lacking social relations and happiness or contentment in situations with adequate social relations. Nonetheless, the strong social relation between individual animals—what we could also refer to as a bond—is only one way of addressing the sociality of animals. A more rudimentary preference towards social company and interaction is revealed in situations where positive emotions are observed in animals interacting with individuals without an adequate time in which to form social bonds, as those described earlier. In these cases, it is not necessarily a specific bond that is of value to the animals but the more basic social connection of being near and associating with other (beneficent/indifferent) animals. Færevik, Jensen, and Bøe have shown that calves separated from their group are calmed significantly by the presence of a calf that they have had time to bond and familiarize themselves with earlier. There is, however, also a noteworthy calming effect if the separated calf is paired with an unfamiliar calf, showing that sociality is important to the animals beyond the strong social relations (Færevik et al. 2006). This is even more apparent in the studies of Kay and Hall in which the researchers addressed the problem of stress in horses during transport by trailer (Kay and Hall 2009). Though they found that traveling with a live companion horse had a considerable calming effect, they achieved almost the same level of stress prevention by using a mirror to emulate the presence of another (unfamiliar) horse.

Telos—Comparisons and Strengths

The cases of boredom and loneliness are examples of a telos-oriented view of animal welfare and highlight some of the problems in traditional utilitarian and deontological approaches to *the good animal life*. An animal-inclusive deontological or rights-based approach would emphasize the individual as ontologically and welfare-wise primary to any given social structure. However, the characterization of farm animals such as cows, pigs, and chicken as individuals is only, at best, a half-truth. The active existence—the being-in-the-world (Zwart 1997)—of a cow is a matter of both individuality and of being part of a sociality that in itself has an existence that is more than the sum of its parts (Harfeld 2011). Thus, a welfare definition must include this good life of the group alongside the good life of the individual. Of course, many animals are housed individually in which case such assessments cannot be achieved. This, on the other hand, only solves an assessment difficulty (a problem for humans) and isolation would, as indicated earlier, further add to the animal welfare problems through its compromise of the animal's social nature—an indispensable part of its telos. The good life of the individual animal is not subordinate to the good life of the collective (whether understood as the sum of individuals—or consisting of but exceeding the sum of individuals). These are parallel approaches to welfare theories and are neither mutually exclusive nor necessarily combinable or comparable. The major concern, however, with rights-based theories in the light of this article is their lack of attentiveness to the whole idea of welfare. When philosophers like Regan (1983) stress the overriding importance of interest based rights and equality, there is very little focus what these interests consist of and the arguments center on what Richard Haynes calls "negative individual rights . . . to be left alone" (Haynes 2008, p. 140). First of all, this kind of argumentation can only have abolition as a conclusion and thereby either impedes or is ineffectual for any work towards welfare improvement within existing systems of animal use, such as, for example, agriculture. Secondly, rights theory's focus on freedom supersedes any appeal to a good life and freedom—or being left alone—does not necessarily lead to a good life for the animal.

[. . .]

Being left alone to fend for yourself in nature neither guarantees nor necessarily facilitates welfare and a good animal life—it only guarantees that you are left alone. Though a life in the freedom of the wild might better the chances of a better and longer life than those of some animals in some agricultural systems, it is by no means assured. Telos, on the other hand, is, as an ethical approach, interested in the good life of those beings living their lives—whether in the wild, in captivity, or

l by humans. When telos-theory stresses the impor-
nderstood as, e.g., *the pigness of the pig*—it is not
natural circumstances as possible. Telos ethics does
s tantamount to faring well with ones life; it does,
ned and extended by the natural facts about a certain
—has a specific sort of nature "which is genetically
low certain interests and needs . . ." (Rollin 1998b,
the framework within which any credible normative
dation of capabilities and potentials that can enable

oriented view, has an elaborate theory of welfare
of animal agriculture. Certainly notions of pain and
mals are essential to understanding animal welfare
ncerning animals. But similar to the just described
uth. Especially hedonistic utilitarianism encounters
e sums of different qualitative experiences. To add up
ings in question have to be of the same general type.
humans and animals alike are of such a qualitative
of comparison or adding together of such things as
er's day and the deep satisfaction of having finished
rianism avoids some of these problems by opening
fy the preferences or desires of the individual. The
a yard stick for welfare is that the beings doing the
he sense that they have arrived at these preferences
animals and humans" (Nussbaum 2007, p. 344) or
taught to presuppose lives with severe limitations.
assessment reflect have been artificially lowered or
oitation (Sumner 1996, p. 166) are lives in which the
nort. In cases of, for example, learned helplessness,
where the observed preferences of the animal are no
nimal can continue to have its preferences satisfied
onger in accordance with the species specific nature
d animal, it is no longer authentically itself to such a

mal agriculture would have several claims to make,
in the housing systems currently used. The Danish
must be "housed [. . .] and cared for in consideration
ated needs . . ."[11] This phrasing is, I argue, very much
ken seriously, radically change way Danish animal
rameter founded in the telos of the animals housing
ic social relations for longer periods and relevantly
and other appropriate considerations. In such group
directed at overall herd/group/flock welfare as well
es and configurations of housing facilities would also
d choice enabling environments and enough space
nce function adequately. The telos approach argues
rn to animal agriculture as it was done before 1950,
a modern framework: A welfare oriented husbandry

of the twenty-first century in which animals can actively live flourishing lives in accordance with the kind of beings that they are.

[. . .]

Notes

1. These numbers originate from the database Infomedia which includes all the major Danish newspapers.
2. http://www.zoo.dk/BesogZoo/OmZoo/~/media/Files/dyrebestanden%202008.ashx (accessed Match 15th 2010).
3. http://www.dst.dk/pukora/epub/Nyt/2000/NR499.pdf (accessed March 15th 2010).
4. Broiler chicken production is by far the most significant, but this number also includes ducks, geese, and turkeys.
5. http://www.landbrug.dk/smcms/Landburg/Baggrund/Tal_om_landburget__1/Statistik/Index.htm?ID=6491 (accessed March 15th 2010).
6. Originally a Heideggerian term which was solely attributed to humans, Hub Zwart (1997) employs it to cover the aspects of animal existence.
7. There appears to be a certain four-step progression of human to animal experiential terminology in the animal science literature. At the very first stage is the outright rejection of the experience in animals. This is followed later by a stage throughout which the experience is explained without suing the human as well as animals, but when addressing animals the defining word is put in quotation marks to indicate that it is not really the right definition. Finally, at the fourth stage, the word come into general acceptance and is used more or less freely and without quotation marks.
8. Thus I choose to differentiate it from the acute "loneliness emotions" of short termed social isolation which, when not repetitive and cumulative, have few lasting effects on the animal.
9. If an animal, which belongs to a social species, has never had any social contacts, it is still a social animal. It is the difference between Aristotle's first and second potentialities (Haynes 2008, p. 123). At the first potentiality level, the animal is born with a capability for socialness. It is, as Rollin puts it, "genetically imprinted" (Rollin 2006, p. 100) and is there from the beginning of the individual's life. The second potentiality level is the actual active socialization of the animal and this requires development through practice and use. The innate social animal that is without the possibility of expressing its secondary social potentialities will have its telos thwarted and will not be able to flourish as the being that it is, even though it does not have preferences towards (or misses) something that it has never known. See also the argument against preferences in the conclusion.
10. Calves that are regrouped too often give up trying to form relationships—and in effect become lonely while having potential social relations around them.
11. Law #386 of June 6th 1991.

References

Alstrup, A. K. O., & Hansen, A. K. (2009). Status over forbruget af forsøgsdyr siden år 2000. *Ugeskrift for Laeger, 171*(43), 3088.

Aristotle, (2004). *On the parts of animals* (*originally around 350 BC*). Whitefish, MT: Kessinger Publication Co.

Arnold, G. W. (1985). Associations and social behaviour. In A. F. Fraser (Ed.), *Ethology of farm animals* (pp. 233–248). New York: Elsevier.

Bekoff, M. (2000). Animal emotions: Exploring passionate natures. *BioScience, 50*, 861–870.

Broom, D. M., & Johnson, K. G. (1993). *Stress and animal welfare*. London: Chapman & Hale.

Færevik, G., Jensen, M. B., & Bøe, K. E. (2006). Dairy calves social preferences and the significance of a companion animal during separation from the group. *Applied Animal Behaviour Science, 99*, 205–211.

Harfeld, J. (2011). Philosophical ethology: On the extents of what it is to be a pig. *Society and Animals, 19*, 83–101.

Haynes, R. P. (2008). *Animal welfare—competing conceptions and their ethical implications*. Dordrecht: Springer Science.

Hermes, G. L., Delgado, B., Tretiakova, M., Cavigelli, S. A., Krausz, T., Conzen, S. D., et al. (2009). Social isolation dysregulates endocrine and behavioral stress while increasing malignant burden of spontaneous mammary tumors. In *Proceedings of the National Academy of Sciences of the United States of America*. http://www.pnas.org/content/early/2009/12/10/0910753106.full.pdf+html. Accessed April 1, 2010.

Kay, R., & Hall, C. (2009). The use of a mirror reduces isolation stress in horses being transported by trailer. *Applied Animal Behaviour Science, 116*, 237–243.

Krebs, J. R. (1979). Optimal foraging: Decision rules for predators. In J. R. Krebs (Ed.), *Behavioural ecology* (pp. 23–63). Guildford, Great Britain: Blackwell Scientific Publications.

MacIntyre, A. (1999). *Dependent rational animals: Why human beings need the virtues*. London: Duckworth.

Manning, A., & Dawkins, M. S. (1998). *An introduction to animal behaviour*. Cambridge: Cambridge University Press.

Martin, M., Sadlo, G., & Stew, G. (2006). The phenomenon of boredom. *Qualitative Research in Psychology, 3*, 193–211.

McEwen, B. S. (2000). The neurobiology of stress: From serendipity to clinical relevance. *Brain Research, 886*, 172–189.

McFarland, D. (1981). *The Oxford companion to animal behaviour*. Oxford: Oxford University Press.

Munksgaard, L., & Simonsen, H. B. (1996). Behavioral and pituitary adrenal axis responses of dairy cows to social isolation and deprivation of lying down. *Journal of Animal Science, 74*, 769–779.

Nussbaum, M. C. (2007). *Frontiers of justice—disability, nationality, species membership*. Cambridge: Belknap Press.

Regan, T. (1983). *The case for animal rights*. Berkeley: University of California Press.

Rollin, B. E. (1998a). On telos and genetic engineering. In A. Holland & A. Johnson (Eds.), *Animal biotechnology and ethics* (pp. 156–172). London: Chapman & Hall.

Rollin, B. E. (1998b). *The unheeded cry—Animal consciousness, animal pain, and science* (1st ed. 1989). Ames: Iowa State University Press.

Rollin, B. E. (2006). *Animals rights and human morality* (1st ed. 1981). New York: Prometheus Books.

Ruis, M. A. W., te Brake, J. H. A., Engel, B., Buist, W. G., Blokhuis, H. J., & Koolhaas, J. M. (2001). Adaptation to social isolation: Acute and long-term stress responses of growing gilts with different coping characteristics. *Physiology and Behavior, 73*, 541–551.

Singer, P. (1993). *Practical ethics*. Cambridge: Cambridge University Press.

Stolba, A., & Wood-Gush, D. G. M. (1981). Behavior of pigs and the design of a new housing system. *Applied Animal Ethology, 8*, 583–585.

Sumner, L. W. (1996). *Welfare, happiness, and ethics*. Oxford: Clarendon Press.

Taylor, C. (1985). *Human agency and language*. Cambridge: Cambridge University Press.

Tuchscherer, M., Kanitz, E., Puppe, B., & Tuchscherer, A. (2006). Early social isolation alters behavioral and physiological responses to an endotoxin challenge in piglets. *Hormones and Behavior, 50*, 753–761.

Van Rooijen, J. (1991). Predictability and boredom. *Applied Animal Behaviour Science, 31*, 283–287.

Veissier, I., Boissy, A., Desire, L., & Greiveldinger, L. (2009). Animals' emotions: Studies in sheep using appraisal theories. *Animal Welfare, 18*, 347–354.

Wemelsfelder, F. (2005). Animal boredom: Understanding the tedium of confined lives. In F. McMillan (Ed.), *Mental health and well-being in animals* (pp. 79–92). Oxford: Blackwell Publishing.

Zwart, H. (1997). What is an animal? A philosophical reflection on the possibility of a moral relationship with animals. *Environmental Values, 6*, 377–392.

De-Extinction

55 Bringing Them Back to Life

The Revival of an Extinct Species Is No Longer a Fantasy

Carl Zimmer

Zimmer outlines some of the most significant recent work in "de-extinction," bringing extinct species back to life. He addresses some of the technical challenges of attempting this work on several species. He also assesses the pros and cons of conducting such work.

On July 30, 2003, a team of Spanish and French scientists reversed time. They brought an animal back from extinction, if only to watch it become extinct again. The animal they revived was a kind of wild goat known as a *bucardo*, or Pyrenean ibex. The bucardo (*Capra pyrenaica pyrenaica*) was a large, handsome creature, reaching up to 220 pounds and sporting long, gently curved horns. For thousands of years it lived high in the Pyrenees, the mountain range that divides France from Spain, where it clambered along cliffs, nibbling on leaves and stems and enduring harsh winters.

Then came the guns. Hunters drove down the bucardo population over several centuries. In 1989, Spanish scientists did a survey and concluded that there were only a dozen or so individuals left. Ten years later, a single bucardo remained: a female nicknamed Celia. A team from the Ordesa and Monte Perdido National Park, led by wildlife veterinarian Alberto Fernández-Arias, caught the animal in a trap, clipped a radio collar around her neck and released her back into the wild. Nine months later, the radio collar let out a long, steady beep: the signal that Celia had died. They found her crushed beneath a fallen tree. With her death, the bucardo became officially extinct.

But Celia's cells lived on, preserved in labs in Zaragoza and Madrid. Over the next few years, a team of reproductive physiologists led by José Folch injected nuclei from those cells into goat eggs emptied of their own DNA, then implanted the eggs in surrogate mothers. After 57 implantations, only seven animals had become pregnant. And of those seven pregnancies, six ended in miscarriages. But one mother—a hybrid between a Spanish ibex and a goat—carried a clone of Celia to term. Folch and his colleagues performed a cesarean section and delivered the 4.5-pound clone. As Fernández-Arias held the newborn bucardo in his arms, he could see that she was struggling to take in air, her tongue jutting grotesquely out of her mouth. Despite the efforts to help her breathe, after a mere ten minutes Celia's clone died. A necropsy later revealed that one of her lungs had grown a gigantic extra lobe, as solid as a piece of liver. There was nothing anyone could have done.

The dodo and the great auk, the thylacine and the Chinese river dolphin, the passenger pigeon and the imperial woodpecker—the bucardo is only one in the long list of animals humans have driven extinct, sometimes deliberately. And with many more species now endangered, the bucardo will have much more company in the years to come. Fernández-Arias belongs to a small but passionate group of researchers who believe that cloning can help reverse that trend.

The notion of bringing vanished species back to life—some call it de-extinction—has hovered at the boundary between reality and science fiction for more than two decades, ever since novelist Michael Crichton unleashed the dinosaurs of Jurassic Park on the world. For most of that time, the science of de-extinction has lagged far behind the fantasy. Celia's clone is the closest that anyone has gotten to true de-extinction. Since witnessing those fleeting minutes of the clone's life, Fernández-Arias, now the head of the government of Aragon's Hunting, Fishing and Wetlands department, has been waiting for the moment when science would finally catch up, and humans might gain the ability to bring back an animal they had driven extinct.

"We are at that moment," he told me.

I met Fernández-Arias last autumn at a closed-session scientific meeting at the National Geographic Society's headquarters in Washington, D.C. For the first time in history, a group of geneticists, wildlife biologists, conservationists and ethicists had gathered to discuss the possibility of de-extinction. Could it be done? Should it be done? One by one, they stood up to present remarkable advances in manipulating stem cells, in recovering ancient DNA, in reconstructing lost genomes. As the meeting unfolded, the scientists became increasingly excited. A consensus was emerging: De-extinction is now within reach.

"It's gone very much further, very much more rapidly than anyone ever would've imagined," says Ross MacPhee, a curator of mammalogy at the American Museum of Natural History in New York. "What we really need to think about is why we would want to do this in the first place, to actually bring back a species."

[. . .]

"If we're talking about species we drove extinct, then I think we have an obligation to try to do this," says Michael Archer, a paleontologist at the University of New South Wales who has championed de-extinction for years. Some people protest that reviving a species that no longer exists amounts to playing God. Archer scoffs at the notion. "I think we played God when we exterminated these animals."

Other scientists who favor de-extinction argue that there will be concrete benefits. Biological diversity is a storehouse of natural invention. Most pharmaceutical drugs, for example, were not invented from scratch—they were derived from natural compounds found in wild plant species, which are also vulnerable to extinction. Some extinct animals also performed vital services in their ecosystems, which might benefit from their return. Siberia, for example, was home 12,000 years ago to mammoths and other big grazing mammals. Back then, the landscape was not moss-dominated tundra but grassy steppes. Sergey Zimov, a Russian ecologist and director of the Northeast Science Station in Cherskiy in the Republic of Sakha, has long argued that this was no coincidence: The mammoths and numerous herbivores maintained the grassland by breaking up the soil and fertilizing it with their manure. Once they were gone, moss took over and transformed the grassland into less productive tundra.

In recent years, Zimov has tried to turn back time on the tundra by bringing horses, muskoxen and other big mammals to a region of Siberia he calls Pleistocene Park. And he would be happy to have woolly mammoths roam free there. "But only my grandchildren will see them," he says. "A mouse breeds very fast. Mammoths breed very slow. Be prepared to wait."

[. . .]

Over the past decade, scientists have improved their success with cloning animals, shifting the technology from high-risk science to workaday business. Researchers have also developed the ability to induce adult animal cells to return to an embryo-like state. These can be coaxed to develop into any type of cell—including eggs or sperm. The eggs can then be further manipulated to develop into full-fledged embryos.

Such technical sleights of hand make it far easier to conjure a vanished species back to life. Scientists and explorers have been talking for decades about bringing back the mammoth. Their first—and so far only—achievement was to find well-preserved mammoths in the Siberian tundra. Now, armed with the new cloning technologies, researchers at the Sooam Biotech Research Foundation in Seoul have teamed up with mammoth experts from North-Eastern Federal University in the Siberian city of Yakutsk. Last summer they traveled up the Yana River, drilling tunnels into the frozen cliffs along the river with giant hoses. In one of those tunnels, they found chunks of mammoth tissue, including bone marrow, hair, skin and fat. The tissue is now in Seoul, where the Sooam scientists are examining it.

"If we dream about it, the ideal case would be finding a viable cell, a cell that's alive," says Sooam's Insung Hwang, who organized the Yana River expedition. If the Sooam researchers do find such a cell, they could coax it to produce millions of cells. These could be reprogrammed to grow into embryos, which could then be implanted in surrogate elephants, the mammoth's closest living relatives.

Most scientists doubt that any living cell could have survived freezing on the open tundra. But Hwang and his colleagues have a Plan B: capture an intact nucleus of a mammoth cell, which is far more likely to have been preserved than the cell itself. Cloning a mammoth from nothing but an intact nucleus, however, will be a lot trickier. The Sooam researchers will need to transfer the nucleus into an elephant egg that has had its own nucleus removed. This will require harvesting eggs from an elephant—a feat no one has yet accomplished. If the DNA inside the nucleus is well preserved enough to take control of the egg, it just might start dividing into a mammoth embryo. If the scientists can get past that hurdle, they still have the formidable task of transplanting the embryo into an elephant's womb. Then, as Zimov cautions, they will need patience. If all goes well, it will still be almost two years before they can see if the elephant will give birth to a healthy mammoth.

"The thing that I always say is, if you don't try, how would you know that it's impossible?" says Hwang.

In 1813, while traveling along the Ohio River from Hardensburgh to Louisville, John James Audubon witnessed one of the most miraculous natural phenomena of his time: a flock of passenger pigeons (*Ectopistes migratorius*) blanketing the sky. "The air was literally filled with Pigeons," he later wrote. "The light of noon-day was obscured as by an eclipse, the dung fell in spots, not unlike melting flakes of snow; and the continued buzz of wings had a tendency to lull my senses to repose."

When Audubon reached Louisville before sunset, the pigeons were still passing overhead—and continued to do so for the next three days. "The people were all in arms," wrote Audubon. "The banks of the Ohio were crowded with men and boys, incessantly shooting at the [pigeons] . . . Multitudes were thus destroyed."

In 1813, it would have been hard to imagine a species less likely to become extinct. Yet by the end of the century, the red-breasted passenger pigeon was in catastrophic decline, the forests it depended upon shrinking, and its numbers dwindling from relentless hunting. In 1900, the last confirmed wild bird was shot by a boy with a BB gun. Fourteen years later, just a century and a year after Audubon marveled at their abundance, the one remaining captive passenger pigeon, a female named Martha, died at the Cincinnati Zoo.

The writer and environmentalist Stewart Brand, best known for founding the *Whole Earth Catalog* in the late 1960s, grew up in Illinois hiking in forests that just a few decades before had been aroar with the sound of the passenger pigeons' wings. "Its habitat was my habitat," he says. Two years ago Brand and his wife, Ryan Phelan, founder of the genetic-testing company DNA Direct, began to wonder if it might be possible to bring the species back to life. One night over dinner with Harvard biologist George Church, a master at manipulating DNA, they discovered that he was thinking along the same lines.

Church knew that standard cloning methods wouldn't work, since bird embryos develop inside shells and no museum specimen of the passenger pigeon (including Martha herself, now in the Smithsonian) would likely contain a fully intact, functional genome. But he could envision a different way of recreating the bird. Preserved specimens contain fragments of DNA. By piecing together the fragments, scientists can now read the roughly one billion letters in the passenger pigeon genome. Church can't yet synthesize an entire animal genome from scratch, but he has invented technology that allows him to make sizable chunks of DNA of any sequence he wants. He could theoretically manufacture genes for passenger pigeon traits—a gene for its long tail, for example—and splice them into the genome of a stem cell from a common rock pigeon.

Rock pigeon stem cells containing this doctored genome could be transformed into germ cells, the precursors to eggs and sperm. These could then be injected into rock pigeon eggs, where they would migrate to the developing embryos' sex organs. Squabs hatched from these eggs would look like normal rock pigeons—but they would be carrying eggs and sperm loaded with doctored DNA.

When the squabs reached maturity and mated, their eggs would hatch squabs carrying unique passenger pigeon traits. These birds could then be further interbred, the scientists selecting for birds that were more and more like the vanished species.

Church's genome-retooling method could theoretically work on any species with a close living relative and a genome capable of being reconstructed. So even if the Sooam team fails to find an intact mammoth nucleus, someone might still bring the species back. Scientists already have the technology for reconstructing most of the genes it takes to make a mammoth, which could be inserted into an elephant stem cell. And there is no shortage of raw material for further experiments emerging from the Siberian permafrost. "With mammoths, it's really a dime a dozen up there," says Hendrik Poinar, an expert on mammoth DNA at McMaster University in Ontario. "It's just a matter of finances now."

Though the revival of a mammoth or a passenger pigeon is no longer mere fantasy, the reality is still years away. For another extinct species, the time frame may be much shorter. Indeed, there's at least a chance it may be back among the living before this story is published.

The animal in question is the obsession of a group of Australian scientists led by Michael Archer, who call their endeavor the Lazarus Project. Archer previously directed a highly publicized attempt to clone the thylacine, an iconic marsupial carnivore that went extinct in the 1930s. That effort managed to capture only some fragments of the thylacine's DNA. Wary of the feverish expectations that such high-profile experiments attract, Archer and his Lazarus Project collaborators kept quiet about their efforts until they had some preliminary results to offer.

That time has come. Early in January, Archer and his colleagues revealed that they were trying to revive two closely related species of Australian frog. Until their disappearance in the mid-1980s, the species shared a unique—and utterly astonishing—method of reproduction. The female frogs released a cloud of eggs, which the males fertilized, whereupon the females swallowed the eggs whole. A hormone in the eggs triggered the female to stop making stomach acid; her stomach, in effect, became a womb. A few weeks later the female opened her mouth and regurgitated her fully formed babies. This miraculous reproductive feat gave the frogs their common names: the northern (*Rheobatrachus vitellinus*) and southern (*Rheobatrachus silus*) gastric brooding frogs.

Unfortunately, not long after researchers began to study the species, they vanished. "The frogs were there one minute, and when scientists came back, they were gone," says Andrew French, a cloning expert at the University of Melbourne and a member of the Lazarus Project.

To bring the frogs back, the project scientists are using state-of-the-art cloning methods to introduce gastric brooding frog nuclei into eggs of living Australian marsh frogs and barred frogs that have had their own genetic material removed. It's slow going, because frog eggs begin to lose their potency after just a few hours and cannot be frozen and revived. The scientists need fresh eggs, which the frogs produce only once a year, during their short breeding season.

Nevertheless, they've made progress. "Suffice it to say, we actually have embryos now of this extinct animal," says Archer. "We're pretty far down this track." The Lazarus Project scientists are confident that they just need to get more high-quality eggs to keep moving forward. "At this point it's just a numbers game," says French.

The matchless oddity of the gastric brooding frogs' reproduction drives home what we lose when a species becomes extinct. But does that mean we should bring them back? Would the world be that much richer for having female frogs that grow little frogs in their stomachs? There are tangible benefits, French argues, such as the insights the frogs might be able to provide about reproduction—insights that might someday lead to treatments for pregnant women who have trouble carrying babies to term. But for many scientists, de-extinction is a distraction from the pressing work required to stave off mass extinctions.

"There is clearly a terrible urgency to saving threatened species and habitats," says John Wiens, an evolutionary biologist at Stony Brook University in New York. "As far as I can see, there is little urgency for bringing back extinct ones. Why invest millions of dollars in bringing a handful of species back from the dead, when there are millions still waiting to be discovered, described, and protected?"

De-extinction advocates counter that the cloning and genomic engineering technologies being developed for de-extinction could also help preserve endangered species, especially ones that don't breed easily in captivity. And though cutting-edge biotechnology can be expensive when it's first developed, it has a way of becoming very cheap very fast. "Maybe some people thought polio vaccines were a distraction from iron lungs," says George Church. "It's hard in advance to say what's distraction and what's salvation."

But what would we be willing to call salvation? Even if Church and his colleagues manage to retrofit every passenger pigeon-specific trait into a rock pigeon, would the resulting creature truly be a passenger pigeon or just an engineered curiosity? If Archer and French do produce a single gastric brooding frog—if they haven't already—does that mean they've revived the species? If that frog doesn't have a mate, then it becomes an amphibian version of Celia, and its species is as good as extinct. Would it be enough to keep a population of the frogs in a lab or perhaps in a zoo, where people could gawk at it? Or would it need to be introduced back into the wild to be truly de-extinct?

"The history of putting species back after they've gone extinct in the wild is fraught with difficulty," says conservation biologist Stuart Pimm of Duke University. A huge effort went into restoring the Arabian oryx to the wild, for example. But after the animals were returned to a refuge in central Oman in 1982, almost all were wiped out by poachers. "We had the animals, and we put them back, and the world wasn't ready," says Pimm. "Having the species solves only a tiny, tiny part of the problem."

Hunting is not the only threat that would face recovered species. For many, there's no place left to call home. The Chinese river dolphin became extinct due to pollution and other pressures from the human population on the Yangtze River. Things are just as bad there today. Around the world, frogs are getting decimated by a human-spread pathogen called the chytrid fungus. If Australian biologists someday release gastric brooding frogs into their old mountain streams, they could promptly become extinct again.

"Without an environment to put re-created species back into, the whole exercise is futile and a gross waste of money," says Glenn Albrecht, director of the Institute for Social Sustainability at Murdoch University in Australia.

Even if de-extinction proved a complete logistical success, the questions would not end. Passenger pigeons might find the rebounding forests of the eastern United States a welcoming home. But wouldn't that be, in effect, the introduction of a genetically engineered organism into the environment? Could passenger pigeons become a reservoir for a virus that might wipe out another bird species? And how would the residents of Chicago, New York, or Washington, D.C., feel about a new pigeon species arriving in their cities, darkening their skies, and covering their streets with snowstorms of dung?

De-extinction advocates are pondering these questions, and most believe they need to be resolved before any major project moves forward. Hank Greely, a leading bioethicist at Stanford University, has taken a keen interest in investigating the ethical and legal implications of de-extinction. And yet for Greely, as for many others, the very fact that science has advanced to the point that such a spectacular feat is possible is a compelling reason to embrace de-extinction, not to shun it.

"What intrigues me is just that it's really cool," Greely says. "A saber-toothed cat? It would be neat to see one of those."

56 Reintroduction and De-Extinction

Dolly Jørgensen

Jørgensen addresses some of the ethical dilemmas associated with work in de-extinction and proposes that the guidelines for reintroducing currently viable species back into former habitat from which they have been extirpated may provide some initial guidelines on reintroducing previously extinct species.

We are entering an age in which species extinction may be reversible. *De-extinction*, as it has been labeled, can apply to any species for which DNA can be recovered, from woolly mammoths of the Pleistocene to thylacines and passenger pigeons from the twentieth century. These developments, which were showcased in March 2013 at a daylong conference called TEDxDe-Extinction, held in Washington, DC, (*http://tedxdeextinction.org*), are exciting to some scientists and terrifying to others. If we are to embark on this de-extinction journey, an act some might label *playing God*, we need to establish the rules of the game. I want to suggest that the well-established standards for species reintroduction projects provide a solid foundation on which de-extinction can be built.

Critics of de-extinction in the popular science media have quickly pointed out drawbacks. From an ethical perspective, they have pointed to potential violations of animal welfare standards, the potential drain on resources that could be used in the conservation of still-existing species, and the implication that species destruction might be seen as permissible if it is reversible. The ecological objections have included the lack of ecosystems in which the re-created creatures could live, the potential invasiveness of the species in the ecosystem, and the potential for new disease vectors. Exploration of de-extinction's ethical dilemmas will require serious scientific and public debate, including a significant contribution from humanities researchers, including philosophers and historians, who have the appropriate theoretical background for conceptualizing what is at stake. I will not tackle those ethical issues here. The solution to the ecological dilemmas, however, may already be at hand through the application of reintroduction standards.

Reintroduction as a Guide

Reintroduction, the release of a species into an area in which it had been indigenous but has since become extinct, is a long-standing practice. The earliest use of the word *reintroduction* in a conservation context is in an article from 1832 about the return of capercaillie (or *capercailzie*) to Scotland (Wilson 1832). The western capercaillie was hunted out in Scotland in the late eighteenth century, and Wilson reported on the first attempt to bring the birds back to Scotland using specimens from Sweden. From these humble beginnings, an entire science of reintroduction has been built up, particularly over the last 30 years.

Reintroduction science has a strong institutional basis in the International Union for Conservation of Nature (IUCN) and in its Species Survival Commission reintroduction specialist group, founded in 1988. The IUCN developed guidelines for reintroduction (IUCN 1998), which are currently under revision (Dalrymple and Moehrenschlager 2013). The guidelines suggest background studies to allow identification of the species' habitat requirements, identification of lessons learned from prior reintroduction projects of similar species, evaluation of potential sites within the former range of the species, selection of appropriately diverse genetic stock, and an assessment of the socioeconomic context of the project. Armstrong and Seddon (2008) extended the guidelines, proposing key questions at the population, metapopulation, and ecosystem levels that should be addressed before reintroduction proceeds. Because the natural extension of de-extinction is the reintroduction of the species to the wild, at a minimum, the species should be targeted for de-extinction only if the original causes of extinction are removed and the habitat requirements of the species are satisfied. Scientific background studies, including the assessment of the socioeconomic aspects of the project, should be undertaken before the technical work on re-creating the species. If the species has nowhere to go, de-extinction should not move forward.

Even before a newly nonextinct species is ready for release, guidelines exist for how it should be handled. From the moment they are born, the animals would be classified as *extinct in the wild* according to the IUCN Red List standards. As such, they should be managed within the guidelines for existing species recovery and conservation paradigms with a focus on captive breeding (IUCN 2002). This would, of course, be crucial in order to build up a viable population of the species. Lessons learned from existing programs for recovery of formerly *extinct in the wild* species, including the California condor, the Arabian oryx, and the European bison, should be incorporated into the management strategies of resurrected species.

Potential Reintroduction Conflicts

Reintroductions of recently extirpated species tend to be relatively uncontested, but when the species have been absent for a long time, applying the *reintroduction* label can be more contentious. Reintroduction plans for species that have been absent for hundreds or thousands of years, such as the beaver and the lynx in Scotland, have stirred up opposition from landholders and special interest groups, who think of these animals as invaders and intruders. Even within scientific circles, the *reintroduction* label has not always been accepted for species absent for an extended period. For example, the Norwegian Black List of invasive species specifically includes musk ox and wild boar present in the country as illegitimate reintroductions, even though the species are known to have existed there thousands of years ago.

Human acceptance of reintroduction projects will be a crucial aspect to consider for de-extinction. Reintroducing brooding frogs, which died out only in the 1980s, will probably be uncontested, because of their recent extinction history. Reintroducing the thylacine, which was hunted to extinction by the 1930s, may prove unproblematic from a species-history standpoint, although it may be rejected by locals because the species is a carnivore, similar to wolf reintroduction plans in North America and Europe. The woolly mammoth, however, will likely invoke a huge opposition based on the thousands of years it has been absent from Earth. We should all remember the significant outcry against the Pleistocene rewilding scheme of Donlan and colleagues (2005); this time, the proposal would be with real mammoths instead of surrogate elephants.

In spite of these conflicts, *reintroduction* is an appropriate label, regardless of the length of time the species has been absent (Jørgensen 2011). Once the technical hurdles of creating viable offspring of extinct animals are overcome, the species becomes a reintroduction candidate. By framing de-extinction as a new kind of reintroduction project, rather than as something entirely novel, a wealth of prior experiences and established guidelines can be drawn on in de-extinction projects.

References

Armstrong DP, Seddon PJ. 2008. Directions in reintroduction biology. *Trends in Ecology and Evolution* 23: 20–25.

486   *Dolly Jørgensen*

Dalrymple SE, Moehrenschlager A. 2013. "Words matter." A response to Jørgensen's treatment of historic range and definitions of reintroduction. *Restoration Ecology* 21: 156–158.

Donlan J. 2005. Re-wilding North America. *Nature* 436: 913–914.

[IUCN] International Union for Conservation of Nature. 1998. IUCN Guidelines for Re-introductions. IUCN.

———. 2002. IUCN Technical Guidelines on the Management of *ex-Situ* Populations for Conservation. IUCN.

Jørgensen D. 2011. What's history got to do with it? A response to Seddon's definition of reintroduction. *Restoration Ecology* 19: 705–708.

Wilson J. 1832. Account of the introduction of the wood-grouse or capercailzie (*Tetrao urogallus*) to the Forest of Braemar. *Edinburgh New Philosophical Journal* 13: 160–165.

Part Seven

Ethics and Wildlife

Introduction to Part Seven

In this part, the authors focus on issues affecting the human relationship to wildlife.

Four authors assess moral issues related to the hunting of wild animals. Aldo Leopold calls for a greater cooperative spirit among protectionists and sportsmen toward common concerns for wildlife and argues that hunting plays an important role in the economics and management of wildlife well-being. Lawrence Cahoone argues that hunting is not a sport but a neo-traditional cultural trophic practice consistent with ecological ethics. Further, some forms of hunting are less damaging to animal populations overall than farming, and even vegetarian diets.

Marti Kheel challenges the morality of sport hunting and offers a number of thoughtful responses to the justifications given for hunting, including psychological, ecological, and spiritual benefits. Using feminist psychoanalytic theory, she offers a more deep-seated basis for the propensity of men to seek to kill animals as part of the hunting ritual. Alastair S. Gunn addresses the morality of hunting generally and then delves more deeply into the issue of trophy hunting and its role in the economy and culture of poorer countries. Despite reservations that he and many feel about trophy hunting, he proposes that it ultimately may be an important strategy to protect the interests of both wildlife and people.

Four papers deal with special wildlife-related issues. Ned Hettinger addresses the arguments surrounding introduction of exotic species to new habitats. He also counters the argument that opposition to exotic species may be comparable to a xenophobic response to various cultural and ethnic groups among humans and concludes that the loss of biological purity and the greater homogenization of the earth's biodiversity are compelling reasons to oppose introduction of exotic species. Schlaepfer, Sax, and Olden note that despite the problems associated with them, non-native species also provide conservation benefits. These may include providing habitat or food to rare species serving as functional substitutes for extinct taxa, and providing desirable ecosystem functions. Dale Peterson addresses the problem of bushmeat in developing countries, especially as it relates to primates, and develops key reasons for conserving primate biodiversity by reducing the use of apes for food. Grace Clement focuses on intrinsic values and advocates going beyond the traditional arguments of justice used by animal rights and animal welfare advocates and incorporating an ethic of care in our relations to nonhuman animals.

Further Reading

Cohn, Priscilla (ed.). (1999) *Ethics and Wildlife*. Lewiston, New York: Edwin Mellen Press.
Conover, Michael. (2002) *Resolving Human-wildlife Conflicts*. Lewis Publishers (A CRC Company) Boca Raton, Florida: CRC Press. 440 pp.
Curnutt, J. 1996. How to argue for and against sport hunting. *Journal of Social Philosophy* 27(2): 65–89.
Curtis, John A. (2002) Ethics in wildlife management: What price? *Environmental Values* 11: 145–61.

Dickson, Paul, and William M. Adams. 2009. Science and uncertainty in South Africa's elephant culling debate. *Environment and Planning C: Government and Policy* 27: 110–123.

Everett, Jennifer. (2001) Environmental ethics, animal welfarism, and the problem of predation: A Bambi lover's respect for nature. *Ethics & The Environment* 6(1): 42–66.

Houston, P. 1995. Women on hunting. Hopewell, NJ: Ecco Press.

Leopold, 1966. *A Sand County Almanac with Essays from Round River*. Oxford: Oxford University Press.

List, C. J. 1997. Is hunting a right thing? *Environmental Ethics* 19: 405–416.

Lombard, A. T., C. F Johnson, R. M. Cowling, and R. L. Pressey (2001) Protecting plants from elephants: Botanical reserve scenarios within the Addo Elephant National Park, South Africa. *Biological Conservation* 102(ER2): 191–203.

Luke, B. 1997. A critical analysis of hunters' ethics. *Environmental Ethics* 19: 25–44.

Michelfelder, D. P. 2003. Valuing wildlife populations in urban environments. *Journal of Social Philosophy* 34: 79–90.

Morgan, William J. (ed.). 2007. *Ethics in Sport* (2nd ed). Human Kinetics, Champaign, Illinois, 474 pp.

Moriarty, P. V., and M. Woods. 1997. Hunting =/= Predation. *Environmental Ethics* 19: 391–404.

Palmer, C. 2003. Placing animals in urban environmental ethics. *Journal of Social Philosophy* 34: 64–78.

Sagoff, Mark (1999) *What's Wrong with Exotic Species?* Institute for Philosophy and Public Policy. www.puaf.umd.edu//IPPP/fall1999/exotic_species.htm. Defends non-native species.

Shafer, Craig L. (2000) The northern Yellowstone elk debate: Policy, hypothesis, and implications. *Natural Areas Journal* 20(4): 342–359.

Shah, N. J. (2000) Eradication of alien predators in the Seychelles: An example of conservation action on tropical islands. *Biodiversity and Conservation* 10(7): 1219–1220.

Seal Hunt Controversy

Butterworth, Andrew, and Mary Richardson. 2013. A review of animal welfare implications of the Canadian commercial seal hunt. *Marine Policy* 38: 457–469.

Butterworth, Andrew, and Mary Richardson. 2014. A review of animal welfare implications of the Canadian commercial seal hunt—A response to critique of paper MP13 172. *Marine Policy* 43: 379–381.

Daoust, Pierre-Yves, Mike Hammill, Garry Stenson, and Charles Caraguel. 2014. A review of animal welfare implications of the Canadian commercial seal hunt: A critique. *Marine Policy* 43: 367–371.

Livernois, John. 2010. The economics of ending Canada's commercial harp seal hunt. *Marine Policy* 34: 42–53.

Study Questions

1. Give the conditions under which you believe that sport hunting might be morally acceptable and the conditions where you believe it might not. Give your reasoning.

2. Do you agree with Gunn's assertion that trophy hunting is justified in Zimbabwe under the conditions he describes? Give your reasoning.

3. Based on Hettinger's and Schlaepfer et al.'s discussions, what is your view of exotic species, including those that are naturally dispersing and apparently nondamaging? Explain your perspective.

4. What is your response to the tension between the role of bushmeat among some subsistence communities and the severe impact hunting has on some primate populations. Is it feasible for both concerns to be addressed? If so, how might that be approached?

5. Give some examples of how an ethic of care Clement proposes might be extended to wild animals.

Hunting Controversies

57 Game and Wild Life Conservation

Aldo Leopold

Leopold emphasizes the importance of both preservationist and sportsperson perspectives in the struggle to enhance the well-being of wildlife; he further calls for more cooperative efforts between these factions. He also affirms the importance of hunting as an important connection between humans and nature as well as an essential economic foundation for managing wildlife.

This is a reply to Mr. T. T. McCabe's well written and persuasive *exposé* of two recent manifestations of the sportsman's movement: my *Game Survey of the North Central States*, and the several publications issued by More Game Birds in America. Both are, I take it, inclusively condemned as "a framework of pernicious doctrines, too often speciously glossed over."

Mr. McCabe's attitude raises what seems to me a fundamental issue. I hope that it may provoke some badly needed cerebration among both protectionists and sportsmen, and especially among those intergrades like myself, who share the aspirations of both.

There are many sportsmen who laugh at any attempt to embody the protectionist point-of-view in any game program. "Whatever you do the protectionists will be against it." Mr. McCabe's paper furnishes scant comfort to those of us who have been holding out against this attitude, because we see in it the indefinite continuation of the present deadlock, from which the sharpest pens gain much glory, but the game gains nothing except a further chance to disappear.

[. . .]

I realize that every time I turn on an electric light, or ride on a Pullman, or pocket the unearned increment on a stock, or a bond, or a piece of real estate, I am "selling out" to the enemies of conservation. When I submit these thoughts to a printing press, I am helping cut down the woods. When I pour cream in my coffee, I am helping to drain a marsh for cows to graze, and to exterminate the birds of Brazil. When I go birding or hunting in my Ford, I am devastating an oil field, and re-electing an imperialist to get me rubber. Nay more: when I father more than two children I am creating an insatiable need for more printing presses, more cows, more coffee, more oil, and more rubber, to supply which more birds, more trees, and more flowers will either be killed, or what is just as destructive, evicted from their several environments.

What to do? I see only two courses open to the likes of us. One is to go live on locusts in the wilderness, if there is any wilderness left. The other is surreptitiously to set up within the economic Juggernaut certain new cogs and wheels whereby the residual love of nature, inherent even in Rotarians, may be made to recreate at least a fraction of those values which their love of "progress" is destroying. A briefer way to put it is: if we want Mr. Babbitt to rebuild outdoor America, we must let him use the same tools wherewith he destroyed it. He knows no other.

I by no means imply that Mr. McCabe should agree with this view. I do imply that to accept the economic order which is destroying wild life disqualifies us from rejecting any and all economic tools for its restoration, on the grounds that such tools are impure and unholy.

With what other than economic tools, for instance, can we cope with progressive eviction of game (and most other wild life) from our rich agricultural lands by clean farming and drainage?

Does anyone still believe that restrictive game laws alone will halt the wave of destruction which sweeps majestically across the continent, regardless of closed seasons, paper refuges, bird-books-for-school-children, game farms, Izaak Walton Leagues, Audubon Societies, or the other feeble palliatives which we protectionists and sportsmen, jointly or separately, have so far erected as barriers in its path? Does Mr. McCabe know a way to induce the average farmer to leave the birds some food and cover without paying him for it? To raise the fund for such payment without in some way taxing sportsmen?

I have tried to build a mechanism whereby the sportsmen and the Ammunition Industry could contribute financially to the solution of this problem, without dictating the answer themselves. The mechanism consists of a series of game fellowships, set up in the agricultural colleges, to examine the question of whether slick-and-clean agriculture is really economic, and if not, to advise farmers how they can, by leaving a little cover and food, raise a game crop, and market the surplus by sale of shooting privileges to sportsmen. This mechanism is, I take it, specious. Have the protectionists a better one to offer?

Another mechanism which I have tried to build is the committee of sportsmen and protectionists charged with setting forth a new wild life policy. Has Mr. McCabe read it?

These things I have done, and I make no apology for them. Even if they should ultimately succeed, they will not restore the good old days of free hunting of wholly natural wild life (which I loved as well as Mr. McCabe), but they may restore something. That something will be more native to America, and available on more democratic terms, than More Game Birds pheasants, even though it be less so than Mr. McCabe's dreams of days gone by.

Let me admit that my cogs and wheels are designed to perpetuate wild life to shoot, as well as wild life to look at. This is because I believe that hunting takes rank with agriculture and nature study as one of three fundamentally valuable human contacts with the soil. Secondly, because hunting revenue offers the only available "coin of the realm" for buying from Mr. Babbitt the environmental modifications necessary to offset the inroads of industry.

I admit the possibility that I am wrong about hunting. The total cessation of it would certainly conserve some forms of wild life in some places. Any ecologist must, however, admit that the resulting distribution and assortment of species would be very irregular and arbitrary, and quite unrelated to human needs. The richest lands would be totally devoid of game because of the lack of cover, and the poorer lands nearly so because of the lack of food. The intermediate zones might have a great deal of game. Each species would shrink to those localities where economic accident offered the requisite assortment of environmental requirements. That same condition—namely the fortuitous (as distinguished from purposeful) make-up of wild life environments—shares, with overshooting, the credit for our present deplorable situation.

The protectionists will, at this point, remind me of the possibilities of inviolate sanctuaries, publicly owned, in which habitable environments are perpetuated at public expense. Let us by all means have as many as possible. But will Mr. Babbitt vote the necessary funds for the huge expansion in sanctuaries which we need? He hasn't so far. It is "blood money" which has bought a large part of what we have. Moreover, sanctuaries propose to salvage only a few samples of wild life. I, for one, demand more. I demand of Mr. Babbitt that game and wild life be one of the normal products of every farm, and the enjoyment of it a part of the normal environment of every boy, whether he live next door to a public sanctuary or elsewhere.

Mr. McCabe taxes me with omitting any mention of game production on public lands, where the one-gallus hunter will have free access to it. I can only infer that he has not read the American Game Policy. Has any group ever proposed a larger public land program, and called for more wild life production thereon? The Policy admits, to be sure, the unpleasant fact that lands must be cheap in order to be public. It advocates the paid-hunting system only for those lands too expensive for the public to own.

Finally Mr. McCabe taxes me with too much interest in exotics. Modesty forbids me to refute this charge in detail. I have persuaded two states to go out of the pheasant business, and several others to limit it to half their area. I devised the "glaciation hypothesis" which seems to exclude pheasants from about a third of the United States. On the other hand, I have recommended the continuation of pheasants and Hungarians in certain regions where economic changes have so radically altered the environment as to make the restoration of native game prohibitive in cost. Just what native species would Mr. McCabe recommend for east-central Wisconsin, or for northern Iowa, or for farm land in Massachusetts?

Let it by no chance be inferred that because I speak as a sportsman I defend the whole history of the sportman's movement. Hindsight shows that history contains any number of blunders, much bad ecology, and not a few actions which must be construed as either stubbornness or hypocrisy. For every one of these, one could point out a counterpart in the history of the protectionists, only there has been no "Emergency Committee" with either the means or the desire to compile and advertise them. Fifteen years ago, for instance, the protectionists closed the prairie chicken in Iowa, and then sat calmly by while plow and cow pushed the species almost to the brink of oblivion. Was this a blunder? Yes—but what of it? Is there any human aspiration which ever scored a victory without losing to some extent its capacity for self-criticism? The worthiness of any cause is not measured by its clean record, but by its readiness to see the blots when they are pointed out, and to change its mind. Is there not some way in which our two factions can point out each other's sophistries and blunders without losing sight of our common love for what Mr. Babbitt is trampling under foot? Must the past mistakes of each group automatically condemn every future effort of either to correct them?

To me, the most hopeful sign in the sportsman's movement is that several little groups have publicly avowed that the old program is a failure. Each is struggling to devise a new formula. I am conceited enough to believe that the formula my little group is trying to put together comes as near meeting the ugly realities of economics on the one hand, and the ideals of the protectionists on the other, as any yet devised. [. . .]

In short, I beg for a little selectivity in weighing the new departures proposed by the other fellow. I also pray for the day when some little group of protectionists will publicly avow that their old formula of restriction is not the whole Alpha-to-Omega of conservation. With both sides in doubt as to the infallibility of their own past dogmas, we might actually hang together long enough to save some wild life. At present, we are getting good and ready to hang separately.

58 Hunting as a Moral Good

Lawrence Cahoone

Rather than a sport, Cahoone views hunting as a neo-traditional cultural trophic practice consistent with ecological ethics. He notes that death by hunter generally is less painful than death in the natural world. Cahoone points out that hunting achieves goods, including trophic responsibility, ecological expertise, and a unique experience of animal inter-dependence. He argues that hunting should be considered a moral good wherever preservation of ecosystems or species requires hunting or if animal deaths per unit of nutrition is lower than that caused by farming practices.

Contemporary hunting is commonly condemned in ethical literature as: (a) the killing of animals for sport; (b) by cruel means that cause excessive suffering; (c) thereby immorally violating our obligations to honour animals' rights or intrinsic goods; (d) whose only practical benefit, i.e. nutrition, is achievable without killing animals, i.e. agriculture; and (e) whose practice embodies no redeeming virtues. I will argue that each of these clauses is dubious or false regarding most contemporary legal hunting in the United States. I leave open whether other types of hunting, or meat-eating, are permissible, as well as what overall ethical theory is most justifiable. In what follows we will discuss ecological ethics versus animal rights and animal welfare ethics (section one), the nature of hunting as currently practised (sections two and three), the relative harms to wildlife of hunting and farming (section four), and some possible virtues of hunting practice (section five).[1]

Which Ethics Applies?

Most current arguments against hunting are based in either the utilitarian animal welfare perspective, which aims to maximise the welfare and minimise the pain of sentient beings, or the deontological animal rights perspective, which endows animals with rights not to be intentionally harmed. The most famous formulators of these views are, respectively, Peter Singer and Tom Regan (Regan 1983; Singer 2002a). The crucial point for each theory is the ascription to individual animals of a morally considerable value comparable, but not equivalent, to that of individual humans, so that any human activity that harms them requires a moral justification in terms of countervailing human rights or interests, i.e., that the activity is truly necessary or achieves a greater good. Each restricts his claim to only some animals; for Singer, those that can suffer, which he claims for mammals and birds, suggests in reptiles and fish, and considers possible in crustaceans and molluscs; for Regan, those that apprehend their identity and welfare, hence are the 'subject of a life,' a capacity he describes only in mammals, although he suggests that killing birds and fish is also wrong. Both take killing such animals for food to be unnecessary, hence immoral. This naturally makes what is called sport hunting, although perhaps not subsistence hunting, immoral.

   [. . .]

   Ecological ethics joins Singer and Regan in finding morally relevant value outside human society, and in ascribing to individual animals goods that potentially generate moral obligations. But they also diverge. Unlike the animal rights/welfare views, ecological ethics must hold that: the ecosystem, on which all members depend, and the species-roles in that ecosystem, are more valuable than the individuals occupying them; the good of a complex organism, e.g., its ability to feel pain or be a 'subject' of its life, can be tramped by the ecosystem role of less complex organisms, including vegetation and terrain or aquatic ecosystem features; wildness, as opposed to domestication, is a good; and even death, as the transfer of chemical energy among organisms, can be a good. Ecology recognises that organisms live at each other's expense. Not only predators, but scavengers, fungi, fruit-eating animals, and autotrophs (e.g. green plants) eliminate competitors by monopolising resources. They may not kill to eat but their eating kills. Ecological ethics recognises that *this is good*; for the good of the ecosystem, maintained by those individual goods and ills, trumps them all. However else ecological ethics differs from animal rights/welfare views, it differs in accepting a kind of holism.[2]

In practice, of course, animal rights/welfare theories are concerned not with the rights, interests, or suffering of animals *per se*, but with *humanly caused* pain and rights-violations, with 'the evil that men do.' They demand that human activities that harm animals be justified before an ethical bar that honours the value of each animal. Ecological ethics can agree. This concern could be captured by a meliorist, secondary principle that would not condemn predation, namely, that *humanly caused animal death and suffering should be reduced as much as possible*, hence allowed *only if necessary*. 'Necessary' must refer to goods of ecosystems, or human goods or rights, sufficient to justify the animal death or harm. How this principle is to be grounded we can leave open for present purposes.

It is reasonable to ask if hunting can justify itself with respect to this meliorist principle. Its fundamental argument against hunting would be: harming or killing animals unnecessarily is wrong; hunting kills animals unnecessarily; so hunting is wrong. Note the major premise is potentially a charge against all animal-killing activities, while the minor premise singles out hunting for lack of 'necessity.' That implies the existence of alternative activities which accomplish any goods or benefits ascribed to hunting without killing animals. Before addressing this basic charge, we have to clarify the nature of contemporary hunting and address less fundamental criticisms made against it.

Is Contemporary Hunting a Sport?

Most anti-hunting criticisms distinguish sport hunting from the subsistence hunting of indigenous peoples, and some accept the latter if a people inhabit a traditional hunting culture *and* must hunt to live.[3] Such hunters can plausibly claim natural necessity: sport may be cultural, but starvation is awfully natural. The condemnation of a sport of killing is presumably less difficult. Not much of a sport, Camilla Fox says, since sport 'implies two players on an equal playing field,' whereas the only equality in hunting is, according to Joy Williams, 'Bam, bam, bam. I get to shoot you and you get to be dead' (Williams 1995: 248; Fox 2002: 2). One can understand the judgment of sport killing as a paradigmatic form of cruelty, 'the perfect type of that pure evil for which metaphysicans have sometimes sought,' according to Joseph Wood Krutch (1957).

Holmes Rolston and Ned Hettinger have separately argued that while hunting would be immoral under a human social morality, that is the wrong morality to apply to relations with wild animals (Rolston 1988; Hettinger 1994). Since hunting is continuous with the natural process of non-human predation, the right morality to apply is the ecological ethics of preserving ecosystems. In contrast, Paul Veatch Moriarity and Mark Woods insist that hunting is not comparable to animal predation. They write, 'There is nothing natural about meat-eating and hunting in our culture. Meat-eating and hunting are cultural activities, not natural activities' (Moriarity and Woods 1997: 399). While subsistence hunters might be considered part of a natural or ecological morality, contemporary American hunters are sportsmen, engaged in a cultural activity that pretends to be natural so as to take a moral holiday.

[. . .]

The 'sport' appellation has its own varied history. In America its mantle was donned by wealthy hunters as a class distinction to mark themselves off from rural 'pot' hunters (List 2004).[4] In the central European or Germanic tradition hunters were never considered sportsmen, but woodsmen, pliers of the forest trades and conservators of its bounty. Contemporary American hunting ethics dictates that prey must be eaten, and an activity whose end is the provision of necessity cannot be a sport. As Fox correctly stated, sport implies equal contenders, but as José Ortega y Gasset pointed out, predator and prey cannot be equals, they must belong to sufficiently dissimilar species bearing a definite venatic relationship (Ortega 1972). The challenge is not who 'wins' but whether predator can defeat the wiles of prey. The 'sporting' aspect of contemporary hunting is 'fair chase,' the renuncia- tion of technical advantages that would negate the prey's strategies of avoidance. This self-imposed limitation does sound like sport, and it is something we perhaps cannot ask of the subsistence hunter, that she sacrifice her child's dinner to fair chase. However, as Charles List points out, indigenous hunting contains many such ethical or ritual rules, fealty to which is crucial to the hunter's social status (List 2004). Thus, even this one apparently distinctive feature of 'sport' hunting does not clearly distinguish it from 'subsistence' hunting.

[. . .]

So is contemporary hunting cultural or natural? The obvious answer is that it is both. The anti- hunters are right: contemporary hunting is not a sport. It is a *cultural trophic practice*.[5] Traditional hunting was a cultured form of food acquisition. Many millennia down the road from her hunter- gatherer origins, now an agro-industrialist, for cultural reasons the human creature elects selectively to strip herself of features of modernity to effect a limited re-occupation of our phylogenetic and archaic niche in wild nature. That means hunting for meat. As Rolston puts it, 'Mere killing for sport is not justified but must join its ancient function . . . the quarry should not be sacrificed outside the paradigm of meat-hunting . . .' (Rolston 1988: 89). If in indigenous societies hunting is a traditional trophic practice, then in contemporary America hunting is a *neo-traditional* trophic practice whereby agro-industrialists elect to approximate the pre-agrarian skill of procuring meat by taking individual wild prey. This is no pretended primitivism, but a practical approximation of an archaic activity.[6] Whether it is a morally permissible practice, of course, remains to be seen.

The Practice of Contemporary Hunting

Hunting practice is unfamiliar to most people, including, to judge by their published work, many of its critics. Its realities are relevant to assessing several moral objections to the *way* contemporary hunters hunt.

Hunting in North America is regulated by the state to ensure the conservation of game and human safety. Open seasons are legally specified by species and weapon. Some are quite brief; the most popular game animal in America is deer (whitetail and mule deer), and in many states the modern gun season is less than two weeks per year (although there are additional seasons for bow and 'primi- tive' firearms). Some states and counties prohibit the use of rifles altogether because of the danger posed by their range. Public hunting lands are few and remote in some states, effectively restricting hunting to landowners, their friends, and clients of commercial hunting operations.

Method varies with weapon, habitat, game laws, but above all with the species hunted. Typically, grouse, pheasants, quail, and rabbits (upland game) are flushed from grass or brush by a moving hunter (or dog) and shot while fleeing with a cartridge-loaded shotgun (which shoots a cluster of metal pellets or 'shot'). The same weapon is used to take waterfowl in flight, from a blind at water's edge or a stationary boat. Deer, elk, and other large herbivores are shot by a modern rifle (long gun with spiral ridge in barrel), muzzle-loading rifle (round and gunpowder loaded separately with a ramrod, also called 'primitive' firearms), slug-loaded shotgun (solid slug instead of cartridge), or bow ('traditional' long or recurve bow, or compound bow, which has cams to decrease the force necessary to hold at full draw). Some game are stalked (tracking a particular animal), or still-hunted (searching by slowly walking), or awaited in hiding at a fixed position along a game trail (in ground blind or tree stand), or driven (a moving partner scares prey toward a stationary hunter), or vocally called during the mating season.

[. . .]

While critics argue that contemporary firearm and bow technologies eliminate fair chase, making hunting too easy, almost all technical advances address convenience, safety, and comfort rather than effectiveness. Modern muzzleloaders and compound bows reduce effort, but do little to make the taking of prey more likely.[7] Only in the use of scoped rifles have technological improvements made a significant difference, because their accuracy at several hundred yards can allow a practised hunter to take game from beyond the prey's sensory range. But this is mainly relevant to hunting large game in unforested, hilly environments; in the woods, or grassy plains, even large game can rarely be seen as much as one hundred yards away. In the field, cartridge-loaded shotguns have an effective range of 30 yards; muzzle-loaders 50 to 100 yards; slug-loaded shotguns about 75; and compound bows about 30 yards. The average distance at which deer, for example, are taken by firearms is 50 yards; by bow, 20 yards. Rifles and shotguns with magazines permit follow-up shots; reloading time makes muzzleloaders and bows normally single shot weapons. So, with all these 'improvements,' still only about 25 per cent of American deer hunters succeed in taking a deer in a given year.

[. . .]

The climax of the scouting, searching, and the seeing is striking game with a deadly projectile. Anti-hunters object to the pain caused by the hunter's strike. Guns kill by massive trauma and shock. Hunting small game with shotguns, any direct hit is likely to be instantly lethal. The same is generally true, or nearly so, for larger game hunted with rifles or slug-loaded shotguns. The hunters' target is usually the heart/lung area or head. If another part of the animal is hit, death can take longer, and a second shot at a moving animal may be required. Arrows are different. They kill by blood loss, denying oxygen to the brain. The time this takes varies widely, depending on the spot hit and the animal's state before being struck. If heart or lungs are hit, death will come in minutes. In fact, modern broadheads (the cutting blades on an arrow) are so sharp the animal may feel only the impact but not the presence of the blades in its body, until it collapses. If the strike has missed heart and lungs, however, bow hunters are unsurprised at having to wait an hour after the stricken animal has run off to find it has bled to death in hiding.

Let us accept that non-instantaneous hunting death involves suffering and/or pain. The question is, how much? Neither hunters nor anti-hunters can answer that question with certainty, but both can, and do, make guesses. It is likely that for animals struck in heart/lung or head by gunshots, and who thus die within moments, shock masks most of the pain, as it would for us. Bow-shot animals who die quickly from the cutting of razor sharp blades also probably feel some, but little, pain. Bow-shot animals who take an hour to bleed to death, even secreted and undisturbed, are *certainly* suffering in some sense.

Does such a level of pain and suffering make the hunter's strike immoral? What is the criterion of morally acceptable pain in hunting? Rolston argues that the criterion is the pain of the prey's likely death in the wild from starvation, disease, or predation:

> Humans are not bound to inflict no innocent suffering. That is contrary to nature. . . . No predator can live without causing pain. . . . The wild animal has no right or welfare claim to have from humans a kinder treatment than in nonhuman nature. . . . The strong ethical rule is this: Do not cause inordinate suffering, beyond those orders of nature from which the animals were taken
>
> (Rolston 1988: 58–61)

We may say that ethically the hunter must strive to inflict the least pain necessary for a successful hunt, but that the suffering is not a moral violation unless it exceeds the pain of the animal's likely wild death. It is difficult to imagine that most forms of natural death—by starvation, disease, expiration in weakened conditions (e.g. in winter, or after injury), and being eaten alive by a predator—involve *less* pain and suffering than most hunting deaths. The suffering of death-by-hunter likely lies below the level of natural death but above the nearly painless euthanasia methods today used in the beef industry (which methods, of course, presuppose human control and the prior elimination of the animal's wildness).

The final phase of the hunting act proper is securing or taking possession of the prey.

[. . .]

The exception to the generally unproblematic nature of securing is the 'wounding' issue, that is, failing to recover mortally stricken prey. Hunters deny its frequency, but it is a significant concern for them; second only to a serious accident to self or other hunters, it is the worst thing that can happen while hunting. Hunters practice to minimise the chance of wounding. How often does non-recovery occur? Bowhunting has been charged with extravagant non-recovery rates, but the most scientific study found that 13 per cent of that minority of bowhunters who actually shot and killed a deer failed to recover it (Krueger 1995)[8] Such a rate is, I believe, below whatever figure would make the underlying activity immoral. For to claim that an activity can only be morally permissible if it is always successful is to declare it immoral.

A fundamental feature of contemporary hunting is that hunters and hunting organisations claim to follow ethical and legal rules specific to hunting. Critics of hunting find hunting ethics a contradiction in terms, or even evidence of the immoral nature of the underlying practice (Luke 1997). Certainly the fact that a practice has an ethics does not make it ethical in the sense of showing it ought to be done. But in the case of hunting, its current ethics has additional historical significance. Contemporary North American hunting evolved in the twentieth century in response to the extinction and near extinction of game species by unregulated hunting—especially commercial hunting—in the nineteenth and early twentieth centuries. Hunting nearly obliterated game species in the United States and lower Canada. Most (not all) were re-established by environmentalists and hunting organisations through hard-won legislation which stipulated an end to commercial hunting and a ban on traffic in wild animal products. An integrated system of wildlife management and hunting was established on several key principles: maintenance of species populations near a healthy level as regulated by scientific wildlife management; maintenance of wide opportunities for public hunting open to non-landowners; reservation of un-hunted wild lands to preserve unaffected gene pools; and licensing and taxation of hunters to support all the above (Geist 1995, 2000). The resulting return of game species in the last 50 years, Geist claims, is the greatest environmental success of the twentieth century (Petersen 2003, 2004). The point is, contemporary hunting was re-invented by activists and government in concert with the evolving field of wildlife management to accord with environmental concerns.[9]

With this came a revised ethics of hunting. The hunter must hunt so as to preserve the local prey species for the future ('bag limits'), renounce technical advances that overwhelm the prey's capacities ('fair chase'), and approximate pre-agrarian use of the dead animal (consume prey). Neo-traditional hunting thus has special social and ecological responsibilities that legitimately compromise its approximation of traditional models. It must balance the competing values of: (a) preserving the health of prey species and ecosystems; (b) reasonable likelihood of hunting success; (c) fair chase; (d) causing minimum pain to prey; and (e) human safety.[10] The form and methods of neo-traditional hunting will legitimately change as each value alters its demands with social, technological, and ecological circumstances.[11]

None of this implies a pristine picture. Hunting is certainly capable of unethical performance, for example, elimination of fair chase or taking shots that invite wounding. Commercial hunting operations that offer hunters with money but not patience an opportunity on enclosed land with winter-fed deer, nearly 'guaranteeing' a trophy animal, partially domesticated prey. Domestic animals cannot be hunted, by definition. Likewise, killing without utilising the dead animal is not immoral hunting, it is *not hunting at all* given that, as I have argued, neo-traditional hunting by nature seeks to approximate archaic hunting practice. Last are those who travel the world to shoot rare game for the sake of international competition.

[. . .]

As such, hunting plays a crucial role in our current system of wildlife management. Hunters substitute for absent natural predators (primarily wolves, but also cougars) in keeping game populations in check and in supporting wildlands financially. Critics claim that the problem to which hunters are offered as the solution has itself been created for hunters' benefit; that is, deer populations are kept artificially large by wildlife managers for the sake of hunters' dollars through regulations encouraging hunters to take bucks, which has allowed deer herds to exceed carrying capacity, creating a self-maintaining deer 'problem' annually solved by hunting. This criticism is partly correct. However, it speaks not to an end of hunting, but to a change in regulations. Many states are now encouraging the taking of antlerless deer, and doubtless this trend should continue (Petersen 2000: 158–69).

Wildlife management supplies an important moral defence of hunting. Some anticipate chemical contraception for wild deer and other species to circumvent this need for hunting. Only time will tell if such can be practicable, but as Gary Varner has argued, in our current technological state 'the defenders of hunting have it right' (Varner 2003: 103). If without such hunting, species populations and/or ecosystems will suffer great harm, then hunting *is* necessary, and even the meliorist, hence environmentally sensitive, version of the animal rights/welfare views ought to endorse limited hunting in those circumstances.[12]. However, this argument defends only what Varner calls 'therapeutic' hunting, tailored solely to cull herds. Contemporary hunting does accomplish that aim, but so would deadly culling by professional wildlife managers.[13] The question would then be which method—expert culling or neo-traditional hunting—is most practicable in technological, social, and financial terms. Thus the wildlife management argument is a legitimate and important, but limited justification of contemporary hunting.

Least Harm: Hunting Versus Farming

The meliorist animal rights/welfare argument holds that hunting kills animals unnecessarily. This claim hangs on the existence of alternative activities that accomplish hunting's goods or effects with less or no animal killing. As noted, neo-traditional hunting is a return to the archaic pursuit of meat, and contemporary hunting ethics dictates that prey must be eaten. Such nutrition cannot justify hunting, it is claimed, because we have an alternative source of nutrition, agriculture, which does not kill animals. This is indifferently an argument against all meat-eating. Although my aim is not to justify meat-eating in general, any argument to justify hunting for meat will inevitably argue for the morality of meat-eating. For the following inferences are, if not irresistible, yet hard to avoid: *if* it is wrong for humans to eat meat, then hunting for meat is wrong too; *if* meat-eating is acceptable, hunting that consumes prey must also be. It would be difficult to argue that an animal suffers more from hunting than from contemporary animal husbandry.[14] Thus, if we may eat domestic cattle, we may eat wild deer; if we may not eat wild deer, we cannot eat domestic cattle either. The point is: by the meliorist principle, hunting (like meat-eating) is immoral because agriculture and vegetarian diets do not kill animals.

[. . .]

Farming harms or kills wild animals in at least five ways. First, clearing land kills animals outright and destroys habitat, hence causes starvation or disruption of reproduction. Second, modern intensive agriculture uses pesticide and nitrogenous fertiliser whose run-off pollutes ground water on which animals depend. Third, modern farming uses machinery to break through the soil, and in each passage ground-nesting amphibians, reptiles, birds, and small mammals are maimed or killed. Fourth, crops must be protected from opportunistic wildlife. Richard Nelson, tracking farmers who routinely kill deer to save crops, claims that, 'Whenever any of us sit down for breakfast, lunch, dinner, or a snack, it's likely that deer were killed to protect some of the food we eat and the beverages we drink' (Nelson 1997: 310). Fifth are a host of indirect harms by modern agriculture's supporting technologies. Vegetable nutrition is wrung from the Earth by diesel-burning machinery and nitrogen- and oil-based fertilisers, processed and refrigerated with power from river-altering, coal-burning, or nuclear-waste-producing plants, driven thousands of miles over asphalt by fossil-fueled tracks.

The meliorist animal rights/welfare view must take into account that *agriculture kills animals*. Hence, so does a vegetarian diet. We now see that hunting must be judged not only relative to the animals hunting kills, but relative to the *animal cost of the agrarian activity that would replace the meat from the animals it kills*. Where a type of hunting has a lower death/nutrition ratio than a type of farming, and where the pain of death by hunter is arguably no greater than death by farmer, the meliorist version of the animal welfare/animal rights argument must morally prefer hunting to farming.

Comprehensive data on wildlife deaths by farming are lacking. The comparison of the animal death/nutrition ratio for farming and hunting will vary, on the farming side, according to crop yield, climate, level of technological intensity, distance from market, etc., and, on the hunting side, with the species and size of animal hunted. All we can do here is to note two comparisons based on two of agriculture's potential harms to wildlife.

Regarding fossil fuel use, Ted Kerasote, using data from David Pimentel, analysed the fossil fuel costs of killing one elk near his Wyoming home versus the same calories of produce (Kerasote 1993: 234ff). The 150 pounds of meat from one elk cost 79,000 kilocalories of fossil fuel energy in producing his gun and ammunition, driving to the field, etc. The caloric equivalent in store bought potatoes cost 151,000 kilocalories; rice and canned beans cost 477,000 kilocalories. Organically growing the 360 pounds of potatoes locally, on .02 hectares, would cost 42,000 kilocalories in seed and other requirements. So, considering fossil fuel use alone, local organic-sustainable farming did undercut the elk meat, although any non-local or processed produce was *far* more costly. That is, *ceteris paribus*, local organic-sustainable farmed vegetable nutrition may be less harmful than locally hunted animal nutrition, but locally hunted animal nutrition was far less harmful than industrially or non-locally farmed vegetable nutrition.

Let us consider the animals killed by farm machinery. In a widely noted essay, Steven Davis argued against universal vegetarianism by claiming that agriculture might produce less nutrition per animal death than animal husbandry, using a figure of 15 animal deaths per hectare from farm machinery (Davis 2003).

[. . .]

Thus, while precise data are lacking, if Davis's figure is even remotely accurate, *it is very likely that agricultural production kills more animals than deer hunting per unit of nutrition*, hence must kill more animals for the same meal. And in terms of animal suffering, it would be difficult to show that death from being maimed, crushed, cut to pieces, poisoned, or starved is less painful than the average death by hunter as described in the preceding section.

As for local organic-sustainable farming, it undoubtedly harms wildlife less per hectare than intensive farming with respect to pesticide/fertiliser use, and presumably less regarding machinery passes and indirect effects of transportation/refrigeration, but it may not with respect to habitat loss and crop protection. Indeed, because its efficiency of production is inevitably lower than that of intensive agriculture, there is a possibly off-setting downward pressure on its nutrition per animal death, requiring more acreage to be put into production to achieve the same nutrition. Whether this prevents it from undercutting hunting's nutrition/death ratio is unclear.

Now, it might be argued that the agrarian killing of animals is unintended, hence moral, or less immoral than the hunter's intended killing. The role of intent, or better, purposiveness in the harm of non-humans is an interesting moral question that cannot be adequately addressed here. But it should be noted that such an argument would undermine much of both animal rights/welfare views and ecological ethics, whose contribution to ethical treatment of non-human creatures calls attention to unintended effects. Do we really want to say that unintended—more precisely, 'unsought'—animal deaths *predictably caused* by an act or policy are not to count against it morally? In some animal experimentation, death is not sought but is a predictable by-product. Are we to say that a *greater* anticipated but unsought harm to animals is morally preferable to a *lesser* but sought harm? Legislation against habitat destruction is morally based on *not* making that distinction.[15]

Thus, at least some forms of hunting are very probably less deadly to animals than farming and the vegetarian diets depending on it. Remember that the meliorist version of the animal rights/welfare views, which is compatible with ecological ethics, holds that humanly caused animal death and suffering should be reduced as much as possible, hence allowed only if necessary. Eating is a necessity. Consequently, in those cases where ethical hunts kill fewer animals for the same nutrition than do farming and vegetarianism, eating hunted meat would be not only morally justified but morally preferred. The lesson is that there is virtually no free lunch; that is, free of moral culpability for animal death. Whatever answer we can give to the 'triangulated' moral argument between vegetarianism, animal husbandry, and hunting as to their respective animal harms, it will be complex, circumstantial, and a matter of *degree*. The mantle of least harm will shift among particular types and circumstances of farming or hunting, or pasturing, each with its own animal cost.

Does Hunting Embody Goods?

Even if hunting is morally permissible, or not immoral, is there anything good about it? Ethically regulated hunting arguably manifests virtues, of which a few can be mentioned. First, like home brewers, vegetable gardeners, and amateur wood-workers, hunters achieve *anachronistic self-sufficiency*. As Leopold said of 'hobbies,' the attempt to maintain pre-modern skills that are markedly less efficient than contemporary modes of production or acquisition, is valuable (Leopold 1970). Hunting shares with raising your own produce some virtue not embodied in buying produce at the store. Second, this self-sufficiency manifests what we could call *trophic responsibility*. Ignorance of food is ignorance of our most basic relation to nature. What Michael Pollan calls 'facing your food' is, particularly in contemporary society, an ecological virtue (Pollan 2002). Hunters face the animal they are to eat in its natural life, they see the wild life it loses when it dies, personally kill and eviscerate it, and sometimes butcher it themselves. Hunting is a personally responsible form of human carnivory. Third, is local *ecological expertise*. Hunters' ability to find game rests on their knowledge of local habitats and species. Long-time hunters typically become experts on their hunting grounds; hunters commonly receive queries from government agencies about non-game species of concern. They are one of the few non-professional groups that routinely canvas local wild habitats off-trail and in harsh weather.

It is an historical fact that hunting has carried special meaning for its practitioners and their societies. As Paul Shepard points out, hunting had metaphysical significance for most pre-agrarian, pre-literate peoples, which is to say, for all of us until five to ten thousand years ago (Shepard 1973). In their ecological cosmologies, the predator-prey relation was conceived as a moral relationship. Animal food was not a *what* but a revered and mysterious *who*, pursuable only by the discerning seeker, a who that dies and becomes the seeker, transforming the latter in the process. This was understood as an exchange in which the human provided the animal respect and thanks, a cultural immortality, and a predatory limit on species populations, while the animal provided humans food and a lesson in the secrets of reality. In evolutionary terms, the hunter, like any predator, serves prey as a messenger of the genetic information that constitutes its species' future; for while the predator uses the prey, it is equally true that the prey-species uses the predator and the ecosystem uses them both (Shepard 1996: 24).[16]

Although modern agro-industrial hunters are not animists, they do engage that archaic practice. Hunting renews their membership both in our archaic human lineage and in the animal sphere. Hunting alone plunges us into the wild on wild business, to pursue our existence by its rules, where every life lives at the expense of others, which is the bargain of animal existence. As Rolston writes, 'In ways that mere watchers of nature can never know, hunters know their ecology. The hunter's success is not conquest but submission to the ecology . . .' (Rolston 1988: 92). Or as Kerasote puts it,

The elk in the forest, the myriad of small creatures lost as the combines turn the fields, and the Douglas fir hidden in the walls of our homes—every day we foreclose one life over another. . . .

> Given this condition and my final inability to escape from it, I decided to go back to hunting . . . because it attaches me to this place and the animals I love, asking me to own what each of us ought to own in some personal way—the pain that runs the world . . .
>
> (Kerasote 1993: 240)

This is less romance, or animism, than a kind of animal honesty. And that may be the virtue most reliably embodied by hunting.

The critic of hunting, left cold by such claims, is likely to say that even if pain 'runs the world,' that is no justification for choosing to *add* to it. True enough. But, as argued, much contemporary hunting does *not* add to but *replaces* some part of the massive, anonymous animal suffering caused unseen by consumers, omnivores, and vegetarians, with pain caused personally and directly, in which the animal's life and death are intimately recognised and responsibility taken. If so, then in a modern society where both meat-eaters and vegetarians are ever more distant from the trophic sources of their existence, it is arguably good that some choose temporarily to return to the archaic practice, common to many animals and essential to their ecosystems, so that participatory awareness of the way life uses death in animal nature does not vanish from human society.

Conclusion

We may summarise. Contemporary hunting is not a sport; it is a neo-traditional cultural practice in which contemporaries re-enter an archaic pursuit of meat. Wild animal death by hunter is on average less painful than death by farmer or by nature, and while more painful than death by enlightened animal husbandry, death by hunter allows the animal its wild life. Regulated, ethical hunting embodies the goods of trophic responsibility, ecosystem expertise, anachronistic self-sufficiency, a rare experience of animal inter-dependence, and a kind of honesty. Whether or not one credits those goods as balancing the animal lives it takes, hunting must still be moral wherever either of two conditions hold: (a) preservation of species or ecosystems requires neo-traditional hunting as the only viable wildlife management tool; or (b) the animal cost of farming per unit of nutrition is equal to or greater than that of hunting. These conditions obtain at least some of the time.

Notes

1. This paper has benefited from the criticism of Elizabeth Baeten, Phil Cafaro, Valerius Geist, Holmes Rolston, and George White, the most skilled and ethical hunter I know.
2. The holism can be variously conceived, e.g. biocentrically (Rolston 1988), an- thropocentrically (Norton 1984, 1987), or in a communitarian fashion (Callicott 1989, 1998).
3. I am not addressing forms of hunting where prey is not consumed, e.g., English fox hunting (Scruton 2001) or indigenous ritualised hunts (Aaltola and Okasanen 2002).
4. J. Claude Evans, in his book on the ecological ethics of hunting and fishing, quotes his own father's pub- lished analysis of the 'decline' of hunting in America. As J. Claude Evans Sr. put it, 'We grew up when hunting was a food-producing skill, and lived through its moving into a sport' (Evans 2005: xxi).
5. As Rolston puts it, 'In this sense, hunting is not sport; it is a sacrament of the fundamental, mandatory seeking and taking possession of value that characterizes an ecosystem and from which no culture ever escapes' (Rolston 1988: 91).
6. Varner distinguishes hunting to protect ecosystems ('therapeutic' hunting), from 'subsistence' hunting for food, and from sport/cultural hunting 'aimed at maintaining religious or cultural traditions, reenacting national or evolutionary history, honing certain skills or just securing a trophy' (Varner 2003: 98). His third category recognises the cultural nature of hunting, which he rightly says can equally apply to Inuit hunters and 'hill country Texans.' What is less right is that, as he admits but does not explore, contempo- rary hunting overlaps all three, being *in principle* a combination of cultural hunting for meat regulated by wildlife-ecosystem management.
7. Compound bows are much less demanding on the skill of the archer and achieve much higher arrow speed, but, given the intrinsic inefficiency of bowhunting, one suspects their main impacts are to put more archers in the field and to reduce woundings.

8. Krueger's study supplemented the usual surveys of hunter self-reports with infrared scanning by helicopter, ground recovery of downed deer, and autopsies. Her findings show that wounding estimates based solely on hunters' self-reports greatly inflate the number of wounded deer.

9. Hunting is one of the few activities in modern society in which killing of un-endangered species is regulated. Nobody is fined or jailed for killing wild animals by backhoe, combine, or sedan.

10. Notice that fair chase and minimal suffering can conflict; reducing the hunter's probability of success can increase the possibility of wounding. The goal is to balance the right kind of inefficiency—the challenge of achieving a makeable shot opportunity—with the right kind of efficiency—shots resulting in a quick death.

11. Hunters' ethical self-restrictions have been used to critique hunting. 'The sportsman's code raises an unmet moral case against hunting,' Luke writes, 'The only moral choice left is to renounce hunting as such' (Luke 1997: 43). Luke's argument is not merely that hunting ethics fails to justify the ethics of hunting—which is *true*—it is that the need for ethical restraints reveals the immoral nature of the activity. Well, sex is subjected to ethical restrictions in most cultures. Do such codes, accepted by the practitioners of sex, raise an 'unmet moral case' against sex? Is the only moral choice to renounce sex as such?

12. For one account of hunting and deer overpopulation, see (Dizard 1994).

13. Varner imagines hunting confined to bait stations where hunters wait with high-powered rifles. Since he does not consider any benefits of neo-traditional hunting other than wildlife management, he naturally defends a hunting that could as easily, and more efficiently, be performed by paid government agents.

14. Regarding modern, high-density animal husbandry, the case is unarguable. Regarding low-density pasturing, the case is less clear, but even here the animal is deprived of its wild life and species-characteristic behaviours.

15. One might suggest (as an anonymous reader of this essay did suggest) that the *law of double effect* might be used to defend farming's unsought killing of animals (this excludes crop-protection kills). But double effect is a two-edged sword. In its historical home in just war theory, the doctrine serves to say that when I bomb a factory, the deaths of the children in the school next door—which I anticipated but did not seek—do not make my act immoral. But in just war theory that doctrine was supplemented by others, notably *proportionality*, which rules out disproportionate harm whether or not it is purposely sought. So the anticipated deaths of the children, *not* immoral under double-effect, could still make the bombing immoral if the total harm caused is disproportionately high relative to the good it achieves (e.g. hastening an end to the war). Double-effect by itself may not be salutary in animal treatment or environmental ethics.

16. The individual dies but the species lives. Roger Scruton is probably right that the totemic hunter did not make a strict distinction between the individual and the species—hence the spirit of the prey continues in the species (see Shepard's example, from the Haida people, 1985: 58–9)—whereas we do. Theirs may have been sloppy metaphysics, but it was fairly accurate ecology. However, with Shepard, I think Scruton wrong in claiming hunting, archaic or contemporary, is sacrificial (Scruton 1997: 477).

References

Aaltola, Elisa and Markku Okasanen. 2002. 'Species conservation and minority rights: The case of springtime bird hunting in Åland'. *Environmental Values* **11**: 443–460.

Callicot, J. Baird. 1989. *In Defense of the Land Ethic: Essays in Environmental Philosophy*. Albany: State University of New York.

Callicot, J. Baird. 1998. '"Back together again" again'. *Environmental Values* **7**: 461–475.

Davis, Steven L. 2003. 'The least harm principle may require that humans consume a diet containing large herbivores, not a vegan diet'. *Journal of Agricultural and Environmental Ethics* **16**: 387–394.

Dizard, Jan. 1994. *Going Wild: Hunting, Animal Rights, and the Contested Meaning of Nature*. Amherst, MA: University of Massachusetts Press.

Evans, J. Claude. 2005. *With Respect for Nature: Living as Part of the Natural World*. Albany, NY: State University of New York Press.

Fox, Camilla. "The Case Against Sport Hunting," *Animal Protection Institute's Animal Issues: Volumes 33–35*, Sacramento: The Institute, 2004. (Originally published vol. 33, no. 2, Summer 2002.

Geist, Valerius. 1995. 'North American policies of wildlife management'. In Valerius Geist and I. McTaggart-Cowan eds., *Wildlife Conservation Policy* (Calgary: Detselig), pp. 77–129.

Geist, Valerius. 2000. 'Under what system of wildlife management are ungulates least domesticated?' In Elisabeth Vrba and George Schaller eds., *Antelopes, Deer, and Relatives: Fossil Record, Behavioral Ecology, Systematics, and Conservation* (New Haven: Yale University Press), pp. 310–319.

Hettinger, Ned. 1994. 'Valuing predation in Rolston's environmental ethics: Bambi lovers versus tree huggers'. *Environmental Ethics* **16**: 3–20.

Kerasote, Ted. 1993. *Bloodties: Nature, Culture, and the Hunt*. New York: Kodansha International.

Krueger, Wendy J. 1995. Aspects of Wounding of White-tailed Deer by Bowhunters. Thesis. West Virginia University, Morgantown, West Virginia. Rpt, Farmland Wildlife Populations & Research Group, Madelia MN.

Krutch, Joseph Wood. 1957. 'The sportsman or the predator? I. A damnable pleasure'. Pp. 8–10, 39–40 in *The Saturday Review*, August 17.

Leopold, Aldo. 1970. *A Sand County Almanac with Essays on Conservation from Round River*. New York: Ballantine Books.

List, Charles. 2004. 'On the moral distinctiveness of sport hunting'. *Environmental Ethics* **26**: 155–169.

Luke, Brian. 1997. 'A critical analysis of hunters' ethics'. *Environmental Ethics* **19**: 25–44.

Moriarity, Paul Veatch and Mark Woods. 1997. 'Hunting≠Predation'. *Environmental Ethics* **19**: 391–405.

Nelson, Richard. 1997. *Heart and Blood: Living with Deer in America*. New York: Vintage.

Norton, Bryan G. 1984. 'Environmental ethics and weak anthropocentrism'. *Environmental Ethics* **6**: 131–148.

Norton, Bryan G. 1987. *Why Preserve Natural Variety?* Princeton: Princeton University Press.

Ortega y Gasset, José. 1972. *Meditations on Hunting*. trans. Howard Wescott. New York: Scribner.

Petersen, David. 2000. *Heartsblood: Hunting, Spirituality, and Wildness in America*. Boulder, CO: Johnson Books.

Petersen, David. 2003. 'Valerius Geist'. *Bugle: The Journal of the Rocky Mountain Elk Foundation* **20**(6): 87–96, November/December 6.

Petersen, David. 2004. 'The future of wild elk, elk country, and the hunt: A conversation with Valerius Geist'. *Bugle: The Journal of the Rocky Mountain Elk Foundation* **21**(1): 46-58, January/February 1.

Pollan, Michael. 2002. 'An animal's place'. *New York Times Magazine*, November 10.

Regan, Tom. 1983. *The Case for Animal Rights*. Berkeley: University of California Press.

Rolston III, Holmes. 1988. *Environmental Ethics: Duties to and Values in the Natural World*. Philadelphia: Temple University Press.

Scruton, Roger.1997. 'From a view to a death: culture, nature and the huntman's art'. *Environmental Values* 6: 471–481.

Scruton, Roger. 2001. *On Hunting*. South Bend, IN: St. Augustine's Press.

Shepard, Paul. 1973. *The Tender Carnivore and the Sacred Game*. Athens, GA: University of Georgia Press.

Shepard, Paul. 1996. *Traces of an Omnivore*. Washington, DC: Island Press/Shearwater.

Shepard, Paul and Barry Sanders. 1985. *The Sacred Paw: The Bear in Nature, Myth, and Literature*. New York: Viking Press.

Singer, Peter. 2002a. *Animal Liberation*. New York: Ecco Press.

Singer, Peter. 2002b. 'Letter to the editor: "An animal's place"'. *New York Times Magazine*, November 24.

Varner, Gary E. 2003. 'Can animal rights activists be environmentalists?' In Andrew Light and Holmes Rolston eds., *Environmental Ethics: An Anthology* (Oxford: Blackwell Publishers), pp. 95–113.

Williams, Joy. 1995. 'The killing game'. In Pam Houston ed., *Women on Hunting* (Hopewell, NJ: Ecco Press), pp. 248–265.

59 The Killing Game

An Ecofeminist Critique of Hunting

Marti Kheel

Kheel addresses the morality of sport hunting and concludes that it lacks justification as a moral activity. She goes on to address the flaws she finds in the various justifications of hunting often cited, including the psychological, moral, and social benefits; ecological benefits; and spiritual benefits. Using feminist psychoanalytic theory, Kheel then proposes that the killing of animals allows the hunter to ritually enact the death of his longing for a return to a primordial female/animal world through death of the animal.

Hunting is an act of violence. And for some, it is a sport. Increasingly, these two facts present hunters with a major public relations problem. While at the turn of the century hunting was considered a praiseworthy activity, today 63 percent of the American public disapproves of hunting for recreation or sport (9).

[. . .]

Hunters have responded to the new public climate by taking refuge in a discourse designed to present what they do as morally laudable. Using a confused amalgam of arguments, they have represented hunting simultaneously as a cultural and spiritual asset, a biological drive, a management tool, and a return to the natural world.

[. . .]

A note about terminology is in order. A growing number of hunters eschew the words *sport hunting*, claiming that they hunt for "ecological" or "spiritual" reasons, not merely for "sport." Although I make distinctions among types of hunters based on their self-professed motives for hunting, I hope to demonstrate that these differences are not as pronounced as many hunters would have us believe. Because, in addition, I challenge the validity of the very notion of hunting as a "sport," generally I use the term *hunting* without the qualifying word *sport*. My use of the word *hunter*, however, does not encompass subsistence hunters. Although I do not rule out the possibility that subsistence hunters share some of the characteristics of the hunters in this study, the more complicated nature of their motives places subsistence hunters beyond the scope of this article. This study examines those who hunt out of desire.

Is Hunting a Sport?

[. . .]

The distinction between sport and play is generally thought to reside in the greater complexity of sport. According to Thomas, "Sport has elements of play but goes beyond the characteristics of play in its rule structure, organization, and criteria for the evaluation of success" (29: p. 18). In addition, although sport is thought to have its basis in play, according to Thomas it has a second distinguishing feature, that is, its agonistic quality. Play, by contrast, is viewed as an inherently "co-operative interaction that has no explicit goal, no end point, and no winners" (11: p. 481).

Caillois (3: pp. 3–10) developed a framework listing six features common to play: (a) Its outcome is uncertain; (b) it is an activity that is freely engaged in; (c) it is unproductive; (d) it is regulated;

(e) it takes place in a separate area; and (f) it is make-believe. Although these features are not universally agreed upon, they provide a helpful starting point for evaluating whether hunting conforms to common conceptions of play and sport.

The first of Caillois's features, the notion that play must not have a predetermined outcome, is inherent in the very nature of hunting as an activity. According to Cartmill, hunting is, by definition, "the deliberate, violent killing of unrestrained, wild animals" (4: p. 30).

[. . .]

The notion of competing with an animal, however, raises a moral problem. Because the animal has not consented to the competition, the game lacks symmetry of structure. [. . .] As Schmitz points out, hunting is more like a contest in which there is only one contestant (i.e., the hunter) (25: p. 30). The morality of a sport in which there is only one participant, however, is highly problematic. The animal's experience is obliterated, subsumed under the rules of a game that require the animal's death.

This relates to the second feature of play (i.e., that it is freely engaged in). Sport hunting is, by definition, an activity that is freely engaged in by hunters. The sport hunter typically is contrasted with the subsistence hunter, who hunts out of need, not out of "desire." [. . .] Yet, there is a major logical flaw in the notion of sport hunting as a voluntary activity, in that only one of the "participants" has chosen to compete.

[. . .]

The notion of hunting as a voluntary activity is also closely allied with the third of Caillois's features, that is, the notion of play as unproductive. Sport hunting, like play or sport in general, is an activity that is thought to be its own reward. Unlike work, it is not undertaken for any external reason.

[. . .]

Although this notion may accurately portray the attitude of many hunters (i.e., they may hunt more for the experience of pursuing the animal than for the moment of the kill), there is a moral problem entailed in the idea of pursuing the death of another living being for the opportunity it affords one to engage in an enjoyable experience.

Hunters frequently invoke the fourth of Caillois's features of play (i.e., that hunting has rules, to defend their "sport" from the charge of cruelty). Hunters, it is said, do not hunt indiscriminately: they conform to rules of good conduct (i.e., limitations on the number of animals killed, the season, and the weapons used). Such rules are said to give the animal a "fair chance." [. . .] [A]ccording to Leopold, the ethical value of hunting resides in the fact that hunters are bound not only to the laws about hunting but to their conscience as well (10: p. 212).

The fifth feature of play, that it takes place in a separate area, clearly applies to sport hunting. [. . .] [H]unting must occur outside and, traditionally, in an area that is considered "wild."

The last feature of Caillois's framework, the make-believe aspect of play, interestingly applies to hunting. For many hunters, sport hunting imaginatively recaptures a time when it is believed that men had to hunt for reasons of survival. In their attempt to lure their prey, hunters often describe an imaginary experience in which they feel as though they have become the animal they intend to kill.

[. . .]

The moral problem with the make-believe aspect of hunting is glaring, for the goal of the hunter's "game" is deadly serious. While hunters may play a "game" in which they imaginatively seek to understand another animal, this game has irrevocable consequences that extend beyond the world of make believe. The hunter does not pretend to kill the animal; the death of the animal is quite real.

Whereas the competitive, goal-oriented nature of hunting fits the notion of a sport, the nonvoluntary conscription of the animal into this "game" casts doubt on the validity of this idea. Both the willingness to "play" and the amusement derived from the activity are one sided. Although hunters may *experience* the activity of hunting as a sport, the skewed symmetry of the "game" renders this notion unintelligible. Hunters thus face a conceptual problem. On the one hand, hunting can exist as a sport only by conferring subjective identity on the animal. On the other hand, hunters can only pursue the death of an animal as playful activity by denying the animal's subjective experience and focusing exclusively on their own experience.

Most hunters ignore the question of the animal's subjective experience, defending their actions by reference to the purity of their own motives and desires, and, in particular, by presenting their *desire* to hunt as a *need*. Hunters have used several strategies to justify hunting, which I have categorized by means of a tripartite typology that distinguishes hunters according to the particular need they argue hunting fulfills: the "happy hunter" hunts for the purpose of enjoyment and pleasure, as well as character development (psychological need); the "holist hunter" hunts for the purpose of maintaining the balance of nature (ecological need); and the "holy hunter" hunts in order to attain a spiritual state (religious need). Whereas the happy hunter once gained status by calling hunting a sport, today's holist and holy hunters seek to distance themselves from the notion of sport. What unites the three types of hunters is their claim that hunting provides some redeeming social, moral, or personal value that is not just desirable but necessary.

The Happy Hunter: Psychological Need

The happy hunter is an unabashed sport hunter who freely admits to the pleasure that he derives from this "sport." Significantly, the animal is literally called "game." As one hunter proclaimed, "I hunt because it is something I like to do" (cited in 17: p. 20). Or, as another states, "The adrenalin flows. It's a good feeling" (cited in 17: p. 34). And, in Ernest Hemingway's inimitable words, "I think they (birds) were made to be shot and some of us were made to shoot them and if that is not so well, never say we did not tell you that we like it" (8: p. 152). In the United States, the conception of hunting as a pleasurable, recreational activity emerged in the middle of the nineteenth century in response to increased urbanization and leisure time. Like other forms of recreation, sport hunting was also thought to confer particular moral and social benefits. This notion of hunting as a beneficial activity stood in stark contrast to the ideas of the colonial period in New England, where hunting was considered a frivolous pastime of irresponsible young men, permissible only insofar as it was necessary for livelihood.

[. . .]

In the late 1800s, happy hunters helped to institutionalize "rules of fair play" in the form of laws designed to stop the decimation of wildlife by commercial and sport hunters. These laws, which included limitations on time, place, and type of weaponry, were seen as necessary not to preserve the animals in and of themselves, but rather to preserve their "sport."

The early conservationist hunters saw hunting as useful in building character, that is, male character. They argued that hunting was a necessary corrective for men who had become overly feminized by the encroaches of civilization. Theodore Roosevelt represents this view (22: p. 1236). [. . .] Messner explains this turn to competitive sports: "With no frontier to conquer, with physical strength becoming less relevant in work, and with urban boys being raised and taught by women, it was feared that males were becoming 'soft,' that society itself was becoming 'feminized' " (15: p. 14). Thus, sport hunting came to be seen as a necessary release for "man's" instinctual and aggressive drives. The point, however, was not for men to be reduced to the level of the animal world. By complying with the rules of "fair play," sport hunters felt they were able to express their "animal instincts," while also demonstrating their superiority to the animal world.

The notion that hunting is a psychologically beneficial release for man's aggression has persisted into this century. Aldo Leopold claimed that hunting is an instinctual urge, in contrast to golf (10: p. 227). [. . .] The value of hunting, for Leopold, resides in the exercise of this aggressive impulse as well as in its control. Leopold's concern is not the preservation of individual animals, but, rather, the "inalienable right" to hunt and kill them (p. 227). Leopold derives this right from a "fact" of nature, which modern hunting is intended to preserve, namely, the Darwinian notion of conflict or survival of the fittest. As Leopold states, "Physical combat between men and beasts was [once] an economic fact, now preserved as hunting and fishing for sport" (10: p. 269). According to Leopold,

"An individual's instincts prompt him to compete for his place in the community, but his ethics prompt him also to cooperate (*perhaps in order that there may be a place to compete for*)" [emphasis added] (10: p. 239).

[. . .]

Happy hunters claim hunting provides a variety of additional psychological benefits. According to Leopold, it stimulates an awareness of history. That is, the hunter is "reenacting the romance of the fur trade." And it promotes a sense of "our dependency on the soil-plant-animal-man food chain, and of the fundamental organization of the biota" (10: p. 212). Another sportsman claims that hunting "renews the traditional kinship between men, wild things, and the land" (13: p. 71). All of these purported benefits have in common the claim that sport hunting helps men to become morally mature.

The Holist Hunter: Ecological Need

Whereas the happy hunter is unabashedly anthropocentric, extolling hunting for its psychological benefits for human beings (and in particular for men), the holist hunter claims more altruistic motives. Although hunting journals still openly extol the pleasures of the hunt, increasing numbers of hunters feel compelled to cite less self-serving reasons for hunting. Holist hunters claim that without their services, the animals they kill would die from starvation. Hence, they are performing a laudable ecological role.

Relinquishing the realm of recreation and pleasure, holist hunters have entered the world of business management and science. Using terms such as "population density," "sustainable yield," and the necessity of "culling" or "harvesting" the "excess" animals that would otherwise starve, holist hunters claim the title of "managers" for the biotic community. Their management partners in this undertaking are the federal and state fish and wildlife agencies, which manage both the animals and the hunters themselves. While hunters claim to be responding to nature's unfortunate excesses, the game management journals reveal another story. For example, according to an article in the *Journal of Wildlife Management.* "The primary management plan has been the one directed at increasing the productivity of the whitetail deer through habitat manipulation and harvest regulation . . . to produce optimum sustained deer yields . . . and hunter satisfaction" (16: p. 92). In short, holist hunters are intent on "managing" animals so that sufficient numbers will remain for them to kill.

For holist hunters, it is not the hunter who is the agent of death, but rather nature or ecology. The hunter is merely carrying out nature's inexorable directives, a participant in a "drama" not of his own making. The violence that hunting inflicts merely expresses the reality of violence in the natural world and thus is beyond ethical reproach. The holist hunter believes that not only should hunting not be shunned, but that it should be embraced.

Holist hunters, however, overlook the vast differences between human predation and natural predation. Whereas natural predators prey on the old, the weak, and the sick, human hunters typically select the biggest and healthiest animals to kill. As a consequence, hunters promote what Teale has called a kind of "evolution in reverse" (28: p. 161). Moreover, sport hunters overlook the extent to which their own actions have produced the problems that they claim to resolve. Sport hunters have pursued a deliberate policy of eliminating natural predators in numerous areas throughout the country, precisely so that they can claim the status of predators for themselves.

The alliance between hunting and the science of ecology has been a fortuitous partnership for modern hunters. Responding to a modern public that rejects the conjunction of pleasure and violence, happy hunters have found in the world of science and business a convenient refuge from attack. Armed with the claim that their mental state has been purified of the taint of pleasure, holist hunters contend that their motives are beyond rebuke. Although their official trade journals continue to enumerate the multiple pleasures to be found in the hunt, increasing numbers of happy hunters assume the camouflage of the holist hunt.

The Holy Hunter: Spiritual Need

For the holy hunter, hunting is not a means of recreation, nor is it a form of work. For the holy hunter, hunting is a religious or spiritual experience. As James Swan has stated, for many it is their religion (27: p. 35). Holy hunters contrast their spiritual attitude of reverence and respect with the crass and superficial mentality of the typical sportsman or happy hunter. Although they too emphasize the notion of emotional self-restraint, they see it as a by-product of a transformed world view. Hunting is akin to a religious rite. In the words of Holmes Rolston, "Hunting is not *sport*: it is a *sacrament* of the fundamental, mandatory seeking and taking possession of value that characterizes an ecosystem and from which no culture ever escapes" (21: p. 91).

The spiritual nature of the hunt is thought to derive from a particular type of awareness, often described as a meditative state. As Richard Nelson states, "Hunting for me can be almost hypnotic. It's like a walking meditation" (18: p. 89). And for Ortega y Gassett, "The hunter is the alert man" who achieves a "universal attention, which does not inscribe itself on any point and tries to be on all points" (19: p. 91). [. . .] And according to Ortega y Gassett, hunting entails a "mystical union with the animal" (19: p. 124).

[. . .]

Like the holist hunters, holy hunters draw on the science of ecology not for a management policy, but for the spiritual lessons that it is thought to inspire. As Young explains, "What is religious about hunting is that it leads us to remember and accept the violent nature of our condition, that every animal that eats will in turn one day be eaten" (32: p. 139). Holy hunters claim a humble and submissive attitude, seeking not to conquer nature, but rather to "submit to ecology" (21: p. 92). Once again, desire and necessity are elided. Hunting is seen not as manifestly the desire to kill, but rather as an ecological necessity.

Holy hunters frequently draw on the spiritual traditions of native cultures to bolster the notion of the holy hunt. James Swan cites the "wisdom of native peoples" that claims that "under the right conditions, the success of the hunter is not just a reflection of skill but the choice of the animal" (27: p. 21). [. . .] The association of hunting with spirituality does, in fact, have a long history among subsistence hunters in native cultures. Some, but by no means all, of these cultures promoted the notion of saying a prayer before killing an animal, as well as the idea that the animal "gives" her or his life as a gift to the hunter. However, there are a number of ethical problems with invoking the traditions of native cultures.

First, the spiritual teachings of diverse native cultures cannot accurately be treated as a monolithic model from which to draw on for our own interactions with animals. Second, it is ethically questionable to extirpate a narrative from one cultural context and to graft it onto another. To the extent that native cultures hunted for subsistence reasons, their experience cannot be applied to a culture where this is no longer the case.

[. . .]

In place of the notion of an inherently aggressive drive that must be contained through adherence to a code of conduct, the holy hunter claims to restrain his aggression to the point of nonexistence at least within the holy hunter's mind. Holy hunters do not "kill" animals according to this world view: rather, animals "give" their lives. Nor do holy hunters perpetrate violence; instead they are passive participants in nature's cycles.

The Hunt for Psychosexual Identity

It is time to ask if there are common underlying themes in all three categories of hunters. The association between hunting and masculine self-identity has been a recurring theme throughout history. Many cultures require a young boy to hunt and kill an animal as a symbolic rite of passage into manhood. Significantly, the young boy is frequently sequestered from the world of women as well. Although hunting is not an exclusively male activity, the vast majority of hunting has been performed by men.

[. . .]

The connection between hunting and masculinity is also commonly expressed in the notion that hunting provides an outlet for men's sexual energy. Thus, according to the holy hunter proponent Dudley Young, there is "an almost erotic connection between hunter and hunted," with the emotion-filled kill being analogous to "sexual ecstasy" (32: pp. 138, 134). And, for the holist environmental writer Holmes Rolston, hunting is viewed as a safety valve for sexual energy. In his words, "the sport hunt sublimates the drive for conquest, a drive without which humans could not have survived, without which we cannot be civilized." He concludes that "perhaps the hunting drive, like the sexual urge, is dangerous to suppress and must be reckoned with" (21: p. 91). For these writers, hunting is not simply a desire, but a biological need.

Hunting is also frequently conceptualized as having a narrative structure that resembles a sexual encounter. There is the initial build up of tension in the course of the chase, leading ultimately to the climax of the kill. Hunters can no more eliminate the kill from the narrative structure of the hunt than it would seem that many men can eliminate orgasm as the goal of sex.

[. . .]

Hunters, however, do not typically depict their sport as the crass expression of a sexual drive. More frequently, hunting is portrayed as an urge to achieve intimacy with nature and as the quintessential act of connection. The priest Theodore Vitali argues that "hunting is a direct participation in nature and has the potential of deepening the spiritual and moral bonds between human and subhuman communities" (30: p. 210). Vitali contrasts hunting with activities such as nature photography and hiking, which he considers "virtually voyeuristic" in that they "lack the intimacy with nature that hunting achieves" (p. 211).

[. . .]

The ingestion of the flesh of the conquered animal is also described by a number of writers as an erotic act. According to Shepard, whereas the "ecstatic consummation of love is killing," the "formal consummation is eating" (26: p. 173). Similarly. Nelson states that "I get a great deal of pleasure from knowing that my body is made in no small measure from deer. I am passionately in love with deer but I also kill them. I appreciate the fact that I am made out of the animal I love" (18: p. 92).

[. . .]

The analogy with sex is instructive, however. Sex is both a biological urge and a socially constructed activity. A man who rapes a woman cannot credibly defend his actions by saying he was simply following his "animal instincts." Nor can he claim that the rape provided a much needed outlet for his sexual energy, nor that it builds (male) character, nor that the rape was performed according to rules of good conduct. Rape is wrong because it is a violation of another living being. Significantly, the literature on rape argues that rapists are not motivated by the urge to fulfill a sexual drive, nor are they out of control. On the contrary, rape is designed to establish men's dominance and control (1). Similarly, hunting may be seen as a symbolic attempt to assert mastery and control over the natural world.

[. . .]

Feminist psychoanalytic theory has sought to explain men's greater propensity for violence. According to object relations theorists, the development of identity in boy children is established through a process of negative identification. Unlike girls, who are able to continue the initial, primary identification with the mother figure, boys must not only disidentify with the mother figure, but they must deny all that is female within themselves, as well as their involvement with the female world (5: p. 167). As a consequence, according to Chodorow, "girls emerge from this period with a basis for 'empathy' built into their primary definition of self in a way that boys do not" (p. 167).

Dorothy Dinnerstein extends this analysis to all of nature. As she argues, boys not only establish their identity in opposition to women, but to all of the natural world (6). Having established a second and alienated nature, it appears that men then face a lifelong urge to return to the original state of oneness that they left behind. The return to an original undifferentiated state, however, is precisely what must be avoided because such a return would constitute an annihilation of the masculine self.

The conflict between these two drives may shed light on the hunter's urge to achieve intimacy in death. The pursuit of the animal expresses the hunter's yearning to repossess his lost female and animal nature. The death of the animal ensures that this oneness with nature is not genuinely attained. Violence becomes the only way in which the hunter can experience this sense of oneness while asserting his masculine self-identity as an autonomous human being. By killing the animal, the hunter ritually enacts the death of his longing for a return to a primordial female/animal world.

Beyond the Killing Game: Toward a Life-Giving Play/Sport

Psychologists and philosophers note that one of the functions of play is to facilitate the maturation process and the development of self-identity. Significantly, hunters claim this is characteristic of hunting. They argue that hunting helps humans (mostly men) to attain full status as human beings. Like play in general, hunting is thought to be particularly useful for young (male) children, aiding them to attain skills that will help them as adults. According to Shepard, the "play" activity of hunting prepares the young boy for future religious experience (26: p. 200).

Another function of children's games often discussed in the literature is their role in developing feelings of empathy for others. According to George Herbert Mead (14) and Jean Piaget (20), games provide children with a means by which to learn to take the role of the other and to come to see themselves through another's eyes.

Interesting differences appear at a young age between the play of boys and girls, which may shed light on men's propensity to hunt. Building on Piaget's studies on rules of the game, Lever found that boys tended to play far more competitively than girls and were more likely to play at structured games, which accorded importance to being proclaimed the winner (11: p. 479). By contrast, girls tended to "keep their play loosely structured [and played] until they [were] bored" (p. 479). Lever's study also found that girls' games were "mostly spontaneous, imaginative, and free of structure or rules. Turn-taking activities like jump rope may be played without setting explicit goals" (p. 481). In addition, "disputes are not likely to occur" and when they do, the game tends to be stopped (p. 479). Playing in smaller, more intimate groups, Lever found that girls' play tended to foster the development of empathy and sensitivity necessary for taking the role of "the particular other," and pointed toward knowing the other as different from the self.

Hunters claim that in the course of stalking their prey, they imaginatively enter into the life of the animal. But whereas hunters claim that this exercise in imagination helps them develop feelings of empathy for the animal, it is their inability to understand the experience of nonhuman animals that is a prerequisite of their hunt. As we have seen, hunters also emphasize the keen sense of alertness and attention that characterizes their state of mind. It is apparent, however, that if hunters were truly attending to nature, instead of to their own amorphous feelings of "love" and "connection," they would feel the terror and fright of the animal they seek to kill.

[. . .]

Ecofeminist philosophy recognizes a crucial distinction that hunters overlook: it is one thing to accept the reality and necessity of death, and quite another to deliberately kill a living being.

The notion of "attentive love," first used by Simone Weil (31), has been employed by a number of feminist philosophers as a central idea in the development of caring interactions toward others. For Weil, attentive love was a certain form of pure, receptive perceiving, as contrasted to egoistic perception, whereby one asks of the other, "What are you going through?" As Ruddick develops this idea, even the notion of empathy is not devoid of egoistic perception. As she explains, "The idea of empathy, as it is popularly understood, underestimates the importance of knowing another *without* finding yourself in her" (23: p. 121). By contrast, "attention lets difference emerge without searching for comforting commonalities, dwells upon the *other* and lets otherness be (23: p. 122).

The ability to achieve this form of attention entails a kind of playful leap of imagination into another's world. Maria Lugones develops this idea in her notion of an imaginative, playful world traveling, in which we can learn to "travel" into different worlds and realities, identifying with others so that "we can understand what it is to be them and what it is to be ourselves in their eyes" (12: p. 17). Sara Ebenreck has suggested that "awareness of imaginative activity may be especially important for environmental ethics, in which the guidelines for action have to do with response to others who are not human, for whom respectful attention may require of us the probing work of imaginative perception" (7: p. 5).

According to Burke, play is "an activity which is free, complete in itself, and artificial or unrealistic" (2: p. 38). As he elaborates, play's "true significance" lies in the fact that it develops our "creative, imaginative ability," enabling us to "live not only in the 'real' world but also in countless symbolic worlds of [our] own making" (2: p. 42). A problem arises, however, when living beings are forcibly conscripted into an artificial world to play the role of symbols themselves. All too often, women and animals have been relegated to the status of symbols, objects, or props for the construction of masculine self-identity. It is one thing to transcend the reality of the mundane world, and quite another to transcend the experience of other living beings.

Modern Western culture has achieved an unprecedented alienation from nature. For many, the urge to reconnect with nature is, in fact, experienced as a deep spiritual or psychological need. Killing is not the best way, however, to fulfill this need, and certainly not the most compassionate. The cooperative play of young girls would appear to provide a more mature and compassionate model for attaining intimacy with nature than hunting. The Council of All Beings workshops developed by John Seed and Joanna Macy (24) provide an example of a playful and imaginative connection with animals that conforms to the cooperative nature of girls' play. In these councils, participants are asked to imaginatively enter into the world of another species and to then bring their experience back to the group. People express profound feelings of empathy, grief, and rage when they realize the impact of deforestation, factory farming, and hunting on nonhuman animals. Through the expression and sharing of such feelings, people become motivated for a larger context of action.

The root of the word *sport* is "to leap joyously." Perhaps, through playful leaps of imagination such as these, we can learn to engage in a play/sport that affirms with love and compassion a genuine connection to all of life.

Bibliography

1. Brownmiller, Susan. *Against Our Will: Men, Women and Rape*. New York: Simon and Schuster, 1975.
2. Burke, Richard. "Work and Play." *Ethics*, 88 (1971), 33–47.
3. Caillois, Roger. *Man, Play, and Games*. Translated by Meyer Barash. New York: The Free Press of Glencoe, 1961.
4. Cartmill, Matt. *A View to a Death in the Morning: Hunting and Nature through History*. Cambridge and London: Harvard University Press, 1993.
5. Chodorow, Nancy. *The Reproduction of Mothering*. Berkeley: University of California Press, 1978.
6. Dinnerstein, Dorothy. *The Mermaid and the Minotaur: Sexual Arrangements and Human Malaise*. New York: Harper, 1967.
7. Ebenreck, Sara. "Opening Pandora's Box: The Role of Imagination in Environmental Ethics." *Environmental Ethics*, 18:1 (1996), 3–18.
8. Hemingway, Ernest. "Remembering Shooting-Flying." *Esquire* (February 1935), pp. 21, 152.
9. Kellert, Stephen. *The Value of Life: Biological Diversity and Human Society*. Washington, DC: Island Press, 1996.
10. Leopold, Aldo. *A Sand County Almanac: With Essays on Conservation from Round River*. Oxford: Oxford University Press, 1966.
11. Lever, Janet. "Sex Differences in the Complexity of Children's Play and Games." *American Sociological Review*, 43 (1978), 471–83.
12. Lugones, Maria. "Playfulness, 'World-Traveling' and Loving Perception." *Hypatia*, 2 (1987), 3–19.
13. Madson, Chris. "State Wildlife Agencies and the Future of Hunting." *Second Annual Governor's Symposium*. Pierre, SD. August 24–26, (1993), pp. 64–71.
14. Mead, George Herbert. *Mind, Self, and Society*. Chicago: University of Chicago Press, 1934.
15. Messner, Michael A. *Power at Play: Sports and the Problem of Masculinity*. Boston: Beacon, 1992.

16. Mirarchi, Ralfe, Scanloni, Patrick, and Kirkpatrick, Roy L. "Annual Changes in Spermatozoan Production and Associated Organs of White-Tailed Deer." *Journal of Wild-Life Management*, 41:1 (1977), 92–9.

17. Mitchell, John G. *The Hunt*. Harmondsworth, England: Penguin, 1981.

18. Nelson, Richard. "Life Ways of the Hunter." In *Talking on the Water: Conversations about Nature and Creativity*. Edited by Jonathan White. San Francisco: Sierra Club Books, 1994, pp. 79–97.

19. Ortega y Gasset, José. *Meditations on Hunting*. Translated by Howard B. Wescott, with a forward by Paul Shepard. New York: Scribner's, 1985.

20. Piaget, Jean. *The Moral Judgement of the Child*. New York: The Free Press, 1968.

21. Rolston, Holmes, III. *Environmental Ethics: Duties to and Values in the Natural World*. Philadelphia: Temple University Press, 1988.

22. Roosevelt, Theodore. "The Value of an Athletic Training." *Harper's Weekly*, 37 (23 December, 1893), p. 1236.

23. Ruddick, Sara. *Maternal Thinking: Toward a Politics of Peace*. New York: Ballantine, 1989.

24. Seed, John, Macy, Joanna, Flemming, Pat, and Naess, Arne. *Thinking Like a Mountain: Toward a Council of All Beings*. Philadelphia: New Society Publishers, 1988.

25. Schmitz, Kenneth L. "Sport and Play: Suspension of the Ordinary." In *Sport and the Body: A Philosophical Symposium*. Edited by Ellen W. Gerber. Philadelphia: Lea & Febiger, 1972, pp. 25–32.

26. Shepard, Paul. *The Tender Carnivore and the Sacred Game*. New York: Scribner's, 1973.

27. Swan, James A. *In Defense of Hunting*. San Francisco: Harper Collins, 1995.

28. Teale, Edwin Way. *Wandering through Winter*. New York: Dodd, Mead and Company, 1966.

29. Thomas, Carolyn E. *Sport in a Philosophic Context*. Philadelphia: Lea & Febiger, 1983.

30. Vitali, Theodore R. "The Dialectical Foundation of the Land Ethic." *Proceedings, Governor's Symposium on North America's Hunting Heritage*, Montana State University. Bozeman, July 16–18, (1992), pp. 203–14.

31. Weil, Simone. "Reflections on the Right Use of School Studies with a View to the Love of God." Pp. 57–66, in *Waiting for God*. Translated by E. Craufurd. New York: Harper, 1951.

32. Young, Dudley. *Origins of the Sacred: The Ecstasies of Love and War*. New York: St. Martin's Press, 1991.

60 Environmental Ethics and Trophy Hunting

Alastair S. Gunn

Gunn addresses the morality of hunting, including trophy hunting, in relation to animal death, animal suffering, hunting ethics, biodiversity and ecosystems, and human needs. Despite sharing with many sport hunters a distaste for trophy hunting, he argues that from broad-based economic and human survival values, trophy hunting is justified. Using Zimbabwe as a case study, he argues that trophy hunting successfully integrates both conservation and development and may be the only feasible strategy to protect the interests of both wildlife and people.

Introduction

The publication in 1980 of J. Baird Callicott's "Animal Liberation: A Triangular Affair" introduced the conflict for environmental management and policy between animal liberation and environmental ethics. Hunting provides a prime example of this still unresolved controversy.

I have found no published source that condemns hunting per se. There is a spectrum in the environmental literature. At one end is the view that hunting is justified only for self protection and for food, where no other reasonable alternative is available. Most writers also agree that hunting is sometimes justified in order to protect endangered species and threatened ecosystems where destructive species have been introduced or natural predators have been exterminated. Others accept hunting as part of cultural tradition or for the psychological well being of the hunter, sometimes extended to include recreational hunting when practiced according to "sporting" rules. Nowhere in the literature, so far as I am aware, is hunting for fun, for the enjoyment of killing, or for the acquisition of trophies defended. However, as I argue towards the end of this paper, trophy hunting is essential in parts of Africa for the survival of both people and wildlife.

Throughout this paper, I assume that animals have interests, and that we have an obligation to take some account of those interests: roughly, that we are entitled to kill animals only in order to promote or protect some nontrivial human interest and where no reasonable alternative strategy is available. This position is roughly that presented by Donald VanDeVeer (1979). Versions of it are widely defended in the literature, though there are different views about *which* human interests are sufficiently significant to justify killing. I restrict my discussion to cases where the interest in question cannot reasonably be achieved without killing animals.

[. . .]

Wildlife Management: The Conventional Western View

[. . .]

Anti-hunting organizations present a number of arguments against both hunting in general and specifically the hunting of marine mammals, elephants, large carnivores, great apes, rhinos, and other large ungulates. In this paper, I concentrate particularly on elephants.

Some common arguments against hunting include the following, each of which is discussed in more detail later.

- Hunting wrongfully deprives animals of something that is valuable to them—their lives (Regan 1983; Taylor 1986). Killing, and not merely successful stalking, is recognized by both supporters and opponents as a central feature of hunting. As Roger King (1991) notes, for proponents of hunting such as José Ortega y Gasset (1972) and Paul Shepherd (1973), the central meaning of hunting is killing, and killing is essential to "Participation in the life cycle of nature" (King 1991, 80). Ann Causey says, "The one element that stands out as truly essential to the authentic hunting experience is the kill" (Causey 1989, 332). Some ecofeminists believe that hunting is a prime example of patriarchal oppression of nature: in Mary Daly's terms, of a "necrophiliac" culture (Daly 1978).
- Hunting causes suffering. [. . .] A high proportion of land mammals and ducks are injured rather than being killed instantly; these "cripples" may suffer for days before either recovering or dying.
- Great apes, elephants, whales, and dolphins are special animals. They are highly intelligent; many species have developed elaborate social systems; they exhibit altruistic behavior toward each other and apparently suffer grief at the death of group members; members of some species including the great apes, orca, and some dolphins are sociable towards humans and are even recorded as having saved human lives; some (humpbacked whales) compose and perform music.
- Hunting is unworthy of civilized beings: "The hunter . . . as a 'redneck,' bloodthirsty villain storming the woods each fall with a massive arsenal . . . hunting [as] a disgusting sport that recalls and rehearses the worst in human behavior" (Vitali 1990, 69).
- Hunting is a threat to biodiversity. It threatens the existence of target species, many of which are already rare, threatened, or endangered. Sport hunting also degrades the gene pool of ungulate species because the most valued targets, dominant males, are the individuals "most fit to pass on the best genes" (Loftin 1984, 69).
- Hunting is not necessary for the fulfillment of important human interests; these interests can be satisfied by other means that do not require killing. Hunting is not economically necessary nor even particularly useful. There are substitutes for all marine and most land mammal products and because whaling, in particular, is probably not a sustainable industry, it cannot make a long-term contribution to the economy (Clark 1973).

Animal Deaths

[. . .] The question for sport hunting advocates to address, if it is admitted that the life of an animal is valuable to it and that animals have an interest in continued life, is whether this interest may justly be overridden. The most obviously persuasive argument is that sustainable hunting kills only animals that would die anyway—or more precisely, since we don't know which animals will die from "natural causes," a proportion of the population will die each year, usually much more slowly and painfully through predation, starvation, or disease.

[. . .]

Animal Suffering

It is inevitable that some animals that are hunted will suffer. [. . .] Where the target is animals whose numbers are widely agreed to be in need of control, supporters of hunting claim that it causes less suffering than alternative methods. Causey believes that "The genuine sport hunter, due to his earnest regard for his prey, is usually highly sensitive to the animal's pain and suffering, and makes every effort to minimize both. Proper weaponry and hunter training can minimize both" (Causey 1989, 335).

[. . .]

Special Status of Major Target Species

The mammals which Western environmentalists especially wish to protect from hunting, and trophy hunters especially wish to bag, are often referred to as "charismatic megafauna." Large land and marine mammals certainly have an appeal to many people, because of their sheer size and presence and in some cases because of special qualities they are said to have.

[. . .]

Claims of intelligence, social structure, altruism, and artistic ability that are comparable to humans, must however be met with some skepticism. Decades of research on humans have failed to obtain widespread agreement on the nature of human intelligence or even on whether there is such a thing as "general intelligence," let alone on how to test it.

[. . .]

Perhaps a case could be made (though not consistently with animal liberation) for giving special protection to species that are particularly intelligent or social or altruistic or which meet a particular standard of aesthetics, but it would need to be a consistent one. Since many species of "lower" mammals, birds, reptiles, fish, and invertebrates meet one or more of these criteria, it follows that we should oppose killing them too.

Hunting as Uncivilized

[. . .] "Shooters" who kill for an extrinsic goal are not necessarily blameworthy. They may, for instance, kill pests or overabundant animals in order to protect ecosystems or endangered species, or to feed their families, and this may be morally justifiable or even a duty. From the idealized hunting perspective shooters do not exhibit the virtues promoted by Ortega y Gasset (1972), Shepherd (1973), and Vitali (1990), but this does not make them vicious. Trophy hunters, however, who kill purely for the sake of acquiring prestigious evidence that they have killed an animal, surely act immorally, because they achieve a trivial benefit for themselves at the expense of the life of an animal. Unlike professional cullers, they may also be considered to exhibit serious character defects. They want to control, to have power, to reduce animals to easy targets, to kill, and to brag about it.

[. . .]

Biodiversity and Ecosystems

It is certainly true that many hunters seek to kill trophy animals which are precisely the animals that the species can least afford to lose: the "genetically prime animals," as Vitali (1990) puts it. However, he believes that most hunters are "opportunistic . . . They take what they can get, and oftentimes this amounts to the young, the weak, and the disabled," as do stalking animal predators. He also points out that opportunistic predators such as lions kill a large number of prime animals "precisely because of the opportunities the animals themselves provide"—for instance, prime male wildebeest are usually alone and, "during the rut . . . tend to be incautious and thus vulnerable to attack" (Vitali 1990, 70). In any case, controlled trophy hunting that is part of an ecologically sound wildlife management program will not unduly affect the gene pool. This is in contrast to the uncontrolled hunting of the past, which in the case of elephants has led to an alarming increase in tusklessness in many parts of Africa.

[. . .]

Hunting in general is not a major threat to biodiversity. In the past, a number of species have become extinct due to hunting pressure—palaeolithic hunters contributed to the extermination of many species of megafauna (Martin and Klein 1984; Uetz and Johnson 1974), while in recent centuries species such as the great auk appear to have died out entirely due to hunting (Halliday 1980). But the millions of species around the world that are currently at risk are threatened not by hunting but by habitat destruction and pollution, loss of food sources, and human disturbance. Opposition to hunting, on its own, will do little to protect biodiversity. The comparatively few species that are commercially hunted—mostly large mammals—can be sustainably managed. Nor is hunting necessarily a threat to ecosystems. In most of Europe and the United States, for instance, humans have exterminated large predators, but are able to control the populations of ungulates by culling and sustainable hunting. We should not allow opposition to hunting to deflect us from the much greater threat to biodiversity posed by habitat loss and degradation.

[. . .]

Protecting existing wilderness may not require any killing, but the restoration of degraded environments is very different. Conservation agencies in New Zealand have killed literally millions of introduced pests, including rodents, goats, deer, possums, and predators in order to restore damaged environments on both the mainland and off-shore islands.

[. . .]

Gary Varner (1994) has argued that what he calls therapeutic hunting ("hunting motivated by and designed to secure the aggregate welfare of the target species and/or the integrity of its ecosystem") is justified in the case of an obligatory management species ("one that has a fairly regular tendency to overshoot the carrying capacity of its range, to the detriment of future generations of it and other species"). Therapeutic hunting is not merely consistent with animal liberation: it is morally required under certain circumstances, where fewer animals would die "than if natural attrition is allowed to take place" (Varner 1994, 257–8). Animal liberationists, obviously, prefer non-lethal methods of control, but "Wildlife requires management, and hunting is at this time the most efficient means to do it" (Vitali 1990, 70).

Opponents of hunting (and trapping) as methods of pest control often advocate contraception. However, at the time of writing, no such methods exist except for a few species on a small scale. Even if effective methods did exist, the costs would be phenomenal and for years to come the contracepted animals would continue to destroy vegetation and to compete with and prey on other animals.

[. . .]

In many areas that were colonized by Europeans, native animals have suffered from predation, competition, and habitat destruction by feral introduced animals. [. . .] *In these and many other cases the conflict between animal liberation and environmental protection is quite inescapable*: Foxes and lyrebirds, feral dogs and kiwis, mallards and their close relatives absolutely cannot coexist, so whatever we do, we will be responsible for some animals living and others dying. The "do-nothing" option is effectively a choice to allow the introduced animals to kill, directly or indirectly, the native animals, as well as upsetting ecological equilibrium.

[. . .]

I conclude that it is legitimate to kill introduced animals that threaten the livelihood of native species, and that sport hunting, where it is an effective means of control (at no cost to society) is legitimate. More controversially, perhaps. I also believe that trophy hunting is also legitimate in these circumstances, even though I also share sports hunters' low opinion of trophy hunting.

Hunting and Human Needs

Writers who identify or sympathize with animal liberation (Varner 1994, 1998 is an exception) usually accept killing only in situations where human survival is at stake. In this view, hunting is regrettable because it causes major harm to animals, or violates their rights, or fails to respect them for their intrinsic or inherent value or intrinsic worth, or deprives them of something (life) that is valuable to them (e.g., Regan 1983; Singer 1975; Taylor 1986). But, as Paul Taylor notes, to insist that even subsistence hunting is wrong is to expect people to sacrifice "their lives for the sake of animals, and no requirement to do that is imposed by respect for nature" (Taylor 1986, 294).

Self-defense is established as a full justification for killing a human attacker, typically by appeal to rights. [. . .] Wild elephants killed 358 people in Kenya between 1990 and 1995 and 53 people in one area of Sri Lanka in 1995; the killing of 43 elephants by the local people in the same year is regrettable, and regretted by the villagers themselves, but hardly blameworthy (Sugg 1996). I take it that this case is uncontroversial.

The self-defense justification is very narrowly conceived where the attacker is human. In contrast, almost everyone would accept the killing of a less direct threat from an animal such as a plague-infected rat or a swarm of locusts, but not an equally infectious human plague sufferer or a crop devastating polluter, which suggests that we don't consider animals' interests to be equal to the like interests of humans. Following Donald VanDeVeer (1979), we might accept that hunting animals (but not humans) to protect one's livelihood is also justified. Laura Westra (1989), who advocates an ethic of respect for animals, accepts that we may kill animals if it is necessary for our survival—it is by restricting our utilization to the meeting of needs that we show respect for both animals and ecosystems. Traditional subsistence hunters are commonly said to show respect for their prey, for instance by refraining from killing totem animals even when food is scarce, explaining to animals why the hunter needs to kill them, asking for their forgiveness, and even mourning their deaths, and are praised for their complete usage of every part of the animal (e.g., Mails 1972).

[. . .]

Conservation: Rich and Poor Nations

The remainder of this paper is concerned with broadly economic issues: I argue that economic considerations (at the extreme, the survival of thousands of people) justify commercial trophy hunting.

First, however, I wish to draw attention to the global economic context in which wildlife management must be discussed. Calls from the North to preserve rainforests, set up national parks, and save endangered species might be more effective if local communities within nations of the South were agreed to have property rights over their fauna and flora (Gunn 1994). Typically, however, genetic resources are appropriated by multinational companies and countries that can afford to research their potential to develop food and industrial and pharmaceutical products. Thus there is little incentive for poor countries to forego the advantages of immediate exploitation (Tietenberg 1990).

[. . .]

Conventional preservation measures will not help poor countries to deal with pressing problems such as malnutrition, poverty, disease, and overcrowding. Indeed, protecting large areas from human encroachment often exacerbates social and economic problems. Nowhere is this more evident than in Africa.

[. . .]

The social and economic costs of preservation are often allocated quite unfairly. For instance, India's "Project Tiger" has possibly—just possibly—saved the species, but according to one report (Chippindale 1984), on average about one person per week is killed by tigers in India. The Amboseli National Park, in Southern Kenya, illustrates the injustice (and also the ineffectiveness) of viewing national parks as "biological islands" which must be preserved from all human use except scientific study and limited tourism. The nomadic Maasai who had traditionally used this region were excluded from it for the benefit of others.

[. . .]

Over the next few decades, wildlife numbers in the "protected" park actually declined, mainly due to illegal hunting. However, a change in land use philosophy in Amboseli NP in the mid 1970s improved both the numbers of wildlife and the economic position of the Maasai. Revenue sharing was introduced; the central government absorbed developmental and recurrent costs of the park; local Maasai were granted title to land outside the Park, to be owned cooperatively as group ranches; and cash compensation was paid for loss of grazing, to cover livestock losses from wildlife migrating outside the Park borders. The Maasai became less dependent on cattle because of these measures and, more importantly, because of the revenue they received from tourist campsites and employment in the Park, with which they were able to build community facilities. Reduction in livestock numbers meant less competition with wildlife, and because the Maasai were now part of the enterprise, illegal hunting greatly declined. As a result, within ten years wildlife numbers had greatly increased (Western 1984).

The Economics of Hunting

Commercial and sport hunting are economically significant activities in many developed countries. For instance, according to the BFSS (n.d.) 33,000 jobs in the United Kingdom depend on hunting. [. . .] However, the economies of rich countries do not depend significantly on hunting and if it was banned, recreational hunters would simply switch their discretionary spending, thus creating jobs in other sectors of the economy.

The situation is quite different in poorer countries, where wildlife has always been used as a resource and "Use or non-use is not the issue; sustainable use is" (Makombe 1993, 17). The colonial powers, after reducing many species to rarity or extinction, generally adopted policies of strict preservation of wildlife. This was done without regard to the needs of local people who were regarded as poachers even when they engaged in traditional subsistence hunting (Makombe 1993, 18).

Poor countries gain considerable revenue from trophy hunting. The impoverished Mongolian government charges $10,000 for a permit to shoot a snow leopard and a 16-day hunt with one snow leopard costs $25,000 per person; any wolves shot along the way are thrown in for $600. Bulgarian dealers sell falcons in the West for $10,000. Orangutan were sold in Taiwan in the 1980s at $30,000 each, though the local traders in Indonesia received less than $200 each for them—still a very considerable sum by local standards (information from Anon. 1993, 1994; Ghazi 1994). None of these cases is part of a sustainable management program, but other countries which manage their wildlife effectively have achieved substantial revenues from trophy hunting while maintaining or increasing their wildlife populations.

Zimbabwe: A Case Study

Wild resources are vital to the survival of millions of Africans. One study estimated that wild resources contributed over $120 million to the Tanzanian economy in 1988 (Kiss 1990); hunting licenses alone yielded $4.5 million in 1990. [. . .] Before Kenya imposed a ban on hunting, the total revenue from sport hunting contributed about 6.5 percent to the total foreign exchange from tourism (Makombe 1993, 28). [. . .] In some countries, a large proportion of household income is derived from wildlife based enterprises—in Malawi, for instance, rural communities derive 2.5 times more cash from wildlife than the market value of their subsistence agricultural products (Makombe 1993, 22). In Zimbabwe, local people are allowed to hunt sustainably both for their own families and to take to market, and a limited number of trophy hunting permits are sold. Zimbabwe—12.7 percent of whose area is devoted to national parks and reserves—also has some of the toughest anti-poaching (in the sense of illegal hunting) units in Africa and spends 0.60 percent of its budget on wildlife (whereas the United States spends only 0.15 percent). This is a substantial commitment in a country which cannot afford to provide adequate health care and education for much of its population and in which 50 percent of the population is unemployed.

[. . .]

Rich countries such as the United States, Australia, and New Zealand which oppose hunting of large animals including whales, and especially trophy hunting, have a very bad reputation in Zimbabwean conservation circles such as Africa Resources Trust (ART) and Zimbabwe Trust (ZIM-TRUST). These private organizations strongly support the government CAMPFIRE Association (an acronym for Communal Areas. Management Programme for Indigenous Resources) which was set up by the Zimbabwean Department of National Parks and Wildlife Management in 1986, with the support of the Worldwide Fund for Nature, the Office of USAID, Harare, and the Centre for Applied Social Sciences (CASS) at the University of Zimbabwe. The objectives of CAMPFIRE, "based on the rationale that communities will invest in environmental conservation if they can use their resources on a sustainable basis," are:

- to initiate a programme for the long-term development, management and sustainable utilisation of the natural resources in the communal areas;
- to achieve management of resources by placing their custody and responsibility with the resident communities;
- to allow communities to benefit directly from the exploitation of natural resources within the communal areas; and
- to establish the administrative and institutional structures necessary to make the programme work.

(ZIMTRUST 1993)

The communal areas are the marginal and submarginal lands which were created early in the twentieth century when the British colonists "took over the most fertile lands and forced much of the indigenous population into arid and semi-arid areas" which are unsuitable for agriculture because they have insufficient or unreliable rainfall. However, they make excellent wildlife habitat" (Anon 1996). The 1975 Parks and Wildlife Act gave ownership of wildlife (including hunting rights) to all property owners, and in 1982 this was extended to the communal areas through their Rural District Councils (Murphree 1991, 8). Over five million people—almost half the population—live in communal areas, which make up 42 percent of the country. Communities may decide to participate in CAMPFIRE, which around half had done in August 1996.

In 1995, CAMPFIRE generated $2.5 million, a substantial sum given that game wardens are paid as little as $80 per month (CAMPFIRE News 1996). This revenue is gained from hunting safaris, tourism such as photographic safaris, sales of products such as animal products and crocodile eggs (for sale to crocodile farmers), and rafting licenses (CAMPFIRE News 1996; ZIMTrust 1993). Around 90 percent of the revenue is generated from the sale of big game hunting licenses, and 64 percent of this is derived from elephant trophy hunting licenses which in March 1996 cost $9,000 (CAMPFIRE News 1996). Over the period 1989–93, 22 percent of revenue was reinvested in wildlife management and 54 percent devolved to the participating communities on the communal lands. Communities spent their shares on infrastructure development such as water supply, clinic and school development, farm fencing (to keep out crop-destroying elephants, hippos, buffalo, and kudu) and roading, income generating projects, and cash distributions to families for their own use. In some areas, this income amounts to 50 percent of a household's annual income and enables families to pay for items such as school fees (CAMPFIRE News 1996). Masoka Ward, a formerly impoverished area, earned $100,000 in 1994 from a safari hunting concession organized through CAMPFIRE. The ward used the money to build a health clinic, pay game guards, and fund a football team, and each of the 140 households also received more than four times their annual income for drought relief, either in cash or maize (CAMPFIRE News 1996). This revenue, of course, would not be available without the sale of hunting licences. It would be even greater were it not for the ban on international trade in elephant products under the Convention on International Trade in Endangered Species and Their Products (CITES) since 1990.

Zimbabwe's policies are a conservation success. Whereas the total population of African elephants fell by half between 1975 and 1990 (from 160,000 to 16,000 in Kenya), Zimbabwe's elephants have increased steadily—32,000 in 1960, 52,000 in 1989, and over 70,000 in 1993 (Ricciutti 1993). The national trophy off-take is restricted to no more than 0.7 percent per year, which is clearly sustainable. For instance, the elephant population density of the Omay Communal

Land, a CAMPFIRE participant, is the same as that in the adjacent Matusadona NP, where hunting is strictly prohibited, and the Omay population grew at 3–4 percent per year from 1982 to 1992, even though, counting "problem" elephants shot by villagers, the average annual off-take was 1.03 percent (Taylor n.d.).

Because they have a stake in sustaining populations of economically valuable game animals, Zimbabweans have a commitment to conservation. As a result, species such as elephants which are rare or extinct in many other countries are thriving in Zimbabwe, along with populations of other animals which benefit from protection of big game habitat. It is sadly ironic that governments of the same European nations that reduced Zimbabwe's elephants to around 4,000 in 1900 (Thomas n.d.) are now highly critical of Zimbabwe's effective and socially equitable sustainable management policies.

It may be claimed that economic benefits could be obtained without the deaths of big game animals by encouraging wilderness tourism and big game viewing. Norman Myers, who has played an important role in protecting East African wildlife, has argued that live animals such as lions are actually much more valuable, economically, than dead ones. He notes (Myers 1981) that a trophy hunter will pay $8,500 to shoot a lion in Kenya, whereas the same animal will generate $7¾ million over its lifetime from people such as myself who wish to view and photograph wildlife, not to kill it. But this is unsound economics, for several reasons. First, each lion is substitutable by another lion. Wildlife tourists want to see lions, not any particular lion. So long as there is a reasonably good chance of seeing lions, people will continue to visit parks. Second, the viability of lions as a species, or of a given population, is not threatened by the carefully controlled issue of permits to trophy hunters. Lions reproduce rapidly and the revenue that would have been generated by Myers's hypothetical lion over its lifetime will continue to be generated by other lions. Third, and most importantly, the number of lions—which the tourists want to view and the trophy hunters want to kill—is limited by the carrying capacity of the environment. The available environment is restricted to National Parks and other protected wildlife areas, such as private game lands. When the human population of Africa (and other areas where lions used to live) was small, lions and humans coexisted, if not necessarily happily on the part of either. With rising human populations, and different expectations, it is utterly impossible that lions will ever again exist in any numbers outside protected areas. Therefore, lion numbers will have to be regulated, and if this can be done for the economic benefit of impoverished local people by the issuing of game licenses, why not?

Conclusion

As Africa's population continues to grow, and habitat shrinks, pressure on wildlife will increase. Africans, like Western environmentalists, are entitled to a materially adequate standard of life. They can not and should not be expected to protect wildlife if it is against their interests to do so. The only feasible strategy to protect the interests of both wildlife and people is one that integrates conservation and development, as in Zimbabwe. Whatever we may think of trophy hunting—and I share the distaste of serious sports hunters for it—at present it is a necessary part of wildlife conservation in Southern Africa.

References

Africa Resources Trust website, Website www.art.org.uk.
Anon. 1993. "Back to Nature's Bosom." *New Zealand Herald*, September 22.
———. 1994. "Cash Quest Could Mean End of Snow Leopard." *New Zealand Herald*, October 10.
———. 1996. *Zimbabwe's CAMPFIRE: Empowering Rural Communities for Conservation and Development.* Harare: Africa Resources Trust and CAMPFIRE Association.
British Field Sports Society. n.d. "Hunting: The Facts." Website www.countryside-alliance.org/country/foxhunting.html.

CAMPFIRE News. 1996. Issue 12. Harare: CAMPFIRE Association.

Causey, Anne S. 1989. "On the Morality of Hunting." *Environmental Ethics* 11: 327–43.

Chippindale, Peter. 1984. "Tigers Too Safe Now." *New Zealand Herald*, March 24.

Clark, Collin W. 1973. "Profit Maximization and the Extinction of Animal Species." *Journal of Political Economy* 81: 950–61.

Daly, Mary. 1978. *Gyn/Ecology: The Meta Ethics of Radical Feminism.* Boston: Beacon Press.

Ghazi, Polly. 1994. "Illegal Help at Circuses." *New Zealand Herald*, December 28.

Gunn, Alastair S. 1994. "Environmental Ethics and Tropical Rainforests: Should Greens Have Standing?" *Environmental Ethics* 16: 21–40.

Halliday, Tim. 1980. *Vanishing Birds.* Harmondsworth: Penguin Books.

King, Roger J.H. 1991. "Environmental Ethics and the Case for Hunting." *Environmental Ethics* 13: 59–85.

Kiss, A., 1990. *Living with Wildlife: Wildlife Resource Management with Local Participation in Africa.* Washington, DC: World Bank Technical Paper No. 130, Africa Technical Department Series.

Loftin, Robert F. 1984. "The Morality of Hunting." *Environmental Ethics* 6: 241–50.

Mails, T.E. 1972. *The Mystical Warriors of the Plains.* Garden City, NY: Doubleday.

Makombe, Kudzai (ed). 1993. *Sharing the Land: Wildlife, People and Development in Africa.* IUCN/ROSA Environmental Series No. 1. Harare: IUCN/ROSA, and Washington DC: IUCN/SUWP.

Martin, Paul and R.G. Klein (eds). 1984. *Quaternary Extinctions: A Prehistoric Revolution.* Tucson: University of Arizona Press.

Murphree, M.W. 1991. *Communities as Institutions for Resource Management.* Occasional Paper Series. Harare: Centre for Applied Social Studies, University of Zimbabwe.

Myers, Norman. 1981. "The Exhausted Earth." *Foreign Policy* 42: 141–55.

Ortega y Gasset, José. 1972. *Meditations on Hunting.* New York: Charles Scribner's Sons.

Regan, Tom. 1983. *The Case for Animal Rights.* Berkeley: University of California Press.

Ricciuti, Edward. 1993. "The Elephant Wars." *Wildlife Conservation*, March/April.

Shepherd, Paul. 1973. *The Tender Carnivore and the Sacred Game.* New York: Charles Scribner's Sons.

Singer, Peter. 1975. *Animal Liberation.* New York: New York Review.

Sugg, Ike G. 1996. "Selling Hunting Rights Saves Animals." *Wall Street Journal*, July 24.

Taylor, Paul. 1986. *Respect for Nature.* Princeton: Princeton University Books.

Taylor, Russell. 1995. From Liability to Asset: Wildlife in the Omay Communal Land of Zimbabwe. Wildlife and Development Series No. 8. London: International Institute for Environment and Development (IIED). 15 pages.

Thomas, Stephen. 1995. The Legacy of Dualism in Decision-Making within CAMPFIRE. Wildlife and Development Series No. 4. London: International Institute for Environment and Development (IIED). 24 pages.

Tietenberg, T.N. 1990. "The Poverty Connection to Environmental Policy." *Challenge*, September/October: 26–32.

Uetz, G. and D.L. Johnson. 1974. "Breaking the Web." *Environment* 16: 31–9.

VanDeVeer, Donald. 1979. "Interspecific Justice." *Inquiry* 22: 55–70.

Varner, Gary E. 1994. "Can Animal Rights Activists be Environmentalists?" In Christine Pierce and Donald VanDeVeer (eds), *People, Penguins, and Plastic Trees.* Belmont, CA: Wadsworth, 2nd ed: 254–73.

———. 1998. *In Nature's Interests? Interests, Animal Rights, and Environmental Ethics.* New York: Oxford University Press.

Vitali, Theodore. 1990. "Sport Hunting: Moral or Immoral?" *Environmental Ethics* 12: 69–82.

Western, David. 1984. "Amboseli National Park: Human Values and the Conservation of a Savanna Ecosystem." In Jeffrey A. McNeely and Kenton R. Miller (eds), *National Parks, Conservation, and Development: The Role of Protected Areas in Sustaining Society: Proceedings of the World Congress on National Parks, Bali, Indonesia, 11–22 October 1982.* Washington, DC: Smithsonian Institution Press: 93–9.

Westra, Laura. 1989. "Ecology and Ethics: Is There a Joint Ethic of Respect?" *Environmental Ethics* 11: 215–30.

ZIMTRUST. 1993. *Historical Overview and Background to CAMPFIRE.* Unpublished report. Harare: Zimbabwe Trust.

Special Problems

61 Exotic Species, Naturalisation, and Biological Nativism

Ned Hettinger

Hettinger addresses arguments both in favor of and in opposition to the continued introduction of exotic species to many habitats. He concludes that there are good reasons for opposing their intro-duction; even the presence of species that are naturally dispersing and nondamaging leads to a loss of biological purity and to a greater global homogenization of plants and animals.

IT IS WELL-KNOWN that the spread of exotic species has caused—and continues to cause—significant environmental degradation, including extinction of native species and massive human influence on natural systems. What is less clear, however, is how we are to conceptualise exotic species. Consider, for example, [. . .] wild pigs (*Sus scrofa*) in the Hawaiian rainforest, whose ancestors were brought to Hawaii by Polynesians perhaps 1500 years ago. Are they still an exotic species or have they 'naturalised' despite constituting an ongoing threat to the native biota in this extinction capital of the world? One commentator put his finger on the problem of understanding exotic species when he said, 'The terms "exotic" and "native" . . . are . . . about as ambiguous as any in our conservation lexicon (except perhaps "natural")' (Noss 1990: 242).

This essay sifts through the mix of biological theorising and philosophical evaluation that constitutes this controversy over understanding, evaluating, and responding to exotic species. I propose a precising definition of exotics as any species significantly foreign to an ecological assemblage, whether or not the species causes damage, is human introduced, or arrives from some other geographical location. My hope is to keep separate the distinct strands typically woven into this concept while still capturing most of our fundamental intuitions about exotics.

[. . .]

What Is an Exotic Species?

[. . .]

The fundamental idea underlying the concept of an exotic species is a species that is alien or foreign. Such a species is foreign in the sense that it has not significantly adapted with the local species and to local abiotic environment. [. . .] Geographical considerations are typically taken as what distinguishes natives from exotics. [. . .] On this account, exotics are species that originally evolved in some other place. Woods and Moriarty (2001) call this the 'evolutionary criterion.'

Specifying the natives of a region as those that originally evolved there is both too stringent a requirement and perhaps overly broad. Too stringent because, by this criterion, humans would be native only to Africa. But all species move around. Species evolve in one locale, then migrate or expand their range to other places, and thrive for thousands of years perfectly at home in these new regions. Few species in a region would be natives if we accepted this evolutionary origin criterion of native species.

[. . .]

I do not think we should require that natives fit an ecosystem, much less be good fits. There might be 'native misfits' as well as 'exotic fits.' [. . .] Consider that the Asian long-horned beetle (*Anoplophora glabripennis*) recently discovered devouring trees in Chicago is also an important threat to trees in its native range (Corn et al. 1999). Barnacles are an example of species that proliferate wildly in their native ranges. [. . .] Unless one accepts an idyllic conception of perfectly-harmonious natural systems, one must admit that native species can wreak havoc in their native ranges.

Similarly, we should not assume that natives are well-integrated into 'balanced' and 'self-regulating communities.' [. . .] Presupposing a tightly integrated and balanced, community conception of natural systems is highly controversial given the recent emphasis in ecology on disequilibrium, instability, disturbance, and heterogeneous patchy landscapes (Hettinger and Throop 1999).

[. . .]

Native species will have significantly adapted with resident species and the local abiotic environment, not in the sense that they necessarily have become good fits or are controlled by others, but in the sense that native species will have 'forged ecological links' (Vermeij 1996: 4) with some other natives. Natives will have 'responded to each other ecologically' and frequently evolutionary (Vermeij 1996: 5). Natives are established species (i.e., more or less permanent residents) tied to some other residents via predation, parasitism, mutualism, commensalism, and so on. Often native species will have affected the abundance of other native individuals, perhaps altering the frequencies of alleles in the gene pool of native populations and thus exerting selective pressure on other natives. A native species will also likely have adapted to the abiotic features of the local environment.

Let me stress again that by 'adapted' I do not mean 'positively fit in.' A species has adapted when it has changed its behaviour, capacities, or gene frequencies in response to other species or local abiota. Aggressively competing is as much adapting as is establishing symbiotic relationships. By adapted, I also do not mean fit or well-suited to survive in an environment. Species that have historically adapted in my sense may go extinct and species that have never actually adapted to a local assemblage may nonetheless be suited to survive there.

In contrast with native species, an exotic species is one that is foreign to an ecosystem in the sense that it has not significantly adapted to the resident species and/or abiotic elements that characterise this system and, perhaps more importantly, the system's resident species have not significantly adapted to it. On the account defended here, species that are introduced to new geographical locations by humans, or that migrate or expand their ranges without such assistance, may or may not be exotics in these new regions. Species are exotic in new locations only when the species movement is ecological and not merely geographical. That is, if a species moves into a type of ecological assemblage that is already present in its home range(s), then the immigrant species is not exotic (foreign) in this new locale: it will already have adapted with the species and types of abiotic features there. If, on the other hand, the species movement results in its presence in a type of ecological assemblage with which it has not previously adapted, then the species is an exotic in this new location.

[. . .]

When the first finches appeared on the Galapagos Islands, they were exotics because they had not adapted with the local species and to the local environment (Woods and Moriarty 2001). [. . .] In contrast, when bison (*Bison bison*) expand their range north or west out of Yellowstone National Park into the surrounding grasslands, they are not exotics because they enter a habitat with species with which they have adapted. [. . .] What counts is ecological difference, not geographical distance.

Whether a species is exotic to an assemblage is a matter of degree. The greater the differences between the species, the abiota, and their interrelationships in the old and new habitats, the more exotic an immigrant will be. After passing a certain threshold of difference, we can be quite comfortable with judgements about a species being exotic. [. . .] But there will be borderline cases where neither the designation exotic nor nonexotic is clearly appropriate. For example, the mountain goats that are moving into Yellowstone Park from the north would be neither clearly exotic nor nonexotic to the Yellowstone assemblages they join, if the flora, fauna, and abiota in their native habitat is somewhat but not all that similar to those they encounter in Yellowstone.

By requiring that a native species has actually adapted to (some of) the other natives in an ecological assemblage, we allow for the possibility of 'exotic fits'; that is, aliens that arrive in new ecosystems but are well-suited to them. Westman (1990: 254) calls this phenomenon 'pre-adaptation' and says it is possible because different species can play functionally similar roles. For example, even if Asian snow leopards (*Panthera uncia*) could play the same ecological roles that the restored grey wolves (*Canis lupus*) play in the Yellowstone assemblage, this would not make them native.

[. . .]

Exotics and Human-Introduced Species

Although exotics are often defined as human-introduced species, the examples of cattle egrets moving to South America and the Galapagos' first finches show that exotic species need not be introduced by humans. Nor need human-introduced species be exotics. Species that humans place into an assemblage as part of a restoration project are often not exotics. For example, the restoration of grey wolves to Yellowstone Park is not exotic introduction, even though humans captured wolves from Canada and released them in regions (Wyoming and Montana) hundreds of miles south of their home. Despite the fact that the individual organisms involved were not previously in the recipient assemblages and despite the fact that they were put there by humans, on the account given here, the released wolves are not an exotic species.

[. . .]

Even human introduction of species to locations where they have never previously existed need not count as exotic introduction. As long as the resident species have adapted with the introduced species, the immigrant will not be exotic. Consider [. . .] introducing a fish species into a high mountain lake previously devoid of that species of fish because a waterfall blocks its dispersal pathway. This need not count as exotic introduction, if the life forms in the lake had adapted with that species of fish and if that species had adapted to abiotic conditions like those in the lake.

[. . .]

Disvaluing Human-Introduced Exotics and U.S. Park Service Policy

Although exotics need not be human introduced, recently many—likely most—are introduced by humans, including those that are the most exotic in their new habitats. Modern humans regularly transport exotics distances, with speeds, and between ecological assemblages that do not frequently occur (or are impossible) with naturally-dispersing exotics. When an exotic species is introduced by humans, whether directly or indirectly, intentionally or nonintentionally, this provides one reason for the negative appraisal commonly levelled at such species. This negative evaluation is justified independently of whether the human-introduced exotic causes damage. Negatively evaluating human-assisted immigrant species—and not those arriving on their own—is a controversial value judgement. It is supported by a number of reasons, briefly outlined below.

Massive human alteration of the earth is ongoing (Vitousek 1997). Perhaps half of the planet's surface is significantly disturbed by humans, and half of that is human dominated (Hannah et al. 1993). Humans are increasingly influencing, altering, and controlling the planet's natural systems. The result is a radical diminution in the sphere of wild nature on earth. An important reason to value natural areas and entities is because they are relatively free of human influence.

[. . .]

The presence of human-introduced species diminishes the wildness of natural systems and thus provides a reason for disvaluing exotic species when they are human introduced.

[. . .]

Some charge that there is misanthropy behind such a distinction in value between human-introduced and naturally-dispersed exotics (Scherer 1994: 185). But valuing humans, even loving humanity, is quite compatible with not wanting humans or their works everywhere, especially in National Parks and wilderness areas.

One of the mandates of U.S. National Parks like Yellowstone is to let nature take its course. [. . .] As a natural area where human influences should be minimised, the negative evaluation of human-introduced exotics is especially compelling and Yellowstone has a strong reason to remove human-introduced exotics. For closely related reasons, the Park has a strong rationale for welcoming naturally-dispersing aliens. The presence of such exotics is a manifestation of wild nature, a world that made us rather than one we have made. Removing naturally-dispersing exotics would (typically) increase human control and manipulation over natural systems.

[. . .]

[H]owever, [i]f naturally-dispersing exotics cause sufficient damage, they may warrant control. The policy of letting nature take its course is not absolute. Respect for wild natural processes can be outweighed by concern for certain outcomes in nature. For example, the protozoan parasite (*Myxobolus cerebralis*) that causes whirling disease (an affliction that cripples some fish species) is a recent European immigrant to Yellowstone's ecosystems. If this species somehow travelled from Europe into Yellowstone without the aid of humans, the Park would be hard pressed to justify welcoming such a naturally-dispersing exotic. If the parasite threatened to destroy the entire Yellowstone cutthroat population, the Park would have strong reasons not to let nature take its course.

Exotics and Damaging Species

Some define exotic species as those that damage the new regions they occupy (Scherer 1994: 185). Indeed, exotics have caused massive amounts of damage, both ecologically and economically. [. . .] Pimentel et al. (1999) estimate that there are about 50,000 species of non-U.S. origin in the country, a fifteenth of the estimated total of 750,000 species. [. . .] According to Pimentel *et al.*, the yearly quantifiable damage these species cause is at least $138 billion.

[. . .]

Exotics have caused the extinction of native species. [. . .] Approximately 40 percent of threatened or endangered species on the U.S. Endangered Species lists are at risk primarily because of exotic species (Pimentel et al. 1999).

Despite the massive ongoing harm such species cause, we should not identify exotics with damaging species. We have already noted that some native species also cause damage. Furthermore, not all immigrants to new ecosystems are harmful. Most get extirpated before they become established. [. . .] According to the 'tens rule,' 10 percent of exotics that are introduced into an area succeed in establishing breeding populations and 10 percent of those will become highly invasive (Bright 1998: 25). Even if only 1 percent of exotics typically cause serious problems, this is of little comfort, for as Bright argues, 'since the global economy is continually showering exotics over the earth's surface, there is little consolation in the fact that 90 percent of these impacts are "duds" and only 1 percent of them really detonate. The bombardment is continual, and so are the detonations' (1998: 24).

[. . .]

Exotics can even be beneficial in the new habitats they occupy. Vermeij speaks of the 'potentially crucial role invasions and invaders have played in stimulating evolution' and says that 'in the absence of invasions, communities and species and interactions comprising them may stagnate, especially if the economic base of energy and nutrients remains fixed' (1996: 7). Exotics sometimes provide habitat for native species. A species of *Eucalyptus* tree introduced into California from Australia over 120 years ago benefits Monarch butterflies (*Danaus plexippus*) who rely on them during annual migrations (Woods and Moriarty 2001). Eucalyptus also benefits native birds and salamanders (Westman 1990: 255). There are also examples of exotics benefiting endangered species: grizzly bears consume substantial amounts of nonnative clover in Yellowstone Park (Reinhart et al.

1999) and, in some locations in the U.S., nutria (*Myocastor coypus*) (a South American relative of the beaver) are a principal food source for the endangered red wolf (*Canis niger*).

[. . .]

Still, there are good reasons for being suspicious of the disruptive potential of exotic species. Exotics often arrive without the predators, parasites, diseases, or competitors that are likely to limit their proliferation in their native habitat. Local prey, hosts, and competitors of exotics have not had a chance to evolve defensive strategies. Past experience, [. . .] is another reason for suspicion. Nevertheless, as with the connection between human introduction and exotics, one ought not to move from an empirical correlation between the presence of exotics and damaging results to a conceptual connection between exotic species and those that cause damage.

When an exotic species causes serious damage or harm, we have a reason for a negative appraisal of this exotic. When exotics cause harm to human interests, the ground for a negative evaluation of these exotics is fairly straightforward. [. . .] When exotic species harm or impoverish nonhuman nature, the justification for a negative evaluation is less straightforward. Many worry about whether it makes sense to harm natural systems and they challenge us to provide a principled distinction between harming a natural system and changing it (Throop 2000). (For example, in what sense did the chestnut blight harm or damage eastern U.S. forests as opposed to merely changing them?) But when an exotic species invades a diverse native community and changes it into a virtually uniform stand of a single species vastly diminished in suitability for wildlife habitat or forage (e.g., *Phragmites* in eastern U.S. wetlands, *Melaleuca* in Florida), a negative appraisal on nonanthropocentric grounds seems straightforward. Such an appraisal is also clearly called for when an exotic species, plentiful in its native habitat and present as an alien around the world, causes large numbers of extinctions of other species (e.g., brown tree snakes). The damage to humans and to nonhuman nature that some exotic species have caused is a significant reason to be worried about exotic species.

Naturalisation of Exotics

[. . .]

I suggest that the process of naturalising and becoming native is neither arbitrary nor purely scientific. [. . .] To become native, an exotic species must not only naturalise ecologically (i.e., adapt with local species and to the local environment), but it must also naturalise evaluatively. This means that for an exotic to become a native, human influence, if any, in the exotic's presence in an assemblage must have sufficiently washed away for us to judge that species to be a natural member of that assemblage.

Ecological Naturalisation

An exotic species naturalises in an ecological sense when it persists in its new habitat and significantly adapts with the resident species and to the local abiota. This is a matter of degree and typically increases over time. Immigrant species will immediately casually interact with elements of the local ecological assemblage, but significant adaptation between the immigrant and residents and between the immigrant and the local abiota takes time and increases over time. Exertion of evolutionary pressure between the immigrant, the residents, and the abiota will also not be immediate.

Determining what is to count as significant adaptation requires context-sensitive judgement. Adaptation can continue indefinitely. Whether adaptation is sufficient for ecological naturalisation may depend on the adaptive potential of a particular species/ecosystem complex. If a great deal of adaptation is going to take place (perhaps including co-evolution of the exotic and several resident species), then until this occurs, we likely would not judge the exotic to have ecologically naturalised. On the other hand, if the exotic tends to employ resources and modes of living that were not previously exploited in the recipient habitat, then perhaps not much adaptation need take place before we judge the species to have ecologically naturalised. In highly individualistic and loose assemblages, where few ecological or evolutionary links exist between members and where many species have wide-ranging tolerances to a diversity of abiotic factors (and so are unlikely to have adapted much to local conditions), a newcomer may be no more exotic (that is, unadapted to the local species and abiotic conditions) than are the resident species. Perhaps very little adaptation is sufficient to ecologically naturalise to such an assemblage. Ecological naturalisation can also occur in assemblages where the vast majority of species are human-introduced exotics (e.g., Hawaiian forests, or cities and suburbs where people have eradicated the natives and planted exotics). Over a sufficient time period, a large group of exotics would ecologically naturalise with each other and the surviving natives would also adapt with the new assemblage.

[. . .]

Evaluative Naturalisation

Should ecological naturalisation be all that is required before an exotic species is to be considered native? I think not. Many immigrant species have been in their new habitats long enough to ecologically naturalise (i.e., significantly adapt with local species) and yet we justifiably hesitate to consider them natives. Consider [. . .] Holmes Rolston's claim that mustangs on the western range are not natives even though they (and the ecological assemblages with which they interact) have had several hundred years to adapt. Many still consider Hawaiian feral pigs nonnative even after some 1500 years. It is hard to believe that significant ecological naturalisation has not occurred during that time span. The judgements that these species are not yet natives—despite having significantly adapted with resident species and to local abiota—can be explained by treating judgements about naturalisation and the resultant nativity as involving an evaluative component in addition to the ecological one.

Onetime exotic species that are judged to have naturalised and become full-fledged natives are ones that we take to be 'natural' members of their ecological assemblages. For this to be the case, we must judge their presence in these assemblages as not representing significant, ongoing human influence. [. . .] This is true even if the immigrant species has significantly ecologically naturalised and is thus no longer exotic.

We do not prevent human-introduced exotics from becoming native when we require that they not only significantly adapt but also become natural members of their new assemblages. For exotics can evaluatively naturalise as well as ecologically naturalise. Human influence on natural systems and species 'washes out' over time, like bootprints in the spring snow. Natural processes can once again take control, as when old mining roads erode and vegetation overgrows them. This washing away of human influence over time constitutes evaluative naturalisation and it allows human-introduced exotics that have ecologically naturalised to become full-fledged natives.

A number of factors affect the washing away of human influence and the resultant evaluative naturalisation (Hettinger and Throop 1999: 20–21). First, the greater the human influence, the longer it takes to wash out. Perhaps this is why we are reluctant to think of feral animals as capable of naturalising and becoming natives even over long time-periods. Domestication of animals constitutes significant human influence over them, and so even after several hundred years we might think that feral horses, for example, are still not native (fully naturalised) on the American range, despite having significantly ecologically naturalised. Withholding the judgement that they have evaluatively naturalised reflects the view that the human influence on those species is of ongoing significance.

[. . .]

Increasing temporal distance from human influence is another factor that contributes to the washing away of such influence. For an exotic species to naturalise ecologically, it must significantly adapt with other natives and the local abiota, and this ensures that it will have some temporal longevity in an assemblage. This longevity may—but need not—be sufficient to ensure evaluative naturalisation.

[. . .]

A third factor affecting the washout of human influence is the extent to which a natural system becomes similar to what it would have been absent that influence. [. . .] Mountain goats would be in Yellowstone if humans had not influenced natural systems. In contrast, [. . .] it is likely that Hawaiian nature would have remained without pigs virtually forever but for human intervention. Thus it is reasonable to view pigs on Hawaii as representing continuing human influence in this respect.

A fourth factor affecting washout of human influence is the extent to which natural forces have reworked a human-influenced system (independently of whether the result is similar to what it would have been absent human intervention). For example, if humans introduce coyotes into an area with significant wolf presence, human influence on the assemblage resulting from coyote introduction would be lessened quickly because wolves significantly dominate coyotes. When a human-introduced exotic has naturalised in the ecological sense, natural forces have reworked the affects of human action to some degree. Thus ecological naturalisation contributes to evaluative naturalisation in this dimension as well, though again there is no reason to think that it is sufficient for it.

[. . .]

Let me summarise the implications of my account of naturalisation for the distinction between exotics and natives. Exotics are species that have not significantly adapted with the local ecological assemblage. Once a species has significantly adapted (ecologically naturalised), it is no longer exotic. But such a species might still not be native. If it was human introduced and if its presence in the assemblage represents significant and ongoing human influence, then it is not a natural member of this assemblage and so is not native. Perhaps kudzu, western mustangs, and Hawaiian pigs are such examples of species that are no longer exotic (because they have ecologically naturalised), but are not yet natives either (because the human influence on their presence is still significant).

Although human introduction is not part of my account of exotics, it is a factor in my account of native species. Are the problems I identified with the human-introduced account of exotics applicable to my account of natives? Although I need not count the restored Yellowstone wolves as exotics (as must the human-introduced account of exotics), it might seem that I cannot say that they are natives either, given the significant human involvement in their return to Yellowstone. But because this is return of a species that humans had previously eradicated, the restoration of wolves to Yellowstone is, in one important respect, a lessening of human influence over both Yellowstone and the wolf as a species. Yellowstone with wolves is now like it would be had humans never eradicated them. Similarly, by returning the wolf to its former range, humans are, in one respect, lessening their overall impact on wolves. Thus, in these respects, wolves are natural and hence native members of Yellowstone, despite being restored by humans.

Xenophobia, Biodiversity, and Disvaluing Exotics as Exotics

Nativists are those who favour native inhabitants over immigrants and/or want to preserve indigenous cultures. Biological nativists favour native flora and fauna, and they combat the introduction and spread of exotic species in order to preserve native assemblages.

[. . .]

Such an opposition to exotic species has been compared to a xenophobic prejudice toward immigrant peoples. [. . .] Jonah Peretti argues that 'nativist trends in Conservation Biology have made environmentalists biased against alien species' and he wants to 'protect modern environmentalists from reproducing the xenophobic and racist attitudes that have plagued nativist biology in the past' (1998: 183, 191).

In contrast, David Ehrenfeld thinks that comparing the antagonism toward exotics with real biases such as racial profiling of African Americans and Hispanics 'deserves ridicule.' [. . .] After noting some exceptions, Ehrenfeld concludes, 'There are more than enough cases in which exotic species have been extremely harmful to justify using the stereotype' (1999: 11).

Ehrenfeld is on shaky ground if the 'ten's rule' is accurate. If only one in one hundred exotics cause serious problems, then stereotypes about the damaging nature of exotic species may be no more statistically grounded than are some of the morally-obnoxious, racial, and sexual stereotypes about humans.

[. . .]

When exotics are also distinguished from human-introduced species (as I have done), what justification for a negative evaluation of exotics remains? Those who oppose naturally dispersing, nondamaging exotics seem to be doing so because these species are alien, and negatively evaluating a species simply because it is foreign does suggest a xenophobic attitude and a troubling nativist desire to keep locals pure from foreign contamination.

[. . .]

Biological nativists' opposition to exotic species can be defended by distinguishing between types of nativism and purism and the reasons for them. While nativisms based on irrational fear, hatred, or feelings of superiority are morally objectionable, I will argue that some versions of both cultural nativism and biological nativism are rational and even praise-worthy. For example, I believe the protection and preservation of indigenous peoples and cultures is desirable. This may involve favouritism for local peoples and opposition to the dilution of local cultures (a kind of purism), but it is based on an admirable attempt to protect the diversity of human culture. Similarly, biological nativism is laudatory because it supports a kind of valuable biodiversity that is increasingly disappearing.

It might seem strange to oppose exotic species on grounds of biodiversity, for the presence of alien species seems to enhance a region's biodiversity, not decrease it. [. . .] But this argument takes too narrow a view of biodiversity. Since the breakup of the supercontinent Pangaea some 180 million years ago, the earth has developed into isolated continents with spectacularly diverse ecological regions. Biological nativists value and want to preserve this diversity of ecological assemblages. This diversity is in jeopardy due to modern humans' wanton mixing of species from around the globe. The objection biological nativists can have to exotic species as exotics—at least in the current context—is that although they immediately add to the species count of the local assemblage and increase biodiversity in that way, the widespread movement of exotic species impoverishes global and regional biodiversity by decreasing the diversity between types of ecological assemblages on the planet. For example, adding a dandelion (*Taraxacum officinale*) to a wilderness area where it previously was absent diminishes the biodiversity of the planet by making this place more like everyplace else. Adding a mimosa tree to Sullivan's Island makes the Lowcountry of South Carolina more like some Asian assemblages. When this is done repeatedly, as humans are now doing and at an ever increasing rate, the trend is toward a globalisation of flora and fauna that threatens to homogenise the world's ecological assemblages into one giant mongrel ecology. Bright calls the spread of exotics 'evolution in reverse' (1998: 17) as the branches of the evolutionary bush are brought back together creating biosimilarity instead of biodiversity.

The loss of biodiversity resultant from the presence of exotics is greatly exacerbated by damaging exotics that invade, extirpate endemic species, or turn diverse native assemblages into near monocultures of themselves. But such causal diminishment in diversity is distinct from the conceptual diminution identified here: the mere presence of massive numbers of exotics in a great number of assemblages diminishes the diversity between ecological assemblages independently of whether they physically replace or diminish natives. Note that opposition to exotics on these conceptual grounds avoids the unfair stereotyping charge that must be addressed by those who oppose exotics because they are likely to cause damage.

It might be objected that presence of exotic species can enhance inter-assemblage biodiversity in certain respects, as well as decreasing it in others, and thus that the spread of exotics may not be a threat to overall biodiversity. For example, the movement of Asian snow leopards into Yellowstone Park would not only increase Yellowstone's species count but it would also make Yellowstone's assemblages differ from those of the Absoroka-Beartooth wilderness to the north in a way they previously did not: now they diverge in the types of mammals present. While snow leopards in

Yellowstone would make Yellowstone's assemblages more like some Asian assemblages, it would also increase differences between Yellowstone and the wilderness areas to the north.

It is true that the presence of exotics can increase inter-assemblage biodiversity in the way suggested. More generally, species movement into new assemblages need not be a threat to overall biodiversity. In evolutionary history, such movement has frequently enriched ecosystems, brought on speciation, and enhanced global biodiversity. Careful planned and monitored human introduction of exotics into selected assemblages might be able to enhance biodiversity as well. But this is no defence for the blind and large-scale human introduction of exotics that is taking place on the planet today. In today's world, the increase in inter-assemblage diversity due to snow leopards' presence in Yellowstone would not last. Snow leopards would quickly find their way (or be introduced) into the Absoroka-Beartooth wilderness, and the increase in regional biodiversity would be lost. If we focus on individual cases of exotic introduction—without considering the cumulative impact of massive numbers of exotic introductions over time—we may be able to convince ourselves that the presence of exotics is benign (or even beneficial) in terms of biodiversity. But in the context of the current flood of exotics, such a focus is myopic. The logical end point of the ongoing, massive spread of exotics is that ecological assemblages in similar climatic and abiotic regions around the world will be composed of the same species. This is a clear case of biotic impoverishment.

[. . .]

In addition to this tragic loss in biodiversity, the spread of exotics also helps to undermine an important feature of human community. Globalisation of flora and fauna contributes to the loss of a human sense of place. As Mark Sagoff perceptively argues, native species 'share a long and fascinating natural history with neighbouring human communities. . . . Many of us feel bound to particular places because of their unique characteristics, especially their flora and fauna. By coming to appreciate, care about, and conserve flora and fauna, we, too, become native to a place' (1999: 22). Using knowledge of—and love for—local native species to help ground a sense of place will no longer make sense in a world where most of these species are cosmopolitan.

Just as the spread of exotic species threatens to homogenise the biosphere and to intensify the loss of a human sense of place, so too economic globalisation and the cosmopolitanisation of humans threaten to impoverish the diversity of the earth's human cultures and to undermine people's senses of community.

[. . .]

[T]he mass importation of exotics does significantly threaten biodiversity and biological nativists typically do not believe in the superiority of the species native to their lands. The charge that biological nativists are xenophobic ignores their admiration of foreign flora and fauna in their native habitats. Although biological nativists favour native biotic purity, they do so in the name of global biodiversity, the preservation of the spectacular diversity between earth's ecological assemblages. Ironically, it is those who favour the cosmopolitanisation of plants and animals that support purity of an invidious sort: in that direction lies a world with the same mix of species virtually everywhere.

Opposition to exotics as exotic can thus be both rational and praiseworthy. Being a foreign species is a disvalue when humans are flooding the earth's ecological assemblages with exotics. Given the significant and ongoing homogenisation and cosmopolitanisation of the biosphere by humans, we may justifiably oppose exotic species even if they have arrived under their own power and cause no physical damage.

Conclusion

Exotic species are best characterised as species that are foreign to an ecological assemblage in the sense that they have not significantly adapted with the biota and abiota constituting that assemblage. Contrary to frequent characterisations, exotics need not cause damage, be introduced by humans, or be geographically remote. Exotic species become natives when they have ecologically naturalised and when human influence over their presence in ecological assemblages (if any) has washed away.

Although the damaging nature and anthropogenic origin of many exotic species provide good reasons for a negative evaluation of such exotics, in today's context, even naturally-dispersing, non-damaging exotics warrant opposition. Biological nativists' antagonism toward exotics need not be xenophobic nor involve unfair stereotyping, and it can be justified as a way of preserving the diversity of ecological assemblages from the homogenising forces of globalisation.

References

Bright, Christopher 1998. *Life Out of Bounds: Bioinvasion in a Borderless World.* New York: W. W. Norton & Co.

Corn, M.L., Buck E.H., Rawson J., and Fischer, E. 1999. *Harmful Non-Native Species: Issues for Congress.* Washington, DC: Congressional Research Service. Library of Congress. Available at http://www.cnie.org/nle/biodv26.html.

Ehrenfeld, David 1999. 'Andalusian Bog Hounds'. *Orion* Autumn: 9–11.

Hannah, Lee, Lohse, David, Hutchinson, Charles, Carr, John L., and Lankerani, Ali 1993. 'A Preliminary Inventory of Human Disturbances of World Ecosystems', *Ambio* **23**: 246–50.

Hettinger, Ned and Throop, Bill 1999. 'Refocusing Ecocentrism: De-Emphasizing Stability and Defending Wildness', *Environmental Ethics* **21**: 3–21.

Noss, Reed 1990. 'Can We Maintain Our Biological and Ecological Integrity?' *Conservation Biology* **4**: 241–3.

Peretti, Jonah H. 1998. 'Nativism and Nature: Rethinking Biological Invasion', *Environmental Values* **7**: 183–92.

Pimentel, D., Lach, L., Zuniga R., and Morrison D. 1999. *Environmental and Economic Costs Associated with Non-indigenous Species in the United States.* Presentation at American Association for the Advancement of Science, Anaheim, CA, January 1999. For text, see http://www.news.cornell.edu/releasesljan99/species_costs.html.

Reinhart, D., Haroldson, M., Mattson, D., and Gunther, K. 1999. *The Effect of Exotic Species on Yellowstone's Grizzly Bears.* Paper delivered at the Yellowstone National Park Conference on Exotic Organisms in Greater Yellowstone: Native Biodiversity under Siege, Mammoth Hot Springs. October 11–13.

Sagoff, Mark 1999. 'What's Wrong with Exotic Species?' *Report from the Institute for Philosophy and Public Policy* **19** (Fall): 16–23.

Scherer, Donald 1994. 'Between Theory and Practice: Some Thoughts on Motivations Behind Restoration', *Restoration and Management Notes* **12**: 184–8.

Throop, William 2000. 'Eradicating the Aliens', in William Throop (ed.) *Environmental Restoration: Ethics, Theory, and Practice*, pp. 179–91. Amherst, NY: Humanity Books.

Vermeij, Geerat 1996. 'An Agenda for Invasion Biology', *Biological Conservation* **7**: 83–9.

Vitousek, Peter 1997. 'Human Domination of Earth's Ecosystems', *Science* **277**: 494–9.

Westman, Walter 1990. 'Park Management of Exotic Species: Problems and Issues'. *Conservation Biology* **4**: 251–60.

Woods, Mark and Moriarty, Paul 2001. 'Strangers in a Strange Land: The Problem of Exotic Species', *Environmental Values* **10**: 163–91.

62 The Potential Conservation Value of Non-Native Species

Martin A. Schlaepfer, Dov F. Sax, and Julian D. Olden

Schlaepfer, Sax, and Olden note that despite the problems associated with them, non-native species also provide conservation benefits. These may include providing habitat or food to rare species serving as functional substitutes for extinct taxa and providing desirable ecosystem functions. Non-native species also may contribute to some conservation goals because they may be more adaptable to changing ecosystems than native species. They may evolve into new taxa that will be unique to their new regions. The authors predict that non-native species will become more accepted over time.

Introduction

Non-native species present a range of threats to native ecosystems and human well-being. Non-native predators and herbivores can cause extinctions of native species, particularly on islands and in freshwater ecosystems (Wilcove et al. 1998; Mooney & Hobbs 2000; Sax & Gaines 2008). Furthermore, they can alter the functioning of ecosystems and can carry infectious diseases that can endanger native species and human health (Vitousek et al. 1996; Daszak et al. 2000; Ehrenfeld 2003). By damaging commercial crops and interfering with industrial activities, non-native species are responsible for annual economic losses on the order of billions of U.S. dollars per year (Pimentel et al. 2005). As a result governmental agencies and nongovernmental organizations are frequently mandated or have chosen to prevent the introduction of non-native species and minimize their negative effects (Millennium Ecosystem Assessment 2005; Lodge et al. 2006).

Not all non-native species cause biological or economic harm, and only a fraction become established and have an effect that is considered harmful (Williamson & Fitter 1996; Davis 2009). But non-native species can also have desirable effects on an ecosystem. For example, numerous species have been repeatedly and deliberately introduced outside their native range for agricultural, ornamental, and recreational purposes (Ewel et al. 1999). As a result non-native species are integral to the culture and economies of most countries. There have also been numerous recent examples of non-native species contributing to achievement of conservation objectives (e.g., Westman 1990; D'Antonio & Meyerson 2002; Gozlan 2008).

Subjective Views of Non-Native Species

Scientific and societal perceptions of non-native species have likely impeded consideration of the potential beneficial effects of non-native species. Most scientists investigating the effects of non-native species try to conduct their work objectively; nevertheless, several authors have demonstrated that a bias persists against non-native species among scientists (Slobodkin 2001; Gurevitch & Padilla 2004; Stromberg et al. 2009). These biases are reflected in the assumptions commonly made about the intrinsic and instrumental values of non-native species, the language used when describing them, and in the types of studies conducted (Sagoff 2005). For example, in a landmark study in which the response of biological diversity (encompassing genetic, species, and ecosystem diversity) to several natural and anthropogenic drivers were predicted, Sala et al. (2000) considered non-native species only as potential threats, not as contributors to a region's species richness. Furthermore, in studies in which an index of biotic integrity was used, the presence of non-native species decreases the index value even if the non-native species have no or little detectable biological effect (Parker et al. 1999). Finally, the language used to describe non-native species in the scientific literature is frequently scattered with militarized and xenophobic expressions (e.g., "war on aliens" and "American ecosystems under siege by alien invaders") (e.g., Peretti 1998; Krajick 2005; Larson 2005).

The consequences of these biases are difficult to quantify, but they almost certainly have resulted in an emphasis on documenting the negative economic and biological effects of non-native species (Pyšek et al. 2008). Studies that fail to find a negative effect (e.g., Nielsen et al. 2008) are likely underreported. Furthermore, numerous researchers have evaluated the economic costs associated with non-native species, and syntheses that estimate the total economic effect of non-native species (e.g., Pimentel et al. 2005; McIntosh et al. 2009) attract substantial attention. By contrast, relatively few researchers have quantified the economic benefits (e.g., value of pollination by non-native bees, fees paid to hunt non-native game) derived from non-native species (but see Southwick & Southwick 1992; Ackefors 1999; Pascual et al. 2009). As a result, there has not been a comprehensive review of the economic benefits, provided by non-native species. The direct economic costs associated with wild and feral non-native species may well be greater than the income they generate, but we think both costs and income should be quantified.

We had two aims here. First, we sought to catalog the possible ways in which non-native species can help achieve conservation objectives. We did not review all the known negative effects of non-native species because these have been described exhaustively (e.g., Mooney & Hobbs 2000; Lodge et al. 2006). We also did not focus on economic or human-health effects. Instead, we considered examples of unplanned and intentional introductions of non-native species that contributed to achieving conservation objectives. We use the term *non-native* for species that occur outside of their historic range and *invasive* for cases in which these species cause biological, social, or economic harm.

Second, we investigated the role of non-native species in the broader context of setting conservation objectives. Traditionally, conservation goals have been defined by historical, static benchmarks aimed at protecting flagship species and "pristine" ecosystems and their putative integrity and stability (Forum 2004). But many non-native species are firmly established in their recipient ecosystems and cannot be eradicated; thus, novel approaches are required to manage them (Schlaepfer et al. 2005; Norton 2009). Furthermore, the negative and positive effects of non-native species vary over time, as will the manner in which these effects are perceived by humans, which in turn will have large effects on how non-native species are managed (Maris & Béchet 2010).

Current Uses of Non-Native Species to Conserve and Restore Species and Ecosystems

Many conservation efforts focus on the protection of genes, species, ecosystems, and their interactions. Numerous researchers have documented the various ways in which non-native species positively contribute to achieving conservation goals either serendipitously (Table 62.1) or intentionally (Table 62.2). Conservation benefits include providing habitat, food, or trophic subsidies for native species, serving as catalysts for the restoration of native species, serving as substitutes for extinct ecosystem engineers, and providing ecosystem services.

Shelter and Food for Native Species

Non-native species can provide shelter (e.g., Wonham et al. 2005; Severns & Warren 2008) or be a nutritional resource (e.g., Bulleri et al. 2006; Carlsson et al. 2009) for native species. The potential role of non-native species in providing resources for rare native species is likely to be particularly

Table 62.1 Examples of positive (+) and negative (−) roles of non-native species that were not intentionally introduced for conservation purposes.*

Purpose	Example	Reference
Habitat, shelter, and food for native species	+ non-native tamarisk (*Tamarix* spp.) provides nesting habitat for Southwestern Willow Flycatcher (*Empidonax traillii extimus*)	Sogge et al. 2008; Stromberg et al. 2009
	+ native butterflies oviposit or feed on non-native plants in California, U.S.A.	Graves & Shapiro 2003
	+ non-native mudsnail (*Potamopyrgus antipodarum*) abundant prey item for native fish in western U.S.A.	Vinson & Baker 2008
	− non-native mudsnail are food for native rainbow trout (*Oncorhynchus mykiss*) but when fish feed exclusively on mudsnails they lose 0.5% of body weight per day	Vinson & Baker 2008
	+ native avian predators in Spain increase in abundance as a result of foraging on non-native crayfish (*Procambarus clarkii*)	Tablado et al. 2010
	+ non-native plant (*Casuarina*) protects native snails (*Ogasawarana optima* and *O. discrpans*) in Japan from predation by non-native black rats (*Rattus rattus*)	Chiba 2010
Catalysts for restoration	+ non-native guava trees (*Psidium guajava*) support native frugivorous birds and promote forest regeneration via seed dispersal in Kenya	Berens et al. 2008
	+ non-native trees established on abandoned pastures facilitate restoration of native tree species in Puerto Rico	Lugo 2004
Ecosystem engineers	+ non-native birds in Hawaii disperse native plant seeds	Foster & Robinson 2007
	+ non-native Pacific oyster (*Crassostrea gigas*) colonizes unvegetated tideflats and forms hard reefs thereby increasing densities of native invertebrate species relative to native oyster beds	Ruesink et al. 2005
Ecosystem services	+ non-native African honey bees (*Apis mellifera*) pollinate native plants in fragmented forest landscapes in Brazil and Australia	Dick 2001; Gross 2001
	+ pollination of the ieie vine (*Freycinetia arborea*) in Hawaii by non-native Japanese White-eye (*Zosterops japonica*) replaces the role formerly held by now-extinct native birds	Cox 1983

* Negative roles listed are not exhaustive and include only those that directly oppose the listed positive roles. Many of the non-native species listed have other negative effects on conservation objectives.

Table 62.2 Examples of positive (+) and unintended negative (−) roles of non-native species that were intentionally introduced for conservation purposes.*

Purpose	Example	Reference
Habitat, shelter, and food for native species	+ American shad (*Alosa sapidissima*) introduced into the Columbia River Basin and California as a forage fish for Pacific salmonids	Petersen et al. 2003
	+ non-native crayfish introduced across North America to provide forage for recreational fishes (e.g., largemouth bass [*Micropterus salmoides*])	Kats & Ferrer 2003
	− introduced non-native crayfish resulted in declines of several native amphibian taxa	Kats & Ferrer 2003
Catalysts for native species	+ non-native trees planted on abandoned pastures to facilitate restoration of native tree restoration species in Puerto Rico	Lugo 1997
	+ non-native cattle maintain early-successional vegetation that favors native fishes and reptiles	Brown & McDonald 1995; Tesauro & Ehrenfeld 2007
	− removal of cattle may result in proliferation of non-native grasses, which would have detrimental effects on the vulnerable (IUCN Red List) native skink (*Cyclodina whitakeri*)	Norton 2009
	+ non-native black locust (*Robinia pseudoacacia*) provides cover and restores soil fertility on mined lands	Ashby 1987
Taxon substitution	+ Aldabra giant tortoise (*Aldabrachelys gigantea*) replaces the ecological role of extinct giant *Cylindraspis* tortoises in the Mascarene Islands	Griffiths & Harris 2010
Ecosystem services	+ non-native *Chrysolina* beetles control invasive St. John's wort (*Hypericum perforatum*) in Australia and North America	Morrison et al. 1998
	− failed biocontrol of non-native cane beetle (*Dermolepida albohirtum*) through introduction of non-native cane toad (*Bufo marinus*) in Australia	Lever 2001
Preservation of species	+ species are transplanted to islands outside their historical range to mediate threats from non-native predators or transplanted poleward to mediate concerns about species' ability to shift their distributions in response to changing climate	Jolly & Colbourne 1991; Fontenot et al. 2006; Richardson et al. 2009; Willis et al. 2009

* Negative roles listed here are not exhaustive and include only those that directly oppose the listed positive roles. Many of the non-native species listed have other negative effects on conservation objectives.

important in situations when restoration of the native species that formerly provided shelter or an energy source is impractical due to limited economic resources or changes in the physical environment (e.g., Zavaleta et al. 2001; Hershner & Havens 2008). In the case of the non-native tamarisk (*Tamarix* spp.), preconceived notions appear to have contributed to an underestimation of its potential contributions to conservation. Tamarisk is a non-native woody plant that has become relatively common in riparian areas throughout the southwestern United States as a result of human activity and changes in hydrology (Stromberg et al. 2009). Initial reports suggested tamarisk were causing a drop in water table levels and reducing habitat quantity and quality for native riparian species, including the Southwestern Willow Flycatcher (*Empidonax traillii extimus*), which is listed as endangered under the U.S. Endangered Species Act. As a result, millions of U.S. dollars were spent removing tamarisk with mechanical treatments, herbicides, and a herbivorous beetle (*Diorabda elongate*) (DeLoach et al. 2006). Nevertheless, results of recent field studies reveal that in some areas up to 75% of the Southwestern Willow Flycatchers nest in tamarisk and that fledgling success associated with nests built in tamarisk was indistinguishable from success associated with nests built in native trees (Ellis et al. 2008; Sogge et al. 2008). In a recent review Stromberg et al. (2009) argue that many undesirable changes to water tables and displacement of native biota attributed to tamarisk are exaggerated or unfounded.

Given the substantial modification to flooding regimes by dams throughout the southwestern United States, it may be difficult in many areas to reestablish native taxa that formerly supported the Flycatcher. Thus, although removing tamarisk may provide a step toward restoring historic vegetation in these regions, doing so may unexpectedly cause direct harm to an endangered native species that now depends in part on tamarisk (Zavaleta et al. 2001; Shafroth et al. 2008). In locations with multiple non-native species, the control or eradication of one species will not necessarily result in the desired outcome because species interactions may be altered (Courchamp et al. 2003; Norton 2009; Chiba 2010).

Catalysis for Restoration

Non-native species that increase structural heterogeneity or complexity of an area are positively correlated with increases in abundance or species richness (Crooks 2002), and in some instances non-native species may therefore be useful catalysts for ecosystem restoration (Ewel & Putz 2004) (Tables 62.1 and 62.2). For example, former pastures with sparse vegetation and eroded soils in Puerto Rico (U.S.A.) are not readily recolonized by native trees. By contrast, non-native plantation trees are able to survive and subsequently attract seed dispersers and establish microclimates in which native plants can reestablish (Lugo 1997; Rodriguez 2006). In one study, 20 native woody species recolonized deforested land eight years after non-native trees were planted, whereas only one native woody species colonized unplanted control plots (Parrotta 1999).

Substitutes for Extinct Taxa

Non-native species are sometimes deliberately introduced to fill an ecological niche formerly occupied by a closely related species (Donlan et al. 2006; Griffiths et al. 2010) (Table 62.2). Non-native species do not have the same cultural and historical value as native species, but they have been used as acceptable ecological substitutes in cases where the benefits of their ecological function are perceived to exceed the potential risks of introducing a non-native species. For example, Aldabra giant tortoises (*Aldabrachelys gigantea*) have been introduced to several small islands surrounding Mauritius, where they appear to have successfully substituted the herbivory and seed-dispersal functions of native tortoises that recently became extinct (Griffiths et al. 2010).

[. . .]

In other cases, the substitute roles provided by non-native species have been more serendipitous (Table 62.1). For example, in Hawaii (U.S.A.), non-native species of birds are now the primary dispersers of seeds and fruits of some native plant species with native dispersers that have become extinct or been extirpated from lowland vegetation (Foster & Robinson 2007). Non-native birds may have contributed to the extinction of several native bird species (by serving as vectors of avian malaria to which native bird species are susceptible (Kilpatrick 2006)), but the remaining native species of plants and current ecosystems may now depend on the ecological roles of such substitute species.

Augmenting Ecosystem Services

Non-native species can alter and degrade ecosystem services, but in other cases they can also provide or augment ecosystem services (Pejchar & Mooney 2009). For instance, non-native species can serve as plant pollinators, especially in fragmented landscapes. Dick (2001) found that native pollinators are absent from forest fragments in Amazonia, Brazil, but that non-native African honey bees (*Apis mellifera scutellata*) move between forest fragments. Honey bees therefore not only pollinate the tall, native, canopy-emergent trees but also ensure long-distance gene flow between forest fragments. In Utah (U.S.A.) non-native plants provide nectar and pollen to insects, thereby increasing the carrying capacity of both generalist and specialist native pollinators (Tepedino et al. 2008). In a review of the ecological effects of two non-native wetland plant species (*Hydrilla verticillata* and *Phragmites australis*) in North America, Hershner and Havens (2008) suggest these plants provide as much or more waterfowl habitat, biomass production, and nitrogen retention than native wetland plant species, although *H. verticillata* also decreases habitat quality for native fishes (Hershner & Havens 2008).

Non-native species can function as biocontrol agents to limit undesirable effects of invasive non-native species in both agricultural and natural settings. Introduced natural enemies have prevented the loss of billions of dollars and has saved human lives by limiting the abundance of agricultural pests such as cottony cushion scale (*Icerya purchasi*) and cassava mealybug (*Phaenococcus manihoti*) (Messing & Wright 2006). Biocontrol agents, however, are sometimes less host-specific than initially thought and may parasitize native species. There is also the potential that novel host preferences may evolve over time (Messing & Wright 2006; Thomas & Reid 2007).

Future Role of Non-Native Species

A subset of non-native species will undoubtedly continue to cause biological, economic, and social harm. But we venture that other non-native species could become increasingly appreciated for their tolerance and adaptability to novel ecological conditions and their contributions to ecosystem resilience and to future speciation events.

Ecological Boles in Rapidly Changing Ecosystems

Non-native species could come to fill important ecosystem and aesthetic functions, particularly in places where native species cannot persist due to environmental changes. Indeed, some non-native species may be preadapted or adapt rapidly to the novel ecological conditions (Byers 2002). Furthermore, the ability of non-native species to tolerate and adapt to a broad range of biotic and abiotic conditions, as well as to expand their ranges rapidly, suggests they may persist under a variety of future climate scenarios (Dukes & Mooney 1999; Muth & Pigliucci 2007; Williams & Jackson 2007).

Non-native species contribute to local species richness (Sax & Gaines 2008) and thus may also contribute to ecosystem resilience and stability. Research has focused on species interactions (e.g., predation, herbivory) that can lead to declines in abundance of native species. Nevertheless, much less attention has been given to how food webs may be altered by the presence of non-native species (although see Byrnes et al. 2007) and whether long periods of time are necessary for strong positive links to form among species. Certainly, ecosystems that are composed mostly of non-native species can have complex species interactions and community structure (Wilkinson 2004). Therefore, it seems likely that non-native species will often contribute to some of the putative benefits of species-rich ecosystems, such as increased productivity and stability (Hooper et al. 2005; Cardinale et al. 2007), but this proposition has not been tested.

Novel Evolutionary Lineages

Given sufficient time, non-native species can increase global species richness through speciation. In situations in which gene flow is absent or low between a species' native and introduced populations, the combination of adaptation to novel selective regimes in the introduced region and drift (particularly with small founder populations) is expected to result in genetic divergence between native and introduced populations (Hendry et al. 2007). Divergent selective pressures can also rapidly arise among introduced populations (Lee 2002). For example, distinct subpopulations of European house sparrows (*Passer domesticus*) have evolved since 1850 in ecosystems in North America that range from deserts to moist, temperate forests (Johnston & Selander 1964).

Non-native species can also contribute to the formation of novel evolutionary lineages among native species. For instance, native soapberry bugs (*Jadera haematoloma*) have colonized non-native plants in the soapberry family in North America, where their lineages have diverged from bugs that remained on the original host (Carroll et al. 1997). Ultimately, such distinct lineages are likely to give rise to reproductively isolated, endemic species. Although speciation is generally believed to occur over centuries or longer, evidence of reproductive isolation was documented in allopatric populations of introduced salmonids after fewer than 13 generations (Hendry et al. 2000).

Non-native species can also catalyze hybridization events between native species that result in novel evolutionary lineages. For example, the *Lonicera* fly is a novel native species that resulted from the hybridization of two native *Rhagoletis* fly species. The parental fly species normally specialize on different native host plants and so rarely encounter each other. But both parental species occasionally visit the invasive honeysuckle (from the *Lonicera tatarica* complex) since its introduction to North America (Schwarz et al. 2007). Thus, the invasive plant provides a location for hybridization to occur. The plant now also serves as a resource on which the novel *Rhagoletis* hybrid species has become specialized.

Speciation events can also result from hybridization between certain non-native and native species and between pairs of non-native species (Vellend et al. 2007). For example, repeated speciation events of salsify (*Tragopogon* spp.) plants have occurred following their hybridization with multiple species introduced to the United States (e.g., Tate et al. 2006). Thus, although non-native species initially contribute to the homogenization of the world's biota (Olden et al. 2004) and may cause a delayed extinction debt (Jackson & Sax 2010), they also represent the source material for future speciation events and could eventually result in instances of evolutionary diversification. A conservation strategy that eradicates species simply because they are non-native could undermine the very biological entities that may be the most likely to succeed in a rapidly changing world.

Managing Non-Native Species

Efforts to manage non-native species generally focus on two approaches that have proven effective: preventing the introduction of novel species that are likely to become invasive and, in the event a non-native species is introduced and rapidly detected, controlling or eradicating the species (Lodge et al. 2006). Challenges to managing non-native species that are firmly established include uncertainties over future effects of a non-native species, divergent values among stakeholders, varying interpretations of sometimes sparse historical records, and dynamic conservation goals.

The future effects of a non-native species are uncertain because biotic interactions are notoriously difficult to predict and because current and future environmental conditions may differ substantially (Walther et al. 2009). For example, expected positive effects will not necessarily be realized. In addition, non-native species may become invasive at some point in the future and potentially result in the extirpation or extinction of other species. These uncertainties have led some to assume all non-native species undesirable until proven otherwise (e.g., Ricciardi & Simberloff 2009). We disagree with this perspective because it assumes the magnitude of negative effects will always be greater than the positive effects. Risk analyses may reveal that some non-native species are more likely to have positive impacts.

Major sources of uncertainty are not only whether a species will become invasive in the future but also for how long negative effects will persist. Theoretically, there will be strong selective advantage for species that exploit an abundant non-native species; thus, initial negative effects are not expected to endure indefinitely. Empirically, the abundance of some non-native species declines after a period of initial growth (Simberloff & Gibbons 2004; Hawkes 2007), but there is insufficient data to predict how long this growth period will last.

Cost-benefit analyses of any management option for non-native species must include the subjective valuation of species (Evans et al. 2008; Sandler 2010). Stakeholders frequently have different value systems and prefer different management outcomes. There may be strong differences in opinion even among individual conservation professionals. For example, some place a premium on the integrity of native ecosystems or fear the future negative effects of non-native species (Ricciardi & Simberloff 2009), whereas others may value the ecosystem function provided by a non-native species (Dudgeon & Smith 2006) or the potential of translocation to preserve species in the wild (Hoegh-Guldberg et al. 2008).

A recurring issue in the valuation of non-native species is whether a species "belongs" to a given region. Strong opposition to non-native species comes from those who wish to retain the historical character of a region. We argue that the character of a region is likely to change over time as a non-native species becomes naturalized and humans grow accustomed to its presence. Evidence of such changes in normative values is already apparent in citizen groups that mobilize for the protection of non-native species such as the dingo (*Canis lupus dingo*) in Australia and *Eucalyptus* trees and Red-masked Parakeets (*Aratinga erythrogenys*) in California (U.S.A.). Philosophically, we question how human actions differ from those of other species. In other words, why is a dispersal event that is facilitated by, say, a migratory bird or storm event (e.g., Censky et al. 1998) considered natural, whereas a human-transported species is non-native and thus undesirable (Brown & Sax 2005; Cassey et al. 2005)? Furthermore, the past distributions and dispersal events of most species are poorly known, and this reduces one's ability to clearly distinguish native from non-native species, especially for lesser-known taxonomic groups (Carlton 1996). Because of these uncertainties and philosophical differences, we believe it is preferable to distinguish species on the basis of how long they have been present with terms such as *long-term resident species, recently arrived species*, and *new species* (Pyšek et al. 2004; Davis 2009). We surmise that species will increasingly be evaluated for reasons independent of their recent range distributions.

Because communities and species characteristics are so dynamic (e.g., Mace & Purvis 2008; Hobbs et al. 2009), we anticipate that conservation professionals will increasingly look toward the future rather than to the past when setting benchmarks and devising strategies. Instead of determining what species formerly occurred in an area and how to restore these species, they might determine what they want the area to look like in the future. Species that are economically or biologically damaging will likely be controlled, regardless of their historic origin. Conversely, species that are considered desirable for their aesthetic beauty, rarity, economic or intrinsic value will likely be protected, subsidized, or left alone, regardless of whether their former status was native or non-native (Briggs 2008; Hoegh-Guldberg et al. 2008). In the past, risk analyses focused on negative events associated with non-native species, and a species was termed invasive if any significant negative effect was documented. Here, we suggest that both negative and positive potential effects of non-native species should be tallied. We also suggest that a more meaningful definition of an invasive species would be one for which there is a *net* negative effect. A dynamic view of nature that recognizes that species characteristics and human valuations thereof change over time not only reflects ongoing evolutionary processes but also leads to a more balanced and objective approach to the management of non-native species.

Acknowledgments

We thank B. Blossey and his laboratory group, K. Schulz and the Aqua-lunch group, T.A. Gavin, P. Kareiva, K. Smith, J. Fridley, J. Stella, and two anonymous reviewers for discussion and comments on previous versions of this manuscript.

Literature Cited

Ackefors, H. 1999. The positive effects of established crayfish introductions in Europe. Pages 49–61 in F. Gherardi and D. M. Holdich, editors. *Crayfish in Europe as alien species.* A.A. Balkema, Rotterdam, The Netherlands.

Ashby, W. C. 1987. Forests. Pages 89–108 in W. R. Jordan III, M. E. Gilpin, and J. D. Aber, editors. *Restoration ecology.* Cambridge University Press, New York.

Berens, D. G., N. Farwig, G. Schaab, and K. Böhning-Gaese. 2008. Exotic guavas are foci of forest regeneration in Kenyan farmland. *Biotropica* **40**:104–112.

Briggs, J. C. 2008. The North Atlantic Ocean: Need for proactive management. *Fisheries* **33**:180–185.

Brown, J. H., and W. McDonald. 1995. Livestock grazing and conservation on southwestern rangelands. *Conservation Biology* **9**:1644–1647.

Brown, J. H., and D. F. Sax. 2005. Biological invasions and scientific objectivity: Reply to Cassey et al. *Austral Ecology* **30**:481–483.

Bulleri, F., L. Airoldi, G. M. Branca, and M. Abbiati. 2006. Positive effects of the introduced green alga, *Codium fragile* ssp. *tomentosoides,* on recruitment and survival of mussels. *Marine Biology* **148**: 1213–1220.

Byers, J. E. 2002. Impact of non-indigenous species on natives enhanced by anthropogenic alteration of selection regimes. *Oikos* **97**:449–458.

Byrnes, J. E., P. L. Reynolds, and J. J. Stachowicz. 2007. Invasions and extinctions reshape coastal marine food webs. *Public Library of Science ONE* **2**:e295. DOI:10.1371/journal.pone.0000295.

Cardinale, B. J., J. P. Wrigh, M. W. Cadotte, I. T. Carroll, A. Hector, D. S. Srivastava, M. Loreau, and J. J. Weis. 2007. Impacts of plant diversity on biomass production increase through time because of species complementarity. *Proceedings of the National Academy of Sciences of the United States of America* **104**:18123–18128.

Carlsson, N. O., O. Sarnelle, and D. L. Strayer. 2009. Native predators and exotic prey—An acquired taste? *Frontiers in Ecology and the Environment* **7**:525–532.

Carlton, J. T. 1996. Biological invasions and cryptogenic species. *Ecology* **77**:1653–1655.

Carroll, S. P., H. Dingle, and S. P. Klassen. 1997. Genetic differentiation of fitness-associated traits among rapidly evolving populations of the soapberry bug. *Evolution* 51:1182–1188.

Cassey, P., T. M. Blackburn, R. P. Duncan, and S. L. Chown. 2005. Concerning invasive species: reply to Brown and Sax. *Austral Ecology* **30**:475–480.

Censky, E. J., K. Hodge, and J. Dudley. 1998. Over-water dispersal of lizards due to hurricanes. *Nature* **395**:556.

Chiba, S. 2010. Invasive non-native species' provision of refugia for endangered native species. *Conservation Biology* **24**:1141–1147.

Courchamp, F., J.-L. Chapuis, and M. Pascal. 2003. Mammal invaders on islands: Impact, control and control impact. *Biological Reviews* **78**:347–383.

Cox, P. A. 1983. Extinction of the Hawaiian avifauna resulted in a change of pollinators for the ieie, *Freycinetia arborea. Oikos* **41**:195–199.

Crooks, J. A. 2002. Characterizing ecosystem-level consequences of biological invasions: The role of ecosystem engineers. *Oikos* **97**:153–166.

D'Antonio, C., and L. A. Meyerson. 2002. Exotic plant species as problems and solutions in ecological restoration: A synthesis. *Restoration Ecology* **10**:703–713.

Daszak, P., A. A. Cunningham, and A. D. Hyatt. 2000. Emerging infectious diseases of wildlife-threats to biodiversity and human health. *Science* **287**:443–449.

Davis, M. A. 2009. *Invasion biology.* Oxford University Press, Oxford, United Kingdom.

DeLoach, C. J., L. R.. Milbrath, R. Carruthers, A. E. Knutson, F. Nibling, D. Eberts, D. C. Thompson, D. J. Kazmer, T. L. Dudley, D. W. Bean, and J. B. Knight. 2006. Overview of saltcedar biological control. Pages 92–99 in C. Aguirre-Bravo, P. J. Pellicane, D. P. Burns, and S. Draggan, editors. *Monitoring science and technology symposium: Unifying knowledge for sustainability in the Western Hemisphere: Proceedings RMRS-P-42CD.* Department of Agriculture, Forest Service, Rocky Mountain Research Station, Fort Collins, Colorado.

Dick, C. W. 2001. Genetic rescue of remnant tropical trees by an alien pollinator. *Proceedings of the Royal Society B–Biological Sciences* **268**:2391–2396.

Dionisio Pires, L. M., B. W. Ibelings, and E. van Donk. 2009. Zebra mussels as a potential tool in the restoration of eutrophic shallow lakes, dominated by toxic cyanobacteria. Pages 361–372 in G. Van der Velde, S. Rajagopal, and A. A. bij de Vaate, editors. *The zebra mussel in Europe.* Backhuys Publishers, Leiden, The Netherlands.

Donlan, C. J., J. Berger, C. E. Bock, J. H. Bock, D. A. Burney, J. A. Estes, and M. E. Soulé. 2006. Pleistocene rewilding: an optimistic agenda for twenty-first century conservation. The American Naturalist **168**:660–681.

Dudgeon, D., and R. E. W. Smith. 2006. Exotic species, fisheries and conservation of freshwater biodiversity in tropical Asia: The case of the Sepik River, Papua New Guinea. *Aquatic Conservation: Marine and Freshwater Ecosystems* **16**:203–215.

Dukes, J. S., and H. A. Mooney. 1999. Does global change increase the success of biological invaders? *Trends in Ecology & Evolution* **14**:135–139.

Ehrenfeld, J. G. 2003. Effects of exotic plant invasions on soil nutrient cycling processes. *Ecosystems* **6**:503–523.

Ellis, L. A., D. M. Weddle, S. D. Stump, H. C. English, and A. E. Graber. 2008. *Southwestern willow flycatcher final survey and monitoring report.* Research technical guidance bulletin 10. Arizona Game and Fish Department, Phoenix.

Evans, J. M., A. C. Wilkie, and J. Burkhardt. 2008. Adaptive management of nonnative species: Moving beyond the "either-or" through experimental pluralism. *Journal of Agricultural & Environmental Ethics* **21**:521–539.

Ewel, J. J., and F. E. Putz. 2004. A place for alien species in ecosystem restoration. *Frontiers in Ecology and the Environment* **2**:354–360.

Ewel, J. J., D. J. O'Dowd, J. Bergelson, C. C. Daehler, C. M. D'Antontio, L. D. Gómez, D. R. Gordon, R. J. Hobbs, A. Holt, K. R. Hopper, C. E. Hughes, M. LaHart, R. R. B. Leakey, W. G. Lee, L. L. Loope, D. H. Lorence, S. M. Louda, A. E. Lugo, P. B. McEvoy, D. M. Richardson, and P. M. Vitousek. 1999. Deliberate introductions of species: Research needs. *BioScience* **49**:619.

Fontenot, D. K., S. P. Terrel, K. Malakooti, and S. Medina. 2006. Health assessment of the Guam rail (*Gallirallus owstoni*) population in the Guam Rail Recovery Program. *Journal of Avian Medicine and Surgery* **20**:225–233.

Forum. 2004. Restoration ecology: The challenge of social values and expectations. *Frontiers in Ecology and the Environment* **2**:43–48.

Foster, J. T., and S. K. Robinson. 2007. Introduced birds and the fate of Hawaiian rainforests. *Conservation Biology* **21**:1248–1257.

Gozlan, R. E. 2008. Introduction of non-native freshwater fish: Is it all bad? *Fish and Fisheries* **9**:106–115.

Graves, S. D., and A. M. Shapiro. 2003. Exotics as host plants of the California butterfly fauna. *Biological Conservation* **110**:413–433.

Griffiths, C.J., and S. Harris. 2010. Prevention of secondary extinctions through taxon substitution. *Conservation Biology* **24**:645–646.

Griffiths, C. J., C. G. Jones, D. M. Hansen, M. Puttoo, R. V. Tatayah, C. B. Müller, and S. Harris. 2010. The use of extant non-indigenous tortoises as a restoration tool to replace extinct ecosystem engineers. *Restoration Ecology* **18**:1–7.

Gross, C. L. 2001. The effect of introduced honeybees on native bee visitation and fruit-set in *Dillwynia juniperina* (Fabaceae) in a fragmented ecosystem. *Biological Conservation* **102**:89–95.

Gurevitch, J., and D. K. Padilla. 2004. Are invasive species a major cause of extinctions? *Trends in Ecology & Evolution* **19**:470–474.

Hawkes, C. V. 2007. Are invaders moving targets? The generality and persistence of advantages in size, reproduction, and enemy release in invasive plant species with time since introduction. *The American Naturalist* **170**:832–843.

Hendry, A. P., P. Nosil, and L. H. Rieseberg. 2007. The speed of ecological speciation. *Functional Ecology* **21**:455–464.

Hendry, A. P., J. K. Wenburg, P. Bentzen, E. C. Volk, and T. P. Quinn. 2000. Rapid evolution of reproductive isolation in the wild: Evidence from introduced salmon. *Science* **290**:516–518.

Hershner, C., and K. J. Havens. 2008. Managing invasive aquatic plants in a changing system: Strategic consideration of ecosystem services. *Conservation Biology* **22**:544–550.

Hobbs, R. J., E. Higgs, and J. A. Harris. 2009. Novel ecosystems: Implications for conservation and restoration. *Trends in Ecology & Evolution* **24**:599–605.

Hoegh-Guldberg, O., L. Hughes, S. McIntyre, D. B. Lindenmayer, C. Parmesan, H. P. Possingham, and C. D. Thomas. 2008. Assisted colonization and rapid climate change. *Science* **321**:345–346.

Hooper, D. U., F. S. Chapin, III, J. J. Ewel, A. Hector, P. Inchausti, S. Lavorel, J. H. Lawton, D. M. Lodge, M. Loreau, S. Naeem, B. Schmid, H. Setälä, A. J. Symstad, J. Vandermeer, and D. A. Wardle. 2005. Effects of biodiversity on ecosystem functioning: a consensus of current knowledge. Ecological Monographs **75**:3–35.

Jackson, S. T., and D. F. Sax. 2010. Balancing biodiversity in a changing environment: Extinction debt, immigration credit and species turnover. *Trends in Ecology & Evolution* **25**:131–198.

Johnston, R. F., and R. K. Selander. 1964. House Sparrows: Rapid evolution of races in North America. *Science* **144**:548–550.

Jolly, J. N., and R. M. Colbourne. 1991. Translocations of the little spotted kiwi (*Apteryx owenii*) between offshore islands of New Zealand. *Journal of the Royal Society of New Zealand* **21**:143–149.

Kats, L. B., and R. P. Ferrer. 2003. Alien predators and amphibian declines: Review of two decades of science and the transition to conservation. *Diversity and Distributions* **9**:99–110.

Kilpatrick, A. M. 2006. Facilitating the evolution of resistance to avian malaria in Hawaiian birds. *Biological Conservation* **128**:475–485.

Krajick, K. 2005. Winning the war against island invaders. *Science* **310**:1410–1413.

Larson, B. M. H. 2005. The war of the roses: Demilitarizing invasion biology. *Frontiers in Ecology and the Environment* **3**:495–500.

Lee, C. E. 2002. Evolutionary genetics of invasive species. *Trends in Ecology & Evolution* **17**:386–391.

Lever, C. 2001. *The cane toad: The history and ecology of a successful colonist*. Westbury Academic and Scientific, Yorkshire, United Kingdom.

Lodge, D. M., S. Williams, H. J. MacIsaac, K. R. Hayes, B. Leung, S. Reichard, R. N. Mack, P. B. Moyle, M. Smith, D. A. Andow, J. T. Carlton, and A. McMichael. 2006. Biological invasions: Recommendations for U.S. policy and management. *Ecological Applications* **16**:2035–2054.

Lugo, A. E. 1997. The apparent paradox of re-establishing species richness on degraded lands with tree mono-cultures. *Forestry Ecology and Management* **99**:9–19.

Lugo, A. E. 2004. The outcome of alien tree invasions in Puerto Rico. *Frontiers in Ecology and the Environment* **2**:265–273.

Mace, G., and A. Purvis. 2008. Evolutionary biology and practical conservation: Bridging a widening gap. *Molecular Ecology* **17**:9–19.

Maris, V., and A. Béchet. 2010. From adaptive management to adjustive management: A pragmatic account of biodiversity values. *Conservation Biology* **24**:966–973.

McIntosh, C. R., D. C. Finnoff, C. Settle, and J. F. Shogren. 2009. Economic valuation and invasive species. Pages 151–179 in R. P. Keller, D. M. Lodge, M. A. Lewis, and J. F. Shogren, editors. *Bioeconomics of invasive species*. Oxford University Press, Oxford, United Kingdom.

Messing, R. H., and M. G. Wright. 2006. Biological control of invasive species: Solution or pollution. *Frontiers in Ecology and the Environment* **4**:132–140.

Millennium Ecosystem Assessment. 2005. *Ecosystems and well-being: Biodiversity synthesis*. World Resources Institute, Washington, DC.

Mooney, H. A., and R. J. Hobbs. 2000. *Invasive species in a changing world*. Island Press, Washington, DC.

Morrison, K. D., E. G. Reekie, and K. I. N. Jensen. 1998. Biocontrol of common St. Johnswort (*Hypericum perforatum*) with *Chrysolina hyperici* and a host-specific *Colletotrichum gloeosporioides*. *Weed Technology* **12**:426–435.

Muth, N. Z., and M. Pigliucci. 2007. Implementation of a novel framework for assessing species plasticity in biological invasions: Responses of *Centaurea* and *Crepis* to phosphorus and water availability. *Journal of Ecology* **95**:1001–1013.

Nielsen, C., C. Heimes, and J. Kollmann. 2008. Little evidence for negative effects of an invasive alien plant on pollinator services. *Biological Invasions* **10**:1353–1363.

Norton, D. A. 2009. Species invasions and the limits to restoration: Learning from the New Zealand experience. *Science* **325**:569–571.

Olden, J. D., N. LeRoy Poff, M. R. Douglas, M. E. Douglas, and K. D. Fausch. 2004. Ecological and evolutionary consequences of biotic homogenization. *Trends in Ecology & Evolution* **19**:18–24.

Parker, I. M., D. Simberloff, W. M. Lonsdale, K. Goodell, M. Wonham, P. M. Kareiva, M. H. Williamson, B. Von Holle, P. B. Moyle, J. E. Byers, and L. Goldwasser. 1999. Impact: Toward a framework for understanding the ecological effects of invaders. *Biological Invasions* **1**:3–19.

Parrotta, J. A. 1999. Productivity, nutrient cycling, and succession in single- and mixed-species plantations of *Casuarina equisetifolia*, *Eucalyptus robusta*, and *Leucaena leucocephala* in Puerto Rico. *Forest Ecology and Management* **124**:45–77.

Pascual, M. A., J. L. Lancelotti, B. Ernst, J. E. Ciancio, E. Aedo, and M. García-Asorey. 2009. Scale, connectivity, and incentives in the introduction and management of non-native species: The case of exotic salmonids in Patagonia. *Frontiers in Ecology and the Environment* **7**:533–540.

Pejchar, L., and H. A. Mooney. 2009. Invasive species, ecoystem services and human well-being. *Trends in Ecology & Evolution* **24**:497–504.

Peretti, J. H. 1998. Nativism and nature: Rethinking biological invasion. *Environmental Values* **7**:183–192.

Petersen, J. H., R. A. Hinrichsen, D. M. Gadomski, D. H. Feil, and D. W. Rondorf. 2003. American shad in the Columbia River. Pages 141–155 in K. E. Limburg and J. R. Waldman, editors. *Biodiversity, status, and conservation of the world's shads.* American Fisheries Society, Bethesda, Maryland.

Pimentel, D., R. Zuniga, and D. Morrison. 2005. Update on the environmental and economic costs associated with alien-invasive species in the United States. *Ecological Economics* **52**:273–288.

Pyšek, P., D. M. Richardson, J. Pergl, V. Jarosík, Z. Sixtová, and E. Weber. 2008. Geographical and taxonomic biases in invasion ecology. *Trends in Ecology & Evolution* **23**:237–244.

Pyšek, P., D. M. Richardson, M. Rejmánek, G. L. Webster, M. Williamson, and J. Kirschner. 2004. Alien plants in checklists and floras: Towards better communication between taxonomists and ecologists. *Taxon* **53**:131–143.

Ricciardi, A., and D. Simberloff. 2009. Assisted colonization is not a viable conservation strategy. *Trends in Ecology & Evolution* **24**:248–253.

Richardson, D. M., J. J. Hellman, J. S. McLachlan, D. F. Sax, M. W. Schwartz, P. Gonzalez, E. J. Brennan, A. Camacho, T. L. Root, O. E. Sala, S. H. Schneider, D. M. Ashe, J. R. Clark, R. Early, J. R. Etterson, E. D. Fielder, J. L. Gill, B. A. Minteer, S. Polasky, H. D. Safford, A. R. Thompson, and M. Vellend. 2009. Multidimensional evaluation of managed relocation. *Proceedings of the National Academy of Sciences* **107**:9721–9724.

Rodriguez, L. F. 2006. Can invasive species facilitate native species? Evidence of how, when, and why these impacts occur. *Biological Invasions* **8**:927–939.

Ruesink, J. L., H. S. Lenihan, A. C. Trimble, K. W. Heiman, F. Micheli, J. E. Byers, and M. C. Kay. 2005. Introduction of non-native oysters: Ecosystem effects and restoration implications. *Annual Review of Ecology, Evolution, and Systematics* **36**:643–689.

Sagoff, M. 2005. Do non-native species threaten the natural environment? *Journal of Agricultural & Environmental Ethics* **18**:215–236.

Sala, O. E., F. S. Chapin III, J. J. Armesto, E. Berlow, J. Bloomfield, R. Dirzo, E. Huber-Sanwald, L. F. Huenneke, R. B. Jackson, A. Kinzig, R. Leemans, D. M. Lodge, H. A. Mooney, M. Oesterheld, N. L. Poff, M. T. Sykes, B. H. Walker, M. Walker, and D. H. Wall. 2000. Global biodiversity scenarios for the year 2100. *Science* **287**:1770–1774.

Sandler, R. 2010. The value of species and ethical foundations of assisted colonization. *Conservation Biology* **24**:424–431.

Sax, D. F., and S. D. Gaines. 2008. Species invasions and extinction: The future of native biodiversity on islands. *Proceedings of the National Academy of Sciences* **105**:11490–11497.

Schlaepfer, M. A., P. W. Sherman, B. Blossey, and M. C. Runge. 2005. Introduced species as evolutionary traps. *Ecology Letters* **8**:241–246.

Schwarz, D., K. D. Shoemaker, N. L. Botteri, B. A. McPheron, and M. Noor. 2007. A novel preference for an invasive plant as a mechanism for animal hybrid speciation. *Evolution* **61**:245–256.

Severns, P. M., and A. D. Warren. 2008. Selectively eliminating and conserving exotic plants to save an endangered butterfly from local extinction. *Animal Conservation* **11**:476–483.

Shafroth, P. B., V. B. Beauchamp, M. K. Briggs, K. Lair, M. L. Scott, and A. A. Sher. 2008. Planning riparian restoration in the context of *Tamarix* control in western North America. *Restoration Ecology* **16**:97–112.

Simberloff, D., and L. Gibbons. 2004. Now you see them, now you don't! Population crashes of established introduced species. *Biological Invasions* **6**:161–172.

Slobodkin, L. B. 2001. The good, the bad, and the reified. *Evolutionary Ecology Research* **3**:1–13.

Sogge, M. K., S. J. Sferra, and E. H. Paxton. 2008. Tamarix as habitat for birds: Implications for riparian restoration in the southwestern United States. *Restoration Ecology* **16**:146–154.

Southwick, E. E., and L. Southwick. 1992. Estimating the economic value of honey bees as agricultural pollinators in the United States. *Economic Entomology* **85**:621–633.

Stromberg, J. C., M. K. Chew, P. L. Nagler, and E. P. Glenn. 2009. Changing perceptions of change: The role of scientists in *Tamarix* and river management. *Restoration Ecology* **17**:177–186.

Tablado, Z., J. L. Tella, J. A. Sanchez-Zapata, and F. Hiraldo. 2010. The paradox of long-term positive effects of a North American crayfish on a European community of predators. *Conservation Biology* DOI: 10.1111/j.1523-1739.2010.01483.x.

Tate, J. A., Z. Ni, A.-C. Scheen, J. Koh, C. A. Gilbert, D. Lefkowitz, Z.J. Chen, P. S. Soltis, and D. E. Soltis. 2006. Evolution and expression of homeologous loci in *Tragopogon miscellus* (Asteraceae), a recent and reciprocally formed allopolyploid. *Genetics* **173**:1599–1611.

Tepedino, V., B. Bradley, and T. Griswold. 2008. Might flowers of invasive plants increase native bee carrying capacity? Intimations from Capitol Reef National Park, Utah. *Natural Areas Journal* **28**:44–50.

Tesauro, J., and D. Ehrenfeld. 2007. The effects of livestock grazing on the bog turtle *Glyptemys* (= *Clemmys*) *muhlenbergii*. *Herpetological* **63**:293–300.

Thomas, M. B., and A. M. Reid. 2007. Are exotic natural enemies an effective way of controlling invasive plants? *Trends in Ecology & Evolution* **22**:447–453.

Vellend, M., L. J. Harmon, J. L. Lockwood, M. M. Mayfield, A. R. Hughes, J. P. Wares, and D. F. Sax. 2007. Effects of exotic species on evolutionary diversification. *Trends in Ecology & Evolution* **22**:481–488.

Vinson, M. R., and M. A. Baker. 2008. Poor growth of rainbow trout fed New Zealand mud snails *Potamopyrgus antipodarum*. *North American Journal of Fisheries Management* **28**:701–709.

Vitousek, P. M., C. M. D'Antonio, L. L. Loope, and R. Westbrooks. 1996. Biological invasions as global environmental change. *American Scientist* **84**:468–478.

Walther, G.-R., A. Roques, P. E. Hulme, M. T. Sykes, P. Pyšek, I. Kühn, and M. Zobel. 2009. Alien species in a warmer world: risks and opportunities. *Trends in Ecology & Evolution* **24**:686–693.

Westman, W. E. 1990. Park management of exotic plant species: Problems and issues. *Conservation Biology* **4**:251–260.

Wilcove, D. S., D. Rothstein, J. Dubow, A. Phillips, and E. Losos. 1998. Quantifying threats to imperiled species in the United States. *Bio-Science* **48**:607–615.

Wilkinson, D. M. 2004. The parable of Green Mountain: Ascension Island, ecosystem construction and ecological fitting. *Journal of Biogeography* **31**:1–4.

Williams, J. W., and S. T. Jackson. 2007. Novel climates, no-analog communities, and ecological surprises. *Frontiers in Ecology and the Environment* **5**:475–482.

Williamson, M., and A. Fitter. 1996. The varying success of invaders. *Ecology* **77**:1661–1666.

Willis, S. G., J. K. Hill, C. D. Thomas, D. B. Roy, R. Fox, D. S. Blakeley, and B. Huntley. 2009. Assisted colonization in a changing climate: A test-study using two U.K. butterflies. *Conservation Letters* **2**:46–52.

Wonham, M. J., M. O'Connor, and C. D. G. Harley. 2005. Positive effects of a dominant invader on introduced and native mudflat species. *Marine Ecology Progress Series* **289**:109–116.

Zavaleta, E. S., R. J. Hobbs, and H. A. Mooney. 2001. Viewing invasive species removal in a whole-ecosystem context. *Trends in Ecology & Evolution* **16**:454–459.

63 To Eat the Laughing Animal

Dale Peterson

Dale Peterson addresses the problem of bushmeat in developing countries, especially as it relates to primates, and calls for conserving primate biodiversity by reducing the use of apes for food. He acknowledges the importance bushmeat plays in subsistence diets but also points out how bushmeat hunting has developed a strong commercial component in some areas and its severe impact on some primates and other species. He develops a number of arguments that can be made to reduce the use of primates for food.

I first heard an ape laugh while following a large group of wild chimpanzees in the great Tai Forest of Côte d'Ivoire, West Africa, as they moved on their daily circuit, a complex progression from food to food to food, from obscure fruits to tender herbs to hard nuts.

These West African chimpanzees are well known for their stone- and hardwood-tool-using culture, and at two or three moments during the day I paused to watch a large number of the nomadic apes assemble in a glade of African walnut trees (*Coula edulis*), pick up the stone and wood hammers they had previously left lying about on the ground, place individual ripe walnuts on top of stone and wood anvils, and then methodically crack open the hard walnut shells to get at the meat inside. That whole procedure was astonishing, particularly since the hammers seemed indistinguishable from rough human artifacts and also since the apes themselves (looking about, picking up walnuts in their hands, walking upright to carry them over to the tools, and squatting intently while they hammered away) seemed to me then hardly distinguishable from people. But my biggest shock that day came from watching a couple of juvenile chimps wrestling, teasing each other, tumbling and chasing—and laughing, laughing their heads off. It was not an action that simply *reminded* me of human laughter or merely *seemed* like human laughter. It was without question genuine laughter, virtually identical to human laughter minus some of the vocalized overlay (producing a gasping, panting, frenetic sort of wood-sawing sound).

Since then, I have observed chimpanzee laughter at other times, in other places. I have also seen wild-born bonobos and gorillas laugh, again apparently as a frantic expression of delight and mirth. And I have been told by experts that orangutans, too, sometimes laugh.

Animal play is not surprising, and one can easily believe that neurologically complex animals experience complex pleasure, something akin to "mirth" or, perhaps, an irresistible sensation of emotional lightness. But laughter? The laughter of apes is entirely different from any mere facial upturn of pleasure: a dog's smile, for instance. And it is another thing altogether from the high-pitched hyena vocalizations, sometimes described as "laughter" but completely unassociated with play or pleasure. Laughter may be among the most fragile and fleeting of vocal utterances. What does it mean? That apes laugh is undeniable. That their laughter means anything significant is a matter of opinion. Still, the laughter of apes provokes us to consider the possibility of an underlying complexity of cognition and intellect, to wonder about the existence of an ape mind.

The great apes—the three species commonly known as chimpanzees, bonobos, and gorillas in Africa, and orangutans in Southeast Asia—are special animals because they are so close to human.

[. . .]

The four nonhuman apes, our closest relatives, mirror our faces and bodies, our hands and fingers, our fingernails and fingerprints. They make and use tools, are capable of long-term planning and deliberate deception. They seem to share our perceptual world. They appear to express something very much like the human repertoire of emotions. They look into a mirror and act as if they recognize themselves as individuals, are manifestly capable of learning symbolic language, share with us several recognizable expressions and gestures—and they laugh in situations that might cause us to laugh, too.

So people living in the Western tradition have recently come to accept, to a significant degree, a special bridge of kinship between apes and humans (or to understand that from the professional biologist's point of view humans are actually a fifth member of the ape group). Perhaps it is because of this recent cultural perception that Westerners are sometimes particularly surprised to learn that the three African apes—chimpanzees, bonobos, and gorillas—have long been a food source for many people living in Central Africa's Congo Basin (a largely forested region claimed by the nations of Cameroon, Central African Republic, Congo, Democratic Republic of Congo, Equatorial Guinea, and Gabon).

The fact, however, should surprise no one. Around the globe, people living in or on the edges of the world's great forests have traditionally taken the protein offered by wild animals: as true in Asia, Europe, and the Americas as it is in Africa. Moreover, the exploitation of wild forest animals for food is really no different from the widespread reliance on seafood, commonly accepted around the world.

But the African tropical forests are particularly rich in variety and have provided Central Africans with a very diverse wealth of game species—collectively known as *bushmeat*—consumed within a very complex milieu of traditions, tastes, habits, and cultural preferences and prohibitions. Some religious prohibitions (notably, the Muslim prohibition against eating primate meat) and a number of village or tribal traditions have kept apes off the menu in a scattered patchwork across the continent. [. . .]

And yet the very quality—human resemblance—that places apes on the prohibited list for some traditions actually lands them on the preferred list in others. Apes look like humans but possess a superhuman strength. The combination of human resemblance and superhuman strength may help explain why apes are, in some places, culturally valued as a food for ambitious men who would like to acquire the strength, and perhaps also the supposed virility, of an ape. [. . .]

These food preferences, based partly upon symbolic value, blend into the preferential logic expressed by symbolic medicine. Symbolic (or "fetish") medicine is a thriving business in the big cities of Central Africa; my own experience suggests that a person can rather easily locate ape parts in the city fetish markets. In Brazzaville, Congo's capital, I once looked over gorilla heads and hands. The hands, so the fetish dealer explained, are used especially by athletes who would like to be stronger. They boil pieces of the flesh until the water is all gone. Then they grind the remnants at the bottom of the pot down to a powder and press the powder into a cut in the skin, thus magically absorbing great strength from the great ape. Likewise, according to Mbongo George, an active commercial meat hunter in southeastern Cameroon, rubbing pulverized gorilla flesh into your back will cure a backache, and chimp bones tied to the hips of a pregnant young girl will ease the process of labor when her own hips are narrow.

Yes, there are many domestic alternatives to bushmeat in Central Africa, particularly in the urban areas. City markets offer domestic meat, both imported and home-grown—and indeed at least some of the bushmeat sold in the city markets is more expensive than some domestic meats. I am persuaded this is true for chimpanzee and elephant meat compared to beef and pork, at least, because I once asked an ordinary citizen in Cameroon's capital city of Yaoundé to buy—bargaining as he would in ordinary circumstances—equivalent-by-weight amounts of chimpanzee, elephant, beef, and pork. In that way, I acquired a strange collection of flesh in my hotel room (severed hand of chimp, slice of elephant trunk, cube of cow, etc.), which I weighed and otherwise compared, and concluded that city people were paying approximately twice as much for chimpanzee and elephant as for beef and pork. Why would anyone pay more for chimp and elephant? Taste is clearly an important but not the only factor in people's food preferences. Many Central Africans still prefer the taste of bushmeat, in all its prolific variety, but millions of recent urbanites also value bushmeat as a reminder of their cultural identity and roots in traditional villages.

In the rural areas where people are in many cases still living in a style close to traditional village life, the market cost hierarchy is reversed, with domestic meats more and bushmeat less expensive. For many rural Africans, then, bushmeat is also attractive simply because it's cheaper.

The standard dynamics of supply and demand mean that this pattern of consumption is about to hit a wall. While Africa is by far the most impoverished continent on the planet, it is also (and not coincidentally) the fastest growing. A natural rate of increase of 3.1 percent per year for Middle Africa indicates that human numbers are doubling every twenty-three years in this part of the world. If food consumption habits continue, in short, demand for bushmeat as a source of dietary protein will double in little more than two decades.

While the demand increases so rapidly, the supply is simply collapsing as a result of at least three factors. First, traditional hunting technologies are being replaced by ever more efficient modern ones, including wire snares, shotguns, and military hardware, and as a direct consequence animals across the Basin are being very efficiently *mined*, rather than *harvested*, out of the forests. Wire snares are particularly devastating because they kill indiscriminately; and, since snare lines are only periodically checked, they allow for considerable waste from rot. Wire snares tend to maim rather than kill bigger animals like the apes, but modern shotguns loaded with large-ball *chevrotine* cartridges enable many of today's hunters to target such larger and more dangerous species with impunity. Apes, who would have been unapproachably dangerous quarry for many (though certainly not all) hunters even a few years ago, are now attractive targets offering a very good deal in hunting economics: ratio of meat to cartridge.

Second, a $1 billion per year commercial logging industry, run primarily by European and Asian firms to supply 10 million cubic meters per year of construction, marine, and finish hardwoods primarily for the pleasure and benefit of European and Asian consumers, has during the last two decades cast a vast network of roads and tracks and trails into profoundly ancient and previously remote forests across the Congo Basin. Loggers degrade these forests, haul in large numbers of workers and families, and often hire hunters to supply the bushmeat to feed the workers and their dependents. Most seriously, though, for the first time in history (and the ecological history of these great forests takes us back to the era of the dinosaurs), the loggers' roads and tracks and trails allow hunters in and meat out. Vast areas of forest that even a decade ago were protected by their remoteness are no longer protected at all.

Third, as a result of the new hunting technologies and the new opportunity offered by all those roads and tracks and trails cut by the European and Asian loggers, a small army of African entrepreneurs has found new economic opportunity in the bushmeat trade, which has quite suddenly become efficient and utterly commercialized. Bushmeat is now big business. It is no longer merely feeding the people in small rural villages and other subsistence communities but instead reaching very deeply into the forests and then stretching very broadly out to the towns and big cities throughout Central Africa. In Gabon alone, the trade currently amounts to a $50 million per year exchange. Altogether, this commerce today draws out of Central Africa's Congo Basin forests an estimated and astonishing 5 million metric tons of animal meat per year. That amount is absolutely unsustainable. The depletion of the supply of wild animals and their meat is not even remotely balanced by the replenishment offered via natural reproduction in a stable ecosystem.

A generally accepted estimate holds that around 1 percent of the total bushmeat trade involves the meat of the great apes: chimpanzees, bonobos, and gorillas. A blind and drunk optimist might imagine that 1 percent even of 5 million metric tons is a somewhat tolerable amount. It is not, of course. And even in the best of circumstances, where apes happen to inhabit legally protected forests (that is, national parks and reserves), a recent survey based on responses from professional fieldworkers tells us that chimpanzees are hunted in 50 percent of their protected areas, bonobos in 88 percent, and gorillas in 56 percent.

The impact of the current explosion in market hunting across the Congo Basin is threatening the existence of several wild animal species—but it disproportionately devastates the great apes. Biologists theoretically examining the sustainability of hunting consider, among other things, the ability of a species to replenish itself. A species with a quick rate of replenishment can likely, other factors being equal, withstand a high rate of depletion from hunting. Thinking about the impact hunting has on the survival of any particular species, in other words, requires us to examine that species' reproduction rates; and the great apes are unfortunately very slow reproducers. Perhaps because they are intelligent animals requiring extended periods of immature dependency while the young learn from their elders, apes wean late, reach independence and puberty late, and produce surprisingly few offspring. Altogether, the apes show about one quarter the reproduction rate of most other mammals.

Given such a slow reproduction rate, biologists calculate that chimpanzees and bonobos can theoretically withstand a loss of only about two percent of their numbers per year and still maintain a steady population. Gorillas may be able to tolerate losses of four percent per year. Monkeys have about the same low tolerance for loss, ranging from one to four percent, depending on the species. Ungulates, depending on the species, should be able to withstand yearly losses ranging most typically around 25 percent; and rodents can do just fine with losses from 13 percent to 80 percent per year, again depending on the species. In an ideal world, hunters would be equipped with pocket calculators to keep track on how sustainable their hunting is. In the real world, commercial hunters usually shoot whatever happens to wander in front of their guns. As a result, active hunting in a forest tends to deplete the fauna in a predictable progression. Apes and monkeys go first. Ungulates next. Rodents last. Indeed, it ought to be possible to measure the faunal disintegration of a forest by comparing the ratio of monkeys to rats sold in local markets.

[. . .]

Based on the "informed consensus of experts," the commercial hunting of apes for meat is "out of control and unsustainable," and it continues "to spread and accelerate" (Buytinksi 2001: 27). With the current levels and patterns of demand for apes as food, how long can they last?

One measure of how fast commercial hunting can reduce an ape population has been provided by the recent history of eastern Democratic Republic of Congo's Kahuzi-Biega National Park, supposedly protected as a UNESCO World Heritage Site but not protected well enough to keep out the professional hunters. In only three years during the last decade, hunters in Kahuzi-Biega earned a living by transforming into meat ("if our worst fears prove founded," so one investigator writes cautiously—Redmond 2001: 3) some 80 to 90 percent of the 17,000 individuals who until then comprised the subspecies *Gorilla gorilla grauerai*.

In sum, conserving biodiversity—saving the apes from extinction—amounts to one argument against using apes as a human food. A second argument has to do with public health. [. . .]

In fact, apes are susceptible to an enormous variety of diseases that will also infect humans, including bacterial meningitis, chicken pox, diphtheria, Epstein–Barr virus, hepatitis A and B, influenza, measles, mumps, pneumonia, rubella, smallpox, whooping cough, and so on. Far more serious, however, is the possible scenario of a person already infected with HIV 1 or HIV 2 coming into intimate contact (through butchering, for instance) with one of several related viruses, the several SIVs endemic among several monkey species, thereby producing a successful cross, a recombinant virus that could become HIV 3. The government of Cameroon recently sponsored an extended study on primate viruses where researchers tested the blood of 788 monkeys kept as pets or sold as meat and discovered that around one-fifth of those samples were infected with numerous varieties of SIV, including five previously unknown types. So the potential for new epidemics based on recombinants should be taken very seriously.

The public health threat is not, of course, limited to Central Africa. Rather, it is a global threat that still tends to be vastly underappreciated by those in the West who are most capable of doing something about it—even as the threat grows with ever-expanding human numbers, international migration, and commerce. In the year 2003, for example, an estimated 11,600 tons of bushment (from antelopes, camels, monkeys, snails, snakes, as well as chimpanzees and gorillas) was illegally smuggled into Great Britain.

The final argument against apes as food is perhaps the one many people think of first but often have trouble describing fully or convincingly, and that is the ethical one: the special case against eating the animal who laughs. Many ethical vegetarians refuse to eat animals capable of suffering, thus drawing a distinction between plants and, at least, vertebrate animals, while possibly giving some invertebrates the benefit of the doubt. Indeed, I believe that most thoughtful people maintain an examined or unexamined hierarchy of value in their vision of the natural world that includes distinctions within the vertebrates—recognizing humans, for example, as among the most complex of the vertebrates with the most compelling capacity for suffering, a perception that possibly accounts for our common and particular horror at the idea of nutritional cannibalism. To the degree that we now see humans as surprisingly closely related to apes, or as belonging taxonomically within the larger group of apes, that makes eating the laughing animal also worthy of our special concern.

References

Buytinski, Tom (2001) "Africa's Great Apes," in Benjamin B. Beck, Tara S. Stoinksi, Michael Hutchins, Terry L. Maple, Bryan Norton, Andrew Rowan, Elizabeth F. Stevens, and Arnold Arluke (eds), *Great Apes: The Ethics of Coexistence*, Washington, D.C.: Smithsonian Institution Press, pp. 3–56.

Redmond, Ian (2001) Coltan Boom, Gorilla Bust: The Impact of Coltan Mining on Gorillas and Other Wildlife in Eastern D. R. Congo. Private report sponsored by the Dian Fossey Gorilla Fund and the Born Free Foundation.

64 The Ethic of Care and the Problem of Wild Animals

Grace Clement

Clement addresses traditional reasons for extending moral concern to animals and argues that these arguments are beneficial but incomplete and inadequate. She challenges the arguments of animal defense theories made by Peter Singer and Tom Regan and argues in favor of extending an ethic of care to human relations with nonhuman animals. Clement addresses potential arguments on why a theory of care may be more pertinent to domestic than wild animals but concludes that an ethic of care and an ethic of justice are appropriate for both wild and domestic animals.

Recently, a number of feminists concerned with the welfare of nonhuman animals have challenged the prevailing approaches to animal defense theory. A collection of essays, *Beyond Animal Rights: A Feminist Caring Ethic for the Treatment of Animals*, challenges the "rights" or "justice" approaches usually taken by animal defense theories, most notably those of Peter Singer and Tom Regan, and argues in favor of an ethic of care for our relations to nonhuman animals. This work arises out of feminist discussions over the past 15 years of the "feminine" ethic of care and its relationship to the "masculine" ethic of justice. Those writing in *Beyond Animal Rights* have extended this discussion by recognizing that the care–justice debate is important not only for relationships among humans but for human relationships to nonhumans as well. [. . .]

In this essay, I will examine the claim that an ethic of care is preferable to an ethic of justice for our relationships with nonhuman animals. To limit my discussion, I will focus on our obligations to animals, even though there are obviously important questions about our obligations to nonanimal members of the biotic community, and I will focus on the morality of eating animals, even though this is only one of many important moral questions about our treatment of nonhuman animals. While I regard the care proposal as promising, I will argue that the distinction between domestic and wild animals raises an important problem for it: while the ethic of care seems to fit our interactions with domestic animals well, it is at best unclear how it might guide our interactions with wild animals. I will consider three different alternative moral approaches to wild animals: a holistic environmentalist approach, an individualistic justice approach, and a justice approach in interaction with and influenced by a care approach. By drawing on the lessons of the recent care/justice debate regarding human-to-human relations, I will show that the third of these alternatives works best. Because I do not regard care and justice as dichotomous, I see this not as a rejection of the thesis of *Beyond Animal Rights* but as a sympathetic extension of it. The "Introduction" to *Beyond Animal Rights* provides four reasons for thinking that an ethic of care is more appropriate for our relationships to nonhuman animals than an ethic of justice (or, what is generally considered the same thing, a rights theory).

First, an ethic of justice "envisages a society of rational, autonomous, independent agents whose property is entitled to protection from external agents" (Donovan and Adams 1996, 14), and thus uses rationality as a test of moral considerability, a test which nonhumans are likely to fail. On the other hand, the ethic of care focuses on relationships *between* individuals rather than on separate individual identities, and thus requires no such test of rationality for moral considerability. Second, an ethic of justice "presumes a society of equal autonomous agents, who require little support from others, who need only that their space be protected from others' intrusions" (Donovan and Adams 1996, 15). But humans and animals are in most ways *unequals*, and thus better fit into the care model which assumes an inherent inequality between carer and cared-for. Third, an ethic of justice is a rationalistic approach, prioritizing reason and suppressing emotion-based appeals for animal welfare. However, feelings play a central role in human relationships to animals, and the ethic of care regards feelings as morally relevant and informative. Finally, an ethic of justice tends to be abstract and formalistic, focusing on universal rules of morality, while our complex relationships with nonhuman animals seem better accounted for by the ethic of care's contextual approach focusing on the particulars of given situations.

These objections to exclusively justice-oriented approaches are valuable. The extent to which prevailing approaches to animal welfare are *exclusively* justice-oriented and thus problematic is evident in Singer's and Regan's insistence that moral arguments must not appeal to our feelings about animals. [. . .] Our feelings may not provide infallible moral guidance, but sometimes they are all we have to appeal to. Perhaps, then, we ought to proceed not by banishing feelings from our moral considerations on the grounds that they are unreliable, but by paying *more* attention both to our feelings *and* to the mechanisms by which they are and can be socially manipulated (Luke 1995, 1996). As the authors of *Beyond Animal Rights* point out, this is an approach that the ethic of care is much more attuned to than the ethic of justice.

While the ethic of care is certainly a promising approach to our relationships with nonhuman animals in this and other ways detailed in *Beyond Animal Rights*, there is a difficulty with this approach left largely unaddressed by these authors. That is, the arguments in this book make domestic animals the paradigm, and it seems at least possible that they work *only* for domestic animals. We can see this by returning to the four arguments offered in the book's "Introduction."

First, the ethic of justice is said to be inappropriate for our dealings with nonhuman animals because it "envisages a society of rational, autonomous, independent agents whose territory or property is entitled to protection from external agents" (Donovan and Adams 1996, 14). Without addressing the difficult issue of the rationality of nonhuman animals, the autonomy and independence of at least wild animals can be and has been defended. In fact, environmental ethicists have long emphasized the difference between wild and domestic animals along these lines: Aldo Leopold wrote that the essence of environmental ethics was "reappraising things unnatural, tame, and confined in terms of things natural, wild, and free" (Callicott 1992, 67). According to environmental ethicist J. Baird Callicott, wild animals are autonomous and independent, while domestic animals are human creations which are *metaphysically* unfree. By this Callicott means that domestic animals are nothing but what we have selectively bred them to be, such that it is as meaningless to speak of *setting free* domestic animals as it would be to speak of setting free a chair. Callicott and other environmental ethicists may be speaking of autonomy in a different sense than the rational autonomy used as a criterion by those defending an ethic of justice, but in any case it seems at least somewhat appropriate to think of human relationships with *wild* animals in terms of a society of independent agents whose territory is entitled to protection from others. The second argument against the justice approach to nonhuman animals likewise seems to apply to domestic rather than to wild animals. Again, the ethic of justice "presumes a society of equal autonomous agents, who require little support from others, who need only that their space be protected from others' intrusions." The editors of *Beyond Animal Rights* continue: "But domestic animals, in particular, are dependent for survival upon humans. We therefore have a situation of unequals, and need to develop an ethic that recognizes this fact" (Donovan and Adams 1996, 15). Clearly, in this argument domestic animals are taken as paradigmatic, for wild animals are certainly not dependent for survival upon humans, at least not upon human *support*. Instead, they are dependent upon humans' putting an end to destruction of natural habitats, or on humans' *restraint*. In fact, just as the ethic of justice would say, it seems that they *do* need only that their space be protected from others' intrusions. While domestic animals depend upon human support, wild animals would most benefit from the disappearance of humans entirely.

Even the argument about the role of emotion in moral argument seems to work better in domestic than in wild contexts. This is evident in "The Caring Sleuth: Portrait of an Animal Rights Activist," in which Kenneth Shapiro discusses the crucial role of sympathy in moral considerations about animals. He quotes Helen Jones, founder of the International Society for Animal Rights, who wrote that:

> My first awareness of animal suffering was at the age of four or five. My mother took me to a zoo. As we entered we saw a large white rabbit, transfixed with fear, in a cage with a snake. Within a second or two the snake began swallowing the rabbit . . . My mother never again entered a zoo. I did, many years later, only to collect evidence for a legal case.
>
> (Shapiro 1996, 130)

Jones experienced a sympathy for the rabbit that many of us share. But in a certain sense this sympathy is odd. After all, snakes *do* eat rabbits, however upsetting it is for us to see a rabbit be eaten, and we certainly cannot legitimately condemn snakes for this behavior, nor can we hope to protect rabbits from this fate. Or, we can only protect rabbits from this fate in places like zoos, when they are rabbits we take into our protection. But it does not seem that our sympathetic reaction to the rabbit in this situation is dependent on the fact that this rabbit is in a zoo. That is, it seems as if the sympathies to which the ethic of care appeals might be more relevant for domestic than for wild animals. As Callicott puts it, in the wild, the fundamental fact of life is eating *and being eaten*, but our sympathies would seem to be out of line with this fact, such that there are good reasons *not* to act on our sympathies for wild animals. This suggests that the fourth argument cited above also works better for domestic animals than for wild animals: at least when it comes to wild animals, a *contextual* approach focusing on particular situations seems less appropriate than an *abstract* approach focusing on the general facts of environmental biology. From these considerations, it seems possible that the claims on behalf of the ethic of care in *Beyond Animal Rights* apply to domestic but not to wild animals. [. . .]

I will first address an objection to this proposal that would be raised by environmental ethicists. Environmentalists would begin by pointing out that the focus on domestic animals I have identified is present not only in the care approach to animal defense theory, but in standard (or "justice") approaches as well, and that *neither* approach works for wild animals. For instance, Mark Sagoff asks, "If the suffering of animals creates human obligation to mitigate it, is there not as much an obligation to prevent a cat from killing a mouse as to prevent a hunter from killing a deer?" (Sagoff 1993, 88). Similarly, if nonhuman animals are said to have certain rights, such as a right to life, then we have a corresponding obligation to protect those rights. While it might be appropriate to endeavor to protect domestic animals' rights to life, it would be absurd, not to mention ecologically disastrous, to endeavor to protect wild animals' right to life (Sagoff 1993, 88–89).

Environmental ethicists would argue that animal defense theories, whether of the justice or care variety, fail in the context of wild animals because they are individualistic in the sense that it is *individual* beings that are considered morally important. What is needed, they would say, is an approach which is holistic in its focus, in that it is *wholes* such as biotic communities and species that are considered morally important. As Aldo Leopold put it, "a thing is right when it tends to preserve the integrity, stability, and beauty of the biotic community. It is wrong when it tends otherwise" (Leopold 1995, 152). [. . .]

According to environmental ethicists, in the context of wild animals, advocates of the ethic of care and advocates of the ethic of justice are *equally* mistaken in their moral attention to individual beings. These considerations suggest that perhaps within the realm of domestic animals, it is appropriate to focus on individual animals, while outside that realm, it is appropriate to think more holistically. In fact, Callicott defends a version of this view in his most recent account of the relationship between animal liberation and environmental ethics (Callicott 1995). He develops an account of "nested communities" that reflect our degree of relationship to various beings and thereby provide the basis for our moral obligations. According to Callicott, we have the greatest moral obligations to those closest to us—to our immediate family—and gradually lesser obligations to those in our more distant communities—such as to neighbors, to citizens, to human beings in general, and to animals in general. One of the ways this account differs from traditional hierarchies which place nonhuman animals last in our moral consideration is by incorporating Mary Midgley's argument that domestic animals are and have always been members of one of our more intimate communities, the "mixed community" (Midgley 1995). For Callicott, humans' close relationships with domestic animals means that domestic animals have a corresponding moral priority.

I will have something to say about Callicott's position on domestic animals shortly, but first I will challenge the claim that, in relation to wild animals at least, humans are morally bound only by holistic concerns about the health of the ecosystem. This would mean that in relation to members of well-populated species, there would be no moral problem with, say, torturing an animal for the fun of it. Environmentalists do not make a point of this, and, in fact, when the environmentalist Holmes Rolston defends meat eating, he says that "when eating [humans] ought to minimize animal suffering" (Rolston 1993, 140). Such a claim is uncontroversial enough that we might not notice that he doesn't say *why* humans ought to minimize animal suffering. In fact, he *can't* provide a reason for this claim within a system that only takes holistic concerns into account. That is, a "moral" approach that focuses *exclusively* on holistic concerns such that suffering becomes morally irrelevant violates some of our most basic moral convictions. [. . .] Since Callicott's environmental ethic for human-wild animal relations is too holistic to allow for some of our basic moral convictions, it might seem to follow that human-wild animal relations should be understood in terms of the individualism of the ethic of justice. That is, it might be argued that while we share with wild animals a *biotic* community, we do not share with them a *moral* community of a kind that would be necessary to ground the claim that we have positive responsibilities to them. While environmental critics of justice ethics point out the absurdity of extending the right to life to wild animals, an ethic of justice need not affirm that wild animals have a right to life. Instead, it can affirm that our primary obligation to wild animals is *noninterference*.

While there is something right about this view, I want to show that it also oversimplifies and distorts matters in important ways. Difficulties with this view are revealed by recent discussions among feminist ethicists of the analogous view that the "private sphere" of family and friends ought to be governed by the ethic of care, while the "public sphere" of government and business ought to be governed by the ethic of justice. According to this view, the partialist ethic of care should be confined to the private sphere, and the rights-oriented ethic of justice should be confined to the public sphere. One reason to be wary of this view is that the public/private dichotomy is strongly gender-coded—the private sphere is regarded as feminine and the public sphere as masculine—and serves to reinforce gender divisions. Moreover, the boundary between public and private spheres is itself at issue, as the private and public sphere are not as different from one another as is commonly assumed. For instance, power relations, which are usually considered the distinguishing feature of the political, are also present in personal relations, as evidenced by widespread domestic violence. Also, dependence and vulnerability, which are usually considered distinctive of personal relations, are also present in public relations. Such overlapping features suggest that the private sphere should be not only caring but just, and that the public sphere should be not only just but caring. In fact, when the two ethics are dichotomized, they tend to take on distorted and damaging forms. For instance, an ethic of care which does not value autonomy tends to result in forms of "caring" which are oppressive to either the caregiver or the recipient of care. Likewise, an ethic of justice which does not value caring tends to result in forms of "justice" that are indifferent to individual suffering (Clement 1996).

These conclusions have clear implications for the present discussion. First, just as the public/private dichotomy is gender-coded, so too is the wild/domestic animal dichotomy. Karen Davis has shown that the wild/domestic animal dichotomy is analogous to the public/private dichotomy, such that these dichotomies serve in similar ways to justify the devaluation of women and domestic animals. [. . .] It might be thought that Callicott does not fit this model because his view of nested communities claims to give domestic animals a higher moral priority than wild animals. However, he clearly does not regard domestic animals with the respect he has for wild animals. Above all, Callicott prizes the natural and the wild, and his deepest moral conviction seems to be that humans ought to overcome their alienation from nature and become more wild.

This leads to a second difficulty revealed by the feminist discussion of the public/private dichotomy. Like that dichotomy, the distinction between domestic and wild animals is not as clear as it is often made out to be. [. . .]

If wild and domestic animals are not completely different, this suggests that our moral stances toward them should not be completely separate, and that when they are, they will tend to be distorted. We can see that this is the case in Callicott's discussion of our obligations toward domestic animals. With his discussion of the mixed community and the trust established between humans and domestic animals, Callicott defends something like an ethic of care toward domestic animals. Yet this ethic is consistent with raising farm animals to kill and eat them, on the grounds that, as a result of selective breeding, farm animals are nonautonomous beings who exist only for this purpose. To the extent that this claim is true, the introduction of justice considerations is important because it reveals that this is a distorted version of the ethic of care. Just as there is a moral problem with caring for persons in a way that undermines their autonomy, there is a moral problem with caring for animals in a way that undermines their autonomy (to whatever extent they can be autonomous). In this way the ethic of justice and its emphasis on autonomy plays an important role in evaluating the ethic of care toward domestic animals.

Just as the ethic of justice has a role to play in an ethic of care toward domestic animals, the ethic of care should play a role in an ethic of justice toward wild animals. First, even if an ethic of justice does not affirm that wild animals have a right to life, there are clearly problems with the individualism of the ethic of justice in the context of wild animals. For instance, for such an ethic, moral claims are based exclusively on characteristics of individual beings, such that environmental concerns about the stability and integrity of the biotic community become morally irrelevant. For instance, an individual member of a well-populated or even overpopulated species is no less valuable than an individual member of an endangered species, or even the *last* members of an endangered species. Taken to this extreme, such individualism seems to threaten the environmental considerations that are essential to the continuance of the individual lives protected. Thus, like the extreme holism of environmental ethics, the extreme individualism of the ethic of justice is morally problematic.

While environmental holists and individualist justice theorists debate whether individuals or wholes should be prioritized, the ethic of care reveals a third possibility. The ethic of care is individualistic in one sense: its moral attention is to *individuals* in virtue of their particular needs. However, it is holistic in another sense: it understands the basic reality to be relationships *between* individuals rather than individuals with their own separate characteristics. Thus, relationships, rather than individuals' characteristics, define the moral realm, but the particularities of individuals dictate the appropriate moral response.

One way in which this middle ground between holism and individualism affects an ethic of justice toward wild animals is the following. In general, we ought to adopt an ethic of noninterference with regard to wild animals because we are unaware of the negative effects our attempts to help animals might have on the natural environment. However, to understand our relationship with wild animals *exclusively* in terms of noninterference suggests that humans are *unnatural* beings who should not in any way be involved in the natural world. The ethic of care helps us avoid this moral distortion by understanding human moral responsiveness to individual animals as arising from the relationship between humans and nonhumans, namely our shared participation in nature. Consider a situation in which an individual encounters a wild animal who is suffering. Should one refuse to alleviate the animal's suffering on the grounds that doing so would be interfering with natural processes that we cannot understand? To do so, I think, would be contrary to one of our most basic moral convictions. This is not to claim that there ought to be public policy devoted to the alleviation of wild animal's suffering, only that when an *individual* human being is confronted by the suffering of an *individual* animal, it would be morally unacceptable to say that we have a moral obligation *not* to relieve that suffering.

[. . .]

There are good reasons to believe that the sympathy we feel toward a suffering animal is at least as natural as, or in fact *more natural than* the hunting "instinct" championed by environmentalists (Luke 1995, 309). For instance, children's sympathies for animals often lead them to refuse to eat meat when they learn that it comes from slaughtered animals, at least until they are given "good" reasons not to act on these sympathies. More generally, the naturalness of our sympathies for animals is supported by the fact that elaborate social mechanisms are necessary to distance us from or to deny the reality of the animal suffering we cause, even, significantly, the suffering that hunting causes (Luke 1995).

Animal welfare advocates who operate from an exclusively justice approach share environmentalists' distrust of our sympathies for animals. However, contrary to Callicott's view that we need to abandon our sympathies and become more "natural," Singer and Regan in effect seek to "tame" us through appeals to reason. Again, the ethic of care reveals a third possibility, in which we recognize the moral importance of our *natural* sympathies toward animals, valuing, like Callicott, participation in nature, but disagreeing with Callicott's account of what is natural and what is artificial. As Luke puts it, instead of "taming ourselves," this involves "going feral" (Luke 1995). I have suggested that, in general, our moral obligations toward wild animals can be understood in terms of noninterference. However, such an approach can easily lead to the morally distorted view that we ought not be involved in nature at all, or that we are unnatural beings, and the ethic of care is necessary as a check against such a distortion. In this essay I have considered a problem raised by the suggestion that the ethic of care, rather than the ethic of justice, is the appropriate ethic for our interactions with nonhuman animals. The problem is that this suggestion seems to make more sense for domestic than for wild animals, and that in fact, for the most part, the ethic of justice *does* seem to make sense for wild animals. That is, the ethic of care seems to "fit" our relations to domestic animals, while the ethic of justice seems to "fit" our relations with wild animals. However, I have shown that these "fits" are only approximate, and that to develop a moral approach to both domestic and wild animals that does justice to our most basic moral convictions, we need to understand the two ethics not dichotomously, but as working together. This means that while the ethic of care will not work as the exclusive or predominant moral approach to wild animals, a satisfactory moral approach to wild animals must include the ethic of care.

Bibliography

Callicott, J. Baird. 1992. Animal Liberation: A Triangular Affair. In *The Animal Rights/Environmental Ethics Debate: The Environmental Perspective*, ed. Eugene C. Hargrove, 37–69. Albany: State University of New York Press.

Callicott, J. Baird. 1995. Animal Liberation and Environment Ethics: Back Together Again. In *Earth Ethics*, ed. James P. Sterba, 190–198. Englewood Cliffs, NJ: Prentice Hall.

Clement, Grace. 1996. *Care, Autonomy, and Justice: Feminism and the Ethic of Care*. Boulder: Westview.

Donovan, Josephine and Carol J. Adams eds. 1996. *Beyond Animal Rights: A Feminist Caring Ethic for the Treatment of Animals*. New York: Continuum.

Leopold, Aldo. 1995. The Land Ethic; Conservation as a Moral Issue, Thinking Like a Mountain. In *Earth Ethics*, ed. James P. Sterba, 147–156. Englewood Cliffs, NJ: Prentice Hall.

Luke, Brian. 1995. Taming Ourselves or Going Feral? Toward a Nonpatriarchal Metaethic of Animal Liberation. In *Animals and Women: Feminist Theoretical Explorations*, ed. Carol J. Adams and Josephine Donovan, 290–319. Durham: Duke University Press.

Luke, Brian. 1996. Justice, Caring, and Animal Liberation. In *Beyond Animal Rights: A Feminist Caring Ethic for the Treatment of Animals*, ed. Josephine Donovan and Carol J. Adams, 77–102. New York: Continuum.

Midgley, Mary. 1995. The Mixed Community. In *Earth Ethics*, ed. James P. Sterba, 80–90. Englewood Cliffs, NJ: Prentice Hall.

Rolston, Holmes III. 1993. Challenges in Environmental Ethics. In *Environmental Philosophy: From Animal Rights to Radical Ecology*, ed. Michael Zimmerman and J. B. Callicott, 135–157. Englewood Cliffs, NJ: Prentice Hall.

Sagoff, Mark. 1993. Animal Liberation, Environmental Ethics: Bad Marriage, Quick Divorce. In *Environmental Philosophy: From Animal Rights to Radical Ecology*, ed. Michael Zimmerman and J. B. Callicott, 84–94. Englewood Cliffs, NJ: Prentice Hall.

Shapiro, Kenneth. 1996. The Caring Sleuth: Portrait of an Animal Rights Activist. In *Beyond Animal Rights: A Feminist Caring Ethic for the Treatment of Animals*, ed. Josephine Donovan and Carol J. Adams, 126–146. New York: Continuum.

Part Eight

Zoos and Aquariums

Introduction to Part Eight

In this part, the authors address some of the important moral issues associated with the long history of use of animals for purposes of human entertainment. In particular, there is a focus on zoos and marine mammal aquaria, with references to a few others.

Lori Marino points out that capture, handling, and confinement produce changes in stress hormone levels similar to that experienced by humans. She gives numerous examples, noting that orcas in particular are seriously affected. Marc Scheff and Kristin Vehrs address the issue of simply freeing all elephants and orcas in captivity.

Dale Jamieson assesses both the strengths and weaknesses of zoos, and makes the argument that the overall balance is tipped against zoos. Michael Hutchins et al. note that the entertainment value of zoos for the public is just one part of a larger set of values, including the scientific research conducted by zoos to gain greater knowledge of nature that is essential to wildlife conservation, particularly to endangered species management. Zoo animals are important as ambassadors for their species, securing public support for wildlife and their habitats. Zoos also help educate the public about wildlife and help generate greater public interest in and support for wildlife conservation. Chris Wemmer goes on to assess the responsibilities and directions of zoos and aquariums in light of the global diversity crisis and calls for a greater emphasis among zoo professionals on science and conservation efforts.

Ben A. Minteer and James P. Collins address the ethical concerns about human intervention in populations and ecosystems, including the proper role of zoos and aquariums as centers for animal research and conservation. They advocate that zoos and aquariums should be less the final stops of endangered/threatened species and become more full partners in integrated conservation strategies across captive, wild, and semi-wild contexts. This also may reduce traditional roles such as the display of exotic animals for public entertainment.

Further Reading

Bostock, Stephen St. C. (1993) *Zoos and Animal Rights: The Ethics of Keeping Animals*, London: Routledge.

"Conference on 'Cetacean rights: Fostering moral and legal change,' Providing the collective rationale for the declaration issued at the end of the meeting." 2011. *Journal of International Wildlife Law & Policy*. 14:78–80. www.cetaceanrights.org.

Gruen, Lori. (2014) *The ethics of captivity*, New York: Oxford University Press, 276 pp.

Hancocks, D. (2001) *A Different Nature: The Paradoxical World of Zoos and Their Uncertain Future*, Berkeley: University of California Press.

Hargrove, John, and Howard Chua-Eoan. (2015) *Beneath the surface: SeaWorld, and the truth beyond blackfish*, New York: Palgrave MacMillan Trade (St. Martin's Press LLC), 264 pp.

Hosey, G. R. (2000) "Zoo animals and their human audiences: What is the visitor effect?" *Animal Welfare* 9: 343–357.

Hutchins, M, B. Smith, R. Fulk, L. Perkins, G. Reinartz, and D. Wharton. (2001) Rights or welfare: A response to the Great Ape Project. Pp. 329–366, in *Great Apes and Humans: Ethics of Coexistence*, B.B. Beck, T. Stoinski, M. Hutchins, T.L. Maple, B. Norton, A. Rowan, E.F. Stevens, and A. Arluke (eds). Washington, DC: Smithsonian Institution Press.

Lin, Doris. (2014) Arguments for and against zoos. http://animalrights.about.com/od/animalsinentertainment/a/Arguments-For-And-Against-Zoos.htm

Marino, Lori. (2014) Cetacean captivity. Pp. 22–37, in *The Ethics of Captivity*, Lori Gruen (ed). New York, NY: Oxford University Press.

Masci, David. (2000) "Zoos in the 21st century." *CQ Researcher, CQ on the Web*. www.cq.com. 28 April 2000, pp. 355–364.

Midgley, Mary. (1999) Should we let them go? Chapter 11. Pp. 152–163, in *Attitudes to Animals: Views in Animal Welfare*, F. L. Dolins (ed.). Cambridge, UK: Cambridge University Press.

Norton, B. G., M. Hutchins, E. F. Stevens, and T. L. Maple (eds.). (1995) *Ethics of the Ark: Zoos, Animal Welfare and Wildlife Conservation*, Washington DC: Smithsonian Institution Press.

Ross, Stephen R. (2014) Captive chimpanzees. Pp. 57–76, in *The ethics of captivity*, Lori Gruen (ed.). New York, NY: Oxford University Press.

Smith, B., and M. Hutchins. (2000). "The value of captive breeding programmes to field conservation: Elephants as an example. *Pachyderm* 28: 101–109.

Stoinski, Tara S., Jacqueline Ogden, Kenneth C. Gold, and Terry L. Maple. (2001) "Captive apes and zoo education." Chapter 5. Pp. 113–132, in *Great Apes and Humans: The Ethics of Coexistence*, B. B. Beck, T. S. Stoinski, M. Hutchins, T. L. Maple, B. Norton, A. Rowan, E. F. Stevens, and A. Arluke (eds.). Washington, DC, Smithsonian Institution Press.

Study Questions

1. In light of Marino's descriptions, what would be your response to a proposal to prohibit any future retention of marine mammals in captivity? How does the exchange between Scheff and Vehrs affect your perspective? Give your reasoning and, where possible, examples to support your position.

   More broadly, how does the work of Hutchins et al. influence your perception of this issue for zoos and aquariums generally? To what degree, if any, do the arguments of Jamieson influence this issue?

2. Wemmer believes that zoo professionals, in contrast to continuing focusing a major emphasis on public recreation and education, should place greater emphasis on supporting science and conservation efforts. Compare and contrast Wemmer's position with that developed by Minteer and Collins. Justify your position.

65 Cetacean Captivity

Lori Marino

Lori Marino notes that cetaceans have a human-like awareness and are among the most culturally sophisticated animals on earth. She points out that capture, handling, and confinement produce changes in stress hormone levels similar to that experienced by humans. She gives numerous examples, noting that orcas in particular are seriously affected. She identifies recent proposals advocating for the rights of cetaceans to life, liberty, and well-being.

Who Are Cetaceans?

Cetaceans (dolphins and whales) are a diverse order of aquatic marine mammals comprising two modern suborders, the Odontoceti (toothed whales, dolphins, and porpoises) and the Mysticeti (the large rorqual and baleen whales). Cetaceans have been subjects of fascination and adulation by humans since ancient times (Marino 2007), likely because of their combination of physical beauty and elegance in a mysterious aquatic environment and their obvious intelligence, sociality, and curiosity. Indeed, many dolphins and whales have the second highest encephalization level (a measure of relative brain size) next to modern humans and significantly above even our closest primate relatives, the great apes (Marino 1998). Their cognitive and communicative abilities are prodigious (see Marino et al. 2008 for a review), and bottlenose dolphins are one of the few species to demonstrate human-like levels of self-awareness (Reiss and Marino 2001). We now know as well that cetaceans are among the most culturally sophisticated beings on the planet (Rendell and Whitehead 2001; Whitehead 2011).

With all that said, our relationship to cetaceans has been, at best, fraught with inconsistencies. Captivity represents one of the ways that humans have objectified and exploited cetaceans in the name of adulation. Humans have at various times, and still do today, both venerated and slaughtered cetaceans. White (2007) suggests that cetaceans are subject to such a wide range of treatments because they, more than any other animal, are the most similar and dissimilar to us at the same time. According to White, cetacean intelligence, self-awareness, emotionality, and social complexity mean that they, like us, experience life as persons. But they look and move very differently, live in an exotic milieu, lack clear facial expressions, communicate in unfamiliar modalities, and always seem to be smiling (although this is just an anatomical illusion). These differences make it challenging for humans to recognize the similarities to us and their ability to suffer like us, and, thus, make it easier to objectify and exploit them (Marino 2013).

The history of cetacean captivity is the history of our simultaneous veneration and exploitation of cetaceans. The exploitation and abuses of cetaceans in captivity are, arguably, worse today for many cetaceans than ever before. Here is how it started.

History of Cetacean Captivity

Despite a long historical relationship with dolphins and other cetaceans (Aristotle is said to have observed and written on their behavior), one of the first documented cases of cetacean captivity and display derives from the 1860s, when circus mogul P. T. Barnum paid to have several beluga whales (*Delphinapterus leucas*) captured from the St. Lawrence River. They were shipped by train in boxes of seaweed and housed in Barnum's American Museum in small enclosures, where most of them died shortly afterwards (Mountain 2012). By the late 1870s, belugas and dolphins were being caught and supplied to aquariums and zoological gardens throughout the eastern United States, Europe, and Asia, where they were trained to perform (Rose 2009). The mortality rate during capture and confinement in these facilities was so high and the survival durations so short that it created a habitual revolving door of replacement by capture from the wild. Collectors expected the animals to die frequently, and they simply went about replacing their "stock" on a continual basis. Barnum himself started with two whales, and by the time his museum burned down in 1985, the ninth captive whale had died (New York Tribune 1861).

Another milestone in the history of cetacean captivity in the United States came in 1938 when a Hollywood film company, Marine Studios, built a seawater tank in Florida in which to film dolphins for movies. The place eventually became Marineland of Florida in the 1970s, the oldest operating cetacean park in the United States. The program's success led to the proliferation of dolphinariums across the world during the 1940s and 1950s, including the Miami Seaquarium and the first inland facility, Seven Seas Panorama in Chicago (Frontline 1997). By this time, the public was generally accustomed to the idea of keeping dolphins and whales captive for amusement, and these early facilities were not afraid to promote this idea, marketing themselves as places of entertainment and distraction. But at the same time, the public was also becoming aware of the prodigious abilities and intelligence of dolphins.

The major impetus for cetacean captivity and popularity came in the early to mid 1960s with the movie and TV series *Flipper*, about a friendly dolphin who saved humans from danger through his extraordinary cunning and anthropomorphic motivations. The show launched a dolphin frenzy with new dolphin facilities, paraphernalia, and products bursting forth globally. But there were no regulations for the welfare of the captive dolphins.

When *Flipper* ended in 1968 and the production was shut down, another pivotal point was reached when one of the dolphins' trainers, Ric O'Barry, reported that after the show was over and one of the dolphins, Kathy, was relegated to a small pool in the back of the studio, she became depressed and took her own life by holding her breath (O'Barry and Coulbourn 2000). That event changed O'Barry forever and launched his career as a tireless and unwithering activist for cetacean protection and freedom from captivity. His conversion mirrored the beginnings of public opinion against cetacean captivity, as the death toll at many hastily constructed facilities rose. Concurrently, the international campaign against whaling was mounting, and people were developing ethical and philosophical arguments against not only hunting whales and other marine mammals but also keeping them in captivity.

With growing public concern, several regulations were put into place to address cetacean welfare and protection. The Animal Welfare Act (AWA), which originated in 1964, provides for inspection of marine parks and other facilities holding captive marine mammals by government-employed veterinarians. But the AWA has been consistently criticized because actual inspections of parks happen infrequently and with little rigor.

The period of 1962–1970 saw some of the most egregious abuses of marine mammals as theme parks and aquaria scrambled to obtain one of the largest dolphins, the orca (*Orcinus orca*), or killer whale, for shows. During this period, orca captures off British Columbia, Washington State, and California were completely unregulated. Capture is a "violent affair" (Rose 2009), and many orcas died during capture, suffocating in nets and drowning from immobilization. In August 1970, Ted Griffin and Don Goldsberry captured 80 orcas from the Washington southern resident population, leading to a devastating decline from which the orca population is still recovering. Four juveniles were accidentally killed. Public reports of these atrocities led to residents pushing for legislation to ban or control orca capture, and in 1971 Washington State passed regulating laws (Frontline 1997).

Among the orcas that were captured from the southern resident population in 1970 was a very young female named Tokitae (Lolita), who was transferred to the Miami Seaquarium, where she was housed with another orca, Hugo, captured earlier from the same pod until his death in 1980. Lolita, who is now over 43 years old, has remained the only orca in her tiny tank to this day. She is the focus of intense animal advocacy efforts to rehabilitate and release her back into the same area she was captured from, where her pod, including her mother, lives to this day.

In 1972, more specific legislation, the Marine Mammal Protection Act (MMPA), was passed, forcing a number of the very worst of the dolphinariums to close. The MMPA, overseen by the National Marine Fisheries Service (NMFS), prohibits the taking of any marine mammals from US waters or by US citizens in international waters except by special permit. Permits are issued for the purposes of scientific work, public display, or strandings or accidental captures by fishermen (Marine Mammal Protection Act 1972). The grave results of the Washington orca captures eventually led to a total ban on capturing orcas from that state in 1976. At the same time, partly as a result of the "Save the Whales" campaign in the mid to late 1970s, the International Whaling Commission (IWC) banned whaling in international waters, but, in actual practice, it excluded dolphins and smaller cetaceans. There were also many legal loopholes for whaling nations. The MMPA provided a patina of protection for marine mammals and has been a positive force in many ways, but exceptions to the regulations and little oversight allowed for the marine theme park industry to operate essentially unfettered and without accountability.

Seeing the writing on the wall and the "green-leaning" zeitgeist of the day, marine mammal theme parks rebranded themselves as centers of education, science, and conservation. But while the public message had changed, the marine parks were still operating in a covert mindset that had the commercial interests of their facilities as the priority. The message seemed new and more ethically focused, but it was a superficial makeover at best.

Through the 1980s and early 1990s, marine parks still took dolphins and whales from the wild for their facilities but drew increasing public ire for doing so. In 1989, the NMFS called for a voluntary moratorium on the capture of bottle-nose dolphins (*Tursiops truncatus*) in the Gulf of Mexico and along the Atlantic coast primarily due to the uncertainty about how captures would affect wild populations (Rose, Parsons, and Farinato 2009). In 1990, SeaWorld contracted a team of orca hunters to capture three to six juvenile killer whales from Puget Sound. Marine mammal activists and the state attorney general at the time were able to ban transportation of captive whales in the State [of Washington], and SeaWorld withdrew. Shortly thereafter, following a media firestorm, British Columbia banned orca captures (Frontline 1997). The last capture of a cetacean from US waters was in 1993, when the Shedd Aquarium took three Pacific white-sided dolphins (*Lagenorhynchus obliquidens*) from the coast of California for display. The public outcry put an end to this activity in the United States once and for all.

Since the moratorium, marine parks have focused on captive breeding to maintain their populations for display. However, the infant mortality rate for captive cetaceans is generally too high to be self-sustaining (Rose 2004). This has led many captive facilities to argue for a return to wild captures. One particular example is the recent request to NMFS by the Georgia Aquarium to import 18 wild-caught belugas from Russian seas. The captive beluga population is dwindling because these animals do not breed or survive well in captivity. Therefore, under the guise of education and conservation, the Georgia Aquarium, SeaWorld, and, ironically, the Shedd Aquarium are all driving an effort to bring these whales, who are already caught, into their facilities for public display. The request has been met with vociferous opposition from many marine mammal scientists, cetacean advocates, and much of the general public. If approved, this request would represent a full-circle return to outdated times when P. T. Barnum captured, exhibited, and caused the death of so many beluga whales.

Current Captive Conditions

At least 19 cetacean species are currently held in captivity around the world; the most commonly held are orcas, beluga whales, bottlenose dolphins, and Pacific white-sided dolphins. The total number of captive bottlenose dolphins around the world is about 800, with the majority at popular tourist attractions in the United States, Mexico, and the Caribbean (Born Free Foundation n.d.). And because captive numbers are not sustainable, many facilities around the world regularly take individuals from the wild.

The ways in which dolphins and whales in captivity are exploited have expanded to increasingly more extravagant circus-like shows to swim-with-dolphin (SWD) programs to the burgeoning industry of dolphin-assisted therapy (DAT), in which dolphins are marketed as "therapeutic agents." Unlike these highly lucrative and growing commercial avenues, the use of captive cetaceans for scientific research has declined precipitously because of the untimely death of so many of the captive dolphins who were used in research throughout the 1980s to the early 2000s (see below). Moreover, the US Navy maintains several cetaceans and other marine mammals to conduct invasive research on them and deploy them in dangerous military situations. But not much is disclosed about these secretive projects.

Given that the overwhelming majority of dolphins and whales around the world are held captive for entertainment and recreation, I will focus here on the commercial venues: aquarium and theme park displays and shows, SWD programs, and DAT. Often these are found in the same facility and are offered as adjunct programs.

The public fascination with dolphins and whales continues to fuel the enthusiasm for visiting aquariums and theme parks. In the United States alone, more than 50 million people visit captive facilities every year (Kestin 2004a). Few animals have the revenue-earning potential of dolphins and whales (Kestin 2004b). Shows have become increasingly commercialized, involving increasingly risky in-water contact between the animals and trainer/performers. As a result, there have been many injuries of trainers during these shows and rehearsals and several well-publicized deaths of both trainers and animals. One particularly pivotal incident occurred when a male orca, Tilikum, killed his trainer, Dawn Brancheau, at SeaWorld Orlando in 2010. Tilikum has been involved in the deaths of three humans over the years. Male orcas normally stay with their mother for a lifetime, but Tilikum was taken from his family group in the wild when he was only three years old (Kirby 2012; Zimmerman 2010) and this maternal deprivation contributed to years of trauma and behavioral abnormalities. The deaths that Tilikum caused, as well as a number of other incidents at marine parks with orcas, have led to much public criticism of keeping orcas in captivity. Unfortunately, Tilikum and the orcas remain in confinement, and marine parks like SeaWorld are fighting legally to maintain in-water work with them. Trainer lives continue to be put at considerable risk when working in the water with orcas, a species that has never injured a human in the wild but is responsible for multiple injuries and deaths in captivity.

It is apparently no longer satisfying to marine park visitors to simply watch dolphins and whales perform when they can get up close and personal with them in the water. Swim-with-dolphin (SWD) programs in captivity, where paying park customers interact and swim with dolphins in their tanks, emerged in the 1980s but have become a ubiquitous offering on the marine theme park circuit. SWD programs are enormously popular as the parks compete for customers. In 1990 there were only four SWD programs in the United States, but now there are as many as 18 facilities offering dolphin "encounter" programs of one kind or another (Stewart and Marino 2009).

Admission to these programs can range from $200 above general park admission fees to even $500 for "trainer of the day" sessions. The closer the visitors are allowed to get to the animals, the higher the ticket price. Often these SWD attractions are touted as educational. Captive facilities claim that visitors learn about the behavior and protection of these animals during these activities and that this knowledge leads to an increase in conservation attitudes. But most of these facilities focus exclusively on husbandry and captive activities to the exclusion of information about the natural lives of dolphins and whales. And there is no evidence to support the claim that dolphin and whale shows or SWD attractions lead to greater or lasting knowledge about the animals or that visitors become more conservation-minded as a result (Marino et al. 2010; Stewart and Marino 2009). In addition, SWD programs can be dangerous for both humans and dolphins. There are numerous reports of swimmers being seriously injured by frustrated and aggressive dolphins in these programs.

And exposure to humans can also increase susceptibility of dolphins to pathogens (Geraci and Ridgway 1991; Mazet, Hunt, and Ziccardi 2004).

Dolphin-assisted therapy (DAT) is actually just a type of SWD disguised as legitimate animal-assisted therapy in which dolphins are marketed as therapeutic agents for a variety of psychological and physical illnesses (Brakes and Williamson 2007). It began in the 1970s by Betsy Smith, who later denounced it publicly as exploitive. Children with autism and their needful parents are a strongly targeted population (Marino and Lilienfeld 2007a). Despite the many claims of this industry, there is no existing evidence that DAT has any therapeutic value (Humphries 2003; Marino and Lilienfeld 1998, 2007b). Actual therapy is treatment for a specific condition and, importantly, is verifiable by outcomes (improvement in some measure of the condition). No such criteria are applicable to DAT and, thus, there is no evidence that it meets even the minimal criteria for therapy.

DAT typically involves several sessions either swimming or interacting with captive dolphins often along with more conventional therapeutic tasks, such as puzzles and motor activities. The standard price of DAT, whose practitioners are not required by law to receive special training or certification, is exorbitant, reaching into the thousands of dollars. Thus, DAT has become a highly lucrative business with facilities all over the world, including the United States. DAT is not regulated by any health and safety standards for either humans or dolphins. Yet there are many risks to both humans and dolphins during DAT that include, but are not limited to, injury, disease transmission, and the potential loss of opportunities for real treatment (Marino 2011). Risks to swimmers and dolphins in DAT are the same for any SWD program. Moreover, the risks to participants in DAT are emotional. Often desperate parents of sick children are led to believe they will receive some kind of lasting improvement from DAT. When they return home to the same problems as before, the disappointment can be devastating, not to mention the financial cost and opportunity loss to engage more mainstream and efficacious treatments.

Effects of Captivity on Cetaceans

Current captive conditions for cetaceans are certainly better than they were in Barnum's day, but despite the higher quality food, improved veterinary care, and advanced water filtration systems, the basic experience of captivity is the same for cetaceans today as it always was. Captivity for both wild-caught and captive-born cetaceans is devastating on several levels. And it is critically important to recognize that although some cetaceans fare better than others, *no cetaceans thrive in captivity*. The effects go beyond the serious welfare problems that plague individual animals when confined in tanks. And these larger effects are more insidious. One significant effect of keeping cetaceans in captivity is that it promotes perceptions of cetaceans that lead to further exploitation and abuse. There is a close ongoing connection between the global marine mammal display industry and dolphin slaughters such as those in Taiji, Japan (Batt 2013). In addition, the effects of removal of even small numbers of animals from a wild population for display can be more devastating than anticipated for the group (Lusseau 2007) because individuals within the group have differentiated social roles and the removal of key socially connected individuals could unravel the entire social network.

The scientific evidence for the damaging effects of captivity on individual dolphin and whale physical and psychological health is overwhelming. Captive cetaceans are considerably challenged by the constraints of their artificial enclosures (Couquiaud 2005). Confinement impacts not only physical freedom but social relationships, degrades autonomy through the imposition of enforced schedules of activity and behavior, causes boredom, induces frustration, and inhibits incentives and abilities to carry out natural behaviors such as hunting and traveling.

There is abundant evidence for stress, disease, and increased mortality in captive cetaceans as an inevitable outcome of confinement, loss of control, and deprivation in captive situations (Marino and Frohoff 2011). Captive cetaceans display physiological and behavioral abnormalities indicative of psychological distress and emotional disturbance. These include stereotypies, for example, repetitious maladaptive behaviors such as head-bobbing and pacing (Fowler 1978; Greenwood 1977), unresponsiveness, excessive submissiveness, hyper-sexual behavior (towards humans or other dolphins), self-inflicted physical trauma and mutilation (Sweeney 1988), stress-induced vomiting (Sweeney 1990), and excessive aggressiveness towards other dolphins and humans as has been seen in Tilikum and others (Stewart and Marino 2009).

The drivers of stress for captive dolphins and whales derive from every aspect of their existence, including capture and transportation from one facility to the next. The US Marine Mammal Inventory Report (2010) lists numerous stress-related disorders, such as ulcerative gastritis, perforating ulcer, cardiogenic shock, and psychogenic shock as "cause of death" in captive cetaceans, confirming that stress is a critical issue for captive marine mammals. Stress derives from many aspects of captivity, not the least of which is the social deprivation associated with loss of one's natal group or transfer from one facility to another, housing with artificially constructed groups of dolphins, the taking of dependent juveniles from their mothers at early ages for transfer from one facility to the next, the lack of space needed for successful conflict-resolution, loss of autonomy, and boredom.

Capture, handling, and confinement produce a demonstrable change in stress hormone levels similar to changes occurring during increased stress in humans (St. Aubin and Geraci 1988). And it is well established that chronic stress leads to immunosuppression and susceptibility to disease in marine mammals (Noda et al. 2007; Spoon and Romano 2011; St. Aubin and Geraci 1988). The result is high mortality rates for both captive-born and wild-caught cetaceans.

For orcas in particular, captivity is catastrophic, as evidenced by their abnormal aggression towards humans and other whales and their very high mortality rates in captivity compared with their natural habitat. A recent review of orca health in captivity substantiates the many health risks by reporting two cases of deaths from mosquito-borne illnesses (St. Louis encephalitis and West Nile) in captive orcas. Unlike their wild counterparts, who are rarely stationary and spend a significant amount of time under water, captive orcas are often confined in pools too shallow for their body length and typically spend hours every day floating motionless on the surface, leaving them vulnerable to biting mosquitoes and, therefore, a variety of blood-borne illnesses (Jett and Ventre 2012). Moreover, most captive orcas are not provided shade from ultraviolet radiation and are often subject to its immunosuppressing effects (Jett and Ventre 2012)

[. . .]

Most captive orcas do not survive past the age of 20 years (Williams 2001). The natural average life span for male and female orcas is 29.2 and 50.2 years, respectively, with a maximum longevity of 60 and 90 years respectively (Ford 2009; Ford, Ellis, and Balcomb 1994; Olesiuk, Bigg, and Ellis 1990; Wells and Scott 1990). DeMaster and Drevenak (1988) estimated the annual mortality rate for captive orcas at seven percent, and two additional studies by Small and DeMaster (1995) and Woodley, Hannah, and Lavigne (1997) both estimated captive annual mortality rates at 6.2 percent (excluding calves) considerably higher than the 2.3 percent annual mortality rate figure for wild populations (DeMaster and Drevenak 1988).

Beluga whales seem to fare no better than orcas. Wild beluga whales may live as long as 50 to 60 years (Stewart et al. 2006), but captive beluga whales routinely die before the age of 30. Likewise, mortality rates for belugas in captivity are higher than in the wild (DeMaster and Drevenak 1988; Small and DeMaster 1995; Woodley et al. 1997). And, as mentioned above, the fact that the dwindling captive population has prompted some theme parks to capture and try to import more of them is evidence of the low survivorship and difficult breeding conditions for belugas in captivity.

Bottlenose dolphins do somewhat better in captivity than orcas and beluga whales but still suffer from stress-related diseases brought about by confinement and loss of autonomy. Only recently have survivorship statistics in captivity (6.4 percent) reached a level not statistically significantly different from that thought to exist in the wild (3.9 percent) (DeMaster and Drevenak 1988; Duffield and Wells 1991; Olesiuk, Bigg, and Ellis 1990; Small and DeMaster 1995). The best estimate of average and maximum life span for captive and wild bottlenose dolphins is about

25 and 45 years, respectively (Small and DeMaster 1995). But there are biases in these data that make it doubtful that bottlenose dolphins live as long in captivity as in the wild. Survivorship statistics from captive facilities often exclude periods of sharply increased mortality—those associated with capture and transfer. Bottlenose dolphins face a sixfold increase in risk of mortality immediately after capture from the wild and immediately after every transfer between facilities (Small and DeMaster 1995). According to Small and DeMaster (1995) the first 60 days of captivity should not be taken into account when calculating survival rates for captured individuals, since the mortality during this time is so high. Further, remote locations and many non-Western or developing countries were not included in these studies; hence it is likely that the worst of these facilities were omitted from these data. These biases can easily lead to artificially inflated survivorship data.

I personally experienced the toll captivity takes on dolphins with the life and untimely deaths of Presley and Tab, two young male dolphins housed at the New York Aquarium in Brooklyn. Presley and Tab were made famous internationally by demonstrating that they recognized themselves in a mirror in a study Diana Reiss and I conducted. The study was the first to provide definitive evidence that at least one cetacean species, bottlenose dolphins, was capable of a complex level of self-awareness indicated by mirror self-recognition (Reiss and Marino 2001). But after all the media coverage died down, the more important story, in my view, unfolded. Presley and Tab were captive born and 13 and 17 years old, respectively, when they were subjects in our study. Not long after our study, Presley and Tab were dead. Each of them was transferred to another facility and met an untimely death from two diseases related to stress and immune-system dysfunction. Presley succumbed to fungal encephalitis and Tab to gastroenteritis. Of course, they had other maladies, and all added up to a foreshortened life.

Presley and Tab are not alone in their fate. All of the dolphins who were subjects of the famed experiments by Lou Herman at Kewalo Basin, that is, Phoenix, Akeakamai, Hiapo, and Elele, died prematurely. A dolphin at another facility, Natua, who demonstrated a complex capacity for metacognition, that is, the ability to think about his own thoughts (Smith et al. 1995), was dead by the age of 18. In fact, none of these "research superstars" lived to the age of 30, with four of them dying earlier than the average, not maximum, life span for *Tursiops*. These outcomes lead inevitably to the question: If captivity involves state-of-the-art veterinary care, protection from external threats, and all the good fish one could eat, why don't these individuals live to their maximum life span? The only conclusion is that there is something inherently incompatible between cetacean well-being and captivity.

What Does the Future Hold for Cetaceans?

The future for cetaceans in captivity is precarious. On the one hand, there are increasing numbers of dolphinariums budding across the globe because the attractions these places offer are still very popular and lucrative. And as long as the public continues to make it profitable to keep dolphins and whales in captivity, it will continue. But at the same time, there are forces working in opposition to cetacean captivity. The death of Dawn Brancheau at SeaWorld in 2010 drew an outpouring of media criticism, and the public has developed a more negative attitude towards orca captivity, if not cetacean captivity in general. Moreover, the incident has resulted in legal challenges and pressures for SeaWorld from the Occupational Safety and Health Administration. David Kirby's book *Death at SeaWorld* and the documentary *Blackfish* continue to contribute greatly to the public's awareness of the problems of orca captivity and both send a disparaging and revealing message about SeaWorld and cetacean captivity in general.

[. . .]

In May 2011, the nonprofit organization Whale and Dolphin Conservation (WDC) became the first NGO to sign the Declaration of Rights for Cetaceans: Whales and Dolphins (http://www.cetacean rights.org/), a historic manifesto that lays out a list of principles promoting the right of cetaceans to life, liberty, and well-being. Currently the Nonhuman Rights Project (http://www.nonhumanrights project.org/) is working toward actual legal rights for members of species other than our own. The NhRP's mission is to change the common-law status of at least some nonhuman animals from mere "things," which lack the capacity to possess any legal right, to "persons," who possess such fundamental rights as bodily integrity and bodily liberty. The NhRP includes cetaceans on its list of potential candidates for legal personhood and will bring lawsuits to bear on this issue in the near future.

These are exciting times for cetacean advocacy and rights. Never before have concepts of rights and personhood for nonhuman animals been taken so seriously in this country. The marine mammal captivity industry is most certainly on the defensive and is losing ground. One can almost feel the tide going out on these abusive spectacles. It is a matter of time before this industry follows Barnum into the void.

References

Batt, E. 2013. "Dolphins Driven into Cove Heading for Highest Numbers in Four Years." Accessed February 1, 2013. http://digitaljournal.com/article/342232.

Born Free Foundation. n.d. "Captive Whales and Dolphins." Accessed November 18, 2013. http://www.bornfree.org.uk/campaigns/zoo-check/captive-whales-dolphins/.

Brakes P., and C. Williamson. 2007. "Dolphin Assisted Therapy: Can You Put Your Faith in DAT?" *Report for the Whale and Dolphin Conservation Society*, October. Accessed November 18, 2013. http://www.wdcs.org/submissions_bin/datreport.pdf.

Couquiaud, E. 2005. "A Survey of the Environments of Cetaceans in Human Care." *Aquatic Mammals* 31(3): 279–280.

DeMaster, D. P., and J. K. Drevenak. 1988. "Survivorship Patterns in Three Species of Captive Cetaceans." *Marine Mammal Science* 4(4): 297–311.

Duffield, D. A., and R. S. Wells. 1991. "The Combined Application of Chromosome, Protein, and Molecular Data for Investigation of Social Unit Structure and Dynamics in *Tursiops truncates*." In A. R. Hoelzel (ed.), *"Genetic Ecology of Whales and Dolphins," special issue of Reports of the International Whaling Commission* 13: 155–169.

Ford, J. K. B. 2009. "Killer Whale." In W. F. Perrin, B. Wursig, and J. G. M. Thewissen (eds.), *Encyclopedia of Marine Mammals*, 2nd ed., 650–657. Boston: Academic Press.

Ford, J. K. B., G. M. Ellis, and K. C. Balcomb. 1994. *Killer Whales: The Natural History and Genealogy of Orinus Orca in British Columbia and Washington*. Seattle: University of Washington Press; Vancouver: UBC Press.

Fowler, M. E. 1978. "A Stereotyped Behavior Pattern in Dolphins." In M. E. Fowler (ed.), *Zoo and Wild Animal Medicine*, 33–34. Philadelphia: W.B. Saunders.

Frontline. 1997. "A Whale of a Business." Accessed March 1, 2013. http://www.pbs.org/wgbh/pages/frontline/shows/whales/man/mancron.html.

Geraci, J. R., and S. H. Ridgeway. 1991. "On Disease Transmission between Cetaceans and Humans." *Marine Mammal Science* 7(2): 191–194.

Greenwood, A. G. 1977. "A Stereotyped Behavior Pattern in Dolphins." *Aquatic Mammals* 5:15–17.

Humphries, T. L. 2003. "Effectiveness of Dolphin-Assisted Therapy as a Behavioral Intervention for Young Children with Disabilities." *Bridges: Practice-Based Research Synthesis* 1:1–9.

Jett, J., and J. Ventre. 2012. "Orca Captivity (*Orcinus orca*) and Vulnerability to Mosquito-Transmitted Viruses." *Journal of Marine Animals and Their Ecology* 5(2): 9–16.

Kestin, S. 2004a. "Not a Perfect Picture: Part I of the Special Report 'Marine Attractions: Below the Surface'." *Sun-Sentinel*. Accessed June 15, 2004. http://www.sun-sentinel.com/news/sfi-dolphins-parksdec31,30.791.1694 story.

Kestin, S. 2004b. "Captive Mammals Can Net Big Profits for Exhibitors: Part III of the Special Report 'Marine Attractions: Below the Surface'." *Sun-Sentinel*. Accessed June 15, 2004. http://www.sun-sentinel.com/news/sfi-dolphins-parksdec31,30.791.1694 story.

Kirby, D. 2012. *Death at Sea World: Shamu and the Dark Side of Killer Whales in Captivity*. New York: St. Martin's Press.

Lusseau, D. 2007. "Evidence for Social Role in a Dolphin Social Network." *Evolution and Ecology* 21: 357–366.

Marino, L. 1998. "A Comparison of Encephalization between Odontocete Cetaceans and Anthropoid Primates." *Brain, Behavior, and Evolution* 51: 230–238.

Marino, L. 2007. "Dolphin Mythology." In M. Bekoff (ed.), *The Encyclopedia of Human-Animal Relationships*, 491–495. Westport, CT: Greenwood.

Marino, L. 2011. "Dolphin Assisted Therapy: From Ancient Myth to Modern Snake Oil." *Phi Kappa Phi Forum* 91(1): 4–6.

Marino, L. 2013. "Dolphins, Humans and Moral Inclusivity." In R. Corbey and A. Lanjouw (eds.), *The Politics of Species: Reshaping our Relationships with Other Animal*, 95–105. Cambridge: Cambridge University Press.

Marino, L., C. Butti, R. C. Connor, R. E. Fordyce, L. M. Herman, P. R. Hof, L. Lefebvre, D. Lusseau, B. McCowan, E. A. Nimchinsky, A. A. Pack, J. S. Reidenberg, D. Reiss, L. Rendell, M. D. Uhen, E. Van der Gucht, and H. Whitehead. 2008. "A Claim in Search of Evidence: Reply to Manger's Thermogenesis Hypothesis of Cetacean Brain Structure." *Biological Reviews of the Cambridge Philosophical Society* 83:417–440.

Marino, L., and T. Frohoff. 2011. "Towards a New Paradigm of Non-Captive Research on Cetacean Cognition." *Public Library of Science ONE* 6(9): e24121. doi:10.1371/journal.pone.0024121.

Marino, L., and S. Lilienfeld. 1998. "Dolphin-Assisted Therapy: Flawed Data, Flawed Conclusions." *Anthrozoos* 11(4): 194–199.

Marino, L., and S. Lilienfeld. 2007a. "Dolphin Assisted Therapy for Autism and Other Developmental Disorders: A Dangerous Fad." *Psychology in Intellectual and Developmental Disabilities* (*Division 33*), *American Psychological Association* 33(2): 2–3.

Marino, L., and S. Lilienfeld. 2007b. "Dolphin Assisted Therapy: More Flawed Data, More Flawed Conclusions." *Anthrozoos* 20: 239–249.

Marino, L., S. O. Lilienfeld, R. Malamud, N. Nobis, and R. Broglio. 2010. "Do Zoos and Aquariums Promote Attitude Change in Visitors? A Critical Evaluation of the American Zoo and Aquarium Study." *Society and Animals* 18:126–138.

Mazet, J. A., T. D. Hunt, and M. H. Ziccardi. 2004. "Assessment of the Risk of Zoonotic Disease Transmission to Marine Mammal Workers and the Public: Survey of Occupational Risks." Final report prepared for United States Marine Mammal Commission, Research Agreement Number K005486–01. Accessed November 18, 2013. http://swfsc.noaa.gov/uploadedFiles/Divisions/PRD/Programs/Photogrammetry/Marine_Mammal_Zoonoses_Final_Report-2.pdf.

Mountain, M. 2012. "How the Beluga Business Began." *Earth in Transition*. September 5. Accessed March 1, 2013. http://www.earthintransition.org/2012/09/how-the-beluga-business-began/.

New York Tribune. 1861. "The Whales." August 9. Accessed March 1, 2013. http://chnm.gmu.edu/lostmuseum/lm/190/.

Noda, K., H. Akiyoshi, M. Aorki, T. Shimada, and F. Ohashi. 2007. "Relationship between Transportation Stress and Polymorphonuclear Functions in Bottlenose Dolphins (*Tursiops truncatus*)." *Journal of Veterinary Medical Science* 69:379–383.

O'Barry, R., and K. Coulbourn. 2000. *Behind the Dolphin Smile*. Los Angeles: Renaissance Book.

Olesiuk, P., M. Bigg, and G. M. Ellis. 1990. "Life History and Population Dynamics of Resident Killer Whales (*Orcinus orca*) in the Coastal Waters of British Columbia and Washington State." *Reports of the International Whaling Commission Special Issue* 12:209–244.

Reiss, D., and L. Marino. 2001. "Self-Recognition in the Bottlenose Dolphin: A Case of Cognitive Convergence." *Proceedings of the National Academy of Sciences USA* 98(10): 5937–5942.

Rendell, L. E., and H. Whitehead. 2001. "Culture in Whales and Dolphins." *Behavioural and Brain Sciences* 24: 309–324.

Rose, N. A. 2004. "Captive Cetaceans: The Science behind the Ethics." Paper presented to the European Cetacean Society 18th Annual Conference, Kolmården, Sweden.

Rose, N. A. 2009. "Do Marine Mammals Belong in Captivity in the 21st Century?" Accessed April 3, 2013. http://www.humanesociety.org/issues/captive_marine/facts/do_marine_mammals_belong_in_captivity.html.

Rose, N. A., E. C. M., Parsons, and R. Farinato. 2009. *The Case Against Marine Mammals in Captivity*. Washington, DC: Humane Society of the United States.

Small, R. J., and D. P. DeMaster. 1995. "Survival of Five Species of Captive Marine Mammals." *Marine Mammal Science* 11(2): 209–226.

Smith, J. D., J. Schull, J. Strote, K. McGee, R. Egnor, and L. Erb. 1995. "The Uncertain Response in the Bottle-nosed Dolphin (*Tursiops truncatus*)." *Journal of Experimental Psychology: General* 124: 391–408.

Spoon, T. R., and T. A. Romano. 2011. "Neuroimmunological Response of Beluga Whales (*Delphinapterus leucas*) to Translocation and a Novel Social Environment." *Brain, Behavior and Immunity* 26(1): 122–131.

St. Aubin, D. J., and J. R. Geraci. 1988. "Capture and Handling Stress Suppresses Circulating Levels of Thyroxine (T4) and Triiodothyronine (T3) in Beluga Whales *Delphinapterus leucas*." *Physiological Zoology* 61(2): 170–175.

Stewart, K. L., and L. Marino. 2009. "Dolphin-Human Interaction Programs: Policies, Problems, and Practical Alternatives." Policy paper for Animals and Society Institute.

Stewart, R. E. A., and S. E. Campana, C. M. Jones, B. E. Stewart. 2006. "Bomb radiocarbon dating calibrates beluga (*Delphinapterus leucas*) age estimates." *Canadian Journal of Zoology* 84(12): 1840–1852.

Sweeney, J. C. 1988. "Specific Pathologic Behavior in Aquatic Mammals: Self-Inflicted Trauma." *Soundings: Newsletter of the International Marine Animal Trainers Association* 13(1): 7.

Sweeney, J. C. 1990. "Marine Mammal Behavioral Diagnostics." In L. A. Dierauf (ed.), *CRC Handbook of Marine Mammal Medicine: Health, Disease, and Rehabilitation*, 53–72. Boston: CRC Press.

US Marine Mammal Inventory Report. 2010. National Marine Fisheries Service, Office of Protected Resources.

Wells, R. S., and M. D. Scott. 1990. "Estimating Bottlenose Dolphin Population Parameters from Individual Identification and Capture-Release Techniques." In P. S. Hammond, S. A. Mizroch, and G. P. Donovan (eds.), *"Individual Recognition of Cetaceans: Use of Photo-Identification and Other Techniques to Estimate Population Parameters,"* special issue of *Reports of the International Whaling Commission* 12:407–415.

White, T. I. 2007. *In Defense of Dolphins: The New Moral Frontier*. Oxford: Blackwell.

Whitehead, H. 2011. "The Culture of Whales and Dolphins." In P. Brakes and M. P. Simmonds (ed.), *Whales and Dolphins: Cognition, Culture, Conservation and Human Perceptions*, 149–165. London: Earthscan.

Williams, V. 2001. *Captive Orcas: Dying to Entertain You*. Chippenham, UK: Whale arid Dolphin Conservation Society.

Woodley, T. H., J. L. Hannah, and D. M. Lavigne. 1997. "A Comparison of Survival Rates for Captive and Free-Ranging Killer Whales (*Orcinus orca*)." International Marine Mammal Association Inc. Draft Technical Report no 93–01.

Zimmerman, T. 2010. "The Killer in the Pool." *Outside*. Accessed November 18, 2013. http://www.outsideonline.com/outdoor-adventure/nature/The-Killer-in-the-Pool.html.

66 Free Willy—and All His Pals

Marc Scheff

Representing the publishers of the magazine Scientific American, *Scheff argues quite broadly that elephants, orcas, and chimps (and other closely related species) should no longer be held in captivity, citing the unique and complex human-like characteristics of these animals. Examples are given to illustrate their intelligence and complex social systems. The shorter life-spans and psychological damage experienced are also noted.*

Science Agenda

Opinion and analysis from *Scientific American*'s Board of Editors
Orcas and elephants are smart, social and way too large for captivity

Having finally joined the rest of the world in severely restricting medical testing on chimpanzees, the U.S. is currently relocating hundreds of government-managed chimps to sanctuaries. One reason for these changes is that the animals are not as essential to biomedical research as they used to be—we have learned to use genetically engineered mice and cell cultures instead. For many people, an even more persuasive argument is that performing medical research on chimpanzees is inhumane because, like us, they are highly intelligent, emotional and self-aware.

As with chimps, the intelligence of orcas and elephants is undeniable. Boasting some of the most intricate brains around, all three animals have recognized themselves in mirrors, indicating that they, too, have a concept of self. All are cooperative problem solvers. Teams of orcas sometimes hunt by producing and directing waves at icebergs to knock seals and penguins into the water. Elephants are also adept toolmakers, fashioning switches with which to shoo flies and chewing bark into balls to plug small drinking holes, thereby preventing evaporation.

Chimps, killer whales and elephants are just as dependent on companionship as we are. A killer whale mother stays with most of her descendants throughout life, sometimes shepherding as many as four generations. Related matrilines, each of which has its own dialect, unite in pods, which merge into clans, which intermingle in large communities—akin to tribes and nations.

Likewise, related elephant mothers and their offspring form tight-knit clans in which they share parenting duties and shield children from predators. When a clan member dies, elephants mourn—there is no other word for it. At Kenya's Samburu National Reserve, zoologist Iain Douglas-Hamilton and his team witnessed elephants from various families tending to an ailing matriarch named Eleanor. Another matriarch used her tusks to lift Eleanor to her feet when she collapsed. Even after Eleanor died, elephants repeatedly visited and caressed her body. Cynthia Moss and other researchers have also reported elephants sprinkling their dead with soil and covering them with branches and leaves.

A number of other species share similar humanlike traits, among them gorillas, orangutans, dolphins and porpoises. What distinguishes orcas and elephants—what makes holding them in captivity so uniquely fraught—is one of the same features that makes them so attractive to zoo-goers: their immense size. African elephants can weigh as much as 15,000 pounds and are used to traveling between watering holes and feeding sites hundreds of miles apart. Confined elephants often spend their time standing around in cramped quarters. Killer whales can reach a length of 32 feet and a weight of 22,000 pounds. The approximately four dozen orcas now in captivity are forced to trade the ocean for a bathtub. At Miami Seaquarium, the aging Lolita lives in a tank that is not even twice as wide as she is long.

These tortuous conditions inflict serious physical and psychological damage on such smart and sensitive animals. Zoo elephants die young, often after becoming obese and infertile. They frequently develop psychological tics such as swaying and head bobbing. Citing ethical reasons, several large zoos in the U.S., Canada, the U.K. and India have closed their elephant exhibits.

Captive orcas are unusually aggressive, biting and ramming one another as well as trainers. Many researchers think the animals behave this way because they are so stressed; some have suggested that longtime confinement makes cetaceans psychotic. In February 2010 SeaWorld orca Tilikum pulled 40-year-old senior trainer Dawn Brancheau underwater, shook her violently, scalped her and severed her spine. It was the second time he had killed a trainer. Wild orcas have never killed anyone.

Orcas and elephants are not the only intelligent species that deserve our respect and attention, but they face unique hardships in captivity. Even though many zoos and sea parks raise awareness about the plight of animals in the wild, the suffering of captive orcas and elephants in particular overshadows this worthy goal. Some currently confined individuals may not survive if released, but the ones that can be, should be, and captive breeding programs should be terminated.

[. . .]

67 Elephants in Captivity

Kristin L. Vehrs

Vehrs responds directly to Scheff, pointing out that the Association of Zoos and Aquariums (AZA) has very high (and rising) standards for animal care and welfare, especially as pertaining to elephants and orcas. She argues that releasing captive animals is more detrimental than providing them with enriching habitats, good nutrition, etc. She emphasizes the roles AZA has taken in combatting elephant poaching and in promoting protection of marine ecosystems.

Your editorial, "Free Willy—And All His Pals" [Science Agenda], fails to accurately reflect the facts about elephants and orcas in human care and reaches the wrong conclusion in asserting elephants and orcas that "can be, should be" released.

The Association of Zoos and Aquariums (AZA) sets high and rising standards for animal care and welfare, which is especially important for elephants and orcas. AZA's science-based accreditation standards are the best way to make sure large and intelligent animals receive the higher level of care they need. Not surprisingly, the only specific example of poor care you note comes from a non-AZA-accredited facility.

There is no solid science to show that captive elephants and whales can or should be released into the wild. For whales and dolphins, the few attempted releases have resulted in suffering and death. A proved solution is to provide these animals with enriching habitats, appropriate social interaction, high-quality veterinary care and nutritious diets—all mandated by AZA standards.

AZA-accredited zoos and aquariums are also taking a leading role in fighting illegal elephant poaching and in promoting protection of our marine ecosystems. The animals at these facilities play a key role in educating and inspiring 180 million people to take conservation action. AZA-accredited institutions have spent more than $1 billion on field conservation projects over the past 10 years. AZA and its members have made considerable efforts to advance animal welfare and conserve wildlife, and we invite your readers to take a second look.

Kristin L. Vehrs
Executive Director
Association of Zoos and Aquariums

THE EDITORS REPLY: There is considerable and increasing evidence that orcas and elephants suffer even in institutions accredited by AZA. Results announced last year from a three-year study on 255 of the roughly 300 elephants in North American AZA-approved zoos found that 74 percent of the elephants were overweight or obese; 25 percent had joint problems in 2012; 67 percent had foot problems in 2012; and nearly 80 percent displayed behavioral tics, such as pacing and head bobbing.

68 Against Zoos

Dale Jamieson

Jamieson reviews a number of the arguments for and against zoos. He points out that while there are a number of arguments made in favor of zoos such as preservation, research, amusement, and education, these often are not compatible interests and thus only some benefits can occur in any one zoo. Further, he addresses the moral problems of keeping wild animals in captivity, the detrimental impacts of captivity, and the implicit message of a false sense of the human place in the natural order.

We can start with a rough-and-ready definition of zoos: they are public parks that display animals, primarily for the purposes of recreation or education. Although large collections of animals were maintained in antiquity, they were not zoos in this sense. Typically, these ancient collections were not exhibited in public parks, or they were maintained for purposes other than recreation or education.
[. . .]
Today in the United States alone there are hundreds of zoos, and they are visited by millions of people every year. They range from roadside menageries run by hucksters to elaborate zoological parks staffed by trained scientists.
[. . .]

Animals and Liberty

Before we consider the reasons that are usually given for the survival of zoos, we should see that there is a moral presumption against keeping wild animals in captivity. What this involves, after all, is taking animals out of their native habitats, transporting them great distances, and keeping them in alien environments in which their liberty is severely restricted. It is surely true that in being taken from the wild and confined in zoos, animals are deprived of a great many goods. For the most part, they are prevented from gathering their own food, developing their own social orders, and generally behaving in ways that are natural to them. These activities all require significantly more liberty than most animals are permitted in zoos. If we are justified in keeping animals in zoos, it must be because there are some important benefits that can be obtained only by doing so.

Against this, it might be said that most mammals and birds added to zoo collections in recent years are captive-bred. Since these animals have never known freedom, it might be claimed that they are denied nothing by captivity. But this argument is far from compelling. A chained puppy prevented from playing or a restrained bird not allowed to fly still have interests in engaging in these activities. Imagine this argument applied to humans. It would be absurd to suggest that those who are born into slavery have no interest in freedom since they have never experienced it. Indeed, we might think that the tragedy of captivity is all the greater for those creatures who have never known liberty.

The idea that there is a presumption against keeping wild animals in captivity is not the property of some particular moral theory; it follows from most reasonable moral theories. Either we have duties to animals or we do not. If we do have duties to animals, surely they include respecting those interests which are most important to them, so long as this does not conflict with other, more stringent duties that we may have. Since an interest in liberty is central for most animals, it follows that if everything else is equal, we should respect this interest.

[. . .]

Arguments for Zoos

What might [. . .] important benefits be? Four are commonly cited: amusement, education, opportunities for scientific research, and help in preserving species.

Amusement was certainly an important reason for the establishment of the early zoos, and it remains an important function of contemporary zoos as well. Most people visit zoos in order to be entertained, and any zoo that wishes to remain financially sound must cater to this desire. Even highly regarded zoos have their share of dancing bears and trained birds of prey. But although providing amusement for people is viewed by the general public as a very important function of zoos, it is hard to see how providing such amusement could possibly justify keeping wild animals in captivity. *[margin note: have to cater to aud.]*

Most curators and administrators reject the idea that the primary purpose of zoos is to provide entertainment. Indeed, many agree that the pleasure we take in viewing wild animals is not in itself a good enough reason to keep them in captivity. Some curators see baby elephant walks, for example, as a necessary evil, or defend such amusements because of their role in educating people, especially children, about animals. It is sometimes said that people must be interested in what they are seeing if they are to be educated about it, and entertainments keep people interested, thus making education possible.

This brings us to a second reason for having zoos: their role in education. This reason has been cited as long as zoos have existed. For example, in its 1898 annual report, the New York Zoological Society resolved to take "measures to inform the public of the great decrease in animal life, to stimulate sentiment in favor of better protection, and to cooperate with other scientific bodies . . . [in] efforts calculated to secure the perpetual preservation of our higher vertebrates." Despite the pious platitudes that are often uttered about the educational efforts of zoos, there is little evidence that zoos are very successful in educating people about animals. Indeed, a literature review commissioned by the American Zoo and Aquarium Association (available on their website) concludes that "[l]ittle to no systematic research has been conducted on the impact of visits to zoos and aquariums on visitor conservation knowledge, awareness, affect, or behavior." The research that is available is not encouraging. Stephen Kellert has found that zoo-goers display the same prejudices about animals as the general public. [. . .] One reason why some zoos have not done a better job in educating people is that many of them make no real effort at education. In the case of others, the problem is an apathetic and unappreciative public. *[margin note: paradoxical]*

Edward G. Ludwig's (1981) study of the zoo in Buffalo, New York, revealed a surprising amount of dissatisfaction on the part of young, scientifically inclined zoo employees. Much of this dissatisfaction stemmed from the almost complete indifference of the public to the zoo's educational efforts. Ludwig's study indicated that most animals are viewed only briefly as people move quickly past cages. The typical zoo-goer stops only to watch baby animals or those who are begging, feeding, or making sounds. [. . .]

Of course, it is undeniable that some education occurs in some zoos. But this very fact raises other issues. What is it that we want people to learn from visiting zoos? Facts about the physiology and behavior of various animals? Attitudes towards the survival of endangered species? Compassion for the fate of all animals? To what degree does education require keeping wild animals in captivity? Couldn't most of the educational benefits of zoos be obtained through videos, lectures, and computer simulations? Indeed, couldn't most of the important educational objectives better be achieved by exhibiting empty cages with explanations of why they are empty? *[margin note: experiential learning]*

A third reason for having zoos is that they support scientific research. This, too, is a benefit that was pointed out long ago. [. . .] Zoos support scientific research in at least three ways: they fund field research by scientists not affiliated with zoos; they employ other scientists as members of zoo staffs; and they make otherwise inaccessible animals available for study.

We should note first that very few zoos support any real scientific research. Fewer still have staff scientists with full-time research appointments. Among those that do, it is common for their scientists to study animals in the wild rather than those in zoo collections. Much of this research, as well as other field research that is supported by zoos, could just as well be funded in a different way—say, by a government agency. The question of whether there should be zoos does not turn on the funding for field research which zoos currently provide. The significance of the research that is actually conducted in zoos is a more important consideration.

Research that is conducted in zoos can be divided into two broad categories: studies in behavior and studies in anatomy and pathology.

Behavioral research conducted on zoo animals is controversial. Some have argued that nothing can be learned by studying animals that are kept in the unnatural conditions that obtain in most zoos. Others have argued that captive animals are more interesting research subjects than are wild animals: since captive animals are free from predation, they exhibit a wider range of physical and behavioral traits than do animals in the wild, thus permitting researchers to view the full range of their genetic possibilities. Both of these positions are surely extreme. Conditions in some zoos are natural enough to permit some interesting research possibilities. But the claim that captive animals are more interesting research subjects than those in the wild is not very plausible. Environments trigger behaviors. No doubt a predation-free environment triggers behaviors different from those of an animal's natural habitat, but there is no reason to believe that better, fuller, or more accurate data can be obtained in predation-free environments than in natural habitats.

Studies in anatomy and pathology have three main purposes: to improve zoo conditions so that captive animals will live longer, be happier, and breed more frequently; to contribute to human health by providing animal models for human ailments; and to increase our knowledge of wild animals for its own sake.

 The first of these aims is surely laudable if we concede that there should be zoos in the first place. But the fact that zoo research contributes to improving conditions in zoos is not a reason for having them. If there were no zoos, there would be no need to improve them.

The second aim, to contribute to human health by providing animal models for human ailments, appears to justify zoos to some extent, but in practice this consideration is not as important as one might think. There are very severe constraints on the experiments that may be conducted on zoo animals. [. . .]

Finally, there is the goal of obtaining knowledge about animals for its own sake. Knowledge is certainly something which is good and, everything being equal, we should encourage people to seek it for its own sake. But everything is not equal in this case. There is a moral presumption against keeping animals in captivity. This presumption can be overcome only by demonstrating that there are important benefits that must be obtained in this way if they are to be obtained at all. It is clear that this is not the case with knowledge for its own sake. There are other channels for our intellectual curiosity, ones that do not exact such a high moral price. Although our quest for knowledge for its own sake is important, it is not important enough to overcome the moral presumption against keeping animals in captivity.

In assessing the significance of research as a reason for having zoos, it is important to remember that very few zoos do any research at all. Whatever benefits result from zoo research could just as well be obtained by having a few zoos instead of the hundreds which now exist. The most this argument could establish is that we are justified in having a few very good zoos. It does not provide a defense of the vast majority of zoos which now exist.

A fourth reason for having zoos is that they preserve species that would otherwise become extinct. As the destruction of habitat accelerates and as breeding programs become increasingly successful, this rationale for zoos gains in popularity. There is some reason for questioning the commitment of zoos to species preservation: it can be argued that they continue to remove more animals from the wild than they return. In the minds of some skeptics, captive breeding programs are more about the preservation of zoos than the preservation of endangered species. Still, without such programs, the Pere David Deer, the Mongolian Wild Horse, and the California Condor would all now be extinct.

Even the best of such programs face difficulties, however. A classic study by Katherine Ralls, Kristin Brugger, and Jonathan Ballou (1979) convincingly argues that lack of genetic diversity among captive animals is a serious problem for zoo breeding programs. In some species, the infant mortality rate among inbred animals is six or seven times that among noninbred animals. In other species, the infant mortality rate among inbred animals is 100 percent.

Moreover, captivity substitutes selection pressures imposed by humans for those of an animal's natural habitat. After a few years in captivity, animals can begin to diverge both behaviorally and genetically from their relatives in the wild. After a century or more, it is not clear that they would be the same animals, in any meaningful sense, that we set out to preserve.

There is also a dark side to zoo breeding programmes: they create many unwanted animals. In some species (lions, tigers, and zebras, for example) a few males can service an entire herd. Extra males are unnecessary to the program and are a financial burden. Some of these animals are sold and end up in the hands of individuals and institutions which lack proper facilities. Others are shot and killed by Great White Hunters in private hunting camps. [. . .] In order to avoid the "surplus" problem, some zoos have considered proposals to "recycle" excess animals: a euphemism for killing them and feeding their bodies to other zoo animals.

The ostensible purpose of zoo breeding programs is to reintroduce animals into the wild. In this regard, the California Condor is often portrayed as a major success story. From a low of 22 individuals in 1982, the population has rebounded to 219, through captive breeding. Since 1992 condors have been reintroduced, but most have not survived and only six eggs have been produced in the wild. Most eggs have failed to hatch, and only one chick has fledged. Wolf reintroductions have also had only limited success. Wolves, even when they have learned how to hunt, have often not learned to avoid people. Familiarity with humans and ignorance about their own cultures have devastated reintroduced populations of big cats, great apes, bears, rhinos, and hippos. According to the philosopher Bryan Norton, putting a captive-bred animal in the wild is "equivalent to dropping a contemporary human being in a remote area in the eighteenth or nineteenth century and saying, 'Let's see if you can make it' " (quoted in Derr 1999). In a 1995 review, Ben Beck, Associate Director of the National Zoological Park in Washington, found that of 145 documented reintroductions involving 115 species, only 16 succeeded in producing self-sustaining wild populations, and only half of these were endangered species.

Even if breeding programs were run in the best possible way, there are limits to what can be done to save endangered species in this way. At most, several hundred species could be preserved in the world's zoos, and then at very great expense. For many of these animals the zoo is likely to be the last stop on the way to extinction. Zoo professionals like to say that they are the Noahs of the modern world and that zoos are their arks, but Noah found a place to land his animals where they could thrive and multiply. If zoos are like arks, then rare animals are like passengers on a voyage of the damned, never to find a port that will let them dock or a land in which they can live in peace. The real solution, of course, is to preserve the wild nature that created these animals and has the power to sustain them. But if it is really true that we are inevitably moving towards a world in which mountain gorillas can survive only in zoos, then we must ask whether it is really better for them to live in artificial environments of our design than not to be born at all.

Even if all these questions and difficulties are overlooked, the importance of preserving endangered species does not provide much support for the existing system of zoos. Most zoos do very little breeding or breed only species which are not endangered. Many of the major breeding programs are run in special facilities which have been established for that purpose. They are often located in remote places, far from the attention of zoo-goers. (For example, the Wildlife Conservation Society [formerly the New York Zoological Society] operates its Wildlife Survival Center on St. Catherine's

Island off the coast of Georgia, and the National Zoo runs its Conservation and Research Center in the Shenandoah Valley of Virginia.) If our main concern is to do what we can to preserve endangered species at any cost and in any way, then we should support such large-scale breeding centers rather than conventional zoos, most of which have neither the staff nor the facilities to run successful breeding programs.

The four reasons for having zoos which I have surveyed carry some weight. But different reasons provide support for different kinds of zoo. Preservation and perhaps research are better carried out in large-scale animal preserves, but these provide few opportunities for amusement and education. Amusement and perhaps education are better provided in urban zoos, but they offer few opportunities for research and preservation. Moreover, whatever benefits are obtained from any kind of zoo, we must confront the moral presumption against keeping wild animals in captivity. Which way do the scales tip? There are two further considerations which, in my view, tip the scales against zoos.

First, captivity does not just deny animals liberty but is often detrimental to them in other respects as well. The history of chimpanzees in the zoos of Europe and America is a good example.

Chimpanzees first entered the zoo world in about 1640 when a Dutch prince, Frederick Henry of Nassau, obtained one for his castle menagerie. The chimpanzee didn't last very long. In 1835, the London Zoo obtained its first chimpanzee; he died immediately. Another was obtained in 1845; she lived six months. All through the nineteenth and early twentieth centuries, zoos obtained chimpanzees who promptly died within nine months. It wasn't until the 1930s that it was discovered that chimpanzees are extremely vulnerable to human respiratory diseases, and that special steps must be taken to protect them. But for nearly a century, zoos removed them from the wild and subjected them to almost certain death. Even today there are chimpanzees and other great apes living in deplorable conditions in zoos around the world.

Chimpanzees are not the only animals to suffer in zoos. It is well known that animals such as polar bears, lions, tigers, and cheetahs fare particularly badly in zoos. A recent (2003) report in *Nature* by Ros Clubb and Georgia Mason shows that repetitive stereotypic behavior and high infant mortality rates in zoos are directly related to an animal's natural home range size. For example, polar bears, whose home range in the wild is about a million times the size of its typical zoo enclosure, spend 25 percent of their days in stereotypic pacing and suffer from a 65 percent infant mortality rate. These results suggest that zoos simply cannot provide the necessary conditions for a decent life for many animals. Indeed, the Detroit Zoo has announced that, for ethical reasons, it will no longer keep elephants in captivity. The San Francisco Zoo has followed suit.

Many animals suffer in zoos quite unnecessarily. In 1974, Peter Batten, former director of the San Jose Zoological Gardens, undertook an exhaustive study of 200 American zoos. In his book *Living Trophies* he documented large numbers of neurotic, overweight animals kept in cramped, cold cells and fed unpalatable synthetic food. Many had deformed feet and appendages caused by unsuitable floor surfaces. Almost every zoo studied had excessive mortality rates, resulting from preventable factors ranging from vandalism to inadequate husbandry practices. Batten's conclusion was: "The majority of American zoos are badly run, their direction incompetent, and animal husbandry inept and in some cases non-existent" (1976: ix).

Many of these same conditions are documented in Lynn Griner's (1983) review of necropsies conducted at the San Diego Zoo over a 14-year period. This zoo may well be the best in the country, and its staff are clearly well trained and well intentioned. Yet this study documents widespread malnutrition among zoo animals; high mortality rates from the use of anesthetics and tranquilizers; serious injuries and deaths sustained in transport; and frequent occurrences of cannibalism, infanticide, and fighting almost certainly caused by overcrowded conditions.

The director of the National Zoo in Washington resigned in 2004 when an independent review panel commissioned by the National Academy of Sciences found severe deficiencies at the zoo in animal care, pest control, record keeping, and management that contributed to the deaths of 23 animals between 1998 and 2003, including, most spectacularly, the loss of two pandas to rat poison.

Despite the best efforts of its well-paid public relations firm, it is difficult to trust an institution that cannot avoid killing its most charismatic and valuable animals in such a stupid and unnecessary way.

The second consideration which tips the scales against zoos is more difficult to articulate but is, to my mind, even more important. Zoos teach us a false sense of our place in the natural order. The means of confinement mark a difference between humans and other animals. They are there at our pleasure, to be used for our purposes. Morality and perhaps our very survival require that we learn to live as one species among many rather than as one species over many. To do this, we must forget what we learn at zoos. Because what zoos teach us is false and dangerous, both humans and other animals will be better off when they are abolished.

References

Batten, P. (1976) *Living Trophies*, New York: Thomas Y. Crowell Co.

Clubb, R., and Mason, G. (2003) "Animal Welfare: Captivity Effects on Wide-Ranging Carnivores," *Nature*, October 2; 425(6957), 473–4.

Derr, M. (1999) "A Rescue Plan for Threatened Species," *New York Times*, January 19.

Griner, L. (1983) *Pathology of Zoo Animals*, San Diego: Zoological Society of San Diego.

Ludwig, E. G. (1981) "People at Zoos: A Sociological Approach," *International Journal for the Study of Animal Problems* 2(6), 310–16.

Ralls, K., Brugger, K., and Ballou, J. (1979) "Inbreeding and Juvenile Mortality in Small Populations of Ungulates," *Science* 206, 1101–3.

69 In Defense of Zoos and Aquariums

The Ethical Basis for Keeping Wild Animals in Captivity

Michael Hutchins, Brandie Smith,
and Ruth Allard

Hutchins and his coauthors argue that a strong commitment to wildlife conservation and animal welfare provide powerful ethical justifications for accredited zoos and aquariums. They note that zoo animals play an increasingly important role as ambassadors for their species in securing a future for wildlife and their habitats. They note the strong financial contribution of zoos to conservation efforts and have been effective at increasing quality of life for captive animals through exhibit design, scientifically based animal programs, and policy. They argue that the benefits of exhibiting animals in zoos are greater than the costs in individual animal welfare.

America's zoos and aquariums have been the focus of recent criticism by some animal rights and welfare advocates and in print and electronic media.[1-7] These critics have characterized zoos and aquariums as animal prisons or, even worse, as exploiters and traffickers of wildlife. These accusations have fueled growing public and governmental concern about the welfare of zoo and aquarium animals and the appropriate use of these animals by public institutions.

Critics often generalize their claims to include all zoologic facilities, regardless of their quality or accomplishments. It is important to understand that there are two different kinds of wildlife facilities in the United States: those that are accredited by the American Zoo and Aquarium Association (AZA) and those that are not. The AZA is the only zoo and aquarium association in the world with an effective accreditation program that helps ensure quality animal care, a code of professional ethics that helps guide and regulate its members' actions, and a dedicated conservation vision.[8-10] Of the more than 2,300 animal exhibitors licensed by the USDA's Animal and Plant Health Inspection Service (APHIS), fewer than 10% are qualified to be AZA members. Our comments are restricted to zoos and aquariums accredited by the AZA.

Although critics of zoos and aquariums tend to receive plenty of media attention, their generalizations about public perceptions of accredited zoologic facilities are not supported by the facts: more than 135 million people visit AZA-accredited institutions annually,[11] more than 58,000 people volunteer more than 5 million hours annually at AZA facilities,[12] a 1992 Roper poll identified zoos and aquariums as the third most trusted messenger on wildlife conservation and environmental issues (trailing only National Geographic and Jacques Cousteau),[13] and reputable print and electronic media outlets produce numerous positive reports about the conservation, scientific, and educational efforts of AZA institutions.[14-17] Given these often disparate perspectives, how should ethically mature, caring people view accredited zoos and aquariums today? Are accredited zoos and aquariums justifiable? If so, under what conditions are they justifiable?

Some zoo and aquarium opponents are more extreme in their criticism than others. For example, some animal rights advocates are vehemently opposed to all forms of captivity, arguing that individual sentient animals have an intrinsic right to liberty.[2] For some people, even domestic pets are subjugated by their human owners; in their view, animals should interact with humans only as voluntary companions. It is highly unlikely that arguments presented here will change the minds of those who currently believe that zoos and aquariums are inherently wrong and should be eliminated.

More mainstream animal welfare advocates are not intrinsically opposed to zoos and aquariums; instead, they contend that the welfare of wild animals is diminished under human care and that it is impossible for zoos and aquariums to provide the richness of experience, freedom of movement, and quality of life animals would experience if left in nature.[1] They have also challenged zoos' and aquariums' reasons for existence, contending that, by itself, recreation is not a sufficient justification for maintaining captive wild animals, especially endangered species. The basis of the argument is that zoos and aquariums and their captive breeding programs do little to support wildlife and habitat conservation. Being conservationists and animal welfare advocates, we believe these arguments provide the most valid and difficult ethical challenges to zoos and aquariums today and, as such, they will be the focus of this report.

It is not our intent to provide a final answer to these complex questions. One cannot resolve moral questions for others, as different people have different opinions, depending on their own experiences, attitudes, and vantage points. Our intent is to contribute to the continual process of critical discussion and deliberation by providing an ethical justification for the existence of accredited zoos and aquariums at the beginning of the twenty-first century.

[. . .]

Conservation Role of Zoos and Aquariums

Zoos and aquariums that value biological diversity have a clear moral obligation to support wildlife and habitat conservation efforts worldwide. The missions of professionally managed zoos and aquariums are complex, but generally include conservation, education, research, and recreation.[18] Although providing wholesome recreational opportunities for the public is important, most people would likely agree that recreation (entertainment) alone is not sufficient justification for the existence of zoos and aquariums or for holding wild animals in captivity.[19] In fact, many animals held by zoos and aquariums are endangered in the wild, and their commercial use exclusively for entertainment purposes would be distasteful, if not illegal. Entertainment is an even less convincing justification if one assumes that the welfare of individual animals may be compromised to some degree as a result of captivity.[1,2]

Conservation, education, and research are other matters. If zoos and aquariums demonstrate an ability to study, manage, preserve, and restore wild animals and their habitats in nature, it would provide a powerful ethical justification for their continued existence.[20–22] This is particularly true given the many serious and pervasive threats facing wildlife and nature today. Wild animals in zoos and aquariums are ambassadors for their species, helping to raise public awareness and funds to support education, research, on-the-ground conservation activities in range countries, and a host of other relevant activities.[20–22] Zoos and aquariums must display and sustainably breed some animals to meet their conservation goals.

The following is a brief overview of some of the numerous conservation activities in which AZA and its members are currently engaged. In 1999 and 2000, AZA and its member institutions supported more than 1,400 field conservation and related scientific research and educational initiatives in more than 80 countries worldwide.[23]

Reintroduction

Zoos and aquariums of the 1980s and early 1990s viewed and described themselves as modern Noah's Arks and organized cooperative breeding programs to sustain populations of endangered species until they could be reintroduced to nature.[24] During the past several years, zoo and aquarium professionals have begun to question this notion, adopting a much broader definition of zoo- and aquarium-based conservation. Central to this concept is the assumption that zoos and aquariums must do more to support in situ conservation in range countries.[20–22, 25, 26] There are far too many endangered species and not nearly enough space to breed them all in captivity and, in many cases, far too little habitat remaining in which to reintroduce them. In addition, reintroduction programs are difficult and expensive, and they amount to treating the symptoms of species loss rather than the causes.[27-29] Though this shift in focus has been well documented,[21-23] critics imply that zoos and aquariums are not active conservation organizations, because they are not releasing a steady stream of animals into the wild. This argument reflects an ignorance of the breadth, scope, and goals of conservation itself.

[. . .]

Endangered Species Recovery

In nature, living organisms are interconnected, and ecosystems cannot function unless they retain most of their essential parts. Endangered species must persist until essential habitat can be restored, better protected, or expanded. Because there are so many species in need of help, zoo and aquarium efforts are often focused on flagship species (those that have the ability to capture the public's attention and help preserve habitat and other taxa). Examples of the many zoo-and aquarium-sponsored efforts to recover endangered species include the Toledo Zoos for the Mona/Virgin Islands boa[30]; Atlanta, National, and San Diego Zoos for the giant panda in China[31]; Fort Worth Zoos for the Jamaican iguana[32]; and Minnesota Zoos for the Sumatran tiger.[33]

Habitat Restoration

Many of the world's natural habitats have been fragmented, altered, or lost because of human activity, with devastating effects on wildlife. In some cases, attempts to conserve biological diversity can be aided through habitat restoration. Restoration activities by zoos and aquariums have, among other things, involved the reestablishment of native vegetation and elimination or control of invasive exotic species.[34]

[. . .]

Scientific Research

Scientific research is critical to wildlife conservation and for improving zoo and aquarium animal management. In situ and ex situ conservation efforts cannot succeed in the absence of knowledge.[35] Unfortunately, our knowledge of most wild animals and their habitats is far from complete. Contemporary zoos and aquariums are investing enormous resources in research, estimated at $50 million annually.[12] Zoos and aquariums offer unique opportunities to study animal behavior, physiology, reproduction, growth, and development of a wide variety of taxa under semicontrolled conditions. Many of these studies would be difficult, if not impossible, to conduct in nature, because of practical or ethical limitations. For example, much of what we know about the biology of arboreal, fossorial, and wide-ranging aquatic species has come from studies[35] of captive animals.

Development of Relevant Technologies

Many technologies developed or tested by zoo and aquarium biologists are relevant to field conservation, a largely unrecognized benefit of maintaining collections of wild animals.[21] As remaining wildlife habitats become progressively smaller and more isolated, the need for active management of wildlife and their habitats grows. Consequently, technologies developed by zoos and aquariums, including those for small population management, ecologic restoration, contraception, and veterinary care, are becoming increasingly relevant to the conservation of wildlife and their habitats.[20-21]

[. . .]

Support of Protected Areas

Habitat loss and lack of law enforcement in and around protected areas are major factors contributing to species endangerment around the world, especially in developing countries.[36] Consequently, there is a recognized need for North American zoos and aquariums to increase their support for conservation on a landscape level.[20–22,29] The AZA and its member institutions are moving in this direction, both individually and collectively.

[. . .]

Conservation Education

Raising public awareness about endangered species and other environmental issues is an important aspect of conservation. If conservation efforts are to be successful, people must be interested in nature and be made aware of the problems and potential solutions facing wildlife and their habitats. With 135 million visitors each year, accredited zoos and aquariums are unique among conservation organizations, because they have a direct connection to the public.

The educational efforts of AZA members are numerous, and accredited zoos and aquariums are continually striving to evaluate their impact on visitors behavior. Evidence indicates that zoo and aquarium educational programs are effective, at least in the short term, in building public appreciation and understanding of wildlife and wildlife conservation issues.[37] The AZA Conservation Education Committee (CEC) has initiated a major study[38] to assess the impact of zoo- and aquarium-based educational efforts on public knowledge, attitudes, and perceptions, with the goal of ensuring that critical conservation messages and concepts are reaching visitors in the most effective way.

Fundraising to Support Conservation

For conservation to succeed, it is critical that it be put on a solid financial base. The AZA and its member institutions are developing improved mechanisms to support conservation and the related scientific and educational activities of its members and collaborators. In this regard, the AZA was the first zoologic association to establish a fund dedicated to supporting wildlife and nature conservation.[39] During the past decade, the AZA Conservation Endowment Fund has provided over $2.5 million to support 164 projects in more than 30 countries. Furthermore, 14 accredited zoos and aquariums have developed their own grant programs to support local and global conservation.

Conservation Planning and Coalition Building

The AZA and its member institutions are becoming increasingly active in conservation planning and coalition building, which are the first steps in effective conservation. Partnerships can greatly enhance organizations' abilities to take action, because expertise and expenses can be shared.

The AZA and its members have been involved in creating two major conservation coalitions: the Bushmeat Crisis Task Force (BCTF) and the Butterfly Conservation Initiative (BFCI). The BCTF is a coalition of 34 conservation and animal protection organizations and accredited zoos committed to curbing illegal commercial trade of wild animals for meat in Africa.[40] The coalition was created as the result of a 1998 meeting organized by the AZA. In just over two short years, BCTF's accomplishments have been substantial and too numerous to list here. To learn more about this project, please visit the BCTF website at www.bushmeat.org.

[. . .]

Animal Welfare—The Critical Caveat

The evidence presented here illustrates that zoo and aquarium contributions to wildlife and habitat conservation are substantial. However, the crux of the debate over zoos and aquariums comes down to a question of focus. Animal rights advocates believe in the intrinsic rights of individual animals, whereas conservationists focus their attention on populations, species, and ecosystems.[41] While we believe that individual animals are morally considerable, we also believe that conservation must be our highest priority. The irreversible loss of populations, species, or ecosystems will not only result in the untold suffering of many individual animals (including humans), it will also result in the loss of millions of future lives. We acknowledge that this broader perspective might appear callous to those who are strict adherents to animal rights philosophy, but zoos' and aquariums' commitment to conservation is matched by an equally strong commitment to animal welfare.[22,42–44] This increased focus on animal welfare helps ensure that the collective benefits derived from wildlife conservation outweigh the costs to individual animals. No reputable zoo or aquarium professional would defend an institution that contributed to conservation, but abused or provided substandard care for its animals. A conservation-oriented mission and staunch commitment to maintaining the highest standards of animal care are the core values of accredited zoos and aquariums.[43,44]

One of the founding fathers of animal rights, Tom Regan, refers to any attempt to usurp the rights of individual sentient animals (be they endangered or common) to preserve populations, species, or ecosystems as "environmental fascism."[45] Several prominent environmental ethicists and conservationists have challenged this view. For example, Warren[46] writes, "It is less important to maintain that other animals have moral rights than to maintain that we have moral obligations to them," and Norton[47] argues, on ethical grounds, that we must balance our obligations to individual animals with our obligations to perpetuate and conserve natural processes. Because there is often a conflict between what is good for individual animals and what is good for populations, species, or ecosystems, this will sometimes mean compromising the welfare of some individuals for the greater good.[47,48]

The following are some examples of how accredited zoos and aquariums are addressing ethical issues related to animal care and propagation.

Providing Appropriate Environments

One of the biggest criticisms from zoo and aquarium detractors is that animal welfare is diminished in captivity, simply because the wild can never be duplicated exactly. This is true. However, zoos and aquariums make up for these inadequacies by creating an environment that offers some of the accouterments of the wild while providing shelter from some of the stresses, such as predation and starvation.[44] Some accredited zoos and aquariums have been criticized for having older, inadequate facilities and care programs for specific taxa.

The comparatively new science of environmental enrichment has been embraced by accredited zoos and aquariums and provides numerous techniques for improving the lives of captive animals.[49] Enrichment is the species-appropriate enhancement of the physical and social environment. Accreditation by the AZA now requires that all member institutions develop and implement an environmental enrichment plan that improves the quality of life of captive animals by providing novel experiences and a variety of stimuli that encourage a range of natural behaviors.[43] These programs demonstrate accredited zoos' and aquariums' commitment to continually improving the welfare of animals in their care.

Ensuring Quality Animal Care

Animal care is being improved and standardized through creation and distribution of husbandry manuals and thorough, scientifically based animal care standards that define appropriate management practices. The AZA Board of Directors approved management and care standards for elephants in 2001,[50] and the AZA Animal Welfare Committee is formulating standards for all remaining mammals.[43] Experts on reptile, amphibian, bird, and invertebrate husbandry have been called on to develop resources for captive management of these taxa as well. Ultimately, standards will be developed for all major taxa in AZA institutions' collections.

[. . .]

Training and Use of Animals in Public Education

Training and the use of animals in education pose some difficult animal care issues for zoos and aquariums. When does training compromise or enhance animal welfare? [. . .] The zoo and aquarium community is continually assessing the impact of professional practices on the animals under our care, and these questions are the subject of considerable debate among the members of the AZA and its Animal Welfare Committee. The Committee is currently working on a draft policy on animals in entertainment to be considered by the AZA Board. If they are to be justified, animal shows, training programs, and exhibit design must contribute to the overall conservation and education goals of the association and not diminish animal welfare.

Surplus Animals

The zoo and aquarium profession uses the term *surplus* to refer to animals that are not needed to meet the population management or conservation goals of an institution or program. It is not that these animals are unwanted or neglected, and despite the penchant of certain critics for misinterpreting the word, surplus does not mean superfluous. All AZA facilities dedicate themselves to providing quality care to all animals in their custody for as long as necessary. Zoos and aquariums make known the availability of their surplus animals in case they can be of conservation or education value to another institution. The AZA also requires that all accredited facilities complete an institutional collection plan to ensure that populations stay within the captive carrying capacity (ie, the available holding space). Institutional collection plans also help zoos and aquariums define the conservation goals for all of the species in their collections.[51]

[. . .]

Beyond AZA

Discussions of zoo and aquarium relevance in today's world often come down to issues of individual animal welfare versus overall species and ecosystem conservation. While we believe that conservation must be the primary mission of modern zoos and aquariums, we also contend that to be morally defensible, zoos and aquariums must demonstrate an equally unwavering commitment to maintaining high standards of animal welfare.

Conclusions

In this report, we have argued that a strong commitment to wildlife conservation and animal welfare provides a powerful ethical justification for accredited zoos and aquariums. As true ambassadors for their species, zoo and aquarium animals play an increasingly important role in securing a future for wild animals and their habitats in nature. This is particularly true given the current global context. The future of wildlife and the ecosystems on which it depends is in grave and immediate danger, and as we have documented in this report, zoos and aquariums contribute to conservation efforts in a wide variety of ways.

One question that must be resolved is how much conservation is enough, and how can these contributions be measured? What is a reasonable investment in conservation: 1, 5, or 10% or more of zoos' and aquariums' budgets? Even a 1% investment in conservation out of an estimated combined budget of over $1 billion would mean that accredited zoos and aquariums contribute $10 million per year to conservation. However, factoring in personnel time, facility costs, and all funds currently being spent on projects, the cumulative investment in conservation, research, and education by accredited zoos and aquariums would easily exceed that amount.[12] Regardless of their financial contribution, how do we measure the quality and impact of zoo- and aquarium-based conservation efforts? We must be committed to evaluating proposed and ongoing projects if zoos and aquariums are to spend their limited conservation resources wisely.

Also, how much should zoos and aquariums be required to improve animal welfare, short of completely replicating the wild? Zoos and aquariums are in a position to greatly increase quality of life for captive animals through improvements in exhibit design, scientifically based animal care programs, and policy. As we expand our accomplishments in these areas, the benefits of exhibiting animals in zoos and aquariums are increasingly likely to vastly outweigh the costs, as measured in terms of individual animal welfare. There will always be a gray area where costs and benefits are arguably equal, and it is here that ethical considerations should be carefully weighed when deciding whether a captive program is necessary. This is similar to the ethical considerations used by biomedical researchers when weighing the benefits of the research against the costs to individual animal welfare,[52] but in those cases, the cost to the animals is weighed against the benefit to humans and other animals. In this case, the cost to the individual animals is weighed against the benefit of the very survival of their species and the habitats on which they depend.

Like evolutionary change in any profession, the complex transformation of accredited zoos and aquariums into conservation and animal welfare organizations is being fueled in part by self-preservation, need, changing societal expectations, our increasing knowledge, and internal pressures. While external critics have certainly played a role in this process, much recent change has been generated from within. There has been a vast influx of talented, extremely well-educated people into accredited zoos and aquariums during the past decade. Some have come directly out of graduate school and others from responsible positions in academia, business, government, or the military. They have come to the zoologic profession with a love for animals and nature and a strong commitment to conservation and animal welfare. One consequence of this recent migration of new, highly trained personnel has been a growing professionalism, which has also led to an abundance of critical thinking and self-evaluation, including useful debate on the ethical basis for keeping wild animals in captivity.[53] We hope this report will continue the growth process by spurring additional discussion and debate throughout and beyond the zoologic community.

References

1. Jamieson D. Zoos revisited. In: Norton BG, Hutchins M, Maples T, and Stevens EF eds. *Ethics on the Ark: Zoos, animal welfare and wildlife conservation.* Washington, DC: Smithsonian Institution Press, 1995; 52–66.
2. Regan T. Are zoos morally defensible? In: Norton BG, Hutchins M, Maples T, and Stevens EF eds. *Ethics on the Ark: Zoos, animal welfare and wildlife conservation.* Washington, DC: Smithsonian Institution Press, 1995; 38–51.
3. Malamud R. *Reading zoos: Representations of animals and captivity.* Washington Square, NY: New York University Press, 2000.
4. Goldston L. Animals to go. *San Jose Mercury News* 1999; Feb:7–10.
5. Farinato R. Another view of zoos. In: *The state of the animals 2001.* Washington, DC: Humane Society of the United States, 2001; 145–147.
6. Satchell M. Investigative report: Cruel and usual. *US News and World Report* 2001; 133:26–33.
7. Green A. *Animal underworld: Inside America's black market for rare and exotic species.* New York: Center for Public Integrity, 1999.
8. *Guide to certification and standardized guidelines.* Silver Spring, MD: American Zoo and Aquarium Association, 2001.
9. Taylor S. Why accreditation? in *Proceedings.* Annual Conference of the American Zoo and Aquarium Association 2000; 7–12.
10. *AZA long-range plan 2001–2006.* Silver Spring, MD: American Zoo and Aquarium Association, 2001.

11. Ballentine J ed. *The 2003 AZA membership directory.* Silver Spring, MD: American Zoo and Aquarium Association, 2003.

12. *The collective impact of America's zoos and aquariums.* Silver Spring, MD: American Zoo and Aquarium Association, 1999.

13. *Public attitudes towards aquariums, theme parks and zoos.* Storrs, CT: The Roper Center for Public Opinion Research, 1992.

14. Tarpy C. New zoos: Taking down the bars. *National Geographic* 1993; Jul:2–37.

15. Sundquist F. End of the Ark? Captive breeding is out; conservation in the wild is in. *Int Wildl* 1995; Nov/Dec:22–29.

16. Cohn JP. Working outside the box: Zoos and aquariums are shifting their conservation focus to the wild. *Bioscience* 2002; 50:564–569.

17. Ebersole, RS. The new zoo. *Audubon* 2001; Nov/Dec:64–70.

18. Croke V. *The modern Ark: The story of zoos: Past, present and future.* New York: Scribner, 1997.

19. Hancocks D. *A different nature: The paradoxical world of zoos and their uncertain future.* Berkeley, CA: University of California Press, 2001.

20. Conway W, Hutchins M. Introduction. In: Conway WG, Hutchins M, Souza M, and Kapetanakos Y eds. *AZA field conservation resource guide.* Atlanta, GA: Zoo Atlanta and Wildlife Conservation Society, 2001; 1–7.

21. Hutchins M, Conway WG. Beyond Noah's Ark: The evolving role of modern zoological parks and aquariums in field conservation. *Int Zoo Yearbook* 1995; 34:117–130.

22. Hutchins M, Smith B. Characteristics of a world class zoo or aquarium in the twenty-first century. *Int Zoo Yearbook* 2003; 38:130–141.

23. Lankard J, ed. *Annual report on conservation and science, 1999–2000.* Silver Spring, MD: American Zoo and Aquarium Association, 2000.

24. Foose TJ. Riders of the last Ark: The role of captive breeding in conservation strategies. In: Kaufman L, Mallory K eds. *The last extinction.* Cambridge, MA: The MIT Press, 1986; 141–165.

25. Wiese R, Willis K, Hutchins M. Is genetic and demographic management conservation? *Zoo Biol* 1994; 13:297–299.

26. Smith B, Hutchins M. The value of captive breeding programmes to field conservation: Elephants as an example. *Pachyderm* 2000; 28:101–109.

27. Hutchins M, Willis K, Wiese R. Author's response. *Zoo Biol* 1995; 14:67–80.

28. Hutchins M, Wiese R, Willis K. Why we need captive breeding, in *Proceedings.* Conference of the American Zoo and Aquarium Association, Wheeling, West Virginia, 1996; 77–86.

29. Snyder NFR, Derrickson SR, Beissinger SR, Wiley, JW, Smith TB, Toone WD, and Miller B. Limitations of captive breeding in endangered species recovery. *Conservation Biology* 1996; 10:338–348.

30. Tolson P. The Mona/Virgin Islands boa SSP, the US Fish and Wildlife Service and the Departmento de Recursos Naturales de Pureto Rico. In: Conway WG, Hutchins M, Souza M, and Kapetanakos Y eds. *AZA field conservation resource guide.* Atlanta, GA: Zoo Atlanta and Wildlife Conservation Society, 2001; 177–180.

31. Hudson R. The Jamaican iguana recovery story: Rediscovery to recovery, 1990–1998. In: Conway WG, Hutchins M, Souza M, and Kapetanakos Y eds. *AZA field conservation resource guide.* Atlanta, GA: Zoo Atlanta and Wildlife Conservation Society, 2001; 42–48.

32. Maple TL. *Saving the giant panda.* Atlanta, GA: Longstreet Press, 2000.

33. Tilson R, Franklin N, Nyhus P, Sriyanto, B, Siswomartono, D., and Manansang J. In situ conservation of the Sumatran tiger in Indonesia. *International Zoo News* 1996; 316–323.

34. Tolson P. Partnering to restore biodiversity: A vision for AZA institutions. *AZA Communique* 2002; Jan:7–8.

35. Hutchins M. Research. In: Bell CE ed. *Encyclopedia of the world's zoos.* Vol 3. Chicago: Fitzroy Dearborn, 2001; 1076–1080.

36. Wilson EO. *The future of life.* Cambridge, MA: Harvard University Press, 2001.

37. Stoinski YT, Ogden J, Gold KC, and Maple TL. Captive apes and zoo education. In: Beck BB, Stoinski TS, Hutchins M, et al. eds. *Great apes and humans: The ethics of coexistence.* Washington, DC: Smithsonian Institution Press, 2001; 113–132.

38. Ogden J. Measuring our impact: What MIRP can mean to you. *AZA Communique* 2002; Sep:23–24.

39. Hutchins M, Souza M. AZA Conservation Endowment Fund: Zoos and aquariums supporting conservation action. In: Conway WG, Hutchins M, Souza M, and Kapetanakos Y eds. *AZA field conservation resource guide.* Atlanta: Zoo Atlanta and Wildlife Conservation Society; 2001; 281–297.

40. Eves H, Hutchins M. The Bushmeat Crisis Task Force: Cooperative efforts to curb the illegal commercial bushmeat trade in Africa. In: Conway WG, Hutchins M, Souza M, and Kapetanakos Y eds. *AZA field conservation resource guide.* Atlanta, GA: Zoo Atlanta and Wildlife Conservation Society, 2001:181–186.

41. Vrijenhook R. Natural processes, individuals, and units of conservation. In: Norton BG, Hutchins M, Stevens EF, and Maple TL eds. *Ethics on the Ark: Zoos, animal welfare and wildlife conservation.* Washington, DC: Smithsonian Institution Press, 1995; 74–92.

42. Hutchins M. Zoo and aquarium animal management and conservation: Current trends and future challenges. *Int. Zoo Yearbook* 2003; 38:14–28.

43. Hutchins M. What is AZA doing to enhance the welfare of captive animals? In *Proceedings.* Annu Conf Am Zoo Aquar Assoc 2001; 117–129.

44. Maple TL, McManamon R, Stevens E. Defining the good zoo: Animal care, maintenance and welfare. In: Norton BG, Hutchins M, Stevens EF, and Maple TL eds. *Ethics on the Ark: Zoos, animal welfare and wildlife conservation.* Washington, DC: Smithsonian Institution Press, 1995; 219–234.

45. Regan T. *The case for animal rights.* Berkeley, CA: University of California Press, 1988.

46. Warren MA. The moral status of great apes. In: Beck BB, Stoinski T, Hutchins M, and Maple TL eds. *Great apes and humans: Ethics of coexistence.* Washington, DC: Smithsonian Institution Press, 2002; 313–328.

47. Norton B. Caring for nature: A broader look at animal stewardship. In: Norton BG, Hutchins M, Stevens EF, and Maple TL eds. *Ethics on the Ark: Zoos, animal welfare and wildlife conservation.* Washington, DC: Smithsonian Institution Press, 1995; 102–121.

48. Hutchins M, Wemmer C. Wildlife conservation and animal rights: Are they compatible? In: Fox MW, Mickley LD eds. *Advances in animal welfare science 1986/87.* Boston, MA: Martinus Nijhoff Publishing, 1987; 111–137.

49. Shepherdson D, Mellen J, Hutchins M eds. *Second nature: Environmental enrichment for captive animals.* Washington, DC: Smithsonian Institution Press, 1999.

50. *AZA standards for elephant management and care.* Silver Spring, MD: American Zoo and Aquarium Association, 2001.

51. Thompson SD, Bell KJ. Institutional collection planning. *Zoo Biol* 1998; 17: 55–57.

52. Orlans B, Beauchamp TL, Dresser R, Morton DB, and Gluck, JP eds. *The human use of animals: Case studies in ethical choice.* New York: Oxford University Press, 1998.

53. Norton B, Hutchins M, Stevens EF, and Maple TL eds. *Ethics on the Ark: Zoos, animal welfare and wildlife conservation.* Washington, DC: Smithsonian Institution Press, 1995.

70 Opportunities Lost

Zoos and the Marsupial that Tried to Be a Wolf

Chris Wemmer

Wemmer assesses the responsibilities and directions of zoos and aquariums following identification of the global diversity crisis. He contrasts the conflicting pressures between providing recreational opportunities for the public, providing education to the visiting public, and providing a greater service to society through science and conservation activities. He advocates greater emphasis on using zoos to support science and conservation efforts.

In the archives of the National Zoo there is a story of an opportunity lost. As zoo stories go, it is not unique. There are many others like it. Such stories sometimes tell us about ourselves.

It started sometime in early 1902. Zoo director William Hornaday wanted to exhibit a thylacine: *Thylacinus cynocephalus*—the pouched beast with a dog's head. Depicted by Patterson as "a species perfectly distinct from any of the animal creation hitherto known . . ." (Quammen, 1997:281), the thylacine had been described almost 100 years earlier. Though sometimes called the Tasmanian tiger because of its striped coat, this strange marsupial was actually a "wannabe" wolf. The long-muzzled head with its short ears, the deep chest, and the feet and legs were distinctively dog-like, but the rear end and long tail hinted of marsupial ancestry. True dogs can wag their tails. This one could not. All the same, the thylacine remains a remarkable example of convergent evolution, and the largest carnivorous marsupial to survive into the twentieth century.

[. . .]

In due course, a Tasmanian trapper caught a female, which was shipped to the states. [. . .]

Over a period of about 90 years some 13 zoos on three continents exhibited about 55 thylacines (Guiler, 1986) (Jones, personal communication). Farmers killed nearly 2,200 for bounties during a 21-year period starting in 1888. The last recorded shooting of a thylacine was in 1930. Six years later the last captive animal died in the Hobart Zoo (Beresford and Bailey, 1981). Even in recent times footprints allegedly have been sighted, but irrefutable evidence of the thylacine's survival is lacking. In reality, the thylacine seems to be gone forever (Quammen, 1997).

What did we learn from the thylacines that lived in zoos? Almost nothing. Guiler (1986:66) commented that "[t]here was an extraordinary apathy shown by the various zoos for the fate of the thylacine." String their lives together and you have more than 100 thylacine years in captivity—ample opportunity for some keen observer to note a few details. [. . .] But the zoo legacy to knowledge and conservation of this species is scant. It is recorded in some amateur movie footage, and a few photographs. The rest is stored in a few museum cabinets.

I feel a nostalgic longing when I think of thylacines. But I feel the same way when I visit a zoo and look at any mysterious creature or endangered species. Will they too become opportunities lost to the institutions that celebrate their uniqueness? How many species we now exhibit will share the planet with us in 25 years, when our numbers reach 10 billion? I don't believe zoos are apathetic about the fate of their charges, but I am concerned about their ability to have a lasting and meaningful impact in a rapidly changing world. The biodiversity crisis is on our lips, but our actions send another message. We know zoos can't change the world, but many of us believe we can have a far greater impact than we do at present.

Zoological institutions have clearly acted upon the calls of their visionary leaders to heed the global biodiversity crisis. In the 1980s, the conservation movement added a challenging new dimension to our profession. We saw a remarkable convergence of purpose among the rank and file of our association. Directors, curators, and keepers from different zoos found themselves working together on American Zoo and Aquarium Association (AZA) Species Survival Plan (SSP) committees. Talented keepers and curators discovered latent skills. For many curators, humdrum jobs suddenly became more interesting. New friendships emerged based on a shared vision. The movement grew into a groundswell. The AZA's conservation movement, embodied in the SSP, Taxon Advisory Groups, Scientific Advisory Groups, and Conservation Action Partnerships are extraordinary examples of planning and cooperation among institutions (Hutchins and Conway, 1995). The IUCN/ Species Survival Commission's Conservation Breeding Specialist Group was born as a parallel movement in the international realm.

But not everyone was ready to ride the new wave. More midlevel zoo personnel were committed to the movement than directors, and some of the latter believed that "the tail was wagging the dog." When the AZA examined its mandate in the late 1980s, the board of directors consulted with institutional directors, and determined that the association's highest purpose was to provide members with services. While these services were seen clearly by the directors as serving the conservation mandate, the decision was disappointing for those who had been lifted by the surge of the new wave. Many midlevel members of the AZA had hoped for a declaration of commitment to a higher cause. They acknowledged that the AZA had made great advances in developing a conservation ethic, but their perception was that the organization's leaders were unable to agree that, as a unifying principle, conservation transcended the need for services.

[. . .]

Until we adopt a unifying philosophy for zoos and aquariums, our collective potential will not be achieved. We have all said it: "The public goes to the zoo to have a good time. Sure we 'do education,' but the hook is recreation." It's that familiar notion of service. We serve the public what it wants (entertainment) and at the same time we give it what it needs (education). But the word "entertainment" somehow doesn't do justice as a reason for keeping wild animals in captivity. Think about it. Isn't education the highest service zoos and aquariums can offer the visiting public? Surely, as a means of achieving conservation, it deserves to be our highest institutional mandate.

But there is another defect in what many perceive to be mainstream thinking about zoos and aquariums, and that is the notion that our visitors represent the ultimate target audience. Looking back, we can honestly say that the 18 zoos that exhibited thylacines certainly served their visitors, but did they serve society as a whole? They might have, had they been able to work together to prevent the thylacine's extinction. Serving society is a lot different from entertaining the public. Here is where science, captive breeding, reintroduction, education, and in situ conservation play a role. Unfortunately, the public doesn't always understand the benefits to society from zoos and aquariums. That's our responsibility, and that is what zoo and aquarium education should be all about.

Zoos and aquariums of the past didn't have the resources to study and conserve every species in their collections. The biodiversity crisis didn't loom darkly on the horizon. Nevertheless, people like Hornaday knew what was happening in the world, and took decisive action to save the American bison from extinction (Rorabacher, 1970). A lot has happened since then. Time is of the essence, and if we don't act soon, the world will lose much of its biota, including many of the most charismatic and engaging life forms we exhibit. Conway (2000) recently cited a prevailing excuse for inaction voiced by some of our colleagues: "Zoos and aquariums were not designed to be conservation organizations." Zoological institutions have unique and rich resources, staff with diverse skills and talents, and prominence in society. But do the leaders of our profession have the foresight and will to retrofit their organizations for a higher cause, and to make conservation and science their primary reasons for being? Let us think deeply about it, and resolve not to witness another opportunity lost.

References

Beresford Q., Bailey G. 1981. *Search for the Tasmanian Tiger*. Hobart: Blubber Head Press. 81 p.

Conway W.G. 2000. *The Changing Role of Zoos in the 21st Century*. AZA Communique, January: 11–12.

Guiler E.R. 1986. *Thylacine: the Tragedy of the Tasmanian Tiger*. Melbourne, Australia: Oxford University Press. 207 p.

Hutchins M., Conway W.G. 1995. Beyond Noah's ark: the evolving role of modern zoological parks and aquariums in field conservation. *Int. Zoo Year b.* 34:117–130.

Quammen D. 1997. *The Song of the Dodo: Island Biogeography in an Age of Extinctions*. New York: Simon and Schuster. 702 p.

Rorabacher J.A. 1970. *The American Buffalo in Transition: An Historical and Economic Survey of the Bison in America*. St Cloud, MN: North Star Press. 142 p.

71 Ecological Ethics in Captivity

Balancing Values and Responsibilities in Zoo and Aquarium Research under Rapid Global Change

Ben A. Minteer and James P. Collins

Minteer and Collins note that there are less clear boundaries between zoo- and aquarium-based conservation and field based approaches as zoos and aquariums become more active in field conservation work and as researchers and managers consider more intensive interventions in wild populations and ecosystems to meet key conservation. These new trends raise significant ethical concerns about human intervention in populations and ecosystems, including the proper role of zoos and aquariums as centers for animal research and conservation.

Introduction

Responsibilities to wildlife in field research and conservation projects have always been complicated because ethical duties to animals, populations, and ecosystems can pull wildlife scientists and managers in different directions (Minteer and Collins 2005a, 2005b, 2008). In recent years, this situation has been made even more complex by the impacts of global change (especially climate change), which, in many quarters, has forced a reassessment of research practice and conservation policy. Scientists and managers wrestle with understanding and protecting species and ecosystems in a rapidly changing environment (Hannah 2012; Marris 2011). In parallel, conservation ethics and values are being reexamined and adapted to fit dynamic ecological and institutional contexts in which traditional models of protecting the environment are being replaced by more pragmatic and interventionist approaches less wedded to historical systems and static preservationist ideals (Camacho et al. 2010; Minteer and Collins 2012). Furthermore, as we acknowledge the history and extent of human influence and impact on ecological systems—even for the most remote parts of the planet—we are confronted with a changing vision of nature. Instead of a stark contrast between "wild" and "managed," we now encounter a continuum of systems more or less impacted by human activity, a scale of degrees and increments (rather than absolutes) of anthropogenic influence that upends many customary divisions in conservation science, policy, and ethics (see, e.g., Dudley 2011).

A case in point is the weakening division between ex situ, or zoo- and aquarium-based research and conservation, and in situ, or field-based biological research and conservation practice. Global climate change, along with other drivers of rapid environmental transformation (e.g., accelerating habitat loss and the spread of invasive species and infectious diseases), is increasingly being viewed as requiring a more proactive and intensive philosophy of conservation and ecological management (Hobbs et al. 2011). One consequence of this shift is that the conceptual and empirical boundaries separating "the field" from "the animal holding facility" are growing hazy: zoos and aquariums are becoming more engaged in field conservation programs, while preserves and natural areas are becoming more intensively managed and designed for a diverse mix of conservation and resource management outputs (Cole and Yung 2010; Dickie et al. 2007; Pritchard et al. 2011).

At the same time, there are new calls within conservation science and management circles to think differently about the connections between captive and wild populations. Indeed, many wildlife scientists are recognizing that captive and wild populations should be seen not as separate biological and management domains but viewed instead as linked metapopulations (e.g., Lacy 2012). They argue that the sustainability of the former requires exchange of animals and DNA from the wild, whereas the viability of the latter may require contributions from ex situ populations as well as the refinement of small-population research and management techniques (Lacy 2012; Redford et al. 2012). Such techniques, however, may only be feasible in the controlled environment of the zoo or aquarium.

The softening of the distinction between ex situ and in situ, the quickening pace of biodiversity loss, and the parallel rise of a more interventionist ecological ethic have significant implications for how we understand and make tradeoffs among values and responsibilities in conservation research and practice. These include the concerns of animal welfare and animal rights as well as species-level and ecosystem-level conservation values. Although all of these obligations remain an important part of the ethical landscape of conservation research and practice, they are being reshaped by the need to respond to rapid environmental change as well as by the research demands of a more interventionist conservation effort.

A good example of this trend is the Amphibian Ark Project (AArk), a global consortium of zoos, aquariums, universities, and conservation organizations that has organized itself around the goal of slowing global amphibian declines and extinctions, which by all accounts have reached historic levels over the last several decades (Collins and Crump 2009; Gewin 2008; Zippel et al. 2011). Zoos and aquariums in the AArk serve as conservation way stations for amphibian populations facing possible extinction because of the combined forces of habitat loss, infectious disease, and climate change. But they also function as centers of research into the drivers of population decline, the possibilities of disease mitigation, and the prospect of selecting for biological resistance to a lethal amphibian pathogen (Woodhams et al. 2011). With the mission of rescuing, housing, and breeding hundreds of amphibian species to return them eventually to native localities, the AArk is emerging as a hybrid or "pan situ" approach to biodiversity protection, a project that integrates (and blurs the borders between) ex situ and in situ conservation (Dickie et al. 2007; Gewin 2008).

In addition, the breeding and research activities within the AArk evoke questions of animal welfare and conservation ethics, including the tensions between and within these commitments. Amphibian research can be invasive and even lethal to individual animals, raising significant and familiar welfare and rights-based concerns in zoo and aquarium research. Moreover, infectious disease research, a significant part of the AArk research portfolio, carries the risk of an infected host or the pathogen itself infecting other animals in a captive-breeding facility or even escaping into local populations. In fact, just such a case occurred when the often-lethal pathogen the amphibian chytrid fungus moved from a common species in a captive-breeding facility to an endangered species. When the latter was introduced into Mallorca to establish a population in the wild, subsequent research revealed that animals were infected by the pathogen from the breeding facility before transfer (Walker et al. 2008). Still, it is clear that many amphibian species will experience further declines or go extinct in the wild if dramatic measures such as the AArk are not pursued until a sustainable recovery and conservation strategy is developed.

In what follows, we examine the ethical and policy-level aspects of research and conservation activities that involve captive wildlife in zoos and aquariums, focusing on some of the implications of accelerating biodiversity decline and rapid environmental change. As we will see, the most pressing ethical issues surrounding zoo- and aquarium-based wildlife in this era of rapid global change are not best described as traditional animal rights versus conservation dilemmas but instead concern what we believe are far more complicated and broad-ranging debates within conservation ethics and practice. These debates include devising an ethically justified research and recovery strategy for wildlife across evolving in situ and ex situ conservation contexts that may require a more interventionist approach to biodiversity management. Zoo and aquarium researchers in a time of rapid global change must find creative ways to integrate and steer the expanding biodiversity research efforts of their facilities. In doing so, they will need to provide the ethical justification and scientific guidance for responding to the plight of those globally endangered species that can benefit from controlled and often intensive analysis in ex situ centers.

Debating the Moral Standing of Animals and the Environment

Ethicists and environmental advocates have often found themselves deeply divided over the moral status of and duties owed to nonhuman animals—a division that has existed despite the common effort among environmental and animal philosophers to expand societal thinking beyond a narrow anthropocentrism (e.g., Callicott 1980; Regan 2004; Sagoff 1984; Singer 1975). The dispute is usually attributed to different framings of moral considerability and significance. Animal welfare and animal rights approaches prioritize the interests or rights of individual animals, whereas environmental ethics typically embraces a more holistic view that focuses on the viability of populations and species and especially the maintenance of ecological and evolutionary processes. The difference between these two views can be philosophically quite stark. For example, animal-centered ethicists such as Peter Singer believe that it makes little sense to talk about nonsentient entities such as species, systems, or processes as having their own "interests" or a good of their own (as environmental ethicists often describe them), although they can be of value to sentient beings and thus objects of indirect moral concern.

In the view of ecocentric ethicists such as J. Baird Callicott and Holmes Rolston, however, an ethics of the environment is incomplete if it does not accord direct moral status to species and ecosystems and the evolutionary and ecological processes that produced and maintain them. Most environmental ethicists are sensitive to animal welfare considerations and are certainly aware that many threats to populations, species, and ecosystems impact animal welfare either directly or indirectly. Typically, however, they advocate focusing moral concern and societal action on such ends as the protection of endangered species and the preservation of wilderness rather than reducing the pain and suffering (or promoting the rights or dignity) of wild animals. Domestic animals are even further outside the traditional ambit of environmental ethicists; indeed, their comparative lack of wildness and autonomy has for some suggested a lower moral status as "artifacts" of human technology rather than moral subjects (see, e.g., Katz 1991).

It is important to point out here that although "animal rights" is often used as a blanket term for ethical and advocacy positions defending the humane treatment or rights of animals, philosophers and others often make an important distinction between animal rights and animal welfare arguments. The former is generally seen as a nonconsequentialist view of an animal's moral status (i.e., a view on which the covered class of individuals is entitled to fair treatment following ascriptions of moral personhood or inherent worth similar to the logic of entitlement we ideally accord individual human persons). Alternatively, the welfare position is traditionally rooted in consequentialist moral reasoning whereby the impacts of decisions and actions affecting the interests or good of the animal are weighed against other goods (including the interests and preferences of humans), and decisions are made based on an assessment of the aggregate good of a particular action, all things being equal. What this means is that, although in many cases both animal rights and animal welfare philosophies will justify similar policy and practical outcomes, in some instances the welfare position may be more accommodating to animal harms when these are offset by the net benefits produced by a particular action or rule. It bears emphasizing, however, that calculations of these benefits and harms must be fair and consistent; they cannot give arbitrary weight to human preferences simply because they are anthropocentric in nature, and all interests—including those of the animal—must be considered.

Not surprisingly, these different approaches to moral consideration have often produced sharp disagreements at the level of practice, especially in wildlife management and biological field research. For example, animal rights proponents regularly condemn wildlife research and management practices that inflict harm or even mortality upon individual animals, such as the lethal control of invasive species, the culling of overabundant native wildlife, and the use of invasive field research techniques; practices that have for decades been widely accepted among wildlife and natural resource managers (e.g., Gustin 2003; Smith 2007). Controversial cases such as the reduction of irruptive whitetail deer populations threatening forest health in New England (Dizard 1999), amphibian toe clipping in capture-mark-recapture field studies (May 2004), the hot branding of sea lions for identification in marine research projects (Minteer and Collins 2008), and the culling of black-throated blue warblers for an ecological field experiment (Vucetich and Nelson 2007) illustrate the ethical conflicts characterizing much of the environmental/conservation ethics and animal welfare/rights debate in wildlife field research.

Despite attempts by some ethicists and scientists to find common ground between animal- and environmental-centered values at either the philosophic or pragmatic level (e.g., Jamieson 1998; Minteer and Collins 2008; Minteer 2012; Perry and Perry 2008; Varner 1998), many observers believe that the gulf separating ethically individualistic, animal-centered commitments and conservationists' more holistic commitment to promoting the viability of populations and communities is simply too wide to bridge, even in cases where animal-centered and biodiversity-centered advocates have common cause (Hutchins 2008; Meffe 2008).

This division has recently been reinforced by public stances taken by wildlife conservation organizations such as The Wildlife Society (TWS), which in 2011 released a position statement on animal rights and conservation that underscored what the organization described as the incompatibility between these two ethical and policy orientations (http://wildlife.org/policy/position-statements). Animal-centered views perceived as more moderate in nature, such as the commitment to the humane treatment of animals in research and management (i.e., a weaker animal welfare position) are ostensibly accepted by TWS, although the organization's position here probably still falls short of what animal welfare ethicists such as Singer would argue is demanded by a principled concern for animal well-being in research and management contexts.

The Ethical Complexity of Zoo and Aquarium Conservation

The practice of keeping animals in zoos and aquariums is one of the more intriguing areas of conflict within the animal ethics-conservation ethics debate. The presumption that the keeping of animals in captivity in zoos and aquariums is morally acceptable has long been questioned by animal rights-oriented philosophers who believe that such facilities by definition diminish animals' liberty and dignity as beings possessing inherent worth (e.g., Jamieson 1985, 1995; Regan 1995). Such critiques either implicitly or explicitly evoke the unpleasant history (from both the contemporary welfare and wildlife conservation perspective) of zoos as wildlife menageries designed primarily for public titillation and entertainment, including notorious cases of animal abuse and the exploitation of captive wildlife for profit. Zoo advocates, however, argue that modern zoos and aquariums have a vital societal mission to educate zoo visitors regarding the necessity of wildlife conservation and the dilemma of global biodiversity decline and that they contribute (and could contribute even more) significantly to fundraising efforts to support conservation projects in the field (e.g., Christie 2007; Hutchins et al. 1995; Zimmerman 2010).

This broad ethical debate over zoos and aquariums in society and the various trade-offs it evokes regarding animal welfare, conservation, scientific research, and entertainment have been complicated by particular high profile cases, such as the keeping of elephants or large carnivores in zoos (Clubb and Mason 2003; Wemmer and Christen 2008) and whales or dolphins (cetaceans) in aquariums and marine parks (Bekoff 2002; Grimm 2011; Kirby 2012). Among other issues, these cases often reveal disagreements among scientists about conditions for housing some of the more charismatic, large, and popular animals in zoos away from in-range conditions as well as differences in assessments of species-specific welfare impacts and requirements across a range of taxa (Hosey et al. 2011). They also exemplify the welfare-entertainment-education-conservation nexus that forms much of the normative and ethical discourse around zoos in modern society (Hancocks 2001; Hanson 2002).

Zoos and aquariums therefore raise a number of ethical issues, from the basic question of the moral acceptability of keeping animals in captivity to more specific arguments and debates over practices such as captive (conservation) breeding, zoo-based research, wild animal acquisition, habitat enrichment, and the commercialization of wildlife (see, e.g., Davis 1997; Kreger and Hutchins 2010; Norton et al. 1995). Clearly, these practices provoke a set of complicated questions about our responsibilities to captive animals and the conservation of species and habitats in the wild.

Perhaps one of the strongest conservation-based arguments supporting housing animals in zoos and aquariums today is that these facilities provide the ability to create "captive assurance populations" through ex situ breeding, with the goal of reintroducing some individuals back into the wild to restore or expand lost or declining populations (Beck et al. 1994; Reid and Zippel 2008). This technique, described earlier in our discussion of the AArk, has produced some notable conservation successes in recent decades, including the recovery of (among other species) the Arabian oryx, the black-footed ferret, and the California condor. On the other hand, many animal rights-oriented critics of conservation breeding and the reintroduction efforts of zoos, such as the advocacy organization People for the Ethical Treatment of Animals (PETA), argue that captive breeding efforts are biased toward the breeding of "cute" animals of value to the public (rather than breeding for conservation purposes) and that such practices create surplus animals that are subsequently transferred to inferior facilities and exploited (www.peta.org/about/why-peta/zoos.aspx). PETA questions as well the broader goal of releasing captive-born and raised animals to the wild, pointing out the inherent difficulties surrounding reintroductions, including the risks they pose to the reintroduced animals and other wildlife in situ. Although these sorts of challenges have also been noted by wildlife biologists and biodiversity scientists, many advocates of conservation breeding and reintroduction programs have argued that further research and improved biological assessment and monitoring efforts can improve the likelihood of success for the release or reintroduction of captive animals to the wild (Earnhardt 2010; Fa et al. 2011).

The data suggest that zoos and aquariums are playing an increasingly significant role in field conservation programs and partnerships. In its 2010 Annual Report on Conservation Science, the Association of Zoos and Aquariums (AZA) lists zoos engaged in more than 1,970 conservation projects (i.e., activities undertaken to benefit in situ wildlife populations) in over 100 countries (www.aza.org/annual-report-on-conservation-and-science/). The AZA coordinates taxon advisory groups and species survival plans to manage conservation breeding, develop in situ and ex situ conservation strategies, and establish management, research, and conservation priorities (www.aza.org/). These experts (which include biologists, veterinarians, reproductive physiologists, and animal behaviorists, among other researchers) also contribute to the development of taxon-specific animal care manuals that provide guidance for animal care based on current science and best practices in animal management (www.aza.org/animal-care-manuals).

As part of their expanding efforts in field conservation, ex situ wildlife facilities are also becoming more significant players in biodiversity research. As Wharton (2007) notes, systematic, zoo-based research on reproduction, behavior, genetics, and other biological dimensions has made many important contributions to the improvement of animal husbandry practice over the past three decades. Moreover, ex situ animal research conducted to inform field conservation is seen as a growing priority for zoos and aquariums, especially in light of worrying trends in global biodiversity decline and the widely acknowledged potential of the extensive zoo and aquarium network to carry out studies that can provide conservation-relevant knowledge for field projects (WAZA 2005; MacDonald and Hofer 2011).

Applied research in zoological institutions (i.e., research motivated by the goal of improving conservation and/or veterinary science) is not the only research contribution of zoos and aquariums, however. Basic research on captive wildlife is also conducted throughout the system and is highly valued by many wildlife scientists, both within and outside of zoological institutions. At Zoo Atlanta, for example, researchers are presently conducting a number of studies designed to inform our understanding of wildlife biology, including the biomechanics of sidewinding locomotion in snakes, social behavior and acoustic communication in giant pandas, and taxonomic and phylogenetic studies of frogs, among other taxa (J. Mendelson, Zoo Atlanta, personal communication, 2012). Such research is often impossible to conduct in the wild, and thus captive populations can hold great value as specimens for basic scientific study.

Although not every zoo and aquarium has the capacity to conduct extensive animal research (focused on either veterinary/animal care or conservation purposes), the larger and better-equipped facilities such as the Bronx Zoo, the San Diego Zoo, Zoo Atlanta, the Monterey Bay Aquarium, and the St. Louis Zoo have become active wildlife and conservation research centers in addition to being popular educational and entertainment facilities. For all these reasons, zoos, aquariums, and other ex situ facilities (e.g., botanic gardens) are being championed by organizations such as the World Association of Zoos and Aquariums as potential models of "integrated conservation" given their ability to participate in a wide range of conservation activities, from ex situ research, education, and breeding of threatened species to field projects in support of animals in the wild to serving (in the case of the AArk) as temporary conservation rescue centers to protect animals threatened by rapid environmental change (WAZA 2005; Zippel et al. 2011). Whether these facilities can develop successful reintroduction programs that will lead to the ultimate recovery of populations they are holding temporarily (such as the AArk program) or whether these "temporary" efforts become de facto and permanent ex situ "solutions" to particular wildlife conservation problems in the field, however, remains to be seen.

For many wildlife biologists and conservationists, then, breeding and conservation-oriented research on captive wildlife are seen as essential activities that should not be halted on the basis of animal welfare and animal rights objections. The ethical imperative to save threatened species from further decline and extinction in the wild has for them a priority over concerns regarding individual animal welfare. Humane treatment of animals (both ex situ and in the field), however, remains a clear ethical obligation of zoo-based scientists and professionals as well as field researchers. It is an obligation formalized in the ethical codes of the major professional and scientific societies, such as the AZA and the Society for Conservation Biology.

Yet not everyone is convinced that this reinvigorated conservation justification for keeping animals in captivity is a compelling rationale for such facilities. For example, some critics have argued in the past that actual conservation-relevant research conducted in or by zoos and aquariums is, in fact, a relatively minor part of their mission and that it cannot justify keeping animals in captivity (see, e.g., Jamieson 1995). Such criticisms are, however, slowly losing their bite as we witness the more recent growth of zoo-based research for conservation purposes (Stanley Price and Fa 2007). Still, it is true that much of the research conducted by zoos today remains focused on animal husbandry rather than conservation of animals in the wild (Fa et al. 2011).

This situation may be changing, however. Indeed, research on captive wildlife in zoos and aquariums (including that driven by conservation concerns) is predicted to continue to grow in significance in the coming decades. Perhaps the most obvious reason for this is access. As mentioned above, scientists in ex situ facilities have the ability to carry out potentially high-impact research projects on captive animals that may be too costly, risky, or logistically impossible to perform on small, wild populations in situ (Barbosa 2009). This research can be valuable for improving animal husbandry in zoos and aquariums, but it can also be useful for augmenting field conservation projects because biological data from captive animals is incorporated in the planning and implementation of field interventions (Wharton 2007). Data collected from animals drawn from populations that only exist in small numbers in the wild are particularly valuable; therefore, captive populations afford important opportunities to collect data on rare species in a controlled and safe environment.

To the degree that research on zoo and aquarium wildlife is used to inform and improve efforts to conserve and manage vulnerable wildlife populations in the field, it may be defended as an ethically justified activity according to the more holistic obligation to promote species viability and ecosystem health—even if it includes techniques that disrupt or harm captive wildlife in the process. Yet, these activities could still be challenged by more animal rights-based arguments that claim that such harms, including the fundamental loss of freedom and the degradation of an animal subject's dignity associated with captivity, can never be offset by the production of beneficial biological consequences at the population or species level (i.e., "good consequences" in the aggregate cannot justify the violation of the moral duty to respect the worth of the individual animal).

For an animal welfare proponent willing to take a more pragmatic position, however, unavoidable harms or disvalues in zoo and aquarium research projects that directly lead to the promotion of the good of the species in the wild may be viewed as ethically tolerable in light of the collective benefit for sentient animals. This view could follow from the utilitarian principle to evaluate an action based on its consequences for all sentient beings impacted by the action or from a more integrated ethical system in which both animal welfare and conservation ethics are operant in moral decision making (see, e.g., Minteer and Collins 2005a, 2005b). Indeed, we suspect that most informed animal welfare supporters also see the value of wildlife conservation and landscape protection (or at least are not opposed to these activities). Therefore, they should not dismiss the real population, species, and ecosystem benefits of research on captive wildlife, especially in a time of global change.

The ethical evaluation of research on captive wildlife, however, can become even more complicated, especially if one holds the foundational view that it is wrong to place animals in captivity in the first place. Research undertaken primarily to improve animal care in ex situ facilities, for example, would appear to be a morally justifiable activity, especially if it produces results than can help zoo managers enrich habitats and improve the health and well-being of wildlife in their care. That is, the research would seem to produce a positive value that deserves to be weighed against any disvalue produced by harming or stressing an animal during the research process. And yet, this research could still be seen as morally unacceptable even if it improves the welfare of captive animals because it destroys the animal's freedom or treats them as a "mere means" to some anthropocentric end. Therefore, according to this abolitionist position, zoo and aquarium wildlife research conducted under the banner of improving animal care or husbandry makes the mistake of assuming that keeping animals in zoos and aquariums is itself defensible, a stance that many arguing from a strong animal rights framework flatly reject (e.g., Jamieson 1985, 1995; Regan 1995).

But what about the case where research on captive wildlife is demonstrated to be necessary to obtain information relevant to the conservation and management of threatened populations in the wild? In such situations, strong ethical objections to the keeping of animals in ex situ facilities, to interfering in their lives, and so forth arguably have comparatively less normative force. To reject this claim, one would have to argue that the well-being of captive animals is and should be a completely separate moral issue from the welfare of wild populations—a position that, as mentioned earlier, is difficult to hold in our increasingly integrated conservation environment. This does not entail the rejection of animal welfare considerations in research design and conduct; these remain compelling at all stages of the research process. But it provides a powerful and morally relevant consideration for undertaking that research rather than ruling it out on moral grounds.

We should underscore that this conclusion does not hold for poorly designed or weakly motivated research projects that promise to shed little new scientific light on wildlife biology and behavior relevant to conservation or that appear to essentially reproduce studies already performed on either captive or wild animals in the field (Minteer and Collins 2008). Determining the conservation value of the proposed research and its scientific necessity is thus a critical activity bearing on the welfare and conservation of animals across in situ and field settings. Yet it is an analysis that necessarily contains a measure of uncertainty that can complicate evaluations and proposed trade-offs among animal welfare, scientific discovery, and the potential for the research to produce results with a direct application to the conservation, management, or recovery of populations in the wild (Parris et al. 2010).

Improved husbandry and conservation value in the field are not the only potential benefits of zoo and aquarium research for wildlife, however. As Lewis (2007) notes, research on captive animals in ex situ facilities may also yield results that can pay dividends in the form of improved animal welfare in field research projects. This is especially true in the case of zoos and aquariums with extensive veterinary departments with the capacity to develop equipment and protocols that minimize research impacts on wildlife in field studies. Such projects might include research on novel, less-invasive animal marking and sampling techniques, the development of safer forms of darting and the use of anesthesia, and the creation of new breeding techniques for recovering particular wild animal populations (Lewis 2007). Although it is not always entirely clear which interventions should be considered invasive in the animal research context or what exactly constitutes harm in these analyses (see, e.g., Goodrowe 2003; Parris et al. 2010; Pauli et al. 2010), it does seem to be the case that wildlife researchers in both ex situ and field study environments are increasingly adopting noninvasive sampling and study techniques for wildlife research, signifying, perhaps, a growing sensitivity to animal welfare in field biology and conservation (Robbins 2009).

If ex situ research on animals can lead to the development of less-invasive technologies and research protocols, then some of the welfare concerns raised by the manipulation or harm of zoo and aquarium animals in the research process that produces these technologies may be offset, at least to a degree and at the aggregate (i.e., population, species, and ecosystem) level, by the net welfare benefits of adopting these less-invasive tools and techniques in biological field research. It is important to note once again, however, that this judgment will likely still not satisfy strict animal rightists who typically resist such attempts at "value balancing" (see e.g., Regan 2004). Furthermore, and as mentioned above, acceptance of animal harms in such research should hold only as long as the research in question is judged to be scientifically sound and well-designed (i.e., as long as it does not run afoul of the "reduction, refinement, and replacement" directives of the use of animals in the life sciences, which are designed to minimize the impact of research activities on animal welfare and screen out research designs that are not ethically justified, scientifically necessary, or efficient (Russell and Burch 1959).

Rapid Global Change and the Evolving Ethics of Ex Situ Research

It is clear that ex situ facilities such as zoos and aquariums will continue to increase in importance as centers of scientific research and conservation action in the twenty-first century (Conde et al. 2011; Conway 2011; Fa et al. 2011). The forces of global environmental change, including climate change, accelerating habitat loss, and the spread of infectious diseases and invasive species, along with the synergies among these and other threats, are currently exerting great pressure on wild species and ecosystems. This pressure is expected to only increase in the coming decades (Rands et al. 2010; Stokstad 2010; Thomas et al. 2004). These dynamics have suggested to many zoo scientists and conservationists an expanding role for many zoos and aquariums in wildlife protection. They can function as safe havens for the more vulnerable species threatened in the wild, as research institutions seeking to understand the impact of global environmental change on wildlife, and as active players in the increasingly intensive process of wildlife conservation in situ, including population management and veterinary care (Conway 2011). As Swaisgood (2007) points out, with the requirement of more intensive managerial interventions in the field because of human encroachment, habitat modification, and other changes, many of the issues central to zoo research and conservation (including animal welfare, the impacts of human disturbance on wildlife, and the consequences of the introduction of animals into novel environments) are increasingly drawing the interest of wildlife researchers and managers in natural areas and in situ conservation projects.

All of these conditions speak to the necessity of wildlife research in zoos and aquariums for informing conservation science under conditions of rapid environmental change, including (most notably) research on the effects of climate change on animal health (MacDonald and Hofer 2011). For example, aquariums can simulate climate change impacts such as shifts in temperature and salinity, the effects of which can be studied on fish growth, breeding, and behavior (Barbosa 2009). Such research could contribute to our understanding of the stresses exerted by global change on wildlife and consequently inform and improve conservation and management efforts in situ.

Another line of research in the domain of global change biology (and wildlife adaptation to environment change) includes studies of captive animals' responses to pathogens and emergent diseases, such as the work undertaken as part of the aforementioned AArk (Woodhams et al. 2011). Notably, these investigations could allow scientists to gain a better grasp of the consequences of temperature variations and disease transmission for the health of wild populations before any effects take hold (Barbosa 2009). The AArk example illustrates the kind of ethical balancing that needs to be performed for claims surrounding animal and species-level welfare and the health and historic integrity of ecosystems. For many amphibian species, AArk is a place of last resort. Once the amphibian chytrid enters an ecosystem, at least some susceptible species will not be able to return to their native habitats without an intervention strategy such as selective breeding for infectious-disease tolerance. An alternative tactic is managed relocation (i.e., the translocation of populations from their native habitat to novel environments that may be well outside their historic range) (e.g., Schwartz et al. 2012). Both approaches, however, involve ethical decisions that balance the welfare of individual frogs and salamanders against that of populations and species as well as the historic integrity of ecosystems (i.e., the particular mix of species and communities that have evolved in these systems over time) (Winston et al. [2014]).

Health- and disease-oriented wildlife research in zoos and aquariums may not only be targeted at wildlife conservation. The public health community, for example, may also have a significant role to play in zoo research in the near term. Epidemiologists and others have noted the value of zoo collections for biosurveillance (i.e., as biological monitoring stations that can be studied to understand and plan for the emergence of future infectious diseases posing public health risks) (McNamara 2007). This proposal raises two further interesting ethical questions regarding the evaluation of zoo- and aquarium-based research under global change: (1) the acceptability of wildlife health research motivated by improving field conservation of the species and (2) wildlife health research that enlists captive wildlife as "sentinels" (McNamara 2007) to provide an early warning system for infectious diseases that might impact human welfare. Both research projects could be pursued under the banner of "wildlife, health, and climate change," yet each would differ in its underlying ethical justification. One program would likely be more species-centered or nonanthropocentric (wildlife health research for conservation purposes), whereas the other would presumably be defended on more anthropocentric grounds, given the focus on safeguarding public health. This philosophic division, however, is not always that well defined, especially if wildlife health research in zoos and aquariums has benefits for both in situ conservation and more human-centered interests (e.g., the provision of ecosystem services). Still, the different research foci would be expected to evoke some differences in ethical analysis regarding their implications for animal welfare, conservation, and human welfare ethics.

For a swelling number of cases, then, scientific study and refinement of conservation breeding techniques, wildlife health research, and so forth will likely be necessary to save focal species in the wild under dynamic and perhaps unprecedented environmental conditions (Gascon et al. 2007). Ethical objections to conservation breeding or to the impacts of high-priority conservation research on captive wildlife motivated by animal welfare and rights concerns will, we believe, become less compelling as the need for captive assurance populations increases (because of the impacts of global change). These ethical objections will also weaken as we see the rise of additional partnerships between ex situ and field conservation organizations and facilities and especially as the former become more directly engaged in recovery and reintroduction efforts that benefit animals in the wild. It is one thing to evaluate captive-breeding programs designed to provide a steady supply of charismatic animals for zoo display. These have rightly drawn the ire of animal advocacy organizations as discussed earlier. It is another thing to assess those activities with the goal of recovering wildlife populations threatened in the field because of accelerating environmental change.

This does not mean that the ethical challenges of recognizing and promoting animal welfare concerns in ex situ research and conservation will or should be swept aside but rather that the more significant (and often more demanding) ethical questions, at least in our view, will take place on the species conservation side of the ethical ledger. These challenges will include the task of accommodating a philosophy of scientific and managerial interventionism in wildlife populations and ecological systems as rapidly emerging threats to species viability and ecosystem health move wildlife researchers and biodiversity managers into a more aggressive and preemptive role in conservation science and practice (Hobbs et al. 2011; Minteer and Collins 2012). The risks attached to this shift include creating further ecological disruption by intervening in biological populations and systems, and a more philosophic consequence—the transgression of venerable preservationist ideals that have long inspired and motivated the efforts of conservationists and ecologists to study and protect species and ecosystems.

For example, ethical dilemmas surrounding the translocation of wildlife populations from native habitats to new environments, including temporary relocations to ex situ facilities such as zoos and aquariums, raise a set of difficult technical, philosophic, and ethical questions for conservation scientists and wildlife biologists (Minteer and Collins 2010). Beyond the animal welfare or animal rights concerns about handling and moving animals that may experience considerable stress (or even mortality) during this process, such practices will also have implications for (1) the original source ecosystems (i.e., the community-level impacts of removing individuals from populations stressed by climate change), (2) the temporary ex situ facility that houses the animals (including shifts in resources and collection space as well as risks of disease transmission) (e.g., Greenwood et al. 2012), and (3) the native species present in the eventual "recipient" ecosystems once the wildlife are introduced (Ricciardi and Simberloff 2009).

Another example is the practice of ecological engineering for species conservation in the wild, which can involve the significant modification (and even invention) of habitat to improve field conservation efforts. Along these lines, Shoo et al. (2011) have proposed considering and testing a number of interventionist approaches to the conservation of amphibian populations threatened by climate change. These include activities such as the manipulation of water levels and canopy cover at breeding sites as well as the creation of new wetland habitat able to support populations under variable rainfall scenarios. The investigators suggest employing an adaptive management protocol to experimentally determine whether and to what extent such manipulations are effective in the field.

Such conservation challenges and others like them ultimately compel us to rethink our responsibilities to safeguard declining species and promote ecosystem integrity and health in an increasingly dynamic environment. We believe that this analysis will also require a reassessment of wildlife research priorities and protocols (including the relative significance of animal welfare concerns in research and conservation) for some time to come.

Conclusions

The ethical terrain of zoo and aquarium research and conservation is experiencing its own rapid and unpredictable shifts that mirror the accelerating pace of environmental and societal change outside these facilities. What is required, we believe, is a more concentrated engagement with a range of ethical and pragmatic considerations in the appraisal of animal research under these conditions. The growing vulnerability of many species to the often lethal combination of climate change, habitat degradation, emerging infectious diseases, and related threats has created a sense of urgency within the biodiversity science community. We need to respond with research agendas that can help to understand and predict the impact of these forces on the viability of populations and species in the wild and to inform actions and policies designed to conserve these populations and species.

Part of this ethical appraisal will require asking some hard questions of zoos and aquariums regarding their priorities and abilities to assume this more demanding position in conservation science, especially because some observers have suggested a need for greater planning and research capacity in these facilities (Anderson et al. 2010; Hutchins and Thompson 2008). Zoological institutions are idiosyncratic entities, and thus there is often a great deal of variability in how particular zoos and aquariums interpret their conservation mission (J. Mendelson, Zoo Atlanta, personal communication, 2012). The divide between mission and practice can produce significant challenges for these institutions as they take on a more aggressive conservation role. For example, and as mentioned above, many would argue that it is critical for zoos and aquariums to avoid becoming the final stop for species threatened in the wild. Instead, they should be true partners in what we have called an integrated, pan situ conservation management strategy across captive, wild, and semiwild contexts. The development by zoos and aquariums of more explicit reintroduction plans in such cases would therefore help ensure that their conservation ethic remains compatible with that of the wider community, which generally favors the maintenance of wild populations (i.e., in situ conservation) whenever possible.

One implication of this move by zoos and aquariums toward a more expanded research and conservation mission is that it will likely affect other zoo programs that have long dominated the culture and activities of zoo keeping. The display of exotic animals for public entertainment, for example, may be impacted as zoos and aquariums attempt to carve out more space for research and conservation activities, both in their facilities and in their budgets. On this point, Conway (2011) proposes that zoos will need to commit to creating more "conservation relevant zoo space" as they make wildlife preservation (and not simply entertainment and exhibition) their primary public goal. Yet such a shift in mission and programs could undercut public support for zoos, especially to the extent that the traditional displays of charismatic wildlife are reduced to accommodate a stronger conservation and research agenda.

An increased emphasis on climate change and its biodiversity impacts, too, could pose a challenge to zoos and aquariums wary of promulgating a negative or doom-and-gloom message to their visitors. Although some facilities are embracing this challenge and making climate change a part of their conservation education programming, some zoos and aquariums are struggling to incorporate this message within their more traditional educational and entertainment aims. For example, the Georgia Aquarium has apparently assured visitors that they will not be subjected to material about "global warming," a concession, according to the aquarium's vice president for education and training to the conservative political leanings of many of the facility's guests (Kaufman 2012). This example speaks to the larger challenge of moving zoos and aquariums into a stronger position of global leadership in conservation education, research, and practice under global change and other major threats to habitat and population viability in the coming decades.

Animal rights and welfare concerns will continue to be relevant to the evaluation of research and conservation activities under global change, but ultimately a more sophisticated and candid analysis of the trade-offs and the multiple imperatives of conservation-driven research on captive populations is required. Our understanding of these responsibilities—and especially the requirement of balancing animal well-being in practice in wildlife management and conservation policy—must evolve along with rapid climate change, extensive habitat fragmentation and destruction, and related forces threatening the distribution and abundance of wildlife around the globe. Unavoidable animal welfare impacts produced as a result of high-priority and well-designed conservation research and conservation activities involving captive animals will in many cases have to be tolerated to understand the consequences of rapid environmental change for vulnerable wildlife populations in the field. It will allow recovery and promote the good of vulnerable species in the wild more effectively under increasingly demanding biological conditions. Inevitably, these changes will continue to blur the boundaries of in situ and ex situ conservation programs as a range of management activities are adopted across more or less managed ecological systems increasingly influenced by human activities.

[. . .]

References

Anderson US, Maple TL, Bloomsmith MA. 2010. Factors facilitating research: A survey of zoo and aquarium professionals. *Zoo Biol* 29:663–675.

Barbosa A. 2009. The role of zoos and aquariums in research into the effects of climate change on animal health. *Int Zoo Yearb* 43:131–135.

Beck BB, Rapaport LG, Stanley MR, Wilson AC. 1994. Reintroduction of captive-born animals. In: Olney PS, Mace G, Feistner ATC, eds. *Creative Conservation: Interactive Management of Wild and Captive Animals.* London: Chapman & Hall. pp. 265–286.

Bekoff M. 2002. Ethics and marine mammals. In: Perri W, Würsig B, Thewissen H, eds. *Encyclopedia of Marine Mammals.* San Diego CA: Academic Press, pp. 398–404.

Callicott JB. 1980. Animal liberation: A triangular affair. *Environ Ethics* 2:311–338.

Camacho AE, Doremus H, McLachlan J, Minteer BA. 2010. Reassessing conservation goals in a changing climate. *Issues Sci Technol* 26:21–26.

Christie S. 2007. Zoo-based fundraising for in situ conservation. In Zimmerman A, Hatchwell M, Dickie L, West C, eds. *Zoos in the 21st Century: Catalysts for Conservation?* Cambridge UK: Cambridge University Press, pp 257–274.

Clubb R, Mason G. 2003. Animal welfare: Captivity effects on wide-ranging carnivores. *Nature* 425:473–174.

Cole DN, Yung L. 2010. *Beyond Naturalness: Rethinking Park and Wilderness Stewardship in an Era of Rapid Change.* Washington DC: Island Press.

Collins JP, Crump ML. 2009. *Extinction in Our Times: Global Amphibian Decline.* Oxford UK: Oxford University Press.

Conde DA, Flesness N, Colchero F, Jones OR, Scheuerlein A. 2011. An emerging role of zoos to conserve biodiversity. *Science* 331:1390–1391.

Conway WG. 2011. Buying time for wild animals with zoos. *Zoo Biol* 30:1–8.

Davis SG. 1997. *Spectacular Nature: Corporate Culture and the Sea World Experience.* Berkeley: University of California Press.

Dickie LA, Bonner JP, West C. 2007. In situ and ex situ conservation: Blurring the boundaries between zoos and the wild. In: Zimmerman A, Hatchwell M, Dickie L, West C, eds. *Zoos in the 21st Century: Catalysts for Conservation?* Cambridge UK: Cambridge University Press. pp. 220–235.

Dizard JE. 1999. *Going Wild: Hunting, Animal Rights, and the Contested Meaning of Nature.* Amherst: University of Massachusetts Press.

Dudley N. 2011. *Authenticity in Nature: Making Choices about the Naturalness of Ecosystems.* New York: Earthscan.

Earnhardt JE. 2010. The role of captive populations in reintroduction programs. In: Kleinman DG, Thompson KV, Baer CK, eds. *Wild Mammals in Captivity: Principles and Techniques for Zoo Management,* 2nd ed. Chicago: University of Chicago Press, pp 268–280.

Fa JE, Funk SM, O'Connell D. 2011. *Zoo Conservation Biology.* Cambridge UK: Cambridge University Press.

Gascon C, Collins JP, Moore RD, Church DR, McKay JE, Mendelson JR 3rd, eds. 2007. *Amphibian Conservation Action Plan.* Gland, Switzerland, and Cambridge UK: IUCN/SSC Amphibian Specialist Group.

Gewin V. 2008. Riders of a modern-day ark. *PLoS Biol* 6:18–21.

Goodrowe KL. 2003. Programs for invasive research in North American zoos and aquariums. *ILAR J* 44:317–323.

Greenwood AD, Tsangaras K, Ho SYW, Szentiks CA, Nikolin VM, Ma G, Damiani A, East ML, Lawrenz A, Hofer H, Osterrieder N. 2012. A potentially fatal mix of herpes in zoos. *Curr Biol* 22:1727–1731.

Grimm D. 2011. Are dolphins too smart for captivity? *Science* 332:526–529.

Gustin G. 2003. Two sides of the swan: Graceful beauty or invasive species. *New York Times.* August 10, 2003. Available online (www.nytimes.com/2003/08/10/nyregion/two-sides-of-the-swan-graceful-beauty-or-inva sive-species.html?pagewanted=all&src=pm), accessed on April 16, 2013.

Hancocks D. 2001. *A Different Nature: The Paradoxical World of Zoos and Their Uncertain Future.* Berkeley: University of California Press.

Hannah L, ed. 2012. *Saving a Millions Species: Extinction Risk from Climate Change.* Washington DC: Island Press.

Hanson E. 2002. *Animal Attractions: Nature on Display in American Zoos.* Princeton NJ: Princeton University Press.

Hobbs RJ, Hallett LM, Ehrlich PR, Mooney HA. 2011. Intervention ecology: Applying ecological science in the twenty-first century. *BioScience* 61:442–450.

Hosey G, Melfi V, Pankhurst S. 2011. *Zoo Animals: Behavior, Management, and Welfare.* Oxford UK: Oxford University Press.

Hutchins M. 2008. Animal rights and conservation. *Conserv Biol* 22:815–816.

Hutchins M, Dresser B, Wemmer C. 1995. Ethical considerations in zoo and aquarium research. In: Norton BG, Hutchins M, Stevens E, Maple T, eds. *Ethics on the Ark: Zoos, Animal Welfare, and Wildlife Conservation*. Washington DC: Smithsonian Institution Press. pp. 253–276.

Hutchins M, Thompson SD. 2008. Zoo and aquarium research: Priority setting for the coming decades. *Zoo Biol* 27:488–497.

Jamieson D. 1985. Against zoos. In: Singer P, ed. *In Defence of Animals*. Oxford UK: Basil Blackwell. pp. 108–117.

Jamieson D. 1995. Zoos revisited. In: Norton BG, Hutchins M, Stevens E, Maple T, eds. *Ethics on the Ark: Zoos. Animal Welfare, and Wildlife Conservation*. Washington DC: Smithsonian Institution Press, pp. 52–66.

Jamieson D. 1998. Animal liberation IS an environmental ethic. *Environ Value* 7:41–57.

Katz E. 1991. Defending the use of animals by business: Animal liberation and environmental ethics. In: Hoffman WM, Frederick R, Petry ES Jr, eds. *Business, Ethics and the Environment: The Public Policy Debate*. New York: Quorum Books, pp. 223–232.

Kaufman L. 2012. Intriguing Habitats, and Careful Discussions of Climate Change. *New York Times*. August 26, 2012. Available online (www.nytimes.com/2012/08/27/science/earth/zoos-and-aquariums-struggle-with-ways-to-discuss-climate-change.html?ref=lesliekaufman). Accessed on April 16, 2013.

Kirby D. 2012. *Death at SeaWorld: Shamu and the Dark Side of Killer Whales in Captivity*. New York: St. Martin's Press.

Kreger MD, Hutchins M. 2010. Ethics of keeping mammals in zoos and aquariums. In: Kleinman DG, Thompson KV, Baer CK, eds. *Wild Mammals in Captivity: Principles and Techniques for Zoo Management*, 2nd ed. Chicago: University of Chicago Press, pp. 3–10.

Lacy RC. 2012. Achieving true sustainability of zoo populations. *Zoo Biol* 32:19–26.

Lewis JCM. 2007. Conservation medicine. In: Zimmerman A, Hatchwell M, Dickie L, West C, eds. *Zoos in the 21st Century: Catalysts for Conservation?* Cambridge UK: Cambridge University Press, pp. 192–204.

MacDonald AA, Hofer H. 2011. Editorial: Research in zoos. *Int Zoo Yearb* 45:1–6.

Marris E. 2011. *Rambunctious Garden: Saving Nature in a Post-Wild World*. New York: Bloomsbury.

May RM. 2004. Ethics and amphibians. *Nature* 431:403.

McNamara T. 2007. The role of zoos in biosurveillance. *Int Zoo Yearb* 41:12–15.

Meffe GK. 2008. A pragmatic ethic for the twenty-first century—Commentary on "From environmental to ecological ethics: Toward a practical ethics for ecologists and conservationists." *Sci Engin Ethics* 14:503–504.

Minteer BA. 2012. *Refounding Environmental Ethics: Pragmatism, Principle, and Practice*. Philadelphia PA: Temple University Press.

Minteer BA, Collins JP. 2005a. Ecological ethics: Building a new tool kit for ecologists and biodiversity managers. *Conserv Biol* 19:1803–1812.

Minteer BA, Collins JP. 2005b. Why we need an "ecological ethics." *Front Ecol Environ* 3:332–337.

Minteer BA, Collins JP. 2008. From environmental to ecological ethics: Toward a practical ethics for ecologists and conservationists. *Sci Eng Ethics* 14:483–501.

Minteer BA, Collins JP. 2010. Move it or lose it? The ecological ethics of relocating species under climate change. *Ecol Appl* 20:1801–1804.

Minteer BA, Collins JP. 2012. Species conservation, rapid environmental change, and ecological ethics. *Nat Educ Ethics* 3:14.

Norton BG, Hutchins M, Stevens E, Maple T, eds. 1995. *Ethics on the Ark: Zoos, Animal Welfare, and Wildlife Conservation*. Washington DC: Smithsonian Institution Press.

Parris KM, McCall SC, McCarthy MA, Minteer BA, Steele K, Bekessy S, Medvecky F. 2010. Assessing ethical trade-offs in ecological field studies. *J Appl Ecol* 47:227–234.

Pauli JN, Whiteman JP, Riley MD, Middleton AD. 2010. Defining noninvasive for sampling vertebrates. *Conservation Biology* 24:349–352.

Perry D, Perry G. 2008. Improving interactions between animal rights groups and conservation biologists. *Conserv Biol* 22:27–35.

Pritchard DJ, Fa JE, Oldfield S, Harrop SR. 2011. Bring the captive closer to the wild: Redefining the role of ex situ conservation. *Oryx* 46:18–23.

Rands MRW, Adams WM, Bennun L, Butchart SHM, Clements A, Coomes D, Entwistle A, Hodge I, Kapos V, Scharlemann JPW, Sutherland WJ, Vira B. 2010. Biodiversity conservation: Challenges beyond 2010. *Science* 329:1298–1303.

Redford KH, Jensen DB, Breheny JJ. 2012. Integrating the captive and the wild. *Science* 338:1157–1158.

Regan T. 1995. Are zoos morally defensible? In: Norton BG, Hutchins M, Stevens E, Maple T, eds. *Ethics on the Ark: Zoos, Animal Welfare, and Wildlife Conservation.* Washington DC: Smithsonian Institution Press. pp. 38–51.

Regan T. 2004. *The Case for Animal Rights, updated ed.* Berkeley: University of California Press.

Reid GM, Zippel KC. 2008. Can zoos and aquariums ensure the survival of amphibians in the 21st century? *Int Zoo Yearb* 42:1–6.

Ricciardi A, Simberloff D. 2009. Assisted colonization is not a viable conservation strategy. *Trends Ecol Evol* 24:248–253.

Robbins J. 2009. Tools that leave wildlife unbothered widen research horizons. *New York Times.* March 9, 2009. Available online (www.nytimes.com/2009/03/10/science/10wild.html). Accessed on April 16, 2013.

Russell WMS, Burch RL. 1959. *The Principles of Humane Experimental Technique.* London: Methuen.

Sagoff M. 1984. Animal liberation and environmental ethics: Bad marriage, quick divorce. *Osgoode Hall Law J* 22:297–307.

Schwartz MW, Hellmann JJ, McLachlan JM, Sax DF, Borevitz JO, Brennan J, Camacho AE, Ceballos G, Clark JR, Doremus H, Early R, Etterson JR, Fielder D, Gill JL, Gonzalez P, Green N, Hannah L, Jamieson DW, Javeline D, Minteer BA, Odenbaugh J, Polasky S, Richardson DM, Root TL, Safford HD, Sala O, Schneider SH, Thompson AR, Williams JW, Vellend M, Vitt P, Zellmer S. 2012. Managed relocation: Integrating the scientific, regulatory and ethical challenges. *BioScience* 62:732–743.

Shoo LP, Olson DH, McMenamin, Murray KA, Van Sluys M, Donnelly MA, Stratford D, Terhivuo J, Andres Merino-Viteri A, Herbert SM, Bishop PJ, Corn PS, Dovey L, Griffiths RA, Lowe K, Mahony M, McCallum H, Shuker JD, Simpkins C, Skerratt LF, Williams SE, Hero J-M. 2011. Engineering a future for amphibians under climate change. *J Appl Ecol* 48:487–492.

Singer P. 1975. *Animal Liberation: A New Ethics for Our Treatment of Animals.* New York: New York Review/Random House.

Smith MM. 2007. The deer departed. *High Country News.* May 28, 2007. Available online (www.hcn.org/issues/347/17030). Accessed on April 16, 2013.

Stanley Price MR, Fa JE. 2007. Reintroductions from zoos: A conservation guiding light or a shooting star. In: Zimmerman A, Hatchwell M, Dickie L, West C, eds. *Zoos in the 21st Century: Catalysts for Conservation?* Cambridge UK: Cambridge University Press. pp. 155–177.

Stokstad E. 2010. Despite progress, biodiversity declines. *Science* 329:1272–1273.

Swaisgood RR. 2007. Current status and future directions of applied behavioral research for animal welfare and conservation. *Applied Animal Behaviour Science* 102:139–162.

Thomas CD, Cameron A, Rhys RE, Bakkenes M, Beaumont LJ, Collingham YC, Erasmus BFN, Marinez FDS, Agrainger A, Hannah L, Hughes L, Huntley B, van Jaarsveld AS, Midgley GF, Miles L, Ortega-Huerta MA, Peterson AT, Phillips OL, Williams SE. 2004. Extinction risk from climate change. *Nature* 427:145–148.

Varner GE. 1998. *In Nature's Interests? Interests, Animal Rights and Environmental Ethics.* Oxford UK: Oxford University Press.

Vucetich JA, Nelson MP. 2007. What are 60 warblers worth? Killing in the name of conservation. *Oikos* 116:1267–1278.

Walker SF, Bosch J, James TY, Litvintseva AP, Valls JAO, Piña S, Garcia G, Rosa GA, Cunningham AA, Hole S, Griffiths R, Fisher MC. 2008. Invasive pathogens threaten species recovery programs. *Curr Biol* 18: R853–R854.

WAZA [World Association of Zoos and Aquariums]. 2005. *The World Zoo and Aquarium Conservation Strategy: Building a Future for Wildlife.* Liebefeld-Bern Switzerland: WAZA.

Wemmer C, Christen C, eds. 2008. *Elephants and Ethics: Toward a Morality of Coexistence.* Baltimore MD: Johns Hopkins University Press.

Wharton D. 2007. Research by zoos. In: Zimmerman A, Hatchwell M, Dickie L, West C, eds. *Zoos in the 21st Century: Catalysts for Conservation?* Cambridge UK: Cambridge University Press. pp. 178–191.

Winston JM, Minteer BA, Collins JP. 2014. Old wine, new bottles? Using history to inform the assisted colonization debate. *Oryx* 48(2): 186–194

Woodhams DC, Bosch J, Briggs CJ, Cashins S, Davis LR, Lauer A, Muths E, Puschendorf R, Schmidt BR, Sheafor B, Voyles J. 2011. Mitigating amphibian disease: Strategies to maintain wild populations and control chytridiomycosis. *Front Zool* 8:1–23.

Zimmerman A. 2010. The role of zoos in contributing to in situ conservation. In: Kleinman DG, Thompson KY Baer CK, eds. *Wild Mammals in Captivity: Principles and Techniques for Zoo Management*, 2nd ed. Chicago: University of Chicago Press, pp. 281–287.

Zippel K, Johnson K, Gagliardo R, Gibson R, McFadden M, Browne R, Martinez C, Townsend E. 2011. The amphibian ark: A global community for ex situ conservation of amphibians. *Herpetol Conserv Biol* 6:340–352.

Part Nine

Animal Companions

Introduction to Part Nine

What moral responsibilities do we have to our animal companions? In the essay "Affection's Claim," Konrad Lorenz relates some wonderful stories of friendships between dogs and human beings, and asserts that a dog's fidelity imposes a responsibility upon us which is as morally important as our responsibilities to a human friend.

Paul Shepard describes the sequence leading from the sacredness of wild animal life in early human societies to our current situation in which wild animals are confined in zoos and seen as equivalent to pets and stuffed toys. Pets were created by selective breeding and cannot restore us to wholeness with the natural world. They are "deficient animals," "monsters," "biological slaves." Wild animals, on the other hand, are the last remaining riches of the planet.

Sometimes the bond with a wild animal can approach that experienced with our domesticated animal companions. Anna Merz relates her remarkable experience of raising the wild rhino Samia in a rhino sanctuary in Africa. Merz and Samia experienced a bond of deep love, trust, and friendship over 10 years, illustrating that beings of two wholly different species can reach out to each other for understanding.

Freya Mathews asserts that the company of both wild and domesticated nonhuman animals is a necessary part of human life, important for us and for our relationship with the environment. She defends domestication of animals and suggests that we need to find new ways to increase urban habitat for wildlife. Mathews describes her experience of how human psychological intimacy with the "unknowable subjectivity" of other animals helps open us to the world "astir with presence" vastly exceeding just human experience.

Clare Palmer discusses the complex issues involved in killing healthy animals in animal shelters. She considers three common claims about humane killing based on minimizing pain, as well as Tom Regan's rejection of painless killing. Palmer finds both approaches troubling, and she recommends a relational approach. According to this approach the relations of dependence and independence between humans and animals should be taken into account. In the reading, Diane Leigh and Marilee Geyer, former shelter workers, provide their recommendations based on their long experience with homeless animals. They discuss companion animal overpopulation as well as the pressing need to reaffirm the preciousness of life itself.

Mark Rowlands discusses the nature of moral evil. He maintains that humans are uniquely evil, in that we make things weak so that we may treat them badly. Bernard Rollin points out the emergence of a social ethic for animals since 1980. With regard to euthanasia, he affirms that the goal should be immediate unconsciousness without pain or distress. In discussing animal-assisted therapy, Tzachi Tamir maintains that therapy which relies on horses and dogs is often beneficial for all involved, but that therapy relying on rodents, birds, monkeys, reptiles and dolphins should be abolished.

Further Reading

Beck, Alan and Aaron Kather (1996) *Between Pets and People*, West Lafayette, IN: Purdue University Press.

Fine, A. (ed.) (2006) *Handbook on Animal-Assisted Therapy, Second Edition: Theoretical Foundations and Guidelines for Practice*, San Diego: Academic Press.

Grandin, Temple and Catherine Johnson (2005) *Animals in Translation: Using the Mysteries of Autism to Decode Animal Behavior*, Orlando, FL: Harcourt, Inc.

Podeberscek, A. L., Paul, E. S., and Serpell, J. A. (eds) (2005) *Companion Animals and Us: Exploring the Relationships between People and Pets*, Cambridge: Cambridge University Press.

Sheldrake, R. (1999) *Dogs That Know When Their Owners Are Coming Home and Other Unexplained Powers of Animals*, New York: Crown.

Slater, M. R. (2002) *Community Approaches to Feral Cats*, Washington, DC: Humane Society Press.

Study Questions

1. Konrad Lorenz maintains that "having" an animal companion involves serious moral responsibilities. What responsibilities do you believe should be associated with having an animal companion?

2. Do you agree with Paul Shepard that pets cannot connect us to the natural world? Explain why, or why not.

3. How does Anna Merz's experience with a wild rhino affect your view of the intelligence or emotional capacity of wild animals?

4. Is Freya Mathews's description of the psychological intimacy she has experienced with animals supported by your own experience of animals? Explain any similarities or differences.

5. Do you believe that we should keep animals as companions? Explain the possible benefits and disadvantages to such animals, as well as to humans.

6. If you live in an urban setting, what are some interactions you have had with wild or feral animals? What recommendations might you suggest for changing urban habitat for the benefit of animals?

7. Reflect on your experience of observing (or using) animals for assistance and therapy. Have you observed stress or suffering? What suggestions do you have to improve the welfare of animals performing these services?

8. Clare Palmer discusses several approaches to the killing of healthy dogs and cats in animal shelters. To what extent do you agree that relations of dependence/independence are morally relevant to this issue? How do you respond to the assertion that both de-sexing and killing are results of human domination of pets?

9. Leigh and Geyer argue for ordinances requiring the spaying and neutering of dogs and cats, with limited exceptions. Do you agree with their view? In "Afterword" they argue that ultimately we need to transcend the current shelter system in the U.S. What are some of the reasons they provide?

10. Do you agree with Rollin's approach to euthanasia of animals? Explain your reasoning.

11. Do you think that Rowlands is right in maintaining that motives are irrelevant in assessing the morality of actions?

12. Based on the interview with Brantley, a former FBI agent, what steps might be taken in early childhood education to avoid animal abuse?

13. Provide an example in which the interests of a rodent are more important than the interests of human beings.

14. Do you agree with Zamir that therapy with animals such as dolphins is inherently exploitative? Explain your answer.

72 Affection's Claim

Konrad Lorenz

Konrad Lorenz describes several memorable dogs and affirms that he has always taken very seriously the responsibility imposed by a dog's fidelity and love. He believes that all love rises from instinctive feeling and that we have obligations to our dogs which are "no less binding" than those to our human friends.

> Knowing me in my soul the very same—
> One who would die to spare you touch of ill!—
> Will you not grant to old affection's claim
> The hand of friendship down Life's sunless hill?
> Thomas Hardy

I once possessed a fascinating little book of crazy tales called 'Snowshoe Al's Bedtime Stories.' It concealed behind a mask of ridiculous nonsense that penetrating and somewhat cruel satire which is one of the characteristic features of American humour, and which is not always easily intelligible to many Europeans. In one of these stories Snowshoe Al relates with romantic sentimentality the heroic deeds of his best friend. Incidents of incredible courage, exaggerated manliness and complete altruism are piled up in a comical parody of Western American romanticism culminating in the touching scenes where the hero saves his friend's life from wolves, grizzly bears, hunger, cold and all the manifold dangers which beset him. The story ends with the laconic statement, 'In so doing, his feet became so badly frozen that I unfortunately had to shoot him.'

If I ask a man who has just been boasting of the prowess and other wonderful properties of one of his dogs, I always ask him whether he has still got the animal. The answer, then, is all too often strongly reminiscent of Snowshoe Al's story, 'No, I had to get rid of him—I moved to another town—or into a smaller house—I got another job and it was awkward for me to keep a dog,' or some other similar excuse. It is to me amazing that many people who are otherwise morally sound feel no disgrace in admitting such an action. They do not realize that there is no difference between their behaviour and that of the satirized egoist in the story. The animal is deprived of rights, not only by the letter of the law, but also by many people's insensitivity.

The fidelity of a dog is a precious gift demanding no less binding moral responsibilities than the friendship of a human being. The bond with a true dog is as lasting as the ties of this earth can ever be, a fact which should be noted by anyone who decides to acquire a canine friend. It may of course happen that the love of a dog is thrust upon one involuntarily, a circumstance which occurred to me when I met the Hanoverian Schweisshund, 'Hirschmann,' on a skiing tour. He was at the time about a year old and a typical masterless dog; for his owner the head forester only loved his old Deutscher Rauhaar (German Pointer) and had no time for the clumsy stripling which showed few signs of ever becoming a gun-dog. Hirschmann was soft and sensitive and a little shy of his master, a fact which did not speak highly for the training ability of the forester. On the other hand I did not think any the better of the dog for coming out with us as early as the second day of our stay. I took him for a sycophant, quite wrongly as it turned out, for he was following not us but me alone. When one morning I found him sleeping outside my bedroom door, I began to reconsider my first opinion and to suspect that a great canine love was germinating. I realized it too late: the oath of allegiance had been sworn nor would the dog recant on the day of my departure. I tried to catch him in order to shut him up and prevent him from following us, but he refused to come near me. Quivering with consternation and with his tail between his legs he stood at a safe distance saying with his eyes, 'I'll do anything at all for you—except leave you!' I capitulated. 'Forester, what's the price of your dog?' The forester, from whose point of view the dog's conduct was sheer desertion, replied without a moment's consideration, 'Ten shillings.' It sounded like an expletive and was meant as such. Before he could think of a better one, the ten shillings were in his hand and two pairs of skis and two pairs of dog's paws were under way. I knew that Hirschmann would follow us but surmised erroneously that, plagued by his conscience, he would slink after us at a distance, thinking that he was not allowed to come with us. What really did happen was entirely unexpected. The full weight of the huge dog hit me broadsides on like a cannon ball and I was precipitated hip foremost on to the icy road. A skier's equilibrium is not proof against the impact of an enormous dog, hurled in a delirium of excitement against him. I had quite underestimated his grasp of the situation. As for Hirschmann, he danced for joy over my extended corpse.

I have always taken very seriously the responsibility imposed by a dog's fidelity, and I am proud that I once risked my life, though inadvertently, to save a dog which had fallen into the Danube at a temperature of −28°C. My Alsatian, Bingo, was running along the frozen edge of the river when he slipped and fell into the water. His claws were unable to grip the sides of the ice so he could not get out. Dogs become exhausted very quickly when attempting to get up too steep a bank. They get into an awkward, more and more upright swimming position until they are soon in imminent danger of drowning. I therefore ran a few yards ahead of the dog which was being swept downstream; then I lay down and, in order to distribute my weight, crept on my belly to the edge of the ice. As Bingo came within my reach, I seized him by the scruff of the neck and pulled him with a jerk towards me on to the ice, but our joint weight was too much for it—it broke, and I slid silently, head first into the freezing cold water. The dog, which, unlike myself, had its head shorewards, managed to reach firmer ice. Now the situation was reversed; Bingo ran apprehensively along the ice and I floated downstream in the current. Finally, because the human hand is better adapted than the paw of the dog for gripping a smooth surface, I managed to escape disaster by my own efforts. I felt ground beneath my feet and threw my upper half upon the ice.

We judge the moral worth of two human friends according to which of them is ready to make the greater sacrifice without thought of recompense. Nietzsche who, unlike most people, wore brutality only as a mask to hide true warmness of heart, said the beautiful words, 'Let it be your aim always to love more than the other, never to be the second.' With human beings, I am sometimes able to fulfil this commandment, but in my relations with a faithful dog, I am always the second. What a strange and unique social relationship! Have you ever thought how extraordinary it all is? Man, endowed with reason and a highly developed sense of moral responsibility, whose finest and noblest belief is the religion of brotherly love, in this very respect falls short of the carnivores. In saying this I am not indulging in sentimental anthropomorphization. Even the noblest human love arises, not from reason and the specifically human, rational moral sense, but from the much deeper age-old layers of instinctive feeling. The highest and most selfless moral behaviour loses all value in our estimation when it arises not from such sources but from the reason. Elizabeth Browning said,

> If thou must love me, let it be for nought
> Except for love's sake only.

Even to-day man's heart is still the same as that of the higher social animals, no matter how far the achievements of his reason and his rational moral sense transcend theirs. The plain fact that my dog loves me more than I love him is undeniable and always fills me with a certain feeling of shame. The dog is ever ready to lay down his life for me. If a lion or a tiger threatened me, Ali, Bully, Tito, Stasi, and all the others would, without a moment's hesitation, have plunged into the hopeless fight to protect my life if only for a few seconds. And I?

73 The Pet World

Paul Shepard

Paul Shepard traces the dramatic change from wild and sacred animal life through domestication, stuffed animal toys for children, pet dogs and cats, and finally to zoos. He describes pets as "civilized paraphernalia," created by selective breeding and hence unable to restore us to wholeness with the Others. Pets only confuse our perception of the wild universe, an outer wilderness which we need to become aware of in our own selves.

[. . .]

Against the indifference of the wild animals, the impetuous affection of our pets seems like an enormous boon. In a world so full of problems and suffering, only the worst curmudgeonly cynic would sneer at our indulgence, their simple pleasure in us, and our joy in them. Something, however, is profoundly wrong with the human/animal pet relationship at its most basic level. Given the obvious benefits of that affiliation, one has to poke very carefully into its psychology and ecology before its fragile core can be exposed.

[. . .]

During the rise of [the] biological void in urban existence in the industrial world from 1850 to 1950, the middle classes began to have fewer children, for whom the household could be a lonely place. In fiction, such a child who represented childhood without siblings and without easy access to street friends was Christopher Robin, for whom Winnie the Pooh was the substitute. Pooh Bear is an animated and storied teddy bear. In this way the Anglo-American concept of animal friends is prefigured in childhood, with the aid of "bedtime" stories, by pretending that one's stuffed toys are alive. This scenario creates a very different childhood orientation toward the living pets than in earlier times, when household animals like rabbits might be eaten, cats caught mice, and dogs served as guards or hunters. From Pooh Bear it is not very far to the doggy friend and but a step from the doggy friend to an imaginary relationship with or among wild animals—animals which, for the first time in history, are almost completely lacking in the child's experience. This sequence is a drama in five acts.

Act I is an outer circle of wild animal life which was a major focus of human attention, establishing the expectation of a rich, surprising, meaningful, and beautiful diversity of life around us. Some animals were sacred. All were conscious, unique, and different in spiritual power.

In Act II people took certain animals into captivity, manipulated their reproduction, and altered their biological natures to conform to human dominance, reconstructing them as members of the household. These became the domestic animals. The wild forms, reduced in number and diversity, literally receded.

Act III begins not with animals but with a class of things called "transitional objects." These are toted around by anxious three-year-old children who are having difficulty becoming independent from their mothers and who are comforted by a soft object that is subjectively intermediate between themselves and the outside world. The children who do not seem to require the security of such objects are those who are surrounded by abundant other forms of life. The exact reason for this is not entirely clear, but apparently animals in their diversity model a world of likeness and difference which makes the child's impending separation less frightening and also resonates with internal, psychic structures which can best be described metaphorically as a fauna. The stuffed toys are simultaneously huggable, transitional objects and "animals." They appeared in large numbers in the industrial, nuclear-family era, compensating children for their lonesome social and ecological situations and preparing them for lifelong pet keeping. The mode of this preparation is pretend-play, the self-dramatization of all life as a happy playground.

Act IV is the transfer of this affection from effigies to dogs and cats. As the toys had been pets, the pets became toys. Even "wild" animal manikins, such as stuffed bears and lions, are little people in the imagination, who participate in a household society, who have expectations, reasons, worries, expressions, voices, tastes, and complicated affinities and antipathies toward each other and their human companions.

Act V extends the equivalence of the living domestic pet and the stuffed wild toy to living nature. If the domestic forms have all along been substitutes for the wild and the latter have become unavailable and unknown, it is easy to fuse the domestic and wild. The wild are simply those potential pets who do not happen to live with us. They are each other's pets, or perhaps creatures whose friendship we have lost. Zoos seem to affirm this identity. The zoo has "toy verisimilitude," foreshadowing the modern child's menagerie of stuffed animals and friendly pets, each zoo creature enduring in blind lethargy, withdrawn except in moments of hyperactivity when the feeder comes, like the puppets waiting in the closet to be flung into tea parties or wagons by a child.

[. . .]

Pets are not part of human evolution or the biological context out of which our ecology comes. They are civilized paraphernalia whose characteristic combination of accompaniment and accommodation is tangled in an ambiguous tyranny. Constance Perrin, an anthropologist, calls it "attachment theory." The animal triggers nurturant behavior and serves as a kind of intermediate object between the owner and a more or less alien world, but at the same time it is dragged about like a tattered security blanket. Indeed, the domestication of animals has never ensured their tender care. In recent Anglo American tradition the dog is "man's best friend," but it is abhorred in the Bible. In Muslim tradition the dog's saliva is noxious, and contact between people and dogs requires ritual cleansing. Over most of the planet the dog is a cur and mongrel scavenger, feral, half-starved, the target of the kick and thrown rock, often cruelly exploited as a slave. Although looked upon with affection, even modern pets are property that is bought, sold, "put down," and neutered. Pets are deliberately abandoned by the millions and necessitate city-run slaughterhouses, shelters, and "placement" services. This paradox of frenetic emotion and casual dismissal reveals our deep disappointment in the pet's ability to do something, be something, that we cannot quite identify. Yi-Fu Tuan considers our behavior to be exercises in casual domination that symbolize human control of nature.[1] In an earlier book I argued that pets were unacknowledged surrogates for human companionships or substitutes for the resolution of interpersonal social problems, and therefore impaired normal human sociality by enabling people to avoid mending, maturing, or otherwise dealing with their personal relationships.[2] Pets can cause family conflict, even divorce, and may become bridges of unhealthy transference relationships and regression to infantile human behavior.

Even so, I now see that the pet may be more than a human replacement. "Pet-facilitated therapy," casual or institutionalized, reduces human suffering. It is truly an astonishing solace. The "companion animal" is a medical miracle to which we should be kind and grateful. But like all psychotherapy its presence is not a true healing. It cheers, modulates pain, and helps the owner/patient to cope.

Domestic animals were "created" by humans by empirical genetic engineering over the past ten thousand years. They are vestiges and fragments from a time of deep human respect for animals, whose abundance dazzled us in their many renditions of life, helping us to know ourselves by showing all that we had not become. The pet cannot restore us to that wholeness any more than an artificial limb renews the original; nor can it do more than simulate the Others among whom our ancestors lived for so long, the Others that constituted for them a cosmos. They and all captive animals are like organ transplants: healthy for us but cut out of their own organic fabric.

What is wrong at the heart of the keeping of pets is that they are deficient animals in whom we have invested the momentum of two million years of love of the Others. They are monsters of the order invented by Frankenstein except that they are engineered to conform to our wishes, biological slaves who cringe and fawn or perform or whatever we wish. As embodiments of trust, dependence, companionship, esthetic beauty, vicarious power, innocence, or action by command, they are wholly unlike the wild world. In effect, they are organic machines conforming to our needs.

No one now doubts that pets can be therapeutic. But they are not a glorious bonus on life; rather they are compensations for something desperately missing, minimal replacements for friendship in all of its meanings. Mass society isolates us in ways and degrees that seem to contradict our population density. Pets occupy by default an equally great human need for others who are not part of our personal lives. The diversity that nourishes the mind extends to the whole realm of life and nature. Pets, being our own creations, do not replace that wild universe. But as living animals they confuse our perception and hide the lack of a wild, nonhuman comity of players on a grand scale—a spectacular drama of life to which our human natures commit our need and expectation.

Wild animals are not our friends. They are uncompromisingly not us nor mindful of us, just as they differ among themselves. They are the last undevoured riches of the planet, what novelist Romain Gary called "the roots of heaven." We cannot comprehend the world as it is experienced by a bat, a termite, or a squid; we cannot force them into barnyard conviviality or household banality without destroying them. More than bearded prophets and great goddesses they are the mediators between us and plants, the rock and suns around us, the rest of the universe. Wild animals connote the wildness in us which cannot be equated to our domestic affairs or reconciled with the petty tyrannies of "dwellers in houses," domesticates, from the same root word that gives "constrain" or "subdue." As a fauna only the wild are a mirror of the multifold strangeness of the human self. We know this. It is why we scrutinize and inspect and remark on them, make them the subject of our art and thought, and sometimes kill and eat them with mindful formality, being in place with our own otherness.[3]

Notes

1. Yi-Fu Tuan, *Dominance and Affection: The Making of Pets* (New Haven: Yale University Press, 1984).
2. Paul Shepard, *Thinking Animals* (New York: Viking, 1978).
3. James O. Breeden (ed.), *Advice among Masters: The Ideal in Slave Management in the Old South* (Westport: Greenwood Press, 1980).

74 Hand-Raising a Rhino in the Wild

Anna Merz

Anna Merz describes how she raised Samia, a female black rhino abandoned by her mother. The tiny baby rhino slept in her bed. When Samia matured and integrated with wild rhinos, she protected Merz in dangerous situations and returned to visit with her daily. Merz's story is so evocative that the reader grieves with her at the tragic death of Samia and her baby.

Samia, the female black rhino who was my pride and my joy, was born ten years ago in the Ngare Sergoi Rhino Sanctuary on the western side of Lewa Downs, a 45,000-acre cattle ranch situated on the northern slopes of Mt. Kenya. I have lived all my life with animals and I have handraised many, but Samia was truly unique. Between us there existed a love, a trust, a reaching out for understanding unlike anything I had known in a relationship before. With her there was none of the usual relationship between man and beast. I never tried to discipline or hold her; she lived as a wild rhino. Yet of her own free will, she kept alive with me the bonds of love, trust, and friendship until her death.

Early in 1984 the sanctuary received its first rhinos, including Samia's mother, Solia. At the present time there are nineteen white and twenty-two black rhinos. Twenty calves have been born here. Not all have survived, but those that died, died of natural causes; none have been poached.

On February 15, 1985, Solia gave birth to a calf, Samia, and promptly deserted her. At that time I knew virtually nothing about rhinos, and certainly nothing about raising rhino babies, not even the proper composition of black rhino milk. Over weeks and months I battled with Samia's unending bouts of diarrhea, dehydration, and abnormal temperatures. As a tiny baby, she slept in my bed, causing matrimonial complications with the amazing messes she produced. Raising her was a series of crises, but at about six months, she started to stabilize.

Each day I walked her over ever-increasing distances to introduce her to the world of which she would be a part and its inhabitants. I remember our first encounter with a group of giraffes; long black eyelashes aflutter, they peered at us with astonishment, this strange combination of old woman, baby rhino, and black dog. Samia didn't see them until they moved and then, in terror at their size, dashed between my legs for safety. This was not a practical proposition and I sat down with a thud. Unable to get under me she compromised by sitting on my prostrate form, snorting her disapproval.

Samia learned quickly that I did not really appreciate being knocked over, even in play, and as her strength grew so her gentleness with me increased. As we walked, she would, of her own accord, offer a helping tail to pull me up the steeper trails. When I weaned her at three and a half years, I expected the bond between us to loosen, as would be only natural, but it never did. For ten years, Samia and I were companions, and even when she was mature and integrated with the wild rhinos, she usually returned to visit with me at least once a day.

During our time together, she taught me so much about the world of the rhino that I could never have learned otherwise. I also tried to teach Samia what I thought she would need to know in order to survive. But I was not always successful. To help Samia develop her sense of smell, I hid, hoping she would put her nose to the ground and search after me. Instead, she went to the garden gate, opened it to let the dogs out, then galloped after them straight to me. By no stretch of the imagination can this be described as instinctive behavior.

Rhinos are not, as reputed, solitary, bad-tempered, stupid animals. I had been warned that after my experience with chimps in Ghana, I would find them dangerous and boring. Rather the opposite. Rhino intelligence is close to that of chimps and their outstanding characteristics are curiosity and nervousness rather than aggression. Through her incredible intelligence, Samia was able to reveal a great deal about the social structure of rhino society and much of the complex methods of communication her species uses, including a wide variety of noises and the regulation of breathing to form a sort of Morse code of sound.

In the beginning of our relationship, I was the teacher and the protector. As she matured our roles reversed, and she showed herself capable of teaching and protecting me. A few weeks before the birth of Samia's own calf, she joined me, which was not unusual, when I was walking the dogs one evening. The thick tropical dusk was falling when three rhinos emerged on the track ahead of us. To avoid them I would have to make a long detour through the thorny bush in the dark. Samia, sensing both my fear and my indecision, realized my predicament and took charge of the situation. She knew these three white rhinos well and would normally have ignored them. Now, she trotted up to them, ears laid flat, huffing and hurrumphing angrily, and they retreated in astonishment at her aggressive behavior. Satisfied that they were routed, she returned to me and the dogs and escorted us safely past where they had been. When she was satisfied that we were safe, she left us to resume her own affairs.

When Samia was mated it was by the wild and violent-tempered bull Kenu. He was a small but immensely powerful rhino and many times he came near my house. On one occasion, Samia saw I was in danger and moved very quickly between us with the intention of stopping his charge. Another day Samia and Kenu visited me together. I went to the gate to greet her not realizing he was there. She stood between us and I could sense his rage and hatred of me, his desire to obliterate both me and that gate that stood between us. For forty long minutes we three stood together and I could both see and hear the breathing patterns by which they were communicating with one another. I could literally see the control that Samia was exercising over his behavior. The first time she protected me, I thought it was chance and good luck, but the second and subsequent times revealed her focus and intention. From running to me for safety, she had come to act as my protector against buffalo and her own kind, but never had I expected her to actually protect me from her own mate.

On the morning of April 11, 1995, I learned, via a radio call, that Samia had had a baby. With both joy and terror, I and a tracker crept to where I could see her, feeding quietly. Deep in the long grass near her flickered the tips of two long ears. There was no sound but that of Samia's munching. I was relieved because I knew from painful experience that baby rhinos cry only if they are in trouble. Half an hour later, the tiny creature staggered to its feet, wobbled round Samia's hind legs, thrust its wee nose into her flank, and started to suckle. Samia stopped feeding and stood quietly while it drank from first one teat and then the other. There was no doubt that she had milk, nor was there any doubt as to the baby's sex—Samia had a son.

Two days later, I was watching her with two trackers and was so absorbed that I did not notice the change in the wind. The trackers moved back but she had got my scent. Now what? These long years of observation have taught me that rhinos are fiercely protective mothers and very solitary for the first year of their baby's life. My knees were shaking so much I had to sit down. Then Samia came to me and, as she had in the past, rested her great head in my lap. While her baby stood a scarce foot away wearing a bewildered expression, I rubbed behind her ears and gently told her how clever she was and how beautiful her son was with his huge ears, blunt nose, big feet, and pearl satin skin. Obviously the bond we had created over the past ten years had withstood his birth.

When Samuel was still a few days old, Samia came to me, leaving him sleeping under a nearby bush. She was standing beside me when he awoke and cried out in fear at finding himself alone. Samia's action was swift and wholly instinctive. She swiped me sideways with her head, knocking me to the ground, and ran to him. Seeing that no harm had befallen him, she returned to me, still sitting where I had fallen. She thrust her nose at me and I assured her that I was unhurt. Then she turned and, as often in days gone by, presented me with her tail for a pull up!

I never attempted to touch her baby, but slowly he got used to my scent and his inborn fear of me lessened. Almost daily at dawn, Samia would come to visit me with him at heel. Each day would start with the knowledge that they were well and safe and that she knew how to raise and protect her child. Frequently, hand-raised animals do not.

I had worried whether Samia would appreciate the dangers surrounding her baby; there was so much I had not been able to teach her. But after some time, I realized that these fears were groundless. Samia had also always been fully aware that I only pretended to eat thornbushes and had not been able to teach her how to manipulate the thorn in her mouth. But at four months, Samuel browsed on these same thornbushes alongside his mother. It was something very beautiful to behold. I watched Samia's affection for her baby, saw how the bond between them became stronger, and felt quite ridiculously proud of her.

Because our April rains virtually failed, I started to supplement Samia's natural browse with a small quantity of alfalfa so her milk wouldn't fail. Almost daily at dawn, she came to my garden fence with her baby. As soon as she heard me open the door, she called to tell me that she was there and hopeful of being fed. The rest of the day she spent in the bush. Seeing her thus was my greatest joy.

Then tragedy struck. Samia did not come to visit me one morning. I went down the valley with Patrick, a tracker, to look for her and found her dead. She was lying on her back below the cliff from which she and her child had fallen. Her death must have been instantaneous. Her baby lay nearby, still alive. I tried to help him rise, but being unable to do so, sent Patrick with the radio to call for help. For two hours, I knelt beside little Samuel, offering what poor comfort I could. Nearby a leopard was grunting, but I could not see it. The valley was beautiful, full of birds and color, and I thought of the many happy hours and days that Samia and I had spent there.

Ian Craig, who came with ropes and other people, realized what I had not, that the baby rhino's back was broken low down near his tail. A merciful shot ended his suffering. Later, after the local Game Warden had come to remove Samia's horns, the trackers laid Samuel beside his mother and I went to say good-bye to them and to cover them with a sackful of flowers.

Samia's death has to me been a tragedy. There was real love and friendship between us and I miss her all the time. Beyond that it was my dearest hope that through her life and that of her child, awareness of and caring for her species could be awakened. In her life, she had proved beyond all doubt that there can be a meeting between two wholly disparate species.

75 Living with Animals

Freya Mathews

Freya Mathews argues that we need to find ways to restore animals to our day-to-day urban reality and suggests ways in which we can increase the amount of urban habitat for wildlife. Mathews also recounts her own childhood, during which she learned to engage with the unknowable subjectivities of animals and found that this experience is "the principal bridge" to communication with the unknowable subjectivity of the wider world beyond human selfhood.

'Without animals,' says Peter, a Maasai nomad interviewed in the *New Internationalist*,[1] 'life isn't worth living.'

Sitting here in my inner-city backyard writing this, with a circle of attentive little upturned canine and feline faces surrounding me, and my cranky duck tugging at my shoelaces, I could not be in more heartfelt agreement. But how many people today would share this sentiment? For how many would it be football that makes life worth living, or cars, or opera, or ice-skating? Is there anything to ground the conviction that I want to defend here, that the company of non-human animals is a necessary part of human life, in a way that football, cars, opera and ice-skating manifestly are not, and that we relinquish or forego it at our peril?

There are two parts to this question. The first is, is it important for *us*, for our own well-being or the realization of our human potential, that we live in intimate commensal relations with animals? The second is, is it important for the *environment* that we live in such relations? Does the *world* need us to continue to live in our ancestral communalism with animals?

My view is that our present estrangement, as human beings, from both the natural world (as evidenced in the environmental crisis) and from ourselves (as evidenced in the intense neuroticization of life in contemporary "advanced" societies) is due at least in part to the progressive removal of animals from our day-to-day urban reality; consequently I shall argue that, in order to address both the environmental crisis and our own crisis of consciousness, we need to find ways of restoring animals to the human household.

[. . .]

If it is accepted that companion animals do induce in us a new moral seriousness about animals generally, then a question arises concerning the status of domestic animals used for productive purposes. Does this new moral seriousness condemn the utilization of animals for such purposes?

[. . .]

The short answer to this question is, I think, that such reconciliation of empathy and use is possible to the extent that utilization is of net benefit to the animals concerned.

[. . .]

To reconcile utilization with empathy, we need to be assured that the life that our exploitative intentions bestow on an individual domestic animal affords both the experiential opportunities and the requisite life span to enable it to achieve a significant degree of the form of self-realization appropriate to its particular kind. This implies that the use we may justifiably make of animals will vary according to their species.

[. . .]

In short, I think the fact that domestic utilization affords evolutionary niches for certain species, in a world of disappearing niches, is a prima facie reason for regarding such utilization as compatible with respect. However, a full-blown attitude of empathy—such as we develop through intimate association with animal companions—requires that the forms of utilization we countenance be compatible with the self-realization of the animals used, where this implies that different forms and degrees of utilization will be appropriate for different species. I would also add that, once we have acknowledged the subjectivity and moral significance of the animals we use, and the moral gravity of our practices of utilization, it becomes incumbent on us to develop cultural expressions of respect, gratitude and indebtedness for the lives we have thus dedicated to our own ends. In this way, our attitude towards domestic animals can develop more affinity with the familial attitudes of hunter-gatherer peoples towards the wild species that constitute their prey.

When domestic utilization of animals is subject to the qualifications I have outlined above, I think it is not only consistent with empathetic concern for the interests of animals: it is actually required by such concern. As environmentalists, committed to the maximal preservation of non-human life on earth, yet facing the cold, hard fact that in the twenty-first century, the processes of urbanization and industrialization that have been synonymous with the disenchantment and tragic devastation of the non-human world are only going to accelerate and intensify, don't we have to admit that one of our best chances for 'saving Nature' is by bringing Nature back into the human domain? We have, for the last few centuries, witnessed the runaway humanization of Nature; now let us inaugurate the wholesale naturalization of human habitat. Our cities are one of the major biological habitats of the future, and our task, as environmentalists, is to ensure that they provide the best opportunities for non-human life that we can devise. We can do this partly by increasing the amount of urban habitat for wildlife. Such habitat can be created by way of indigenous plantings and by permacultural programs of food production in the city. Buildings can also be designed or adapted to create, rather than exclude, habitat opportunities for wild animals (by way of stork-friendly chimneys, for instance, and roofs that accommodate bats and nesting birds). However we can also increase the urban opportunities for non-human life by finding new ways for animals to 'earn their living' in the city.

[. . .]

The possibilities for reintegrating animals productively into urban life are as limitless as our imaginations. However, the principal way in which animals can 'earn their living' in the city is still, I think, via their companionate role. The exclusive reign of the dog and the cat in this connection needs to be challenged, and the adaptability of other species to the human hearth and home investigated.

[. . .]

The 'green' city of the future, then, would be a mixed community rich in habitat opportunities for a great diversity of animal species. This reintegration of animals into human life would also help to expand human imaginative and empathetic horizons, undermining anthropocentrism and reinforcing commitment to the protection of the non-human world. At the same time, the multiple contacts with animals that it would afford would enhance the health and sanity of the human population.

[. . .]

These then are some of the reasons why I think that our living with animals is important both for us and for them. However, this commensality shapes not only our ethical attitudes towards non-human individuals and species but our very sense of the world. I have not yet brought this larger significance of the relationship fully to light, nor can I hope to do so with any pretence of completeness. In order to capture a little of this cosmological significance however, I would like to recount, in these concluding pages, the experiential origins of my own conviction that 'without animals, life isn't worth living.'

I grew up surrounded by loving animals on what today would be described as a hobby farm, situated on the rural outskirts of Melbourne, Australia. These animals included dogs and cats, ducks, geese, hens, and, at one stage, a turkey. There were brief episodes with sheep and cows. The main focus of my entire childhood, however, was my ponies. My first pony, and the horses that came after her, were my day-long playmates and confidants. It was to them that I recited my earliest poems, and to them that I ran when I was hurt or excited. They nuzzled me in the same soft, considerate way whatever the occasion. I chose their company not for want of family and friends, but for its own sake. The form of intimacy that grew up between us was qualitatively different from anything that could have developed between myself and human persons. It was a kind of uncluttered closeness, or being-with, which existed despite the fact that our subjectivities were, in terms of content, mutually unknowable. We took it for granted, on either side, that this unknowability did not matter, that our psyches could touch and pervade each other, without need for explanations or self-disclosures, such as those conveyable by language. These animals were, for me, 'primary others,' in the psychoanalytic sense; they were not substitutes for, but additional to, significant humans, nor could humans substitute for them. My subjectivity—my sense of self and world—was constituted through my 'object relations' with these animals just as fundamentally as it was through my relations with primary human others.[2]

[. . .]

Looking back on my early years now, it seems more plausible to me to assume that the ample opportunities for close communion with animals that were available to me throughout my childhood had opened me to a larger world, a world astir with presence or presences that vastly exceeded the human. It was this direct contact with unknowable but pervasive presence which instilled in me a sense of the sacredness or enchantment of the world, and the potentiality for 'magic' within it. 'Magic' was, in this context, just the possibility of the world's response—the possibility, indeed probability, that the world, when invoked in good faith, *will* respond, though not necessarily in the manner one anticipates or with the results for which one hopes. One should certainly not, in my view, rely on this world to fulfil requests or afford protection, but if one entreats it simply to reveal itself, to engage in an act of communication, then, in my experience, it will generally do so, though in its own ever-unpredictable way. I learned this as a child, through the receptiveness that my animal familiars created in me, and it filled my whole being with a sense of being accompanied, of never being alone, a sense of background love, akin to the background radiation of which physicists speak. This is a 'love' which has nothing to do with saving us from death and suffering or with making us happy. From the viewpoint of the world, death and suffering are just inevitable concomitants of individual life. The point for individuals, from this perspective, is not to seek to evade these inevitabilities, but to reach beyond them—to call into the silence beyond human selfhood in search of a reply. This is the moment for which the world has been waiting, and in which it will rejoice: the moment when we ask it to speak. To receive its reply is to enter a love far greater than the kind of protection and indulgence that our traditional importunate forms of prayer expect, for that reply signifies that we belong to an animate order, a pattern of meaning, from which death cannot separate us, and to which suffering only summons us.

I offer these concluding reflections, not as argument, but as testimony relating to my own personal sense of the larger import of human-animal commensality, especially when that commensality is established in childhood. To engage with the unknowable subjectivities of animals, and to experience their response to us, is perhaps the principal bridge to communication with the unknowable subjectivity of the wider world. To experience the world thus, as an ensouled or spiritual thing, will not only direct the course of our own self-realization in the most fundamental way; it will also ensure an attitude of profound mutuality and awed protectiveness towards the world itself.

Notes

1. Nikkivan der Gaag, 'The Maasai and the Travellers', *New Internationalist*, 266 (1995), pp. 24–5.
2. The term 'object relations' is deployed in a branch of psychoanalytic theory, known as 'object relations theory,' to designate the kinds of relations with primary others that an infant internalizes in the process of developing its individual sense of self. It is associated with the work of D.W. Winnicott, and later feminist theorists, such as Nancy Chodorow.

76 Killing Animals in Animal Shelters

Clare Palmer

Clare Palmer addresses the important topic of killing healthy, unwanted animals in animal shelters. She notes that a utilitarian approach of "humane killing" finds painless killing acceptable. Tom Regan's rights approach, on the other hand, rejects painless killing as harmful in that the animal experiences the ultimate loss of future satisfaction. Palmer recommends instead a relational approach which both values the duties of care for dependent domesticated animals and respects the independence of feral cats and dogs.

Introduction

[. . .]

I want, in this essay, to consider the painless killing of healthy animals (primarily cats and dogs) in animal shelters.[1] Although no completely reliable statistics exist, it is estimated that between 6 and 10 million dogs and between 7 and 10 million cats were humanely killed in pet shelters in the United States in 1990.[2] In particular, I will be exploring the ethical debate around this practice, not with the intention of proposing any definitive "solution," but in order to clarify existing arguments and to suggest some new perspectives on the issues raised. It should also be noted that this essay focuses on ethical, rather than economic, issues about killing animals in animal shelters. Clearly, there is a sense in which financial expedience is the primary reason for the killing of such animals. It would be extremely expensive to house indefinitely all the healthy animals that currently come into animal shelters. But that such killing is accepted and tolerated socially is an ethical issue worthy of investigation in its own right.

Animal Shelters: Context and Practices

Animal shelters take several forms. Some are provided and run by local or city authorities, others by animal protection charities. Almost all of the former, and many of the latter, regularly humanely kill healthy animals. A small number of animal charity shelters and adoption organizations have no-kill policies (except in cases where animals are seriously ill and suffering). Organizations of this kind often select "adoptable" animals from local authority pounds and hold them until they can place them in a home. However, the majority of animal shelters do kill. Statistics suggest that on average, six out of ten stray dogs and eight out of ten stray cats never make it out of an animal shelter alive.[3] [. . .]

Several different methods of humane killing are routinely used in animal shelters. The most widely advocated and commonest method is by injection of barbiturates. The Report of the American Veterinary Medical Association (AVMA) Panel on Euthanasia in 2000 recommended this as the preferred method of humanely killing dogs and cats (some animal welfare organizations consider this to be the only acceptable way)[4] on the grounds that it works very quickly with minimal discomfort to the animals and is relatively inexpensive. There are disadvantages: those administering the barbiturate injection must be trained and skilled in doing so; a second member of staff is always required to restrain the animal; the drugs are dangerous to humans; the animal may produce "an aesthetically objectionable terminal gasp"; and the drugs linger in the carcass and may be hazardous if eaten by another animal. The other main alternatives used for humane killing in animal shelters are gases, primarily carbon monoxide and carbon dioxide.[5] Animals may be gassed together in larger numbers in gas chambers (though it is recommended that animals be separated from one another during the process) and no specialist training is required, though correct gas flow levels must be maintained. Carbon monoxide is particularly effective; the AVMA reports that it "induces loss of consciousness without pain and with minimal discernible discomfort" and that at correct levels, death follows rapidly. However, the chambers must be well maintained and sealed, both to get the flow level right and to avoid affecting nearby humans.

The AVMA report—although contested in some quarters—maintains that these methods of killing, if correctly administered, are painless to animals. For the purposes of this essay, I am going to accept this judgment and assume that killing in animal shelters can be carried out without pain or significant distress to the animals. This, obviously, does not mean that no ethical issues are involved; indeed, it is these issues that I will now move on to consider more closely.

Common Claims about Humane Killing

Arguments in support of humane killing in animal shelters tend to maintain that it is the best option for unadopted or unadoptable animals, given the complex of circumstances that brought them there. Specifically, such arguments usually put forward some or all of the following claims (they may be mutually reinforcing):

1. Humane killing is best for the individual animal concerned.
2. Humane killing of such individual animals is required because of animal overpopulation.
3. Humane killing of such individual animals is best for human beings.

Claim 1, that humane killing is best for the individual animal concerned, rests on the judgment that continued life for that animal would be worse than death. Such arguments are commonly found among those who surrender animals to shelters and among shelter workers. Stephanie Frommer and Arnold Arluke report that many who surrender animals to animal shelters "consider euthanization a better solution for their pets than allowing them to live in poor situations. . . . Death was preferable to sacrificing the quality of life that the animal deserved and had come to expect."[6] Similarly, Frommer and Arluke found that shelter workers also used this argument: "By assuming that animals would meet a worse fate as a stray or with uncaring people, shelter workers enable themselves to view euthanasia as merciful."[7] Some shelter workers also maintained that the lives of animals in shelters are of such low quality that humane killing just helps along a process of dying already under way. Although Frommer and Arluke consider these responses only in the context of guilt-displacement strategies, they may be taken as ethical arguments in their own right. That is to say, in terms of the animal's own welfare, humane killing in animal shelters is ethical because it is in the interests of the animal concerned. The alternatives are likely to be poor living conditions that may include abandonment, ferality, hunger, lack of shelter, and ill-health or killing that might be far less humane than that practiced in the animal shelter. Any of these things, so the argument runs, would be worse for the animal than a painless, if premature, death. I will return to this claim later.

Claim 2, that humane killing of individual animals is required because of animal overpopulation, is usually located in the context of a broader discourse about animal overpopulation. The fundamental problem is understood as being the constant production of surplus dogs and cats—more than there can be homes for with human beings. Such surplus animals are likely to be unsterilized and to have a high fecundity rate, thus multiplying the problem.[8] Overpopulation of dogs and cats, it is argued, leads to the creation of feral cat colonies and dog packs (this rests on the assumption that those who take unwanted animals to animal shelters would abandon them if shelters were not available). Alongside poor individual welfare (as in claim 1), diseases and infestations may be carried beyond feral populations into homed populations (though homed populations can at least be vaccinated against some diseases). Even as it is, as fast as animals are killed in animal shelters, new animals are produced to take their place. Without animal shelters, feral populations would rapidly expand, and without killing, animal numbers in animal shelters would quickly grow far beyond the ability of the shelters to deal with them. This view tends to rest on the idea of total animal population welfare rather than on the welfare of specific individuals, as in claim 1. It may thus be argued that even if in the case of any particular individual animal, humane killing may not seem to be in its interests, from the perspective of the total, accumulated welfare of all the individual animals in that population—say, cats in New York—humane killing is required to keep the remaining cats reasonably healthy and with sufficient access to food and shelter. Some individuals must be sacrificed for the welfare of the cat population as a whole.

Claim 3, that humane killing of individual animals is good for human beings, is a further step from claim 2—now the limiting of animal populations is good for humans as well as for animal populations. This is usually explained in terms of hygiene, possible disease, and nuisance. Abandoned and feral animals and colonies of such animals are often seen as health hazards to humans as well as to homed animals. Dog and cat waste, for instance, may harbor parasitic diseases such as toxoplasmosis, which can cause eye or brain damage to infants and the immunosuppressed. The animals may also be considered as the cause of mess and noise and to be of unsightly appearance. [. . .]

These common arguments are consequentialist in nature: that is, they rest on the view that humane killing in animal shelters brings about the *best consequences* for individual humans and animals and/or for human and animal populations. Central to this kind of consequentialist position is the idea of *welfare*, construed with particular attention to the avoidance of pain to individual animals and to the health of populations as a whole. Humane killing is seen as maximizing animal and human welfare. Although not usually couched in philosophical terms, these arguments assume a form similar to classical utilitarianism, sometimes used as a basis for philosophical arguments for "animal liberation." Utilitarian arguments of this kind usually maintain that the ability to feel pain is the basic characteristic that determines whether a being should be taken into account when making moral decisions and that the central principle of moral decision-making should be the minimization of total pain in the world, whether that pain is human or animal.[9] Such arguments, while militating against the painful transportation and killing of animals for food and against pain inflicted in experimentation, have nothing obviously negative to say about painless killing in animal shelters. Indeed, guided by pain-minimization alone, practices involving painless killing with a view to promoting total welfare would seem (at first sight, at least) morally laudable. If no pain is involved, and if the continuing life of the animal would be a painful one or contribute to greater pain in animal or human populations, the killing feeds nothing negative into a decision-making calculus.[10] So the common claims I have outlined above and philosophical utilitarian positions associated with animal liberation can be, paradoxically, quite close to one another.[11]

However, very different ethical perspectives can be taken on humane killing in animal shelters. I want now to move on to consider just one, the animal rights position taken by philosopher Tom Regan.

Regan, Rights, and Humane Killing

Tom Regan's book *The Case for Animal Rights*, published in 1983, is a sustained philosophical defense of the argument that we should think of animals (he focuses primarily on mammals) as bearers of particular kinds of rights, primarily rights to respect and to freedom from harm. These rights, he argues, rest on the inherent value possessed by animals, independent of their usefulness to or relationships with human beings; this value is equally present in all animals (and humans).

Animals possess such value by virtue of being "subjects of a life"—that is, in Regan's words, as beings displaying the following characteristics:

> beliefs and desires; perception, memory and a sense of the future, including their own future; an emotional life together with feelings of pleasure and pain; preference and welfare interests; the ability to initiate actions in pursuit of their desires and goals; a psychophysical unity over time and an individual welfare in the sense that their experiential life fares well or ill for them, logically independently of their utility for others and logically independently of their being the object of anyone else's interests.[12]

Resting on this theoretical basis, Regan's view is thus rather different from the pain-minimizing, consequentialist positions considered above. He argues that an animal's (or, indeed, a human's) welfare can be harmed without causing pain. Harms to welfare may involve deprivations, even where the individual concerned does not know that or of what they are being deprived.[13] One might, for instance, rear a child in a cage from birth while maintaining the child in a pain-free state; the child would still be harmed, even if he or she did not know what he or she was missing (and, Regan points out, part of the harm is actually *that* the child does not know what he or she is missing). Further, Regan goes on to argue, killing painlessly is just such a harm by deprivation. Indeed, it is fundamental and irreversible; it forecloses all possibilities of finding future satisfaction; it is thus "the ultimate harm because it is the ultimate loss" (although it may not be the worst harm there is—living a life of relentless physical agony would be worse).[14] So, he maintains, "to bring about the untimely death of animals will not hurt them if this is done painlessly; but they will be harmed."[15] Thus there is an immediate contrast with the earlier view, where, since pain is all that is to be taken into account, painless killing does not seem to be a harm at all.[16]

Regan's view that painless killing is a harm clearly has a bearing on the killing of animals in animal shelters. He does not explicitly discuss moral decision-making in this context. However, he makes one point about such killing very clear: the killing of healthy animals in animal shelters should not be regarded as euthanasia (a term I have avoided using until now for just this reason). Regan maintains that euthanasia of animals must have the following characteristics: (a) killing must be by the most painless means possible; (b) killing must be believed to be in the animal's interests, and this must be a true belief; and (c) the one who kills must be motivated out of concern for the interest, good, or welfare of the particular animal involved.[17] Even where (a) applies in animal shelters, according to Regan (b) and (c) usually do not. As we have seen, often the reasons offered for painlessly killing animals are based on the consequences for whole populations, not on the interests, good, or welfare of the particular animal being killed. This may, Regan suggests, be called "well-intentioned killing," but it is not appropriately called euthanasia. [. . .]

As a nonconsequentialist, Regan takes the view that some actions are morally unacceptable, even if they are aimed at bringing about a greater good. And killing any being with inherent value and a right to respect in order to further any other purpose at all, including minimizing the pain of other animals, humans, or populations of animals and humans, is just such an unacceptable action. For Regan, the only grounds on which killing an animal is morally acceptable is if it is in the interests of the animal concerned, and that could only be if the animal were to be in acute pain with no prospect of that pain ever ceasing.[18] Humane killing of healthy animals in animal shelters does not fall into this category; it is thus an ethically unacceptable practice and should be ceased.

A Relational Approach

Two conflicting ways of thinking about painless killing in animal shelters have so far been identified. One is the broadly consequentialist view that painless killing is the best solution, in terms of minimizing pain, to the perceived problem of dog and cat overpopulation. The second is that painless killing is an unethical, harmful practice that takes the lives of beings entitled to respect. Yet there seems something troubling about both perspectives, taken alone. On the one hand, looking at the issue from a consequentialist, pain-minimization perspective, painless killing does not seem problematic at all. And yet surely the killing of cats and dogs on such a scale does merit, at least, some ethical unease. The rights view, on the other hand, seems excessively demanding, both philosophically, in terms of human responsibilities for animal lives, and in practice, with its implication that all abandoned cats and dogs should be treated, in terms of the provision of essentials, as members of what is almost an animal welfare state.

As I said at the beginning, the purpose of this essay is not to propose any straightforward "solution" to the problem of killing animals in animal shelters. Rather, I want to suggest another possible perspective that I think is at least worth considering alongside the two I have already outlined. This perspective could be thought of as a "relational approach." That is to say, rather than focusing on the outcomes of particular actions or on the value-giving qualities or abilities possessed by animals in themselves, the focus is on the nature of the relationships *between* humans and animals. While not denying the significance of the pain-minimizing, consequentialist view and the rights view, such a relational approach can highlight other moral questions that arise. It can look broadly at the context of human relationships with domestic cats and dogs, seeing painless killing in animal shelters as emerging from a whole nexus of historical and cultural relationships and practices. [. . .]

Dependence and Independence

Dogs and cats kept as pets are domesticated species, bound into historical relationships with human beings. Exactly how such relationships began is contested, and how "domesticated" should be defined is also an area of dispute.[19] But it is undisputed that one key element of domestication is human intervention in animal breeding, in particular in the selection of mates in order to produce offspring that manifest characteristics desired by humans. Domesticated dogs and cats bear witness to these human desires in the shapes and forms of their bodies and in particular in their neotonization (that is, their retention of infantile characteristics). One consequence of this intervention in breeding is the diminished ability of many domesticated dogs and cats to live independently of humans.

It is, though, important to be careful here. Only some dogs and cats are fully dependent on humans (especially when bred in particular bodily shapes that make hunting, scavenging, or reproducing difficult). If abandoned, they would die, perhaps in painful ways. But other dogs and cats can survive partially, or wholly, independent of human beings. Studies of feral dogs, for instance, have suggested that they can live reasonably well, although they are indirectly dependent on scavenging from human settlements.[20] Colonies of feral cats may also scavenge but can live by hunting for birds and rodents. Certainly, such animals may be more vulnerable to disease and injury than homed animals and do not have access to veterinary care; but nonetheless their lives in general do not seem to be ones of unremitting pain such that they might be considered to be lives not worth living.

Significant issues arise from these relations of dependence/independence. First, where domestic cats and dogs are wholly dependent on humans, a special relationship, created by humans, has been established. By relationship here, I do not mean a relationship of affect, though such a relationship may exist in some cases. Rather, I mean that humans have acted to create animals that are constituted such that they are unable to be independent.

[. . .] At the individual level, one could maintain that along with an individual's decision to produce or adopt pets comes a duty to care and provide for them.[21] This is a commonplace, of course, which often forms one part of an animal welfare organization's educational campaign. The second level, though, follows a broader, social obligation arising out of the social creation of dependent domesticated animals. That there is a population of domestic dogs and cats, whether homed, unwanted, abandoned, or feral, is due to human action and human relations with these animals. On this basis, it can be argued that humans have *acquired* ethical responsibilities toward humanly originating dependent animals that do not exist toward, say, urban rat populations (where the rats are wild in origin).[22] The existence of animal shelters at all may indicate some basic recognition of this (after all, no such shelters exist for urban rat populations, for which painless killing is rarely considered to be of ethical significance). But it is questionable whether painless killing is an appropriate way of discharging responsibilities to unwanted but dependent animals humans have themselves created.

On the other hand, though, some domesticated cats and dogs do manage to live lives that appear to be satisfactory, outside the context of a home with an owner. They may live as individual hunters and scavengers; they may form colonies and packs with others; they may take up residence in abandoned buildings or the grounds of institutions, allotments, cemeteries, and other backwaters of human development. For these animals, either indirectly reliant on human beings or largely independent of them, being taken to an animal shelter for painless killing seems to be a denial of their *lack* of relationship with particular human beings rather than the failure, as in the previous case, to recognize the ethical force of dependence. Animals that have strayed for some time, or which are feral, are regarded as "unadoptable"; they are likely to be quickly dispatched in a shelter.

The question then arises whether it is better to live a life of ferality, provided that it is not one of interminable agony, or to be painlessly killed. How one answers this question depends on a number of factors, including whether cats and dogs are thought of as the kinds of beings that have any sense of themselves as beings that exist over time and whether they have nonmomentary future-oriented desires that entail continued existence in order to be fulfilled.[23] (Regan obviously thinks they do, and Peter Singer, a utilitarian, suggests in recent editions of *Practical Ethics* that dogs and cats may be self-conscious with a sense of themselves as beings that exist over time, such that killing them, however painlessly, is wrong).[24] In any case, it may be that some sort of double-bind is in operation here. Domestic dogs and cats are recognized in Western urban settings, in particular, as properly living in relationship to particular human owners. This relationship is not regarded as so binding that painless killing—often merely for convenience—is thought of as morally unacceptable, not just by the individuals who surrender animals but at a broader social level where the collective and historical responsibility for having created dependent animals is not taken seriously. But, on the other hand, the relationship is regarded as binding enough that individual animals living outside such a relationship are regarded as inevitably unable to cope, out of place, and (perhaps) better off dead.[25] On both counts, this leads to an increase in the number of animals being humanely killed in animal shelters.

So I am suggesting that greater *collective* responsibility needs to be taken for the existence of all domestic animals (rather than the responsibility being regarded as one attaching solely to individual owners). This may mean both that there are duties of provision and care for dependent domesticated animals and obligations to respect the independent lives of those cats and dogs that succeed in surviving outside the context of a human home; their lives should not be regarded as lives not worth living. These domesticated animals are in particular situations substantially as a result of their relationships to humans and human society; having deliberately put animals into these situations, the appropriate ethical response is to do what is best for the animals concerned within the context in which they are located.

Power and Instrumentalism

[. . .] Pets are, generally, viewed with what might be called an "attitude of instrumentalism." Of course, this attitude is to be expected in the relations humans have with animals kept for food and experimental purposes. But it is unsettling in a relationship described, as we have seen, in terms of companionship or the familial. Yet this attitude not only seems widespread with respect to pets but also is at least plausible that educational campaigns about responsible pet-ownership can actually promote just such a perspective. At the same time, it is this attitude of instrumentalism that makes the surrender of dogs and cats to animal shelters more, rather than less, likely.

One good example of how this attitude of instrumentalism plays out is with respect to de-sexing. Almost all animal welfare organizations advocate de-sexing; they pay for it, encourage it, and campaign for it. The main arguments presented in favor of it are that it prevents the production of unwanted offspring and reduces roaming and other unwanted behaviors in pets themselves. That is to say, it is better both for animal populations and for human owners if pets are de-sexed. But what of the animal itself? We cannot know whether de-sexing matters to a cat or dog, and if it does, how much and in what ways. But it might be the case that there is a way in which de-sexing harms animals, even if it does not matter to them in the sense of being aware of what they are missing. Perhaps the pursuit of sex and the interactions involved in that pursuit, the practice of sex, and the process of producing young would be rich experiences for cats and dogs, so that once de-sexed their lives are less rich, even though they do not know it.

However one might regard animals' *loss* by de-sexing, it is rarely the case that de-sexing is carried out solely for the *benefit* of the animal concerned. When animals are de-sexed, they are, in most cases, being treated as instruments, as a means to an end, where the end is the good of the whole population or, more frequently, an easier life with the owner. So, animals are anesthetized and made to undergo surgery that will change their lives, a process of human domination—understood here as a power relation that they are unable to resist—for reasons not usually to do with their own welfare but as instrumental to other ends. And while there are occasions in many dependent relationships where dominating behavior toward the dependent being seems ethically appropriate or necessary, such occasions are usually in the interests of the one being dominated; that is to say, they are a form of paternalism. This, however, is rarely the case with pet de-sexing, where domination combines with instrumentalism, not paternalism.[26]

But this description—a process of human domination that they are unable to understand or resist, for reasons not to do with their own welfare but as instrumental to other ends—might equally be used to describe much painless killing in animal shelters. What I am suggesting is that both de-sexing and killing in animal shelters flow from the same underlying attitude toward pets. This attitude is one of willingness to adopt dominating practices that treat animals as means to other ends. If this is right, campaigns to promote de-sexing, while at one level being successful in reducing the number of kittens and puppies born[27] at another level actually promote dominating and instrumentalist underlying attitudes and relationships that make people more likely to surrender animals to animal shelters. Removal of the sex of a domesticated animal (unless that sex can be used for other instrumentalist purposes, such as pedigree breeding) is seen as being good for animal populations and as making the animal into a better, more amenable companion. Precisely the same arguments, as I have already maintained—the need to manage animal populations and problems in "companionship" with animals—lead to the surrender of animals to animal shelters. Rather than seeing the killing of animals in animal shelters as an aberration resulting from overpopulation and some irresponsible owners, it can be viewed instead as the inevitable outcome of a widespread set of human-pet relationships, flowing from an underlying human attitude of instrumentalism, an attitude sometimes promoted by animal welfare organizations themselves.

Conclusion

In this essay, I have considered some of the ethical issues around the practice of painless killing of cats and dogs in animal shelters. I have looked at the most prominent ethical approaches to such killing—that is, a kind of pain-minimizing consequentialism and an animal rights approach. I have suggested that another way of framing the situation would be to explore aspects of the human-animal relations involved, focusing on the relations of dependence/independence between humans and domesticated cats and dogs, and the underlying human relational attitude toward these animals. I have suggested, first, that the ethical responsibilities of the creation of dependence where it exists should be taken more seriously; second, that, on the other hand, relative independence where it exists should be respected; and third, that an underlying cause of the high death toll in animal shelters is an attitude toward pet animals of instrumentalism, an attitude that can actually be promoted by some attempts to reduce the number of animals coming into animal shelters.

Only the second of these points constitutes any kind of practical recommendation at all: that cats and dogs leading feral lives that do not seem to be lives of interminable pain should be left alone to live out their lives, even if their presence seems messy and unhygienic to nearby humans.[28] Aside from this, I have merely attempted to think through some of the underlying relationships, attitudes, and responsibilities that lead to the painless killing of so many animals in animal shelters. Such deep-seated relationships and attitudes are not amenable to simple educational campaigns about "snipping and chipping"—indeed, as I have suggested, such campaigns may serve to reinforce, not undercut, existing attitudes. To change the practices of killing in animal shelters will require a substantial cultural change in attitudes toward those animals humans increasingly like to call "companions."

Notes

1. I am, in this essay, interested in the special case of killing healthy animals rather than sick and suffering animals. There is a degree of ambiguity about this, but the broad distinction will suffice here.
2. P. N. Olson and C. Moulton, "Pet (Dog and Cat) Overpopulation in the United States," *Journal of Reproduction and Fertility* supp. 47 (1993): 433–38. These statistics, though, are contested. See Bernard Rollin and Michael Rollin, "Dogmatisms and Catechisms: Ethics and Companion Animals," *Anthrozoos* 14, no. 1 (2001): 6. I am using the expression "humanely killed" rather than "euthanized" because, as will be seen later, some object to this name for the practice.
3. SAFE 2003 at http://www.safeanimals.com/euthanasia.
4. See R. H. Schmidt "2000 Report of the AVMA Panel on Euthanasia," *Journal of the American Veterinary Medical Association,* 218, no. 5 (March 2001): 669–96. The US Animal Protection Institute, for instance, maintains barbiturate injection to be the only acceptable method of animal euthanasia in a shelter. See Jean Hofve, "Euthanasia and the Animal Shelter," *Animal* 32, no. 2 (Summer 2001), http://www.api4animals./org.
5. Methods deemed unacceptable by the AVMA still seem to be used in some places: there is, for instance, a report that in Enoch, Utah, stray animals are killed by exhaust fumes from a truck.
6. Stephanie Frommer and Arnold Arluke, "Loving Them to Death: Blame-Displacing Strategies of Animal Shelter Workers and Surrenderers," *Society and Animals* 7, no. 1 (1999): 5.
7. Ibid., 8.
8. Olson and Moulton, "Pet Overpopulation," 434.
9. This view is often associated with Peter Singer in *Animal Liberation* (1975; repr., London: Jonathan Cape, 1984). Although Singer is well known for being a utilitarian (though more recently a preference utilitarian rather than a classical utilitarian), as has been pointed out by Keith Burgess-Jackson, the book *Animal Liberation* is not explicitly utilitarian. It is compatible with utilitarianism but does not presuppose it. See Burgess-Jackson's Web log at http://analphilosopher.blogspot.com/2003_12_01_analphilosopher_archive.html.
10. Of course, this is a somewhat simplified position, since there are a range of other factors involved—for instance, the well-documented distress caused to those working in animal shelters at having to carry out the humane killing. I will discuss other possible consequentialist verdicts later.
11. This, though, is not the only possible utilitarian "take" on the situation. See Peter Singer, "Killing Humans and Killing Animals," *Inquiry* 22 (1979): 145–55, and his more recent discussion in Peter Singer, *Practical Ethics,* 2nd ed. (Cambridge: Cambridge University Press, 1993), 132, where he suggests that dogs and cats may be self-conscious and, if so, should not be killed, however painlessly, as noted on p. 181.
12. Tom Regan, *The Case for Animal Rights* (Berkeley: University of California, 1983), 243. Obviously, very many difficulties exist with this argument at all stages; it is not necessary to go into these difficulties here.
13. Ibid., 98–9. This is a view that could be shared by some utilitarians, since one would expect deprivation to mean that an individual's experiences were less happy or less rich than they would otherwise be.
14. Ibid., 100, 113, 117.
15. Ibid., 103.
16. Painless killing, though, ends the possibility of a particular individual having future happy experiences, which (unless replaced) would matter in some forms of utilitarianism as affecting the total happiness in the world. There isn't space to pursue this issue here; Singer discusses it further in *Practical Ethics.*
17. Regan, *Case for Animal Rights*, 114.
18. Regan, in fact, does make a couple of exceptions to this, in particular in what he calls the "miniride" principle. I do not think that the miniride principle applies in this case, though it would be an interesting study to explore this in more detail. See ibid., 305.
19. See, for instance, Stephen Budiansky's *Covenant of the Wild: Why Animals Chose Domestication* (London: Wiedenfeld and Nicholson, 1992), where it is argued that animals connived in their own domestication, a view that is in contrast with more traditional accounts where domestication is presented as humans capturing or confining animals (that is to say, humans were the only active agents in the process).

20. See Joanna Newby, *The Pact for Survival* (Sydney: Australian Broadcasting Corporation, 1977), 61.

21. Just this case has already been convincingly argued by Keith Burgess-Jackson, and I will not argue for it further here. See Keith Burgess-Jackson, "Doing Right by Our Animal Companions," *Journal of Ethics* 2 (1998): 159–85.

22. I recognize that significant philosophical difficulties exist with the idea of collective or social responsibilities and that many philosophers will find this claim unsatisfactory. There is not, however, space to consider expanded senses of responsibility in more detail here.

23. Nel Noddings raises this question as part of her discussion of caring. She asks, "Does one who cares choose swift and merciful death for the object of her care over precarious and perhaps painful life?," and answers that "it depends on our caretaking abilities, on traffic conditions where we live, on the physical condition of the animal." See Nel Noddings, *Caring* (London: University of California Press, 1984), 13.

24. Singer, *Practical Ethics*, 110–34.

25. The idea that feral animals—specifically cats—are often regarded as being "out of place" is explored by H. Griffiths, J. Poulter, and D. Sibley, "Feral Cats in the City," in *Animal Spaces, Beastly Places*, eds. Chris Philo and Chris Wilbert (London: Routledge, 2000), 56–70.

26. A recent study of websites advocating spaying and neutering in fact does uncover paternalistic arguments. It is claimed that de-sexed animals are less susceptible to disease (since they are not mating), are less likely to be harmed by fighting, and do not suffer from thwarted sexual urges. See, for instance, http://www.ktvu.com/family/2003733/detail.html. I don't think that the presence of such paternalistic arguments invalidates my claims here, since the same kinds of paternalistic arguments also exist for humane killing, as I have pointed out.

27. Though this may not be achieved: see Olson and Moulton, "Pet Overpopulation," 43.

28. It might be, for instance, that development of the policy implications of ideas in this essay would lead to advocacy of a much more stringent licensing scheme for pet ownership.

77 The Structure of Evil

Mark Rowlands

Rowlands provides striking examples of the pain caused by electric shock for a wolf and for dogs. He then discusses the nature of moral evil, arguing that such evil does not reside only in a failure to protect those whom you have a duty to protect or in the entertaining of "fundamentally stupid" beliefs. In addition, it requires that the victim be helpless. Rowlands maintains that humans are uniquely evil, in that we make things weak so that we may treat them badly.

1. Do you think that Rowlands is right in maintaining that motives are irrelevant in assessing the morality of actions?
2. In your view, what relevance does the story of the wolf have for understanding the structure of evil?

I

Brenin was a wolf with whom I was fortunate to spend a decade or so of my life. I mention him because there are two episodes from his life that are peculiarly relevant to this chapter. The first occurred when he was a young wolf, and we were living in the United States. We used to go running together most days. But Brenin had been a little off-colour for the past couple of days, and I didn't want to risk him in the heat of an Alabama summer. So, today, I left him behind—a decision with which he vehemently disagreed and about which he made his displeasure known.

Brenin apparently managed to open the garden gate, and charged off after me. About ten minutes into my run, I heard a screeching of brakes following by a loud, sickening, thud. I turned to see Brenin lying in the road, having been hit by a Chevrolet Blazer. A Blazer, for those of you who are not American, is an SUV. It had passed seconds earlier, travelling at—I would estimate—somewhere in the region of forty to fifty miles per hour. Brenin lay in the road for a few heart-stopping seconds, howling, and then he picked himself up and ran off into the woods. It took me nearly an hour to find him. But when I did, he was largely okay. In a day or so he was back to normal. In fact, the Chevy came off distinctly worse.

The Blazer would have killed me. But Brenin's physical scars healed in just a few days. And, psychologically, there didn't seem to be any scarring at all. The very next day, he was pestering me to take him running, and never showed any subsequent fear of the cars that would fly past him on the road. Brenin was a very tough and together animal, both physically and psychologically. I want you to bear this in mind when I tell you the next story.

We are out running again, but this time it is a few years later. We have moved to Ireland and are running together along the banks of the River Lee in Cork. When we were on the return leg of the run, I grabbed hold of Brenin's collar, since I had seen, up ahead, Paco, a big St Bernard. Brenin was officially hostile to all large male dogs, and I didn't fancy having to step in to separate those two.

As I grabbed his collar, we ducked under one of the electric cattle fences. My elbow brushed the fence, and the shock passed through to Brenin. Brenin took off, scorching straight past a somewhat mystified Paco. And he didn't stop until he reached the car, a couple of miles away. He was there waiting for me when I eventually got back, anxious and breathless. We had gone on that same run most days, rain or shine, for the best part of a year. But he never went back again. He refused point blank, and his decision would remain unchanged no matter what the form of begging, bribery or coercion I employed. That, apparently, is how horrible electricity is for wolves.

Perhaps, you might think Brenin was just being a little histrionic. It was, after all, only a mild electric shock. If you are tempted to think this, just remember the Chevy Blazer. On balance, it seems that for a wolf a mild electric shock is a lot worse than being hit by an SUV!

II

With this in mind, consider some famous experiments conducted by experimental psychologists at a world-renowned university. The experiments involved a shuttlebox. This box consists in two compartments separated by a barrier. The floor of each compartment is an electrified grid. The psychologist and his collaborators would put a dog in one compartment, and then give an intense electric shock to its feet. Instinctively, the dog jumps over from one compartment to the other. They would then repeat this procedure over and over—several hundred times in a typical experiment. Each time, however, the jump is more and more difficult for the dog because the experimenters are gradually making the barrier higher and higher. Eventually the dog can't make the jump, and falls to the electrified grid beneath it. In a variation, the experimenters electrify the floor on both sides of the barrier. No matter where the dog jumps, it is going to be shocked. Nevertheless, the pain of the shock is intense, and the dog tries to escape, no matter how futile the attempt. And so the dog jumps from one electrified grid to the other. The researchers, when they wrote up the experiment, described the dog as giving a 'sharp anticipatory yip which turned into a yelp when he landed on the electrified grid.' The end result is the same. Exhausted, the dog lies on the floor urinating, defecating, yelping, shrieking, trembling. After ten to twelve days of these sorts of trials, the dog ceases to resist the shock. In these experiments, I think, we find an instructive distillation of the concept of human evil.

III

Evil has fallen on hard times lately—not in the sense that there isn't much of it around but, rather, in that most people are loathe to admit its existence. Evil, they will insist, is either a medical issue—the result of some form of mental illness—or it is a social issue—the result of some societal malaise or other. The guiding assumption is that evil deeds require evil people; and evil people must act from evil motives. And if you have no control over your motives—because you are medically ill or socially maladapted—then you have no control over the deeds. This connection between evil deeds and evil motives is no accident. It goes back to a distinction originally made in the middle ages—between moral and natural evil. Medieval philosophers noted that evil—which they thought of as pain, suffering and associated ilk—could be caused by two different sorts of thing: natural events and human agency. Pain and suffering caused by earthquakes, floods, hurricanes, disease, and so on, they called natural evil. This they distinguished from the pain and suffering caused by human agency, which they called moral evil. But the idea of agency—of acting—involves the notion of a motive or intention. Therefore, people have inferred—though it doesn't strictly follow—morally evil acts require evil motives. And an evil person, therefore, is someone who acts from evil motives.

The result is a highly intellectualized concept of moral evil. A good example of this is provided by Colin McGinn, a friend and one of the best philosophers around, who understands moral evil as essentially a kind of *Schadenfreude*—taking delight in the pain, suffering or misfortune of someone else.[1] This may seem like a good way of understanding evil. Surely it is evil to delight in the pain, suffering or misfortune of someone else? And surely the sort of person who does this is as good an example as any of an evil person? I want to undermine whatever confidence you have in this idea.

Here is a real case. A young girl is the victim of long-term abuse as a child, being regularly raped by her father from a very young age. Horrified, you might ask what her mother was doing in all of this. Didn't she realize what was happening? Her reply chilled me to the bone, and still does. When her father came back drunk, abusive and spoiling for a fight her mother would tell her to, as she put it, go in there and keep him quiet! Whenever I need to keep an image of human evil firmly in my mind, I just think of this woman telling her daughter to go in there and keep him quiet.

There are two acts of evil involved here; the repeated episodes of rape by the father and the active complicity of the mother. And it is not easy to see which is worse. The mother was a victim—certainly—but was she any less evil? Her evil was, we must assume, fuelled by her terror—and not by any delight she took in the suffering of her daughter. But this doesn't change the fact that her actions were as evil as it is possible to imagine. Just think about that when you assume that victims can't be evil.

Who knows the motives of the man who called himself her father? Perhaps he understood that what he was doing was evil. But suppose he didn't. Suppose he thought it was a perfectly natural aspect of family life—maybe because he grew up in similar circumstances. All I can say is: who cares what he thought? There is no need to speculate about his motives. Even if he thought he was doing nothing wrong—even if he thought he was doing right—that diminishes his evil not one bit.

You can be evil—as was the mother—because you fail in your duties of protection, and whatever terror you feel here does not alter the evil of your acts or omissions. And you can be evil—as was the father in our wholly speculative reconstruction of his motives—because you are an irredeemably stupid man. But in neither case does your evil have anything to do in taking delight in the pain, suffering or misfortune of others. Deliberate malice has, I think, little to do with the essence of evil. Let's now flash forward a few years, at least in our imagination. Let's suppose the father and mother were eventually caught and punished. I'm not sure what, in these circumstances, the daughter's emotional reaction would be. Probably a little mixed, I would expect.

But suppose it wasn't mixed. Suppose she was absolutely delighted. Moreover, suppose she was delighted for one very simple reason: vengeance. She wanted her parents to suffer. Would this be an evil desire? I don't think so. I think her desire for vengeance may be regrettable. It may be evidence of permanent psychological scarring. Maybe. But it isn't evil. And is the woman evil for having this desire? This charge would be implausible. Delighting in the misfortune of evil people—especially when you have personally suffered at their hands—may not be a shining example of moral development. But it is a long way from being evil.

So, contrary to what McGinn—and the philosophical tradition—claims, I think *Schadenfreude* is neither a necessary nor a sufficient condition for being an evil person. It is not necessary because you can be evil even if you don't delight in the pain, suffering or misfortune of others. You can be evil, as was the mother, because you don't do your duty. And you can be evil, as was the father in our reconstruction of his motives, because you have fundamentally stupid beliefs. And *Schadenfreude* is not sufficient for being an evil person. Taking delight in the pain of evil others, when you have suffered at their hands, does not automatically make you evil.

IV

Many people would be appalled if I mentioned the animal experiments in the same breath as the abused child—as if that in some way diminishes her suffering. But, I've argued, the best way of understanding evil is not in terms of the motives of the person who acts, but in terms of the structure of the situation in which they act. So, with this in mind, let's look at the shared structure of the shuttlebox experiments and the abused child.

In both cases, of course, we might find fundamentally stupid beliefs on the part of the perpetrators: for example, the belief that torturing dogs with electricity is going to reveal anything at all about the nature of human depression—with its multifarious causes, etiologies and syndromes. We often also find derogation of moral duty: for example, the duty to protect those who are defenceless against those who deem them inferior and therefore expendable. Stupidity and derogation are typically centrally involved in evil acts. However, there is one further ingredient, and without this neither stupidity nor derogation is of any consequence: the helplessness of the victim. In this regard, I think Milan Kundera said something fundamentally important and correct about the nature of human goodness:

> True human goodness cannot show itself in all its purity and liberty except in regard to those who have no power. The true moral test of humanity (the most radical, situated on a level so profound that it escapes our notice) lies in its relations with those who are at its mercy: the animals. And it is here that exists the fundamental failing of man, so fundamental that all others follow from it.[2]

In effect, I am making the converse point about human evil. When the other—whether human or animal—is powerless, you have no self-interested motive for treating them with decency or respect. You do not fear them, nor do you covet their assistance. The only motive you can have for treating them with decency and respect is a moral one: you treat them in this way because that is the right thing to do. And you do this because that is the sort of person you are. And if you do not . . . that is when evil gains a foothold in the world. Stupidity of belief and derogation of duty can do their work only when the victim is powerless—helplessness is the canvas on which the portrait of human evil is painted.

If this is correct, then there are more evil acts, and more evil people, than we would care to imagine or admit. When we think of evil in terms of medical illness or social breakdown, then we assume that evil is exceptional; evil is something that resides at the margins of society. But, in fact, evil pervades society all the way in. It attaches to abusive fathers and complicit mothers. But it attaches no less to privileged and happy psychologists—supposed experts in the domain of mental health who acted, we can suppose, only out of the best intentions towards humanity.

Ultimately, there are more evil acts and more evil people than we would care to admit, because humans stand in a unique relationship to evil. Humans are not unique in that they treat the helpless badly. All animals do so—life is profoundly cruel. Humans are the animals that manufacture weakness. The abused child was naturally helpless. But the researchers' dogs were the product of 20,000 years of social and genetic engineering that led them, eventually but inexorably, to a shuttlebox. In this, we have taken the cruelty of life, refined it, and intensified it. Humans don't merely treat the weak badly. Humans make things weak precisely so that they may treat them badly. If we wanted a one-sentence definition of humans, this one would do: humans are the animals that engineer the possibility of their own evil.

Notes

1. Colin McGinn, *Ethics, evil and fiction* (Oxford: Oxford University Press, 1999).
2. Milan Kundera, *L'insoutenable légèreté de l'être* (Paris: Gallimard, 1984), p. 421. Translation mine.

78 An FBI Perspective on Animal Cruelty

Alan C. Brantley

Brantley explains threat assessment as it pertains to the link between animal abuse and violent crime. Other factors are also relevant, such as violence toward other children and property. He indicates that hurting animals and children is often considered by prisoners to be significantly worse than crimes against adults. Brantley points out the significance of an escalating pattern of abuse against pets. Cases of animal cruelty might be connected to homicide.

Animal cruelty is not as serious as killing human beings, but it is very serious. One reason for the lack of willingness to be involved in such cases is fear for one's own safety. Rehabilitation is very unlikely.

1. In your view, what steps might be taken in early childhood education to avoid animal abuse?
2. There are a number of programs which team up abandoned dogs and prisoners. How important do you believe such programs to be?

Q: What is the history of the Behavioral Science Unit/Investigative Support Unit?

Brantley: The Behavioral Science Unit originated in the 1970s and is located at the FBI Academy. Its purpose is to teach behavioural science to FBI trainees and National Academy students. The instructors were often asked questions about violent criminals, such as, 'What do you think causes a person to do something like this?' The instructors offered some ideas, and as the students went out and applied some of these ideas, it was seen that there might be some merit to using this knowledge in field operations. In the mid-1980s, the National Center for the Analysis of Violent Crime was founded with the primary mission of identifying and tracking serial killers, but it also was given the task of looking at any violent crime that was particularly vicious, unusual, or repetitive, including serial rape and child molestation. We now look at and provide operational assistance to law enforcement agencies and prosecutors worldwide who are confronted with any type of violent crime.

Q: You have said that the FBI takes the connection between animal cruelty and violent crime very seriously. How is this awareness applied on a daily basis?

Brantley: A lot of what we do is called threat assessment. If we have a known subject, we want as much information as we can obtain from family members, co-workers, local police, and others, before we offer an opinion about this person's threat level and dangerousness. Something we believe is prominently displayed in the histories of people who are habitually violent is animal abuse. We look not only for a history of animal abuse, torment, or torture, but also for childhood or adolescent acts of violence toward other children and possibly adults, and for a history of destructiveness to property.

Sometimes this violence against animals is symbolic. We have had cases where individuals had an early history of taking stuffed animals or even pictures of animals and carving them up. That is a risk indicator.

You can look at cruelty to animals and cruelty to humans as a continuum. We first see people begin to fantasize about these violent actions. If there is escalation along this continuum, we may see acting out against inanimate objects. This may also be manifest in the writings or drawings of the individual affected. The next phase is usually acting out against animals.

Q: When did the FBI first begin to see this connection?

Brantley: We first quantified it when we did research in the late 1970s interviewing 36 multiple murderers in prison. This kind of theme had already emerged in our work with violent criminals. We all believed this was an important factor, so we said, 'Let's go and ask the offenders themselves and see what they have to say about it.' By self report, 36 per cent described killing and torturing animals as children and 46 per cent said they did this as adolescents. We believe that the real figure was much higher, but that people might not have been willing to admit to it.

Q: You mean that people who commit multiple, brutal murders might be reluctant to admit to killing animals?

Brantley: I believe that to be true in some cases. In the inmate population, it's one thing to be a big-time criminal and kill people—many inmates have no empathy or concern for human victims—but they might identify with animals. I've worked with prisoners who kept pets even though they weren't supposed to. They would consider someone else hurting their pet as reason enough to commit homicide. Also, within prisons, criminals usually don't want to talk about what they have done to animals or children for fear that other inmates may retaliate against them or that they may lose status among their peers.

Q: Where is violence against animals coming from? Are criminals witnessing it in others? Convicted serial killer Ted Bundy recounted being forced to watch his grandfather's animal abuse.

Brantley: For the most part, in my experience, offenders who harm animals as children pretty much come up with this on their own. Quite often they will do this in the presence of others and teach it to others, but the ones with a rich history of violence are usually the instigators. Some children might follow along to be accepted, but the ones we need to worry about are the one or two dominant, influential children who initiate the cruelty.

Q: What components need to be present for you to think a child or adolescent is really in trouble?

Brantley: You have to look at the quality of the act and at the frequency and severity. If a child kicks the dog when somebody's been aggressive toward him, that's one issue, but if it's a daily thing or if he has a pattern of tormenting and physically torturing the family dog or cat, that's another. I would look to see if the pattern is escalating. I look at any type of abuse of an animal as serious to begin with, unless I have other information that might explain it. It should not be dismissed. I've seen it too often develop into something more severe. Some types of abuse—for example, against insects—seem to be fundamentally different. Our society doesn't consider insects attractive or worthy of affection. But our pets are friendly and affectionate and they often symbolically represent the qualities and characteristics of human beings. Violence against them more likely indicates violence that may well escalate into violence against humans.

You also need to look at the bigger picture. What's going on at home? What other supports, if any, are in place? How is the child doing at school? Is he drinking or doing drugs?

Q: We are familiar with the 'classic' cases of serial killers, like Jeffrey Dahmer, who had early histories of animal abuse (see the Summer 1986 *HSUS News*). Are there any recent cases you have worked on?

Brantley: The Jason Massey case jumps out as being a prominent one. This was a case from 1993 in Texas. This individual, from an early age, started his career killing many dogs and cats. He finally graduated, at the age of 20, to beheading a 13-year-old girl and shooting her 14-year-old stepbrother to death.

He was convicted of murder. I was brought in for the sentencing phase to testify as to his dangerousness and future threat to the community. The prosecutors knew that he was a prolific killer of animals, and that he was saving the body parts of these animals. The prosecutor discovered a cooler full of animal remains that belonged to Massey and brought it to the courtroom for the sentencing hearing. It caused the jurors to react strongly, and ultimately the sentence was death.

Q: Mr Massey had been institutionalized at his mother's request two years before the murders since she was aware of his diaries, which recorded his violent fantasies, and his animal killings, yet he was released. Do you think that mental health officials have been slower than law enforcement agencies in taking animal abuse seriously?

Brantley: We've made this a part of a lot of our training for local police, and I think most police recognize that when they see animal mutilation or torture that they need to check it out; but police have to triage and prioritize their cases. We try to tell people that investigating animal cruelty and investigating homicides may not be mutually exclusive.

We are trying to do the same for mental health professionals. We offer training to forensic psychiatrists through a fellowship programme and provide other training to the mental health community. I think psychiatrists are receptive to our message when we can give them examples and case studies demonstrating this connection. The word is getting out.

Q: Do you think more aggressive prosecution of animal-cruelty cases can help get some people into the legal system who might otherwise slip through?

Brantley: I think that it is a legitimate way to deal with someone who poses a threat. Remember, Al Capone was finally imprisoned for income-tax evasion rather than for murder or racketeering—charges which could never be proven.

Q: Have you ever encountered a situation where extreme or repeated animal cruelty is the only warning sign you see in an individual, where there is no other violent behaviour? Or does such abuse not occur in a vacuum?

Brantley: I would agree with that last concept. But let's say that you do have a case of an individual who seems not to have had any other adjustment problems but is harming animals. What that says is that while, up to that point, there is no documented history of adjustment problems, there are adjustment problems now and there could be greater problems down the road. We have some kids who start early and move toward greater and greater levels of violence, some who get into it starting in adolescence, and some who are adults before they start to blossom into violent offenders.

Q: Do you find animal cruelty developing in those who have already begun killing people?

Brantley: We know that certain types of offenders who have escalated to human victims will, at times, regress back to earlier offences such as making obscene phone calls, stalking people, or killing animals. Rarely, if ever, do we see humans being killed as a precursor to the killing of animals.

Q: How would you respond to the argument that animal cruelty provides an outlet that prevents violent individuals from acting against people?

Brantley: I would disagree with that. Animal cruelty is not as serious as killing human beings, we have to agree to that, but certainly it's moving in a very ominous direction. This is not a harmless venting of emotion in a healthy individual; this is a warning sign that this individual is not mentally healthy and needs some sort of intervention. Abusing animals does not dissipate those violent emotions; instead, it may fuel them.

Q: What problems do you have in trying to assess the dangerousness of a suspect or a known offender?

Brantley: Getting background information is the main problem. People know this person has done these things, but there may be no record or we haven't found the right people to interview.

Q: That's one of the reasons why we have put an emphasis on stronger anti-cruelty laws and more aggressive enforcement—to get such information in the record.

Brantley: A lot of the time people who encounter this kind of behaviour are looking for the best in people. We also see cases where people are quite frankly afraid to get involved, because if they are dealing with a child or adult who seems to be bizarre or threatening, they are afraid that he or she may no longer kill animals but instead come after them. I've seen a lot of mental health professionals, law enforcement officers, and private citizens who don't want to get involved because they are afraid—and for good reason. There are very scary people out there doing scary things. That's largely why they are doing it and talking about it: they want to intimidate and shock and offend, sometimes regardless of the consequences.

Q: Is there hope for such an individual?

Brantley: The earlier you can intervene, the better off you'll be. I like to be optimistic. I think in the vast majority of cases, especially if you get to them as children, you can intervene. People shouldn't discount animal abuse as a childish prank or childish experimentation.

Q: Have you ever seen any serial killers who have been rehabilitated?

Brantley: I've seen no examples of it and no real efforts to even attempt it! Even if you had a programme that might work, the potential consequences of being wrong and releasing someone like that greatly outweigh the benefits of attempting it, in my opinion.

Q: There is also a problem in trying to understand which acts against animals and others are associated with the escalation of violence, since police records, if they exist, are often unavailable or juvenile offences are expunged. Sometimes only local humane societies or animal-control agencies have any record. The Humane Society of the United States (HSUS) hopes to facilitate consolidating some of these records.

Brantley: That would be great. If animal-cruelty investigators are aware of a case such as a sexual homicide in their community and they are also aware of any animal mutilation going on in the same area, I would encourage them to reach out to us.

Note: *Alan C. Brantley was interviewed by Dr Randall Lockwood and Ann Church. The Interview was originally published in HSUS News (Fall 1996) and is reproduced with the permission of Mr Brantley and the HSUS.*

79 Ethics and Euthanasia

Bernard E. Rollin

Rollin points out that animals anticipate at least the short-term future. In addition, it is important to most of us that the ends of their lives not involve fear, horror, pain or suffering, because of the finality of killing.

He asserts that questions of animal welfare are partly questions of ethical obligation, to which science can add relevant data. Rollin refers to the "five freedoms" articulated in Britain during the 1970s and contrasts it with the CAST report in the 1980s written by U.S. agricultural scientists. For Rollin, the CAST report in effect says that only productivity matters.

He points out the emergence of a social ethic for animals since 1980, as seen in the proliferation of laws regarding animal welfare. With regard to euthanasia, Rollin affirms the Canadian Council of Animal Care according to which welfare principles of immediate unconsciousness without pain or distress should be followed. A device which seems able to create hypoxia in small rodents is under development.

The death of an animal at human hands, be it a companion animal, food animal, or research animal, is an important element of an animal's welfare. Aristotle pointed out, with regard to humans, "count no man happy until he is dead." This is easy to understand with regard to human life, for the circumstances of one's death can considerably alter one's gestalt on everything else in life that has come before. Consider, for example, a man on his deathbed, who overhears what he thought was his loving wife for 40 years, say to another man, "I can't wait until the old bastard is gone. Then we can at last be together on his money." In that instant, what he thought was a good life is suddenly transfigured into a nightmare. Or, as an alternative example, imagine a Jewish citizen of Germany who served as a hero in World War I and as a pillar of the community, suddenly rousted by the Nazis, dragged to a concentration camp, and executed. Again, his life's history is colored irrevocably and negatively by the nature of his death.

In the case of an animal, the nature of its life seems at first blush different. After all, as Heidegger points out, a human being's life is futural in orientation, defined by goal-directed futural projects such as getting one's degree, seeing one's children graduate, finishing one's novel, and so on, all of which require the ability to think about long-term futural and possible events. This, in turn, requires a language and its syntax, which allow a linguistic being to think in counterfactual terms—"I will meet you in the park, but if the weather is foul, I will meet you in the restaurant"; universal terms, "all black widow spiders are dangerous"; possible terms, "my book might garner critical acclaim," or negative terms, "there are no unicorns in the library," or in combinations of these. Animals, lacking language, seem to be unable to think in that way. For these reasons, it is widely believed that ending an animal's life painlessly doesn't harm the animal—one is not aborting its life's goal or project. One has treated an animal well if one has given it a life consisting of pleasant "nows." For these reasons, many people, including myself, have argued that involuntary euthanasia is not only permissible for suffering animals but indeed obligatory. Lacking hope, because hope requires futurally oriented concepts, an animal that lives in the now becomes its suffering, while a human can anticipate modalities for relief, or look forward to fulfilling his or her futural life-defining goal.

On the other hand, it appears that Aristotle's point about how life ends could apply to an animal. Imagine a faithful dog, accustomed to love, being beaten to death by its master. In addition to the physical pain involved, there must also be emotional pain growing out of the dissonance between the animal's past and what it currently experiences. (We have of course every reason to believe animals can remember.) Thus, I feel comfortable suggesting that end-of-life experiences may have special significance to animals as well, since they color the sum total of the animal's previous experiences. A painful or stressful death may eclipse or negatively color all that came before. At least we can suggest that something like this insight underlays the high degree of human concern about how an animal dies, since the actual death is usually only a tiny fraction of the animal's life.

It is important to realize that we cannot be absolutely certain of the claim that animals do not anticipate the future. In fact, it seems obvious that they definitely anticipate the short-term future, as when a cat waits outside a mouse hole or a lion intercepts a gazelle. Anticipating the long-term future seems more problematic for the reasons given above, but it is far from clear where one draws the line between short and long term, and thus we may well be aborting future projects when we kill an animal.

If pressed to do so, I would make the distinction between an animal's ability to anticipate the short-term future versus the long-term future as follows: cases like the cat's anticipatory waiting outside the mouse hole can be explained by reference to innate or hard-wired predatory tendencies, which are given real-world content by the animal's experience. That is to say, the cat has had one or many associative experiences of mice emerging from holes, so the next time it expects another mouse. On the other hand, it cannot anticipate the end of life or playing with its as yet unborn grandchild, since it has experienced neither and lacks the linguistic capability discussed above.

I invoke this element of doubt to provide yet another reason we must address euthanasia as a social-ethical issue. It is evident that society is very much concerned about how an animal's life is ended. A few years ago, I received the following query from the *The Canadian Veterinary Journal* for me to address in the monthly column I have written for the *Journal* since 1990.

> *Why does society [demand] scrupulous rules to prevent relatively momentary suffering in animals being killed for food and research, while overlooking the much greater suffering that the same animals may experience in life if they are food or research animals?*

My reply was in part as follows:

> *Given our uncertainty about death, we approach it with profound concern. I recall team-teaching a course in the proper use of laboratory animals. One week, we taught euthanasia, using animals (rats) that needed to die for a research protocol. I recall the profound experience of uncertainty and regret I experienced when my colleague injected them with pentobarbital, and I watched the little life-flame flicker and die. I recall feeling "Who am I to do this, given the struggle these little creatures had engaged in to survive?" My only consolation, for want of a better word, was that they went to sleep peacefully, unaware that what they struggled to preserve had ended.*

It is important to us that the summation, or consummation, of their lives not involve fear, horror, pain, or suffering as the final encapsulation of their lives, particularly given that we cannot provide compensation or remedy after death. The finality of killing makes us tread lightly.

Concern for these last moments is, in my view, an affirmation of decency in the face of inflicting irreversible termination of the creatures whose lives seem to be metaphysically their own, not ours to dispose of. This is a primordial emotion, more primordial than the reflective thought required to worry about how they live. One can hope that society will continue to develop its reflective concern about how we in fact make these animals expend their lives.

Plainly, society has evidenced an ever-increasing awareness of animal welfare for animals in all areas of human use, most recently agricultural animals—for example, 2008's Proposition 2 in California, overwhelmingly passed by voters, that banned battery cages, veal crates, and gestation stalls; Colorado's law, SB 201 of May 2008 eliminating gestation crates and veal crates; the Arizona and Florida referenda abolishing sow stalls; and the Oregon law doing the same. Unfortunately, US organized veterinary medicine, like the US agricultural industry, simply does not understand the concept of animal welfare, and correlatively, the concept of euthanasia, since euthanasia (that is, how an animal dies) is surely one aspect of its welfare.

When one discusses animal welfare with industry groups or with the American Veterinary Medical Association, one finds the same response—animal welfare is solely a matter of "sound science." Those of us serving on the Pew Commission, better known as the National Commission on Industrial Farm Animal Production, encountered this response regularly during our dealings with industry representatives. This commission studied intensive animal agriculture in the US (1). One representative of the National Pork Producers, testifying before the Commission, affirmed that while people in her industry were quite "nervous" about the Commission, their anxiety would be allayed were we to base all of our conclusions and recommendations on "sound science." Hoping to rectify the error in that comment, as well as educate the numerous industry representatives present, I responded to her as follows: "Madam, if we on the Commission were asking the question of how to raise swine in confinement, science could certainly answer that question for us. But that is not the question the Commission, or society, is asking. What we are asking is, ought we to raise swine in confinement? And to this question, science is not relevant." Judging by her puzzled response, "huh?" I assume I did not make my point.

Questions of animal welfare are at least partly "ought" questions, questions of ethical obligation. The concept of animal welfare is an ethical concept to which, once understood, science brings relevant data. When we ask about an animal's welfare under humanly imposed conditions, we are asking about what we owe the animal, and to what extent. When a document called the CAST (Council on Agricultural Science and Technology) report, first published by US agricultural scientists in the early 1980s, discussed animal welfare, it affirmed that the necessary and sufficient conditions for attributing positive welfare to an animal were represented by the animal's productivity. A productive animal enjoyed positive welfare; a non-productive animal enjoyed poor welfare (2).

This notion was fraught with many difficulties. First of all, productivity is an economic notion predicated of a whole operation; welfare is predicated of individual animals. An operation such as caged laying hens may be quite profitable if the cages are severely overcrowded; yet the individual hens do not enjoy good welfare. Second, as we shall see, equating productivity and welfare is, to some significant extent, legitimate under husbandry conditions, where the producer does well if and only if the animals do well, and square pegs, as it were, are fitted into square holes with as little friction as possible (as when pigs live outside). Under industrial conditions, however, animals do not naturally fit in the niche or environment in which they are kept, and are subjected to "technological sanders" that allow for producers to force square pegs into round holes—antibiotics, feed additives, hormones, air handling systems—so the animals do not die and produce more and more kilograms of meat or milk. Without these technologies, the animals could not be productive. We will return to the contrast between husbandry and industrial approaches to animal agriculture.

The key point to recall here is that even if the CAST Report definition of animal welfare did not suffer from the difficulties we outlined, it is still an ethical concept. It essentially says "what we owe animals and to what extent is simply what it takes to get them to create profit." This in turn would imply that the animals are well-off if they have only food, water, and shelter, something the industry has sometimes asserted. Even in the early 1980s, however, there were animal advocates and others who would take a very different ethical stance on what we owe farm animals. Indeed, the famous "five freedoms" articulated in Britain by the Farm Animal Welfare Council (3) during the 1970s (even before the CAST Report) represents quite a different ethical view of what we owe animals, when it affirms that:

The welfare of an animal includes its physical and mental state and we consider that good animal welfare implies both fitness and a sense of well-being. Any animal kept by man must at least be protected from unnecessary suffering.

We believe that an animal's welfare, whether on farm, in transit, at market, or at a place of slaughter should be considered in terms of "five freedoms":

1. Freedom from Hunger and Thirst—by ready access to fresh water and a diet to maintain full health and vigor.
2. Freedom from Discomfort—by providing an appropriate environment including shelter and a comfortable resting area.
3. Freedom from Pain, Injury, or Disease—by prevention or rapid diagnosis and treatment.
4. Freedom to Express Normal Behavior—by providing sufficient space, proper facilities, and company of the animal's own kind.
5. Freedom from Fear and Distress—by ensuring conditions and treatment which avoid mental suffering.

Clearly, the two definitions contain very different notions of our moral obligation to animals (and there is an indefinite number of other definitions). Which definition is correct, of course, cannot be decided by gathering facts or doing experiments—indeed *which ethical framework one adopts will in fact determine the shape of science studying animal welfare!*

To clarify: suppose you hold the view that an animal is well-off when it is productive, as per the CAST Report. The role of your welfare science in this case will be to study what feed, bedding, temperature, and so on, are most efficient at producing the most meat, milk, or eggs for the least money—much what animal and veterinary sciences do today. On the other hand, if you take the Farm Animal Welfare Council view of welfare, your efficiency will be constrained by the need to acknowledge the animals' natural behavior and mental state, and to assure that there is minimal pain, fear, distress, and discomfort—not factors in the CAST view of welfare unless they have a negative impact on economic productivity. Thus, in a real sense, sound science does not determine your concept of welfare; rather, your concept of welfare determines what counts as sound science!

The failure to recognize the inescapable ethical component in the concept of animal welfare leads inexorably to those holding different ethical views talking past each other. Thus, producers ignore questions of animal pain, fear, distress, confinement, truncated mobility, bad air quality, social isolation, and impoverished environment unless any of these factors impacts negatively on the "bottom line." Animal advocates, on the other hand, give such factors primacy, and are totally unimpressed with how efficient or productive the system may be.

A major question obviously arises here. If the notion of animal welfare is inseparable from ethical components, and people's ethical stance on obligations to farm animals differ markedly across a highly diverse spectrum, whose ethic is to predominate and define, in law or regulation, what counts as "animal welfare"? This is of great concern to the agriculture industry, worrying as they do about "vegetarian activists hell-bent on abolishing meat." In actual fact, of course, such concern is misplaced, for the chance of such an extremely radical thing's happening is vanishingly small. By and large, however, the ethic adopted in society reflects a societal consensus, what most people either believe to be right and wrong or are willing to accept upon reflection.

All of us have our own personal ethics which rule a goodly portion of our lives. Fundamental questions such as what we read, what we eat, to whom we give charity, what political and religious beliefs we hold, and myriad others are answered by our personal ethics. These derive from many sources—parents, religious institutions, friends, books, movies, and television. One is certainly entitled to believe ethically, as do some PETA members, that "meat is murder," that one should be a vegetarian, that it is immoral to use products derived from animal research, and so on.

Clearly, a society, particularly a free society, contains a bewildering array of such personal ethics, with the potential for significant clashes between them. If my personal ethic is based in fundamentalist religious beliefs and yours is based in celebrating the pleasures of the flesh, we are destined to clash, perhaps violently. For this reason, social life cannot function simply by relying on an individual's personal ethics, except perhaps in singularly monolithic cultures where all members share overwhelmingly the same values. One can find examples of something resembling this in small towns in rural farming areas, where there is no need to lock one's doors, remove one's keys from the car, or fear for one's personal safety. But of course such places are few, and probably decreasing in number. In larger communities, the extreme case being New York City or London, one finds a welter of diverse cultures and corresponding diverse personal ethics crammed into a small geographical locus. For this reason alone, as well as to control those whose personal ethic may entail taking advantage of others, a social consensus ethic is required, one which transcends personal ethics. This social consensus ethic is invariably articulated in law, with manifest sanctions for its violation. As societies evolve, different issues emerge, leading to changes in the social ethic.

My claim then, is that beginning roughly in the late 1960s, the treatment of animals has moved from being a paradigmatic example of personal ethics to ever-increasingly falling within the purview of societal ethics and law.

Exactly the same logic holds regarding euthanasia. The concept of a "good death" is inherently valuational in general and a matter of ethics in particular. Thus we must look to our current societal ethic for animal treatment to grasp what society expects of euthanasia.

I have done a great deal of writing explicating the emerging social ethic for animals since 1980, and many of my predictions (for example, of legislative pro-animal referenda) have come to pass. In bare bones, the ethic for animals has moved beyond the traditional anti-cruelty ethic and laws that prohibit deliberate, sadistic, willful, intentional infliction of pain and suffering on animals, or outrageous neglect. The point of that ethic was largely to ferret out sadists and psychopaths who begin with animals and "graduate" to people. (Animal abuse by children is sentinel behavior for subsequent psychopathy.) Nothing involved in "ministering to the necessities of man," or that is standard industry practice can count as cruelty. That in turn means that only a tiny amount of animal suffering is capturable by the anti-cruelty ethic—over 99% of animals' suffering is the result of normal and decent motivations advancing knowledge, supplying cheap and plentiful food, making a legal profit. All the suffering that animals experience in research and agriculture, for example, is immune to the anti-cruelty ethics and laws.

It is for this reason that we have seen a proliferation of laws and proposed laws pertaining to animal welfare in areas traditionally exempt from anti-cruelty laws. The 1985 laws for laboratory animals, which I helped draft, represented a watershed in this regard, since it became mandatory to control pain and distress, something the research community had not done before. In a 1982 literature search on laboratory animal analgesia, I was unable to find papers on the topic. Today there are thousands.

The new ethic demands legislatively encoded guarantees that animals not suffer pain or distress, and live under conditions approximating what their biological and psychological natures demand. As Dale Schwindaman, head of the United States Department of Agriculture's (USDA) Animal and Plant Health Inspection Service (APHIS), said to me when the laboratory animal laws passed, "we have just witnessed the birth of some legally encoded rights for animals," though technically animals remain property. In 2004, 2100 laws were proposed regarding animal welfare across the US, and the momentum for farm animal protection illustrates our point.

This societal ethic should determine how we think about euthanasia. Historically, and not that long ago, "euthanasia" was accomplished in many ways unthinkable today: curariform drugs, strychnine, use of car exhaust, bludgeoning, drowning, electro-shock, suffocating birds using thoracic compression (crushing the chest) thereby suffocating them, some of which were accepted by the AVMA and some of which are still accepted, as we shall see.

The best succinct encapsulation of social-ethical requirements for euthanasia may be found in the Canadian Council on Animal Care (CCAC) module, "Euthanasia of Experimental Animals" (4).

> The humane killing of animals requires knowledge, skill, respect for the animal, and an understanding of the many factors that are part of choosing a humane method. The primary welfare principles for a humane method of killing an animal require that there should be very rapid (immediate) unconsciousness and subsequent death and there should be no pain or distress accompanying the procedure.

We will call this statement the Welfare Principle. Since the CCAC represents the opinions of scientists and veterinarians using animals, this statement cannot be viewed as utopian, though it is in fact violated in CCAC's

[. . .]

This discussion leads me to draw an ethical/welfare logical corollary from the Welfare Principle: In the absence of certainty about animal pain and distress, the animals should be given the benefit of the doubt.

[. . .]

Clearly the main ethical points of the statement are immediacy of loss of consciousness and the absence of pain and distress in the process of euthanasia. These are the primary values that should guide choice of method. There are, however, secondary values which, while not as weighty, are relevant to choosing euthanasia methods.

Practicality

The "gold standard" for euthanasia of all mammalian species is probably barbiturate injection after sedation and placement of a catheter. Having witnessed this many times, I can attest to its humaneness. Most US humane societies now use it, and virtually all veterinarians. This notwithstanding, it would be practically impossible to do this in a research setting, where it may be necessary to kill 1,000 mice at one time. Similarly, it could not be used for slaughter because it is too time-consuming, and even more importantly, because it would render the carcass inedible. Thus, such euthanasia may be problematic for a horse if the animal is to be placed in a landfill, where scavengers may eat the meat and ingest the barbiturates. Eagles have been killed by such carcasses.

Psychological Effect on the Operator

In normal people, prolonged periods of killing animals, even when necessary (as in the case of disease outbreak), can have a profound and negative psychological effect. In technicians, researchers, laboratory animal veterinarians, or humane society or shelter personnel, killing can create what I have called "moral stress" arising from the paradox that those who care a great deal about animals, and who sometimes chose their job out of a desire to help animals, end up in an assembly line of killing. This often creates both physical and psychological distress, the onset of psychogenic afflictions such as asthma and irritable bowel, substance abuse, alienation from family, and job dissatisfaction. (Even the sadists of the Nazi killing machine were so affected.) While some of this is inevitable, some methods are better than others, and obviously the methods most gentle for the animal create the least stress. When improper high-altitude chambers were used in humane societies, intra-nasal and intra-ocular pressure in young animals suffering from infections could cause bleeding from eyes, nose, and ears, with both the animals and workers suffering. Similarly, the actual slaughterers in slaughterhouses are often seen as "scary" by the other workers, are shunned by them, and tend to interact primarily with each other.

[...]

These considerations led me to look for a more humane method for euthanizing small rodents and, with the help of wonderful, equally concerned colleagues in a variety of fields, we began to investigate creating hypoxia (brain death) without asphyxia or suffocation. We began to study hypobaric hypoxia. The basis for my idea was old World War II movies where a pilot flies too high without oxygen and "blacks out." This led me to look at the US Air Force website.

Hypoxia (loss of oxygen to the brain) is a potential problem for pilots, so all pilots must, as part of their training, experience high-altitude loss of oxygen pressure in a chamber. They report a dissolution of consciousness and a pleasant euphoria equivalent to ingesting 6 ounces of alcohol, before going unconscious, which I confirmed with former pilots. We also possess notebooks of late 18th-century French balloonists who ascended to great heights, wrote of the pleasantness of the experience, and said they planned to go higher, did so, and expired. Knowing that high altitude hypoxia had been used prior to the 1980s for euthanasia in pounds and shelters and that that had been disastrous because defective equipment lead to depressurization and repressurization as a result of leakage, and to suffering in animals with naso-pharyngeal infection, we started from scratch. With the help of a number of mechanical engineers, we built a precise, computer-controlled, leak-proof chamber. We then tested it on rats and mice that showed no signs of pain or distress, merely a period of excitation (described by some as "popcorn mice") before falling asleep. Best of all, we saw no sign of respiratory distress or escape behavior. We are currently having the device tested at a major medical school to get physiological evidence supporting our observations. . . .

1. Pew Commission on Industrial Farm Animal Production [Last accessed August 11, 2009]. Available from <http://ncifap.org/>
2. CAST (Council for Agricultural Science and Technology) Scientific Aspects of the Welfare of Food Animals. 1981;19.
3. FAWC (Farm Animal Welfare Council) [Last accessed August 10, 2009]; The Five Freedoms. 1979 <http://www.fawc.org.uk/freedoms.htm>
4. CCAC (Canadian Council on Animal Care) Guide for the Care and Use of Experimental Animals, Section XII, Euthanasia. Ottawa. 1993.[Last accessed August 10, 2009]. Available from <http://www.ccac.ca/en/ccac_programs/guidelines_policies/guides/english/toc_v1.htm>

80 The Miracle of Life and Afterword

Diane Leigh and Marilee Geyer

Leigh and Geyer highlight unintentional breeding, intentional breeding based on ignorance, and "puppy mills" as important causes of companion animal overpopulation. They commend mandatory spaying and neutering of most dogs and cats. They urge the long-range goal of elimi- nating the disconnection of humans from other beings so that animals are never considered to be trash. Solving the problem of homeless animals is a step toward expanding our caring to all living beings.

For decades, shelters have been fighting a battle against companion animal overpopulation, the tragedy of too many puppies and kittens born into a world that cannot provide homes for them all. The statistics, however familiar to many people, are still staggering: a female dog and her puppies are theoretically capable of multiplying to over 67,000 in just six years, and a female cat and her kittens can result in over 400,000 offspring in only seven years.

The reasons for companion animal overpopulation are varied. Unintentional breeding is part of the problem—the mating of animals whose guardians didn't realize they were old enough, or didn't realize they were in heat, or just didn't take any action to prevent it. There are those who don't know about overpopulation and the need to prevent the births of more animals, and those who can't afford to spay or neuter their animal.

Intentional breeding also contributes to overpopulation by those who let their animal have a litter because they want their children to witness the "miracle of birth," or those who are still under the outdated impression that animals *should* have one litter before being spayed.

The breeders who create and supply a market for a variety of purebred animals, and those who create non-purebred, "designer" dogs and cats, each contribute, as do those who breed their purebred as a way to recoup the purchase price of the animal or just to bring in some extra cash.

The demand in this country for purebred animals has also created a lucrative and horrific trade in living beings. It is estimated that 300,000 to 500,000 purebred puppies are sold in pet stores each year, and that 90% of those animals come from large-scale commercial breeders commonly referred to as "puppy mills." These mills mass-produce puppies for profit, typically keeping dozens to hundreds of female dogs in crude, cramped cages, or tied, for their entire lives. The dogs are bred incessantly, then disposed of—killed—after four or five years, when their bodies are worn out and they are no longer "productive." Their puppies are sold to brokers who ship them to other parts of the country to be resold in pet stores. The largest concentrations of puppy mills are found in the states of Arkansas, Iowa, Kansas, Missouri, Nebraska, Oklahoma, and Pennsylvania. And while the demand for purebred cats is significantly smaller than for purebred dogs, there are "kitten mills" churning out the most popular breeds: Persians, Himalayans, and Siamese.

Commercial breeders are required to be licensed, although some ignore this requirement, by the United States Department of Agriculture (USDA), and are subject to the provisions of the Animal Welfare Act, the laws which regulate the care the animals are supposed to receive. But the USDA is notoriously understaffed and inspections of puppy mills are infrequent at best. Fewer than 100 inspectors oversee over 11,000 animal facilities nationwide, which include research laboratories, circuses, zoos, and about 4,100 commercial dog breeders.

Reports of hideous conditions found in puppy mills are shockingly frequent, detailing conditions of unimaginable suffering: wire cages stacked on top of each other, feces and urine from animals on top dripping down on animals in cages below; no shelter from heat or cold; filthy, matted dogs malnourished and near starvation, with open sores and skin worn bare from rubbing against their cages, feet wounded from standing on wire for months, even years; rampant disease and illness.

The puppies born in these abysmal conditions have a high incidence of genetic defects due to careless breeding. Surveys have found that half of the puppies sold in pet stores are sick or incubating a disease. Many of the pups have behavior problems due to lack of socialization and the horrendous conditions they endure during some of the most formative weeks of their lives.

American Kennel Club (AKC) "papers" are no guarantee that a puppy did not come from a puppy mill. Contrary to what many people believe, and according to the AKC itself, it does not guarantee the health or "quality" of a dog, and does not assure that the dog came from humane conditions. The AKC is simply a registry, recording the births and lineages of dogs. The AKC does, however, take in millions of dollars each year from the registrations they process to create the papers that accompany purebred dogs, including puppy mill pups. It also opposes new legislation intended to strengthen the laws regulating puppy mills and protecting puppy mill dogs.

All of this while millions of other dogs are waiting in shelters, and dying there, for simple lack of homes. The answer is simple: when the public no longer buys into the notion that purebred dogs are the "best" dogs, when they refuse to buy puppies from pet stores, the puppy mill industry will no longer be profitable and there will be no incentive to perpetuate this brutality.

At its most basic level, as long as there are not enough homes for them all, any animal added to the existing population, for *whatever* reason, helps feed companion animal overpopulation, with devastating results. Puppies and kittens for whom homes cannot be found are brought to shelters in droves and fill the facilities beyond capacity, contributing to the euthanasia of millions. A secondary impact is borne by the adult animals in the shelter, who are in desperate need of homes but who suffer very reduced chances of getting them when they must compete with adorable puppies and kittens. Disproportionate numbers of adult animals end up as euthanasia statistics because of this disadvantage.

Spay and neuter, the solution to the companion animal overpopulation tragedy, is the impassioned battle cry of shelter workers. These routine surgical procedures sterilize dogs and cats by removing the reproductive organs of female animals (spaying) or the testicles of males (neutering). In addition to helping stop overpopulation, the animals also benefit: studies show spayed and neutered animals live longer, healthier lives with fewer medical and behavioral problems.

Animal advocates have done everything imaginable to make spay/neuter operations inexpensive, easy to obtain and desirable. Millions of flyers have been distributed extolling the many health and behavioral benefits of spaying and neutering. Countless articles have been published, and even more countless media interviews have been given. National campaigns and events have centered around the idea—a U.S. postal stamp promoting sterilization has even been released. Shelters have built low cost and free spay/neuter clinics, and some have even created mobile clinics to bring these services to the streets.

Responsible shelters also work to ensure that the animals they adopt into the community are spayed and neutered. Some collect a monetary deposit from the adopter which is refunded upon proof of sterilization, although this requires diligent and time-consuming follow-up to ensure that every adopted animal does, in fact, get spayed or neutered. Other shelters have their own clinics to perform the surgeries on site, or arrange to have the surgeries done by local veterinarians, to guarantee that adopted animals are spayed and neutered before being released to their new homes.

More recently, a new tool has been added to the arsenal fighting companion animal overpopulation: many communities across the country have adopted ordinances requiring the spaying and neutering of all dogs and cats except in very limited, designated cases.

In some areas of the country, this battle has seen some success. Some shelters that once handled seemingly endless litters are finally seeing fewer, as the flood of incoming puppies and kittens has slowed. In those areas, although not completely eliminated, companion animal overpopulation is no longer the primary source of homeless animals. [. . .]

Afterword

[. . .] Shelters should be leaders in the battle to end the homeless animal tragedy, but they cannot end it for us. Shelters should, and must, create programs that reach out beyond their walls to prevent animals from becoming homeless—identification and microchipping programs, low cost spay/neuter, pet parenting classes and animal behavior help, for instance—but we must use these programs. We are the ones who must make the commitment, and take the actions, to ensure we never cause an animal to be in an animal shelter. We must understand: as soon as this country stops filling animal shelters with homeless animals, the killing can stop.

Ultimately, though, we need to transcend sheltering and the current shelter system in this country. The shelter system, as it exists today, and has existed for decades, has as one of its primary functions the processing of living beings—either by recycling them to new homes or destroying them, but disposing of them somehow and relieving people and communities of their responsibility for them. It is a tangible sign of our society's deep disconnection from other beings, a disconnection so profound and damaging that we could legitimately categorize it as a sickness.

We need to acknowledge this sickness and how it plays out in our shelters, and never make excuses for it or believe that it is acceptable. The truth is, there should not be a need in a civilized society for a system that disposes of animals as if they were trash. We need to tell this truth, as an act of respect to the animals, and because the truth cannot be changed until it can be seen.

At the deepest level, the only thing that will heal this sickness, and alleviate the pain we feel over this issue, is to end the killing, by creating communities that no longer have overwhelming homeless animal problems and have, therefore, no need to kill animals. By creating communities that find killing to be an unacceptable answer, and that see animals as having value and beauty, as beings with a sacred spark of life and spirit.

People sometimes ask, in light of the devastating and important issues that face us in our modern times, why the homeless animal issue is important, why we should be concerned about it. The answer to this question is critical, as the underlying societal values that enable the homeless animal problem also enable and are deeply connected to other social issues of our time—issues which exist on a continuum created by our attitudes toward our fellow beings and the planet we share.

The homeless animal problem is a reflection of a society that has lost touch with other living beings, with the natural world, and with the very web of life. It is but one tragic symptom of a culture that does not see its connections to others, does not see others as having inherent value, and instead sees them as put here for our use, as disposable or somehow lesser, as somehow not worthy of reverence, compassion and respect. This same societal thinking, this way of separating ourselves from "others," allows for the possibility of the destruction of ancient forests, damage to our environment and the animals in it, of racism and exploitation of third world peoples, of poverty and human homelessness, of children going hungry in a land of plenty, of devaluing our elders . . . this way of viewing the "others" in our world enables and underlies a continuum of issues.

The systematic mass destruction and disposal of millions of living creatures every year constitutes a kind of violence in our society that is no less violent because it is institutionalized and mostly overlooked. When killing those who are closest to, and most dependent upon us becomes an unquestioned fact of daily life, we have set a very dangerous and damaging precedent as to what is ethically acceptable, what we are willing to tolerate, and what we are capable of doing to others. How much easier is it to deny consideration and compassion to one group when we have learned to accept the mass killing of another—and especially, of beings whom we call our "friends"?

The homeless animal issue is critically important because it is so fundamental: dogs and cats are the closest most people ever get to other species and the natural world. If our concern and compassion are so weak and limited that we are unable to save those animals closest to us, how will we ever be able to save the more distant beings—the endangered species we may never see, the redwoods and mountains and wilderness we may never visit, the suffering people we may never meet and whose misery we may never experience directly?

And yet, there is unique power in this issue. Solving this problem offers us the chance to take a first step toward healing our relationship with the natural world, to reawaken and embrace our connection with other living beings, to reaffirm the preciousness of life itself. It offers us the potent opportunity to become better human beings, to call forward the finest parts of ourselves and express the very best of our humanity. If we are able, as a society, to find the compassion and dedication to save our companion animals, to treat them with the love and respect they deserve, to solve this problem in an ethical way, then perhaps we can extend that compassion and dedication to others in need.

Perhaps this issue can be a stepping stone toward an expanding circle of compassion and action, toward creating a society that is just and caring to all living beings—beginning with the precious ones "right in our own backyards."

The two cats who live with me, Otto and Raphael, walk into the room as I write. They swirl around my feet, nibble at some food, look out the window. One huge black cat, one skinny orange one, each with his own unique, quirky personality, each with his own story.

They are ordinary cats: six years old now, they have lived in my home since their kittenhoods, and are healthy, safe and happy. They play and pick on each other, follow the sun each day from window to window, sleep in deep peace.

And they are extraordinary cats: they shine into my life their unconditional love, share with me their in-the-moment wisdom, show me how to live with generosity, gentleness and joy. Their innocent presence is a constant reminder of the preciousness of all life.

Our companion animals live with us in our world, but they bring with them gifts from their animal worlds. It is a privilege to have them near. They are our link to the wild animals we will never see except in books or on television. They are the animal fur we get to stroke, and the paws we get to touch. They are the wild, mysterious eyes we get to gaze into. They give us a glimpse into "other nations." They are messengers, bringing us a critical, sacred message of connection; they are teachers, showing us back to our place in the web of life, showing us the way back home.

Can there be any doubt of what we owe them in return?

81 The Moral Basis of Animal-Assisted Therapy

Tzachi Zamir

Is nonhuman animal-assisted therapy (AAT) a form of exploitation? After exploring possible moral vindications of AAT and after establishing a distinction between "use" and "exploitation," the essay distinguishes between forms of animal-assisted therapy that are morally unobjectionable and those modes of it that ought to be abolished.

Nonhuman animal-assisted therapy (AAT)[1] is becoming increasingly popular. Expositors claim that its roots go back to the eighteenth century when Tuke, one of the originators of modern psychiatry, introduced its use in his work with his patients. Nowadays, AAT encompasses interventions incorporating dogs, cats, rodents, birds, reptiles, horses, monkeys, and even dolphins. The goals of such therapy are extremely varied, including psychological, therapeutic objectives as well as other forms of assistance.[2]

In this essay, I will ignore the prudential questions that plague almost all AAT literature that I have come across; that is, whether the benefits of AAT can be shown conclusively over and against more conventional modes of therapy. I will assume—what is in fact highly controversial—that AAT is therapeutically effective generally and, for some individuals, is advantageous when compared with other forms of therapy. Can such uses of nonhuman animals be morally justified from a "liberationist" perspective, a perspective that acknowledges that animals are not merely a resource to be exploited by humans?[3] Practitioners of AAT often say that they work with animals rather than "use" them. The primary distinction that this essay formulates is the one between use and exploitation. I then pursue the implications of this distinction to the moral status of AAT.

The Case Against AAT

AAT literature does not ignore the moral dimension of the work that it advocates. Yet the remarks on ethics appear to be limited to considerations of welfare. The *Delta Society's* website, for example, warns its readers that AAT may be inappropriate for the animals when

1. injuries from rough handling or from other animals may occur;
2. basic animal welfare cannot be assured (this includes veterinary care and access to water and exercise areas); and
3. the animal does not enjoy visiting.

In a different publication by the same organization, it is maintained that, "At all times the rights of the animals shall be respected and ensured. This includes humane treatment, protection from undue stress, and availability of water and exercise area" (Grammonley et al., 1997, p. 2). One proposed code of ethics for animal-assisted therapy includes requirements:

1. the animal's welfare must be the priority of the therapy facilitator;
2. the therapy animal must "never be forced to leave the home to go to work" or to perform actions that it is reluctant to perform; and

3. animals are to be given adjustment time and quiet time periods before sessions and be protected from individuals carrying diseases that may be transmitted to them.

(Preziosi, 1997, pp. 5–6)

Yet from a broader liberationist perspective, such remarks barely scratch the surface of the moral
questions that AAT raises. A liberationist stance ascribes value not only to the life of the animal but
also to the quality of such a life—as well as to the value of the animal's freedom—in the sense that
lack of freedom requires a moral justification. For liberationists, using animals to treat humans is
potentially immoral in five distinct ways:

Limitations of Freedom

Companion animals need to be kept by the therapists or be temporary companion animals of the
individual being treated. In some cases, when the animals are in effect modified pets (like guide
dogs), the limitations of freedom are the same as those involved in all pet-owner relationships (relationships that are themselves immoral for some liberationists, regardless of their quality). In the case
of animals who are not pets or modified pets (rabbits, hamsters, chinchillas, snakes, birds, all of
whom respond to human beings but, unlike alarm or service dogs, do not appear to derive pleasure
from such interaction and seem incapable of transferring their social needs onto humans), the loss
of freedom may be much more severe.

Life Determination

Freedom can be curtailed for a temporary period (confining a wounded animal in the wild and then
releasing the animal once the animal has healed). But unlike limitation-of-freedom actions, some
actions with regard to animals are total and life-determining. Turning an animal into a companion
animal; into an animal in the zoo; into a race horse, a jumper, or an event horse are life-determining
actions. The decision to employ an animal therapeutically involves making such a total decision
regarding a particular animal.

Training

Getting dogs or monkeys to assist humans efficiently in numerous tasks involves a prolonged period
of training, which itself includes various violations of the animal's well being. Creating horses for
therapy (therapy-horses) requires "breaking" them. Moreover, unlike cats and dogs, many of the
other animals used in AAT are frightened by human presence, and they have to undergo periods in
which they get accustomed to humans around them.

Simians live in packs. By turning them into nursing entities, one disconnects them from
whatever it is that they maintain through their social context. The same holds for rabbits or
other rodents who are isolated from their kin. There is, to be sure, a certain degree of mystery here both regarding the nature of the social needs and the way they might be internally
experienced as a loss by the animal. Yet it is morally safe to make the probable assumption
that such disconnection (or bringing up the animal without contact with the animal's kin) is a
form of deprivation.

Injury

Animals for therapy (therapy-animals) can be (and are) routinely manhandled. Even when gently
handled, exposing them to strangers who pet them can itself create anxieties in them. A small percentage of such animals are injured during these sessions.[4]

Instrumentalization

Liberationists tend to tacitly or explicitly model ideal human-nonhuman relations on analogies with human-human ethics. While few extend to animals—the same range of moral considerability that befits humans—liberationists turn the human-nonhuman model from the thoughtless instrumentalization that is typical of human relations with objects into forms of interaction that approximate human-human relations. From this perspective, since it is unimaginable to retain a sub-group of human beings as therapeutic aids of other human beings even if proved as facilitating extremely effective therapy (say that the tactile quality of touching members of this subgroup is proved to have therapeutic merits), doing this to animals is wrong in a similar way. Animals are not out there to be used, even when the use is important or worthy.

Liberationists would be quick to identify these five potential violations of the moral status of animals and would accordingly be concerned about the moral legitimacy of AAT as such. The fact that much more serious violations than the five noted above occur does not abrogate the moral questions that relate to the five violations. It matters not that billions of animals are routinely killed for negligible reasons or that they are institutionally used and exploited in large-scale industries all over the world. If these five violations cannot be vindicated, liberationists should censor these modalities of therapy and assistance.

A Paternalistic Case for AAT?

Analyzing the moral status of the five potential violations invites an exploration of the pet-owner relationship. If pet-owner relationships can be morally justified, some of the therapeutic uses of animals sketched above might be vindicated as well.[5] I have elsewhere proposed a utilitarian-based justification of the pet-owner relationship that can morally legitimize the practice of keeping some animals as pets. In a nutshell, my claim was that the hands-off approach advocated by some liberationists—the idea that the lives of animals are better the less paternalistic they are—is morally sound though, ironically, not always in the interest of the animals themselves. Accordingly, I urged liberationists to avoid the hands-off approach.[6] With regard to companion animals, some pet-owner relationships are an overall good for human as well as for nonhuman animals. The paternalistic framework of such relations is a potential wrong but is exonerated because it makes for a better world for small animals: it is an overall better alternative for them than a life in the wild. Success stories of feral populations of horses and dogs would modify such an impression only in few examples but are less impressive when thinking about highly populated countries in which such animals would turn into "pests" and would be treated accordingly. Cats and dogs get to lead longer, safer, and more comfortable lives. While they lose through this exchange too (loss of freedom, being subjected to various operative interventions), such losses are offset by the benefits to them in the long run (limiting movement can prolong the life of the pet since it diminishes the risks of accidents and injury from fighting other animals—a neutered animal lives longer).[7]

In other cases, such losses help preserve the pet-owner relations as such (most owners would refuse to keep animals who can freely reproduce), relations the existence of which is an overall good for the pets. Such welfare-based thinking can also generate welfare-based distinctions that can tell us when pet abuse takes place and can guide some moral decision-making within small animal veterinary medicine. Some paternalistic, invasive, owner actions are justified on welfare ground, as the overall good for companion animals trumps their inability to understand the action (vaccination). Other such actions are obviously immoral, as they do not promote any animal interest and advance a marginal interest of the owner (ear docking). Most other actions fall in the middle and should be assessed in terms of the overall good for the animal, the owner, and in terms of available alternatives to the examined action.

For some animals, turning them into companion animals is not a benefit to them in any obvious way (wild animals and birds); so, welfare considerations urge us to banish the attempt to keep such animals as pets. Yet the same considerations suggest that the practice of keeping companion animals is not objectionable as such: an ideal liberationist world will include pet-owner relationships, and such relations—at their best—also show us that a paternalistic, yet non-exploitative, human-animal relation is both possible and actual.

Can animal-therapy be justified in a similar way? "Service" animals such as signal and guide dogs easily fall into the pet-owner category; so, such practices are, in principle, justified. Dogs do pay a price for such lives: they are spayed or neutered, trained for long periods (in the case of guide dogs much longer than other dogs), and isolated from their kin. But dogs seem to be able to transfer their social needs onto humans, and some of the prolonged training can arguably be an advantage, providing important (and pleasurable) mental stimulation to these dogs. If humanity were to endorse a hands-off approach with regard to animals, such dogs would appear to lead qualitatively inferior (and probably shorter) lives in the wild—even in the few countries in the world in which the notion of "the wild" still makes sense.

Some AAT programs strive to connect animal interests and human needs by placing shelter-abandoned animals with elderly people, thus benefiting particular animals in an even more immediate way.[8] Is a capuchin monkey, captured in the wild, isolated from the pack, trained using electric shocks, had teeth extracted—all of these prior to placing the monkey as a nurse of a handicapped person—better off than living in the wild?[9] The answer is here negative. Such an animal is better off having nothing to do with humans. In such examples, the hands-off approach is not only morally sound but is also continuous with the animal's welfare. The same holds for other forms of AAT: maintaining stressed rodents in petting areas in educational and therapeutic institutions for the projected benefit of children, psychiatric patients, or prisoners who may enjoy various therapeutic benefits through this connection does not appear to promote any of the rodent's own interests.[10] The lives of these rodents apart from humans appear to be a better alternative for them.

The same considerations help make sense of horse-assisted therapy. Justifying hippotherapy brings up the range of moral issues relating to equine husbandry and the moral status of the diverse practices it involves (racing, show jumping, hunting, riding as such). Horses require lengthy training periods and demand the use of bits and harnesses. Many of them are then kept in very small locks. They are subjected to all of the medical interventions that cats and dogs undergo. All of these practices would disturb liberationists. Yet where and how would horses exist in an ideal liberationist world? Reserves might be an option in some countries in which feral populations of horses might be feasible. But in many parts of the world, a puritanical decision to let horses be would boil down to a horseless environment.

Liberationists would know that the argument from the animal's projected welfare is a risky one to make, since the idea that the animal's existence justifies exploiting the animal is routinely used in various forms, supposedly vindicating all kinds of animal abuse. However, I believe that in the context of AAT this justification is viable.[11] I do, however, wish to add that since equine husbandry appears to be economically driven through and through, the idea that some relations between humans and horses are justified in the sense that they ultimately benefit horses does not morally cleanse all such relationships. It is not obvious to me that practices such as racing, dressage, or show jumping are morally justified, as they involve pain and risk of injury to the animal, and—according to one veterinarian I have consulted, Orit Zamir DVM—they can radically curtail the life-span of the horses and diminish its quality. Hippotherapy, by contrast, is not a form of human-animal connection that appears detrimental to the horse. The utilitarian benefits for such horses—they get to exist,[12] lead safe and relatively comfortable lives, are not abused or exploited—outweigh the prices they pay.

Use Versus Exploitation

I have so far argued that for some animals AAT cannot be vindicated through appeals to the overall good for the animal through the animal's forced participation in a paternalistic relationship with humans. Could some other framework justify using animals for therapeutic purposes? In this section,

I will discuss (and reject) two such possible justifications: Cartesianism and Kantianism. Later in this essay, I address Utilitarianism and Speciesism.

Cartesians claim that animals lack moral considerability. For a Cartesian, it is senseless to draw a morally relevant distinction between animals and objects (for Descartes, this also involved a denial of animal pain). Since animals lack moral considerability, any action done to them—AAT included—is morally permissible. Kantians are fig-leaf Cartesians. They agree with Cartesians that animals lack any kind of intrinsic moral status. But they also claim that some actions with respect to animals are morally reprehensible. This stems not from anything having to do with the animal but from how such actions determine the agents that performed them:—from what these actions say about them or about humanity in general. Cartesians would have no problem with any form of AAT since, for them, animals are no more than means to an end. Kantians would concur with this, adding the restriction that no abuse or cruelty should take place as part of AAT (consistent Cartesians would have no problem with cruelty to therapy animals, if it is shown to be therapeutically beneficial to human patients.[13])

The more general issue of the moral considerability of animals cannot be broached here. Liberationists have offered detailed criticisms of the Cartesian and Kantian frameworks. My own arguments against these positions, as well as my own position regarding the moral considerability of animals as such, is available elsewhere.[14] In our context, both positions constitute a theoretical, not a practical, opposition. By this, I mean that judging by the literature that they produce and by their concern with animal welfare, people involved in offering AAT appear to be both sensitive and concerned about the well being of the animals on whom they rely. They would find it odd to think that one may do anything one likes to an animal (Cartesianism) or that torturing a dog is wrong, not because of the dog but only because of what this says about the torturer (Kantianism).[15]

Short of a categorical denial of moral status, AAT advocates may favor weaker forms of these positions. They might try to defend the idea that using animals is permissible, even when detrimental to their welfare, so long as no abuse takes place. They will argue that such use does not constitute exploitation. The liberationism I have outlined above, in which some instrumental human-animal relations are morally legitimate, although they constitute a use of animals, is close to this position—but importantly different not only in general moral categories but also in terms of the consequences for particular species in the context of AAT.

To palpably perceive this difference, we need to draw some distinctions regarding instrumentalization. We now approach the conceptual heart of this essay: the distinction between use and exploitation and the manner by which this distinction affects the moral status (or lack of it) of AAT.

Actual practice pressurizes those who would like to relate to avoiding instrumentalization as a morally meaningful value. We routinely use our friends and relations for emotional or physical support. We use other people for their abilities, knowledge, and work power. And since give-and-take relations are a legitimate part of life, the relevant moral distinction is not the one between instrumentalization and noninstrumentalization but the one between use and exploitation. Kant was unhelpful regarding this, holding that whereas in some contexts it is permissible to treat another person as a means, it is immoral to perceive another person *merely* as a means. This position is notoriously vague, since it appeals to private motivations that are easily given to manipulation and rationalization. People can and do exploit others while commending themselves for negligible concessions that they make for the benefit of the exploited party.

Fortunately, the distinction between use and exploitation is not hard to draw. X uses Y when X perceives Y as a means of furthering X's own financial (or other) well being. This turns into exploitation when X is willing to act in a way that is substantially detrimental to Y's own well being in order to further X's own. By "substantial," I mean that the action predictably carries consequences such as shortening Y's life, damaging Y's health, limiting Y's freedom, abusing what Y is (some forms of prostitution), systematically thwarting Y's potential (child labor), and subjecting Y to pain or to a strongly undesired life (demanding inhuman workloads and thus creating human-slavery).

In addition, exploitation usually suggests lack of consent by the exploited party (or a consent predicated on a highly limited choice or on choosing among impossible alternatives). Exploitation is also mostly related to the existence of unequal power-relations or some dependency relations between the parties, favoring the exploiting party in an institutional and systematic way.

To know for certain that X is not exploiting Y, merely using Y, X must repeatedly make choices that substantively further Y's welfare even when in conflict with X's own prudential motives. This need not mean that X is to become irrational or altruistic. It merely suggests how persons can actually verify that they are not involved in an exploitative relationship. I believe that people can legitimately fall short of this ideal. That is, they can be uncertain as to whether a particular relationship that they have is exploitative. Give-and-take relations can be vague in this sense. For example, immigrants in well-off countries sometimes offer to overwork themselves so as to provide for the families in their home countries. Fantasizing about global justice is nice as a thought-experiment, but it does not help one when compelled to choose between cooperating with such requests or not. One does not always know. And provided that one does not knowingly participate in, or cooperate with, clear-cut exploitative relations, I believe that it is morally permissible to have relations over which one has some misgivings.

How can one tell whether one is in a "clear-cut" exploitative relationship? Generally, you are exploiting an entity if your relationship with it predictably benefits you and harms the entity. More specifically and in light of the various characterizations of exploitative relationships mentioned above, the answer is both quantitative and qualitative: relationships become more exploitative if they share more of the characteristics spelled out above (this is the "quantitative" answer). At the same time, a relationship can manifest only one of the characteristics mentioned above in some substantial way and be clearly exploitative (the "qualitative" answer). If, for example, I provide an entity with a comfortable life in which it is not abused in any way yet aim to kill it when it is very young, the relationship is clearly exploitative. If, on the other hand, I intend to terminate the entity's life only if it becomes old or incurably ill, I am not exploiting it, even if I would not act in the same way with regard to a human being. This is why pet-owner relationships can be non-exploitative (although they might constitute use) and why the same cannot be said concerning the lamb industry. I am not claiming that distinguishing between use and exploitation is always simple. Indeed, animal-ethics provide many vague cases (free roaming, de-beaked hens, for instance). But the considerations that could lead us in deciding these issues are not mysterious and many times indicate decisive answers.

We are now in a position to assess the modified Cartesian /Kantian counterargument to my proposal. I have argued that animals may be used but may not be exploited and have tried to unpack this distinction. Applied to AAT, this means that service dogs are used, though not exploited, since their welfare is promoted by the relationship. Horses too gain much from their relations with humans. The same cannot be said for rodents, snakes, birds, aquarium-kept dolphins, or monkeys who gain little or nothing through AAT and lose a lot.[16] Unlike horses or dogs, all of these creatures can easily exist in the wild in large numbers; by turning them into vehicles for therapy, both their freedom and their social needs are radically curtailed. Counter to my opponent's claims, AAT that uses these creatures is exploitative, even if no abuse takes place.

Two Objections

Before examining whether exploiting animals can be defended as such, I need to respond to two counterarguments to what I have just said. The first is that I am downplaying the significance of the price horses and dogs pay for their existence in the company of humans. Watching a horse struggle with the bit in his mouth is a difficult sight. "Breaking" horses or the prolonged training periods that service dogs undergo can boil down to painful activities and deprivation, especially when the training system is not (or is not only) reward-based. Moreover, the import of thwarting the procreative potential of these animals by neutering them cannot be ignored.

The second objection has to do with the argument from nonexistence on which I relied when claiming that dogs and horses gain from their relations with humans, since this relationship means that they exist. I have said that I defend the metaphysical plausibility of such an argument elsewhere. In a nutshell, I argue that a nonexistent entity cannot be harmed by not bringing "it" into existence, yet it—now without the quotes—can benefit from a decision to bring it into existence. There is nothing contradictory about an entity having both these properties. But there is a nonmetaphysically based objection to this move having to do with species as opposed to particular entities. I have said that, in most countries, horses and dogs are not likely to exist outside of use-based human relations and that abrogating all such relations will, in any case, imply a radical reduction in the number of such beings. But an AAT therapist can choose to breed particular rodents for the purpose of using them in therapeutic sessions, claiming that—like horses or dogs—these *particular* animals gain their existence from entering this exchange. Why, then, am I legitimating the former relations and prohibiting the latter?

Beginning with the substantial prices that horses and dogs pay for living their lives with humans, here a liberationist is compelled to factor in moral, political, and strategic considerations. Consider two versions of a liberationist ideal world: the first is based on the hands-off approach. Here, human animals live alongside nonhuman animals. Some interaction between the species might occur, but it would never be achieved through coercing animals. Pet-owner relations would probably not exist as such. People may take in injured animals for short periods, or, if they can afford the space needed, may allow animals to live and breed in an unlimited way in their homes. Cows, sheep, horses, dogs, cats, and pigs would roam freely in large areas that are fenced off from humans. They would never be killed for their flesh or hides. Nor would they be used to obtain eggs and milk: protein substitutes would replace these, since collective moral veganism would make such replacement mandatory (and affordable). This ideal obviously involves a radical shrinking in numbers for these creatures, as there will be no financial incentive to breed them. But the ones who will exist would lead uninterrupted lives. Humans will occasionally visit these reserves (zoos would be abolished) so as to watch those animals from afar.

Here is another, less serene, liberationist ideal world: in this world, animals are never killed in order to satisfy human interests (including culinary, scientific, or recreational interests). Protein substitutes and alternative research models have been devised, activities like hunting or fishing have been outlawed, and zoos have been banished. Yet animals do live with humans in various relationships that promote some human interests. Free-roaming animals are maintained by humans so as to obtain milk and eggs. When such animals die, their flesh and hides are used. Cats, dogs, and horses are kept by humans; this does mean that they are spayed and neutered, vaccinated, and subjected to training. The animals are well kept, and some cosmetic interventions done to them today are banned.

I submit that this second ideal world is overall better for animals than the first. Many more animals would exist (millions more would exist), the lives they would lead would be qualitatively good ones and would not constitute a debasing of what having a life means—a debasement that exists when animals are perceived merely as means for producing this or that. And it is such a world that liberationists should strive to create. This does not obviously legitimize everything done to dogs or horses. Aesthetic surgery for dogs cannot be legitimated, and some modes of keeping and using horses will disappear. But this position involves embracing a quasi-paternalistic relationship with these beings, holding that doing so is beneficial to them. For a liberationist, the moral price of accepting this position is upholding the moral legitimacy of bits, harnesses, and invasive surgery. Yet for liberationists such as I, the moral price that the first world implies, although more abstract in nature, is higher: One has to, in this case, swallow the implication of a petless world, both in terms of ourselves and of these beings. And since the lives of many horses and pets are qualitatively good ones, I do not subscribe to the morally purer stance, which will make all of these disappear.

Responding to the second counter-argument requires specifying when and where the argument from nonexistence can be legitimately employed. Merely bringing a being into existence is not, *ipso facto*, a benefit to it. Two additional considerations have to be brought into play before one can conclude that an entity benefits from bringing it into existence. First, the qualitative consideration: if the entity's future life is predicted to be qualitatively bad in a significant way, then bringing it into existence is not a benefit to it. The negative quality has to, of course, be significant. An obvious example is that of bringing a person into a long life of perpetual torture.[17] The second consideration is "teleological." Bringing a being into a life form, which debases the very idea of having a life, is wrong, even if the life offered is qualitatively reasonable. For example, bringing some people into the world with the sole purpose of using them as organ banks later (while providing them with a qualitatively reasonable existence) abuses what having a life means. I call this abuse "teleological," because here the problem is the distorted, projected goal for a life.

I have claimed that in the case of rodents, birds, reptiles, fish, and monkeys, there is no species-related, welfare-based justification that enables perceiving AAT as a practice that helps these beings *qua* members of a potentially extinct species. The counter-argument has granted this, yet claimed that bringing a particular member of these animals into existence for the purpose of AAT benefits the member. In response, I admit that the AAT therapist who brings a particular rodent to life for the purpose of AAT does not necessarily abuse the rodent. The life of the rodent may be comfortable, and it need not constitute a debasement of what having a life means in the same manner in which, say, factory farming abuses the lives of the animals whose lives it takes.

However, that a particular rodent does benefit from the decision to bring the rodent into existence should not change the conclusion for a liberationist. The reason for this is that when a particular AAT animal's welfare is genuinely considered, it seems overall best for the animal to be set free after being brought into existence by the therapist. And so, if the technician is truly concerned with the particular animal's welfare, the technician should hypothetically release the animal from captivity as soon as possible.

Unlike dogs or horses—the release of whom either is not feasible in most areas (horses) or appears to compromise their welfare—mice, hamsters, and chinchillas on the whole express no particular attachment to human contact (unlike dogs) or seek their company (unlike some cats). And so, a particular, welfare-based justification from nonexistence can only work if one is willing to accept the implication that the same welfare considerations, which justify bringing the particular animal into existence, would then undermine maintaining an AAT-based relationship with this particular animal, since releasing the animal is overall better for the animal.

An Exploitation-Based Case for AAT?

A defender of AAT may now concede that some forms of AAT are exploitative but assert that it is morally permissible to exploit animals. This position need not be coupled with a Cartesian or a Kantian categorical denial of moral considerability to animals. The defender of AAT will here follow what appears to be the consensus in many countries: animals are entitled to some moral considerability (and this basically means that cruelty to animals ought to be prevented). Yet nothing stands in the way of exploiting animals for all kinds of purposes, AAT included. The response to this argument ("But if it is wrong to be cruel to an entity, how can it be right to exploit it"?) will be rejected by this defender of AAT by adopting a "degrees" view of moral considerability: the defender of AAT will claim that animals have some degree of moral considerability, which justifies preventing abuse of them—but not enough to prohibit exploiting them.

Yet the degrees view cannot be accepted. First, it is questionable whether it can be successfully formulated at all, though this is less important for our purposes.[18] Moreover, the morally relevant properties that generate the prohibition on cruelty—the animal's capacity to suffer as well as the animal's possession of an interest/desire not to be subjected to some actions—are shared by humans, too. In the case of humans, it is partly these properties that underlie the condemnation of exploiting them. It would therefore appear mysterious why, if one is willing to admit these properties into an analysis (and condemnation) of one kind of conduct, one dismisses these very same properties when analyzing another. If, for example, one opposes cruelty to animals because their suffering is morally relevant (and not just because cruelty is reprehensible as such), one is obligated to avoid actions that create such suffering.

What this means, morally, is that when human interests appear to require animal suffering, one cannot just allow these interests to trump one's obligation to avoid creating suffering. One is morally required to seriously strive at first to devise alternatives to these conflicts of interests. Many (not all) human-animal conflicts of interests can be finessed, meaning that it is possible to meet the human need in a substantial—though sometimes not maximal—way without compromising the well being of animals. Recognizing this makes it possible to avoid a host of second-order questions regarding the relative importance of human interests as well as the plausibility (or lack of it) of mobilizing this importance in order to thwart particular animal interests.[19]

One does not have to exploit animals so as to have eggs or milk. The same applies to AAT: there are numerous effective modes of therapy that do not exploit animals; so there is no reason to institutionalize the latter. Moreover, since this essay's analysis justifies some modes of AAT—while disallowing others—if therapeutic considerations favor the use of animals, this can still be done through deploying dogs or horses. It seems strained to claim that the value of using, specifically, rodents or birds for some patients is of such additional therapeutic value (over, say, employing dogs) as to render void the desire to avoid exploitation.

Two Further Objections (and Conclusion)

The argument I have just used regarding the moral obligation to circumvent either-or conflicts of interests between humans and animals, applies also to speciesist or utilitarian objections to my general claim. "Speciesism" is a confused term and, under most of its renderings, is not opposed to liberationism.[20] In our context, a speciesist rejoinder would boil down to saying that since human interests are more important than the interests of animals, various forms of exploitation (such as the forms of AAT that rely on rodents, birds, dolphins, reptiles, and monkeys) are morally legitimate. The argument in *Two Objections* above adequately answers this objection: the question is not whose interests are more important but whether a particular conflict of interests can be avoided. Since the either-or nature of the question of some forms of AAT is a mirage, speciesism is continuous with abrogating forms of AAT that involve exploitation and can be easily replaced.

Utilitarian objections to the foregoing conclusion are similar, basically claiming that the overall good achieved in a world in which exploitative forms of AAT occur is greater than the overall good in a world that does not contain such therapeutic options. Unpacking "overall good" shows that, in the AAT context, there are three possible variants of the utilitarian claim, two of which are speciesist; the third, liberationist. The two speciesist variants of this utilitarian argument would hold that human interests are more important than animal interests. They would differ on what "more important" should mean in practice, the first variant holding that any human interest categorically trumps any animal one. The second variant maintains that some human interests trump some (though not all) animal ones.[21] The liberationist variant of a utilitarian objection, which is actually continuous with classical utilitarianism, is that human and nonhuman interests count equally; yet it may be the case that some disutility to animals, caused by exploitative forms of AAT, substantially promotes the well being of some humans in a way that makes for a better world than one in which exploitation does not occur.

Responding to these objections need not invoke the complex evaluation of utilitarianism as such or the difficulties involved in weighing interests. If my previous argument is sound, considerations of an overall good only superficially imply that anyone's interests should be compromised, so all three utilitarian variants miss the mark. The therapeutic benefits to humans could be met without exploitation. Accordingly, avoiding some forms of AAT does not diminish the projected, overall good.

In conclusion: Forms of AAT that rely on horses and dogs are continuous with the welfare of these animals. Without a relationship with humans, an overwhelming number of these beings would not exist. Their lives with human beings exact a price from them. But given responsible human owners, such lives are qualitatively comfortable and safe, and they need not frustrate the social needs of these creatures. A world in which practices like AAT exist is an overall better world for these beings than one that does not include them, and this provides a broad, moral vindication of forms of AAT that rely on these beings. On the other hand, rodents, birds, monkeys, reptiles, and dolphins gain little by coercing them into AAT. Such practices are therefore exploitative. Since the human interests that are involved can be easily met without exploiting these beings, the moral conclusion is that such forms of AAT should be abolished.

Notes

1. The literature deploys a finer terminology here, distinguishing AAT from AAA (animal-assisted activities), the latter covering nontherapeutic work done with animals, which is nevertheless deemed as potentially beneficial for humans. This distinction is not pertinent to the following analysis, so I will use AAT as an umbrella term covering various modalities of therapy and assistance incorporating the use of animals.

2. Psychologically oriented AAT includes child-oriented interventions that rely on animals to achieve wide-ranging goals. These include boosting the self-esteem of insecure children; therapeutic horseback riding (hippotherapy); creating oblique communication over the child's own problems through her interaction with animals; cultivating self-control and curtailing impulsive behavior in children with ADHD; enhancing empathy, responsibility, and furthering the child's capacity to nurse through creating controlled child-animal relationships. Aside from children, psychological branches of AAT also include interventions with clinically depressed individuals, with the elderly, and with incarcerated inmates in some prisons. In all, advocates of AAT claim that the ability of the animal to generate what is many times perceived as unconditional acceptance and to facilitate dialogue that is nonthreatening, their capacity to enforce on depressives or recuperating individuals a compelling "here and now," even the tactile sensations that their touch induces, turn animals into invaluable helpers in creating therapeutically meaningful interventions. Apart from allowing people to relate to themselves through projection, some psychotherapists believe that the animals tap into various unconscious drives that they embody or archetypically signify, thus creating analytically deep therapy that could not be achieved through nonanimal targeted projections. Apart from psychology, forms of AAT have been introduced in assisting the handicapped ("service animals," such as dogs for the hearing impaired, guide dogs for the blind, monkeys for quadriplegic individuals). Animals feature in programs designed to assist the mentally handicapped. They are deployed as part of new modalities of speech therapy. Animals are also relied upon to function as organic alarm systems (dogs) who can help with specific medical conditions such as epilepsy and diabetes by alerting the owner to an oncoming seizure. Specialized animal-assisted therapy programs exist for special needs individuals; for autistic people; and for patients suffering from fatal, incurable diseases. There are many available expositions of the current extent of AAT, as well as summaries of research that attempts to validate it. For some of these, see Shalev (1996), Grammonley et al. (1997), Cusack (1988), and Gilshtrom (2003).

3. The terms "liberationist perspective" or "liberationist stance" are my own (drawing from Peter Singer's *Animal Liberation*). Throughout this essay such terms stipulate what I believe to be a shared consensus among various pro-animal advocates (who, needless to say, differ on many details), who would agree that the status of nonhuman animals today demands immediate reform, stemming from a prior belief that animals are not merely a resource for human usage.

4. Most surveys on AAT given above (see note 3) describe cases of manhandling and injury.

5. A different possible moral extension of considerations, which I will not attempt, relates to zoos. If keeping animals in zoos is not immoral, curtailing their movement when they are in pet centers and making life-determining decisions for them when turning them into therapeutic means will surely pass as moral, too. I will avoid this direction because reversing these transitive relations does not work: a justification of animal therapy is not, *a fortiori*, a vindication of zoos, and I wish to retain the possibility that animal therapy is a justified practice, whereas the other is not.

6. My argument was made in the context of the debate among liberationists whether moral veganism or moral vegetarianism is the morally adequate response to current exploitative practice. See Zamir (2004).

7. This claim and some of the assertions regarding horses in the next section are based on a conversation with Orit Zamir, DVM.
8. A program discussed in Lannuzi and Rowan (1991).
9. For details of this program, see Lannuzi and Rowan (1991).
10. The surveys on AAT above usually comment on the stress and anxiety that may be involved in such programs (see, in particular on this, Lannuzi and Rowan, 1991). Animals have desires and needs, though some philosophers doubt whether these constitute interests. This subtlety does not affect my argument throughout this paper.
11. In Zamir (2004a), I argue why the use of this argument in order to justify raising animals and killing them for their flesh is wrong. In Zamir (2004, p. 1) I suggest three restrictions on the use of this argument, which could distinguish between right and wrong applications of this argument.
12. Some philosophers would oppose this, saying that existence cannot be a benefit since this assumes a meaningless position, prior to its present existence, in which the nonexistent animal could be harmed or helped by human decisions. See Zamir (2004), for a reply to this. Later in this essay, I summarize this reply.
13. While Cartesians seem to be more hostile than Kantians to the liberationist cause, it is interesting to note that Descartes's own position, resting as it did on the denial of animal pain, is thus conditional on an empirical belief which, when informed (and transformed) by our modern understanding regarding pain, would change the moral attitude to animals. By contrast, the Kantian indirect duties approach thoroughly repudiates the moral status of animals, and this dismissal is unconnected to the existence or nonexistence of animal pain. The awareness that animals produce, and respond to, endorphins, that they respond to pain-relievers would have probably persuaded Descartes to modify his position. Kant, on the other hand, would have been unimpressed. Yet for the purposes of this essay, "Cartesians" covers all who deny that animals possess moral standing (with or without connection to pain).
14. See Zamir (2004b) "Why Animals Matter?," forthcoming in *Between the Species*.
15. Kantians and Cartesians would (rightly) charge me with an *ad hominem* reasoning here, claiming that even if AAT practitioners are likely to avoid Kantianism and Cartesianism, this predilection is no argument against these positions as being right. I admit the topical nature of my argument here and refer readers who may be interested in a more detailed response to these to Zamir (2000b).
16. It was pointed out to me that in some dolphin-related AAT programs the dolphins are actually free and the therapeutic objectives are obtained without moving the dolphins from their natural habitat and without coercion. My remarks throughout this essay regarding dolphins do not apply to such programs.
17. This claim has no implication for discussions of euthanasia (assuming that animal-ethics discussions carry over into human-ethics). The considerations that pertain to a future life that no one yet has are different from those that are relevant to a life already possessed by a particular person. One cannot be said to benefit a future, potential life by bringing it into a projected life of perpetual fear, isolation, and pain. This does not imply that someone who already lives such a life is better off dead. The claim is also disconnected from the abortion debate, which includes its own claims regarding the relative quality of a future life. An existing zygote is a particular, potential/actual life, while we are here considering abstract, potential ones. Moreover, the negative quality of a future life of disability, of being adopted (since one's natural parents cannot responsibly function as parents), the two considerations that prompt future quality-of-a-life arguments within the abortion debate are categorically distinct from issues of projected future exploitation that are relevant here.
18. For arguments against the plausibility of a degrees view, see Regan (1985, Ch. 7, p. 2), DeGrazia (1996, Ch. 3), Rowland (2002, Ch. 2, 3).
19. For discussion of the dubiousness of this move, see Zamir (2006).
20. See Zamir (forthcomings).
21. The terminology, which has been suggested for this distinction (by Brody, 2001), is "lexical priority" of human over nonhuman interests (any human interest overmasters any animal interest) and "discounting of interests" (extremely important animal interests can take preference over negligible human interests).

References

Brody, B. A. (2001). Defending animal research: An international perspective. In E. F. Paul & J. Paul (Eds.), *Why animal experimentation matters: The use of animals in medical research* (pp. 131–148). New Brunswick: Transaction Publishers.

Cusack, O. (1988). *Pets and mental health,* New York: Haworth Press.

DeGrazia, D. (1996). *Taking animals seriously: Mental life and moral status,* New York: Cambridge University Press.

Gilshtrom, R. (2003). *Special pets for special needs population,* Israel: Ach (Hebrew).

Grammonley, J., Howie, A. R., Kirwin, S., Zapf, S., Frye, J., Freeman, G., Stuart-Lannuzi, D. & Rowan, A. N. (1991). Ethical issues in animal-assisted therapy programs, *Anthrozoös,* 4 (3), 154–163.

Preziosi, R. J. (1997). For your consideration: A pet-assisted therapist facilitator code of ethics, *The Latham Letter,* Spring, 5–6.

Regan, T. (1985). *The case for animals rights,* Berkeley: University of California Press.

Rowland, M. (2002). *Animals like us,* London: Verso.

Shalev, A. (1996). *The furry healer: Pets as a therapeutic means: Theory, research and practice,* Tel-Aviv: Tcherikover Publishers (Hebrew).

Zamir, T. (2004). Veganism, *Journal of Social Philosophy,* September, 35 (3), 367–379.

———— (2004a, June). Killing for pleasure, *Between the Species,* (web-journal).

———— (2004b). Why animals matter? *Between the Species* (web-journal).

———— (2006). Killing for knowledge, *Journal of Applied Philosophy* 23.1 (2006): 1–40.

———— (forthcomingb). *Is speciesism opposed to liberationism?*

Part Ten

Animal Law/Animal Activism

Introduction to Part Ten

Should animals have legal rights? How can the situations of animals be improved? Is civil disobedience morally justified? The authors in this part present widely diverging answers to these questions. In "A Great Shout," attorney Steven Wise notes that we have assigned ourselves the exalted status of legal persons and consider every other animal as merely legal things which can be owned. Wise argues for fundamental legal rights for the great apes based on their possession of autonomy.

In a book review of Wise's book *Rattling the Cage*, Richard Posner critiques Wise's analysis. He points out that Wise does not show that having cognitive capacity is a necessary or sufficient condition of having legal rights. Wise downplays the fact that such legal rights would be a drastic departure from existing law. Posner argues that making wild animals property is the best way to increase animal protection, given that "aggressive implementations" of animal-rights thinking are not likely to prevail.

In "The Dangerous Claims of the Animal Rights Movement," Richard Epstein points out a number of important differences between human beings and animals which support the view that human welfare is more important than animal welfare. He maintains that treating animals as the moral and legal peers of human beings would undermine the liberty and dignity of human beings. It is appropriate that animals remain our property.

In "Every Sparrow That Falls," Wesley Jamison, Caspar Wenk, and James Parker analyze animal rights activism as a movement that functions like a religion, based on their research in Switzerland and the United States. They identify five components of animal rights activism which fulfill the definition of "functional religion" stated by the U.S. Supreme Court.

Several essays discuss strategies by which to improve the condition of animals. In "Understanding Animal Rights Violence" Tom Regan explores the split between "immediatists" and "gradualists." The diversity of views within the animal rights movement means that it is accurately characterized neither as nonviolent nor as terrorist. Regan proposes incremental abolitionist change, in which one use of animals at a time is completely stopped.

Courtney Dillard examines the effectiveness of two organized protests and acts of civil disobedience against the largest pigeon shoot in the United States. Her findings suggest that the effectiveness of civil disobedience is increased when it is enacted in nonviolent and nonthreatening ways and when participants demonstrate both a willingness to suffer for their beliefs and an interest in communicating that suffering to onlookers.

In "Ten Ways to Make a Difference," Peter Singer draws on the work of Henry Spira, an activist who has had remarkable successes in reducing animal suffering. He presents Spira's life as an example of finding meaning by living in accord with one's own values. The ten suggestions are the result of Spira's experience in changing public opinion. Ball and Friedrich affirm that suffering is the greatest barrier to happiness. Accordingly, they believe that the best way to proceed is to practice vegetarianism.

Christine Korsgaard maintains that the traditional division of entities into persons and things is inadequate. She states that the best way to treat animals is to treat them as ends in themselves, who have rights to not be mistreated by human beings. Stephen Latham critics U.S. law as having gaps. He believes, however, that the existing regulatory structure can accommodate changes which will reduce unnecessary animal suffering.

Further Reading

Datta, A. (1998) *Animals and the Law: A Review of Animals and the State*, Chichester, England: Chichester Institute of Higher Education.

Favre, D. (1996) "Legal Rights for Our Fellow Creatures," *Contemporary Philosophy* 28(4–5): 7–10.

Francione, G. (2000) *Introduction to Animal Rights: Your Child or the Dog?* Philadelphia: Temple University Press.

Garner, R. (1998) *Political Animals: Animal Protection Politics in Britain and the United States*, New York: St. Martin's.

Hall, Lee (2006) *Capers in the Churchyard: Animal Rights Advocacy in the Age of Terror*, Darien, CT: Nectar Bat Press.

Jasper, M.C. (1997) *Animal Rights Law*, Dobbs Ferry, NY: Oceana.

Munro, L. (2001) *Compassionate Beasts: The Quest for Animal Rights*, Westport, CT: Praeger.

Singer, P. (1998) *Ethics into Action: Henry Spira and the Animal Rights Movement*, Lanham, MD: Rowman and Littlefield.

——— (ed.) (2006) *In Defense of Animals: The Second Wave*, Malden, MA: Blackwell.

Sunstein, Cass R. and Nussbaum, Martha C. (eds.) (2004) *Animal Rights: Current Debates and New Direction*, New York: Oxford University Press.

Waisman, Sonia S., Frasch, Pamela D., and Wagman, Bruce A. (2006) *Animal Law: Cases and Materials*, Durham, NC: Carolina Academic Press.

Wise, S.M. (2000) *Rattling the Cage: Toward Legal Rights for Animals*, Cambridge, MA: Perseus Books.

——— (2002) *Drawing the Line: Science and the Case for Animal Rights*, Cambridge, MA: Perseus Books.

Study Questions

1. Steven Wise and Richard Posner disagree concerning the role of an animal's cognitive capacity as a basis for legal rights. Which position do you find more convincing? Justify your position.

2. Wise proposes that we recognize "practical autonomy" as sufficient to justify the attribution of basic legal rights. To what degree do you support Wise's proposal? To what degree do the positions of Gómez and Cavalieri in Part Three support such a concept?

3. Richard Epstein discusses a number of negative consequences which follow from the recognition of animal rights. Do you believe that such consequences are likely? Give your reasoning.

4. Both Posner and Epstein point out that the current legal situation of treating animals as the property of human beings often has a positive effect on animal welfare. To what extent does your own experience ratify this claim?

5. Which of the five characteristics of a religion discussed by Jamison, Wenk, and Parker are characteristic of the animal rights movement, in your experience? Which do not appear to be characteristic? Justify your positions. Can you cite other social reform movements which also share some or all of these religious characteristics?

6. Tom Regan describes the current abolition/reform split in the animal rights movement. Explain which approach you believe to be more effective, and why. Under what circumstances, if any, do you believe that violence against property on behalf of animal welfare is morally acceptable?

7. Tom Regan proposes a solution to the abolition/reform split at the end of his article. Do you believe that his solution is workable? Give your reasons.

8. Courtney Dillard analyzes effective civil disobedience. How might the strategies she describes be used in social reform movements not involving animals?

9. In your own words, explain Korsgaard's statements that law is why the other animals are completely at our mercy.

10. In your view, what is the most powerful argument offered by Ball and Friedrich in the Animal Activist's Handbook?

82 A Great Shout
Legal Rights for Great Apes

Steven M. Wise

[handwritten: // stringently adhere to the tenants of the Bible]

Steven M. Wise argues that legal rules that may have made good sense in the past may make good sense no longer. As the scientific evidence of the capacities of nonhuman animals such as the great apes continues to mount, it is apparent that treating animals as things is unjust. Wise argues on both legal and philosophical grounds that the "practical autonomy" exhibited by many animals is sufficient to justify the attribution of basic legal rights.

The earliest known law is preserved in cuneiform on Sumerian clay tablets. These Mesopotamian law codes, 4,000 years old, the Laws of Ur-Nammu, the Lipit-Ishtar Lawcode, the Laws of Eshunna, and the Laws of Hammurabi, assumed that humans could own both nonhuman animals and slaves (Wise 1996). It took most of the next 4,000 years for subjective legal rights to develop. Even in Republican and Imperial Rome, legal rights were understood to exist only in the objective sense of being "the right thing to do" (Wise 1996, 799). Subjective legal rights, claims that one person could make on another, first glimmered in twelfth-century writings. It was only in the fourteenth century that the notion that one's legal rights were one's property began to root (Wise 1996).

Not until the nineteenth century was slavery abolished in the West and every human formally cloaked with the legal personhood that signifies eligibility for fundamental legal rights. So the final brick of a great legal wall, begun millennia ago, was cemented into place. Today, on one side of this legal wall reside all the natural legal persons, all the members of a single species, *Homo sapiens*. We have assigned ourselves, alone among the millions of animal species, the exalted status of legal persons, entitled to all the rights, privileges, powers, and immunities of "legal personhood" (Wise 1996). [margin handwritten: metaphorical wall]

On the other side of this wall lies every other animal. They are not legal persons but legal things. During the American Civil War, President Abraham Lincoln was said to have spurned South Carolina's peace commissioners with the statement, "As President, I have no eyes but Constitutional eyes; I cannot see you" (*Oxford Dictionary of Quotations* 1979, 313). In this way, their "legal thinghood" makes nonhuman animals invisible to the civil law. Civil judges have no eyes for anyone but legal persons.

[...]

The legal thinghood of nonhuman animals has a unique history. An understanding of this history is instrumental to what Oliver Wendell Holmes Jr. called the "deliberate reconsideration" to which every legal rule must eventually fall subject (Holmes 1897). Alan Watson has concluded from his studies of comparative law that "to a truly astounding degree the law is rooted in the past" (Watson 1993, 95). The most common sources from which we quarry our law are the legal rules of earlier times. But when we borrow past law, we borrow the past. Legal rules that may have made good sense when they were fashioned may make good sense no longer. Raised by age to the status of self-evident truths they may perpetrate ancient ignorance, ancient prejudices, and ancient injustices that may once have been less unjust because we knew no better.

[...]

To Think About It Was to Condemn It

The wall's foundations have rotted. Because its intellectual foundations are unprincipled and arbitrary, unfair and unjust, its greatest vulnerability, at least in the English-speaking countries, is to the unceasing tendency of the common law "to work itself pure," to borrow a phrase from Lord Mansfield, the great eighteenth-century English judge.[1] Once a great injustice is brought to their attention, common law judges have the duty to place the legal rules that are its source alongside those great overarching principles that have been integral to Western law and justice for hundreds of years—equality, liberty, fairness, and reasoned judicial decision making—to determine if, in light of what are believed to be true facts and modern values, those rules should be found wanting.

[. . .]

Recall that the abomination of human slavery was finally abolished in the West little more than 100 years ago. It continues in a few countries to this day. The first thinking about the justice of the legal thinghood of nonhuman animals occurred just as slavery was flickering in the West. To date it has resulted mostly in the enactment of pathetically inadequate anticruelty statutes. But as the scientific evidence of the true natures of such nonhuman animals as chimpanzees continues to mount, that thinking will be its undoing. Because to think about the legal thinghood of such creatures as the great apes will be finally to condemn such a notion.

This process has begun. Modern law has begun slowly to disassemble the radical incommensurability said to exist between all human and all nonhuman animals from both the top down and the bottom up. The intrinsic value of human beings is now seen in law as commensurable with other legal values. This was reflected, for example, in the enactment in the English-speaking countries of wrongful death statutes in the middle of the nineteenth century. These statutes were intended to alter the ancient, and unfair, common law rule that the loss of human life, understood to be incommensurable with anything else, could never be compensated by money (Wise 1998b). The lives of at least some nonhuman animals have begun to be infused with a degree of intrinsic and not merely instrumental value. The preamble to the United Nations World Charter for Nature states that "every form of life is unique, warranting respect regardless of its worth to man" (World Charter 1982, 992). Respected international law commentators have argued that the legal right of individual whales to life may be becoming a part of binding international law (D'Amato and Chopra 1991). While interpreting the federal Endangered Species Act, the U.S. Supreme Court was guided in its decision by the declaration of the American Congress that endangered species were of "incalculable value."[2]

[. . .]

Liberty: The Supreme Value of the Western World

Today liberty "stands unchallenged as the supreme value of the Western world" (Patterson 1991, ix). Out of the more than 200 recorded senses of "liberty," Sir Isaiah Berlin famously identified two central senses: negative and positive (Berlin 1969). One's negative liberty, with which we are concerned, is often described as "freedom from" and depends on being able to do what one wishes without human interference (Berlin 1998). On the other hand, one's positive liberty may be described as "freedom to" (Berlin 1969, lvi; McPherson 1990, 61).

[. . .]

I refer to these fundamental negative liberty rights as "dignity-rights." International and domestic courts and legislatures around the world recognize that for a human being to have a minimal opportunity to flourish, such dignity-rights as bodily integrity and bodily liberty must be protected by sturdy barriers of negative liberty rights that form a protective legal perimeter around our bodies and personalities (Berlin 1969; Dworkin 1977; Feinberg 1966).

Anglo American common law recognizes a general negative liberty right. The constitutions of most modern nations protect fundamental negative liberty rights (Allan 1991).[3]

[. . .]

Fundamental Rights Derive From a Practical Autonomy

It is true, as the Kansas Supreme Court has said, that "Anglo American law starts with the premise of thorough-going self determination."[4] But what kind of autonomy is required? Philosophers often understand autonomy to mean what the German philosopher Immanuel Kant intended it to mean 200 years ago. We will call Kant's notion of autonomy "full autonomy." Though whole books have been written about what Kant meant, I will try to catch much of his core meaning in a single sentence: I have autonomy if, in determining what I ought to do in any situation, I have the ability to understand what others can and ought to do, I can rationally analyze whether it would be right for me to act in some way or another, keeping in mind that I should act only as I would want others to act and as they can act, and then I can do what I have decided is right.

My ability to perform something like this calculus is what makes me autonomous, gives me dignity, and requires that I be treated as a person. If I cannot do this, I lack autonomy and dignity and can justly be treated as a thing, according to Kant.

Whether I have summarized Kant's idea perfectly or not is irrelevant. What is important is that anything that resembles this analysis demands an ability to reason at an almost inhumanly high level. Perhaps our Aristotles, Kants, Freuds, and Einsteins achieved it some of the time. But it is only a glimmering possibility for infants and children, most normal adults never reach it, and the severely mentally limited and the permanently vegetative do not even begin. How did Kant deal with them? Well, he did not, and his "deep silence" on the moral status of children and nonrational adults has not gone unnoticed (Herman 1993). Even Aristotle and company pass significant portions of their lives on automatic pilot or often act out of desire, and not reason, which is precisely how Kant argued nonhuman animals act (Herman 1993; Langer 1997). Were judges to demand full autonomy as a prerequisite for dignity, they would exclude most of us, themselves included, from eligibility for dignity-rights.

Beings may possess a much simpler ability that allows them to act to fulfill their intended purposes. They may have varying capacities for mental flexibility and responsiveness. Autonomy can encompass a range of capacities for consciousness from the most simple awareness of one's present experience to a much broader and deeper self-awareness, self-reflection, and an awareness of the past, present, and future. The full autonomy of, say, Plato might be said to approximate the high end of full Kantian autonomy, whereas the consciousness of a typical preschooler might approximate the low end of a practical autonomy.

A full Kantian autonomy is too narrow a prerequisite for dignity-rights. Not all humans possess it to any degree. Most possess it only in varying degrees. No humans possess it all the time and no one expects them to. Many more humans, though still not anencephalic or even normal infants, the most severely retarded adults, or adults in persistent vegetative comas, possess a practical autonomy than possess full Kantian autonomy (Russell 1996; Wright 1993). A practical autonomy merely recognizes that a being has a somewhat "less than perfect ability to choose appropriate actions" (Cherniak 1985, 5). Any being capable of desires and beliefs has a practical autonomy if she can have beliefs and desires and is able to make "some, but not necessarily all of the sound inferences from the belief set that are apparently appropriate" (Cherniak 1985, 10; Rachels 1990; Regan 1983; Wright 1993). A practical autonomy, therefore, much more closely coincides with the way in which human beings are normally understood to be autonomous.

Perhaps most important for our purposes, fundamental common law and constitutional rights were not designed to protect only the fully autonomous. Courts are exquisitely sensitive to autonomy's practical sense.[5] Once some minimum capacity is attained, courts generally respect the choices made within exceedingly wide parameters, at least with respect to human adults. Practical autonomy acts as a trip wire for dignity-rights. This is because a choice emanating from even a flickering autonomy is more highly valued, regardless of whether the actions are rational, reasonable, or even inimical to one's own best interests, than is any specific choice.[6] That is why the judges of the California Court of Appeals said that "respect for the dignity and autonomy of the individual is a value universally celebrated in free societies. . . . Out of fidelity to that value defendant's choice must be honored even if he opts foolishly to go to hell in a handbasket."[7]

American courts routinely hold that incompetent human beings are entitled to the same dignity-rights as competent human beings. For example, the U.S. Supreme Court held that a man with an I.Q. below 10 and the mental capacity of an 18-month-old child had an inextinguishable liberty right to personal security.[8]

[. . .]

Now comes the exceedingly odd part: Even humans who have always lacked autonomy and self-determination are said to possess the requisite dignity for legal personhood.[9] "Can it be doubted," state the judges of high courts rhetorically, "that the value of human dignity extends to both (competent and incompetent humans)?"[10] Undoubting courts grant competent, incompetent, and never-competent humans the same common law dignity-rights and the rights to protect their powers to use them as well.[11] The result is that humans with minimal, or even no, capacity for autonomy and self-determination, even terminally ill infants who lack all cognition, possess not just protected dignity-rights but the right to use their power to enforce them.[12]

[. . .]

Courts recognize human dignity-rights in the complete absence of autonomy only by using an arbitrary legal fiction that controverts the empirical evidence that no such autonomy exists. Conversely, courts refuse to recognize dignity-rights of the great apes only by using a second arbitrary legal fiction in the teeth of empirical evidence that they possess it (Nino 1993; Rachels 1990). But legal fictions can only be justified when they harmonize with, or at least do not undermine, the overarching values and principles of a legal system. Thus the legal fiction that a human who actually lacks autonomy has it is benign, for at worst it extends legal rights to those who might not need them. At best it protects the bodily integrity of the most helpless humans alive. But the legal fiction that great apes are not autonomous when they actually are undermines every important principle and value of Western justice: liberty, equality, fairness, and reasoned judicial decision making. It is pernicious.

[. . .]

Equality: Likes Should be Treated Alike

Equality is the axiom of Western justice that likes be treated alike. [. . .] Equality's logical component requires that dissimilar treatment rests on some relevant and objectively ascertainable difference between a favored and disfavored class with respect to the harm to be avoided or the benefit to be promoted (Simons 1989).[13]

[. . .]

Equality's normative component means that no matter how perfect the relationship between ends and means may be, some means and some ends are unacceptable solely because they are arbitrary, irrelevant, invidious, or are otherwise normatively illegitimate.[14]

Together, the logical and normative elements of equality mean that only qualities that are objectively ascertainable and normatively acceptable should be compared. Actual and relevant likenesses that are examined in light of current knowledge and normative understandings that are not false, assumed, unprovable, or anachronistic assumptions or contain "fixed notions" about likeness should be the measure.[15] These are the teachings of the fundamental value of equality.

Closely related to equality rights are proportionality rights. Proportionality requires that unalikes be treated proportionately to their unalikeness (Simons 1989).

[. . .]

At least three independent equality or proportionality arguments support fundamental legal rights for the great apes (Wise 1998a). First, great apes who possess Kant's full autonomy should be entitled to dignity-rights *if* humans who possess full autonomy are entitled to them. To do otherwise would be to undermine the major principled arguments against racism and sexism.

Second, great apes who possess a practical autonomy should be entitled to dignity-rights in proportion to the degree to which they approach full Kantian autonomy *if* humans who possess a practical autonomy are entitled to dignity-rights in proportion to the degree to which *they* approach full Kantian autonomy. Thus if a human is entitled to fewer, narrower, or partial legal rights as their capabilities approach the quality Q, so should nonhuman animals whose capabilities also approach the quality Q.

Third, in perhaps the clearest argument for equality, great apes who possess either full Kantian autonomy or a practical autonomy should be entitled to the same fundamental rights to which humans who entirely lack autonomy are entitled. Placing the rightless legal thing, the bonobo Kanzi, beside an anencephalic 1-day-old human with the legal right to choose to consent or withhold consent to medical treatment highlights the legal aberration that is Kanzi's legal thinghood.

Probably the strongest argument that just being human is necessary for the possession of fundamental equality rights has been offered by Carl Cohen, who has argued that at least moral rights should be limited to all and only human beings. "The issue," said Cohen, "is one of kind" (Cohen 1986, 866). He acknowledged that some humans lack autonomy and the ability to make moral choices. However, because humans as a "kind" possess this ability, it should be imputed to all humans, regardless of their actual abilities. But Cohen's argument can succeed only if the species, *H. sapiens*, can nonarbitrarily be designated as the boundary of a relevant "kind." That is doubtful. Other classifications, some wider, such as animals, vertebrates, mammals, primates, and apes, and at least one narrower—normal adult humans—also contain every fully autonomous human.

As well as being logically flawed, Cohen's argument for group benefits is normatively flawed. It "assumes that we should determine how an individual is to be treated, not on the basis of *its* qualities but on the basis of *other* individuals' qualities" (Rachels 1990, 187). Rachels calls the opposing moral idea "moral individualism" and defines it to mean that "how an individual may be treated is to be determined, not by considering his group memberships, but by considering his own particular characteristics" (Rachels 1990, 173). It is individualism, and not group benefits, that is more consistent with the overarching principles and values of a liberal democracy and that has the firmer basis in present law.

[...]

Will We Affirm or Undermine Our Commitment to Fundamental Human Rights?

The destruction of the legal thinghood even of the great apes, our closest cousins, will necessarily involve a long and difficult struggle. It is the nature of great change to stimulate great opposition. But the anachronistic legal thinghood of the great apes so contradicts outright the overarching principles of equality, liberty, fairness, and rationality in judicial decision making that it will eventually be denied only by those in whom a narrow self-interest predominates.

[...]

Notes

1. *Omichund v. Barker*, 1 Atk. 21, 33 (K.B. 1744).
2. *Tennessee Valley Authority v. Hill*, 437 U.S. 153, 188 (1978). The Endangered Species Act, 16 U.S.C. §§ 1531–43 (1973).
3. *E.g., Youngberg v. Romeo*, 457 U.S. 307, 317 (1982); *Bowers v. Devito*, 686 F.2d 616, 618 (7th Cir. 1982).
4. *Natanson v. Kline*, 350 P.2d 1093, 1104 (Kan. 1960). *See also Stamford Hospital v. Vega*, 674 A.2d 821, 831 (Conn. 1996).
5. *E.g., Rivers v. Katz*, 495 N.E.2d 337, 341, *reargument denied*, 498 N.E.2d 438 (N.Y. 1986); *Schmidt v. Schmidt*, 450 A.2d 421, 422–23 (Pa. Super. 1983) (a 26-year-old woman with Down syndrome with the mental ability of a child between 4 ½ and 8 years can rationally decide whether to choose to visit a parent).

6. *E.g., Thornburgh v. American College of Obstetricians and Gynecologists*, 476 U.S. 747, 778 n.5 (Stevens, J., concurring); *Application of President & Directors of Georgetown College*, 331 F.2d 1010, 1017 (D.C. Cir. 1964); *State v. Wagner*, 752 P.2d 1136, 1178 (Ore. 1988).
7. *People v. Nauton*, 34 Cal. Rptr. 2d 861, 864 (Ct. App. 1994).
8. *Youngberg, supra* note 3, at 315–16.
9. *E.g., Gray v. Romeo*, 697 F. Supp. 580, 587 (D.R.I. 1987); *Conservatorship of Drabick*, 245 Cal. Rptr. 840, 855, *cert. denied sub nom., Drabick v. Drabick*, 488 U.S. 958 (1988); *Superintendent of Belchertown State School v. Saikewicz*, 370 N.E.2d 417, 427, 428 (Mass. 1977); *Eichner v. Dillon*, 426 N.Y.S.2d 517, 542 (App. Div.), *modified* 52 N.Y.2d 363 (1980); *see Conservatorship of Valerie N.*, 707 P.2d 760, 776 (Cal. 1985), citing *Matter of Moe*, 432 N.E.2d 712, 720 (Mass. 1982).
10. *Matter of Guardianship of L.W.*, 482 N.W.2d 60, 69 (Wis. 1992), quoting *Eichner, supra* note 16, at 542. *See also Gray, supra* note 16, at 587; *Matter of Moe, supra* note 16, at 719; *Delio v. Westchester County Medical Center*, 516 N.Y.S.2d 677, 686 (N.Y. App. Div. 1987).
11. *E.g., Gray, supra* note 16, at 587; *Conservatorship of Drabick, supra* note 16, at 855; *Foody v. Manchester Memorial Hospital*, 482 A.2d 713, 718 (Conn. Sup. Ct. 1984); *Matter of Tavel*, 661 A.2d 1061, 1069 (Del. 1995); *Severns v. Wilmington Medical Center, Inc.*, 421 A.2d 1334, 1347 (Del. 1980); *John F. Kennedy Memorial Hospital v. Bludworth*, 452 So.2d 921, 921, 923, 924 (Fla. 1985); *In re Guardianship of Barry*, 445 So.2d 365, 370 (Fla. Dist. Ct. App. 1984); *DeGrella by and through Parrent v. Elston*, 858 S.W.2d, 698, 709 (Ky. 1993); *In re L.H.R.*, 321 S.E.2d 716, 722 (Ga. 1984); *Care and Protection of Beth*, 587 N.E.2d 1377, 1382 (Mass. 1992); *Matter of Conroy*, 486 A.2d 1209, 1229 (N.J. 1985); *In re Grady*, 426 A.2d. 474–75 (N.J. 1981); *In re Quinlan*, 355 A.2d 647, 664 (N.J.), *cert. denied sub nom., Garger v. New Jersey*, 429 U.S. 922 (1976); *Eichner, supra,* note 16, at 546; *Matter of Guardianship of Hamlin*, 689 P.2d 1372, 1376 (Wash. 1984); *In re Colyer*, 660 P.2d 738, 774 (Wash. 1983); *Matter of Guardianship of L.W., supra* note 17, at 67, 68.
12. *E.g., In re L.H.R., supra* note 18 (4-month-old in chronic vegetative state); *Care and Protection of Beth, supra* note 18 (10-month-old in irreversible coma); *Strunk v. Strunk*, 445 S.W.2d 145 (Ky. 1969) (27-year-old with an I.Q. of 35 and a mental age of 6 years); *In re Grady, supra* note 18; *In re Penny N.*, 414 A.2d 541 (N.H. 1980); *Saikewicz, supra* note 16 (67-year-old with an I.Q. of 10 and a mental age of 31 months); *Matter of Guardianship of L.W., supra* note 18, at 68; *In re Guardianship of Barry, supra* note 18 (anencephalic 10-month-old with no cognitive brain function).
13. *E.g., Logan v. Zimmerman Brush Co.*, 455 U.S. 422, 442 (1982) (plurality opinion); *Rinaldi v. Yeager*, 384 U.S. 305, 308–309 (1966); *McLaughlin v. Florida*, 379 U.S. 184, 191 (1964).
14. *E.g., Romer v. Evans*, 116 S. Ct. 1620, 1627–29 (1996); *Skinner, supra* note 34. *See Thoreson v. Penthouse International, Ltd.*, 563 N.Y.S.2d 968, 975 (Sup. Ct. 1990).
15. *E.g., United States v. Virginia*, 116 S. Ct. 2264, 2277–78 (1996), quoting *Mississippi University for Women v. Hogan*, 458 U.S. 718, 725 (1985); *Craig v. Boren*, 429 U.S. 190, 197 (1976). *See Romer, supra* note 35, at 1628.

References

Berlin, I. 1969. Two concepts of liberty. In *Four essays on liberty* (pp. 117–72). Oxford: Oxford University Press.
———. 1998. My intellectual path. *New York Review of Books*, May 14, 53–60.
Cherniak, C. 1985. *Minimal rationality*. Cambridge: MIT Press.
Cohen, C. 1986. The case for the use of animals in biomedical research. *New England Journal of Medicine* 317: 867–70.
D'Amato, A., and Chopra, S. K. 1991. Whales: Their emerging right to life. *American Journal of International Law* 85: 21–62.
Dworkin, R. 1977. *Taking rights seriously*. Cambridge, MA: Harvard University Press.
Feinberg, J. 1966. Duties, rights, and claims. *American Philosophy Quarterly* 3: 37.
Herman, B. 1993. *The practice of moral judgment*. Cambridge, MA: Harvard University Press.
Holmes, O. W., Jr. 1897. The path of the law. *Harvard Law Review* 10: 457–78.
Langer, E. 1997. *The power of mindful learning*. Reading, MA: Addison-Wesley.
McPherson, J. M. 1990. *Abraham Lincoln and the second American revolution*. Oxford: Oxford University Press.
Nino, C. S. 1993. *The ethics of human rights*. Oxford: Oxford University Press.
Oxford Dictionary of Quotations. 1979. (3rd ed.). Oxford: Oxford University Press.
Patterson, O. 1991. *Freedom: Freedom in the making of Western culture*. New York: Basic Books.

Rachels, J. 1990. *Created from animals*. Oxford: Oxford University Press.

Regan, T. 1983. *The case for animal rights*. Berkeley: University of California Press.

Russell, J. 1996. *Agency—Its role in mental development*. Hove, UK: Erlbaum.

Simons, K. W. 1989. Overinclusion and underinclusion: A new model. *UCLA Law Review* 36: 447–89.

Watson, A. 1993. *Legal transplants—An approach to comparative law*. Athens: University of Georgia Press.

Wise, S. M. 1996. The legal thinghood of nonhuman animals. *Boston College Environmental Affairs Law Review* 23(3): 471–546.

———. 1998a. Hardly a revolution—The eligibility of nonhuman animals for dignity-rights in a liberal democracy. *Vermont Law Review* 22: 793–915.

———. 1998b. Recovery of common law damages for emotional distress, loss of society, and loss of companionship for the wrongful death of a companion animal. *Animal Law* 4: 33.

World Charter for Nature. 1982. GA Res. 37/7 Annex UNGAOR, 37th Sess. Suppl. No. 51, UNDO A/37151 (Oct. 28) (preamble). In H. W. Wood, Jr., The United Nations World Charter for Nature: The developing nations' initiative to establish protections for the environment. *Ecology* 12: 977–92.

Wright, W. A. 1993. Treating animals as ends. *Journal of Value Inquiry* 27: 353–66.

83 Book Review of *Rattling the Cage: Toward Legal Rights for Animals* by Steven M. Wise

Richard A. Posner

Richard Posner responds to Wise's arguments by pointing out that Wise has not shown that having cognitive capacity is necessary or sufficient for having legal rights. In Posner's view, Wise is not urging judges to develop doctrines already implicit in legal tradition but rather to "set sail on an uncharted sea without a compass." Posner recommends instead that we build on the liberating potential of legal property, because people tend to protect what they own, and that we extend and more vigorously enforce laws designed to prevent cruelty to animals.[1]

The "animal rights" movement is gathering steam, and Steven Wise is one of the pistons. A lawyer whose practice is the protection of animals, he has now written a book in which he urges courts in the exercise of their common-law powers of legal rulemaking to confer legally enforceable rights on animals, beginning with chimpanzees and bonobos (the two most intelligent primate species).[2]

[. . .]

If Wise is to persuade his chosen audience, he must show how courts can proceed incrementally, building on existing cases and legal concepts, toward his goal of radically enhanced legal protection for animals. Recall the process by which, starting from the unpromising principle that "separate but equal" was constitutional, the Supreme Court outlawed official segregation. First, certain public facilities were held not to be equal; then segregation of law schools was invalidated as inherently unequal because of the importance of the contacts made in law school to a successful legal practice; then segregation of elementary schools was outlawed on the basis of social scientific evidence that this segregation, too, was inherently unequal; then the "separate but equal" principle itself, having been reduced to a husk, was quietly buried and the no-segregation principle of the education cases extended to all public facilities, including rest rooms and drinking fountains.

That is the process that Wise envisages for the animal-rights movement, although the end point is less clear. We have, Wise points out, a robust conception of human rights, and we apply it even to people who by reason of retardation or other mental disability cannot enforce their own rights but need a guardian to do it for them. The evolution of human-rights law has involved not only expanding the number of rights but also expanding the number of rights-holders, notably by adding women and blacks. (Much of Wise's book is about human rights and about the methodology by which judges enlarge human rights in response to changed understandings.) We also have a long history of providing legal protections for animals that recognize their sentience, their emotional capacity, and their capacity to suffer pain; these protections have been growing too.

Wise wants to merge these legal streams by showing that the apes that are most like us genetically, namely the chimpanzees and the bonobos, are also very much like us in their mentation, which exceeds that of human infants and profoundly retarded people. He believes that they are enough like us to be in the direct path of rights expansion. So far as deserving to have rights is concerned, he finds no principled difference between the least mentally able people and the most mentally able animals, as the two groups overlap—or at least too little difference to justify interrupting, at the gateway to the animal kingdom, the expansive rights trend that he has discerned. The law's traditional dichotomy between humans and animals is a vestige of bad science and of a hierarchizing tendency that put men over animals just as it put free men over slaves. Wise does not say how many other animal species besides chimpanzees and bonobos he would like to see entitled, but he makes clear that he regards entitling those two species as a milestone, not as the end of the road.

[. . .]

From his principle of equality Wise deduces that chimpanzees should have the same constitutional rights and other legal rights that small children and severely retarded adults have: the rights to life, to bodily integrity, to subsistence, and to some kind of freedom (how much is unclear), but not the right to vote. He does not discuss whether they should have the right to reproduce. But he is emphatic that since we would not permit invasive or dangerous medical experimentation on small children or severely retarded adults, neither can we permit such experimentation on chimpanzees, no matter how great the benefits for human health.

The framework of Wise's analysis, as we have seen, is the history of extending rights to formerly excluded persons. Working within that conventional lawyerly framework, he seeks to convince his readers that chimpanzees have the essential attribute of persons, which he believes is the level of mentation that we call consciousness, but (to avoid a *reductio ad absurdum*) that computers do not have it. In short, anyone who has consciousness should have rights; chimpanzees are conscious; therefore, chimpanzees should have rights.

How convincing is the analysis? [. . .] It is the major premise that presents the immediate difficulty with this syllogistic approach to the question of animal rights. Cognitive capacity is certainly *relevant* to rights; it is a precondition of some rights, such as the right to vote. But most people would not think it either a necessary or a sufficient condition of having legally enforceable rights, and Wise has not attempted to take on their arguments. Many people believe, for example, that a one-day-old human fetus, though it has no cognitive capacity, should have a right to life; and, after the first trimester, the Supreme Court permits the fetus to be accorded a qualified such right, though the cognitive capacity of a second- or even third-trimester fetus is very limited. And Wise is not distressed at the thought of destroying a "conscious" computer,[3] showing that even he does not take completely seriously the notion that rights follow cognitive capacity. Most people would think it distinctly odd to proportion animal rights to animal intelligence, as Wise wishes to do, implying that dolphins, parrots, and ravens are entitled to more legal protection than horses (or most monkeys), and perhaps that the laws forbidding cruelty to animals should be limited to the most intelligent animals, inviting the crack, "They don't have syntax, so we can eat them."[4] And most of us would think it downright offensive to give greater rights to monkeys, let alone to computers, than to retarded people, upon a showing that the monkey or the computer has a greater cognitive capacity than a profoundly retarded human being, unless perhaps the human being has no brain function at all above the autonomic level, that is, is in a vegetative state. Cognition and rights-deservedness are not interwoven as tightly as Wise believes, though he is not, of course, the first to believe this.[5]

There is a related objection to his approach. Wise wants judges, in good common-law fashion, to move step by step, and for the first step simply to declare that chimpanzees have legal rights. But judges asked to step onto a new path of doctrinal growth want to have some idea of where the path leads, even if it would be unreasonable to insist that the destination be clearly seen. Wise gives them no idea.

[. . .]

But what is meant by liberating animals and giving them the rights of human beings of the same cognitive capacity? Does an animal's right to life place a duty on human beings to protect animals from being killed by other animals? Is capacity to feel pain sufficient cognitive capacity to entitle an animal to at least the most elementary human rights? What kinds of habitats must we create and maintain for all the rights-bearing animals in the United States? Does human convenience have *any* weight in deciding what rights an animal has? Can common-law courts actually work out a satisfactory regime of animal rights without the aid of legislatures? When human rights and animal rights collide, do human rights have priority, and if so, why? And what is to be done when animal rights collide with each other, as they do with laws that by protecting wolves endanger sheep? Must entire species of animals be "segregated" from each other and from human beings, and, if so, what does "separate but equal" mean in this context? May we "discriminate" against animals, and if so, how much? Do species have "rights," or just individual animals, and if the latter, does this mean that according special legal protection for endangered species is a denial of equal protection? Is domestication a form of enslavement? Wise does not try to answer any of these questions. He is asking judges to set sail on an uncharted sea without a compass.

The underlying problem is the practitioner-oriented framework of Wise's discussion, with its heavy reliance on argument from analogy and on the syllogism described above. Analogy gives him his major premise, and the syllogism takes him from there to his conclusion. Chimpanzees are like human beings; therefore, so far as Wise is concerned,[6] giving animals rights is like giving black people the rights of whites. But chimpanzees are like human beings in some respects but not in others that may be equally or more relevant to the question of whether to give chimpanzees rights, and legal rights have been designed to serve the needs and interests of human beings having the usual human capacities and so make a poor fit with the needs and interests of animals.

Wise's book illustrates the severe limitations of legal reasoning. Because judges (and therefore the lawyers who argue to them) are reluctant for political and professional reasons to acknowledge that they are expanding or otherwise changing the law, rather than just applying it, departures from existing law are treated as applications of it guided by analogy or deduction. Wise either is playing this game, or has been fooled by it. He makes it seem that animal rights in the expansive form that he conceives them are nothing new—they just plug a hole unaccountably left in the existing case law on rights. Animals just got overlooked, as blacks and women had once been overlooked. But correcting a logical error, removing an inconsistency—in short, tidying up doctrine—is not what would be involved in deciding that chimpanzees have the same rights as three-year-old human beings. What Wise's book really does, rather than supplying the reasons for change, is supply the rationalizations that courts persuaded on other grounds to change the law might use to conceal the novelty of their action. Judges are not easily fooled by a lawyer who argues for a change in the law on the basis that it is no change at all but is merely the recognition of a logical entailment of existing law. The value of such an argument lies in giving judges a professionally respectable ground for rationalizing the change, a ground that minimizes its novelty. But judges must have reasons for wanting to make the change, and this is where a lawyer's brief, of which Wise's book is an extension, tends to fall down.

[. . .]

There is a sad poverty of imagination in an approach to animal protection that can think of it only on the model of the civil rights movement. It is a poverty that reflects the blinkered approach of the traditional lawyer, afraid to acknowledge novelty and therefore unable to think clearly about the reasons pro or con a departure from the legal status quo. It reflects also the extent to which liberal lawyers remain in thrall to the constitutional jurisprudence of the Warren Court and insensitive to the "liberating" potential of commodification. One way to protect animals is to make them property, because people tend to protect what they own.

[. . .]

Wise has overlooked not only the possibilities of commodification, but also, and less excusably, an approach to the question of animal welfare that is more conservative, methodologically as well as politically, but possibly more efficacious, than rights-mongering. That is simply to extend, and more vigorously to enforce, laws designed to prevent gratuitous cruelty to animals.

[. . .]

No doubt we should want to do more than merely avoid gratuitous cruelty to animals. [. . .] But neither philosophical reflection nor a vocabulary of rights is likely to add anything to the sympathetic emotions that narratives of the mistreatment of animals are likely to engender in most of us.

I close with a recent judicial opinion by one of our ablest federal judges, Michael Boudin, in a heart-rending "animal rights" case.[7] The plaintiff had rescued an orphaned raccoon, whom she named Mia and raised as a pet. Mia lived in a cage attached to the plaintiff's home for seven years until she was seized and destroyed by the state in the episode that provoked the suit. A police officer noticed Mia in her cage and reported her to the local animal control officer, who discovered that the plaintiff did not have a permit for the animal, as required by state law. The police then forcibly seized Mia from her cage after a struggle with the plaintiff, carried her off, and had her killed and tested for rabies. Testing for rabies in a raccoon requires that the animal be killed, and a supposed epidemic of raccoon rabies had led the state (Rhode Island) to require the testing of raccoons to whom humans (in this case the plaintiff) had been exposed.[8] Mia tested negative, but of course it was too late for Mia.

The plaintiff claimed that the state had deprived her of property, namely Mia, without notice and an opportunity for a hearing and thus had violated the Due Process Clause of the Fourteenth Amendment. Property for these purposes depends on state law, and the court found, undoubtedly correctly, that Rhode Island does not recognize property rights in wild animals unless a permit has been granted,[9] and fear of rabies had deterred the authorities from granting permits for raccoons. To be owned is the antithesis of being a rights-holder. But if Rhode Island had a more generous conception of property in wild animals, the police might have been deterred from what appears to have been the high-handed, indeed arbitrary, treatment of Mia. As the court explained, it does not seem that the plaintiff had been "exposed" to Mia in the relevant statutory sense: There was no indication that the raccoon had bitten the plaintiff or that its saliva had otherwise entered the plaintiff's bloodstream.[10] And since Mia had been in a cage for seven years,[11] it was unlikely, to say the least, that she was infected with rabies. Moreover, from the standpoint of controlling the spread of rabies, there was no reason to worry about Mia infecting the plaintiff, since people do not spread rabies. Mia was dangerous, if at all, only to the plaintiff, who was happy to assume the risk. The refusal to allow her to keep Mia made no sense at all, but there was no constitutional issue because Mia was not the plaintiff's "property" within the meaning of the Due Process Clause of the Fourteenth Amendment.

This is just one example, and it does not prove that animals benefit less by having human-type "rights" and thus being "free" than by being "imprisoned" and by being "reduced" to "mere" property. I note in this connection that the average life span of an "alley cat" is only about two years, and that of a well-cared-for pet cat at least 12 years, but that is just another example, and against it may be placed the sad fate of the laboratory animal, who is the laboratory's property. The most aggressive implementations of animal-rights thinking would undoubtedly benefit animals more than commodification and a more determined program of enforcing existing laws against cruelty to animals. But those implementations are unlikely, so the modest alternatives are worth serious consideration. We may overlook this simple point, however much we love animals, if we listen too raptly to the siren song of "animal rights."

Notes

1. Steven M. Wise. *Rattling the Cage: Toward Legal Rights for Animals* (2000).
2. These are closely related species, and Wise discusses them more or less interchangeably. For the sake of brevity, I will generally refer only to chimpanzees, but what I say about them applies equally to bonobos.
3. *See* Wise, *supra* note 1 p. 268.
4. *See* Richard Sorabji. Animal Minds and Human Morals: The Origins of the Western Debate (1993) note 3, p. 2.
5. E.g., Bruce A. Ackerman. Social Justice in the Liberal State 80 (1980) ("The rights of the talking ape are more secure than those of the human vegetable.") *But cf.* Wise, pp. 262–3.
6. *See* Wise, *supra* note 2 pp. 123–4.
7. Bilida v. McCleod, 211 F.3d 166 (1st Cir. 2000).
8. *Id.* p. 169.
9. *Id.* pp. 173–4.
10. *Id.* p. 169 n.2.
11. *Id.* p. 169.

84 The Dangerous Claims of the Animal Rights Movement

Richard A. Epstein

Richard Epstein is unconvinced by the arguments of Wise and others for the personhood of great apes. Animals lack the capacity for higher cognitive language and thought that characterizes human beings as a species. Epstein points out a number of unfortunate consequences which would ensue if we accepted the claims of the animal rights movement. He concludes that it is appropriate for animals to be treated as property.

The Separation of the Species

Behind [the] traditional debates lies one key assumption that today's vocal defenders of animal rights brand as "species-ist." Descriptively, they have a point. Sometimes the classical view treated animals as a distinctive form of property; at other times animals became the object of public regulation. In both settings, however, the legal rules were imposed largely for the benefit of human beings, either in their role as owners of animals or as part of that ubiquitous public-at-large that benefitted from their preservation. None of our laws dealing with animals put the animal front and center as the *holder* of property rights in themselves—rights good against the human beings who protect animals in some cases and slaughter them in others.

Our species-ist assumption is savagely attacked by the new generation of animal rights activists, whose clarion call for *person*hood—the choice of terms is telling—is a declaration of independence of animals from their human owners. Their theme generates tremendous resonance, but it is often defended on several misguided grounds.

First, they claim that we now have a greater understanding of the complex behaviors and personalities of animals, especially those in the higher orders. Even though the fields of sociobiology and animal behavior have made enormous strides in recent years, the basic point is an old one. Descartes got it wrong when he said that animals moved about like the ghost in the machine. The older law understood that animals can be provoked or teased; that they are capable of committing deliberate or inadvertent acts. Sure, animals may not be able to talk, but they have extensive powers of anticipation and rationalization; they can form and break alliances; they can show anger, annoyance, and remorse; they can store food for later use; they respond to courtship and aggression; they can engage in acts of rape and acts of love; they respect and violate territories. Indeed, in many ways their repertoire of emotions is quite broad, rivaling that of human beings.

But one difference stands out: through thick and thin, animals do not have the capacity of higher cognitive language and thought that characterizes human beings as a species, even if not shared at all times by all its individual members. We should never pretend that the case against recognizing animal rights is easier than it really is. But by the same token, we cannot accept the facile argument that our *new* understanding of animals leads to a new appreciation of their rights. The fundamentals have long been recognized by the lawyers and writers who fashioned the old legal order.

Second, animal activists such as Wise remind us of the huge overlap in DNA between human beings and chimpanzees. The fact itself is incontrovertible. Yet the implications we should draw from that fact are not. The observed behavioral differences between humans and chimpanzees are still what they have always been; they are neither increased nor decreased by the number of common genes. The evolutionary biologist should use this evidence to determine when the lines of chimps separated from that of human beings, but the genetic revelation does not establish that chimps and bonobos are able to engage in the abstract thought that would enable them to present on their own behalf the claims for personhood that Wise and others make on their behalf. The number of common genes humans have with other primates is also very high, as it is even with other animals that diverged from human beings long before the arrival of primates. The question to answer is not how many genes humans and chimpanzees have in common; it is how many traits they have in common. The large number of common genes helps explain empirically the rapid rate of evolution. It does not narrow the enormous gulf that a few genes are able to create.

Third, Wise and other defenders of personhood for animals have line-drawing problems of their own. If that higher status is offered to chimps and bonobos, then what about orangutans and gorillas? Or horses, dogs, and cows? All of these animals have a substantial level of cognitive capacity, and wide range of emotions, even if they do not have the same advanced cognitive skills of the chimps and bonobos. Does personhood extend this far, and if not, then why does it extend as far as Wise and others would take it? The frequent analogy of chimpanzees to slaves hardly carries the day, given the ability of individuals from different human populations to interbreed with each other and to perform the same set of speech and communicative acts. Nor is it particularly persuasive to note that individuals with serious neurological or physical impairments often have far less cognitive and emotional capacity than normal chimpanzees or dogs. For one, we in fact *do* recognize that different rules apply to individuals in extreme cases, allowing, for example, the withdrawal of feeding tubes from individuals in a permanent vegetative state. In addition, important human relations intrude into the deliberations. These human beings, whatever their impairments, are the fathers, mothers, sisters, and brothers of other human beings in ways that chimpanzees and bonobos are not.

Fourth, the animal rights activists often attack the question from the other side by offering bland assurances that people today do not need to rely on animal labor and products in order to survive as human beings. Typically, animal rights activists put their claims in universalistic terms. But in so doing they argue as though in primitive times animals and agriculture fell into separate compartments, when in truth they were part of a seamless enterprise. Animal power was necessary to clear the woods, to fertilize and plow the fields, and to harvest the crop. Meat and dairy products were an essential part of primitive diets. The early society that did not rely on animals for food, for labor, for warfare was the society that did not survive to yield the heightened moral sensibilities of today. It was the society that perished from its want of food, clothing, and shelter—a high price to pay for a questionable moral principle. And, if this new regime is implemented, the animal rights movement condemns millions of less fortunate people around the globe to death today. Just this past March the *New York Times* ran a painful story about the question of whether the preservation of gorillas in Africa placed at risk the subsistence economies of the nearby tribes.

Today, perhaps people fortunate enough to live in prosperous lands could live without having to use animals for consumption or labor, but the long-term agenda, if not the immediate demands, of the animal rights activists cut far deeper. For activists such as Gary Francione of Rutgers-Newark Law School, the mere ownership of animals is a sin: no pets, no circuses, no milk, no cheese, no horses to ride, no dogs, cats, birds, or fish around the house. These relationships are condemned in good Marxist terms as being based on power differentials, and thus are barred: the animals who seem to like being pandered to suffer from, as it were, a form of false consciousness.

Fifth, more ominously, if pets are out, so too is the use of animals for medical science. In dealing with this issue, Wise is brutally explicit in describing what it is for chimpanzees to suffer in isolation the final effects of the ravages of AIDS. No one could argue that this conduct did not cry out for justification. Yet by the same token, the question is could the conduct itself be justified? To answer that question in human terms, one has to look at the other side of the equation, and ask what has been learned from these experiments, what wonder drugs have been created, what scourges of human (and animal) kind have been eliminated. I do not pretend to be an expert on this subject, but so long as the vaccine for smallpox comes from cows or the insulin for treating diabetes comes from pigs, then I am hard pressed to defend any categorical rule that bans all use of animals in medical experimentation. One has to have an accurate accounting of what is on the other side, and on that issue the silence of the animal rights activists is deafening.

The argument here has its inescapable moral dimension. No matter what one's intellectual orientation, no one would—or should—dispute the proposition that animals should not be used in research if the same (or better) results could be achieved at the same (or lower) cost by test tubes and computer simulations alone. Nor would any one want future surgeons to try out new techniques on animals if they could be risklessly performed on human beings the first time out. But, alas, neither of these happy eventualities come close to being a partial truth. It is easy to identify many situations where human advancement comes only at the price of animal suffering. How to proceed then turns on the balance between these two unquantifiable considerations.

[. . .]

Sixth, medical research is not all that is at stake once the asserted parity between animal rights and human rights is acknowledged. Our entire system of property allows owners to transform the soil and to exclude others. Now if the first human being may exclude subsequent arrivals, what happens when animals are given similar rights? Their dens, burrows, nests, and hives long antedate human arrival. The principle of first possession should therefore block us from clearing the land for farms, homes, and factories unless we can find ways to make just compensation to each individual animal for its own losses. But I fail to see how this system would work, for to transfer animals from one habitat to another only unlawfully displaces animals at the second location. The blunt truth is that the arrival of human beings necessarily results in the death of some earlier animal occupants, even if it increases the welfare of others who learn to live in harmony with us. So if prior in time is higher in right, then we should fold up our tents right now and let the animals fight it out for territory, just as if we had never arrived on the face of the globe.

[. . .]

The Current Legal Scene

Animal owners have recovered large awards for the malpractice of veterinarians. The damages paid are meant to cover not only the market value of the animal but the loss of companionship to the owner. This is simply solid economics—for what the defenders of animal rights do not tell is that this outcome derives its power from recognizing that the actual losses *to the owner* exceed the market value of the animal, precisely because they include these nonmonetary elements. [. . .] These cases therefore gain their resonance from a traditional property rights conception.

[. . .]

A similar logic also applies to a 1998 decision in the District of Columbia, *Animal Legal Defense Fund, Inc. v. Glickman.* Here a zoo visitor was held to have "standing" to sue under the Animal Welfare Act of 1985, which provided generally that animals' keepers must meet conditions of confinement that ensure "the psychological well being of primates." That objective is certainly laudable in simple human terms, even if the new animal rights activists would shut down all zoos. But allowing a zoo visitor to sue to protect the zoo animals made it crystal clear that the rights vindicated by the action were those of the individual plaintiff, and not those of the animal. And no one doubts that Congress could reverse that decision by a statutory amendment that allows only for public inspection and enforcement of the provisions of the Act.

In sum, no one can deny the enormous political waves created by animal rights activists. [. . .] It is, however, one thing to raise social conscience about the status of animals. It is quite another to raise the status of animals to asserted parity with human beings. That move, if systematically implemented, would pose a mortal threat to human society that few human beings would, or should, accept. We have quite enough difficulty in persuading or coercing human beings to respect the rights of their fellow humans to live in peace with each other. [. . .] We should not undermine, as would surely be the case, the liberty and dignity of human beings by treating animals as their moral equals and legal peers. [. . .] Animals are properly property. It is not, nor has it ever been, immoral for human beings, as a species, to prefer their own kind. What lion would deny it?

85 U.S. Law and Animal Experimentation
A Critical Primer

Stephen R. Latham

Every country's law permits medical experimentation on animals. While some countries protect particular kinds of animals from being subject to experimentation—notably great apes and endangered species—very few place concrete limitations on what researchers may cause animals to suffer, given sufficient scientific justification. What laws do, instead, is establish standards for the humane treatment and housing of animals in labs, and they encourage researchers to limit or seek alternatives to the use of animals, when doing that is consistent with the scientific goals of their research. The result, of course, is that no existing regulatory scheme is satisfactory to opponents of animal research. The law, in their view, does nothing more than make the animal research scientist into a sort of James Bond villain: superficially polite, offering fine housing and well-prepared cuisine even to those whom he intends, eventually, to kill.

Of course, the goals of animal experimentation law seem much more reasonable if one accepts that research on animals is both important for medical progress and morally permissible. On those assumptions, it makes a great deal of sense for the law to aim primarily at limiting unnecessary animal suffering even as it licenses scientifically justified experimentation. U.S. law accepts those assumptions and adopts that aim.

The system that has evolved in the United States combines elements of sometimes competing regulatory philosophies. The result is a complex, multilayered system that addresses the most important concerns, but, partly because of historical accident, also leaves some gaps. Even proponents of medical research on animals can see obvious ways in which the regulatory structure could be changed to benefit animals. Perhaps more important, though, is the fact that the existing regulatory structure, imperfect though it may be, is elastic enough to accommodate substantial changes that could reduce unnecessary animal suffering.

Multiple Regulatory Approaches

Animal welfare laws must address three main ways in which unnecessary animal suffering can occur in the context of medical experimentation. First, such suffering can occur when a given research protocol is not well justified scientifically. An experiment that was so badly designed that it could never generate any useful scientific knowledge would never warrant animal suffering. Harder cases result when the amount of suffering is ratcheted down, or the experiment's potential to generate useful knowledge is ratcheted up. A legal regime concerned with avoiding this kind of unnecessary suffering can opt to trust in the judgment of each individual research scientist, or empower someone besides the researcher to make at least some baseline assessment of the scientific value of each new animal research protocol. It can also provide information and guidance to researchers or overseers to improve their decisions.

Second, unnecessary suffering can occur when the amount of animal suffering induced by an experiment is not strictly required to conduct the experiment—perhaps because more animals are used than are necessary; or because less sentient animals could be substituted for more sentient ones, or computer or tissue models substituted for animals entirely; or because crude experimental procedures are producing avoidable stress or pain. A legal framework seeking to avoid these kinds of unnecessary suffering will encourage or require researchers to use the three Rs: *reduce* (the number of animals used in experiments), *replace* (animals with nonanimals, higher-order animals with lower), and *refine* (experimental procedures causing pain or distress).[1]

Third, unnecessary suffering can occur outside the actual research protocol yet still in the research setting because of inappropriate animal handling, housing, and feeding practices. A legal regime seeking to avoid this kind of suffering will dictate humane standards for animal housing and care.

Given these goals, what sort of regulatory scheme would be best at realizing them? One can imagine a variety of available approaches, from strong, centralized state regulation and monitoring of all experimentation to a hands-off reliance on professional self-regulation among laboratory researchers. On the world stage, the United Kingdom is closest to taking the former approach, Japan to the latter. U.S. law falls somewhere in the middle, in part because U.S. law in this area is in fact the result of a gradual, decades-long merging of the government regulatory and professional self-regulatory approaches.[2]

The government regulatory approach is embodied in the sprawling, strange, and often amended Animal Welfare Act of 1966. In its original form, the AWA was designed to control pet breeding and sale practices; it was passed, in part, as a result of public outcry about the mistreatment of dogs sold to laboratories. As amended, it governs the treatment of animals in a wide range of settings, from pet shops to circuses and from zoos to laboratories. Its enforcement is delegated to the U.S. Department of Agriculture's Animal and Plant Health Inspection Service, whose inspectors make unannounced site visits to research facilities. Violations uncovered on such visits can result in fines and even, in extreme cases, criminal prosecution. The most common complaint about enforcement under the AWA is that it is rigid and mechanistic.

Because of its historical roots in concern for pets, the AWA's reach is confined to warm-blooded animals, and it contains special regulations addressed to certain animal favorites: dogs, cats, rabbits, and monkeys. Its animal experimentation regulations apply to any school or research facility that purchases or transports live animals in interstate commerce or that receives federal funding. But in fact the law has never reached the bulk of warm-blooded animals actually used in research. Concern about high regulatory costs—and about possible delay in creating guidelines for other, more popular animals—led the USDA to exclude laboratory rats and mice from its oversight from as early as 1970. In spite of lobbying efforts in the 1980s by proanimal groups, a congressional amendment to the AWA in 2002 legally formalized the agency's longtime practice, excluding rats, mice, and birds from the definition of "animal."[3]

In general, the law and its implementing regulations have focused on setting demanding, detailed standards for animal housing and basic standards for pain control. It supports only minimal review of the scientific merit of research protocols, bur it requires researchers to make efforts to "reduce, replace, and refine."

The self-regulatory approach to animal research regulation is embodied in the National Institutes of Health's *Guide for the Care and Use of Laboratory Animals*.[4] The *Guide* has existed in some version since 1963, when it was introduced as a voluntary set of professional standards for laboratory animal research. Today, the *Guide's* standards are mandatory for all research facilities receiving federal funds. The *Guide* covers the treatment of all vertebrates, which means that, at least in federally funded research, it closes many of the gaps left open by the AWA. Not only are rats, mice, and birds covered, but also cold-blooded vertebrates like zebra fish—currently the go-to animal for laboratory studies of pain and nerve function.

The change in the *Guide's* status to a rulebook has altered its content somewhat. Earlier editions' expansive aspirational goals have given way in later editions to more readily applicable rules. There has also been considerable pressure to get the AWA's regulatory requirements and the *Guide's* standards to match, since all federally funded researchers are bound by both. Indeed, today, the two sets of standards are, if not identical, at least compatible with one another. But in general, where the AWA regulations are more rigidly prescriptive, the *Guide* permits lab veterinarians to use their professional judgment in applying general standards to particular species or protocols.

> Clearly there is room for reform. If the AWA were amended to include rats, mice, and birds, for example, that would be a major step toward ensuring the humane treatment of all animals in public and private labs.

Since the 1980s, both the AWA and the *Guide* have attempted to assure oversight of animal research primarily by mandating the establishment, at each research institution, of an institutional animal care and use committee. The law mandates that each IACUC include among its members a veterinarian who will attend to the needs of the animals on site, an expert in the scientific use of lab animals, a person (from within the research institution or outside it) without such scientific expertise, and a community member who is unaffiliated with the research institution and can represent the views of the public. The IACUC is charged with reviewing all proposed animal research protocols, with ensuring that researchers make efforts to employ the three Rs, with overseeing and reporting on laboratory compliance with regulations relating to animal housing and care, and with answering complaints about the treatment of animals. Each IACUC is also empowered to require changes to experimental protocols or to laboratory animal care procedures and even to suspend research activities.

Federal standards are full of specific requirements for different kinds of studies, but in general, it is fair to say that they offer the most concrete guidance on questions of animal housing and care. The regulations include detailed discussions of square footage, exercise requirements, room temperature, and more. Considerably less guidance is offered on issues of protocol evaluation and implementation of the three Rs.

Of course, this is exactly what might be expected given the incredible volume and variety of animal research in the United States. A central authority can say a lot about how to house and feed monkeys, mice, and zebra fish, and expert advice on those issues will apply to all monkeys, mice, and zebra fish in every lab, no matter what protocols they are being used for. But questions about the other possible sources of unnecessary animal suffering—the scientific justification of a given protocol, or the ways in which animal suffering connected to a given protocol might be avoided or reduced—are too numerous and varied to be answerable in advance by a central authority. With regard to those highly fact-specific questions, U.S. law relies on the expert judgment of local IACUCs.

It is no coincidence that this kind of reliance on decentralized expert committees is also the salient feature of U.S. law governing research on human subjects. The federal Common Rule,[5] faced with a similar diversity of research protocols to evaluate, regulate, and modify, uses the same tactics as the AWA: it mandates creating research oversight committees (institutional review boards), specifies that their membership should include both relevant expertise and community representation, and empowers them to make and enforce a range of judgments about particular experimental protocols.

While the many IACUCs are expected to exercise independent judgment with regard to the scientific issues brought before them, the U.S. government does its best to inform the judgment by providing them with educational resources. The Public Health Service and the Department of Agriculture websites are full of guidance documents and educational resources for laboratory researchers and for IACUC members. There are documents, for example, with specific ideas about how and when to substitute lower-order animals for higher-order animals, and other documents providing up-to-date scientific news about newly developed computer models that can substitute, in some cases, for animal experimentation.

Finally, just as in the human subjects research world, federal regulations are quite commonly supplemented by private education and accreditation. Many research facilities seek accreditation by the Association for the Assessment and Accreditation of Laboratory Animal Care, a professional association of veterinarians and laboratory scientists. AAALAC provides education and does prearranged site inspections of labs once every three years. Educational and inspection standards are built largely around the requirements of the *Guide,* and the NIH accepts AAALAC accreditation as prima facie evidence of a facility's compliance with the *Guide's* requirements.

Toward Reform: Accountability, Uniformity, Balance

The system of decentralized oversight by local IACUCs has several obvious advantages: it permits oversight by people with knowledge of the local researchers and laboratory facilities; it allows IACUCs to develop specialized knowledge, well tailored to the research being done at their facilities; and it is likely more speedy than any alternative program of centralized governmental research oversight would be. On the other hand, the decentralization of oversight has given rise to a number of problems—which, not surprisingly, are similar to those that beset the IRB system in human subjects research.

First, there is a problem of transparency and accountability. IACUCs are for the most part fairly anonymous. Hardly anyone not directly involved in animal research knows that they exist, much less who their members are. And of course, their members are not elected or in any other way publicly accountable for the decisions they make. Most IACUC decisions do not take the form of opinions or any other form of substantive, publishable decision, but of recommendations to researchers for piecemeal alteration of protocols. A central repository of IACUC minutes, and of policies adopted by different IACUCs, might both increase accountability and stimulate new ideas by creating cross talk between IACUCs. But any such repository would have to be created with an eye toward preserving researchers' intellectual property.

Second, decentralization almost necessarily gives rise to a lack of uniformity in decision-making and in quality of research oversight. One IACUC may conclude that a protocol involves unnecessarily harsh treatment of animals or presents an opportunity for substitution of nonanimal models; another may view the original protocol as unproblematic and requiring no amendment. A number of studies have shown that similar protocols are treated quite differently by different IACUCs.[6] It is unclear what the implications of such findings are. Do they reveal that IACUCs have differing standards relating to animal welfare? That they judge similar protocols differently when they are presented by different researchers? Or some combination of these factors? In any case, enforced uniformity across IACUCs is a dangerous solution to propose for the problem of varying standards, in the absence of clear knowledge about whose standards are appropriate—and whose would be enforced.

A third complaint about the decentralized approach to animal-research regulation involves the perception that the U.S. government is too deferential to local IACUCs and does not take the task of auditing labs sufficiently seriously. In the early 2000s, there were some high-profile allegations made by whistleblowers from the USDA's Animal and Plant Health Inspection Service (APHIS) that audit findings were deliberately being watered down to be less critical than the field officers originally intended them to be.[7] U.S. audits of APHIS confirmed allegations of lax auditing in some regions of the country.[8] The obvious reform here is to better fund and train both the regulatory overseers and those who audit their performance.

There are other important criticisms of the U.S. regulatory regime not directly connected to its choice of decentralized decision-making. First, there is the question of scientific justification for animal suffering. The AWA does not ask IACUCs to balance animal suffering against the scientific merit or promise of any given experiment. Instead, it asks IACUCs to ensure only that any given protocol has scientific merit and that any animal suffering the protocol induces is strictly necessary to that science. The result is that any study that will advance science, even in a very small way, can be used to justify tremendous amounts of animal suffering, as long as the suffering is necessary to the advance. Though they do seek to modify studies via use of the three Rs, IACUCs almost never reject protocols.

Finally, and most importantly, there is the issue of which animals are protected. As already mentioned, the hundreds of thousands of rats, mice, and birds used in private, nonfederally funded labs are not subject to any federal regulation. (Some individual states' anticruelty statutes may apply in some cases, but there is very limited case law in the area.) Excluded, also, are cold-blooded animals. This means that there is no federal legal pressure on private firms such as drug companies to reduce or refine animal use, or to replace animals with computer or tissue models—a strategy that may be particularly feasible in studies of toxicology or drug metabolization.

Even in federally funded facilities, the living conditions of rats, mice, and birds are not subject to the USDA's APHIS inspection; only in AAALAC-accredited facilities is there oversight beyond self-reporting, and AAALAC does scheduled inspections only once every three years. Rats and mice, it should be stressed, are the most commonly used laboratory animals. In addition, U.S. law offers no protection for invertebrate, cold-blooded animals such as cephalopods. By contrast, Europe has recently moved to protect cephalopods in light of their manifest intelligence and sentience. Nor does U.S. law prevent research on great apes, or ban (though it does regulate) the use of wild-caught animals. And the United States is one of only two governments in the world that still permits invasive research on chimpanzees, though the scope of federal funding for chimp research has recently been sharply limited.[9]

Clearly there is room for reform. Some needed reform involves stepping up research oversight. If the AWA were amended to include rats, mice, and birds, for example, that would be a major step toward ensuring the humane treatment of all animals in public and private labs. In addition, the inspection rate for facilities could be more frequent. Publicly funded U.S. labs are inspected by APHIS about once a year, by their own IACUCs twice a year, and by AAALAC (if they choose to be AAALAC-certified) once every three years. Compare this to the U.K. system of inspecting about once a month. Other reforms could involve improving rigid and not-terribly-useful existing regulations, like cage-size requirements currently based on animals' body size rather than on their behavioral needs. Most significantly, the law could be reformed to permit a more explicit balancing of harms to animals (including both suffering and death) against the scientific gains at which the research aims. Empowering IACUCs to engage in such balancing is hardly radical; IRBs, for example, are already empowered to engage in such balancing in the human subjects research area, and this has not caused research to grind to a halt. Such a reform would require us to confront directly the question of how much suffering humans can impose on other species in return for small but real gains in knowledge.

Finally, a great deal can be accomplished even within an unchanged legal regime. The most urgent need is for more to be done to implement the three Rs. The familiar calls for better education about replacement techniques and more aggressive IACUC intervention on behalf of reduction and refinement are, of course, well justified. But even more dramatic reduction might be achieved if the goal of reduction were pursued not only within but also across protocols. There might be significant gains from putting animal-sharing procedures in place at the institutional level. At the moment, animals are commonly euthanized whenever the particular research project they're involved in comes to an end, without regard to the animal's age or health status. If a protocol involves attempts to breed, for example, mice with particular genetic traits, the pups born without those traits are routinely euthanized. If research facilities could work with researchers to use healthy animals from one study in another, rather than default to their euthanization, then fewer animals would need to be bred for suffering.

Notes

1. The widely accepted "Three Rs" terminology was first introduced into the animal research literature in W. M. S. Russell and R. L. Burch, *The Principals of Human Experimentation Technique* (London: Methuen, 1959).
2. A detailed account of the confluence of these two streams of regulation (to which my brief discussion here is heavily indebted) is provided by L. Carbone, *What Animals Want: Expertise and Advocacy in Laboratory Animal Welfare Policy* (Oxford, UK: Oxford University Press, 2004), p. 34ff.

3. Wild-caught rats and mice are included in the regulations. For more detail, see Carbone, *What Animals Want,* p. 69ff.

4. National Research Council, *Guide for the Care and Use of Laboratory Animals*, 8th ed. (Washington, DC: National Academics Press, 2011).

5. U.S. Department of Health and Human Services, 45 CFR 46.

6. See, for example, S. Plous and H. Herzog, "Reliability of Protocol Reviews for Animals Research," *Science* 293 (2001): 608–9.

7. See, for example, the statement of Dr. Isis Johnson-Brown, USDA whistleblower, alleging regulatory inaction on her report criticizing cage conditions at the Oregon Primate Center, at http://www.all-creatures.org/saen/articles-statementofijb.html, accessed October 2, 2012.

8. USDA Office of Inspector General, Western Region, "Audit Report: APHIS Animal Care Program Inspection and Enforcement Activities," Report No. 33002–3-SF, September 2005, p. i, http://www.usda.gov/oig/webdocs/33002–03-SF.pdf.

9. See Institute of Medicine, *Committee on the Use of Chimpanzees in Biomedical and Behavioral Research: Assessing the Necessity* (Washington, DC: National Academies Press, 2011); B. M. Altevogt et al., "Guiding Limited Use of Chimpanzees in Research," *Science* 335 (2012): 41–2.

86 Personhood, Animals, and the Law

Christine M. Korsgaard

The idea that all the entities in the world may be, for legal and moral purposes, divided into the two categories of "persons" and "things" comes down to us from the tradition of Roman law. In the law, a "person" is essentially the subject of rights and obligations, while a thing may be owned as property. In ethics, a person is an object of respect, to be valued for her own sake, and never to be used as a mere means to an end, while a thing has only a derivative value, and may be used as a means to some person's ends. This bifurcation is unfortunate because it seems to leave us with no alternative but to categorize everything as either a person or a thing. Yet some of the entities that give rise to the most vexing ethical problems are exactly the ones that do not seem to fit comfortably into either category. For various, different kinds of reasons, it seems inappropriate to categorize a fetus, a non-human animal, the environment, or an object of great beauty, as a person, but neither does it seem right to say of such things that they are to be valued only as means.

In the law, the bifurcation between persons and things or persons and property leaves non-human animals in an especially awkward position. Animals, or at least many of them, are sentient beings with lives of their own and capacities for enjoyment and suffering that seem to make some sort of claim on us. Some have very sophisticated cognitive capacities, including some sense of self. But because animals are classified as property, efforts to secure them some legal protections have been of mixed success and have introduced a certain level of incoherence into the laws. In the face of this, some animal rights advocates have suggested that all cognitively sophisticated animals, or all animals generally, ought to be re-categorized as legal persons.

But it may be argued that those who make this proposal are ignoring something important about the concept of a person. It has generally been assumed that "personhood," whatever it is, is, or is based on, an attribute that is characteristic of human beings, and not of the other animals. In the philosophical tradition, the most common candidate for the attribute that establishes "personhood" is rationality, but understood in a specific sense. Rationality is sometimes loosely identified with the ability to choose intelligently between options or to solve problems by taking thought, but those are attributes that human beings arguably share with many other animals. The more specific sense of "rationality" refers to a normative capacity, a capacity to assess the grounds of our beliefs and actions, and to adjust them accordingly. On the side of action, for instance, it is the capacity to ask whether something that would potentially motivate you to perform a certain action is really a *reason* for doing that action—and then to be motivated to act in accordance with the answer that you get. Rationality, in this sense, is normative self-government, the capacity to be governed by thoughts about what you *ought* to do or to believe.

In fact, even some thinkers who would deny that *rationality* is the distinctive characteristic of humanity would still agree that normative self-government is both definitive of personhood and distinctive of humanity. In the empiricist tradition, the tradition of Locke, Hume, and Hutcheson, it has been common to attribute to human beings, and human beings alone, a capacity to form so-called "second-order" attitudes—for instance, attitudes towards our own desires—that make them liable to normative assessment. Though I may desire to do something, I may also disapprove of that desire, and reject its influence over me. According to empiricists, second-order attitudes are what make human beings subject to an "ought." So many philosophers have agreed that it is in virtue of normative self-government that human beings count as persons in the legal and moral sense.

Certainly, if something along these lines is correct, it is natural to think that only human beings can have obligations. In order to have obligations, you need to be able to think about whether what you are doing is right, and to adjust your conduct accordingly. This requires a highly developed "theory of mind," as ethologists call it. An animal has a theory of mind when the animal knows that animals (herself included) have mental attitudes, such as beliefs and desires. But in order to be rational in the sense I just described, an animal must not only know that she and other animals have mental attitudes. She must also know that her attitudes are connected in certain ways—for instance, that she is inclined to perform a certain action *because* she has a certain desire. To ask whether you have a good reason for doing what you propose to do, or whether it is right, is to think about and evaluate that connection, and it seems likely that only human beings can do that.

But it is a much harder question whether being rational in this sense is necessary for having *rights,* and that is the question most pressing from the point of view of those who seek legal protections for animals. The traditional distinction between persons and things groups the ability to have rights and the liability to having obligations together. One common view about why that should be so is that rights are grounded in some sort of agreement that is reciprocal: I agree to respect certain claims of yours, provided that you respect certain similar claims of mine. The view of society as based on a kind of social contract supports such a conception of rights. But in fact our laws do not merely protect those who as citizens are involved in making its laws: rather, they protect anyone who shares the interests that the laws were made to protect. So for instance, foreigners on our soil have rights not to be robbed or murdered, regardless of the fact that they are not parties to our own social contract. The laws that we make against murder and robbery are intended to protect certain human interests that foreigners share with citizens, and that is sufficient to give them the relevant rights. Of course, foreigners on our soil can also be made to conform to our laws—reciprocity can be required of them. But when we speak of universal human rights, we speak of interests that are shared by every human being and that we think ought to be protected, not merely of the interests protected under some actual social contract. So it makes sense to raise the question whether the other animals share the kinds of interests that our laws—either legal or moral—are meant to protect.

Animal rights advocates urge that the other animals, like human beings, do have interests. Let me do a little philosophizing about why this is so. Animals have interests because of the way in which things can be good or bad for them. Generally speaking, we use the concepts of good-for and bad-for when we regard objects functionally. Something is good for an object when it enables the object to function well, and bad for it when it interferes with its ability to function. So we might say that riding the brakes is bad for your car, while a regular oil change is good for it. Organisms may be regarded as functional objects, "designed" by the evolutionary process to survive and reproduce. We are thinking of things that way when we say that plenty of water and sunshine are good for the plants. Because a car is an artifact made for human purposes, the ways in which things are good or bad for the car are derivative from human interests. But the way in which things are good or bad for organisms is non-derivative: things are good or bad for the organisms themselves.

What is distinctive of animal life is the *way* that it functions, which is by means of perception and action. Through perception, an animal forms some sort of representation of her environment. As a result of instinct, learning, and in the case of some animals, intelligent thought, objects in the animal's environment are represented as desirable or aversive in specific ways: as something to eat, or to flee from, or to mate with, or to take care of. Or some sort of practical representation may arise from within, as when you get hungry and find yourself irresistibly thinking about a sandwich. The animal then acts in accordance with these practical representations. The practical representations serve, though very imperfectly of course, to enable an animal to get what is good for her and avoid what is bad for her. In other words, when animals evolved, a kind of entity came into existence which actually *experiences* the goodness or badness of its own condition, or at least of some aspects of its own condition, in a positive or negative way—as something desirable or aversive. An animal experiences its own good or ill.

So the way in which things are good or bad for animals is distinctive in that it is both non-derivative and capable of being experienced. We can describe these things by saying that animals have interests, or that there are facts about their welfare. Although our own welfare is more complex than that of the other animals, it is because we are animals, not because we are human beings or persons, that we ourselves have interests or a welfare. Animal rights advocates argue that having a welfare or interests is sufficient to ground rights. We should ask on what basis we claim rights for ourselves, and demand respect for them from each other, if it is not that we ourselves are beings with interests or a welfare?

Well, here is one possible answer. Immanuel Kant, who made the concept of a person central to his ethics, argued that a person is an end in himself, to be valued and respected for his own sake, and never to be used merely as a means. Kant claimed that the basis of that value is the capacity for rational choice, or autonomy. He also claimed that it is because of our autonomy that human beings have rights. Because human beings are rational beings, Kant argued, human beings, unlike the other animals, are able to choose our own way of life. We reflect about what counts as a good life, decide the question for ourselves, and live accordingly. In the liberal tradition, with its strong emphasis on toleration, and its antagonism to paternalism, this kind of autonomy has often been regarded as the basis of rights. We have the basic rights of personal liberty, liberty of conscience, and freedom of speech and association, because each of us has the right to determine for himself or herself what counts as a worthwhile life, and to live that life, so long as the way we act is consistent with a like right for everyone else. Because the other animals do not choose their own way of life, they do not have rights grounded in this kind of autonomy.

But this response is not wholly satisfactory. I think we do have specifically human rights grounded in our autonomy. But the trouble with leaving it at that, is that what makes it important *to us* that our rights should be respected is not just that we value our autonomy. It is also that we value, to speak almost circularly, our welfare, our interests, or our good. Rights grounded in autonomy may often give us an *indirect* way to protect what we regard as our good. If someone cannot interfere with your freedom of speech, for example, he cannot interfere with your saying your prayers. It is in part because you care about saying your prayers, and not just because you care about your autonomy, that you care about your right to say them. This is where it becomes clear that there is a problem with dividing the world into persons and things. The other animals, who do not have autonomy, are left with no legal means of protecting their interests or their welfare. If they have no rights, they are not persons, and that leaves them to be things. But animals are not mere things, since they are beings with interests and lives of their own. Insofar as they come within the purview of human laws at all, it is because they are a subject population, and the only way to afford any effective protection for their welfare is through human laws.

It is worth emphasizing that last thought. The idea of animal rights sounds silly to some people, because it seems to suggest an insane desire to moralize nature: to imply that we should declare predation to be murder and to make it illegal, or perhaps to turn battles over territory into property disputes that get settled in court. But an advocate of animal rights need not be in favor of our trying to protect non-human animals from each other. Rather, the point is to protect them from us, from human beings. The reason only the law can do that effectively is because in a sense, the law is the reason why many of the other animals are so completely at our mercy. What I mean is this: it is not just because we are individually smarter than the other animals that human beings are able to do as we will with them. It is because human beings are so cooperative and therefore so organized. And the way that we organize ourselves is by making laws, which set the terms of our interactions and so unite us into an effective whole. If the law says it is permissible for a person to inflict torments on an animal in order to test a product, for instance, then there is nothing anyone can do to protect that animal. So it is one of those cases—and there are certainly others—in which the only thing that can afford protection against the power of the law is the law itself.

The fact that we have any anti-cruelty laws at all embodies the idea that the welfare of any being who has a welfare—a non-derivative and experienced good—is worthy of regard for its own sake. It should be protected unless there is some good reason why not. It is a further step to say that all animals are ends in themselves, never to be used as mere means to someone else's ends. But once we agree that their welfare is to be regarded, then we do need a good reason for disregarding it. And what is that reason supposed to be? Why should our interests prevail over theirs?

The reason most frequently offered is that human beings just *are* more valuable and important than the other animals. Some theological traditions have claimed this: human beings are supremely valuable, and the world and all its contents, including the other animals, were made for our use. But in the absence of such a context, importance must be importance *to* or *for* someone or something. Perhaps we are more important to ourselves. But, then, each of us has some small circle of loved ones who are the most important people in the world to him, and we do not take that as a reason to do experiments on strangers, or eat them, or steal their organs. Something more must be said to explain the precedence that we give to ourselves.

But mainly I think we should ask ourselves, on what grounds do we ourselves claim to be valuable in the way that we claim to be—ends in ourselves, never to be used as a mere means to someone else's ends? Is it really because we have the capacity for rational choice, or is it also more simply because we have a welfare of our own? If it is the latter, simple consistency demands that, as far as we possibly can, we should treat the other animals as ends in themselves. The other animals lack normative self-government, and in that sense they are not persons; but we need not accept the idea that the world is divided into persons and property, or persons and things. Without reclassifying them as persons, we may still regard all animals as ends in themselves, and, as such, the proper subjects of rights against human mistreatment.

87 Every Sparrow That Falls

Understanding Animal Rights Activism as Functional Religion

*Wesley V. Jamison, Caspar Wenk,
and James V. Parker*

Wesley Jamison, Caspar Wenk, and James Parker have found that the goals of animal rights activists in Switzerland and the United States often require extremely high levels of commitment and conviction. An analysis of the movement as a functional religion demonstrates some of the sources of this commitment. The analysis uses Yinger's five categories: intense and memorable conversion experiences, newfound communities of meaning, normative creeds, elaborate and well-defined codes of behavior, and cult formation. The authors predict changes within the movement should it evolve into a mainstream political force.

The [. . .] goals of animal rights activists often require extraordinary levels of personal commitment and conviction (Jasper and Nelkin, 1992; Herzog, 1993; McAllister, 1997). What are the sources of this intensity and commitment? Once mobilized, what keeps an animal rights activist motivated toward the transformation of society's relationship with animals? And what course of action will the movement take should it fail to redeem society? A guide for activists who object in conscience to classroom vivisection and dissection advises that their objection is a constitutionally protected exercise of religious belief (Francione and Charlton, 1992). The authors' claim that such activists are acting out of religious belief may surprise many observers. Social science data indicate that most animal rights activists are not members of traditional churches; indeed, they think of themselves as atheist or agnostic (Richards, 1990).[1] Nonetheless, social scientists have argued that animal rights may serve as a cosmological buttress against anomie and bewilderment in modern society (Sutherland and Nash, 1994; McAllister, 1997; Franklin, 1999).[2]

Francione and Charlton (1992) argue that . . . "The law does not require a belief to be 'theistic' or based on faith in a 'God' or 'Supreme Being' " in order to be protected.

[. . .]

The United States Supreme Court, the authors point out, has adopted a "functional" definition of religion:

> The Court has recognized that in order to determine whether a set of beliefs constitutes a religion, the appropriate focus is not the substance of a person's belief system (i.e., whether a person believes in a personal God of the Jewish, Christian or Muslim traditions), but rather, what function or role the belief systems plays in the person's life.
>
> (Francione and Charlton, 1992, p. 4)

Yinger (1970) articulated the distinction between substantive and functional definitions of religion for social scientists. It is a distinction that allows us to analyze seemingly secular movements as religions because they function as religions; that is, they provide meaning around which individuals coalesce, interpreting life through a system of beliefs, symbols, rituals, and prescriptions for behavior. Indeed, Berger (1992, 1999) has noted the emergence of such functional, secular religiosity as an alternative expression of "repressed transcendence." Berger argues that in response to modernity's cultural delegitimization of traditional religions and objective truth, individuals, rather than ending their quest for religious truth, shift the foci of their quest toward other outlets.

[. . .]

We drew the data for this article from long interviews with informants in both the United States and Switzerland. Although the political manifestations of animal rights ideology are context dependent, social scientists have hypothesized that mass movement activism (e.g. animal rights) may be a reaction to sociological factors that transcend culture and thus share relatively uniform causes (Giddens, 1990, 1991; Beck, 1992; Sutherland and Nash, 1994). Switzerland and the United States share similar representative, federal political systems that are highly decentralized and shunt many political issues toward the lowest levels of political participation where, over time, intensity in citizen involvement is emphasized. Likewise, democracy in the United States resembles Swiss democracy in that citizens have the opportunity to pass or amend legislation through direct democracy, and this similarly emphasizes political intensity among political participants. The Swiss and U.S. systems are similar in that multiple checks and balances thwart radical political movements and cause incremental change (Linder, 1994).

[. . .]

The animal rights movements in both countries differ in significant ways. The U.S. movement has diverged into a reformist arm that allows for humane use of animals and a radical arm that seeks to protect them from all human use through the extension of inalienable rights. In Switzerland, the *Tierschutz* movement similarly contains reformist and radical branches, but because of political history the Swiss movement tends to shy away from the language of rights. Another difference is that the U.S. system is intentionally confrontational, pitting interest groups against each other in perpetual conflict, whereas the Swiss system is by intent more consensual and cooperative (Berry, 1994; Linder, 1994). One manifestation of this difference is that in the United States the animal rights movement has sought confrontation outside the boundaries of political legislation both to shock citizens and to bring about strategic legislative change (Francione, 1996), while in Switzerland the animal rights movement has sought redress through primarily political means and has stayed relatively non-confrontational (Linder, 1994).

[. . .]

Results: The Elements of Functional Religion

Conversion

Morally persuasive religious belief often originates in an experience of conversion. Coming from a biblical expression meaning "to be turned around," conversion can reverse a person's life.

[. . .]

Our informants reported having had formative events that sensitized them to movement rhetoric and images and began the process of dissonance. Our informants confirmed Jasper and Poulsen's (1995) hypothesis concerning activist recruitment. For our informants, awareness of incongruence between behavior and feelings remained a vivid but nebulous reality coupled to a vague sense of guilt over not doing more. Their unease grew until it eventually became manifest in a single emotional epiphany. One informant noted:

> I received literature, [that was] doing an exposé on dog-meat markets in Asia; I still remember it vividly. I was reading this mailing postcard while eating a ham sandwich. There was a picture of this dog, his legs tethered, a tin cup over his muzzle; then it hit me! I made the connection between the being in the picture and the being in my mouth. Before, everything seemed to be OK, but now, I realized that treating animals as objects was bad. It was like someone had opened

a door. I felt incredible sadness, and at the same time incredible joy. I knew that I would never be the same again, that I was leaving something behind . . . that I would be a better person, that I had been cleansed.

[. . .]

Community

Converts create communities. [. . .] [One] informant experienced separation from her previous relationships: "I had a sense of being 'called out.' I had trouble relating to some people. People would stare when I would order [vegetarian food] in restaurants. It was embarrassing for me, and very uncomfortable." Indeed, some of our informants attributed their divorces to their newfound beliefs. After their conversion, our informants uniformly experienced feelings of social isolation, which in turn led them to seek out others who believed. Our informants often faced ostracism and scorn from family and friends as they tried to relate to their conversion.

[. . .]

Creed

Although most animal rights activists do not recite a formal profession of faith (Richards, 1990), they have beliefs that may be compared to traditional religious doctrines. At first glance, their creed seems obvious and simple: animals either have the right to live their lives without human interference or have the right to be considered equally with humans in the ethical balance that weighs the right and wrong of any action or policy (Singer, 1975; Regan, 1983). Nevertheless, the commitment of our informants to political guarantees of rights for animals is part of a larger system of beliefs about life and the human–nonhuman animal relationship. That system includes several beliefs about nature, suffering, and death and is typified by creedal doctrinaire beliefs. Our informants agreed that active inclusion in the movement carries with it certain proscribed beliefs such as the assertion of the moral righteousness of the movement and the necessity of spreading that revelation. Believing entails spreading the faith, and animal rights activists are proselytizers. Herzog (1993) has found that the involvement of almost all animal rights activists contains an evangelical component.

[. . .]

In our informants' creed, suffering is evil, and its alleviation is good; humans are at once derived from, and unique in, the natural world. In other words, people are related through evolution to animals but ethically constrained from using them because we, alone, are conscious of the suffering such use causes and can exercise free will to end it.

[. . .]

To our informants, nature acquires normative value and is the repository of nobility and virtue, while humans acquire negative and even evil attributes (Chase, 1995; Dizard, 1999). [. . .] Certainly, animals are part of nature, but to our informants their goodness lies in their perceived moral innocence. [. . .] Indeed, for our informants it appeared that people were the problem, that innocence could be found only in animals, and that humans just by existing—are detrimental to animals.

[. . .]

An all-encompassing statement of faith professed by some of our informants demonstrated the codified edicts of animal rights: "Animals are not ours to eat, wear, experiment on, or use in any way!" Finding its ultimate expression in the form of veganism, this lifestyle consciously forgoes the use of materials that have, in any way, caused animal suffering. Our informants defined vegans as "a person who doesn't use, to the greatest extent possible, any products that come from animals . . . it's impossible to get away from animal use . . . but if an alternative is available, they use it."

Unlimited in scope, veganism provides an elaborate superstructure with which activists support their lives. Bordering on asceticism, the constraints placed on personal behavior and the resultant emotional demands of compliance can be extraordinary (Sperling, 1988; Herzog, 1993).

[. . .]

Cult (Collective Meanings Expressed as Symbols and Rituals)

Substantive religions often organize their worship around the teachings of sacred texts/inspired narrative or the consumption of a holy food. Although nothing so formal as listening to the inspired text or eating a sacred meal characterizes the gatherings of animal rights partisans, elements of those gatherings nevertheless resemble the ritual behavior of traditional religions. An informant reflected this repetitive reification of belief:

> [I] was shy . . . I don't classify myself as an activist, but I went along with a friend. When we got there, the meeting began with people introducing themselves and talking about the problems [professing the creed and keeping the behavioral code] they had had.

[. . .]

Animal rights activists often share news clippings, letters, and personal stories that tell of recent conversions and encourage participants in their commitment. The introduction and welcoming of new and potential members often are an integral part of animal rights meetings.

[. . .]

During such moments of epistemological challenge, symbols helped to remind and rejuvenate our informants. [. . .] Animal rights activists use pictures of monkeys strapped in chairs, cats wearing electrodes, and rabbits with eye or flesh ulceration in much the same way: that is, as symbolic representations of human values and the corresponding affronts to those values. Looking on and identifying with those innocent victims, just as Christians look upon and identify a lamb as the propitiatory sacrifice of Jesus, can bring about conversion and redemption (Sperling, 1988; Jasper and Nelkin, 1992). Indeed, most of our informants had such symbols in their social environments.

[. . .]

[T]he thesis may explain how our informants retain enthusiasm and how the movement retains its cohesion in the face of seemingly insurmountable obstacles posited by the incremental U.S. and Swiss political systems. Central to the stories of our informants was a profound sense of guilt at discovering personal complicity in the suffering of animals. The movement places moral culpability squarely upon their shoulders, and its rhetoric exacerbates this. Then, in the tradition of all purposive mass movements, it offers itself as the ultimate form of absolution. With a creed that presents a disheartening picture of their world and a code of behavior that at once is unattainable and noble, believers are drawn into further activism as a source of penance.

[. . .]

Predictive Power

[. . .] We can look to the course run by religious and secular movements to find answers to intriguing questions about the animal rights movement's future.

[. . .]

We might ask how the movement, should it evolve into a mainstream political force, might retain its distinctive redemptive flavor? First, while maintaining its transcendent goal, it could pick and choose its battles, settling for those it can win: not the end of animal use in agriculture, but the end of raising calves for veal; not the end of all animal products, but the end of wearing furs; not the end of using animals in medical research, but the end of research that can be presented as an affront to decency. Second, the movement might develop two distinctive and separable tiers of membership.

694 *Wesley V. Jamison et al.*

[. . .]

An elite would hold out for the original vision of societal transformation, keep themselves from any compromise, and pursue a prophetic course. Others entangled in earning a living, rearing a family, and enjoying friendships do what they can: adopt a dog, write a protest letter to a shampoo manufacturer, or buy synthetic clothes.

A parallel with the early Christian church is instructive. The Church moved in this direction during the second, third, and fourth centuries. An elite chose to move into isolation and live by the evangelical counsels. With their vows of poverty, chastity, and obedience, they foreswore personal property and wealth, family responsibilities, and even personal autonomy. The way of these monks was declared the way of perfection. For those who were not able to live so purely a second tier of citizenship developed. Gradually, the word *laos*, which in earliest times referred to all Christians (as in the expression *laos theou* or 'the people of God'), came to refer to those who did not follow the monks—the laity. In other words, the animal rights movement may develop a secularized monastic system as a means to assuage the schismatic tension between pragmatism and purity implicit within an incremental political system.

[. . .]

It is no mistake that the movement has had success—although each of the informants was disheartened by the glacial rate of change. The modern movement to protect animals, whether it be in Switzerland or the United States, has, at the least, sensitized non-believers to the plight of animals and perhaps even continued to sow the seeds of epistemological discontent that led our informants to convert to the cause.

Notes

1. For a relevant discussion of animal rights as a derivative of modernity, see Franklin (1999).
2. It could be argued that cultural differences between the Swiss and Americans confound any useful examination of animal rights activism. On the contrary, a central theme in modernity and the study of pluralization is that "modern" post-industrial Western nations are buffeted by the same effects of modernity. Our data showed little cultural differences between informants from the two countries.

References

Beck, U. (1992). *Risk society: Towards a new modernity*. London: Sage Publishers.

Berger, P. (1992). *A far glory: The quest for faith in an age of credulity*. New York: Basic.

——— (1999). *The desecularization of the world: Resurgent religion and world politics*. New York: Eerdmans Publishing Company.

Berry, J. (1994). *The interest group society*. Boston: Scott, Foresman/Little, Brown.

Chase, A. (1995). *In a dark wood: The fight over forests and the rising tyranny of ecology*. New York: Free Press.

Dizard, J. (1999). *Going wild: Hunting, animal rights, and the contested meaning of nature*. Amherst: University of Massachusetts Press.

Francione, G. (1996). *Rain without thunder: The ideology of the animal rights movement*. Philadelphia: Temple University Press.

Francione, G., and Charlton, A. (1992). *Vivisection and dissection in the classroom: A guide to conscientious objection*. Jenkintown: The American Anti-Vivisection Society.

Franklin, A. (1999). *Animals in modern culture: A sociology of human–animal relations in modernity*. London: Corwin Publishers.

Giddens, A. (1990). *The consequences of modernity*. Stanford: Stanford University Press.

——— (1991). *Modernity and self-identity: Self and society in the late modern age*. Stanford: Stanford University Press.

Herzog, H. (1993). "The movement is my life": The psychology of animal rights activism. *The Journal of Social Issues, 49*, 103–19.

Jasper, J., and Nelkin, D. (1992). *The animal rights crusade: Growth of a moral protest*. New York: Free Press.

Jasper, J., and Poulsen, J. (1995). Recruiting strangers and friends: Moral shocks and social networks in animal rights and anti-nuclear protests. *Social Problems*, *42*, 493–512.

Linder, W. (1994). *Swiss democracy*. London: Sage Publishers.

McAllister, J. (1997). *Hearts and minds: The controversy over laboratory animals*. Philadelphia: Temple University Press.

Regan, T. (1983). *The case for animal rights*. Berkeley: University of California Press.

Richards, R. (1990). *Consensus mobilization through ideology, networks, and grievances: A study of the contemporary animal rights movement*. Ann Arbor: University Microfilms.

Singer, P. (1975). *Animal liberation*. New York: New York Book Review.

Sperling, Susan (1988). *Animal liberators: Research and morality*. Berkeley: University of California Press.

Sutherland, K., and Nash, W. (1994). Animal rights as new environmental cosmology. *Qualitative Sociology*, *17*, 171–86.

Yinger, M. (1970). *The scientific study of religion*. New York: Macmillan Publishing Company.

88 Understanding Animal Rights Violence

Tom Regan

Tom Regan draws connections between two social justice movements: the nineteenth-century anti-slavery movement in the United States and the contemporary animal rights movement. Both exhibit the split between those who insist on the immediate end to unjust practice (abolitionists) and those who are gradualists or reformists. It is the abolitionists who include those who are willing to commit acts of violence. A second split is between those who work with the government and those who refuse to do so, and a third is between those who condone violence against property in defense of animals and those who do not. Regan recommends "incremental abolitionist change" as a shared agenda.

Those people who view themselves as advocates of animal rights—and I certainly include myself among them—also see themselves as part of a social justice movement: the animal rights movement. In this respect, animal rights advocates believe that common bonds unite them with those who have worked for justice in other quarters: for example, for women, people of color, the poor, and gays and lesbians. The struggle for equal rights for and among these people is hardly complete; the struggle for the rights of animals has only begun, and this latter struggle promises to be, if anything, more difficult and protracted than any of its social justice relatives. For while demands for equal rights for many historically disfranchised people face formidable obstacles, they have one advantage over the struggle for animal rights. None of the other movements I have mentioned challenges the conception of the moral community that has dominated Western thought and traditions, the one that includes *humans only*; rather, all these struggles work with rather than against this conception, demanding only (and I do not mean to minimize the enormous difficulties such a demand inevitably faces) that the boundaries of the moral community expand to include previously excluded human beings—Native Americans, for example, or humans who suffer from various physical or mental disabilities.

The struggle for animal rights is different; it calls for a deeper, more fundamental change in the way we think about membership in the moral community. It demands not an expansion but a dismantling of the for-humans-only conception, to be replaced by one that includes other-than-human animals.

Not surprisingly, therefore, any obstacle that stands in the way of greater justice for people of color or the poor, for example, also stands in the way of greater justice for chimpanzees and chickens, whereas the struggle for justice for chimpanzees and chickens encounters obstacles at once more fundamental and unique, including the resistance or disdain of people who are among the most enlightened when it comes to injustice done to humans. Any doubt about this can be readily dispelled by gauging the indifference and hostility showered on the very idea of animal rights by both many of the leaders and most of the rank and file in any human rights movement, including, for example, those committed to justice and equality for women and racial minorities.

Despite these differences, those of us involved in the struggle for animal rights need to remember that we share many of the challenges other social justice movements face. [. . .] By way of illustration, I want to explore a few of the similarities between the nineteenth-century antislavery movement in America and today's animal rights movement.

Before doing this, I want to try to defuse a possible misunderstanding. I am not in any way suggesting that the animal rights movement and the antislavery movement are in every respect the same (clearly, they are not), any more than I would be suggesting that all African Americans must be either gay or lesbian because there are similarities between the movement to liberate slaves, on the one hand, and the gay and lesbian movement, on the other. Similarities are just that: similarities. And one thing similarities are not is sameness.

[. . .]

Animal Rights Versus Animal Welfare

When it comes to what we humans are morally permitted to do to other animals, it is safe to say that opinion is divided. Some people (abolitionists) believe that we should stop using nonhuman animals, whether as sources of food, as trained performers, or as models of various diseases, for example. Others (welfarists) think such utilization is permissible as long as it is done humanely. Those who accept the former outlook object to such utilization in principle and believe it should end in practice. Those who accept the latter outlook accept such utilization in principle and believe it may continue in practice, provided the welfare of animals is not unduly compromised, in which case these practices will need to be appropriately reformed. Clearly real differences separate these two ways of thinking, one abolitionist at its core, the other not. Anyone who would deny or attempt to minimize these differences would distort rather than describe the truth.

[. . .]

One area where these differences can make a difference is the particular matter before us. For it is among abolitionists, not reformists—among animal rightists, not animal welfarists—that we find those willing to commit acts of violence in the name of animal liberation. Nevertheless—and this is of great importance—not all animal rightists are prepared to go this far. That is, within the animal rights movement one finds deep, protracted, principled disagreements about the limits of protest in general and the permissibility of using violence in particular.

Analogous ideological and tactical themes are to be found in the antislavery movement. That movement was anything but monolithic. True, all abolitionists shared a common goal: slavery in America had to end. Beyond their agreement concerning this unifying goal, however, partisans of emancipation divided over a rich, complex fabric of well-considered, passionately espoused, and irreconcilable disagreements concerning the appropriate means of ending it. For my purposes, reference to just three areas of disagreement will suffice.

Abolition First Versus Abolition Later

Following the lead of William Lloyd Garrison (1831), some abolitionists called for the unconditional emancipation of slaves, insisting as well that former slave owners not receive compensation for their financial losses. "Immediatists" (as they were called) wanted to end slavery first and then go forward with various plans to educate and in other ways prepare the newly freed slaves for the responsibilities of full citizenship. Other abolitionists (Channing 1835) favored a "gradualist" approach: complete emancipation was the eventual goal, but only after various alternatives to slave labor and improvements in the life of the slaves were in place. Thus, some gradualists sought freedom for slaves after (not before) those in bondage had received at least a rudimentary education or acquired a marketable skill or after (not before) a plan of financial compensation to former slave owners, or another plan calling for voluntary recolonization, had been implemented.

[. . .]

This split between slavery's immediatists and gradualists is mirrored in today's animal rights movement. Some people who profess belief in the movement's abolitionist goals also believe that these goals can be achieved by using gradualist means—for example, by supporting protocols that aim to reduce or refine animal use in a scientific setting, with replacement possibly achieved later on, or by decreasing the number of hens raised in cages today as a step along the way to emptying cages tomorrow. In this way, it is believed, we can succeed both in making the lives of some animals better today and in ending all animal exploitation in the future.

Other animal rights abolitionists are cut from more Garrison-like cloth. For these animal rightists, *how* we get to the abolitionist goal, not just *that* we get there, matters morally (Francione and Regan 1992). Following the higher moral law that we are not to do evil that good may come, these activists believe that they should not tacitly support violating the rights of some animals today in the hope of freeing others tomorrow. For these activists, as was true of their counterparts in the antislavery movement, it is not a question of first finding an alternative to the evil being done before deciding whether to stop doing it; instead, one must first decide to end the evil and then look for another way to achieve the goals one seeks. For these animal rights activists, then, our first obligation is to stop using animals as we do; after we have satisfied this obligation, there will be plenty of time to search for alternative ways of doing what it is we want to do. To end evil now rather than later is what conformity to the higher moral law requires.

Working with the Government Versus Working Independently

A second common theme concerns the role of government. The antislavery movement once again was sharply divided. Whereas Garrison and his followers refused to cooperate with the government, others insisted on the necessity of working with elected representatives; among this latter group, Frederick Douglass was unquestionably the most illustrious representative (see Douglass 1845).

[. . .]

The Constitution contains no ambiguous language concerning nonhuman animals that might occasion a split among today's animal rights advocates like that between Garrison and Douglass. Cows and pigs, chimpanzees and dolphins, ospreys and squirrels—all are total nonpersons as far as the Constitution is concerned. Even so, what we might term the *political sensibilities* of Garrison and Douglass live on in today's animal rights movement.

Douglass's faith in the role of government is represented by those animal rights advocates who look to the government—laws, enforcement mechanisms, and the courts—as essential elements in realizing the abolitionist goal for which they labor. In contrast, Garrison's disdain for the government is mirrored by today's animal rights activists who have lost faith in the progressive role current or foreseeable laws, enforcement mechanisms, or court proceedings might play in the struggle for animal liberation. For these activists, the government is not only historically rooted in and constitutionally committed to the ideology of speciesism but also daily subject to the influence of powerful special interests that perpetuate speciesist practices as a matter of law. These activists see the government as part of the problem, not part of the solution.

Violence Versus Nonviolence

Despite his belief in the necessity of working with the government, Douglass was to his dying day a staunch supporter of "agitation," a commitment poignantly captured by Philip Foner's description of a meeting that took place some weeks before Douglass's death.

> In the early days of 1895, a young Negro student living in New England journeyed to Providence, Rhode Island, to seek the advice of the aged Frederick Douglass who was visiting that city. As the interview drew to a close the youth said, "Mr. Douglass, you have lived in both the old and new dispensations. What have you to say to a young Negro just starting out? What should he do?" The patriarch lifted his head and replied, "Agitate! Agitate! Agitate!"
>
> (Foner 1950:371)

To our ears, Douglass's prescription might sound like a license to lawlessness, but this is not what he meant. For most of his life, Douglass, like the vast majority of abolitionists, favored only nonviolent forms of agitation: peaceful assemblies, rallies, the distribution of pamphlets and other materials depicting the plight of slaves, and petitions—measures that collectively were referred to as "moral suasion." People were to be persuaded that slavery was wrong and ought to be abolished through appeals to their reason, their sense of justice, and their human compassion, not coerced to agree through violence or intimidation.

On this point Garrison and Douglass, who disagreed about much, spoke with one voice. When Garrison said abolitionists were not to do evil that good may come, he meant that they were not to do evil *even to slaveholders, even in pursuit of emancipation.* As he saw it, respect for the higher moral law requires that all efforts made in the name of emancipation, whether immediatist or gradualist and whether in concert with the Union or apart from it, treat all persons respectfully and thus nonviolently.

[. . .]

On this matter, today's animal rightists, if not unanimously then at least solidly, align themselves with Garrison and Douglass. Evil, in the form of violence, should not be done to any human being, even in pursuit of animal liberation, and anyone who would perform such an act, whatever that person might say or believe, would not be acting according to the higher moral law that should guide and inform the animal rights movement.

This prohibition against violence to human and other forms of sentient life, however, does not necessarily carry over to property. Most of slavery's opponents understood this. If the cost of freeing a slave was damaged, destroyed, or in the case of slaves themselves, stolen property, then Garrison, Douglass, and most (but not all) of their abolitionist peers were prepared to accept such violence.

The same is true of many of today's animal rights advocates. Let me be perfectly honest. Some animal rightists obviously believe that violent acts against property carried out in the name of animal liberation, as well as the liberation of animals themselves (the theft of property, given current law), are perfectly justified. Other animal rightists disagree, believing that a principled commitment to the "higher moral law" of nonviolence must be maintained even in the treatment of property.

How many believe the one, how many believe the other, no one, I think, can say. What we can say, and what we should say, is this: it is just as false, just as misleading, and possibly just as dishonest to say that the animal rights movement is a nonviolent movement as it is to say that it is a terrorist movement.

[. . .]

How to Lessen Animal Rights Violence

This violence is something that everyone, both friend and foe of animal rights, must lament, something we all wish could be prevented. The question is how to do so.

[. . .]

My own (very) modest proposal is this. Although Garrison-like abolitionists cannot support reformist measures, they can support *incremental abolitionist change*, change that involves stopping the utilization of nonhuman animals for one purpose or another. One goal, for example, might be not fewer animals used in cosmetic or industrial testing but no animals used for this purpose. Other goals might be not fewer dogs "sacrificed" in dog labs, or fewer primates "studied" in maternal deprivation research, or fewer goats shot and killed in weapons testing, but no animals used in each of these (and an indefinite number of other possible) cases.

A shared agenda of this type could set forth objectives that animal rights abolitionists, scientific policy makers, and biomedical researchers, for example, could agree on and work collaboratively to achieve; as such, it would go a long way toward reducing animal rights violence. It would demonstrate that it is possible to achieve incremental abolitionist goals by acting nonviolently within the system. This in turn would help defuse the idea that such goals can be achieved only by acting violently outside the system.

[. . .]

[U]nless we practice preventive ethics in this quarter, animal rights violence will increase in the coming months and years. Indeed, as things stand at present, the wonder of it is not that there is animal rights violence but that there is not more of it.

[. . .]

Works cited

Channing, William Ellery. 1835. "Essay on Slavery." In *The Works of William E. Channing*, 6 vols., 2:123–33. Boston: Anti-Slavery Office.

Douglass, Frederick. 1845. *Narrative of the Life of Frederick Douglass: An American Slave. Written by Himself.* Boston: Anti-Slavery Office.

Foner, Philip S. 1950. *Frederick Douglass: A Biography*. New York: Citadel.

Francione, Gary, and Tom Regan. 1992. "A Movement's Means Create Its Ends." *The Animals' Agenda*, January/February, pp. 40–3.

Garrison, William Lloyd. 1831. "Immediate Emancipation." *The Liberator*, September 3, pp. 1–2.

89 Civil Disobedience

A Case Study in Factors of Effectiveness

Courtney L. Dillard

Courtney Dillard presents her observations of two protests against the largest pigeon shoot in the United States. In the second protest, activists lay flat on the ground, bound themselves to one another at the neck, remained silent, and remained calm. In being bound together, they attempt to represent the helplessness of the birds. The onlookers who were interviewed indicated that this approach was very effective in changing attitudes.

Advocating for animals in this country dates as far back as the colonial period. In 1641, legal arguments were put forth that made cruelty to domestic animals unlawful in the Massachusetts Bay Colony. By the mid-1800s, several social movement organizations, such as the American Society for the Prevention of Cruelty to Animals (ASPCA) and the Philadelphia Society for the Prevention of Cruelty to Animals were created to advocate for animal welfare in the wider courts of public opinion. Over time, the numbers of people and organizations arguing on behalf of animals grew substantially. In addition, the tactics and strategies employed in such advocacy became more varied and creative.

Such changes perhaps are most notable in surveying the activities of social movement organizations in the last two decades. The 1980s witnessed not only major ideological shifts from welfare to rights but also tactical shifts from behind-the-scenes negotiation in the courtroom or legislative bodies to very public acts of protest and civil disobedience. As the media, particularly television, quickly became an essential part of educating and persuading the public on animal issues, tactics that gained media coverage were often employed. Because one of the enduring news values is controversy and conflict (Stephens, 1980), the potential for acts of civil disobedience often ensured media attention. Today, some activists and organizations wholly embrace the use of civil disobedience.

[. . .]

Instead of wrestling with the question of whether civil disobedience is an effective advocacy tool in general, I ask if the effectiveness of civil disobedience may be determined in part by the way it is enacted. To pursue this question, I analyze a specific case study of a long-term animal advocacy campaign—The Fund for Animals' campaign to abolish the Hegins pigeon shoot. In this article, I compare the enactment of civil disobedience in two years of protest that differed considerably from one another.

[. . .]

Hegins: A Case Analysis

The Event

The Fred Coleman Memorial Shoot, the shoot's official name, began more than a half century ago in the early 1930s. Pigeon shooting is a rather common sport in the rural counties of Pennsylvania, but the shoot at Hegins quickly grew to become the largest event of its kind in the country. Each Labor

Day weekend, people from a number of surrounding counties and states descended on the town to shoot over 5,000 birds. Funds from the event were used to raise money to continue maintenance on the park and subsidize such local services as the firehouse (B. Tobash, personal communication, February 20, 1997).

The rules surrounding the shoot and the manner in which it is conducted haven't changed since the event's earliest days. Organizers of the shoot purchase pigeons from breeders or those who have trapped the birds in the wild. They then keep the pigeons in cages, often cramped together for days or even weeks before the event. Participants in the shoot, limited to 250 at Hegins, pay an entry fee, typically $75, for a chance to shoot as many pigeons as possible. The shooter with the largest number of hits at the end of the weekend wins the event.

During the shoot, participants stand ready with their guns and then shout "Pull," ordering the strings tied to the cage doors to be pulled and the doors opened, releasing the pigeons one at a time. Pigeons either fly out or, having been weakened by their captivity, walk out of the cages. At that moment, the shooter fires, attempting to kill the pigeon (H. Prescott, personal communication, October 25, 1996). If the shooter misses, the bird may fly out of the park boundaries to safety. If wounded, the pigeon often lands in the shooting field. While the shooters aim to kill, they often only wound the birds. One field estimate suggested that only 30 percent of the birds died instantly (Fund Press Release, 1996). It is the duty of the trapper boys, typically about age 12, to retrieve the wounded birds from the shooting field and kill them by decapitating them over the rim of a barrel or with their bare hands. Although it is not advocated, birds also are killed by being jumped upon, left to suffocate in the barrel of bodies, or occasionally ripped apart. Once the shoot ends, the dead birds are thrown away as trash (Becker, 1996).

[. . .]

The Protest in 1992

Before the event in 1992, The Fund encouraged activists to protest the shoot, running advertisements in animal activist magazines and networking through other national and local groups. The organization created a press release promising to stage "what is likely to be the nation's largest ever protest on behalf of animals" (Fund Press Release, 1992). The goal was to have as many people as possible engage in protest activities and willingly be arrested for breaking various laws. Though The Fund had been successful in attracting 1,500 protestors, it did little to organize protest activity before the event. A workshop in civil disobedience was optional, and no specific acts were arranged.

Because there had been no attempt to regulate the behavior of the activists, the overall context for the protest was one of chaos and tension. Several incidents led to a feeling of threat and anger. Videos of the event show the Black Berets, an animal rights militia of sorts, taunting spectators, calling them "pigeon sucking perverts," and trying to elicit a response. All people interviewed, including Prescott, agree that there were obscenities, insults, and screaming matches "breaking out all over the park" (H. Prescott; Media representatives 1–4, personal communications, February 20, 1997). [. . .] Most of the 114 activists were arrested on charges of disorderly conduct, criminal trespass, theft and harassment (Helgeson, 1992).

Period of Reconsideration

Following the protests of 1992, leaders at The Fund assessed their situation. It was clear that despite many acts of civil disobedience, they had not been able to gain much public support. The most disturbing trend that Fund leaders noticed was the media's approach to the protest. Only minimal attention was given to the actual plight of the pigeons. Reporters chose to focus on the more controversial conflict between supporters and protesters of the shoot.

[. . .]

In 1996, The Fund decided to reinstate some form of civil disobedience. Leaders at The Fund focused on developing an approach to civil disobedience that would better communicate their objections to the shoot and generally be more effective in persuading both the local and national audience to speak out against the event. In so doing, they tried to better understand their audience and more clearly represent themselves.

[. . .]

Protests 1996

The correspondence with activists before the event in 1996 differs notably from that in 1992. Instead of encouraging large numbers to attend, The Fund solicited only a small group of activists. As "peacekeepers," they were told that their job was to assure that "public attention—including media attention—is not distracted from the cruelty of the event by loud and potentially violent confrontations between activists and shoot supporters" (H. Prescott, personal communication, October 25, 1996).

[. . .]

In the midst of this context, those participating in the civil disobedience followed the plans that were carefully constructed prior to their arrival. Twelve activists in two groups of six entered the shooting fields before the event began. Locking steel bicycle locks together, they bound themselves to one another at the neck and then lay down. Their goal was twofold: (a) to prevent the start of the shoot for as long as possible and (b) to make the argument, with their bodies, that the shoot was unjust and should be discontinued (H. Prescott, personal communication, February 21, 1997).

In conducting the civil disobedience, the activists remained silent and at a distance from the crowd. They lay flat on the ground, putting their "health and safety in jeopardy" (Police representative, personal communication, February 20, 1997). Even when the crowd tried to provoke the disobedients, they remained calm and did not respond in any way. When finally they were cut free from the kryptonite octopus, they did not resist arrest and were quietly removed from the field. The shoot was held up for close to two hours. The disobedients acted totally without violence (physical or verbal). In being bound together, they attempted to represent the captivity and helplessness of the birds. This small act of suffering was put forth as a type of representation for the ultimate suffering of the pigeons who were to be wounded and killed.

[. . .]

Discussion

At the protests of the pigeon shoot in Hegins, leaders of The Fund wanted to communicate a message about the suffering of the birds. Initially, this suffering aroused their anger, and they represented themselves in anger. At the protest in 1992, those involved in the protest often hurled insults at the crowd, which included a number of children. [. . .] In 1992, the protesters and those engaged in civil disobedience were neither nonviolent nor able to demonstrate clearly a willingness to suffer.

[. . .]

The most important aspect of civil disobedience that was recognized and respected by the activists in 1996 was nonviolence. The disobedients realized that their argument could not be put forth in violence, as those who were threatened would be unlikely to acknowledge some common ground and therefore could not be persuaded. Almost everyone interviewed agreed that the protesters were more effective when they engaged in "true" civil disobedience and abandoned the angry and violent tone set early on (Media representative 2, personal communication, February 20, 1997). One representative from the local media even suggested that if "they [the protesters] keep it toned down, at a low level, they can win over a good majority of the solid decent people in the town" (Media representative 2, personal communication, February 20, 1997).

The second key aspect of civil disobedience activists acknowledged in 1996 was a willingness to suffer for their beliefs and to communicate that suffering to onlookers. Instead of showing anger at the treatment of the pigeons during the shoot, the disobedients and other activists tried to represent the suffering of the pigeons through their own suffering.

[. . .]

In many ways, 1996 was the turning point in the battle over pigeon shoots in Hegins, Pennsylvania. In 1997 and 1998, The Fund basically stayed away from the event, choosing to capitalize on growing support for its position. The Fund pursued cruelty cases in court and lobbied for bills in the state legislature. After a series of legal rounds, supporters of the shoot agreed to discontinue the event. In 1999, and for every Labor Day since then, the shooting fields in Hegins have been silent. After 10 years and various approaches to the tactic of civil disobedience, the activists are finally sounding victory.

[. . .]

Civil disobedience can be an empowering activity for both activists and the general public. Activists join together and publicly advocate their position. The general public witnesses commitments and challenges to the system that extend beyond the voting booth and individual consumer choices. When civil disobedience is truly effective, it can change society's relationship to animals and even revitalize our public sphere.

References

Becker, C. (1996). [Videotape] *Gunblast, culture clash.*
The Fund. (1996). *Guidelines for animal protection activists at Hegins, 1996.* Unpublished document.
Fund Press Release. (September 2, 1992). Silver Spring, MD: Author.
Fund Press Release. (September 6, 1996). Silver Spring, MD: Author.
Glaser, B. and Stauss, A. (1967). *The discovery of grounded theory.* Chicago: Aldine.
Stephens, M. (1980). *Broadcast news.* New York: Holt, Rinehart & Winston.

90 Ten Ways to Make a Difference

Peter Singer

Peter Singer builds on the work of Henry Spira (1927–98) in suggesting 10 effective strategies to use on behalf of animals. To many, Henry Spira was the most effective activist of the modern animal rights movement. He put the issue of cosmetics testing on the political map, and convinced the USDA to abandon a face-branding requirement slated to include all cattle imported from Mexico. His success shows that one person can still make a difference.

1. Try to Understand the Public's Current Thinking and Where It Could Be Encouraged to Go Tomorrow. Above All, Keep in Touch with Reality

Too many activists mix only with other activists and imagine that everyone else thinks as they do. They start to believe in their own propaganda and lose their feel for what the average person in the street might think. They no longer know what is achievable and what is a fantasy that has grown out of their own intense conviction of the need for change.

[. . .]

Henry Spira grabs every opportunity to talk to people outside the animal movement. He'll start up a conversation with the person sitting next to him on a bus or train, mention an issue he is concerned about, and listen to their responses. How do they react? Can they feel themselves in the place of the victim? Are they outraged? What in particular do they focus on?

2. Select a Target on the Basis of Vulnerabilities to Public Opinion, the Intensity of Suffering, and the Opportunities for Change

Target selection is crucial. Henry knows that he can run an effective campaign when he feels sure that, as he said about the New York state law allowing laboratories to take dogs and cats from shelters, "it just defies common sense that the average guy in the street would say, 'Hey, that's a real neat thing to do.'"

You know that you have a good target if, by merely stating the issue, you put your adversary on the defensive. During the museum campaign, for example, Henry could ask the public: "Do you want your tax monies spent to mutilate cats in order to observe the sexual performance of crippled felines?" The museum was immediately in a very awkward position. Cosmetic testing made another good target, because you only had to ask, "Is another shampoo worth blinding rabbits?" to put Revlon officials on the defensive.

Keeping in touch with reality is a prerequisite for selecting the right target: If you don't know what the public currently thinks, you won't know what they will find acceptable and what will revolt them.

The other elements of point 2 suggest a balance between the good that the campaign can do and its likelihood of success. When Henry selected the cat experiments at the American Museum of Natural History as his first target, he knew that he would directly affect, at best, about sixty cats a year—a tiny number compared to many other possible targets. But the opportunity for change was great because of the nature of the experiments themselves and the location and vulnerability of the institution carrying out the experiments. In 1976, it was vital for the animal movement to have a victory, no matter how small, to encourage its own supporters to believe in the possibility of change and to gain some credibility with the wider world.

[. . .]

3.   Set Goals That Are Achievable. Bring about Meaningful Change One Step at a Time. Raising Awareness Is Not Enough

When Henry first took an interest in opposing animal experimentation, the antivivisection movement had no goal other than the abolition of vivisection and no strategy for achieving this goal other than "raising awareness"—that is, mailing out literature filled with pictures and descriptions of the horrors of vivisection. This was the strategy of a movement that talked mainly to itself. It had no idea how to get a hold on the levers of change, or even where those levers might be located. It seemed unaware of its own image as a bunch of ineffective cranks and did not know how to make vivisection an issue that would be picked up by the media. Henry's background in the civil rights movement told him that this was not the way to succeed:

> One of the first things that I learned in earlier movements was that nothing is ever an all-or-nothing issue. It's not a one-day process, it's a long process. You need to see the world—including individuals and institutions—as not being static but in constant change, with change occurring one step at a time. It's incremental. It's almost like organic development. You might say, for instance, that a couple of blacks demanding to be seated at a lunch counter really doesn't make a hell of a lot of difference because most of them don't even have the money to buy anything at a lunch counter. But it did make a difference, it was a first step. Once you take that first step and you have that same first step in a number of places, you integrate a number of lunch counters, you set a whole pattern, and it's one of the steps that would generate the least amount of resistance. It's something that's winnable, but it encourages the black struggle and it clearly leads to the next step and the next step. I think that no movement has ever won on the basis of all or none.[1]

Some activists think that accepting less than, say, the total abolition of vivisection is a form of compromise that reduces their chances of a more complete victory. Henry's view is: "I want to abolish the use of animals as much as anybody else, but I say, let's do what we can do today and then do more tomorrow."[2] That is why he was willing to support moves to replace the LD50 with tests like the approximate lethal dose test, which still uses animals, but far fewer of them.

Look for targets that are not only winnable in themselves, but where winning will have expanding ripple effects. Ask yourself if success in one campaign will be a stepping stone toward still-bigger targets and more significant victories. The campaign against Revlon is an example: Because it made research into alternatives respectable, its most important effects have been felt beyond Revlon and even beyond the cosmetics industry as a whole.

While raising awareness is essential if we are to bring about change, Henry does not usually work directly at raising awareness. (His advertisements against meat are an exception.) Awareness follows a successful campaign, and a successful campaign will have achievable goals.

4.   Establish Credible Sources of Information and Documentation. Never Assume Anything. Never Deceive the Media or the Public. Maintain Credibility, Don't Exaggerate or Hype the Issue

Before starting a new campaign, Henry spends several months gathering information. Freedom of information legislation has helped enormously, but a lot of information is already out there, in the public domain. Experimenters report their experiments in scientific journals that are available in major libraries, and valuable data about corporations may also be a matter of public record. Henry is never content simply to quote from the leaflets of animal rights groups, or other opponents of the institution or corporation that he is targeting. He always goes to the source, which is preferably a publication of the target itself, or else a government document. Newspapers like the *New York Times* have been prepared to run Henry's advertisements making very specific allegations of wrongdoing against people like Frank Perdue because every allegation has been meticulously checked.

Some organizations describing experiments will conveniently omit details that make the experiments less shocking than they would otherwise appear. They may, for example, neglect to tell their readers that the animals were anesthetized at the time. But those who do this eventually lose credibility. Henry's credibility is extraordinarily high, both within the animal movement and with its opponents, because he regards it as his most important asset. It is therefore never to be sacrificed for a short-term gain, no matter how tempting that may be at the time.

5. Don't Divide the World into Saints and Sinners

When Henry wants to get someone—a scientist, a corporate executive, a legislator, or a government official—to do something differently, he puts himself in the position of that person:

> [The question to ask yourself is:] If I were that person, what would make me want to change my behavior? If you accuse them of being a bunch of sadistic bastards, these people are not going to figure, "Hey, what is it I could do that's going to be different and make those people happy?" That's not the way the real world works.

Being personally hostile to an opponent may be a good way of letting off steam, but it doesn't win people over. When Henry wanted to persuade scientists working for corporations like Procter & Gamble to develop nonanimal alternatives, he saw their situation as similar to that of people who eat animals:

> How do you change these people's behavior best? By saying you've never made a conscious decision to harm those animals. Basically you've been programmed from being a kid: "Be nice to cat and doggy, and eat meat." And I think some of these researchers, that's how they were taught, that's how they were programmed. And you want to reprogram them, and you're not going to reprogram them by saying we're saints and you're sinners, and we're going to clobber you with a two-by-four in order to educate you.

As Susan Fowler, editor of the trade magazine *Lab Animal* at the time of the Revlon campaign, put it:

> There is no sense in Henry's campaign of: "Well, this is Revlon, and no one in Revlon is going to be interested in what we are doing, they're all the enemy." Rather . . . he looks for—and kind of waits for, I think—someone to step out of the group and say: "Well, I understand what you're saying.[3]

Without this attitude, when Roger Shelley came along ready to listen to what Henry wanted Revlon to do, the opportunity to change the company's approach could easily have been missed.

Not dividing the world into saints and sinners isn't just sound tactics, it is also the way Henry thinks. "People can change," he says. "I used to eat animals and I never considered myself a cannibal."[4]

6. Seek Dialogue and Attempt to Work Together to Solve Problems. Position Issues as Problems with Solutions. This Is Best Done by Presenting Realistic Alternatives

Because he doesn't think of his opponents as evil, Henry has no preconceptions about whether they will or will not work with him to reduce animal suffering. So he opens every campaign with a polite letter to the target organization—whether the American Museum of Natural History, Amnesty

International, Revlon, Frank Perdue, or a meatpacker—inviting them to discuss the concerns he has. Sometimes Henry's invitations have been ignored, sometimes they have received an equally polite response from a person skilled in public relations who has no intention of doing anything, and sometimes they have led directly to the change he wanted without any public campaigning at all. But the fact that he suggests sitting down to talk about the problem before he does any public campaigning shows that he isn't just stirring up trouble for the fun of it, or as a way of raising funds for his organization.

Henry puts considerable thought into how the person or organization he is approaching could achieve its goals while eliminating or substantially reducing the suffering now being caused. The classic example of an imaginative solution was Henry's proposal to Revlon and other cosmetics manufacturers that they should fund research into alternatives to the Draize eye test. For more than a year before his campaign went public, Henry had been seeking a collaborative, rather than a confrontational, approach with Revlon. In the end, after the campaign finally did go public, Revlon accepted his proposal and, together with other companies, found that for a very small expenditure, relative to their income, they could develop an alternative that enabled them to have a more precise, cheaper form of product safety testing that did not involve animals at all.

Having a realistic solution to offer means that it is possible to accentuate the positive, instead of running a purely negative campaign. In interviews and leaflets about the Draize test, for example, Henry always emphasized that in vitro testing methods offered the prospect of quicker, cheaper, more reliable, and more elegant ways of testing the safety of new products.

[. . .]

In terms of offering a positive outcome, the difference between the campaigns against the cat experiments and those against the Draize test was one of degree, not kind. If your tube of toothpaste is blocked, whether you will be able to get any toothpaste out of it will depend on how badly blocked the tube is and on how much pressure is exerted on it. So, too, whether an institution or corporation will adopt an alternative will depend on how negatively it views the alternative and how much pressure it is under. The more realistic the alternative is, the less pressure will be needed to see it adopted.

7. Be Ready for Confrontation If Your Target Remains Unresponsive. If Accepted Channels Don't Work, Prepare an Escalating Public Awareness Campaign to Place Your Adversary on the Defensive

If point 6 is about making it easy for the toothpaste to come out of the tube, point 7 is about increasing the pressure if it still won't come. A public awareness campaign may take various forms. At the American Museum of Natural History, it started with an article in a local newspaper, then it was kept up by pickets and demonstrations, and finally it spread through the national media and specialist journals like *Science*. The Revlon campaign went public with a dramatic full-page advertisement in the *New York Times*, which itself generated more publicity. The campaign continued with demonstrations outside Revlon's offices. The Perdue and face-branding campaigns relied much more heavily on advertising and the use of the media. Advertising takes money, on which, see point 8.

8. Avoid Bureaucracy

Anyone who has been frustrated by lengthy committee meetings that absorb time and energy will sympathize with Henry's desire to get things done rather than spend time on organizational tangles. Worse still, bureaucratic structures all too often divert energy into making the organization grow, rather than getting results for the cause. Then when the organization grows, it needs staff and an office. So you get a situation in which people who want to make a difference for animals (or for street kids, or for rain forests, or for whatever cause) spend 80 percent of their time raising money just to keep the organization going. Most of the time is spent ensuring that everyone in the organization gets along with one another, feels appreciated, and is not upset because he or she expected to be promoted to a more responsible position or given an office with more windows.

Henry has been able to avoid such obstacles by working, essentially, on his own. That isn't a style that will suit everyone, but it has worked well for Henry. Animal Rights International has no members. It has a long list of advisers and its board consists of trusted close friends whom Henry can rely upon for support without hassles. Henry doesn't need a lot of money, but he does need some. He has been fortunate in finding two donors who support him regularly because they like to see their money making a difference.

When Henry needs more clout, he puts a coalition together—as he did on the repeal of the Metcalf-Hatch Act, in fighting against the Draize and LD50 tests, and now, to persuade McDonald's to take a leading role in improving the welfare of farm animals. Since his early success at the American Museum of Natural History, other organizations have been eager to join his coalitions. At their height, these coalitions have included hundreds of organizations, with memberships in the millions. Here, too, though, Henry keeps hassles to a minimum. Organizations are welcome to participate at whatever level they wish. Some get their supporters out to demonstrate or march, while others don't. Some pay for full-page advertisements, and others ask them to write letters to newspapers, where they may reach millions without spending a cent. What no organization can do is dictate policy. Henry consults widely, but in the end, he makes his own decisions, thus avoiding the time-consuming and sometimes divisive process of elections and committee meetings. Clearly, in the case of major disagreements, organizations have the option of leaving; but if the coalition is making progress, organizations will generally swallow the disagreements in order to be part of a successful team.

9. Don't Assume That Only Legislation or Legal Action can Solve the Problem

Henry has used elected representatives in his campaigns to put pressure on government agencies and to gain publicity. But the only campaign in which he achieved his aim through legislation was the repeal of the Metcalf-Hatch Act. Here, since bad legislation was the target of the campaign, he had no choice. Otherwise, as far as he can, Henry stays out of conventional political processes and keeps away from the courts: "No congressional bill, no legal gimmickry, by itself, will save the animals." No doubt there are other situations, and other issues, on which legislation will make a difference. But on the whole, Henry sees laws as maintaining the status quo. They will be changed only in order to keep disturbance at a minimum. The danger of getting deeply involved in the political process is that it often deflects struggles into what Henry calls "political gabbery." There is a lot of talk, but nothing happens. Political lobbying or legal maneuvering becomes a substitute for action.

10. Ask Yourself: "Will It Work?"

All of the preceding points are directed toward this last one. Before you launch a campaign, or continue with a campaign already begun, ask yourself if it will work. If you can't give a realistic account of the ways in which your plans will achieve your objectives, you need to change your plans. Keeping in touch with what the public is thinking, selecting a target, setting an achievable goal, getting accurate information, maintaining credibility, suggesting alternative solutions, being ready to talk to adversaries or to confront them if they will not talk—all of these are directed toward creating a campaign that is a practical means of making a difference. The overriding question is always: *Will it work?*

[. . .]

Notes

1. "Singer Speaks with Spira," *Animal Liberation*, January–March 1989, p. 5.
2. Ibid., p. 6.
3. Susan Fowler, videotaped interview with author, New York, December 1996.
4. "Singer Speaks with Spira," p. 5.

91 The Animal Activist's Handbook

Maximizing Our Positive Impact in Today's World

Matt Ball and Bruce Friedrich

Choosing Meaningful Action

Is there a reason to care about how we live?

In his book *How Are We To Live?* (1995), Peter Singer describes how the collapse of religious traditions has left a void in many people's lives: "When Sartre realized that life has no meaning, it was a shocking contention. Now, it is simply the normal understanding." Most Americans wouldn't agree that life has no meaning, and the vast majority claim to believe in God and a higher purpose. Observing actual behavior, however, one wonders whether people are living lives that can be reconciled with their belief in meaning.

More than fifty years ago, Catholic Worker Movement founder Dorothy Day argued that we show our faith in a deeper meaning by living our lives in a way that speaks to our values. Like Gandhi and many other great spiritual teachers from a variety of faiths, she believed that our actions indicate both our values and whether we actually believe in a higher meaning.

It seems to us that "getting ahead"—accumulating material wealth and possessions for oneself and/or one's family—has become many people's *de facto* meaning of life, regardless of what they say they believe. For many others, life appears to be only about getting to the finish line, about filling up time with television, sports, and whatever else. For many (if not most) people, life has become a race to acquire more stuff and a fight against boredom.

But are those who live for possessions or simply to pass time really happy? Is this the best way to live? And more critically, how should we evaluate *our* lives? We hope you'll agree that answers to these questions are important enough to pursue with honesty and humility. Our struggle with these questions is the starting point of this book.

Evolution and Insatiability

The first step in our quest for a meaningful life is to break down assumptions and dig to the roots of our motivation, i.e., why do we make the choices we do? Sometimes our choices seem to be consciously considered; we might even make lists, "pro" on one side and "con" on the other. But there's always more going on—there are aspects of our nature as human beings that point us in one direction or another. With a general understanding of our evolutionary baggage, we can better understand why we often find ourselves pursuing material goods and simply passing time. From there, we may be able to make some rational assessments of whether these pursuits truly are the path to happiness.

Simply put, it's human nature to desire *more*, to strive for a greater share, regardless of what we already have. Over the millennia, those who were satisfied with what they had were erased from the gene pool by our unfulfilled ancestors. Individuals who pursued and obtained the most (e.g., food, partners, children, and other signs of "wealth") were the ones who prospered. The connection between "having" and the continuation of one's genes wasn't conscious, but was manifested in the individual's drives and desires for more, a discontent with the status quo, and envy of those with more. As Robert Wright summarizes in *The Moral Animal* (1995), "People weren't, of course, designed to be relentlessly happy in the ancestral environment; there, as here, anxiety was a chronic motivator, and happiness was the always pursued, often receding, goal."

These innate desires, built into our genes over the course of many millions of years, haven't disappeared; they remain a part of the human genetic makeup. Sadly, there really is no such thing as "enough," since our bodies are programmed with a view toward possible, unpredictable scarcity. Much of humanity has reached a point that our genetic programming could not have predicted—we can be reasonably sure we will survive and provide for future generations.

The fact that human programming to acquire doesn't have an "off" switch can be verified by even a cursory look at the world's millionaires and billionaires. In fact, it would appear that nothing satiates the drive for accumulating—there's always more to have, and there are always those who are better off with whom we feel we must compete. If you're Donald Trump, you can simply compete with yourself to acquire even more. Evolution has left us with a nature that *pursues* without end.

Americans are now about twice as rich as we were in the 1970s, and the Japanese are about six times richer than they were in the 1950s, but neither population is happier now, according to scientific studies (see, for example, imomus.livejournal.com/175376.html). Similarly, even lottery winners revert to their former baseline of happiness (Gilbert, 2007; Haidt, 2006). The phrase isn't "the *pursuit* of happiness" for nothing! Ultimately, the perhaps counterintuitive (and hard to accept) fact is that happiness simply isn't to be found in possessions or wealth.

Once we recognize our ancient, innate drives, we can more clearly and logically pursue what's really important—what it can and should mean to be human. Rational analysis reveals the pitfalls of our evolutionary heritage and can free us from desires that prevent us from achieving sustainable peace and happiness—drives that leave us striving toward, but never achieving, lasting happiness.

As rational beings, we can make decisions about how to live our lives based on logical and consistent derivations from first principles—concepts that we rationally agree are important, defensible, and fundamental—rather than evolutionary baggage, inherent prejudices, or current societal norms. In other words, we can choose to author our life's story, rather than following the narrative set by our genes.

[. . .]

Throughout history, many have claimed to know the meaning of life. They set forth their particular philosophy, rules, and dogma. Looking at options today, we find dozens of competing approaches from philosophers, preachers, psychologists, etc., each convinced that theirs is the right way.

If we are to make rational choices as the basis of our life, we not only have to understand our genetic heritage, but we also have to recognize our cultural programming. If we want to be free of encumbrances that keep us from true fulfillment, it's important that we seek to understand what is fundamental, rather than accepting the dogma *du jour*, the beliefs of our parents, the preaching at the local church, current social views, the most recent best-seller. Just as reason shows us the biological baggage we've accumulated over evolutionary time scales, reason also shows us our cultural encumbrances.

Reason allows us to rise above all of this by showing us a larger perspective, revealing a "rule of the universe," where no one's interests count for more than anyone else's. Putting aside inherent prejudices leads to equal consideration of interests. Interestingly, this is summarized by "The Golden Rule," which can be seen as a core tenet of many ethical and religious traditions. "Love your neighbor as yourself," said Jesus. "What is hateful to you do not do to your neighbor," said Rabbi Hillel, the great Jewish teacher from just before Jesus' time. Confucius summed up his teaching in similar terms: "What you do not want done to yourself, do not do to others." The *Mahabharata*, the great Hindu epic, says: "Let no person do to another that which would be repugnant to her/himself."

Over the course of history, through endless human explanations, proclamations, and interpretations, many ethical systems have lost whatever connection they once had to fundamental principles like the Golden Rule. Most ethical systems have become a list of dos and (more often) don'ts. Those that have thrived have often come with large helpings of protection for the powerful and the status quo. It is an abdication of our rationality and humanity to accept the rules and laws of our day and our society as settled truths. We rightfully shudder at past persecutions of people like Galileo, Susan B. Anthony, Frederick Douglass, and Martin Luther King, Jr., all of whom questioned the dogma of the day. It would be naïve to think that today's society has all the right answers.

Where are we led when we pursue an objective perspective? Honestly and thoroughly considering a universal view shows that, if you dig far enough, virtually all actions can be traced to a desire for fulfillment or happiness and a need to avoid or alleviate suffering. In other words, when push comes to shove, thousands of years of philosophy can be summarized in nineteen words: Something is "good" if it leads to more happiness, and something is "bad" if it leads to more suffering. This is simplistic, of course. Not every situation lends itself to a clear analysis of consequences. Some things may seem intuitively "right" and actually be "right," even if the immediate consequences aren't obviously better than the consequences of different actions. Yet, despite the fact that some situations are difficult to analyze thoroughly, in general, focusing on the *consequences* of the actions is the most consistent way to maximize good outcomes.

Similarly, some things simply *seem* wrong, regardless of any consequential analysis. People come up with examples that seem to defy simple utilitarian analysis as well. But if we are to make rational, defensible decisions that are free of biases, utilitarianism offers a useful, straightforward, objective perspective that can help us avoid being distracted by personal or societal prejudices.

Given that pain—physical, emotional, or psychological—is generally the single greatest barrier to happiness, alleviating pain and suffering is a reasonable first priority for people who want to devote themselves to making the world a kinder place. We are in no way discounting the value of pleasure, but in the end we agree with Richard Ryder, who states in *Painism: A Modern Morality*, "At its extreme, pain is more powerful than pleasure can ever be. Pain overrules pleasure within the individual far more effectively than pleasure can dominate pain." In short, an objective ethics argues that we should make decisions based on what leads to the least amount of suffering.

Once we recognize that suffering is fundamentally bad, and thus eliminating suffering is the ultimate good, we can each dedicate our life to reducing as much suffering as possible. From these primary principles, we can give up the futile *pursuit* of happiness and, instead, live our lives beyond ourselves, for what is truly important. We can transcend our genetic and cultural programming and experience the full potential of our humanity and the richness possible in our existence. From a rational, universal starting point, we can choose to author our life's story, rather than following the narrative set for us by our genes and our culture. We can rise above the self-centered and immediate. We can be a part of something *greater*. . . .

Striving for Morality: Our Influence More Than Our Actions

[. . .]

It's logical that a fundamental ethic involves the reduction of suffering, but often ethics aren't thought of in practical, applied, consequential terms. Rather, "ethics" are thought of only as rules and regulations. It's because of human weakness and prejudice that so much philosophy and religion have become associated with commands and dictates, if we want to be free to live fully, to write our own narrative, we can reject the norms of today and the prejudices of our biology and recognize the fundamental wrong of suffering in the world. We don't need some formal structure to tell us right from wrong; we don't need a priest, rabbi, imam, or philosophy professor to tell us that it's bad to let someone starve to death, that genocide is wrong, that it's a tragedy when children are orphaned by AIDS.

More importantly, however, a complete ethic isn't just about minimizing the bad impact *we* have in the world. The needed change isn't simply *personal.* Although our decisions regarding what to eat and wear, what kind of car to drive, or for whom we should cast our vote are important, they're not as important as our influence on others. That is our *real* impact on the world.

Think of it this way: if we buy only vegan food, or we vote for the candidate of our choice, or we buy only coffee, clothing, etc., that's been produced fairly and responsibly, that's one unit of goodness in that area. If, however, we advocate for our position, each person we influence to do the same thing will *double* the good that our choices cause! Once we have ten people on board, our impact on the world is ten times greater than the choices that we, personally, have made *or that we will ever make*! In just *one* day, with just *one* interaction, we can do as much good for the world with our influence as we can do with our personal decisions and choices over the course of *our entire lives.*

To make the world better, we can—must—do much more than just make good, ethical choices ourselves. We can expose injustice, solicit kindness from others, and work for widespread change and the adoption of moral policies. Every person we meet is a potential major victory. Our power to change the world is much more than we imagine; our potential is mind-blowing!

We have no excuse for waiting. Living ethically—pursuing meaningful action toward a better world by alleviating and preventing suffering—doesn't require any consensus. If we were the one suffering—imprisoned unjustly, enslaved with no rights, exploited because of our race or species—we wouldn't want concerned, thoughtful people to put off taking action until the next election or until a large group endorsed our cause. We don't have to change the government to change the world. We don't have to start a group or organize a campaign. We can each act today and every day.

How Will We Focus Our Energy?

If we agree that the meaning of life is to make the world a better place by exposing and eliminating as much suffering as possible, then the most critical question of our lives is this: how do we do the most possible good in a world where suffering is so widespread?

Again, a basic understanding of human nature can show us potential prejudices and blind spots that might impede us from being optimally effective. Each of us has a bias of concern toward self-interest, the known, and the immediate. This applies to activists just as much as to the general population. Most people working for a better world concentrate on others who are most like them or who are closest to them geographically and/or biologically. It's almost too obvious to warrant mention, but most people working on gay rights issues are gay, on women's rights issues are women, on civil rights are African American, on anti-Semitism are Jewish, etc.

These causes are important, but they're also issues of self-interest for many. Even with causes such as child abuse, cancer, domestic violence, and so on, leaders are often individuals with personal experience (e.g., when celebrities experience a disease, either personally or through a loved one, they often become spokespeople). Charities working within the U.S. get much more funding than those who do work overseas. Work on behalf of exploited or suffering human beings receives exponentially more funding and attention than work on behalf of non-human animals, and demonstrations for human rights attract more people and more moral outrage than demonstrations on behalf of animals.

Some people point to dogs and cats as an exception. In 2007, when investigators pulled sixty abused animals, dozens of animals' corpses, and truckloads of dog fighting paraphernalia from Atlanta Falcons quarterback Michael Vick's property, there were loud and vigorous demonstrations denouncing his cruelty to animals. At the same time, though, there were demonstrations supporting Vick, both on the field and in the community. Many commentators argued that the issue was not worthy of the concern and attention it was getting; others argued he shouldn't be suspended from playing football. Obviously, no one would have been pro-Vick if dead and battered human beings had been found on his property, or if the rape racks had been for humans, rather than dogs. Of course, the numbers protesting his actions were still a tiny fraction of the numbers that turn out for an anti-abortion or anti-war rally.

Some have expressed surprise or even envy at PETA's multi-million-dollar annual budget. This, too, shows the degree of our species bias—as if we're surprised an animal protection organization could take in such a "lofty" sum. Think about it: the largest animal rights organization in the world has a budget of some tens of millions of dollars per year to work against all of the combined injustices against the more than ten billion land animals who are killed annually in the United States. Planned Parenthood took in thirty times that much for work on women's health; Catholic Charities took well over a hundred times more to work on poverty issues. One human disease—cancer—gets thousands and thousands of times more money devoted to it than is contributed to every single issue related to animal rights. Indeed, our entire government is focused on human needs, and spends billions each year subsidizing animal agriculture.

Guiding Principles

An understanding of human nature, along with the recognition of the primacy of suffering, leads to two guiding principles that we've found useful in freeing our advocacy from prejudice.

First, to maximize the amount of good we can accomplish, we should strive to set aside personal biases as much as possible. We should challenge ourselves to approach advocacy through a straightforward analysis of the world as it is, motivated *solely* by a desire to alleviate suffering to the greatest extent possible. If the amount of suffering in the world weren't so vast, other considerations would be warranted (e.g., maximizing pleasure). But as long as so many are suffering so horribly, eliminating as much suffering as possible must be our primary motivating factor.

Second, it's vital we recognize that we all have limited resources and time. It's a simple fact that when we choose to do one thing, we're choosing not to do another—there's no way around it. Instead of choosing to "do something, do anything," we must challenge ourselves to pursue actions that will likely lead to the greatest reduction in suffering. There are a myriad of worthy pursuits, and of course we appreciate anyone working to make the world a kinder place. However, given the above principles, we challenge everyone—including ourselves—to constantly strive to maximize the efficacy of our actions.

Striking at the Root

> There are a thousand hacking at the branches of evil to one who is striking at the root.
> —Henry David Thoreau, *Walden*

Perhaps you've heard the story of the person who finds babies floating down the river a few times per day, day after day after day—saving some, missing most of them. Every day, she waits by the river, knowing there'll be babies to save. Sure enough, every day she pulls some of the drowning babies out of the river, and she feels good about her efforts—saving lives, every day—even as she mourns the many who drown. Finally, one day she thinks, "Who on earth keeps tossing these babies into the river?"

She walks upstream, finds the person doing it, and stops him. In that moment, she's saved all of the babies who would have been tossed into the river in the future, and becomes free to dedicate herself to something else that would be helpful in the world. There's much triage work to be done in our society—there are many drowning babies, as it were. And obviously the work of saving them is good. But we're convinced that if we can stop people from tossing babies into the water in the first place, we'll be more effective.

In concrete terms, we choose not to focus our incredibly limited time and resources on individual animals, however valuable and rewarding that work is. Rather, we seek to challenge the very structures of oppression against animals, and to work to dismantle the system that says animals are commodities we can eat. To do this as effectively as possible, we must set priorities and, given our limited resources, make some difficult, rational choices.

Setting Priorities

Peter Singer asks us in "The Singer Solution to World Poverty" (utilitarian.net/singer/by/19990905.htm) to consider the case of a man who just bought a new car. He paid $50,000 for the car and doesn't have it insured yet. His car stalls on a set of railroad tracks, and, before he can push the car off, he sees a small girl also on the tracks, oblivious to an oncoming train. He has to choose between moving his car or saving the girl. Obviously, if he chose the car, all of us would hold him in moral contempt. Singer asks: what is the real difference between this scenario and buying the car in the first place, when you could buy a perfectly acceptable car for $20,000 or less, leaving $30,000 to dedicate to poverty relief, which would save far more than one child.

Similarly, consider the example of someone who has just bought an extra pair of two-hundred-dollar shoes. She sees a child drowning in the river. If the person chooses not to jump in for fear of destroying her shoes, again, all of us would find her morally reprehensible. Yet the same moral conclusion can be drawn when it comes to buying a pair of expensive shoes that aren't needed in the first place, rather than giving the money to charity.

When applying this to animals, the comparison becomes even more stark, since, for just a few coins, you can put an illustrated, detailed, documented booklet in someone's hands, show someone *Meet Your Meat* (meat.org) through online advertising, or show them a thirty-second vegetarian commercial. It takes so little to be the animals' voice, yet few of us even consider utilizing the power we have.

Even though U.S. society is composed mainly of professed Christians, most ignore Christ's words to the rich man: "Go, sell all that you have, and give to the poor" (Matthew 19). In an attempt to update the principle for our often selfish society, Singer makes the case that a reasonable standard for most of us would be to give away twenty percent of our income. Will that hurt, given that we've grown accustomed to our current level of income? For most of us, it will. At the very least, it will require an adjustment. But can we do it without actual physical harm coming to us? For most of us, yes, we can. Organizations dedicated to reducing as much suffering as possible can use that money to make the world better—far more so than whatever we might otherwise spend it on. . . .

[. . .]

We Can Do It

Consider this: the people we admire are not those who went along with the crowd, who did whatever was allowed by the norms of their times. Rather, the people we rightly respect are those who stood up to the prejudices of their society. Dr. Martin Luther King, Jr., Dorothy Day, Mohandas Gandhi, Susan B. Anthony, and so many other individuals changed their world. We are all called to do no less.

In the face of so much suffering, it can become easy to become despondent and to think that we can't change the world. But if we break our work into chunks, celebrate the "small" victories for what they really mean (e.g., turning one person vegetarian changes their entire life forever and makes a massive, positive impact in the world), and keep ourselves focused on our goals, we can realize what significant progress we're making. After decades of experience as activists, we're deeply and profoundly optimistic. Every day, we take inspiration in a review of the progress that has been won for social justice and animal protection (as we discuss at greater length in Chapter Five).

There are, of course, many potential targets for our activism: two billion people live without access to clean water; a billion don't have enough calories to sustain themselves; women in many parts of the world suffer unjust treatment and violence; our fellow creatures are abused and slaughtered.

These are a few of our society's current practices that, we're convinced, future generations will look back on with the same sense of incredulity we reserve for past atrocities like slavery and witch burnings. We are called to be like those we admire for standing up against the prejudices of their day.

Why Vegetarian Advocacy?

Because our singular goal is to have the greatest impact on the amount of suffering in the world, we've chosen to dedicate our lives to exposing the cruelties of factory farms and industrial slaughterhouses while promoting a vegetarian diet.

Emphasizing factory farms and dietary change is not our "personal issue." We have no special affinity to farmed animals over other animals (or human beings). Rather, this conscious choice follows directly from our fundamental guiding principles: 1) We want to maximize the reduction of suffering, and 2) We know that, by choosing to do one thing, we're choosing not to do other things.

Our experience has shown that promoting vegetarianism offers the most effective and efficient way of decreasing overall suffering, for three basic reasons—the sheer number of animals, the enormous amount of suffering involved, and the opportunity the issue presents.

The Numbers

The number of animals raised and killed for food *each year* in the U.S. alone *vastly* exceeds any and all other forms of exploitation. The numbers are *far* greater than the total human population of the entire world: more than ten billion land animals are consumed in the U.S. each year, while the human global population is just over six billion. Approximately ninety-nine out of every hundred animals killed in the U.S. each year are slaughtered for human consumption. From a statistical standpoint, every animal killed in the U.S. dies to be eaten.

The Suffering

Of course, if these billions of animals lived happy, healthy lives and had quick and painless deaths, then our concern for suffering might lead us to focus our efforts elsewhere. But animals raised for food in the U.S. must endure unimaginable suffering. Indeed, perhaps the most difficult aspect of advocating on behalf of these animals is trying to describe the indescribable: the overcrowding and confinement, the stench, the racket, the extremes of heat and cold, the attacks and even cannibalism, the hunger and starvation, the illness, the mutilation, the drugging and breeding that create animals who can't even walk (e.g., "Farmed Chickens Can't Walk; Just Grow Them in Vats Already," blog. wired.com/wiredscience/2008/02/chickens-cant-w.html)—in short, the near-constant suffering and horror of every day of their lives. Indeed, every year, hundreds of millions of animals—*many times more* than the total number killed for fur, housed in shelters, and locked in laboratories combined—don't even make it to slaughter. They actually *suffer to death*.

The Opportunity

If there were nothing we could do about these animals' suffering—if it all happened in a distant land beyond our influence—then, again, our focus would be different. But anti-factory-farming/pro-vegetarianism advocacy is the most readily accessible option for making a better world. We don't have to overthrow a government. We don't have to forsake modern life. We don't have to win an election or convince Congress of the validity of our argument. We don't have to start a group or organize a campaign. Rather, every day, *every single person* makes decisions that affect the lives of these farmed animals. Helping people change leads to fewer animals suffering in factory farms. By choosing to expose the horrors of modern agribusiness and promote vegetarianism, every person we meet is a potential victory.

All thoughtful people want to see the world become more just and peaceful. Nearly everyone is worried about injustice and violence and wishes they could do something to stop it. What can we do about starvation and AIDS in sub-Saharan Africa? We can donate money, write letters, or try to get the government to intervene and give more aid. But all of those actions, though well-meaning, are far removed from having a measurable effect. On the other hand, three times each and every day, we make a concrete decision about who we are in the world. We each answer the question: "Do I want to add to the level of violence and misery and bloodshed in the world, or do I want to make a kind and compassionate choice?"

Simply put, the meat industry is violence we can either support or help stop. Every time we sit down to eat, we have the opportunity to have a profound impact on the world. Every meat-free meal is a blow against factory farms. Every time someone notices we don't eat meat, we're providing the animals a voice. It's hard to imagine any other choice we can make with such far-reaching effects.

It's very powerful to realize that following a vegetarian diet and setting a cruelty-free example allow us to take a stand against violence and suffering. *Every single time* we order from a menu, go shopping, or open up the refrigerator, we stand up for compassion. It is even more powerful to realize that every day, we can multiply that impact through our advocacy.

Seeing the Unseen

Our goal is to put aside our personal affinities, and instead focus solely on the suffering of others. In doing so, we've found that the above three points—the numbers, the suffering, and the opportunity—when taken together, are a logically compelling and, indeed, an irrefutable argument for working to end factory farming and promote vegetarianism.

Paul McCartney has pointed out that, "If slaughterhouses had glass walls, everyone would be a vegetarian." This concisely captures the main problem of vegetarian advocacy: people don't have to see the animals they eat being imprisoned in factory farms and butchered in industrial slaughterhouses. Someone can order a chicken sandwich, and to that person, it's just a sandwich. Even detailed, take-home illustrations, videos, and information about factory farms don't always stick with every individual. Society is set up not only to conceal the realities behind meat and divorce it from the actual animal, but to celebrate inanimate pieces of meat in and of themselves.

Similarly, if the realities of factory farms and slaughterhouses were as visible as the meat they produce, all thoughtful, compassionate individuals would be vegetarian advocates. Strip away the elaborate concealment and we'd see that nearly all animals exploited in this country suffer and die to be eaten. With the animals visible, it would be apparent that every single person can make a direct and massive positive impact, simply by choosing to eat kind foods, rather than cruel foods.

Our inherent prejudice in favor of familiar animals (and for those whose suffering is immediately in front of us) has led those concerned with animals to spend hundreds of millions of dollars on cats and dogs each year, while focusing very little on the billions of domesticated animals slaughtered to be eaten. This is why one email plea about homeless pets in New Orleans is able to bring in much more money than any fundraiser for vegetarian promotion. Our hearts go out to familiar animals ("pets") who suffer through wars, natural disasters, and who are killed in shelters. We are, of course, glad that many people are compassionate toward these animals. Similar compassion and level of concern, exhibited efficiently and without prejudice, however, could have an exponentially greater impact.

For example, assuming only a very conservative one percent rate of change from the booklets that groups like Vegan Outreach and PETA distribute, there are tens of thousands of vegetarians in the world who would otherwise have eaten meat for the rest of their lives. Since the average American consumes about three dozen factory-farmed birds and mammals a year (and even more aquatic animals), distribution of these booklets has led to *many hundreds of millions* of birds and mammals being completely spared from the horrors of factory farms over the next fifty years. And that's assuming only a one percent total rate of influence and no multiplier effect (i.e., that each of these new vegetarians doesn't influence anyone else)!

In fact, there's reason to believe that the conversion rate is quite a bit higher, and that the multiplier effect is very powerful. PETA surveyed people who received their vegetarian starter guide, and responses indicated that more than eighty percent of non-vegans changed their diet, with twenty-three percent going from meat eater to an entirely vegetarian or vegan diet after reading the guide. Clearly there's some self-selection in survey responses, but these results indicate that the rate of change is probably greater than one percent, and that even those who don't immediately go entirely vegetarian may be cutting back on their meat consumption (please see animaladvocacybook.com for more details).

Because there are so few of us who look beyond the familiar and immediate, recognize the magnitude of the suffering caused by eating meat, and understand the opportunity vegetarian outreach presents, we have a special obligation to do the hard, intangible, and often unrewarding work of removing the walls that hide the atrocities of factory farms and industrial slaughterhouses. We need to be the vanguard, working as much as possible to abolish, totally and forever, the horrors of modern animal agriculture.

Index

abolitionists 697–8; *see also* slavery
Abram, David 444
Abravanel 291
absent referents 45, 243, 281–2, 281–5;
  objectification, fragmentation, and consumption
  for 284–5; overlapping 282–3; racism and 283;
  sexual violence and meat eating and 283–4
acetaminophen 315
acetylsalicylic acid 315
Adams, Carol J. 45, 243, 281–5
ADMET (absorption, distribution, metabolism,
  excretion, and toxicity) data 316
Advanced Cell Technology (ACT) 410
Advertising Standards Authority (UK) 354
Africa Resources Trust (ART) 519
African grey parrots, communication by 145
After Christianity 294
aggressive intergroup encounters 189
agribusiness, goal of 246
agriculture: confinement 243; husbandry, origin of
  1; improving research in animal 265–6; intensive,
  elimination of 272; killing animals 499–500;
  no-till 271, 272; pre- 1; *telos* and 449–51; *see also*
  farming
Alam, Mohamed 243, 301
alarm calling 146
Allard, Ruth 582
Allen, Colin 65, 130–2
American Academy of Religion 298
American Association of Zoos and Aquariums
  (AZA) 199, 575, 577, 582–7, 592, 598
American Kennel Club (AKC) 647
American Meat Institute 254
American Medical Association 322, 359
American Museum of Natural History 480
American Society for the Prevention of Cruelty to
  Animals (ASPCA) 6–7, 701
American Society for the Prevention of Cruelty to
  Children 7
American Veterinary Medical Association
  622–3, 644
Ammann, Karl 198
anachronistic self-sufficiency and hunters 501
analogy, reasoning by 219
Andrews, Kristin 161, 181–94
anesthetics and analgesics 111, 350–1

Angel, George 6–7
Angulo, E. 388–9
animacy 176
animal-assisted therapy (AAT): exploitation-based
  case for 657–8; moral basis of 650–9; objections
  to 655–9; paternalistic case for 652–3; swim-with-
  dolphins programs 566–7; use versus exploitation
  and 653–5
animal-to-animal embryonic, fetal, or adult
  chimeras 405
Animal Behavior 343
animal-harm scales 370–1
animal-to-human embryonic, fetal, or adult
  chimeras 405
Animal Legal Defense Fund, Inc. v. Glickman 678
Animal Liberation 8, 349
"Animal Liberation" 274
"Animal Liberation: A Triangular Affair" 514
Animal Liberation Front 8–9, 322
Animal Machines 8
Animal Plant and Health Inspection
  Service (aphis) 263
Animal Protection Act (Germany) 368
Animal Reform Movement 8
Animal Rights and Human Morality 349, 465
Animal Rights Theory (ART) 269; critics of 58;
  premise of 53, 55–6; rejection of 56–7; *see also*
  rights, animal
Animal Welfare Act (US) 341, 366, 367, 368, 564,
  681–2
Animal Welfare Institute 7
animals: ancient views of 1–3; beliefs on 51–2;
  compassion for 4, 292; complex behaviors of 65;
  connection between gods and 1; cruelty toward
  5, 635–8; desires, intentions, and feelings in 13;
  dialogical ethic of care for treatment of 45–7;
  differences between humans and 33–4; direct
  duties and 26; eating of, by other animals 38–9; as
  genuine thinkers 65, 100; medieval views of 3–4;
  prehistoric 1; sacred 1; slavery of 4; souls in 290;
  viewed as being-less 285
Animals, Men and Morals 8
Animals (Scientific Procedures) Act (UK) 352
Animals and Why They Matter 1
Animals as Persons 56
Animals Voice 9

Anthes, Emily 10
Anthony, Susan B. 7, 713, 716
anthropocentrism 4–5, 9, 91
anthropomorphism 65; argument by analogy 91–3;
    argument from experimental data 93–7; confusion
    with anthrocentrism 91; consciousness and 230;
    cross-species modeling and 89–97; defined
    91; fate in contemporary science 97; logical
    objections to 90–1
antibiotics 90, 259
antifactual consciousness 134
antimicrobial resistance 258–60, 263
anxiety 71
Ape Alliance 198
apes, great 515; concept of death in 93;
    consciousness in 173; eye contact by 178; as food
    548–52; humanizing of 179; importance of second
    person and 161; language and 168–72; legal rights
    for 665–9; linguistic capacities and self-awareness
    in 161; metarepresentations and 178–9; mutual
    awareness in 178; personhood of 57, 175–83;
    representation in 177; second-person attitude in
    178–9; social life of 156; theory of mind in 93;
    see also chimpanzees
appraisal theory 74–7
approach process systems 73
Aquinas, Thomas 2, 26, 295
Archer, Michael 480, 482, 483
Aristotle 26–7, 113, 216, 291, 295, 349, 449, 667; on
    meat-eating and vegetarianism 2; *telos* of animals
    and 464, 465, 467
Arluke, Arnold 340, 341, 623
Armstrong and Seddon 485
artificial intelligence 121
Ascione, F. R. 380
associative conditioning 99, 130
associative learning 100
atonement doctrine 296–7
Atwood, Margaret 434, 435, 437, 438, 440, 442–3
Audubon, John James 481
Augustine, St. 2, 295
Australia 7
autism 251–2
autoneotic memory 144
avoidance process 73
Ayer, Alfred Jules 348

baboons 83–5, 155–6
Balfour, D. 380
Ball, Matt 711
Ballou, Jonathan 579
Bardot Foundation, Brigitte 200
Barnum, P. T. 563–4
Barry, Kathy 282
Barth, Karl 296
Bate, Jonathan 45
Bateson, Gregory 46
Bateson, Mary Catherine 46
bats 134, 137, 230
Batten, Peter 580
battered women 282–5

Baylis, Françoise 395, 405, 415–17
bear-baiting 3–5, 115
Beatrix Potter syndrome 135
Beck, Ben 579
bees 217
behavior: culture as determinant of 205; non-
    psychological explanations of 99–100;
    psychological explanations of 100
behavioral activation 73
behavioral inhibition system 73
behaviorism 100, 144
belief attribution 191–3
beluga whales *see* cetacean captivity
Bentham, Jeremy 5, 27, 32, 54, 278, 400
Benvenisty et al. 405
Berger, P. 690
Bergh, Henry 6–7
Bergson, Henri-Louis 347
Berlin, Isaiah 666
Bermond, Bob 116
Bermúdez, José Luis 65, 99
bestiality 3
*Beyond Animal Rights: A Feminist Caring Ethic for
    the Treatment of Animals* 553–4, 555
bias: human 168–72; judgment 78
biblical view of animal rights 3, 290–2; Christianity
    and 3, 294–9; Judaism and 289–92; *see also*
    theology
Bill of Rights (US) 349
binocular rivalry 142, 146
biodiversity: ecological ethics of research in
    zoos and aquariums and 594–604; ecological
    integrity and 459–60; exotic species and 531–3;
    managers and ecological ethics 387–92; trophy
    hunting and 516–17; xenophobia and 531–3;
    zoos and 591–2
bioethicists 360
biological species concept 407
biology: conservation 206, 209–10, 212;
    population 206
Biology 348
biomedicine *see* research, animal
biotechnology, animal 395; benefits of genetic
    manipulation in 397–8; culture and scientific
    attitude 428–31; ethical issues in 397–401;
    failure of standard ethical critiques of 426–8;
    future of 401; inevitability of 425–32; public
    opinion and 415; regulation 431–2; *see also*
    genetic engineering
birds 115, 136, 218–19
Birke, Lynda 305, 339
black Americans 283
Blackfish 569
Blair Brothers Ranch 276
Bleich, David 291
blind rage 118
blindsight 118, 142
bluenose 208
Boesch, C. 181
bonobos (pigmy chimpanzees): communication
    by 145, 169–72; language competency

in 169–72; self-recognition with mirrors 154; social life of 156

Book of the Dead 1

boredom 467–70

bottlenose dolphins 157, 207, 210–11, 221–6

Bovenkirk, Bernice 395, 456

bovine growth hormone (BGH) 430

bovine somatotropin (BST) 255, 430

bowhunting 498

Bowring 436, 438, 444–5

Boyd, R. 407

Brambell Report 8

Brancheau, Dawn 566, 569, 574

Brand, Stewart 481

branding 36

Brantley, Alan C. 635

Brave New World 358, 453

Brazzaville Zoo 200

breeding: programs in zoos 579–80, 592, 595; puppy mills and 646–9

Bright, Christopher 532

British Institute of Medical Ethics 334

British Toxicological Society 355

Brody, Baruch A. 305, 330

Brom, Frans 395, 456

Bronx Zoo 599

Brugger, Kristin 579

bucardo 479

Buddhism 400

bull-baiting 3, 5, 115

Bundy, Ted 636

Burch, R. L. 331, 369, 401

Burke, Richard 512

Burkhardt, Jeffrey 395, 425, 430

Burman, Oliver H. P. 65, 71

Burt, J. 344

Busch, L. 430

Bush, George W. 275

bushmeat 198, 548–52

Bushmeat Crisis Task Force (BCTF) 198, 585

butchering imagery 284

Butterfly Conservation Initiative (BFCI) 585

cage-birds 4

Cahoone, Lawrence 487, 494

Caillois, Roger 505–6

Callicott, J. Baird 391, 514, 554, 555–6, 558, 596

Calvin, John 4

CAMPFIRE Association 519–21

Canada 370, 639, 644; contemporary hunting practice in 497–9

Canadian Council on Animal Care 644

Canadian Veterinary Journal 640

captivity: cetacean 563–70; ecological ethics in 594–604; effects on animals 567–9, 573–4; elephants in 573–4, 575; history of 563–5; *see also* zoos and aquariums

"Caring Sleuth: Portrait of an Animal Rights Activist, The" 555

Carruthers, Peter 311, 323

Cartesianism 4, 654

Case for Animal Rights, The 269, 349, 624–5

castration 36

cat flaps 4

cats 3; dependence and independence of 626–7; killed in animal shelters 622–9

cattle/cows: bovine growth hormone (BGH) and 430; bovine somatotropin (BST) and 255, 430; branding 36; chute system for handling 251–3; in factory farms 246, 247; fear in 251–2; handling and stunning practices for 254–5; as model for power and fertility 1; transport problems 255; vocalizations by 254–5

causal isomorphism 94, 97

Causey, Ann 515

Cavalieri, Paola 13, 26, 54, 161, 235, 278

ceiling effect 76

Central Africa 549–50, 551–2

cephalopods as food 250

cetacean captivity 563–70; current conditions 565–7; effects on cetaceans 567–9; future of 569–70; history of 563–5

cetaceans: conservation and 208–9; culture of 206–8; study of 206; vocalization in 238

charismatic megafauna 516

Charles River Laboratories 340

Charlton, A. 690

Cheeke, Peter 272

chickens: eggs of 35; in factory farms 245, 247; in family farms 249

chimeras and hybrids 405–6; moral confusion over 410–12

Chimpanzee FACS (Facial Action Coding System) 190

chimpanzees 83, 548, 549–50; ability to coordinate behavior 188–9; aggressive intergroup encounters in 189; anthropomorphism and 89; behavior of 89, 95; belief attribution and 191–3; in captivity 573–4, 580; communication by 145; conservation of 205; culture in 181–3; exploratory behavior in 189–91, 193–4; facial expressions in 192; field studies of 181; as folk psychologists 161, 185, 186–7, 193–4; gaze-following behavior in 95; goal-directed behavior in 155; growth of human populations as problem 197; hiding of facial expressions 192; intellectual abilities of 196; language in 168–72; legal rights of 673; medical research labs and 199; observations of wild 161; physical interactions in 278; planning and deceit in 126; problems faced by wild 196–8; production of human-like vocal sounds by 171–2; pursuit of goals by 151; sanctuaries for 198–9, 201; second-order beliefs in 94, 95; self-recognition with mirrors and 154, 220–1; social cognition in 186; social explanation-seeking behavior in 185; social life of 156; Species Survival Plan for 199; suggestive behavior in 155; surplus 200–1; theory of mind in, 89, 161, 185–6, 193; tool use by 145; understanding of agency 187–8; understanding of goals 187; in zoos 199; *see also* bonobos (pigmy chimpanzees)

Chodorow, Nancy 510

Chomsky, N. 112
choosing, *telos* and 467–70
Chopra, Sudhir 236, 239
Christianity 2, 5, 400, 694; compatibility with feminism 294; ethic of compassion towards animals in 3; human dominion over animals in 56; speciesism and 294–9; view of animals 3, 4, 5; women in 294
Church, George 481–2, 483
civil disobedience 701–4
classical conditioning 99
Clement, Grace 487, 553
Clioquinol 314
cloning 399; extinct animals 479, 480–1
Clubb, Ros 580
cock-fighting 4, 115
codified killing 29
cognition, animal: capacity 65, 274, 673; complexity and versatility of 140; defined 140; study of 99–107
cognitive ethnology 89, 93, 99, 150
cognitive science 237
coherence motivation 123
Cohen, Carl 13, 22–5, 309, 311, 669
Cohen, Shear-Yashuv 292
Collins, James 305, 387, 561, 594
Committee on the Status of Endangered Wildlife in Canada (COSEWIC) 211
communication, animal 65; in bonobos 145, 169–72; linguistic 169; natural 146; symbolic 169; types of 145–6; in whales 235; *see also* vocalization
companions, animal 3, 4, 609; animal-assisted therapy and 650–9; dogs as 611–12; domestication of wild animals into 613–15; hand-raising a rhino in the wild as 616–18; instrumentalism and 627–8; killed in animal shelters 622–9; living with 619–21; overpopulation of 646–9
Compassion in World Farming 8
competition, livestock market 265
Comstock, Gary 456
conditional reasoning 106
conditioned stimulus 99
conditioning: associative 99, 130; classical 99; fear 131; instrumental 99; observational 153–4; operant 99; Pavlovian 99, 220
confinement 243, 468–9
conformist cultures 212
congenital insensitivity to pain 130
congenital pain indifference 121
Congo Basin 549–51
conscious information processing 123–4
conscious/sentient being 55
consciousness, animal 53, 65, 133–9; as all-or-nothing phenomenon 65; communication in reporting subjective experience 145–6; defined 167; episodic memory 143–4; evidence of 140–6; explicit learning and 143–4; fitness function of suffering and 124–6; goal-directed desires and actions in 144; importance of bodily emotions for 142; intrinsic intentionality and 172–3; metacognition and 216; as natural emergent property of increasing complexity 121; neural correlates of 141–3; pain and 278–80; phenomenal 138, 217; primary 144; suffering and 121–4; tools in 145; versatility and 143
consequentialist critiques of animal biotechnology 427–8
conservation: biology 206, 206–10, 212, 388–9; cultural 208–9; defined 205; education by zoos and aquariums 585; ethical complexity of zoo and aquarium 597–601; focus on genetic diversity 205; fundraising to support 585; game and wildlife 491–3; horizontal culture and 208; integrated 599; interaction with culture 209; non-native species used for 536–40; planning and coalition building 585; role of zoos and aquariums 583, 594–604; trophy hunting and 518–19; vertical culture and 208–9
Conservation of Well-Being, Principle of 452–5
contingency checking behaviors 223
contract model, impact of 40
Convention on International Trade in Endangered Species and Their Products (CITES) 198, 520
Conway, W. G. 592
Cooke, B. 388–9
cooperative hunting 157
Cordovero, Moshe 292
core affect: causes of longer-term on mood states 76; functional view of 73–4; influence of discrete emotions on 75–6; location in 75; position in space 73–4; subjective emotional experience and 72–3
core consciousness 142
Corea, Gena 284
cortical dominance 118
cortisone 315
cosmetics testing 289, 292
Costello, Elizabeth 84
Cotman, Graziella 198, 200
Council of All Beings 512
Council of Europe 247
Cousteau, Jacques 582
cowbirds, 218–19
Cowper, William 295
coyotes, 146
Craig, Ian 618
Crichton, Michael 479
critter psychologist, 185–94
Cronus, Age of 1–2
cross-modal transfer of information 196
cross-species ignorance claim 333, 334
cross-species modeling, 89–97
crossing of species boundaries 405–12; moral confusion over 410–12; moral relevance of species boundaries and 415–16; moral unrest with 409–10; yuck factor and 416–17
cruelty, animal 5–6, 635–8
cults 693
cultural conservation 208–9
cultural evolution, maladaptive behavior and 209
cultural evolutionarily significant units 212
cultural expectations 168–72

Cultural Survival 205, 212
cultural trophic practice, hunting as 496
culture: biodiversity and 211–12; of biotechnology
    430–1; in chimpanzees 181–3; defined 167,
    181, 238; in determining behavior 205; genetic
    inheritance and 205–6; horizontal 205, 206, 207,
    208; interaction with conservation 209; material
    208; oblique 208; patriarchal 243, 281; social
    learning and 205; vertical 205, 206, 208
Curtin, Deanne 46
cyborg manifesto 445

Daggett, Hermann 5
Dahmer, Jeffrey 636
dairy industry: lameness in cows in 255; transport
    problems 255
Daly, Mary 284, 515
D'Amato, Anthony 236, 239
Darwin, Charles 71, 89, 89, 216, 349, 465
Darwinism 115
da Vinci, Leonardo 4
Davis, H. 380
Davis, Karen 556
Davis, Steven L. 243, 269, 500
Day, Dorothy 711, 716
death: to animals in the field 270–1; as comparable
    harm 19; concept of, for apes 93; intended versus
    unintended 272; for native people 25; painless 13;
    in pasture-forage model 271; in pasture/ruminant
    model 271; *see also* killing
Death at SeaWorld 569
deception and animal self-awareness 155–6
decision making: ethical criteria for 370; influence
    of mood states on 76–7
deep ecology theory 42
de-extinction: as no longer a fantasy 479–83;
    reintroduction and 484–5
deGrazia, David 10, 243, 245, 305, 321, 330, 337
de Lauretis, Teresa 281
deliberative communities of researchers and
    managers 390
Delta Society 650
DeMaster, D. P. 568–9
de Montaigne, Michel 4
Denmark 463
deontological ethics 435–7, 441
depo-provera 315
Descartes, Rene 3, 114, 133, 134, 216, 218, 400
desert bighorn sheep 389
de-sexing of domesticated animals 628
desires and animal self-awareness 150–2
de Waal, Francs 120
Dewey, John 389
dialects: in sperm whales 238; in songbirds 181
dialogical ethic of care, 45–7
dialogical theory 43
Diamond, Cora 56
Dick, C. W. 540
diethylstilbesterol (DES) 313
digitalis 315
Dillard, Courtney 663, 701

dimensional approach 71; integrating with discrete
    emotions approach 74–8; value of 71
Dinnerstein, Dorothy 510
discounting: further issues in 336–7; lexical priority
    versus 333–5; rationale for 335–6
discrete emotions 71; causes and functions of 74;
    core affective characteristics of 75; influence of
    mood states on 76–7; influence on location in core
    affect space 75–6; integrating with dimensional
    approach 74–8
disease monitoring and tracking 263–4
dis/integrating animals 434–45; virtue of 435–7
displacement thesis 6
disruptive species 528–9
DNA Direct 481
Dobzhansky, T. 407
"Dog's Mess: Theology as if Animals Mattered,
    The" 298
dogs: alarm calls of 146; association with death and
    healing 1; as companions 611–12; dependence
    and independence of 626–7; desires and
    intentional actions in 150–1; electric shock
    pain experienced by 631–4; fighting 6, 115;
    killed in animal shelters 622–9; lifeboat case
    and 20; overpopulation 646; puppy mill 646–9;
    vocalization in 45
dolphins 83, 515; ability to imitate 154; ability
    to repeat behavior 153; -assisted therapy
    566–7; body image in 218; broker 157; captivity
    563–70; characterization and interpretation of
    consciousness in 216–20; cognitive abilities
    in 230; consciousness in 229–31; culture as
    determinant of behavior in 161; episodic memory
    in 144, 230; feeding habits of 210; horizontal head
    movements in 223; learning in 219; metacognition
    studies in 226–9; metamemory in 229; mirror
    self-recognition by 221–6; personhood in 57;
    problem-solving in 151–2; request for assistance
    152; self-recognition with mirrors and 154,
    220–6, 229; sensitivity to human expectations
    230; social life of 157; as sympatric population
    211; vertical head movements in 223; *see also*
    bottlenose dolphins; cetaceans
Dombrowski, D. A. 2
domestic animals: in animal-assisted therapy
    650–9; dependence and independence of 626–7;
    de-sexing of 628; evolution of 613–15; homeless
    648–9; killed in shelters 622–9; killing of family
    pet in 284; overpopulation of 646–9; *telos* and
    453; *see also* companions, animal
domestic violence 283–4
*Dominion: The Power of Man, the Suffering of
    Animals, and the Call to Mercy* 275
Donaldson, Sue 53
Donlan, J. 485
Donnelley, S. 378
Donovan, Josephine 13, 42–7
double othering of lab rats 344–5
Douglas, M. 409
Douglas-Hamilton, Iain 573
Douglass, Frederick 698, 699, 713

Dovid of Lelov 292
Dow Chemical 430
Draize test 36, 37
Dreaded Comparison: Human and Animal Slavery, The 283
dreams 167
Dresser, R. 378
Dretske, F 104
Driesch, Hans 347
drug testing in animals 313–19
dualistic thoughts 251
Dworkin, Andrea 284
Dworkin, Ronald 53

Ebenreck, Sara 512
echolocation 230
ecological ethics 387–92, 427–8; in captivity 594–604
ecological naturalization 529–30
ecology, ethical dilemmas in 388–9
economics of hunting 519, 521
ecosystems: augmented by non-native species 539–40; integrity 459–60; non-native species used for restoring 536–40; role of non-native species in rapidly changing 540
Edge, W. D. 270
education, animal use in: effects on animals 378–80; humane 375–81; (human) social issues in 380–1; issues in teaching and learning and 376–8; in zoos and aquariums 577–8, 587
eggs, chicken 35
Ehrenfeld, David 531
Einstein, Albert 347, 358, 667
Eisenberg, L. 408
Eisnitz, Gail 246
elephants 515, 518, 520–1, 549–50; arguments against release from captivity 575; in captivity 573–4, 575; conservation of 205; crop-raiding by 208; personhood in 57; self-recognition with mirrors 154; tool use by 145
Ellman, M. 344
emotions and mood, animal 65; conscious subjective experience of 72; discrete 72; hypothesis-driven measures of 72; integrative and functional framework for study of 71–9; measurement of 77–8; similarities between autistic emotions and 251–6; triggering of 119
empathy 13, 46–7
Empedocles 2
encephalization 237–8
endangered species: choosing between protected and 389; recovery in zoos and aquariums 584
Endangered Species Act 666
end/means docrinte 27, 28
endorphins 111
Engel, Mylan 305, 309
Enlightenment, the 42
episodic memory 143–4
epistemic seeing 104
Epstein, Richard 663, 676
equality 33, 668–9

equal-significance position 333
Erskine, Thomas 5
ethanology 116
ethic-of-care theorists 44
ethical force 425
ethical norms 27
ethical sensitivity to animals 295
ethical vegetarianism 243
ethicists 360, 555; ecological ethics and 387–92; on moral standing of animals and the environment 596–7
ethics 10, 28, 32–41; ambivalence in 9; of animal farming, *telos* and 463–74; animal integrity in 456–61; of animal research 321–8, 352–6; applicability of 359; applied to hunting 494–5; bans on certain activities and 368–9; basis for keeping wild animals in captivity 582–8; biotechnology 397–401; of care and problem of wild animals 553–8; choosing between endangered and protected species 389; control of animal pain and suffering 366–7; criteria for decision making 370; current laws and 365–71; deontological 435–7, 441; dialogical ethic of care for treatment of 45–7; dilemmas in ecology and conservation biology 388–9; ecological 387–92, 427–8; euthanasia and 639–45; of genetic engineering of animals for human consumption 434–45; husbandry standards, inspections, and record keeping 366; inevitability of animal biotechnology and 426–8; logical positivism and 348; mechanomorphosis and 443–5; reasons scientists avoid thinking about 358–62; sensitivity to animals 295; specification of investigator competency 367–8; Three R alternatives and 369–70; tools for ecological problem solving 389–92; training in 358–9; trophy hunting and environmental 514–21; use of animal-harm scales and 370–1; viewed as arbitrary 359–60; virtue 10, 28; Western 26; *see also* morality
"Ethics of Animal Research, The" 330
Europe: bans on certain activities 368–9; position on animal research 331–3; *see also* United Kingdom, the
European Union 9, 247, 262; *see also* United Kingdom, the
Europeans for Medical Progress (EMP) 353
euthanasia: in animal shelters 622–9; ethics and 639–45; gold standard for 644; psychological effect on the operator 644–5
evaluative naturalization 530–1
evil 631–4
evolution: of domesticated animals 613–15; evolution of theory of mind 185; human insatiability and 711–14
evolutionary lineages, role of non-native species in 540–1
evolutionary significant units 210–12
evolutionary species concept 407
exotic species: as damaging species 528–9; defined 525–7; and disvaluing human-introduced exotics and U.S. Park Service policy 527–8; and

human-introduced species 527; naturalization of 529–31; xenophobia, biodiversity, and disvaluing exotics as 531–3
experience in scientific research 347–51
experimentation, animal 6, 34, 36–7, 305; alternatives to 316–17; common ground on 310–11, 323–6; commonsense case against 309–18; defense of 309–10, 322, 330–7; electric shock pain in 631–4; ethical themes of national regulations governing 365–71; points on which agreement between two sides is unlikely 326–7; scientific case against 311–16; U.S. law and 680–4; what can be done now to build upon points of agreement over 327–8; *see also* research, animal
explicit learning 143–4
Extension Thesis 6
extraordinary vacillations of movement 136
eye contract 177–8

facial expressions in chimpanzees 192
factory farming 8, 245–50; antibiotic use in 258–60; cruelties of 275; disease monitoring and tracking 263–4; employees 248; genetic engineering used in 440–1; institution of 246–7; moral evaluation of 247–9; Pew Commission report on 258–66; pollution and 260, 276
falconry 115
family farming 249–50, 262, 274
Farm Animal Reform Movement 8
farming: disease monitoring and tracking 263–4; factory 8, 9, 35–6, 38, 245–9, 258–66, 275, 440–1; family 249–50, 262, 274; versus hunting 499–501; lack of legal protection for animals 245; Pew Commission report on 258–66; *telos* and ethics of 463–74; traditional family 249–50, 262
fear 71–2, 152, 251; conditioning 131
fearful-banana paradigm 190, 193
Federal Bureau of Investigation 635–8
feminism 6, 284; Christianity and 294; ecofeminist view of hunting and 505–12
feminist animal care theory 13, 42–5
Fernández-Arias, Alberto 479–80
Festing, Simon 305, 352
Fields, William Mintz 167–73
fight flight flee system (FFFS) 73
Finland 370
Finsen, L. and S. 6, 10
fish as food 250
Flint, Caroline 354
Flipper 564
fluoride 315
Flury-Roversi, M. 312
Folch, José 479
folk psychologists, chimpanzees as 161, 185, 186–7, 193–4
Foner, Philip 698
food, animals for 35–6, 41, 243; animals as absent referents and 281–5; apes 548–52; auditing of plants for compliance with industry guidelines and 254–6; basic argument for vegetarianism and

274–80; ethical dimensions of genetic engineering of 434–45; factory farming and 245–9; hunting 495; Islamic law on 301–2; least harm principle and 269–72; Pew Commission report on industrial farm animal production and 258–66; seafood 250; thinking like animals and 251–3; traditional family farming and 249–50; *see also* vegetarianism
food additives 36
Food Security Act (US) 347
Fort Worth Zoos 584
Forward, Martin 243, 301
Fossey, Dian 85
Fowler, Susan 707
Fox, Camilla 495, 496
Fox, M. 426
fox-hunting 115
Francione, G. L. 56, 59, 271, 677, 690
Frankenstein's Cat 10
Frankenstein Syndrome, The 456
free-floating moods 71, 72, 76
Freedom of Information Act (UK) 353
French, Andrew 482–3
Frey, Ray 13, 50–2, 322
Friedrich, Bruce 711
friendship 85
Frommer, Stephanie 623
frontal lobotomy 121
functional view of core affect 73–4
Fund for Animals 7; Fund, The 701–4
Fund for the Replacement of Animals in Medical Experiments 356
fur trade 37
future anticipation by animals 152–3

Galapagos Islands 526
Galdikas, Birute 253
Galileo 113, 217, 713
game and wildlife conservation 491–3, 518–19
Game Survey of the North Central States 491
Gandhi, Mohandas 711, 716
Gardner, H. 376
Garrison, William Lloyd 697–8, 699
Gary, Romain 615
Geist, Valerius 498
genetic engineering: animal genetic manipulation 418–24; bringing end of animal suffering and end of animals 441–3; crossing species boundaries 405–12; defense of moral relevance of species boundaries 415–17; dis/integrating animals 434–45; in factory farms 440–1; mechanomorphosis and other ethical consequences of 443–5; moral confusion over 410–12; promises of failure and risks of success with 439–40; species identity and 406–8; *telos* and 449–55; *see also* biotechnology, animal
genetic manipulation 397–8, 418–24; background to 418; deontological ethics and 435–7; moral objections to 420–3; process 418–19; promises of failure and risks of success with 439–40
Genetic Savings & Clone (GSC) company 399

genetically modified organisms (GMO) 388–9, 434, 437
Geneva Conventions 239
GenPharm 341
genuine thinkers, identification of 99
Georgia Aquarium 565
Germany 5, 368
Gewirth, Alan 29
Geyer, Marilee 609, 646
Gilligan, Carol 42, 43
Glaspell, Susan 284
goal-desires 104
goal emulation 153
Golden Rule, the 28, 712–13
Goldsberry, Don 564
Gombe National Park 196, 197, 199
Goodall, Jane 155, 161, 181–3, 196–201
gorillas 83, 176
Gould, J. L. 348
GP Net 353
Graham, S. 434
Grandin, Temple 243, 251, 254
"Great Ape Project" 278
Great Britain *see* United Kingdom, the
Greek, C. Ray 313–14, 315
Greek, Jean Swindle 313–14, 315
Greely, Hank 483
Gregory, Dick 283
Griffin, Donald R. 65, 140–6
Griffin, Susan 284
Griffin, Ted 564
Griffiths, P. 407
Grinnell, Frederick 429, 432
Guide for the Care and Use of Laboratory Animals 681–3
Guide for the Perplexed, The 291
Guiding Principles for Biomedical Research involving Animals 365
Guiler, E. R. 591
Guinan, Michael 350
Guither, H. D. 7
Gunn, Alastair S. 487, 514

habitat restoration by zoos and aquariums 584
Hale, Matthew 4
halibut 208
Hamdress, Ursula 282
Hampson, Daphne 294, 297
haNasi, Yehudah 291
hand-raising of wild animals 616–18
handling and stunning practices 254–6
Hansen's disease 112
happy hunters 507–8
Haraway, Donna 340, 341, 436–7, 445
Harding, Sandra 47
Harding, Vincent 283
Hardy, Thomas 611
Harfeld, Jes Lynning 395, 463
Harley, Heidi E. 216
Harlow, H. F. 36–7
Harrison, Ruth 8

Hazlitt, William 285
Health Research Extension Act (US) 347
Hegins pigeon shoot 701–4
Hemingway, Ernest 507
hepatitis 399
Hepner, L. A. 380
herds, breaking of 36
Herman, Lou 569
Hershner and havens 540
Herzog, H. 692
Hesiod 1
Hettinger, Ned 487, 495, 525
higher-order thoughts 102–3
HIV/AIDS 399, 401, 551, 713, 718
Hodges, John 9
holist hunters 508
Hollander, Xaviera 284
Holmes, Oliver Wendell, Jr. 665
holy hunters 509
homeless animals 648–9
homeostatic property cluster 407, 408
homo sapiens, definition of 408, 665
Hood, G. A. 270
Hopko, Thomas 10
horizontal culture, 205–8
Hornaday, William 591
Houghton, Douglas 8
How Are We To Live? 711
human-to-animal embryonic chimeras 405–6
human-to-animal fetal or adult chimeras 405
human embryonic stem cell research 417; as moral good 494–502
human-introduced species 527
human nature 408
human-priority position 333
human rights 26–30, 54–8
Human Society of the United States 7, 322, 638
humane education: concept of 375–6; effects on animals 378–80; (human) social issues in 380–1; issues in teaching and learning and 376–8
Humane Innovations and Alternatives 380
Humane Slaughter Act (US) 245–7, 264
Humane Society of the United States 7
humans: animal cruelty by 635–8; bias in 168–72; boredom in 467–70; definition of *homo sapiens* and 408; development through play 511–12; differences between animals and 33–4; DNA 398, 409, 410; equality of 668–9; equal rights with animals 55; evolution and insatiability 711–14; fundamental rights derived from practical autonomy 667–8; human-to-animal embryonic chimeras 405–6; hunter-gatherer stage of 1; integrity 458–9; legal rights of 55, 665–9; liberty rights 666; living with animals 619–21; needs and hunting 517–18; personhood 686–9; psychological effects of animal euthanasia on 644–5; psychosexual identity and hunting 509–11; rights of adult 55; risks of genetic manipulation being applied to 421; slavery 283, 310, 666; species identity 407–8; Universal Declaration of Human Rights and 239; xenophobia in 531–3

humanocentric prejudices about animals 297–8

Hume, David 114, 686

humpback whales 207

hunter-gatherer stage of human societies 1, 274

hunting 487; advocates of sustainable 515; as contemporary sport 495–6; conventional western view of wildlife management and 514–15; as cultural trophic practice 496; ecofeminist critique of 505–12; ecological need of "holist hunters" and 508; economics of 519, 521; embodying goods 501–2; environmental ethics and trophy 514–21; ethics applied to 494–5; versus farming 499–501; game and wildlife conservation and 491–3, 518–19; Hegins pigeon shoot 701–4; human needs and 517–18; minimizing animal suffering and 515–16; as neo-traditional trophic practice 496, 499; practice of contemporary 496–9; psychological need of "happy hunters" and 507–8; psychosexual identity and 509–11; self-defense justification for 518; special status of major target species and 516; spiritual need of "holy hunters" and 509; threat to biodiversity 516–17; as uncivilized 516; viewed as a sport 505–7; viewed as life-giving play/sport for human development 511–12; in Zimbabwe 519–21

hunting-gathering, local 272, 274

husbandry: origin of 1; research 600–1; standards, inspections, and record keeping laws 366

Hutcheson, Francis 686

Hutchins, Michael 582

Huxley, Aldous 358

hybrids, interspecies 405, 410–12, 440; non-native species and 541

hygiene movement 6

hypoanalgesia 131

hypoxia 645

Ibn Ezra 291

ibuprofen 315

ICM 353

identity, species 406–8

imitation and animal self-awareness 153–4

In Defense of Animals 8

incommensurability claim 333–4

Individuals, value and respect for 16–17, 54

industrial farm animal production 258–66; air quality degradation in 260; animal wastes in 260; as energy intensive 260–1; environmental impact of 260; feed formulation in 259; greenhouse gases in 260; groundwater contamination in 260; health risks from 259–60; improving regulations in 264; improving research in 265–6; intensive confinement in 261–2, 264–5; runoff in 260; toxic gases and dusts associated with 260; unintended consequences of 259, 266

industrial food animal production (IFAP) system 258–66

Industrial Revolution 5

inferential role of thoughts 102–3

information: conscious processing of 123–4; cross-modal transfer of 196

inherent values 16, 18, 22–5

innate releasing mechanisms 99–100

Inner Eye 125

instinctive hostility 409

Institute for Animals and Society 9

Institutional Review Boards 359

instrumental conditioning 100

instrumentalism 627–8

integrated conservation 599

integrity, animal 456–61; ecosystem integrity and 459–60; as flawed but workable solution 460–1; human integrity versus 458–9; objections to 457–8; reasons for using 456–7

intended vs. unintended death 272

intensive confinement, phasing out of 264–5

intentional agriculture, elimination of 272

intentional agency 175, 187–8

intentional ascent 102–5

intentional misleading 156

intentionality 173

International Fund for Animal Welfare 8

International Genetic Standard CD Rat 340–1

International Guiding Principles for Biomedical Research Involving Animals 327

International Society for Animal Rights 7, 555

International Union for Conservation of Nature (IUCN) 484–5

International Whaling Commission 239, 240

interspecies hybrids 405, 410–12, 440

intersubjective recognition 59

intersubjectivity, human-baboon 83

intra-human egalitarian paradigm 27

intrinsic intentionality and consciousness 172–3

intrinsic values 16

introspective awareness 149–50, 158

invasive species 485

inviolability 53, 55

irreflexive consciousness 117–20

irreversibility arguments against animal biotechnology 427–8

Islam and animal-human relationship 56, 301–2

isomorphism, causal 94, 97

isolation, pain of 470–2

Isuprel 314

Jaggar, Alison 46

Jamieson, Dale 561, 576

Jamison, Wesley 663, 690

Japan 681, 712

Japanese macaques 181

Jasper, J. 691

Jesus Christ *see* Christianity and speciesism

Jewish tradition, animal rights in 289–92, 400

Jones, Helen 555

Jørgensen, Dolly 395, 484

Journal of the American Medical Association 309, 322, 359

Journal of Wildlife Management 508

judgment bias 78

"Jury of Her Peers, A" 284
justice 18–20, 55

Kabbalah 291–2
Kac, Eduardo 10
Kaldewaij, Frederike 13
Kalechofsky, R. 6
Kant, Immanuel 13, 26, 43–4, 112–13, 667,
    668–9, 688
Kantianism 654, 667, 668–9
Kay, James 459
Keeton, W. T. 348
Kellert, Stephen 577
Kempner, J. 361
Kenya Wildlife Service 200
Kerasote, Ted 270, 272, 500, 501–2
Kheel, Marti 487, 505
Kibale National Park 189
killing: of animals for food 35–6, 243, 245–302;
    in animal shelters 622–9; codified 29; of family
    pets 284; of non-self-conscious animals 40–1;
    of wild animals 41; wrongness from 421–2;
    see also death
King, Martin Luther, Jr. 713, 716
King, Roger 515
Kingsford, Anna 7
Kingsolver, B. 269
Kirby, David 569
Kirmayer, Laurence 439
Kitchell, Ralph 350
Kleinig, J. 378
Kook, Abraham Isaac 292
Krutch, Joseph Wood 495
Kundera, Milan 634
Kymlicka, Will 53–61

laboratory rodents *see* rodents
Lacy, W. 430
Lana Project 168
language 5; in apes 168–72; dependence of logical
    thought on 105–8; dialect and 181, 238; facial
    expressions and 192; in humans 112; sign 154;
    thought based on 251; universal grammar and 45;
    verbal apprehension and 238
Language, Truth, and Logic 348
language-based thoughts 251
Latour, B. 343
laughter, ape 548–52
law: animal activism and animal 663; animal
    experimentation and U.S. 680–4; animal rights
    and current 678–9; anti-cruelty 6, 638, 643, 689;
    lack of protection for farm animals 245; legal
    rights for great apes and 665–9; legal rights of
    adult humans 55, 665–9; personhood, animals,
    and the 686–9; *Rattling the Cage: Toward Legal
    Rights for Animals* 663, 672–5; reforms 683–4;
    see also regulations
Lazarus Project 482
LD50 test 36, 37
learning: associative 100; in dolphins 219; explicit
    143–4; in marine snails 131; nociception-related

130; in scrub jays 143–4; trial and error 126;
    see also social learning
least harm principle 243, 269–72; applied
    to hunting 499–501
Lee, Ronnie 8
Le Gallois, J. J. C. 311
Leiber, Justin 133
Leigh, Diane 609, 646
Lemons, John 460
Leopold, Aldo 487, 491, 507–8, 554
Lever, Janet 511
Levin, Mark 315–16
Lewis, J.C.M. 600
lexical priority versus discounting 333–5
liberal democracy 54
liberal rights doctrine 42
liberty rights 666
lifeboat case 20
Lincoln, Abraham 665
Lindsey, G. D. 270
linguistic communication 169
linguistic self-report 72
Linzey, Andrew 243, 294–9
List, Charles 496
live animal trade 198
lived life, *telos* and the 466–7
Living Trophies 580
Lock, R. 378
Locke, John 4, 216, 237, 686
Lockwood, Michael 125
logical positivism 347–8
logical thought dependence on language 105–6
logos 2
London Zoo 580
loneliness 470–2
Lorenz, Konrad 609, 611
Lovelace, Linda 284
Ludwig, Edward G. 577
Lugones, Maria 511–12
Luke, Brian 46
Lukes, Stephen 429
Luther, Martin 4
Luzzato, Chayyim 292
Lynch, M. 342

Macdonald, D. W. 270
MacIntyre, Alasdair 298–9
MacPhee, Ross 480
Macy, Joanna 512
Mader, Sylvia 348
Maimonides 291
Maine Mammal Protection Act (US) 565
Major, John 8
maladaptive behavior, 209, 212
mammoths 480–1, 485
manipulation, genetic *see* genetic manipulation
manure and pollution 260–1, 276
marine snails 131
Marine Studios 564
Marineland of Florida 564
Marino, Lori 561, 563

Marks, Jonathan 278
Martin, Richard 5
Marxism 677
Mason, Georgia 580
Massey, Jason 636–7
material culture 208
Mathews, Freya 609, 619
Mayr, E. 407
McCabe, T. T. 491–3
McCartney, Paul 718
McCoy, E. D. 391
McGinn, Colin 632–3
McGinnis, J. R. 381
McGrew, W. C. 181
Mead, George Herbert 511
meat-eating; *see* food, animals for; vegetarianism
mechanomorphosis 443–5
medieval thought on animal rights 291–2
Meet Your Meat 716
Mellor, D. J. 370–1
Melton, Douglas 359
Melville, Herman 135–6
memory, 143–4, 153
Mendl, Michael 65, 71–9
mental maps 102
mental states, 112–14
mentation 112
Merleau-Ponty, Maurice 444
Merz, Anna 609, 616
Merz, J. F. 361
metacognition 157–8, 216; in dolphins 226–9; in monkeys 157–8, 228
metamemory 228–9
metarepresentations 175, 178–9
Metcalf-Hatch Act 709
Methodism 5
Miami Seaquarium 564–5, 574
microdosing technology 317, 355–6
Middle Ages, 3
Midgley, Mary 1, 133, 323, 337, 556
Midrashim 290
Mill, John Stuart 453
Millennium Pharmaceuticals 315
mind-reading abilities of animals 104–5, 107
minimalist approach 101
minimize harm principle 270
miniride principle 19–20
Minteer, Ben 305, 387, 561, 594
mirrors, self-recognition studies with 154, 220–6, 229, 238
Mitchell, Sandra D. 65, 89–97
Mobilization for Animals 8
Moby Dick, 135–6
modus ponens 106
monkeys: alarm calls of 146; anticipation of future and 153; binocular rivalry and 146; cortical lesions in 142; deafferented 112; goal-directed behavior in 155; metacognition in 157–8, 228; radiation experiments on 36; self-recognition with mirrors and 154; social life of 156; *see also* Rhesus monkeys

mono-culture-confinement farm animal production 263
Monsanto 430
Montaigne, Michel de 4, 133, 135
Monterey Bay Aquarium 599
mood states: causes of longer-term core affect 76; influence on decision making, appraisals and discrete emotions 76–7
moral agents 15–16, 27–8; inherent value of 16, 17
Moral Animal, The 712
moral blindness 9
moral certainty 133
moral colonialism 44
moral ecology 378–9
moral reasoning, 59–60
moral rights of animals 15–16, 50–2
moral self-control 57–8
moral significance 101
morality 236–7, 349, 441; animal-assisted therapy and 650–9; ethic of care and 555–7; evaluation of factory farming 247–9; evil and 631–4; human striving for 713–14; hunting as moral good and 494–502; moral ecology and 378–9; moral relevance of species boundaries and 415–17, 437–9; perception of mental states and 113–14; *telos* and 449–55; tools for ecological problem solving and 389–92; unrest with crossing species boundaries 409–10; *see also* ethics; ethics of animal research
Morals, Reason, and Animals 349
Morgan, Lloyd 112
MORI 353
Moriarity, Paul Veatch 495, 525
Morton, David 395, 397
Moss, Cynthia 573
mother, separation of young and 36
"Mouse Research Bolsters Controversial Theory of Aging" 434
Muhammad *see* Muslim view of animal-human relationship
Mumford, K. 391
Murphy, Caroline 441
Murphy, Patrick 45
Muslim view of animal-human relationship 301–2
mutual awareness 175, 178

Nachmanides 291
Nagel, Thomas 134–7
Nass, R. D. 270
National Academies of Science (NAS) 263, 580
National Animal Identification System 263
National Anti-Vivisection Society 7
National Beef Plan 276
National Cancer Institute 315
National Centre for the Replacement, Refinement and Reduction of Animals in Research (UK) 354
National Geographic Society 480, 582
National Institutes of Health (US) 358–9, 681–3
National Marine Fisheries Service (US) 211, 565
National Pork Producers Council 275
National Research Council (US) 379

National Zoological Park 579, 580
Native Americans 283
native species 525–7
naturalization of exotic species 529–31
Nature 580
Ndoke National Park 196
negative activation 73
Nelson, Leonard 50, 51
Nelson, Richard 499, 509
neo-Darwinism 125
neo-traditional trophic practice, hunting as 496, 499
Netherlands, the 368, 369, 370, 457; Constitution and human integrity 459
neural correlates of animal consciousness 141–3
neurophysiology and denial of pain 111
neuropsychological and evolutionary approach to animal consciousness and suffering 116–26
neuropsychology 116
neuroscience 71
New Caledonian crows 145, 152
New England Biolabs 340
New England Journal of Medicine 322
New Mexico Department of Game and Fish 389
New York Review of Books 274
New York Times 677
New York Times Magazine 276
New York Zoological Society 577
New Zealand 369, 370, 371, 517
Newton, Isaac 4, 347
Nishida, T. 181–3
nociception 119, 130, 279
Noddings, Nel 46
Nonhuman Rights Project 570
nonhumans, equality of 29, 33
non-linguistic thoughts 100–3
non-native species: augmenting ecosystem services 539–40; as catalysis for restoration 539; current uses to conserve and restore species and ecosystems 536–40; ecological role in rapidly changing ecosystems 540; exotic species as 527–31; future role of 540; management of 541–2; novel evolutionary lineages and 540–1; potential conservation value of 535–42; providing shelter and food for native species 536–9; subjective views of 535–6; as substitutes for extinct taxa 539
non-self-conscious animals, killing of 40–1
No Other Gods 429
norms, ethical 27
Norton, Bryan 579
Norwegian Black List 485
no-till agriculture 271, 272
nuclear-cytoplasmic hybrids 405

O'Barry, Ric 564
objectification 284–5
oblique culture 208
observational conditioning 153–4
odontocetes, 208
Office of Technology Assessment (US) 415
Olden, Julian D. 535
opaque-barrier test 96

open-heartedness/mindedness 296
operant conditioning 99
opinio juris 236, 239
oppression 284–5
Opren 314
optimum pressure concept 252
orangutans 253, 548
orcas *see* whales
Orlans, F. Barbara 305, 365
orphans, sanctuary care of 198–9
Ortega y Gasset, José 496, 509, 515, 516
Oryx and Crake 434, 435, 437, 440, 442–3
Osborne, Richard W. 205
overlapping absent referents 282–3
overpopulation, animal 646–9
Ovid 2

pack behavior 156
pain, animal 65, 111–15, 274; alleged unobservability of mental states and 112; anesthesia and analgesia for 111, 350–1; animal cruelty 635–8; animals' understanding of 350; capacities for 32–3, 38, 65; congenital indifference to 121; congenital insensitivity to 130; consciousness and 278–80; contemporary hunting and 497–8; correlation of vocalization with 254–5; distinction between nociception and 119; distinction between suffering and 138; by electric shock in experimentation 631–4; extending mentation to 114–15; factory farming and 275; feeling of 38; functions of 130–2; of isolation 470–2; killing in animal shelters without 625–6; laws regarding control of suffering and 366–7; measures of reactivity 130; mental states as perceptual category and 112–13; morality and perception of mental states 113–14; neurophysiology and 111; scientific incoherence of denying 111–12; study of 71, 278–80; vocalization with 254–5; *see also* suffering
Paine, Thomas 5
Painism: A Modern Morality 713
painless death 13
Palmer, Clare 609, 622
Park Service, U.S. 527–8
Parker, James 663, 690
pasture/ruminant model 271
Patagonian tooth-fish 208
paternalistic case for AAT 652–3
patriarchal culture 243, 281
Paul, Elizabeth 65, 71
Pavlovian conditioning 99, 220
People for the Ethical Treatment of Animals (PETA) 8, 598, 715, 718–19
Perdue, Frank 707, 708
Perlis, C. S. 361
person(s): apes as 175–83; criteria to distinguish 175; defined 237; as intentional agents 175; as term, 86n
personhood 686–9; in obscuring moral reasoning 59–60; passing test of 57; in rejecting inviolable rights for animals 58–9; rejection of animal

rights theory by appeal to 56–7; as synonym for selfhood 59–60; of whales 161, 235–40
Peterson, Dale 487, 548
pets *see* companions, animal
Petto, Andrew 305, 375, 377
Pew Commission report on industrial farm animal production 258–66, 641
Phelan, Ryan 481
phenomenal consciousness 138, 217
Philadelphia Society for the Prevention of Cruelty to Animals 701
phylogenetic proximity 93
phylogenetic relatedness 93
Piaget, Jean 511
pictorial models 102
pictorial representations 103
pigs: in factory farms 245, 247, 275; handling and stunning practices for 254–5; as "pigoons" in *Oryx and Crake* 437–9, 440; transport problems 255; vocalizations 255
"Pigs *Will* Fly" 438
Pimentel, David 500, 528
Pippin, John 317
Plato 2, 667
Plea for Vegetarianism 7
Plotinus 2
Pluhar, Evelyn 322
Plumwood, Val 436
Pluralistic Folk Psychology (PFP) approach 185, 187, 194
Plutarch 2
Pogge, Thomas 29
Poinar, Hendrik 482
Poky Feeders 276
Political Animal, The 10
Pollan, Michael 276
pollution and factory farming 260, 276
population biology 206
Porphyry 2
positive activation 73
positivism, logical 347–8
positivistic-behavioristic ideology 112
Posner, Richard 663, 672
Poulsen, J. 691
Povinelli, Daniel J. 89, 92, 97, 278
practical ethics 32–41
prairie dogs 146
Prednisone 315
prefrontal cortex 120, 121, 124, 129
Premack, David 186
prepositional attitudes 151
Prescott, H. 702
Preziosi, R. J. 651
prevention cases, miniride principle in 20
primates intersubjectivity versus theory of mind 175–83
Primatt, Humphry 5
"Promises of Monsters: A Regenerative Politics for Inappropriate/d Others, The" 436–7
propositional and non-propositional thought in non-linguistic creatures 100–1

protected species, choosing between endangered and 389
proto-thoughts 101
proximity, evolutionary and phylogenetic 93
psychological and non-psychological explanations, of behavior 99–100
psychology 217; neuro 116; pluralistic folk 185, 187, 194; standard folk 191
psychopharmacology 71
psychosexual identity and hunting 509–11
public opinion: on animal welfare 463–4; biotechnology and 415; ethics and 360–1
puppy mills 646–9
Pythagoras 2

qualia 117, 118, 218
Quine, W. V. O. 102
Qur'an 301–2

rabbits, genetically modified 388–9
Rachels, James 243, 274
racism 27, 33, 283, 337, 416, 531; absent referents and 283
Radford, Rosemary 47
radical feminist theory 284
Ralls, Katherine 579
rape 282–5
rationality 105, 686–7
rats *see* rodents
Rattling the Cage: Toward Legal Rights for Animals 663, 672–5
Rawls, John 28, 54
reasoning 105, 219
receptive understanding 168
reciprocity and ethics 39–40
record keeping laws 366
Regan, Tom 8, 13, 23–5, 42, 243, 269, 270, 271, 309–10, 322, 426, 494, 586, 663; on animal rights violence 696; *Case for Animal Rights, The* 269, 349, 624–5; on ethic of care and wild animals 553–4, 558; on moral ecology 378
regulations: animal biotechnology 431–2; animal experimentation 680–3; animal-harm scales and 370–1; bans on certain activities 368–9; controls on animal pain and suffering 366–7; countries with and without animal protection 365; critical review of protocols 367; ethical criteria for decision making and 370; ethical issues in current 365–71; husbandry standards, inspections, and record keeping 366; IFAP 264; specifications of investigator competency 367–8; Three R alternatives and 369–70; *see also* law
Reid, C. S. W. 370–1
reintroduction and de-extinction 209, 484–5; role of zoos and aquariums 583–4
Reiss, Diana 569
religion *see* theology
Renaissance, the 3–4
Rendell, Luke 205
research, animal 305; agriculture 265–6; alternatives to 316–17; background on debate over 321–3;

common ground on 310–11, 323–6; commonsense case against 309–18; defense of 309–10, 322, 330–7; ethics of 321–8, 348, 352–6; further issues in discounting and 336–7; laboratory rodents in 339–45; lexical priority versus discounting 333–5; points on which agreement between two sides is unlikely 326–7; rapid global change and evolving ethics of ex situ 601–3; rationale for discounting and 335–6; scientific case against 311–16; scientific ideology and 347–51; U.S. and European positions on 331–3; what can be done now to build upon points of agreement over 327–8; in zoos and aquariums 598–601; *see also* experimentation, animal

Research Defence Society (UK) 353
respect principle 18–19
restoration, habitat 584
Revlon 708
rewards acquisition 73–4
Reynolds, V. 181
rhesus monkeys: goal-directed behavior in 155; metacognition in 228; radiation experiments on 36; *see also* monkeys
rhinos, hand-raised 616–18
Rifkin, J. 427
rights, animal 22–5, 50, 53, 90; activism as functional religion 690–4; activists' handbook 711–19; activists working with government 698; animal biotechnology and 426–7; as argument for vegetarianism 274–80; arguments for 15–21; in Christian tradition 294–9, 400; civil disobedience 701–4; current legal scene 678–9; ethic of care and wild 553–8; genetic manipulation of animals and 435–7; hunting and 494–5; ideology 278; in Jewish tradition 289–92, 400; moral standing of animals and 596; movement, dangerous claims of 676–9; strategies 705–9; violence 696–700; *see also* animal rights
Robert, Jason Scott 395, 405, 415–17
Rodd, Rosemary 323
rodents: changing meanings of 340; created in the laboratory 339–40; doubly othered 344–5; experimentation on 36, 153, 312–13, 315; inherent value of 24, 25; labeled as not quite an animal 341–4; mapping metaphors and 340–1
role specialization 157
Rollin, Bernard E. 9, 10, 22, 23, 65, 111–15, 243, 305, 323, 347, 395; *Animal Rights and Human Morality* 349, 465; on ethics and euthanasia 639; *Frankenstein Syndrome* 456; new social ethic for animals 441–2; on *telos* 449; *telos* of animals and 465–7; on welfare interests of animals 456–7
Rolston, Holmes 495, 496, 497, 510, 530, 556, 596
Roosevelt, Theodore 507
Rosen, David 292
Rosenberg, C. E. 428, 429
Ross, W. D. 335
Rowlands, Mark 631
Royal Society for the Prevention of Cruelty to Animals (RSPCA) 6
Russell, Karla 305, 369, 375, 401

Russell, W. M. S. 331
Rutgers, Bart 457
Ryder, Richard 1, 5, 8, 9, 10, 438, 713; on animal welfare movement versus animal rights movement 9; *The Political Animal* 10; on speciesism 8
Ryle, Gilbert 101

sablefish 208
sacred animals 1
sadness 72
Sagoff, Mark 533
Salisbury, Joyce 3
Salt, Henry 7, 115
San Diego Zoo 599
San Jose Zoological Gardens 580
sanitary movement 6
Sapontzis, Steve 10, 22, 23, 323, 349
Savage-Rumbaugh, Sue 161, 167–73, 186
Sax, Dov F. 535
Scheff, Marc 561, 573
Scheler, Max 45
Schlaepfer, Martin A. 535
Schmitz, Kenneth L. 506
Schwartz, Richard 292
Schweitzer, Albert 298
Scientific American 434, 573–4
Scientific Attitude, The 429
scientific community: attitude and biotechnology culture 428–31; avoidance of thinking about ethics 358–62; deliberative 390; ecological ethics and 387–92
scientific ideology 243; animal research and 347–51; biotechnology culture and 428–31
scientism 428, 429–30
scrub jays 143–4
Scully, Matthew 275, 276, 280
sea otters 209–10
seafood 250
Sears, David 292
SeaWorld 565, 566, 569, 574
second-person modality 175, 178
second-personal attitude in apes 178–9
Seed, John 512
seeing 191; distinction between simple and epistemic 104
Sefer Chasidim 292
Seidenberg, David Mevorach 289
self-awareness, animal 149–58; bodily 149–50, 154, 157, 158; complex social understanding and 156–7; deception and 155–6; fear and 152; future anticipation in 152–3; imitation and 153–4; metacognition and 157–8; self-recognition with mirrors and 154; spatial perspective and 155; types of 149–50, 157
self-defense justification for hunting 518
selfhood 53, 59–60
self-perception with mirrors 154, 220–6, 229, 238
semantic ascent 102–3
Seneca 2
sensorimotor intelligence 176, 218
sentience 2, 22, 55–6, 103

Serpell, J. A. 1
Seven Seas Panorama 564
sexism 337
sexual violence 632–3; absent referents and 283–4;
    meat eating and 283–4
Shakespeare, William 4
Shapiro, Kenneth 380, 555
Shaw, George Bernard 7
Shedd Aquarium 565
Shelley, Percy Bysshe 7
Shelley, Roger 707
shellfish 250
shelters, animal: animal overpopulation and 646–9;
    killing in 622–9
Sheng 405
Shepard, Paul 511, 515, 516, 609, 613
Shrader-Frechette, K. 391
sign language 154
silicon consciousness 134
simple seeing 104
Simpson, G. G. 407
Singer, Peter 13, 32, 61, 133, 137, 243, 249, 274,
    275, 278, 309–10, 322, 335, 494, 596, 663, 711,
    716; *Animal Liberation* 8, 349; on ethic of care
    and wild animals 553–4, 558; on Henry Spira
    705–9; right to life of animals and 466; on self-
    consciousness in dogs and cats 627
"Singer Solution to World Poverty, The" 716
Singleton, R. 378
situation-desires 104
slavery 32, 39, 283, 310, 666, 697–8; of animals 4
Slicer, Deborah 44–5
sliding-scale model of moral status 249–50
slum clearance 6
Small, R. J. 568–9
Smith, Betsy 567
Smith, Brandie 582
Smith, Kevin 395
Smuts, Barbara 83–5
snakes 1
social learning 206–7, 238; culture and 205;
    types of 207
social mongoose 146
social self-awareness 149, 157, 158
Society for Animal Protective Legislation 7
Society for the Prevention of Cruelty to Animals
    (SPCA) 5–6
Socrates 2, 453
Somerville, Margaret 59
Sontag, Susan 46
souls: in animals 290; transmigration of 2
Southwestern Willow Flycatcher 538–9
special problems: apes as food 548–52; ethic of
    care and problem of wild animals 553–8; exotic
    species 525–34; potential conservation value of
    non-native species 535–42
species: damaging 528–9; defense of moral
    relevance of boundaries between 415–17,
    437–9; endangered 389, 584; exotic 525–7;
    human-introduced 527; hybrids 405, 410–12,
    541; identity 406–8; invasive 485; native

525–7; non-native 527–31, 535–42; separation
    of 676–8
Species Survival Commission 484
speciesism 8, 27, 33, 35–7, 61, 654, 676–8, 715;
    Christianity and 294–9
Speck, Gayle B. 140
sperm whales: culture in 209; dialect in 238;
    hierarchies in 207; horizontal culture of 208; as
    sympatric population 211
Spiegel, Marjorie 283
spinner dolphins 206–7
Spira, Henry 8, 321, 663, 705–9
spirituality *see* religious issues
sport, characteristics of 505–6
squirrel monkeys 153
Standard Folk Psychology 191
starlings 218–19
Steiner, Gary 56
St. Louis Zoo 599
St Francis of Assisi 3
Stiegman, Emero 290
Stoics 2
Stout, J. 409–10
Streiffer, Robert 395, 415
streptomycin 315
Strunden, George 197
subject-of-a-life criterion 13, 18, 22, 24, 25, 269
subjective experiences: communications in reporting
    145–6; core affect and 72–3
subsistence hunting 198
suffering 117, 138, 468, 717; consciousness and
    121–4; contemporary hunting and 497–8, 515–16;
    genetic engineering and end of animals and
    441–3; wrongness from 422–3; *see also* pain
Sugiyama, Y. 181
surplus animals 587
Swaisgood, R.R. 601
Swan, James 509
Sweden 369
swim-with-dolphins programs 566–7
Switzerland 369, 370, 690–4
symbiosis 253
symbolic communications 169
symbolism, animal 3
symmetry thesis 186
sympathy 13, 43–4
sympatric cultural variants 209–12

TACARE (Lake Tanganika Catchment Reforestation
    and Education Project) 197
tactical deception 104–5
Taglialatela, Jared 167
tail docking 275
Talmud, the 289–92
tamarin monkeys: goal-directed behavior in 155;
    self-recognition with mirrors 154
Taylor, A. 272
Taylor, Charles 470
Taylor, Paul 517–18
Tchimpounga Sanctuary 198–200
teaching *see* education, animal use in

Teale, Edwin Way 508
technology development in zoos and aquariums 584
telepathy 57–8
telos 449–55; boredom, choosing, and 467–70; comparisons and strengths 472–3; ethics of animal farming and 463–74; and the lived life 466–7; and the nature of an animal 464; pain of isolation and 470–2; Rollin and animal 465–6
Temerlins, Jane and Maurice 200
temporal self-awareness 157
territoriality 209
tetracycline-fermentation by-products 259
Tew, T. E. 270
thalidomide 313
Thatcher, Margaret 8
theocentrism 9
theology: ancient beliefs and 2–3; and animal rights activism as functional religion 690–4; animal rights in Jewish tradition 289–92, 400; Christianity as speciesist 294–9, 400; Christian views of animals 3, 4, 5; connections between gods and animals 1; "holy hunters" and 509; humanocentric 298; Islam and animal-human relationship 301–2; souls in animals and 290; transmigration of souls 2, 114; vegetarianism and 2; *see also* biblical view of animal rights
Theology and Feminism 294
Theory of Justice, A 54
theory of mind 155, 157, 161; in apes 93; in chimpanzees 89, 161, 185–6, 193; evolution of 185; primate intersubjectivity versus 175–6
There Is a River: The Black Struggle for Freedom in America 283
thinking and thoughts: dualistic 251; higher-order 102–3; inferential role of 102–3; language-based 251; like animals 251–3; non-linguist 102–3; proto- 101; visual 251
Thinking Without Words 99–107
third-person modality 175, 178
Thomas, Carolyn E. 505
Thomas, Keith 3–5, 283
Thomist conception of hierarchy 295
Thompson, Paul 9
Thoreau, Henry David 7, 715
Three R program 331–2, 401; alternatives 369–70
thylacine 485, 591–2
Thyron, Thomas 4
tip-of-the-tongue phenomenon 226
Tobash, B. 702
Toledo Zoos 584
tools for ecological problem solving 389–92
Torah, the 289–92
traditional family farming 249–50, 262
transgenesis: ethical dimensions of domesticated animals' 434–45; methods of 423–4; moral objections to 420–3; outcomes of 420, 424; process of 418–19
transgenic organisms 405
translocations as conservation tool 209
transmigration of souls 2, 114
transport problems 255

Trans-Species Unlimited 8
trial and error learning 126
Tronto, Joan 46
trophy hunting and environmental ethics 514–21; *see also* hunting
Trump, Donald 712
trust as component of friendship 85
turkeys 249
Tutin, C. E. G. 181
tylosin 260
Tyndale-Briscoe 389
Tyron, Thomas 4

unconditioned response 99
unconditioned stimulus 99
unconscious driving 217
UNICEF 197
unintended death 272
Union of Concerned Scientists 259
United Kingdom, the 370; Advertising Standards Authority 354; animal experimentation law in 681; Animals (Scientific Procedures) Act 352; British Institute of Medical Ethics 334; British Toxicological Society 355; early views on cruelty to animals 4–5; Ethical Review Process in 352–3; ethics of animal research and 352–6; factory farming in 246–7; Freedom of Information Act 353; growth of animal welfare movement in 7–9; meat eating culture of 285; National Centre for the Replacement, Refinement and Reduction of Animals in Research 354; origins of the animal welfare movement in 5–6; Research Defence Society 353; Yorkshire Cancer Research 355
United Nations: Convention on the Rights of Persons with Disabilities (2006) 58; Universal Declaration of Human Rights 239
United States, the 369; Animal Identification Number 263; Animal Welfare Act 341, 366, 367, 368, 564, 681–2; Armed Forces Radiobiology Institute 36; Bill of Rights 349; deregulation of meat industry in 248–9; factory farming in 246–7; Food Security Act 347; growth of animal welfare movement in 7–9; Health Research Extension Act 347; Humane Slaughter Act 245–7, 264; Humane Society of 322, 638; law and animal experimentation 680–4; Maine Mammal Protection Act 565; meat eating culture of 285; National Institutes of Health 358–9; National Research Council 379; Office of Technology Assessment 415; origins of the animal welfare movement in 6–7; Park Service 527–8; position on animal research 331–3; practice of hunting in 496–9; voluntary animal tracking systems 263; Wild Horses Act of 1959 7
Universal Declaration of Human Rights 239
universal grammar 45
universalizability 44
"U.S. Government Principles for the Utilization and Care of Vertebrate Animals Used in Testing, Research, and Training" 331

US Department of Agriculture 246–7, 431, 646; Animal and Plant Health Inspection Service (APHIS) 582, 643, 681
US Food and Drug Administration 275, 314, 315, 430
utilitarianism 5, 13, 28, 32, 42, 43, 453, 473, 654; for animals 54; beliefs on inviolable rights 53–4; value in 17; vegetarianism and 275

Vance, Richard 309
van den Bergh, Babs 395, 456
VanDeVeer, Donald 514, 518
Varner, Gary 279, 499, 517
veal, factory farming and 247
Vegan Outreach 718
veganism: animal rights activism and 692–3; death to animals in the field and 270–1; least harm principle and 269–72
vegetarianism 1–3, 5, 7, 35–6, 243; advocacy 717–18; argument against 500; basic argument for 274–80; Jewish religious thought and 292; least harm principle and 269–72; origins of 1–2, 7; *see also* food, animals for
Vehrs, Kristin 561, 575
verbal language apprehension 238
vertical culture 205, 206, 208; conservation and 208–9
vervet monkeys: alarm calls of 146; social life of 156
Vick, Michael 714
Victoria, Queen of England 6
violence: animal rights 696–700; against animals 635–8; hunting and 510–11; sexual 283–4, 632–3; against women 282–5, 632–3
virtue ethics 10, 28
visual thoughts 251
vital interests, protection of 28
Vitali, Theodore 510, 516
vivisection 3, 6, 7, 115
vocalization 131; correlation with pain 254–5; in dogs 45; scores 254–5; *see also* communication, animal
von Eschenbach, Andrew C. 314

Waldau, Paul 298
Walden 715
Walker, Margaret Urban 44
Warkentin, Traci 395, 434
Warren, M. A. 586
Washoe (chimpanzee) 154, 168
Watson, Alan 665
Weatherill, A. 380
Webster, John 255
Weissman, I. 405
welfare, animal 90, 254, 426–7; animal rights versus 697; attitude changes toward productivity and 256; boredom and 467–70; Conservation of Well-Being and 452–5; ethics of hunting and 494–5; loneliness and 470–2; movement growth 7–9; movement origins 5; public opinion on 463–4;

roles of zoos and aquariums in 586; *telos* and 463–74; *see also* animal rights
Wemelsfelder, Françoise 468–70
Wemmer, Chris 561, 591
Wenk, Caspar 663, 690
Wesley, John 5
Western ethics 26
Western political theory 55
Westra, Laura 459, 460, 518
Whale and Dolphin Conservation (WDC) 569
whales 515; arguments against release from captivity 575; attribution of "person" to 57, 161, 235–40; in captivity 563–70, 573–4; communication skills in 235; culture in 161, 209; feeding habits of 210–11; fish stealing by 208; hierarchies among 207; horizontal culture of 208; neurological complexity of 235, 238; opposition to hunting of 235; social learning in 207; *see also* cetaceans
whaling 236; commercial 208–9; extirpation due to 208; International Whaling Commission and 239
Wharton 598
What It Means to Be 98% Chimpanzee 278
white 563
Whitehead, Hal 161, 205
Whiten, Andrew 161, 181
Whole Earth Catalog 481
Wiens, John 482–3
wild animals: ethic of care and 553–8; hand-raising of 616–18; killing of 41
Wild Horses Act of 1959 (US) 7
wildlife 487; conservation 491–3, 518–19; management, conventional western view of 514–15
Wildlife Conservation Society 579–80
Wildlife Society, The (TWS) 597
Wiley, E. O. 407
Wilkinson, Robin 305, 352
willed ignorance 276
Williams, Howard 7
Williams, Joy 495
Williams, M. B. 408
Wilson, J. 484
Wilson, R. A. 407
Wise, Steven 161, 663, 672; *Rattling the Cage: Toward Legal Rights for Animals* 663, 672–5
Wittgenstein, Ludwig 45, 216, 348
Wolpe, Paul Root 305, 358
wolves, electric shock pain experienced by 631–4
women: as absent referents 282–3; battered 282–5; in Christianity 294; Christianity and 294; employment in slaughter plants 252; mapping metaphors with rodents 340–1; violence against 282–5, 510–11, 632–3; women's liberation and 274; women's movement and 6; *see also* feminism
Woods, Mark 495, 525
World Association of Zoos and Aquariums 599
World Health Organization (WHO): *Guiding Principles for Biomedical Research involving Animals* 365; Report on Infectious Diseases 259
World Trade Organization (WTO) 9

worse-off principle 20
Wrangham, R. W. 181
Wright, Robert 712
wrongness: from killing 421–2; from suffering
      422–3
Würsig, Bernd 205

xenophobia 531–3

Yellowstone Park 526–7, 528, 531, 532–3
Yinger, M. 690
Yorkshire Cancer Research (UK) 355
YouGov 353
Young, Dudley 510
young, separation of mother and 36
yuck factor 416–17

Zair, Orit 653
Zamir, Tzachi 650
Zbinden, G. 312
Zimbabwe 519–21
Zimbabwe Trust (ZIMTRUST) 519
Zimeldine 314
Zimmer, Carl 395, 479

Zimov, Sergey 480
Zoo Atlanta 599
zoomorphic gods 1
zoos and aquariums 561; animal liberty and
      576–7; animal welfare and 586; arguments
      against 573–4; arguments for 575, 577–81,
      582–8; balancing values and responsibilities in
      research under rapid global change 594–604;
      breeding programs 579–80, 592, 595; cetaceans in
      563–70; conservation education 585; conservation
      planning and coalition building 585; conservation
      role of 583; development of relevant technologies
      in 584; ecological ethics in captivity and 594–604;
      education through 577–8, 587; endangered
      species recovery by 584; ensuring quality animal
      care in 586–7; ethical complexity of conservation
      in 597–601; fundraising to support conservation
      585; global diversity crisis and 591–2; habitat
      restoration by 584; knowledge obtained from
      animals in 578; preservation of species in
      578–9; providing appropriate environments 586;
      reintroduction of species by 583–4; scientific
      research in 577–8, 598–603; support of protected
      areas 585; surplus animals in 587